THE
STRATEGY PROCESS

Concepts, Contexts, Cases

SECOND EDITION

HENRY MINTZBERG
McGill University
and
JAMES BRIAN QUINN
Dartmouth College

PRENTICE HALL
Englewood Cliffs, New Jersey 07632

Library of Congress Cataloging-in-Publication Data

Quinn, James Brian,
  The strategy process : concepts, contexts, cases / James Brian
Quinn and Henry Mintzberg.—2nd ed.
    p.   cm.
  Includes bibliographical references and index.
  ISBN 0-13-851916-1
  1. Strategic planning.   2. Strategic planning—Case studies.
I. Mintzberg, Henry.   II. Title.
HD30.28.Q53   1991
658.4'012—dc20
                                            90-20781
                                               CIP

Editorial/production supervision: **Karen Bernhaut**
Interior design: **Linda Rosa**
Cover design: **Ray Lundgren**
Manufacturing buyers: **Trudy Pisciotti and Robert Anderson**
Acquisitions Editor: **Alison Reeves**

 © 1991 and 1988 by Prentice-Hall, Inc.
A Paramount Communications Company
Englewood Cliffs, New Jersey 07632

Printed in the United States of America
10   9   8   7   6   5

ISBN   0-13-851916-1

Prentice-Hall International (UK) Limited, *London*
Prentice-Hall of Australia Pty. Limited, *Sydney*
Prentice-Hall Canada Inc., *Toronto*
Prentice-Hall Hispanoamericana, S.A., *Mexico*
Prentice-Hall of India Private Limited, *New Delhi*
Prentice-Hall of Japan, Inc., *Tokyo*
Simon & Schuster Asia Pte. Ltd., *Singapore*
Editora Prentice-Hall do Brasil, Ltda., *Rio de Janeiro*

To All Our Thoughtful Students Past and Future

With a Special Appreciation to Allie
For her unique patience, kindness, beauty, and intelligence.

BRIAN

CONTENTS

v

SECTION TWO ORGANIZATION

SECTION THREE CONTEXT

ACKNOWLEDGMENTS

We have been involved in the teaching and practice of strategy formation since the 1960s. What originally brought this book together was our firm belief that this field badly needed a new kind of text. We wanted one that looked at process issues as well as analysis; one that was built around critical strategy concepts and contexts instead of the overworked dichotomy of formulation and implementation; and one that accomplished these aims with writing that was intelligent, eclectic, and lively. We sought to combine theory and practice, and description and prescription, in new ways that offered insights none could achieve alone. All of these goals remain exactly the same in this second edition, except that here we set out to fine tune a basic formula that we feel worked well in the first one. Our own work on the first edition took far longer and was more difficult than we could have imagined, and the same holds true for this second edition. We hope that good students of management will think it worthwhile.

In any work of this scope, there are far too many people involved to thank each one individually. We would, however, like to acknowledge the special assistance given us by those who went especially out of their way to be helpful. In the academic community, several people deserve special mention. Deans John Hennessey and Colin Blaydon at the Tuck School kindly arranged for time and funding support to develop the many complex cases contained in the book. Mr. Bohdan Hawrylyshyn of the Institute for Management Development of Lausanne, Switzerland generously contributed funding and contacts for cases made in Europe and Japan. At INSEAD, Sumantra Goshal offered especially valuable advice on new readings to consider.

The people who really make such a major project as this happen are the competent research associates and secretaries who undertake the major burden of the work. At the Amos Tuck School of Business Administration, Penny C. Paquette, Suzanne Sweet, and Tammy Stebbins deserve special praise. Ms. Paquette was researcher and co-author of many of the cases for the book and oversaw the endless problems of coordinating clearances and production logistics for major portions of the book. Mrs. Sweet and Stebbins very professionally managed thousands of pages of original text and revisions with secretarial and computer skills that were invaluable. At McGill David Myles helped in all kinds of little ways, while Kate Maguire-Devlin's untold numbers of little contributions, important though they were, do not stand up to her big one—to provide a good-natured order without which the readings portion of this book could never have been finished.

At Prentice Hall, Karen Bernhaut and other professionals worked industriously on this edition to integrate the pieces into a comprehensive text, and took charge of the production, no easy task but one they carried out with skill and diligence. But our experience at Prentice Hall started much earlier, with Alison Reeves, who championed this book from the beginning and then worked vigorously to see it through to the publication of the original and this second edition. It was never easy, and we appreciate her extensive efforts.

A special thanks must also be offered to those who worked with the book in both its preliminary stages and in revision and offered invaluable feedback: in Montreal, those 1985-86 "guinea pig" McGill MBA students, and for this edition, Jan Jorgensen, Cynthia Hardy, and Tom Powell, who made many useful suggestions based on their teaching. Pierre Brunet and Bill Taylor at Concordia gave helpful comments on both editions, as did Fritz Reiger at Windsor. Bill Joyce and Rich D'Aveni at Tuck and Bill Davidson at the University of Southern California made significant contributions through their sophisticated teaching of the cases on an experimental basis. Further feedback of great use was provided by those users of the first edition book who returned the Prentice Hall questionnaire. We are deeply indebted to all of these people. A special mention should be made of John Voyer at the University of Southern Maine, whose excellent advice, provided since the beginning, has helped to shape this book. We are particularly grateful to him, not only for that feedback and his key role in the Teaching Manual, but for his capacity to get inside the book—to appreciate it for exactly what it is—and so to have provided us with the best indication of what it might be able to accomplish.

Among those who provided invaluable help on individual cases were Charles H. Bell, James McFarland, Verne Johnson, and John Gerlach of General Mills, Inc.; Thomas Murphy, E. M. Estes, Henry Duncombe, and F. Alan Smith of General Motors Corporation; Alastair Pilkington, Lord Pilkington, and B. N. Tyler of Pilkington Bros. Ltd.; William Spoor, Jack Stafford, E. H. Wingate, and G. Dunhowe of The Pillsbury Company; Helen Boehm of The Studios of Edward Marshall Boehm; Fred Middleton and Robert Swanson of Genentech, Inc.; Dr. Robert Noyce and Dr. Gordon Moore of Intel Corporation; Fred Smith, James Barksdale, and Thomas Oliver of Federal Express Corporation; Masaru Ibuka, Akoi Morita, Dr. Nobutoshi Kihara, and Dr. Makoto Kikuchi of Sony Corporation; Nobuhiko Kawamoto, Yasuhito Sato, T. Yashiki, and F. Kikuchi of Honda Motor Company, Ltd.; Bob O. Evans and Vincent Learson of IBM Corp.; Dr. Norton Belknap, Thomas Barrow, and George Piercy of Exxon Corp.; Dr. Richard Young, William McCune, I. M. Booth, and Peter Wensberg of Polaroid Corp.; Warren Bull, Rowland Frazee, and Alan Taylor of the Royal Bank of Canada; Stanley Feldberg, Sumner Feldberg, Maurice Segall, and Herschel Denker of Zayre Corporation; and Anthony Frank of First Nationwide Financial Corporation; Lew Veraldi and Charles Gumushian at Ford Motor Company; Arthur Sulzberger (Sr. and Jr.), and Warren Hoge of *The New York Times*. To each person who kindly contributed valuable time to this project, we are deeply grateful.

One last word; this book is not "finished." Our text, like the subject of so much of its content, is an ongoing process, not a static statement, as we believe the reader will find reflected in this new edition. So much of this book is so different from conventional strategy textbooks, indeed from our own text last time, that there are bound to be all kinds of opportunities for improvement. We would like to ask you to help us in this regard. We shall revise the text again to improve it to keep up with this exciting field. Please write to any of us with your suggestions on how to improve the readings, the cases, and the organization of the book at large and its presentation. Strategy making, we believe, is a learning process; we are also engaged in a learning process. And for that we need your feedback. Thank you and enjoy what follows.

Henry Mintzberg
James Brian Quinn

INTRODUCTION

In our first edition, we set out to produce a different kind of textbook in the field of business policy or, as it is now more popularly called, strategic management. We tried to provide the reader with a richness of theory, a richness of practice, and a strong basis for linkage between the two. We rejected the strictly case study approach, which leaves theory out altogether, or soft-pedals it, and thereby denies the accumulated benefits of many years of careful research and thought about management processes. We also rejected an alternate approach that forces on readers a highly rationalistic model of how the strategy process *should* function. We collaborated on this book because we believe that in this complex world of organizations a range of concepts is needed to cut through and illuminate particular aspects of that complexity. There is no "one best way" to create strategy, nor is there "one best form" of organization. Quite different forms work well in particular contexts. We believe that exploring a fuller variety systematically will create a deeper and more useful appreciation of the strategy process. In this revised edition, we remain loyal to these beliefs and objectives, having concentrated our efforts on improving the material we have included to reflect them. While maintaining the basic outline of the book, we replaced, added, and revised a great many of its specific components. In particular, 14 of the readings are new to this edition and 13 have been revised; about one-third of the cases are likewise new, while another one-third more have been shortened, revised, or updated based on the last few years' teaching experience and professors' suggestions. Most important, all the new cases contain a strong international competitive focus representing the global dimensions of today's major strategy issues. There are new cases involving both Japanese and European companies, as well as the new joint ventures used in worldwide competition in both professional services and manufacturing companies. You will find that cases on Honda Motor, Ford: Team Taurus, New Steel Corp., Biogen N.V., and PRA&D raise issues on the cutting edge of strategy for the 1990s.

This text, unlike most others, is therefore eclectic. Presenting published articles and portions of other books in their original form, rather than filtered through our minds and pens, is one way to reinforce this variety. Each author has his or her own ideas and his or her own best way of expressing them (ourselves included!). Summarized by us, these readings would lose a good deal of their richness.

We do not apologize for contradictions among the ideas of leading thinkers. The world is full of contradictions. The real danger lies in using pat solutions to a nuanced reality, not in opening perspectives up to different interpretations. The effective strategist is one who can live with contradictions, learn to appreciate their causes and effects, and reconcile them sufficiently for effective action. The readings have, nonetheless, been ordered by chapter to suggest some ways in which that reconciliation can be considered. Our own chapter introductions are also intended to assist in this task and to help place the readings themselves in perspective.

ON THEORY

A word on theory is in order. We do not consider theory a dirty word, nor do we apologize for making it a major component of this book. To some people, to be theoretical is to be detached, impractical. But a bright social scientist once said that "there is nothing so practical as a good theory." And every successful doctor, engineer, and physicist would have to agree: they would be unable to practice their modern work without theories. Theories are useful because they shortcut the need to store masses of data. It is easier to remember a simple framework about some phenomenon that it is to consider every detail you ever observed. In a sense, theories are a bit like cataloging systems in libraries: the world would be impossibly confusing without them. They enable you to store and conveniently access your own experiences as well as those of others.

One can, however, suffer not just from an absence of theories, but also from being dominated by them without realizing it. To paraphrase the words of John Maynard Keynes, most "practical men" are the slaves of some defunct theorist. Whether we realize it or not, our behavior is guided by the systems of ideas that we have internalized over the years. Much can be learned by bringing these out in the open, examining them more carefully, and comparing them with alternative ways to view the world—including ones based on systematic study (that is, research). One of our prime intentions in this book is to expose the limitations of conventional theories and to offer alternate explanations that can be superior guides to understanding and taking action in specific contexts.

Prescriptive Versus Descriptive Theory

Unlike many textbooks in this field, this one tries to explain the world as it is, rather than as someone thinks it is *supposed* to be. Although there has sometimes been a tendency to disdain such *descriptive* theories, *prescriptive* (or normative) ones have often been the problem, rather than the solution, in the field of management. There is no one best way in management; no prescription works for all organizations. Even when a prescription seems effective in some context, it requires a sophisticated understanding of exactly what that context is and how it functions. In other words, one cannot decide reliably what should be done in a system as complicated as a contemporary organization without a genuine understanding of how that organization really works. In engineering, no student ever questions having to learn physics, in medicine, having to learn anatomy. Imagine an engineering student's hand shooting up in a physics class: "Listen, prof, it's fine to tell us how the atom does work. But what we really want to know is how the atom *should* work." Why should a management student's similar demand in the realm of strategy or structure be considered any more appropriate? How can people manage complex systems they do not understand?

Nevertheless, we have not ignored prescriptive theory when it appears useful. A number of prescriptive techniques (industry analysis, portfolio analysis, experience curves, etc.) are discussed. But these are associated both with other readings and with cases that will help you understand the context and limitations of their usefulness. Both cases and readings offer opportunities to pursue the full complexity of strategic situations. You will find a wide range of issues and perspectives addressed. One of our main goals is to integrate a variety of views, rather than allow strategy to be fragmented into just "human issues" and "economics issues." The text and cases provide a basis for treating the full complexity of strategic management.

ON SOURCES

How were all the readings selected and edited? One popular textbook boasted a few years back that all its readings were published since 1980 (except one dated 1979!). We make no such claim; indeed we would like to make quite a different boast; many of our readings have been around quite a while, long enough to mature, like fine wine. Our criterion for inclusion was not the newness of the article so much as the quality of its insight—that is, its ability to explain some aspect of the strategy process better than any other article. Time does not age the really good articles. Quite the opposite—it distinguishes their quality (but sometimes it brings us back to the old habits of masculine gender; we apologize to our readers for this). We are, of course, not biased toward old articles—just toward good ones. Hence, the materials in this book range from classics of the 1950s to some published just before our final selection was made (as well as a few hitherto unpublished pieces). You will find articles from the most serious academic journals, the best practitioner magazines, books, and some very obscure sources. The best can sometimes be found in strange places!

We have opted to include many shorter readings rather than fewer longer ones, and we have tried to present as wide a variety of good ideas as possible while maintaining clarity. To do so we often had to cut within readings. We have, in fact, put a great deal of effort into the cutting in order to extract the key messages of each reading in as brief, concise, and clear a manner as possible. Unfortunately, our cutting sometimes forced us to eliminate interesting examples and side issues. (In the readings, as well as some of the case materials from published sources, dots . . . signify portions that have been deleted from the original, while square brackets [ ] signify our own insertions of minor clarifications into the original text.) We apologize to you, the reader, as well as to the authors, for having done this, but hope that the overall result has rendered these changes worthwhile.

We have also included a number of our own works. Perhaps we are biased, having less objective standards by which to judge what we have written. But we have messages to convey, too, and our own writings do examine the basic themes that we feel are important in policy and strategy courses today.

ON CASES

A major danger of studying the strategy process—probably the most enticing subject in the management curriculum, and at the pinnacle of organizational processes—is that students and professors can become detached from the basics of the enterprise. The "Don't bore me with the operating details; I'm here to tackle the really big issues" syndrome has been the death of many business policy or strategy courses (not to mention managerial practices!). The big issues *are* rooted in little details. We have tried to recognize this in both the readings and the cases. Effective strategy processes always come down to specifics. The cases and the industry reference notes provide a rich soil for investigating strategic realities. Their complexities always extend well below the surface. Each layer peeled back can reveal new insights and rewards.

As useful as they are, however, cases are not really the ideal way to understand strategy: involving oneself in the hubbub of life in a real organization is. We harbor no illusions that reading 20 pages on an organization will make you an expert. But cases remain the most convenient way to introduce practice into the classroom, to tap a wide variety of experiences, and to involve students actively in analysis and decision making. Our cases consciously contain both their prescriptive and descriptive aspects. On the one hand, they provide the data and background for making a major decision. Students can appraise the situation in its full context, suggest what future directions would be best for the organization in question, and discuss how their solutions can realistically be implemented. On the other hand, each case is also an opportunity to understand the dynamics of an organization—the historical context of the problems it faces, the influence of its culture, its probable reactions to varying solutions, and so on. Unlike many cases which focus on only the analytical aspects of a decision, ours constantly force you to consider the messy realities of arriving at decisions in organizations and obtaining a desired response to any decision. In these respects, case study involves a good deal of descriptive *and* prescriptive analysis.

Linking Cases and Readings

The cases in this book are not intended to emphasize any particular theories, any more than the theoretical materials are included because they explain particular cases. Each case presents a slice of some specific reality, each reading a conceptual interpretation of some phenomenon. The readings are placed in particular groupings because they approach some common aspects or issues in theory.

We have provided some general guidelines for relating particular cases to sets of readings. But do not push this too far: analyze each case for its own sake. Cases are intrinsically richer than readings. Each contains a wide variety of issues—many awfully messy—in no particular order. The readings, in contrast, are usually neat and tidy, professing one or a few basic conceptual ideas, and providing some specific vocabulary. When the two connect—sometimes through direct effort, more often indirectly as conceptual ideas are recalled in the situation of a particular case —some powerful learning can take place in the form of clarification or, we hope, revelation.

Try to see how particular theories can help you to understand some of the issues in the cases and provide useful frameworks for drawing conclusions. Perhaps the great military theorist, Von Clausewitz, said it best over a century ago (to borrow a quotation from one of our readings of Chapter 1):

> All that theory can do is give the artist or soldier points of reference and standards of evaluation . . . with the ultimate purpose not of telling him how to act but of developing his judgment. (1976:15)

In applying the theory to cases, please do not assume that it is only the readings cross referenced with the case that matter. We have designed the book so that the textual materials develop as the chapters unfold. Concepts introduced in earlier chapters become integrated in the later ones. And early cases tend to build knowledge for those appearing later. Problems and their organizational context move from the simple to the more complex. Space limitations and the structured nature of theories require some compartmentalization. But don't take that compartmentalization too literally. In preparing each case, use whatever concepts you find helpful both from chapters of this book and from your personal knowledge. The cases themselves deal with real people in real companies. The reality they present is enormously complicated; their dynamics extend to today's newspaper, and *Who's Who,* or any other reference you can imagine. Use any sound source of information that helps you to deal with them. Part of the fun of policy or strategy courses is understanding how major decisions happened to be made and what were their subsequent consequences—local, national, even international.

These are all living cases. In the strictest sense they have no beginning or end. They have been written in as lively a style as possible; we do not believe business school cases need be dull! Each case deals with a major transition point in the history of an enterprise. Each can be used in a variety of ways to emphasize a particular set of concepts at a particular time in the course. Many lend themselves to sophisticated financial, industry, portfolio, and competitive analyses as well as discerning organizational, behavioral, and managerial practice inquiries. And many contain entrepreneurial and technological dimensions rarely found in strategy cases. Trying to figure out what is going on should be challenging as well as fun!

Case Discussion

Management cases provide a concrete information base for students to analyze and share as they discuss management issues. Without this focus, discussions of theory can become quite confusing. You may have in mind an image of an organization or situation that is very different from that of other discussants. As a result, what appars to be a difference in theory will—after much argument—often turn out to be simply a difference in perception of the realities surrounding these examples.

In this text we try to provide three levels of learning: *first,* a chance to share the generalized insights of leading theoreticians (in the readings); *second,* an opportunity to test the applicability and limits of these theories in specific (case) situations; *third,* the capacity to develop one's own special amalgam of insights based upon empirical observations and inductive reasoning (from case analyses). All are useful approaches; some students and professors will find one mix more productive for their special level of experience or mind set. Another will prefer a quite different mix. Hence, we include a wide selection of cases and readings.

The cases are not intended as *examples* of either weak or exceptionally good management practices. Nor, as we noted, do they provide *examples* of the concepts in a particular reading. They are discussion vehicles for probing the benefits and limits of various approaches. And they are analytical vehicles for applying and testing concepts and tools developed in your education and experience. Almost every case has its marketing, operations, accounting, financial, human relations, planning and control, external environmental, ethical, political, and quantitative dimensions. Each dimension should be addressed in preparations and classroom discussions, although some aspects will inevitably emerge as more important in one situation than another.

In each case you should look for several sets of issues. First, you should understand what went on in that situation. Why did it happen this way? What are the strong or weak features of what happened? What could have been changed to advantage? How? Why? Second, there are always issues of what should be done next. What are the key issues to be resolved? What are the major alternatives available? What outcomes could the organization expect from each? Which alternative should it select? Why? Third, there will almost always be "hard" quantitative data and "soft" qualitative impressions about each situation. Both deserve attention. Because the cases deal with real companies, and real people, in real situations, their data bases can be *extended* as far as students and professors wish. They only have to consult their libraries and daily newspapers.

But remember, no realistic strategy situation is *just* an organization behavior problem or *just* a financial or economic analytical one. Both sets of information should be considered, and an *integrated* solution developed. Our cases are consciously constructed for this. Given their complexity we have tried to keep the cases as short as possible. And we have tried to capture some of the flavor of the real organization. Moreover, we have sought to mix product and services cases, technological and "nontech" cases, entrepreneurial, small company, and large enterprise situations. In this cross section, we have tried to capture some of the most important and exciting issues, concepts, and products of our times. We believe management is fun, and important. The cases try to convey this.

There is no "correct" answer to any case. There may be several "good" answers and many poor ones. The purpose of a strategy course should be to help you understand the nature of these "better" answers, what to look for, how to analyze alternatives, and how to see through the complexities of reaching solutions and implanting them in real organizations. A strategy course can only improve your probability of success, not ensure it. The total number of variables in a real strategy situation is typically beyond the control of any one person or group. Hence another caveat: don't rely on what a company actually did as a guide to effective action. The company may have succeeded or failed not because of its specific decisions, but because of luck, an outstanding personality, the bizarre action of an opponent, international actions over which it had no control, and so on. One of the products of a successful strategy course should be a little humility.

Case Study Guides

We have posed a few questions at the end of each case as discussion guides. Students have generally found these helpful in organizing their thinking about each case. If you answer these questions well, you can probably deal with anything that comes up in class. But each professor may conduct his or her class in a quite different fashion. The questions should help you see relevant issues, but they should not limit your thinking. From time to time there are intermediate "decision points" in a case. Work on the material up to that point just as you would a short case. The case materials immediately following these decision points consciously leave out much detail on what might have happened so that you can arrive at your own specific solutions. Later you can see them in the context of a longer time horizon, much like a mystery story unfolding in phases. Analyze the specific situations, consider alternatives, and arrive at specific conclusions—understanding that later events might have looked a bit different if your solution had been implemented. Like any good mystery story, a case provides many clues, never all, but, surprisingly, sometimes more than executives might have had time to absorb in the real situation.

Believing that no "canned approach" is viable for all strategic situations, we have selected cases that cut across a variety of issues and theoretical constructs. Almost any of these cases is so complex that it can be positioned at a number of different spots in a good strategy course. We have clustered them around the three major segments of the text for convenience to students and professors. But the cases could equally well be taught in a number of other sequences. We leave the final case selection to the style and wisdom of the professor and his or her students.

Not Formulation, Then Implementation

The first edition of this text offered a chapter format that was new to the policy or strategy field. Unlike most others, it had no specific chapter or section devoted to "implementation" per se. The assumption in other texts is that strategy is formulated and then implemented, with organizational structures, control systems, and the like following obediently behind strategy. In this text, as in reality, formulation and implementation are intertwined as complex interactive processes in which politics, values, organizational culture, and management styles determine or constrain particular strategic decisions. And strategy, structure, and systems mix together in complicated ways to influence outcomes. While strategy formulation and implementation may be separated in some situations—perhaps in crises, in some totally new ventures, as well as in organizations facing predictable futures—these events are rare. We certainly do not believe in building a whole book (let alone a whole field) around this conceptual distinction.

But Concepts, Then Contexts

The readings are divided roughly into two different parts. The first deals with *concepts,* the second with *contexts.* We introduce strategy and structure as well as power, culture, and several other concepts early in the text as equal partners in the complex web of ideas that make up what we call "the strategy process." In the second half of the text we weave these concepts together in a number of distinct situations, which we call *contexts.*

Our theme diagram illustrates this. Concepts, shown on top, are divided into two groups—strategy and organization—to represent the first two sections of the book. Contexts draw all these concepts together, in a variety of situations—covered in the third section—which we consider the key ones in the field of strategy today (though hardly the only ones). The outline of the text, chapter by chapter, proceeds as follows:

Section I: Strategy

The first section is called "*Strategy*"; it comprises five chapters (two introductory in nature and three on the processes by which strategy making takes place). Chapter 1 introduces *the strategy concept* and probes the meaning of this important word to broaden your view of it. Here the pattern is set of challenging you to question conventional views, especially when these act to narrow perspectives. The themes introduced in this chapter carry throughout the book and are worth care in understanding.

Chapter 2 introduces a very important character in this book, *the strategist* as general manager. This person may not be the only one who makes strategy in an organization, but he or she is clearly a key player. In examining the work of the general manager and the character of his or her job, we shall perhaps upset a number of widely accepted notions. We do this to help you understand the very real complexities and difficulties of making strategy and managing in contemporary organizations.

Chapters 3, 4, and 5 take up a theme that is treated extensively in the text—to the point of being reflected in its title: the development of an understanding of the *processes* by which strategies are made. Chapter 3 looks at *formulating strategy,*

STRATEGY PROCESS THEME DIAGRAM

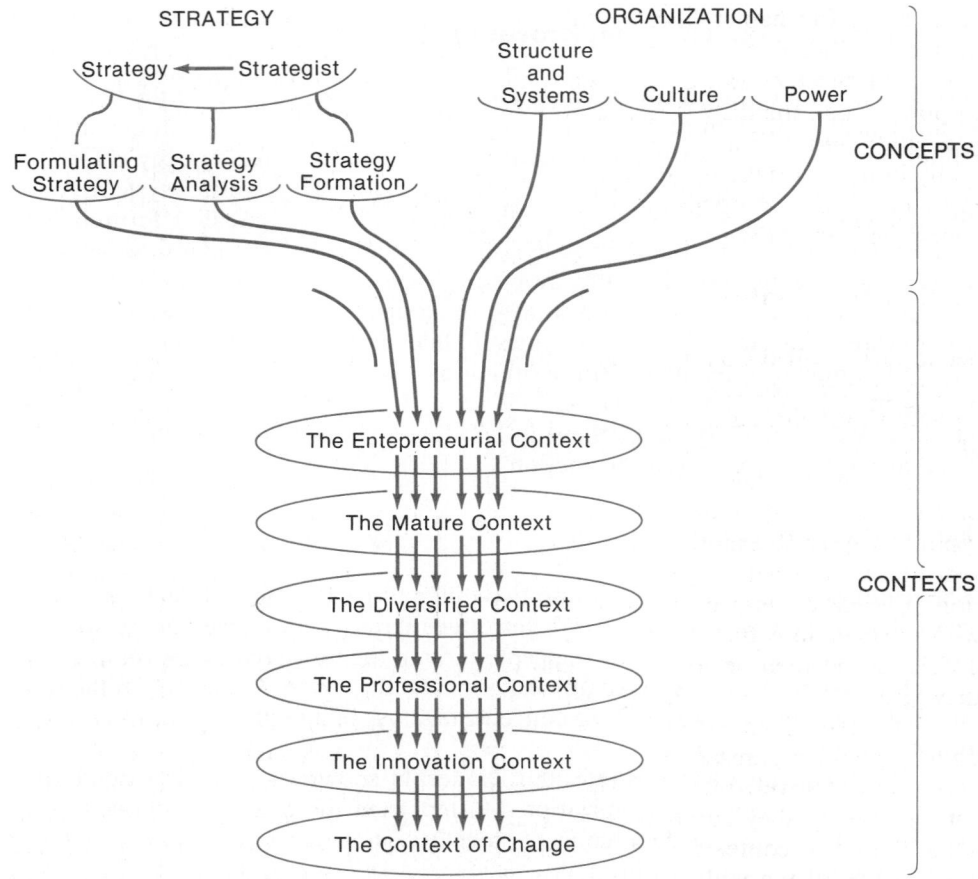

specifically at some widely accepted prescriptive models for how organizations should go about developing their strategies. Chapter 4 extends these ideas to more formal ways of doing *strategy analysis* and considering what, if any, "generic" forms a strategy can take. While readings in later chapters will challenge some of these precepts, what will not be questioned is the importance of having to understand them. They are fundamental to appreciating the strategy process today.

Chapter 5 switches from a prescriptive to a descriptive approach. Concerned with understanding *strategy formation,* it considers how strategies actually *do* form in organizations (not necessarily by being formulated) and *why* different processes may be effective in specific circumstances. This text takes an unconventional stand by viewing planning and other formal approaches as not the only—and often indeed not even the most desirable—ways to make strategy. You will find our emphasis on the descriptive process—as an equal partner with the more traditional concerns for technical and analytical issues—to be one of the unifying themes of this book.

Section II: Organization

In Section I, the readings introduced strategy, the strategist, and various ways in which strategy might be formulated and does in fact form. In Section II, entitled *Organization,* we introduce other concepts that constitute part of the strategy process.

In Chapter 6, we consider *structure and systems,* where particular attention is paid to the various forms that structure can take as well as the mechanisms that comprise it. In Chapter 7, we consider *culture,* especially how strong systems of beliefs, called "ideologies," impact on organizations and their strategies and so influence their effectiveness. In Chapter 8, *power* is the focus. We consider two aspects of power: first, the distribution of power among the various actors within the organization and its links to political activity; second, the organization as a political entity in its own right and its power to pursue its own ends, whether or not responsibly, in the face of opposing forces in society. Both aspects will be seen to influence significantly the processes by which strategies are formulated or form.

Section III: Context

Section III is called *Context.* We consider how all of the elements introduced so far —strategy, the processes by which it is formulated and gets formed, the strategist, structure, systems, culture and power—combine to suit particular contexts, six in all.

Chapter 9 deals with the *entrepreneurial context,* where a rather simple organization comes under the close control of a strong leader, often a person with vision. Chapter 10 examines the *mature context,* one common to many large business and government organizations involved in the mass production or distribution of goods or services. Chapter 11 introduces the *diversified context,* and deals with organizations that have diversified their product or service lines and usually divisionalized their structures to deal with the greater varieties of environments they face.

Chapters 12 and 13 develop the contexts of professionalism and innovation, both involving organizations of high expertise. In the professional context, the experts work relatively independently in rather stable conditions, while in the innovation context, they combine in project teams under more dynamic conditions. What these two contexts have in common, however, is that they act in ways that upset many of the widely accepted notions about how organizations should be structured and make strategy.

In considering each of these widely different contexts, we seek to discuss (where appropriate material is available) the situations in which each is most likely to be found, the structures most suited to it, the kinds of strategies that tend to be pursued, the processes by which these strategies tend to be formed and might be formulated, and the social issues associated with the context.

Chapter 14 is devoted not so much to a specific context as to *managing change* between contexts, or within a context (which we can, of course, characterize as the context of change). The major concerns are how organizations can cope with crises, turnarounds, revitalizations, and new stages in their own life cycles or those of their key products.

The readings end in Chapter 15 on a provocative note, designed to encourage *thinking strategically,* about strategy itself and the whole process of management.

Well, there you have it. We have worked hard on this book, in both the original and this revised edition, to get it right. We have tried to think things through from the basics, with a resulting text that in style, format, and content is unusual for the field of policy or strategy. Our product may not be perfect, but we believe it is good—indeed better than any other text available. Now it's your turn to find out if you agree. Have fun doing so!

STRATEGY

THE STRATEGY CONCEPT

We open this text on its focal point: strategy. The first section is called "Strategy," the first chapter, "the Strategy Concept." Later chapters in this section describe the role of the general manager as strategist and consider the processes by which strategies get made from three perspectives: deliberate formulation, systematic analysis, and emergent formation. But in its opening chapter, we consider the central concept—strategy itself.

What is strategy anyway? There is no single, universally accepted definition. Different authors and managers use the term differently; for example, some include goals and objectives as part of strategy while others make firm distinctions between them. Our intention in including the following readings is not to promote any one view of strategy, but rather to suggest a number that seem useful. As will be evident throughout this text, our wish is not to narrow perspectives but to broaden them by trying to clarify issues. In pursuing these readings, it will be helpful to think about the meaning of strategy, to try to understand how different people have used the term, and, later, to see if certain definitions hold up better in particular contexts.

We have taken the opportunity to include in this first chapter readings by each of us, the two coauthors of the book. They set the tone for the material that follows and provide an indication of our own thinking. As you will see, our views are similar but certainly not identical; indeed in places we differ somewhat (for example, on the word "tactics"). But overall, we believe you will find these views complementary.

The first reading, by James Brian Quinn of the Amos Tuck Business School of Dartmouth College, provides a general overview by clarifying some of the vocabulary in this field and introducing a number of the themes that will appear throughout the text. In this reading from his book *Strategies for Change: Logical Incrementalism,* Quinn places special emphasis on the military uses of the term and draws from this domain a set of essential "dimensions" or criteria for successful strategies. To derive these, he goes back to Philip and Alexander of Macedonia for his main example; he also provides a brief kaleidoscope of how similar concepts have influenced later military and diplomatic strategists.

Discussion of the military aspects of strategy must surely be among the oldest continuous literatures in the world. In fact, the origins of the word "strategy" go back even farther than this experience in Macedonia, to the Greeks whom Alexander and his father defeated. As Quinn notes and Roger Evered, in another article, elaborates,

> Initially *strategos* referred to a role (a general in command of an army). Later it came to mean "the art of the general," which is to say the psychological and behavioral skills with which he occupied the role. By the time of Pericles (450 B.C.) it came to mean managerial skill (administration, leadership, oration, power). And by Alexander's time (330 B.C.) it referred to the skill of employing forces to overcome opposition and to create a unified system of global governance. (1980:3)

The second reading, by Henry Mintzberg who teaches policy in the Faculty of Management at McGill University in Montreal, serves to open up the concept of strategy to a variety of views, some very different from traditional military or business writings (but suggested briefly in the Quinn reading). Mintzberg focuses on various distinct definitions of strategy—as plan (as well as ploy), pattern, position, and perspective. He uses the first two of these definitions to take us beyond *deliberate* strategy—beyond the traditional view of the term—to the notion of *emergent* strategy. This introduces the idea that strategies can *form* in an organization without being consciously intended, that is, without being *formulated*. This may seem to run counter to the whole thrust of the strategy literature, but Mintzberg argues that many people implicitly use the term this way even though they would not so define it.

Upon completion of these readings, we hope that you will be less sure of *the* use of the word strategy, but more ready to tackle the study of the strategy *process* with a broadened perspective and an open mind. There are no universally right answers in this field (any more than there are in most other fields), but there are interesting and constructive orientations.

Several cases relate well to the concepts developed in this chapter. The Guns of August picks up the military and formally derived concepts of strategy discussed in the two articles. Cases such as Boehm, Intel, New Steel Corp., and Genentech offer opportunities to consider the concepts of strategy analytically, while IBM (A), Honda Motor, and Biogen deal with the processes through which organizations arrive at strategies.

● ## STRATEGIES FOR CHANGE*

BY JAMES BRIAN QUINN

SOME USEFUL DEFINITIONS

Because the words *strategy, objectives, goals, policy,* and *programs* . . . have different meanings to individual readers or to various organizational cultures, I [try] to

---

* Excerpted from James Brian Quinn, *Strategies for Change: Logical Incrementalism* (copyright © Richard D. Irwin, Inc., 1980), Chaps. 1 and 5; reprinted by permission of the publisher.

use certain definitions consistently . . . For clarity—not pedantry—these are set forth as follows:

A **strategy** is the *pattern* or *plan* that *integrates* an organization's *major* goals, policies, and action sequences into a *cohesive* whole. A well-formulated strategy helps to *marshal* and *allocate* an organization's resources into a *unique and viable posture* based on its relative *internal competencies* and *shortcomings,* anticipated *changes in the environment,* and contingent moves by *intelligent opponents.*

Goals (or **objectives**) state *what* is to be achieved and *when* results are to be accomplished, but they do not state *how* the results are to be achieved. All organizations have multiple goals existing in a complex hierarchy (Simon, 1964): from value objectives, which express the broad value premises toward which the company is to strive; through overall organizational objectives, which establish the intended *nature* of the enterprise and the *directions* in which it should move; to a series of less permanent goals that define targets for each organizational unit, its subunits, and finally all major program activities within each subunit. Major goals —those that affect the entity's overall direction and viability—are called *strategic goals.*

Policies are rules or guidelines that express the *limits* within which action should occur. These rules often take the form of contingent decisions for resolving conflicts among specific objectives. For example: "Don't exceed three months' inventory in any item without corporate approval." Like the objectives they support, policies exist in a hierarchy throughout the organization. Major policies—those that guide the entity's overall direction and posture or determine its viability—are called *strategic policies.*

Programs specify the *step-by-step sequence of actions* necessary to achieve major objectives. They express *how* objectives will be achieved within the limits set by policy. They ensure that resources are committed to achieve goals, and they provide the dynamic track against which progress can be measured. Those major programs that determine the entity's overall thrust and viability are called *strategic programs.*

Strategic decisions are those that determine the overall direction of an enterprise and its ultimate viability in light of the predictable, the unpredictable, and the unknowable changes that may occur in its most important surrounding environments. They intimately shape the true goals of the enterprise. They help delineate the broad limits within which the enterprise operates. They dictate both the resources the enterprise will have accessible for its tasks and the principal patterns in which these resources will be allocated. And they determine the effectiveness of the enterprise—whether its major thrusts are in the right directions given its resource potentials—rather than whether individual tasks are performed efficiently. Management for efficiency, along with the myriad decisions necessary to maintain the daily life and services of the enterprise, is the domain of operations.

Strategies Versus Tactics

Strategies normally exist at many different levels in any large organization. For example, in government there are world trade, national economic, treasury department, military spending, investment, fiscal, monetary supply, banking, regional development, and local reemployment strategies—all related to each other somewhat hierarchically yet each having imperatives of its own. Similarly, businesses have numerous strategies from corporate levels to department levels within divisions. Yet if strategies exist at all these levels, how do strategies and tactics differ? Often the primary difference lies in the scale of action or the perspective of the leader. What appears to be a "tactic" to the chief executive officer (or general) may be a "strategy" to the marketing head (or lieutenant) if it determines the ultimate success and viability of his or her organization. In a more precise sense, tactics can occur at either level. They are the short-duration, adaptive, action-interaction re-alignments that opposing forces use to accomplish limited goals after their initial contact. Strategy defines a continuing basis for ordering these adaptations toward more broadly conceived purposes.

A genuine strategy is always needed when the potential actions or responses of intelligent opponents can seriously affect the endeavor's desired outcome—regardless of that endeavor's organizational level in the total enterprise. This condition almost always pertains to the important actions taken at the top level of competitive organizations. However, game theorists quickly point out that some important top-level actions—for example, sending a peacetime fleet across the Atlantic—merely require elaborate coordinative plans and programs (Von Neumann and Morgenstern, 1944; Shubik, 1975; McDonald, 1950). A whole new set of concepts, a true strategy, is needed if some people or nations decide to oppose the fleet's purposes. And it is these concepts that in large part distinguish strategic formulation from simpler programmatic planning.

Strategies may be looked at as either a priori statements to guide action or a posteriori results of actual decision behavior. In most complex organizations . . . one would be hard pressed to find a complete a priori statement of a total strategy that actually is followed. Yet often the existence of a strategy (or strategy change) may be clear to an objective observer, although it is not yet apparent to the executives making critical decisions. One, therefore, must look at the actual emerging *pattern* of the enterprise's operant goals, policies, and major programs to see what its true strategy is (Mintzberg, 1972). Whether it is consciously set forth in advance or is simply a widely held understanding resulting from a stream of decisions, this pattern becomes the real strategy of the enterprise. And it is changes in this pattern —regardless of what any formal strategic documents may say—that either analysts or strategic decision makers must address if they wish to comprehend or alter the concern's strategic posture. . . .

THE CLASSICAL APPROACH TO STRATEGY

Military-diplomatic strategies have existed since prehistoric times. In fact, one function of the earliest historians and poets was to collect the accumulated lore of these successful and unsuccessful life-and-death strategies and convert them into wisdom and guidance for the future. As societies grew larger and conflicts more complex, generals, statesmen, and captains studied, codified, and tested essential strategic concepts until a coherent body of principles seemed to emerge. In various forms these were ultimately distilled into the maxims of Sun Tzu (1963), Machia-velli (1950), Napoleon (1940), Von Clausewitz (1976), Foch (1970), Lenin (1927), Hart (1954), Montgomery (1958), or Mao Tse-Tung (1967). Yet with a few excep-tions—largely introduced by modern technology—the most basic principles of strategy were in place and recorded long before the Christian era. More modern in-stitutions primarily adapted and modified these to their own special environments.

Although one could choose any number of classical military-diplomatic strat-egies as examples, Philip and Alexander's actions at Chaeronea (in 338 B.C.) con-tain many currently relevant concepts (Varner and Alger, 1978; Green, 1970). . . .

A Grand Strategy

Philip and his young son, Alexander, had very *clear goals*. They sought to rid Macedonia of influence by the Greek city-states and to *establish dominance* over what was then essentially northern Greece. They also wanted Athens to *join a coalition* with them against Persia on their eastern flank. *Assessing their resources,* they *decided to avoid* the overwhelming superiority of the Athenian fleet and *chose to forego* attack on the powerful walled cities of Athens and Thebes where their superbly trained phalanxes and cavalry would not *have distinct advantages.*

Philip and Alexander *used an indirect approach* when an invitation by the Amphictyonic Council brought their army south to punish Amphissa. In a *planned sequence of actions and deceptive maneuvers,* they cut away from a direct line of march to Amphissa, *bypassed the enemy,* and *fortified a key base,* Elatea. They then took steps to *weaken their opponents politically and morally* by pressing restoration of the Phoenician communities earlier dispersed by the Thebans and by having Philip declared a champion of the Delphic gods. Then *using misleading messages* to make the enemy believe they had moved north to Thrace and also *using developed intelligence sources,* the Macedonians in a *surprise attack* annihilated the Greeks' positions near Amphissa. This *lured their opponents away from their defensive positions* in the nearby mountain passes to *consolidate their forces* near the town of Chaeronca.

There, *assessing the relative strengths* of their opponents, the Macedonians first *attempted to negotiate* to achieve their goals. When this was unsuccessful they had a *well-developed contingency plan* on how to *attack and overwhelm* the Greeks. Prior to this time, of course, the Macedonians had *organized* their troops into the famed phalanxes, and had *developed the full logistics* needed for their field support including a longer spear, which helped the Macedonian phalanxes penetrate the solid shield wall of the heavily massed Greek formations. *Using the natural advantages* of their grassy terrain, the Macedonians had developed cavalry support for their phalanxes' movements far beyond the Greek capability. Finally, using a *relative advantage*—the *command structure* their hierarchical *social system* allowed—against the more democratic Greeks, the Macedonian nobles had *trained their personnel* into one of the most *disciplined and highly motivated forces* in the world.

The Battle Strategy

Supporting this was the battle strategy at Chaeronea, which emerged as follows. Philip and Alexander first *analyzed their specific strengths and weaknesses and their opponents' current alignments and probable moves.* The Macedonian strength lay in their new spear technology, the *mobility* of their superbly disciplined phalanxes, and the powerful cavalry units led by Alexander. Their weaknesses were that they were badly outnumbered and faced—in the Athenians and the Theban Band—some of the finest foot troops in the world. However, their opponents had two weak points. One was the Greek left flank with lightly armed local troops placed near the Chaeronean Acropolis and next to some more heavily armed—but hastily assembled—hoplites bridging to the strong center held by the Athenians. The famed Theban Band anchored the Greek right wing near a swamp on the Cephissus River. [See Figure 1.]

Philip and Alexander *organized their leadership to command key positions;* Philip took over the right wing and Alexander the cavalry. They *aligned their forces* into *a unique posture* which *used their strengths* and *offset their weaknesses.* They decided on those spots at which they would *concentrate their forces,* what *positions to concede,* and what *key points* they *must take and hold.* Starting with their units angled back from the Greek lines (see map), they developed a *focused major thrust* against the Greek left wing and *attacked their opponents' weakness*—the troops near Chaeronea—with the most disciplined of the Macedonian units, the guards' brigade. After building up pressure and stretching the Greek line to its left, the guards' brigade abruptly began a *planned withdrawal.* This *feint* caused the Greek left to break ranks

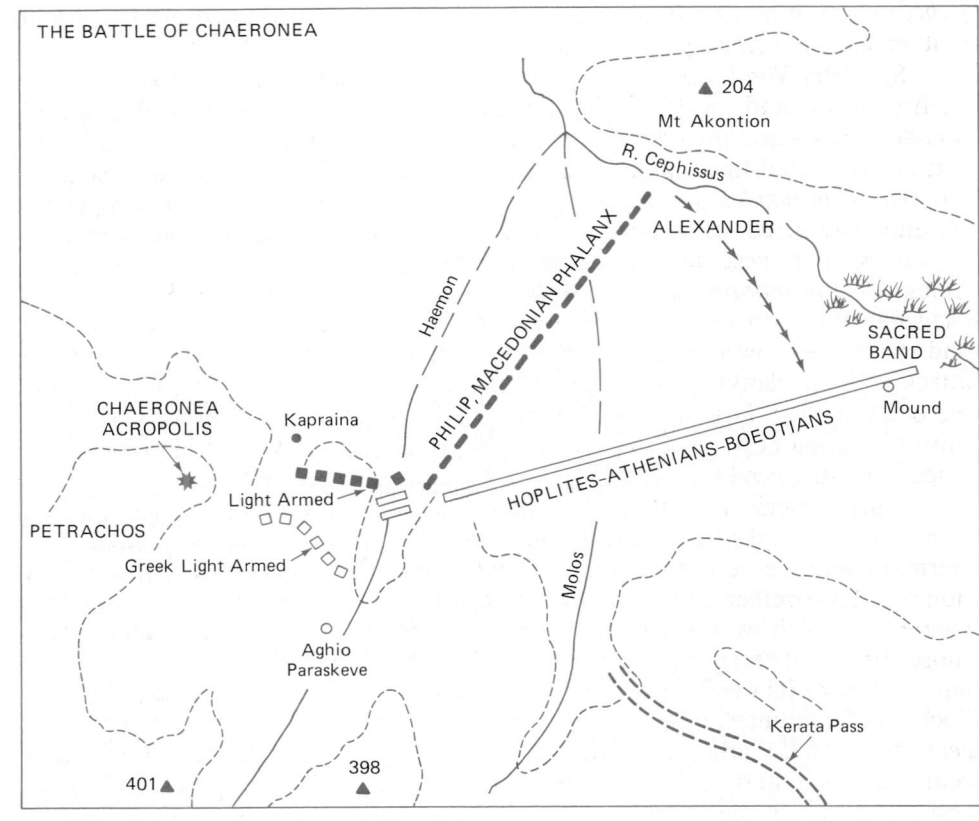

FIGURE 1

The Battle of Chaeronea
Source: Modified with permission from P. Green, Alexander the Great, *Praeger Publishers, New York, 1970.*

THE BATTLE OF CHAERONEA

and rush forward, believing the Macedonians to be in full retreat. This *stretched the opponents' resources* as the Greek center moved left to *maintain contact* with its flank and to attack the "fleeing" Macedonians.

Then *with predetermined timing,* Alexander's cavalry *attacked the exposure* of the stretched line at the same moment Philip's phalanxes *re-formed as planned* on the high ground at the edge of the Heamon River. Alexander *broke through* and *formed a bridgehead* behind the Greeks. He *refocused his forces against a segment* of the opponents' line; his cavalry *surrounded and destroyed* the Theban Band as the *overwhelming power* of the phalanxes poured through the gap he had created. From its *secured position,* the Macedonian left flank then turned and *attacked the flank* of the Athenians. With the help of Philip's *planned counterattack,* the Macedonians *expanded their dominance and overwhelmed the critical target,* i.e., the Greek center. . . .

Modern Analogies

Similar concepts have continued to dominate the modern era of formal strategic thought. As this period begins, Scharnhorst still points to the need to *analyze social forces and structures* as a basis for *understanding effective command styles* and *motivational stimuli* (Von Clausewitz, 1976:8). Frederick the Great proved this point in the field. Presumably based on such analyses, he adopted *training, discipline,* and *fast maneuvers* as the central concepts for a tightly disciplined German culture that had to be constantly ready to fight on two fronts (Phillips, 1940). Von Bülow (1806) continued to emphasize the dominant strategic roles of *geographical positioning* and *logistical support systems* in strategy. Both Jomini (1971) and Von Bülow (1806) stressed the concepts of *concentration, points of domination,* and *ra-*

pidity of movement as central strategic themes and even tried to develop them into mathematically precise principles for their time.

Still later Von Clausewitz expounded on the paramountcy of *clear major objectives* in war and on developing war strategies as a component of the nation's *broader goals* with *time horizons* extending beyond the war itself. Within this context he postulated that an effective strategy should be focused around a relatively *few central principles,* which can *create, guide,* and *maintain dominance* despite the enormous frictions that occur as one tries to position or maneuver large forces in war. Among these he included many of the concepts operant in Macedonian times: *spirit or morale, surprise, cunning, concentration in space, dominance of selected positions, use of strategic reserves, unification over time, tension and release,* and so on. He showed how these broad principles applied to a number of specific attack, defense, flanking, and retreat situations; but he always stressed the intangible of *leadership.* His basic positioning and organizational principles were to be mixed with boldness, perseverance, and genius. He constantly emphasized—as did Napoleon—the need for *planned flexibility* once the battle was joined.

Later strategic analysts adapted these classic themes for larger-scale conflicts. Von Schlieffen linked together the huge numerical and production *strengths* of Germany and the vast *maneuvering capabilities* of Flanders fields to pull the nation's might together conceptually behind a *unique alignment of forces* ("a giant hayrake"), which would *outflank* his French opponents, *attack weaknesses* (their supply lines and rear), capture and *hold key political centers* of France, and *dominate or destroy* its weakened army in the field (Tuchman, 1962). On the other side, Foch and Grandmaison saw *morale* ("élan"), *nerve* ("cran"), and continuous *concentrated attack* ("attaque à outrance") as *matching the values* of a volatile, recently defeated, and vengeful French nation, which had decided (for both moral and *coalition* reasons) to *set important limits* on its own actions in World War I— that is, not to attack first or through Belgium.

As these two strategies lost shape and became the head-on slaughter of trench warfare, Hart (1954) revitalized the *indirect approach,* and this became a central theme of British strategic thinking between the wars. Later in the United States, Matloff and Snell (1953) began to stress planning for *large-scale coalitions* as the giant forces of World War II developed. The Enigma group *moved secretly to develop the intelligence network* that was so crucial in the war's outcome (Stevenson, 1976). But once engaged in war, George Marshall still saw the only hope for Allied victory in *concentrating overwhelming forces* against one enemy (Germany) first, then after *conceding early losses* in the Pacific, *refocusing Allied forces* in a gigantic *sequential coordinated movement* against Japan. In the eastern theater, MacArthur first *fell back, consolidated a base* for operations, *built up his logistics, avoided his opponent's strengths, bypassed* Japan's established defensive positions, and in a *gigantic flanking maneuver* was ready to invade Japan after *softening its political and psychological will* through saturation bombing (James, 1970).

All these modern thinkers and practitioners utilized classical principles of strategy dating back to the Greek era, but perhaps the most startling analogies of World War II lay in Patton's and Rommel's battle strategies, which were almost carbon copies of the Macedonians' concepts of planned concentration, rapid breakthrough, encirclement, and attack on the enemy's rear (Essame, 1974; Farago, 1964; Irving, 1977; Young, 1974).

Similar concepts still pervade well-conceived strategies—whether they are government, diplomatic, military, sports, or business strategies. What could be more direct than the parallel between Chaeronea and a well-developed business strategy that first probes and withdraws to determine opponents' strengths, forces opponents to stretch their commitments, then concentrates resources, attacks a clear exposure, overwhelms a selected market segment, builds a bridgehead in that market, and then regroups and expands from that base to dominate a wider field? Many companies have followed just such strategies with great success. . . .

DIMENSIONS OF STRATEGY

Analysis of military-diplomatic strategies and similar analogies in other fields provides some essential insights into the basic dimensions, nature, and design of formal strategies.

First, effective formal strategies contain three essential elements: (1) the most important *goals* (or objectives) to be achieved, (2) the most significant *policies* guiding or limiting action, and (3) the major *action sequences* (or programs) that are to accomplish the defined goals within the limits set. Since strategy determines the overall direction and action focus of the organization, its formulation cannot be regarded as the mere generation and alignment of programs to meet predetermined goals. Goal development is an integral part of strategy formulation. . . .

Second, effective strategies develop around a *few key concepts and thrusts,* which give them cohesion, balance, and focus. Some thrusts are temporary; others are carried through to the end of the strategy. Some cost more per unit gain than others. Yet resources must be *allocated in patterns* that provide sufficient resources for each thrust to succeed regardless of its relative cost/gain ratio. And organizational units must be coordinated and actions controlled to support the intended thrust pattern or else the total strategy will fail. . . .

Third, strategy deals not just with the unpredictable but also with the *unknowable.* For major enterprise strategies, no analyst could predict the precise ways in which all impinging forces could interact with each other, be distorted by nature or human emotions, or be modified by the imaginations and purposeful counteractions of intelligent opponents (Braybrooke and Lindblom, 1963). Many have noted how large-scale systems can respond quite counterintuitively (Forrester, 1971) to apparently rational actions or how a seemingly bizarre series of events can conspire to prevent or assist success (White, 1978; Lindblom, 1959). . . .

Consequently, the essence of strategy—whether military, diplomatic, business, sports, (or) political . . .—is to *build a posture* that is so strong (and potentially flexible) in selective ways that the organization can achieve its goals despite the unforeseeable ways external forces may actually interact when the time comes.

Fourth, just as military organizations have multiple echelons of grand, theater, area, battle, infantry, and artillery strategies, so should other complex organizations have a number of hierarchically related and mutually supporting strategies (Vancil and Lorange, 1975; Vancil, 1976). Each such strategy must be more or less complete in itself, congruent with the level of decentralization intended. Yet each must be shaped as a cohesive element of higher-level strategies. Although, for reasons cited, achieving total cohesion among all of a major organization's strategies would be a superhuman task for any chief executive officer, it is important that there be a systematic means for testing each component strategy and seeing that it fulfills the major tenets of a well-formed strategy.

The criteria derived from military-diplomatic strategies provide an excellent framework for this, yet too often one sees purported formal strategies at all organizational levels that are not strategies at all. Because they ignore or violate even the most basic strategic principles, they are little more than aggregates of philosophies or agglomerations of programs. They lack the cohesiveness, flexibility, thrust, sense of positioning against intelligent opposition, and other criteria that historical analysis suggests effective strategies must contain. Whether formally or incrementally derived, strategies should be at least intellectually tested against the proper criteria.

11

THE STRATEGY
CONCEPT

Criteria for Effective Strategy

In devising a strategy to deal with the unknowable, what factors should one consider? Although each strategic situation is unique, are there some common criteria that tend to define a good strategy? The fact that a strategy worked in retrospect is not a sufficient criterion for judging any strategy. Was Grant really a greater strategist than Lee? Was Foch's strategy better than Von Schlieffen's? Was Xerxes's strategy superior to that of Leonidas? Was it the Russians' strategy that allowed them to roll over the Czechoslovaks in 1968? Clearly other factors than strategy—including luck, overwhelming resources, superb or stupid implementation, and enemy errors —help determine ultimate results. Besides, at the time one formulates a strategy, one cannot use the criterion of ultimate success because the outcome is still in doubt. Yet one clearly needs some guidelines to define an effective strategic structure.

A few studies have suggested some initial criteria for evaluating a strategy (Tilles, 1963; Christensen et al., 1978). These include its clarity, motivational impact, internal consistency, compatibility with the environment, appropriateness in light of resources, degree of risk, match to the personal values of key figures, time horizon, and workability. . . . In addition, historical examples—from both business and military-diplomatic settings—suggest that effective strategies should at a minimum encompass certain other critical factors and structural elements. . . .

- *Clear, decisive objectives:* Are all efforts directed toward clearly understood, decisive, and attainable overall goals? Specific goals of subordinate units may change in the heat of campaigns or competition, but the overriding goals of the strategy for all units must remain clear enough to provide continuity and cohesion for tactical choices during the time horizon of the strategy. All goals need not be written down or numerically precise, but they must be understood and be decisive—that is, if they are achieved they should ensure the continued viability and vitality of the entity vis-à-vis its opponents.

- *Maintaining the initiative:* Does the strategy preserve freedom of action and enhance commitment? Does it set the pace and determine the course of events rather than reacting to them? A prolonged reactive posture breeds unrest, lowers morale, and surrenders the advantage of timing and intangibles to opponents. Ultimately such a posture increases costs, decreases the number of options available, and lowers the probability of achieving sufficient success to ensure independence and continuity.

- *Concentration:* Does the strategy concentrate superior power at the place and time likely to be decisive? Has the strategy defined precisely what will make the enterprise superior in power—that is, "best" in critical dimensions—in relation to its opponents. A distinctive competency yields greater success with fewer resources and is the essential basis for higher gains (or profits) than competitors. . . .

- *Flexibility:* Has the strategy purposely built in resource buffers and dimensions for flexibility and maneuver? Reserved capabilities, planned maneuverability, and repositioning allow one to use minimum resources while keeping opponents at a relative disadvantage. As corollaries of concentration and concession, they permit the strategist to reuse the same forces to overwhelm selected positions at different times. They also force less flexible opponents to use more resources to hold predetermined positions, while simultaneously requiring minimum fixed commitment of one's own resources for defensive purposes.

- *Coordinated and committed leadership:* Does the strategy provide responsible, committed leadership for each of its major goals? . . . [Leaders] must be so chosen and motivated that their own interests and values match the needs of their roles. Successful strategies require commitment, not just acceptance.

- *Surprise:* Has the strategy made use of speed, secrecy, and intelligence to attack exposed or unprepared opponents at unexpected times? With surprise and correct timing, success can be achieved out of all proportion to the energy exerted and can decisively change strategic positions. . . .

- *Security:* Does the strategy secure resource bases and all vital operating points for the enterprise? Does it develop an effective intelligence system sufficient to prevent surprises by opponents? Does it develop the full logistics to support each of its major thrusts? Does it use coalitions effectively to extend the resource base and zones of friendly acceptance for the enterprise? . . .

These are critical elements of strategy, whether in business, government, or warfare.

• FIVE Ps FOR STRATEGY*

HENRY MINTZBERG

Human nature insists on *a* definition for every concept. But the word *strategy* has long been used implicitly in different ways even if it has traditionally been defined in only one. Explicit recognition of multiple definitions can help people to maneuver through this difficult field. Accordingly, five definitions of strategy are presented here—as plan, ploy, pattern, position, and perspective—and some of their interrelationships are then considered.

STRATEGY AS PLAN

To almost anyone you care to ask, **strategy is a plan**—some sort of *consciously intended* course of action, a guideline (or set of guidelines) to deal with a situation. A kid has a "strategy" to get over a fence, a corporation has one to capture a market. By this definition, strategies have two essential characteristics: they are made in advance of the actions to which they apply, and they are developed consciously and purposefully. A host of definitions in a variety of fields reinforce this view. For example:

- in the military: Strategy is concerned with "draft[ing] the plan of war . . . shap[ing] the individual campaigns and within these, decid[ing] on the individual engagements" (Von Clausewitz, 1976:177).
- in Game Theory: Strategy is "a complete plan: a plan which specifies what

* Originally published in the *California Management Review* (Fall 1987), © 1987 by the Regents of the University of California. Reprinted with deletions by permission of the *California Management Review*.

choices [the player] will make in every possible situation" (von Newman and Morgenstern, 1944:79).

in management: "Strategy is a unified, comprehensive, and integrated plan . . . designed to ensure that the basic objectives of the enterprise are achieved" (Glueck, 1980:9).

As plans, strategies may be general or they can be specific. There is one use of the word in the specific sense that should be identified here. As plan, **a strategy can be a ploy,** too, really just a specific "maneuver" intended to outwit an opponent or competitor. The kid may use the fence as a ploy to draw a bully into his yard, where his Doberman pinscher awaits intruders. Likewise, a corporation may threaten to expand plant capacity to discourage a competitor from building a new plant. Here the real strategy (as plan, that is, the real intention) is the threat, not the expansion itself, and as such is a ploy.

In fact, there is a growing literature in the field of strategic management, as well as on the general process of bargaining, that views strategy in this way and so focuses attention on its most dynamic and competitive aspects. For example, in his popular book, *Competitive Strategy,* Porter (1980) devotes one chapter to "Market Signals" (including discussion of the effects of announcing moves, the use of "the fighting brand," and the use of threats of private antitrust suits) and another to "Competitive Moves" (including actions to preempt competitive response). And Schelling (1980) devotes much of his famous book, *The Strategy of Conflict,* to the topic of ploys to outwit rivals in a competitive or bargaining situation.

STRATEGY AS PATTERN

But if strategies can be intended (whether as general plans or specific ploys), surely they can also be realized. In other words, defining strategy as a plan is not sufficient; we also need a definition that encompasses the resulting behavior. Thus a third definition is proposed: **strategy is a pattern**—specifically, a pattern in a stream of actions (Mintzberg and Waters, 1985). By this definition, when Picasso painted blue for a time, that was a strategy, just as was the behavior of the Ford Motor Company when Henry Ford offered his Model T only in black. In other words, by this definition, strategy is *consistency* in behavior, *whether or not* intended.

This may sound like a strange definition for a word that has been so bound up with free will ("strategos" in Greek, the art of the army general[1]). But the fact of the matter is that while hardly anyone defines strategy in this way, many people seem at one time or another to so use it. Consider this quotation from a business executive: "Gradually the successful approaches merge into a pattern of action that becomes our strategy. We certainly don't have an overall strategy on this" (quoted in Quinn, 1980:35). This comment is inconsistent only if we restrict ourselves to one definition of strategy: what this man seems to be saying is that his firm has strategy as pattern, but not as plan. Or consider this comment in *Business Week* on a joint venture between General Motors and Toyota:

> The tentative Toyota deal may be most significant because it is another example of how GM's strategy boils down to doing a little bit of everything until the market decides where it is going. (*Business Week,* October 31, 1983)

---

[1] Evered (1983) discusses the Greek origins of the word and traces its entry into contemporary Western vocabulary through the military.

A journalist has inferred a pattern in the behavior of a corporation and labeled it strategy.

The point is that every time a journalist imputes a strategy to a corporation or to a government, and every time a manager does the same thing to a competitor or even to the senior management of his own firm, they are implicitly defining strategy as pattern in action—that is, inferring consistency in behavior and labeling it strategy. They may, of course, go further and impute intention to that consistency—that is, assume there is a plan behind the pattern. But that is an assumption, which may prove false.

Thus, the definitions of strategy as plan and pattern can be quite independent of each other: plans may go unrealized, while patterns may appear without preconception. To paraphrase Hume, strategies may result from human actions but not human designs (see Majone, 1976–77). If we label the first definition *intended* strategy and the second *realized* strategy, as shown in Figure 1, then we can distinguish *deliberate* strategies, where intentions that existed previously were realized, from *emergent* strategies, where patterns developed in the absence of intentions, or despite them (which went *unrealized*).

For a strategy to be truly deliberate—that is, for a pattern to have been intended *exactly* as realized—would seem to be a tall order. Precise intentions would have had to be stated in advance by the leadership of the organization; these would have had to be accepted as is by everyone else, and then realized with no interference by market, technological, or political forces and so on. Likewise, a truly emergent strategy is again a tall order, requiring consistency in action without any hint of intention. (No consistency means *no* strategy, or at least unrealized strategy.) Yet some strategies do come close enough to either form, while others—probably most—sit on the continuum that exists between the two, reflecting deliberate as well as emergent aspects. Table 1 lists various kinds of strategies along this continuum.

Strategies About What?

Labeling strategies as plans or patterns still begs one basic question: *strategies about what?* Many writers respond by discussing the deployment of resources, but the question remains: which resources and for what purposes? An army may plan to reduce the number of nails in its shoes, or a corporation may realize a pattern of

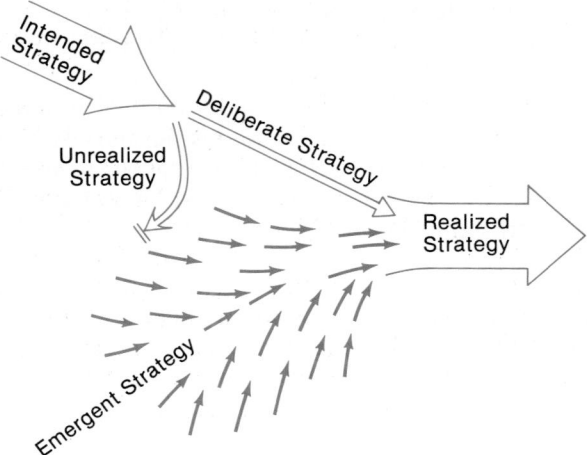

FIGURE 1
Deliberate and Emergent Strategies

TABLE 1   Various Kinds of Strategies, from Rather Deliberate to Mostly Emergent*

Planned Strategy: Precise intentions are formulated and articulated by a central leadership, and backed up by formal controls to ensure their surprise-free implementation in an environment that is benign, controllable, or predictable (to ensure no distortion of intentions); these strategies are highly deliberate.

Entrepreneurial Strategy: Intentions exist as the personal, unarticulated vision of a single leader, and so are adaptable to new opportunities; the organization is under the personal control of the leader and located in a protected niche in its environment; these strategies are relatively deliberate but can emerge too.

Ideological Strategy: Intentions exist as the collective vision of all the members of the organization, controlled through strong shared norms; the organization is often proactive vis-à-vis its environment; these strategies are rather deliberate.

Umbrella Strategy: A leadership in partial control of organizational actions defines strategic targets or boundaries within which others must act (for example, that all new products be high priced and at the technological cutting edge, although what these actual products are to be is left to emerge); as a result, strategies are partly deliberate (the boundaries) and partly emergent (the patterns within them); this strategy can also be called deliberately emergent, in that the leadership purposefully allows others the flexibility to maneuver and form patterns within the boundaries.

Process Strategy: The leadership controls the process aspects of strategy (who gets hired and so gets a chance to influence strategy, what structures they work within, etc.), leaving the actual content of strategy to others; strategies are again partly deliberate (concerning process) and partly emergent (concerning content), and deliberately emergent.

Disconnected Strategy: Members or subunits loosely coupled to the rest of the organization produce patterns in the streams of their own actions in the absence of, or in direct contradiction to the central or common intentions of the organization at large; the strategies can be deliberate for those who make them.

Consensus Strategy: Through mutual adjustment, various members converge on patterns that pervade the organization in the absence of central or common intentions; these strategies are rather emergent in nature.

Imposed Strategy: The external environment dictates patterns in actions, either through direct imposition (say, by an outside owner or by a strong customer) or through implicitly preempting or bounding organizational choice (as in a large airline that must fly jumbo jets to remain viable); these strategies are organizationally emergent, although they may be internalized and made deliberate.

* Adapted from Mintzberg and Waters (1985:270).

marketing only products painted black, but these hardly meet the lofty label "strategy." Or do they?

As the word has been handed down from the military, "strategy" refers to the important things, "tactics" to the details (more formally, "tactics teaches the use of armed forces in the engagement, strategy the use of engagements for the object of the war," von Clausewitz, 1976:128). Nails in shoes, colors of cars; these are certainly details. The problem is that in retrospect details can sometimes prove "strategic." Even in the military: "For want of a Nail, the Shoe was lost; for want of a Shoe the Horse was lost . . . ," and so on through the rider and general to the battle, "all for want of Care about a Horseshoe Nail" (Franklin, 1977:280). Indeed one of the reasons Henry Ford lost his war with General Motors was that he refused to paint his cars anything but black.

Rumelt (1979) notes that "one person's strategies are another's tactics—that what is strategic depends on where you sit." It also depends on *when* you sit; what seems tactical today may prove strategic tomorrow. The point is that labels should not be used to imply that some issues are *inevitably* more important than others. There are times when it pays to manage the details and let the strategies emerge for themselves. Thus there is good reason to refer to issues as more or less "strategic," in other words, more or less "important" in some context, whether as intended before acting or as realized after it. Accordingly, the answer to the question, strategy about what, is: potentially about anything. About products and processes, customers and citizens, social responsibilities and self interests, control and color.

Two aspects of the content of strategies must, however, be singled out because they are of particular importance.

15

The fourth definition is that **strategy is a position**—specifically, a means of locating an organization in what organization theorists like to call an "environment." By this definition, strategy becomes the mediating force—or "match," according to Hofer and Schendel (1978:4)—between organization and environment, that is, between the internal and the external context. In ecological terms, strategy becomes a "niche"; in economic terms, a place that generates "rent" (that is "returns to [being] in a 'unique' place" (Bowman, 1974:47)); in management terms, formally, a product-market "domain" (Thompson, 1967), the place in the environment where resources are concentrated.

Note that this definition of strategy can be compatible with either (or all) of the preceding ones; a position can be preselected and aspired to through a plan (or ploy) and/or it can be reached, perhaps even found, through a pattern of behavior.

In military and game theory views of strategy, it is generally used in the context of what is called a "two-person game," better known in business as head-on competition (where ploys are especially common). The definition of strategy as position, however, implicitly allows us to open up the concept, to so-called n-person games (that is, many players), and beyond. In other words, while position can always be defined with respect to a single competitor (literally so in the military, where position becomes the site of battle), it can also be considered in the context of a number of competitors or simply with respect to markets or an environment at large. But strategy as position can extend beyond competition too, economic and otherwise. Indeed, what is the meaning of the word "niche" but a position that is occupied to *avoid* competition. Thus, we can move from the definition employed by General Ulysses Grant in the 1860s, "Strategy [is] the deployment of one's resources in a manner which is most likely to defeat the enemy," to that of Professor Richard Rumelt in the 1980s, "Strategy is creating situations for economic rents and finding ways to sustain them,"[2] that is, any viable position, whether or not directly competitive.

Astley and Fombrun (1983), in fact, take the next logical step by introducing the notion of "collective" strategy, that is, strategy pursued to promote cooperation between organizations, even would-be competitors (equivalent in biology to animals herding together for protection). Such strategies can range "from informal arrangements and discussions to formal devices such as interlocking directorates, joint ventures, and mergers" (p. 577). In fact, considered from a slightly different angle, these can sometimes be described as *political* strategies, that is strategies to subvert the legitimate forces of competition.

STRATEGY AS PERSPECTIVE

While the fourth definition of strategy looks out, seeking to locate the organization in the external environment, and down to concrete positions, the fifth looks inside the organization, indeed inside the heads of the collective strategist, but up to a broader view. Here, **strategy is a perspective,** its content consisting not just of a chosen position, but of an ingrained way of perceiving the world. There are organizations that favor marketing and build a whole ideology around that (an IBM); Hewlett-Packard has developed the "H-P way," based on its engineering culture,

---

[2] Expressed at the Strategic Management Society Conference, Montreal, October 1982.

while McDonald's has become famous for its emphasis on "quality, service, cleanliness, and value."

Strategy in this respect is to the organization what personality is to the individual. Indeed, one of the earliest and most influential writers on strategy (at least as his ideas have been reflected in more popular writings) was Philip Selznick (1957:47), who wrote about the "character" of an organization—distinct and integrated "commitments to ways of acting and responding" that are built right into it. A variety of concepts from other fields also capture this notion; anthropologists refer to the "culture" of a society and sociologists to its "ideology"; military theorists write of the "grand strategy" of armies; while management theorists have used terms such as the "theory of the business" and its "driving force" (Drucker, 1974; Tregoe and Zimmerman, 1980); and Germans perhaps capture it best with their word "Weltanschauung," literally "worldview," meaning collective intuition about how the world works.

This fifth definition suggests above all that strategy is a *concept.* This has one important implication, namely, that all strategies are abstractions which exist only in the minds of interested parties. It is important to remember that no one has ever seen a strategy or touched one; every strategy is an invention, a figment of someone's imagination, whether conceived of as intentions to regulate behavior before it takes place or inferred as patterns to describe behavior that has already occurred.

What is of key importance about this fifth definition, however, is that the perspective is *shared.* As implied in the words Weltanschauung, culture, and ideology (with respect to a society), but not the word personality, strategy is a perspective shared by the members of an organization, through their intentions and/or by their actions. In effect, when we are talking of strategy in this context, we are entering the realm of the *collective mind*—individuals united by common thinking and/or behavior. A major issue in the study of strategy formation becomes, therefore, how to read that collective mind—to understand how intentions diffuse through the system called organization to become shared and how actions come to be exercised on a collective yet consistent basis.

INTERRELATING THE Ps

As suggested above, strategy as both position and perspective can be compatible with strategy as plan and/or pattern. But, in fact, the relationships between these different definitions can be more involved than that. For example, while some consider perspective to *be* a plan (Lapierre, 1980, writes of strategies as "dreams in search of reality"), others describe it as *giving rise* to plans (for example, as positions and/or patterns in some kind of implicit hierarchy). But the concept of emergent strategy is that a pattern can emerge and be recognized so that it gives rise to a formal plan, perhaps within an overall perspective.

We may ask how perspective arises in the first place. Probably through earlier experiences: the organization tried various things in its formative years and gradually consolidated a perspective around what worked. In other words, organizations would appear to develop "character" much as people develop personality—by interacting with the world as they find it through the use of their innate skills and natural propensities. Thus pattern can give rise to perspective too. And so can position. Witness Perrow's (1970:161) discussion of the "wool men" and "silk men" of the textile trade, people who developed an almost religious dedication to the fibers they produced.

No matter how they appear, however, there is reason to believe that while plans and positions may be dispensable, perspectives are immutable (Brunsson,

1982). In other words, once they are established, perspectives become difficult to change. Indeed, a perspective may become so deeply ingrained in the behavior of an organization that the associated beliefs can become subconscious in the minds of its members. When that happens, perspective can come to look more like pattern than like plan—in other words, it can be found more in the consistency of behaviors than in the articulation of intentions.

Of course, if perspective is immutable, then change in plan and position within perspective is easy compared to change outside perspective. In this regard, it is interesting to take up the case of Egg McMuffin. Was this product when new—the American breakfast in a bun—a strategic change for the McDonald's fast-food chain? Posed in MBA classes, this earth-shattering (or at least stomach-shattering) question inevitably evokes heated debate. Proponents (usually people sympathetic to fast food) argue that of course it was: it brought McDonald's into a new market, the breakfast one, extending the use of existing facilities. Opponents retort that this is nonsense; nothing changed but a few ingredients: this was the same old pap in a new package. Both sides are, of course, right—and wrong. It simply depends on how you define strategy. Position changed; perspective remained the same. Indeed —and this is the point—the position could be changed easily because it was compatible with the existing perspective. Egg McMuffin is pure McDonald's, not only in product and package, but also in production and propagation. But imagine a change of position at McDonald's that would require a change of perspective—say, to introduce candlelight dining with personal service (your McDuckling à l'Orange cooked to order) to capture the late evening market. We needn't say more, except perhaps to label this the "Egg McMuffin syndrome."

THE NEED FOR ECLECTICISM IN DEFINITION

While various relationships exist among the different definitions, no one relationship, nor any single definition for that matter, takes precedence over the others. In some ways, these definitions compete (in that they can substitute for each other), but in perhaps more important ways, they complement. Not all plans become patterns nor are all patterns that develop planned; some ploys are less than positions, while other strategies are more than positions yet less than perspectives. Each definition adds important elements to our understanding of strategy, indeed encourages us to address fundamental questions about organizations in general.

As plan, strategy deals with how leaders try to establish direction for organizations, to set them on predetermined courses of action. Strategy as plan also raises the fundamental issue of cognition—how intentions are conceived in the human brain in the first place, indeed, what intentions really mean. The road to hell in this field can be paved with those who take all stated intentions at face value. In studying strategy as plan, we must somehow get into the mind of the strategist, to find out what is really intended.

As ploy, strategy takes us into the realm of direct competition, where threats and feints and various other maneuvers are employed to gain advantage. This places the process of strategy formation in its most dynamic setting, with moves provoking countermoves and so on. Yet ironically, strategy itself is a concept rooted not in change but in stability—in set plans and established patterns. How then to reconcile the dynamic notions of strategy as ploy with the static ones of strategy as pattern and other forms of plan?

As pattern, strategy focuses on action, reminding us that the concept is an empty one if it does not take behavior into account. Strategy as pattern also introduces the notion of convergence, the achievement of consistency in an organization's behavior. How does this consistency form, where does it come from? Realized strategy, when considered alongside intended strategy, encourages us to consider the notion that strategies can emerge as well as be deliberately imposed.

As position, strategy encourages us to look at organizations in their competitive environments—how they find their positions and protect them in order to meet competition, avoid it, or subvert it. This enables us to think of organizations in ecological terms, as organisms in niches that struggle for survival in a world of hostility and uncertainty as well as symbiosis.

And finally as perspective, strategy raises intriguing questions about intention and behavior in a collective context. If we define organization as collective action in the pursuit of common mission (a fancy way of saying that a group of people under a common label—whether a General Motors or a Luigi's Body Shop —somehow find the means to cooperate in the production of specific goods and services), then strategy as perspective raises the issue of how intentions diffuse through a group of people to become shared as norms and values, and how patterns of behavior become deeply ingrained in the group.

Thus, strategy is not just a notion of how to deal with an enemy or a set of competitors or a market, as it is treated in so much of the literature and in its popular usage. It also draws us into some of the most fundamental issues about organizations as instruments for collective perception and action.

To conclude, a good deal of the confusion in this field stems from contradictory and ill-defined uses of the term strategy. By explicating and using various definitions, we may be able to avoid some of this confusion, and thereby enrich our ability to understand and manage the processes by which strategies form.

CHAPTER

2

THE STRATEGIST

Every conventional strategy or policy textbook focuses on the job of the general manager as a main ingredient in understanding the process of strategy formation. The discussion of emergent strategy in the last chapter suggests that we do not take such a narrow view of the strategist. Anyone in the organization who happens to control key or precedent setting actions can be a strategist; the strategist can be a *collection* of people as well. Nevertheless, managers—especially senior general managers—are obviously prime candidates for such a role because their perspective is generally broader than any of their subordinates and because so much power naturally resides with them. Hence we focus in this chapter on the general manager as strategist.

We present three readings that describe the work of the manager. The one by Mintzberg challenges the conventional view of the manager as planner, organizer, coordinator, and controller. The point is not that managers do not do these things; it is that these words are too vague to capture the daily reality of managerial work. The image presented in this article is a very different one; a job characterized by pressure, interruption, orientation to action, oral rather than written communication, and working with outsiders and colleagues as much as with so-called subordinates. While the issue is not addressed at this point in any detail, one evident and important conclusion is that managers who work in such ways cannot possibly function as traditionally depicted strategists supposedly do—as leaders directing their organizations the way conductors direct their orchestras (at least the way it looks on the podium). We shall develop this point further in Chapter 5, when we consider how strategies really are formed in organizations.

The article by Edward Wrapp, of the University of Chicago and well known in management development circles, provides at least one widely referenced model illustrating how this does happen in large organizations. He depicts managers as somewhat political animals, providing broad guidance, but facilitating or pushing through their strategies, bit by bit, in rather unexpected ways. They rarely state specific goals. They practice "the art of imprecision," trying to "avoid policy strait-jackets," while concentrating on only a few really significant issues. They move whenever possible through "corridors of comparative indifference" to avoid undue opposition, at the same time they are trying to ensure that the organization has a cohesive sense of direction. Wrapp's observations challenge the more prescriptive views of strategy formulation, but elements of them can be observed in many of the cases, notably IBM (A), Pillsbury Co., Continental Group, General Mills, and Mountbatten and India.

Philip Selznick, a famous Berkeley sociologist, offers another perspective on the manager as strategist in the third reading. It is not just his or her role in the *creation* of strategy so much as in its *institutionalization* that counts—the establishment of commitment among the people who make up the organization. In this reading, the full meaning of the view of strategy as perspective emerges—not as a calculated position but as a deep-rooted perspective. Selznick's brief but brilliant essay, written in the 1950s, introduced a number of concepts that subsequently became the foundation for much of our current thinking about business strategy (which, incidentally, both he and Wrapp refer to as "policy")—the selection of mission, the notion of distinctive competence, the definition of "organization character," and so on. Note also the differences between Selznick's and Wrapp's view of the manager, especially with regard to the articulation of purpose, or direction. Are they describing different contexts in which managers work? Might the two views sometimes be compatible in the same managerial job?

Selznick also discusses the role of values in managerial work, specifically the manager's role to "infuse [the organization] with value." Much strategy-making behavior is heavily influenced by values; individual managers looking at the same data may choose quite different strategies based on what they believe, that is, their values. Values provide the perceptive screen or "prism" through which individual managers sift and weigh different options, opportunities, or threats. They provide the "utility system" of the economist and the expectations of desired or unacceptable behavior that become the "culture" of an organization.

We introduce some of these concepts in our brief excerpts from Selznick's book to try to capture in his words ideas that will recur throughout the readings and cases of this book. This reading is not always an easy one, and our editing of it may make it somewhat disjointed. But it is well worth your effort. The reading is brief, but it is an important premier statement on the role of leadership values in organizations. Peters and Waterman, in their book *In Search of Excellence,* refer to this "often-overlooked" book as "beautifully describ[ing]" these and other traits "basic to the success of the excellent companies" (1982:85, 98).

The impact of values in strategic decision making shows up most clearly in the cases on Gallo Wineries, New York Times, Hewlett-Packard, Genentech, Sony, Pilkington, and Matsushita. But values issues pervade virtually all the cases, including the military strategies in The Guns of August and the diplomatic strategies in Mountbatten and India. They are a major issues in designing or carrying out any real life strategy.

● THE MANAGER'S JOB: FOLKLORE AND FACT*

BY HENRY MINTZBERG

If you ask managers what they do, they will most likely tell you that they plan, organize, coordinate, and control. Then watch what they do. Don't be surprised if you can't relate what you see to these four words.

---

* Originally published in the *Harvard Business Review* (July–August 1975) and winner of the McKinsey prize for the best article in the *Review* in 1975. Copyright © 1975 by the President and Fellows of Harvard College; all rights reserved. Reprinted with deletions by permission of the *Harvard Business Review.*

When they are called and told that one of their factories has just burned down, and they advise the caller to see whether temporary arrangements can be made to supply customers through a foreign subsidiary, are they planning, organizing, coordinating, or controlling? How about when they present a gold watch to a retiring employee? Or when they attend a conference to meet people in the trade? Or on returning from that conference, when they tell one of their employees about an interesting product idea they picked up there?

The fact is that these four words, which have dominated management vocabulary since the French industrialist Henri Fayol first introduced them in 1916, tell us little about what managers actually do. At best, they indicate some vague objectives managers have when they work.

My intention in this article is simple: to break the reader away from Fayol's words and introduce him or her to a more supportable, and what I believe to be a more useful, description of managerial work. This description derives from my review and synthesis of the available research on how various managers have spent their time.

In some studies, managers were observed intensively ("shadowed" is the term some of them used); in a number of others, they kept detailed diaries of their activities; in a few studies, their records were analyzed. All kinds of managers were studied—foremen, factory supervisors, staff managers, field sales managers, hospital administrators, presidents of companies and nations, and even street gang leaders. These "managers" worked in the United States, Canada, Sweden, and Great Britain.

A synthesis of these findings paints an interesting picture, one as different from Fayol's classical view as a cubist abstract is from a Renaissance painting. In a sense, this picture will be obvious to anyone who has ever spent a day in a manager's office, either in front of the desk or behind it. Yet, at the same time, this picture may turn out to be revolutionary, in that it throws into doubt so much of the folklore that we have accepted about the manager's work.

I first discuss some of this folklore and contrast it with some of the findings of systematic research—the hard facts about how managers spend their time. Then I synthesize those research findings in a description of ten roles that seem to describe the essential content of all managers' jobs. In a concluding section, I discuss a number of implications of this synthesis for those trying to achieve more effective management.

SOME FOLKLORE AND FACTS ABOUT MANAGERIAL WORK

There are four myths about the manager's job that do not bear up under careful scrutiny of the facts.

Folklore: The manager is a reflective, systematic planner. The evidence on this issue is overwhelming, but not a shred of it supports this statement.

Fact: Study after study has shown that managers work at an unrelenting pace, that their activities are characterized by brevity, variety, and discontinuity, and that they are strongly oriented to action and dislike reflective activities. Consider this evidence:

- Half the activities engaged in by the five [American] chief executives [that I studied in my own research (Mintzberg, 1973a)] lasted less than nine minutes, and only 10% exceeded one hour. A study of 56 U.S. foremen found that they averaged 583 activities per eight-hour shift, an average of 1 every 48 seconds (Guest, 1956:478). The work pace for both chief executives and foremen was unrelenting. The chief executives met a steady stream of callers and mail from the moment they arrived in the morning until they left in the evening. Coffee breaks and lunches were inevitably work related, and ever-present subordinates seemed to usurp any free moment.

A diary study of 160 British middle and top managers found that they worked for a half hour or more without interruption only about once every two days (Stewart, 1967).

Of the verbal contacts of the chief executives in my study, 93% were arranged on an ad hoc basis. Only 1% of the executives' time was spent in open-ended observational tours. Only 1 out of 368 verbal contacts was unrelated to a specific issue and could be called general planning. Another researcher finds that "in *not one single case* did a manager report the obtaining of important external information from a general conversation or other undirected personal communication" (Aguilar, 1967:102).

No study has found important patterns in the way managers schedule their time. They seem to jump from issue to issue, continually responding to the needs of the moment.

Is this the planner that the classical view describes? Hardly. How, then, can we explain this behavior? The manager is simply responding to the pressures of the job. I found that my chief executives terminated many of their own activities, often leaving meetings before the end and interrupted their desk work to call in subordinates. One president not only placed his desk so that he could look down a long hallway but also left his door open when he was alone—an invitation for subordinates to come in and interrupt him.

Clearly, these managers wanted to encourage the flow of current information. But more significantly, they seemed to be conditioned by their own work loads. They appreciated the opportunity cost of their own time, and they were continually aware of their ever-present obligations—mail to be answered, callers to attend to, and so on. It seems that no matter what he or she is doing, the manager is plagued by the possibilities of what he or she might do and must do.

When the manager must plan, he or she seems to do so implicitly in the context of daily actions, not in some abstract process reserved for two weeks in the organization's mountain retreat. The plans of the chief executives I studied seemed to exist only in their heads—as flexible, but often specific, intentions. The traditional literature not-withstanding, the job of managing does not breed reflective planners; the manager is a real-time responder to stimuli, an individual who is conditioned by his or her job to prefer live to delayed action.

Folklore: The effective manager has no regular duties to perform. Managers are constantly being told to spend more time planning and delegating, and less time seeing customers and engaging in negotiations. These are not, after all, the true tasks of the manager. To use the popular analogy, the good manager, like the good conductor, carefully orchestrates everything in advance, then sits back to enjoy the fruits of his or her labor, responding occasionally to an unforeseeable exception. . . .

Fact: In addition to handling exceptions, managerial work involves performing a number of regular duties, including ritual and ceremony, negotiations, and proc-

essing of soft information that links the organization with its environment. Consider some evidence from the research studies:

- A study of the work of the presidents of small companies found that they engaged in routine activities because their companies could not afford staff specialists and were so thin on operating personnel that a single absence often required the president to substitute (Choran in Mintzberg, 1973a).
- One study of field sales managers and another of chief executives suggest that it is a natural part of both jobs to see important customers, assuming the managers wish to keep those customers (Davis, 1957; Copeman, 1963).
- Someone, only half in jest, once described the manager as that person who sees visitors so that everyone else can get his or her work done. In my study, I found that certain ceremonial duties—meeting visiting dignitaries, giving out gold watches, presiding at Christmas dinners—were an intrinsic part of the chief executive's job.
- Studies of managers' information flow suggest that managers play a key role in securing "soft" external information (much of it available only to them because of their status) and in passing it along to their subordinates.

Folklore: The senior manager needs aggregated information, which a formal management information system best provides. In keeping with the classical view of the manager as that individual perched on the apex of a regulated, hierarchical system, the literature's manager was to receive all important information from a giant, comprehensive MIS.

But this never proved true at all. A look at how managers actually process information makes the reason quite clear. Managers have five media at their command—documents, telephone calls, scheduled and unscheduled meetings, and observational tours.

Fact: Managers strongly favor the verbal media—namely, telephone calls and meetings. The evidence comes from every single study of managerial work: Consider the following:

- In two British studies, managers spent an average of 66% and 80% of their time in verbal (oral) communication (Stewart, 1967; Burns, 1954). In my study of five American chief executives, the figure was 78%.
- These five chief executives treated mail processing as a burden to be dispensed with. One came in Saturday morning to process 142 pieces of mail in just over three hours, to "get rid of all the stuff." This same manager looked at the first piece of "hard" mail he had received all week, a standard cost report, and put it aside with the comment, "I never look at this."
- These same five chief executives responded immediately to 2 of the 40 routine reports they received during the five weeks of my study and to four items in the 104 periodicals. They skimmed most of these periodicals in seconds, almost ritualistically. In all, these chief executives of good-sized organizations initiated on their own—that is, not in response to something else—a grand total of 25 pieces of mail during the 25 days I observed them.

An analysis of the mail the executives received reveals an interesting picture —only 13% was of specific and immediate use. So now we have another piece in the puzzle: not much of the mail provides live, current information—the action of a competitor, the mood of a government legislator, or the rating of last night's television show. Yet this is the information that drove the managers, interrupting their meetings and rescheduling their workdays.

Consider another interesting finding. Managers seem to cherish "soft" information, especially gossip, hearsay, and speculation. Why? The reason is its timeliness; today's gossip may be tomorrow's fact. The manager who is not accessible for the telephone call informing him or her that the firm's biggest customer was seen golfing with its main competitor may read about a dramatic drop in sales in the next quarterly report. But then it's too late.

Consider the words of Richard Neustadt, who studied the information-collecting habits of Presidents Roosevelt, Truman, and Eisenhower:

> It is not information of a general sort that helps a President see personal stakes; not summaries, not surveys, not the *bland amalgams*. Rather . . . it is the odds and ends of *tangible detail* that pieced together in his mind illuminate the underside of issues put before him. To help himself he must reach out as widely as he can for every scrap of fact, opinion, gossip, bearing on his interests and relationships as President. He must become his own director of his own central intelligence (1960:153–154; italics added).

The manager's emphasis on the verbal media raises two important points:

First, verbal information is stored in the brains of people. Only when people write this information down can it be stored in the files of the organization—whether in metal cabinets or on magnetic tape—and managers apparently do not write down much of what they hear. Thus the strategic data bank of the organization is not in the memory of its computers but in the minds of its managers.

Second, the managers' extensive use of verbal media helps to explain why they are reluctant to delegate tasks. When we note that most of the managers' important information comes in verbal form and is stored in their heads, we can well appreciate their reluctance. It is not as if they can hand a dossier over to someone; they must take the time to "dump memory"—to tell that someone all they know about the subject. But this could take so long that the managers may find it easier to do the task themselves. Thus the managers are damned by their own information systems to a "dilemma of delegation"—to do too much themselves or to delegate to their subordinates with inadequate briefing.

Folklore: Management is, or at least is quickly becoming, a science and a profession. By almost any definitions of *science* and *profession,* this statement is false. Brief observation of any manager will quickly lay to rest the notion that managers practice a science. A science involves the enaction of systematic, analytically determined procedures or programs. If we do not even know what procedures managers use, how can we prescribe them by scientific analysis? And how can we call management a profession if we cannot specify what managers are to learn?

Fact: The managers' programs—to schedule time, process information, make decisions, and so on—remain locked deep inside their brains. Thus, to describe these programs, we rely on words like *judgment* and *intuition,* seldom stopping to realize that they are merely labels for our ignorance.

I was struck during my study by the fact that the executives I was observing —all very competent by any standard—are fundamentally indistinguishable from their counterparts of a hundred years ago (or a thousand years ago, for that matter). The information they need differs, but they seek it in the same way—by word of mouth. Their decisions concern modern technology, but the procedures they use to make them are the same as the procedures of the nineteenth-century manager. In fact, the manager is in a kind of loop, with increasingly heavy work pressures but no aid forthcoming from management science.

Considering the facts about managerial work, we can see that the manager's job is enormously complicated and difficult. The manager is overburdened with obligations; yet he or she cannot easily delegate tasks. As a result, he or she is driven to overwork and is forced to do many tasks superficially. Brevity, fragmentation, and verbal communication characterize the work. Yet these are the very characteristics of managerial work that have impeded scientific attempts to improve it. As a result, the management scientists have concentrated their efforts on the specialized functions of the organization, where they could more easily analyze the procedures and quantify the relevant information. Thus the first step in providing managers with some help is to find out what their job really is.

BACK TO A BASIC DESCRIPTION OF MANAGERIAL WORK

Now let us try to put some of the pieces of this puzzle together. Earlier, I defined the manager as that person in charge of an organization or one of its subunits. Besides chief executive officers, this definition would include vice presidents, bishops, foremen, hockey coaches, and prime ministers. Can all of these people have anything in common? Indeed they can. For an important starting point, all are vested with formal authority over an organizational unit. From formal authority comes status, which leads to various interpersonal relations, and from these comes access to information. Information, in turn, enables the manager to make decisions and strategies for his or her unit.

The manager's job can be described in terms of various "roles," or organized sets of behaviors identified with a position. My description, shown in Figure 1, comprises ten roles.

Interpersonal Roles

Three of the manager's roles arise directly from formal authority and involve basic interpersonal relationships.

1. First is the *figurehead* role. By virtue of his or her position as head of an organizational unit, every manager must perform some duties of a ceremonial nature. The president greets the touring dignitaries, the foreman attends the wedding of a lathe operator, and the sales manager takes an important customer to lunch.

The chief executives of my study spend 12% of their contact time on ceremonial duties; 17% of their incoming mail dealt with acknowledgments and requests related to their status. For example, a letter to a company president requested free merchandise for a crippled schoolchild; diplomas were put on the desk of the school superintendent for his signature.

Duties that involve interpersonal roles may sometimes be routine, involving little serious communication and no important decision making. Nevertheless, they are important to the smooth functioning of an organization and cannot be ignored by the manager.

2. Because he or she is in charge of an organizational unit, the manager is responsible for the work of the people of that unit. His or her actions in this regard constitute the *leader* role. Some of these actions involve leadership directly—for

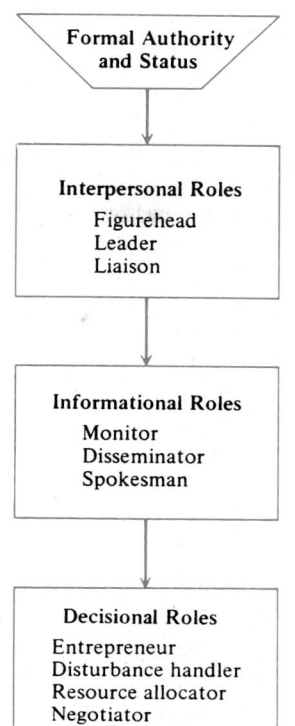

FIGURE 1
The Manager's Roles

example, in most organizations the manager is normally responsible for hiring and training his or her own staff.

In addition, there is the indirect exercise of the leader role. Every manager must motivate and encourage his or her employees, somehow reconciling their individual needs with the goals of the organization. In virtually every contact the manager has with these employees, subordinates seeking leadership clues probe his or her actions: "Does he approve?" "How would she like the report to turn out?" "Is he more interested in market share than high profits?"

The influence of managers is most clearly seen in the leader role. Formal authority vests them with great potential power; leadership determines in large part how much of it they will realize.

3. The literature of management has always recognized the leader role, particularly those aspects of it related to motivation. In comparison, until recently it has hardly mentioned the *liaison* role, in which the manager makes contacts outside his or her vertical chain of command. This is remarkable in light of the finding of virtually every study of managerial work that managers spend as much time with peers and other people outside their units as they do with their own subordinates —and, surprisingly, very little time with their own superiors (generally on the order of 45%, 45%, and 10% respectively).

The contacts the five CEOs made were with an incredibly wide range of people: subordinates; clients, business associates, and suppliers; and peers—managers of similar organizations, government and trade organization officials, fellow directors on outside boards, and independents with no relevant organizational affiliations. The chief executives' time with and mail from these groups is shown in Figure 2.

27

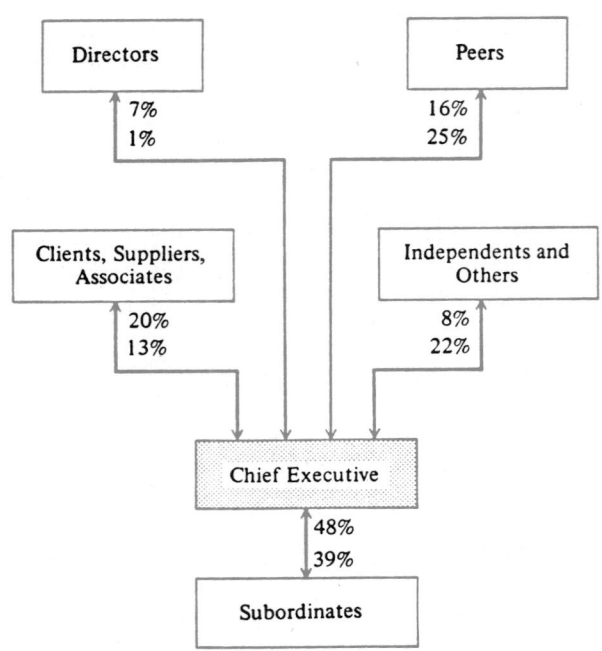

FIGURE 2
The Chief Executives'
Contacts

As we shall see shortly, the manager cultivates such contacts largely to find information. In effect, the liaison role is devoted to building up the manager's own external information system—informal, private, verbal, but, nevertheless, effective.

Informational Roles

By virtue of their interpersonal contacts, both with subordinates and with their network of contacts, managers emerge as the nerve centers of their organizational units. They may not know everything, but they typically know more than any other member of their unit.

Studies have shown this relationship to hold for all managers, from street gang leaders to U.S. presidents. In *The Human Group,* George C. Homans (1950) explains how, because they were at the center of the information flow in their own gangs and were also in close touch with other gang leaders, street gang leaders were better informed than any of their followers. And Richard Neustadt describes the following account from his study of Franklin D. Roosevelt:

> The essence of Roosevelt's technique for information-gathering was competition. "He would call you in," one of his aides once told me, "and he'd ask you to get the story on some complicated business, and you'd come back after a couple of days of hard labor and present the juicy morsel you'd uncovered under a stone somewhere, and *then* you'd find out he knew all about it, along with something else you *didn't* know. Where he got this information from he wouldn't mention, usually, but after he had done this to you once or twice you got damn careful about *your* information." (1960:157).

We can see where Roosevelt "got this information" when we consider the relationship between the interpersonal and informational roles. As leaders, managers have formal and easy access to every member of their units. Hence, as noted earlier, they tend to know more about their own unit than anyone else does. In addition, their liaison contacts expose the managers to external information to which their subordinates often lack access. Many of these contacts are with other managers of equal status, who are themselves nerve centers in their own organization. In this way, managers develop powerful data bases of information.

The processing of information is a key part of the manager's job. In my study, the chief executives spent 40% of their contact time on activities devoted exclusively to the transmission of information; 70% of their incoming mail was purely informational (as opposed to requests for action). The manager does not leave meetings or hang up the telephone in order to get back to work. In large part, communication *is* his or her work. Three roles describe these informational aspects of managerial work.

4. As *monitor,* the manager perpetually scans the environment for information, interrogates his or her liaison contacts and subordinates, and receives unsolicited information, much of it as a result of the network of personal contacts he or she has developed. Remember that a good part of the information the manager collects in the monitor role arrives in verbal form, often as gossip, hearsay, and speculation. By virtue of his or her contacts, the manager has a natural advantage in collecting this soft information.

5. Managers must share and distribute much of this information. Information gleaned from outside personal contacts may be needed within the unit. In their *disseminator* roles, managers pass some of their privileged information directly to their subordinates, who would otherwise have no access to it. When their subordinates lack easy contact with one another, managers will sometimes pass information from one to another.

6. In their *spokesperson* roles, managers send some of their information to people outside their units—a president makes a speech to lobby for an organization cause, or a foreman suggests a product modification to a supplier. In addition, as part of their roles as spokesperson, every manager must inform and satisfy the influential people who control his or her organizational unit. Chief executives especially may spend great amounts of time with hosts of influencers. Directors and shareholders must be advised about financial performance; consumer groups must be assured that the organization is fulfilling its social responsibilities, and so on.

Decisional Roles

Information is not, of course, an end in itself; it is the basic input to decision making. One thing is clear in the study of managerial work: managers play the major role in their unit's decision-making system. As its formal authority, only they can commit the unit to important new courses of action; and as its nerve center, only they have full and current information to make the set of decisions that determine the unit's strategy. Four roles describe the manager as decision maker.

7. As *entrepreneur,* the manager seeks to improve the unit, to adapt it to changing conditions in the environment. In the monitor role, the president is constantly on the lookout for new ideas. When a good one appears, he or she initiates a development project that he or she may supervise himself or delegate to an employee (perhaps with the stipulation that he or she must approve the final proposal).

There are two interesting features about these development projects at the chief executive level. First, these projects do not involve single decisions or even unified clusters of decisions. Rather, they emerge as a series of small decisions and actions sequenced over time. Apparently, chief executives prolong each project so that they can fit it bit by bit into their busy, disjointed schedules and so that they can gradually come to comprehend the issue, if it is a complex one.

Second, the chief executives I studied supervised as many as 50 of these projects at the same time. Some projects entailed new products or processes; others involved public relations campaigns, improvement of the cash position, reorganization of a weak department, resolution of a morale problem in a foreign division, integration of computer operations, various acquisitions at different stages of development, and so on.

The chief executive appears to maintain a kind of inventory of the development projects that he or she supervises—projects that are at various stages of development, some active and some in limbo. Like a juggler, he or she keeps a number of projects in the air; periodically, one comes down, is given a new burst of energy, and is sent back into orbit. At various intervals, he or she puts new projects onstream and discards old ones.

8.   While the entrepreneur role describes the manager as the voluntary initiator of change, the *disturbance handler* role depicts the manager involuntarily responding to pressures. Here change is beyond the manager's control. A strike looms, a major customer has gone bankrupt, or a supplier reneges on his contract.

It has been fashionable, I noted earlier, to compare the manager to an orchestra conductor, just as Peter F. Drucker wrote in *The Practice of Management:*

> The manager has the task of creating a true whole that is larger than the sum of its parts, a productive entity that turns out more than the sum of the resources put into it. One analogy is the conductor of a symphony orchestra, through whose effort, vision and leadership individual instrumental parts that are so much noise by themselves become the living whole of music. But the conductor has the composer's score; he is only interpreter. The manager is both composer and conductor. (1954:341–342)

Now consider the words of Leonard R. Sayles, who has carried out systematic research on the manager's job:

> [The manager] is like a symphony orchestra conductor, endeavouring to maintain a melodious performance in which the contributions of the various instruments are coordinated and sequenced, patterned and paced, while the orchestra members are having various personal difficulties, stage hands are moving music stands, alternating excessive heat and cold are creating audience and instrument problems, and the sponsor of the concert is insisting on irrational changes in the program. (1964:162)

In effect, every manager must spend a good part of his or her time responding to high-pressure disturbances. No organization can be so well run, so standardized, that it has considered every contingency in advance. Disturbances arise not only because poor managers ignore situations until they reach crisis proportions, but also because good managers cannot possibly anticipate all the consequences of the actions they take.

9.   The third decisional role is that of *resource allocator.* To the manager falls the responsibility of deciding who will get what in his or her organizational unit. Perhaps the most important resource the manager allocates is his or her own time. Access to the manager constitutes exposure to the unit's nerve center and

decision-maker. The manager is also charged with designing the unit's structure, that pattern of formal relationships that determines how work is to be divided and coordinated.

Also, in his or her role as resource allocator, the manager authorizes the important decisions of the unit before they are implemented. By retaining this power, the manager can ensure that decisions are interrelated; all must pass through a single brain. To fragment this power is to encourage discontinuous decision making and a disjoined strategy.

10. The final decisional role is that of *negotiator*. Studies of managerial work at all levels indicate that managers spend considerable time in negotiations: the president of the football team is called in to work out a contract with the holdout superstar; the corporation president leads her company's contingent to negotiate a new stock issue; the foreman argues a grievance problem to its conclusion with the shop steward. As Leonard Sayles puts it, negotiations are a "way of life" for the sophisticated manager.

These negotiations are duties of the manager's job; perhaps routine, they are not to be shirked. They are an integral part of the job, for only the manager has the authority to commit organizational resources in "real time," and only he or she has the nerve center information that important negotiations require.

The Integrated Job

It should be clear by now that the ten roles I have been describing are not easily separable. In the terminology of the psychologist, they form a gestalt, an integrated whole. No role can be pulled out of the framework and the job be left intact. For example, a manager without liaison contacts lacks external information. As a result, he or she can neither disseminate the information employees need nor make decisions that adequately reflect external conditions. (In fact, this is a problem for the new person in a managerial position, since he or she cannot make effective decisions until he or she has built up his network of contacts.)

To say that the ten roles form a gestalt is not to say that all managers give equal attention to each role. In fact, I found in my review of the various research studies that

> . . . sales managers seem to spend relatively more of their time in the interpersonal roles, presumably a reflection of the extrovert nature of the marketing activity;
> . . . production managers give relatively more attention to the decisional roles, presumably a reflection of their concern with efficient work flow;
> . . . staff managers spend the most time in the informational roles, since they are experts who manage departments that advise other parts of the organization.

Nevertheless, in all cases the interpersonal, informational, and decisional roles remain inseparable.

CONCLUSION

No job is more vital to our society than that of the manager. It is the manager who determines whether our social institutions serve us well or whether they squander our talents and resources. It is time to strip away the folklore about managerial work, and time to study it realistically so that we can begin the difficult task of making significant improvements in its performance.

GOOD MANAGERS DON'T MAKE POLICY DECISIONS*

BY H. EDWARD WRAPP

The upper reaches of management are a land of mystery and intrigue. Very few people have ever been there, and the present inhabitants frequently send back messages that are incoherent both to other levels of management and to the world in general. This may account for the myths, illusions, and caricatures that permeate the literature of management—for example, such widely held notions as these:

- Life gets less complicated as a manager reaches the top of the pyramid.
- The manager at the top level knows everything that's going on in the organization, can command whatever resources he may need, and therefore can be more decisive.
- The general manager's day is taken up with making broad policy decisions and formulating precise objectives.
- The top executive's primary activity is conceptualizing long-range plans.
- In a large company, the top executive may be seen meditating about the role of his organization in society.

I suggest that none of these versions alone, or in combination, is an accurate portrayal of what a general manager does. Perhaps students of the management process have been overly eager to develop a theory and a discipline. As one executive I know puts it, "I guess I do some of the things described in the books and articles, but the descriptions are lifeless, and my job isn't."

What common characteristics, then, do successful executives exhibit *in reality?* I shall identify five skills or talents which, in my experience, seem especially significant. . . .

KEEPING WELL INFORMED

First, each of my heroes has a special talent for keeping himself informed about a wide range of operating decisions being made at different levels in the company. As he moves up the ladder, he develops a network of information sources in many different departments. He cultivates these sources and keeps them open no matter how high he climbs in the organization. When the need arises, he bypasses the lines on the organization chart to seek more than one version of a situation.

In some instances, especially when they suspect he would not be in total agreement with their decision, his subordinates will elect to inform him in advance, before they announce a decision. In these circumstances, he is in a position to defer the decision, or redirect it, or even block further action. However, he does not insist on this procedure. Ordinarily he leaves it up to the members of his organization to decide at what stage they inform him.

Top-level managers are frequently criticized by writers, consultants, and lower levels of management for continuing to enmesh themselves in operating

---

* Originally published in the *Harvard Business Review* (September–October 1967) and winner of the McKinsey prize for the best article in the *Review* in 1967. Copyright © 1967 by the President and Fellows of Harvard College; all rights reserved. Reprinted with deletions by permission of the *Harvard Business Review.*

problems, after promotion to the top, rather than withdrawing to the "big picture." Without any doubt, some managers do get lost in a welter of detail and insist on making too many decisions. Superficially, the good manager may seem to make the same mistake—but his purposes are different. He knows that only by keeping well informed about the decisions being made can he avoid the sterility so often found in those who isolate themselves from operations. If he follows the advice to free himself from operations, he may soon find himself subsisting on a diet of abstractions, leaving the choice of what he eats in the hands of his subordinates. As Kenneth Boulding puts it, "The very purpose of a hierarchy is to prevent information from reaching higher layers. It operates as an information filter, and there are little wastebaskets all along the way" (in *Business Week,* February 18, 1967:202). . . .

FOCUSING TIME AND ENERGY

The second skill of the good manager is that he knows how to save his energy and hours for those few particular issues, decisions, or problems to which he should give his personal attention. He knows the fine and subtle distinction between keeping fully informed about operating decisions and allowing the organization to force him into participating in these decisions or, even worse, making them. Recognizing that he can bring his special talents to bear on only a limited number of matters, he chooses those issues which he believes will have the greatest long-term impact on the company, and on which his special abilities can be most productive. Under ordinary circumstances he will limit himself to three or four major objectives during any single period of sustained activity.

What about the situations he elects *not* to become involved in as a decision maker? He makes sure (using the skill first mentioned) that the organization keeps him informed about them at various stages; he does not want to be accused of indifference to such issues. He trains his subordinates not to bring the matters to him for a decision. The communication to him from below is essentially one of: "Here is our sizeup, and here's what we propose to do." Reserving his hearty encouragement for those projects which hold superior promise of a contribution to total corporate strategy, he simply acknowledges receipt of information on other matters. When he sees a problem where the organization needs his help, he finds a way to transmit his know-how short of giving orders—usually by asking perceptive questions.

PLAYING THE POWER GAME

To what extent do successful top executives push their ideas and proposals through the organization? The rather common notion that the "prime mover" continually creates and forces through new programs, like a powerful majority leader in a liberal Congress, is in my opinion very misleading.

The successful manager is sensitive to the power structure in the organization. In considering any major current proposal, he can plot the position of the various individuals and units in the organization of a scale ranging from complete, outspoken support down to determined, sometimes bitter, and oftentimes well-cloaked opposition. In the middle of the scale is an area of comparative indifference. Usually, several aspects of a proposal will fall into this area, and *here is where he knows he can operate.* He assesses the depth and nature of the blocs in the organization. His perception permits him to move through what I call *corridors* of comparative indifference. He seldom challenges when a corridor is blocked, preferring to pause until it has opened up.

Related to this particular skill is his ability to recognize the need for a few trial-balloon launchers in the organization. He knows that the organization will tolerate only a certain number of proposals which emanate from the apex of the pyramid. No matter how sorely he may be tempted to stimulate the organization with a flow of his own ideas, he knows he must work through idea men in different parts of the organization. As he studies the reactions of key individuals and groups to the trial balloons these men send up, he is able to make a better assessment of how to limit the emasculation of the various proposals. For seldom does he find a proposal which is supported by all quarters of the organization. The emergence of strong support in certain quarters is almost sure to evoke strong opposition in others.

Value of Sense of Timing

Circumstances like these mean that a good sense of timing is a priceless asset for a top executive. . . . As a good manager stands at a point in time, he can identify a set of goals he is interested in, albeit the outline of them may be pretty hazy. His timetable, which is also pretty hazy, suggests that some must be accomplished sooner than others, and that some may be safely postponed for several months or years. He has a still hazier notion of how he can reach these goals. He assesses key individuals and groups. He knows that each has its own set of goals, some of which he understands rather thoroughly and others about which he can only speculate. He knows also that these individuals and groups represent blocks to certain programs or projects, and that these points of opposition must be taken into account. As the day-to-day operating decisions are made, and as proposals are responded to both by individuals and by groups, he perceives more clearly where the corridors of comparative indifference are. He takes action accordingly.

THE ART OF IMPRECISION

The fourth skill of the successful manager is knowing how to satisfy the organization that it has a sense of direction *without ever actually getting himself committed publicly to a specific set of objectives.* This is not to say that he does not have objectives—personal and corporate, long-term and short-term. They are significant guides to his thinking, and he modifies them continually as he better understands the resources he is working with, the competition, and the changing market demands. But as the organization clamors for statements of objectives, these are samples of what they get back from him:

> "Our company aims to be number one in its industry."
> "Our objective is growth with profit."
> "We seek the maximum return on investment."
> "Management's goal is to meet its responsibilities to stockholders, employees, and the public."

In my opinion, statements such as these provide almost no guidance to the various levels of management. Yet they are quite readily accepted as objectives by large numbers of intelligent people.

Why does the good manager shy away from precise statements of his objectives for the organization? The main reason is that he finds it impossible to set down specific objectives which will be relevant for any reasonable period into the future. Conditions in business change continually and rapidly, and corporate strategy must be revised to take the changes into account. The more explicit the statement of strategy, the more difficult it becomes to persuade the organization to turn to different goals when needs and conditions shift.

The public and the stockholders, to be sure, must perceive the organization as having a well-defined set of objectives and clear sense of direction. But in reality the good top manager is seldom so certain of the direction which should be taken. Better than anyone else, he senses the many, many threats to his company— threats which lie in the economy, in the actions of competitors, and, not least, within his own organization.

He also knows that it is impossible to state objectives clearly enough so that everyone in the organization understands what they mean. Objectives get communicated only over time by a consistency or pattern in operating decisions. Such decisions are more meaningful than words. In instances where precise objectives are spelled out, the organization tends to interpret them so they fit its own needs.

Subordinates who keep pressing for more precise objectives are in truth working against their own best interests. Each time the objectives are stated more specifically, a subordinate's range of possibilities for operating are reduced. The narrower field means less room to roam and to accommodate the flow of ideas coming up from his part of the organization.

Avoiding Policy Straitjackets

The successful manager's reluctance to be precise extends into the area of policy decisions. He seldom makes a forthright statement of policy. He may be aware that in some companies there are executives who spend more time in arbitrating disputes caused by stated policies than in moving the company forward. The management textbooks contend that well-defined policies are the sine qua non of a well-managed company. My research does not bear out this contention. For example,

> The president of one company with which I am familiar deliberately leaves the assignments of his top officers vague and refuses to define policies for them. He passes out new assignments with seemingly no pattern in mind and consciously sets up competitive ventures among his subordinates. His methods, though they would never be sanctioned by a classical organization planner, are deliberate—and, incidentally, quite effective.

Since able managers do not make policy decisions, does this mean that well-managed companies operate without policies? Certainly not. But the policies are those which evolve over time from an indescribable mix of operating decisions. From any single operating decision might have come a very minor dimension of the policy as the organization understands it; from a series of decisions comes a pattern of guidelines for various levels of the organization.

The skillful manager resists the urge to write a company creed or to compile a policy manual. Preoccupation with detailed statements of corporate objectives and departmental goals and with comprehensive organization charts and job descriptions—this is often the first symptom of an organization which is in the early stages of atrophy.

The "management by objectives" school, so widely heralded in recent years, suggests that detailed objectives be spelled out at all levels in the corporation. This method is feasible at lower levels of management, but it becomes unworkable at the upper levels. The top manager must think out objectives in detail, but ordinarily some of the objectives must be withheld, or at least communicated to the organization in modest doses. A conditioning process which may stretch over months or years is necessary in order to prepare the organization for radical departures from what it is currently striving to attain.

Suppose, for example, that a president is convinced his company must phase out of the principal business it has been in for 35 years. Although making this change of course is one of his objectives, he may well feel that he cannot disclose the idea even to his vice presidents, whose total know-how is in the present business. A blunt announcement that the company is changing horses would be too great a shock for most of them to bear. And so he begins moving toward this goal but without a full disclosure to his management group.

A detailed spelling out of objectives may only complicate the task of reaching them. Specific, detailed statements give the opposition an opportunity to organize its defenses.

MUDDLING WITH A PURPOSE

The fifth, and most important, skill I shall describe bears little relation to the doctrine that management is (or should be) a comprehensive, systematic, logical, well-programmed science. Of all the heresies set forth here, this should strike doctrinaires as the rankest of all!

The successful manager, in my observation, recognizes the futility of trying to push total packages or programs through the organization. He is willing to take less than total acceptance in order to achieve modest progress toward his goals. Avoiding debates on principles, he tries to piece together particles that may appear to be incidentals into a program that moves at least part of the way toward his objectives. His attitude is based on optimism and persistence. Over and over he says to himself, "There must be some parts of this proposal on which we can capitalize."

Whenever he identifies relationships among the different proposals before him, he knows that they present opportunities for combination and restructuring. It follows that he is a man of wide-ranging interests and curiosity. The more things he knows about, the more opportunities he will have to discover parts which are related. This process does not require great intellectual brilliance or unusual creativity. The wider ranging his interests, the more likely that he will be able to tie together several unrelated proposals. He is skilled as an analyst, but even more talented as a conceptualizer.

If the manager has built or inherited a solid organization, it will be difficult for him to come up with an idea which no one in the company has ever thought of before. His most significant contribution may be that he can see relationships which no one else has seen. . . .

Contrasting Pictures

It is interesting to note, in the writings of several students of management, the emergence of the concept that, rather than making decisions, the leader's principal task is maintaining operating conditions which permit the various decision-making systems to function effectively. The supporters of this theory, it seems to me, overlook the subtle turns of direction which the leader can provide. He cannot add purpose and structure to the balanced judgments of subordinates if he simply rubberstamps their decisions. He must weigh the issues and reach his own decision. . . .

Many of the articles about successful executives picture them as great thinkers who sit at their desks drafting master blueprints for their companies. The successful top executives I have seen at work do not operate this way. Rather than produce a full-grown decision tree, they start with a twig, help it grow, and ease themselves out on the limbs only after they have tested to see how much weight the limbs can stand.

In my picture, the general manager sits in the midst of a continuous stream of operating problems. His organization presents him with a flow of proposals to deal with the problems. Some of these proposals are contained in voluminous, well-documented, formal reports; some are as fleeting as the walk-in visit from a subordinate whose latest inspiration came during the morning's coffee break. Knowing how meaningless it is to say, "This is a finance problem," or, "That is a communications problem," the manager feels no compulsion to classify his problems. He is, in fact, undismayed by a problem that defies classification. As the late Gary Steiner, in one of his speeches, put it, "He has a high tolerance for ambiguity."

In considering each proposal, the general manager tests it against at least three criteria:

1. Will the total proposal—or, more often, will some part of the proposal—move the organization toward the objectives which he has in mind?

2. How will the whole or parts of the proposal be received by the various groups and sub-groups in the organization? Where will the strongest opposition come from, which group will furnish the strongest support, and which group will be neutral or indifferent?

3. How does the proposal relate to programs already in process or currently proposed? Can some parts of the proposal under consideration be added on to a program already under way, or can they be combined with all or parts of other proposals in a package which can be steered through the organization? . . .

CONCLUSION

To recapitulate, the general manager possesses five important skills. He knows how to

1. *Keep open many pipelines of information*—No one will quarrel with the desirability of an early warning system which provides varied viewpoints on an issue. However, very few managers know how to practice this skill, and the books on management add precious little to our understanding of the techniques which make it practicable.

2. *Concentrate on a limited number of significant issues*—No matter how skillful the manager is in focusing his energies and talents, he is inevitably caught up in a number of inconsequential duties. Active leadership of an organization demands a high level of personal involvement, and personal involvement brings with it many time-consuming activities which have an

infinitesimal impact on corporate strategy. Hence this second skill, while perhaps the most logical of the five, is by no means the easiest to apply.

3. *Identify the corridors of comparative indifference*—Are there inferences here that the good manager has no ideas of his own, that he stands by until his organization proposes solutions, that he never uses his authority to force a proposal through the organization? Such inferences are not intended. The message is that a good organization will tolerate only so much direction from the top; the good manager therefore is adept at sensing how hard he can push.

4. *Give the organization a sense of direction with open-ended objectives*—In assessing this skill, keep in mind that I am talking about top levels of management. At lower levels, the manager should be encouraged to write down his objectives, if for no other reason than to ascertain if they are consistent with corporate strategy.

5. *Spot opportunities and relationships in the stream of operating problems and decisions*—Lest it be concluded from the description of this skill that the good manager is more an improviser than a planner, let me emphasize that he is a planner and encourages planning by his subordinates. Interestingly, though, professional planners may be irritated by a good general manager. Most of them complain about his lack of vision. They devise a master plan, but the president (or other operating executive) seems to ignore it, or to give it minimum acknowledgment by borrowing bits and pieces for implementation. They seem to feel that the power of a good master plan will be obvious to everyone, and its implementation automatic. But the general manager knows that even if the plan is sound and imaginative, the job has only begun. The long, painful task of implementation will depend on his skill, not that of the planner. . . .

● LEADERSHIP IN ADMINISTRATION*

BY PHILIP SELZNICK

The nature and quality of leadership, in the sense of statesmanship, is an elusive but persistent theme in the history of ideas. Most writers have centered their attention on *political* statesmen, leaders of whole communities who sit in the high places where great issues are joined and settled. In our time, there is no abatement of the need to continue the great discussion, to learn how to reconcile idealism with expediency, freedom with organization.

But an additional emphasis is necessary. Ours is a pluralist society made up of many large, influential, relatively autonomous groups. The U.S. government itself consists of independently powerful agencies which do a great deal on their own initiative and are largely self-governing. These, and the institutions of industry, politics, education, and other fields, often command large resources; their leaders are inevitably responsible for the material and psychological well-being of numerous constituents; and they have become increasingly *public* in nature, attached to such interests and dealing with such problems as affect the welfare of the entire community. In our society the need for statesmanship is widely diffused and beset

* Excerpted from Philip Selznick, *Leadership in Administration: A Sociological Interpretation* (copyright © by Harper & Row, 1957); reprinted by permission of Harper & Row, Publishers, Inc.

by special problems. An understanding of leadership in both public and private organizations must have a high place on the agenda of social inquiry. . . .

The argument of this essay is quite simply stated: *The executive becomes a statesman as he makes the transition from administrative management to institutional leadership.* This shift entails a reassessment of his own tasks and of the needs of the enterprise. It is marked by a concern for the evolution of the organization as a whole, including its changing aims and capabilities. In a word, it means viewing the organization as an institution. To understand the nature of institutional leadership, we must have some notion of the meaning and significance of the term "institution" itself.

ORGANIZATIONS AND INSTITUTIONS

The most striking and obvious thing about an administrative organization is its formal system of rules and objectives. Here tasks, powers, and procedures are set out according to some officially approved pattern. This pattern purports to say how the work of the organization is to be carried on, whether it be producing steel, winning votes, teaching children, or saving souls. The organization thus designed is a technical instrument for mobilizing human energies and directing them toward set aims. We allocate tasks, delegate authority, channel communication, and find some way of coordinating all that has been divided up and parceled out. All this is conceived as an exercise in engineering; it is governed by the related ideals of rationality and discipline.

The term "organization" thus suggests a certain bareness, a lean, no-nonsense system of consciously coordinated activities (Barnard, 1938:73). It refers to an *expendable tool,* a rational instrument engineered to do a job. An "institution," on the other hand, is more nearly a natural product of social needs and pressures —a responsive, adaptive organism. This distinction is a matter of analysis, not of direct description. It does not mean that any given enterprise must be either one or the other. While an extreme case may closely approach either an "ideal" organization or an "ideal" institution, most living associations resist so easy a classification. They are complex mixtures of both designed and responsive behavior. . . .

In what is perhaps its most significant meaning, "to institutionalize" is to *infuse with value* beyond the technical requirements of the task at hand. The prizing of social machinery beyond its technical role is largely a reflection of the unique way in which it fulfills personal or group needs. Whenever individuals become attached to an organization or a way of doing things as persons rather than as technicians, the result is a prizing of the device for its own sake. From the standpoint of the committed person, the organization is changed from an expendable tool into a valued source of personal satisfaction. Some manifestations of this process are quite obvious; others are less easily recognized. It is commonplace that administrative changes are difficult when individuals have become habituated to and identified with long-established procedures. For example, the shifting of personnel is inhibited when business relations become personal ones and there is resistance to any change that threatens rewarding ties. A great deal of energy in organizations is expended in a continuous effort to preserve the rational, technical, impersonal system against such counterpressures. . . .

The test of infusion with value is *expendability.* If an organization is merely an instrument, it will be readily altered or cast aside when a more efficient tool becomes available. Most organizations are thus expendable. When value infusion takes place, however, there is a resistance to change. People feel a sense of personal loss; the "identity" of the group or community seems somehow to be violated; they bow to economic or technological considerations only reluctantly, with regret. A case in point is the perennial effort to save San Francisco's cable cars from replacement by more economical forms of transportation. The Marine Corps has this institutional halo, and it resists administrative measures that would submerge its identity. . . .

To summarize: organizations are technical instruments, designed as means to definite goals. They are judged on engineering premises; they are expendable. Institutions, whether conceived as groups or practices, may be partly engineered, but they have also a "natural" dimension. They are products of interaction and adaptation; they become the receptacles of group idealism; they are less readily expendable. . . .

THE DEFAULT OF LEADERSHIP

When institutional leadership fails, it is perhaps more often by default than by positive error or sin. Leadership is lacking when it is needed; and the institution drifts, exposed to vagrant pressures, readily influenced by short-run opportunistic trends. This default is partly a failure of nerve, partly a failure of understanding. It takes nerve to hold a course; it takes understanding to recognize and deal with the basic sources of institutional vulnerability.

One type of default is the failure to set goals. Once an organization becomes a "going concern," with many forces working to keep it alive, the people who run it can readily escape the task of defining its purposes. This evasion stems partly from the hard intellectual labor involved, a labor that often seems but to increase the burden of already onerous daily operations. In part, also, there is the wish to avoid conflicts with those in and out of the organization who would be threatened by a sharp definition of purpose, with its attendant claims and responsibilities. Even business firms find it easy to fall back on conventional phrases, such as that "our goal is to make profit," phrases which offer little guidance in the formulation of policy.

A critique of leadership, we shall argue, must include this emphasis on the leader's responsibility to define the mission of the enterprise. This view is not new. It is important because so much of administrative analysis takes the goal of the organization as given, whereas in many crucial instances this is precisely what is problematic. We shall also suggest that the analysis of goals is itself dependent on an understanding of the organization's social structure. In other words, the purposes we have or can have depend on what we are or what we can be. In statesmanship no less than in the search for personal wisdom, the Socratic dictum—know thyself—provides the ultimate guide.

Another type of default occurs when goals, however neatly formulated, enjoy only a superficial acceptance and do not genuinely influence the total structure of the enterprise. Truly accepted values must infuse the organization at many levels, affecting the perspectives and attitudes of personnel, the relative importance of staff activities, the distribution of authority, relations with outside groups, and many other matters. Thus if a large corporation asserts a wish to change its role in the community from a narrow emphasis on profit making to a larger social responsibility (even though the ultimate goal remains some combination of survival and profit-making ability), it must explore the implications of such a change for decision making in a wide variety of organizational activities. We shall stress that the task of building special values and a distinctive competence into the organization is a prime function of leadership. . . .

Finally, the role of the institutional leader should be clearly distinguished from that of the "interpersonal" leader. The latter's task is to smooth the path of human interaction, ease communication, evoke personal devotion, and allay anxiety. His expertness has relatively little to do with content; he is more concerned with persons than with policies. His main contribution is to the efficiency of the enterprise. The institutional leader, on the other hand, *is primarily an expert in the promotion and protection of values.* The interpretation that follows takes this idea as a starting point, exploring its meaning and implications. . . .

It is in the realm of policy—including the areas where policy formation and organization building meet—that the distinctive quality of institutional leadership is found. Ultimately, this is the quality of statesmanship which deals with current issues, not for themselves alone but according to their long-run implications for the role and meaning of the group. Group leadership is far more than the capacity to mobilize personal support; it is more than the maintenance of equilibrium through the routine solution of everyday problems; it is the function of the leader-statesman—whether of a nation or a private association—to define the ends of group existence, to design an enterprise distinctively adapted to these ends, and to see that that design becomes a living reality. These tasks are not routine; they call for continuous self-appraisal on the part of the leaders; and they may require only a few critical decisions over a long period of time. "Mere speed, frequency, and vigor in coming to decisions may have little relevance at the top executive level, where a man's basic contribution to the enterprise may turn on his making two or three significant decisions a year" (Learned, Ulrich, and Booz, 1951:57). This basic contribution is not always aided by the traits often associated with psychological leadership, such as aggressive self-confidence, intuitive sureness, ability to inspire. . . .

CHARACTER AS DISTINCTIVE COMPETENCE

In studying character we are interested in the *distinctive competence or inadequacy* that an organization has acquired. In doing so, we look beyond the formal aspects to examine the commitments that have been accepted in the course of adaptation to internal and external pressures. . . . Commitments to ways of acting and responding are built into the organization. When integrated, these commitments define the "character" of the organization. . . .

THE FUNCTIONS OF INSTITUTIONAL LEADERSHIP

We have argued that policy and administration are interdependent in the special sense that certain areas of organizational activity are peculiarly sensitive to policy matters. Because these areas exist, creative men are needed—more in some circumstances than in others—who know how to transform a neutral body of men into a committed polity. These men are called leaders; their profession is politics. . . .

Leadership sets goals, but in doing so takes account of the conditions that have already determined what the organization can do and to some extent what it must do. Leadership creates and molds an organization embodying—in thought and feeling and habit—the value premises of policy. Leadership reconciles internal strivings and environmental pressures, paying close attention to the way adaptive behavior brings about changes in organizational character. When an organization lacks leadership, these tasks are inadequately fulfilled, however expert the flow of paper and however smooth the channels of communication and command. And this fulfillment requires a continuous scrutiny of how the changing social structure affects the evolution of policy.

The relation of leadership to organizational character may be more closely explored if we examine some of the key tasks leaders are called on to perform:

1. *The definition of institutional mission and role.* The setting of goals is a creative task. It entails a self-assessment to discover the true commitments of the organization, as set by effective internal and external demands. The failure to set aims in the light of these commitments is a major source of irresponsibility in leadership.

2. *The institutional embodiment of purpose.* The task of leadership is not only to make policy but to build it into the organization's social structure. This, too, is a creative task. It means shaping the "character" of the organization, sensitizing it to ways of thinking and responding, so that increased reliability in the execution and elaboration of policy will be achieved according to its spirit as well as its letter.

3. *The defense of institutional integrity.* The leadership of any polity fails when it concentrates on sheer survival: institutional survival, properly understood, is a matter of maintaining values and distinctive identity. This is at once one of the most important and least understood functions of leadership. This area (like that of defining institutional mission) is a place where the intuitively knowledgeable leader and the administrative analyst often part company, because the latter has no tools to deal with it. The fallacy of combining agencies on the basis of "logical" association of functions is a characteristic result of the failure to take account of institutional integrity.

4. *The ordering of internal conflict.* Internal interest groups form naturally in large-scale organizations, since the total enterprise is in one sense a polity composed of a number of suborganizations. The struggle among competing interests always has a high claim on the attention of leadership. This is so because the direction of the enterprise as a whole may be seriously influenced by changes in the internal balance of power. In exercising control, leadership has a dual task. It must win the consent of constituent units, in order to maximize voluntary cooperation, and therefore must permit emergent interest blocs a wide degree of representation. At the same time, in order to hold the helm, it must see that a balance of power appropriate to the fulfillment of key commitments will be maintained.

FORMULATING STRATEGY

Most of what has been published in this field deals with how strategy *should* be designed or consciously *formulated*. On the prescription of how this should be accomplished, there has been a good deal of consensus, although, as we shall see later, this is now eroding. Perhaps we should more properly conclude that there have been two waves of consensus. The first, which developed in the 1960s, is presented in this chapter; the second, which emerged around 1980, did not challenge the first so much as build on it. This is presented in Chapter 4.

Ken Andrews of the Harvard Business School is the person most commonly associated with the first wave, although Bill Newman of Columbia wrote on some of these issues much earlier and Igor Ansoff simultaneously outlined very similar views while he was at Carnegie-Mellon. But the Andrews text became the best known, in part because it was so simply and clearly written, in part because it was embodied in a popular textbook (with cases) emanating from the Harvard Business School.

We reproduce parts of the Andrews text (as revised in its own publication in 1980, but based on the original 1965 edition). These serve to introduce the basic point that strategy, ultimately, requires the achievement of fit between the external situation (opportunities and threats) and internal capability (strengths and weaknesses). Note how the Andrews approach builds directly on some of the military concepts outlined earlier. Both seek to leverage the impact of resources by concentrating efforts within a defined zone of dominance while attempting to anticipate the effects of potentially damaging external forces. In reading the Andrews excerpts, you may also be struck by the relationship in spirit—and indeed sometimes in detail—to the Selznick material of the last chapter.

As you read the Andrews text, a number of basic premises will quickly become evident. Among these are: the clear distinction made between strategy formulation and strategy implementation (in effect, between thinking and action); the belief that strategy (or at least intended strategy) should be made explicit; the notion that structure should follow strategy (in other words, be designed in accordance with it); and the assumption that strategy emanates from the formal leadership of the organization. Similar premises underlie most of the prescriptive literature of strategic management.

This model (if we can call it that) has proven very useful in many circumstances as a broad way to analyze a strategic situation and to think about making strategy. A careful strategist should certainly touch all the bases suggested in this approach. But in many circumstances the model cannot or should not be followed to the letter, as shall be discussed in Chapter 5 and later ones.

The Rumelt reading elaborates on one element in this traditional model—the evaluation of strategies. While the Andrews text contains a similar discussion, Rumelt, a graduate of the Harvard Business School and policy professor at UCLA, develops it in a particularly elegant way, helping to round out this chapter on the classical view of formulating strategy.

A number of cases allow us to apply and understand the value and limitations of this approach. The Boehm, Intel, New Steel Corp., Genentech, and Zayre cases provide particularly useful examples of where it has a high payoff. Other cases like Biogen, Honda Motor, and IBM (A) suggest its limitations.

• THE CONCEPT OF CORPORATE STRATEGY*

BY KENNETH R. ANDREWS

THE STRATEGY CONCEPT

What Strategy Is

Corporate strategy is the pattern of decisions in a company that determines and reveals its objectives, purposes, or goals, produces the principal policies and plans for achieving those goals, and defines the range of business the company is to pursue, the kind of economic and human organization it is or intends to be, and the nature of the economic and noneconomic contribution it intends to make to its shareholders, employees, customers, and communities. . . .

The strategic decision contributing to this pattern is one that is effective over long periods of time, affects the company in many different ways, and focuses and commits a significant portion of its resources to the expected outcomes. The pattern resulting from a series of such decisions will probably define the central character and image of a company, the individuality it has for its members and various publics, and the position it will occupy in its industry and markets. It will permit the specification of particular objectives to be attained through a timed sequence investment and implementation decisions and will govern directly the deployment or redeployment of resources to make these decisions effective.

Some aspects of such a pattern of decision may be in an established corporation unchanging over long periods of time, like a commitment to quality, or high technology, or certain raw materials, or good labor relations. Other aspects of a strategy must change as or before the world changes, such as product line, manu-

* Excerpted from Kenneth R. Andrews, *The Concept of Corporate Strategy,* rev. ed. (copyright © by Richard D. Irwin, Inc., 1980), Chaps. 2 and 3; reprinted by permission of the publisher.

facturing process, or merchandising and styling practices. The basic determinants of company character, if purposefully institutionalized, are likely to persist through and shape the nature of substantial changes in product-market choices and allocation of resources. . . .

It is important, however, not to take the idea apart in another way, that is, to separate goals from the policies designed to achieve those goals. The essence of the definition of strategy I have just recorded is *pattern.* The interdependence of purposes, policies, and organized action is crucial to the particularity of an individual strategy and its opportunity to identify competitive advantage. It is the unity, coherence, and internal consistency of a company's strategic decisions that position the company in its environment and give the firm its identity, its power to mobilize its strengths, and its likelihood of success in the marketplace. It is the interrelationship of a set of goals and policies that crystallizes from the formless reality of a company's environment a set of problems an organization can seize upon and solve.

What you are doing, in short, is never meaningful unless you can say or imply what you are doing it for: the quality of administrative action and the motivation lending it power cannot be appraised without knowing its relationship to purpose. Breaking up the system of corporate goals and the character-determining major policies for attainment leads to narrow and mechanical conceptions of strategic management and endless logic chopping. . . .

Summary Statements of Strategy

Before we proceed to clarification of this concept by application, we should specify the terms in which strategy is usually expressed. A summary statement of strategy will characterize the product line and services offered or planned by the company, the markets and market segments for which products and services are now or will be designed, and the channels through which these markets will be reached. The means by which the operation is to be financed will be specified, as will the profit objectives and the emphasis to be placed on the safety of capital versus level of return. Major policy in central functions such as marketing, manufacturing, procurement, research and development, labor relations, and personnel, will be stated where they distinguish the company from others, and usually the intended size, form, and climate of the organization will be included.

Each company, if it were to construct a summary strategy from what it understands itself to be aiming at, would have a different statement with different categories of decision emphasized to indicate what it wanted to be or do. . . .

Formulation of Strategy

Corporate strategy is an organization process, in many ways inseparable from the structure, behavior, and culture of the company in which it takes place. Nevertheless, we may abstract from the process two important aspects, interrelated in real life but separable for the purposes of analysis. The first of these we may call *formulation,* the second *implementation.* Deciding what strategy should be may be approached as a rational undertaking, even if in life emotional attachments . . . may complicate choice among future alternatives. . . .

The principal subactivities of strategy formulation as a logical activity include identifying opportunities and threats in the company's environment and attaching some estimate or risk to the discernible alternatives. Before a choice can be made, the company's strengths and weaknesses should be appraised together with the resources on hand and available. Its actual or potential capacity to take advantage of perceived market needs or to cope with attendant risks should be estimated as objectively as possible. The strategic alternative which results from matching opportunity and corporate capability at an acceptable level of risk is what we may call an *economic strategy.*

The process described thus far assumes that strategists are analytically objective in estimating the relative capacity of their company and the opportunity they see or anticipate in developing markets. The extent to which they wish to undertake low or high risk presumably depends on their profit objectives. The higher they set the latter, the more willing they must be to assume a correspondingly high risk that the market opportunity they see will not develop or that the corporate competence required to excel competition will not be forthcoming.

So far we have described the intellectual processes of ascertaining what a company *might do* in terms of environmental opportunity, of deciding what it *can do* in terms of ability and power, and of bringing these two considerations together in optimal equilibrium. The determination of strategy also requires consideration of what alternatives are preferred by the chief executive and perhaps by his or her immediate associates as well, quite apart from economic considerations. Personal values, aspirations, and ideals do, and in our judgment quite properly should, influence the final choice of purposes. Thus what the executives of a company *want to do* must be brought into the strategic decision.

Finally strategic choice has an ethical aspect—a fact much more dramatically illustrated in some industries than in others. Just as alternatives may be ordered in terms of the degree of risk that they entail, so may they be examined against the standards of responsiveness to the expectations of society that the strategist elects. Some alternatives may seem to the executive considering them more attractive than others when the public good or service to society is considered. What a company *should do* thus appears as a fourth element of the strategic decision. . . .

The Implementation of Strategy

Since effective implementation can make a sound strategic decision ineffective or a debatable choice successful, it is as important to examine the processes of implementation as to weigh the advantages of available strategic alternatives. The implementation of strategy is comprised of a series of subactivities which are primarily administrative. If purpose is determined, then the resources of a company can be mobilized to accomplish it. An organizational structure appropriate for the efficient performance of the required tasks must be made effective by information systems and relationships permitting coordination of subdivided activities. The organizational processes of performance measurement, compensation, management development—all of them enmeshed in systems of incentives and controls—must be directed toward the kind of behavior required by organizational purpose. The role of personal leadership is important and sometimes decisive in the accomplishment of strategy. Although we know that organization structure and processes of compensation, incentives, control, and management development influence and constrain the formulation of strategy, we should look first at the logical proposition that structure should follow strategy in order to cope later with the organizational reality that strategy also follows structure. When we have examined both tendencies, we will understand and to some extent be prepared to deal with the interdependence of the formulation and implementation of corporate purpose. Figure 1 may be useful in understanding the analysis of strategy as a pattern of interrelated decisions. . . .

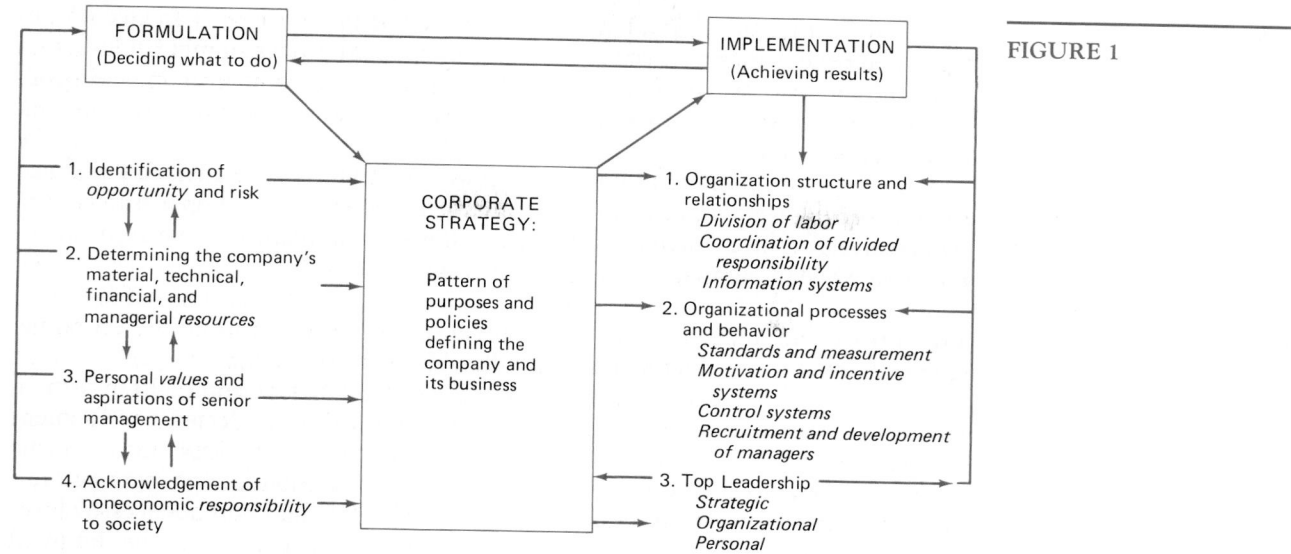

FIGURE 1

FORMULATION
(Deciding what to do)

IMPLEMENTATION
(Achieving results)

1. Identification of *opportunity* and risk

2. Determining the company's material, technical, financial, and managerial *resources*

3. Personal *values* and aspirations of senior management

4. Acknowledgement of noneconomic *responsibility* to society

CORPORATE STRATEGY:

Pattern of purposes and policies defining the company and its business

1. Organization structure and relationships
Division of labor
Coordination of divided responsibility
Information systems

2. Organizational processes and behavior
Standards and measurement
Motivation and incentive systems
Control systems
Recruitment and development of managers

3. Top Leadership
Strategic
Organizational
Personal

RELATING OPPORTUNITIES TO RESOURCES

Determination of a suitable strategy for a company begins in identifying the opportunities and risks in its environment. This [discussion] is concerned with the identification of a range of strategic alternatives, the narrowing of this range by recognizing the constraints imposed by corporate capability, and the determination of one or more economic strategies at acceptable levels of risk. . . .

The Nature of the Company's Environment

The environment of an organization in business, like that of any other organic entity, is the pattern of all the external conditions and influences that affect its life and development. The environmental influences relevant to strategic decision operate in a company's industry, the total business community, its city, its country, and the world. They are technological, economic, physical, social, and political in kind. The corporate strategist is usually at least intuitively aware of these features of the current environment. But in all these categories change is taking place at varying rates—fastest in technology, less rapidly in politics. Change in the environment of business necessitates continuous monitoring of a company's definition of its business, lest it falter, blur, or become obsolete. Since by definition the formulation of strategy is performed with the future in mind, executives who take part in the strategic planning process must be aware of those aspects of their company's environment especially susceptible to the kind of change that will affect their company's future.

Technology: From the point of view of the corporate strategist, technological developments are not only the fastest unfolding but the most far-reaching in extending or contracting opportunity for an established company. They include the discoveries of science, the impact of related product development, the less dramatic machinery and process improvements, and the progress of automation and data processing. . . .

Ecology: It used to be possible to take for granted the physical characteristics of the environment and find them favorable to industrial development. Plant sites were chosen using criteria like availability of process and cooling water, accessibility to various forms of transportation, and stability of soil conditions. With the increase in sensitivity to the impact on the physical environment of all industrial activity, it becomes essential, often to comply with law, to consider how planned expansion and even continued operation under changing standards will affect and be perceived to affect the air, water, traffic density, and quality of life generally of any area which a company would like to enter. . . .

Economics: Because business is more accustomed to monitoring economic trends than those in other spheres, it is less likely to be taken by surprise by such massive developments as the internationalization of competition, the return of China and Russia to trade with the West, the slower than projected development of the Third World countries, the Americanization of demand and culture in the developing countries and the resulting backlash of nationalism, the increased importance of the large multinational corporations and the consequences of host-country hostility, the recurrence of recession, and the persistence of inflation in all phases of the business cycle. The consequences of world economic trends need to be monitored in much greater detail for any one industry or company.

Industry: Although the industry environment is the one most company strategists believe they know most about, the opportunities and risks that reside there are often blurred by familiarity and the uncritical acceptance of the established relative position of competitors. . . .

Society: Social development of which strategists keep aware include such influential forces as the quest for equality for minority groups, the demand of women for opportunity and recognition, the changing patterns of work and leisure, the effects of urbanization upon the individual, family, and neighborhood, the rise of crime, the decline of conventional morality, and the changing composition of world population.

Politics: The political forces important to the business firm are similarly extensive and complex—the changing relations between communist and noncommunist countries (East and West) and between prosperous and poor countries (North and South), the relation between private enterprise and government, between workers and management, the impact of national planning on corporate planning, and the rise of what George Lodge (1975) calls the communitarian ideology. . . .

Although it is not possible to know or spell out here the significance of such technical, economic, social, and political trends, and possibilities for the strategist of a given business or company, some simple things are clear. Changing values will lead to different expectations of the role business should perform. Business will be expected to perform its mission not only with economy in the use of energy but with sensitivity to the ecological environment. Organizations in all walks of life will be called upon to be more explicit about their goals and to meet the needs and aspirations (for example, for education) of their membership.

In any case, change threatens all established strategies. We know that a thriving company—itself a living system—is bound up in a variety of interrelationships with larger systems comprising its technological, economic, ecological, social, and political environment. If environmental developments are destroying and creating business opportunities, advance notice of specific instances relevant to a single company is essential to intelligent planning. Risk and opportunity in the last quarter of the twentieth century require of executives a keen interest in what is going on outside their companies. More than that, a practical means of tracking developments promising good or ill, and profit or loss, needs to be devised. . . .

For the firm that has not determined what its strategy dictates it needs to know or has not embarked upon the systematic surveillance of environmental change, a few simple questions kept constantly in mind will highlight changing opportunity and risk. In examining your own company or one you are interested in, these questions should lead to an estimate of opportunity and danger in the present and predicted company setting.

1. What are the essential economic, technical, and physical characteristics of the industry in which the company participates? . . .

2. What trends suggesting future change in economic and technical characteristics are apparent? . . .

3. What is the nature of competition both within the industry and across industries? . . .

4. What are the requirements for success in competition in the company's industry? . . .

5. Given the technical, economic, social, and political developments that most directly apply, what is the range of strategy available to any company in this industry? . . .

Identifying Corporate Competence and Resources

The first step in validating a tentative choice among several opportunities is to determine whether the organization has the capacity to prosecute it successfully. The capability of an organization is its demonstrated and potential ability to accomplish, against the opposition of circumstance or competition, whatever it sets out to do. Every organization has actual and potential strengths and weaknesses. Since it is prudent in formulating strategy to extend or maximize the one and contain or minimize the other, it is important to try to determine what they are and to distinguish one from the other.

It is just as possible, though much more difficult, for a company to know its own strengths and limitations as it is to maintain a workable surveillance of its changing environment. Subjectivity, lack of confidence, and unwillingness to face reality may make it hard for organizations as well as for individuals to know themselves. But just as it is essential, though difficult, that a maturing person achieve reasonable self-awareness, so an organization can identify approximately its central strength and critical vulnerability. . . .

To make an effective contribution to strategic planning, the key attributes to be appraised should be identified and consistent criteria established for judging them. If attention is directed to strategies, policy commitments, and past practices in the context of discrepancy between organization goals and attainment, an outcome useful to an individual manager's strategic planning is possible. The assessment of strengths and weaknesses associated with the attainment of specific objectives becomes in Stevenson's (1976) words a "key link in a feedback loop" which allows managers to learn from the success or failures of the policies they institute.

Although [a] study by Stevenson did not find or establish a systematic way of developing or using such knowledge, members of organizations develop judgments about what the company can do particularly well—its core of competence. If consensus can be reached about this capability, no matter how subjectively arrived at, its application to identified opportunity can be estimated.

Sources of Capabilities: The powers of a company constituting a resource for growth and diversification accrue primarily from experience in making and marketing a product line or providing a service. They inhere as well in (1) the developing strengths and weaknesses of the individuals comprising the organization, (2) the degree to which individual capability is effectively applied to the common task, and (3) the quality of coordination of individual and group effort.

The experience gained through successful execution of a strategy centered upon one goal may unexpectedly develop capabilities which could be applied to different ends. Whether they should be so applied is another question. For example, a manufacturer of salt can strengthen his competitive position by offering his customers salt-dispensing equipment. If, in the course of making engineering improvements in this equipment, a new solenoid principle is perfected that has application to many industrial switching problems, should this patentable and marketable innovation be exploited? The answer would turn not only on whether economic analysis of the opportunity shows this to be a durable and profitable possibility, but also on whether the organization can muster the financial, manufacturing, and marketing strength to exploit the discovery and live with its success. The former question is likely to have a more positive answer than the latter. In this connection, it seems important to remember that individual and unsupported flashes of strength are not as dependable as the gradually accumulated product and market-related fruits of experience.

Even where competence to exploit an opportunity is nurtured by experience in related fields, the level of that competence may be too low for any great reliance to be placed upon it. Thus a chain of children's clothing stores might well acquire the administrative, merchandising, buying, and selling skills that would permit it to add departments in women's wear. Similarly, a sales force effective in distributing typewriters might gain proficiency in selling office machinery and supplies. But even here it would be well to ask what *distinctive* ability these companies could bring to the retailing of soft goods or office equipment to attract customers away from a plethora of competitors.

Identifying Strengths: The distinctive competence of an organization is more than what it can do; it is what it can do particularly well. To identify the less obvious or by-product strengths of an organization that may well be transferable to some more profitable new opportunity, one might well begin by examining the organization's current product line and by defining the functions it serves in its markets. Almost any important consumer product has functions which are related to others into which a qualified company might move. The typewriter, for example, is more than the simple machine for mechanizing handwriting that it once appeared to be when looked at only from the point of view of its designer and manufacturer. Closely analyzed from the point of view of the potential user, the typewriter is found to contribute to a broad range of information processing functions. Any one of these might have suggested an area to be exploited by a typewriter manufacturer. Tacitly defining a typewriter as a replacement for a fountain pen as a writing instrument rather than as an input-output device for word processing is the explanation provided by hindsight for the failure of the old-line typewriter companies to develop before IBM did the electric typewriter and the computer-related input-output devices it made possible. The definition of product which would lead to identification of transferable skills must be expressed in terms of the market needs it may fill rather than the engineering specifications to which it conforms.

Besides looking at the uses or functions to which present products contribute, the would-be diversifier might profitably identify the skills that underlie whatever success has been achieved. The qualifications of an organization efficient at performing its long-accustomed tasks come to be taken for granted and considered humdrum, like the steady provision of first-class service. The insight required to identify the essential strength justifying new ventures does not come naturally. Its cultivation can probably be helped by recognition of the need for analysis. In any case, we should look beyond the company's capacity to invent new products. Product leadership is not possible for a majority of companies, so it is fortunate that patentable new products are not the only major highway to new opportunities. Other avenues include new marketing services, new methods of distribution, new values in quality-price combinations, and creative merchandising. The effort to find or to create a competence that is truly distinctive may hold the real key to a company's success or even to its future development. For example, the ability of a cement manufacturer to run a truck fleet more effectively than its competitors may constitute one of its principal competitive strengths in selling an undifferentiated product.

Matching Opportunity and Competence: The way to narrow the range of alternatives, made extensive by imaginative identification of new possibilities, is to match opportunity to competence, once each has been accurately identified and its future significance estimated. It is this combination which establishes a company's economic mission and its position in its environment. The combination is designed to minimize organizational weakness and to maximize strength. In every case, risk attends it. And when opportunity seems to outrun present distinctive competence, the willingness to gamble that the latter can be built up to the required level is almost indispensable to a strategy that challenges the organization and the people in it. Figure 2 diagrams the matching of opportunity and resources that results in an economic strategy.

Before we leave the creative act of putting together a company's unique internal capability and opportunity evolving in the external world, we should note that —aside from distinctive competence—the principal resources found in any company are money and people—technical and managerial people. At an advanced stage of economic development, money seems less a problem than technical competence, and the latter less critical than managerial ability. Do not assume that managerial capacity can rise to any occasion. The diversification of American industry is marked by hundreds of instances in which a company strong in one endeavor lacked the ability to manage an enterprise requiring different skills. The right to make handsome profits over a long period must be earned. Opportunism without competence is a path to fairyland.

Besides equating an appraisal of market opportunity and organizational capability, the decision to make and market a particular product or service should be accompanied by an identification of the nature of the business and the kind of company its management desires. Such a guiding concept is a product of many considerations, including the managers' personal values. . . .

Uniqueness of Strategy: In each company, the way in which distinctive competence, organizational resources, and organizational values are combined is or should be unique. Differences among companies are as numerous as differences among individuals. The combinations of opportunity to which distinctive compe-

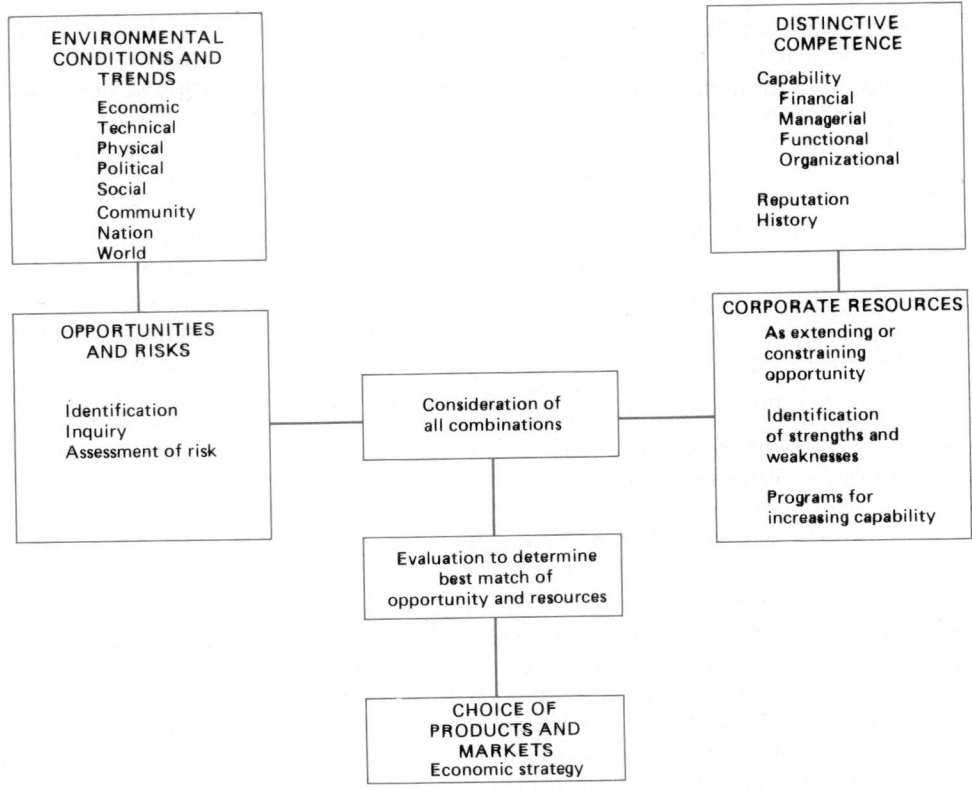

FIGURE 2
Schematic Development of
Economic Strategy

ENVIRONMENTAL
CONDITIONS AND
TRENDS
Economic
Technical
Physical
Political
Social
Community
Nation
World

DISTINCTIVE
COMPETENCE

Capability
Financial
Managerial
Functional
Organizational

Reputation
History

OPPORTUNITIES
AND RISKS

Identification
Inquiry
Assessment of risk

CORPORATE RESOURCES
As extending or
constraining
opportunity

Identification
of strengths and
weaknesses

Programs for
increasing capability

Consideration of
all combinations

Evaluation to determine
best match of
opportunity and resources

CHOICE OF
PRODUCTS AND
MARKETS
Economic strategy

tences, resources, and values may be applied are equally extensive. Generalizing about how to make an effective match is less rewarding than working at it. The effort is a highly stimulating and challenging exercise. The outcome will be unique for each company and each situation.

THE EVALUATION OF BUSINESS STRATEGY*

BY RICHARD RUMELT

Strategy can neither be formulated nor adjusted to changing circumstances without a process of strategy evaluation. Whether performed by an individual or as part of an organizational review procedure, strategy evaluation forms an essential step in the process of guiding an enterprise.

For many executives strategy evaluation is simply an appraisal of how well a business performs. Has it grown? Is the profit rate normal or better? If the answers to these questions are affirmative, it is argued that the firm's strategy must be sound. Despite its unassailable simplicity, this line of reasoning misses the whole point of strategy—that the critical factors determining the quality of current results are often not directly observable or simply measured, and that by the time strategic opportunities or threats do directly affect operating results, it may well be too late

* Originally published in William F. Glueck, *Business Policy and Strategic Management,* 3rd ed. (McGraw-Hill, 1980); reprinted with deletions by permission of the publisher.

for an effective response. Thus, strategy evaluation is an attempt to look beyond the obvious facts regarding the short-term health of a business and appraise instead those more fundamental factors and trends that govern success in the chosen field of endeavor.

THE CHALLENGE OF EVALUATION

However it is accomplished, the products of a business strategy evaluation are answers to these three questions:

1. Are the objectives of the business appropriate?
2. Are the major policies and plans appropriate?
3. Do the results obtained to date confirm or refute critical assumptions on which the strategy rests?

Devising adequate answers to these questions is neither simple nor straightforward. It requires a reasonable store of situation-based knowledge and more than the usual degree of insight. In particular, the major issues which make evaluation difficult and with which the analyst must come to grips are these:

- Each business strategy is unique. For example, one paper manufacturer might rely on its vast timber holdings to weather almost any storm while another might place primary reliance in modern machinery and an extensive distribution system. Neither strategy is "wrong" nor "right" in any absolute sense; both may be right or wrong for the firms in question. Strategy evaluation must, then, rest on a type of situational logic that does not focus on "one best way" but which can be tailored to each problem as it is faced.

- Strategy is centrally concerned with the selection of goals and objectives. Many people, including seasoned executives, find it much easier to set or try to achieve goals than to evaluate them. In part this is a consequence of training in problem structuring. It also arises out of a tendency to confuse *values,* which are fundamental expressions of human personality, with objectives, which are *devices* for lending coherence to action.

- Formal systems of strategic review, while appealing in principle, can create explosive conflict situations. Not only are there serious questions as to who is qualified to give an objective evaluation, the whole idea of strategy evaluation implies management by "much more than results" and runs counter to much of currently popular management philosophy.

THE PRINCIPLES OF STRATEGY EVALUATION

. . . For our purposes a strategy is a set of objectives, policies, and plans that, taken together, define the scope of the enterprise and its approach to survival and success. Alternatively, we could say that the particular policies, plans, and objectives of a business express its strategy for coping with a complex competitive environment.

One of the fundamental tenets of science is that a theory can never be proven to be absolutely true. A theory can, however, be declared absolutely false if it fails to stand up to testing. Similarly, it is impossible to demonstrate conclusively that a particular business strategy is optimal or even to guarantee that it will work. One can, nevertheless, test it for critical flaws. Of the many tests which could be justifiably applied to a business strategy, most will fit within one of these broad criteria:

- *Consistency:* The strategy must not present mutually inconsistent goals and policies.
- *Consonance:* The strategy must represent an adaptive response to the external environment and to the critical changes occurring within it.
- *Advantage:* The strategy must provide for the creation and/or maintenance of a competitive advantage in the selected area of activity.
- *Feasibility:* The strategy must neither overtax available resources nor create unsolvable subproblems.

A strategy that fails to meet one or more of these criteria is strongly suspect. It fails to perform at least one of the key functions that are necessary for the survival of the business. Experience within a particular industry or other setting will permit the analyst to sharpen these criteria and add others that are appropriate to the situation at hand.

Consistency

Gross inconsistency within a strategy seems unlikely until it is realized that many strategies have not been explicitly formulated but have evolved over time in an ad hoc fashion. Even strategies that are the result of formal procedures may easily contain compromise arrangements between opposing power groups.

Inconsistency in strategy is not simply a flaw in logic. A key function of strategy is to provide coherence to organizational action. A clear and explicit concept of strategy can foster a climate of tacit coordination that is more efficient than most administrative mechanisms. Many high-technology firms, for example, face a basic strategic choice between offering high-cost products with high custom-engineering content and lower-cost products that are more standardized and sold at higher volume. If senior management does not enunciate a clear consistent sense of where the corporation stands on these issues, there will be continuing conflict between sales, design, engineering, and manufacturing people. A clear consistent strategy, by contrast, allows a sales engineer to negotiate a contract with a minimum of coordination—the trade-offs are an explicit part of the firm's posture.

Organizational conflict and interdepartmental bickering are often symptoms of a managerial disorder but may also indicate problems of strategic inconsistency. Here are some indicators that can help sort out these two different problems:

- If problems in coordination and planning continue despite changes in personnel and tend to be issue rather than people based, they are probably due to inconsistencies in strategy.
- If success for one organizational department means, or is interpreted to mean, failure for another department, the basic objective structure is inconsistent.
- If, despite attempts to delegate authority, operating problems continue to be brought to the top for the resolution of *policy* issues, the basic strategy is probably inconsistent.

A final type of consistency that must be sought in strategy is between organizational objectives and the values of the management group. Inconsistency in this area is more of a problem in strategy formulation than in the evaluation of a strategy that has already been implemented. It can still arise, however, if the future direction of the business requires changes that conflict with managerial values. The most frequent source of such conflict is growth. As a business expands beyond the scale that allows an easy informal method of operation, many executives experience a sharp sense of loss. While growth can of course be curtailed, it often will require special attention to a firm's competitive position if survival without growth is desired. The same basic issues arise when other types of personal or social values come into conflict with existing or apparently necessary policies: the resolution of the conflict will normally require an adjustment in the competitive strategy.

Consonance

The way in which a business relates to its environment has two aspects: the business must both match and be adapted to its environment and it must at the same time compete with other firms that are also trying to adapt. This dual character of the relationship between the firm and its environment has its analog in two different aspects of strategic choice and two different methods of strategy evaluation.

The first aspect of fit deals with the basic mission or scope of the business and the second with its special competitive position or "edge." Analysis of the first is normally done by looking at changing economic and social conditions over *time*. Analysis of the second, by contrast, typically focuses on the differences across firms at a given time. We call the first the "generic" aspect of strategy and the second "competitive" strategy. Table 1 summarizes the differences between these concepts.

The notion of consonance, or matching, therefore, invites a focus on generic strategy. The role of the evaluator in this case is to examine the basic pattern of economic relationships that characterize the business and determine whether or not sufficient value is being created to sustain the strategy. Most macroanalysis of changing economic conditions is oriented toward the formulation or evaluation of generic strategies. For example, a planning department forecasts that within 10 years home appliances will no longer use mechanical timers or logic. Instead, microprocessors will do the job more reliably and less expensively. The basic message here for the makers of mechanical timers is that their generic strategies are becoming obsolete, especially if they specialize in major home appliances. Note that the threat in this case is not to a particular firm, competitive position, or individual approach to the marketplace but to the basic generic mission.

One major difficulty in evaluating consonance is that most of the critical threats to a business are those which come from without, threatening an entire

TABLE 1   Generic Versus Competitive Strategy

	GENERIC	COMPETITIVE
Measure of success	Sales growth	Market share
Return to the firm	Value added	Return on investment
Function	Provision of value to the customer	Maintaining or obtaining a defensible position
Basic strategic tasks	Adapting to change and innovation	Creating barriers and deterring rivals
Method of expressing strategy	Product/market terms, functional terms	Policies leading to defensible position
Basic approach to analysis	Study of group of businesses over time	Comparision across rivals at a given time

group of firms. Management, however, is often so engrossed in competitive thinking that such threats are only recognized after the damage has reached considerable proportions. . . .

The key to evaluating consonance is an understanding of why the business, as it currently stands, exists at all and how it assumed its current pattern. Once the analyst obtains a good grasp of the basic economic foundation that supports and defines the business, it is possible to study the consequences of key trends and changes. Without such an understanding, there is no good way of deciding what kinds of changes are most crucial and the analyst can be quickly overwhelmed with data.

Advantage

It is no exaggeration to say that competitive strategy is the art of creating or exploiting those advantages that are most telling, enduring, and most difficult to duplicate.

Competitive strategy, in contrast with generic strategy, focuses on the differences among firms rather than their common missions. The problem it addresses is not so much "how can this function be performed" but "how can *we* perform it either better than, or at least instead of our rivals?" The chain supermarket, for example, represents a successful generic strategy. As a way of doing business, of organizing economic transactions, it has replaced almost all the smaller owner-managed food shops of an earlier era. Yet a potential or actual participant in the retail food business must go beyond this generic strategy and find a way of competing in this business. As another illustration, American Motors' early success in compact cars was generic—other firms soon copied the basic product concept. Once this happened, AMC had to try to either forge a strong competitive strategy in this area or seek a different type of competitive arena.

Competitive advantages can normally be traced to one of three roots:

- Superior resources
- Superior skills
- Superior position

The nature of the advantages produced by the first two are obvious. They represent the ability of a business to do more and/or do it better than its rivals. The critical analytical issue here is the question of which skills and resources represent advantages in which competitive arenas. The skills that make for success in the aerospace electronics industry, for instance, do not seem to have much to do with those needed in consumer electronics. Similarly, what makes for success in the early phases of an industry life cycle may be quite different than what ensures top performance in the later phases.

The idea that certain arrangements of one's resources can enhance their combined effectiveness, and perhaps even put rival forces in a state of disarray, is at the heart of the traditional notion of strategy. This kind of "positional" advantage is familiar to military theorists, chess players, and diplomats. Position plays a crucial role in business strategy as well. . . .

Positional advantage can be gained by foresight, superior skill and/or resources, or just plain luck. Once gained, a good position is defensible. This means that it (1) returns enough value to warrant its continued maintenance and (2) would be so costly to capture that rivals are deterred from full-scale attacks on the core of the business. Position, it must be noted, tends to be self-sustaining as long as the basic environmental factors that underlie it remain stable. Thus, entrenched firms can be almost impossible to unseat, even if their raw skill levels are only average. And when a shifting environment allows position to be gained by a new entrant or innovator, the results can be spectacular.

The types of positional advantage that are most well known are those associated with size or scale. As the scale of operations increases, most firms are able to reduce both the marginal and the total cost of each additional unit produced. Marginal costs fall due to the effects of learning and more efficient processes, and total costs per unit fall even faster as fixed overheads are spread over a larger volume of activity. The larger firm can simply take these gains in terms of increased profitability or it can invest some of the extra returns in position-maintaining activities. By engaging in more research and development, being first to go abroad, having the largest advertising budget, and absorbing the costs involved with acting as an industry spokesman, the dominant business is rechanneling the gains obtained from its advantages into activities designed to maintain those advantages. This kind of positive feedback is the source of the power of position-based advantages —the policies that act to enhance position do not require unusual skills; they simply work most effectively for those who are already in the position in the first place.

While it is not true that larger businesses always have the advantages, it is true that larger businesses will tend to operate in markets and use procedures that turn their size to advantage. Large national consumer-products firms, for example, will normally have an advantage over smaller regional firms in the efficient use of mass advertising, especially network TV. The larger firm will, then, tend to deal in those products where the marginal effect of advertising is most potent, while the smaller firms will seek product-market positions that exploit other types of advantage.

Not all positional advantages are associated with size, although some type of uniqueness is a virtual prerequisite. The principal characteristic of good position is that it permits the firm to obtain advantage from policies that would not similarly benefit rivals without the position. For example, Volkswagen in 1966 had a strong, well-defined position as the preeminent maker of inexpensive, well-engineered, functional automobiles. This position allowed it to follow a policy of not changing its body styling. The policy both enhanced VW's position and reduced costs. Rivals could not similarly benefit from such a policy unless they could also duplicate the other aspects of VW's position. At the other end of the spectrum, Rolls-Royce employed a policy of deliberately limiting its output, a policy which enhanced its unique position and which could do so only because of that position in the first place. Mintzberg (1973b) calls strongly defensible positions and the associated policies "gestalt strategies," recognizing that they are difficult to either analyze or attack in a piecemeal fashion.

Another type of positional advantage derives from successful trade names. These brands, especially when advertised, place retailers in the position of having to stock them which, in turn, reinforces the position and raises the barrier to entry still further. Such famous names as Sara Lee, Johnson & Johnson, and Kraft greatly reduce, for their holders, both the problems of gaining wide distribution for new products and obtaining trial use of new products by the buying public.

Other position-based advantages follow from such factors as:

- The ownership of special raw material sources or long-term supply contracts
- Being geographically located near key customers in a business involving significant fixed investment and high transport costs

- Being a leader in a service field that permits or requires the building of a unique experience base while serving clients
- Being a full-line producer in a market with heavy trade-up phenomena
- Having a wide reputation for providing a needed product or service trait reliably and dependably

In each case, the position permits competitive policies to be adopted that can serve to reinforce the position. *Whenever* this type of positive-feedback phenomena is encountered, the particular policy mix that creates it will be found to be a defensible business position. The key factors that sparked industrial success stories such as IBM and Eastman Kodak were the *early* and rapid domination of strong positions opened up by new technologies.

Feasibility

The final broad test of strategy is its feasibility. Can the strategy be attempted within the physical, human, and financial resources available? The financial resources of a business are the easiest to quantify and are normally the first limitation against which strategy is tested. It is sometimes forgotten, however, that innovative approaches to financing expansion can both stretch the ultimate limitations and provide a competitive advantage, even if it is only temporary. Devices such as captive finance subsidiaries, sale-leaseback arrangements, and tying plant mortgages to long-term contracts have all been used effectively to help win key positions in suddenly expanding industries.

The less quantifiable but actually more rigid limitation on strategic choice is that imposed by the individual and organizational capabilities that are available.

In assessing the organization's ability to carry out a strategy, it is helpful to ask three separate questions.

1. Has the organization demonstrated that it possesses the problem-solving abilities and/or special competences required by the strategy? A strategy, as such, does not and cannot specify in detail each action that must be carried out. Its purpose is to provide structure to the general issue of the business' goals and approaches to coping with its environment. It is up to the members and departments of the organization to carry out the tasks defined by strategy. A strategy that requires tasks to be accomplished which fall outside the realm of available or easily obtainable skill and knowledge cannot be accepted. It is either infeasible or incomplete.

2. Has the organization demonstrated the degree of coordinative and integrative skill necessary to carry out the strategy? The key tasks required of a strategy not only require specialized skill, but often make considerable demands on the organization's ability to integrate disparate activities. . . .

3. Does the strategy challenge and motivate key personnel and is it acceptable to those who must lend their support? The purpose of strategy is to effectively deploy the unique and distinctive resources of an enterprise. If key managers are unmoved by a strategy, not excited by its goals or methods, or strongly support an alternative, it fails in a major way. . . .

. . . In most medium- to large-size firms, strategy evaluation is not a purely intellectual task. The issues involved are too important and too closely associated with the distribution of power and authority for either strategy formulation or evaluation to take place in an ivory tower environment. In fact, most firms rarely engage in explicit formal strategy evaluation. Rather, the evaluation of current strategy is a continuing process and one that is difficult to separate from the normal planning, reporting, control, and reward systems of the firm. From this point of view, strategy evaluation is not so much an intellectual task as it is an organizational process.

As process, strategy evaluation is the outcome of activities and events which are strongly shaped by the firm's control and reward systems, its information and planning systems, its structure, and its history and particular culture. Thus, its performance is, in practice, tied more directly to the quality of the firm's strategic management than to any particular analytical scheme. In particular, organizing major units around the primary strategic tasks and making the extra effort required to incorporate measures of strategic success in the control system may play vital roles in facilitating strategy evaluation within the firm.

Ultimately, a firm's ability to maintain its competitive position in a world of rivalry and change may be best served by managers who can maintain a dual view of strategy and strategy evaluation—they must be willing and able to perceive the strategy within the welter of daily activity *and* to build and maintain structures and systems that make strategic factors the object of current activity.

CHAPTER 4

STRATEGY ANALYSIS

As noted in the introduction to Chapter 3, there is a second prescriptive view on the way strategy should be formulated, which developed in the 1980s. Its contribution is less as a new conceptual model—in fact it embraces most of the premises of the traditional model—than in carefully structuring the kinds of formal analyses that should be undertaken to develop a successful strategy. One outcome of this more formal approach is that its adherents have come to see many strategies as fitting certain "generic" classifications—not being created so much individually as selected from a limited set of options based on systematic study of the firm and the industry conditions it faces. This approach has proved to be powerful and useful in many situations.

A leader of this approach is Michael Porter of the Harvard Business School, who studied at the doctoral level in Harvard's economics department. By building intellectual bridges between the fields of management policy and industrial organization—the latter a branch of economics concerned with the performance of industries as a function of their competitive characteristics—Porter elaborated on the earlier views of Andrews, Ansoff, Newman, et al.

We open this chapter with Porter's basic model of competitive and industry analysis, probably his best known work in the area of strategy analysis. As presented in this award-winning *Harvard Business Review* article, it proposes a framework of five forces which in his view define the basic posture of competition in an industry—the bargaining power of existing suppliers and buyers, the threat of substitutes and new entrants, and the intensity of existing rivalry. The model is a powerful one, as you shall see in references to it in subsequent readings as well as in applications of it in the case studies.

Porter is known for several other frameworks as well, for example, his concept of "generic strategies," of which he argues there are three in particular—cost leadership, differentiation, and focus (or scope); his discussion of the "value chain" as a way of decomposing the activities of a business to apply strategy analyses of various kinds; his notion of strategic groups, where firms with like sets of strategies compete in subsegments of an industry; and his concept of "generic industry environments," such as "fragmented" or "mature," which reflect similar characteristics.

We shall hear from Porter again on the last of these in our context section. But his three generic strategies as well as his value chain will be summarized in a second reading in this chapter, by Mintzberg, that seeks to present a more comprehensive picture of the various strategies that firms commonly pursue. Mintzberg's framework considers these at five levels—strategies concerned with locating the core business, distinguishing the core business (the heart of what is often referred to as "business"-level strategy, and where Porter's three generic strategies are found and where his value chain is best introduced), elaborating the core business, extending the core business (where so-called "corporate" level strategies are found), and reconceiving the core business(es).

Our third reading of this chapter, entitled "Developing Competitive Advantage" and authored by Xavier Gilbert and Paul Strebel, two professors at the International Institute for Management Development in Lausanne, Switzerland, draw on Porter's concept of industry analysis, generic strategies, and strategic groups (also including something akin to the value chain, which they call the "business system"), but knit them together in a unique way to suggest an integrated framework to formulate strategy. When Porter introduced his three generic strategies, he made a specific case for not being "stuck in the middle," particularly between cost leadership and differentiation. Gilbert and Strebel, in contrast, introduce "outpacing" strategies designed to do just that—get the best of both these worlds. They believe that over time, through a "dynamic path," some truly successful firms manage to be both efficient in their delivery of low-cost products and services and effective in their capacity to create high received value through differentiation. In reading the various cases, you may wish to consider this specific contradiction and these general views of strategy formulation, to help you decide for yourself which view better captures the realities of strategy.

In some ways, the strategy analysis frameworks of this chapter parallel those of Andrews. But these authors add a number of new systematic and analytical elements, often creating a result that is less broad, more focused. You should consider which approach will be more effective, at least under specific circumstances.

The New Steel Corp., Intel (when combined with the Semiconductor Industry Reference Note found in the Instructor's Manual), and Gallo Wineries cases offer excellent opportunities for industry analyses. The Federal Express, Honda Motor, Ford: Team Taurus, General Motors (B), and Royal Bank of Canada cases present powerful vehicles for competitive analyses. And the Exxon, New York Times, Honda Motor, IBM (C), Matsushita, Sony, and Genentech cases raise many issues about the "value chain" and "outpacing strategy" concepts. We hope these cases will teach you how to conduct such analyses, but at the same time will create some doubts about any specific analytical framework's capacity to capture the full richness of any major corporation's total strategy.

● HOW COMPETITIVE FORCES SHAPE STRATEGY*

BY MICHAEL E. PORTER

The essence of strategy formulation is coping with competition. Yet it is easy to view competition too narrowly and too pessimistically. While one sometimes hears

* Originally published in the *Harvard Business Review* (March–April, 1979) and winner of the McKinsey prize for the best article in the *Review* in 1979. Copyright © 1979 by the President and Fellows of Harvard College; all rights reserved. Reprinted with deletions by permission of the *Harvard Business Review*.

executives complaining to the contrary, intense competition in an industry is neither coincidence nor bad luck.

Moreover, in the fight for market share, competition is not manifested only in the other players. Rather, competition in an industry is rooted in its underlying economics, and competitive forces exist that go well beyond the established combatants in a particular industry. Customers, suppliers, potential entrants, and substitute products are all competitors that may be more or less prominent or active depending on the industry.

The state of competition in an industry depends on five basic forces, which are diagrammed in Figure 1. The collective strength of these forces determines the ultimate profit potential of an industry. It ranges from *intense* in industries like tires, metal cans, and steel, where no company earns spectacular returns on investment, to *mild* in industries like oil field services and equipment, soft drinks, and toiletries, where there is room for quite high returns.

In the economists' "perfectly competitive" industry, jockeying for position is unbridled and entry to the industry very easy. This kind of industry structure, of course, offers the worst prospect for long-run profitability. The weaker the forces collectively, however, the greater the opportunity for superior performance.

FIGURE 1
Elements of Industry Structure

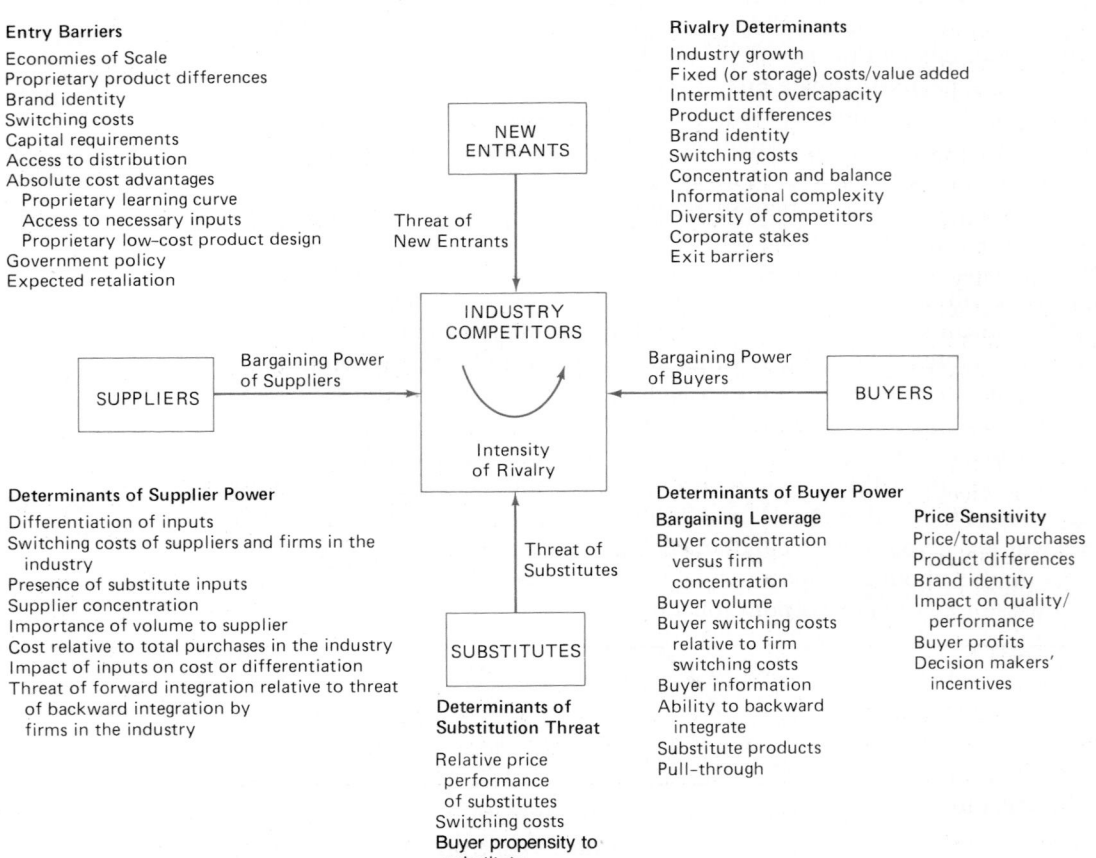

Entry Barriers

Economies of Scale
Proprietary product differences
Brand identity
Switching costs
Capital requirements
Access to distribution
Absolute cost advantages
  Proprietary learning curve
  Access to necessary inputs
  Proprietary low-cost product design
Government policy
Expected retaliation

Rivalry Determinants

Industry growth
Fixed (or storage) costs/value added
Intermittent overcapacity
Product differences
Brand identity
Switching costs
Concentration and balance
Informational complexity
Diversity of competitors
Corporate stakes
Exit barriers

Threat of
New Entrants

NEW
ENTRANTS

INDUSTRY
COMPETITORS

Bargaining Power
of Suppliers

SUPPLIERS

Bargaining Power
of Buyers

BUYERS

Intensity
of Rivalry

Threat of
Substitutes

SUBSTITUTES

Determinants of Supplier Power

Differentiation of inputs
Switching costs of suppliers and firms in the
  industry
Presence of substitute inputs
Supplier concentration
Importance of volume to supplier
Cost relative to total purchases in the industry
Impact of inputs on cost or differentiation
Threat of forward integration relative to threat
  of backward integration by
  firms in the industry

**Determinants of
Substitution Threat**

Relative price
  performance
  of substitutes
Switching costs
Buyer propensity to
  substitute

Determinants of Buyer Power

Bargaining Leverage

Buyer concentration
  versus firm
  concentration
Buyer volume
Buyer switching costs
  relative to firm
  switching costs
Buyer information
Ability to backward
  integrate
Substitute products
Pull-through

Price Sensitivity

Price/total purchases
Product differences
Brand identity
Impact on quality/
  performance
Buyer profits
Decision makers'
  incentives

Whatever their collective strength, the corporate strategist's goal is to find a position in the industry where his or her company can best defend itself against these forces or can influence them in its favor. The collective strength of the forces may be painfully apparent to all the antagonists; but to cope with them, the strategist must delve below the surface and analyze the sources of each. For example, what makes the industry vulnerable to entry? What determines the bargaining power of suppliers?

Knowledge of these underlying sources of competitive pressure provides the groundwork for a strategic agenda of action. They highlight the critical strengths and weaknesses of the company, animate the positioning of the company in its industry, clarify the areas where strategic changes may yield the greatest payoff, and highlight the places where industry trends promise to hold the greatest significance as either opportunities or threats. Understanding these sources also proves to be of help in considering areas for diversification.

CONTENDING FORCES

The strongest competitive force or forces determine the profitability of an industry and so are of greatest importance in strategy formulation. For example, even a company with a strong position in an industry unthreatened by potential entrants will earn low returns if it faces a superior or lower-cost substitute product—as the leading manufacturers of vacuum tubes and coffee percolators have learned to their sorrow. In such a situation, coping with the substitute product becomes the number one strategic priority.

Different forces take on prominence, of course, in shaping competition in each industry. In the oceangoing tanker industry the key force is probably the buyers (the major oil companies), while in tires it is powerful OEM buyers coupled with tough competitors. In the steel industry the key forces are foreign competitors and substitute materials.

Every industry has an underlying structure, or a set of fundamental economic and technical characteristics, that gives rise to these competitive forces. The strategist, wanting to position his company to cope best with its industry environment or to influence that environment in the company's favor, must learn what makes the environment tick.

This view of competition pertains equally to industries dealing in services and to those selling products. To avoid monotony in this article, I refer to both products and services as "products." The same general principles apply to all types of business.

A few characteristics are critical to the strength of each competitive force. I shall discuss them in this section.

Threat of Entry

New entrants to an industry bring new capacity, the desire to gain market share, and often substantial resources. Companies diversifying through acquisition into the industry from other markets often leverage their resources to cause a shakeup, as Philip Morris did with Miller beer.

The seriousness of the threat of entry depends on the barriers present and on the reaction from existing competitors that the entrant can expect. If barriers to entry are high and a newcomer can expect sharp retaliation from the entrenched competitors, obviously he will not pose a serious threat of entering.

There are six major sources of barriers to entry:

1. *Economies of scale*—These economies deter entry by forcing the aspirant either to come in on a large scale or to accept a cost disadvantage. Scale economies in production, research, marketing, and service are probably the key barriers to entry in the mainframe computer industry, as Xerox and GE sadly discovered. Economies of scale can also act as hurdles in distribution, utilization of the sales force, financing, and nearly any other part of a business.

2. *Product differentiation*—Brand identification creates a barrier by forcing entrants to spend heavily to overcome customer loyalty. Advertising, customer service, being first in the industry, and product differences are among the factors fostering brand identification. It is perhaps the most important entry barrier in soft drinks, over-the-counter drugs, cosmetics, investment banking, and public accounting. To create high fences around their businesses, brewers couple brand identification with economies of scale in production, distribution, and marketing.

3. *Capital requirements*—The need to invest large financial resources in order to compete creates a barrier to entry, particulary if the capital is required for unrecoverable expenditures in up-front advertising or R&D. Capital is necessary not only for fixed facilities but also for customer credit, inventories, and absorbing start-up losses. While major corporations have the financial resources to invade almost any industry, the huge capital requirements in certain fields, such as computer manufacturing and mineral extraction, limit the pool of likely entrants.

4. *Cost disadvantages independent of size*—Entrenched companies may have cost advantages not available to potential rivals, no matter what their size and attainable economies of scale. These advantages can stem from the effects of the learning curve (and of its first cousin, the experience curve), proprietary technology, access to the best raw materials sources, assets purchased at preinflation prices, government subsidies, or favorable locations. Sometimes cost advantages are legally enforceable, as they are through patents. . . . [Editor's note: See Chapter 11 of this text for a discussion of the experience curve.]

5. *Access to distribution channels*—The new boy on the block must, of course, secure distribution of his product or service. A new food product, for example, must displace others from the supermarket shelf via price breaks, promotions, intense selling efforts, or some other means. The more limited the wholesale or retail channels are and the more that existing competitors have these tied up, obviously the tougher that entry into the industry will be. Sometimes this barrier is so high that, to surmount it, a new contestant must create its own distribution channels, as Timex did in the watch industry in the 1950s.

6. *Government policy*—The government can limit or even foreclose entry to industries with such controls as license requirements and limits on access to raw materials. Regulated industries like trucking, liquor retailing, and freight forwarding are noticeable examples; more subtle government restrictions operate in fields like ski-area development and coal mining. The government also can play a major indirect role by affecting entry barriers through controls such as air and water pollution standards and safety regulations.

The potential rival's expectations about the reaction of existing competitors also will influence its decision on whether to enter. The company is likely to have second thoughts if incumbents have previously lashed out at new entrants or if:

- The incumbents possess substantial resources to fight back, including excess cash and unused borrowing power, productive capacity, or clout with distribution channels and customers.

- The incumbents seem likely to cut prices because of a desire to keep market shares or because of industrywide excess capacity.

- Industry growth is slow, affecting its ability to absorb the new arrival and probably causing the financial performance of all the parties involved to decline.

Changing Conditions: From a strategic standpoint there are two important additional points to note about the threat of entry.

First, it changes, of course, as these conditions change. The expiration of Polaroid's basic patents on instant photography, for instance, greatly reduced its absolute cost entry barrier built by proprietary technology. It is not surprising that Kodak plunged into the market. Product differentiation in printing has all but disappeared. Conversely, in the auto industry economies of scale increased enormously with post–World War II automation and vertical integration—virtually stopping successful new entry.

Second, strategic decisions involving a large segment of an industry can have a major impact on the conditions determining the threat of entry. For example, the actions of many U.S. wine producers in the 1960s to step up product introductions, raise advertising levels, and expand distribution nationally surely strengthened the entry roadblocks by raising economies of scale and making access to distribution channels more difficult. Similarly, decisions by members of the recreational vehicle industry to vertically integrate in order to lower costs have greatly increased the economies of scale and raised the capital cost barriers.

Powerful Suppliers and Buyers

Suppliers can exert bargaining power on participants in an industry by raising prices or reducing the quality of purchased goods and services. Powerful suppliers can thereby squeeze profitability out of an industry unable to recover cost increases in its own prices. By raising their prices, soft drink concentrate producers have contributed to the erosion of profitability of bottling companies because the bottlers, facing intense competition from powdered mixes, fruit drinks, and other beverages, have limited freedom to raise *their* prices accordingly. Customers likewise can force down prices, demand higher quality or more service, and play competitors off against each other—all at the expense of industry profits.

The power of each important supplier or buyer group depends on a number of characteristics of its market situation and on the relative importance of its sales or purchases to the industry compared with its overall business.

A *supplier* group is powerful if:

- It is dominated by a few companies and is more concentrated than the industry it sells to.

- Its product is unique or at least differentiated, or if it has built up switching costs. Switching costs are fixed costs buyers face in changing suppliers. These arise because, among other things, a buyer's product specifications tie it to particular suppliers, it has invested heavily in specialized ancillary equipment or in learning how to operate a supplier's equipment (as in computer software), or its production lines are connected to the supplier's manufacturing facilities (as in some manufacture of beverage containers).

- It is not obliged to contend with other products for sale to the industry. For instance, the competition between the steel companies and the aluminum companies to sell to the can industry checks the power of each supplier.

- It poses a credible threat of integrating forward into the industry's business. This provides a check against the industry's ability to improve the terms on which it purchases.

- The industry is not an important customer of the supplier group. If the industry *is* an important customer, suppliers' fortunes will be closely tied to the industry, and they will want to protect the industry through reasonable pricing and assistance in activities like R&D and lobbying.

A *buyer* group is powerful if:

- It is concentrated or purchases in large volumes. Large-volume buyers are particularly potent forces if heavy fixed costs characterize the industry—as they do in metal containers, corn refining, and bulk chemicals, for example —which raise the stakes to keep capacity filled.

- The products it purchases from the industry are standard or undifferentiated. The buyers, sure that they can always find alternative suppliers, may play one company against another, as they do in aluminum extrusion.

- The products it purchases from the industry form a component of its product and represent a significant fraction of its cost. The buyers are likely to shop for a favorable price and purchase selectively. Where the product sold by the industry in question is a small fraction of buyers' costs, buyers are usually must less price sensitive.

- It earns low profits, which create great incentive to lower its purchasing costs. Highly profitable buyers, however, are generally less price sensitive (that is, of course, if the item does not represent a large fraction of their costs).

- The industry's product is unimportant to the quality of the buyers' products or services. Where the quality of the buyers' products is very much affected by the industry's product, buyers are generally less price sensitive. Industries in which this situation obtains include oil field equipment, where a malfunction can lead to large losses, and enclosures for electronic medical and test instruments, where the quality of the enclosure can influence the user's impression about the quality of the equipment inside.

- The industry's product does not save the buyer money. Where the industry's product or service can pay for itself many times over, the buyer is rarely price sensitive; rather, he is interested in quality. This is true in services like investment banking and public accounting, where errors in judgment can be costly and embarrassing, and in businesses like the logging of oil wells, where an accurate survey can save thousands of dollars in drilling costs.

- The buyers pose a credible threat of integrating backward to make the industry's product. The Big Three auto producers and major buyers of cars have often used the threat of self-manufacture as a bargaining lever. But sometimes an industry engenders a threat to buyers that its members may integrate forward.

Most of these sources of buyer power can be attributed to consumers as a group as well as to industrial and commercial buyers; only a modification of the frame of reference is necessary. Consumers tend to be more price sensitive if they are purchasing products that are undifferentiated, expensive relative to their incomes, and of a sort where quality is not particularly important.

The buying power of retailers is determined by the same rules, with one important addition. Retailers can gain significant bargaining power over manufacturers when they can influence consumers' purchasing decisions, as they do in audio components, jewelry, appliances, sporting goods, and other goods.

Strategic Action: A company's choice of suppliers to buy from or buyer groups to sell to should be viewed as a crucial strategic decision. A company can improve its strategic posture by finding suppliers or buyers who possess the least power to influence it adversely.

Most common is the situation of a company being able to choose whom it will sell to—in other words, buyer selection. Rarely do all the buyer groups a company sells to enjoy equal power. Even if a company sells to a single industry, segments usually exist within that industry that exercise less power (and that are therefore less price sensitive) than others. For example, the replacement market for most products is less price sensitive than the overall market.

As a rule, a company can sell to powerful buyers and still come away with above-average profitability only if it is a low-cost producer in its industry or if its product enjoys some unusual, if not unique, features. In supplying large customers with electric motors, Emerson Electric earns high returns because its low-cost position permits the company to meet or undercut competitors' prices.

If the company lacks a low-cost position or a unique product, selling to everyone is self-defeating because the more sales it achieves, the more vulnerable it becomes. The company may have to muster the courage to turn away business and sell only to less potent customers.

Buyer selection has been a key to the success of National Can and Crown Cork & Seal. They focus on the segments of the can industry where they can create product differentiation, minimize the threat of backward integration, and otherwise mitigate the awesome power of their customers. Of course, some industries do not enjoy the luxury of selecting "good" buyers.

As the factors creating supplier and buyer power change with time or as a result of a company's strategic decisions, naturally the power of these groups rises or declines. In the ready-to-wear clothing industry, as the buyers (department stores and clothing stores) have become more concentrated and control has passed to large chains, the industry has come under increasing pressure and suffered falling margins. The industry has been unable to differentiate its product or engender switching costs that lock in its buyers enough to neutralize these trends.

Substitute Products

By placing a ceiling on prices it can charge, substitute products or services limit the potential of an industry. Unless it can upgrade the quality of the product or differentiate it somehow (as via marketing), the industry will suffer in earnings and possibly in growth.

Manifestly, the more attractive the price-performance trade-off offered by substitute products, the firmer the lid placed on the industry's profit potential. Sugar producers confronted with the large-scale commercialization of high-fructose corn syrup, a sugar substitute, are learning this lesson today.

Substitutes not only limit profits in normal times; they also reduce the bonanza an industry can reap in boom times. In 1978 the producers of fiberglass insulation enjoyed unprecedented demand as a result of high energy costs and severe winter weather. But the industry's ability to raise prices was tempered by the plethora of insulation substitutes, including cellulose, rock wool, and styrofoam. These substitutes are bound to become an even stronger force once the current round of plant additions by fiberglass insulation producers has boosted capacity enough to meet demand (and then some).

Substitute products that deserve the most attention strategically are those that (1) are subject to trends improving their price-performance trade-off with the industry's product, or (2) are produced by industries earning high profits. Substitutes often come rapidly into play if some development increases competition in their industries and causes price reduction or performance improvement.

Jockeying for Position

Rivalry among existing competitors takes the familiar form of jockeying for position—using tactics like price competition, product introduction, and advertising slugfests. Intense rivalry is related to the presence of a number of factors:

- Competitors are numerous or are roughly equal in size and power. In many U.S. industries in recent years foreign contenders, of course, have become part of the competitive picture.
- Industry growth is slow, precipitating fights for market share that involve expansion-minded members.
- The product or service lacks differentiation or switching costs, which lock in buyers and protect one combatant from raids on its customers by another.
- Fixed costs are high or the product is perishable, creating strong temptation to cut prices. Many basic materials businesses, like paper and aluminum, suffer from this problem when demand slackens.
- Capacity is normally augmented in large increments. Such additions, as in the chlorine and vinyl chloride businesses, disrupt the industry's supply-demand balance and often lead to periods of overcapacity and price cutting.
- Exit barriers are high. Exit barriers, like very specialized assets or management's loyalty to a particular business, keep companies competing even though they may be earning low or even negative returns on investment. Excess capacity remains functioning, and the profitability of the healthy competitors suffers as the sick ones hang on. If the entire industry suffers from overcapacity, it may seek government help—particularly if foreign competition is present.
- The rivals are diverse in strategies, origins, and "personalities." They have different ideas about how to compete and continually run head on into each other in the process. . . .

While a company must live with many of these factors—because they are built into industry economics—it may have some latitude for improving matters through strategic shifts. For example, it may try to raise buyers' switching costs or increase product differentiation. A focus on selling efforts in the fastest-growing segments of the industry or on market areas with the lowest fixed costs can reduce the impact of industry rivalry. If it is feasible, a company can try to avoid confrontation with competitors having high exit barriers and can thus sidestep involvement in bitter price cutting.

Once the corporate strategist has assessed the forces affecting competition in his industry and their underlying causes, he can identify his company's strengths and weaknesses. The crucial strengths and weaknesses from a strategic standpoint are the company's posture vis-à-vis the underlying causes of each force. Where does it stand against substitutes? Against the sources of entry barriers?

Then the strategist can devise a plan of action that may include (1) positioning the company so that its capabilities provide the best defense against the competitive force; and/or (2) influencing the balance of the forces through strategic moves, thereby improving the company's position; and/or (3) anticipating shifts in the factors underlying the forces and responding to them, with the hope of exploiting change by choosing a strategy appropriate for the new competitive balance before opponents recognize it. I shall consider each strategic approach in turn.

Positioning the Company

The first approach takes the structure of the industry as given and matches the company's stengths and weaknesses to it. Strategy can be viewed as building defenses against the competitive forces or as finding positions in the industry where the forces are weakest.

Knowledge of the company's capabilities and of the causes of the competitive forces will highlight the areas where the company should confront competition and where avoid it. If the company is a low-cost producer, it may choose to confront powerful buyers while it takes care to sell them only products not vulnerable to competition from substitutes. . . .

Influencing the Balance

When dealing with the forces that drive industry competition, a company can devise a strategy that takes the offensive. This posture is designed to do more than merely cope with the forces themselves; it is meant to alter their causes.

Innovations in marketing can raise brand identification or otherwise differentiate the product. Capital investments in large-scale facilities or vertical integration affect entry barriers. The balance of forces is partly a result of external factors and partly in the company's control.

Exploiting Industry Change

Industry evolution is important strategically because evolution, of course, brings with it changes in the sources of competition I have identified. In the familiar product life-cycle pattern, for example, growth rates change, product differentiation is said to decline as the business becomes more mature, and the companies tend to integrate vertically.

These trends are not so important in themselves; what is critical is whether they affect the sources of competition. . . .

Obviously, the trends carrying the highest priority from a strategic standpoint are those that affect the most important sources of competition in the industry and those that elevate new causes to the forefront. . . .

The framework for analyzing competition that I have described can also be used to predict the eventual profitability of an industry. In long-range planning the task is to examine each competitive force, forecast the magnitude of each underlying cause, and then construct a composite picture of the likely profit potential of the industry. . . .

The key to growth—even survival—is to stake out a position that is less vulnerable to attack from head-to-head opponents, whether established or new, and less vulnerable to erosion from the direction of buyers, suppliers, and substitute goods. Establishing such a position can take many forms—solidifying relationships with favorable customers, differentiating the product either substantively or psychologically through marketing, integrating forward or backward, establishing technological leadership.

● GENERIC STRATEGIES*

BY HENRY MINTZBERG

Almost every serious author concerned with "content" issues in strategic management, not to mention strategy consulting "boutique," has his, her, or its own list of strategies commonly pursued by different organizations. The problem is that these lists almost always either focus narrowly on special types of strategies or else aggregate arbitrarily across all varieties of them with no real order.

In 1965, Igor Ansoff proposed a matrix of four strategies that became quite well known—market penetration, product development, market development, and diversification (1965:109). But this was hardly comprehensive. Fifteen years later, Michael Porter (1980) introduced what became the best known list of "generic strategies": cost leadership, differentiation, and focus. But the Porter list was also incomplete: while Ansoff focused on *extensions* of business strategy, Porter focused on *identifying* business strategy in the first place. This article seeks to outline in an orderly fashion the families of strategies widely represented in organizations in general, divided into five groupings:

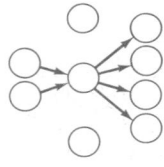

1. *locating* the core business, which will be shown as a single node—one circle—in a matrix of circles

2. *distinguishing* the core business, by looking inside that circle

3. *elaborating* the core business, considering how the circle may be enlarged or developed in various ways

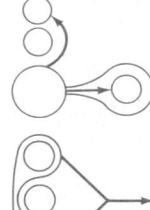

4. *extending* the core business, leading the circle to link up with other circles (other businesses)

5. *reconceiving* the core business(es), in effect changing or combining the circles.

These will be presented as a logical hierarchy, although it should be emphasized that strategies do not necessarily develop that way in organizations.

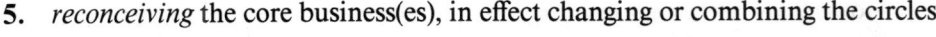

* Abbreviated version prepared for this book of Henry Mintzberg, "Generic Strategies: Toward a Comprehensive Framework," in *Advances in Strategic Management,* Vol. 5 (Greenwich, CT: JAI Press, 1988), pp. 1–67.

A business can be thought to exist at a junction in a network of industries that take raw materials and through selling to and buying from each other produce various finished products (or services). Figure 1, for example, shows a hypothetical canoe business in such a network. Core location strategies can be described with respect to the stage of the business in the network and the particular industry in question.

Strategies of Stage of Operations

Traditionally, industries have been categorized as being in the primary (raw materials extraction and conversion), secondary (manufacturing), or tertiary (delivery or other service) stage of operations. More recently, however, stage in the "stream" has been the favored form of description:

Upstream Business Strategy: Upstream businesses function close to the raw material. As shown in the little figure, the flow of product tends to be divergent, from a basic material (wood, aluminum) to a variety of uses for it. Upstream business tends to be technology and capital intensive rather than people intensive, and more inclined to search for advantage through low costs than through high margins and to favor sales push over market pull (Galbraith, 1983:65–66).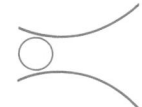

Midstream Business Strategy: Here the organization sits at the neck of an hourglass, drawing a variety of inputs into a single production process out of which flows the product to a variety of users, much as the canoe business is shown in Figure 1.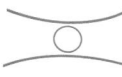

Downstream Business Strategy: Here a wide variety of inputs converge into a narrow funnel, as in the many products sold by a department store.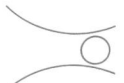

Strategies of Industry

Many factors are involved in the identification of an industry, so many that it would be difficult to develop a concise set of generic labels. Moreover, change continually renders the boundaries between "industries" arbitrary. Diverse products get bundled together so that two industries become one while traditionally bundled products get separated so that one industry becomes two. Economists in government and elsewhere spend a great deal of time trying to pin these things down, via SIC codes and the like. In effect, they try to fix what strategists try to change: competitive advantage often comes from reconceiving the definition of an industry.

Having located the circle that identifies the core business, the next step is to open it up—to distinguish the characteristics that enable an organization to achieve competitive advantage and so to survive in its own context.

The Functional Areas

This second level of strategy can encompass a whole host of strategies in the various functional areas. As shown in Figure 2, they may include input "sourcing"

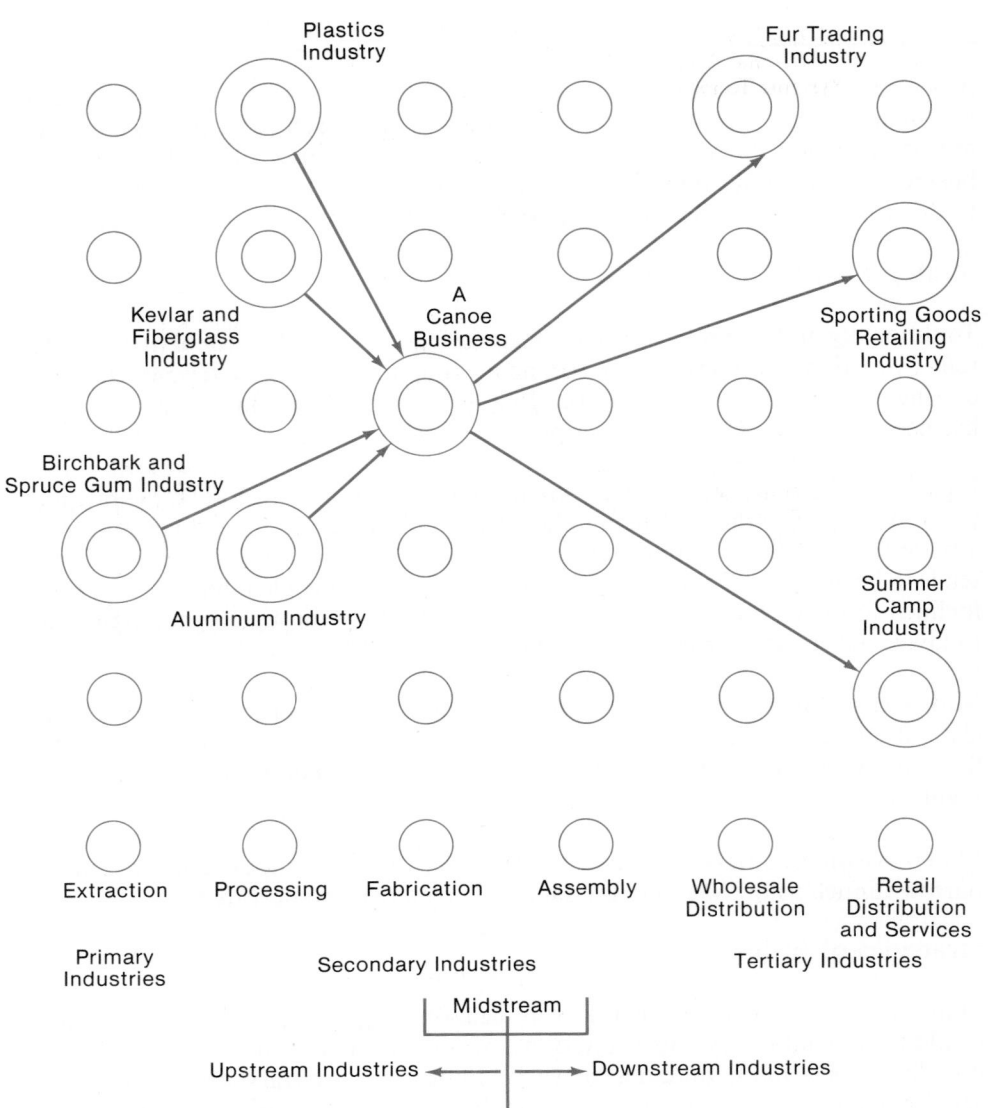

Plastics
Industry

Fur Trading
Industry

Kevlar and
Fiberglass
Industry

A
Canoe
Business

Sporting Goods
Retailing
Industry

Birchbark and
Spruce Gum Industry

Aluminum Industry

Summer
Camp
Industry

Extraction   Processing   Fabrication   Assembly   Wholesale
Distribution

Retail
Distribution
and Services

Primary
Industries

Secondary Industries

Tertiary Industries

Midstream

Upstream Industries ◄──────► Downstream Industries

strategies, throughput "processing" strategies, and output "delivery" strategies, all reinforced by a set of "supporting" strategies.

It has been popular of late to describe organizations in this way, especially since Michael Porter built his 1985 book around the "generic value chain," shown in Figure 3. Porter presents it as "a systematic way of examining all the activities a firm performs and how they interact . . . for analyzing the sources of competitive advantage" (1985:33). Such a chain, and how it performs individual activities, reflects a firm's "history, its strategy, its approach to implementing its strategy, and the underlying economies of the activities themselves" (p. 36). According to Porter, "the goal of any generic strategy" is to "create value for buyers" at a profit. Accordingly,

The value chain displays total value, and consists of *value activities* and *margin*. Value activities are the physically and technologically distinct activities a firm performs. These are the building blocks by which a firm creates a product valuable to its

FIGURE 2
**Functional Areas, in
Systems Terms**

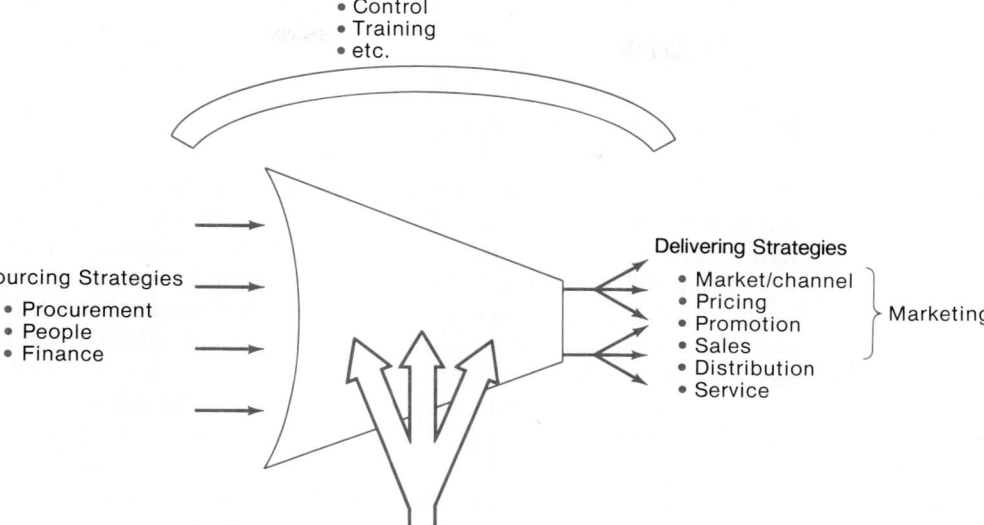

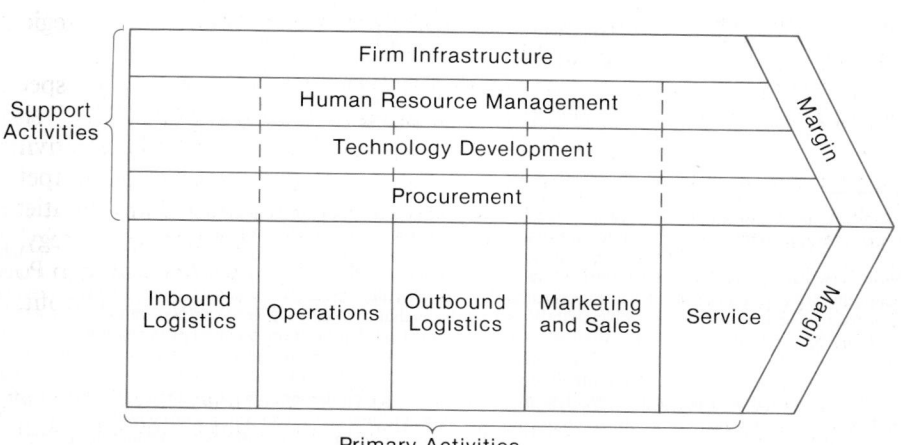

FIGURE 3
The Generic Value Chain
From Porter (1985:37).

buyers. Margin is the difference between total value and the collective cost of performing the value activities. . . .

Value activities can be divided into two broad types, *primary* activities and *support* activities. Primary activities, listed along the bottom of Figure 3 are the activities involved in the physical creation of the product and its sale and transfer to the buyer as well as after-sale assistance. In any firm, primary activities can be divided into the five generic categories shown in Figure 3. Support activities support the primary activities and each other by providing purchased inputs, technology, human resources, and various firmwide functions. (p. 38)[1]

Porter's Generic Strategies

Porter's framework of "generic strategies" has also become quite widely used. In our terms, these constitute strategies to distinguish the core business. Porter believes there are but two "basic types of competitive advantage a firm can possess: low cost or differentiation" (1985:11). These combine with the "scope" of a firm's operations (the range of market segments targeted) to produce "three *generic strategies* for achieving above-average performance in an industry: cost leadership, differentiation, and focus" (namely, narrow scope), shown in Figure 4.

To Porter, firms that wish to gain competitive advantage must "make a choice" among these: "being 'all things to all people' is a recipe for strategic mediocrity and below-average performance" (p. 12). Or in words that have become more controversial, "a firm that engages in each generic strategy but fails to achieve any of them is 'stuck in the middle'" (p. 16).

FIGURE 4
Porter's Generic Strategies
From Porter (1985:12)

---

[1] Our figure differs from Porter's in certain ways. Because he places his major emphasis on the flow of physical materials (for example, referring to "inbound logistics" as encompassing "materials handling, warehousing, inventory control, vehicle scheduling, and returns to suppliers"), he shows procurement and human resource management as support activities, whereas by taking more of a general system orientation, our Figure 2 shows them as inputs, among the sourcing strategies. Likewise, he considers technology development as support whereas Figure 2 considers it as part of processing. (Among the reasons Porter gives for doing this is that such development can pertain to "outbound logistics" or delivery as well as processing. While true, it also seems true that far more technology development pertains to operations than to delivery, especially in the manufacturing firms that are the focus of Porter's attention. Likewise, Porter describes procurement as pertaining to any of the primary activities, or other support activities for that matter. But in our terms that does not make it any less an aspect of sourcing on the inbound side.) In fact, Porter's description would relegate engineering and product design (not to mention human resources and purchasing) to staff rather than line activities, a place that would certainly be disputed in many manufacturing firms (with product design, for example, being mentioned only peripherally in his text (p. 42) alongside other "technology development" activities such as media research and servicing procedures).

The strategies we describe in this section take their lead from Porter, but depart in some respects. We shall distinguish scope and differentiation, as Porter did in his 1980 book (focus being introduced as narrow scope in his later book), but we shall include cost leadership as a form of differentiation (namely with regard to low price). If, as Porter argues, the intention of generic strategies is to seize and sustain competitive advantage, then it is not taking the leadership on cutting costs that matters so much as using that cost leadership to underprice competitors and so to attract buyers.[2]

Thus two types of strategies for distinguishing a core business are presented here. First is a set of increasingly extensive strategies of *differentiation,* shown on the face of the circle. These identify what is fundamentally distinct about a business in the marketplace, in effect as perceived by its customers. Second is a set of decreasingly extensive strategies of *scope,* shown as a third dimension, which converts the circle into a cylinder. These identify what markets the business is after, as perceived by itself.

Strategies of Differentiation

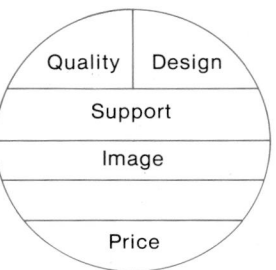

As is generally agreed in the literature of strategic management, an organization distinguishes itself in a competitive marketplace by differentiating its offerings in some way—by acting to distinguish its products and services from those of its competitors. Hence, differentiation fills the face of the circle used to identify the core business. An organization can differentiate its offerings in six basic ways:

Price Differentiation Strategy: The most basic way to differentiate a product (or service) is simply to charge a lower price for it. All things being equal, or not too unequal, some people at least will always beat a path to the door of the cheaper product. Price differentiation may be used with a product undifferentiated in any other way—in effect, a standard design, perhaps a commodity. The producer simply absorbs the lost margin, or makes it up through a higher volume of sales. But other times, backing up price differentiation is a strategy of design intended to create a product that is intrinsically cheaper.

Image Differentiation Strategy: Marketing is sometimes used to feign differentiation where it does not otherwise exist—an image is created for the product. This can also include cosmetic differences to a product that do not enhance its performance in any serious way, for example, putting fins on an automobile or a fancier package around yogurt. (Of course, if it is the image that is for sale, in other words if the product is intrinsically cosmetic, as, say, in "designer" jeans, then cosmetic differences would have to be described as design differentiation.)

Support Differentiation Strategy: More substantial, yet still having no effect on the product itself, is to differentiate on the basis of something that goes alongside the product, some basis of support. This may have to do with selling the product (such as special credit or 24-hour delivery), servicing the product (such as exceptional after-sales service), or providing a related product or service alongside the

---

[2] In other words, it is the differentiation of price that naturally drives the functional strategy of reducing costs just as it is the differentiation of product that naturally drives the functional strategies of enhancing quality or creating innovation. (To be consistent with the label of "cost leadership," Porter would have had to call his differentiation strategy "product leadership.") A company could, of course, cut costs while holding prices equivalent to competitors. But often that means less service, lower quality, fewer features, etc., and so the customers would have to be attracted by lower prices. [See Mintzberg (1988:14–17) for a fuller discussion of this point.]

basic one (paddling lessons with the canoe you buy). In an article entitled "Marketing Success Through Differentiation—of Anything," Theodore Levitt has argued the interesting point that "there is no such thing as a commodity" (1980:83). His basic point is that no matter how difficult it may be to achieve differentiation by design, there is always a basis to achieve another substantial form of differentiation, especially by support.

Quality Differentiation Strategy: Quality differentiation has to do with features of the product that make it better—not fundamentally different, just better. The product performs with (1) greater initial reliability, (2) greater long-term durability, and/or (3) superior performance.

Design Differentiation Strategy: Last but certainly not least is differentiation on the basis of design—offering something that is truly different, that breaks away from the "dominant design" if there is one, to provide unique features. While everyone else was making cameras whose pictures could be seen next week, Edwin Land went off and made one whose pictures could be seen in the next minute.

Undifferentiation Strategy: To have no basis for differentiation is a strategy too, indeed by all observation a common one, and in fact one that may be pursued deliberately. Hence there is a blank space in the circle. Given enough room in a market, and a management without the skill or the will to differentiate what it sells, there can be place for copycats.

Scope Strategies

Customization
•standardized
•tailored
•pure

Increasing Selectivity

Unsegmented

Segmentation
•comprehensive
•selective
•focussed (niche)

The second dimension to distinguish the core business is by the *scope* of the products and services offered, in effect the extent of the markets in which they are sold. Scope is essentially a demand-driven concept, taking its lead from the market—what exists out there. Differentiation, in contrast, is a supply-driven concept, rooted in the nature of the product itself—what is offered to the market (Smith, 1956). Differentiation, by concentrating on the product offered, adopts the perspective of the customer, existing only when that person perceives some characteristic of the product that adds value. And scope, by focusing on the market served, adopts the perspective of the producer, existing only in the collective mind of the organization—in terms of how it diffuses and disaggregates its markets (in other words, what marketing people call segmentation).

Scope is shown here as a third dimension on our circle, converting it into a cylinder.

The disks of this figure represent the variety and range of products offered; arrows emanating from the cylinder, as shown, can represent the variety and range of markets served, as we shall do later. Scope strategies include the following:

Unsegmentation Strategy: "One size fits all": the Ford Model T, table salt. In fact, it is difficult to think of any product today that is not segmented in some way. What the unsegmented strategy really means then is that the organization tries to capture a wide chunk of the market with a basic configuration of the product.

Segmentation Strategies: The possibilities for segmentation are limitless, as are the possible degrees. We can, however, distinguish a range of this, from a simple segmentation strategy (three basic sizes of paper clips) to a hyperfine segmentation strategy (as in designer lighting). Also, some organizations seek to be *comprehen-*

sive, to serve all segments (department store, large cigarette manufacturers), others to be *selective,* targeting carefully only certain segments (e.g., "clean" mutual funds).

Niche Strategy: Niche strategies focus on a single segment. Just as the panda bear has found its biological niche in the consumption of bamboo shoots, so too is there the canoe company that has found its market niche in the fabrication of racing canoes, or the many firms which are distinguished only by the fact that they provide their highly standardized offerings in a unique place, a geographical niche— the corner grocery story, the regional cement producer, the national Red Cross office. All tend to follow "industry" recipes to the letter, providing them to their particular community. In a sense, all strategies are in some sense niche, characterized as much by what they exclude as by what they include. No organization can be all things to all people. The all-encompassing strategy is no strategy at all.

Customizing Strategies: Customization is the limiting case of segmentation: disaggregation of the market to the point where each customer constitutes a unique segment. *Pure* customization, in which the product is developed from scratch for each customer, is found in the architecturally designed house and the special purpose machine. It infiltrates the entire value chain: the product is not only delivered in a personalized way, not only assembled and even fabricated to order, but is also designed for the individual customer in the first place. Less ambitious but probably more common is *tailored* customization: a basic design is modified, usually in the fabrication stage, to the customer's needs or specifications (certain housing, protheses modified to fit the bone joints of each customer, and so on). *Standardized* customization means that final products are assembled to individual requests for standard components—as in automobiles in which the customer is allowed to choose color, engine, and various accessories. Advances in computer-aided design and manufacturing (CAD, CAM) will doubtlessly cause a proliferation of standardized customization, as well as tailored customization.

ELABORATING THE CORE BUSINESS

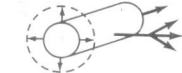

Given a core business with a distinguishing competitive posture, in terms of differentiation and scope, we now come to the question of what strategies of a generic nature are available to elaborate that core business.

An organization can elaborate a business in a number of ways. It can develop its product offerings within that business, it can develop its market via new segments, new channels, or new geographical areas, or it can simply push the same products more vigorously through the same markets. Back in 1965, Igor Ansoff showed these strategies (as well as one to be discussed in the next section) as presented in Figure 5.

	Existing Product	New Product
Existing Market	Penetration Strategies	Product Development Strategies
New Market	Market Development Strategies	Diversification Strategies

FIGURE 5

Ways to Elaborate a Given Business
From Ansoff (1965:109), with minor modifications; see also Johnson and Jones (1957:52).

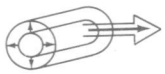

Penetration Strategies: Penetration strategies work from a base of existing products and existing markets, seeking to penetrate the market by increasing the organization's share of it. This may be done by straight *expansion* or by the *takeover* of existing competitors. Trying to expand sales with no fundamental change in product or market (buying market share through more promotion, etc.) is at one and the same time the most obvious thing to do and perhaps the most difficult to succeed at, because, at least in a relatively stable market, it means extracting market share from other firms, which logically leads to increased competition. Takeover, where possible, obviously avoids this, but perhaps at a high cost. The harvesting strategy, popularized in the 1970s by the Boston Consulting Group, in some ways represents the opposite of the penetration strategies. The way to deal with "cash cows"—businesses with high market shares but low growth potential—was to harvest them, cease investment and exploit whatever potential remained. The mixing of the metaphors may have been an indication of the dubiousness of the strategy, since to harvest a cow is, of course, to kill it. (See the Seeger reading in Chapter 11).

Market Development Strategies: A predominant strategy here is *market elaboration,* which means promoting existing products in new markets—in effect broadening the scope of the business by finding new market segments, perhaps served by new channels. Product substitution is a particular case of market elaboration, where uses for a product are promoted that enable it to substitute for other products. *Market consolidation* is the inverse of market elaboration, namely reducing the number of segments. But this is not just a strategy of failure. Given the common tendency to proliferate market segments, it makes sense for the healthy organization to rationalize them periodically, to purge the excesses.

Geographic Expansion Strategies: An important form of market development can be geographic expansion—carrying the existing product offering to new geographical areas, anywhere from the next block to across the world. When this also involves a strategy of geographic rationalization—locating different business functions in different places—it is sometimes referred to as a "global strategy." The IKEA furniture company, for example, designs in Scandinavia, sources in Eastern Europe among other places, and markets in Western Europe and North America.

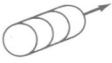

Product Development Strategies: Here we can distinguish a simple *product extention* strategy from a more extensive *product line proliferation* strategy, and their counterparts, *product line rationalization.* Offering new or modified products in the same basic business is another obvious way to elaborate a core business—from cornflakes to bran flakes and rice crispies, eventually offering every permutation and combination of the edible grains. This may amount to differentiation by design, if the products are new and distinctive, or else to no more than increased scope through segmentation, if standardized products are added to the line. Product line proliferation means aiming at comprehensive product segmentation—the complete coverage of a given business. Rationalization means culling products and thinning the line to get rid of overlaps or unprofitable excesses. Again we might expect cycles of product extension and rationalization, at least in businesses (such as cosmetics and textiles) predisposed to proliferation in their product lines.

EXTENDING THE CORE BUSINESS

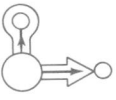

Now we come to strategies designed to take organizations beyond their core business. This can be done in so-called vertical or horizontal ways, as well as combinations of the two. "Vertical" means backward or forward in the operating chain, the strategy being known formally as "vertical integration," although why this has been designated vertical is difficult to understand, especially since the flow of product and the chain itself are almost always drawn horizontally! Hence this will here be labeled chain integration. "Horizontal" diversification (its own geometry no more evident), which will be called here just plain diversification, refers to encompassing within the organization other, parallel businesses, not in the same chain of operations.

Chain Integration Strategies: Organizations can extend their operating chains downstream or upstream, encompassing within their own operations the activities of their customers on the delivery end or their suppliers on the sourcing end. In effect, they choose to "make" rather than to "buy" or sell. *Impartation* (Barreyre, 1984; Barreyre and Carle, 1983) is a label that has been proposed to describe the opposite strategy, where the organization chooses to buy what it previously made, or sell what it previously transferred.

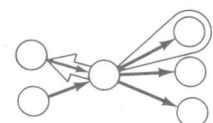

Diversification Strategies: *Diversification* refers to the entry into some business not in the same chain of operation. It may be *related* to some distinctive competence or asset of the core business itself (also called *concentric* diversification); otherwise, it is referred to as *unrelated* or *conglomerate,* diversification. In related diversification, there is evident potential synergy between the new business and the core one, based on a common facility, asset, channel, skill, even opportunity. Porter (1985:323–324) makes the distinction here between "intangible" and "tangible" relatedness. The former is based on some functional or managerial skill considered common across the businesses, as in a Philip Morris using its marketing capabilities in Kraft. The latter refers to businesses that actually "share activities in the value chain" (p. 323), for example, different products sold by the same sales force. It should be emphasized here that no matter what its basis, every related diversification is also fundamentally an unrelated one, as many diversifying organizations have discovered to their regret. That is, no matter what *is* common between two different businesses, many other things are not.

Strategies of Entry and Control: Chain integration or diversification may be achieved by *internal development* or *acquisition.* In other words, an organization can enter a new business by developing it itself or by buying an organization already in that business. Our little diagrams show the former as a circle growing out from the core business to envelope the new business, the latter as an arrow coming out from the core business to connect to the new but already established business. Both internal development and acquisition involve complete ownership and formal control of the diversified business. But there are a host of other possible strategies, as follows:

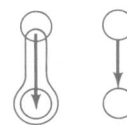

Strategies of Entry and Control

Full ownership and control
- Internal Development
- Acquisition

Partial ownership and control
- Majority, minority
- Partnership, including
  - Joint venture
  - Turnkey (temporary control)

Partial control without ownership
- Licencing
- Franchising
- Long-term contracting

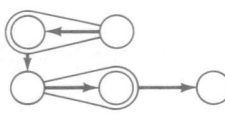

Combined Integration-Diversification Strategies: Among the most interesting are those strategies that combine chain integration with business diversification, sometimes leading organizations into whole networks of new businesses. *By-product diversification* involves selling off the by-products of the operating chain in separate markets, as when an airline offers its maintenance services to other carriers. The new activity amounts to a form of market development at some intermediate point in the operating chain. *Linked diversification* extends by-product diversification: one business simply leads to another, whether integrated "vertically" or diversified "horizontally." The organization pursues its operating chain upstream, downstream, sidestream; it exploits preproducts, end products, and by-products of its core products as well as of each other, ending up with a network of businesses, as illustrated in the case of a supermarket chain in Figure 6. *Crystalline diversification* pushes the previous strategy to the limit, so that it becomes difficult and perhaps irrelevant to distinguish integration from diversification, core activities from peripheral activities, closely related businesses from distantly related ones. What were once clear links in a few chains now metamorphose into what looks like a form of crystalline growth, as business after business gets added literally right and left as well as up and down. Here businesses tend to be related, at least initially, through internal development of core competences, as in the "coating and bonding technologies" that are common to so many of 3M's products.

Withdrawal Strategies: Finally there are strategies that reverse all those of diversification: organizations cut back on the businesses they are in. "Exit" has been one popular label for this, withdrawal is another. Sometimes organizations *shrink* their activities, canceling long-term licenses, ceasing to sell by-products, reducing their crystalline networks. Other times they abandon or *liquidate* businesses (the

FIGURE 6
Linked Diversification on a Time Scale—the Case of the Steinberg chain
From Mintzberg and Waters (1982:490).

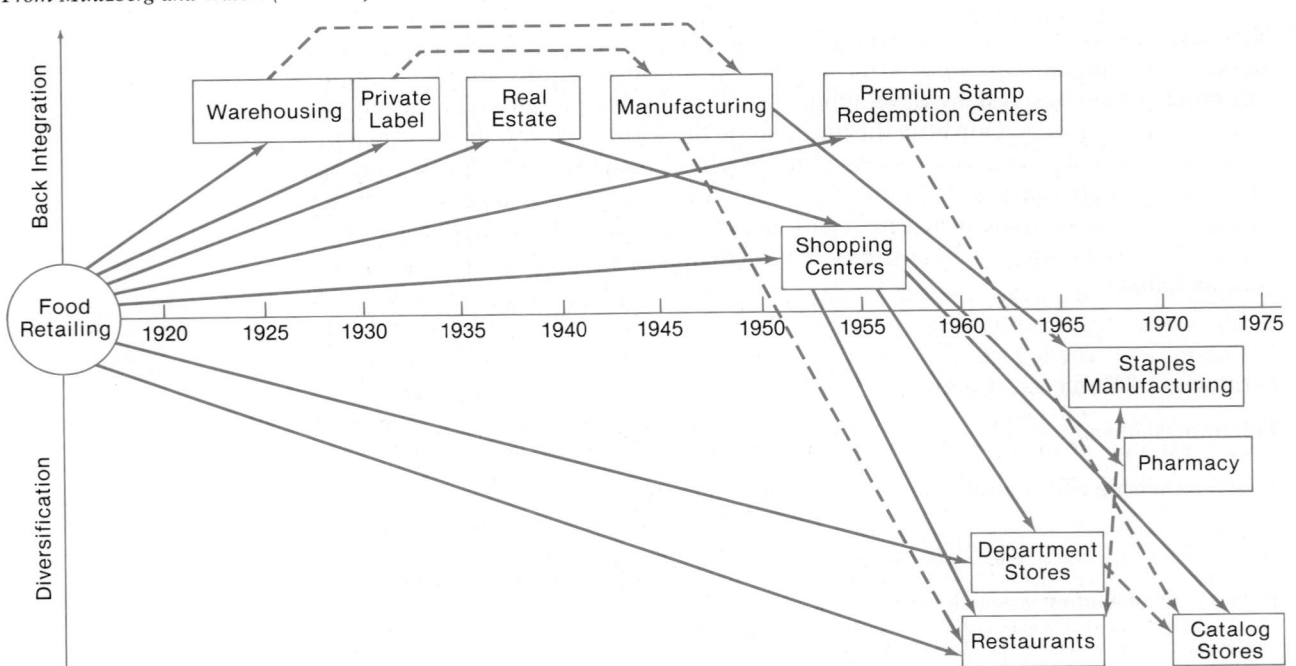

opposite of internal development), or else they *divest* them (the opposite of acquisition).

RECONCEIVING THE CORE BUSINESS(ES)

It may seem strange to end a discussion of strategies of ever more elaborate development of a business with ones involving reconception of the business. But in one
important sense, there is a logic to this: after a core business has been identified,
distinguished, elaborated, and extended, there often follows the need not just to
consolidate it but also to redefine it and reconfigure it—in essence, to reconceive
it. As they develop, through all the waves of expansion, integration, diversification,
and so on, some organizations lose a sense of themselves. Then reconception becomes the ultimate form of consolidation: rationalizing not just excesses in product offerings or markets segments or even new businesses, but all of these things
together and more—the essence of the entire strategy itself. We can identify three
basic reconception strategies:

Business Redefinition Strategy: A business, as Abell (1980) has pointed out,
may be defined in a variety of ways—by the function it performs, the market it
serves, the product it produces. All businesses have popular conceptions. Some are
narrow and tangible, such as the canoe business, others broader and vague, such as
the financial services business. All such definitions, no matter how tangible, are ultimately concepts that exist in the minds of actors and observers. It therefore becomes possible, with a little effort and imagination, to *redefine* a particular
business—reconceive the "recipe" for how that business is conducted (Grinyer and
Spender, 1979; Spender, 1989)—as Edwin Land did when he developed the Polaroid camera.[3]

Business Recombination Strategies: As Porter notes, through the waves of diversification that swept American business in the 1960s and 1970s, "the concept of
synergy has become widely regarded as passé"—a "nice idea" but one that rarely
occurred in practice" (1985:317–318). Businesses were elements in a portfolio to
be bought and sold, or, at best, grown and harvested. Deploring that conclusion,
Porter devoted three chapters of his 1985 book to "horizontal strategy," which we
shall refer to here (given our problems with the geometry of this field) as *business
recombination* strategies—efforts to recombine different businesses in some way, at
the limit to reconceive various businesses as one. Businesses can be recombined
tangibly or only conceptually. The latter was encouraged by Levitt's "Marketing
Myopia" (1960) article. By a stroke of the pen, railroads could be in the transportation business, ball bearing manufacturers in the friction reduction business. Realizing some practical change in behavior often proved much more difficult,
however. But when some substantial basis exists for combining different activities,
a strategy of business recombination can be very effective. There may never have
been a transportation business, but 3M was able to draw on common technological
capabilities to create a coating and bonding business.[4] Business recombination can

---

[3] MacMillan refers to the business redefinition strategy as "reshaping the industry infrastructure" (1983:18), while
Porter calls it "reconfiguration" (1985:519–523), although his notion of product *substitution,* (273–314) could sometimes also constitute a form of business redefinition.

[4] Our suspicion, we should note, is that such labels often emerge after the fact, as the organization seeks a way to rationalize the diversification that has already taken place. In effect, the strategy is emergent. (See Chapter 1 on "Five Ps
for Strategy.")

also be more tangible, based on shared activities in the value chain, as in a strategy of *bundling,* where complementary products are sold together for a single price (e.g., automobile service with the new car). Of course, *unbundling* can be an equally viable strategy, such as selling "term" insurance free of any investment obligation. Carried to their logical extreme, the more tangible recombination strategies lead to a "systems view" of the business, where all products and services are conceived to be tightly interrelated.

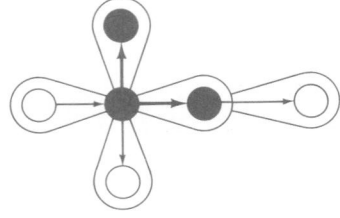

Core Relocation Strategies: Finally we come full circle by closing the discussion where we began, on the location of the core business. An organization, in addition to having one or more strategic positions in a marketplace, tends to have what Jay Galbraith (1983) calls a single "center of gravity" (see his article in Chapter 6), some conceptual place where is concentrated not only its core skills but also its cultural heart, as in a Procter & Gamble focusing its efforts on "branded consumer products," each "sold primarily by advertising to the homemaker and managed by a brand manager" (1984:13). But as changes in strategic position take place, shifts can also take place in this center of gravity, in various ways. First, the organization can move *along the operating chain,* upstream or downstream, as did General Mills "from a flour miller to a related diversified provider of products for the homemaker"; eventually the company sold off its flour milling operation altogether (Galbraith, 1983:76). Second, there can be a shift *between dominant functions,* say from production to marketing. Third is the shift *to a new business,* whether or not at the same stage of the operating chain. Such shifts can be awfully demanding, simply because each industry is a culture with its own ways of thinking and acting. Finally, is the shift *to a new core theme,* as in the reorientation from a single function or product to a broader concept, for example when Procter & Gamble changed from being a soap company to being in the personal care business.

This brings us to the end of our discussion of generic strategies—our loop from locating a business to distinguishing it, elaborating it, extending it, and finally reconceiving it. We should close with the warning that while a framework of generic strategies may help to think about positioning an organization, use of it as a pat list may put that organization at a disadvantage against competitors that develop their strategies in more creative ways.

● DEVELOPING COMPETITIVE ADVANTAGE*

BY XAVIER GILBERT AND PAUL STREBEL

Different industries offer different competitive opportunities and, as a result, successful strategies vary from one industry to another. Identifying which strategies can lead to competitive advantages in an industry may be done in three main steps:

1. *Industry definition:* This involves defining the boundaries of the industry, learning its rules of the game and identifying the other players.

---

* This article was prepared especially for the first edition of this book, and was also published with modifications in *The Handbook of Business Strategy: 1986–1987 Year Book,* William D. Guth (ed.), (Warrer, Gorham and Lamont, 1986), used with the permission of Xavier Gilbert and Paul Strebel.

2. *Identification of possible competitive moves:* Competitive moves exploit the possible sources of competitive advantages in the industry. Their degree of effectiveness evolves with the industry life cycle and is influenced by the moves of other competitors.

3. *Selecting among generic strategies:* Successful strategies rely on a sequence of competitive moves. There are only a few such successful sequences corresponding to different industry situations.

We shall discuss each of these steps in turn.

INDUSTRY DEFINITION

The arena of competition within which an industry member should fight will be described in terms of its boundaries, its rules of the game, and its players.

Identifying the Boundaries of the Industry

In identifying what constitutes the industry, we must take into account all the activities that are necessary to deliver a product or service that meets the expectations of a market. In this regard, many definitions of a company's business, or of its industry, have been too narrow: there is more to its business than a product, a process, and a market; there is in fact an entire chain of activities, from product design to product utilization by the final customer, that must be mobilized to meet certain market expectations.

The most commonly accepted term to designate this chain of activities is the *business system.* The concept, or some variation of it, has been used frequently under different names, such as "industry dynamics" or "value chain"; the term "business system" was coined in the Seventies by the consulting firm McKinsey & Company, from whom we borrow it. Some examples will illustrate why it is important to take into account the entire chain of activities represented by the business system when deciding how to compete.

The first example is provided by the personal computer industry (Figure 1). The business system of the personal computer industry includes a wide range of activities: product design, component manufacturing, different stages of assembly, software development, marketing, selling, distribution, service and support to the customer, and the utilization of the product by the customer. Each of these activities is expected to add value to the product so that it meets the needs of the customer. A view of all the activities necessary to serve customer expectations, as provided by the industry's business system, is thus the starting point of industry analysis.

Different competitors have made different choices with respect to how these activities should be dealt with. Some have designed their product around the "IBM industry standard" in order to have access to software, while others have been using a proprietary operating system. Some are designing their own components, while others are finding sources for them outside. Some have selectively authorized dealers to sell their products, while others use mass-retailing channels and others again sell directly to the final customer. This shows that there may be different ways to use the activities in the business system to provide value to the final customer.

Rather than considering the company as competing *in an industry,* it should thus be seen as competing *within a business system,* in the same way as a chess player uses the resources of a chessboard. A chess player does not try to win by

FIGURE 1
The PC Industry

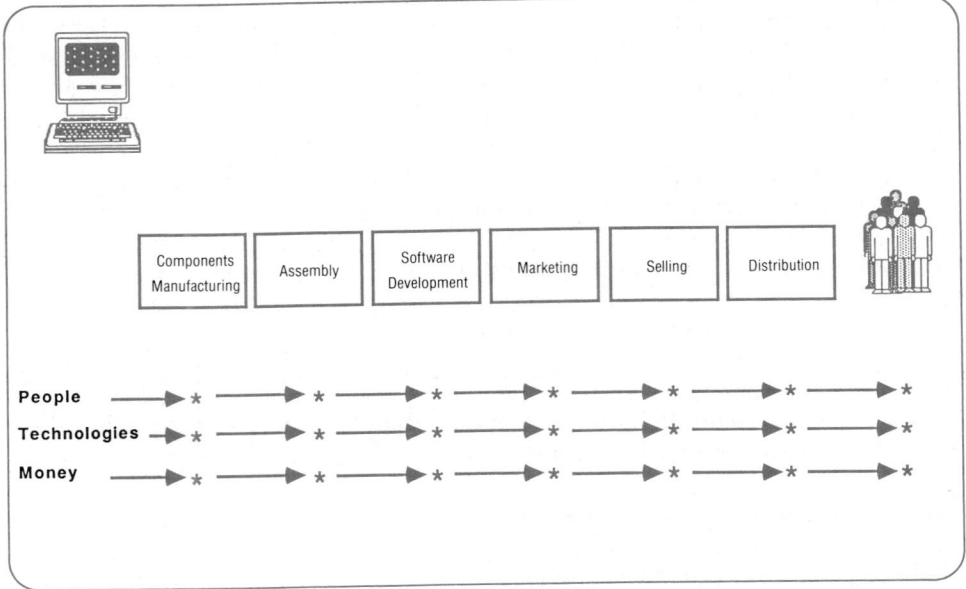

asking simply, "How do I win at chess?" Instead, the player asks, "How should I use my pawns, my rooks, my knights, my bishops, my queen, and even my king?" Similarly, each personal computer company should see itself as competing with other companies on design, on component manufacturing, on assembly of specific configurations, on software development, on marketing, on selling, on distribution, and on service support to the customer, and not simply as competing "in the personal computer industry."

Learning the Rules of the Game

Each activity in the business system adds perceived value to the product or service. Value,[1] for the customer, is the perceived stream of benefits that accrue from obtaining the product or service. Price is what the customer is willing to pay for that stream of benefits. If the price of a good or service is high, it must provide high value, otherwise it is driven out of the market. If the value of a good or service is low, its price must be low, otherwise it is also driven out of the market. Hence, in a competitive situation, and over a period of time, the price customers are willing to pay for a good or service is a good proxy measure of its value.

The "game" is to create a disequilibrium between the perceived value offered and the price asked by either increasing the former or by reducing the latter. This modifies the terms of competition and potentially drives competitors out of the market. Competitors will have to respond by either offering more perceived value for the same price or by offering the same value at a lower price.

At the same time, each activity in the business system is performed at a cost. Getting the stream of benefits that accrue from the good or service to the customer is thus done at a certain "delivered cost" which sets a lower limit to the price of the good or service if the business system is to remain profitable. Decreasing the price will thus imply that the delivered cost be first decreased by adjusting the business system. As a result, the rules of the game may also be described as providing the highest possible perceived value to the final customer, at the lowest possible delivered cost.

84

---

[1] "Value" is used here with the meaning it is given by economists in the utility theory.

In addition, the intrinsic logic of the business system must also be taken into account. This logic is dictated by the fact that the business-system activities must be coordinated to provide a specific final product. This requirement is best examined at the level of the resources needed for each activity: people, technologies and money.

The personal computer industry again illustrates the point. Among the resources needed to perform the various activities of the business system, the technologies will be used as an example. First, the final customers are not supposed to be computer experts. Their technological know-how might be in the areas of financial analysis, accounting or text processing, not in programming or establishing communication protocols with peripherals. This implies technological choices at the level of product and software design that will make the machine user friendly. It also implies that the technology required to service the machine and to assist customers, also selected at the time of product design, be compatible with the technology available in the distribution channels.

Similar consistency requirements could be observed with respect to the other resources: people and money. If these rules of the game were not respected, the business system could not deliver a product or service of desired perceived value. Laying out the activities of the business system and the resources required by each of them is thus necessary before the game can be played effectively.

Identifying the Other Players

"Players" in a business system do not consist only of competitors; they may be other participants in the business system that perform vital activities. For the provider of a product or service, managing the business system can be complicated by players up- and downstream in the system. By playing an optimal game from their perspective, these other participants may suboptimize the whole business system and put pressure on other activities.

Consider for example the Swiss watch industry (Figure 2). As long as competition was limited, the Swiss watch manufacturers, who were essentially fragmented assemblers, enjoyed satisfactory margins, even though their value added

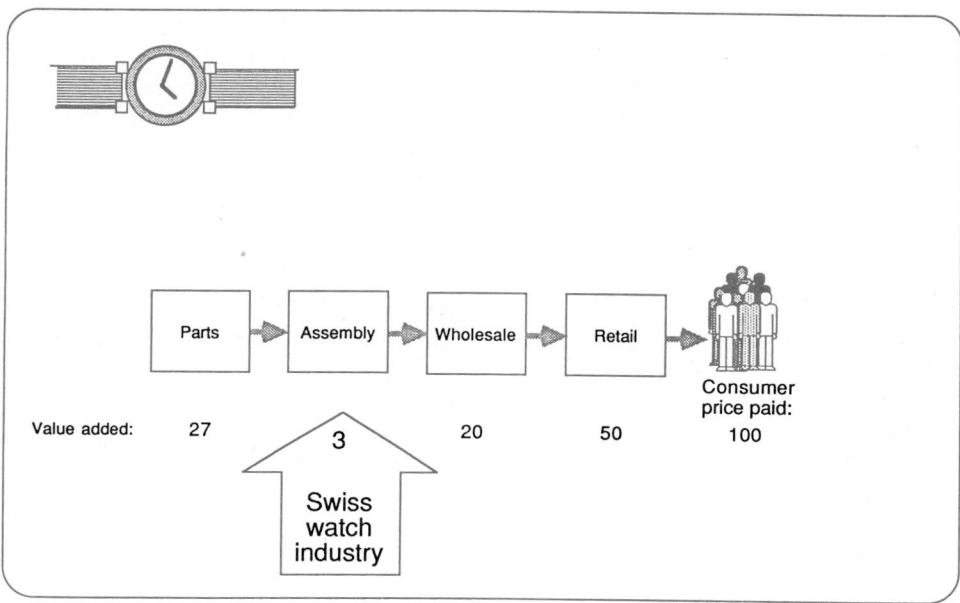

FIGURE 2
The Swiss Watch Industry

was small relative to the entire business system. But the industry experienced intense global competition during the Seventies and Eighties, leading to sharp price decreases. The first reaction was to believe that competition among watchmakers was the source of these difficulties. Attempts were made to restructure the Swiss watch industry so as to obtain economies of scale similar to those of global competitors.

However, the business system shows clearly that competition among watchmakers was not the biggest problem. Producing cheaper watches was necessary, but not sufficient. The Swiss watchmakers were competing fiercely for the consumers' money with costly distribution channels whose added value was questionable for a fast growing mass market. Developing a watch which would not only be inexpensive, but could also be sold through low-margin distribution channels with no service, such as the Swatch, was the way to circumvent this form of competition effectively.

COMPETITIVE MOVES

Competitive advantages are built on the ability to utilize the business system to provide final customers with the desired perceived value, at the lowest delivered cost. However, not all the activities of a business system offer the same potential to build these competitive advantages. In addition, their choice is affected by the stage of development of the industry as well as by the moves of other competitors. This leads to the identification of a limited number of generic moves to gain competitive advantages.

Competitive Advantages Offered by the Business System

Superior profitability requires either higher perceived value and/or lower delivered cost than the competition. This is achieved either through superior performance in at least one of the business-system activities, or through a creative and innovative combination of several activities. Such *competitive formulas* are the basis of all successful strategies.

For example, in the watch industry the main activities of the business system include design, manufacturing of movement parts, movement assembly, case manufacturing and assembly, wholesaling, and retail. Each of these activities can be performed to maximize the perceived value for the final user, or to minimize the delivered cost. Design, for example, can emphasize luxury and elegance, or it can ensure low-cost manufacturing. Traditional distribution channels through wholesalers and specialty stores will provide more perceived value, while mass distribution directly through low-margin outlets will contribute to a low delivered cost. A range of competitive formulas can thus be developed, combining the various activities of the business system in a manner that will provide the desired perceived value at the desired delivered cost.

Two observations, however, suggest that this range of possible competitive formulas is not very wide. The first one is that there is an internal logic to each business system. The balance between perceived value and delivered cost cannot be established for one activity independently of the others. For example, it is not possible to use traditional distribution channels to distribute the Swatch. Because of the high distribution margins and of the limited volume the delivered cost would be higher than the perceived value. This is indeed what is meant by a competitive formula. The various activities of the business system must combine high perceived value and low delivered cost in a coherent manner.

The second observation is that high perceived value and low delivered cost constitute the only possible generic competitive moves. Experience shows that there are no other possibilities. There are only variations around these two main themes, as allowed by the expectations of different market segments. Strategic advantages are obtained by combining them in a sequence, one being implemented preferably in a way that prepares the implementation of the other at a later time.

Many failures have been caused by the inability to put together coherent business systems, with respect to low delivered cost and high perceived value. This was exactly how the Swiss watch industry got into trouble, trying to compete in markets expecting low delivered cost with a business system designed for high perceived value. When the promoters of the Swatch saw that the biggest revolution in the industry was not a technological one, but a distribution one, they engineered a fine-tuned competitive formula in which each business-system activity contributed to delivering a watch for less than SFr50 (about $25). Even though the Swatch is very precise and carries an element of snobbish appeal, the move was quite clearly a low-delivered-cost one, with a formula that provided maximum perceived value within the low-delivered-cost constraint.

Stage of Development of the Industry

Although it would be theoretically feasible to choose either of these two moves—high perceived value or low delivered cost—at any point in time, the actual possibilities are in fact strongly influenced by the stage of industry development. The personal computer industry will be used as an example of the inferences that can be drawn from an industry life cycle to assist in the diagnosis of potential competitive advantages.

Consider first the personal computer industry in the second half of the Seventies. The characteristics of the product were in a state of flux, with many competing versions. The manufacturing process was not yet a matter of real concern, as the technology was still evolving. The business system of the industry had not stabilized. Competition was restricted to product innovation and development. These characteristics are typical of an *emerging industry* offering *high perceived value* to a limited market (Figure 3).

Consider now the personal computer industry after IBM's entry. Even though IBM's product was not regarded by seasoned users as particularly innovative on the technological side, it had the perhaps unintended advantage of embodying an acceptable common denominator of characteristics desired by a wide cross section of the market. Not the least of these characteristics was the image of IBM's reliability. The IBM PC was soon perceived as the industry standard.

Standardization marks the first important transition to another phase of industry evolution during which competitive advantages shift to *low delivered cost*. This new phase is characterized by *rapid market development*. The personal computer industry was no exception as it moved into a period of very rapid growth in unit sales. Attention had to be shifted to the production process, while most manufacturers were adopting the "IBM standard." Rather than further product development, resources were now directed towards the entire business system: process technology, market positioning, and distribution efficiency were key.

When IBM and others began to use prices strategically, many of the early competitors could not follow. Those who did survive had joined the industry-standard bandwagon and had the necessary resources to invest in the manufacturing process. The key competitors were now large, professional firms which followed a similar, low-delivered-cost industry discipline.

FIGURE 3
Industry Life Cycle

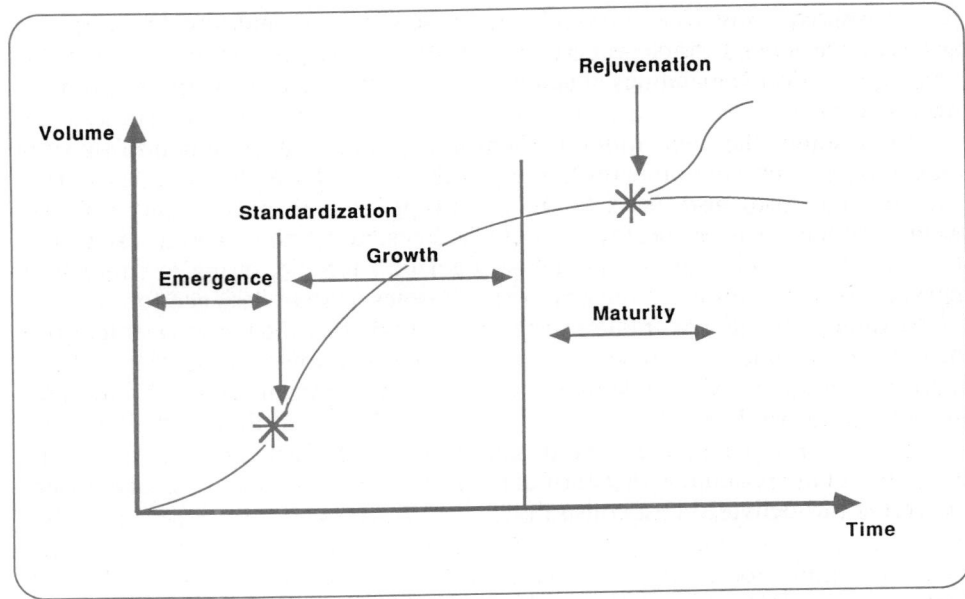

At the end of 1984 and in 1985, however, a new turn took place in the industry. Signs of *industry maturity* were appearing in the United States, while activity was starting again on the side of product improvement. IBM itself launched its PC-AT and the need for networks was receiving increasing attention from competitors. Such renewed interest in the perceived value of the product is typical at this stage of an industry's evolution, often called rejuvenation (Figure 3). However, the entire process that made the business system work was still getting much attention. Resources were now channeled both to the process and to a new product generation: integrated computer networks. These developments were in the hands of a few large competitors who could be active on two fronts, process and product.

In a *maturing industry, rejuvenation* is the second important evolutionary transition. It marks the shift to product differentiation and innovation, in addition to cost reduction and process efficiency. At this stage, competitive advantages must be maintained on two fronts: *low delivered cost* and, again, *high perceived value.* As a result of this combination, however, perceived-value advantages can only be marginal and short lived. This is a time when marketing activity is at its peak.

The effectiveness of high-perceived-value and low-delivered-cost advantages thus varies with the stage of development of the industry. The two generic moves that lead to these advantages must be implemented at the right stage of development of the industry, either to accelerate its evolution, or to follow it.

Identifying Strategic Groups

The competitors in an industry can be positioned according to which generic moves they are making at a given time. The resulting mapping may be examined for signs of strategic groups of competitors.

Identifying strategic groups can serve several purposes. An important one is to assess how the moves of competitors may affect the evolution of the industry. The life cycle of an industry is not only pulled by changes in market expectations. It is also pushed by the move of some of the competitors. For example, IBM's entry in the personal computer industry accelerated the transition to market development. Subsequently, IBM's low-delivered-cost move accompanied with decreasing prices accelerated the transition to maturity. As we have seen, assessing the industry evolution is an important input in deciding which competitive move to implement next.

In addition, the identification of strategic groups can serve two other purposes. First, by observing how the key competitors are playing the business system to obtain their competitive advantages, it is possible to develop a better understanding of the business system and of the possible competitive advantages it offers. Second, identifying which competitive positions are occupied and by whom helps decide which competitors may be confronted or avoided.

Although the movements of competitors can be assessed quantitatively, since both perceived value and delivered cost can be measured, an example of how it can be done qualitatively will be provided here. This example is based on the personal computer industry (Figure 4).

Three main groups could be identified in early 1986. The first group included the industry-standard competitors, of course led by IBM. A low-delivered-cost obsession was clear with this group, as indicated by the price decreases that marked 1985 and were continuing in 1986. In addition to IBM, the group included Compaq, Zenith, for example in the United States, Sharp, Epson and Toshiba from Japan, and Olivetti from Europe. All were offering basically the same commodity-like product. All were seeing low price as a necessary condition to stay in the game. However, and this is characteristic of a mature industry, all were also trying to offer something else in addition to low price, such as more speed, more capacity, more user friendliness, wider distribution. But none of these features could yield a lasting advantage.

There was a second group that was trying to exploit the fact that the rules of the game could perhaps be changed. If networking of personal computers, with each other and with mainframes, became critical, which seemed to be the case, the personal computer would become a standard workstation in a decentralized data processing system. It would no longer be the "force de frappe" and future competitive advantages would accrue from the ability to provide communication hardware and software.

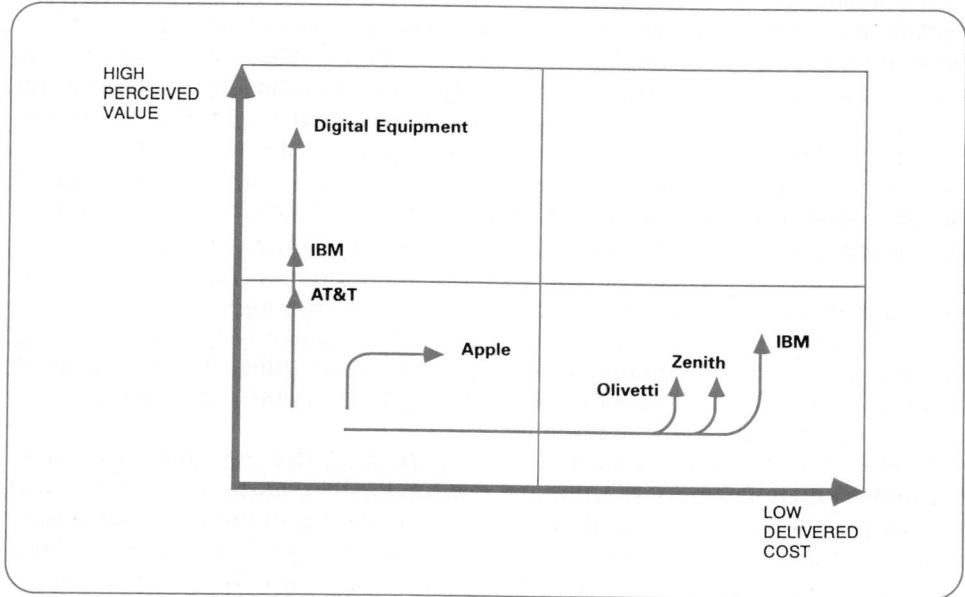

FIGURE 4
Strategic Groups: The PC Industry

Among the companies competing effectively in this direction were Digital Equipment and other minicomputer vendors, who had traditionally networked their machines. IBM was also trying to compete on this front, with its usual follower approach, but it was hampered by its traditionally centralized approach to data processing. AT&T and other telecommunication companies were other credible contenders. The strategies in this group were clearly on the side of the high perceived value. The battle of communication standards that was taking place at that time was characteristic of these strategies.

There was finally a third group of those who were beginning to look as if they had missed the boat. Apple was still its most successful member, fighting with low prices and product uniqueness, but a uniqueness of increasingly questionable relevance. However, Apple's statements of intention concerning a future compatibility of the Macintosh with IBM's personal-computer standard and with Digital Equipment's network architecture, demonstrated some understanding of the emerging new rules of the game.

GENERIC STRATEGIES

Two generic moves, leading either to high perceived value, or to low delivered cost advantages, have been identified and their relevance at different stages of evolution of an industry has been discussed. Successful competitors, however, appear to be combining these moves within overall strategies that allow them to maintain a superior competitive position throughout the evolution of their industry. Two types of generic strategies can be identified:

> One-dimensional strategies, either high perceived value or low delivered cost.
> Outpacing strategies, either preemptive or proactive.

One-dimensional Strategies

One-dimensional strategies rely on the continued repetition of one move, either a high-perceived-value one, or low-delivered-cost one. The situations where this seems possible are not numerous. Only in industries with very short life cycles, like fashion, is it possible to pursue indefinitely a high-perceived-value strategy. Only in industries with very long life cycles, like commodities, is it possible to stick continuously to a low-delivered-cost strategy. In other instances, one-dimensional strategies often hide an inability to implement a new move at the right time and lead to disasters.

The Japanese entry into Western automobile markets is an illustration. In the Sixties, Western manufacturers were pursuing high-perceived-value strategies. In the United States, this led to yearly model changes. In Europe, ingenious, overengineered small cars were being produced with rather primitive processes. In the late Sixties, Japanese manufacturers began to sell basic and very inexpensive cars thanks to their highly efficient way of playing the business system, of which the manufacturing process was only a part. Success was almost immediate. Western manufacturers failed to see the need for a radical change in their competitive thrust and several were never able to respond.

However, this was not the end of the story. Both the price umbrella offered by Western manufacturers and the superior productivity of the Japanese allowed the latter to reinvest their cash-flow into product improvements and to offer more value for the same price. In Europe, this shift towards higher perceived value was welcomed because it brought new attraction to a standardizing product entering the maturity stage. In the United States, it essentially met an unsatisfied need for a lower-value, lower-price car to which U.S. manufacturers could never respond. This is evidenced by the instant success achieved by Hyundai by providing the same value as a Japanese car maker, but for less money.

Outpacing Strategies

The example of the automobile industry showed clearly that the formulation of a successful strategy rarely relies on the repeated implementation of the same move to maintain a static position. Successful strategies generally consist of a planned sequence of moves from one position to another, at the right time. The sequential implementation of competitive moves should not be seen as strategy changes. It must be planned, one move creating the conditions for the implementation of the next. The dynamic nature of successful strategies is reflected in their description as *outpacing* strategies (Figure 5). Outpacing strategies can be preemptive or proactive.

A preemptive strategy is needed by an industry leader to prevent the occurrence of a situation such as the one in the automobile industry. If successful, this strategy will shift the industry life cycle from the emergence stage to the growth stage. Its purpose is to prevent followers from developing secure low-price positions. This is achieved by shifting at the right time from a high-perceived-value position to a low-delivered-cost one. This implies the establishment of a product standard and the development of a *pricing reserve*.

Establishing a standard is not only a matter of technology, as was well demonstrated by the IBM Personal Computer. It is rather a question of business system: establishing a formula that meets the expectations of a larger number of potential customers than do other competitive formulas. It is the desired outcome of a high-perceived-value move.

Developing a pricing reserve simply means investing in process improvements to enable the shift to a low-delivered-cost strategy, as soon as a standard is

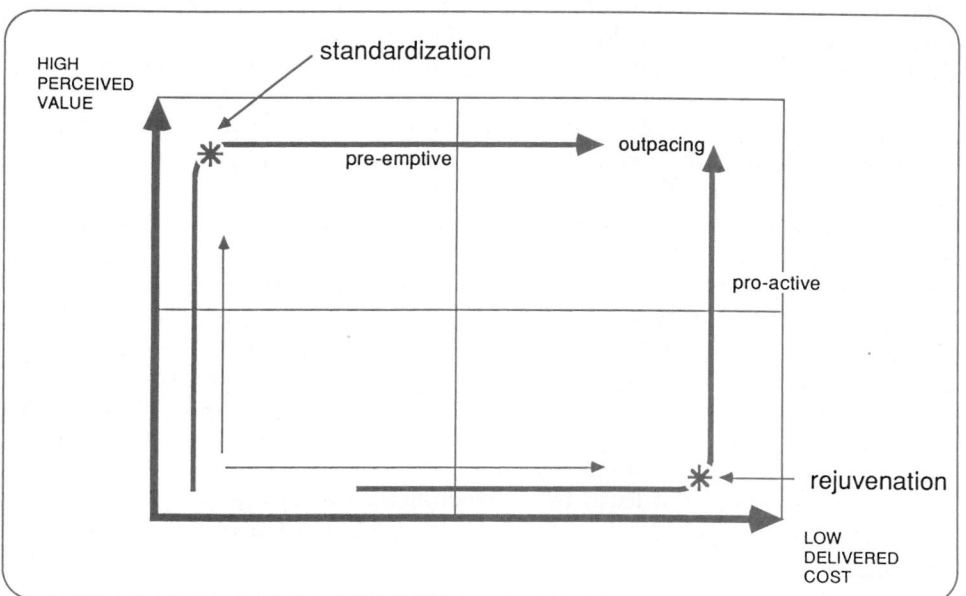

FIGURE 5
Outpacing Strategies

accepted. Experience shows that very few companies can make this shift effectively. It is nevertheless the condition for the tactical use of prices to prevent followers from generating the cash flow that will be necessary to go through the next industry transition, from low delivered cost, back to high perceived value, when the industry matures, if not to discourage them from entering at all. Such a strategy was followed by IBM, immediately after the IBM PC was accepted as a standard.

The timing of a preemptive, outpacing strategy is clearly critical. Launched too early, considerable investments in process improvement will be started before the formula is accepted as a standard. Should another standard emerge rapidly, the company will not be able to write off its previous process investments. Launched too late, further investments will have been made into product improvements which the market will not be willing to pay for. This will make it difficult to defend market share against the lower-priced standards and will waste resources that would otherwise be needed for process investments.

Proactive, outpacing strategies are required after the industry transition to lower growth and maturity. Their purpose is to escape the stalemate of maturity, so characteristic of many industries, where price wars often equate with self destruction. Often implemented by followers, they consist in building a solid low-delivered-cost position from which to launch a high-perceived-value move. While a preemptive strategy focuses on a mass market, a proactive one focuses on selected market segments to which more perceived value can be offered through a range of possibilities, from simple formula differentiation to rejuvenation of the industry. All these possibilities imply essentially the same approach: changing the rules of the game of the business system.

This is done by "unbundling" the perceived value added by each activity of the business system: what does each activity really provide to the selected market segment, and at what cost? The process of unbundling will identify elements of perceived value that are not worth their delivered cost. Then additional elements of perceived value, desirable for the market segment, can be included in the formula at an acceptable cost.

An example of this approach is the way in which the Swedish firm, IKEA, redesigned its business system in order to compete effectively in furniture mass distribution. IKEA eliminated or modified the activities that increased the delivered cost and did not add essential perceived value from the consumer point of view. Carefully monitored subcontracting of production to specialized manufacturers ensured quality at a lower cost. The furniture was no longer assembled, but flat-packed. It was not displayed in city-center stores, but in hyperstores, outside cities. A trade-off was made between minimum inventories, to decrease the delivered cost, and immediate availability. Furthermore, by doing its own product design, IKEA could ensure a low-delivered cost consistency throughout its business system.

On the other hand, perceived value was added where this could be done for a low-delivered cost. A very wide range of home products was offered under the same roof and could be looked at and tried by the consumer in the display section of the stores, rather than only seen in different stores or in catalogues. The furniture was normally available immediately and could be taken back home by car. Doing its own design, IKEA could offer a homogeneous, modular product range. The desirable image of Scandinavian furniture was skillfully exploited to add perceived value. Last but not least, by redesigning its entire business system, IKEA built an additional powerful competitive advantage: the know-how necessary to operate this formula.

Analysis of competitive advantage is thus an intrinsic part of strategic management, rather than a separate exercise, as it is often presented. Indeed, it cannot be performed linearly in a way that leads to one end product, the "knowledge of the industry." It is performed through an iterative process, leading to hypotheses concerning possible strategies, testing them against the company's capabilities and against the positions of competition, and going back to the drawing board to assess other possibilities. This iterative process is the foundation on which each move can lead to sustainable competitive advantages by being part of an overall strategy to fight in the dynamic battlefield of an industry. Bringing this iterative process to life is a permanent responsibility of the general manager of a business unit.

CHAPTER

5

STRATEGY FORMATION

The readings of the last two chapters described how strategies are supposed to be made and thereby illustrated the *pre*scriptive side of the field. This chapter presents readings that describe how strategies really do seem to be made, the *de*scriptive side. We title this chapter "Strategy Formation" to emphasize the point introduced in Chapter 1 that strategies can *form* implicitly as well as be *formulated* explicitly.

The preceding chapters may seem to deal with an unreachable utopia, this one with an imperfect reality. But there may be a better conclusion: that *pre*scription offers useful guidelines for thinking about ends and how to order physical resources efficiently to achieve them, while *de*scription provides a useful frame of reference for considering how this must be related to real-world patterns of behavior in organizations. Another way to say this is that while the analytical tools and models prescribed earlier are vital to thinking about strategy intelligently, they must also be rooted in a genuine understanding of the realities of organizations. Unfortunately, management writers, especially in traditional strategy textbooks, have often been quick to prescribe without offering enough appreciation of why managers and organizations act in the ways they do.

Brian Quinn opens with a sharp focus on how managers really do seem to behave when they create strategy. This reading is drawn from his book *Strategies for Change, Logical Incrementalism,* and it develops a particular view of the strategy-making process based on intensive interviews in some of America's and Europe's best known corporations. Planning does not capture the essence of strategy formation, according to Quinn, although it does play an important role in developing new data and in confirming strategies derived in other ways. The traditional view of incrementalism does not fit observed behavior patterns either. The processes Quinn observed seem incremental on the surface, but a powerful logic underlies them. And, unlike the other incremental processes, these are not so much *re*active as subtly *pro*active. Executives use incremental approaches to deal simultaneously with the informational, motivational, and political aspects of creating a strategy.

Above all, Quinn depicts strategy formation as a managed interactive *learning* process in which the chief strategist gradually works out strategy in his or her own mind and orchestrates the organization's acceptance of it. In emphasizing the role of a central strategist—or small groups managing "subsystems" of strategy—Quinn often seems close to Andrews's view. But the two differ markedly in other important respects. In his emphasis on the political and motivational dimensions of strategy, Quinn may be closer to Wrapp whose managers "don't make policy decisions." In fact, Quinn attempts to integrate his views with the traditional one, noting that while the strategies themselves "emerge" from an incremental process, they have many of the characteristics of the highly deliberate ones of Andrews's strategists. A number of cases, notably those on IBM (A), Honda Motor, Sony, Pillsbury, General Mills, Continental Group, and Mountbatten and India offer opportunities to investigate the interaction of analytical and incremental processes in strategy formation.

The following reading by Mintzberg complements that of Quinn. Called "Crafting Strategy," it shows how managers mold strategies the way craftsmen mold their clay. This reading also builds on Mintzberg's reading of Chapter 1 on the different forms of strategy, developing further the concept of emergent strategy.

As you will see, the two authors of this book share a basic philosophy about how organizations must go about the difficult process of setting basic direction in a complex world. They also share a basic belief in the key role of the actual strategy-making process in organizations. Hence the title of the book, *The Strategy Process* and the particular importance of this chapter in it.

In a chapter that challenges many of the accepted notions about how strategy should be made, the next reading may be the most upsetting of all. In it Richard Pascale, a well-known consultant, writer, and lecturer at Stanford Business School, challenges head on not only the whole approach to strategy analysis (as represented in the last chapter), especially as practiced by the Boston Consulting Group (one of the better known "strategy boutiques" whose ideas will be discussed in Chapters 10 and 11), but also the very concept of strategy formulation itself.

As his point of departure, Pascale describes a BCG study carried out for the British government to explain how manufacturers in that country lost the American motorcycle market to the Japanese, and to the Honda Company in particular. The analysis seems impeccable and eminently logical: The Japanese were simply more clever, by thinking through a brilliant strategy before they acted. But then Pascale flew to Japan and interviewed those clever executives who pulled off this coup. We shall save the story for Pascale, who tells it with a great deal of color, except to note here its basic message: An openness to learning and a fierce commitment to an organization and its markets may count for more in strategy making than all the brilliant analysis one can imagine. (Ask yourself while reading these accounts how the strategic behavior of the British motorcycle manufacturers who received the BCG report might have differed if they had instead received Pascale's second story.) Pascale in effect takes the arguments for incrementalism and strategy making as a crafting and learning process to their natural conclusions (or one of them, at least).

No one who reads Pascale's account can ever feel quite so smug about rational strategy analysis again. We include this reading, however, not to encourage rejection of that type of analysis, or the very solid thinking that has gone into the works of Porter, Ansoff, and others. Rather, we wish to balance the message conveyed in so much of the strategy literature with the practical lessons from the field. The point is that successful strategists can no more rely exclusively on such analysis than they can do without it. Effective strategy formation, one must conclude from all these readings, is a sometimes deceptive and multifaceted affair, its complexity never to be underestimated.

We have mentioned the complementarity of the Quinn and Mintzberg views of strategy making. But there is one difference that is worth addressing. While both view the process as one of evolution and learning, Quinn tends to place greater emphasis on the role of the chief executive, and senior management team in general, as central strategist, while Mintzberg tends to place a little more emphasis on others who can feed strategy up the hierarchy, especially in his discussion of a "grass-roots" approach to the process. In effect, organizations may have senior managers sending their strategic visions down the hierarchy, while below creative people may be sending strategic initiatives back up. Effective organizations seem to do both, but that raises a major problem in the strategy process: the middle managers may get caught in the middle, between these two. How to reconcile the two opposing pressures? The Honda case and reading gives some indication of how they may deal with it, but it is restricted largely to a set of events in one part of a company. Thus we close this chapter on process with a reading that addresses in a rather sophisticated way this very issue. Written by Ikujiro Nonaka, dean of the Japanese strategy researchers and professor of management at Hitotsubashi University, it proposes as a reconciliation a form of "middle-up-down management."

● STRATEGIC CHANGE: "LOGICAL INCREMENTALISM"*

BY JAMES BRIAN QUINN

> When I was younger I always conceived of a room where all these [strategic] concepts were worked out for the whole company. Later I didn't find any such room. . . . The strategy [of the company] may not even exist in the mind of one man. I certainly don't know where it is written down. It is simply transmitted in the series of decisions made. (Interview quote)

When well-managed major organizations make significant changes in strategy, the approaches they use frequently bear little resemblance to the rational-analytical systems so often touted in the planning literature. The full strategy is rarely written down in any one place. The processes used to arrive at the total strategy are typically fragmented, evolutionary, and largely intuitive. Although one can usually find embedded in these fragments some very refined *pieces* of formal strategic analysis, the real strategy tends to *evolve* as internal decisions and external events flow together to create a new, widely shared consensus for action among key members of the top management team. Far from being an abrogation of good management practice, the rationale behind this kind of strategy formulation is so powerful that it perhaps provides the normative model for strategic decision making—rather than the step-by-step "formal systems planning" approach so often espoused.

THE FORMAL SYSTEMS PLANNING APPROACH

A strong normative literature states what factors *should* be included in a systematically planned strategy and how to analyze and relate these factors step by step. While this approach is excellent for some purposes, it tends to focus unduly on

* Excerpted from an article originally published in *Sloan Management Review* I, no. 20 (Fall 1978), pp. 7–21. Copyright © 1978 by Sloan Management Review; reprinted by permission of the Review.

measurable quantitative factors and to underemphasize the vital qualitative, or- ganizational, and power-behavioral factors which so often determine strategic suc- cess in one situation versus another. In practice, such planning is just one building block in a continuous stream of events that really determine corporate strategy.

THE POWER-BEHAVIORAL APPROACH

Other investigators have provided important insights on the crucial psychological, power, and behavioral relationships in strategy formulation. Among other things, these have enhanced understanding about: the *multiple goal structures* of organiza- tions, the *politics* of strategic decisions, executive *bargaining* and *negotiation* proc- esses, *satisficing* (as opposed to maximizing) in decision making, the role of *coalitions* in strategic management, and the practice of "muddling" in the public sphere. Unfortunately, however, many power-behavioral studies have been con- ducted in settings far removed from the realities of strategy formulation. Others have concentrated solely on human dynamics, power relationships, and organiza- tional processes and ignored the ways in which systematic data analysis shapes and often dominates crucial aspects of strategic decisions. Finally, few have offered much normative guidance for the strategist.

THE STUDY

Recognizing the contributions and limitations of both approaches, I attempted to document the dynamics of actual strategic change processes in some ten major companies as perceived by those most knowledgeably and intimately involved in them. These companies varied with respect to products, markets, time horizons, technological complexities, and national versus international dimensions. . . .[1]

SUMMARY FINDINGS

Several important findings have begun to emerge from these investigations.

- Neither the "power-behavioral" nor the "formal systems planning" paradigm adequately characterizes the way successful strategic processes operate.
- Effective strategies tend to emerge from a series of "strategic subsystems," each of which attacks a specific class of strategic issue (e.g., acquisitions, di- vestitures, or major reorganizations) in a disciplined way, but which is blended incrementally and opportunistically into a cohesive pattern that be- comes the company's strategy.
- The logic behind each "subsystem" is so powerful that, to some extent, it may serve as a normative approach for formulating these key elements of strategy in large companies.
- Because of cognitive and process limits, almost all of these subsystems—and the formal planning activity itself—must be managed and linked together by an approach best described as "logical incrementalism."

---

[1] Cooperating companies included General Motors Corp., Chrysler Corp., Volvo (AB), General Mills, Pillsbury Co., Xerox Corp., Texas Instruments, Exxon, Continental Group, and Pilkington Brothers.

- Such incrementalism is not "muddling." It is a purposeful, effective, proactive management technique for improving and integrating *both* the analytical and behavioral aspects of strategy formulation.

CRITICAL STRATEGIC ISSUES

Although certain "hard data" decisions (e.g., on product-market position or resource allocations) tend to dominate the analytical literature (Ansoff, 1965; Katz, 1970), executives identified other "soft" changes that have at least as much importance in shaping their concern's strategic posture. Most often cited were changes in the company's

1. Overall organizational structure or its basic management style
2. Relationships with the government or other external interest groups
3. Acquisition, divestiture, or divisional control practices
4. International posture and relationships
5. Innovative capabilities or personnel motivations as affected by growth
6. Worker and professional relationships reflecting changed social expectations and values
7. Past or anticipated technological environments

When executives were asked to "describe the processes through which their company arrived at its new posture" vis-à-vis each of these critical domains, several important points emerged. First, few of these issues lent themselves to quantitative modeling techniques or perhaps even formal financial analyses. Second, successful companies used a different "subsystem" to formulate strategy for each major class of strategic issues, yet these "subsystems" were quite similar among companies even in very different industries (see Figure 1). Finally, no single formal analytical process could handle all strategic variables simultaneously on a planned basis. Why?

Precipitating Events

Often external or internal events, over which managements had essentially no control, would precipitate urgent, piecemeal, interim decisions which inexorably shaped the company's future strategic posture. One clearly observes this phenomenon in: the decisions forced on General Motors by the 1973–1974 oil crisis, the shift in posture pressed upon Exxon by sudden nationalizations, or the dramatic opportunities allowed for Haloid Corporation and Pilkington Brothers, Ltd. by the unexpected inventions of xerography and float glass.

In these cases, analyses from earlier formal planning cycles did contribute greatly, as long as the general nature of the contingency had been anticipated. They broadened the information base available (as in Exxon's case), extended the options considered (Haloid-Xerox), created shared values to guide decisions about precipitating events in consistent directions (Pilkington), or built up resource bases, management flexibilities, or active search routines for opportunities whose specific nature could not be defined in advance (General Mills, Pillsbury). But no organization—no matter how brilliant, rational, or imaginative—could possibly foresee the timing, severity, or even the nature of all such precipitating events. Further, when these events did occur there might be neither time, resources, nor information enough to undertake a full formal strategic analysis of all possible options

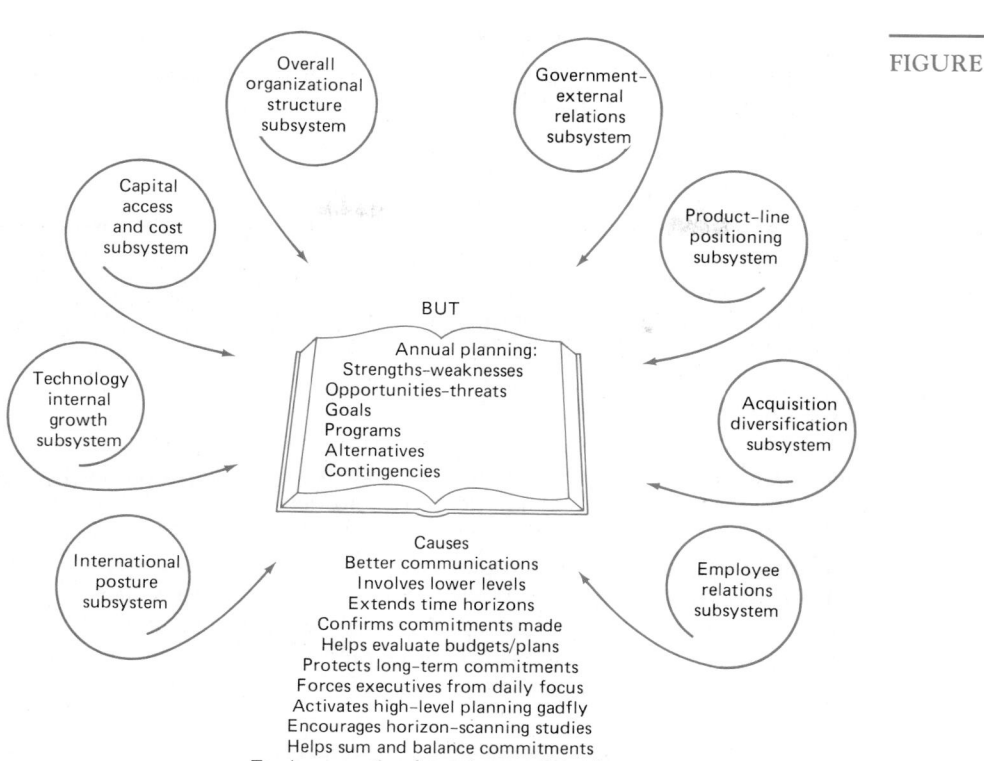

FIGURE 1

Overall organizational structure subsystem

Government-external relations subsystem

Capital access and cost subsystem

Product-line positioning subsystem

Technology internal growth subsystem

Acquisition diversification subsystem

BUT

Annual planning:
Strengths-weaknesses
Opportunities-threats
Goals
Programs
Alternatives
Contingencies

International posture subsystem

Employee relations subsystem

Causes
Better communications
Involves lower levels
Extends time horizons
Confirms commitments made
Helps evaluate budgets/plans
Protects long-term commitments
Forces executives from daily focus
Activates high-level planning gadfly
Encourages horizon-scanning studies
Helps sum and balance commitments
Teaches executives future impact of decisions
Provides a vehicle for negotiating operating goals
Coordinates tactical, divisional, corporate, strategic plans
etc.

and their consequences. Yet early decisions made under stress conditions often meant new thrusts, precedents, or lost opportunities that were difficult to reverse later.

An Incremental Logic

Recognizing this, top executives usually consciously tried to deal with precipitating events in an incremental fashion. Early commitments were kept broadly formative, tentative, and subject to later review. In some case neither the company nor the external players could understand the full implications of alternative actions. All parties wanted to test assumptions and have an opportunity to learn from and adapt to the others' responses. Such behavior clearly occurred during the 1973–1974 oil crisis; the ensuing interactions improved the quality of decisions for all. It .also recurred frequently in other widely different contexts. For example,

Neither the potential producer nor user of a completely new product or process (like xerography or float glass) could fully conceptualize its ramifications without interactive testing. All parties benefited from procedures which purposely delayed decisions and allowed mutual feedback. Some companies, like IBM or Xerox, have formalized this concept into "phase program planning" systems. They make concrete decisions only on individual phases (or stages) of new product developments, establish interactive testing procedures with customers, and postpone final configuration commitments until the latest possible moment.

Similarly, even under pressure, most top executives were extremely sensitive to organizational and power relationships and consciously managed decision processes to improve these dynamics. They often purposely delayed initial decisions, or

99

kept such decisions vague, in order to encourage lower-level participation, to gain more information from specialists, or to build commitment to solutions. Even when a crisis atmosphere tended to shorten time horizons and make decisions more goal oriented than political, perceptive executives consciously tried to keep their options open until they understood how the crisis would affect the power bases and needs of their key constituents. . . .

Conscious incrementalism helps to (1) cope with both the cognitive and process limits on each major decision, (2) build the logical-analytical framework these decisions require, and (3) create the personal and organizational awareness, understanding, acceptance, and commitment needed to implement the strategies effectively.

The Diversification Subsystem

Strategies for diversification, either through R&D or acquisitions, provide excellent examples. The formal analytical steps needed for successful diversification are well documented (Mace and Montgomery, 1962). However, the precise directions that R&D may project the company can only be understood step by step as scientists uncover new phenomena, make and amplify discoveries, build prototypes, reduce concepts to practice, and interact with users during product introductions. Similarly, only as each acquisition is sequentially identified, investigated, negotiated for, and integrated into the organization can one predict its ultimate impact on the total enterprise.

A step-by-step approach is clearly necessary to guide and assess the strategic fit of each internal or external diversification candidate. Incremental processes are also required to manage the crucial psychological and power shifts that ultimately determine the program's overall direction and consequences. These processes help unify both the analytical and behavioral aspects of diversification decisions. They create the broad conceptual consensus, the risk-taking attitudes, the organizational and resource flexibilities, and the adaptive dynamism that determine both the timing and direction of diversification strategies. Most important among these processes are:

- *Generating a genuine, top-level psychological commitment to diversification.* General Mills, Pillsbury, and Xerox all started their major diversification programs with broad analytical studies and goal-setting exercises designed both to build top-level consensus around the need to diversify and to establish the general directions for diversification. Without such action, top-level bargaining for resources would have continued to support only more familiar (and hence apparently less risky) old lines, and this could delay or undermine the entire diversification endeavor.

- *Consciously preparing to move opportunistically.* Organizational and fiscal resources must be built up in advance to exploit candidates as they randomly appear. And a "credible activist" for ventures must be developed and backed by someone with commitment power. All successful acquirers created the potential for "profit-centered" divisions within their organizational structures, strengthened their financial-controllership capabilities, took action to create low-cost capital access, and maintained the shortest possible communication lines from the "acquisitions activist" to the resource-committing authority. All these actions integrally determined which diversifications actually could be made, the timing of their accession, and the pace they could be absorbed.

- *Building a "comfort factor" for risk taking.* Perceived risk is largely a function of one's knowledge about a field. Hence well-conceived diversification programs should anticipate a trial-and-error period during which top managers reject early proposed fields or opportunities until they have analyzed enough trail candidates to "become comfortable" with an initial selection. Early successes tend to be "sure things" close to the companies' past (real or supposed) expertise. After a few successful diversifications, managements tend to become more confident and accept other candidates—farther from traditional lines—at a faster rate. Again the way this process is handled affects both the direction and pace of the actual program.

- *Developing a new ethos.* If new divisions are more successful than the old—as they should be—they attract relatively more resources and their political power grows. Their most effective line managers move into corporate positions, and slowly the company's special competency and ethos change. Finally, the concepts and products which once dominated the company's culture may decline in importance or even disappear. Acknowledging these ultimate consequences to the organization at the beginning of a diversification program would clearly be impolitic, even if the manager both desired and could predict the probable new ethos. These factors must be handled adaptively, as opportunities present themselves and as individual leaders and power centers develop.

Each of the above processes interacts with all others (and with the random appearance of diversification candidates) to affect action sequences, elapsed time, and ultimate results in unexpected ways. Complexities are so great that few diversification programs end up as initially envisioned. Consequently, wise managers recognize the limits to systematic analysis in diversification, and use formal planning to build the "comfort levels" executives need for risk taking and to guide the program's early directions and priorities. They then modify these flexibly, step by step, as new opportunities, power centers, and developed competencies merge to create new potentials.

The Major Reorganization Subsystem

It is well recognized that major organizational changes are an integral part of strategy (Chandler, 1962). Sometimes they constitute a strategy themselves, sometimes they precede and/or precipitate a new strategy, and sometimes they help to implement a strategy. However, like many other important strategic decisions, macroorganizational moves are typically handled incrementally *and* outside of formal planning processes. Their effects on personal or power relationships preclude discussion in the open forums and reports of such processes.

In addition, major organizational changes have timing imperatives (or "process limits") all their own. In making any significant shifts, the executive must think through the new roles, capabilities, and probable individual reactions of the many principals affected. He may have to wait for the promotion or retirement of a valued colleague before consummating any change. He then frequently has to bring in, train, or test new people for substantial periods before he can staff key posts with confidence. During this testing period he may substantially modify his original concept of the reorganization, as he evaluates individuals' potentials, their performance in specific roles, their personal drives, and their relationships with other team members.

Because this chain of decisions affects the career development, power, affluence, and self-image of so many, the executive tends to keep close counsel in his discussions, negotiates individually with key people, and makes final commitments as late as possible in order to obtain the best matches between people's capabilities, personalities, and aspirations and their new roles. Typically, all these events do not come together at one convenient time, particularly the moment annual plans are due. Instead the executive moves opportunistically, step by step, selectively moving people toward a broadly conceived organizational goal, which is constantly modified and rarely articulated in detail until the last pieces fit together.

Major organizational moves may also define entirely new strategies the guiding executive cannot fully foresee. For example:

When Exxon began its regional decentralization on a worldwide basis, the Executive Committee placed a senior officer and board member with a very responsive management style in a vaguely defined "coordinative role" vis-à-vis its powerful and successful European units. Over a period of two years this man sensed problems and experimented with voluntary coordinative possibilities on a pan-European basis. Only later, with greater understanding by both corporate and divisional officers, did Exxon move to a more formal "line" relationship for what became Exxon Europe. Even then the move had to be coordinated in other areas of the world. All of these changes together led to an entirely new internal power balance toward regional and non-U.S. concerns and to a more responsive worldwide posture for Exxon. . . .

In such situations, executives may be able to predict the broad direction, but not the precise nature, of the ultimate strategy which will result. In some cases, such as Exxon, the rebalance of power and information relationships *becomes* the strategy, or at least its central element. In others, organizational shifts are primarily means of triggering or implementing new strategic concepts and philosophies. But in all cases, major organizational changes create unexpected new stresses, opportunities, power bases, information centers, and credibility relationships that can affect both previous plans and future strategies in unanticipated ways. Effective reorganization decisions, therefore, allow for testing, flexibility, and feedback. Hence, they should, and usually do, evolve incrementally.

FORMAL PLANNING IN CORPORATE STRATEGY

What role do classical formal planning techniques play in strategy formulation? All companies in the sample do have formal planning procedures embedded in their management direction and control systems. These serve certain essential functions. In a process sense, they

Provide a discipline forcing managers to take a careful look ahead periodically.

Require rigorous communications about goals, strategic issues, and resource allocations.

Stimulate longer-term analyses than would otherwise be made.

Generate a basis for evaluating and integrating short-term plans.

Lengthen time horizons and protect long-term investments such as R&D.

Create a psychological backdrop and an information framework about the future against which managers can calibrate short-term or interim decisions.

Fine-tune annual commitments.

Formalize cost reduction programs.

Help implement strategic changes once decided on (for example, coordinating all elements of Exxon's decision to change its corporate name).

In fact, formal planning practices actually institutionalize incrementalism. There are two reasons for this. *First,* in order to utilize specialized expertise and to obtain executive involvement and commitment, most planning occurs "from the bottom up" in response to broadly defined assumptions or goals, many of which are long standing or negotiated well in advance. Of necessity, lower-level groups have only a partial view of the corporation's total strategy, and command only a fragment of its resources. Their power bases, identity, expertise, and rewards also usually depend on their existing products or processes. Hence, these products or processes, rather than entirely new departures, should and do receive their primary attention. *Second,* most managements purposely design their plans to be "living" or "ever green." They are intended only as "frameworks" to guide and provide consistency for future decisions made incrementally. To act otherwise would be to deny that further information could have a value. Thus, properly formulated formal plans are also a part of an incremental logic.

In each case there were also important precursor events, analyses, and political interactions, and each was followed by organizational, power, and behavioral changes. But interestingly, such special strategic studies also represent a "subsystem" of strategy formulation distinct from both annual planning activities and the other subsystems exemplified above. Each of these develops some important aspect of strategy, incrementally blending its conclusions with those of other subsystems, and it would be virtually impossible to force all these together to crystallize a completely articulated corporate strategy at any one instant.

Total Posture Planning

Occasionally, however, managements do attempt very broad assessments of their companies' total posture. James McFarland of General Mills did this through taking the company's topmost managers away for a three day retreat to answer the questions on what defined a "great company" from the viewpoints of stockholders, employees, suppliers, the public, and society; how did the company's strengths and weaknesses compare with the defined posture of "greatness;" and finally how should they proceed to overcome the company's weaknesses and move it from "goodness to greatness." The strategies that characterized the McFarland era at General Mills flowed from these assessments.

Yet even such major endeavors are only portions of a total strategic process. Values which have been built up over decades stimulate or constrain alternatives. Precipitating events, acquisitions, divestitures, external relations, and organizational changes develop important segments of each strategy incrementally. Even the strategies articulated leave key elements to be defined as new information becomes available, polities permit, particular opportunities appear, or major product thrusts prove unsuccessful. Actual strategies therefore evolve as each company overextends, consolidates, makes errors, and rebalances various thrusts over time. And it is both logical and expected that this should be the case.

Strategic decisions do not lend themselves to aggregation into a single massive decision matrix where all factors can be treated relatively simultaneously in order to arrive at a holistic optimum. Many have spoken of the "cognitive limits" (March and Simon, 1958) which prevent this. Of equal importance are the "process limits"—that is, the timing and sequencing imperatives necessary to create awareness, build comfort levels, develop consensus, select and train people, and so on—which constrain the system, yet ultimately determine the decision itself.

A Strategy Emerges

Successful executives link together and bring order to a series of strategic processes and decisions spanning years. At the beginning of the process it is literally impossible to predict all the events and forces which will shape the future of the company. The best executives can do is to forecast the most likely forces which will impinge on the company's affairs and the ranges of their possible impact. They then attempt to build a resource base and a corporate *posture* that are so strong in selected areas that the enterprise can survive and prosper despite all but the most devastating events. They consciously select market/technological/product segments which the concern can "dominate" given its resource limits, and place some "side bets" (Ansoff, 1965) in order to decrease the risk of catastrophic failure or to increase the company's flexibility for future options.

They then proceed incrementally to handle urgent matters, start longer-term sequences whose specific future branches and consequences are perhaps murky, respond to unforeseen events as they occur, build on successes, and brace up or cut losses on failures. They constantly reassess the future, find new congruencies as events unfurl, and blend the organization's skills and resources into new balances of dominance and risk aversion as various forces intersect to suggest better—but never perfect—alignments. The process is dynamic, with neither a real beginning nor end. . . .

CONCLUSION

Strategy deals with the unknowable, not the uncertain. It involves forces of such great number, strength, and combinatory powers that one cannot predict events in a probabilistic sense. Hence logic dictates that one proceed flexibly and experimentally from broad concepts toward specific commitments, making the latter concrete as late as possible in order to narrow the bands of uncertainty and to benefit from the best available information. This is the process of "logical incrementalism."

"Logical incrementalism" is not "muddling," as most people use that word. It is conscious, purposeful, proactive, good management. Properly managed, it allows the executive to bind together the contributions of rational systematic analyses, political and power theories, and organizational behavior concepts. It helps the executive achieve cohesion and identity with new directions. It allows him to deal with power relationships and individual behavioral needs, and permits him to use the best possible informational and analytical inputs in choosing his major courses of action. . . .

• CRAFTING STRATEGY*

BY HENRY MINTZBERG

Imagine someone planning strategy. What likely springs to mind is an image of orderly thinking: a senior manager, or a group of them, sitting in an office formulating courses of action that everyone else will implement on schedule. The keynote is reason—rational control, the systematic analysis of competitors and markets, of company strengths and weaknesses, the combination of these analyses producing clear, explicit, full-blown strategies.

Now imagine someone *crafting* strategy. A wholly different image likely results, as different from planning as craft is from mechanization. Craft evokes traditional skill, dedication, perfection through the mastery of detail. What springs to mind is not so much thinking and reason as involvement, a feeling of intimacy and harmony with the materials at hand, developed through long experience and commitment. Formulation and implementation merge into a fluid process of learning through which creative strategies evolve.

My thesis is simple: the crafting image better captures the process by which effective strategies come to be. The planning image, long popular in the literature, distorts these processes and thereby misguides organizations that embrace it unreservedly.

In developing this thesis, I shall draw on the experiences of a single craftsman, a potter, and compare them with the results of a research project that tracked the strategies of a number of corporations across several decades. Because the two contexts are so obviously different, my metaphor, like my assertion, may seem farfetched at first. Yet if we think of a craftsman as an organization of one, we can see that he or she must also resolve one of the great challenges the corporate strategist faces: knowing the organization's capabilities well enough to think deeply enough about its strategic direction. By considering strategy making from the perspective of one person, free of all the paraphernalia of what has been called the strategy industry, we can learn something about the formation of strategy in the corporation. For much as our potter has to manage her craft, so too managers have to craft their strategy.

At work, the potter sits before a lump of clay on the wheel. Her mind is on the clay, but she is also aware of sitting between her past experiences and her future prospects. She knows exactly what has and has not worked for her in the past. She has an intimate knowledge of her work, her capabilities, and her markets. As a craftsman, she senses rather than analyzes these things; her knowledge is "tacit." All these things are working in her mind as her hands are working the clay. The product that emerges on the wheel is likely to be in the tradition of her past work, but she may break away and embark on a new direction. Even so, the past is no less present, projecting itself into the future.

In my metaphor, managers are craftsmen and strategy is their clay. Like the potter, they sit between the past of corporate capabilities and a future of market opportunities. And if they are truly craftsmen, they bring to their work an equally intimate knowledge of the materials at hand. That is the essence of crafting strategy.

---

* Originally published in the *Harvard Business Review* (July–August 1987) and winner of McKinsey prize for second best article in the *Review* 1987. Copyright © 1987 by the President and Fellows of Harvard College; all rights reserved. Reprinted with deletions by permission of the *Harvard Business Review*.

Ask almost anyone what strategy is, and they will define it as a plan of some sort, an explicit guide to future behavior. Then ask them what strategy a competitor or a government or even they themselves have actually pursued. Chances are they will describe consistency in *past* behavior—a pattern in action over time. Strategy, it turns out, is one of those words that people define in one way and often use in another, without realizing the difference.

The reason for this is simple. Strategy's formal definition and its Greek military origins not withstanding, we need the word as much to explain past actions as to describe intended behavior. After all, if strategies can be planned and intended, they can also be pursued and realized (or not realized, as the case may be). And pattern in action, or what we call realized strategy, explains that pursuit. Moreover, just as a plan need not produce a pattern (some strategies that are intended are simply not realized), so too a pattern need not result from a plan. An organization can have a pattern (or realized strategy) without knowing it, let alone making it explicit.

Patterns, like beauty, are in the mind of the beholder, of course. But finding them in organizations is not very difficult. But what about intended strategies, those formal plans and pronouncements we think of when we use the term *strategy?* Ironically, here we run into all kinds of problems. Even with a single craftsman, how can we know what her intended strategies really were? If we could go back, would we find expressions of intention? And if we could, would we be able to trust them? We often fool ourselves, as well as others, by denying our subconscious motives. And remember that intentions are cheap, at least when compared with realizations.

Reading the Organization's Mind

If you believe all this has more to do with the Freudian recesses of a craftsman's mind than with the practical realities of producing automobiles, then think again. For who knows what the intended strategies of an organization really mean, let alone what they are? Can we simply assume in this collective context that the company's intended strategies are represented by its formal plans or by other statements emanating from the executive suite? Might these be just vain hopes or rationalizations or ploys to fool the competition? And even if expressed intentions do exist, to what extent do various people in the organization share them? How do we read the collective mind? Who is the strategist anyway?

The traditional view of strategic management resolves these problems quite simply, by what organizational theorists call attribution. You see it all the time in the business press. When General Motors acts, it's because its CEO has made a strategy. Given realization, there must have been intention, and that is automatically attributed to the chief.

In a short magazine article, this assumption is understandable. Journalists don't have a lot of time to uncover the origins of strategy, and GM is a large, complicated organization. But just consider all the complexity and confusion that gets tucked under this assumption—all the meetings and debates, the many people, the dead ends, the folding and unfolding of ideas. Now imagine trying to build a formal strategy-making system around that assumption. Is it any wonder that formal strategic planning is often such a resounding failure?

To unravel some of the confusion—and move away from the artificial complexity we have piled around the strategy-making process—we need to get back to some basic concepts. The most basic of all is the intimate connection between thought and action. That is the key to craft, and so also to the crafting of strategy.

2. STRATEGIES NEED NOT BE DELIBERATE—THEY CAN ALSO EMERGE, MORE OR LESS.

Virtually everything that has been written about strategy making depicts it as a deliberate process. First we think, then we act. We formulate, then we implement. The progression seems so perfectly sensible. Why would anybody want to proceed differently?

Our potter is in the studio, rolling the clay to make a waferlike sculpture. The clay sticks to the rolling pin, and a round form appears. Why not make a cylindrical vase? One idea leads to another, until a new pattern forms. Action has driven thinking: a strategy has emerged.

Out in the field, a salesman visits a customer. The product isn't quite right, and together they work out some modifications. The salesman returns to his company and puts the changes through; after two or three more rounds, they finally get it right. A new product emerges, which eventually opens up a new market. The company has changed strategic course.

In fact, most salespeople are less fortunate than this one or than our craftsman. In an organization of one, the implementor is the formulator, so innovations can be incorporated into strategy quickly and easily. In a large organization, the innovator may be ten levels removed from the leader who is supposed to dictate strategy and may also have to sell the idea to dozens of peers doing the same job.

Some salespeople, of course, can proceed on their own, modifying products to suit their customers and convincing skunkworks in the factory to produce them. In effect, they pursue their own strategies. Maybe no one else notices or cares. Sometimes, however, their innovations do get noticed, perhaps years later, when the company's prevalent strategies have broken down and its leaders are groping for something new. Then the salesperson's strategy may be allowed to pervade the system, to become organizational.

Is this story farfetched? Certainly not. We've all heard stories like it. But since we tend to see only what we believe, if we believe that strategies have to be planned, we're unlikely to see the real meaning such stories hold.

Consider how the National Film Board of Canada (NFB) came to adopt a feature-film strategy. The NFB is a federal government agency, famous for its creativity and expert in the production of short documentaries. Some years back, it funded a filmmaker on a project that unexpectedly ran long. To distribute his film, the NFB turned to theaters and so inadvertently gained experience in marketing feature-length films. Other filmmakers caught onto the idea, and eventually the NFB found itself pursuing a feature-film strategy—a pattern of producing such films.

My point is simple, deceptively simple: strategies can *form* as well as be *formulated*. A realized strategy can emerge in response to an evolving situation, or it can be brought about deliberately, through a process of formulation followed by implementation. But when these planned intentions do not produce the desired actions, organizations are left with unrealized strategies.

Today we hear a great deal about unrealized strategies, almost always in concert with the claim that implementation has failed. Management has been lax, controls have been loose, people haven't been committed. Excuses abound. At times, indeed, they may be valid. But often these explanations prove too easy. So some people look beyond implementation to formulation. The strategists haven't been smart enough.

While it is certainly true that many intended strategies are ill conceived, I believe that the problem often lies one step beyond, in the distinction we make between formulation and implementation, the common assumption that thought must be independent of and precede action. Sure, people could be smarter—but not only by conceiving more clever strategies. Sometimes they can be smarter by allowing their strategies to develop gradually, through the organization's actions and experiences. Smart strategists appreciate that they cannot always be smart enough to think through everything in advance.

Hands and Minds

No craftsman thinks some days and works others. The craftsman's mind is going constantly, in tandem with her hands. Yet large organizations try to separate the work of minds and hands. In so doing, they often sever the vital feedback link between the two. The salesperson who finds a customer with an unmet need may possess the most strategic bit of information in the entire organization. But that information is useless if he or she cannot create a strategy in response to it or else convey the information to someone who can—because the channels are blocked or because the formulators have simply finished formulating. The notion that strategy is something that should happen way up there, far removed from the details of running an organization on a daily basis, is one of the great fallacies of conventional strategic management. And it explains a good many of the most dramatic failures in business and public policy today.

Strategies like the NFB's that appear without clear intentions—or in spite of them—can be called emergent. Actions simply converge into patterns. They may become deliberate, of course, if the pattern is recognized and then legitimated by senior management. But that's after the fact.

All this may sound rather strange, I know. Strategies that emerge? Managers who acknowledge strategies already formed? Over the years, we have met with a good deal of resistance from people upset by what they perceive to be our passive definition of a word so bound up with proactive behavior and free will. After all, strategy means control—the ancient Greeks used it to describe the art of the army general.

Strategic Learning

But we have persisted in this usage for one reason: learning. Purely deliberate strategy precludes learning once the strategy is formulated; emergent strategy fosters it. People take actions one by one and respond to them, so that patterns eventually form.

Our craftsman tries to make a freestanding sculptural form. It doesn't work, so she rounds it a bit here, flattens it a bit there. The result looks better, but still isn't quite right. She makes another and another and another. Eventually, after days or months or years, she finally has what she wants. She is off on a new strategy.

In practice, of course, all strategy making walks on two feet, one deliberate, the other emergent. For just as purely deliberate strategy making precludes learning, so purely emergent strategy making precludes control. Pushed to the limit, neither approach makes much sense. Learning must be coupled with control. That is why we use the word *strategy* for both emergent and deliberate behavior.

Likewise, there is no such thing as a purely deliberate strategy or a purely emergent one. No organization—not even the ones commanded by those ancient Greek generals—knows enough to work everything out in advance, to ignore learning en route. And no one—not even a solitary potter—can be flexible enough to leave everything to happenstance, to give up all control. Craft requires control just as it requires responsiveness to the material at hand. Thus deliberate and emergent strategy form the end points of a continuum along which the strategies that are crafted in the real world may be found. Some strategies may approach either end, but many more fall at intermediate points.

3. EFFECTIVE STRATEGIES DEVELOP IN ALL KINDS OF STRANGE WAYS.

Effective strategies can show up in the strangest places and develop through the most unexpected means. There is no one best way to make strategy.

The form for a ceramic cat collapses on the wheel, and our potter sees a bull taking shape. Clay sticks to a rolling pin, and a line of cylinders results. Wafers come into being because of a shortage of clay and limited kiln space while visiting a studio in France. Thus errors become opportunities, and limitations stimulate creativity. The natural propensity to experiment, even boredom, likewise stimulates strategic change.

Organizations that craft their strategies have similar experiences. Recall the National Film Board with its inadvertently long film. Or consider its experiences with experimental films, which made special use of animation and sound. For 20 years, the NFB produced a bare but steady trickle of such films. In fact, every film but one in that trickle was produced by a single person, Norman McLaren, the NFB's most celebrated filmmaker. McLaren pursued a *personal strategy* of experimentation, deliberate for him perhaps (though who can know whether he had the whole stream in mind or simply planned one film at a time?) but not for the organization. Then 20 years later, others followed his lead and the trickle widened, his personal strategy becoming more broadly organizational.

While the NFB may seem like an extreme case, it highlights behavior that can be found, albeit in muted form, in all organizations. Those who doubt this might read Richard Pascale's account of how Honda stumbled into its enormous success in the American motorcyle market [the following article in this book].

Grass-roots Strategy Making

These strategies all reflect, in whole or part, what we like to call a grass-roots approach to strategic management. Strategies grow like weeds in a garden. They take root in all kinds of places, wherever people have the capacity to learn (because they are in touch with the situation) and the resources to support that capacity. These strategies become organizational when they become collective, that is, when they proliferate to guide the behavior of the organization at large.

Of course, this view is overstated. But it is no less extreme than the conventional view of strategic management, which might be labeled the hothouse approach. Neither is right. Reality falls between the two. Some of the most effective strategies we uncovered in our research combined deliberation and control with flexibility and organizational learning.

Consider first what we call the *umbrella strategy*. Here senior management sets out broad guidelines (say, to produce only high-margin products at the cutting edge of technology or to favor products using bonding technology) and leaves the specifics (such as what these products will be) to others lower down in the organization. This strategy is not only deliberate (in its guidelines) and emergent (in its specifics), but it is also deliberately emergent, in that the process is consciously managed to allow strategies to emerge en route. IBM used the umbrella strategy in the early 1960s with the impending 360 series, when its senior management approved a set of broad criteria for the design of a family of computers later developed in detail throughout the organization. [See the IBM case in this section.]

Deliberately emergent, too, is what we call the *process strategy*. Here management controls the process of strategy formation—concerning itself with the design of the structure, its staffing, procedures, and so on—while leaving the actual content to others.

Both process and umbrella strategies seem to be especially prevalent in businesses that require great expertise and creativity—a 3M, a Hewlett-Packard, a National Film Board. Such organizations can be effective only if their implementors are allowed to be formulators, because it is people way down in the hierarchy who are in touch with the situation at hand and have the requisite technical expertise. In a sense, these are organizations peopled with craftsmen, all of whom must be strategists.

4. STRATEGIC REORIENTATIONS HAPPEN IN BRIEF, QUANTUM LEAPS.

The conventional view of strategic management, especially in the planning literature, claims that change must be continuous: the organization should be adapting all the time. Yet this view proves to be ironic because the very concept of strategy is rooted in stability, not change. As this same literature makes clear, organizations pursue strategies to set direction, to lay out courses of action, and to elicit cooperation from their members around common, established guidelines. By any definition, strategy imposes stability on an organization. No stability means no strategy (no course to the future, no pattern from the past). Indeed, the very fact of having a strategy, and especially of making it explicit (as the conventional literature implores managers to do), creates resistance to strategic change!

What the conventional view fails to come to grips with, then, is how and when to promote change. A fundamental dilemma of strategy making is the need to reconcile the forces for stability and for change—to focus efforts and gain operating efficiencies on the one hand, yet adapt and maintain currency with a changing external environment on the other.

Quantum Leaps

Our own research and that of colleagues suggest that organizations resolve these opposing forces by attending first to one and then to the other. Clear periods of stability and change can usually be distinguished in any organization: while it is true that particular strategies may always be changing marginally, it seems equally true that major shifts in strategic orientation occur only rarely.

In our study of Steinberg, Inc., a large Quebec supermarket chain headquartered in Montreal, we found only two important reorientations in the 60 years from its founding to the mid-1970s: a shift to self-service in 1933 and the introduction of shopping centers and public financing in 1953. At Volkswagenwerk, we saw only one between the late 1940s and the 1970s, the tumultuous shift from the traditional Beetle to the Audi-type design. And at Air Canada, we found none over the airline's first four decades, following its initial positioning.

Our colleagues at McGill, Danny Miller and Peter Friesen (1984), found this pattern of change so common in their studies of large numbers of companies (especially the high-performance ones) that they built a theory around it, which they labeled the quantum theory of strategic change. Their basic point is that organizations adopt two distinctly different modes of behavior at different times.

Most of the time they pursue a given strategic orientation. Change may seem continuous, but it occurs in the context of that orientation (perfecting a given retailing formula, for example) and usually amounts to doing more of the same, perhaps better as well. Most organizations favor these periods of stability because they achieve success not by changing strategies but by exploiting the ones they have. They, like craftsmen, seek continuous improvement by using their distinctive competencies on established courses.

While this goes on, however, the world continues to change, sometimes slowly, occasionally in dramatic shifts. Thus gradually or suddenly, the organization's strategic orientation moves out of sync with its environment. Then what Miller and Friesen call a strategic revolution must take place. That long period of evolutionary change is suddenly punctuated by a brief bout of revolutionary turmoil in which the organization quickly alters many of its established patterns. In effect, it tries to leap to a new stability quickly to reestablish an integrated posture among a new set of strategies, structures, and culture.

But what about all those emergent strategies, growing like weeds around the organization? What the quantum theory suggests is that the really novel ones are generally held in check in some corner of the organization until a strategic revolution becomes necessary. Then, as an alternative to having to develop new strategies from scratch or having to import generic strategies from competitors, the organization can turn to its own emerging patterns to find its new orientation. As the old, established strategy disintegrates, the seeds of the new one begin to spread.

This quantum theory of change seems to apply particularly well to large established, mass-production companies, like a Volkswagenwerk. Because they are especially reliant on standardized procedures, their resistance to strategic reorientation tends to be especially fierce. So we find long periods of stability broken by short disruptive periods of revolutionary change. Strategic reorientations really are cultural revolutions.

In more creative organizations we see a somewhat different pattern of change and stability, one that is more balanced. Companies in the business of producing novel outputs apparently need to run off in all directions from time to time to sustain their creativity. Yet they also need to settle down after such periods to find some order in the resulting chaos—convergence following divergence.

Whether through quantum revolutions or cycles of convergence and divergence, however, organizations seem to need to separate in time the basic forces for change and stability, reconciling them by attending to each in turn. Many strategic failures can be attributed either to mixing the two or to an obsession with one of these forces at the expense of the other.

The problems are evident in the work of many craftsmen. On the one hand, there are those who seize on the perfection of a single theme and never change. Eventually the creativity disappears from their work and the world passes them by —much as it did Volkswagenwerk until the company was shocked into its strategic revolution. And then there are those who are always changing, who flit from one idea to another and never settle down. Because no theme or strategy ever emerges in their work, they cannot exploit or even develop any distinctive competence.

And because their work lacks definition, identity crises are likely to develop, with neither the craftsmen nor their clientele knowing what to make of it. Miller and Friesen (1978: 921) found this behavior in conventional business too; they label it "the impulsive firm running blind." How often have we seen it in companies that go on acquisition sprees?

5. TO MANAGE STRATEGY, THEN, IS TO CRAFT THOUGHT AND ACTION, CONTROL AND LEARNING, STABILITY AND CHANGE.

The popular view sees the strategist as a planner or as a visionary, someone sitting on a pedestal dictating brilliant strategies for everyone else to implement. While recognizing the importance of thinking ahead and especially of the need for creative vision in this pedantic world, I wish to propose an additional view of the strategist—as a pattern recognizer, a learner if you will—who manages a process in which strategies (and visions) can emerge as well as be deliberately conceived. I also wish to redefine that strategist, to extend that someone into the collective entity made up of the many actors whose interplay speaks an organization's mind. This strategist *finds* strategies no less than creates them, often in patterns that form inadvertently in its own behavior.

What, then, does it mean to craft strategy? Let us return to the words associated with craft: dedication, experience, involvement with the material, the personal touch, mastery of detail, a sense of harmony and integration. Managers who craft strategy do not spend much time in executive suites reading MIS reports or industry analyses. They are involved, responsive to their materials, learning about their organizations and industries through personal touch. They are also sensitive to experience, recognizing that while individual vision may be important, other factors must help determine strategy as well.

Manage stability: Managing strategy is mostly managing stability, not change. Indeed, most of the time senior managers should not be formulating strategy at all; they should be getting on with making their organizations as effective as possible in pursuing the strategies they already have. Like distinguished craftsmen, organizations become distinguished because they master the details.

To manage strategy, then, at least in the first instance, is not so much to promote change as to know *when* to do so. Advocates of strategic planning often urge managers to plan for perpetual instability in the environment (for example, by rolling over five-year plans annually). But this obsession with change is dysfunctional. Organizations that reassess their strategies continuously are like individuals who reassess their jobs or their marriages continuously—in both cases, they will drive themselves crazy or else reduce themselves to inaction. The formal planning process repeats itself so often and so mechanically that it desensitizes the organization to real change, programs it more and more deeply into set patterns, and thereby encourages it to make only minor adaptations.

So-called strategic planning must be recognized for what it is: a means, not to create strategy, but to program a strategy already created—to work out its implications formally. It is essentially analytic in nature, based on decomposition, while strategy creation is essentially a process of synthesis. That is why trying to create strategies through formal planning most often leads to extrapolating existing ones or copying those of competitors.

This is not to say that planners have no role to play in strategy formation. In addition to programming strategies created by other means, they can feed ad hoc analyses into the strategy-making process at the front end to be sure that the hard data are taken into consideration. They can also stimulate others to think strategically. And of course people called planners can be strategists too, so long as they are creative thinkers who are in touch with what is relevant. But that has nothing to do with the technology of formal planning.

Detect discontinuity: Environments do not change on any regular or orderly basis. And they seldom undergo continuous dramatic change, claims about our "age of discontinuity" and environmental "turbulence" notwithstanding. (Go tell people who lived through the Great Depression or survivors of the siege of Leningrad during World War II that ours are turbulent times.) Much of the time, change is minor and even temporary and requires no strategic response. Once in a while there is a truly significant discontinuity or, even less often, a gestalt shift in the environment, where everything important seems to change at once. But these events, while critical, are also easy to recognize.

The real challenge in crafting strategy lies in detecting the subtle discontinuities that may undermine a business in the future. And for that, there is no technique, no program, just a sharp mind in touch with the situation. Such discontinuities are unexpected and irregular, essentially unprecedented. They can be dealt with only by minds that are attuned to existing patterns yet able to perceive important breaks in them. Unfortunately, this form of strategic thinking tends to atrophy during the long periods of stability that most organizations experience. So the trick is to manage within a given strategic orientation most of the time yet be able to pick out the occasional discontinuity that really matters. The ability to make that kind of switch in thinking is the essence of strategic management. And it has more to do with vision and involvement than it does with analytic technique.

Know the business: Note the kind of knowledge involved in strategic thinking: not intellectual knowledge, not analytical reports or abstracted facts and figures (though these can certainly help), but personal knowledge, intimate understanding, equivalent to the craftsman's feel for the clay. Facts are available to anyone; this kind of knowledge is not. Wisdom is the word that captures it best. But wisdom is a word that has been lost in the bureaucracies we have built for ourselves, systems designed to distance leaders from operating details. Show me managers who think they can rely on formal planning to create their strategies, and I'll show you managers who lack intimate knowledge of their businesses or the creativity to do something with it.

Craftsmen have to train themselves to see, to pick up things other people miss. The same holds true for managers of strategy. It is those with a kind of peripheral vision who are best able to detect and take advantage of events as they unfold.

Manage patterns: Whether in an executive suite in Manhattan or a pottery studio in Montreal, a key to managing strategy is the ability to detect emerging patterns and help them take shape. The job of the manager is not just to preconceive specific strategies but also to recognize their emergence elsewhere in the organization and intervene when appropriate.

Like weeds that appear unexpectedly in a garden, some emergent strategies may need to be uprooted immediately. But management cannot be too quick to cut off the unexpected, for tomorrow's vision may grow out of today's aberration. (Europeans, after all, enjoy salads made from the leaves of the dandelion, America's most notorious weed.) Thus some patterns are worth watching until their effects have more clearly manifested themselves. Then those that prove useful can be made deliberate and be incorporated into the formal strategy, even if that means shifting the strategic umbrella to cover them.

To manage in this context, then, is to create the climate within which a wide variety of strategies can grow. In more complex organizations, this may mean building flexible structures, hiring creative people, defining broad umbrella strategies, and watching for the patterns that emerge.

Reconcile change and continuity: Finally, managers considering radical departures need to keep the quantum theory of change in mind. As Ecclesiastes reminds us, there is a time to sow and a time to reap. Some new patterns must be held in check until the organization is ready for a strategic revolution, or at least a period of divergence. Managers who are obsessed with either change or stability are bound eventually to harm their organizations. As pattern recognizer, the manager has to be able to sense when to exploit an established crop of strategies and when to encourage new strains to displace the old.

While strategy is a word that is usually associated with the future, its link to the past is no less central. As Kierkegaard once observed, life is lived forward but understood backward. Managers may have to live strategy in the future, but they must understand it through the past.

Like potters at the wheel, organizations must make sense of the past if they hope to manage the future. Only by coming to understand the patterns that form in their own behavior do they get to know their capabilities and their potential. Thus crafting strategy, like managing craft, requires a natural synthesis of the future, present, and past.

• THE HONDA EFFECT*

BY RICHARD T. PASCALE

At face value, "strategy" is an innocent noun. Webster defines it as the large-scale planning and direction of operations. In the business context, it pertains to a process by which a firm searches and analyzes its environment and resources in order to (1) select opportunities defined in terms of markets to be served and products to serve them and (2) make discrete decisions to invest resources in order to achieve identified objectives. (Bower, 1970: 7–8).

But for a vast and influential population of executives, planners, academics, and consultants, strategy is more than a conventional English noun. It embodies an implicit model of how organizations should be guided and consequently, proconfigures our way of thinking. Strategy formulation (1) is generally assumed to be driven by senior management whom we expect to set strategic direction, (2) has been extensively influenced by empirical models and concepts, and (3) is often associated with a laborious strategic planning process that, in some companies, has produced more paper than insight.

A $500-million-a-year "strategy" industry has emerged in the United States and Europe comprised of management consultants, strategic planning staffs, and business school academics. It caters to the unique emphasis that American and Eu-

---

* Excerpted from an article originally entitled "Perspectives on Strategy: The Real Story Behind Honda's Success," *California Management Review XXVI*, no. 3, pp. 47–72. Copyright © 1984 by the Regents of the University of California. Reprinted by permission of the Regents.

ropean companies place upon this particular aspect of managing and directing corporations.

Words often derive meaning from their cultural context. *Strategy* is one such word and nowhere is the contrast of meanings more pronounced than between Japan and the United States. The Japanese view the emphasis we place on "strategy" as we might regard their enthusiasm for Kabuki or sumo wrestling. They note our interest not with an intent of acquiring similar ones but for insight into our peculiarities. The Japanese are somewhat distrustful of a single "strategy" for in their view any idea that focuses attention does so at the expense of peripheral vision. They strongly believe that *peripheral vision* is essential to discerning changes in the customer, the technology or competition, and is the key to corporate survival over the long haul. They regard any prospesity to be driven by a single-minded strategy as a weakness.

The Japanese have particular discomfort with strategic concepts. While they do not reject ideas such as the experience curve or portfolio theory outright they regard them as a stimulus to perception. They have often ferreted out the "formula" of their concept-driven American competitors and exploited their inflexibility. In musical instruments, for example (a mature industry facing stagnation as birthrates in the United States and Japan declined), Yamaha might have classified its products as "cash cows" and gone on to better things (as its chief U.S. competitor, Baldwin United, had done). Instead, beginning with a negligible share of the U.S. market, Yamaha plowed ahead and destroyed Baldwin's seemingly unchallengeable dominance. YKK's success in zippers against Talon (a Textron division) and Honda's outflanking of Harley-Davidson (a former AMF subsidiary) in the motorcycle field provide parallel illustrations. All three cases involved American conglomerates, wedded to the portfolio concept, that had classified pianos, zippers, and motorcycles as mature businesses to be harvested rather than nourished and defended. Of course, those who developed portfolio theory and other strategic concepts protest that they were never intended to be mindlessly applied in setting strategic direction. But most would also agree that there is a widespread tendency in American corporations to misapply concepts and to otherwise become strategically myopic—ignoring the marketplace, the customer, and the problems of execution. This tendency toward misapplication, being both pervasive and persistent over several decades, is a phenomenon that the literature has largely ignored [for exceptions, see Hayes and Abernathy, 1980:67; Hayes and Garvin, 1982:71]. There is a need to identify explicitly the factors that influence how we conceptualize strategy —and which foster its misuse.

HONDA: THE STRATEGY MODEL

In 1975, Boston Consulting Group (BCG) presented the British government its final report: *Strategy Alternatives for the British Motorcycle Industry.* This 120-page document identified two key factors leading to the British demise in the world's motorcycle industry:

- Market share loss and profitability declines
- Scale economy disadvantages in technology, distribution, and manufacturing

During the period 1959 to 1973, the British share of the U.S. motorcycle industry had dropped from 49% to 9%. Introducing BCG's recommended strategy (of targeting market segments where sufficient production volumes could be attained to be price competitive) the report states:

> The success of the Japanese manufacturers originated with the growth of their domestic market during the 1950s. As recently as 1960, only 4 percent of Japanese motorcycle production was exported. By this time, however, the Japanese had developed huge production volumes in small motorcycles in their domestic market, and volume-related cost reductions had followed. This resulted in a highly competitive cost position which the Japanese used as a springboard for penetration of world markets with small motorcycles in the early 1960s (BCG, 1975:xiv).

The BCG study was made public by the British government and rapidly disseminated in the United States. It exemplifies the necessary (and, I argue, insufficient) strategist's perspective of

- examining competition primarily from an intercompany perspective,
- at a high level of abstraction,
- with heavy reliance on microeconomic concepts (such as the experience curve).

Case writers at Harvard Business School, UCLA, and the University of Virginia quickly condensed the BCG report for classroom use in case discussions. It currently enjoys extensive use in first-term courses in business policy.

Of particular note in the BCG study, and in the subsequent Harvard Business School rendition, is the historical treatment of Honda.

> The mix of competitors in the U.S. motorcycle market underwent a major shift in the 1960s. Motorcycle registrations increased from 575,000 in 1960 to 1,382,000 in 1965. Prior to 1960 the U.S. market was served mainly by Harley-Davidson of U.S.A., BSA, Triumph and Norton of U.K. and Moto-Guzzi of Italy. Harley was the market leader with total 1959 sales of $16.6 million. After the second world war, motorcycles in the U.S.A. attracted a very limited group of people other than police and army personnel who used motorcycles on the job. While most motorcyclists were no doubt decent people, groups of rowdies who went around on motorcycles and called themselves by such names as "Hell's Angels," "Satan's Slaves" gave motorcycling a bad image. Even leather jackets which were worn by motorcyclists as a protective device acquired an unsavory image. A 1953 movie called "The Wild Ones" starring a 650cc Triumph, a black leather jacket and Marlon Brando gave the rowdy motorcyclists wide media coverage. The stereotype of the motorcyclist was a leather-jacketed, teenage troublemaker.
>
> Honda established an American subsidiary in 1959—American Honda Motor Company. This was in sharp contrast to other foreign producers who relied on distributors. Honda's marketing strategy was described in the 1963 annual report as "With its policy of selling, not primarily to confirmed motorcyclists but rather to members of the general public who had never before given a second thought to a motorcycle. . . ." Honda started its push in the U.S. market with the smallest, lightweight motorcycles. It had a three-speed transmisson, an automatic clutch, five horsepower (the American cycle only had two and a half), an electric starter and step through frame for female riders. And it was easier to handle. The Honda machines sold for under $250 in retail compared with $1,000–$1,500 for the bigger American or British machines. Even at that early date Honda was probably superior to other competitors in productivity.
>
> By June 1960 Honda's Research and Development effort was staffed with 700 designers/engineers. This might be contrasted with 100 engineers/draftsmen employed by . . . (European and American competitors). In 1962 production per man-

year was running at 159 units, (a figure not reached by Harley-Davidson until 1974). Honda's net fixed asset investment was $8170 per employee . . . (more than twice its European and American competitors). With 1959 sales of $55 million Honda was already the largest motorcycle producer in the world.

Honda followed a policy of developing the market region by region. They started on the West Coast and moved eastward over a period of four–five years. Honda sold 2,500 machines in the U.S. in 1960. In 1961 they lined up 125 distributors and spent $150,000 on regional advertising. Their advertising was directed to the young families, their advertising theme was "You Meet the Nicest People on a Honda." This was a deliberate attempt to dissociate motorcycles from rowdy, Hell's Angels type people.

Honda's success in creating demand for lightweight motorcycles was phenomenal. American Honda's sales went from $500,000 in 1960 to $77 million in 1965. By 1966 the market share data showed the ascendancy of Japanese producers and their success in selling lightweight motorcycles. [Honda had 63% of the market.] . . . Starting from virtually nothing in 1960, the lightweight motorcycles had clearly established their lead (Purkayastha, 1981: 5, 10, 11, 12).

Quoting from the BCG report:

The Japanese motorcycle industry, and in particular Honda, the market leader, present a [consistent] picture. The basic philosophy of the Japanese manufacturers is that high volumes per model provide the potential for high productivity as a result of using capital intensive and highly automated techniques. Their marketing strategies are therefore directed towards developing these high model volumes, hence the careful attention that we have observed them giving to growth and market share.

The overall result of this philosophy over time has been that the Japanese have now developed an entrenched and leading position in terms of technology and production methods. . . . The major factors which appear to account for the Japanese superiority in both these areas are . . . (specialized production systems, balancing engineering and market requirements, and the cost efficiency and reliability of suppliers) (BCG, pp. 59, 40).

As evidence of Honda's strategy of taking position as low cost producer and exploiting economies of scale, other sources cite Honda's construction in 1959 of a plant to manufacture 30,000 motorcycles per month well ahead of existing demand at the time. (Up until then Honda's most popular models sold 2,000–3,000 units per month.) (Sakiya, 1982:119)

The overall picture as depicted by the quotes exemplifies the "strategy model." Honda is portrayed as a firm dedicated to being the low price producer, utilizing its dominant market position in Japan to force entry into the U.S. market, expanding that market by redefining a leisure class ("Nicest People") segment, and exploiting its comparative advantage via aggressive pricing and advertising. Rich-

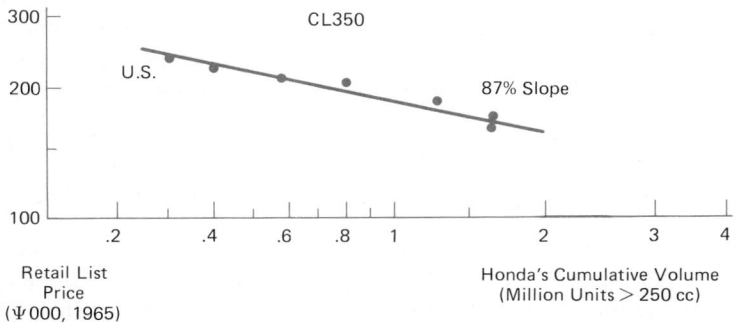

FIGURE 1
Source: BCG (1975) "Strategy Alternatives for the British Motorcycle Industry."

ard Rumelt, writing the teaching note for the UCLA adaptation of the case states: "The fundamental contribution of BCG is not the experience curve per se but the ever-present assumption that differences in cost (or efficiency) are the fundamental components of strategy." (Rumelt, 1980:2).

THE ORGANIZATIONAL PROCESS PERSPECTIVE

On September 10, 1982, the six Japanese executives responsible for Honda's entry into the U.S. motorcycle market in 1959 assembled in Honda's Tokyo headquarters. They had gathered at my request to describe in fine grain detail the sequence of events that had led to Honda's ultimate position of dominance in the U.S. market. All were in their sixties; three were retired. The story that unfolded, greatly abbreviated below, highlights miscalculation, serendipity, and organizational learning—counterpoints to the streamlined "strategy" version related earlier. . . .

Any account of Honda's successes must grasp at the outset the unusual character of its founder, Sochiro Honda, and his partner, Takeo Fujisawa. Honda was an inventive genius with a large ego and mercurial temperament, given to bouts of "philandering" (to use his expression) (Sakiya, 1979). . . .

Postwar Japan was in desperate need of transportation. Motorcycle manufacturers proliferated, producing clip-on engines that converted bicycles into makeshift "mopeds." Honda was among these but it was not until he teamed up with Fujisawa in 1949 that the elements of a successful enterprise began to take shape. Fujisawa provided money as well as financial and marketing strengths. In 1950 their first D-type motorcycle was introduced. They were, at that juncture, participating in a fragmented industry along with 247 other manufacturers. Other than its sturdy frame, this introductory product was unnoteworthy and did not enjoy great commercial success. (Sakiya, 1979, 1982).

Honda embodied a rare combination of inventive ability and ultimate self-confidence. His motivation was not primarily commercial. Rather, the company served as a vehicle to give expression to his inventive abilities. A successful company would provide a resource base to pursue, in Fujisawa's words, his "grandiose dream." Fujisawa continues, "There was no end to his pursuit of technology." (Sakiya, 1982).

Fujisawa, in an effort to save the faltering company, pressed Honda to abandon their noisy two-stroke engine and pursue a four-stroke design. The quieter four-stroke engines were appearing on competitive motorcycles, therefore threatening Honda with extinction. Mr. Honda balked. But a year later, Honda stunned Fujisawa with a breakthrough design that doubled the horsepower of competitive four-stroke engines. With this innovation, the firm was off and putting, and by 1951 demand was brisk. There was no organization, however, and the plant was chaotic (Sakiya, 1982). Strong demand, however, required early investment in a simplified mass production process. As a result, *primarily* due to design advantages, and secondarily to production methods, Honda became one of the four or five industry leaders by 1954 with 15 percent market share (data provided by company). . . .

For Fujisawa, the engine innovation meant increased sales and easier access to financing. For Mr. Honda, the higher horsepower engine opened the possibility of pursuing one of his central ambitions in life—to race his motorcycle and win. . . .

Fujisawa, throughout the fifties, sought to turn Honda's attention from his enthusiasm with racing to the more mundane requirements of running an enterprise. By 1956, as the innovations gained from racing had begun to pay off in vastly more efficient engines, Fujisawa pressed Honda to adapt this technology for a commercial motorcycle (Sakiya, 1979, 1982). Fujisawa had a particular segment in mind. Most motorcyclists in Japan were male and the machines were used primarily as an alternative form of transportation to trains and buses. There were, however, a vast number of small commercial establishments in Japan that still delivered goods and ran errands on bicycles. Trains and buses were inconvenient for these activities. The pursestrings of these small enterprises were controlled by the Japanese wife—who resisted buying conventional motorcycles because they were expensive, dangerous, and hard to handle. Fujisawa challenged Honda: Can you use what you've learned from racing to come up with an inexpensive, safe-looking motorcycle that can be driven with one hand (to facilitate carrying packages).

In 1958, the Honda 50cc Supercub was introduced—with an automatic clutch, three-speed transmission, automatic starter, and the safe, friendly look of a bicycle (without the stigma of the outmoded mopeds). Owing almost entirely to its high horsepower but *lightweight 50cc engine* (not to production efficiencies), it was affordable. Overnight, the firm was overwhelmed with orders. Engulfed by demand, they sought financing to build a new plant with a 30,000 unit per month capacity. "It wasn't a speculative investment," recalls one executive. "We had the proprietary technology, we had the market, and the demand was enormous." (The plant was completed in mid-1960.) Prior to its opening, demand was met through makeshift, high cost, company-owned assembly and farmed-out assembly through subcontractors. By the end of 1959, Honda had skyrocketed into first place among Japanese motorcycle manufacturers. Of its total sales that year of 285,000 units, 168,000 were Supercubs.

Fujisawa utilized the Supercub to restructure Honda's channels of distribution. For many years, Honda had rankled under the two-tier distribution system that prevailed in the industry. These problems had been exacerbated by the fact that Honda was a late entry and had been carried as secondary line by distributors whose loyalties lay with their older manufacturers. Further weakening Honda's leverage, all manufacturer sales were on a consignment basis.

Deftly, Fujisawa had characterized the Supercub to Honda's distributors as "something much more like a bicycle than a motorcycle." The traditional channels, to their later regret, agreed. Under amicable terms Fujisawa began selling the Supercub directly to retailers—and primarily through bicycle shops. Since these shops were small and numerous (approximately 12,000 in Japan), sales on consignment were unthinkable. A cash-on-delivery system was installed, giving Honda significantly more leverage over its dealerships than the other motorcycle manufacturers enjoyed.

The stage was now set for exploration of the U.S. market. Mr. Honda's racing conquests in the late 1950s had given substance to his convictions about his abilities. . . .

Two Honda executives—the soon-to-be-named president of American Honda, Kihachiro Kawashima, and his assistant—arrived in the United States in late 1958. Their itinerary: San Francisco, Los Angeles, Dallas, New York, and Columbus. Mr. Kawashima recounts his impressions:

> My first reaction after travelling across the United States was: How could we have been so stupid as to start a war with such a vast and wealthy country! My second reaction was discomfort. I spoke poor English. We dropped in on motorcycle dealers who treated us discourteously and in addition, gave the general impression of being motorcycle enthusiasts who, secondarily, were in business. There were only 3,000 motorcycle dealers in the United States at the time and only 1,000 of them were open five days a week. The remainder were open on nights and weekends. Inventory was

poor, manufacturers sold motorcycles to dealers on consignment, the retailers provided consumer financing; after-sales service was poor. It was discouraging.

My other impression was that everyone in the United States drove an automobile—making it doubtful that motorcycles could ever do very well in the market. However, with 450,000 motorcycle registrations in the U.S. and 60,000 motorcycles imported from Europe each year it didn't seem unreasonable to shoot for 10 percent of the import market. I returned to Japan with that report.

In truth, we had no strategy other than the idea of seeing if we could sell something in the United States. It was a new frontier, a new challenge, and it fit the "success against all odds" culture that Mr. Honda had cultivated. I reported my impressions to Fujisawa—including the seat-of-the-pants target of trying, over several years, to attain a 10 percent share of U.S. imports. He didn't probe that target quantitatively. We did not discuss profits or deadlines for breakeven. Fujisawa told me if anyone could succeed, I could and authorized $1 million for the venture.

The next hurdle was to obtain a currency allocation from the Ministry of Finance. They were extraordinarily skeptical. Toyota had launched the Toyopet in the U.S. in 1958 and had failed miserably. "How could Honda succeed?" they asked. Months went by. We put the project on hold. Suddenly, five months after our application, we were given the go-ahead—but at only a fraction of our expected level of commitment. "You can invest $250,000 in the U.S. market." they said, "but only $110,000 in cash." The remainder of our assets had to be in parts and motorcycle inventory.

We moved into frantic activity as the government, hoping we would give up on the idea, continued to hold us to the July 1959 start-up timetable. Our focus, as mentioned earlier, was to compete with the European exports. We knew our products at the time were good but not far superior. Mr. Honda was especially confident of the 250cc and 305cc machines. The shape of the handlebar on these larger machines looked like the eyebrow of Buddha, which he felt was a strong selling point. Thus, after some discussion and with no compelling criteria for selection, we configured our start-up inventory with 25 percent of each of our four products—the 50cc Supercub and the 125cc, 250cc, and 305cc machines. In dollar value terms, of course, the inventory was heavily weighted toward the larger bikes.

The stringent monetary controls of the Japanese government together with the unfriendly reception we had received during our 1958 visit caused us to start small. We chose Los Angeles where there was a large second and third generation Japanese community, a climate suitable for motorcycle use, and a growing population. We were so strapped for cash that the three of us shared a furnished apartment that rented for $80 per month. Two of us slept on the floor. We obtained a warehouse in a run-down section of the city and waited for the ship to arrive. Not daring to spare our funds for equipment, the three of us stacked the motorcycle crates three high—by hand, swept the floors, and built and maintained the parts bin.

We were entirely in the dark the first year. We were not aware the motorcycle business in the United States occurs during a seasonable April-to-August window—and our timing coincided with the closing of the 1959 season. Our hard-learned experiences with distributorships in Japan convinced us to try to go to the retailers direct. We ran ads in the motorcycle trade magazine for dealers. A few responded. By spring of 1960, we had forty dealers and some of our inventory in their stores—mostly larger bikes. A few of the 250cc and 305cc bikes began to sell. Then disaster struck.

By the first week of April 1960, reports were coming in that our machines were leaking oil and encountering clutch failure. This was our lowest moment. Honda's fragile reputation was being destroyed before it could be established. As it turned out, motorcycles in the United States are driven much farther and much faster than in Japan. We dug deeply into our precious cash reserves to air freight our motorcycles to the Honda testing lab in Japan. Through the dark month of April, Pan Am was the only enterprise in the U.S. that was nice to us. Our testing lab worked twenty-four-hour days bench testing the bikes to try to replicate the failure. Within a month, a redesigned head gasket and clutch spring solved the problem. But in the meantime, events had taken a surprising turn.

Throughout our first eight months, following Mr. Honda's and our own instincts, we had not attempted to move the 50cc Supercubs. While they were a smash success in Japan (and manufacturing couldn't keep up with demand there), they seemed wholly unsuitable for the U.S. market where everything was bigger and more luxurious. As a clincher, we had our sights on the import market—and the Europeans, like the American manufacturers, emphasized the larger machines.

We used the Honda 50s ourselves to ride around Los Angeles on errands. They attracted a lot of attention. One day we had a call from a Sears buyer. While persisting in our refusal to sell through an intermediary, we took note of Sears' interest. But we still hesitated to push the 50cc bikes out of fear they might harm our image in a heavily macho market. But when the larger bikes started breaking, we had no choice. We let the 50cc bikes move. And surprisingly, the retailers who wanted to sell them weren't motorcycle dealers, they were sporting goods stores.

The excitement created by the Honda Supercub began to gain momentum. Under restrictions from the Japanese government, we were still on a cash basis. Working with our initial cash and inventory, we sold machines, reinvested in inventory, and sunk the profits into additional inventory and advertising. Our advertising tried to straddle the market. While retailers continued to inform us that our Supercub customers were normal everyday Americans, we hesitated to target toward this segment out of fear of alienating the high margin end of our business—sold through the traditional motorcycle dealers to a more traditional "black leather jacket" customer.

Honda's phenomenal sales and share gains over the ensuing years have been previously reported. History has it that Honda "*redefined*" the U.S. motorcycle industry. In the view of American Honda's start-up team, this was an innovation they backed into—and reluctantly. It was certainly not the strategy they embarked on in 1959. As late as 1963, Honda was still working with its original Los Angeles advertising agency, its ad campaigns straddling all customers so as not to antagonize one market in pursuit of another.

In the spring of 1963, an undergraduate advertising major at UCLA submitted, in fulfillment of a routine course assignment, an ad campaign for Honda. Its theme: You Meet the Nicest People on a Honda. Encouraged by his instructor, the student passed his work on to a friend at Grey Advertising. Grey had been soliciting the Honda account—which with a $5 million a year budget was becoming an attractive potential client. Grey purchased the student's idea—on a tightly kept nondisclosure basis. Grey attempted to sell the idea to Honda.

Interestingly, the Honda management team, which by 1963 had grown to five Japanese executives, was badly split on this advertising decision. The president and treasurer favored another proposal from another agency. The director of sales, however, felt strongly that the Nicest People campaign was the right one—and his commitment eventually held sway. Thus, in 1963, through an inadvertent sequence of events, Honda came to adopt a strategy that directly identified and targeted that large untapped segment of the marketplace that has since become inseparable from the Honda legend.

The Nicest People campaign drove Honda's sales at an even greater rate. By 1964, nearly one out of every two motorcycles sold was a Honda. As a result of the influx of medium income leisure class consumers, banks and other consumer credit companies began to finance motorcycles—shifting away from dealer credit, which had been the traditional purchasing mechanism available. Honda, seizing the opportunity of soaring demand for its products, took a courageous and seemingly risky position. Late in 1964, they announced that thereafter, they would cease to ship on a consignment basis but would require cash on delivery. Honda braced itself for revolt. While nearly every dealer questioned, appealed, or complained, none relinquished his franchise. In one fell swoop, Honda shifted the power relationship from the dealer to the manufacturer. Within three years, this would become the pattern for the industry.

THE "HONDA EFFECT"

The preceding account of Honda's inroads in the U.S. motorcycle industry provides more than a second perspective on reality. It focuses our attention on different issues and raises different questions. What factors permitted two men as unlike one another as Honda and Fujisawa to function effectively as a team? What incentives and understandings permitted the Japanese executives at American Honda to respond to the market as it emerged rather than doggedly pursue the 250cc and 305 cc strategy that Mr. Honda favored? What decision process permitted the relatively junior sales director to overturn the bosses' preferences and choose the Nicest People campaign? What values or commitment drove Honda to take the enormous risk of alienating its dealers in 1964 in shifting from a consignment to cash? In hindsight, these pivotal events all seem ho-hum common sense. But each day, as organizations live out their lives without the benefit of hindsight, few choose so well and so consistently.

The juxtaposed perspectives reveal what I shall call the "Honda Effect." Western consultants, academics, and executives express a preference for oversimplifications of reality and cognitively linear explanations of events. To be sure, they have always acknowledged that the "human factor" must be taken into account. But extensive reading of strategy cases at business schools, consultants' reports, strategic planning documents as well as the coverage of the popular press, reveals a widespread tendency to overlook the process through which organizations experiment, adapt, and learn. We tend to impute coherence and purposive rationality to events when the opposite may be closer to the truth. How an organization deals with miscalculation, mistakes, and serendipitous events *outside its field of vision is often crucial to success over time.* It is this realm that requires better understanding and further research if we are to enhance our ability to guide an organization's destiny. . . .

An earlier section has addressed the shortcomings of the narrowly defined microeconomic strategy model. The Japanese avoid this pitfall by adopting a broader notion of "strategy." In our recent awe of things Japanese, most Americans forget that the original products of the Japanese automotive manufacturers badly missed the mark. Toyota's Toyopet was square, sexless, and mechanically defective. It failed miserably, as did Datsun's first several entries into the U.S. market. More recently, Mazda miscalculated badly with its first rotary engine and nearly went bankrupt. Contrary to myth, the Japanese did not from the onset embark on a strategy to seize the high-quality small-car market. They manufactured what they were accustomed to building in Japan and tried to sell it abroad. Their success, as any Japanese automotive executive will readily agree, did not result from a bold insight by a few big brains at the top. On the contrary, success was achieved by senior managers humble enough not to take their initial strategic positions too seriously. What saved Japan's near-failures was the cumulative impact of "little brains" in the form of salesmen and dealers and production workers, all contributing incrementally to the quality and market position these companies enjoy today. Middle and upper management saw their primary task as guiding and orchestrating this input from below rather than steering the organization from above along a predetermined strategic course.

The Japanese don't use the term "strategy" to describe a crisp business definition or competitive master plan. They think more in terms of "strategic accommodation," or "adaptive persistence," underscoring their belief that corporate direction evolves from an incremental adjustment to unfolding events. Rarely, in their view, does one leader (or a strategic planning group) produce a bold strategy that guides a firm unerringly. Far more frequently, the input is from below. It is this ability of an organization to move information and ideas from the bottom to the top and back again in continuous dialogue that the Japanese value above all things. As this dialogue is pursued, what in hindsight may be "strategy" evolves. In sum, "strategy" is defined as "all the things necessary for the successful functioning of organization as an adaptive mechanism." . . .

● TOWARD MIDDLE-UP-DOWN MANAGEMENT*

BY IKUJIRO NONAKA

The concepts of "top-down" and "bottom-up" management pervade management research and the popular business literature. Both center on information flow and information processing. Top-down management emphasizes the process of implementing and refining decisions made by top management as they are transmitted to the lower levels of the organization. Bottom-up management emphasizes the influence of information coming up from lower levels on management decision making. The management styles of individual firms are usually seen as located somewhere on the continuum between these two types.

However, organizations must not only process information; they must also create it. If we look closely at R&D activities, we find a pattern in some firms that does not fit on the continuum between top-down and bottom-up. It is a process that resolves the contradiction between the visionary but abstract concepts of top management and the experience-grounded concepts originating on the shopfloor by assigning a more central role to middle managers. This process, which is particularly well suited to the age of fierce market competition and rapid technological change, I call *middle-up-down management.* . . .

If we view the organization as a three-tiered structure—composed of the individual, the group, and the organization as a whole—then we can pinpoint the specific characteristics that are important to information creation at each tier of the organization (see Table 1).

TABLE 1   **Levels of Organizational Information Creation**

Level	Emergent Property	Factors Related to Information Creation
Organization	Structure	Competitive Resource Allocation
Group	Interaction	Direct Dialogue
Individual	Autonomy	Action and Deliberation

* Originally published in the *Sloan Management Review* (Spring 1988). Copyright © 1988 by the *Sloan Management Review;* all rights reserved. Reprinted with deletions by permission of the *Review.*

The Individual Level

The emergent, or critical, property of information creation at the individual level is autonomy. This level is characterized by action and deliberation: Only here is it possible to deliberate and act autonomously. Autonomy begins to be realized when individuals are given the freedom to combine thought and action at their own discretion, and are thereby able to guarantee the unity of knowledge and action. . . .

The Group Level

The emergent property at the group level is interaction—more concretely, open and frank dialogue. Human interaction is best realized within the organization at the group level.

The creation of information is the creation of a new perspective. The dynamic, complementary process that results in a shift to a new point of view requires interaction—a dialogue or debate—among people. The process is convoluted, involving a cycle of affirmation, denial, and resolution before new information is created. Since the significance of information is elastic during this process, individuals have the opportunity to interpret and reinterpret for themselves; this freedom allows group members to organize information individually. Unity and coherence are born from this group action. Coherence itself, however, can serve both to promote and to hinder the creation of information. Coherence often produces a pressure for conformity, and differing opinions are confined or limited with the birth of what Janis (1972) calls "group think." However, this tendency must be balanced against the fact that trust is the precondition for creative dialogue, as well as for the open exchange and cooperative possession of information.

The Organizational Level

The emergent property of the organization as a whole is structure. An organization's structure regulates the depth of the relationship between groups (sections) involved in information creation. From a macro perspective, structure produces the means for the distribution of resources among the various groups in the organization, and thereby contributes to a greater competitive capability. The structure of an organization is designed to be able to mediate between the desires of the group and of the individual in relation to information creation. It thus addresses the problem of allocating resources properly among competing interests. . . .

METHODOLOGIES OF ORGANIZATIONAL INFORMATION CREATION

Top-down management is essentially deductive; bottom-up management is essentially inductive. Let us briefly consider how these two managerial styles affect the "emergent properties" of resource allocation, interaction, and autonomy. Later we will propose middle-up-down management . . . as a methodology for information creation that can incorporate the strengths of both inductive and deductive management.

Deductive Management

Resource Allocation: The management methods used in deductive corporations are premised on the belief that information creation occurs mainly at the top. The role of top management is to clarify decision premises and to design organizational structures that can reduce individual information and decision burdens. Top management also allocates resources using sophisticated analytical techniques. Since decision making is concentrated at headquarters, a common set of clear-cut and measurable criteria that transcends the specific requirements of the various divisions is needed. ROI is typically used as such a criterion, with cash flow within and across individual strategic business units becoming the major concern with respect to resource allocation.

The underlying principle supporting such a management approach is the information-processing paradigm. But the hierarchy designed by top management in a deductive manner is not suited to allow organizational members at lower levels to create information in a flexible manner.

Interaction: Top-down, strong leadership is the basic policy adopted by deductive management. Information is processed; it moves from the upper levels to the lower levels, and variety reduction is the keystone. The elimination of "noise," "fluctuation," and "chaos" is the paramount concern. Information creation at the lower levels proceeds with great difficulty.

Information activity between divisions has a sequential relay pattern; work completed by one division is passed on to another division.

There is a tendency for the transformation of information into knowledge to occur with great intensity within the narrow areas of labor divisions. However, the amount of semantic information and knowledge absorbed and accumulated by the lower levels of the organization is small because of the lack of personal interaction.

Autonomy: Top managers and corporate staff possess the greatest autonomy. They are likely to adopt a hands-off, deductive methodology rather than a hands-on one. Consequently their information creation activities sometimes move far from the individual, shopfloor viewpoint. However, there is a potential for creating visionary concepts at the organizational level that could not be reached based on individual experience.

Inductive Management

Resource Allocation: Inductive management maintains that the organizational creation of information begins with the vision of the individual—the entrepreneurial individual—and that people who have an interest in a project will become the core of any long-term effort.

Technology is seen as the interaction between people and systems of information or knowledge. Thus the concept of synergy is basic to inductive management. Resources are allocated in a way that encourages interaction, allowing new concepts and theories to develop in the most natural way possible. The ideal inductive organization is "self-organizing." Autonomous information creation takes place by expanding from the individual level to the group level and then to the organizational level. At 3M, for example, a project can become a department and then a division if it is sufficiently successful.

Interaction: A supportive leadership that moves in step with the individual, the group, and the organization is necessary for information creation in an inductive-management organization. The support of an influential leader is necessary for individuals or self-organizing groups that have vision, since they will need help overcoming opposition from within the organization.

The need for a supporting sponsor to assist the intracompany entrepreneur is particularly emphasized at 3M. Before a daring and promising idea can stand on its own, it must be defined and supported by a sponsor willing to risk his or her reputation in order to advance or support changes in intracompany values. The leadership style of the sponsor can be summed up in the unspoken maxim, "The captain bites his tongue until it bleeds." On the basis of past experience, the leader relies on his or her own criteria (consciously and unconsciously) to guide the creation of new information.

Autonomy: Autonomy is given to those working as entrepreneurs at every organizational level. In many cases such individuals create meaningful information in the midst of interactive, tense relations, by testing and deepening their intuitive understanding through practice. Their information creation may be based on hunches or intuition, or on the ability to recognize the essence holistically in a moment.

Since the individual internalizes a great deal of tacit understanding, a career-path personnel policy that stresses promotions and transfers is used to support the organizational transfer of understanding. On the other hand, since the unlearning of acquired personal experience is difficult, inductive management may be unsuitable in instances where there are frequent large-scale reorganizations or replacements due to acquisitions or divestitures.

SYNTHESIZING INDUCTIVE AND DEDUCTIVE MANAGEMENT

Today, the intensity of market competition and the speed required for efficient information creation suggest a need to synthesize these two managerial styles. This synthesis involves the conceptualization of symbiotic management (Kagono et al., 1985) or what I call compressive management. . . . [It] can also be called middle-up-down management. The core of this managerial style is not the top managers or the entrepreneurial individuals, but rather the middle managers.

Middle management occupies a key position; it is equipped with the ability to combine strategic macro (context-free) information and hands-on micro (context-specific) information. In other words, middle management is in a position to forge the organizational link between deductive and inductive management.

Middle management is able most effectively to eliminate the noise, fluctuation, and chaos within an organization's information creation structure by serving as the starting point for action to be taken by upper and lower levels. Therefore, middle managers are also able to serve as the agent for change in the organization's self-renewal process.

Resource Allocation: Top management is responsible for determining the overall direction of the company and for establishing the time limits on realizing that vision. Time is the key resource. Each individual performing day-to-day tasks has his or her own vision. It is the middle manager who works, within a certain time limit, as a "translator" in charge of unifying individual visions and creating a larger vision, which will in turn be reflected in future individual visions. The group functions as the field for the realization of this process. In order to achieve this vision, middle managers work with upper- and lower-level personnel. However, it is the top that selects the middle, and selecting the right people becomes the most important foundation of an effective corporate strategy. In addition to deciding who will formulate and implement a strategy, the top serves as a catalyst that creates fluctuation or chaos.

Consequently, in compressive management, the entrepreneurial middle receives broad direction from the top and begins the process of information creation within the group, working to involve relevant individuals and carrying out information creation intensively within a compressed period of time. Through interaction with top management, middle management secures the resources required to achieve its vision. In this process, both deductive strategic planning and inductive emanation of information from the needs of the market are integrated to establish a definite direction for resource deployment and to create a practical concept which follows that direction.

The unit for resource allocation should be designed by the top so that the middle can create meaningful concepts. The structure of this unit can take a variety of forms, but usually consists of a multidisciplinary team led by middle management.

Interaction: Before the entrepreneurial middle can realize its vision, it must first confront and survive the criticism of other members of the group through intensive communication. As a result of this criticism, a more concrete concept will be formed. In order to realize a vision, an idea must successfully challenge the stability of the organization, involving people from both top and bottom, left and right.

This process often involves the following steps. The first stage is establishing creative chaos (Nonaka, 1989). Top management offers a challenging goal and creates tension. As the organization moves in the direction of innovation, creative chaos is amplified to focus on specific contradictions in order to solve the problem. These contradictions produce a demand for a new perspective, speeding up information creation activity. This approach is exemplified by the Honda R&D manager's statement, "Creativity is born by pushing people against the wall and pressuring them almost to the extreme."

The second stage involves the formation of a self-organizing team that tries to create a new order (meaning) out of the chaos. This self-organizing group has the following characteristics: it is autonomous; it is multidisciplinary, so as to encourage cross-fertilization among its members; and it creates challenging goals that force it to transcend the existing contradictions. This team forms the core for an intense level of activity and works independently of other divisions within the corporation.

The third stage is the synchronization of concept creation. This stage is the embodiment of the spiral in which information creation moves from middle management to the top and bottom. These movements resemble the punting and passing that occur in a rugby match as the opposing teams attempt to win ground (Takeuchi and Nonaka, 1986). The realization of a concept is made possible by the intraorganizational divisions pulling together in a "shared division of labor" and by promoting "active cooperative phenomena" (Imai et al., 1985).

The fourth stage involves the transfer of learning and unlearning. Innovation that aims at a distant and vaguely defined goal goes through apparently redundant phases of shared division of labor. The natural consequence of this process is to activate the information creation activities at all levels of the organization. The successful innovation generates a new order and gives birth to organizational learning and unlearning.

Autonomy: A group is given both autonomy (freedom) and a time limitation (constraint). Middle management becomes the logical center for the fusion of the deductive and inductive styles of management. Although it may be possible to balance the use of stored syntactic information and of tacit understanding, the need for a rapid response to changing conditions will not allow middle management to concentrate exclusively on the creation of information. The requirement simultaneously to expand the knowledge base and process information may eventually place an excessive burden upon the middle management group. If these people are not allowed to recharge their batteries from time to time, the long-term capacity for organizational information creation will weaken.

PROPER MANAGEMENT OF ORGANIZATIONAL INFORMATION CREATION

I have spoken of three methodologies for information creation—deductive, inductive, and compressive. Their approximate patterns are sketched in Figure 1 and Table 2.

One cannot make an unqualified choice of methodology until one has considered the special environmental characteristics present. The relationship between the environment and the appropriate management methodology is perhaps best illustrated in Figure 2.

FIGURE 1
A Comparison of
Organizational Information
Creation Patterns

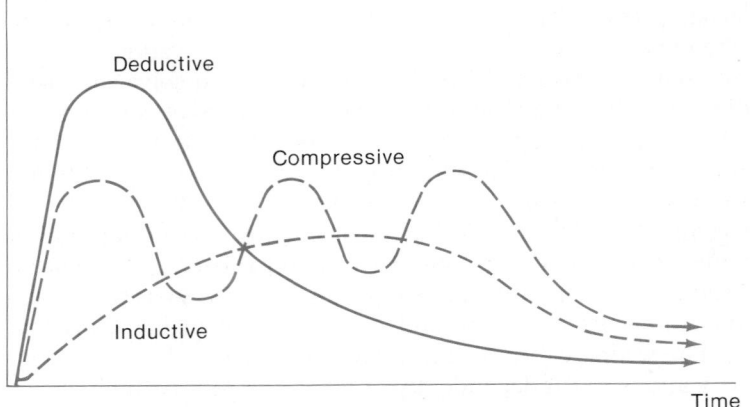

Fluctuation in Organizational
Information Creation Activity

TABLE 2   Comparison of Methodology of Organizational Information Creation

	DEDUCTIVE MANAGEMENT	INDUCTIVE MANAGEMENT	COMPRESSIVE MANAGEMENT
Resource Allocation			
• Key Resource	Money	People	Time
• Time Management	Periodical Planning	Self-management	Deadline
• Unit of Resource Allocation	SBU	Individual	Self-organizing Team
Interaction			
• Top Management	Leader	Sponsor	Catalyst
• Context of Interaction	Within Headquarters	Among Voluntary Individuals	Among Designated Individuals within the Group
• Direction	Top down	Bottom up	Middle up and down
Autonomy			
• Methodology	Deductive, Hands off	Inductive, Hands on	Hands on and off
• Knowledge	Articulate	Tacit	Articulate/Tacit
Problem	Analysis Paralysis	Inductive Ambiguity	Exhaustion

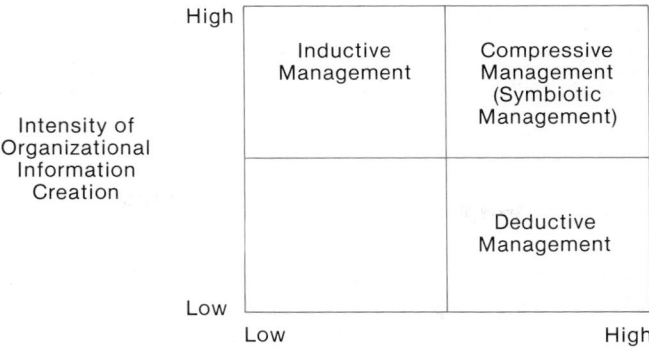

FIGURE 2
The Relationship between
Organizational Information
Creation and
Environmental
Characteristics

As environmental uncertainty increases, the organization can adapt itself more effectively with a high level of information creation occurring at all levels of the organization, rather than with a low level of information creation. In this sense, as the need for information creation increases, companies will probably make a shift from deductive management to inductive or compressive management, which have higher information creativity.

In the meantime, as market reactions speed up as a result of intense competition, companies will likely shift from inductive or deductive management to compressive management to cope with that problem. However, compressive management must come to grips with the problem of placing a great deal of pressure on middle management to process an expanding base of information within a limited time period. Therefore, whether or not information creation that is both high in quality and well coordinated can occur will depend largely on how entrepreneurial middle management really is.

CONCLUSION

The essential logic of compressive management is that top management creates a vision or dream, and middle management creates and implements concrete concepts to solve and transcend the contradictions arising from gaps between what exists at the moment and what management hopes to create. In other words, top management creates an overall theory, while middle management creates a middle-range theory and tests it empirically within the framework of the entire organization.

Mr. Tadashi Kume, president of Honda, expresses the role of middle management as follows: "I continually create dreams, but people run in different directions unless they are able to directly interact with reality. Top management doesn't know what bottom management is doing. The opposite is also true. For example, John at Honda Ohio is not able to see the company's overall direction. We at corporate headquarters see the world differently, think differently, and face a different environment. It is middle management that is charged with integrating the two viewpoints emanating from top and bottom management. There can be no progress without such integration." . . .

Middle-up-down management is a type of organizational information creation that involves the total organization. It may best embody the essence of an organization spontaneously surviving in the business environment's ceaseless generation of changes.

EDWARD MARSHALL BOEHM, INC.

Edward Marshall Boehm—a farmer, veterinarian, and nature lover living near New York City—was convinced by his wife and friends to translate some of his clay animal sculptures into pieces for possible sale to the gift and art markets. Boehm recognized that porcelain was the best medium for portraying his creations because of its translucent beauty, permanence, and fidelity of color as well as form. But the finest of the porcelains, hard paste porcelain, was largely a secret art about which little technical literature existed. Boehm studied this art relentlessly, absorbing whatever knowledge artbooks, museums, and the few U.S. ceramic factories offered. Then after months of experimentation in a dingy Trenton (N.J.) basement, Boehm and some chemist friends developed a porcelain clay equal to the finest in the world.

Next Boehm had to master the complex art of porcelain manufacture. Each piece of porcelain sculpture is a technical as well as artistic challenge. A 52-step process is required to convert a plasticine sculpture into a completed porcelain piece. For example, one major creation took 509 mold sections to make 151 parts, and consumed 8 tons of plaster in the molds. Sculptural detail included 60,000 individually carved feather barbs. Each creation had to be kiln-fired to 2400° where heat could change a graceful detail into a twisted mass. Then it had to be painted, often in successive layers, and perhaps fired repeatedly to anneal delicate colors. No American had excelled in hard paste porcelains. And when Boehm's creations first appeared no one understood the quality of the porcelain or even believed it was hard paste porcelain.

But Boehm began to create in porcelain what he knew and loved best, nature —particularly the more delicate forms of animals, birds, and flowers. In his art

Case copyright © 1976 by James Brian Quinn.
The generous cooperation of Edward Marshall Boehm, Inc. is gratefully acknowledged.

Boehm tried "to capture that special moment and setting which conveys the character, charm, and loveliness of a bird or animal in its natural habitat." After selling his early creations for several years during her lunch hours, his talented wife, Helen, left an outstanding opthalmic marketing career to "peddle" Boehm's porcelains full time. Soon Mrs. Boehm's extraordinary merchandising skills, promotional touch, and sense for the art market began to pay off. People liked Boehm's horses and dogs, but bought his birds. And Boehm agreeably complied, striving for ever greater perfection on ever more exotic and natural bird creations.

By 1968 some Boehm porcelains (especially birds) had become recognized as collectors items. An extremely complex piece like "Fondo Marino" might sell for $28,500 at retail, and might command much more upon resale. Edward Marshall

Snowy Owl
Courtesy of Edward Marshall Boehm, Inc.

Boehm, then 55—though flattered by his products' commercial success—considered his art primarily an expression of his love for nature. He felt the ornithological importance of portraying vanishing species like U.S. prairie chickens with fidelity and traveled to remote areas to bring back live samples of rare tropical birds for study and later rendering into porcelain. A single company, Minton China, was the exclusive distributor of Boehm products to some 175 retail outlets in the U.S. Boehm's line included (1) its "Fledgling" series of smaller somewhat simpler pieces, usually selling for less than $100, (2) its profitable middle series of complex sculptures like the "Snowy Owl" (see picture) selling from $800 to $5,000, and (3) its special artistic pieces (like "Fondo Marino" or "Ivory Billed Woodpeckers") which might sell initially for over $20,000.

Individual Boehm porcelains were increasingly being recognized as outstanding artistic creations and sought by some sophisticated collectors. Production of such designs might be sold out for years in advance, but it was difficult to anticipate which pieces might achieve this distinction. Many of the company's past policies no longer seemed appropriate. And the Boehms wanted to further position the company for the long run. When asked what they wanted from the company, they would respond, "to make the world aware of Mr. Boehm's artistic talent, to help world wildlife causes by creating appreciation and protection for threatened species, and to build a continuing business that could make them comfortably wealthy, perhaps millionaires." No one goal had great precedence over the others.

QUESTIONS

1. What strategy should the Boehms follow?
2. Why?

GENENTECH, INC. (A)

In January 1976, Robert Swanson, a venture capitalist with Kleiner and Perkins in San Francisco called Dr. Herbert Boyer at the University of California (San Francisco) to discuss the potentials of commercializing recombinant DNA technology. The cold call—triggered by one of Boyer's papers that Swanson had read—resulted in a 20-minute planned meeting, which extended into a 4-hour conversation over several beers in a nearby tavern. What emerged from that meeting stands as one of the most exciting partnerships in recent years between entrepreneur and scientist. Their company, Genentech, achieved a number of important technical firsts in the application of genetic technologies for useful purposes. Then in October 1980, when it offered its shares publicly, Genentech's stock exploded within minutes from an initial offering price of $35 to a peak of $89 before subsiding to $71.25 a share—making both Swanson (32) and Boyer (44) millionaires many times over. How did this large-scale venture come into being? What would its role be in this "industry of the future?"

THE PARTNERSHIP

Swanson, a graduate of M.I.T. with a bachelor's degree in chemistry and a master's in management, had worked with Citicorp Venture Capital Ltd. before joining Kleiner and Perkins in 1975. Out of a number of technologies he was actively following, recombinant DNA most intrigued his imagination. He had tried unsuccessfully to interest private biological laboratories in industrial prospects for the

Case copyright © 1982 by James Brian Quinn. Research assistant—Allie J. Quinn.

The generous support of the Adolf H. Lundin Professorship at the International Management Institute, Geneva, Switzerland is gratefully acknowledged, as is the generous cooperation of Genentech, Inc.

technology. They thought it would take at least five years to develop the earliest products, too long when compared to their other priorities. Swanson had also canvassed many academic scientists who were leaders in the field. They too felt the newly emerging science was far from the marketplace. Dr. Boyer was the only eminent scientist who at that time believed the technology was ripe for commercial application. Based upon their mutual interests, Swanson and Boyer formed a partnership soon after their first meeting, each putting up $500 of capital to pursue prospects further. Their backgrounds provided an interesting contrast.

Gene Splicing Begins

In high school Herb Boyer—the scientific half of the team—had played football, served as class president, and dabbled in drama. Presciently perhaps, in his senior yearbook, he had stated his goal in life as: "to become a successful businessman." The young Boyer had studied science, primarily because his football coach taught it. But the exposure took. Taking a Ph.D. in bacteriology from the University of Pittsburgh and a post-doctoral fellowship at Yale, Boyer joined the faculty of the University of California Medical Center in San Francisco in 1966. His true interest was research into DNA, the helix-shaped molecule which carries the genetic information determining hereditary characteristics of all living things.

Boyer's work led to another chance meeting in November 1972. After listening to papers all day at a Hawaii scientific conference, Boyer and Stanley Cohen of Stanford met at a delicatessen for a late snack. As they munched on corned beef sandwiches they discovered that their research merged in a unique way. Cohen had been looking for a way to insert foreign genetic material into an *E. coli* bacterium. He had been experimenting with *E. coli*'s plasmids which contained genetic information in simpler structures than its chromosomes. Boyer had found some restriction enzymes that could cut free DNA structures precisely at predetermined points, leaving some "sticky ends" of the DNA molecule to which (the two reasoned) specific genes similarly cut from other structures might attach themselves. The twin breakthroughs—Cohen's understanding of bacterial plasmids and Boyer's enzymes—soon opened a new era.

In 1973 Dr. Boyer's and Dr. Cohen's teams became the first to perfect the technique called "gene splicing" or "recombinant DNA technique." They transplanted a gene from a South African toad into a bacterium, which then reproduced the toad gene. This confirmed the possibility of transferring specific genes from other living systems into bacteria and using the bacteria as factories for reproducing that genetic material.

Being academic scientists, Drs. Cohen and Boyer quickly published their results in a refereed journal for the science community to scrutinize. Only many months later, just in time to avert the one-year prior-publication limit on U.S. patent applications, did Stanford's patent expert (Niel Reimers) get Boyer and Cohen to apply for a U.S. patent with Stanford as the holding agent. Even then, their early publication of results prohibited patenting in most foreign countries, where any prior (nonpatent) publication normally precludes patentability. Boyer and Cohen assigned their rights to royalties in their initial patents to their respective universities.

During this period of basic research Dr. Boyer, like many other biochemists, was thoroughly absorbed by the fascinating frontiers of his complex science. He even named his Siamese cats Watson and Crick after James Watson and Francis Crick who shared the 1962 Nobel prize for their revelations on the structure of the DNA molecule. Before Swanson approached him about forming a company, Dr. Boyer had reportedly "never considered such a possibility." In fact, he even had to borrow the initial $500 for his share of the partnership. Although well established in academic and professional circles, Boyer was virtually unknown to the public or investment community until Genentech's stock underwent its spectacular opening. Even then he preferred a low-profile role, rarely agreeing to press interviews.

The Seed Capital Era

Between January and April 1976, Boyer and Swanson made more detailed investigations of specific technological and market opportunities. Swanson continued to be supported by Kleiner and Perkins on an informal basis during this period. Then on April 7 Swanson and Boyer incorporated Genentech, each taking 25,000 common shares* in return for the cash and assets of their partnership. Kleiner and Perkins agreed to provide some $200,000 of seed capital in return for 20,000 shares** of A Series convertible preferred stock. During this period Swanson and Boyer worked out a detailed business plan which became the basis of Genentech's early technical development and financial expansion.

DECISION POINT

What should have been the critical considerations in Kleiner and Perkins' strategy at this time? What specific actions should Boyer and Swanson take within the limits of the $200,000 seed capital? What should their early strategy be? Why?

THE BUSINESS PLAN

The business plan Swanson and Boyer drew up called for more extensive financing than the initial seed capital could provide. Initially Genentech had authorized capital of 1,000,000 shares of common stock (2¢ par value) and 100,000 shares of convertible preferred (2¢ par). The Plan called for a secondary financing of $500,000 in convertible preferred stock (at $50 per share for 10,000 shares, or 11% of the company). The resulting financial structure (assuming total dilution) was to be:

NAME	SHARES
Boyer	25,000
Swanson	25,000
Riggs and Itakura[a]	10,000
Kleiner and Perkins	20,000
New Partner	10,000
TOTAL	90,000

[a] Scientists attracted to work with Genentech.
Source: Company records.

The money was to carry Genentech through the development of its first commercial product. At that time more capital would be raised to finish the develop-

---

* Later the initial common split 10 for 1.
** Each then convertible for 1 common share, later 4 shares before the common split.

ment of the second product and to establish production facilities. The Plan read, "With the following sales and earnings estimates for 1980, investors are offered an investment opportunity with more than a 79% compound growth rate."

1980 Estimated Sales	$15,000,000
1980 Estimated Profits	3,140,000

The financing was expanded to $850,074 with negotiations completed in March 1977 for a private placement of 29,496 Class A Preferred shares to five venture capital groups plus Kleiner and Perkins.

Goals for Genentech

The Plan further stated, "It is Genentech's goal to select products that are in great demand and to specifically engineer microorganisms to produce those products. We expect to be the first company to commercialize the technology, and we plan to build a major profitable corporation by manufacturing and marketing needed products that benefit mankind. . . . It is Genentech's initial strategy to design microorganisms that will synthesize products for which there is a large existing market and where economies of production will give the company very substantial cost advantages. . . . The future uses of genetic engineering are far reaching and many. With Genentech's technology, microorganisms could be engineered to produce protein to meet world food needs or to produce antibodies to fight viral infections. Any product produced by a living organism is eventually within the company's reach."

The Plan also provided: a detailed explanation of the recombinant DNA technology itself,* a schedule for the development of products, a broad description of the market opportunity, and more detailed descriptions of the intended first two products (somatostatin and insulin). A copy of Genentech's daring development schedule appears as Exhibit 2.

Initial Products

Mr. Fred Middleton, one of the first eight members of the Genentech team and later chief financial officer of Genentech, said, "One of the challenges of this field is that there are so many different sorts of applications. It is time consuming and all encompassing to work on any particular protein. With limited resources you must be sure that you strategically pick the right things to do." Somatostatin, a relatively small and simple protein was selected as the first targeted product, and human insulin as the second. Somatostatin was a naturally occurring brain hormone with possible uses in a variety of disorders. Insulin—a much more complex structure—was essential to the treatment of diabetes.

In seeking these products, Mr. Swanson repeatedly affirmed Genentech's determination "to build one of the finest scientific teams in this field in the world." Genentech's policy was to remain "a part of the scientific community with responsibilities to both its own scientists and to science at large." Mr. Swanson stressed a philosophy of integrating science and business. Genentech was not to be "just an innovative research and development organization that coordinates major research projects," he said. That might be profitable in its own right, but short-sighted. "We were determined to be a fully integrated business organization."

---

* For a simpler description, see Exhibit 1.

Then in August 1977, little more than a year after the company was founded, Genentech scientists "cloned' DNA in a bacteria culture to produce somatostatin. Somatostatin was the first useful product produced by the recombinant DNA technology. In testimony before the Congress of the United States, Dr. Philip Handler, president of the National Academy of Sciences, hailed the achievement as a "scientific triumph of the first order." Production of somatostatin was to begin in February 1978. Genentech's somatostatin would initially be sold only for use in laboratory research. But its potential markets were very large, including possible uses in the treatment of diabetes, gastric bleeding, and various hormonal disorders. The FDA had already cleared somatostatin produced by other techniques as a chemical for clinical trials. Competitors' somatostatin was selling for between $30,000 and $55,000 per gram in small amounts. Genentech sought to supply large quantities of somatostatin with production costs of under $30 per gram.

In November 1977 Genentech scientists began to work on methods for bacterial production of human insulin. In February 1978 the company leased space in South San Francisco for its headquarters and laboratories for its scientists' experiments aimed at human insulin expression. To complete the second phase of its physical plant expansion program, and to fund the insulin project, Genentech raised additional equity capital of $950,000 through private placements.

At the end of the offering, there were also 758,976 shares of common stock owned by the founders, Genentech's employees, and consultants. Boyer and Swanson each owned 250,000 shares after the 10:1 common split. Wilmington Securities (of Pittsburgh) was the lead group in this third offering. Exhibit 3 provides a summary of all other Genentech financings.

Class A Preferred Stock*

NAME	SEED SHARES	CAPITAL $	MARCH 1977 SHARES	$	APRIL 1978 SHARES	$
Kleiner and Perkins	20,000	100,000	3,470	100,000	—	—
Inco Securities			13,880	400,000	—	—
Innoven			4,338	125,000	2,500	200,000
Mayfield II			4,338	125,000	1,250	100,000
Sofinnova			1,735	50,000	1,000	80,000
Venture Assoc.			1,735	50,000	—	—
Wilmington Securities			—	—	6,250	500,000
Others			—	—	875	70,000
			29,496	850,000	11,875	950,000

* All shares convertible at 4:1 before Genentech's 10:1 common stock split.

Source: Company records.

Human Insulin Achieved

In August 1978 Genentech and City of Hope National Medical Center at Duart, California, jointly announced that they had produced human insulin by recombinant DNA technology. The announcement said, "This achievement may be the most significant advance in the treatment of diabetes since the development of animal insulin for human use in the 1920s. The insulin synthesis is the first laboratory production of a significant widely needed human hormone using recombinant DNA technology." The contributions of Drs. Crea, Itakura, and Riggs at the City of Hope, as well as Drs. Goeddel and Cleid at Genentech, were specifically cited. The announcement noted that approximately 1.5 million diabetics took injections of expensive insulin every day. The new process would permit ample quantities of a product "chemically identical to human insulin" to be produced at substantially lower costs than existing processes. This laboratory success followed a remarkably rapid development of the technology:[1]

- May 1977: Rat insulin gene incorporated in *E. coli* at University of California, San Francisco, with no gene expression occurring.
- November 1977: Stanford University reports *E. coli* takes up DNA from higher cells.
- November 1977: University of California at San Francisco fuses clinically synthesized gene for somatostatin to an *E. coli* enzyme gene; gene expression obtained.
- June 1978: Joslin Diabetes Foundation announces rat insulin gene fused to another gene and incorporated into *E. coli*. The combined protein was excreted from bacteria.
- August 1978: Genentech achieves successful laboratory production of insulin from recombinant DNA technology.

If successfully produced in quantity Genentech's insulin would be "human insulin," with a chemical structure exactly like the insulin naturally occurring within the human body. Unlike bovine or porcine insulin, "human insulin" was not expected to cause allergic reactions in certain individuals. Insulin represented a large existing market (more than $100 million worldwide, with over half the market in the United States). Eli Lilly Co. held over 80% of the domestic market, which at that time was growing at about 6% annually. The existing source for insulin was animal pancreas glands. As the market grew, these were coming into increasingly short supply and were very expensive to process.

Bovine and porcine pancreases had increased in price from 40¢ per pound in 1972 to over $1.25 per pound in 1978. Ten thousand pounds of pancreas were needed for one pound of insulin. Then, large-scale and complicated chemical processing techniques were needed to obtain purified insulin. Genentech's production process was expected to take place in a standard 750-liter laboratory fermentation vessel. A little over $800 worth of growth medium would produce approximately 15 kilograms (net weight) of bacterial cells coded for insulin within an 8-hour shift, and the process could be speeded so that cell mass doubled every 20 minutes. Early estimates were that about 30% of the total protein would be insulin. This would yield approximately one pound of purified insulin per production run.

However, Mr. Swanson cautioned "the technology is a long way from being ready for commercial production. We've set up a pilot manufacturing facility for fermentation and extraction. We have hired key personnel to work on the scale-up process. And we have filed patent applications for the present technology. But the fate of these patents cannot be predicted at this time." Nevertheless, in Swanson's view "the procedure was similar to having the process to make a semiconductor when everyone else was using vacuum tubes."[2]

Development and scale up costs would be "several million dollars" for each product. Clinical tests would require $3–20 million more. (See Exhibit 4 for the typical sequence of steps involved.) Few pharmaceutical products then reached the market with less than $8–10 million in investment, with delays of 3–4 years being common. Even then Genentech would have to meet other potential genetic competitors, existing products in the market, and an unreliable world patent structure in which many countries did not recognize product patents on products for human health. To complicate things further Genentech was supporting other laboratory work which could lead to a highly diverse set of end products. But the company could not be sure which products could ultimately be achieved in the laboratory or cleared for commercial use. Nor did it know the precise sequence in which these events would occur. Against this background, Genentech had to decide the next stage of its strategy. In December 1978 Genentech, whose scientific team had increased to 26 including 12 Ph.D.s, added three laboratories and six new offices to its facilities. A second business plan was developed which projected a doubling of staff and facilities in 1978, a $1.3 million needed capital expansion, and a fully integrated product program for the "post-insulin era."

QUESTIONS

1. What should the venture capitalists' strategy have been with their first $100,000–200,000 investment? Why is the company financed the way it is?

2. What are the major strategic options facing Genentech at the end of the case? What strategy should it follow? Why?

3. Answer the questions interspersed in the case.

EXHIBIT 1
Redesigning Bacteria

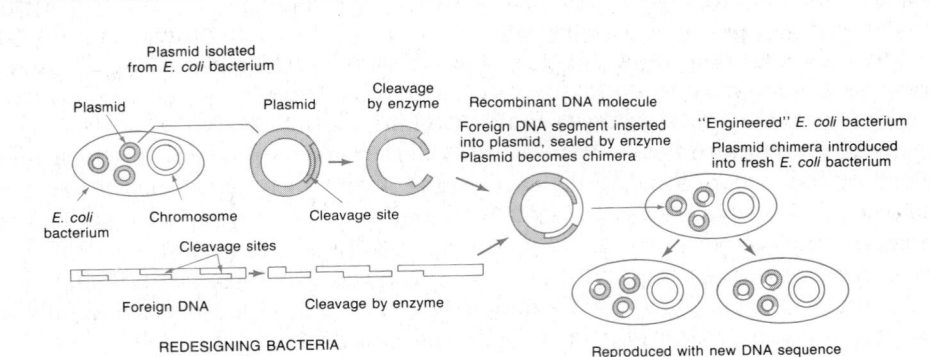

REDESIGNING BACTERIA

The development of the recombinant DNA technique ushered in a new era of genetic engineering—with all of its promise and possible peril. The lowly organism that currently plays the largest role in the process is the *E. coli* bacterium. This microbe—a laboratory derivative of a common inhabitant of the human intestine—lends itself to being engineered because its genetic structure has been so well studied. In the first step of the process, scientists place the bacterium in a test tube with a detergent-like liquid. This dissolves the microbe's outer membrane, causing its DNA strands to spill out in a disorderly tangle. Most of the DNA is included in the bacterium's chromosome, in the form of a long strand containing thousands of genes. The remainder is found in several tiny, closed loops called plasmids, which have only a few genes each and are the most popular vehicles for the recombinant technique.

After the plasmids are separated from the chromosomal DNA in a centrifuge, they are placed in a solution with a chemical catalyst called a restriction enzyme. This enzyme cuts through the plasmids' DNA strips at specific points. It leaves overlapping, mortise-type breaks with "sticky" ends. The opened plasmid loops are then mixed in a solution with genes—also removed by the use of restriction enzymes—from the DNA of a plant, animal, bacterium or virus. In the solution is another enzyme called a DNA ligase, which cements the foreign gene into place in the opening of the plasmids. The result of these unions are new loops of DNA called plasmid chimeras because, like the Chimera—the mythical lion-goat-serpent after which they are named—they contain the components of more than one organism.

Finally, the chimeras are placed in a solution of cold calcium chloride containing normal *E. coli* bacteria. When the solution is suddenly heated, the membranes of the *E. coli* become permeable, allowing the plasmid chimeras to pass through and become part of the microbes' new genetic structure. When the *E. coli* reproduce, they create carbon copies of themselves, new plasmids—and DNA sequences—and all. Thus they become forms of life potentially different from what they had been before—imbued with characteristics dictated not only by their own *E. coli* genes, but also by genes from an entirely different species.

EXHIBIT 2
Development Schedule

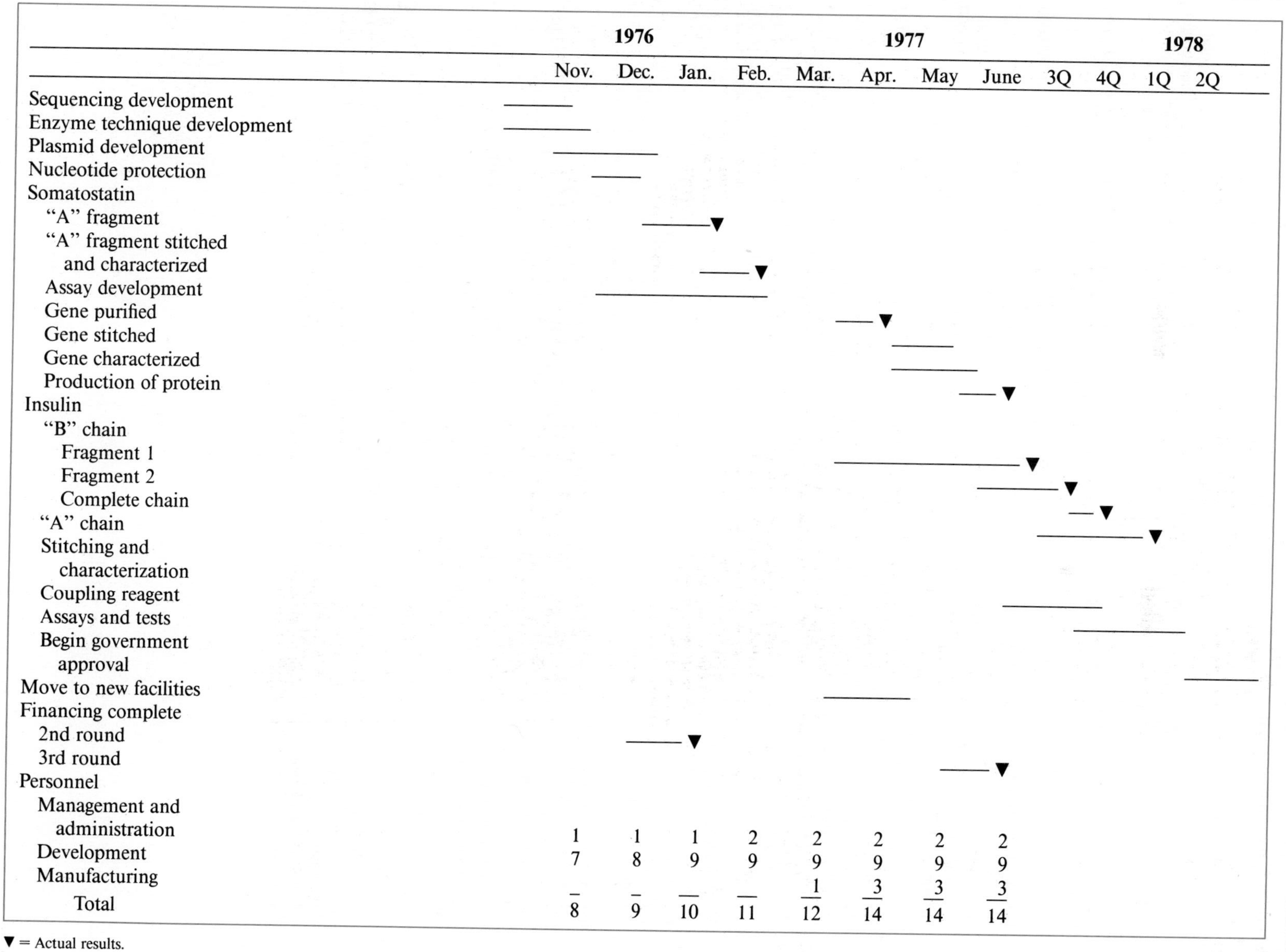

	1976		1977									1978
	Nov.	Dec.	Jan.	Feb.	Mar.	Apr.	May	June	3Q	4Q	1Q	2Q
Sequencing development												
Enzyme technique development												
Plasmid development												
Nucleotide protection												
Somatostatin												
"A" fragment												
"A" fragment stitched and characterized												
Assay development												
Gene purified												
Gene stitched												
Gene characterized												
Production of protein												
Insulin												
"B" chain												
Fragment 1												
Fragment 2												
Complete chain												
"A" chain												
Stitching and characterization												
Coupling reagent												
Assays and tests												
Begin government approval												
Move to new facilities												
Financing complete												
2nd round												
3rd round												
Personnel												
Management and administration	1	1	1	2	2	2	2					
Development	7	8	9	9	9	9	9					
Manufacturing	—	—	—	—	1	3	3					
Total	8	9	10	11	12	14	14					

▶ = Actual results.
Source: Company records.

141

EXHIBIT 3
Statement of Shareholders' Equity

	Preferred Stock	Common Stock	Series B Restricted Stock	Series C Restricted Stock	Capital in Excess of Par Value	Retained Earnings (Deficit)	Less Notes Receivable Sale of Stock	Total Shareholders' Equity
Balance at December 31, 1978	$1,227	$ 14,465	—	—	$ 1,937,580	$(888,368)	$ (24,749)	$ 1,040,155
Issuance of Preferred stock (25,000 shares)	500	—	—	—	9,999,500	—	—	10,000,000
Issuance of Common stock (45,726 shares)	—	915	—	—	29,678	—	(20,500)	10,093
Stock issuance costs	—	—	—	—	(11,000)	—	—	(11,000)
Repurchase of Common stock (3,750 shares)	—	(75)	—	—	(1,050)	—	—	(1,125)
Ten-for-one conversion of Preferred stock (863,710 shares)	(1,727)	17,274	—	—	(15,547)	—	—	—
Payments on notes receivable	—	—	—	—	—	—	9,954	9,954
Net income	—	—	—	—	—	116,336	—	116,336
Balance at December 31, 1979	—	32,579	—	—	11,939,161	(772,032)	(35,295)	11,164,413
Four-for-one conversion of Common stock (4,885,134 shares)	—	97,702	—	—	(97,702)	—	—	—
Issuance of Common stock (1,124,608 shares)	—	22,493	—	—	39,209,596	—	—	39,232,089
Issuance of Series B Restricted stock (224,250 shares)	—	—	$4,485	—	342,015	—	(301,330)	45,170
Stock issuance costs	—	—	—	—	(2,945,579)	—	—	(2,945,579)
Repurchase of Common stock (48,236 shares)	—	(965)	—	—	(15,875)	—	—	(16,840)
Payments on notes receivable	—	—	—	—	—	—	20,182	20,182
Donated equipment	—	—	—	—	36,450	—	—	36,450
Tax benefit from employee stock plan	—	—	—	—	10,998	—	—	10,998
Net income	—	—	—	—	—	236,292	—	236,292

EXHIBIT 3 (Continued)

	Preferred Stock	Common Stock	Series B Restricted Stock	Series C Restricted Stock	Capital in Excess of Par Value	Retained Earnings (Deficit)	Less Notes Receivable Sale of Stock	Total Shareholders' Equity
Balance at December 31, 1980	—	151,809	4,485	—	48,479,064	(535,740)	(316,443)	47,783,175
Issuance of Common stock (163,684 shares)	—	3,274	—	—	5,047,378	—	—	5,050,652
Issuance of Series B Restricted Stock (71,980 shares)	—	—	1,440	—	358,460	—	(317,250)	42,650
Issuance of Series C Restricted Stock (69,500 shares)	—	—	—	$1,390	241,860	—	(200,150)	43,100
Stock issuance costs	—	—	—	—	(328,800)	—	—	(328,800)
Repurchase of Common stock (7,903 shares)	—	(158)	—	—	(10,558)	—	—	(10,716)
Conversion of Series B Restricted Stock (296,230 shares)	—	5,925	(5,925)	—	—	—	—	—
Payments on notes receivable	—	—	—	—	—	—	26,680	26,680
Tax benefit from employee stock plan	—	—	—	—	23,000	—	—	23,000
Net income	—	—	—	—	—	503,010	—	503,010
Balance at December 31, 1981	—	$160,850	—	$1,390	$53,810,404	$ (32,730)	$(807,163)	$53,132,751

See accompanying notes provided in company's annual report.

Source: Genentech, Inc., *Annual Report,* 1981.

EXHIBIT 4
The Product Development
Process

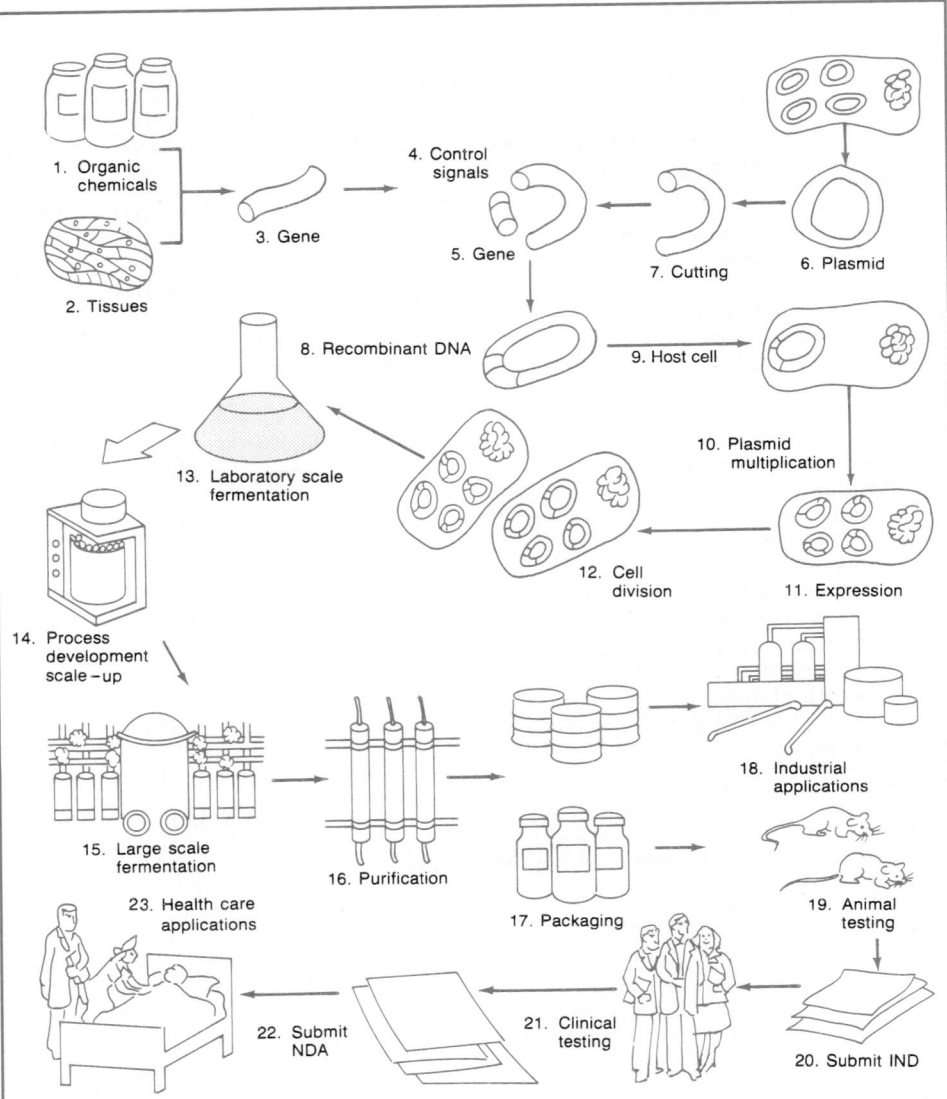

1. Organic chemicals
2. Tissues
3. Gene
4. Control signals
5. Gene
6. Plasmid
7. Cutting
8. Recombinant DNA
9. Host cell
10. Plasmid multiplication
11. Expression
12. Cell division
13. Laboratory scale fermentation
14. Process development scale-up
15. Large scale fermentation
16. Purification
17. Packaging
18. Industrial applications
19. Animal testing
20. Submit IND
21. Clinical testing
22. Submit NDA
23. Health care applications

The development process begins by obtaining DNA either through organic synthesis (1) or derived from biological sources such as tissues (2). The DNA obtained from one or both sources is tailored to form the basic "gene" (3) which contains the genetic information to "code" for a desired product, such as human interferon or human insulin. Control signals (4) containing instructions are added to this gene (5). Circular DNA molecules called plasmids (6) are isolated from micro-organisms such as *E. coli,* cut open (7) and spliced back (8) together with genes and control signals to form "recombinant DNA" molecules. These molecules are then introduced into a host cell (9).

Each plasmid is copied many times in a cell (10). Each cell then translates the information contained in these plasmids into the desired product, a process called "expression" (11). Cells divide (12) and pass on to their offspring the same genetic information contained in the parent cell.

Fermentation of large populations of genetically engineered micro-organisms is first done in shaker flasks (13), and then in small fermenters (14)

EXHIBIT 4 (Continued)

to determine growth conditions, and eventually in larger fermentation tanks (15). Cellular extract obtained from the fermentation process is then separated, purified (16), and packaged (17) either for industrial use (18) or health care applications.

Health care products are first tested in animal studies (19) to demonstrate a product's pharmacological activity and safety. In the United States, an investigational new drug application (IND) (20) is submitted to begin human clinical trials to establish safety and efficacy. Following clinical testing (21), a new drug application (NDA) (22) is filed with the Food and Drug Administration (FDA). When the NDA has been reviewed and approved by the FDA the product may be marketed in the United States (23).

Source: Genentech, Inc.

EXHIBIT 5
Potential Markets for the Gene-Splicers

Product category	Number of compounds	Current market value	Selected compound or use	Time needed to implement genetic production
AMINO ACIDS	9	$1,703,000,000	Glutamate Tryptophan	5 years 5 years
VITAMINS	6	667,700,000	Vitamin C Vitamin E	10 years 15 years
ENZYMES	11	217,700,000	Pepsin	5 years
STEROID HORMONES	6	367,800,000	Cortisone	10 years
PEPTIDE HORMONES	9	269,700,000	Human growth hormone Insulin	5 years 5 years
VIRAL ANTIGENS	9	N/A	Hoof-and-mouth disease virus Influenza viruses	5 years 10 years
SHORT PEPTIDES	2	4,400,000	Aspartame	5 years
MISCELLANEOUS PROTEINS	2	300,000,000	Interferon	5 years
ANTIBIOTICS	4*	4,240,000,000	Penicillins Erythromycins	10 years 10 years
PESTICIDES	2*	100,000,000	Microbial Aromatics	5 years 10 years

EXHIBIT 5 **(Continued)**

Product category	Number of compounds	Current market value	Selected compound or use	Time needed to implement genetic production
METHANE	1	$12,572,000,000	Methane	10 years
ALIPHATICS (Other than methane)	24	2,737,500,000	Ethanol Ethylene glycol Propylene glycol Isobutylene	5 years 5 years 10 years 10 years
AROMATICS	10	1,250,900,000	Aspirin Phenol	5 years 10 years
INORGANICS	2	2,681,000,000	Hydrogen Ammonia	15 years 15 years
MINERAL LEACHING	5	N/A	Uranium Cobalt Iron	
BIODEGRADATION	N/A	N/A	Removal of organic phosphates	

N/A = not available.

* Number indicates classes of compounds, rather than number of compounds.

Source: Industry Week, September 7, 1981.

EXHIBIT 5 (Continued)

Applications of Genetic Engineering Technologies

Microbial Product or Process	End Use	Microbial Product or Process	End Use
AGRICULTURE		**FOOD PROCESSING**	
Amino acids, vitamins	Feed additives (e.g., lysine)	Amino acids, vitamins	Food enrichment and flavoring agents
Antibiotics	Feed additives and prophylactics	Aromatic compounds	Food additives
		Aliphatic compounds	Food additives
Short peptides	Feed additives and growth promoters	Short peptides	Artificial sweeteners
		Enzymes	Manufacturing processes
Viral Antigens	Vaccines	Cellulose conversion	Sugar production
Insecticides	Pest control	**PHARMACEUTICALS**	
Nitrogen fixation	Fertilizer and legume inoculants	Amino acids, vitamins	Intravenous solutions
		Aromatic compounds	Analgesics, narcotics, etc.
Biodegradation	Organic phosphate removal		
		Steroid hormone modification	Various therapeutics and prophylactics
CHEMISTRY			
Aromatic compounds	Chemical intermediates	Antibiotics, antibiotic modification	Control of infectious diseases
Aliphatic compounds	Chemical intermediates		
Enzymes	Manufacturing processes		Control of hemoglobin disorders
Biodegradation	Organic phosphate and arylsulfonate removal	Short peptides	
			Control of metabolic disorders
Mineral leaching	Metal extraction	Peptide hormones	
ENERGY			Various diagnostic (e.g., glucose oxidase) and therapeutic (e.g., urokinase) procedures
Enzymes	Manufacturing processes	Enzymes	
Biodegradation	Petroleum by-products removal		
Sewage conversion	Methane production		Vaccines (e.g., hepatitis vaccine)
Cellulose conversion	Alcohol production	Viral antigens	
Mineral leaching	Uranium concentration		Various therapeutics (e.g., interferon, human serum albumin)
Coal conversion	Methane production	Other proteins	
Biophotolysis	Hydrogen production		
			Control of hereditary disorders
		Gene preparations	

Source: Genex Corporation in *Chemical & Engineering News,* March 17, 1980, p. 23.

THE GUNS OF AUGUST: GERMAN AND FRENCH STRATEGY IN 1914

THE GERMAN VIEW

Count Alfred von Schlieffen, Chief of the German General Staff from 1891 to 1906 was, like all German officers, schooled in Clausewitz's precept, "The heart of France lies between Brussels and Paris." It was a frustrating axiom because the path it pointed to was forbidden by Belgian neutrality, which Germany, along with the other four major European powers, had guaranteed in perpetuity. Believing that war was a certainty and that Germany must enter it under conditions that gave her the most promise of success, Schlieffen determined not to allow the Belgian difficulty to stand in Germany's way. Of the two classes of Prussian officer, the bullnecked and the wasp-waisted, he belonged to the second. Monocled and effete in appearance, cold and distant in manner, he concentrated with such single-mindedness on his profession that when an aide, at the end of an all-night staff ride in East Prussia, pointed out to him the beauty of the river Pregel sparkling in the rising sun, the General gave a brief, hard look and replied, "An unimportant obstacle." So too, he decided, was Belgian neutrality.

The Belgian Question

A neutral and independent Belgium was the creation of England, or rather of England's ablest Foreign Minister, Lord Palmerston. Belgium's coast was England's frontier; on the plains of Belgium, Wellington had defeated the greatest threat to

Reprinted with permission of Macmillan Publishing Company and Russell & Volkening, as agents for the author, from *The Guns of August* by Barbara W. Tuchman. Copyright © 1962 by Barbara W. Tuchman. Subheadings and questions at end inserted by James Brian Quinn to aid students.

England since the Armada. Thereafter England was determined to make that patch of open, easily traversable territory a neutral zone and, under the post-Napoleon settlement of the Congress of Vienna, agreed with the other powers to attach it to the Kingdom of the Netherlands. Resenting union with a Protestant power, burning with the fever of the nineteenth-century nationalism, the Belgians revolted in 1830, setting off an international scramble. The Dutch fought to retain their province; the French, eager to reabsorb what they had once ruled, moved in; the autocratic states—Russia, Prussia, and Austria—bent on keeping Europe clamped under the vise of Vienna, were ready to shoot at the first sign of revolt anywhere.

Lord Palmerston outmaneuvered them all. He knew that a subject province would be an eternal temptation to one neighbor or another and that only an independent nation, resolved to maintain its own integrity, could survive as a safety zone. Through nine years of nerve, of suppleness, of never swerving from his aim, of calling out the British fleet when necessary, he played off all contenders and secured an international treaty guaranteeing Belgium as an "independent and perpetually neutral state." The treaty was signed in 1839 by England, France, Russia, Prussia, and Austria.

Ever since 1892, when France and Russia had joined in military alliance, it was clear that four of the five signatories of the Belgian treaty would be automatically engaged—two against two—in the war for which Schlieffen had to plan. Europe was a heap of swords piled as delicately as jackstraws; one could not be pulled out without moving the others. Under the terms of the Austro-German alliance, Germany was obliged to support Austria in any conflict with Russia. Under the terms of the alliance between France and Russia, both parties were obliged to move against Germany if either became involved in a "defensive war" with Germany. These arrangements made it inevitable that in any war in which she engaged, Germany would have to fight on two fronts against both Russia and France.

What part England would play was uncertain; she might remain neutral; she might, if given cause, come in against Germany. That Belgium could be the cause was no secret. In Franco-Prussian War of 1870, when Germany was still a climbing power, Bismarck had been happy enough, upon a hint from England, to reaffirm the inviolability of Belgium. Gladstone had secured a treaty from both belligerents providing that if either violated Belgian neutrality, England would cooperate with the other to the extent of defending Belgium, though without engaging in the general operations of the war. Although there was something a little impractical about the tail of this Gladstonian formula, the Germans had no reason to suppose its underlying motive any less operative in 1914 than in 1870. Nevertheless, Schlieffen decided, in the event of war, to attack France by way of Belgium.

France First

His reason was "military necessity." In a two-front war, he wrote, "the whole of Germany must throw itself upon *one* enemy, the strongest, most powerful, most dangerous enemy, and that can only be France." Schlieffen's completed plan for 1906, the year he retired, allocated six weeks and seven-eighths of Germany's forces to smash France while one-eighth was to hold her eastern frontier against Russia until the bulk of her army could be brought back to face the second enemy. He chose France first because Russia could frustrate a quick victory by simply withdrawing within her infinite room, leaving Germany to be sucked into an endless campaign as Napoleon had been. France was both closer at hand and quicker to mobilize. The German and French armies each required two weeks to complete mobilization before a major attack could begin on the fifteenth day. Russia, according to German arithmetic, because of her vast distances, huge numbers, and meager railroads, would take six weeks before she could launch a major offensive, by which time France would be beaten.

The risk of leaving East Prussia, hearth of Junkerdom and the Hohenzollerns, to be held by only nine divisions was hard to accept, but Frederick the Great had said, "It is better to lose a province than split the forces with which one seeks victory," and nothing so comforts the military mind as the maxim of a great but dead general. Only by throwing the utmost numbers against the West could France be finished off quickly. Only by a strategy of envelopment, using Belgium as a pathway, could the German armies, in Schlieffen's opinion, attack France successfully. His reasoning, from the purely military point of view, appeared faultless.

The German Army of a million and a half that was to be used against France was now six times the size it had been in 1870, and needed room to maneuver. French fortresses constructed along the frontiers of Alsace and Lorraine after 1870 precluded the Germans from making a frontal attack across the common border. A protracted siege would provide no opportunity, as long as French lines to the rear remained open, of netting the enemy quickly in a battle of annihilation. Only by envelopment could the French be taken from behind and destroyed. But at either end of the French lines lay neutral territory—Switzerland and Belgium. There was not enough room for the huge German Army to get around the French armies and still stay inside France. The Germans had done it in 1870 when both armies were small, but now it was a matter of moving an army of millions to outflank an army of millions. Space, roads, and railroads were essential. The flat plains of Flanders had them. In Belgium there was both room for the outflanking maneuver which was Schlieffen's formula for success as well as a way to avoid the frontal attack which was his formula for disaster.

Clausewitz, oracle of German military thought, had ordained a quick victory by "decisive battle" as the first object in offensive war. Occupation of the enemy's territory and gaining control of his resources was secondary. To speed an early decision was essential. Time counted above all else. Anything that protracted a campaign Clausewitz condemned. "Gradual reduction" of the enemy, or a war of attrition, he feared like the pit of hell. He wrote in the decade of Waterloo, and his works had been accepted as the Bible of strategy ever since.

The New Cannae

To achieve decisive victory, Schlieffen fixed upon a strategy derived from Hannibal and the Battle of Cannae. The dead general who mesmerized Schlieffen had been dead a very long time. Two thousand years had passed since Hannibal's classic double envelopment of the Romans at Cannae. Field gun and machine gun had replaced bow and arrow and slingshot, Schlieffen wrote, "but the principles of strategy remain unchanged. The enemy's front is not the objective. The essential thing is to crush the enemy's flanks . . . and complete the extermination by attack upon his rear." Under Schlieffen, envelopment became the fetish and frontal attack the anathema of the German General Staff.

Schlieffen's first plan to include the violation of Belgium was formulated in 1899. It called for cutting across the corner of Belgium east of the Meuse. Enlarged with each successive year, by 1905 it had expanded into a huge enveloping right-wing sweep in which the German armies would cross Belgium from Liège to Brussels before turning southward, where they could take advantage of the open country of Flanders, to march against France. Everything depended upon a quick decision against France, and even the long way around through Flanders would be quicker than laying siege to the fortress line across the common border.

Schlieffen did not have enough divisions for a double envelopment of France à la Cannae. For this he substituted a heavily one-sided right wing that would spread across the whole of Belgium on both sides of the Meuse, sweep down through the country like a monstrous hayrake, cross the Franco-Belgian frontier along its entire width, and descend upon Paris along the Valley of the Oise. The German mass would come between the capital and the French armies which, drawn back to meet the menace, would be caught, away from their fortified areas, in the decisive battle of annihilation. Essential to the plan was a deliberately weak German left wing on the Alsace-Lorraine front which would tempt the French in that area forward into a "sack" between Metz and the Vosges. It was expected that the French, intent upon liberating their lost provinces, would attack here, and it was considered so much the better for the success of the German plan if they did, for they could be held in the sack by the German left wing while the main victory was obtained from behind. In the back of Schlieffen's mind always glimmered the hope that, as battle unfolded, a counterattack by his left wing could be mounted in order to bring about a true double enevelopment—the "colossal Cannae" of his dreams. Sternly saving his greatest strength for the right wing, he did not yield to that vaulting ambition in his plan. But the lure of the left wing remained to tempt his successors.

Thus the Germans came to Belgium. Decisive battle dictated envelopment, and envelopment dictated the use of Belgian territory. The German General Staff pronounced it a military necessity; Kaiser and Chancellor accepted it with more or less equanimity. Whether it was advisable, whether it was even expedient in view of the probable effect on world opinion, especially on neutral opinion, was irrelevant. That it seemed necessary to the triumph of German arms was the only criterion. Germans had imbibed from 1870 the lesson that arms and war were the sole source of German greatness. They had been taught by Field Marshal von der Goltz, in his book *The Nation in Arms,* that "We have won our position through the sharpness of our sword, not through the sharpness of our mind." The decision to violate Belgian neutrality followed easily.

National Character

Character is fate, the Greeks believed. A hundred years of German philosophy went into the making of this decision in which the seed of self-destruction lay embedded, waiting for its hour. The voice was Schlieffen's, but the hand was the hand of Fichte who saw the German people chosen by Providence to occupy the supreme place in the history of the universe, of Hegel who saw them leading the world to a glorious destiny of compulsory *Kultur,* of Nietzsche who told them that Supermen were above ordinary controls, of Treitschke who set the increase of power as the highest moral duty of the state, of the whole German people, who called their temporal ruler the "All-Highest." What made the Schlieffen plan was not Clausewitz and the Battle of Cannae, but the body of accumulated egoism which suckled the German people and created a nation fed on "the desperate delusion of the will that deems itself absolute."

The goal, decisive battle, was a product of the victories over Austria and France in 1866 and 1870. Dead battles, like dead generals, hold the military mind in their dead grip, and Germans, no less than other peoples, prepare for the last war. They staked everything on decisive battle in the image of Hannibal, but even the ghost of Hannibal might have reminded Schlieffen that though Carthage won at Cannae, Rome won the war.

Old Field Marshal Moltke in 1890 foretold that the next war might last seven years—or thirty—because the resources of a modern state were so great it would not know itself to be beaten after a single military defeat and would not give up. His nephew and namesake who succeeded Schlieffen as Chief of Staff also had moments when he saw the truth as clearly. In a moment of heresy to Clausewitz, he said to the Kaiser in 1906, "It will be a national war which will not be settled by a decisive battle but by a long wearisome struggle with a country that will not be overcome until its whole national force is broken, and a war which will utterly exhaust our own people, even if we are victorious." It went against human nature, however—and the nature of General Staffs—to follow through the logic of his own prophecy. Amorphous and without limits, the concept of a long war could not be scientifically planned for as could the orthodox, predictable, and simple solution of decisive battle and a short war. The younger Moltke was already Chief of Staff when he made his prophecy, but neither he nor his Staff, nor the Staff of any other country, ever made any effort to plan for a long war. Besides the two Moltkes, one dead and the other infirm of purpose, some military strategists in other countries glimpsed the possibility of prolonged war, but all preferred to believe, along with the bankers and industrialists, that because of the dislocation of economic life a general European war could not last longer than three or four months. One constant among the elements of 1914—as of any era—was the disposition of everyone on all sides not to prepare for the harder alternative, not to act upon what they suspected to be true.

Schlieffen, having embraced the strategy of "decisive battle," pinned Germany's fate to it. He expected France to violate Belgium as soon as Germany's deployment at the Belgian frontier revealed her strategy, and he therefore planned that Germany should do it first and faster. "Belgian neutrality must be broken by one side or the other," his thesis ran. "Whoever gets there first and occupies Brussels and imposes a war levy of some 1,000 million francs has the upper hand."

Indemnity, which enables a state to conduct war at the enemy's expense instead of its own, was a secondary object laid down by Clausewitz. His third was the winning of public opinion, which is accomplished by "gaining great victories and possession of the enemy's capital" and which helps to bring an end to resistance. He knew how material success could gain public opinion; he forgot how moral failure could lose it, which too can be a hazard of war.

It was a hazard the French never lost sight of, and it led them to the opposite conclusion from the one Schlieffen expected. Belgium was their pathway of attack too, through the Ardennes if not through Flanders, but their plan of campaign prohibited their armies from using it until after the Germans had violated Belgium first. To them the logic of the matter was clear: Belgium was an open path in either direction; whether Germany or France would use it depended on which of the two wanted war the more. As a French general said, "The one that willed war more than the other could not help but will the violation of Belgian neutrality."

Schlieffen and his Staff did not think Belgium would fight and add its six divisions to the French forces. When Chancellor Bülow, discussing the problem with Schlieffen in 1904, reminded him of Bismarck's warning that it would be against "plain common sense" to add another enemy to the forces against Germany, Schlieffen twisted his monocle several times in his eye, as was his habit, and said: "Of course. We haven't grown stupider since then." But Belgium would not resist by force of arms; she would be satisfied to protest, he said.

German confidence on this score was due to placing rather too high a value on the well-known avarice of Leopold II, who was King of the Belgians in Schlieffen's time. Tall and imposing with his black spade beard and his aura of wickedness composed of mistresses, money, Congo cruelties, and other scandals, Leopold was, in the opinion of Emperor Franz Josef of Austria, "a thoroughly bad man." There were few men who could be so described, the Emperor said, but the King of the Belgians was one. Because Leopold was avaricious, among other vices, the Kaiser supposed that avarice would rule over common sense, and he conceived a clever plan to tempt Leopold into [an] alliance with an offer of French territory. Whenever the Kaiser was seized with a project he attempted instantly to execute it, usually to his astonishment and chagrin when it did not work. In 1904 he invited Leopold to visit him in Berlin, spoke to him in "the kindest way in the world" about his proud forefathers, the Dukes of Burgundy, and offered to re-create the old Duchy of Burgundy for him out of Artois, French Flanders, and the French Ardennes. Leopold gazed at him "openmouthed," then, attempting to pass it off with a laugh, reminded the Kaiser that much had changed since the fifteenth century. In any event, he said, his Ministers and Parliament would never consider such a suggestion.

That was the wrong thing to say, for the Kaiser flew into one of his rages and scolded the King for putting respect for Parliament and Ministers above respect for the finger of God (with which William sometimes confused himself). "I told him," William reported to Chancellor von Bülow, "I could not be played with. Whoever in the case of a European war was not with me was against me." He was a soldier, he proclaimed, in the school of Napoleon and Frederick the Great who began their wars by forestalling their enemies, and "so should I, in the event of Belgium's not being on my side, be actuated by strategical considerations only."

This declared intent, the first explicit threat to tear up the treaty, dumbfounded King Leopold. He drove off to the station with his helmet on back to front, looking to the aide who accompanied him "as if he had had a shock of some kind."

Although the Kaiser's scheme failed, Leopold was still expected to barter Belgium's neutrality for a purse of two million pounds sterling. When a French intelligence officer, who was told this figure by a German officer after the war, expressed surprise at its generosity, he was reminded that "the French would have had to pay for it." Even after Leopold was succeeded in 1909 by his nephew King Albert, a very different quantity, Belgium's resistance was still expected by Schlieffen's successors to be a formality. It might, for example, suggested a German diplomat in 1911, take the form of "lining up her army along the road taken by the German forces."

"Brush the Channel"

Schlieffen designated thirty-four divisions to take the roads through Belgium, disposing on their way of Belgium's six divisions if, as seemed to the Germans unlikely, they chose to resist. The Germans were intensely anxious that they should not, because resistance would mean destruction of railways and bridges and consequent dislocation of the schedule to which the German Staff was passionately attached. Belgian acquiescence, on the other hand, would avoid the necessity of tying up divisions in siege of the Belgian fortresses and would also tend to silence public disapproval of Germany's act. To persuade Belgium against futile resistance, Schlieffen arranged that she should be confronted, prior to invasion, by an ultimatum requiring her to yield "all fortresses, railways and troops" or face bombardment of her fortified cities. Heavy artillery was ready to transform the threat of bombardment into reality, if necessary. The heavy guns would in any case, Schlieffen wrote in 1912, be needed further on in the campaign. "The great industrial town of Lille, for example, offers an excellent target for bombardment."

Schlieffen wanted his right wing to reach as far west as Lille in order to make the envelopment of the French complete. "When you march into France," he said, "let the man on the right brush the Channel with his sleeve." Furthermore, counting on British belligerency, he wanted a wide sweep in order to rake in a British Expeditionary Force along with the French. He placed a higher value on the blockade potential of British sea power than on the British Army, and therefore was determined to achieve a quick victory over French and British land forces and an early decision of the war before the economic consequences of British hostility could make themselves felt. To that end everything must go to swell the right wing. He had to make it powerful in numbers because the density of soldiers per mile determined the extent of territory that could be covered.

Employing the active army alone, he would not have enough divisions both to hold his eastern frontier against a Russian breakthrough and to achieve the superiority in numbers over France which he needed for a quick victory. His solution was simple if revolutionary. He decided to use reserve units in the front line. According to prevailing military doctrine, only the youngest men, fresh from the rigors and discipline of barracks and drill, were fit to fight; reserves who had finished their compulsory military service and returned to civilian life were considered soft and were not wanted in the battle line. Except for men under twenty-six who were merged with the active units, the reserves were formed into divisions of their own, intended for use as occupation troops and for other rear duty. Schlieffen changed all that. He added some twenty reserve divisions (the number varied according to the year of the plan) to the line of march of the fifty or more active divisions. With this increase in numbers his cherished envelopment became possible.

After retiring in 1906 he spent his last years still writing about Cannae, improving his plan, composing memoranda to guide his successors, and died at eighty in 1913, muttering at the end: "It must come to a fight. Only make the right wing strong."

Von Moltke

His successor, the melancholy General von Moltke, was something of a pessimist who lacked Schlieffen's readiness to concentrate all his strength in one maneuver. If Schlieffen's motto was "Be bold, be bold," Moltke's was, "But not too bold." He worried both about the weakness of his left wing against the French and about the weakness of the forces left to defend East Prussia against the Russians. He even debated with his Staff the advisability of fighting a defensive war against France, but rejected the idea because it precluded all possibility of "engaging the enemy on his own territory." The Staff agreed that the invasion of Belgium would be "entirely just and necessary" because the war would be one for the "defense and existence of Germany." Schlieffen's plan was maintained, and Moltke consoled himself with the thought, as he said in 1913, that "We must put aside all commonplaces as to the responsibility of the aggressor. . . . Success alone justifies war." But just to be safe everywhere, each year, cutting into Schlieffen's dying request, he borrowed strength from the right wing to add to the left.

Moltke planned for a German left wing of 8 corps numbering about 320,000 men to hold the front in Alsace and Lorraine south of Metz. The German center of 11 corps numbering about 400,000 men would invade France through Luxembourg and the Ardennes. The German right wing of 16 corps numbering about 700,000 men would attack through Belgium, smash the famed gateway fortresses of Liège and Namur which held the Meuse, and fling itself across the river to reach the flat country and straight roads on the far side. Every day's schedule of march was fixed in advance. The Belgians were not expected to fight, but if they did the power of the German assault was expected to persuade them quickly to surrender. The schedule called for the roads through Liège to be open by the twelfth day of mobilization, Brussels to be taken by M-19, the French frontier crossed on M-22, a line Thionville-St. Quentin reached by M-31, Paris and decisive victory by M-39.

The plan of campaign was as rigid and complete as the blueprint for a battleship. Heeding Clausewitz's warning that military plans which leave no room for the unexpected can lead to disaster, the Germans with infinite care had attempted to provide for every contingency. Their staff officers, trained at maneuvers and at war-college desks to supply the correct solution for any given set of circumstances, were expected to cope with the unexpected. Against that elusive, that mocking and perilous quantity, every precaution had been taken except one—flexibility.

While the plan for maximum effort against France hardened, Moltke's fears of Russia gradually lessened as his General Staff evolved a credo, based on a careful count of Russian railway mileage, that Russia would not be "ready" for war until 1916. This was confirmed in German minds by their spies' reports of Russian remarks "that something was going to begin in 1916."

In 1914 two events sharpened Germany's readiness to a fine point. In April, England had begun naval talks with the Russians, and in June, Germany herself had completed the widening of the Kiel Canal, permitting her new dreadnoughts direct access from the North Sea to the Baltic. On learning of the Anglo-Russian talks, Moltke said in May during a visit to his Austrian opposite number, Franz Conrad von Hötzendorff, that from now on "any adjournment will have the effect of diminishing our chances of success." Two weeks later, on June 1, he said to Baron Eckhardstein, "We are ready, and the sooner the better for us."

THE FRENCH VIEW

General de Castelnau, Deputy Chief of the French General Staff, was visited at the War Office one day in 1913 by the Military Governor of Lille, General Lebas, who came to protest the General Staff's decision to abandon Lille as a fortified city. Situated ten miles from the Belgian border and forty miles inland from the Channel, Lille lay close to the path that an invading army would take if it came by way of Flanders. In answer to General Lebas' plea for its defense, General de Castelnau spread out a map and measured with a ruler the distance from the German border to Lille by way of Belgium. The normal density of troops required for a vigorous offensive, he reminded his caller, was five or six to a meter. If the Germans extended themselves as far west as Lille, de Castelnau pointed out, they would be stretched out two to a meter.

"We'll Cut Them in Half"

"We'll cut them in half!" he declared. The German active Army, he explained, could deploy some twenty-five corps, about a million men, on the Western Front. "Here, figure it out for yourself," he said, handling Lebas the ruler. "If they come as far as Lille," he repeated with sardonic satisfaction, "so much the better for us."

French strategy did not ignore the threat of envelopment by a German right wing. On the contrary, the French General Staff believed that the stronger the Germans made their right wing, the correspondingly weaker they would leave their center and left where the French Army planned to break through. French strategy turned its back to the Belgian frontier and its face to the Rhine. While the Germans were taking the long way around to fall upon the French flank, the French planned a two-pronged offensive that would smash through the German center and left on either side of the German fortified area at Metz and by victory there, sever the German right wing from its base, rendering it harmless. It was a bold plan born of an idea—an idea inherent in the recovery of France from the humiliation of Sedan.

The Shadow of Sedan

Under the peace terms dictated by Germany at Versailles in 1871, France had suffered amputation, indemnity, and occupation. Even a triumphal march by the German Army down the Champs Elysées was among the terms imposed. It took place along a silent, black-draped avenue empty of onlookers. At Bordeaux, when the French Assembly ratified the peace terms, the deputies of Alsace-Lorraine walked from the hall in tears, leaving behind their protest: "We proclaim forever the right of Alsatians and Lorrainers to remain members of the French nation. We swear for ourselves, our constituents, our children and our children's children to claim that right for all time, by every means, in the face of the usurper."

The annexation, though opposed by Bismarck, who said it would be the Achilles' heel of the new German Empire, was required by the elder Moltke and his Staff. They insisted, and convinced the Emperor, that the border provinces with Metz, Strasbourg, and the crest of the Vosges must be sliced off in order to put France geographically forever on the defensive. They added a crushing indemnity of five billion francs intended to hobble France for a generation, and lodged an army of occupation until it should be paid. With one enormous effort the French raised and paid off the sum within three years, and their recovery began.

The memory of Sedan remained, a stationary dark shadow on the French consciousness. *"N'en parlez jamais; pensez-y toujours"* (Never speak of it; think of it always) had counseled Gambetta. For more than forty years the thought of "Again" was the single most fundamental factor of French policy. In the early years after 1870, instinct and military weakness dictated a fortress strategy. France walled herself in behind a system of entrenched camps connected by forts. Two fortified lines, Belfort-Epinal and Toul-Verdun, guarded the eastern frontier, and one, Maubeuge-Valenciennes-Lille, guarded the western half of the Belgian frontier; the gaps between were intended to canalize the invasion forces.

Behind her wall, as Victor Hugo urged at his most vibrant: "France will have but one thought: to reconstitute her forces, gather her energy, nourish her sacred anger, raise her young generation to form an army of the whole people, to work without cease, to study the methods and skills of our enemies, to become again a great France, the France of 1792, the France of an idea with a sword. Then one day she will be irresistible. Then she will take back Alsace-Lorraine."

Through returning prosperity and growing empire, through the perennial civil quarrels—royalism, Boulangism, clericalism, strikes, and the culminating, devastating Dreyfus Affair—the sacred anger still glowed, especially in the army. The one thing that held together all elements of the army, whether old guard or republican, Jesuit or Freemason, was the *mystique d'Alsace.* The eyes of all were fixed on the blue line of the Vosges. A captain of infantry confessed in 1912 that he used to lead the men of his company in secret patrols of two or three through the dark pines to the mountaintops where they could gaze down on Colmar. "On our return from those clandestine expeditions our columns reformed, choked and dumb with emotion."

Originally neither German nor French, Alsace had been snatched back and forth between the two until, under Louis XIV, it was confirmed to France by the Treaty of Westphalia in 1648. After Germany annexed Alsace and part of Lorraine in 1870 Bismarck advised giving the inhabitants as much autonomy as possible and encouraging their particularism, for, he said, the more Alsatian they felt, the less they would feel French. His successors did not see the necessity. They took no account of the wishes of their new subjects, made no effort to win them over, administered the provinces as *Reichsland,* or "Imperial territory," under German officials on virtually the same terms as their African colonies, and succeeded only in infuriating and alienating the population until in 1911 a constitution was granted them. By then it was too late. German rule exploded in the Zabern Affair in 1913 which began, after an exchange of insults between townspeople and garrison, when a German officer struck a crippled shoemaker with his saber. It ended in the complete and public exposure of German policy in the *Reichsland,* in a surge of anti-German feeling in world opinion, and in the simultaneous triumph of militarism in Berlin where the officer of Zabern became a hero, congratulated by the Crown Prince.

For Germany 1870 was not a final settlement. The German day in Europe which they thought had dawned when the German Empire was proclaimed in the Hall of Mirrors at Versailles was still postponed. France was not crushed; the French Empire was actually expanding in North Africa and Indo-China; the world of art and beauty and style still worshiped at the feet of Paris. Germans were still gnawed by envy of the country they had conquered. "As well off as God in France," was a German saying. At the same time they considered France decadent in culture and enfeebled by democracy. "It is impossible for a country that has had forty-two war ministers in forty-three years to fight effectively," announced Professor Hans Delbrück, Germany's leading historian. Believing themselves superior in soul, in strength, in energy, industry, and national virtue, Germans felt they deserved the dominion of Europe. The work of Sedan must be completed.

"Élan Vital"

Living in the shadow of that unfinished business, France, reviving in spirit and strength, grew weary of being eternally on guard, eternally exhorted by her leaders to defend herself. As the century turned, her spirit rebelled against thirty years of the defensive with its implied avowal of inferiority. France knew herself to be physically weaker than Germany. Her population was less, her birth rate lower. She needed some weapon that Germany lacked to give herself confidence in her survival. The "idea with a sword" fulfilled the need. Expressed by Bergson it was called *élan vital,* the all-conquering will. Belief in its power convinced France that the human spirit need not, after all, bow to the predestined forces of evolution which Schopenhauer and Hegel had declared to be irresistible. The spirit of France would be the equalizing factor. Her will to win, her *élan,* would enable France to defeat her enemy. Her genius was in her spirit, the spirit of *la gloire,* of 1792, of the incomparable "Marseillaise," the spirit of General Margueritte's heroic cavalry charge before Sedan when even Wilhelm I, watching the battle, could not forbear to cry, "*Oh, les braves gens!*"

Belief in the fervor of France, in the *furor Gallicae,* revived France's faith in herself in the generation after 1870. It was that fervor, unfurling her banners, sounding her bugles, arming her soldiers, that would lead France to victory if the day of "Again" should come.

Translated into military terms Bergson's *élan vital* became the doctrine of the offensive. In proportion as a defensive gave way to an offensive strategy, the attention paid to the Belgian frontier gradually gave way in favor of a progressive shift of gravity eastward toward the point where a French offensive could be launched to break through to the Rhine. For the Germans the roundabout road through Flanders led to Paris; for the French it led nowhere. They could only get to Berlin by the shortest way. The more the thinking of the French General Staff approached the offensive, the greater the forces it concentrated at the attacking point and the fewer it left to defend the Belgian frontier.

The doctrine of the offensive had its fount in the Ecole Supérieure de la Guerre, or War College, the ark of the army's intellectual elite, whose director, General Ferdinand Foch, was the molder of French military theory of his time. Foch's mind, like a heart, contained two valves: one pumped spirit into strategy; the other circulated common sense. On the one hand Foch preached a *mystique* of will expressed in his famous aphorisms, "The will to conquer is the first condition of victory," or more succinctly, *"Victoire c'est la volonté,"* and, "A battle won is a battle in which one will not confess oneself beaten."

In practice this was to become the famous order at the Marne to attack when the situation called for retreat. His officers of those days remember him bellowing "Attack! Attack!" with furious, sweeping gestures while he dashed about in short rushes as if charged by an electric battery. Why, he was later asked, did he advance at the Marne when he was technically beaten? "Why? I don't know. Because of my men, because I had a will. And then—God was there."

Though a profound student of Clausewitz, Foch did not, like Clausewitz's German successors, believe in a foolproof schedule of battle worked out in advance. Rather he taught the necessity of perpetual adaptability and improvisation to fit circumstances. "Regulations," he would say, "are all very well for drill but in the hour of danger they are no more use. . . . You have to learn to think." To think meant to give room for freedom of initiative, for the imponderable to win over the material, for will to demonstrate its power over circumstance.

But the idea that morale alone could conquer, Foch warned, was an "infantile notion." From his flights of metaphysics he would descend at once, in his lectures and his prewar books *Les Principes de la Guerre* and *La Conduite de la Guerre,* to the earth of tactics, the placing of advance guards, the necessity of *sureté,* or protection, the elements of firepower, the need for obedience and discipline. The realistic half of his teaching was summed up in another aphorism he made familiar during the war, *"De quoi s'agit-il?"* (What is the essence of the problem?)

Eloquent as he was on tactics, it was Foch's *mystique* of will that captured the minds of his followers. Once in 1908 when Clemenceau was considering Foch, then a professor, for the post of Director of the War College, a private agent whom he sent to listen to the lectures reported back in bewilderment, "This officer teaches metaphysics so abstruse as to make idiots of his pupils." Although Clemenceau appointed Foch in spite of it, there was, in one sense, truth in the report. Foch's principles, not because they were too abstruse but because they were too attractive, laid a trap for France. They were taken up with particular enthusiasm by Colonel Grandmaison, "an ardent and brilliant officer" who was Director of the Troisième Bureau, or Bureau of Military Operations, and who in 1911 delivered two lectures at the War College which had a crystallizing effect.

"Offensive à Outrance"

Colonel Grandmaison grasped only the head and not the feet of Foch's principles. Expounding their *élan* without their *sureté,* he expressed a military philosophy that electrified his audience. He waved before their dazzled eyes an "idea with a sword" which showed them how France could win. Its essence was the *offensive à ou-trance,* offensive to the limit. Only this could achieve Clausewitz's decisive battle which "exploited to the finish, is the essential act of war" and which "once engaged, must be pushed to the end, with no second thoughts, up to the extremes of human endurance." Seizure of initiative is the *sine qua non.* Preconceived arrangements based on a dogmatic judgment of what the enemy will do are premature. Liberty of action is achieved only by imposing one's will upon the enemy. "All command decisions must be inspired by the will to seize and retain the initiative." The defensive is forgotten, abandoned, discarded; its only possible justification is an occasional "economizing of forces at certain points with a view to adding them to the attack."

The effect on the General Staff was profound, and during the next two years was embodied in new Field Regulations for the conduct of war and in a new plan of campaign called Plan 17, which was adopted in May, 1913. Within a few months of Grandmaison's lectures, the President of the Republic, M. Fallières, announced: "The offensive alone is suited to the temperament of French soldiers. . . . We are determined to march straight against the enemy without hesitation."

The new Field Regulations, enacted by the government in October, 1913, as the fundamental document for the training and conduct of the French Army, opened with a flourish of trumpets: "The French Army, returning to its tradition, henceforth admits no law but the offensive." Eight commandments followed, ringing with the clash of "decisive battle," "offensive without hesitation," "fierceness and tenacity," "breaking the will of the adversary," "ruthless and tireless pursuit." With all the ardor of orthodoxy stamping out heresy, the Regulations stamped upon and discarded the defensive. "The offensive alone," it proclaimed, "leads to positive results." Its Seventh Commandment, italicized by the authors, stated: *"Battles are beyond everything else struggles of morale. Defeat is inevitable as soon as the hope of conquering ceases to exist. Success comes not to him who has suffered the least but to him whose will is firmest and morale strongest."*

Nowhere in the eight commandments was there mention of matériel or firepower or what Foch called *sureté.* The teaching of the Regulations became epitomized in the favorite word of the French officer corps, *le cran,* nerve, or less politely, guts. Like the youth who set out for the mountaintop under the banner marked "Excelsior!" the French Army marched to war in 1914 under a banner marked *"Cran."*

Over the years, while French military philosophy had changed, French geography had not. The geographical facts of her frontiers remained what Germany had made them in 1870. Germany's territorial demands, William I had explained to the protesting Empress Eugénie, "have no aim other than to push back the starting point from which French armies could in the future attack us." They also pushed forward the starting point from which Germany could attack France. While French history and development after the turn of the century fixed her mind upon the offensive, her geography still required a strategy of the defensive.

General Michel

In 1911, the same year as Colonel Grandmaison's lectures, a last effort to commit France to a strategy of the defensive was made in the Supreme War Council by no less a personage than the Commander in Chief designate, General Michel. As Vice President of the Council, a post which carried with it the position of Commander in Chief in the event of war, General Michel was then the ranking officer in the army. In a report that precisely reflected Schlieffen's thinking, he submitted his estimate of the probable German line of attack and his proposals for countering it. Because of the natural escarpments and French fortifications along the common border with Germany, he argued, the Germans could not hope to win a prompt decisive battle in Lorraine. Nor would the passage through Luxembourg and the near corner of Belgium east of the Meuse give them sufficient room for their favored strategy of envelopment. Only by taking advantage of "the whole of Belgium," he said, could the Germans achieve that "immediate, brutal and decisive" offensive which they must launch upon France before the forces of her Allies could come into play. He pointed out that the Germans had long yearned for Belgium's great port of Antwerp, and this gave them an additional reason for an attack through Flanders. He proposed to face the Germans along a line Verdun-Namur-Antwerp with a French army of a million men whose left wing—like Schlieffen's right—should brush the Channel with its sleeve.

Not only was General Michel's plan defensive in character; it also depended upon a proposal that was anathema to his fellow officers. To match the numbers he believed the Germans would send through Belgium, General Michel proposed to double French front-line effectives by attaching a regiment of reserves to every active regiment. Had he proposed to admit Mistinguette to the Immortals of the French Academy, he could hardly have raised more clamor and disgust.

"Les réserves, c'est zéro!" was the classic dogma of the French officer corps. Men who had finished their compulsory training under universal service and were between the ages of twenty-three and thirty-four were classed as reserves. Upon mobilization the youngest classes filled out the regular army units to war strength; the others were formed into reserve regiments, brigades, and divisions according to their local geographical districts. These were considered fit only for rear duty or for use as fortress troops, and incapable, because of their lack of trained officers and NCOs, of being attached to the fighting regiments. The regular army's contempt for the reserves, in which it was joined by the parties of the right, was augmented by dislike of the principle of the "nation in arms." To merge the reserves with the active divisions would be to put a drag on the army's fighting thrust. Only the active army, they believed, could be depended upon to defend the country.

The left parties, on the other hand, with memories of General Boulanger on horseback, associated the army with *coups d'état* and believed in the principle of a "nation in arms" as the only safeguard of the Republic. They maintained that a few months' training would fit any citizen for war, and violently opposed the increase of military service to three years. The army demanded this reform in 1913 not only to match an increase in the German Army but also because the more men who were in training at any one time, the less reliance needed to be placed on reserve units. After angry debate, with bitterly divisive effect on the country, the Three-Year Law was enacted in August, 1913.

Disdain of the reserves was augmented by the new doctrine of the offensive which, it was felt, could only be properly inculcated in active troops. To perform the irresistible onslaught of the *attaque brusquée,* symbolized by the bayonet charge, the essential quality was *élan,* and *élan* could not expected of men settled in civilian life with family responsibilities. Reserves mixed with active troops would create "armies of decadence," incapable of the will to conquer.

Similar sentiments were known to be held across the Rhine. The Kaiser was widely credited with the edict "No fathers of families at the front." Among the French General Staff it was an article of faith that the Germans would not mix reserve units with active units, and this led to the belief that the Germans would not have enough men in the front line to do two things at once: send a strong right wing in a wide sweep through Belgium west of the Meuse and keep sufficient forces at their center and left to stop a French breakthrough to the Rhine.

When General Michel presented his plan, the minister of War, Messimy, treated it *"comme une insanité."* As chairman of the Supreme War Council he not only attempted to suppress it but at once consulted other members of the council on the advisability of removing Michel.

Messimy, an exuberant, energetic, almost violent man with a thick neck, round head, bright peasant's eyes behind spectacles, and a loud voice, was a former career officer. In 1899 as a thirty-year-old captain of Chasseurs, he had resigned from the army in protest against its refusal to reopen the Dreyfus case. In that heated time the officer corps insisted as a body that to admit the possibility of Dreyfus's innocence after his conviction would be to destroy the army's prestige and infallibility. Unable to put loyalty to the army above justice, Messimy determined upon a political career with the declared goal of "reconciling the army with the nation." He swept into the War Ministry with a passion for improvement. Finding a number of generals "incapable not only of leading their troops but even of following them," he adopted Theodore Roosevelt's expedient of ordering all generals to conduct maneuvers on horseback. When this provoked protests that old so-and-so would be forced to retire from the army Messimy replied that that was indeed his object. He had been named War Minister on June 30, 1911, after a succession of four ministers in four months and the next day was met by the attack of the German gunboat *Panther* on Agadir precipitating the second Moroccan crisis. Expecting mobilization at any moment, Messimy discovered the generalissimo-designate, General Michel, to be "hesitant, indecisive and crushed by the weight of the duty that might at any moment devolve upon him." In his present post Messimy believed he represented a "national danger." Michel's "insane" proposal provided the excuse to get rid of him.

Michel, however, refused to go without first having his plan presented to the Council whose members included the foremost generals of France: Gallieni, the great colonial; Pau, the one-armed veteran of 1870; Joffre, the silent engineer; Dubail, the pattern of gallantry, who wore his kepi cocked over one eye with the *"chic exquis"* of the Second Empire. All were to hold active commands in 1914 and two were to become Marshals of France. None gave Michel's plan his support. One officer from the War Ministry who was present at the meeting said: "There is no use discussing it. General Michel is off his head."

Whether or not this verdict represented the views of all present—Michel later claimed that General Dubail, for one, had originally agreed with him—Messimy, who made no secret of his hostility, carried the Council with him. A trick of fate arranged that Messimy should be a forceful character and Michel should not. To be right and overruled is not forgiven to persons in responsible positions, and Michel duly paid for his clairvoyance. Relieved of his command, he was appointed Military Governor of Paris where in a crucial hour in the coming test he was indeed to prove "hesitant and indecisive."

Messimy having fervently stamped out Michael's heresy of the defensive, did his best, as War Minister, to equip the army to fight a successful offensive but was in his turn frustrated in his most-cherished prospect—the need to reform the French uniform. The British had adopted khaki after the Boer War, and the Germans were about to make the change from Prussian blue to field-gray. But in 1912 French soldiers still wore the same blue coats, red kepi, and red trousers they had worn in 1830 when rifle fire carried only two hundred paces and when armies, fighting at these close quarters, had no need for concealment. Visiting the Balkan front in 1912, Messimy saw the advantages gained by the dull-colored Bulgarians and came home determined to make the French soldier less visible. His project to clothe him in gray-blue or gray-green raised a howl of protest. Army pride was as intransigent about giving up its red trousers as it was about adopting heavy guns. Army prestige was once again felt to be at stake. To clothe the French soldier in some muddy, inglorious color, declared the army's champions, would be to realize the fondest hopes of Dreyfusards and Freemasons. To banish "all that is colorful, all that gives the soldier his vivid aspect," wrote the *Echo de Paris,* "is to go contrary both to French taste and military function." Messimy pointed out that the two might no longer be synonymous, but his opponents proved immovable. At a parliamentary hearing a former War Minister, M. Etienne, spoke for France.

"Eliminate the red trousers?" he cried. "Never! *Le pantalon rouge c'est la France!*"

"That blind and imbecile attachment to the most visible of all colors," wrote Messimy afterward, "was to have cruel consequences."

In the meantime, still in the midst of the Agadir crisis, he had to name a new prospective generalissimo in place of Michel. He planned to give added authority to the post by combining with it that of Chief of the General Staff and by abolishing the post of Chief of Staff to the War Ministry, currently held by General Dubail. Michel's successor would have all the reins of power concentrated in his hands.

Messimy's first choice was the austere and brilliant general in pince-nez, Gallieni, who refused it because, he explained, having been instrumental in Michel's dismissal he felt scruples about replacing him. Furthermore he had only two years to go before retirement at sixty-four, and he believed the appointment of a "colonial" would be resented by the Metropolitan Army—*"une question de bouton,"* he said, tapping his insignia. General Pau, who was next in line, made it a condition that he be allowed to name generals of his own choice to the higher commands which, as he was known for his reactionary opinions, threatened to wake the barely slumbering feud between rightist army and republican nation. Respecting him for his honesty, the government refused his condition. Messimy consulted Gallieni, who suggested his former subordinate in Madagascar, "a cool and methodical worker with a lucid and precise mind." Accordingly the post was offered to General Joseph-Jacques-Césaire Joffre, then aged fifty-nine, formerly chief of the Engineer Corps and presently Chief of the Services of the Rear.

Massive and paunchy in his baggy uniform, with a fleshy face adorned by a heavy, nearly white mustache and bushy eyebrows to match, with a clear youthful skin, calm blue eyes and a candid, tranquil gaze, Joffre looked like Santa Claus and gave an impression of benevolence and naïveté—two qualities not noticeably part of his character. He did not come of a gentleman's family, was not a graduate of St. Cyr (but of the less aristocratic if more scientific Ecole Polytechnique), had not passed through the higher training of the War College. As an officer of the Engineer Corps, which dealt with such unromantic matters as fortifications and railways, he belonged to a branch of the service not drawn upon for the higher commands. He was the eldest of the eleven children of a petit bourgeois manufacturer of wine barrels in the French Pyrénées. His military career had been marked by quiet accomplishment and efficiency in each post he filled: as company commander in Formosa and Indo-China, as a major in the Sudan and Timbuktu, as staff officer in the Railway Section of the War Ministry, as lecturer at the Artillery

School, as fortifications officer under Gallieni in Madagascar from 1900 to 1905, as general of a division in 1905, of a corps in 1908, and as Director of the Rear and member of the War Council since 1910.

General Joffre

He had no known clerical, monarchist, or other disturbing connections; he had been out of the country during the Dreyfus Affair; his reputation as a good republican was as smooth as his well-manicured hands; he was solid and utterly phlegmatic. His outstanding characteristic was a habitual silence that in other men would have seemed self-deprecatory but, worn like an aura over Joffre's great, calm bulk, inspired confidence. He had still five years to go before retirement.

Joffre was conscious of one lack: he had had no training in the rarefied realms of staff work. On a hot July day when doors in the War Ministry on the Rue St. Dominique were left open, officers glancing out of their rooms saw General Pau holding Joffre by a button of his uniform. "Take it, *cher ami,*" he was saying. "We will give you Castelnau. He knows all about staff work—everything will go of itself."

Castelnau, who was a graduate both of St. Cyr and of the War College, came, like D'Artagnan, from Gascony, which is said to produce men of hot blood and cold brain. He suffered from the disadvantage of family connections with a marquis, of associating with Jesuits, and of a personal Catholicism which he practiced so vigorously as to earn him during the war the name of *le capucin botté,* the Monk in Boots. He had, however, long experience on the General Staff. Joffre would have preferred Foch but knew Messimy to have an unexplained prejudice against him. As was his habit, he listened without comment to Pau's advice, and promptly took it.

"Aye!" complained Messimy when Joffre asked for Castelnau as his Deputy Chief. "You will rouse a storm in the parties of the left and make yourself a lot of enemies." However, with the assent of the President and Premier who "made a face" at the condition but agreed, both appointments were put through together. A fellow general, pursuing some personal intrigue warned Joffre that Castelnau might displace him. "Get rid of me! Not Castelnau," Joffre replied, unruffled. "I need him for six months; then I'll give him a corps command." As it proved, he found Castelnau invaluable, and when war came gave him command of an army instead of a corps.

Joffre's supreme confidence in himself was expressed in the following year when his aide, Major Alexandre, asked him if he thought war was shortly to be expected.

"Certainly I think so," Joffre replied. "I have always thought so. It will come. I shall fight it and I shall win. I have always succeeded in whatever I do—as in the Sudan. It will be that way again."

It will mean a Marshal's baton for you," his aide suggested with some awe at the vision.

"Yes." Joffre acknowledged the prospect with laconic equanimity.

Plan 17

Under the aegis of this unassailable figure the General Staff from 1911 on threw itself into the task of revising the Field Regulations, retraining the troops in their spirit, and making a new plan of campaign to replace the now obsolete Plan 16.

The staff's guiding mind, Foch, was gone from the War College, promoted and shifted to the field and ultimately to Nancy where, as he said, the frontier of 1870 "cuts like a scar across the breast of the country." There, guarding the frontier, he commanded the XXth Corps which he was soon to make famous. He had left behind, however, a "chapel," as cliques in the French Army were called, of his disciples who formed Joffre's entourage. He had also left behind a strategic plan which became the framework of Plan 17. Complete in April, 1913, it was adopted without discussion or consultation, together with the new Field Regulations by the Supreme War Council in May. The next eight months were spent reorganizing the army on the basis of the plan and preparing all the instructions and orders for mobilization, transport, services of supply, areas and schedules of deployment and concentration. By February, 1914, it was ready to be distributed in sections to each of the generals of the five armies into which the French forces were divided, only that part of it which concerned him individually going to each one.

Its motivating idea, as expressed by Foch, was, "We must get to Berlin by going through Mainz," that is, by crossing the Rhine at Mainz, 130 miles northeast of Nancy. That objective, however, was an idea only. Unlike the Schlieffen plan, Plan 17 contained no stated over-all objective and no explicit schedule of operations. It was not a plan of operations but a plan of deployment with directives for several possible lines of attack for each army, depending on circumstances, but without a given goal. Because it was in essence a plan of response, of riposte to a German attack, whose avenues the French could not be sure of in advance, it had of necessity to be, as Joffre said, "a posteriori and opportunist." Its intention was inflexible: Attack! Otherwise its arrangements were flexible.

A brief general directive of five sentences, classified as secret, was all that was shown in common to the generals who were to carry out the plan, and they were not permitted to discuss it. It offered very little for discussion. Like the Field Regulations it opened with a flourish: "Whatever the circumstance, it is the Commander in Chief's intention to advance with all forces united to the attack of the German armies." The rest of the general directive stated merely that French action would consist of two major offensives, one to the left and one to the right of the German fortified area of Metz-Thionville. The one to the right or south of Metz would attack directly eastward across the old border of Lorraine, while a secondary operation in Alsace was designed to anchor the French right on the Rhine. The offensive to the left or north of Metz would attack either to the north, or, in the event the enemy violated neutral territory, to the northeast through Luxembourg and the Belgian Ardennes, but this movement would be carried out "only by order of the Commander in Chief." The general purpose, although this was nowhere stated, was to drive through to the Rhine, at the same time isolating and cutting off the invading German right wing from behind.

To this end Plan 17 deployed the five French armies along the frontier from Belfort in Alsace as far as Hirson, about a third of the way along the Franco-Belgian border. The remaining two-thirds of the Belgian frontier, from Hirson to the sea, was left undefended. It was along that stretch that General Michel had planned to defend France. Joffre found his plan in the office safe when he succeeded Michel. It concentrated the center of gravity of the French forces to this extreme left section of the line where Joffre left none. It was a plan of pure defense; it allowed for no seizing of initiative; it was, as Joffre decided after careful study, "foolishness."

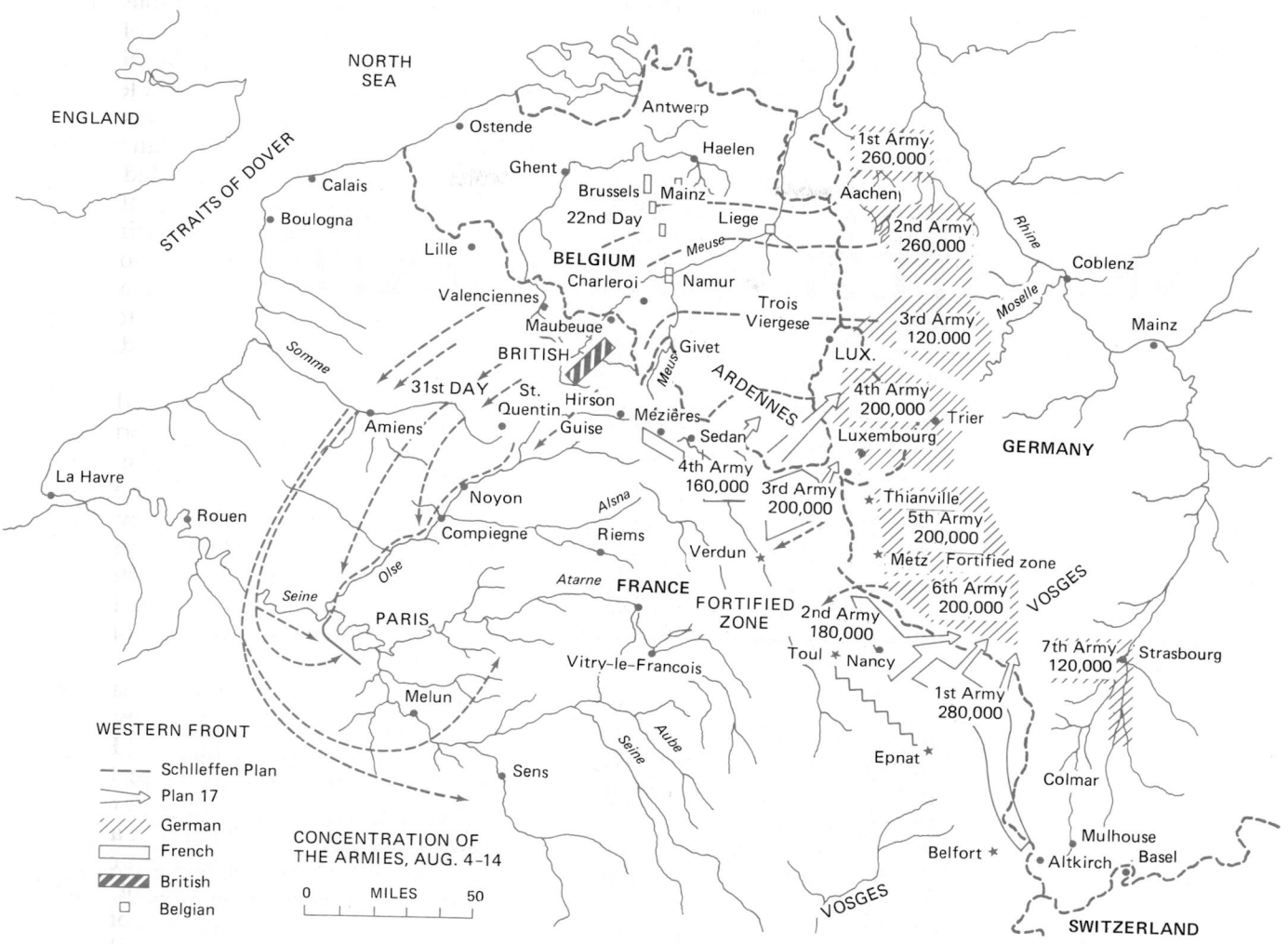

WESTERN FRONT

- - - - Schlieffen Plan
⟶ Plan 17
//// German
☐ French
▨ British
☐ Belgian

CONCENTRATION OF
THE ARMIES, AUG. 4-14

0   MILES   50

QUESTIONS

1. What were the major characteristics (or dimensions) of the French and German strategies in World War I?

2. What were the strong points in these strategies? Weak points? What should have been done differently? Why?

3. What principles of strategy do the success and failures of each side suggest?

1-4

NEW STEEL CORPORATION

In the late 1970s, some young executives—their leader was 35—in a major steel company proposed to the top executive group a way of counteracting the increasingly heavy imports of foreign steel into the company's market places. They suggested that—despite many seemingly unfavorable cost factors in the United States—it would be possible to compete successfully, make high margins, and grow rapidly by producing steel in the United States in competition with foreign sources. Top management was interested but unpersuaded, and the team set out to develop its plan in greater depth and to implement it personally if necessary.

Until about 1960, the U.S. steel industry had been the world's leader in steel production, technology, and marketing. But in 1959 the United States became a net importer of steel, and technological leadership in basic carbon steels began to shift to Japan. The U.S. industry, mired in low profits, was unable to generate the capital to modernize. Meanwhile, the Japanese and Korean industries, with one-half the capital cost of the United States and much lower labor rates (see accompanying exhibits), were able to surge ahead in a wide range of steel products. In 1978 the Japanese had an average cost advantage of 10–15% against U.S. competitors, and this advantage increased as the exchange rate for the U.S. dollar rose against the yen. By the early 1980s, total U.S. capacity for raw steel was 155 million tons annually, with 76% being in the hands of the top 10 integrated producers. The industry's top 15 firms operating 36 integrated mills—located primarily in Pennsylvania, Ohio, Indiana, and Illinois—averaged about 3.2 million tons of steel per year and had plant investment levels of $30,000–45,000 per employee.

Although Japan led in many areas of steel technology, such technologies were generally available to others through licensing. By the early 1980s, the United States had dropped to second place in its steel R&D effort behind Japan, but still led in those special stocks and alloys the U.S. space and defense programs demanded. More detailed figures about the U.S. industry and its competitive posture are contained in the following exhibits.

QUESTIONS

1. How could the team best position the proposed new company for success against foreign competition?

2. What would be the critical factors for success? What target performance levels in these characteristics would ensure success? How could these be achieved?

3. How could the team implement a strategy which would be sure to win against foreign competition?

Year	Carbon	Alloy	Stainless	Total
1965	116,651 (88.8%)	13,318 (10.1%)	1,493 (1.1%)	131,462
1970	117,411 (89.3%)	12,824 (9.7%)	1,279 (1.0%)	131,514
1975	100,360 (86.0%)	15,171 (13.0%)	1,111 (1.0%)	116,642
1976	112,008 (87.5%)	14,308 (11.2%)	1,684 (1.3%)	128,000
1977	108,130 (86.3%)	15,341 (12.2%)	1,862 (1.5%)	125,333
1978	116,916 (85.3%)	18,161 (13.3%)	1,954 (1.4%)	137,031
1979	116,226 (85.3%)	18,008 (13.2%)	2,107 (1.5%)	136,341
1980	94,689 (84.7%)	15,445 (13.8%)	1,701 (1.5%)	111,835

Source: American Iron and Steel Institute, *Annual Statistical Report,* years given, in *The Competitive Status of the U.S. Steel Industry,* National Academy Press, 1985.

EXHIBIT 1
U.S. Raw Steel Output by Grade (thousands of net tons)

	Number of Research Scientists and Engineers in Ferrous Metal R&D				
	1967	1970	1975	1977	1978
Japan	4,450	4,880	5,480	5,710	5,760
U.S.	3,150	3,200	3,330	4,000	—
U.K.	2,880	2,450	1,570	—	—
W. Germany	1,870	1,870	990	—	—
France	585	605	575	—	—

Source: B. S. Old et al., "Brief Technology Assessment of the Domestic Steel Industry," Report to Lehigh University and the U.S. Department of Commerce, January 1981, in *The Competitive Status of the U.S. Steel Industry,* National Academy Press, 1985.

EXHIBIT 2
Comparative National Ferrous Metal R&D Efforts

EXHIBIT 3
Total Costs of Steel Production, 1982
(Dollars Per Metric Ton of Carbon Steel Products Shipped)

	United States		United Kingdom		France		Japan		West Germany	
Capacity utilization[a]	90%	48%	90%	58%	90%	61%	90%	58%	90%	55%
Labor	$172	—	$122	—	$150	—	$72	—	$133	—
Materials	291	372	386	370	299	296	254	285	283	290
Financial exp.[b]	34	74	42	77	84	98	61	101	46	64
Total pretax cost	580	695	493	585	465	546	411	490	430	513
Total pretax profit	23	—	11	—	28	—	72	—	45	—

[a] The first column for each country presents estimates of what production costs would have been if capacity utilization was 90 percent. The second column contains estimates of costs at the rates of capacity utilization that actually existed in 1982.

[b] Depreciation, interest, and miscellaneous taxes.

Source: "World Steel Dynamics," Paine Webber Mitchell Hutchins, Inc., 1983, in *The Competitive Status of the U.S. Steel Industry,* National Academy Press, 1985.

EXHIBIT 4
Costs of Refining (basis: 1 short ton of output)

Cost Category	BOF[a]	EAF (DRI1)[b]	EAF (DRI2)[c]	EAF (scrap)[d]
Process materials	$207.59	$217.53	$186.30	$117.67
Energy	1.58	34.98	34.13	26.25
Direct labor	8.55	15.54	15.54	15.54
Capital	9.73	15.04	15.04	16.26
Other	5.26	7.28	6.90	6.33
Total	$232.71	$290.37	$257.91	$182.05

[a] BOF = Basic oxygen furnace.

[b] EAF (DRI1) = Electric arc furnace using direct reduced iron (gas-based).

[c] EAF (DRI2) = Electric arc furnace using direct reduced iron (coal-based).

[d] EAF (scrap) = Electric arc furnace using scrap.

Source: The Competitive Status of the U.S. Steel Industry, National Academy Press, 1985.

Year	United States	Japan	West Germany	United Kingdom	France
1964	12.32	26.03	22.39	25.43	25.61
1972	10.61	11.85	13.44	19.59	16.32
1973	10.15	9.49	12.08	18.40	15.36
1974	9.97	9.33	11.34	19.99	14.76
1975	10.63	10.08	12.64	23.17	17.15
1976	10.30	9.16	11.89	21.02	15.75
1977	10.62	8.91	11.87	21.69	14.85
1978	9.84	8.39	10.77	20.37	13.34
1979	9.97	7.58	9.79	18.86	12.07
1980	10.37	7.33	9.85	21.45*	11.59
Percentage of average annual change: 1964–1980	−1.08	−7.92	−5.13	−1.06	−4.96

* Estimates for 1980 are based on a comparison of the last 9 months of 1980 with the same period in 1979 because of the nationwide work stoppage in January through March 1980.

Source: U.S. Department of Labor, Bureau of Labor Statistics, unpublished data, in *The Competitive Status of the U.S. Steel Industry,* National Academy Press, 1985.

EXHIBIT 5
Labor Productivity at Actual Operating Rates, 1964–1980 (employee hours required per short ton of carbon steel shipped)

Year	United States	Japan	West Germany	France	United Kingdom
1969	92	78	76	87	85
1970	100	82	86	90	92
1971	106	87	97	97	106
1972	110	90	102	103	109
1973	118	100	125	125	122
1974	157	140	170	168	169
1975	186	167	210	212	213
1976	199	175	208	205	201
1977	215	194	223	211	229
1978	233	218	241	231	265
1979	262	220	262	268	319
1980	298	261	291	302	441
1981	329	290	286	298	387
1982	373	285	290	296	370

Note: This table shows comparative materials cost for the United States and four other major producing countries. An examination of Exhibit 3 reveals that materials costs represent between 50 and 70 percent of the total cost of making steel. The major components of materials costs are (1) iron ore and scrap, (2) coking coal, and (3) other forms of energy (fuel oil, electricity, noncoking coal, natural gas), representing about 45, 35, and 20 percent of the total, respectively.

Source: "World Steel Dynamics," Paine Webber Mitchell Hutchins, Inc., 1981 and 1983, in *The Competitive Status of the U.S. Steel Industry,* National Academy Press, 1985.

EXHIBIT 6
Comparative International Materials Costs, 1969–1982 ($ per Ton at Actual Capacity Utilization)

EXHIBIT 7
Total Imports by Type of Steel, 1970–1982 (Millions of Net Tons)

Year	Carbon		Alloy		Stainless	
	Tonnage	Percentage of Total	Tonnage	Percentage of Total	Tonnage	Percentage of Total
1970	12.83	96.1	0.35	2.6	0.18	1.3
1971	17.69	96.7	0.42	2.3	0.19	1.0
1972	17.09	96.6	0.45	2.5	0.15	0.9
1973	14.60	96.3	0.43	2.9	0.13	0.8
1974	15.61	96.4	0.41	2.6	0.18	1.0
1975	11.39	94.9	0.45	3.7	0.17	1.4
1976	13.65	95.4	0.48	3.4	0.18	1.2
1977	18.21	96.0	0.58	3.1	0.18	0.9
1978	20.09	95.5	0.75	3.5	0.20	1.0
1979	16.62	94.9	0.73	4.2	0.17	1.0
1980	14.78	95.4	0.56	3.6	0.15	1.0
1981	18.62	93.6	1.09	5.5	0.19	1.0
1982	15.38	92.3	1.08	6.5	0.20	1.2

Source: U.S. Bureau of the Census, in *The Competitive Status of the U.S. Steel Industry,* National Academy Press, 1985.

EXHIBIT 8
Percentage of Raw Carbon Steel Production by Furnace Type, 1960–1980

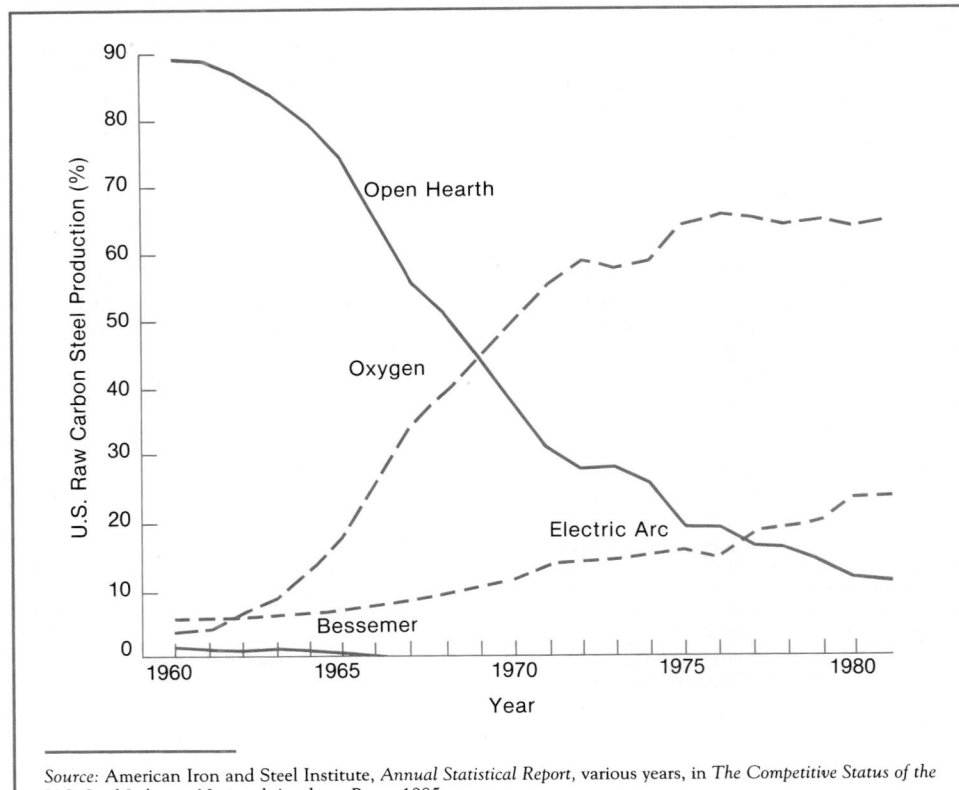

Source: American Iron and Steel Institute, *Annual Statistical Report,* various years, in *The Competitive Status of the U.S. Steel Industry,* National Academy Press, 1985.

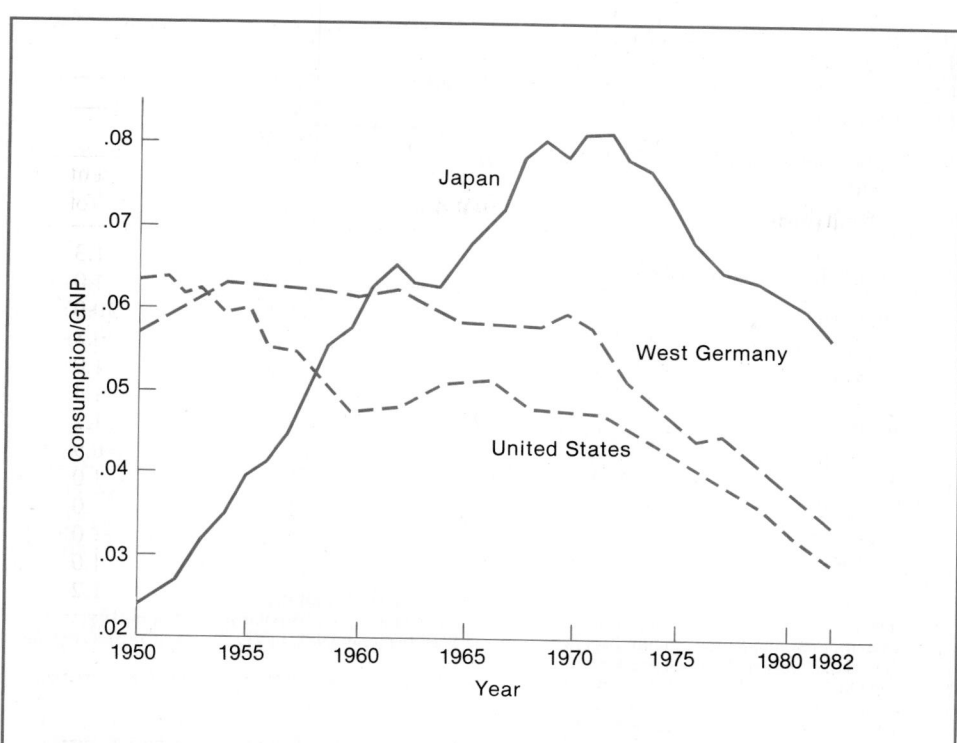

EXHIBIT 9
The Steel Consumption/
Real GNP Ratio over Time
in Some Developed
Countries, 1950–1982

Source: *Steel: Upheaval in a Basic Industry*, Barnett and Schorsch, Ballinger, 1983, in *The Competitive Status of the U.S. Steel Industry*, National Academy Press, 1985.

EXHIBIT 10

Estimated Costs Per Ton of New Integrated Carbon Steel Plants in the United States, 1978–1980

AISI (1978 dollars)[a]	Established Plant	New Plant	Difference
Operating cost	$319	$226	$−93
Capital cost	36	126	+93
Total	355	355	0
Crandall (1978 dollars)[b]			
Operating cost	$324	$264	$−60
Capital cost	30	161	+131
Total	354	425	+71
World Steel Dynamics (1980 dollars)[c]			
Operating cost	$422	$351	$−71
Capital cost	25	176	+151
Total	447	527	+80

[a] "Steel at the Crossroads: One Year Later," American Iron and Steel Institute, 1981.
[b] *The United States Steel Industry in Recurrent Crises . . .*, Crandall, The Brookings Institution, 1981.
[c] Marcus, Presentation to the Latin American Iron and Steel Institute, 1981, in *The Competitive Status of the U.S. Steel Industry,* National Academy Press, 1985.
Note: Only about 10% of the U.S. steel output is produced in plants less than 32 years old. Of the 23 primary technological developments of the last 3 decades, the U.S. and Japan led both in initiation and first commercial use. The Japanese have gained world leadership in integrated mills through heavy capital commitments and experience curve effects. The U.S. leads in the argon-oxygen decarbonization, consumable electrode (electric arc), vacuum induction melting, and powder metallurgy technologies used for specialty steels. Two radical technologies in the early stage of development are direct steelmaking (a one step process for the smelting and reduction of ores to molten steel), and near net shape casting which virtually eliminates machining and scrap. Scrap used in electric arc furnaces is available in higher quality and at lower cost in the U.S. than in any other major industrialized country.

172

INTEL CORPORATION

In 1968 Robert N. Noyce (age 40) and Gordon E. Moore (age 39) broke away from Fairchild Semiconductor to form Intel Corporation. They concentrated on semiconductor memory components for the computer industry. When Intel started, no market existed for its principal product. By the late 1970s Intel's trailblazing technologies had irrevocably restructured the electronics, computer and communications industries. In the 1980s semiconductors were affecting social changes many believed would be as profound as those of the industrial revolution. Not without cause did CEO Moore say, "We're in the business of revolutionizing society."[1] Opportunities seemed boundless. But in the early 1980s continuing technological advances and Japan's massive competitive capabilities presented strategic challenges without precedent for this relatively new and small company in a world of industrial giants.

BUDDING ENTREPRENEURS

Noyce and Moore made an unusual team. Although the future of this revolutionary technology was unknown at that time, Noyce—an inveterate young tinkerer from a small Iowa town—headed for MIT to study about the new field only to find it had no courses on semiconductors. Taking his Ph.D. (in electron physics) at the top of his class, Noyce had joined Philco's semiconductor division. Two and a half years later, he got a call from William Shockley, the inventor of the transistor,

Case copyright © 1985 by James Brian Quinn.

The generous support of the Adolf H. Lundin Professorship at the International Management Institute, Geneva, Switzerland is gratefully acknowledged. The generous cooperation of Intel Corporation is gratefully acknowledged. Numbers in parentheses indicate the reference and page number for material from a previously footnoted source.

who was starting a new semiconductor company in Palo Alto (California). Noyce and Moore, a Ph.D. chemist from Cal Tech, arrived there the same day.[2] Thus began one of the most successful technical partnerships of modern times.

Fairchild Semiconductor

The imaginative Shockley had assembled a group of bright young scientists, but the operation fell apart when eight of them left only a year later. Shockley's managerial shortcomings had totally alienated them.[3] Even while with Shockley the group had looked upon Noyce as a leader. His enthusiasm—and his approach to everything with the idea that it was going to work—easily infected people. One of the members of the group wrote to a friend of his family who worked for Hayden Stone, the New York investment firm. Hayden Stone soon arranged to finance the new semiconductor company the young enterpreneurs wanted to organize. The eight young founders contributed about $500 apiece . . . but most of the start-up money came from Fairchild Camera and Instrument Corporation which also received an option to buy the group's budding company, known as Fairchild Semiconductor. (2,147)

Big Company Blues

The company, which started in a rented building in Mountain View, California, grew fast. By 1968 Noyce was supervising nearly 15,000 employees in the United States and abroad. Both he and Moore achieved major technical advances in semiconductor technology at Fairchild (including the first planar integrated circuit and the first stable MOS transistor).* But both men had begun to find big-company life less and less satisfying.

When Fairchild Camera had exercised its option to buy out Fairchild Semiconductor in 1959 and make it into an operating division, the originators each got about $250,000 worth of stock in Fairchild Camera. But Noyce and Moore began to feel that a company as big as Fairchild could not easily expand into new areas of semiconductor technology. Noyce said, "Fairchild was getting big and clumsy. LSI had been talked about a good deal, but there was no commitment behind it."[4] New ventures in such a complex field initially lose money—sometimes a lot of it—and it is often difficult to justify big losses to directors and stockholders. Moore and Noyce finally left Fairchild Semiconductor (in the summer of 1968). But not before they had built the company into a $150 million enterprise, one of the Big Three in its field along with Texas Instruments and Motorola.

A NEW COMPANY

"We figured LSI (Large Scale Integration) was the kind of business we'd be interested in. We both had started in technology, not in computers or finance. It would be fun for us," said Noyce. Noyce and Moore decided that their new company should try to establish itself as a specialist and leader in the computer memory field, a field where semiconductors had had very little impact and no larger companies were present. As Moore explains, "It's very tempting for a little company to

---

* All technical terms are defined in the glossary at the end of the case.

run in all directions. We went the other way. It was our objective to dominate any market in which we participated."

Venture Capital

The pair knew they would need quite a bit of money to start up. Fortunately, Noyce had already had considerable personal exposure to the investment community. Among his acquaintances was Arthur Rock, who had helped to arrange the original financing for Fairchild Semiconductor while he was at Hayden Stone. Later Rock had become a successful venture capitalist in San Francisco and had helped start Teledyne and Scientific Data Systems. In fact, Rock was among the premier venture capitalists in high technology. (2,149) His major coup was arranging to sell SDS, which he had helped to start with $1 million, to Xerox for $900 million worth of stock. Rock makes it a point not to master the intricate technologies of the companies he backs. He fears that would interfere with his judgment of people as managers. (2,65)

"It was a very natural thing to go to Art and say, 'Incidentally, Art, do you have an extra $2.5 million you would like to put on the crap table?' " said Noyce. Rock had long before become convinced of Noyce's abilities as a manager. But he also knew that men who run big companies for others don't necessarily make good entrepreneurs. So Rock, a cautious man, grilled Noyce on his goals and his emotional and financial commitment to the idea. "My way with people who want to start companies is to talk to them until they are exhausted—and then talk to them some more," said Rock. "Finally, I get an impression what their real objectives are, whether they have integrity, whether they are interested in running a big company, whether their goals are big enough. One of the things I'm interested in is whether the management puts a limit on the company they want. If they do, I get fearful." (2,149) Noyce wanted to grow to $100 million in 10 years.[3] Rock was pleased with Noyce's responses and by the fact that both Noyce and Moore were willing to invest substantial amounts of their own money, about $250,000 each.

Intel (a contraction of "integrated electronics") started in the enviable position of having so many would-be investors that it could choose those it preferred. "People had known Bob and were kind of lined up to invest in the company," said Rock. Rock purchased $300,000 worth of convertible debentures and brought in other investors who took an additional $2.2 million. Later Intel sold 154,000 shares of common stock in private placements for $2.2 million. The common was immediately oversubscribed.[5] Ultimately, paid-in capital for Intel amounted to about $17.5 million. But after its initial debenture issues, Intel did not find it necessary to borrow or to use its line of bank credit. During this period the company owned almost all its facilities.

Total sales growth of integrated circuits (I/Cs) in the 1970s was expected to average 20% per year.[6] I/Cs were expected to have even more impact on electronics than transistors had, although no one knew precisely when or how. It cost millions to develop initial technologies, to build facilities, and to make the first successful chips. But production bugs made yields a miserable 1–5% of each run. Over 100 steps had to be performed perfectly in sequence. With tolerances of a few microns (millionths of a meter) required, a fleck of dust would cause a faulty device. And reliability testing of the circuits had to be meticulous, a million or more tests for each chip. Nevertheless, this miraculous technology, if mastered, could drive the cost of transistors down 10,000-fold or more. (2,151–152) Older vacuum tube companies couldn't cope with these uncertainties.[7] And customers, so-called "systems houses," were often afraid of trusting their design secrets to outside I/C suppliers.[8] This was the business Intel set its cap for.

A Complex Technology

Semiconductor memory chips at that time had only highly specialized, limited applications in computers. They were too slow for main memories where tiny ferrite ringlets (or cores) had to be tediously and expensively hand strung on fine wire networks. In 1970 memory could occupy half the CPU and be 60% of its cost, but memory demand was growing faster than computer demand.[9] If one could succeed, the opportunity could be great. In theory, chips could be mass produced rather than hand assembled; and their compact structures could allow more flexible computer designs and much faster operation with lower electrical power.

To invade the mainframe computer market Noyce and Moore decided to leapfrog existing memories and drive for a 1,000-bit (4,000 transistor) chip no larger than the 200-bit chips then in service. Intel soon had plenty of competition —all small fry. But many failed or sold out to larger companies. Intel was the first small concern to focus specifically on semiconductor memory and concentrated more talent on memories than any of its rivals, including such giants as Texas Instruments.

Intel engineers began work on novel memory chips that utilized a brand-new concept, the so-called "silicon-gate" approach. Before Intel's pioneering, aluminum electrode gates were built into semiconductors. But the use of metal made the manufacturing process so delicate and tricky that only 5% of the devices manufactured were usable. Noyce and Moore decided to substitute polysilicon for metal in the gate, and they were vindicated when they got yields of 10% on their first memory chip.

"They Just Bowled Us Over"

But it was their second MOS product that became famous. The 1103 memory chip held more than 1,000 bits, or more than 4,000 transistors. Intel wasn't the first with a 1,000-bit chip. Advanced Memory Systems (AMS) had started delivery of a similar chip a few months earlier in 1970. But Intel's 1103 quickly grabbed the major share of the market. It became not only the industry standard but also the largest-selling semiconductor component in the world. A crucial element in the acceptance of the 1103 as the industry standard was the cooperation of a Honeywell computer team in testing the device to get rid of hidden bugs and in devising circuit specifications that suited makers of computers.

The 1103 attracted so much attention and looked so promising that Texas Instruments, Fairchild, and almost everyone else in the semiconductor industry initially sought to become a "second source" for the chip. The AMS device was buried in this avalanche. "We had a better design," said Robert H. F. Lloyd, former chairman of AMS. "But Intel just bowled us over with their prestige, salesmanship, and the publicity their device got." Soon Intel drew so far ahead of its competition that most rivals decided it wouldn't be worthwhile to copy the 1103. Even Texas Instruments finally chose not to commit to the 1,000-bit memory-device race. It started working, instead, on an even denser chip.

Meantime, Intel established its own second source. For a $2 million fee, it licensed a Montreal company, Microsystems International, Ltd. (MIL), and taught its engineers how to make the 1103. Royalties came from MIL at a propitious time for Intel. The market for semiconductors slumped in the spring of 1970, but Intel escaped much of the impact because it was not yet in volume production. And Noyce and Moore even convinced their skeptical directors that construction should not be halted on a much needed $2.3 million headquarters and production expansion in Santa Clara.

Success was not easy or straightforward. Two months after the 1103 was introduced, a complex reliability problem cropped up. An excess electrical charge on the surface tended to erase data stored within the chip. Recognizing that the company's whole future might be at stake, Intel's engineers worked at a panicky pace for two months to identify the cause of the problem, and six more to clear it up. How it was done remains a company secret. "This place was a madhouse," recalls Andrew S. Grove, then vice president and director of operations.

"The 1103 was a brand-new circuit-design concept, it brought about a brand-new systems approach to computer memories, and its manufacturing required a brand-new technology," added Grove. "Yet it became, over the short period of one year, a high-volume production item—high volume by any standards in this industry." Making the 1103 concept work at the technology level, at the device level, and at the systems level and successfully introducing it into high-volume manufacturing required . . . a fair measure of orchestrated brilliance. Everybody from technologists to designers to reliability experts had to work to the same schedule toward a different aspect of the same goal, interfacing simultaneously at all levels over quite a long period of time . . . Yet I would wake up at night, reliving some of the fights that took place during the day on how to accomplish various goals." (2,155)

"The operating style that evolved at Intel was based on the recognition of our own identity," said Grove. "The semiconductor industry consisted of companies that typically fell into one of two extremes: technology leaders and manufacturing leaders. Neither of these types of leadership would accomplish what we wanted to do. We wanted to capitalize on new technology and we wanted to sell our technology and our engineering over and over again. This meant high volume. We regarded ourselves as essentially a manufacturer of *high-technology jelly beans.*"

Early Organization

"A manufacturer of high-technology jelly beans needs a different breed of people. The wild-eyed, bushy-haired, boy geniuses that dominate the think tanks and the solely technology-oriented companies will never take their technology to the jelly-bean stage. Similarly, the other stereotype—the straight-laced, crewcut, and moustache-free manufacturing operators of conventional industry—will never generate the technology in the first place." A key question was how to find and mix the two talents. There weren't many experienced engineering or manufacturing people, and top young graduates were sought after by everyone. "In engineering we needed to orient toward market areas and specialized customer needs—such as computer mainframe memories, increasingly sophisticated peripheral capabilities, general purpose I/Cs, and timing circuits." Engineering had to come through *first* with a workable design for what the customer would need most.

But in manufacturing Intel needed to standardize as much as possible. In production, said Grove, "We actually borrowed from a very successful manufacturer of medium technology jelly beans—McDonald's hamburgers. When you thought about their standardized process and standardized module approach, it had much to offer in our technology." But there was also a sociological reason for what became known as the "McIntel" approach. Noyce was convinced that the day of the huge production unit was gone, that modern workers performed better in smaller, more informal production units. And by 1975 Intel had such units in various Santa Clara towns as well as in Oregon, the Philippines, and Malaysia. In each area Grove introduced perhaps the toughest quality control and monitoring systems in the industry and a system of rewards to match Intel's production philosophy.

Finally Intel realized that reliable delivery was perhaps the most important single issue in marketing its chips. Intel quickly evolved its well known motto, "Intel Delivers." But these words had to be backed by careful practices and dramatic policies to be credible to a skeptical market place. For example, at one point early in its history, Intel convinced Honeywell to give it a contract for a custom memory device. Honeywell had already placed contracts with six semiconductor manufacturers including Texas Instruments and Fairchild. "We started about six months later than the others," recalls Grove, "and we were the only ones to deliver the device, about a year later." (2,158)

Living on the Brink of Disaster

"This business lived on the brink of disaster," explained Moore. "As soon as you could make a device with high yield, you calculated that you could decrease costs by trying to make something four times as complex, which brought your yield down again." Overeager technologists could easily miscalculate future yields and pledge deliveries they could not meet or set prices that turned out to be below their costs. Said Noyce, "If you look at our stuff and melt it down for silicon, that's a small fraction of cost—the rest is mistakes. Yet we chose to work on the verge of disaster because that meant doing the job with finesse, not brute strength." Early entry allowed Intel quick recovery of development costs through high prices for unique products. It also meant "experience curve" advantages in costs over those who entered later. Volumes were growing so rapidly that future plant space was a necessity, but the technology was moving so fast that one never knew two years ahead what products would be made in the plants. Still plant construction might easily take more than two years for planning and implementation.

The conflicting strategic requirements of production, engineering, marketing (plus international operations) required some unique policy and organizational solutions for the young Intel. Intel had an insatiable need for skilled personnel and tried some imaginative ways of meeting it. The company hired new employees for its wafer-processing facility at Livermore months before that plant went into operation and bused the employees 35 miles each way daily to Santa Clara to train them. To hang on to skilled people, Grove used a technique that he called "Peter Principle recycling."* Instead of firing foremen and other managers who flopped when promoted to more demanding jobs, he split their tasks, giving them smaller responsibilities. Some of these "recycled" men again advanced to higher positions; only a few left.

Middle managers at Intel were monitored carefully but had considerable operational freedom. "Lots of guys starting new companies are interested in keeping their fingers in every part of the pie," said Moore. "I think Bob and I were relatively willing to relinquish day-to-day details." For example, Intel had streamlined purchasing to the point where the engineer in charge of a project could buy a $250,000 tester, or whatever he needed, by simply signing for it—provided it was in his budget . . ." "(In a big company) you would need seven different signatures on a piece of paper to spend any money," said Moore. Noyce and Moore also tried to keep operations as informal as they could. Spaces in the huge Intel parking lot were not marked with officials' names. . . . "If Bob gets to work late," said Moore,

* The Peter Principle said that an organization kept on promoting its people until they reached a level beyond their competency, where they were held. Thus managements of all organizations became incompetent.

"he parks way out in the corner of the lot. I think this will continue. Sometimes it's a pain in the neck. But the other problem is, once you start marking parking spaces, where do you stop." (2,189–190) The rule still held in the 1980s.

> ### DECISION POINT
>
> What are the key factors for success in each functional area? What specific policies should Intel develop to meet the conflicting requirements of manufacturing, engineering, and the market? What specific organizational form should Intel undertake in its early years?

AN EXPLODING MARKET

In 1973, just as the 1103 reached its production peak, the trade press dubbed it the "DC-3" of the chip field. The 4000-bit (or 4K) chip had arrived, but it was possible for two or three 4K devices to dominate different market segments. Thus, Mostek, TI, Fairchild, and some ten other companies went after the new market. Intel announced its 4K chip a month before TI, but later found its circuitry slower than TI's—fast enough for peripherals, but not the big main-frame market. Intel countered by making a chip "compatible" with TI's and hammering away at volume production and reliability to take market share. About then Gordon Moore came up with "Moore's Law"—a recognition that the number of components one could put on a chip doubled every year. This set implicit targets for future LSI programs.

The Microprocessor

Among the more exciting potentials of the mid-1970s was the emerging impact of another Intel invention—the microprocessor. By 1972 a number of LSI chips capable of significant computation had been produced or were in design for small calculators or intelligent terminals. A Japanese calculator company, Busicom, asked Intel to develop a 12-chip set for a high-performance programmable calculator series. ROM—read-only memory—chips would customize each model for specific uses. As he worked on the problem, Intel's M. E. "Ted" Hoff concluded that Busicom's design was too complex to be cost effective. Hoff had been utilizing a DEC PDP8 and was struck by its lean architecture versus the complexity of the Busicom design. With a relatively primitive instruction set, the PDP8 could perform highly complex control and arithmetic functions because of its large program memory. Hoff proposed to Intel management a program to design a simpler, more general-purpose, more powerful single-chip processor. If successful, such a device might have applications well beyond just calculators.

Intel's management responded quickly and enthusiastically. A small team soon defined a 3-chip design: a 4-bit CPU, a ROM program memory, and a RAM (random access memory) data memory. This design was vastly aided by the concurrent invention of the EPROM (erasable programmable read-only memory) by Dov Frohman at Intel. But it still languished for lack of staffing until Federico Faggin—later cofounder of Zilog—arrived from Fairchild in early 1970. Faggin worked furiously on the silicon design, and in only nine months produced working samples of the chips that would become the MCS-4 microprocessor, the world's first "micro" computer.

In some complex negotiations with Busicom, Intel won the right to sell the MCS-4 chips to others for non-calculator applications. The marketing department saw microprocessors as possibly a 10% slice of the minicomputer market, then at 20,000 units per year. While Intel management thought it might obtain as much as 90% of this market in its early stages, there was considerable debate at the Board level as to whether and how the company should exercise this option. There was widespread skepticism about the microprocessor in the industry. Many saw it as too slow and small to be of much use. But Intel went ahead. As the market finally opened, competitors grew rapidly—to 54 by 1976. And TI, a late entry with its TMW-1000, actually became the leading producer of 4-bit processors.

About that time other fields of application for ICs had begun to loom as interesting possible areas of diversification. A trap Noyce wanted to avoid was becoming so engrossed in existing profitable products that Intel neglected new opportunities. The company looked carefully at Microma, Inc., a manufacturer of electronic watches using Intel chips. This looked like "a unique opportunity for electronics to supplant another technology." And there were a myriad of other application possibilities on the horizon. Eventually, the company bought Microma for $2.8 million. This began a complex of longer term developments that intimately shaped the Intel of the early 1980s.

Even as Intel was working on the MSC-4, a parallel development was underway that would lead to its first 8-bit processor, the 8008. Then in 1974 Intel introduced its much more powerful 8080, which quickly became accepted as the 8-bit standard and was widely second sourced. Faggin, Hoff, and Mazor carefully designed the 8080 to be compatible in software with the earlier 8008. This policy of upward compatibility had been followed for all Intel machines thereafter. The 8080 was the first Intel microprocessor announced before it was actually available, "to give customers lead time to design the part into new products." Now things were moving fast. In only three years, microcomputers had exceeded the population of both minis and mainframe computers combined. (2,189–190) The first 8-bit single-chip computer (CPU, I/O, RAM, and ROM) was Intel's 8048, introduced in 1976. With it a whole new era of computers and automation began.

The 16-Bit Era

Originally, a 16-bit processor had been considered a mini, and all smaller ones were micros. But this distinction began to fade as National Semi-conductor introduced its 1-chip, 16-bit, Pace microprocessor series. Although other entrants were earlier, Intel hit the market in 1978 with its powerful 8086 which had 10 times the through-put and 16 times the memory (one megabyte) of its earlier 8080. By 1979, 75 million microprocessors had been shipped, with an annual compound growth rate of 188% since 1975.

By 1982 microprocessors had created a whole new market for intelligent, user-friendly instruments unavailable ten years previously. Electronic games and toys had become by far the largest current market—suddenly surpassing the sales of any other single form of entertainment in the United States and Japan. Arthur D. Little expected this market to grow sixfold by 1987. But others saw microprocessors and VLSI chips of other sorts restructuring a variety of industries and services in the 1980s. Microprocessors could already be built on a single chip to be as powerful as the room-sized IBM machines of the late 1960s. (See Table 1.) And a 64-bit microprocessor—with even more inherent address and accuracy capabilities than the most powerful mainframes—seemed probable in the not too distant future.

TABLE 1 Microprocessor Functional Classes

Micro System Class	Level of Functionality	Typical Price	PERFORMANCE RELATIVE TO MICROCONTROLLER		MEMORY	
			CPU	I/O	Typical Size (Bytes)	Management
Micromainframe	32 bit	$400–$3,600	20–70	6–45	256K–8M	Dynamic addressing, segmented or paged; adaptive virtual support
Micromaxi	16 or 32 bit	$100–$500	25	12	128K–1M	Structured addressing, segmented or paged; virtual support
Micromini	16 bit	$20–$150	8–10	6	32K–256K	Static addressing, segmented or paged
Microcomputer	8 or 16 bit	$10–$50	1–5	3–5	4K–64K	Segmented or direct
Microcontroller	8 bit	$2–$20	1	1	1K–2K	Direct or absolute

Source: "Intel Takes Aim at the '80s," *Electronics,* February 28, 1980. Copyright © 1980, McGraw-Hill, Inc. All rights reserved.

Cost and Performance

Intel's most radical new offering was its iAPX432 which had a 16-megabyte physical address space and a virtual address of 1 trillion bytes. This 3-chip processor was designed for critical on-line data base management, networking, and switching system management and control. (2,189–190)

The iAPX432 characterized other major changes in the industry. The rule of thumb through the 1970s was that every 10 years one could buy ten times more computing power for the same cost as a decade before. It was also common for LSI and VLSI chip costs to drop 25% yearly. And the early 1980s seemed unlikely to decrease this rate of change. But development costs were also soaring. The 4004 microprocessor was designed by one man in nine months. In contrast the iAPX432 took 6 years and 100 person-years of engineering. Intel—through 1981 —had already spent some $100 million to design its next generation of computers. In the late 1970s it had cost only about $100,000 to produce a typical first LSI chip and the marginal cost of a millionth good chip was close to zero. But as VLSI (very large scale integrated) chips in the early 1980s became more complex, the first chip might cost more than $10–20 million—and later chips were correspondingly expensive. A whole new plant for complex VLSI chips might cost $100–200 million alone.

By 1981 over 100,000 products already had microprocessors built into them. And the quantity and complexity of applications were growing exceedingly rapidly, with virtually every industry and household a potential user. Yet the number of computer programmers to develop these applications was not. In 1980 Andy Grove, then president of Intel, noted, "If the computer industry keeps growing at its current rate, by 1990 it will take a million more qualified programmers to provide the needed software."[10] University output was only in the tens of thousands. In addition, the amount of software for new systems had risen dramatically. Typical customer software for major new applications in the 1970s might have ranged from $250,000 to $300,000. By the mid-1980s similar applications might cost

181

$1–5 million.[11] The cost of marketing a new system had become as expensive as its initial development.

The computer world of the 1980s would be peculiar. Replacing all of IBM's 360s with 8086 micros would occupy only a few days production at Intel. Yet Intel was projecting a growth of 33% per year and was investing over $150 million in capital per year in an industry where domestic competition was popping all around, where the Japanese had targeted national priorities to dominate semiconductors in the 1980s, and where European governments were ready to put up $$\frac{1}{2}$$ billion to ensure their companies a future in the field.

The Japanese Challenge

In 1979 the United States still commanded 67% of the world market for semiconductors, while the Japanese had only 22%. But, led by its large integrated companies—NEC, Fujitsu, and Hitachi—the Japanese moved strongly into the 16K and 64K RAM markets.[12] By 1979 they had 40% of the 16K RAM market. Although Intel had been earlier than the Japanese in introducing its 64K RAM, the company ran into trouble producing it in quantity. Meanwhile the Japanese introduced and perfected production on a 64K RAM that was not as densely packed as the American 64K RAM—that is, it had larger overall dimensions—and shipped some 85% of the market in 1981. By early 1982 Motorola and Intel had solved their problems with 64K chips that had some potential advantages in speed and packaging over the Japanese. But the Japanese were well down the experience curve on their chips and cut prices severely to discourage the entry of others. As a result various sources estimated that the total profit from 64K chips in 1982 would be only $20 million worldwide.

A number of factors made the Japanese challenge upsetting to the U.S. industry. Almost all the basic research and early technical work on semiconductors had been done by U.S. companies. Many claimed that the early Japanese entries in I/Cs had simply copied U.S. designs relying on the U.S. courts' notoriously lax attitudes on patent enforcement to keep them out of legal troubles. Others noted that the Japanese government through its MITI (Ministry for International Trade and Industry) had given Japanese companies some $200 million in development support to invade the semiconductor and computer markets. And Japanese banks financed these entrants with a level of debt that would not be considered prudent—or perhaps legal—in the United States or Europe. Because of high savings rates and low inflation, interest rates were very low (5–6%) in Japan; and satisfactory net profits could thus be correspondingly lower, that is, 1–2% on sales in NEC. The Japanese did not have to carry the overhead burden of a military establishment. And because of post–War World II recovery and high investment rates their suppliers' plants were relatively modern.

In addition to these structural advantages no one denied that a highly disciplined, well-educated, and strongly motivated Japanese worker-manager pool was also at the heart of the Japanese challenge. In fact, Japanese management, worker security, and worker cooperation practices were widely admired. But many resented the overt and covert trade barriers that protected the Japanese market, allowing domestic manufacturers to build volume—and lower costs—without foreign competition. Prior to 1975 semiconductor imports into Japan were reportedly controlled by an informal quota system in which MITI would "suggest" that an importer "consider" a domestic source before MITI would approve an import license. Japan's NT&T (the government-controlled telecommunications company) refused to allow foreigners to bid on its contracts, and so on.[12] The fact that

Japan's biggest semiconductor producers (Hitachi, NEC, Fujitsu) were also among the biggest component users compounded the market control problem. Unknown internal transfer pricing practices made it difficult to substantiate Silicon Valley's claims that the Japanese were "dumping" 16K chips on the U.S. market at half the Japanese price. See Exhibits 1 and 2 for data on the Japanese semiconductor industry.

Acknowledging many of these points in a January 1982 speech, Bob Noyce noted, "The Japanese are smart, patient, and hard working people. And that's unfair competition. We must do something about it. . . . But on the whole to date they are still very much followers in microelectronics. They have yet to produce an innovation in microprocessors."

PRACTICES ATTUNED TO THE TIMES

How could Intel adapt to these challenges? The company had grown larger and more complex in the 1970s. But it had also worked hard to keep its management systems attuned to the times. A few key elements in its approach follow.

The Top Team

By 1982 Intel's "two-headed monster"—Noyce and Moore—had become a three-headed "executive office." Chairman Moore—pensive and more reserved in his habits—was the company's long-range thinker, charting overall product strategies. The more gregarious Noyce, now vice chairman, had become Intel's Mr. Outside and was increasingly recognized as one of the industry's major spokesmen. Andy Grove (age 45), who had headed Fairchild's metal oxide semiconductor (MOS) reseach and joined Intel at its startup, was president and chief operating officer. Although less visible than Noyce and Moore in the early years, Grove was increasingly recognized as the personality driving Intel's internal affairs. "Grove has to be the world's most organized guy," said an admiring Moore. "He sees problems developing much sooner than other people, and he's interested in the people and people interactions needed to solve them."

The three worked well together, respecting each other's technical abilities, and arguing openly and without rancor when they disagreed. To maintain a close touch with the organization each man was in a separate area of Intel's Santa Clara complex. Their offices were indistinguishable from all the other cubicles that secretaries and junior executives worked in. All office walls in Intel were only shoulder high partitions, there were no doors on any offices (including Moore's), no limousines, and no executive dining rooms. Any of the top three was likely to plop down at a table in their building's cafeteria and join in a lunch chat with whomever was there. Said one group of employees, "It's exciting to know you may see and talk to the very top guy at any time. You feel a real part of things."

Councils and Confrontation

Intel had tried hard to avoid communications barriers and structural bureaucracies. While the company was decentralized into relatively small operating units, people might still have several bosses, depending on the problems at hand. Virtually all staff functions—purchasing, operating procedures, employee compensation, and so on—were handled by "councils" of line managers. There were usually several dozen—ninety were once counted—of such councils operating at one time.

On the councils all people participated as equals, with new members free to openly challenge top managers. "The idea," said Grove, "is to remove authority from an artificial spot at the top and place it where the most knowledgeable people are. . . . I can't pretend to know the shape of the next generation of silicon or computer technology any more. People like me need information from those closest to the technology. We can't afford the hierarchical barriers to the exchange of ideas that so many corporations have. The technology is moving too fast."

This free exchange of ideas was reinforced by a policy of "constructive confrontation." Each member of a team was expected to challenge *ideas* openly and aggressively, but never to attack an individual's motives for presenting an idea. Employees said, "Things can get very rough in a meeting. You'd be surprised at the things people can say. But if you are seeking a solution, it's OK." Grove himself set the tone. "When he walks into the room, things can get electric. . . . I've seen him listen to a carefully prepared report for a while and shatter the room with 'I've never heard so much bullshit in my life.' " The company has courses on "constructive confrontation" for all its rising executives and includes the concept in its early training of people in Intel's philosophy.

The World of High Achievers

Like all other groups and individuals in Intel, the councils were required to set performance objectives and be measured against them. Assignments were set by the council and agreed to by each employee and his supervisor. Grove said, "This takes a lot of time but everyone knows exactly whom they report to on each item —and so do their supervisors. We can't afford to leave anything to chance as we grow larger." Performance measurement pervaded everything. When Noyce had joined Shockley, he had said, "I had to test myself, to know if I could hold my own with the best." In 1982 the attitude persisted: "We are seeking high achievers. And high achievers love to be measured because otherwise they can't prove to themselves that they're achieving. Measuring them says that you care about them. . . . (But it must be an honest review.) Many people have never had an honest review before. They've been passed along by school systems and managements that don't want to tell people when they don't measure up. We tell them, 'Here are the things you did poorly. And here are the things you did well.' "

Intel had MBO (management by objectives) everywhere. Each person had multiple objectives. All employees wrote down what they were going to do, got their bosses' agreements and reviewed how well they performed with both their management *and* peer groups. This made the review a communication device among various groups as well. A key to the system was the "one-on-one" meetings between a supervisor and subordinate. The meeting belonged to the subordinate who went to the boss, provided the agenda, told the boss what he was doing, and saw whether there was any assistance the boss could offer. These meetings were required for everyone on a regular basis. They might occur weekly for newcomers, but they were seldom less than monthly for anyone. In any meeting at Intel problems were put forward first, and everyone dug in to solve them.[13]

Formal Organization

There was no large corporate staff in the usual sense. Instead the top division managers formed the "executive staff" whose job was to worry about the whole business, not just their individual portions of it. Expectedly, Intel was leery of formal organization charts. But Exhibit 3 gives some sense of the matrix of management that guided Intel in 1982.

The basic product group organization included: (1) *Components Group*—RAMs, EPROMs, bubble memories, memory products, and all component manufacturing, wafer processing, and assembly; (2) *Microcomputers Group*—microprocessors, microcontrollers, development systems, telecommunication circuits, and military products; and (3) *Systems Group*—single-board computers, integrated systems, OEM and end user memory systems, commercial software, commerical microsystems operations, and systems manufacturing. But within this structure "flexibility" still dominated. Teams were formed for special problems. And planning was performed across all divisions toward a selected set of strategic business segments (SBSs), Intel's version of the strategic business units (SBUs) used in other companies. Noyce said, "Strategic planning is imbedded into the organization. It is one of the primary functions of line managers. They buy into the program. They carry it out. They're determining their own future.[14]

An interesting example of this was the bubble memory group established as a separate entrepreneurial division within Intel. In 1970 Bell Laboratories discovered that in certain materials, it was possible to create small densely packed magnetic bubbles whose location and polarity could be controlled to store enormous quantities of information in a very small space. Although greeted with enthusiasm at first, the technology was difficult to reduce to practice, and most larger companies gave up on it in the late 1970s. A few small entrepreneurial concerns persisted, however; and in 1978 one of these came to Intel with a promising approach ready for scale up and possible introduction. Intel brought the company in as a separate division with a very unusual incentive program to maintain its management's enthusiasm and entrepreneurial flair. In 1982, Intel bubble memories with 1 million bits per chip capacity were commercial and a 4 million–bit chip was announced for release late in the year.

An Innovative Year

Despite the deep recession in 1981, Intel had introduced a chain of impressive new products. Its 64K RAM seemed destined to take back a share of this market where the Japanese had surged to dominance. Intel used a "cell redundancy" design that cost 15–20% in chip area but gave a 2 to 3X yield gain. Rothschild, Unterberg, Towbin estimated Intel's direct chip costs as perhaps the United States' lowest ($8–9 in 1981) in a market where Hitachi was selling 64K chips for $8–9 in quantity. Volume production could bring Intel's costs down to $4.50–4.00 in the future. Other competitors' cost estimates follow:

64K Producer Cost and Production Estimates

MANUFACTURER	EST. AVERAGE 1981 PRODUCTION PER MONTH	EST. AVERAGE 1981 UNIT COST
Intel	75,000	$ 8–9
Motorola	150,000	10–12
Texas Instruments	40,000	12–16
Fujitsu	150,000	9–11
Hitachi	200,000	9–11
NEC	150,000	10–12
AMD	0	—
National Semiconductor	0	—
Mostek	70,000	12–16

Source: Rothschild, Unterberg, Towbin, *Intel Research Report,* August 25, 1981.

Other significant new products were a 64K EPROM (fastest available), the i432X microprocessor (with power equal to IBM's 370/158 main-frame), and the revolutionary E²PROM (electrically erasable programmable read-only memory). The micro-mainframe market could be over $\frac{1}{2}$ billion in the mid 1980s. And Intel thought E²PROMs could replace all EPROM applications in time and open vast new possibilities. E²PROMs could be reprogrammed without removing the chip from its setting and destroying its old programs with ultraviolet light as EPROMs required. These were but a few of the 85–90 new products Intel introduced in 1981, a disaster year for the industry caused by severe price competition and general economic conditions. As a result Rothschild, Unterberg, Towbin was forecasting Intel's growth at 35% per year to 1985 with profit margins of 15–17%. They forecast Intel's overall financials as shown in Tables 2 and 3.

Now Intel could meet its competition with some powerful strengths. Processing technology at Intel was perhaps unmatched in the industry. The density of components on a chip was defined by so called "design rules" which set the minimum spacings which could be reliably met between components. Intel's technology (H-MOS III) was perhaps the most powerful in the industry for this purpose. But the Japanese were pushing hard on this gap. Some comparisons follow:

Process Technology Comparison

COMPANY	NEW PROCESS NAME	MINIMUM NEW PROCESS DESIGN RULE	CURRENT PROCESS DESIGN RULE u = MICRONS	NEW PROCESS STATUS
Intel	H-MOS II	2–3 u	2–4 u	Stable
	H-MOS III*	1–2 u*		
Motorola	H-MOS II	2–2½ u	2½–5 u	Stable
	H-MOS III*	1.4–1.8 u*		
Texas Instruments	S-MOS	3 u	3½–5 u	Improving
National Semi.	X-MOS	2–3 u	3½–5 u	Development
Advanced Micro Devices	N/S 8	2–3 u	3⅓–4 u	Improving
Mostek	SP 5	2.5–2.7 u	4 u	Improving
Nippon Electric	N.A.	N.A	3½–4 u	Stable

* *Planned.*
Source: Rothschild, Unterberg, Towbin, *Intel Research Report,* August 25, 1981.

TABLE 2 **Intel Financial Estimates**

($ MILLIONS, EXCEPT PER SHARE DATA)				
Sales	**1979**	**1980**	**1981E**	**1982E**
Memory				
1K, 4K dynamic	$ 41	$ 32	$ 10	$ 5
16K dynamic	49	86	80	45
64K dynamic	—	6	20	55
1K, 4K, 16K static	66	95	65	90
PROM, EPROM, EEPROM	120	153	100	165
Total memory	$276	$372	$275	$ 360
Microprocessor				
Memory	70	94	85	105
CPU	60	86	125	195
Peripheral	30	49	60	90
Total Microprocessor	$160	$229	$270	$ 390

TABLE 2 (Continued)

($ MILLIONS, EXCEPT PER SHARE DATA)

Sales	1979	1980	1981E	1982E
Board Level	30	37	30	40
Develop. system	95	125	140	160
Memory system	100	92	85	115
Total sales	$663	$855	$800	$1,065

Pretax Income/Margin	1979	1980	1981E	1982E
Memory	$54/19%	$61/16%	$(18)/–%	$30/8%
Microprocessor	53/33	76/33	43/16	91/23
Develop. System	29/30	36/29	27/19	35/22
Other	13/10	10/8	7/6	12/8
Total	$149/22.5%	$183/21.4%	$ 59/7%	$168/16%
Tax rate	47.8%	47.8%	44.4%	44%
Net income	$ 78	$ 95.5	$ 33	$ 94
E.P.S. (43.5 million shares)	$ 1.80	$ 2.21	$.50–1.00	$ 2.15

Source: Rothschild, Unterberg, Towbin, *Intel Research Report,* August 25, 1981.

TABLE 3   Intel Financial Estimates ($ Millions, Except Percentages)

FUNDS FLOW	1979	1980	1981E	1982E	1983E	1984E	1985E
Sources							
Net income	$ 77.8	$ 96.7	$ 33	$ 94	$130	$170	$230
Depreciation	40.4	49.0	70	85	100	135	170
Deferred taxes	6.8	8.0	2	8	10	14	20
Equity sales	19.8	32.9	25	35	45	55	65
Debt financing	—	150.0	—	—	—	—	—
Total	$144.8	$336.7	$130	$222	$285	$374	$485
Uses							
Capital spending	$ 96.7	$152.2	$150	$110	$145	$225	$300
Funds required for working capital	52.0	39.0	(11)	53	75	100	135
Funds provided or (required)	$ (3.9)	$145.4	$ 9	$ 59	$ 65	$ 49	$ 50
Return on average equity	30.6%	26.3%	7.5%	17.7%	19.0%	19.3%	20.1%

Source: Rothschild, Unterberg, Towbin, *Intel Research Report,* August 25, 1981.

Many observers felt that the "Intel culture" would be a major determinant of its success in the wild world of the 1980s. This "culture" was an odd mixture of discipline and flexibility that pervaded the company. So important was this "culture" that all employees were put through a course on it soon after they arrived. This was especially important in a company like Intel where half of the people might have been present only a year or less. The top three executives consistently taught in this course as they did in the complex of other courses set up to maintain Intel's competitiveness for the 1980s. Grove said, "Management must teach to have the courses believed. . . . It takes a lot of time. But nothing could be more important than understanding how we operate and what makes Intel unique. Intel is a complete philosophy not just a job."

At Intel people were expected to be disciplined, to work hard. There are clocks and "sign-in sheets" for all people who arrived after the rigorous 8:00 A.M. starting hour. Even top executives followed this rule. Someone once said, "Intel is the only place I've ever seen where 8 A.M. meetings start at 8." Many people don't like the demands Intel makes and its lack of structure. Some employees said, "Some people can't understand that no one will tell them what to do. They have to define what they are going to do and then live up to it. We've seen lots of people quit in the first month because they can't take the pressure." But those who stay like the atmosphere. "It's great to say you work at Intel. You know you're the best. . . . I guess it's a real pride in being first, in being on the frontier. You know you're really a part of something very big—very important." At Intel employees had put over $60 million of their own money into its stock, which had never paid a dividend.[10] Perhaps this was why Intel was able to meet the 1981 downturn with its "20% solution." Under this program many of the professional staff agreed to work an extra day a week—without extra pay—to get out new products and to break production bottlenecks as necessary. Many participated in the seven-month campaign, which was an outstanding success, allowing Intel to rocket out of the recession with a momentum of new products and processes few enjoyed.

"Quality Circles," Total Quality Control, and Quality Assurance programs had long been present in Intel, along with a monthly cash bonus system for quantity and quality of production output. The latter was announced at a monthly bonus meeting in which performance, suggestions, and solutions were discussed directly with the people doing the job on the production line. But noted Noyce, "In a larger organization there is a frustration. It takes longer to see the results of what you're doing. You push on one thing a year and see some movement. In a small organization you can turn on a dime and change direction. With 10,000 people, you break the organization into small manageable units, so you can change the direction of one unit at a time. . . ."

"But in development you can't afford that. You have to move fast, to be first. But you're in a realm where no one has done before what you're trying to do. You have to measure absolutely everything, so when something goes wrong, you have some idea of what went wrong. You don't change something unless you've proved it on a pilot basis first, so that it won't louse up something else. . . . Yet you have to compete against other people who may not know this—and get lucky. You also have to compete against the massive capacities of the large Japanese companies to change the whole market place if they make a right decision and you don't. None of us—no one—has managed a company in this kind of technology and this competition before. We have to write the book for the future. It's quite a challenge."

Moore stated the ultimate challenge in these terms, "We intend to be the outstandingly successful company in this industry. And we intend to continue to be a leader in the revolutionary technology that is changing the way the world is run."[1] The question was how to do this in an era in which many saw the once almost mystically high technology chip business moving into a commodity era.

Said Noyce, "A company with 16,000 employees and $800 million in sales can't fail to be different than the start up company we were 13 years ago. But in the past we have been first with major innovations like the silicon gate MOS, LSI memory, microprocessor, E^2PROM, HMOS, megabit bubbles, and 32-bit microprocessor. . . . To be recognized as the technological leader in those areas we pursue is still a goal. . . . This and our other stated goals (see Exhibit 4) remain guideposts for our future."

1. Evaluate the past strategy of Intel. What criteria should one use in evaluating a strategy?

2. What new problems do you see for Intel's future? What should it do about these?

3. How should it organize to support its strategy?

EXHIBIT 1

Preliminary Estimated 1981 Versus 1980 Worldwide Semiconductor Shipment Comparisons (millions of dollars)

Company	1980	1981	Annual Growth Percent
Texas Instruments	$1,580	$1,295	(18.0)%
Motorola	1,100	1,185	7.7
Nippon Electric	769	928	20.7
Hitachi	658	824	25.2
Toshiba	629	768	22.1
National Semiconductor	770	730	(5.2)
Fairchild	566	505	(10.8)
Intel	575	500	(13.0)
Fujitsu	419	482	15.0
Philips*	558	480	(14.0)
Matsushita	300	379	21.3
Signetics	384	375	(2.3)
Siemens**	423	337	(20.3)
Mitsubishi	254	308	26.3
RCA	322	293	(9.0)
AMD	282	277	(1.8)
General Instrument	244	264	8.2
Mostek	330	255	(22.7)
Sanyo	180	216	20.0
ITT	241	200	(17.0)
SGS-ATES	170	178	4.7
Harris	185	165	(10.8)
Thomson-CSF	179	156	(12.8)
AEG-Telefunken	180	141	(21.7)
American Microsystems	117	130	11.1
General Electric	137	122	(10.9)
Hewlett-Packard	95	90	(5.3)
International Rectifier	90	90	0.0
Intersil	106	88	(17.0)
Synertek	60	72	20.0
Unitrode	70	70	0.0
Rockwell	70	70	0.0
Total of Above Companies	$12,043	$11,973	(0.6)%

* Excludes Sinergetics subsidiary.

** Excludes U.S. subsidiaries.

Source: DATAQUEST, Inc., March 1982.

EXHIBIT 2
Comparison United States
versus Japan, 1979–1981

Producer	Year	Plant and Equipment Expenditure	Sales	Percent
United States	1979	$ 980 mil.	$6,600 mil.	14.8%
	1980	1,275 mil.	8,400 mil.	15.1
	1981	1,150 mil.	8,900 mil.	12.9
Japan	1979	$ 555 mil.	$3,284 mil.	16.9%
	1980	829 mil.	4,592 mil.	18.1
	1981	900 mil.	5,165 mil.	17.4

Source: Rothschild, Unterberg, Towbin, *Intel Research Report,* August 25, 1981.

EXHIBIT 3
Intel's Organization 1982

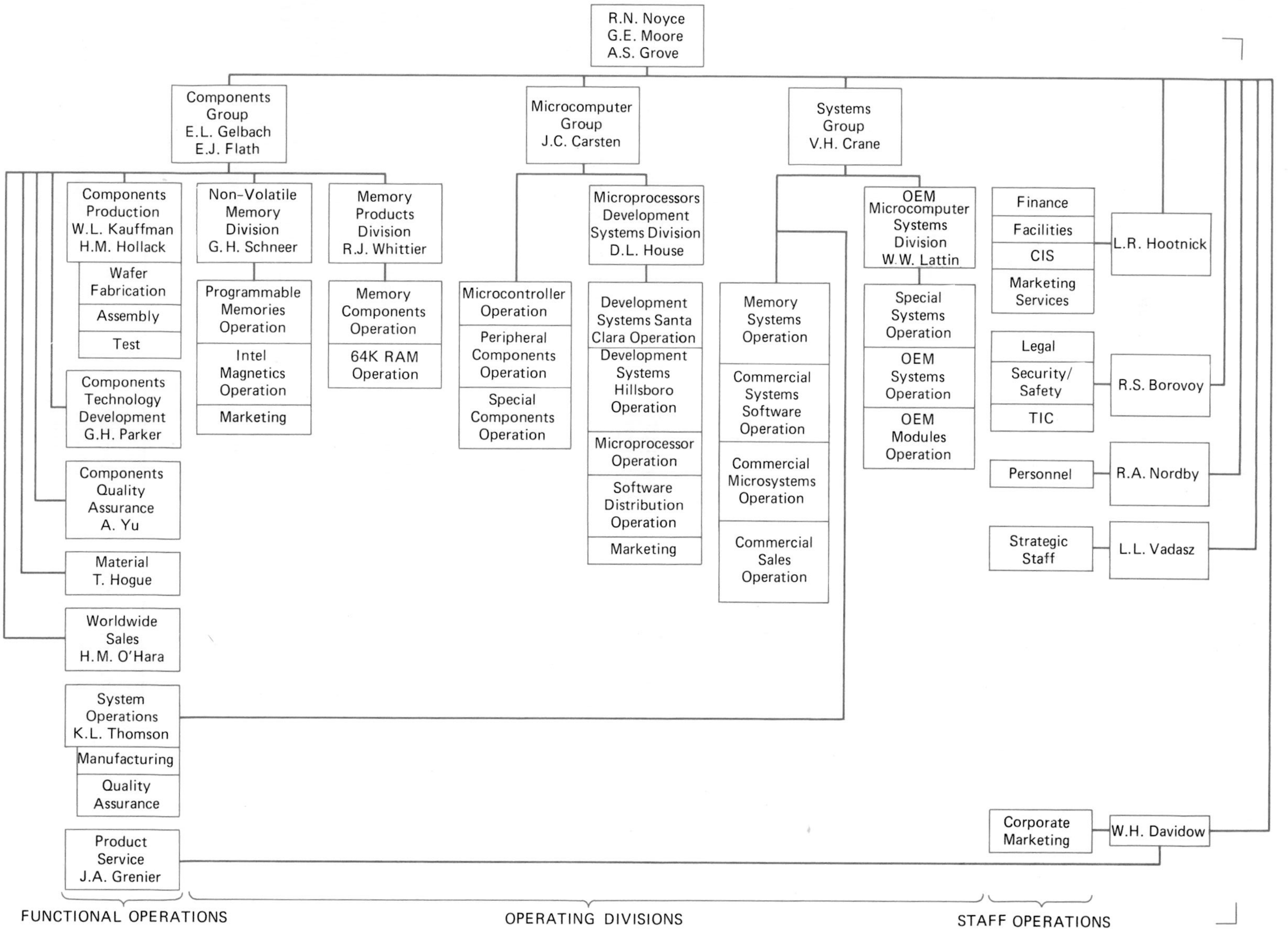

Source: Company records.

191

EXHIBIT 4
Intel Corporation
Corporate Objectives

Intel's basic objective is to be an outstandingly successful business over the long term. We have become accustomed to excellence in everything we undertake. This overall objective can be divided into series of more specific objectives:

1. To grow to a minimum of 250 million dollars in after-tax earnings by 1985 while maintaining an average of at least 10% after-tax margin and, at all times, the highest margins of major companies in our industry.

2. To concentrate on those areas of business where we can have a commanding position (either #1 or #2) and in which our combination of capabilities result in uniquely strong competitive advantages; to maintain a position in other business areas only if it is important to develop or support the commanding positions.

3. To be and be recognized as the technological leader in those areas we pursue.

4. To be and be recognized as the leader in meeting our customers' needs for delivery, reliability, quality and service.

5. To minimize the effects of disruptive fluctuations caused by business cycles and capricious competitors so that our long term commitments to people and programs can be maintained.

6. To seek out, attract and retain the best people possible at all levels and provide them with challenging jobs, training and opportunities for personal growth so that they may share in Intel's success.

7. To conduct our business with customers and vendors and in our internal activities with integrity and professionalism.

8. Be an asset to the countries and communities in which we operate.

Source: Company Records, May 8, 1981.

EXHIBIT 5
Competitor Profiles

The worldwide noncaptive market for semiconductors approximated $13.8 billion in 1980. Discrete devices constituted a large portion of the market and accounted for $4.3 billion or 31% of all semiconductors sold. Integrated circuits, which consist of bipolar and MOS devices, amounted to $9.5 billion or 69% of industry sales. MOS memory devices accounted for the largest portion of integrated circuit sales and comprised about 18% of all semiconductor device sales. Bipolar logic circuits at $2.2 billion and linear devices at $1.8 billion accounted for the next largest portions of the industry.

MOTOROLA

Motorola appears to have the strongest position in the semiconductor industry. It has the best product balance of all the suppliers and is well-positioned in leading-edge, rapidly growing products. The company is the world's

EXHIBIT 5
(Continued)

largest supplier of discrete devices with a 10% market share. Within the discrete category, Motorola dominates the market for power devices. It is the largest factor in power transistors, rectifiers and zener diodes, and second to General Electric in thyristors. The company should also become a major force in power MOS/FETs, an emerging market. The discrete business is highly profitable, very stable, and provides funds which can be invested in faster growing integrated circuit lines.

In bipolar logic, Motorola has emerged as the dominant supplier of high speed emitter coupled logic (ECL), which is used in high performance computers. It also offers a line of ECL gate arrays. The company is one of the top three bipolar linear producers, and appears to be gaining position in this market. . . . Motorola has the broadest range of processors and peripherals next to the industry leader, Intel. In memories, Motorola is the current domestic leader in 64K-bit RAM production and a leading factor in static RAMs, EPROMs and EEPROMs. Finally, as the dominant factor in CMOS, the most important technology for the second half of this decade, the company offers a broad line of CMOS logic circuits and several CMOS microprocessor families.

INTEL

Intel garners the second-place award because of its dominant position in microprocessors and specialty memory products. Intel literally invented the microprocessor in 1971 and exploited its position by continually upgrading its processor and peripheral and support capabilities. The company is unsurpassed in the 8-bit market and is expected to share the top spot with Motorola's 68000 in the 16-bit market. Furthermore, the company was the first to introduce a 32-bit processor, the iAPX-432, which will be available for customer sampling in 1982. Intel also pioneered many new memory products such as the static RAM, EPROM and E^2PROM. The company still maintains its leadership position in these rapidly growing product lines, but is not expected to achieve the dominance of these markets that it did during the 1970s.

ADVANCED MICRO DEVICES

AMD is rapidly emerging as a major force in the integrated circuit market. The company emphasizes proprietary products which account for 40–50% of its revenues and a larger portion of its profits. It pioneered and now dominates the 4-bit slice bipolar microprocessor market, which is used for high speed computation applications, and followed this product with a 16-bit line aimed at the high speed controller market. The company is also a leading factor in high performance bipolar RAMs and PROMs. Key thrusts for the future include a line of MOS and linear telecommunications chips and Ethernet controller circuits. In addition, the company was recently designated as the official domestic second source for Intel's 8086 16-bit microprocessor line.

EXHIBIT 5
(Continued)

TEXAS INSTRUMENTS (TI)

This company was once perceived as the premier semiconductor company. Its position has slipped because of the glittering performances of Intel and Advanced Micro Devices combined with its relatively poor performance in 8-bit and 16-bit microprocessors and CMOS development. We sense that TI is regrouping and preparing for a market onslaught in the 1982–1986 period. It intends to protect its dominant position in digital bipolar markets through extensions of the advanced low-power Shottky (ALS) line and expanded gate array offerings. In the MOS memory area, TI has become a major factor in EPROMs, and is the second largest domestic supplier, next to Motorola, in the 64K-bit dynamic RAM. The company is the leading supplier of 4-bit microprocessors, which are principally used in toys, games and appliances. Its 8-bit effort has stalled, but new thrusts are being made in the single-chip processor area. A very fast, 24-MHz version of the 9900 16-bit microprocessor was recently announced. While this part is the fastest on the market, we do not expect it to be overwhelmingly successful due to its rather turgid, outdated architecture. CMOS is receiving lots of development attention and we would expect numerous product introductions to unfold over the next few years. TI must offer a broad line of CMOS logic circuits in order to protect its flanks in the bipolar logic market.

NATIONAL SEMICONDUCTOR

National is perhaps the most maligned of the semiconductor companies. It is viewed as a strong production house with little technology and thin management. This latter point has been further emphasized by the recent departures of several corporate offices. In our opinion, National is a much better company than is generally perceived. It is the third largest domestic semiconductor company and one of the top five independent vendors in the world. The company offers a very broad product line ranging from discrete devices to high performance integrated circuits. National is one of the leaders in bipolar logic with a strong position in Shottky and ALS, and will soon broaden its bipolar memory participation through the introduction of high speed ECL RAMs. In addition, the company will offer ECL Macrocell arrays. National is the dominant factor in the linear circuit area and has probably introduced more innovative linear devices than all competitors combined. This product line is highly profitable and can be viewed as a cash cow.

National's other strength is CMOS, where it offers a line of logic devices, gate arrays and microprocessors. Moreover, the company has developed several CMOS digital/analog converters and three proprietary telecommunications chips. The company is a leading participant in MOS memories but has not distinguished itself in this area. National's weakest area is MOS microprocessors, where its only success to date has been in the 4-bit processor. The company has not participated heavily in the 8-bit market and is now sampling its 16-bit proprietary processor, the NS16000.

EXHIBIT 5
(Continued)

MONOLITHIC MEMORIES

Monolithic Memories is the second largest supplier of bipolar, programmable read-only memories (PROMs). These devices are used in minicomputer, military electronics and microprocessor applications. The company pioneered this product in the early 1970s and has retained a leadership position. The company was late in developing higher density versions of the PROM, but has made excellent progress in developing the next generation of product in an attempt to overtake the competition. The 16K-bit family will shortly be available in two configurations: $2K \times 8$ and $4K \times 4$. A registered version of the 16K-bit part will be available next year along with a 32K-bit device. Furthermore, faster versions of low density devices have been introduced, such as a 256-bit part with an access time of 17 nanoseconds, and will secure the company's leadership position at the low end of the market.

Source: Hambrecht & Quist Incorporated, *Research Report,* November 1981.

195

EXHIBIT 6
Semiconductor Scorecard ($ millions)

	Discretes	Bipolar Logic	Bipolar Memory	Linear	MOS Memories	MOS Micro-processors	CMOS	Total
Texas Instruments	$200	$530 LS	$50	$180	$300 64K DRAM EPROM	$90	$10	$1,360
Motorola	$420 Power	$170 ECL	$20	$165	$155	$75 6800 68000	$175	$1,180
National Semiconductor	$50	$250	$30	$205	$130	$30	$80 p² process	$775
Intel	—	$5	$30	—	$355 EPROM EEPROM	$220 8080 8086	$5	$615
Advanced Micro Devices	—	$80 Bit Slice	$40 RAM PROM	$30	$90	$50	—	$290
Monolithic Memories	—	$20 PAL	$68 PROM	—	—	—	—	$88
Other Major Competitors	Philips $310 Toshiba $275 NEC $260 Hitachi $250	Fairchild $300 Signetics $250 Fujitsu $125 RCA $100	Signetics $95 Fairchild $70 Harris $50 Fujitsu $25	Fairchild $90 RCA $85 Analog $80 Signetics $70	Mostek $260 Fujitsu $230 NEC $180 Hitachi $150	NEC $75 Hitachi $40 Zilog $30 Fairchild $30	RCA $100 Harris $60 AMI $40 Intersil $30	$3,660
Total	$4,300	$2,200	$600	$1,800	$2,500	$800	$600	$13,800

Source: Hambrecht & Quist Incorporated, *Research Report*, November 1981.

EXHIBIT 7

Financial Statements—Intel Corporation
Consolidated Statement of Income, (*thousands—except per share amounts*)

Three Years ended December 31, 1981	1981	1980	1979
Net Revenues	**$788,676**	**$854,561**	**$660,984**
Cost of sales	458,308	399,438	313,106
Research and development	116,496	96,426	66,735
Marketing, general and administrative	184,293	175,577	131,974
Operating costs and expenses	759,097	671,441	511,815
Income before interest and other and taxes on income	29,579	183,120	149,169
Interest and other	(10,655)	(2,209)	121
Income before taxes on income	**40,234**	**185,329**	**149,048**
Taxes on income	12,875	88,588	71,244
Net Income	**$ 27,359**	**$ 96,741**	**$ 77,804**
Earnings per capital and capital equivalent share	**$ 0.61**	**$ 2.21**	**$ 1.85**
Capital shares and equivalents	**44,700**	**43,720**	**42,145**

Consolidated Statement of Shareholders' Equity, (*thousands*)

Three Years ended December 31, 1981	1981 Capital Stock		1980	1979
	Number of Shares	Amount	Retained Earnings	Total
Balance at December 31, 1978	**39,832**	**$ 70,618**	**$134,444**	**$205,062**
Proceeds from sales of shares through employee stock plans and tax benefit thereof	1,180	19,869	—	19,869
Acquisition of MRI, Inc.	372	4,562	(4,108)	454
Net income	—	—	77,804	77,804
Balance at December 31, 1979	**41,384**	**95,049**	**208,140**	**303,189**
Proceeds from sales of shares through employee plans and tax benefit thereof	1,352	32,930	—	32,930
Net income	—	—	96,741	96,741
Balance at December 31, 1980	**42,736**	**127,979**	**304,881**	**432,860**
Proceeds from sales of shares through employee stock plans and tax benefit thereof	1,030	27,598	—	27,598
Net income	—	—	27,359	27,359
Balance at December 31, 1981	**43,766**	**$155,577**	**$332,240**	**$487,817**

See accompanying notes provided in company's annual report.

Source: Intel Corporation, *Annual Report,* 1981.

197

EXHIBIT 7 (Continued)

Intel Corporation Consolidated Balance Sheet,
(dollars in thousands)

December 31, 1981 and 1980	1981	1980
Assets		
Current assets:		
Cash and short-term investments at cost, which approximates market	$115,260	$127,681
Accounts receivable, net of allowance for doubtful accounts of $3,878 ($4,296 in 1980)	179,604	195,644
Inventories	97,452	91,401
Prepaid taxes on income and other assets	67,454	31,883
Total current assets	**459,770**	**446,609**
Property, plant and equipment:		
Land and buildings	215,519	165,831
Machinery and equipment	279,676	222,140
Construction in progress	80,269	48,417
Equipment leased to others	15,478	10,546
	590,942	446,934
Less: Accumulated depreciation	179,195	126,375
Property, plant and equipment, net	**411,747**	**320,559**
Total Assets	**$871,517**	**$767,168**
Liabilities and Shareholders' Equity		
Current liabilities:		
Notes payable	$ 31,889	$ 11,844
Accounts payable	41,700	30,350
Deferred income on shipments to distributors	52,683	46,033
Accrued liabilities	45,705	39,902
Profit sharing retirement plan accrual	—	15,250
Income taxes payable	—	3,892
Total current liabilities	**171,977**	**147,271**
7% Convertible subordinated debentures	**150,000**	**150,000**
Deferred taxes on income	**44,019**	**23,266**
Unamortized investment tax credits	**17,704**	**13,771**
Shareholders' equity:		
Capital stock, no par value, 75,000,000 shares authorized	155,577	127,979
Retained earnings	332,240	304,881
Total Shareholders' Equity	**487,817**	**432,860**
Total Liabilities and Shareholders' Equity	**$871,517**	**$767,168**

See accompanying notes provided in company's annual report.

Source: Intel Corporation, *Annual Report,* 1981.

EXHIBIT 7 (Continued)

Intel Corporation Financial Summary, 1972–1981
(thousands—except per share amounts)

Ten Years ended December 31, 1981

| | Net Investment in Plant and Equip. | Total Assets | Long-Term Debt | Shareholders' Equity | Working Capital Provided by | | Working Capital Used for Net Additions to Plant and Equip. |
					Operations	Employee Stock Plans	
1981	$411,747	$871,517	$150,000	$487,817	$115,021	$27,598	$154,164
1980	320,559	767,168	150,000	432,860	153,751	32,930	152,151
1979	217,391	500,093	—	303,189	124,961	19,869	96,681
1978	160,140	356,565	—	205,062	78,025	12,025	104,157
1977	80,117	221,246	—	148,942	49,777	7,766	44,881
1976	51,069	156,568	—	109,460	38,018	10,073	32,073
1975	28,474	102,719	—	74,173	24,232	7,100	11,169
1974	22,186	75,410	—	50,799	25,515	3,135	12,783
1973	13,015	50,567	—	27,888	12,402	1,278	9,113
1972	5,376	21,944	—	17,396	3,552	684	2,104

| | Net Revenues | Cost of Sales | Research and Development | Other Costs and Expenses, Net | Net Income | |
					Total	Per Share
1981	$788,676	$458,308	$116,496	$186,513	$27,359	$0.61
1980	854,561	399,438	96,426	261,956	96,741	2.21
1979	660,984	313,106	66,735	203,339	77,804	1.85
1978	399,390	196,376	41,360	117,340	44,314	1.08
1977	282,549	143,979	27,921	78,933	31,716	0.80
1976	225,979	117,193	20,709	62,863	25,214	0.63
1975	136,788	67,649	14,541	38,324	16,274	0.42
1974	134,456	67,909	10,500	36,271	19,776	0.53
1973	66,170	35,109	4,565	17,282	9,214	0.25
1972	23,417	12,425	3,442	4,466	3,084	0.09

Source: Intel Corporation, *Annual Report,* 1981.

APPENDIX A—GLOSSARY

Bit Contraction for binary digit. A bit is a 0 or 1. Bits are usually grouped together to form bytes (8 bits) or words (4, 8, 16, 32, etc., bits).

Byte A group of 8 bits.

CMOS Complementary metal oxide semiconductor technology. CMOS offers the advantages of very low power consumption and high noise immunity. CMOS uses both n-channel and p-channel transistors and has speed and density characteristics between NMOS and PMOS.

CPU The central processing unit. The part of the computer responsible for fetching, decoding, and executing instructions. The CPU contains the control unit, arithmetic logic unit and related support facilities such as clocks, drivers, and registers.

Dynamic RAM (DRAM) A dynamic read/write memory. Each data bit is stored as a charge on a single MOS transistor. This design permits high circuit densities, but the charge "leaks" away. Therefore, in a typical dynamic memory

199

the data must be "refreshed" (recharged) every 2 milliseconds. This process requires additional refresh logic, usually external to the chip. Dynamic memory chips are less expensive than static ones and are frequently preferred for memory size over 16K.

E²PROM (EEPROM or "E-square PROM") A read-only memory that can be electrically reprogrammed in the field (a limited number of times) after the entire memory is erased by an electric field.

EPROM Erasable programmable read-only memory. An EPROM can be reprogrammed several times. EPROM typically refers to an erasable PROM in which all data can be erased by exposing the chip to a powerful ultraviolet light source for several minutes. The IC can then be reprogrammed (by the user) with a PROM-programmer and will retain its data contents for several years. EPROMs that can be erased with electricity are called EEPROMs.

IC Integrated circuit. A device that incorporates a circuit of several electronic components in a single package. The number of components, typically transistors, can range from 2 to several hundred thousand.

Linear (Analog) Having a continuous variable signal as in a radio wave, TV transmission, or telephone signal. Linear ICs accept and manipulate analog signals.

LSI Large-scale integration (incorporating 500 to 10,000–20,000 transistors/chip).

MOS Metal-oxide semiconductor technology. A semiconductor process technology named for the three successive layers of materials used. MOS is used to fabricate most high density (LSI and VLSI) devices such as microprocessors and memories.

PROM A programmable read-only memory (ROM). PROMs may be programmed by the user. PROM programmers are typically external devices used to write bit patterns into the user-programmable ROM. PROMs, like all ROMs, are non-volatile.

RAM Random-access memory. A memory device allowing the repeated storage and retrieval of information (sometimes called "read/write" memory). RAMs are usually volatile, that is, all data are lost when power is removed.

ROM Read-only memory. ROMs include mask-type ROMs, PROMs, EPROMs, and EEPROMs. All ROMs retain their data without power.

SLSI Super-large-scale integration (or ULSI) technology incorporating over 500,000 transistors per IC.

Static RAM Read/write memories not requiring dynamic refresh. Static RAMs offer lower densities but similar speeds to dynamic RAMs (DRAMs). Like dynamic memories, static RAMs retain data only as long as power is supplied.

VLSI Very-large-scale integration incorporating approximately 10,000 to 50,000–100,000 transistors per chip.

Wafer A round slice of silicon ingot upon which integrated circuits are fabricated. The ICs on a wafer (dice) are tested, cut into chips, packaged, further tested, and then sold as finished ICs.

BIOGEN N.V.

In 1976, two major start-ups, Cetus and Genentech, were busily recruiting the top American talent in the newly emerging field of biotechnology. Ray Schaefer of Inco (a Canadian mining and metals company) had been stimulated by Moshe Alafi, a venture capitalist who was then chairman of Cetus, to invest in the industry. Schaefer convinced Inco's venture capital arm to participate in Cetus and later Genentech. But he also saw an opportunity to start another company, Biogen N.V.

While many university chemists and engineers had worked as consultants to industrial corporations, few molecular biologists had done so, especially in Europe where such "commercial" relationships were actively discouraged. With much negotiation and persuasiveness Schaefer and Alafi finally signed up seven outstanding European and three leading American researchers. All were reasonably senior scientists, and many were heads of their university departments. In this tightly knit field most of them already knew each other, and all spoke English. Luring the scientists took more than just stock (which they received at $0.0125 per share). Special relationships had to be set up with the individual scientists and the universities to maintain their academic independence and to honor the fact that virtually all European universities and university research are supported through public funding. These relationships proved to be critical to the whole Biogen strategy.[1]

Although Schaefer and Alafi had originally expected only one or two of the major scientists they contacted to become actively involved with the company's operations (as was the case with other biotech start-ups), they suddenly found they had lined up perhaps the industry's richest international talent pool of academic microbiologists. These key scientists became members of Biogen's Scientific Board

Copyright © 1989 James Brian Quinn. This case was prepared by Penny C. Paquette under the supervision of Professor Quinn using secondary sources only.

which chose its own members and elected one-third (5) of the Board of Supervisory Directors, which managed the business aspects of Biogen—with the notable exception of its research programs. As founding shareholders the members of the Scientific Board also had antidilution rights—that is, the Supervisory Board could not issue more than 10,000 shares in any year without their approval. It was the Scientific Board's role to determine the company's scientific direction by allocating funds within the program, approving projects, and monitoring scientific activities. Each project was directed by one or more members of the Scientific Board.

Biogen Forms

In May 1978, Biogen N.V. was officially created as a Netherlands Antilles corporation with a Swiss operating subsidiary. It started with paid-in capital of $750,000 provided by Inco (in payment for 2,155,000 shares, 1,250,000 at $0.20 per share, the rest for Inco's preincorporation services), a Boston venture capital firm, Moshe Alafi, and some European investors. Until early 1980, the company acted simply as a financial conduit to support the research directed by Biogen's Scientific Board members at their respective universities.

The Board's ten scientists, each of whom was considered a world authority in his particular field, included

- Walter Gilbert, Ph.D., American Cancer Society Professor of Molecular Biology at Harvard University and member of the National Academy of Sciences. Dr. Gilbert later won a Nobel prize for his work on insulin production utilizing bacteria.
- Walter C. Fiers, Ph.D., professor and chairman of the Department of Molecular Biology at the University of Ghent, Belgium, who was working on human fibroblast (beta) and immune (gamma) interferons, tumor necrosis factor and interleukin-2. (See Exhibit 2B for a brief description of these and the other important substances being researched as possible therapeutic agents.)
- Brian S. Hartley, Ph.D., head of the Biochemistry Department at Imperial College in England, who was working on ethanol production using strains of thermophilic microorganisms that ferment biomass efficiently.
- Peter-Hans Hofschneider, M.D., Ph.D., professor of biochemistry at the medical faculty of the Ludwig Maxmillian University of Munich and head of the Virology Department and chairman of the Max Planck Institute for Biochemistry in Munich. He was a specialist in research on foot-and-mouth disease.
- Bernard Mach, M.D., Ph.D., professor and chairman of the Department of Microbiology at the University of Geneva Medical School and a member of the Swiss Science Council. His interests included erythropoietin and the development of a malaria vaccine.
- Kenneth Murray, Ph.D., professor and head of the Department of Molecular Biology at the University of Edinburgh, Scotland, whose work concentrated on hepatitis B vaccine development.
- Heinz Schaller, Ph.D., professor of microbiology and director of the Institute of Microbiology at Heidelberg University.
- Phillip Sharp, Ph.D., associate professor of biology at the Massachusetts Institute of Technology, who was focusing on development of animal growth hormones.

- Daniel Wang, Ph.D., professor of chemical and biochemical engineering at the Massachusetts Institute of Technology. His main area of concentration was biotechnological process development and process scale-up to production levels including computer controls.
- Charles Weissmann, M.D., Ph.D., professor of molecular biology and director of the Institute of Molecular Biology at the University of Zurich. Dr. Weissmann was a recognized world authority on interferon research. Many thought he also would emerge as a Nobel Prize winner.

The Scientific Board—originally conceived primarily as an advisory or consulting board—contained members with an interest in each of the major scientific and technical specialties that comprised the overall biotechnology field. In addition to the application areas described above, these included structure of genes; the expression of proteins in bacteria; the molecular biology of yeasts, viruses, and mammalian cells; ethanol production and host-vector systems; the molecular biology of immune response systems; the development of vaccines against various viruses; enzyme purification and the use of immobilized cells for biological production processes; and biotechnological process development and process scale-up to production levels.

Early Management Issues

At first, Dan Adams of Inco served as the general business manager of Biogen. When Adams left as a result of internal disagreements with Inco, Walter Gilbert (who was then chairman of the Scientific Board and co-chairman of the Supervisory Board) stepped in and ran the business from his office at Harvard until November 1979, when the company found a full-time president and CEO for Biogen S.A.—Robert Cawthorn, former executive vice president of Pfizer/Europe. Meanwhile, efforts were continuing to raise additional capital—a never-ending task in an industry in its research stage where money had to be plowed into projects for years before product revenues might emerge.

After scouring Europe for support and discovering that investing in a "concept" company was considered too risky there, Biogen hit big with the second company it approached in the United States. Schering-Plough, a major pharmaceutical company, put up $8 million for a 16% interest in the company and a worldwide license to market three Biogen products of its choosing. Shareholder agreements stipulated that as many as 5 Supervisory Board directors could be designated by the major corporate shareholders. Schering-Plough reportedly invested in Biogen because of the latter's leadership position in interferon research. As one executive vice president explained, "You just couldn't hire people like that to work in an industrial setting." At this time, Inco also put in another $1.25 million (250,000 shares at $5 per share) raising total paid-in capital to $10 million.

1980 was a pivotal year for Biogen. First, Walter Gilbert won the Nobel prize in chemistry. Then Dr. Weissmann announced that he had cloned and expressed the previously elusive protein interferon, which was expected to provide the most important new drug class since antibiotics. Although the interferon produced was not identical to human interferon and the bacterial cells produced interferon at a rate 1,000 times slower than human cells, the announcement catapulted Biogen into the headlines. Interferon was supposed to be the golden drug of a new era, a $2 billion-a-year product, and Wall Street was obsessed with the question of who would clone interferon first. Finally on June 17, 1980, the U.S. Supreme Court paved the way for patent protection in biotechnology by ruling 5 to 4 that new forms of life which could only be created by imaginative human intervention at the laboratory or mass production level could be patented. Chemicals, products, or life forms occurring in their natural or "true" state are generally not patentable. When natural substances can be reproduced in quantity only by rDNA processes, both the product and the process may be patented. Each individual process based on a different "expression system" (bacterium, yeast, or mammalian cell) can allow patentability. Totally new muteins or analogs may be patented as new "compositions of matter," giving potentially very strong protected positions.

Based on these events, Schering-Plough and Inco each put more capital ($4 million and $4.61 million, respectively) into the company. Monsanto invested another $20 million for a 12.5% interest in Biogen (even though Monsanto was simultaneously establishing its own in-house molecular biology center). Schering-Plough also began paying Biogen R&D fees under its shareholder agreement concerning the three projects it could select for further proprietary development.

Biogen opened small laboratories in both Geneva, Switzerland, and Cambridge, Massachusetts; and the transition from a financial conduit to a real operating entity began. Soon Biogen N.V. (as holding company) had four subsidiaries—each with its own management. Biogen S.A. (Switzerland) was the original operating subsidiary doing contract research for Biogen N.V., which held the rights to all the corporation's technologies. Biogen Research Corporation (U.S.) became an American subsidiary doing contract research. Biogen, Inc. (U.S.) was to become Biogen N.V.'s U.S. marketing and manufacturing arm run by Robert Fildes formerly of the Bristol Labs, a subsidiary of Bristol-Myers. Biogen B.V. (Netherlands) was responsible for licensing the group's technology and obtaining royalties from third parties.

DECISION POINT

1. Evaluate Biogen's actions to date. Why was Biogen developed the way it was? What do you think about the way it was financed? Organized? What arguments could Biogen have most persuasively used to attract researchers and universities to join in this endeavor?

2. How should Biogen position itself in the fledgling biotechnology industry? What pattern of research projects should be undertaken? Why? Assuming a senior researcher and his or her support costs about $200,000 per year, how would you allocate resources among various goals? Stages of R&D? Product versus process development? How should the corporate shareholders influence this positioning?

1981–1983: A GROWTH ERA

During 1981, Grand Metropolitan, a large British conglomerate which hoped that the company would identify and develop biotechnology applications in the food and beverage industry, acquired $10 million worth of preferred stock (a 5.3% interest if converted) in Biogen. Inco also invested another $2.5 million (200,000 shares at $12.50 per share). In August Walter Gilbert took over as CEO of Biogen S.A. from Cawthorn who remained president. Gilbert served as chairman of the Board of Supervisory Directors, the Scientific Board, and was chairman of the Board of Biogen, Inc. and Biogen Research Corp. Harvard forced Gilbert to resign his academic post at this time. When asked why he accepted the company posts instead of staying in academia, Gilbert replied, "I found that I was too much involved behind the scenes, and so I stepped forward to run [Biogen] myself. I found myself very strongly involved in the central management of the company, but as a consultant. I was doing it unofficially and finally I found that role confining."[1]

The company soon had three scientists from its Scientific Board working full time as employees rather than as consultants. Besides Gilbert, two newer members of the board, Julian Davies and Richard Flavell were, respectively, president of Biogen S.A. and Biogen Research Corporation. Each was also director of his entity's research laboratories. Davies was formerly Steenbock Professor of Biomolecular Structure at the University of Wisconsin. The defection of Dr. Flavell in 1981 from his post as head of the Laboratory of Gene Structure at Britain's National Institute for Medical Research caused rumors of a "biotechnology brain drain" in England and at least indirectly led to the creation of Celltech Ltd., a British biotechnology consortium, sponsored in part by the government. Meanwhile many of the top business people recruited earlier moved on to other opportunities—Cawthorn in April 1982 became president of Rorer International Corp., a pharmaceutical company, and Fildes in December 1982 became CEO of Cetus. Mark Skaletsky (age 34), who in 1981 had followed Fildes from Bristol Labs to handle Biogen's product development and licensing, became President of Biogen, Inc. Barrie James from Merck's international division became vice president-director of business development of Biogen B.V. But no one replaced Cawthorn as president of Biogen S.A.

Basic Approaches

The *Economist* in late 1980 compared the biotech industry to the early semiconductor industry:

> Genetic engineering today is at the stage the transistor was in during the early 1950s. In the then budding electronics industry lots of firms were making prototypes of transistorized products in the laboratory—but a single transistor cost $15 and a mass market had still to be found. In the end, many of the pioneers lost out to latecomers. So it is likely to be in genetic engineering. It is too early to say who will be the Texas Instruments of this industry. And, remember, at the stage genetic engineering is now, nobody guessed that the transistor would be overtaken by the integrated circuit.[2]

Dr. Davies described the Geneva Labs' approach at this stage as follows: "We set up the research unit here in the same way as in Cambridge—to allow people the flexibility and time and ideas to be able to express themselves. The labs don't close. We want people to be able to work at night and weekends, and they do." While it is not a scientific utopia because proprietary interests "prevent one from talking as freely with one's scientific colleagues as one might," Biogen was fairly liberal in this respect. The company tried to foster the informality of the academic world, yet keep the company's commercial interests in mind. About half of the researchers were pursuing some projects that at that point had no clear practical value to Biogen.

From the beginning, Biogen had proclaimed its objective was to become a large commercial company—"the Texas Instruments of our field," said Cawthorn. In 1983 Gilbert was quoted as saying, "We have a vision of being a company of a certain size . . . we're not looking for small niches." Dr. Flavell observed: "While in any basic research activity you have clearly defined goals, those goals were now a bit different—to produce a product. This makes it, in a sense, more satisfying, because [such research] begins where I always used to begin, but it ends very much further along than I would ever have ended [in the past]." Biogen's leaders quickly recognized it could not become a major company by merely conducting research or working for clients on a cost-plus contract basis. Yet the company initially had only pilot fermentation facilities—a 300-liter fermenter in Geneva and a 1,000-liter fermenter in Zurich—and no clinical affairs group capable of planning and supervising regulatory testing or sales force to market its products. And many of Biogen's early commercial arrangements involved worldwide licenses giving Biogen only royalties on sales, plus reimbursement of specified research and clinical testing costs.

An Expanded Program

From 1980 to early 1983, Biogen grew rapidly and continued to broaden its research base. By the end of 1982, Biogen had 250 full-time employees, of which 79 held Ph.D. degrees; 13 held other advanced scientific degrees. There were 153 employees in Geneva and Zurich, 92 in Cambridge, and 5 in Ghent. Of the 250 total, 203 were engaged in research and development; 47 in management and administrative capacities. More than 3/4 of Biogen's research activities were now being conducted in its own laboratories. (In 1980, 1981, and 1982 Biogen research conducted in university labs accounted for 48%, 28%, and 16%, respectively, of the company's R&D expenditures.)

Under its investment agreement, Schering-Plough picked up worldwide rights to three products, alpha and beta interferon and erythropoietin, a substance which stimulated the production of red blood cells and might be useful in treating several anemias. It rapidly developed alpha interferon, began clinical trials in September 1981 in both Europe and the United States, planned a production facility in Ireland, and hoped to bring the substance to market by 1984–1985. Genentech and its partner Hoffman LaRoche (a major Swiss pharmaceutical company) began trials of their alpha interferon about six months later. However, results began to indicate that alpha interferon was not effective for some common types of cancer (e.g., advanced colon, breast, and lung cancers) and for certain viral infections. Cancer provides one of the most difficult targets for product development because of the heterogeneity of the disease itself and the variable courses it may follow in different individuals. Animal tests are often not valid predictors of human responses, and *in vivo* human testing is costly and fraught with risks, objective sampling problems, and ethical issues. For example, should "double-blind" protocols be maintained if one believes the drug is the patient's only hope of living?

Nevertheless tests of alpha interferon continued on other cancers and infectious diseases, but flu-like side effects often became severe at high dosages. Schering-Plough moved to clinical trials of alpha interferon (in a nasal spray form) as a cold preventative, a market which some analysts thought could be as large as $200 million a year. The interferons, although natural substances themselves, became the first biotechnology products to be studied for use as true drugs—rather than to augment or replace the patients' shortage of chemicals performing normal physiological functions, such as insulin. But in early 1983, Biogen had not yet produced a beta interferon for preclinical or clinical testing—since it seemed this substance would perform basically the same functions in humans as alpha interferon.

Genentech had been the first to report the synthesis of biologically active immune (or gamma) interferon and file-related patent applications. But Biogen was not far behind and was actively pursuing this product, which it believed could both bolster the human immune response system and serve as a useful anti-tumor agent. By early 1983 Biogen had produced gamma interferon of high purity in amounts sufficient to conduct animal and preclinical trials in tissue. In 1982, Biogen had signed a license and development agreement with Shionogi & Co. Ltd. pursuant to which Shionogi would provide clinical and commercial development of immune interferon in Japan and Taiwan. Biogen was to supply the substance for clinical trials and could, at its option, supply part of all of Shionogi's requirements for later commercialization. No licensing arrangements had been concluded for the product's commercialization in Europe or the United States.

A Broad Spectrum

As of early 1983 Biogen's other research efforts and licensing agreements were as follows:

- In collaboration with Novo Industri A/S—one of the two largest producers of animal-based insulin—Biogen was working toward the production of human insulin using rDNA technology. Genentech's licensee, Eli Lilly, had already begun marketing a recombinant human insulin, the first biotechnology product to gain FDA approval.

- Other human proteins in development included Factor VIII (to be used for blood clotting in the treatment of hemophilia), human serum albumin (for transfusion purposes), and tissue plasminogen activator (TPA) for dissolving blood clots. Biogen had licensed its human serum albumin in Japan and Taiwan to Shionogi and reached an agreement with Fujisawa Pharmaceutical Co. for the development and commercialization of TPA in Japan, Taiwan, and South Korea. Factor VIII was licensed to Teijin Ltd. for most of the southeast Pacific area. And Biogen and KabiVitrum AB would collaborate on development of commercial Factor VIII products with Kabi having the right to market such products in selected countries outside North America.

- Several lymphokines (substances made by white blood cells that serve as signals for the functioning or multiplication of other white blood cell types) were also under development. These included tumor necrosis factor (TNF), interleukin-2 (IL-2) and macrophage activation factor (later referred to as colony stimulating factor). Shionogi and Biogen would collaborate on the development of interleukin-2 under similar arrangements to those for gamma interferon.

- In human vaccines Biogen had concentrated on various types of hepatitis and a malaria vaccine. Biogen scientists were the first to report the synthesis of hepatitis B antigens in *E. coli* bacteria. The company had begun to receive limited revenues from the sale of hepatitis B core antigen for diagnostic kits manufactured by various companies and had a license agreement with Green Cross for a potential vaccine. However, Chiron and Merck were about to begin clinical trials with a yeast-based hepatitis vaccine.

- Biogen had major projects on: (1) a vaccine for foot-and-mouth disease in cattle and pigs, (2) the production of animal growth hormones for cows and pigs under agreements with International Minerals & Chemicals Corporation, and (3) the production of a broad spectrum, biodegradable herbicide for a Japanese company. Work on Biogen's ethanol project had been suspended due to depressed petroleum prices. A joint feasibility study with Inco (testing the use of biotechnology to produce organisms for extraction of non-ferrous metals from low-grade ores and other mineral sources) was continuing.

Biogen had begun receiving research and development fees from its corporate shareholders and others in 1980. While such fees had increased dramatically, so had the amounts being invested in research and development; and plans were already underway to build a $25 million production plant in Cambridge, Massachusetts. Future plans called for creation of major production facilities in Europe since export controls on U.S. companies did not affect non-FDA sanctioned drugs made and approved for use in Europe.

Public or Other Financing?

From 1980 through early 1983, the biotechnology industry had grown substantially. As the industry grew and matured, financing options expanded as well. In October 1980, Genentech became the first biotech company to "go public." Its initial public offering set a new Wall Street record for the fastest ever price increase per share—from $35 to $89 in 20 minutes—and netted the company some $36.6 million. In March 1981 Cetus followed suit and raised $119 million, setting its own Wall Street record—for the most money raised in an initial public offering. By the end of 1981 more than 80 biotechnology firms had been formed, including a specialized new group concentrating on monoclonal antibodies for diagnostic tests and the new forms of drug delivery monoclonals allowed. And Agrigenetics, a firm specializing in agricultural applications of biotechnology, had pioneered the use of R&D limited partnerships as a financing source in the industry. Table 1 summarizes Biogen's financial history through 1982.

Many European governments now recognized the potentials of biotechnology and began trying to expand their domestic biotech industries. But options for private financing in Europe remained quite limited as compared to the United States where by the end of 1982 more than $1.1 billion of non-government investment ($550 million from corporations, $450 million from public sales of stock, and over $100 million from venture capitalists and institutions) had poured into the industry. Table 2 presents summary financials for some of Biogen's competitors—those already publicly held and several then considering possible IPOs. Exhibit 1 shows 1980–1984 trends in both the overall stock market and in biotechnology stocks.

DECISION POINT

1. Given its recent technical progress and its overall strategy and goals, approximately how much more capital does Biogen need in early 1983? For what purposes?

2. What are Biogen's options in terms of financing? What are the major pros and cons of each?

3. What factors should Biogen's management consider in structuring each possible major capital option—that is, an initial public offering? Limited partnerships? Private placements with institutions or corporations? Industrial revenue bonds? Other?

4. If Biogen decides to go public, how should it price its stock? At what price would you buy it? Why?

TABLE 1 **Biogen N.V.:** Selected Statement of Operations Information, 1978–1982 *(in thousands, except per share data)*

	MAY 5 TO DECEMBER 31, 1978	YEAR ENDED DECEMBER 31			
		1979	1980	1981	1982
Revenues					
Research and development fees:					
Affiliates	—	—	$ 1,689	$ 3,940	$ 5,487
Other	—	—	250	1,550	6,655
Total	—	—	1,939	5,490	12,142
Interest	$ 24	$ 83	1,045	7,229	8,482
Total revenues	24	83	2,984	12,719	20,624
Expenses					
Research and development	204	896	3,532	8,932	18,420
General and administrative	81	999	1,339	3,870	5,534
Interest	—	—	—	317	552
Exchange losses (gains)	—	(123)	643	(19)	62
Total expense	285	1,772	5,514	13,100	24,568
Loss before income taxes and extraordinary item	261	1,689	2,530	381	3,944
Income taxes	—	8	228	401	762
Loss before extraordinary item	261	1,697	2,758	782	4,706
Extraordinary item	—	—	—	—	(215)
Net loss	$ 261	$1,697	$ 2,758	$ 782	$ 4,491
Loss per share					
Loss before extraordinary item	$0.04	$0.17	$0.27	$0.05	$0.29
Extraordinary item	—	—	—	—	(0.01)
Net loss	$0.04	$0.17	$0.27	$0.05	$0.28
Weighted average number of shares outstanding	6,340	9,990	10,372	14,792	16,180

Selected Balance Sheet Information, 1978–1982 *(in thousands)*

		AT DECEMBER 31,			
	1978	1979	1980	1981	1982
Working capital	$ 428	$4,635	$29,402	$63,745	$51,667
Property and equipment, net	—	325	1,281	7,106	14,373
Total assets	1,230	5,987	33,885	77,348	73,508
Long-term debt, excluding current portion	—	—	—	7,171	5,860
Shareholders' equity	466	5,060	31,153	65,921	61,876

Other Selected Information

Number of employees at year-end	—	3	41	154	250

TABLE 2 Financial Summaries, 1978–1982 ($000)

	GENENTECH				
	12/78	12/79	12/80	12/81	12/82
Revenues					
R&D	796.5	2,581.6	6,498.6	15,207.4	28,837.7
Interest	56.6	524.2	2,463.5	6,073.3	3,765.5
Other	3.2	300.0			
Total	856.3	3,405.8	8,962.1	21,280.8	32,603.2
Expenses					
R&D					
G&A					
Interest					
Other					
Total	1,229.6	3,278.0	8,691.8	20,702.8	31,911.0
Profit (loss)	(373.3)	127.8	270.3	578.0	692.2
Taxes		46.3	120.0	278.0	67.0
Extraordinary items		86.0	34.8	203.0	
Net profit (loss)	(373.3)	116.3	236.3	503.0	625.2
Working capital		9,943.2	43,191.2	29,109.7	41,376.2
Total assets		12,127.1	50,504.7	66,244.8	101,243.9
Long-term obligations		67.0	47.0	6,766.1	6,285.3
Shareholders' equity		11,164.4	47,783.2	53,132.8	84,295.8

	CHIRON		IMMUNEX	
	4/82	4/83	12/81	12/82
Revenues				
R&D	833.3	1,579.0		940.0
Interest	14.6	139.2	41.3	155.2
Other	30.0			
Total	877.9	1,718.2	41.3	1,095.2
Expenses				
R&D	1,227.2	3,182.6		1,438.5
G&A	307.3	661.0	98.3	502.4
Interest	29.7	104.5		
Other				
Total	1,564.2	3,948.1	101.1	1,981.8
Profit (loss)	(686.3)	(2,229.9)	(59.8)	(886.6)
Taxes				
Extraordinary items				
Net profit (loss)	(686.3)	(2,229.9)	(59.8)	(886.6)
Working capital	(714.3)	1,165.0	762.9	1,131.5
Total assets	1,777.5	4,625.1	1,030.5	4,005.5
Long-term obligations	201.7	742.0	51.7	842.5
Shareholders' equity	300.3	2,973.5	911.1	2,999.2

TABLE 2 (Continued)

211
BIOGEN N.V.

	CETUS				
	6/1978	6/1979	6/1980	6/1981	6/1982
Revenues					
R&D	2,066.2	2,896.7	8,538.5		15,214.5
Interest	315.9	683.3	947.7	5,742.3	16,701.9
Other	24.2	43.9	135.6		972.1
Total	2,406.3	3,623.9	9,621.8	15,621.7	32,603.2
Expenses					
R&D	4,071.2	5,765.4	9,178.3		20,343.4
G&A					7,515.9
Interest	85.3	16.2	367.6		
Other					
Total	4,156.5	5,781.6	9,545.9	15,031.0	27,859.3
Profit (loss)	(1,750.2)	(2,157.7)	75.9	578.0	692.2
Taxes			7.0	278.0	67.0
Extraordinary items			34.8		1,504.8
Net profit (loss)	(1,750.2)	(2,157.7)	86.9	503.0	4,504.8

Notes: **Genentech** went public in October 1980 at $35 per share. Some 1.1 million shares were sold with 7,572,102 shares outstanding after the IPO. Genentech planned to use the proceeds as follows: $4 million for equipment, $14 million for land and building construction, and the rest as working capital for R&D, clinical trials, inventories, and so on. At that time, the only major (owning more than 5%) corporate shareholder was Lubrizol, which had a 24% interest.

Chiron was founded in May 1981 by Drs. Rutter, Penhoet, and Valenzuela, three Ph.D.s in biochemistry. By early 1983 the company had 55 researchers and was considered the industry leader in production of proteins in yeast. Merck, the contract sponsor of Chiron's hepatitis B vaccine, had already filed an IND and would soon begin clinical trials. The company also had a strong portfolio of products at the research and development stage including other vaccines, epidermal growth factor, insulin-like growth factors, superoxide dismutase, growth hormone releasing factor, IL-2, and tissue plasminogen activator.

Immunex was founded in July 1981 by a businessman with no health care background and two scientists at the Fred Hutchinson Cancer Research Center in Seattle, Washington—Dr. Steve Gillis, who became director of R&D at Immunex, and Dr. Christopher Henney, who headed the cancer center's immunology program and was scientific director of the company. The company had 40 employees and did not have manufacturing facilities or a sales force. Immunex had collaborative research agreements with Hoffmann LaRoche for IL-2 and SmithKline for Macrophage Activating Factor. Other products in research and development phases included colony stimulating factors, and IL-1. The company had focused exclusively on immunological substances, especially lymphokines like IL-2 and CSFs. It also had developed a serum-free tissue culture medium which eliminated the problem of impurities in such cultures.

Cetus went public in March 1981 at a price of $23 per share. 5.5 million shares were sold by the company and 224,965 shares by selling shareholders. After the IPO there were 22,478,610 shares outstanding. Cetus planned to use the proceeds as follows: $27 million for production and distribution of Cetus products, $25 million for self-funded research, $24 million for research and administrative facilities, $19 million for equipment, and $12 million for new venture subsidiaries. Major (owning more than 5%) corporate shareholders at that time included National Distillers & Chemical Corp. (14.2%), SOCAL (22.4%), and Standard Oil of Indiana (27.6%).

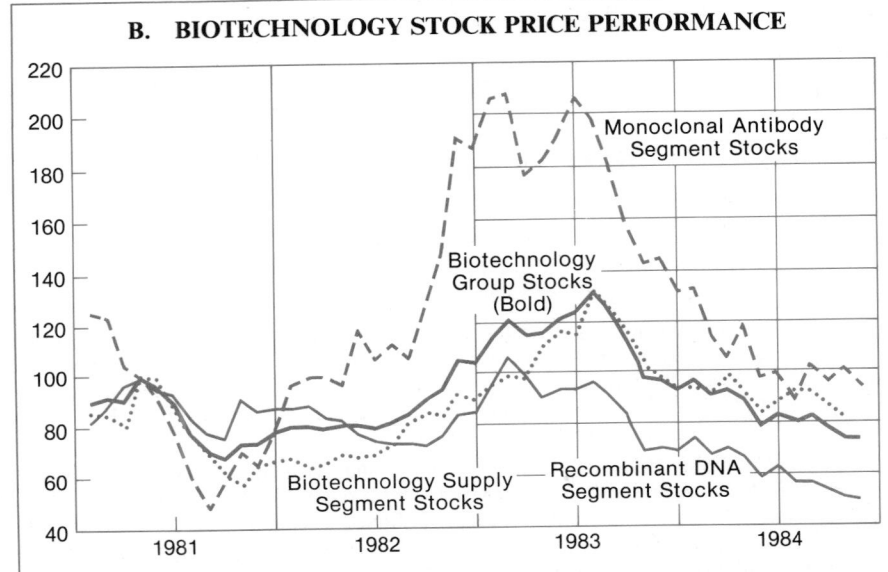

A. LOW-HIGH STOCK PRICE RANGES; 1981–1985
(in dollars per share, rounded)

Company	1981	1982	1983	1984	1985
Genentech	$26–48	$26–49	$26–49	$29–41	$34–73
Cetus	11–23	8–14	11–19	9–14	9–30
Amgen	—	—	6–15	4– 8	5–15
Immunex	—	—	6–14	4– 9	4–15
Chiron	—	—	6–12	4– 8	5–14
Biogen	—	—	—	4–14	6–19

Source: Moody's OTC Industrials, 1986.

B. BIOTECHNOLOGY STOCK PRICE PERFORMANCE

Biotechnology group & individual segments stock price performance relative to the S&P 500 indexed to 100 at 4/81 for comparison.

Source: L. Miller, "Biotechnology: The Good, The Bad, and The Ugly," December 18, 1984, *Industry Analysis,* Paine Webber, Inc.

1985 SITUATION

After arranging for financing, Biogen accelerated its plans to independently develop and market certain selected products. And the company moved into a whole new stage of development. Julian Davies commented,

> There's no doubt that getting into the question of production and [clinical] trials involves a [new] formal and structured aspect of the company that we will have to accept. We now are looking for people who are experts in this kind of area, and they're very, very different from the kind of people we're looking for in research. We need dif-

ferent capabilities, we need different training, and to some extent we need people with totally different attitudes.[5]

In early 1984, Charles Weissmann was elected chairman of the Scientific Board and Mark Skaletsky was made principal operating officer of Biogen worldwide in addition to his position as president of Biogen, Inc. Biogen attempted to maintain a separation of R&D from manufacturing and marketing. While concerned about the need for more marketing guidance, Mark Skaletsky commented: "We have to be very careful about not losing our edge in the technology. If it means investing 15–20% of our revenues in research on an annual basis, we'll do that."[1] Although corporate headquarters were still in Geneva, Skaletsky and Gilbert remained based in Cambridge and spent about one week a month in Geneva. Relations between the scientists and the other experts were reportedly becoming strained, and Geneva scientists complained that the U.S. group got an inordinate share of publicity and credit for Biogen's scientific breakthroughs. Rumors spread of Gilbert's sometimes stormy relations with other scientists at Biogen, both in Cambridge and Geneva.

Competitor Situation 1985–1986

Genentech: By the end of 1985, Genentech had begun marketing of its first product, human growth hormone for which it had received orphan drug status from the FDA. This gave Genentech the distinction of being the first biotechnology company to become a fully integrated pharmaceutical firm. Sales of its human insulin by Eli Lilly were generating a growing stream of royalties for the company. During 1985, Genentech had total revenues of $90 million of which $5 million were from product sales. Net income was $5.6 million and total assets were $239 million.

Cetus: Although Cetus had focused heavily on the cancer market in terms of human therapeutics, it owned in varying degrees several other ventures within and outside of the human health field. These included joint ventures in the agricultural field (Agracetus), in the instruments field, in the *in vitro* diagnostics market (a proprietary DNA probe) and a minority interest in a company testing an ambulatory pump suitable for delivering complex cancer regimens. Cetus had more than 600 employees, two-thirds of whom were in R&D and manufacturing. In advance of the approval of its anticipated cancer therapeutics, Cetus expected to develop a sales force geared to covering the 2,400 registered oncologists. Cetus had made a profit of $1.4 million for 1985 on revenues of $57 million, only $35.8 million of which was represented by R&D fees. Working capital was almost $100 million.

Amgen: By early 1986, Amgen had succeeded in narrowing its losses to little more than $500,000 on revenues of $23.4 million. Amgen was one of the few companies with capabilities in all three systems of protein production (bacteria, yeast, and mammalian cells). The company was gearing up to produce diagnostics, specialty chemicals, and animal hormones as well as human therapeutics.

Genetics Institute: Genetics Institute was founded in late 1980 by two Harvard professors. Until mid-1986, the company's growth was financed through private placements; in May 1986, it raised $85 million in an initial public offering. The company was involved in agricultural products and industrial processing as well as human pharmaceuticals and diagnostics. At the time it went public, Genetics Institute had more than 250 employees, and a loss of $1.7 million for 1985 on revenues of $21 million.

Immunex: By 1986, Immunex had almost 200 employees. During 1985 it lost $4.4 million on revenues of $3.2 million consisting primarily of R&D fees. The firm was continuing its focus on immunology and its announced goal to become a fully integrated pharmaceutical firm. Negotiations were underway with Eastman Kodak to form a 50/50 joint venture which would provide Immunex with the manufacturing capacity it was currently lacking. The possibility also was being discussed of using Immunex's rapid assay process to screen the over 500,000 chemical compounds Kodak had synthesized.

Chiron: In early 1986, Chiron, which was best known for its yeast technology and vaccine design, was also exploring the possibility of a joint venture with Ciba-Geigy to develop a line of vaccines. With close to 200 employees, Chiron planned to develop and market ophthalmic products such as epidermal growth factors on its own. In mid-1986 Chiron had incurred a loss of $4 million on revenues of $8 million.

Biogen Responds

After some disappointments in obtaining financing Biogen was forced to commit more of its own internal resources to development than planned. $22 million was spent on R&D in 1983, while only $10.5 million in fees came in. 1983's loss of $11.6 million (which Gilbert said was acceptable in exchange for the increased competitive advantage Biogen would obtain when its product came to market) was shortly followed by a 1984 loss of $13 million, as more than $35 million sluiced into R&D and construction of production facilities in Geneva. To stanch these losses, dramatic action was taken. In November, 55 of the firm's 400 employees were dismissed. By December, Biogen's stock was trading at $5 per share; and on December 14, Gilbert abruptly resigned his position as CEO (although he remained on the Scientific Board and Supervisory Directors' Board). While company spokesmen maintained that the board had not pushed out Gilbert, internal observers conceded that "his resignation was not something they resisted."[3]

Mark Skaletsky was named acting CEO, and Biogen actively began searching for a permanent successor. Then came the thunderclap. In July 1985, Julian Davies (a key figure in hiring and training the company's young scientists and in negotiating licensing agreements) "sent shockwaves through the biotech community by resigning both his executive post and his position on Biogen's Scientific Board." He commented, "when I go to scientific meetings today, I often hear about the sort of research which I simply cannot do any more. The problem has never been the need for secrecy, as some suspected. . . . I do miss teaching and contacts with students. But the critical factor has been a loss of freedom to pursue studies not tied to immediate sales potentials."[4]

Not until late October 1985 was the search for a new CEO successful. Biogen named James Vincent to succeed Gilbert as chairman and CEO. Vincent, 46, was an experienced executive with a significant health care background and "a first-hand knowledge of the development of biotechnology" (gained when he put Allied Signal's Health and Scientific Products subsidiary into the biotech business by purchasing $10 million of Genetics Institute and negotiating a long-term R&D contract with them). Vincent inherited an organization pursuing many important programs in the human health care field. Exhibits 2–4 provide detailed information on Biogen's products, competitors, and financial status in 1985.

1. What are the main factors that led Biogen to its current position? What might have been done differently and why?

2. What are the key issues facing Vincent as he takes over the company? In what order should he deal with these issues?

3. What should Biogen's strategy be in the future? What, if any, are the unique aspects of strategy and strategy making in the biotechnology industry?

4. How should Biogen position itself relative to its main competitors? What elements of their strategies can you surmise?

EXHIBIT 2A
Biogen's Competitive Status by Product

Product	Major Competitors	Status Phase I	Status Phase II	Status Phase III	Patent Position	Partners/Licensees
ALPHA INTERFERON						
Natural Alpha 2	Biogen		NDA expected 6/86		Overlapping; Genentech	Worldwide, Schering-Plough
Natural Alpha 2	Genentech		NDA expected 6/86		Overlapping; Biogen	Worldwide, Hoffmann LaRoche
Consensus Analog	Amgen		✓	✓	Compos.-of-Matter	None
GAMMA INTERFERON						
Natural Equiv.	Biogen			✓	Filed: Poor Position	Far East, Shionogi
Natural	Genentech			✓	Pending: First To File	Europe, Boehringer; Japan, Daiichi
Natural	Amgen		✓		Pending: First Right Sequence	None
Natural	Suntory		✓		None	US, Schering-Plough
TUMOR NECROSIS FACTOR						
Natural	Biogen	✓			Pending; Behind Genentech	Japan, Suntory; Non-U.S., BASF
Natural	Genentech		✓		Pending; First Right Sequence	Japan, Fujisawa; Europe, Boehringer
Natural	Asahi		✓		First File; Sequence Error	Collaborating With Dainippon
Analog	Cetus		Trials 1986		Possible Good Position	None
INTERLEUKIN-2 (IL-2)						
Natural	Biogen	✓	✓		None	Far East, Shionogi
Natural Equiv.	Cetus		✓		Strong; Possible Pool Immunex	None
Natural	Immunex		✓		Strong; Possible Pool Cetus	Worldwide, Hoffmann LaRoche
Analog	Amgen	✓	✓		Sued by Cetus	Worldwide, Johnson & Johnson
MULLERIAN INHIBITING FACTORS						
Natural	Biogen	✓			Strong—Alone	None
COLONY STIMULATING FACTORS						
GM, G, Natural	Biogen		No Clinicals		None	Japan, Sumitomo
GM	Genetics Inst.		Trials 1986		Good	Worldwide, Sandoz
GM, M, & G	Immunex		Trials 1989/87		Filed After Gen. Inst.	Worldwide, Hoechst
M, Natural, Anal.	Cetus		'87 Maybe		Good	None
G	Amgen		'87 Maybe		Good, First To Clone	Far East, Kirin; US, direct

Product	Major Competitors	I	II	III	Patent Position	Partners/Licensees
TISSUE PLASMINOGEN ACTIVATOR						
Natural & Analog	Biogen	Trials 1986			None	Far East, Fujisawa; US, SmithKline
Natural & Analog	Genentech	IND 1986			Good, First US & UK	Europe, Boehringer; Japan, Mitsubishi
Analog	Chiron	Trials 1986			None	Worldwide, Hoechst
Natural	Genetics Inst.	Trials 1986			None	Worldwide, Burroughs Wellcome
LIPOCORTIN						
Natural	Biogen	Trials 1986–87			Filed After Cal. Bio.	Far East, Yamanouchi
Natural	Calif. Biotech.	No Date Set			Good, First To File	None
INTERLEUKIN-1 (IL-1)						
Alpha, Beta, & Inhibitors	Biogen	Preclinical Res.			?	None
Alpha, Beta, & Inhibitors	Immunex	Preclinical Res.			?	Licensed to Syntex
ERYTHROPOIETIN (EPO)						
Natural	Biogen	Preclinical Res.			?	Worldwide, Schering-Plough
Natural	Amgen		✓		Good	Far East, Kirin; US & Europe, J&J
Natural	Genetics Inst.		Trial 1986		?	Far East, Chugai
HEPATITIS B VACCINE						
Yeast Based	Biogen			✓	Not Applicable	Far East, Green Cross; Rest, Wellcome
Yeast Based	Chiron	✓	Approval 1986		″	Worldwide, Merck
Yeast Based	Amgen		✓ Trials 1986		″	Worldwide, Johnson & Johnson
Mammalian	Genentech	Trials 1986			″	Far East, Mitsubishi; US & Eur., Merieux
Yeast Based	Endotronics	Trials Ongoing			″	SmithKline
PORCINE GROWTH HORMONE						
Natural	Biogen	Animal Trials			″	IMC
Natural	Genentech	Animal Trials			″	SmithKline Beckman
Natural	Amgen	Preclinical Research			″	Monsanto

Source: Compiled from various analysts' reports and public documents of the various companies mentioned.

Sale of Drugs by Product Type

	1984 Worldwide Pharmaceutical Sales (U.S. $millions)	
Prescription of which:		89,730
Anti-infective	15,850	
Cardiovascular	15,540	
Internal Medicine	13,020	
Pain Control	11,870	
Topicals	7,010	
Nutritionals	6,870	
Respiratory	6,270	
Mental Health	6,060	
Other	7,240	
Over-the-Counter		12,210
Total		101,940

Sale of Drugs by Geographic Location

Country	1984 Sales (U.S. $millions)	1985–95 Growth Outlook
United States	22,410	Moderate
Japan	14,670	Moderate
West Germany	6,100	Moderate
France	5,600	Moderate
China	4,550	Low
Italy	4,390	High
United Kingdom	3,150	Low
Canada	1,600	Moderate
South Korea	1,400	High
Spain	1,385	Moderate
India	1,350	High
Mexico	1,220	Declining
Brazil	1,100	Declining
Argentina	800	Declining
Australia	640	Moderate
Indonesia	550	High
Others	31,025	
Total	101,940	

Source: Compiled from various analysts' reports and articles about biotechnology.

A useful distinction can be made between physiologic and pharmacologic use of such naturally occurring substances. Physiologic use is defined as the use of the substance in a manner designed to mimic its natural role as precisely as possible. Pharmacologic use implies that the role of the naturally occurring substance is that of a true drug. Higher doses are usually associated with pharmacologic uses and increase the incidence of toxicity or side effects. More importantly, the ultimate efficacy of the substance as a drug is much less certain than in a physiologic role.

ALPHA INTERFERON

Also known as leukocyte interferon, alpha interferon was the first of the interferons to be widely tested. Used alone, it did not prove to be effective against the more common (solid) cancers but is quite successful against certain rare cancers such as hairy cell leukemia and granulocytic leukemia. It has also been tested as a therapy against various infectious diseases. Annual market size estimates for the early 1990s range from $120 million up to $500 million.

There are some 20 different alpha interferons and Amgen has developed a consensus analog which incorporates the predominant features of many of those. While "natural" alpha interferon creates flu-like side effects which can be a problem with high dosages, Amgen's analog appears to create no such side effects. Competitive products in development include beta and gamma interferon and IL-2.

GAMMA INTERFERON

Gamma interferon is now being tested both as a monotherapy and in combination with Tumor Necrosis Factor (TNF), alpha interferon, and IL-2 against cancer and various infectious diseases. It inhibits cancer cell growth and is reportedly a more powerful stimulator of the immune system than other interferons. It appears to be effective against renal cell carcinoma and may be useful against other more common cancers in combination with TNF. (There seems to be some evidence that the combination of TNF and gamma interferon mimics the effects of IL-2.)

In a complicated multi-shot regimen, gamma interferon has been shown to have symptomatic value against rheumatoid arthritis and possibly other autoimmune diseases like lupus and ulcerative colitis. (Patients receiving gamma interferon have been noted to have high endogenous levels of steroids which suppress the immune system. This is useful for autoimmune diseases but may also suggest that the use of steroid inhibitors might increase gamma interferon's effectiveness against cancers and infections.) It is still unclear whether it acts as a disease-modifying agent as well as relieving symptoms.

Side effects of gamma interferon therapy are similar to those for alpha interferon. Market size estimates for the early 1990s vary from $75 million to $500 million.

219

TUMOR NECROSIS FACTOR (TNF)

Until very recently TNF's very identity was unclear. Rockefeller University showed it to be probably identical to a substance known as cachectin, which is a major mediator of septic shock. This is why several firms are developing monoclonal antibodies against TNF to counteract septic shock and cachexia (withering away or weight loss) in cancer patients. There seem to be at least two different TNFs, one of which is produced by T cells and the other of which is produced by monocytes and interacts with IL-2.

Testing to date has shown TNF alone to have no efficacy against any cancer, so most developers are concentrating on combination therapy. As one analyst said, "TNF may emerge as the monosodium glutamate of biotechnology—worth little by itself but extremely valuable in improving other agents." Meanwhile clinicians must navigate the fine line between TNF's anti-cancer properties and its capacity to induce systemic shock.

INTERLEUKIN-2 (IL-2)

IL-2 is being tested against cancer and various infectious diseases. It has shown to be quite effective against renal cell carcinoma, malignant melanoma, colorectal and ovarian cancers when administered using adoptive immunotherapy techniques developed by the National Cancer Institute. Effectiveness using direct administration has been limited to date. IL-2 may also be an alternative to CSFs in preventing infections in chemotherapy patients.

Annual market size estimates for the early 1990s vary from $75 million to $500 million.

MULLERIAN INHIBITING SUBSTANCE (MIS)

MIS is a protein which causes sexual differentiation. It is produced in fetal testes and causes regression of the Mullerian duct, thereby preventing development of the female reproductive system. Biogen preclinical research and testing indicates that MIS may be useful in treatment of tumors of the female reproductive system. Studies in animals show it to slow the growth of cancer cells but not kill them. Potentially troublesome side effects could be the inhibition of the growth of normal cells within the reproductive tract.

There are no competitive therapies now being developed which seem particularly promising.

COLONY STIMULATING FACTORS (CSFs)

CSFs stimulate the rapid multiplication of blood molecules. CSF-GM and IL-3 appear to have the broadest activity level; CSF-M stimulates the production of monocytes and activates them, and CSF-G (Pluropoetin) which stimulates early stage blood cells. CSF-G was devoid of toxicity in primate studies, but this may not be true of broad acting CSFs.

CSFs are being tested for use in preventing infections in cancer chemotherapy patients, severe burn cases, and AIDS complications. Other possible uses include significantly speeding up the reconstitution process following a bone marrow transplant and controlling infections related to trauma, organ transplantation, and diabetes.

Annual market size estimates in the early 1990s are more than $1 billion for all uses with the main use being by cancer patients and burn victims.

TISSUE PLASMINOGEN ACTIVATOR (TPA)

TPA is a blood clot dissolving agent with potential effectiveness against a variety of serious conditions caused by blood clots including heart attacks, pulmonary embolism, deep vein thrombosis, and unstable angina. Because it accumulates at blood clots where it converts plasminogen into an active molecule which can dissolve the clot, it is preferable to general anticoagulants which have the problem of creating systemic bleeding.

Another clot dissolving agent, Streptokinase, is currently used in similar situations but is not nearly as effective as TPA. Pro-urokinase, which appears to be virtually identical to TPA, should be cheaper to manufacture since it can be made in bacteria as opposed to mammalian cells. Acylated streptokinase is currently being tested and appears to have the possibility to be nearly as effective as TPA while being cheaper to manufacture.

LIPOCORTIN

Lipocortin is an anti-inflammatory agent which is expected to be nearly as potent as steroids but with much lower side effects. The benefits of lower side effects are most striking during longer term use or systemic use, but lipocortin currently has a shorter half-life than steroids and requires parenteral or topical administration.

Annual market size estimates for the early 1990s are about $50 million. Its major value may be as a research tool in the development of other anti-inflammatory agents which could be taken orally and are longer lasting.

INTERLEUKIN-1 (IL-1)

There seem to be at least two distinct IL-1 proteins—IL-1 alpha which stimulates skin cell proliferation and IL-1 beta which induces bone demineralization and cartilage destruction. IL-1 alpha may prove to be useful in accelerating wound healing, for severe burns, as a component in suntan lotions, acne preparations, and toothpaste.

Inhibitors to IL-1 beta may be useful in the treatment of rheumatoid arthritis, lupus, and ulcerative colitis and in the control of the rejection response in transplantation.

ERYTHROPOETIN (EPO)

EPO is a hormone produced mainly by the kidneys to stimulate the production of red blood cells. Testing is now underway for the use of EPO in the treatment of anemia in kidney dialysis patients. These patients now require frequent blood transfusions to increase the percentage of red cells in their blood. EPO therapy means they do not have to have transfusions but also seems to create iron deficiencies which then require modifications to their diets and thus increase dialysis requirements.

221

Other possible uses include treatment of anemia in kidney-impaired patients not yet requiring dialysis, treatment of other types of anemia, and treatment of elective surgery patients to create a stockpile of their own (red cell enriched) blood to reduce dependence on donated blood for transfusions. All of these uses depend on being able to administer EPO other than intravenously.

Annual market size estimates for 1990 are more than $200 million.

HEPATITIS B VACCINE

Hepatitis B vaccines provide immunization against hepatitis B which is a major problem in less developed countries and might well be added to the group of diseases for which immunization is required in developed nations.

The size of the market depends greatly on the price per dose. While immunization will probably still be undertaken in developed nations if the price remains at current levels, penetration of the large market in LDCs depends on achieving a substantially lower price per dose. At a lower price per dose the market could be as large as $200 million.

PORCINE GROWTH HORMONE

Porcine growth hormone has been shown to increase feed efficiency by 15–20% while increasing the leanness of the meat and allowing sows to produce additional milk for their young thus raising survival rates in litters. The market could be $200–400 million worldwide since there are 90 million hogs raised annually in the United States and 250 million elsewhere. That potential is limited by the delivery system, however, since hogs receive less human handling and are less valuable per animal than cows. The system must be reasonably cheap and simple and the market must place a premium on lean pork meat.

Source: Compiled from various analysts' reports and articles about biotechnology.

Persons with Selected Chronic Conditions: 1985

Chronic Condition	# Conditions (1,000)	# Conditions per 1,000 Persons
Arthritis	30,060	128.6
Gout (incl. gouty arthritis)	2,273	9.7
Intervertebral disc disorders	4,049	17.3
Bone spur or tendinitis, unspecified	2,093	9.0
Bursitis, unspecified	4,827	20.7
Deformity or orthopedic impairment	26,314	112.6
Ulcer	4,614	19.7
Enteritis or colitis	2,708	11.6
Gastritis or duodenitis	2,991	12.8
Diabetes	6,134	26.2
Anemias	3,350	14.3

Persons with Selected Chronic Conditions: 1985

Chronic Condition	# Conditions (1,000)	# Conditions per 1,000 Persons
Heart disease	19,295	82.6
Rheumatic fever, with or without heart disease	1,505	6.4
Hypertension (high blood pressure)	29,249	125.1
Chronic bronchitis	11,618	49.7
Asthma	8,612	36.8
Chronic sinusitis	32,492	139.0

Source: "Current Estimates from the National Health Interview Survey for the U.S., 1985," *Vital & Health Statistics/Series,* vol. 10, no. 160, National Center for Health Statistics.

Death Rates for Selected Causes of Death in the United States
(Deaths per 100,000 population)

	1970	1984
All Causes	714.3	545.9
Disease of the heart	253.6	183.6
Cerebrovascular diseases	66.3	33.4
Malignant neoplasms	129.9	133.5
Respiratory System	28.4	38.4
Colorectal	16.8	15.0
Prostrate	13.3	14.5
Breast	23.1	23.2
Chronic obstructive pulmonary diseases	13.2	17.7
Pneumonia and flu	22.1	12.2
Chronic liver disease and cirrhosis	14.7	10.0
Diabetes mellitus	14.1	9.5

Source: Health, United States, 1986, Public Health Service, U.S. Department of Health and Human Services.

Cancer Statistics

	Estimated New Cases, 1985 (1,000)	Five-Year Survival Rates,* 1977–1982 (%)
All sites	910	49
Lung	144	13
Breast	120	74
Colon	96	53
Prostrate	86	71
Rectum	42	50
Bladder	40	76
Corpus uteri	37	84
Oral cavity and pharynx	29	51
Leukemia	25	33
Pancreas	25	2
Stomach	25	16

* Survival rates represent the number of persons who live at least five years after a disease is diagnosed per 100 persons diagnosed with the disease in a given time period.

Source: U.S. National Institutes of Health, National Cancer Institute, *Annual Cancer Statistics Review.*

The 25 Largest Pharmaceutical Companies in the World, 1982[a]

Name	Pharmaceutical Sales			R&D Expenditure	
	$Million	As % Total Sales	As % World[b] Sales	$Million	As % Drug Sales
Bayer (Germany)	2,452	17	3.6		13.5
Merck and Co. (USA)	2,217	72	3.3	300	6.0
American Home Products (USA)	2,144	47	3.1	130	6.0
Hoechst (Germany)	2,071[c]	15	3.0	219	10.6
Ciba-Geiby	2,054	30	3.0		
Pfizer (USA)	1,694	49	2.5	175	10.3
Eli Lilly (USA)	1,532	52	2.2		
Hoffman-Laroche (Swiss)	1,512	42	2.2	300	19.8
Sandoz (Swiss)	1,419	47	2.1	180	12.7
Bristol-Meyers (USA)	1,360	38	2.0	140	10.2
Smithkline Beckman (USA)	1,339	45	2.0	166	12.4
Abbott (USA)	1,300	50	1.9	120	9.2
Takeda (Japanese)	1,291	59	1.9		
Warner Lambert (USA)	1,286	40	1.9	116	9.0
Boehringer Ingelheim (Germany)	1,214	82	1.8	185	15.2
Upjohn (USA)	1,213	66	1.8		
Johnson & Johnson (USA)	1,119	19	1.6	160	14.3
Glaxo (British)	999	83	1.4	90	9.1
Squibb (USA)	978	59	1.4	110	11.2
Rhone-Poulenc (French)	896	16	1.3	125	14.0
American Cynamid (USA)	884	26	1.3		
Schering-Plough (USA)	882	49	1.3	100	11.3
ICI (British)	839	80	1.2	98	11.3
Wellcome (British)	837	80	1.2	117	14.1
Beecham (British)	782	31	1.1	90	11.5

[a] Figures from company reports and from information from Interpharma SA; *Scrip,* various issues; *European Chemical News,* various issues. R&D expenditures are approximate and should be used with caution. They have however been considered as realistic estimates by industrial experts consulted.
[b] Excluding CMFA.
[c] Excluding Roussel-Uclaf.

Source: The Pharmaceutical Industry: Trade Related Issues. Organization for Economic Co-operation and Development, 1985.

Company	Sales (in millions)
Merck	$875
Eli Lilly	850
American Home Products	650
Pfizer	575
Hoffmann-LaRoche	400
Smithkline Beckman	375
Johnson & Johnson	350
Bristol-Myers	325
Upjohn	300
Boehringer-Ingelheim	175
Schering-Plough	175

* Many of the products which had provided the bulk of the profitability of the industry over the 1970s were due to go "off-patent" by the beginning of the 1990s in most major markets. As the patents expired on nearly all of the top 200 prescription drugs in the United States, sales of generic or "off-patent" drugs were expected to soar, reaching close to $9 billion by 1990.

Source: "Molecules and markets: A survey of pharmaceuticals," *The Economist,* February 7, 1987.

EXHIBIT 3B
Estimated 1985 Sales of Drugs with Patent Expiration Dates from 1981 to 1991 by Company*

EXHIBIT 4
Biogen N.V. and Subsidiaries
Summary Financial Information 1983–1985 (in thousands of U.S. dollars)

	12/31/85	12/31/84	12/31/83
INCOME STATEMENT			
Operating revenues			
R&D fees—corp. shareholders	$ 5,476	$ 10,776	$ 3,000
R&D fees—outside sponsors	9,602	12,112	7,536
Derived from			
North America	7,365	15,716	3,500
Europe	2,197	4,648	723
Japan	5,515	2,524	6,313
Interest income	6,372	8,501	7,901
R&D expenses	31,037	35,028	22,054
General and admin. expenses	7,920	8,139	6,921
Loss before income taxes	18,624	12,378	11,016
Net loss after tax	19,062	13,132	11,664
Weighted ave. # shares outst.	18,593	18,610	17,979
BALANCE SHEET			
Cash and interest-bearing invest.	$ 53,452	$ 72,167	$ 79,468
Total current assets	56,956	79,177	85,743
Leasehold improvements	16,109	15,390	14,706
Equipment	17,778	15,373	13,060
Less: Accumulated depreciation	12,920	7,766	4,589
Investment in joint venture	4,959	4,414	—
Patent costs, net of amort.	2,381	2,760	2,145
Total assets	85,833	109,760	111,427
Total current liabilities	7,407	14,937	5,191
Long-term debt	3,562	2,972	3,409
Common stock, par $.01/share	188	188	188
Additional paid-in capital	127,907	127,546	124,463
Deficit	(53,847)	(34,785)	(21,653)
Shareholders' equity	74,864	91,852	102,826

Source: Biogen N.V., *Annual Report,* 1983–1985.

1-7

FEDERAL EXPRESS CORPORATION

In the mid 1970s Federal Express Corporation became the largest start-up venture capital investment in history. Its success revolutionalized package and document delivery in the United States. By the fall of 1985 Federal's highly entrepreneurial management had built sales to $2 billion and launched the company on a visionary new product concept, ZapMail, which utilized the most modern communications technologies and would potentially dwarf in scale the $96 million investment which had initially gotten Federal Express rolling. In 1986, developing this new concept successfully and relating it properly to the company's existing businesses were forefront issues for Federal's top management team.

COMPLEX BEGINNINGS

The myth is that the Federal Express system sprang full blown from the head of young Frederick W. Smith in a 1964 Yale term paper for which he received an unappreciating "C" grade. The facts are much more complicated. Although many of the ideas he put forward in that paper were proved correct by later events, it took years to work out the full mechanics of how to provide overnight delivery of packages and documents. First deliveries were not made until the spring of 1973.

In classic style, Fred Smith's entrepreneurial track record probably began when he was 15 and started the Arden Record Company with a high school class-

Case copyright © 1986 by James Brian Quinn. Case prepared by Penny C. Paquette under the supervision of Professor Quinn.

The generous cooperation of the Federal Express Corporation is gratefully acknowledged.

mate in Memphis. That same year, Smith also learned to fly, beginning a lifetime fascination with advanced technology and flight. At Yale, he helped revitalize the Yale Flying Club. And his first real business venture after college was selling and repairing aircraft. Smith's father was also a self-made millionaire. He had developed the Dixie Greyhound Co. and founded the Toddle House restaurant chain, a forerunner of today's fast-food outlets. Although he died when Fred was only 4, Fred's father left a sizable fortune and a letter admonishing Fred "to put his inheritance to work and use the funds held in trust as a foundation for greater wealth."[1]

After graduating from Yale and serving two tours of duty in Vietnam as a Marine, Smith returned to the South and purchased a Little Rock company, Arkansas Aviation Sales, which provided maintenance services for corporate aircraft and brokered corporate jets. Despite the success of these ventures, from 1969 until 1971 Smith continued to flesh out the concept of an overnight air delivery service. The Federal Reserve System looked like an ideal first customer for such a service. The cost of the Fed's float of checks in its system was about $3 million per day of delay. Smith took his idea to the Fed, which seemed to respond favorably. When he thought the transaction was set, Smith put up $250,000 of his own funds to start his new company and got his family trust to match his equity investment and to guarantee a $3.6 million bank loan to buy two small Falcon jet aircraft.

A few weeks later the Fed backed out, and Smith had two jets and a rejected concept on his hands. But he had incorporated on June 18, 1971 under the name Federal Express, both to support his proposed relationship with the Federal Reserve and to indicate a developing nationwide service.

The Early 1970s Air Freight Industry

Smith felt a number of U.S. life-style and corporate trends strongly supported developing a service for overnight delivery of urgent or high-value packets. At that time shippers were faced with a variety of choices. They could use the U.S. mails; contract directly with various air or ground carriers; or call air forwarding agents who acted as brokers—arranging trucking to the airport, transport as air cargo on freight or passenger airlines, and truck pickup and delivery at the destination. A typical package went through 5 to 10 different corporate hands. In 1972 the top three domestic air forwarders were Emery, Airborne, and UPS. Regulations prohibited forwarders from operating their own aircraft. For a variety of reasons forwarders' delivery was unreliable and generally took 2 to 4 days. United Parcel Service (UPS) with its huge ground network was more dependable, but could not guarantee delivery in anything less than 2 days. And most air carriers were marginally profitable or losing money on their small package businesses.

Smith spent $150,000 on two different market research studies to investigate his concept. They found the airlines posed particular problems as linkages in the priority parcel delivery system. Over 60% of all airline movements occurred between the 25 largest markets, and only 10% of their fleets were flying after 10:00 P.M. By contrast, over 80% of the small urgent shipments originated or terminated outside the top 25 markets. And the purchase of jumbo aircraft by the major airlines seemed likely to further consolidate routes and decrease the flexibility of the system. As Fred Smith said when he was investigating the Federal Reserve System's possibilities, "[The Fed] gives you in microcosm a picture of the flow of U.S. economic activity. Six thousand pounds of checks a day go from New York City to Chicago, and one pound a day might move randomly from Billings, Montana to Jacksonville, Florida."[2] In this complexity, Smith saw his opportunity.

Still he struggled to find a workable concept which would (1) meet the market need his research studies said was there, (2) utilize his Falcon aircraft, and (3) fit into the regulatory structures of the CAB. In December 1971 Smith had signed a contract with Pan Am to buy 23 more Falcons, which were available then at a distress price. However, a CAB regulation—Part 298 under which Smith hoped to operate—posed major problems. Part 298 permitted air taxi services to carry people, property, and mail on chartered flights without CAB's prior approval of their specific routes. However, Smith's Falcons exceeded Part 298's allowed gross takeoff weight (including fuel, etc.) of 12,500 pounds, until the regulation was revised in September 1972 to permit "payload weights" of 7,500 pounds. This change, preceded by much lobbying by Smith and substantial opposition from the airlines, made the Falcons viable.

During the fall of 1972 Smith put together a management team for Federal Express and started to design and put in place certain major logistic elements for his system. The crucial determinations made at this time were (1) to serve only a limited network of cities, (2) to use Memphis, Tennessee as the central sorting point for Federal's proposed "hub and spoke" air system, (3) to establish a van pickup and delivery network to support this system, and (4) to undertake the major modifications to the Falcon aircraft necessary to handle air cargo in volume. As of September 1972, Federal began to fly some contract charters for individual customers, and to service three U.S. mail routes to utilize its aircraft. It also performed several experiments for specific industrial clients to demonstrate that overnight delivery of urgent packages was possible.

Then on March 12, 1973 Federal undertook an operational test with an 11 city network. The results did not bode well for the company, with fewer than 18 packages handled—and one of those was a birthday present from Fred Smith to a close friend. Finally the official "first night" for Federal Express occurred on April 17, 1973. But the number of packages handled was still a discouraging 186. By October the nightly count had risen to only 2,000, despite many experiments to improve operations. And keeping the company alive was a full-time dilemma.

Charles Lea of New Court Securities said that in September 1973 his company's financial studies had come up with a survival financial package "calling for $52 million: $10 million for operating losses, $40 million for aircraft and equipment, $2.5 million for working capital. Fred Smith had already invested $6–9 million. . . . It would be the largest venture capital deal ever undertaken at that time. . . . The worst case scenario called for losses in the first year of $9.3 million with profits climbing close to $9.5 million by 1976." The major question was how could Smith, who had been working feverishly for years on the project, convince investors to put up such enormous sums for a new company, operating in a new market, with a totally new concept, and hemorrhaging cash and operating losses. At the end of its first fiscal year, May 1974, Federal had revenues of $17.3 million and losses of $13.3 million.

228

Through a series of cliffhanging negotiations with banks, venture capitalists, and government regulators Mr. Smith and his team hung doggedly on to their dream and developed a totally new priority delivery system for the United States. Federal's early financial performance and equity financings are summarized in Exhibit 1. Only those bank financings associated with equity offerings are detailed. What had previously been a relatively diffuse, but homogeneous marketplace began a process of segmentation that was accelerated by the gradual deregulation of the transportation industry and the emergence of a few large competitors.

Federal Express grew rapidly to sales of $160 million in 1978 with profits of $19.4 million. The success of Federal Express had both created a new market and attracted numerous new competitors. An estimated 40% of Federal's volume was made up of items which previously might not have been air shipped at all. Kidder Peabody's Transportation Research Group described the size and characteristics of the "expedited package and document delivery market" in a June 1983 report. Exhibits 2–4 show these findings. The following section briefly describes the way competition was emerging in the late 1970s and early 1980s.

The Early 1980s Marketplace

Emery was the largest and most profitable domestic air freight forwarder with a wide geographical distribution system inside and outside the United States. Emery had finally responded to Federal's challenge in late 1978 by offering next day delivery using its own planes. It had evolved from using two separate hubs (for small packages and heavier freight) to a single hub in Dayton, Ohio which sorted light and heavy freight at the same time. Emery offered delivery of either kind of package by noon the next day. Although some 60% of its shipments were under 50 pounds, it was still heavily dependent on larger, heavier cargo. Many felt that Emery was using its high-margin international business to subsidize its lower margin domestic business in its battle with industry leader, Federal Express.

Airborne, Seattle based, was the second largest domestic air freight forwarder and by 1982 also held second place in the air express business. Airborne had a wholly integrated air-ground transportation system modeled after Federal's. But 75% of its revenues came from the highly competitive national accounts sector as opposed to lower volume shippers, and it lacked the overall volume to match Federal's position as low-cost producer. Some 20% of its volume came from international operations.

United Parcel Service had revenues of $4 billion in 1980 and shipped more than 1.8 billion packages in that year, all weighing 70 lb. or less. UPS was privately held by its own management and had some $2 billion in assets. In addition to more than 60,000 ground vehicles driven by 85,000 Teamsters, UPS was the largest single shipper on most railroads and by 1982–1983 owned a fleet of planes itself. At the time Federal began offering its overnight service, UPS had only its "Blue Label" service, a second-day delivery commitment. In late 1982 it introduced a "next day by 3 P.M." service (with no "on-call" pickup) for a limited network of cities. Of its daily volume of between 5 and 10 million packages, only about 150,000 of them went by air. UPS concentrated on gaining productivity through the tight management of its people rather than using automation and in 1986 still handled its enormous sorting process by hand.

Purolator Courier was part of a company which also had an armored car division and manufactured automotive products. The Courier division was the company's largest source of revenues. Like UPS, Purolator Courier provided a scheduled pickup and delivery service moving cancelled checks and general commodities of less than 50 lb. It was the largest and fastest-growing non-union trucking concern in North America—four times the size of its nearest non-union ground-based competitor. In 1976, it had started chartering planes for shipments of more than 400 miles, but in the early 1980s approximately 80% of its shipments still moved by surface, which cost $\frac{1}{6}$ of what air transport did. Seventy percent of Purolator's volume was in machine parts, blood plasma, and film for processing. By the early 1980s, it had teamed up with MCI Communications to act as a delivery arm of MCI Mail, and had added on-call pickup services after the trucking industry was deregulated.

DHL, named after its three American founders, developed a fast delivery service between California and Hawaii in 1969 and expanded to the Far East in 1970–1972. Forced to split its domestic and overseas operations, the foreign unit, now DHL International, was sold to a college friend of one of the founders. Although legally separate, they were run by a joint management committee from both. Operating out of Hong Kong, DHL International controlled some 60–65% of the international fast document delivery business, with 816 stations in 172 countries. It tended to follow a pricing strategy—some 12–25% below its large international competitors, and was on its way to being the largest operator in Europe. Much of DHL's Far Eastern business was focused on packages 150 pounds and over for the retail trade. Privately held, DHL claimed to be the world's largest air express company, yet it had less that 5% of the domestic U.S. business. Its American unit, DHL Worldwide Express, was responsible for both the United States and Latin America.

FEDERAL'S STRUCTURE IN 1985

By late 1985 Federal Express was offering next day service to more than 40,000 communities, or close to 98% of the U.S. population, through a network of more than 720 Full Service Stations and Business Service Centers in major metropolitan areas. These offered customers access to all of Federal's own services and at one time provided xerographic services for a fee. In addition, Federal maintained more than 5,000 overnight delivery counters or drop boxes and was in the process of opening manned kiosk units in suburban areas. Ground and air transport was provided by a fleet of 12,700 ground vehicles (courier vans, line haul trucks, etc.) and 90 aircraft (11 DC-10s, 53 727s, and 26 Cessna 208 Caravans with individual cargo capacities ranging from 148,000 lb. down to 2,960 lb.). The Memphis Superhub with a maximum sorting capacity (for a two-hour sort) of 570,000 packages was being augmented by smaller regional hubs in Newark, New Jersey and elsewhere. Express delivery volume for the quarter ending February 28, 1986 was 37 million units.

Federal's major services included three overnight delivery options ("Priority One" for packages weighing up to 150 lb.; "Courier Pak" for documents, reports, machine parts, and so on generally weighing between 8 oz. and 6 lb. in envelopes, boxes, and tubes; and "Overnight Letter" for 9″ × 12″ envelopes holding up to 30 pages). In addition, Federal offered "Standard Air" for packages weighing up to 150 lb. and scheduled for delivery no later than the close of business on the second day, and "ZapMail" which allowed same-day delivery of documents and graphics via a facsimile transmission network. Federal Express also provided direct service to Canada and "Priority One" and "Courier Pak" services with a second day commitment to major European cities via its European hub in Brussels. A breakdown of operating statistics by each major class of service is provided in Exhibit 5.

By the mid 1980s, the $4.5 billion air express, small package industry was in what one analyst described as "the later stages of the growth phase of its life cycle and was characterized by price discounting, heavy promotion, peaking out of unit profits, and the emergence of many new competitors. . . . Federal Express, however, had not lost any significant market share and continued to show unit volume growth greater than its competitors. In addition, the company (which was the industry's lowest cost producer with an operating profit margin at least twice that of its competitors) continued to lower its costs per package at a rate almost equal to the forecast longer term decline in yield" (i.e., revenues per package).[3] As Mr. Smith commented, "I think in our base business there is about to be an enormous shake out. Not everybody is going to survive. There are ten competitors in this market, and two of them represent 90% of all the growth. You know what that means for the other guys." See the chart below and Exhibit 5 for operating and financial statistics.

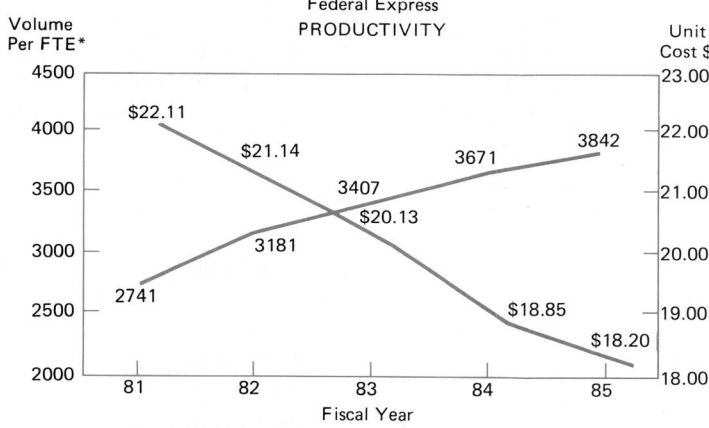

*FTE = Full Time Equivalent Employee

Source: Robinson-Humphrey Company, Inc. Equities Research, *Basic Report-Federal Express Corporation,* November 1, 1985.

Operating Systems and Technology

As one observer commented: "An overnight delivery firm must combine the dispatching capabilities of a nationwide taxi service, the sorting facilities of a postal service without the time margin, the logistics of an airline whose passengers can't get themselves on and off the flights and the customer service function of a bank whose customers can demand immediate confirmation of every transaction."[4] As a consequence, Federal Express had become one of the nation's most highly sophisticated users of electronics and telecommunications technology. As noted by

COO James Barksdale, Federal spent between 6% and 7% of its revenues on tele-communications and computing R&D, excluding ZapMail. In the early 1980s Federal had established an Advanced Systems Development group in Colorado Springs to handle the development of its new systems.

Federal's main operating system was called COSMOS for Customer Oriented Service and Management Operating Systems. Information concerning a customer's order was entered into the system at regional customer service centers as the customer called in. Federal's DADS (Digitally Assisted Dispatch System) tied the couriers into local dispatching centers through CRTs in their vans or hand carried lap computers. These allowed couriers to receive, via radio data links, customer pickup information which was sent electronically to their dispatching centers from regional customer service centers. COSMOS was used to track packages at key points in the system and to develop information for control purposes. COSMOS information could be used to respond to customer inquiries (up to 15,000 per day) and provide data for the company's billing system. The information contained in the COSMOS system was also utilized to plan flight operations, monitor activity levels, and manage work flows within the entire Federal network. Federal's data processing center supported one terminal for every two employees and handled a million transactions per hour.

Federal's package and mail sort systems were based on destination zip code information which through 1986 had to be manually entered at the start of the sort process at the Memphis Superhub. This input activated computer controlled conveyor belts and large sweeping arms that, at the right moment, pushed packets off the line and into their destination bins. Federal's new ZODIAC system, due to be introduced in 1987, would allow automated sorting using a camera activated robotic system to read destination zip codes. In addition, Federal operated its own weather analysis, aircraft ground control, and flight simulator facilities. It had equipped its aircraft with the most sophisticated in-flight electronic systems available for commercial aviation. If necessary, each plane could be flown and controlled via onboard computers from take off to touch down at the Memphis Superhub.

Philosophy and Organization

Amid all this technology Mr. Smith had built what one executive called "A singularly entrepreneurial company." Smith himself was styled, "As close to a true visionary as you can come. He has a tremendous sense of historical perspective, seeing the company in a much bigger and more global way than most senior executives would. Fred sees us playing a key role in the world and in information movement. Any logistical problem or segment for business in those worlds is within our province." The same executive continued:

> Mr. Smith constantly probes the limits of technology and management possibilities by posing "Why can't we" and "What if" questions to the people around him. ZODIAC came about this way. Smith kept saying, "Why can't we do it all electronically? Why not just use bar codes and have a machine to read them?" Once he gets an idea, he's a bulldog; he hangs on until he gets an answer or is convinced it can't be done. But above all, he is concerned about his people, and he generates intense personal loyalties. Some observers have said that if you lined up all Federal Express employees on the bridge across the Mississippi here and Fred said "jump," 99% would leap. He's that kind of person.

In the mid 1980s the Federal Express Manager's Guide instructs every manager to "take care of our people; they, in turn, will deliver the impeccable service demanded by our customers who will reward us with the profitability necessary to secure our future. People-Service-Profit, these three words are the very foundation of Federal Express." Federal's commitment to being a "people-oriented company" goes beyond the lip service paid by many companies. The Senior Vice President and Chief Personnel Officer reports directly to the top. (See Exhibit 6 for a corporate organization chart.) Putting employee considerations first has led Federal to "atomize" stations when they reach 50 vans, rather than to seek greater economies from scale. Its Guaranteed Fair Treatment process means that top executives spend an entire morning most weeks deciding what was "fair" for lower-level employees in what many would consider minor personnel grievances. Every week, the company posts a long list of available positions through its nationwide system. No job can be filled by an outsider unless no one within the company is interested and qualified.

Employee involvement is encouraged by such actions as paying up to $25,000 for productivity improvement suggestions. Candid and extensive communications about every subject are rules at Federal Express, and the philosophy is applied to the financial community as well as employees. Top executives regularly hold brown bag lunches during which they answer employees' questions and listen to suggestions. Every year they hold a companywide "Family Briefing" to discuss issues of concern to Federal's employees. The atmosphere is informal—everyone calls their CEO "Fred," and top executives make it a point to be visible and accessible. Wages, benefits, and profit-sharing opportunities are outstanding. As the Manager's Guide states, "Our people-first philosophy means Federal Express is dedicated to maintaining an employee relations environment which renders unions unnecessary—not because we are anti-union but because we are totally pro-employee." Considered one of "The 10 Best Companies in the U.S. to Work For," not a single one of Federal's more than 38,000 employees belongs to a union. Over 75% of its employees are under 35, and the work pace at its sorting hubs would have made Frederick Taylor beam with pride.

As Jim Barksdale said, "Motivated people move faster. . . . You have to understand our business. Our people philosophy is not out of a spirit of altruism. You have fewer problems and make more money."[5] Federal had invested heavily in training, communications, and management systems to achieve the highest possible service standard, but it also stressed the importance of each individual employee's being committed to that standard. Its Manager's Guide noted harshly, "98% or 99% may be fine for many human endeavors, but our customers expect faultless service—all the time—and there is no acceptable reason in their eyes for our failing to perform in accordance with our commitments."

When asked what the company did internally to foster the spirit of innovation and entrepreneurship which had gotten it to the top of its industry in 1986, Mr. Smith said,

> We try to teach managers that innovation and entrepreneurship at the managerial level is necessary not just to keep everybody interested and to get lots of press. It is essential for the long term success of the organization. I think that is much more important than any particular project or specific thing we might do . . . it's the inculcation of that into the management culture of the company that counts. Another thing that is pretty important is that we let people fail. We give them lots of opportunity to fail and if they do fail, we generally will give them a chance to stay with the company if they want to. We have a fair number of examples of people who have made successful retrograde movements and then gone back up in their careers. We won't kill you if you fail. We won't let you continue in your same position, but we won't fire you. You can't shoot the innovator or you will never develop an entrepreneurial atmosphere inside the company.

"We also just keep pointing out to people that discounted cash flows and rates of return are only as good as the assumptions that are put into them and that qualitative assumptions are often as important as quantitative ones. So we encourage people to advance ideas even if they can't show an immediate payoff and then we make subjective judgments as to whether to adopt them based on our understanding of how the business really works."

THE NEXT GENERATION

As early as 1978/79 Mr. Smith began worrying about the impact the emergence of "electronic mail" might have on the overnight delivery market for documents in which Federal held the dominant position. Said one executive,

> Smith saw electronics as such an important and likely development in the logistics of our business that we should be in the forefront of it. We should lose to ourselves, and not to any competitors. Smith kept saying he wanted the capacity for instantaneous transmission of information in the Federal system, and he saw no reason he couldn't have it. He kept looking for technical people who would say "I can do that." Finally he went outside and hired people who felt that way. He hired Chuck Winston about 1980 from Addressograph Multigraph. Earlier he had bought the heavily computerized insurance division of Cook Industries, a large grain trading company in Memphis that had hit on hard times. This added substantially to the expertise we needed.

Now, Federal could begin more concrete planning for its next generation product, code-named Gemini. Smith hoped Gemini would put Federal Express into the same-day delivery market which he estimated could account for 20,000–40,000 deliveries per business day in the early 1980s. But its ultimate potentials seemed much larger.

Mr. Smith had seen a facsimile machine designed by AM International (formerly Addressograph-Multigraph) for IBM's Satellite Business Systems Division to be used by large companies for overnight intra-company transfers of documents using satellite transmission. The machine helped him crystallize an idea he had been mulling over for some months. This was about the time Federal Express purchased the Cook Industries subsidiary and gained both a future Chief Operating Officer, James Barksdale, and the expertise of some 55 IBM specialists who worked there. Mr. Barksdale joined Federal Express because he was attracted by the challenge of building Federal's existing internal computer systems and people resources into a major new product—first called Gemini, later ZapMail. As Mr. Smith later said,

> We carried more important business correspondence than anybody else in the country . . . so we knew an awful lot about what people were thinking about in terms of their needs for moving high priority documents. In the early part of the 1980s we became very convinced that sometime in the next 10 to 15 years people who had to move documents like that were going to expect to be able to move them from their desk to another instantaneously.

Developing the Technology

In 1980 Vince Fagan, Federal's Marketing head, was assigned the task of researching the telecommunications industry and its trends. Although Fagan had been a skeptic about "electronic mail," he concluded that from a strategic viewpoint Federal Express had two great strengths to apply in support of the Gemini project.

First, its courier network and its COSMOS/DADS systems allowed Federal to offer its customers the instantaneous "connectivity"—the capacity to connect up with virtually anyone anywhere in the country—so critical in telecommunications systems. Second, the company enjoyed a very advanced expertise in telecommunications, software development, and systems operations.

But Federal had never designed or produced electronic equipment for large volume markets. So, working from specifications developed by Mr. Barksdale and its communications laboratories based at the Colorado Advanced Systems Development group, Federal contracted with Nippon Electric Company (NEC) to develop and produce the ZapMailer—the first computerized "store and forward" facsimile machine which offered a high-quality (400 pixel per inch/160,000 pixel per square inch) output, high throughput, and complete telephone system compatability.

Mr. Barksdale explained the ZapMailer and its associated systems as follows:

> If you take an image and you digitize that image at a resolution acceptable to the human eye for a business document, you have x black dots and x white dots. For a standard business page, that is 640,000 bits of information. Regular telephone lines allow you to transmit data at a rate of 4,800–9,600 bits per second and special leased circuits permit rates of 56,000 bits per second. Unfortunately, because of expectations about regular photocopiers, the customer wants to scan a page at a rate of about one page every 3 seconds. So the ZapMailer was designed to scan the document at that speed, digitize its image, store it on a magnetic disk drive, and transmit the image through the phone lines as fast as it could—although to date this has been far slower than the rate the ZapMailer could scan and store the information from a page. We then intend to upgrade slower phone lines to our own high-speed satellite transmission system.

While the ZapMailer was waiting to transmit, it was to be available for other things—to make other images or to receive incoming images from other ZapMailers. Each machine was to be equipped with multiple ports so it could have this desired flexibility. Finally the ZapMailer was to use plain paper as its output medium, rather than the thermal paper other facsimile machines did. The formidable engineering task to bring this machine into being was given to a small team of highly skilled electronics people headed by Ace McInturff, who had come to Federal Express from AM International. Although the ZapMailer development team was in Memphis, the COSMOS group with which it had to coordinate was in Colorado.

THE ZAPMAIL CONCEPT

As the concept for the ZapMailer came into place, Federal Express spent almost $2 million dollars on several market research studies. These studies explained the proposed ZapMail system and its capabilities in detail to various potential customers. The research involved more than 600 users of overnight services and indicated that if such a service existed, demand would be in the tens of thousands of messages per day. Thirty-seven percent of Federal's customers were already using some sort of facsimile transmission equipment, and many of those interviewed indicated they would switch to Gemini. Later when the ZapMail system was publicly announced, the security analysts also responded with enthusiasm. One analyst commented: "Gemini (ZapMail) will quickly set a new standard for fast delivery. Brokerage reports, ad copy, legal briefs, and so on will all be deliverable on a 2-hour basis."[6] Another analyst, for Robinson Humphrey, explained,

Gemini is a natural extension of Federal's asset base, operational systems, market recognition, and technical expertise. [Although] Gemini start-up costs are expected to be $25 to $35 million (including advertising) in fiscal 1984, Gemini leverages Federal's existing assets. The only additional assets required are image transmission machines, packet switching computers and supplementary leased telephone lines.[7]

The company in its meetings with analysts emphasized that Federal was not trying to build a new business with Gemini, but saw it "as a way to launch Federal Express from packages to pages." The range of Gemini services to be offered included (1) *pickup and delivery* (maximum time elapsed from initial call to delivery would be two hours); (2) *pickup to destination* (Federal would pick up the document and transmit it from a Federal Express office directly to a receiving party who had Federal's image processing equipment on its own premises); (3) *premise to delivery* (customer would originate on its own ZapMailer, send the message to a Federal station, where it would be picked up and delivered by a courier to a customer without its own ZapMailer; and (4) *premise to premise* or *machine to machine* (customer with a ZapMailer would send the message directly to someone else who also had one). See Appendix A for a description of the transmission network and some key issues presented by its technology and operations. Federal Express felt that these services would eventually cannibalize up to 20% of its overnight document volume. The *pickup and delivery mode* concept was $\frac{1}{2}$ hour to pick up, 1 hour to transmit and create remote hard copy, and $\frac{1}{2}$ hour to deliver. Before the official start of service, NEC had to deliver more than 1,000 machines; and Federal had to establish remote courier sites called "closets" to cover entire cities within half an hour. An experienced management team, made up primarily of Federal Express personnel from its overnight delivery operations, was given the assignment of bringing ZapMail to the market.

ZapMail Starts Up

Service officially started in July 1984, accompanied by an advertising campaign in the Federal Express tradition (see Exhibit 7). In keeping with past practice, the ads emphasized humor and the nature of Federal's service rather than the technology behind it. The financial community responded enthusiastically. Said one analyst, "We believe Federal Express's two-hour facsimile service could develop $500 million–$1 billion of revenues five years from now with 35% profit margins, and incremental EPS from this could be $2–$4 per share by 1990. . . . However, (the report warned) the major offering in this market to date, *MCI Mail,* has been notoriously unsuccessful."[8]

Estimated ZapMail Profitability

Est. revenue per Transaction		$40
Costs		
Courier time	$10	
Postage and billing	2	
Telecommunications	3	
Management, supervisory	3	
Subtotal, incremental costs		$18
Network: Depr. and maint.		8
Profit		$14

Source: Rooney Pace, Inc., *Research Report-Federal Express Corporation,* June 18, 1984.

Although Federal had consciously forecast demand on the high side to ensure its ability to meet service commitments, ZapMail volume ran 30 to 60 days behind levels initially projected. Nonetheless, by the 11th week of service, ZapMail's average daily volume was 1,679, which on an annualized basis would give Federal more revenue than MCI's electronic mail service—which had been on the market for more than a year.

The reliability of the ZapMailer machines themselves far exceeded expectation, but there were problems with delays in installing high-speed dedicated data lines for some of the ZapMailer machines due to the Bell divestiture. Despite this, service levels (i.e., the percentage of time Federal met its service commitment) quickly went from 70% to more than 90%, and satisfaction levels (as measured by interviews) rose to 95%. An initial breakdown of ZapMail customers by industry indicated that attorneys, ad agencies, real estate firms, and financial service providers were the prime users at this time.

The Second Stage

While the original ZapMailers purchased by Federal were very costly, Federal was able to lower costs rapidly. Costs dropped by a factor of 5 within about two years through increasing volume, falling prices for key technologies, and eliminating some features. Federal was the exclusive marketing agent for the ZapMailer machine for a specified period of time. At first Federal operated only in the pickup and delivery mode. Then, in a second phase rollout, ZapMailers were made available to customers in March 1985. By the middle of September 1985 4,500 machines had been installed, and Federal had firm orders for some 7,000 more. At that point, usage of the ZapMailers by customers who had them in their offices averaged 4.2 pages per ZapMailer day. When machines had been in use for 5 months or more, usage rose to 7.6 pages per day. Although the cost difference between ZapMail and Federal's express document service was minimal for the customer, most ZapMail usage seemed to be in an "emergency" category, and 90% of all volume came from 10% of the customers.

While the ZapMailers themselves exceeded Federal's reliability and quality expectations, the inconsistent quality of the U.S. telephone system created quality problems which customers blamed on Federal. Satellite quality transmission lines had approximately one bit error for every million bits transmitted, but some local lines in less populated areas had as many as one bit error in every 2,000 bits transmitted. But the biggest problems were network hangups. (See Exhibit 8 for details.)

The tables that follow give the financial results for the ZapMail project through early 1986.

ZapMail Losses and Investment

	ZAPMAIL LOSSES ($ millions)	INVESTMENT IN ZAP ASSETS ($ millions)
FY 1984	$ 24.1	$ 75.0
FY 1985	$125.6	$133.0 (estimate)
FY 1985—Q1	31.3	
FY 1985—Q2	29.6	
FY 1985—Q3	31.6	
FY 1985—Q4	33.1	

ZapMail Losses and Investment (Continued)

	ZAPMAIL LOSSES ($ millions)	INVESTMENT IN ZAP ASSETS ($ millions)
FY 1986	$120.2 (estimate)	$200.0 (estimate)
FY 1986—Q1	26.0	
FY 1986—Q2	30.0	
FY 1986—Q3	34.2	
FY 1987	$ 75.0 (estimate)	

Source: Various investment research reports.

ZapMail P & L Structure

FY 1985 ($ millions)

Network Expense	$ 23.1
Depreciation and Equipment Leases	12.3
Sales and Service Expense	31.1
Support Operations and Other Exp.	15.7
Total Electronic Products	$ 82.2
Field Operations	$ 18.5
Customer Service and General Support	4.0
Marketing and Advertising	31.9
Total Operating Costs	$136.6
ZapMail Revenues	14.7
Operating Loss	$121.9
Corporation Overhead	3.2
ZapMail Loss	$125.1

Note: Does not include interest expense or tax benefit.

Source: Robinson Humphrey Company, Inc., Equities Research, *Basic Report-Federal Express Corporation,* November 1, 1985.

ZapMail Operating Data

FY 1986 1st QUARTER		
	ZapMail-Courier	ZapMailer
Volume (thousands)	176	224
Revenue (millions)	$ 6.1	$1.4
Revenue per document	$34.55	$6.42
Pages per document	9.1	4.5

Source: Robinson Humphrey Company, Inc., Equities Research, *Basic Report-Federal Express Corporation,* November 1, 1985.

THE FUTURE

In describing some of the forces shaping the future for Zapmail, Fred Smith noted that the facsimile market itself, telecommunications technologies, and all related costs were changing rapidly. Whereas in the early 1980s only about 10,000 "sub-minute speed" facsimile machines had been sold each year, in 1985 over 100,000 were sold. Telecommunications equipment costs were dropping exponentially. Satellite technologies and their related costs were also changing rapidly. The G Star3 satellite Federal utilized cost about $3,000 per month in 1986 for each circuit leased. If Federal went ahead with its plan to put up its own satellites in the late 1980s, costs would drop to about $600 per month for each circuit. And advances in satellite architecture or software—particularly demand assigned multiplexing—would make it possible to utilize each circuit's capabilities many times over what had been previously possible. The total cost of Federal's proposed two satellites (plus one ground spare) was estimated at $250 million. Federal had been allocated two satellite "slots" or positions, but had to decide in spring 1986 whether to use them. Earth stations for satellite transmission and reception had cost $25 million five to ten years earlier, but in 1986 they cost as little as $4,500 each and had the ability to transmit at 56,000 bits per second. By 1990 Federal Express expected earth station costs to drop to as low as $1,500.

Federal's use of its telecommunications network was also expanding in leaps and bounds. In addition to using the network for its own operations and for Zap-Mail, Federal would soon offer its customers the ability to automate their shipping docks by tying them directly into the COSMOS system. The same field service technicians who serviced couriers' radios, DADS computers, (etc.), also serviced customers' ZapMailers and would soon be handling their COSMOS terminals. As Mr. Tom Oliver, Senior V.P., Electronic Products, put the challenge:

> The whole purpose of this thing is to have a network that offers an extremely high speed end-to-end connectivity that is driven over a satellite network, with low cost but high-quality terminals, and low-cost satellite earth stations. The output of the machine at the other end of the line must be in a form that is as good as the best xerographic copy you can get today. Perhaps the environment is too difficult to allow one to think through all the things that will be important in advance. Dealing with the unexpected is a part of the process of a large scale innovation like this.

But in early 1986, ZapMail's potentials were far from realized, and Federal's management was trying to decide how to best develop ZapMail itself, to relate ZapMail to the rest of Federal's activities. Mr. Smith summarized:

> Our feeling is that we are in two super growth businesses. One is the delivery of high-priority packages, and the other is the transmission of high-priority documents. I think that the forces at work on the high-priority packages are as great, if not greater, than they are on the demand for the transmission of documents. Despite our problems so far with ZapMail, I think we as a management group are still very confident about the concept and committed to making sure Federal is a major player in this next crucial development in our industry.
>
> We have told the stock market that this is an entrepreneurial company, and we've told them what we are trying to do. If people don't like these kinds of uncertainties, they shouldn't own the stock. The company is very long term oriented, and we've forewarned everyone. We've always said we won't make forecasts. We'll give you all the information and be as candid with you as we can, commensurate with our plans. I feel much more responsible to the employees of the company than I do to most of the outside folks. Most of them are big boys—big investment firms.
>
> I'm keenly aware of the money that we're socking into our big projects. After all, I'm a big stockholder, too. But I am very confident that if we didn't do these things, come the early 1990s, our base business would have evolved just like any other industry and go down to a marginal rate of return. If our employees and investors want to have their high value added jobs and opportunities, they've got to take some short-term hits. That's the price of being an entrepreneurial company.

QUESTIONS

1. What special operations problems does ZapMail pose for Federal Express? How should it deal with these?

2. What strategy should Federal Express attempt to utilize in developing Zap-Mail?

3. How should Federal conceptualize the relationship between ZapMail and its traditional services? Possible future services?

4. What specific actions should Mr. Smith and Mr. Barksdale take in 1986 concerning ZapMail? Why?

APPENDIX A

The ZapMail Network

As originally installed, customers' ZapMailers had to be connected into telephone lines leading to one of Federal's 54 "packet switching stations" or "nodes" across the country. Here "packet switching computers" broke the page of data into small packets (of 1,000 bits each) which could be individually identified, transmitted, checked, and reassembled into the original page at its destination. Most often, a message would go from a customer's sending ZapMailer to a "node" over a standard 9600 bit per second (bps) telephone line, be sent over 56,000 bps "trunk line" ground links to the node nearest its destination, then have to go back into a standard 9600 bps telephone line to reach the receiving ZapMailer. Federal started service with a totally ground based network, but soon leased some satellite circuits and by late 1985 had 12 earth stations in place to send and receive messages via satellites between the nodes. Packets could be routed by Federal's computers over ground or satellite circuits independently, so the network could balance itself and adjust for peak loads or failures in the network as necessary.

When Federal's "pick up and delivery" services were used, a courier would take the document(s) to be transmitted to a ZapMailer at the nearest local station, "closet" in a big city, or Service Center—from which it would follow a route similar to the above. If the originating location was also an earth station, its packet switching computer might prepare the packets to be transmitted from a sending "dish" on its grounds or rooftop to a satellite, from which it would be targeted to the right receiving dish at another ground station, and then be sent along ground links to the local station nearest the intended recipient. Individual ZapMailer machines were too small to contain all the routing information needed to connect directly to receiving machines. Consequently—whether the document was originally scanned in the customer's or Federal's ZapMailer—each ZapMail image went first to a "node." There a packet switching computer broke it into packets, identified each packet as to its recipient and later reassembly needs, found the best route over which to send the packet, and sent it on its way. At the receiving point, a Zap-Mailer machine would hold the packets for a document until all were in hand and then reassemble and print them with a quality equal to a xerographic copy. (See diagram.)

By 1986 the network could handle enormous volumes. For example, a large user of packet switched messages might transmit 2 billion packets per month. To maintain the system's integrity despite these volumes, Federal's packet switching computers (designed and built by Tandem) were installed in parallel and with high redundancy. Through clever design the computers could even detect and adjust for a gradual deterioration in their own performance and switch packets elsewhere in

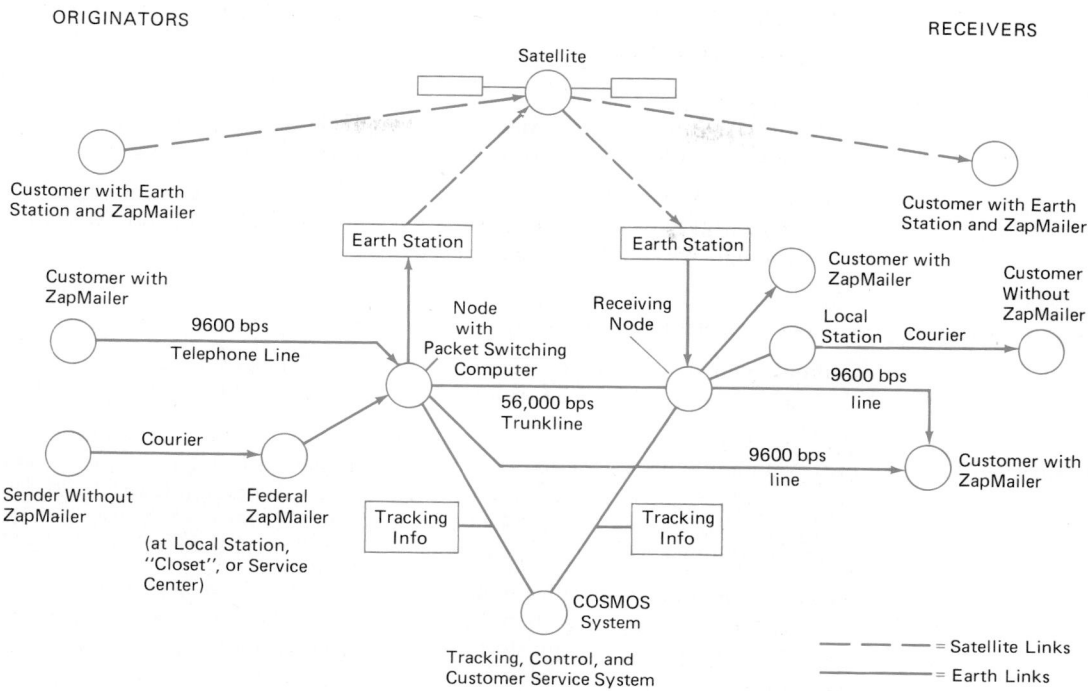

ORIGINATORS   RECEIVERS

the system if necessary. This provided for a "soft fail" as opposed to a "hard fail" capability, crucial to system reliability. As a result, in 1986 Federal's network for ZapMail had not gone "down" since the day it was brought on line (2 years before), despite the fact that it was switching 6 billion packets *a day.*

The combined ground and satellite system was considered a "hybrid system," which Federal hoped to convert into a pure satellite system. Because of new technologies ground station dishes were shrinking in size (and cost) rapidly, with small $4\frac{1}{2}$ foot diameters becoming commercially feasible for high-frequency transmission and reception. Even smaller sizes were predicted for the future. Simultaneously, satellite bandwidths (capacities to receive and transmit information per unit of time) were also expanding at exponential rates. Although a ZapMail page contained an enormous amount of information (640,000 bits of electronic data), communication satellites for television could already handle about 100 television channels simultaneously, each with a *6 million bit per second* requirement. And newer satellites were expected to be able to target their transmissions to very small areas (only a few thousand yards in diameter) at the earth's surface, thus increasing their flexibility even further.

Anticipating these changes. Federal's packet switching technique was designed to allow a "Telehub" in Memphis to coordinate the entire ZapMail system when Federal Express moved to its own satellites. The Telehub was (1) to remember each ZapMailer's unique location, call number, or frequency for transmission and reception; (2) to be directly in touch with all Federal's earth stations; and (3) to pick up, route, and control all Federal packets sent by satellite. Although in 1986 Federal was still leasing satellite space, it hoped that eventually each Zap-Mailer would be tied to its own earth station or at least have direct access to a 56,000 bps ground line connecting it to an earth station.

EXHIBIT 1
Early Equity Financing History Federal Express Corporation

September 1972	FWS Enterprise Co. (family trust) invests $3.25 million.
February 1973	(1) FWS invests $2 million. (2) White, Weld & Co. (Brick Meers) agrees to undertake a private placement attempt to raise $20 million. This placement was not successful.
May 1973	General Dynamics Corp. guarantees $23.7 million loan to FEC from Chase Manhattan Bank (due Sept. 1973). In return, GD received option to acquire 80% of FEC for $16 million. This option was never exercised.
July 1973	White, Weld and New Court Securities (Charles Lea and Richard Stowe) agree to try another private placement.
October 1973	Commitments of $23 million secured from venture capitalists. However, Chase Manhattan backed out of loan commitment, thus preventing completion of private placement.
November 1973	First National Bank of Chicago (Robert Abboud) agreed to replace Chase Manhattan as lead bank in lending pool. First Chicago loans $10 million. Chase lends $10 million, but requires additional $4 million investment from FWS Enterprise Co. This was drawn down as a private placement of $23 million of notes and revolving credit.
March 1974	(1) 64,000 shares of convertible preferred stock issued to raise $6.4 million. (2) Banks agreed to loan additional $5.1 million in exchange for warrants to purchase 226,190 shares of common stock at an average price of $3.07

Ownership of FEC

New Court	21%
FWS & FWS Enterp.	19%
Banks	9%
Citicorp Venture Capital	9%
Other	42%

September 1974	Venture capitalists purchase 1.6 million shares of convertible subordinated notes for $3.9 million

Ownership of FEC

Lenders/Banks	25%
New Court	16%
Prudential	11%
FWS & FWS Enterp.	9%
Other	39%

Source: Company records.

242

EXHIBIT 1 (Continued)

Federal Express Corporation Financial Highlights*
(Fiscal Years 1973–1978)

	1978	1977	1976	1975	1974	1973
Operating results						
Revenues	$160,301	$109,210	$75,055	$43,489	$17,292	$ 6,168
Operating income (loss)	25,237	13,068	9,845	(4,124)	(8,845)	(2,904)
Pretax income (loss)	19,544	7,678	3,635	(11,517)	(13,366)	(4,461)
Net income (loss)	19,498(a)	7,882	3,585	(11,517)	(13,366)	(4,661)
Earnings per share	0.63(a)	0.27	0.12			
Financial Position						
Current assets	$ 30,370	$ 20,349	$14,725	$ 9,481	$ 7,981	$ 3,100
Property and equipment, net	71,813	53,616	55,297	59,276	59,701	51,487
Total assets	106,291	75,321	71,229	70,193	70,697	56,771
Current liabilities	24,315	19,192	12,954	11,818	9,136	44,949
Long-term debt	30,825	46,229	56,186	59,892	51,605	11,533
Common stockholders' investment	37,491	(8,488)	(16,561)	(1,517)	(8,694)	289
Ave. shares outstanding	11,512	10,292	10,064	1,060	164	100

(a) After tax benefit of loss carryforward.
* $ In thousands except earnings per share.
Source: Company records.

EXHIBIT 2
Characteristics of U.S. Intercity Express Package/Document Delivery Market

	Urgent (same day)	Priority (next A.M.) Under 350 Miles	Priority (next A.M.) Over 350 Miles	Semipriority (next P.M.)	Nonpriority (next P.M. or 2nd day)
Principal transport mode(s)	Van; rail; air	Surface	Air	Air	Air or surface
Size of units (approximate)					
Small packages	NA	15 lb. (ave.)	15 lb. (ave.)	15 lb. (ave.)	15 lb. (ave.)
Envelopes	NA	Under 2 lb.	Under 2 lb.	Under 2 lb.	Under 2 lb.
Cartons/tubes	NA	Under 6 lb.	Under 6 lb.	Under 6 lb.	Under 6 lb.
Priority letters	NA	2 to 4 oz.	2 to 4 oz.	2 to 4 oz.	2 to 4 oz.
Illustrative rates (a)					
Small packages	(b)	Surface: $11.35 to $17.40(c) Air: $47.50 to $51.99	Surface: (d) Air: $47.50 to $51.99	Surface: $9.05-to-$19.10(d) Air: Up to $24.00	Surface: $8.25 to $15.39(a) Air: $9.37 to $24.00
Envelopes	(b)	Surface: $13.75 Air: $21.75 to $23.50	Surface: (d) Air: $21.75 to $23.50	Surface: $7.13 to $11.60(e) Air: $9.35 to $12.47	Surface: $2.54 to $13.74(c) Air: $2.70 to $4.00(c)
Cartons/tubes	(b)	Surface: $7.25 to $11.60(c) Air: $34.75 to $36.50	Surface: (d) Air: $34.75 to $36.50	Surface: $7.13 to $10.80(e) Air: $9.35 to $13.44	Surface: $2.54 to $13.74(c) Air: $2.70 to $4.00(c)
Priority letters	(b)	Surface: $8.75 Air: $11.00 to $12.50	Surface: (d) Air: $11.00 to $12.50	Surface: $8.75 Air: $8.75 to $9.35	(e)
Sensitivity	Service	Service	Service	Service, price	Price

NA Not available.
(a) Rates are given for illustrative purposes only. They refer to single units of average weight. They do not reflect volume discounts or any charges that might be added for special services.
(b) It is difficult to categorize same-day delivery rates because they vary with the type of service provided; USPS rates are low ($15.40 for a 14-pound Boston-to-Chicago delivery, for example), but this applies only to airport-to-airport service. Door-to-door pickup and delivery by specialized courier services can easily range up to $100.00, depending on distance.
(c) Depending on distance.
(d) Generally speaking, next-morning deliveries cannot be made by surface to points over 350 miles distant.
(e) Two-ounce letters can move on a 1-to-2 day basis for as little as 37 cents a letter.

Source: U.S. Postal Service, Company Service Guides in Kidder, Peabody & Co., Inc., The Equity Research Department, A. H. Norling. *Company Analysis: Federal Express Corp.*, June 20, 1983.

EXHIBIT 3
Estimated Daily Volume by Carrier in Various Segments of U.S. Intercity Parcel Express/Courier Express Package/Document Delivery Market (units in thousands) (a)

	Priority Market (E)(b)			Semipriority Market (E)(c)	Nonpriority (E)(d)	Total (E)
	Under 350 Miles(e)	Over 350 Miles(f)	Total			
Small package market						
U.S. Postal Service	(g)	(g)	(g)	30(g)	380	410
United Parcel Service	(g)	(g)	(g)	15	130	145
Purolator	107	10	117	—	(h)	117
Federal Express	6	40	46	22	—	68
Airborne Express	1	12	13	—	—	13
Emery Express	1	12	13	(h)	(h)	13
Burlington Northern	(h)	5	5	—	—	5
United Express	(h)	4	4	—	—	4
Others	1	6	7	—	—	7
Total	116	89	205	67	510	782
Envelope/carton market						
U.S. Postal Service	(g)	(g)	(g)	60(g)	420	480
Federal Express	7	67	74	—	—	74
Purolator	16	7	23	—	(h)	23
Airborne Express	1	10	11	—	—	11
Emery Express	(h)	7	7	—	—	7
United Express	—	1	1	—	—	1
Total	24	92	116	60	420	596
Priority letter market						
U.S. Postal Service	18(i)	48(i)	66(i)	—	—	66
Federal Express	4	36	40	—	—	40
Airborne Express	(g)	3	3	—	—	3
Emery Express (j)	(h)	(h)	(h)	(h)	—	(h)
Purolator (j)	4	1	5	—	—	5
Total	26	88	144	—	—	114

EXHIBIT 3 (Continued)

	Priority Market (E)(b)			Semipriority Market (E)(c)	Nonpriority (E)(d)	Total (E)
	Under 350 Miles(e)	Over 350 Miles(f)	Total			
Total market						
U.S. Postal Service	18	48	66	90	800	956
Federal Express	17	143	160	22	—	182
Purolator	127	18	145	—	(h)	145
United Parcel Service	—	—	—	15	130	145
Airborne Express	2	25	27	—	—	27
Emery Express	1	19	20	(h)	(h)	20
Burlington Northern	(h)	5	5	—	—	5
United Express	(h)	5	5	—	—	5
Others	1	6	7	—	—	7
Total	166	269	435	127	930	1,492

(NA) Not available.
(E) Kidder, Peabody & Co. Incorporated estimates.
(a) Average number of shipments per business day (255 days per year).
(b) Next-morning delivery.
(c) Next-afternoon delivery.
(d) Next-afternoon or second-day delivery; all distances; surface or air.
(e) Primarily surface.
(f) Primarily air.
(g) Although some deliveries may be made by noon, service is classified as semipriority because of lack of next morning commitment.
(h) Data either not available or insignificant in volume. Included in other categories.
(i) USPS Express mail letter service is regarded as a priority product despite lack of next morning commitment.
(j) Letter service inaugurated March 1, 1983.

Source: Kidder, Peabody & Co., Inc., The Equity Research Department, A. H. Norling, *Company Analysis: Federal Express Corp.,* June 20, 1983.

EXHIBIT 4
Estimated Carrier Shares in Various Segments of U.S. Intercity Express Delivery Market *(percentage of total revenues)*

Competitors	USPS	Federal Express	UPS	Emery	Purolator	Airborne	BNAF	United	All Others	Annual Value (% millions)
Small Package Market										
Priority under 350 miles (a)	—	21.7	—	4.5	69.0	3.1	(d)	(d)	1.7	290
Priority over 350 miles (a)	—	50.4	—	14.5	8.4	13.7	4.8	3.0	5.2	830
Semipriority market (b)	46.2	36.1	21.3	(d)	—	—	—	—	—	245
Nonpriority (c)	54.3	—	45.7	(d)	(d)	—	—	—	—	530
Envelope/Carton Market										
Priority under 350 miles (a)	—	50.7	—	(d)	42.3	7.0	—	(d)	—	70
Priority over 350 miles (a)	—	76.3	—	6.0	6.6	10.1	—	0.8	—	455
Semipriority market (b)	80.3	—	19.7	(d)	—	—	—	—	—	175
Nonpriority (c)	84.4	—	15.6	(d)	(d)	—	—	—	—	480
Priority Letter Market										
Priority under 350 miles (a)	69.4	17.7	—	(d)	12.9	(d)	—	—	—	60
Priority over 350 miles (a)	50.0	46.5	—	(d)	0.9	2.6	—	—	—	230
Total Market										
Priority under 350 miles (a)	10.2	26.0	—	3.1	56.3	3.3	—	—	1.1	420
Priority over 350 miles (a)	7.5	57.7	—	9.8	6.8	11.0	2.6	1.6	3.0	1,510
Semipriority market (b)	58.5	20.9	20.6	(d)	—	—	—	—	—	420
Nonpriority (c)	68.6	—	31.4	(d)	(d)	—	—	—	—	1,010

(a) Next-morning delivery.
(b) Next-afternoon delivery.
(c) Next-afternoon or second-day delivery.
(d) Data either not available or insignificant in volume. Included in other categories.
Annual value statistics are Kidder Peabody & Co. Inc. estimates.

Source: Kidder, Peabody & Co., Inc., The Equity Research Department, A. H. Norling, *Company Analysis: Federal Express Corp.,* June 20, 1983.

EXHIBIT 5
Federal Express Corporation Product Line Statistics

	FY 1981	FY 1982	FY 1983	FY 1984	FY 1985
Packages (000)					
Priority One and Courier Pak	20,117	24,800	29,221	38,080	51,562
Standard Air	2,029	2,207	4,555	11,136	18,932
Overnight Letter	—	5,093	8,830	18,211	33,048
ZapMail	—	—	—	—	554
Total	22,146	32,100	42,606	67,427	104,096
Yields					
Priority One and Courier Pak	$26.88	$27.86	$28.25	$28.14	$26.62
Standard Air	21.18	22.15	16.99	13.80	13.45
Overnight Letter	—	10.99	10.76	10.60	10.89
ZapMail	—	—	—	—	27.36
Composite	26.29	24.79	23.42	21.03	19.19
Percent of revenues					
Priority One and Courier Pak	91.5%	85.9%	81.9%	74.6%	67.6%
Standard Air	7.3	6.1	7.7	10.7	12.5
Overnight Letter	—	7.0	9.4	13.4	17.7
Other	1.2	1.0	1.0	1.3	2.2
Total	100.0%	100.0%	100.0%	100.0%	100.0%

	FY 1985				FY 1986	
	First Quarter	Second Quarter	Third Quarter	Fourth Quarter	First Quarter	Second Quarter
Total Packages (000)						
Priority One and Courier Pak	11,349	12,319	13,180	14,722	14,488	15,357
Standard Air	4,092	4,487	4,990	5,363	5,317	5,870
Overnight Letter	6,832	7,522	8,513	10,182	10,678	12,075
ZapMail	28	112	168	246	398	629
Total	22,301	24,440	26,851	30,513	30,881	33,931
Yields						
Priority One and Courier Pak	$27.08	$26.96	$25.98	$26.56	$26.52	$25.77
Standard Air	13.11	13.97	13.23	13.49	13.27	13.29
Overnight Letter	10.44	10.91	11.02	11.08	11.04	10.97
ZapMail	26.08	30.50	25.19	25.88	18.86	13.15
Composite	19.42	19.65	18.86	19.09	18.79	18.11
Percent of Revenues						
Priority One and Courier Pak	69.6%	68.5%	66.7%	66.0%	65.2%	63.2%
Standard Air	12.2	12.9	12.9	12.2	12.0	12.5
Overnight Letter	16.2	16.9	18.3	19.0	20.1	21.2
ZapMail	.2	.7	.8	1.1	1.3	1.3
Other	1.8	1.0	1.3	1.7	1.4	1.8
Total	100.0%	100.0%	100.0%	100.0%	100.0%	100.0%

Source: Company records.

EXHIBIT 5 (Continued)

Federal Express Corporation Operating Statistics

	FY 1981	FY 1982	FY 1983	FY 1984	FY 1985
Total costs ($000)					
Salaries and employee benefits	$233,831	$320,345	$419,644	$ 622,675	$ 907,186
Depreciation and amortization	39,195	56,341	77,421	111,956	172,333
Equipment and facility rentals	33,282	44,806	57,751	87,572	146,389
Fuel	57,037	69,282	71,262	93,520	133,473
Maintenance and repairs	22,286	38,795	44,083	59,482	90,992
Communications	14,382	23,304	27,191	37,370	81,872
Advertising	17,159	25,302	34,558	39,345	60,834
Provision for uncollectible accounts	4,290	8,108	11,184	13,927	29,646
Other	68,296	98,166	114,256	205,250	271,213
Total	$489,758	$684,449	$857,350	$1,271,097	$1,893,938
Cost per package					
Salaries and employee benefits	$10.56	$ 9.98	$ 9.85	$ 9.24	$ 8.71
Depreciation and amortization	1.77	1.75	1.82	1.66	1.66
Equipment and facility rentals	1.50	1.39	1.36	1.30	1.41
Fuel	2.58	2.16	1.67	1.39	1.28
Maintenance and repairs	1.01	1.21	1.03	0.88	0.87
Communications	0.65	0.73	0.64	0.55	0.79
Advertising	0.77	0.79	0.81	0.58	0.58
Provision for uncollectible accounts	0.19	0.25	0.26	0.21	0.28
Other	3.08	3.06	2.68	3.04	2.61
Total	$22.11	$21.32	$20.12	$18.85	$18.19
Cost per package by department					
Line haul operations	$ 7.66	$ 6.79	$ 5.44	$ 4.46	$ 3.62
Package support operations	8.58	8.43	8.98	9.26	8.98
Customer support	1.25	1.59	1.33	1.19	1.10
General support	1.73	1.33	1.71	1.54	1.38
Advertising and marketing support	0.99	0.98	0.95	0.70	0.66
General and administrative	1.51	1.75	1.20	1.00	0.94
Electronic products	—	—	0.03	0.19	0.80
Business service centers	0.21	0.21	0.24	0.31	0.44
Provisions for uncollectible accounts	0.18	0.24	0.24	0.20	0.27
	$22.11	$21.32	$20.12	$18.85	$18.19

Source: Company records.

EXHIBIT 5 (Continued)

Federal Express Corporation Financial Highlights
(Fiscal Years 1979–1985)

	1985	1984	1983	1982	1981	1980	1979
Operating results							
Revenues	$2,030,661	$1,436,305	$1,008,087	$803,915	$589,493	$415,379	$258,482
Operating income (loss)	136,723	165,208	150,737	119,466	99,735	67,001	40,112
Pretax income (loss)	83,378	152,260	150,216	131,080	98,044	59,373	33,783
Net income (loss)	76,077	115,430	88,933	78,385	58,136	37,729	20,383
Earnings per share	$1.61	$2.52	$2.03	$1.85	$1.42	$1.00	$.59
Operating margin	6.7%	11.5%	15.0%	14.9%	16.9%		
Pretax margin	4.1%	10.6%	14.9%	16.3%	16.6%		
Excl. aircraft sales	3.7%	10.4%	14.5%	15.4%	15.3%		
Financial position							
Current assets	$ 423,144	$ 328,136	$ 265,171	$194,265	$166,952	$ 85,454	$ 48,975
Property and equipment	1,793,016	1,427,281	817,650	603,598	467,194		
Accumulated depreciation	(466,993)	(314,642)	(221,258)	(146,026)	(93,944)		
Property and equipment, net	1,346,023	1,112,639	596,392	457,572	373,250	277,702	123,844
Total assets	1,899,506	1,525,805	991,717	730,291	570,112	395,030	179,823
Current liabilities	316,878	255,910	175,293	114,596	113,846	64,351	43,681
Long-term debt	607,508	435,158	247,424	223,856	162,705	142,465	45,729
Deferred income taxes	159,810	112,439	59,094	33,874	13,505		
$9.50 cumulative preferred stock	3,043	4,577	6,112	7,646	9,181		
Common stockholders' investment							
Common stock	$ 4,703	$ 4,639	$ 2,197	$ 2,076	$ 1,966		
Add'l paid-in capital	340,753	321,768	222,782	157,489	155,522		
Retained earnings	466,811	391,314	278,815	190,754	113,387		
Total common stockholders' investment	$ 812,267	$ 717,721	$ 503,794	$350,319	$270,875	$168,745	$ 74,946

* $ In thousands except earnings per share.
Source: Company records.

EXHIBIT 6
Federal Express Corporation 1985 Organization

Executive Vice President, Chief Operating Officer — James L. Barksdale
- Ground Operations and Sales
- Telecommunication
- Information Systems
- Central Support Services
- Electronic Products

Senior Vice President, Chief Personnel Officer — James A. Perkins
- Personnel Administration
- Human Resources Analysis
- Human Resource Development
- Corporate Safety, Health, & Fire
- Personnel Information Control Center (PICC)
- Corporate Services

Senior Vice President, Marketing & Customer Service — Carole A. Presley
- Marketing & Customer Service
- Electronic Products
- Express Products
- Customer Service
- Retail Marketing
- Corporate Marketing

Senior Vice President, Chief Financial Officer — David C. Anderson
- Financial Planning
- Revenue & Treasury Operations
- EPD & Telecommunication Finance
- Internal Audit
- Corporate Finance
- Risk Management
- Controller
- Tax

Senior Vice President, Information Systems — Ron J. Ponder
- Information Systems
- Systems Development
- Operations Research
- Computer Operations (Ground)
- Systems Engineering & Design
- Systems Integration
- Computer Operations

Senior Vice President, Electronic Products — Thomas R. Oliver
- Electronic Products Service
- Electronic Products Sales

Senior Vice President, Group Operations — Fred A. Manske
- Corporate Sales
- International Operations & Customs
- Ground Ops Training & Support Services
- Service Systems

Vice President, Corporate Communications — Daniel N. Copp
- Public Relations
- Employee Communications
- Publishing Services

Senior Vice President, General Counsel — Kenneth R. Masterson
- General Counsel
- Litigation
- Corporate Legal Affairs
- Regulatory Affairs
- Legal
- Corporate Security
- Contracts
- Labor/Employment Law

Senior Vice President, Line Haul Operations — James R. Riedmeyer
- Feeder Aircraft
- Flight Operations & Support
- Maintenance Services
- Corporate Aviation
- Aircraft Acquisition & Sales
- System Control/Scheduling
- Engineering & Quality Assurance

Senior Vice President, Telecommunications — T. Allan McArtor
- Systems
- Radio & Voice Systems
- International Telecommunications
- Satellite Systems Ops & Integration
- Telephone & Radio Systems

Senior Vice President, Central Support Services — Theodore L. Weise
- Sort Systems Development
- Hub Operations
- Properties & Facilities
- BSC/Field Sales & Operations
- Logistics

Source: Company records.

EXHIBIT 7

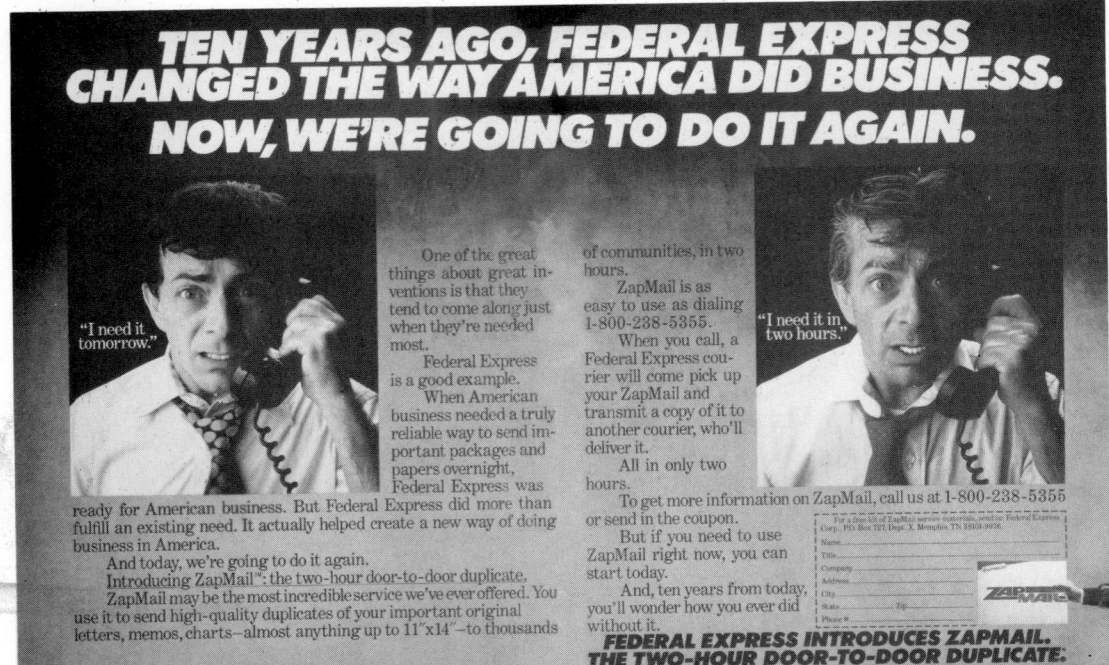

EXHIBIT 8
Network Analysis Report
for 02/28/86

Document First Call Failure Types

Description	Document Count	% of Total Docs. with Failures
Destination Busy	1358	53
Machine / Line Down	434	17
Call Drop	746	29
Destination Disk Full	14	1
Total First Call Failures	2552	100%

* Does not include broadcasts

Detailed Account of Above Groups

First Call Type	Document Count	% of Total Docs. with Failures
Destination Busy Receiving	1233	48
Dest. Busy Transmitting	125	5
All Dest. Lines Are Down	40	2
Dial 8 : Connection Failed	363	14
PMX / 2W : No Answer Tone	31	1
Dial 10 : Collision	121	5
No Data for 120 Seconds	199	8
BT: No Call Accepted	23	1
Dial 6 : Request Timeout	21	1
Origin Line Failed	43	2
Dest Line Failed	142	6
Checksum Error On 1st Page	9	0
Other Failures	934	37
No Destination Disk Space	14	1%

Source: Company records.

1-8

E & J GALLO WINERY

"The winemaker is a warrior" begins an old Italian poem. For nearly 50 years, the two sons of an Italian immigrant have taken those words to heart. Ever since they pooled $5,900 in capital to set up their winery in Modesto, California, in 1933, the brothers have managed their enterprise with a discipline, precision, and success that few companies enjoy. But, in the late 1980s, Ernest and Julio, then in their 70s, had to worry about the future of their remarkable concern. In 1986, *Fortune* magazine published a rare and insightful article on the company. The article, quoted almost in its entirety, follows.

A Will to Dominate

When it comes to business, the brothers Ernest and Julio Gallo brook neither waste nor weakness. Just ask the scores of companies, large and small, that over the past five decades have made the mistake of venturing onto their turf. [Despite their ages, Ernest and Julio Gallo] have not lost their desperate will to dominate. . . . What is Gallo's secret? "A constant striving for perfection in every aspect of our business," says Ernest. That may sound self-serving, but it is in large part true. Plainly put, Ernest and Julio are better at the nuts and bolts of the wine business than anyone else in the world. They are more resourceful, more thorough, more exacting. And they are not afraid to exercise their power over grape growers, distributors, or anyone else. "I sometimes feel like an Olympic runner who gets mad at his coach," says David Terk, an independent distributor in Abilene, Texas. "Gallo pushes so hard you end up working more than you want."

Case copyright © 1989 James Brian Quinn. This case was prepared from secondary sources only with the help of professor Richard D'Aveni. Research associate on this case was Penny C. Paquette. Materials reproduced by special permission from "How Gallo Crushes The Competition," by Jaclyn Fierman, September 1, 1986. Copyright © 1986 *Fortune* magazine.

Not that the Gallos face no challenges. The most unusual by far comes from their younger brother, Joseph, 66. In a drama worthy of the wine-country soap opera *Falcon Crest,* Joseph is suing for a one-third interest in the winery. He claims that the winery is an outgrowth of their father's wine-grape business and that his big brothers cheated him out of his rightful inheritance.

Ernest and Julio's other problems are more mundane. The national obsession with fitness and the crackdown on drunken driving have had a sobering effect on wine production, Gallo included. Americans drank 6.5% less table wine in 1985 than in 1984 and will probably cut consumption 5% more this year, according to *Impact,* an industry newsletter. The wine industry's smartest response to the new abstinence is coolers, fruity beverages with a splash of wine and roughly the alcohol content of beer. Gallo, in typical fashion, has outsmarted everyone: its year-old cooler, Bartles & Jaymes, is number one.

Further challenges come from another trend among wine drinkers—the swing to pricey table wines made from the finest grapes. Americans are demanding better quality than ever before, and premium wines have raised their share of the $8.3-billion-a-year business from 8% in 1980 to 20% today. Gallo sells more premium wine than any other producer, but its growth in this category is limited because it lacks snob appeal. The name *Gallo,* which means "rooster" in Italian, is associated with screw tops and bottles in paper bags (from its earlier marketing history). The brothers are battling to upgrade their image with the same vengeance they bring to every war they wage.

For now they can take heart in making the most, if not the best, wine in the world. The joke goes that Gallo spills more than anyone else sells. The truth is not far off. Last year Gallo shipped over 150 million gallons of wine, according to the *Gomberg-Fredrikson Report,* an authoritative industry newsletter. Its most popular brands are Chablis Blanc, Hearty Burgundy, Carlo Rossi, and other low-priced jug wines, which together account for a commanding 31% of the volume in that end of the market. The brothers also sell more champagne (André), brandy (E&J), sherry, vermouth, and port than anyone else. All told, they buy roughly 30% of California's annual wine-grape harvest and produce one of every four bottles of wine sold in the United States.

They also squeeze profits from the wine business while others come up dry. The winery is privately owned by Ernest, Julio, and their fecund families—between them the brothers have 4 children, 20 grandchildren, and 6 great-grandchildren. Three children, a son-in-law, and 4 grandchildren work for the company, but share little of Ernest and Julio's power. . . . [Ernest and Julio] keep financial details tightly corked. Based on interviews with dozens of current and former employees, industry experts, and competitors, *Fortune* estimated that Gallo earns at least $50 million a year on sales of roughly $1 billion. By comparison, Seagram, the nation's largest distillery and second-largest winery, booked roughly $350 million in wine revenues [in 1984] and lost money on its best-selling table wines, Paul Masson and Taylor California Cellars. Gallo's other main competitors, Almadén, owned by National Distillers & Chemical Corp., and Inglenook, owned by Heublein, are making money, but not much.

Private ownership and staggering volume contribute to Gallo's success. The company can wrest market share from competitors by settling for paper-thin margins and occasional losses that stockholders of publicly held companies might not tolerate for long. Moreover, Gallo does not have disparate claims on its resources and can devote all its energy to wine. "Unlike our major competition," says Ernest, "wine is our only business."

[Few] other companies could afford to replicate the degree of vertical integration Gallo has built up over the years. The brothers own Fairbanks Trucking Co., one of the largest intrastate truckers in California. Its 200 semis and 500 trailers are constantly hauling wine out of Modesto and raw materials back in—including sand from around the state and lime from Gallo's quarry east of Sacramento. Alone among wine producers, Gallo makes bottles—2 million a day—and its Mid-cal Aluminum Co. spews out screw tops as fast as the bottles are filled.

Crusher Power

Most of the country's 1,300 or so wineries concentrate on production to the neglect of marketing. They entrust their fate with consumers to independent distributors who work for several competing producers. Most distributors, in turn, figure their job is done once they take orders and make deliveries to grocery and liquor stores. Gallo, by contrast, participates in every aspect of selling short of whispering in the ear of each imbiber. The company owns its distributors in about a dozen markets and probably would buy many of the more than 300 independents who handle its wines if laws in most states did not prohibit doing so.

Gallo's power elicits emotions from admiration to hate from just about everyone touched by it. "The hate part," says a Sonoma Valley grower, "is getting rejected by Gallo at the crusher"—the place where growers bring their grapes to be graded, sold, and eventually crushed into juice and fermented. Distributors feel hatred or something near it if they are unceremoniously dumped, as many have been for failing to satisfy Ernest's demanding requirements. Competitors hate being singled out as the next rival to be vanquished. Says a cowed Stuart Bewley, who helped start California Cooler five years ago, "They aim all their guns at once." Bewley's brand was the market leader in wine coolers until Gallo stormed into the business. Bewley sold California Cooler to Brown-Forman (in 1984) but still manages the operation. Yet even competitors thank the Gallos for expanding the wine market. While the Gallos may not make the world's best wine, they have lifted the U.S. standard for low-priced table wine well above that served in Italy or France.

A Divided Kingdom

E & J Gallo Winery is a divided kingdom. Julio is president and oversees production. Big brother Ernest is chairman and rules over marketing, sales, and distribution. The two steer clear of each other, conducting business on separate floors. "We don't have everyday contact," says Julio, whose domain is the first floor at the neoclassic headquarters some natives call Parthenon West. Ernest holds court upstairs. The brothers mesh well despite the division: Julio's goal is to make more wine than Ernest can sell, Ernest's to sell more than Julio can make.

Thick fingered and full faced, Julio aptly describes himself as a farmer at heart. "I like to walk in the fields with the old-timers," he says. "I feel at home in the vineyards." Make no mistake, though, Julio is a patrician farmer, dressed not in overalls and work boots but in linen trousers and slightly scuffed wing tips. His office is elegantly appointed, with a solid oak desk and inlaid wooden artworks depicting harvest scenes in the French countryside. His modern ranch house down the road from the winery is festooned with images of grapes, from jade carvings along the walls to the silverware and place mats on his table.

Ernest conducts business in a setting cluttered with mementos not from the fields but from the world of selling. He has a framed New Yorker cartoon that shows two couples drinking wine in a restaurant. The caption reads: "Surprisingly good, isn't it? It's Gallo. Mort and I simply got tired of being snobs." Expressions of fierce pride abound from the Gallo-green crushed-velvet couch to an ambitious collection of glass, metal, and ceramic statuettes of *galli*. Paler, grittier, and less courtly than his brother, Ernest cares little for social or decorative amenities. "We don't socialize much," says the more affable Julio. "There's not much to talk about."

Ernest wouldn't waste time schmoozing anyway. He would rather interrogate than converse. He bridles when questioned and has the habit of answering with questions of his own. He is after all the information he can get and is intolerant when someone does not deliver. "If you try to cover up, he'll expose you," says George Frank, who directed Gallo's East Coast sales for three decades and retired last year.

Ernest's employees toil much harder than most because they know the boss will try to catch them off guard. "I never knew if he was checking on the marketplace or on me," says Frank. On frequent trips around the country, Ernest orders a distributor to pick him up at eight in the morning, map in hand. Mindful of neither distance nor direction, he points to several towns where he wants to check the positioning of his products in stores. "Ernest doesn't want you to take him on a tour," says Laurence Weinstein, a distributor in Madison, Wisconsin. "If he sees you turning left, he'll tell you to turn right."

The distributors behave more like family members than independents because most owe their success to the winery. "Ernest picked distributors who were hungry," says Frank. "They knew if they failed with Gallo, they might be out on the street." Once Ernest chooses a distributor, he or his troops plan strategy with him down to the last detail, analyzing traffic patterns in every store in the district and the number of Gallo cases each should stock.

A Regimented Distribution System

Ernest encourages distributors to hire a separate sales force to sell his products alone. When Texas distributor David Terk decided it wasn't worth the extra money to employ a special Gallo team, he and Ernest severed ties. Terk eventually came around to Gallo's way of thinking and has been reinstated. "If you follow Ernest's advice," Terk says, "he'll make you rich." Ernest also tries to persuade distributors to sell his wines exclusively. "We never told distributors to throw out Gallo competitors," says Frank. "But we might have asked them how they planned to do justice if they carried two competing brands."

The Federal Trade Commission objected to that friendly persuasion 10 years ago, charging Gallo with unfair competition. Gallo signed a consent order that prohibited it from punishing distributors for selling competing brands and from requiring them to disclose sales figures. The FTC set aside the order three years ago after Gallo argued that the market had grown more competitive and that the order was giving other wine makers an unfair advantage: they were freed to set up exclusive deals with distributors.

Now that Gallo can regiment its distributors once again, it rarely hears a grumble out of them. One bold exception: Ohio distributor Bernard Rutman sued Gallo last year, alleging that the company violated antitrust laws when it dumped him for no good reason after 40 years of loyal service. Without Gallo products, which Rutman referred to as "call items" or "door openers," he lost several retail accounts. Rutman claimed that Gallo's action had reduced competition because he could no longer afford the sales force needed to sell a broad range of products. Gallo fought the charges and won, arguing that it was not the winery's responsibility to open doors for competitors. Rutman is appealing.

Ernest finds distributors who will open doors for *him*. Aggressive salesmen are crucial to Gallo's success because they are the winery's link to retailers, and retailers have the last crack at influencing consumers. "Seagram," concedes Edgar Bronfman Jr., "has typically pushed everything to the distributor and left it to him to deal with the stores." Ernest makes certain that his distributors deal with the stores like no others. They build floor displays, lift cases, and dust the bottles on the shelves. "If you turn your back on a Gallo salesman," says a manager of a San Francisco liquor store, "he'll turn the place into a Gallo outlet."

Gallo leaves nothing to chance—and very little to the imagination. Required reading and rereading for new salesmen is Gallo's 300-page training manual. More graphic than the *Kama Sutra,* it describes and diagrams every conceivable angle of the wine business. "As a sales representative of Gallo wine," the tome begins, "you are the man that Ernest and Julio Gallo depend on to sell retailers the merchandising ideas that sell Gallo wine to consumers."

What follow are 16 dizzying chapters, each ending with a quiz. A section on how to display Gallo products in stores spells out which items to place at eye level (the most highly advertised ones) and which to position above the belt (impulse items). Another details how much shelf space Gallo brands should occupy (seven feet on each of five shelves, the largest area the eye can easily scan). Maintaining shelves the Gallo way requires a ten-point checklist (No. 7: "Wherever there is a decided price advantage in buying a larger size, the larger size should be placed to the right of the smaller size.") The "complete sales call" would be incomplete unless all ten steps from another checklist were taken (No. 6: "It's time to think . . . you should know what you'd like to say and how you're going to say it to *this* retailer.").

Among the trove of sales tips: "An off-color joke may be great if you're selling pornography, but it's a little difficult to use this opener . . . to sell the retailer on cold-box placement for wine." The retail world is made up of six types of buyers, the manual explains. They range from "the silent type (he just listens)" to "the aggressive type (he's looking for a fight)." If you run into the silent type, "avoid embarrassing questions." When you meet up with an aggressive one, "let him win the battle, but you win the war."

Gallo hasn't lost a war yet. Even Coca-Cola, no wimp at marketing, surrendered in 1983 after six years of butting barrels with the wine Goliath. When Coke got into the wine business in 1977, consumption had been rising 7% a year. But that trend soon fizzled. The profit margins Coke was used to in soda never materialized for wine, not even close. By the time Coke sold its Wine Spectrum unit to Seagram for more than $200 million, it had overpromoted and underpriced its Taylor California Cellars.

From Plebeian to Snob

Pleasing the plebeian palate in Podunk used to be all that mattered in the wine business, and no one did that better than Gallo. But today even Podunk has wine snobs. Having to prove themselves all over again is a nasty twist of fate for the Gallos, who have devoted decades to upgrading everyday drinking wine for Americans. "We have varietals we think are the very best," Julio insists. Not Chateau Lafite, to be sure, but certainly respectable. Some wine connoisseurs compare Gallo's varietals to competing brands that sell for twice as much.

The screw-top stigma hurts, but the Gallo brothers learned early how bitter the wine business can be. They got their first taste as young boys, toiling in their father Joseph's Modesto vineyard in their spare time. After Julio finished high school and Ernest graduated from Modesto Junior College, they worked full time for their father. "He believed in hard work and no play," says Julio. "None at all."

An immigrant from the Piedmont region in northwest Italy, Joseph Gallo was a small-time grape grower and shipper. Prohibition did not put him out of work: the government permitted wine for medicinal and religious use. But the Depression took a tragic toll. The Gallo business almost went under, and in the spring of 1933 Joseph shot his wife and reportedly chased Ernest and Julio across his fields waving a shotgun. After they escaped, Joseph killed himself. Ernest is reminded of the tragedy daily: his childhood residence, a stucco house with a pillared porch, is on the road from the winery to his present home, a modest bungalow with a security guard out front. Julio relived the horror years later when his second son, Philip, then a teenager, committed suicide.

Prohibition ended the same year that their parents died, and the Gallos, then in their early 20s, decided to switch from growing grapes to producing wine. Problem was, they had no idea how to make the stuff. They found instructions in two thin pamphlets in the Modesto Public Library and, with $5,900.23 to their names, burst out of the post-Prohibition starting gate with 600 other newly formed wineries. "My confidence," recalls Ernest, "was unlimited."

Finding customers was the next hurdle, and Ernest was born with an instinct for that. A Chicago distributor wrote to newly licensed California wineries, inviting them to send him samples. Ernest went the extra mile. He boarded a plane for Chicago, met the man at his office, and sold him 6,000 gallons at 50 cents a gallon. Ernest continued east and sold the rest of the first year's production for a profit of $34,000. The Gallos initially sold wine in bulk to bottlers, but in 1938 they started doing their own bottling under the Gallo label, a far more profitable venture. Sales grew unabated for years.

"Success in life," says the insular Ernest, "depends on who your parents were and what circumstances you grew up in." Hard work was Joseph Gallo's ethic, and it became Ernest's as well. Driving himself and others is a survival instinct for Ernest. But perhaps because his father ultimately failed, Ernest also believes that hard work alone is not enough. "It boils down to luck," he says of his and Julio's success. "Circumstances could have been otherwise."

Growing with Thunder

As luck would have it, the Gallos had their first phenomenal success with a high-alcohol, lemon-flavored beverage they began selling in the late 1950s. A radio jingle sent the stuff to the top of the charts on skid rows across the country: "What the word? Thunderbird. How's it sold? Good and cold. What's the jive? Bird's alive. What's the price? Thirty-twice." But Thunderbird also left Gallo with a gutter image it has been hard pressed to shake.

Each in his own way, the Gallos are fighting to change that. Julio may be more easygoing than Ernest, but he is no pushover when it comes to getting what he wants from growers. Says Frank, Gallo's former East Coast executive: "He works with grapes as if he's pursuing the Holy Grail." With the help of graduates from California's top oenology schools, Julio has experimented with hundreds of varieties over the years. In the 1960s he made an unprecedented offer of 15-year contracts to growers who would rip up their vineyards and replant better grapes. Julio got his better grapes, and he also got an assured supply of his most essential raw material. Unlike small wineries, which grow the bulk of their grapes, Gallo buys more than 95 percent of the grapes it crushes.

Growing for Gallo is a mixed blessing. The 1,500 Gallo growers know they have a home for their grapes every season because Gallo's needs are so vast. But they are never sure how much they will get paid until they get to one of Gallo's three grape-crushing and fermenting operations: the Frei Brothers winery in Sonoma County, which Gallo bought from the Frei family in 1977, or the Livingston and Fresno plants in San Joaquin Valley. If grapes do not meet standards for Gallo's top-quality wines—handpicked, the right color, the proper acid and sugar balance—the winery downgrades them for use in other products and slashes the price. The *Healdsburg Tribune,* a newspaper in Sonoma County, has condemned the Gallos and called for state regulation of grading. An editorial claimed growers had been victimized by "sudden devaluation or outright rejection of their grapes, always with the company's take-it-or-leave-it attitude. . . . Most growers have little choice but to take it."

One who chose not to take it was Steven Sommer, a Sonoma grower who filed a grievance with the California Department of Agriculture in 1984 after Gallo downgraded most of his 50-ton harvest from $475 a ton to $275. Gallo claimed the grapes were off color and therefore would not yield flavorful wine. "It was just the way the sun was shining on them," Sommer insisted. The state ruled in Gallo's favor: since the growers had no written contract stating otherwise, Gallo had the right to judge grapes however it chose. Sommer's protest served a purpose, though. Gallo now gives one-year contracts in Sonoma County that spell out its standards. "The old-timers always did business on a handshake," says Julio. "The young growers want things in writing." Sommer has gone into business for himself, producing wine from the grapes he grows.

Julio insists on rigorous standards in Modesto, where all Gallo products are blended, bottled, and tasted every morning at 11 o'clock. Gallo was among the first producers to store wine in stainless steel containers instead of the usual redwood or concrete casks that can breed bad-tasting bacteria. Like giant thermos bottles, tanks at Gallo's three crushers and at the Modesto headquarters protect 300 million gallons of wine from the searing heat. Passers-by could easily mistake the Modesto plant for an oil refinery. There's no sign anywhere that says Gallo. "We know where the place is," Julio explains.

The refinery image is a sore point with Julio. "It was never my ambition to run the biggest winery in the world," he says. "It doesn't impress me at all." Unlike other wineries, Gallo offers no tours to the public. [Although Gallo has a 3-million-gallon underground cask facility], changing Gallo's image is really an above-ground proposition, and Ernest is throwing more than $40 million into advertising this year to get the quality message to consumers. . . . It features sensuous, slow-moving images of ethnic weddings, sunlit vineyards, and crystal goblets, to a mesmerizing score by Vangelis, the Academy Award–winning composer for the movie *Chariots of Fire.*

The new image is being crafted by Hal Riney, a San Francisco ad man with an agency bearing his name. Riney is also the genius behind those fictional farmers, Frank Bartles and Ed Jaymes, who told us in their early ads about how they put their orchard and vineyard together to make a premium wine cooler. "So Ed took out a second on his house," says poker-faced Frank, "and wrote to Harvard for an MBA." The pair was recently seen in New York City eating "big doughnuts" (the locals call them bagels).

Bartles & Jaymes has hurtled to the top of a high heap—there are over 100 coolers on the market. Cooler sales reached almost 40 million cases in 1984, and Marvin Shanken, publisher of *Impact,* predicted that consumption could swell to 90 million cases and constitute a third of the total wine market by 1990. The wine in most coolers is made from the cheapest grapes, and initially the mix was far more profitable than straight wine. But in typical fashion, Gallo devastated everyone else's profit margins when it entered the war. "We've had to double our ad spending and put our products on promotion a lot more often," says California Cooler's Bewley. Another major accomplishment for Riney has been getting along with Ernest Gallo. Before Riney, scores of agencies tried and failed to hack Ernest's ways. That kind of turnover is legendary at Gallo. A few employees, like Frank, stay forever, but many leave after a few years with whatever tricks they've managed to learn from one of America's best marketing minds.

A Generation Gap

A long-time Gallo executive puts his finger on a problem this has caused: "There's a whole level missing at Gallo in terms of age." The Gallos will not tolerate being crossed, even by family. Their battle with brother Joseph, who raises cattle and grows grapes, started when Joseph began selling cheese under the Gallo name. Ernest and Julio claimed Joseph was violating their trademark and, they say, offered him a royalty-free license to use the name. When Joseph refused, Ernest and Julio sued him for trademark infringement.

Joseph's lawyer says his research for that suit led to the discovery that the trademark dated back to the father's business. He then researched the father's estate to determine whether Joseph, who was 13 when his father killed himself, was an heir to the trademark. That search, the lawyer says, led to the discoveries that Joseph had inherited an interest in the father's business and that E & J Winery is an outgrowth of that business. Ernest and Julio say Joseph's claim is ridiculous, and that they started the winery with their own savings.

Ernest tries to recruit Ivy Leaguers and young MBAs—nearly all of them men. "We look for creativity, compatibility, and a sense of urgency," he says. But he doesn't give the whiz kids room to grow. Gallo graduates say the most frustrating thing about Ernest is his insistence on keeping everything secret. "I never saw a profit-and-loss statement," says Diana Kelleher, 39, who was marketing manager for several products in the early 1980s and one of the few women executives at Gallo. "Ernest wouldn't tell anyone the cost of raw materials, overhead, or packaging." Kelleher now runs a Los Angeles consulting firm.

Julio has begun to pass his scepter: his son, Robert, 52, and son-in-law, James Coleman, 50, oversee much of the day-to-day production. Ernest refuses to give anyone an aerial view of his part of the kingdom. Both his sons, David, 47, and Joseph, 45, work on his side of the business, but neither is heir apparent. Though both graduated from Notre Dame and Joseph has an MBA from Stanford, they lack their father's drive and authority. Those who have worked closely with the family say that Joseph's judgment is uneven and David's behavior occasionally bizarre.

But if Ernest's sons are less prepared to run Gallo than they should be, the problem may have more to do with his management style than their deficiencies. Ernest claims he wants people to be daring, yet his intimidating manner usually produces sycophants. He governs by a committee consisting of his sons and a handful of top executives. On most policy matters, Ernest goes around the table and asks each man for his opinion. But he usually fails to elicit their best because they try to second-guess him. Ernest cannot bear to relinquish control. The deep-rooted need to hold on is understandable: in his world, events can get so wildly out of control that they produce the tragedies of his youth. Call his style shortsighted, even paranoid. Rest assured, though, Ernest has figured out how to sell Gallo products from the grave. He probably is well along on a manual outlining every conceivable war that could break out in the wine world and ten steps to win each one."

Although the U.S. market is growing, the U.S. total consumption of wines is still only sixth in the world, behind much smaller countries like Spain, Italy, and Argentina (see Exhibit 1). Moreover, the United States is a poor ninth in terms of per capita wine consumption among major countries, fortieth if all countries are included.

Production of wine has always been an international phenomenon (see Exhibit 2). France leads the world in quality wine exports, although individual wines from other areas (including a strong new representation from California) enjoy excellent individual reputations. Such wines usually come from individual vineyards, although starting in the mid-1970s, there were innumerable attempts to reproduce the qualities of the great wines—particularly French wines—by using the same varieties of grapes and similar soil conditions. Although the French have dominated with the concept of the "varietal" wines—those made from only one grape variety —the idea is beginning to spread to other areas. The Italians, in particular, are beginning to specialize, exploiting certain well-regarded grape stocks, their favorable growing climate, and low-cost labor.

New technology has also begun to affect the industry. Until recently, mass-produced wines were simply not stable enough to be transportable and had to be drunk within a few months of fermentation. Wines had to be aged in wood, distilled to kill destructive bacteria, or sweet enough to cope with storage and transport. However, modern technologies of wine processing and storage allow world transport of most varieties. But nearly half the cost of most imported wines is in excise duties and local taxes. Customs duties on wine in developed countries are generally specific to the particular wine and increase with the gradations of the wine and whether it is imported in bottles or bulk containers.

Many changes in technology have to do with the development of special grape varieties designed to appeal to the palates of modern consumers. The French call these varieties "noble," but they tend to be less productive per acre than some of the stronger wine grapes, yielding fewer grapes after more attention has been paid to them. Nevertheless, it is the fermentation process that has changed most. White dry wines formerly tended to be unstable unless they were treated with sulfur. The California industry, however, pioneered a revolution in which the juice is fermented at relatively cool temperatures in cylinders made of stainless steel. The temperature is much easier to control than in traditional wooden vats. And the wine can be kept firmly insulated from the air by means of inert gases. For red wines, tradition dictated that they be kept in wood storage for several years to stand the strains of travel and further storage. This led to stronger, tougher wines which provided energy for the drinker. Now stainless steel, temperature- and atmosphere-controlled tanks, and careful measurement and control of the fermentation process allow production and shipment virtually anywhere for markets in which lightness is preferred, fruitiness is desirable, and nourishment is tertiary. (See Exhibit 3.)

The American Market

The American market for imported wines is the world's largest and most competitive. While wines were long the beverage of the elite, the large emerging class of professional people and the extended travel habits of Americans have led to a broad geographic and income distribution for imported wines. As the 1980s began, wine consumption was growing in the United States at an annual rate of 6–7%, with estimates for the 1985–1990 era being an average of 6.7% against an earlier growth rate of less than 4%. Wine purchases were growing at over twice the rate for soft drinks and beer, while sales of distilled spirits remained static. The U.S. wine industry responded by producing high-quality "jug wines" on a massive scale at prices which importers found hard to match. A number of well-to-do Californians also formed new boutique wineries to satisfy the emerging tastes for distinctiveness. Nevertheless, imports took over an increasing share of the total American market. In 1960 they accounted for 7% of the market, 10% in 1970, and 21% in 1980. By 1985 the figure was over 25%. The new market was still dominated by some very large players. In 1985 the approximate market shares were as follows:

E & J Gallo	26.1%
Seagram and Sons	8.3%
Canandaigua	5.4%
Brown Forman	5.1%
National Distillers	4.0%
Heublein	3.7%
Imports	25.0% (approx.)
All others	22.6% (approx.)

Source: Compiled from *Fortune,* September 1, 1986, and import data modified from world data sources.

An estimated 7% of the U.S. population consumed nearly two-thirds of all table wines sold, and nearly half these people lived in five states: California, New York, Florida, Illinois, and Texas. However, table wine was becoming much more widespread geographically in the mid-1980s. A saying persisted that "every time an old bourbon drinker dies, two wine drinkers come of age." The wine and spirits industry journal, *Impact,* estimated that per capita consumption would reach 5.4 gallons a year by 1990, translating into a sales increase of about 80% over the entire decade. While the mid- and low-priced wine markets became more competitive, the premium segment, which accounted for approximately 10% of the $5.5 billion California wine industry, boomed at a 12% growth rate. However, the resulting rush by the boutique vintners to satisfy this market produced a scattered and often inconsistent offering. Consumers who had earlier embraced common, inexpensive wines began to move to these wines, to imported beers, and to wine coolers. Growth of low-priced California wines had flattened since 1980 and actually fell 5% in 1985. In the mid-1980s, the U.S. wine-producing industry was beginning to undergo many mergers and consolidations as firms moved for scale economies and as foreign wineries and producers sought expanded access to U.S. distribution. For many, the industry was notoriously lacking in profits. As one executive of Christian Brothers said, "You want to know how to make a small fortune in the wine business? Start with a large one."

QUESTIONS

1. Why did Ernest and Julio Gallo choose their particular strategy? What are the strengths and weaknesses of their past strategy?

2. What important environmental and business changes must Gallo Winery deal with in the near future? What strategic alternatives exist?

3. If you were a consultant to the Gallos, how would you approach the issues of strategy implementation posed by the new strategy?

4. If you were competing against the Gallos, what actions would you take? What specific actions should the Gallos take in the near future? Why?

EXHIBIT 1

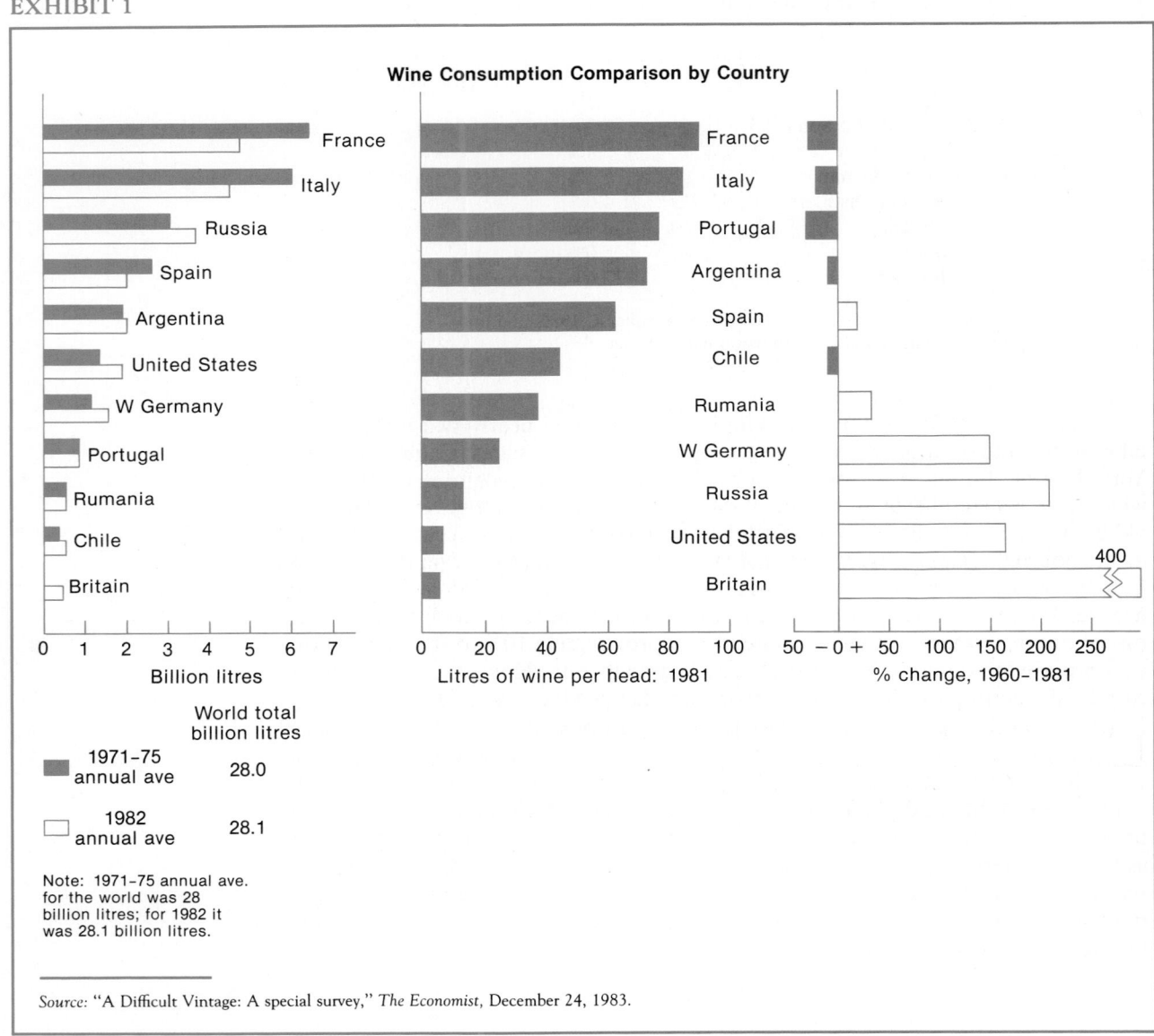

Wine Consumption Comparison by Country

Source: "A Difficult Vintage: A special survey," *The Economist*, December 24, 1983.

EXHIBIT 2

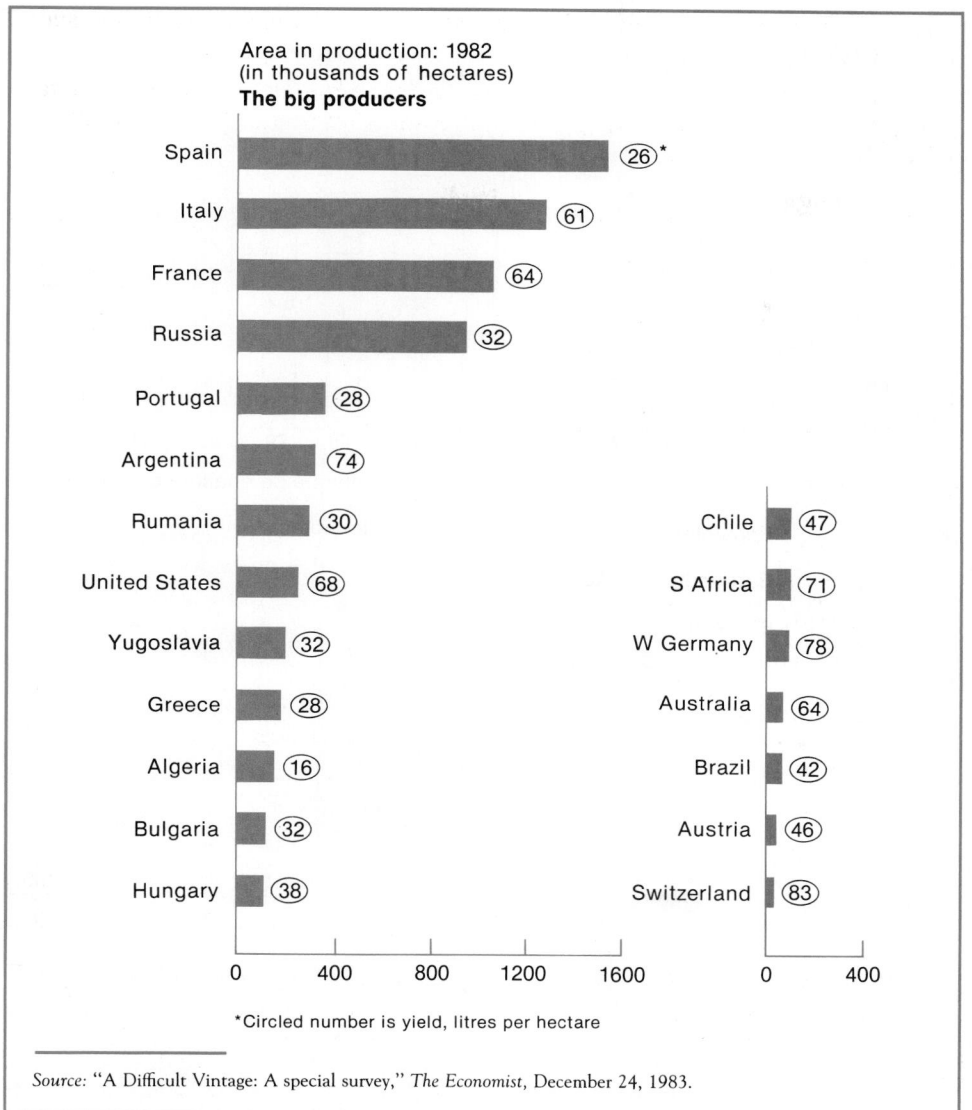

Area in production: 1982
(in thousands of hectares)
The big producers

*Circled number is yield, litres per hectare

Source: "A Difficult Vintage: A special survey," *The Economist*, December 24, 1983.

EXHIBIT 3

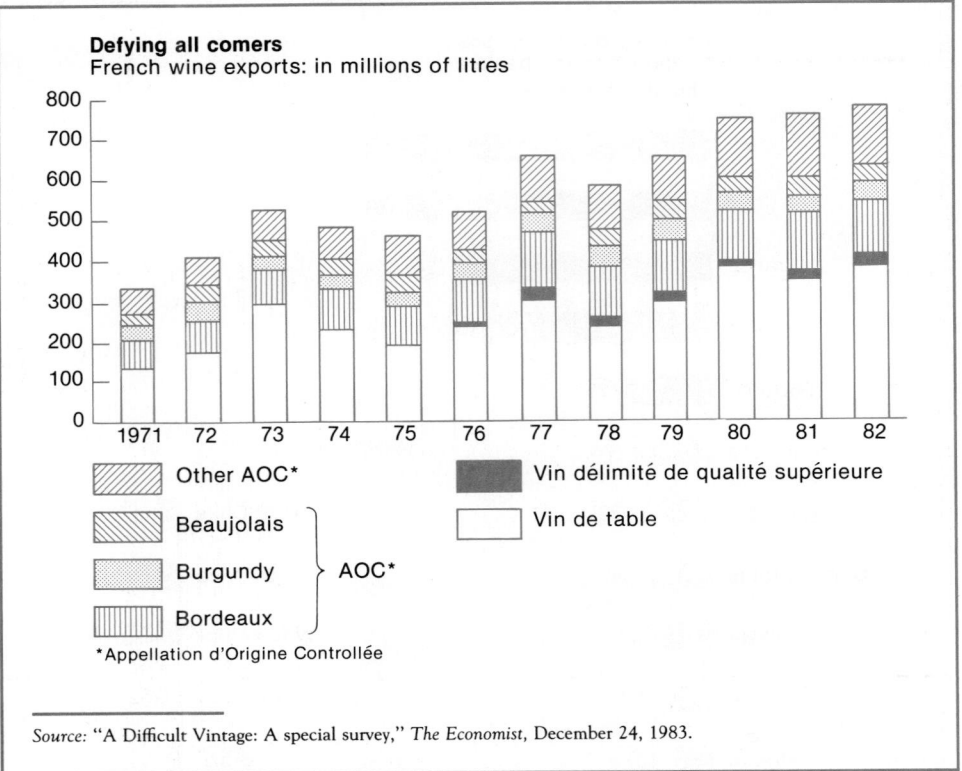

Defying all comers
French wine exports: in millions of litres

Legend:
- Other AOC*
- Beaujolais
- Burgundy } AOC*
- Bordeaux
- Vin délimité de qualité supérieure
- Vin de table

*Appellation d'Origine Controllée

Source: "A Difficult Vintage: A special survey," *The Economist*, December 24, 1983.

IBM (A): THE SYSTEM/360 DECISION

The decision by the management of the International Business Machines Corp. to produce a new family of computers, called the System/360, was one of the most crucial and portentous—as well as perhaps the riskiest—business judgments of recent times. The decision committed IBM to laying out money in sums that read like the federal budget—some $5 billion over a period of four years. To launch the 360, IBM was forced into sweeping organizational changes, with executives rising and falling with the changing tides of battle. The very character of this large and influential company was significantly altered by the ordeal of the 360, and the way it thought about itself changed, too. Bob Evans, the line manager who had the major responsibility for designing this gamble of a corporate lifetime, was only half joking when he said: "We called this project 'You bet your company.' "

Evans insisted that the 360 "was a damn good risk, and a lot less risk than it would have been to do anything else, or to do nothing at all," and there is a lot of evidence to support him. . . . A long stride ahead in the technology of computers in commercial use was taken by the 360. So sweeping were the implications that it required ten years before there was enough data to evaluate the wisdom of the whole undertaking.

The new System/360 was intended to obsolete virtually all other existing computers—including those being offered by IBM itself. Thus, the first and most extraordinary point to note about this decision was that it involved a challenge to the marketing structure of the computer industry—an industry that the challenger itself had dominated overwhelmingly for nearly a decade. It was roughly as though

Case compilation copyright © 1983 by James Brian Quinn. All sections drawn from a two-part series: T. A. Wise, "IBM's $5 Billion Gamble," and "The Rocky Road to the Marketplace," *Fortune,* September–October 1966. Copyright © 1966 Time, Inc. All rights reserved to original copyright holder. Reproduced by permission. Questions at end added by Professor Quinn. Verb tenses have been edited to clarify time relationships. Minor sections have been deleted (. . .) when peripheral.

General Motors had decided to scrap its existing makes and models and offer in their place one new line of cars, covering the entire spectrum of demand, with a radically redesigned engine and an exotic fuel. . . .

[In 1966] there were perhaps 35,000 computers in use, and it was estimated that there would be 85,000 by 1975. IBM sat astride this exploding market, accounting for something like two-thirds of the worldwide business—that is, the dollar value of general-purpose computers then installed or on order. IBM's share of this market [in 1965] represented about 77% of the company's $3.6 billion gross revenues [and $477 million of profits].

Several separate but interrelated steps were involved in the launching of System/360. Each one of the steps involved major difficulties, and taking them all meant that IBM was accepting a staggering challenge to its management capabilities. First, the 360 depended heavily on microcircuitry, an advance technology in the field of computers. In a 1952 vacuum-tube model of IBM's first generation of computers, there were about 2,000 components per cubic foot. In a second-generation machine, which used transistors instead of tubes, the figure was 5,000 per cubic foot. The System/360 model 75 computer, using hybrid microcircuitry, involved 30,000 components per cubic foot. The old vacuum-tube computer could perform approximately 2,500 multiplications per second; the 360 model 75 was designed to perform 375,000 per second. The cost of carrying out 100,000 computations on the first-generation model was $1.38; the 360 reduced the cost to $3\frac{1}{2}$ cents.

The second step was the provision for compatibility—that is, as the users' computer requirements grew they could move up from one machine to another without having to discard or rewrite already existing programs. Limited compatibility had already been achieved by IBM, and by some of its competitors too, for that matter, on machines of similar design but different power. But it had never been achieved on a broad line of computers with a wide range of powers, and achieving this compatibility depended as much on developing compatible programs or "software" as it did on the hardware. All the auxiliary machines—"peripheral equipment" as they are called in the trade—had to be designed so that they could feed information into or receive information from the central processing unit; this meant that the equipment had to have timing, voltage, and signal levels matching those of the central unit. In computerese, the peripheral equipment was to have "standard interface." The head of one competing computer manufacturing company acknowledges that at the time of the System/360 announcement he regarded the IBM decision as sheer folly and doubted that IBM would be able to produce or deliver a line that was completely compatible.

Finally—and this was the boldest and most perilous part of the plan—it was decided that six main units of the 360 line, originally designated models 30, 40, 50, 62, and 70, should be announced and made available simultaneously. (Models at the lower and higher ends of the line were to be announced later.) This meant that all parts of the company would have to adhere to a meticulous schedule.

UP IN MANUFACTURING, DOWN IN CASH

The effort involved in the program was enormous. IBM spent over half a billion dollars on research and development programs associated with the 360. This involved a tremendous hunt for talent: by the end of 1966, one-third of IBM's 190,000 employees had been hired since the new program was announced. Between that time, April 7, 1964, and the end of 1967, the company opened five new plants in the United States and abroad and had budgeted a total of $4.5 billion for rental machines, plant, and equipment. Not even the Manhattan Project, which produced the atomic bomb in World War II, cost so much (the government's costs up to Hiroshima are reckoned at $2 billion), nor, probably, had any other privately financed commercial project in history.

Such an effort changed IBM's nature in several ways:

The company, which was essentially an assembler of computer components and a business-service organization, became a major manufacturing concern as well. It became the world's largest maker of integrated circuits, producing an estimated 150 million of the hybrid variety annually in the late 1960s.

After some ambivalence, IBM abandoned any notion that it was simply another American company with a large foreign operation. The view now is that IBM is a fully integrated international company, in which the managers of overseas units are presumed to have the same capabilities and responsibilities as those in the U.S. The company's World Trade subsidiary stopped trying to develop its own computers; instead, it marketed the 360 overseas, and helped in the engineering and manufacturing of the 360.

The company's table of organization was restructured significantly at least three times during the 360's development cycle. Several new divisions and their executives emerged, while others suffered total or partial eclipse. An old maxim of the IBM organization was that few men rose to line executive positions unless they had spent some time selling. A new group of technically oriented executives came to the forefront for the first time, diluting some of the traditional power of the marketing men in the corporation.

The Missionaries and the Scientists

Oddly enough, the upheaval at IBM went largely unnoticed. The company was able to make itself over more or less in private. It was able to do so partly because IBM is so widely assumed to be an organization in which the unexpected simply doesn't happen. Outsiders viewing IBM presume it to be a model of rationality and order—a presumption related to the company's products which are, of course, instruments that enable (and require) their users to think clearly about management.

This image of IBM, moreover, had been furthered over the years by the styles of the two Watsons. Tom Watson, Sr., combined an intense devotion to disciplined thinking with formal, rather Victorian attitudes about conduct, clothes, and courtesy. The senior Watson's hostility toward drinking, and his demand that employees dedicate themselves totally to the welfare of the corporation, created a kind of evangelical atmosphere. When Tom Watson, Jr., took over from his father in 1956, the manner and style shifted somewhat, but the missionary zeal remained—now overlaid by a new dedication to the disciplines of science. The overlay reinforced the image of IBM as a chillingly efficient organization, one in which plans were developed logically and executed with crisp efficiency. It was hard to envision the company in a gambling role.

The dimensions of the 360 gamble are difficult to state precisely. The company's executives, who are men used to thinking of risks and payoffs in hard quantitative terms, insist that no meaningful figure could ever be put on the gamble—that is, on the odds that the program would be brought off on schedule, or on the costs involved if it failed.

Outsailing the Boss

At the time, it scarcely seemed that any gamble at all was necessary. IBM was way out ahead of the competition, and looked as if it could continue smoothly in its old ways forever. Below the surface, though, IBM's organization didn't fit the changing markets so neatly anymore, and there really was, in Evans's phrase, a risk involved in doing nothing.

No one understood this more thoroughly, or with more sense of urgency, than one of the principal decision makers of the company, T. Vincent Learson. His entire career at IBM, which began in 1935, had been concerned with getting new products to market. In 1954 he was tapped by young Tom Watson as the man to spearhead the company's first big entry into the commercial computer field—with the 702 and 705 models. His success led to his promotion to vice president and group executive in 1956. In 1959 he took over both of the company's computer development and manufacturing operations, the General Products Division and the Data Systems Division.

Learson stood 6 foot 6 and was a tough and forceful personality. When he was managing any major IBM program, he tended to be impatient with staff reports and committees, and to operate outside the conventional chain of command; if he wanted to know why a program was behind schedule, he was apt to call directly on an executive at a much lower level who might help him find out. But he often operated indirectly, too, organizing major management changes without his own hands being visible to the men involved. Though he lacked the formal scientific background that is taken for granted in many areas of IBM, Learson had a reputation as a searching and persistent questioner about any proposals brought before him; executives who had not done their homework might find their presentations falling apart under his questions—and might also find that he would continue the inquisition in a way that made their failure an object lesson to any spectators. And Learson was the most vigorous supporter of the company's attitude that a salesman who had lost an order without exhausting all the resources the company had to back him up deserved to be drawn and quartered.

At IBM, Learson was known as demanding, domineering, and direct—given to calling people anywhere in the company to find out firsthand what was going on. But Learson was also known as a friendly and whimsical man who was IBM's number one cheerleader. He delighted in showing up unannounced, whether in a hospital to cheer up one of his sick secretaries or at a retirement dinner in Boston for a lady who ran a course in keypunching there when Learson was a young salesman. For all the diverging views of Learson, the man, as a top executive the degree of loyalty that Learson inspired was remarkable. Said one former executive, who was forced out of IBM, "I admire the man. He's like General Patton—someone you follow into battle."

Learson's personal competitiveness was something of a legend at IBM. It was significantly demonstrated in the Newport-to-Bermuda yacht race, in which Learson entered his own boat, the *Thunderbird*. He boned up on the history of the race in past years, and managed to get a navigator who had been on a winning boat three different times. He also persuaded Bill Lapworth, the famous boat designer, to be a crewman. Learson traveled personally to California to get one of the best spinnaker men available. All these competitive efforts were especially fascinating to the people at IBM because Tom Watson, Jr., also had an entry in the Bermuda race; he'd, in fact, been competing in it for years. Before the race Watson good-humoredly warned Learson at a board meeting that he'd better not win if he expected to stay at IBM. Learson's answer was not recorded. But Learson won the race. Watson's *Palowan* finished twenty-fourth on corrected time.

When Learson took over the computer group he found himself supervising two major engineering centers that had been competing with each other for some time. The General Products Division's facility in Endicott, New York, produced the low-priced 1401 model, by far the most popular of all IBM's computers—or of anyone else's to that date; something like 10,000 of them had been installed by the mid-1960s. Meanwhile, the Data Systems Division in Poughkeepsie made the more glamorous 7000 series, of which the 7090 was the most powerful. Originally, IBM had intended that the two centers operate in separate markets, but as computer prices came down in the late 1950s and as more versions of each model were offered, their markets came to overlap—and they entered a period in which they were increasingly penetrating each other's markets, heightening the feeling of rivalry. Each had its own development program, although any decision to produce or market a new computer, of course, had to be ratified at corporate headquarters. The rivalry between the two divisions was to become an element in, and be exacerbated by, the decision to produce the 360.

Both the 1401 and the 7000 series were selling well in 1960. But computer engineers and architects are a restless breed; they are apt to be thinking of improvements in design or circuitry five minutes after the specifications of their latest machines are frozen. In the General Products Division, most such thinking in 1960 and 1961 was long term; it was assumed that the 1401 would be on the market until about 1968. The thinking at the Data Systems Division concerned both long-range and more immediate matters.

A $20 Million Stretch

One of the immediate matters was the division's "Stretch" computer, which was already on the market but having difficulties. The computer had been designed to dwarf all others in size and power, and it was priced around $13,500,000. But it never met more than 70 percent of the promised specifications, and not many of them were sold. In May 1961, Tom Watson made the decision that the price of Stretch should be cut to $8 million to match the value of its performance—at which level Stretch was plainly uneconomic to produce. He had to make the decision, it happened, just before he was to fly to California and address an industry group on the subject of progress in the computer field.

Before he left for the coast, an annoyed Watson made a few tart remarks about the folly of getting involved in large and overambitious projects that you couldn't deliver on. In his speech, he admitted that Stretch was a flop. "Our greatest mistake in Stretch," he said, "is that we walked up to the plate and pointed at the left-field stands. When we swung, it was not a homer but a hard line drive to the outfield. We're going to be a good deal more careful about what we promise in the future." Soon after he returned the program was quietly shelved; only seven of the machines were ultimately put in operation. IBM's overall loss on the program was about $20 million.

The Stretch fiasco had two consequences. One was that the company practically ignored the giant-computer field during the next two years—and thereby enabled Control Data to get a sizable headstart in the market. Customers were principally government and university research centers, where the most complex scientific problems are tackled and computers of tremendous power are required. Eventually, in 1963, Watson pointed out that his strictures against overambitious projects had not been meant to exclude IBM from this scientific market, and the company later tried to get back into it. Its entry was to be the 360-90, the most powerful machine of the new line.

A second consequence of the Stretch fiasco was that Learson and the men under him, especially those in the Data Systems Division, were under special pressure to be certain that the next big project was thought out more carefully and that it worked exactly as promised. As it happened, the project the division had in mind in 1960–1961 was a fairly ambitious one: it was for a line of computers, tentatively called the 8000 series, that would replace the 7000 series, and would also provide a limited measure of compatibility among the four models projected. The 8000 series was based on transistor technology, and therefore still belonged to the second generation; however, there had been so much recent progress in circuitry design and transistor performance that the series had considerably more capability than anything being offered by IBM at that time.

The principal sponsor of the 8000 concept was Fred Brooks, head of systems planning for the Poughkeepsie division. An imaginative, enthusiastic 29-year-old North Carolinian with a considerable measure of southern charm, Brooks became completely dedicated to the concept of the new series, and beginning in late 1960 he began trying to enlist support for it. He had a major opportunity to make his case for the 8000 program at a briefing for the division's management, which was held at Poughkeepsie in January 1961.

By all accounts, he performed well: he was relaxed, confident, informed on every aspect of the technology involved, and persuasive about the need for a change. Data Systems' existing product line, he argued, was a mixed bag. The capability of some models overlapped that of others, while still other capabilities were unavailable in any model. The 8000 series would end all this confusion. One machine was already built, cost estimates and a market forecast had been made, a pricing schedule had been completed, and Brooks proposed announcing the series late that year or early in 1962. It could be the division's basic product line until 1968, he added. Most of Brooks' audience found his case entirely persuasive.

Enter the Man from Headquarters

Learson, however, was not ready to be sold so easily. The problems with Stretch must have been on his mind, and probably tended to make him look hard at any big new proposals. Beyond that, he was skeptical that the 8000 series would minimize the confusion in the division's product line, and he wondered whether the concept might not even *contribute* to the confusion. Learson had received a long memorandum from his chief assistant, Don Spaulding, on the general subject of equipment proliferation. Spaulding argued that there were already too many different computers in existence, and that they required too many supporting programs and too much peripheral equipment; some drastic simplification of the industry's merchandise was called for.

With these thoughts in mind, Learson was not persuaded that Brooks' concept was taking IBM in the right direction. Finally, he was not persuaded that the company should again invest heavily in second-generation technology. Along with a group of computer users, he had recently attended a special course on industrial dynamics that was being given at the Massachusetts Institute of Technology. Much of the discussion had been over his head, he later recalled, but from what his classmates were saying he came away with the clear conviction that computer applications would soon be expanding rapidly, and that what was needed was a bold move away from "record keeping" and toward more sophisticated business applications.

There was soon direct evidence of Learson's skepticism about the 8000 series. Shortly after the briefing Bob Evans, who was then manager of processing systems in the General Products Division, was dispatched to Poughkeepsie as head of Data Systems' planning and development. He brought along a number of men who had worked with him in Endicott. Given the rivalry between the two divisions, it is not very surprising that he received a cool welcome. His subsequent attitude toward the 8000 concept ensured that his relations with Brooks would stay cool.

Evans made several different criticisms of the concept. The main one was that the proposed line was "nonhomogeneous"—that is, it was not designed throughout to combine scientific and business applications. Further, he contended that it lacked sufficient compatibility within the line. It would compound the pro-liferation problem. He also argued that it was time to turn to the technologies asso-ciated with integrated circuits.

Blood on the Floor

For various reasons, including timing, Brooks was opposed, and he and Evans fought bitterly for several months. At one point Evans called him and quietly men-tioned that Brooks was getting a raise in salary. Brooks started to utter a few words of thanks when Evans said flatly, "I want you to know I had nothing to do with it."

In March 1961, Brooks had a chance to make a presentation to the corporate management committee, a group that included Tom Watson, his brother, A. K. Watson, who headed the World Trade Corp., Albert Williams, who was then presi-dent of the corporation (later chairman of the executive committee), and Learson. Brooks made another effective presentation, and for a while he and his allies thought that the 8000 might be approved after all.

But early in May it became clear that Evans was the winner. His victory was formalized in a meeting, at the Gideon Putnam Hotel in Saratoga, of all the key people who had worked on the 8000. There, on May 15, Evans announced that the 8000 project was dead and that he now had the tough job of reassigning them all to other tasks. In the words of one participant, "There was blood all over the floor."

Evans now outlined some new programs for the Data Systems Division. His short-term program called for an extension of the 7000 line, both upward and downward. At the lower end of the line there would be two new models, the 7040 and 7044. At the upper end there would be a 7094 and a 7094 II. This program was generally noncontroversial, except for the fact that the 7044 had almost ex-actly the same capabilities as a computer called Scamp, which was being proposed by another part of IBM. It would obviously make no sense to build both com-puters; and, as it happened, Scamp had some powerful support.

Scamp was a small scientific computer developed originally for the European market. Its principal designer was John Fairclough, a young man (he was then 30) working in the World Trade Corp.'s Hursley Laboratory, sixty miles southwest of London. The subsidiary had a sizable stake in Scamp. It had been trying for many years to produce a computer tailored to the needs of its own markets, but had re-peatedly failed, and had therefore been obliged to sell American-made machines overseas.

But Scamp looked especially promising, and the subsidiary's executives, in-cluding Fairclough and A. K. Watson, were confident that it would meet American standards. It had previously tested well and attracted a fair amount of attention in IBM's American laboratories. Evans himself came to Hursley to look at it, and was impressed. But its similarity to the 7044 finally took Fairclough and some asso-ciates to the United States to test their machine against a 7044 prototype.

Mere Equality Won't Do

As things turned out, Scamp did about as well as the 7044—but, also as things turned out, that wasn't good enough. Evans and Learson were resolved to stretch out the 7000 line, but opposed to anything that would add to proliferation. In prin-ciple, A. K. Watson, who had always run World Trade as a kind of personal fief-dom, could have stepped in and ordered the production of Scamp on his own authority. In practice, he decided the argument against proliferation was a valid one. And so, in the end, he personally gave the order to drop Scamp. Fairclough got the news one day soon after he had returned to England, and he found himself with a sizable staff that had to be reassigned. He says that he considered resigning, but instead worked off his annoyance by sipping Scotch and brooding much of the night.

Evans and Learson had also agreed that Data Systems should try its hand at designing a computer line that would blanket the market. The General Products Division was asked to play a role in the new design, but its response was lukewarm, so the bulk of the work at this stage fell to Data Systems. The project was dubbed NPL, for new product line; the name System/360 was not settled on until much later. To head the project, Evans selected his old adversary Brooks—a move that surprised a large number of IBM executives, including Brooks himself.

Still smarting over the loss of the 8000 project, and suspicious that the NPL was just a "window-dressing" operation, Brooks accepted the job only tentatively. To work with him, and apparently to ensure the NPL did not end up as the 8000 under a new name, Evans brought Gene Amdahl, a crack designer whom the company had called on to work on several earlier computers. However, Amdahl's influence was offset by that of another designer, Gerrit Blaauw, a veteran and past supporter of the 8000 project. Brooks' group received enough money to show that the company took NPL seriously (the first-year appropriation was $3,800,000), but Amdahl and Blaauw disagreed on design concepts, and the project floundered until November 1961.

Even to the trained eye IBM's main divisions appeared to be in excellent health in the summer of 1961. The General Products Division, according to Evans, was "fat and dumb and happy" in the lower end of the market, selling the 1401 at a furious rate, and still feeling secure about its line through about 1968. The World Trade Corp. was growing rapidly, although it had suffered its third major setback on getting a computer line of its own. The Data Systems Division was extending its old 7000 line to meet the competition, and working on the NPL.

THE PROLIFERATING PRODUCTS

But it was around this time that Tom Watson and Learson—then a group executive vice president, and nominally at least working under Albert Williams, the company president—developed several large concerns. There was the absence of any clear, overall concept of the company's product line; 15 or 20 different engineering groups scattered throughout the company were generating different computer products, and while the products were in most cases superior, the proliferation was putting overwhelming strains on the company's ability to supply programming for customers. The view at the top was that IBM required some major changes if it expected to stay ahead in the computer market when the third generation came along.

Between August and October 1961, Watson and Learson initiated a number of dialogues with their divisional lieutenants in an effort to define a strategy for the new era. By the end of October, though, neither of them believed that any strategy was coming into focus. At this point Learson made a crucial decision. He decided to set up a special committee, composed of representatives from every major segment of the company, to formulate some policy guidance. The committee was called SPREAD—an acronym for systems programming, research, engineering, and development. Its chairman was John Haanstra, then a vice president of the General Products Division. There were 12 other members, including Evans, Brooks, and Fairclough.

The SPREAD Committee was conducted informally, but with a good amount of spirited discussion. For the same purposes it broke up into separate committees, such as one on programming capability. Haanstra, as one member put it, acted as a hammer on the committee anvil, forcing ideas into debate and demanding definitions. Still, there was some feeling that Haanstra was bothered by the fact that the group was heavily represented by "big machine"–oriented men.

The progress of the committee during November was steady, but it was also, in Learson's view, "hellishly slow." Suddenly Haanstra found himself promoted to the presidency of the General Products Division and Bob Evans took over as chairman of SPREAD. The committee meetings were held in the New Englander Motor Hotel, just north of Stamford, Connecticut. In effect, although not quite literally, Learson locked the doors and told the members that they couldn't get out until they had reached some conclusions.

While Evans accelerated the pace of the sessions somewhat, Fred Brooks increasingly emerged as the man who was shaping the direction of the committee recommendations. This was not very surprising, for he and his group had had a headstart in thinking out many of the issues. By December 28, 1961, the SPREAD Committee had hammered out an 80-page statement of its recommendations. On January 4, 1962, the committee amplified the report for the benefit of the 50 top executives of the corporation.

Brooks was assigned the role of principal speaker on this occasion. The presentation was split into several parts and took an entire day. The main points of the report were:

> There was a definite need for a single, compatible family of computers ranging from one with the smallest existing core memory, which would be below the 1401 line, to one as powerful as IBM's biggest—at that time the 7094. In fact, the needs were said to extend beyond the IBM range, but the report expressed doubt that compatibility could be extended that far.
>
> The new line should not be aimed simply at replacing the popular 1401 or 7000 series, but at opening up whole new fields of computer applications. At that time compatibility between those machines and the new line was not judged to be of major importance, because the original timetable on the appearance of the various members of the new family of computers stretched out for several years.
>
> The System/360 must have both business and scientific applications. This dual purpose was a difficult assignment because commercial machines accept large amounts of data but have little manipulative ability, while scientific machines work on relatively small quantities of data that are endlessly manipulated. To achieve duality the report decided that each machine in the new line would be made available with core memories of varying sizes. In addition, the machine would provide a variety of technical and esoteric features to handle both scientific and commercial assignments.
>
> Information input and output equipment, and all other peripheral equipment, must have "standard interface"—so that various types and sizes of peripheral equipment could be hitched to the main computer without missing a beat. This too was to become an important feature of the new line.

Learson recalled the reaction when the presentation ended. "There were all sorts of people up there and while it wasn't received too well, there were no real objections. So I said to them, 'All right, we'll do it.' The problem was, they thought it was too grandiose. The report said we'd have to spend $125 million on programming the system at a time when we were spending only about $10 million a year for programming. Everybody said you just couldn't spend that amount. The job just looked too big to the marketing people, the financial people, and the engineers. Everyone recognized it was a gigantic task that would mean all our resources were tied up in one project—and we knew that for a long time we wouldn't be getting anything out of it."

APRIL 1964—PUBLIC ANNOUNCEMENT

When Tom Watson, Jr., made what he called "the most important product announcement in the company's history," he created quite a stir. International Business Machines is not a corporation given to making earth-shaking pronouncements casually, and the declaration that it was launching an entirely new computer line, the System/360, was headline news. The elaborate logistics that IBM worked out in order to get maximum press coverage—besides a huge assembly at Poughkeepsie, IBM staged press conferences on the same day in 62 cities in the United States and in 14 foreign countries—underscored its view of the importance of the event. And the fact that the move until then had been a closely guarded secret added an engaging element of surprise. . . . In the scattered locations where IBM plans, builds, and sells its products, there was, on that evening of April 7, 1964, a certain amount of dancing in the streets. . . .

But the managerial and organizational changes that were brought about by the company's struggle to settle on, and then to produce and market, the new line [had very long-term] effects. In each of these several aspects, past, present, and future were closely intertwined.

The Rising Cost of Asking Questions

No part of the whole adventure of launching System/360 was as tough, as stubborn, or as enduring as the programming. Early in 1966, talking to a group of IBM customers, Tom Watson, Jr., said ruefully: "We are investing nearly as much in System/360 programming as we are in the entire development of System/360 hardware. A few months ago the bill for 1966 was going to be $40 million. I asked Vin Learson last night before I left what he thought it would be for 1966 and he said $50 million. Twenty-four hours later I met Watts Humphrey, who is in charge of programming production, in the hall here and said, 'Is this figure about right? Can I use it?' He said it's going to be $60 million. You can see that if I keep asking questions we won't pay a dividend this year."

Watson's concern about programming went back to the beginnings of the System/360 affair. By late 1962 he was sufficiently aware of the proportions of the question to invite the eight top executives of IBM to his ski lodge in Stowe, Vermont, for a three-day session on programming. The session was conducted by Fred Brooks, the corporate manager for the design of the 360 project, and other experts; they went into the programming in considerable detail. While the matter can become highly technical, in general IBM's objective was to devise an "operating system" for its computer line, so that the computers would schedule themselves, without manual interruption, and would be kept working continuously at or near their capacity. At the time it announced System/360, IBM promised future users that it would supply them with such a command system.

Delivery on that promise was agonizingly difficult. Even though Tom Watson and the other top executives knew the critical importance of programming, the size of the job was seriously underestimated. The difficulty of coordinating the work of hundreds of programmers was enormous. The operating system IBM was striving for required the company to work out many new ideas and approaches; as one company executive said, "We were trying to schedule inventions, which is a dangerous thing to do in a committed project." Customers came up with more extensive programming tasks than the company had expected, and there were inevitable delays and slowdowns. The difficulties of programming prevented some users from getting the full benefits from their new machines for years. The company didn't have most of the bugs out of the larger systems' programming until at least mid-1967—well behind its expectations.

The Cold Realities of Choice

In technology, IBM was also breaking new ground. During the formative years of the decisions about the technology of System/360, a lengthy report on the subject was prepared by the *ad hoc* Logic Committee, headed by Erich Bloch, a specialist in circuitry for IBM. Eventually, the Logic Committee report led to the company's formal commitment to a new hybrid kind of integrated-circuit technology—a move that, like many other aspects of the 360 decision, is still criticized by some people in the computer industry, both inside and outside of IBM.

The move, though, was hardly made in haste. The whole computer industry had raced through two phases of electronic technology—vacuum tubes and transistors—between 1951 and 1960. By the late 1950s it was becoming apparent that further technological changes of sweeping importance were in the offing. At that time, however, IBM was not very much of a force in scientific research, its strengths lying in the assembling and marketing of computers, not in their advanced concepts. The company's management at the time had the wit to recognize the nature of the corporate deficiency, and to see the importance of correcting it. In 1956, IBM hired Dr. Emanuel Piore, formerly chief scientist of U.S. naval research. Piore became IBM's director of research and a major figure in the technological direction that the company finally chose for its System/360.

In the end, the choice narrowed to two technologies. One was monolithic integrated circuitry: putting all the elements of a circuit—transistors, resistors, and diodes—on one chip at one time. The other was hybrid integrated circuitry—IBM rather densely termed it "solid logic technology"—which means making transistors and diodes separately and then soldering them into place. In 1961 the Logic Committee decided that the production of monolithic circuits in great quantities would be risky, and in any case would not meet the schedule for any new line of computers to be marketed by 1964.

There was little opposition to this recommendation initially, except among a few engineering purists. Later, however, the opposition strengthened. The purists believed that monolithic circuits were sure to come, and that the company in a few years would find itself frozen into a technology that might be obsolete before the investment could be recovered. However, the Logic Committee's recommendation on the hybrid approach was accepted; since that time, Watson has referred to the acceptance as "the most fortunate decision we ever made."

THE SECRETS CIRCUITS HIDE

The decision to move into hybrid integrated technology accelerated IBM's push into component manufacturing, a basic change in the character of the company. In the day of vacuum tubes and transistors, IBM had designed the components for its circuits, ordered them from other companies (a principal supplier: Texas Instruments), then assembled them to its own specifications. But with the new circuitry, those specifications would have to be built into the components from the outset. "Too much proprietary information was involved in circuitry production," said Watson. "Unless we did it ourselves, we could be turning over some of the essentials of our business to another company. We had no intention of doing that." In addition, of course, IBM saw no reason why it should not capture some of the profit from the manufacturing that it was creating on such a large scale.

The company's turn to a new technology jibed neatly with a previous decision made in 1960 by Watson at the urging of the man who was then IBM president, Al Williams, that the company should move into component manufacturing. By the time the decision to go into hybrid circuits was made, IBM already had started putting together a component manufacturing division. Its general manager was John Gibson, a Johns Hopkins Ph.D. in electrical engineering. Under Gibson, the new division won the authority, hitherto divided among other divisions of the company, to designate and to buy the components for computer hardware, along with a new authority to manufacture them when Gibson thought it appropriate.

This new assignment of responsibility was resented by managers in the Data Systems and General Products divisions, since it represented a limitation of their authority. Also, they protested that they would be unable to compare the price and quality of inhouse components with those made by an outside supplier if they lost their independence of action. But Vincent Learson, then group executive vice president, feared that if they kept their independence they would continue to make purchases outside the company, and that IBM as a consequence would have no market for its own component output. He therefore put the power of decision in Gibson's hands. IBM's board, in effect, ruled in Gibson's favor when, in 1962, it authorized the construction of a new manufacturing plant, and the purchase of its automatic equipment, at a cost of over $100 million.

Systems Design: Worldwide

While IBM was making up its corporate mind about the technology for System/360, the delegation of specific responsibilities was going ahead. Learson designated Bob Evans, now head of the Federal Systems Division, to manage the giant undertaking. Under Evans, Fred Brooks was put in charge of all the System/360 work being done at Poughkeepsie, where four of the original models were designed; he was also made manager of the overall design of the central processors. The plant at Endicott was given the job of designing the model 30, successor to the popular 1401, which had been developed there. And John Fairclough, a systems designer at World Trade, was assigned to design the model 40 at the IBM lab at Hursley, England.

Out of the Hursley experience came an interesting byproduct that had significant implications for IBM's future. With different labs engaged in the 360 design, it was vital to provide for virtually instant communication between them. IBM therefore leased a special transatlantic line between its home offices and the engineers in England, and later in Germany. The international engineering group was woven together with considerable effectiveness, giving IBM the justifiable claim that the 360 computer was probably the first product of truly international design.

In a Tug-of-War, Enough Rope to Hang Yourself

Even in a corporation inured to change, people resist change. By 1963, with the important decisions on the 360 being implemented, excitement about the new product line began to spread through the corporation—at least among those who were privy to the secret. But this rising pitch of interest by no means meant that the struggle inside the company was settled. The new family of computers cut across all the old lines of authority and upset all the old divisions. The System/360 concepts plunged IBM into an organizational upheaval.

Resistance came in only a mild form from the World Trade Corp., whose long-time boss was A. K. Watson, Tom's brother. World Trade managers always thought of European markets as very different from those in the United States, and as requiring special considerations that U.S. designers would not give them. Initially they had reservations about the concept of a single computer family, which they thought of as fitted only to U.S. needs. But when IBM laboratories in Europe were included in the formulation of the design of some of the 360 models, the grumblings from World Trade were muted. Later A. K. Watson was made vice chairman of the corporation and Gilbert Jones, formerly the head of domestic marketing of computers for the company, took over World Trade. These moves further integrated the domestic and foreign operations, and gave World Trade assurance that its voice would be heard at the top level of the corporation.

The General Products Division, for its part, really bristled with hostility. Its output, after all, accounted for two-thirds of the company's revenues for data processing. It had a popular and profitable product in the field, the 1401, which the 360 threatened to replace. The executive in charge of General Products, John Haanstra, fought against some phases of the 360 program. Haanstra thought the new line would hit his division hard. He was concerned, from the time the System/360 program was approved, about the possibility that it would undermine his division's profits. Specifically, he feared that the cost of providing compatibility in the lower end of the 360 line (which would be General Products' responsibility) might price the machines out of the market. Later he was to develop some more elaborate arguments against the program.

Long after the company's SPREAD Committee had outlined the System/360 concept, and it had been endorsed by IBM's top management, there were numerous development efforts going on inside the company that offered continuing alternatives to the concept—and they were taken seriously enough, in some cases, so that there were fights for jurisdiction over them. Early in 1963, for example, there was a row over development work at IBM's San Jose Laboratory, which belonged to the General Products Division. It turned out that San Jose—which had been explicitly told to stop the work—was still developing a low-power machine similar to the one being worked on in World Trade's German lab. When he heard about the continuing effort, A. K. Watson went to the lab, along with Emanuel Piore, and seems to have angrily restated his demand that San Jose cut it out. Some people from San Jose were then transferred to Germany to work on the German machine, and the General Products effort was stopped. In the curious way of organizations, though, things turned out well enough in the end; the German machine proved to be a good one, and the Americans who came into the project contributed a lot to its salability. With some adaptations, the machine was finally incorporated into the 360 line, and, as the model 20 it later sold better than probably any other in the series.

TOP MANAGEMENT SHIFTS

In the fall of 1963, Tom Watson . . . made some new management assignments that reflected the impact of the 360 program on the corporation. Learson was shifted away from supervising product development and given responsibility for marketing, this being the next phase of the 360 program. Gibson took over Learson's former responsibilities. The increasing development of IBM into a homogeneous international organization was reflected in the move up of A. K. Watson from World Trade to corporate vice chairman. He was succeeded by Gilbert Jones, former head of domestic marketing. Piore became a group vice president in charge of research and several other activities.

One reason for Watson's interest in speeding up the 360 program in late 1963 was an increasing awareness that the IBM product line was running out of steam. The company was barely reaching its sales goals in this period. Some of this slowdown, no doubt, was due to mounting rumors about the new line. But there was another, critical reason for the slowdown: major customers were seeking ways of linking separate data-processing operations on a national basis, and IBM had limited capability along that line. Finally, IBM got a distinctly unpleasant shock in December 1963, when the Honeywell Corp. announced a new computer. Its model 200 had been designed along the same lines as the 1401—a fact Honeywell cheerfully acknowledged—but it used newer, faster, and cheaper transistors than the 1401 and was therefore priced 30 percent below the IBM model. To make matters worse, Honeywell's engineers had figured out a means by which customers interested in reprogramming from an IBM 1401 to a Honeywell 200 could do so inexpensively. The vulnerability of the 1401 line was obvious, and so was the company's need for the new line of computers.

It was around this time that some IBM executives began to argue seriously for simultaneous introduction of the whole 360 family. There were several advantages to the move. One was that it would have a tremendous public relations impact and demonstrate the distinctive nature of IBM's new undertaking. Customers would have a clear picture of where and how they could grow with the computer product line, and so would be more inclined to wait for it. Finally, there might be an antitrust problem in introducing the various 360 models sequentially. The Justice Department might feel that an IBM salesman was improperly taking away competitors' business if he urged customers not to buy their products because of an impending announcement of his own company's new model. IBM had long had a company policy under which no employee was allowed to tell a customer of any new product not formally announced by the management. (Several employees have, in fact, been fired or disciplined for violating the rule.) Announcing the whole 360 line at once would dispose of the problem.

Learson Stages a Shoot-Out

Beginning in late 1963, then, the idea of announcing and marketing the 360 family all at once gained increasing support. At the same time, by making the 360 program tougher to achieve, the idea gave Haanstra some new arguments against the program. His opposition now centered on two main points. First, he argued that the General Products manufacturing organization would be under pressure to build in a couple of years enough units of the model 30 to replace a field inventory of the 1401 that had been installed over a five-year period. He said that IBM was in danger of acquiring a huge backlog, one representing perhaps two or three years' output, and that competitors, able to deliver in a year or less, would steal business away.

But Haanstra's argument was countered to some extent by a group of resourceful IBM engineers. They believed that the so-called "read-only" storage device could be adapted to make the 360–30 compatible with the 1401. The read-only technique, which involved the storing of permanent electronic instructions in the computer, could be adapted to make the model 30 act like a 1401 in many respects: the computer would be slowed down, but the user would be able to employ his 1401 programs. IBM executives had earlier been exposed to a read-only device by John Fairclough, the head of World Trade's Hursley Laboratory in England, when he was trying (unsuccessfully) to win corporate approval for his Scamp computer.

Could the device really be used to meet Haanstra's objections to the 360–30? To find out, Learson staged a "shoot-out" in January 1964, between the 1401-S and the model 30. The test proved that the model 30, "emulating" the 1401, could already operate at 80% of the speed of the 1401-S—and could improve that figure with other adaptations. That was good enough for Learson. He notified Watson that he was ready to go, and said that he favored announcing the whole System/360 family at once.

"Going . . . Going . . . Gone!"

Haanstra was still not convinced. He persisted in his view that his manufacturing organization probably could not gear up to meet the production demand adequately. On March 18 and 19, a final "risk-assessment" session was held at Yorktown Heights to review once again every debatable point of the program. Tom Watson, Jr., President Al Williams, and 30 top executives of the corporation attended. This was to be the last chance for the unpersuaded to state their doubts or objections on any aspect of the new program—patent protection, policy on computer returns, the company's ability to hire and train an enormous new work force in the time allotted, and so on. Haanstra himself was conspicuously absent from this session. In February he had been relieved of his responsibilities as president of the General Products Division and assigned to special duty—monitoring a project to investigate the possibility of IBM's getting into magnetic tape. (He later became a vice president of the Federal Systems Division.) At the end of the risk-assessment meeting, Watson seemed satisfied that all the objections to the 360 had been met. Al Williams, who had been presiding, stood up before the group, asked if there were any last dissents, and then, getting no response, dramatically intoned, "Going . . . going . . . gone!"

The April 7, 1964 announcement of the program unveiled details of six separate compatible computer machines; their memories would be interchangeable, so that a total of nineteen different combinations would be available. The peripheral equipment was to consist of forty different input and output devices, including printers, optical scanners, and high-speed tape drives. Delivery of the new machines would start in April 1965.

The Nature of the Risk

The basic announcement of the new line brought a mixed reaction from the competition. The implication that the 360 line would make obsolete all earlier equipment was derided and minimized by some rival manufacturers, who seized every opportunity to argue that the move was less significant than it appeared . . . [or claimed it was unfeasible or uneconomic for customers].

But some of the competition was concerned enough about the System/360 to respond to its challenge on a large scale. During the summer of 1964, General Electric announced that its 600 line of computers would have time-sharing capabilities. The full import of this announcement hit IBM that fall, when MIT, prime target of several computer manufacturers, announced that it would buy a G.E. machine. IBM had worked on a time-sharing program back in 1960 but had abandoned the idea when the cost of the terminals involved seemed to make it uneconomic. G.E.'s success caught IBM off base and in 1964 and 1965 it was scrambling madly to provide the same capability in the 360 line. Late in 1964, RCA announced it would use pure monolithic integrated circuitry (i.e., as opposed to IBM's hybrid circuitry) in some models of its new Spectra 70 line. This development probably led to a certain amount of soul-searching at IBM.

In the end, . . . the company felt that the turn to monolithic circuitry did not involve capabilities that threatened the 360 line; furthermore, if and when monolithic circuitry ever did prove to have decisive advantages over IBM's hybrid circuitry, the company was prepared—the computers themselves and some three quarters of the component manufacturing equipment could be adapted fairly inexpensively to monolithics. As for time sharing, any anxieties IBM had about that were eased in March 1965, when Watts Humphrey, a systems expert who had been given the assignment of meeting the time-sharing challenge, got the job done. . . .

IBM announced additions to the 360 line in 1964 and 1965. One was the model 90, a supercomputer type, designed to be competitive with Control Data's 6800. Another was the 360–44, designed for special scientific purposes. Also, there was the 360–67, a large time-sharing machine. Another, the 360–20, represented a pioneering push into the low end of the market. None of these were fully compatible with the models originally announced, but they were considered part of the 360 family.

System/360 underwent many changes after the concept was originally brought forth back in 1962 and even after Watson's announcement in 1964. More central processors were later offered in the 360 line; some of them had memories that were much faster than those originally offered. The number of input-output machines [increased several times]. . . .

"Major Reshufflements"

IBM had several managers trying to keep the 360 program on track in 1964–1965. Gibson, who had succeeded Learson in the job, was replaced late in 1964. His successor, Paul Knaplund, lasted about another year. . . . In 1965 there was one item of unalloyed bad news: the company had suffered heavy setbacks at the high end of the 360 line—that is, in its efforts to bring forth a great supercomputer in the tradition of Stretch. In 1964 it wrote off $15 million worth of parts and equipment developed specifically for the 360–90.

There were signs at about this time that the 360 program was still generating other reshufflements of divisions and personnel. Dr. Piore had been freed from operational duties and responsibilities and given a license to roam the company checking on just about all technical activities. Some of his former duties were placed in a division headed by Eugene Fubini, a former Assistant Secretary of Defense and the Pentagon's deputy director of research and engineering before he joined IBM in 1965. Fubini was one of the first outsiders ever brought into the company at such a high executive level. Another change represented a comeback for Stephen Dunwell, who had managed the Stretch program and had been made the goat for its expensive failure to perform as advertised. When IBM got into the 360 program, its technical group discovered that the work done on Stretch was immensely valuable to them; and Watson personally gave Dunwell an award as an IBM fellow (which entitled him to work with IBM backing, for five years, on any project of his choosing).

In 1971 58-year-old Tom Watson, Jr., slowed by poor health, turned over the chairmanship of the company to T. Vincent Learson. While Learson was taking on the top job, computer makers were rattled by a recession and shaken by a series of corporate crises. 1970–1972 saw General Electric Co. and RCA withdraw from the field, cutting the number of U.S. computer makers from nine to seven. The industry was struck by a backlash from oversold customers, a new generation of computers, and a switch in government expenditures away from R&D and toward social services. Customers became sales resistant and cost conscious.

Business Week commented,

> The Learson era in the computer business promises to be vastly different from the preceding two decades of frantic growth, during which IBM's yearly revenues increased more than thirty-fold—from $226 million in 1951 to $8.2 billion this year. The outlook for the industry is for a lower rate of growth from a bigger base. But the growth will still be a very healthy 10% to 12% annually, depending on the state of the general economy. If IBM merely holds its present share of the market, this pace of growth would mean annual increments in its revenues of around half a billion dollars. . . .

On his sixtieth birthday in 1972, T. V. Learson surprised nearly everyone by announcing his retirement after only 18 months as chairman. Said Learson, "We believe very strongly that in a business as technical and competitive as this, the interests of IBM will be best served by management teams of younger upcoming men and women. . . ." Learson's successor as chairman, 52-year-old Frank Cary, was a quieter and more amiable executive, yet few observers felt the management shuffle heralded any significant departure from the vigorous marketing oriented practices of the Learson era.

QUESTIONS

1. What stimulated the change in strategy at the time of the 360? Evaluate the process by which change was brought about.

2. Evaluate Mr. Learson as a change manager. Why does he act this way?

3. How could other companies have taken advantage of IBM's 360 strategy? What should IBM do about these?

1-10

HONDA MOTOR COMPANY

In the post World War II era Honda Motor Co. (Ltd.) was a major force in revolutionizing the motorcycle and small car industries of the world. What were the keys to success for this unique Japanese company? What were its relationships to the national planning systems so often given credit for the emergence of the modern Japanese auto industry? And where should Honda look for its future successes in the mid-to-late 1990s?

THE YOUNGEST ENTREPRENEUR

Mr. Soichiro Honda began his career at Arto Shokai, an auto repair shop in Tokyo. At age 16, during the Great Kanto earthquake of 1923, the young apprentice who had never driven a car leapt to the wheel of a customer's vehicle and in a bit of daring-do maneuvered it to safety. Unlike his fellow apprentices Honda stayed on to help Arto Shokai's master mechanic recover from the disaster. Soon the owner-"master" set up the rapidly experienced Honda as head of a branch of Arto Shokai in Hamamatsu, Honda's home town. There Honda patented cast-metal spokes to replace all wooden ones—like those that burned out, almost wrecking his car, during the earthquake episode—and gathered the first of over 100 personal patents in his lifetime. The Japanese trading companies soon began exporting his spokes all over the Far East.

By age 25, Honda was one of the youngest Japanese entrepreneurs around. He became *the* Hamamatsu playboy, not only plying from one geisha house to the next, but piling geishas into his own car for wild drives and drunken revels around the town. In one such escapade his car full of geishas went off a bridge, but landed safely in the mud—no injuries. In another, he tossed a geisha from a second story window. She landed on some electric wires below—from which a suddenly sobered Honda carefully extracted her—again, fortunately, no injuries. These are only some of the many colorful stories about the young Mr. Honda.

Motors and Mechanics

Honda also loved motors and engines. When the head of Arto Shokai suggested Honda might build a racer (on his own time), Honda spent months of midnight hours to build a car from spare parts and war surplus aircraft engines. He soon began to drive his products himself, to win races, and to extend his reputation for wild eccentricity into other areas.

Honda started making basic changes in racing car designs, and soon set new speed records. But in the All Japan Speed Rally of 1936, travelling at 120 kph—a record not exceeded for years—another car jumped in front of Honda, demolishing Honda's car and leaving him with lifetime injuries. This incident as much as anything directed his energies from racing toward engineering. Seeing more opportunities in manufacturing than repairs, Honda formed Tokai Heavy Industries in 1937 to make piston rings for cars.

Piston Rings and War

But Honda knew nothing about the complex casting processes involved. For months he and his assistant lived in their factory, day and night. Honda became a working hermit, complete with uncut hair and bristling chin. His limited savings wasted away. He sold his wife's jewelry to keep on, but he persisted, knowing his family would starve if he failed. After many frustrating failures, Honda sought the specialized technical knowledge he lacked because he had dropped out of school. After painfully gaining entry to the Hamamatsu High School of Technology—ten years older than his classmates, an unprecedented act in age-and-class-conscious Japan—Honda promptly upset the authorities by only attending classes of interest to him, listening carefully to what interested him, and not even taking notes on the rest. He refused to take examinations, saying that a diploma was worth less than a movie ticket; at least the ticket guaranteed you got into the theater.[1]

As Honda began to understand the technicalities of his product, he sold rings to the low end of the market, but could not meet Toyota's high quality standards. When he tried to expand his plant, the government refused to permit him a cement allotment in its carefully controlled pre-war economic strategy. Honda not only figured out how to make his own cement, he developed special automated equipment that let him meet the major manufacturers' quality standards for rings and later for aircraft propellers. But during the war American bombings and an earthquake destroyed much of his operation. Honda sold off the rest of his assets as the war ended. With the proceeds he bought a huge drum of medical alcohol, made his own sake, and spent an inebriated year visiting with friends and trying to decide what to do next.

HONDA MOTORS BEGINS

The post war era was terrible. Japan's cities were destroyed. City dwellers had to sortie into the country to buy their daily food. Trains were overcrowded and gasoline was in short supply. Honda later said, "I happened on the idea of fitting an engine to a bicycle simply because I didn't want to ride the incredibly crowded trains and buses myself, and it became impossible for me to drive my car because of the gasoline shortage."[2] Using small, war-surplus gasoline powered motors which had provided electricity for military radios, Honda made motor bikes that were an instant hit. When Honda exhausted his supply of surplus motors, he designed his own motor which could use an economical pine–resin fuel combination. He bought a pine forest to obtain the resin for his fuel mixture, but almost burned this down while trying to blast a hole in the base of a tree to get the resin.

Honda realized that his simple motorbikes would not last long once Japan began its postwar recovery. In 1949 he raised some $3,800 from friends and designed a longer range two-stroke, 3 hp (98cc) machine—the Type D with a superior stamped metal frame, christened the "Dream." Soon Honda was selling 1,000 bikes and motorcycles a month to black marketeers and small bicycle shops. But Honda's bill collectors often found their customers had disappeared or gone bankrupt before they paid the company. Honda was more interested in the product and its engineering than in profits. Production and sales were doing well, but the company was facing imminent bankruptcy. Honda welcomed the recommendation of an acquaintance that he take on Takeo Fujisawa as his head of finance and marketing. Fujisawa's heavy and ponderous style contrasted sharply with Honda's waspish, impatient, even rude directness, but the two became friends for life.

They moved the company from sleepy, gossipy, Hamamatsu—where the neighbors objected to Honda's flamboyant noisy sake-filled 3 a.m. returns on his motorcycle—to Tokyo and promptly applied for government support to produce 300 motorcycles per month. MITI—Japan's coordinating agency for industry, technology, and trade affairs—thought no one could sell that many motorcycles, and denied its support. Ignoring MITI's skepticism, Fujisawa wrote an impassioned letter to all of the 18,000 bicycle shops in Japan, presenting Honda's product as their wave of the future and promising to train them in its sale and repair. While Japan's largest producers typically had only regional distribution, Honda soon had a national network of 5,000 dedicated dealers.

Next, instead of emulating the 4-stroke, side-valve machine competitors had, Honda created a 146cc 4-stroke, overhead valve (OHV) engine with 5.5 horsepower. The Type E doubled available horsepower with no added weight, and became the basis for Honda's appeal to the high performance marketplace. Honda integrated the production of the key components, engines, frames, chains, and drives essential to such performance. But it outsourced non-critical parts as much as possible, and purchased a relatively small old sewing machine plant for assembly operations. Lacking large scale production facilities, Honda and his people designed special small scale assembly equipment—and simply stayed at work each day as long as it took to meet orders.

Technology and Quality

While other manufacturers milked a single winning design in the domestic marketplace, Honda thought Type E did not hit a wide enough market. "I racked my brain to contrive a two-wheeler with an engine which would be in high demand. I concluded I must make a motorcycle that would substitute for the bicycle."[2] Honda developed a new 50cc engine from the ground up, and coupled this with a small friendly looking frame for informal users. Sensing an untapped market niche for local delivery vehicles for small businesses, he designed in a step-through frame, an automatic transmission, and one-hand controls that allowed riders to carry a package in the other hand. The market for the "Cub" boomed, and Honda moved into large volume manufacturing for the first time.

In 1951, top officials of the larger Japanese manufacturers invited Honda and Fujisawa to attend a private meeting to determine incentive policies for Japanese exporters. Honda refused to attend, thus beginning a long pattern of nonparticipation with the central political and business forces directing Japan's economic recovery. He felt that high quality goods needed no such supports and knew no national boundaries.

Whatever his political prowess, Honda attacked any mechanical problems before him with energy and persistence. If he thought of a new concept in the middle of the night, he would get up and make notes so as not to forget it. Honda was talkative, energetic, gregarious—always excited by the technology and his products, never (according to Mr. Fujisawa) "by the profits we would make next year." But Honda earned the nickname Kaminari-san—"Mr. Thunder"—because of his instantaneous temper and sometimes erratic behavior. He spent most of his time in the factory or development shop working side-by-side with his workers. Employees from his early years remember his shouting at engineers or pounding himself on the head when they made a mistake. On one occasion, after finding some bolts improperly tightened, he grabbed a wrench from a technician, did the job right, and then popped the technician with the wrench while shouting, "You damned fool. This is how you are supposed to tighten bolts."[1,72] People later avoided close contact when Honda was carrying a wrench.

Expanding Investments

Honda's financial problems were solved in a unique way. Once they saw the Honda Cub, dealers were so impressed that they came to the company to buy whatever inventory they could. This was in sharp contrast to their usual practice of selling whatever models the big manufacturers had been able to force on them. Fujisawa cleverly used this demand to his advantage. He allocated production to those who could pay in advance and began weeding out slow paying distributors and dealers. Soon Honda had not only the widest, but the strongest, motorcycle dealer network in Japan.

As sales expanded, Honda Motors pushed investments upward even faster. Fujisawa purchased some large, key plots of land for future expansion. And Soichiro Honda insisted on the highest quality machinery for his plants. The two traveled to the U.S. to evaluate the U.S. industry, and engaged in a machine tool buying spree. Although total corporate capital was only $165,000, they bought over $1 million in imported tools; between 1952 and 1954 Honda's total capital expenditures outweighed those of the much larger Toyota and Nissan units. How did they finance this phenomenon? Unable and unwilling to obtain government financing, and lacking access to Japan's closely controlled equity markets, Mr Fujisawa again had to use clever—though high risk—trade financing to see the company through.

EXPANSION TO WORLD MARKETS

About this time Honda decided that motorcycle racing could assert to the world his company's true expertise in motorcycle design. After some disappointing initial entries in international races, Honda realized that the key to success was lighter, more efficient engines, getting more power from more thorough combustion.

Honda engineers ultimately designed an engine with the cam shaft at the top—the then unique overhead cam (OHC) engine—and made crucial discoveries about mixing gases in the combustion chamber that led to the CVCC engines of its later automobiles. Honda's motorcycles won the Manufacturers' Team Prize for the company in 1959 and the first five places (in both 125 and 255cc sizes) at the Isle of Man races in 1961. These were considered the "Olympics of racing" at the time.

Time for Strategy

While Mr. Honda was mesmerized by the sheer technological questions of these "racing years," Mr. Fujisawa was concerned with the company's longer term strategy. He thought there was a large untapped market for smaller, safer "bikes," geared to customers who resisted larger motorcycles as expensive, dangerous, and associated with the "black leather jacket" crowd. He wanted a small 50cc bike for novices, youthful executives, or young couples. At first Mr. Honda ignored his colleague's unusual vision. Then around 1958, Honda designed and built a full sized example of a "scooter" that would do the trick. Fujisawa was immediately excited by the product and soon predicted sales of 30,000 units per month—a bit ambitious in a Japanese market that then constituted only 20,000 per month for all two-wheelers.

Now considered to be the Model T of two-wheeled vehicles and probably Honda's masterpiece, the new motorbike was called the Super Cub. Revolutionary in design, the Super Cub had a light, carefree image, a step-through configuration which made it easier for women to ride, and a graceful, stylish appearance. But the new model also sported a 3-speed transmission, an automatic clutch, and a 50cc OHC engine which, based on Honda's racing experience, generated 4.5 horsepower.

By the end of 1959 the Super Cub had enabled Honda to assume the number one position among Japanese motorcycle manufacturers, with 60% of its sales being Super Cubs. The company's best selling earlier model had sold only 3,000 units per month. Honda invested 10 billion yen in a single factory to build 30,000 Super Cubs a month, with no guarantee of maintaining that level of sales. Fujisawa intuitively pushed ahead. He described the Super Cub to retailers as "more like a bicycle than a motorcycle," and began to sell the vehicles directly to retailers, mostly bicycle shops. By 1959 Honda was the largest motorcycle producer in the world.

The first Super Cub ("step–through") inaugurated in 1958
Source: Honda Motor Corporation

Honda and Fujisawa thought the time now had come to pursue the world market actively. Honda executives regarded Europe and Southeast Asia as the best markets to target, since Americans were so tied to the automobile and held an unattractive image of motorcycles and their riders. They argued that a small company like Honda would struggle to penetrate the U.S. market where only 60,000 motorcycles were imported yearly and where only 3,000 dealers existed—scarcely 1,000 of which were even open five days a week—took motorcycles on consignment, and gave spotty after-sales service. After several years of trying to pry open the under-developed country markets of Asia, Mr. Fujisawa—thinking that American preferences could set the trends for the rest of the world—targeted the United States as crucial.

Like most foreign producers, Honda at first relied on an agent for distribution in the United States but quickly dropped it as ineffective. Fujisawa established an overseas unit reporting directly to corporate headquarters to give Honda a better presence in the market, especially in post-sale servicing. Despite onerous exchange restrictions by the Japanese government, American Honda Motor Co. was formed in June 1959 with a Los Angeles headquarters and its own executive vice president, Mr. Kihachiro Kawashima.

The company had gone to MITI for a currency allocation, but was rebuffed. MITI reasoned that if the giant Toyota had earlier failed at the same venture, how could Honda succeed? Its meager $110,000 currency allocation meant Honda had to start its U.S. operations with only $250,000 of paid-in capital. Initially, it appeared that the skeptics were right. Honda's cycles did not sell in the U.S.; the negative image associated with motorcycles might be too entrenched for even Honda to overcome. But Kawashima and his two associates dug in, shared an apartment for $80 a month, rented a warehouse in a run-down area of Los Angeles, and personally stacked motorcycle crates, swept the floors, and built and maintained the parts bin.

Early 1960 became disastrous when customers reported Honda's larger motorcycles frequently leaked oil or experienced serious clutch failures on the longer, harder, and faster roads and tracks of the U.S. In a move that presaged later policies, Kawashima air-freighted the motorcycles to Japan where engineering teams, working night and day, found a way to fix the problem in one short month.

Then events took a surprising turn. Up to this point, executives of American Honda had promoted sales of the larger, more luxurious motorcycles because they seemed more suited to the U.S. market. Although they had not attempted to sell the 50cc Super Cubs through U.S. dealers, the executives rode them around Los Angeles themselves and noticed the bikes attracted considerable attention. With the larger bikes facing engineering problems, American Honda decided to increase emphasis on its 50cc line, just to generate cash flows.

The Super Cub created genuine excitement and enthusiasm in the American market primarily because it retailed for less than $250, compared with $1,000 to $1,500 for the bigger American or British motorcycles. American Honda was extremely concerned that it not lose the "black leather jacket" customers which comprised the high margin portion of the business.[3] But Honda's retailers continually reported that Super Cub customers were normal everyday Americans. Because of Japanese government restrictions, however, American Honda had to operate on a cash basis, building its inventory, advertising, and distribution systems without using Japanese generated yen. The division was extremely limited on cash. Yet by 1962–63 Honda's export earnings (from motorcycles) surpassed those of Nissan or Toyota. And by 1965, Honda America's motorcycle sales had jumped to $77 million and a whopping 63% market share.

DECISION POINT

How should Honda develop its U.S. presence? What should its advertising, pricing, distribution, inventory, product, and service policies be in the U.S.? How should these be related to its Japanese prices, production facilities, development activities, and the continuing restriction by the Ministry of Finance on exports of Japanese Yen?

FOUR WHEELS FOR HONDA

In the 1950s Japan had intensified its now famous programs for coordinating the development of selected high priority industries. Early on, MITI had targeted the steel, textile, shipbuilding, and petrochemical industries for such development. In the 1960s it began to encourage selected mass production industries including automobiles and optical devices, although it never "targeted" these as it had other sectors. In later years semiconductors, software, and computers were given priorities.

MITI announced in 1960 that it planned to divide the existing passenger car manufacturers into three groups (a mass-production car group, a mini-car group, and a special-purpose vehicle group) and that no other manufacturers would be permitted to enter. The government reasoned that the move would reduce destructive domestic competition and allow the industry to achieve scale economies for world penetration. But Honda, who would have been foreclosed from the market, was outraged. Fortunately, some leftist riots forced postponement of the hearings on the proposal, and it was never officially enacted. But it did stimulate Mr. Honda, who had dreamed since childhood of building automobiles, to move rapidly.

Racers and Instincts

To enter the auto market, Honda determined that the company must: (1) design and build racing cars capable of competing with the world's best and (2) ensure that any passenger cars derived from these would be of the world's highest quality. Although MITI actively opposed Honda's entry into automobiles, at the 1962 Tokyo Motor Show, Honda revealed a light-duty (T-360) truck and a (S-500) sports car prototype. The T-360 performed like a sports car and was the first truck of its class to permit high speeds. High horsepower, high rpms, and outstanding combustion efficiency comprised the critical engineering technologies which went into these first vehicles.

Mr. Honda's basic approach had always been to develop a special engine to solve each specific problem. Since he was strapped for cash, he had designed efficient small engines which were compact but powerful. As he moved to automobile engines, Honda adapted the technology he had created for his previous motorcycle designs. Replicating their motorcycle strategy, Honda engineers by 1964 had developed a Formula I racer. The company's 1965 Formula I entry won Honda's first Grand Prix victory in Mexico City. In 1966 Britisher Jack Brabham drove to eleven straight victories in a Honda Formula II equipped with a 4 cylinder 1,000cc

(160 HP) water-cooled engine. But within a few years Honda withdrew his cars (and later his motorcycles) from racing, saying the company had gained all the technology and publicity it could from that source.

Honda's auto racing technology was soon transferred to mass production passenger cars—first in the 1967 N–360 mini car, with an air-cooled, two-cylinder engine, and a front wheel drive (FWD) system unprecedented in automobile design. The N–360 was an instant success and captured 31.2% of Japan's total sales in its class, a mere two months after its introduction.

A Clean New Engine

In 1970 the U.S. Congress amended the Clean Air Act, requiring a 90 percent reduction in the emission of hydrocarbons, carbon monoxide, and nitrogen oxides by 1976. Honda executives had begun research on a "clean" automobile engine in the mid–1960s. From the beginning they sought an engine that Mr. Honda demanded, offering both the highest internal efficiency and greatest "external merit" in terms of its cleanliness and safety. Recognizing that any system which used an after-treatment device inherently wasted the potential energy of fuel, Honda had started several major projects on different efficient engines that burned exhaust gases more thoroughly.

Ultimately, in early 1971, the company chose its CVCC (compound vortex controlled combustion) engine, an engineering concept that was surprisingly simple yet decidedly effective. Tasuka Date, a top Honda engineer, had conceived of igniting a much richer fuel mixture (about 4.5:1) in an auxiliary chamber and letting the explosion expand into the main chamber, which had the desired lean (18:1 or 20:1) mixture to keep operating temperature low within the engine, yet minimize exhausts.

The CVCC engine was adaptable to both small and large cars. Detroit executives initially held that such "stratified charge" engines could only be put on small cars. But Honda proved its principle by modifying two 8-cylinder Chevy Impala engines to its design and improving their engine efficiency, gasoline mileage, and emission characteristics sufficiently to meet promulgated 1975 air quality standards. Despite Detroit's continued opposition, the CVCC was the only engine in the world which, operating in its normal mode in the early 1970s, could meet the proposed U.S. Air Quality Standards.

A TECHNOLOGY FOCUS

The parent company backed its strong technological presence in its markets with many times more engineers than its non–Japanese competitors. Yet the company enjoyed the lowest rates of R&D cost to sales among the Japanese majors.

The Expert System

Recognizing that neither he nor Mr. Honda would have prospered in a typical pyramidal organization, Mr. Fujisawa had developed what became known as Honda Motor's "expert system" in which creative people—experts—could fully utilize their skills and be rewarded appropriately. He wanted a flat or "paperweight" organization in which a promising person was not dependent upon or restrained by his immediate superior. He envisioned the organization as a kind of web "with engineers lined up sideways instead of top to bottom." According to Dr. Kowomoto of Honda R&D, any number of people could have top engineering positions based solely on their technical "expert" qualifications, even with no one reporting to them.

Fujisawa's organization recognized that fundamental research was unique. It needed to concentrate on technological understanding, faced many non-commercializable failures, and rarely worked well in a structured environment. By contrast production/development had to be carefully controlled, financially driven, and error free. Honda's researchers could define their own research themes and pursue their projects to conclusion. Research focused on product activities in small teams, typically two to ten people. Engineering was independent of Research and concentrated on process development.

Integrated Designs

Once development began, projects were managed across research, design, product engineering, and early production stages. Each person in a project group both maintained his own specialty and worked directly with other team members. Dr. Kowomoto emphasized that few risks were taken once a product or process was prototyped. Using its special coordination techniques, Honda operated on a two-three year cycle from development to production, as compared with a worldwide average of over four years for the auto industry.

Honda's development process centered on its SED (Sales, Production Engineering, and Development) system. Through constant reviews and their own training, engineers were encouraged to "think like customers." Each group on a team advanced its arguments based on its own analysis of the potentials, requirements, and constraints it saw for the new product. Interactions among the groups was based on a principle that the company characterized as "mutual aggression." Each was strongly encouraged to pursue its individual position all the way until a final decision was reached. Within R&D different subgroups pursued competing technical solutions until the most appropriate one was selected by the team. The R&D organization developing new products had "no pyramidal or hierarchical organization, just engineers and chief engineers." On a project team, titles did not influence decisions; even the newest engineers were to "argue frankly" with senior people, including vice presidents who might be on or visit their team. One person —like a metallurgy specialist—might be on many different teams simultaneously, developing completely different new products in parallel for each.

A very specific schedule was set for each project early on, and no deviations from the schedule were allowed despite problems which might develop. People were expected to work as hard as necessary to maintain planned progress, which was reviewed every 3 months by an SED oversight group where each function presented its views as vigorously as possible. Development people argued for the best technological solution, Engineering for the best quality-cost solution, and Sales to see that the design fitted market trends. Since Honda first introduced its cars in Japan, they had to be successful in the Japanese market. But the same car— modified only for local safety, right hand driving, or environmental standards— had to meet other countries' market demands as well. Although Honda, as a smaller manufacturer, outsourced many of its raw materials, sheet metal, and fabricated parts, through the early 1980s, it had been reluctant to share its design information with outside suppliers until final specifications were set.

Honda Motors was quick to point out that its process was one of "trial and error." For example, in 1970 Honda's 1300cc model introduced with considerable confidence by Marketing had suffered a terrible market failure. In contrast, the Civic had an unstylish look which many feared would not sell well. Instead it became a popular product and Honda's stable-volume production model with a potential for long product life. The first marketed model of the Honda Prelude had so little power that it was sometimes called the "Quaalude." But the company quickly restyled it, increased the power of its engine, gave it a much more "macho" appeal, and made it a success.

A unique aspect of Honda's design process was the fact that workers could suggest and implement process changes themselves right on the production line. A visitor would see small areas (20′ × 20′) out on the factory floor where workers were building their own new prototype processes. When asked if they were supervised by engineers, the answer would be, "No! If they need engineers they will find them." Changes were not limited to single work stations. Workers had automated whole body-panel and body-assembly sections this way. Each year Honda sponsored an "idea contest" and gave awards for its employees' most ingenious ideas, both for company use and for sheer inventiveness. One winner was a three-wheeled "all terrain" powered bike that became a major product line.

Production Organization

Honda enjoyed some unique policies in the production area. In its foreign operations, it encouraged employees to wear uniforms, like its Japanese employees. Most did. Each individual was called an "associate," a term which described how each person related to other members of the organization and conveyed a feeling of respect for the individual. Overseas, Honda preferred to develop its own people in order to reduce the chances of employees bringing bad work habits with them. Newly hired associates were often rotated to other tasks and dispatched to Honda plants in Japan where they learned Honda's methodologies of producing to exact specifications.

Once trained, Honda promoted the best qualified person to do a job. Unlike other companies in Japan, seniority never had a high priority in determining advancement. Even in its U.S. operations, where other companies stressed seniority, young Honda managers often occupied high positions that would take five to ten years more to achieve in other companies.

Everyone was treated as an equal. Even the ubiquitous, identical uniforms of Honda employees emphasized equality, rather than rank. Everyone ate in the same cafeteria. No one had a private office. Honda facilities featured open areas where managers, coordinators, staff, and clerical workers worked side by side at plain desks. Managers and engineers routinely handled parts and equipment on the shop floor. Soichiro Honda believed that good leaders should perform even the most undesirable jobs willingly, and at least once. Accordingly, he was known to sweep factory floors, empty ash trays, and pick up paper towels from restroom floors wherever he went.

On matters which affected them, associates were asked their opinion. In the United States they voluntarily suggested cutting the lunch hour to 30 minutes and shortening the work day. They chose how to expand production during pressing times and which days of a holiday week would be work days or free. Disciplined associates could appeal their cases to a court of peers selected at random from cohorts on another shift. The peer group's decision was by secret ballot and was binding on all parties.

Dr. Robert Guest, a world authority on automotive organizations, described Honda's organization practices this way.

> Almost all members of Honda's operating management started in the shop itself, as did 65% of its Japanese sales personnel. There is frequent movement of workers laterally and through promotions. Everyone understands that automation will be targeted

first at the most onerous tasks. Much of the machinery at Honda is built by a Honda engineering subsidiary, which was set up because of the many new ideas that were originated by the workforce themselves. No one fears problems of technological unemployment, as growth continues.

Work standards are written up by the employees themselves, in conjunction with their foremen. Honda threw out American-style scientific management systems when they found that their workers slowed down while being timed and objected to the process. Mr. Honda, by skill and temperament, was a 'shop man' who was always concerned about the product, production details, and more importantly about the role played by people on the shop floor and their creative potentials.[4]

Organization Structure

True to his stated policy of "proceed always with ambition and youthfulness," Soichiro Honda (age 68) and Takeo Fujisawa (age 62) retired from active management of the company on its 25th anniversary in 1973, becoming "advisors" to the firm. Mr. Kowashima, then Tadashi Kume became president of Honda Motor Company. The top management group was assembled on the third floor of Honda's Tokyo headquarters office—using an open-plan executive suite where 32 directors worked together in a single open room. Just as in Honda's factories, senior executives like Kume occupied desks in an open office with chairs scattered around. Junior managers bustled in and out visiting dealers and suppliers. While decisions at this level were widely discussed in the room, Mr. Kume, an engineer who had earlier opposed and defeated Honda in a showdown over the development of air-cooled engines, was clearly the first among equals. He was "a passionate man in the Honda tradition, a man who, like the founder, sometimes shouted to make himself heard. . . . He listed as his hobby drinking sake, but cars, and more particularly the engines in them were, still his passion."

The company's management structure had three levels. At the top was a board of directors, consisting of 24 company officers, including its two "supreme advisors." Within the board were a senior managing director's group, a decision–making body consisting of the president, two executive vice presidents, and four senior management directors. The president's expertise was in technology; one vice president's was in sales; and the other, responsible for the company's financial policies, was an engineer by training and a generalist by experience at Honda.

At the corporate level, this group controlled three specialist groups, each made up of managing directors and ordinary directors and joined as needed by the heads of semi-independent affiliated companies. The three specialist groups were responsible for matters relating to "people, things, and money." The individual sections and divisions responsible for day-to-day operations and for specific areas of profit-making reported to the "president's office." They were under the general oversight of the specialist groups, which did not represent any specific section with daily responsibilities for profit. Among other things, these specialist groups were responsible for overseeing major new projects of the company. An example was the deployment of a task force in 1977 to select a site for its U.S. motorcycle (and later, automobile) assembly operations.

At the operational level, Honda utilized basically a worldwide functional organization for its line activities. For example, a North American Sales Division reported directly to the headquarters Sales group, overseas Production divisions to the headquarters Manufacturing group, and small overseas R&D units to corporate R&D. However, engine R&D, engine manufacture, and manufacture of some key subassemblies were kept in Japan. Some products were designed and built in Japan directly for export; some were built in Japan and modified for export; others were built entirely in overseas operations.

In the late 1980s Honda had become the fourth largest maker of American cars. Honda decided in 1979 to build a 150,000 unit U.S. auto assembly plant alongside its Marysville, Ohio motorcycle plant. Accords began rolling off in December, 1982. When the plant's capacity became seriously strained in 1985, Honda moved quickly to double it. The new space was used to produce Honda's popular Civic, the smallest and least expensive car Honda sold in the U.S.

Honda had aggressively built its image in the U.S. through a quiet sophisticated advertising program. According to professional analysts, American consumers perceived the Honda name as being synonymous with quality, just as they perceived the Sony brand. The quality of Japanese-made Honda cars was legendary. Engineering and automotive magazine ratings of the world's best cars almost always included the Honda Accord. For example, testers for *Road and Track* had paired the Mercedes-Benz 190E with the Accord SE-i; the Mercedes at $23,000 scored 166 points, the Accord at $13,000 scored 163.[5] And the U.S. operation was determined to equal that record.

Honda in Japan

In 1983 Honda eased past Mazda to take over the number three sales position with 8% of Japan's market, following Toyota's 41% share and Nissan's 26%. While the rest of the Japanese industry was having difficulty in its home market, Honda sales boomed upward by 18%, the highest growth among major auto makers. Honda launched a new mini-car in Japan called the Citi, whose sales immediately soared to 99,000 units, almost double those of the Civic, Honda's next most popular car there. Honda's partly-plastic bodied, CRX two-seater car won the 1983 Car of the Year Award in Japan, leading all contenders by a big margin. And in America, EPA gave the CRX its highest rating for fuel economy—51 miles per gallon.

Although motorcycles accounted for only about 25% of Honda's $10 billion in early 1980s sales, the company was dominated by people who grew up in that fiercely competitive business. The great flexibility and cost consciousness of motorcycle manufacturing penetrated all aspects of Honda. And its top management was the youngest in the Japanese auto industry. Unfortunately however—like its rivals—Honda had not been able to make much money in Japan. In the mid-1980s, the Japanese market was barely growing, and heavy competition among 10 auto makers kept prices low. While Japanese manufacturers discounted their cars heavily in Japan, they sold at premium prices in America. For example, Honda's 1984 Prelude, initially priced at $9,995 in America, went for about half that in Japan. Honda made higher operating profits (8.6% on consolidated sales in 1983) than either Toyota (6.9%) or Nissan (5.8%). But in the voluntary quota system to the United States, Honda was allowed only 350,000 cars for shipment, compared with 500,000 for Toyota and 450,000 for Nissan.

Honda in America

Worldwide, Toyota was clearly Honda's most formidable Japanese competitor. Toyota was the world's third largest car company ($\frac{1}{2}$ the size of Ford and $\frac{1}{3}$ the size of G.M.) and had recently decided to lay down new plants in the U.S. and Canada. (See Table 1.)

Despite its position as the number one foreign auto maker selling in the United States, Toyota had previously made all its cars abroad. Toyota's public reference to its mid-1980s strategy was "Global 10" symbolizing its intent to capture

295

TABLE 1 New Capacity in Canada

COMPANY	START-UP DATE	INVESTMENT ($ MILLIONS)	ANNUAL PLANNED PRODUCTION UNITS
Hyundai	1988	$220	100,000
Toyota	1988	$220	50,000
Suzuki*	1989	$300	300,000

* Joint venture with General Motors.

Source: Business Week, Nov. 4, 1985.

10% of the world vehicle market. But insiders said the company had upped that target to 12%.[6] Toyota backed that intention with a war chest of some $5 billion in cash equivalent assets. Toyota's new U.S. factory, unlike its joint venture with GM in California, would be aimed at the "upscale" U.S. market with its $9,378 Camry. And Toyota brought a number of its most crucial Japanese suppliers to the United States to manufacture near its plants. Backed by the lowest cost production system in Japan, Toyota was adding dealerships, boosting advertising, and lowering its cycle times for model changes. It was also bringing its dealers into its just-in-time inventory systems, pressing ahead with "the same kind of ruthlessness in sales and distribution that it had pioneered in the factory."[6]

Not content with having entered the U.S. market directly, various Asian car makers were also entering through Canada. Lured by huge Canadian incentives, South Korea's Hyundai and Japan's Toyota and Suzuki had announced plans for some $600 million in capacity in Canada. (See Table 1.) These would add 23% to Canada's capacity of 1.1 million units per year by the late 1980s. Under a 1965 U.S.-Canadian agreement, a manufacturer in Canada could ship cars to the United States duty-free as long as 50% of the value had been added in North America.

Canadian provinces competed hotly for the new Asian plants. Experts estimated that Hyundai's tariff exemptions alone would cost the Canadian government $150 million in lost taxes per year. Canadian manufacturing costs had fallen sharply since 1980 because of Canada's weak currency. In addition, Canada's national health system created an (approximately) $8/hour labor cost advantage over the United States.

U.S. Operations

Although some claimed Honda's ultimate goal was to be Japan's biggest auto maker, its top management remained silent on this point. Nevertheless, the press consistently reported that Honda's target was to sell one million cars per year in the United States in the early 1990s. In this competition, the $250 million Honda had invested in its Marysville plant compared favorably with the $660 million Nissan had spent for a similar capacity plant in the United States [7] or the $500 million Toyota was preparing to spend on its new 200,000 unit Camry facility.[6]

Honda had attacked all its costs in the United States aggressively. By using labor practices similar to its Japanese units, it had gotten the total compensation of its nonunionized U.S. workers to about $14/hour compared with some $23 at the Big Three's unionized plants. Honda had also used less expensive components than U.S. makers—and often got better quality for its money. About $\frac{1}{2}$ the value of a Honda's parts was imported from Japan. Some were made to order by the parent company (especially for the Accord) but others were cheaper than U.S. parts or of higher quality. Honda said it had planned to use a higher proportion of U.S. made parts, "But the attitude of some suppliers was that their job was only to give us the parts, and that we must check the quality ourselves. . . . We told them that wasn't enough, we expected 100% good parts." Some suppliers responded, others did not. Honda could build a fully equipped 1985 Accord for about $8,000, some $1,000-$1,500 less than it cost General Motors to build a comparably equipped version of its Buick or Olds line. And by 1988 it could ship the cars to Japan from the United States at a profit.

After some initial problems, (dominantly with paint, rust, brakes, and air conditioning) in early models, Honda's U.S. products were given an overwhelmingly high rating by Consumer's Union. The automobile press said the redesigned 1985 Accord built in America was "a great improvement on one of the classic modern cars," and its successor became the best selling single mark in the United States during the late 1980s.

What is the Future?

Under Mr. Kume, technology continued to receive the same high priority it had under Mr. Honda. For example, while the body of the CRX sports car still contained 60% metal in 1984, Kume said his goal was to build the car with a 100% plastic shell. Further into the future was the possibility of the "ceramic engine," currently being pursued by all Japanese manufacturers because of its high thermal efficiency, high compression ratios, and low fuel consumption. Ceramic engines also offered opportunities for getting rid of water cooled radiators and much of the other weight and complexity associated with the cast steel engine blocks which had been the standby of the industry for years. Automobile design and manufacture were undergoing their most radical changes in some 60 years.

Exhibit 1 offers some comparative and trend data concerning the major U.S. and Japanese automakers' sales, production, and export of cars. Exhibit 2 gives some comparative financials for these companies in the late 1980s. Exhibit 3 indicates the structure of the European and world markets for cars.

Sales of cars in Japan had been limited by government policy constraining credit, by the scarcity of roadways, and the very expensive parking facilities needed in most areas. In 1988 Japan had only 243 cars per 1000 people as compared with 370 in Britain, 454 in West Germany, and 588 in the United States. However, Japan's shift toward a domestic, consumer economy was expected to ease credit restrictions and to expand major motorways (from 2,700 miles to 8,700 miles by 2010). Japan's export of autos was constrained by its "voluntary restraint" agreements with the United States.

Although Honda had been the first Japanese producer to manufacture autos in America, Nissan, Toyota, Mazda, Mitsubishi, Suzuki, and Subaru were expected to follow. Honda's plant expansions would allow it to produce 500,000 cars per year, from which it expected to export 50,000 cars per year by 1991 from America to Japan. Nissan was expanding its Smyrna facility and would be producing some 450,000 cars per year by 1992. Total Japanese auto manufacture in the United States was expected to reach 2.9 million vehicles per year in 1991 in addition to another 2 million direct exports from Japan. Ford and General Motors were expanding their plants to produce over 4.3 million compact and sub-compact cars annually during the early 1990s.

Although U.S. manufacturers had made substantial progress, the average Japanese plant turned out a car with 20.3 hours of labor versus 24.4 hours for the average U.S. facility. The rapidly appreciating Yen had decreased the Japanese domestic manufacturing cost advantages to only $300 on the average. Wages and fringe benefits at the U.S. Big Three cost about $30 per hour versus $24 at even

Toyota's U.S. plants. And experts estimated that some of the Big Three's health care programs alone cost $300–$500 more per car than Japanese manufacturers'. U.S. manufacturers had responded by moving toward the up-market, but government mandated "fleet fuel economy" standards of 27.5 miles per gallon were beginning to create serious problems for American-owned producers.

The European Market

In contrast to its U.S. strategy, Honda had been reluctant to invest heavily in Europe, apart from its motorcycle plants. It had undertaken a joint production arrangement with British Leland for a new 2-liter car, bigger than any Honda had ever built. Total Japanese penetration of European markets was also not nearly as great. (See charts in Exhibit 3.) No one knew how Europe 1992 would affect auto production in the EEC. Quotas had restricted imports of Japanese cars into individual countries in the past. However, Spain and some of the "Mediterranean countries" with low labor costs were pressing to break these quotas in 1992. Building sales in Europe would be difficult against the well-known, high quality, and accepted European brands. However, many European producers had not updated their plants as dramatically as the Americans, and some of the great European cars had not won a "car of the year" award in over a decade.

On the positive side, Japan's auto industry, which had been barely a quarter the size of Britain's in 1965, was now seven times larger. However, like the Japanese and American markets, over-capacity (of about 20%) plagued the European marketplace. Because of such considerations, France, Italy, and Spain (which together accounted for about 40% of total European sales) were virtually closed to Japanese producers, and other countries had applied ceilings to Japanese imports. These were largely offset by exports of the upper-line European cars, like BMW, Daimler-Benz, Jaguar, Saab, and Volvo, mostly to the U.S. Few of the "lower-end" European cars enjoyed a substantial export market.

Cost structures in the automobile industry were changing rapidly in the late 1980s. Components and materials comprised about 50%–60%, and labor about 20%, of an auto's factory cost. Plants for sophisticated components like engines, gear trains, or trans-axles might cost $500–$800 million, while assembly plants were decreasing in size but increasing in the complexity of their flexible automation. In addition, about 30% of the pre-tax price of a car was accounted for by marketing and distribution.

While U.S. owned companies had a strong presence in Europe, individual Japanese companies did not. (See Exhibit 3.) Japanese car companies' strategy problems were compounded by vastly increased price cutting and retail competition in Japan. Toyota and Nissan seemed strong enough to withstand any onslaught, but both Mitsubishi and Mazda were plagued with scale problems, despite some fine individual products.

Given the massive capital requirements of the automobile industry, few would have thought a new entrant like Honda could have survived, much less prospered, in the 1960s and 1970s. But as *Fortune* concluded, "A few years ago when Japanese cars flooded the American market, Detroit appeared frozen by indecision. The established Japanese companies, by comparison, seemed invincible. Now relative newcomer Honda is making the other Japanese car makers look ponderous and timid . . . against a company willing to take risks and move fast."[7] But the markets of the 1990s posed formidable new challenges for Japan's number three auto producer.

1. What important patterns have guided Honda's strategy in the past? How do these affect its future strategy? What do you think of its organizational structure and practices? What lessons can be learned from Honda?

2. What were the critical factors for Honda's success during its early entrepreneurial development? Compare and contrast this pattern with that of other entrepreneurial Japanese and U.S. companies. What are the most important similarities and differences?

3. How should Honda position itself in the early 1990s? Why? How should Detroit respond to this positioning?

4. What implications does Honda's past history have for the future of the auto industry?

EXHIBIT 1
Market Shares of Major Producers

	Honda	Toyota	Nissan	Mazda	Mitsubishi	GM	Ford	Chrysler[a]
U.S. Car Sales (000)								
1978	275	442	339	n/a	n/a	5405	2663	1421
1983	401	556	522	n/a	n/a	4054	1571	1178
1988	769	689	514	n/a	n/a	3822	2290	1191
U.S. Car Production (000)								
1982	2	0	0	0	0	3173	1104	710
1985	145	0	44	0	0	4822	1636	1377
1988	366	19[b]	110	167	0	3427	1807	1073
U.S. Market Share (%)								
1978	2.4	3.9	3.0	n/a	n/a	47.8	23.5	12.6
1983	4.4	6.1	5.7	n/a	n/a	44.2	17.1	12.3
1988	7.2	6.5	4.8	n/a	n/a	35.9	21.5	11.2
Japanese Car Sales (000)								
1977	166	892	755	176	218	7	7	1
1982	240	1174	822	247	226	2	1	<1
1987	337	1454	765	199	158	3	1	<1
Japanese Car Production (000)								
1978	653	2039	1733	493	629	0	0	0
1983	956	2569	1859	815	571	0	0	0
1988	1073	2983	1731	880	640	0	0	0
Japanese Market Share (%)								
1977	10.6	34.7	29.8	9.2	9.0	<.1	<.1	<.1
1982	12.7	31.9	26.6	11.8	8.5	<.1	<.1	<.1
1987	16.2	32.1	21.7	11.5	7.2	<.1	<.1	<.1
Car Exports (000)								
1978	488	900	855	341	321	d	d	d
1983	900	1365	1179	674	432	d	d	d
1988	675	1232	849	643	410	d	d	d
Car Production (000) (outside of home country)								
1987	340	88[c]	213	4	n/a	2002	2170	77

[a] Includes AMC.
[b] Excludes NUMMI.
[c] Includes NUMMI.
[d] 1987 exports of cars from the United Stated totalled only 633,000 (with 562,000 of those being to Canada).

Source: Compiled from *Ward's Automotive Yearbook,* 1989 edition; *World Motor Vehicle Data,* 1989 edition.

EXHIBIT 2
Comparative Financials—FY 1989
($ Millions)

	Honda[a]	Nissan[b]	Mazda[c]	Toyota[d]	Ford[e]
Sales	26,434	36,452	6,532	54,254	82,193
Other income	121	276	12	203	11,148
Total revenues					
Cost of sales	19,274	28,651	5,840	45,032	68,233
S, G&A expense	4,427	6,393	560	5,705	3,452
Interest expense	186	752	39	168	354
Other expenses	70	—	—	—	—
Income before taxes	1,304	1,462	106	4,588	8,343
Income taxes	611	608	69	2,369	2,999
Net income	737	868	54	133	5,300
Cash dividends	85	250	30	371	1,114
Inventories	3,600	3,814	1,254	1,968	4,396
Total assets	17,306	35,922	9,964	40,980	143,367
Long-term debt and other oblig.	2,543	6,163	1,946	4,179	6,175
Shareholder's equity	6,829	12,495	2,614	24,701	21,529

[a] Honda Motor Co., Ltd. manufactures and sells motorcycles, autos, pumps, lawn mowers, power tillers, etc.
[b] Nissan Motor Co., Ltd. manufactures and sells autos, rockets, forklifts, textile machinery, boats, etc.
[c] Mazda Motor Corp. manufactures passenger cars, trucks, buses, machine tools, etc.
[d] Toyota Motor Co., Ltd. manufactures passenger cars, commercial vehicles, prefabricated housing units, etc. Merged with Toyota Motor Sales Co., Ltd. July 1982.
[e] Ford Motor Co. manufactures, assembles, and sells cars, trucks, and related parts and accessories. Subsidiary businesses include Aerospace and Communications, steel, Ford Motor Credit Co., Leasing, Land Development. Ford owns 25% interest in Mazda Motor Corp.

Source: Compiled from Moody's *Industrial Manual* and Moody's *International,* 1989 edition.

EXHIBIT 3

World Vehicle Production (000)

Company	1982		1987	
	Cars	Total	Cars	Total
1. General Motors (USA)	4,870	6,150	5,605	7,497
2. Ford (USA)	2,890	4,027	4,000	5,892
3. Toyota (Japan)	2,258	3,147	2,796	3,730
4. Nissan (Japan)	1,864	2,512	2,017	2,658
5. Peugeot Group (France)	1,673	1,489	2,301	2,512
6. VW Group (W. Germ.)	1,903	2,079	2,338	2,475
7. Chrysler (USA)	789	1,041	1,186	2,188
8. Renault (France)	1,844	2,105	1,742	2,053
9. Fiat Group (Italy)	1,343	1,635	1,675	1,880
10. VAZ (USSR)			725	1,605
11. Honda (Japan)	861	1,022	1,362	1,581
12. Mitsubishi (Japan)	573	969	595	1,231
13. Mazda (Japan)	824	1,110	858	1,202
14. Suzuki (Japan)	114	603	297	868
15. Daimler-Benz (W. Germ.)	466	690	596	823
16. Hyundai (Korea)	78	91	545	607
17. Fuji-Subaru (Japan)	201	514	267	605
18. Daihatsu (Japan)	128	464	142	598
19. Isuzu (Japan)	113	405	204	542
20. Rover Group (UK)	405	509	472	537
Top 40 manufacturers	26,077	34,221	32,727	44,609
North American Cos.	8,689	11,501	10,792	15,663
Western European Cos.	8,432	9,766	10,371	11,759
Japanese Cos.	6,937	10,808	8,536	13,080
Eastern European Cos.	1,925	1,989	2,086	2,975
Korean Cos.	n/a	n/a	790	966
Total World Production	29,776	39,750	33,007	45,914

Source: Compiled by the Motor Vehicle Manufacturers Association of the U.S., Inc. from reports of various overseas motor vehicle associations. Published in *Facts and Figures, 1985 and 1989.*

Free World Passenger Car Demand By Region (Millions)

	1985	1987	1992	1997
U.S.	11.0	10.3	10.5	11.1
Canada	1.1	1.1	1.1	1.2
Europe	10.6	12.4	12.9	13.7
Latin America	1.2	1.1	1.6	2.0
Mid-East	0.4	0.3	0.6	0.7
Africa	0.3	0.3	0.5	0.7
Asia-Pacific	4.2	4.4	5.3	6.1
Total	28.8	29.9	32.5	35.5

Source: 1989 *Ward's Automotive Yearbook,* page 77.

EXHIBIT 3 (Continued)

European New Car Registrations By Manufacturer

	1985		1988	
	Units (thousands)	Percent	Units (thousands)	Percent
VW Group	1,529	14.4	1,930	14.9
Fiat Group	1,304	12.3	1,916	14.8
Ford Total[a]	1,268	11.9	1,466	11.3
Peugeot Group	1,226	11.5	1,672	12.9
GM Total[b]	1,212	11.4	1,375	10.6
Renault	1,139	10.7	1,326	10.2
Mercedes	394	3.7	445	3.4
Austin Rover	420	3.9	448	3.5
Nissan	307	2.9	378	2.9
Toyota	248	2.6	349	2.7
BMW	290	2.7	355	2.7
Volvo	255	2.4	265	2.0
Mazda	203	1.9	245	1.9
Alfa Romeo	161	1.5	213	1.6
Mitsubishi	116	1.1	156	1.2
Honda	n/a	n/a	140	1.1

[a] of which more than 99% is sold by Ford Europe.
[b] of which more than 98% is sold by Opel/Vauxhall.
Source: 1989 *Ward's Automotive Yearbook,* p. 87.

European Car Sales By Country

	New Car Sales (000)	Japanese Import Penetration (%)	
	1988	1977	1987
W. Germany	2,808	2.5	15.1
France	2,217	2.6	2.9
UK	2,216	10.6	11.2
Italy	2,184	0.1	0.7
Spain	877	0.0	0.2
Netherlands	483	19.8	25.9
Belgium	427	19.3	20.8
Sweden	344	10.4	21.7
Switzerland	319	12.1	28.9
Austria	253	5.7	31.2
Portugal	206	15.2	8.5
Finland	174	21.8	41.8
Other	470	n/a	n/a
Total	12,978	n/a	11.2

Source: 1988 Car Sales from 1989 *Ward's Automotive Yearbook,* page 87; Japanese import penetration figures compiled by the Motor Vehicle Manufacturers Association of the U.S., Inc. from reports of various overseas motor vehicle associations. Published in *Facts and Figures, 1989.*

EXHIBIT 3 (Continued)

Europe's Big Six Western European Car Sales By Country, 1988

ªGroup sales

% share of Western European car market by origin	1988 actual	1995 forecast
Western Europe	86.3	74.4
Japanᵇ	11.3	17.8
Eastern Europe	1.8	2.5
United States	0.2	1.5
South Korea	0.2	3.5
Others	0.2	0.3

ᵇIncluding production in Europe and United States

Source: The Economist, September 23, 1989.

ORGANIZATION

DEALING WITH STRUCTURE AND SYSTEMS

Chapter 5 has completed Section 1, which introduced the concepts related to our central theme, strategy—what it is, how it should and does get made, and the nature of the work of one of its key makers, the general manager. Chapter 6 begins Section 2, which deals with another set of concepts that every student of general management must come to understand. We group these under the title *Organization* because they all pertain to the basic design and running of the organization.

In this chapter we examine the design of organizational *structure* and the development of *systems* for coordination and control. In Chapter 7, we consider *culture,* that ideological glue that holds organizations together, enhancing their ability to pursue strategies on one hand, but sometimes impeding strategic change on the other. And in Chapter 8, we turn to the questions of *power*—how it flows within the organization and how the organization uses it in its external environment.

Structure, in our view, no more follows strategy than the left foot follows the right in walking. The two exist *inter*dependently, each influencing the other. There are certainly times when a structure is redesigned to carry out a new strategy. But the choice of any new strategy is likewise influenced by the realities and potentials of the existing structure. Indeed, the classical model of strategy formulation (discussed in Chapter 3) implicitly recognizes this by showing the strengths and weaknesses of the organization as an input to the creation of strategies. Surely these strengths and weaknesses are deeply rooted within the existing structure, indeed often part and parcel of it. Hence, we introduce here structure and the associated administrative systems which make it work as essential factors to consider in the strategy process. Later when we present the various contexts within which organizations function, we shall consider the different ways in which strategy and structure interact.

All of the readings of this chapter reinforce these points. The Waterman, Peters, and Phillips article originally published under the title "Structure Is Not

Organization," introduces the well-known "7-S" framework that was developed at the McKinsey consulting firm, where all three authors worked when this article was published. (This framework was, in fact, one of the antecedents of the best-selling management book *In Search of Excellence* by two of these authors.) This framework explicitly considers how structure, systems, style, and other organizational factors interrelate with strategy; as such, many practicing executives and students have found this a most valuable construct in thinking about organizations. (Note that what the authors call "superordinate goals" were renamed "shared values" in the *Excellence* book. We discuss them in some depth under the label "culture" in Chapter 7, noting that these were first introduced in this book in the Selznick reading of Chapter 2.)

The second reading approaches conventional concepts of strategy and its relationship to structure, but does so in an unconventional way. In his article "Strategy and Organization Planning," Jay Galbraith, a former MIT and Wharton Business School professor who worked as an independent management consultant for several years and now teaches at the University of Southern California, also views structure broadly as encompassing support systems of various kinds. Building on concepts such as "driving force" and "center of gravity," Galbraith links various strategies (of vertical integration and diversification) to forms of structure, ranging from the functional to the increasingly diversified. Galbraith covers a wide body of important literature in the field and uses visual imagery to make his points. The result is one of the best articles in print on the relationship between the strategy of diversification and the structure of divisionalization.

Unconventional, too, but in a very different way, is the following article by Quinn, Doorley, and Paquette. Whereas Galbraith discusses vertical integration and diversification, they focus in a sense on vertical *de*integration; whereas Galbraith discusses moving upstream and downstream, they in a sense recommend taking many internal activities *off*stream. Interestingly, however, these authors focus their discussion on a concept very close to Galbraith's "center of gravity," which they call an organization's "core activities."

The subject here is a rather new concept of organization for the 1990s, facilitated by new information technologies, what the authors call the "intellectual holding company." By concentrating strategic analyses on each element in the value chain, companies can target their own resources towards those things they do best, and outsource those activities others can perform better. In this way they can lower their investments, flatten their organizations, and improve the quality and flexibility of their outputs. (See the associated reading by two of these authors in Chapter 12 on "Spider's Web," "Infinitely Flat," and "Inverted" Organizations.) The authors suggest how these innovative new forms can act to restructure entire industries. When coupled with cases from the service sector and concepts from the Professional Context chapter, this reading provides powerful new insights.

The fourth reading, excerpted originally from Mintzberg's book *The Structuring of Organizations,* comprehensively probes the design of organizational structures, including their formal systems. It seeks to do two things: first to delineate the basic dimensions or organizations and then to combine these to identify various basic types of organizations, called "configurations." The dimensions introduced include mechanisms used to coordinate work in organizations, parameters to consider in designing structures, and situational factors which influence choices among these design parameters. This reading also introduces a somewhat novel diagram to depict organizations, not as the usual organizational chart or cybernetic flow process, but as a visual combination of the critical parts of an organization. This reading then clusters all these dimensions into a set of configurations, each introduced briefly here and discussed at length in later chapters. In fact, the choice of the chapters on context—entrepreneurial, mature, diversified, professional, and innovative (leaving aside the last on strategic change)—was really based on five of these types, so that reading the conclusion to this article will help to introduce you to Section 3.

A number of cases allow students to probe the particular ramifications of these concepts. The Polaroid, Ford: Team Taurus, Royal Bank of Canada, PRA&D, General Mills, Zayre, and Exxon cases most clearly illustrate the principles and controversies these structural and organizational articles raise. But many cases from other sections, as well, develop useful and complementary insights about the interfaces of organization, structure, and strategy.

● THE 7-S FRAMEWORK*

BY ROBERT H. WATERMAN, JR., THOMAS J. PETERS, AND JULIEN R. PHILLIPS

The Belgian surrealist René Magritte painted a series of pipes and titled the series *Ceci n'est pas une pipe:* this is not a pipe. The picture of the thing is not the thing. In the same way, a structure is not an organization. We all know that, but like as not, when we reorganize, what we do is to restructure. Intellectually all managers and consultants know that much more goes on in the process of organizing than the charts, boxes, dotted lines, position descriptions, and matrices can possibly depict. But all too often we behave as though we didn't know it; if we want change we change the structure. . . .

Our assertion is that productive organization change is not simply a matter of structure, although structure is important. It is not so simple as the interaction between strategy and structure, although strategy is critical too. Our claim is that effective organizational change is really the relationship between structure, strategy, systems, style, skills, staff, and something we call superordinate goals. (The alliteration is intentional: it serves as an aid to memory.)

Our central idea is that organization effectiveness, stems from the interaction of several factors—some not especially obvious and some underanalyzed. Our framework for organization change, graphically depicted in Figure 1, suggests several important ideas:

● First is the idea of a multiplicity of factors that influence an organization's ability to change and its proper mode of change. Why pay attention to only one or two, ignoring the others? Beyond structure and strategy, there are at least five other identifiable elements. The division is to some extent arbitrary, but it has the merit of acknowledging the complexity identified in the research and segmenting it into manageable parts.

● Second, the diagram is intended to convey the notion of the interconnectedness of the variables—the idea is that it's difficult, perhaps impossible, to make significant progress in one area without making progress in the others as well. Notions of organization change that ignore its many aspects or their interconnectedness are dangerous.

* Originally published as "Structure is Not Organization" in *Business Horizons* (June 1980); copyright © 1980 by the Foundation for the School of Business at Indiana University; all rights reserved. Reprinted with deletions by permission of the publisher.

FIGURE 1
A New View of
Organization

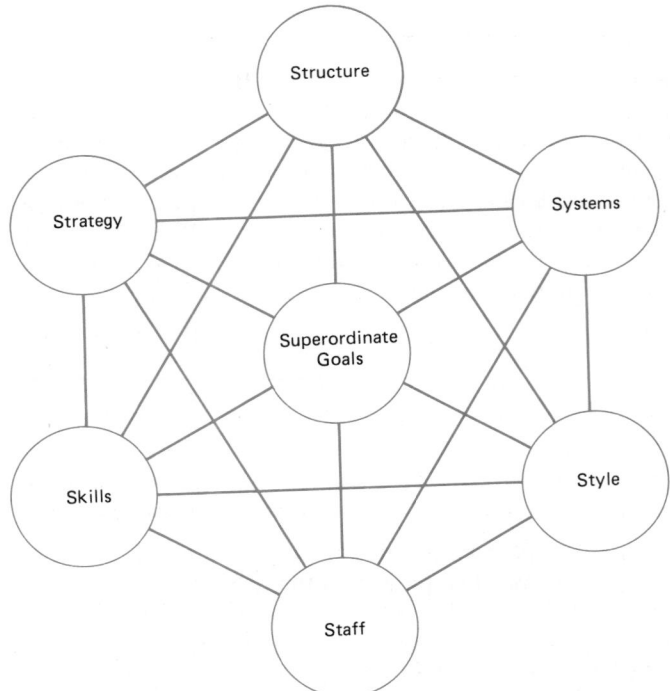

- In [an] article on strategy, *Fortune* commented that perhaps as many as 90% of carefully planned strategies don't work. If that is so, our guess would be that the failure is a failure in execution, resulting from inattention to the other S's. Just as a logistics bottleneck can cripple a military strategy, inadequate systems or staff can make paper tigers of the best-laid plans for clobbering competitors.

- Finally, the shape of the diagram is significant. It has no starting point or implied hierarchy. A priori, it isn't obvious which of the seven factors will be the driving force in changing a particular organization at a particular point in time. In some cases, the critical variable might be strategy. In others, it could be systems or structure.

STRUCTURE

To understand this model of organization change better, let us look at each of its elements, beginning—as most organization discussions do—with structure. What will the new organization of the 1980s be like? If decentralization was the trend of the past, what is next? Is it matrix organization? What will "Son of Matrix" look like? Our answer is that those questions miss the point. . . .

The central problem in structuring today . . . is not the one on which most organization designers spend their time—that is, how to divide up tasks. It is one of emphasis and coordination—how to make the whole thing work. The challenge lies not so much in trying to comprehend all the possible dimensions of organization structure as in developing the ability to focus on those dimensions which are currently important to the organization's evolution—and to be ready to refocus as the crucial dimensions shift.

If structure is not enough, what is? Obviously, there is strategy. It was Alfred Chandler (1962) who first pointed out that structure follows strategy, or more precisely, that a strategy of diversity forces a decentralized structure. Throughout the past decade, the corporate world has given close attention to the interplay between strategy and structure. Certainly, clear ideas about strategy make the job of structural design more rational.

By "strategy" we mean those actions that a company plans in response to or anticipation of changes in its external environment—its customers, its competitors. Strategy is the way a company aims to improve its position vis-à-vis competition—perhaps through low-cost production or delivery, perhaps by providing better value to the customer, perhaps by achieving sales and service dominance. It is, or ought to be, an organization's way of saying: "Here is how we will create unique value."

As the company's chosen route to competitive success, strategy is obviously a central concern in many business situations—especially in highly competitive industries where the game is won or lost on share points. But "structure follows strategy" is by no means the be-all and end-all of organization wisdom. We find too many examples of large, prestigious companies around the world that are replete with strategy and cannot execute any of it. There is little if anything wrong with their structures; the causes of their inability to execute lie in other dimensions of our framework. When we turn to nonprofit and public sector organizations, moreover, we find that the whole meaning of "strategy" is tenuous—but the problem of organizational effectiveness looms as large as ever.

Strategy, then, is clearly a critical variable in organization design—but much more is at work.

By systems we mean all the procedures, formal and informal, that make the organization go, day by day and year by year: capital budgeting systems, training systems, cost accounting procedures, budgeting systems. If there is a variable in our model that threatens to dominate the others, it could well be systems. Do you want to understand how an organization really does (or doesn't) get things done? Look at the systems. Do you want to change an organization without disruptive restructuring? Try changing the systems.

A large consumer goods manufacturer was recently trying to come up with an overall corporate strategy. Textbook portfolio theory seemed to apply: find a good way to segment the business, decide which segments in the total business portfolio are most attractive, invest most heavily in those. The only catch: reliable cost data by segment were not to be had. The company's management information system was not adequate to support the segmentation. . . .

[One] intriguing aspect of systems is the way they mirror the state of an organization. Consider a certain company we'll call International Wickets. For years management has talked about the need to become more market oriented. Yet astonishingly little time is spent in their planning meetings on customers, marketing, market share, or other issues having to do with market orientation. One of their key systems, in other words, remains *very* internally oriented. Without a change in this key system, the market orientation goal will remain unattainable no matter how much change takes place in structure and strategy.

311

To many business managers the word "systems" has a dull, plodding, middle-management sound. Yet it is astonishing how powerfully systems changes can enhance organizational effectiveness—without the disruptive side effects that so often ensue from tinkering with structure.

STYLE

It is remarkable how often writers, in characterizing a corporate management for the business press, fall back on the word "style." . . . The trouble we have with style is not in recognizing its importance, but in doing much about it. Personalities don't change, or so the conventional wisdom goes.

We think it is important to distinguish between the basic personality of a top-management team and the way that team comes across to the organization. Organizations may listen to what managers say, but they believe what managers do. Not words, but patterns of actions are decisive. The power of style, then, is essentially manageable.

One element of a manager's style is how he or she chooses to spend time. As Henry Mintzberg has pointed out managers don't spend their time in the neatly compartmentalized planning, organizing, motivating, and controlling modes of classical management theory. Their days are a mess—or so it seems. There's a seeming infinity of things they might devote attention to. No top executive attends to all of the demands of his time; the median time spent on any one issue is nine minutes.

What can a top manager do in nine minutes? Actually, a good deal. He can signal what's on his mind; he can reinforce a message; he can nudge people's thinking in a desired direction. Skillful management of his inevitably fragmented time is, in fact, an immensely powerful change lever. . . .

Another aspect of style is symbolic behavior. Companies most successful in finding mineral deposits typically have more people on the board who understand exploration or have headed exploration departments. Typically they fund exploration more consistently (that is, their year-to-year spending patterns are less volatile). They define fewer and more consistent exploration targets. Their exploration activities typically report at a higher organizational level. And they typically articulate better reasons for exploring in the first place.

STAFF

Staff (in the sense of people, not line/staff) is often treated in one of two ways. At the hard end of the spectrum, we talk of appraisal systems, pay scales, formal training programs, and the like. At the soft end, we talk about morale, attitude, motivation, and behavior.

Top management is often, and justifiably, turned off by both these approaches. The first seems too trivial for their immediate concern ("Leave it to the personnel department"), the second too intractable ("We don't want a bunch of shrinks running around, stirring up the place with more attitude surveys").

Our predilection is to broaden and redefine the nature of the people issue. What do the top-performing companies do to foster the process of developing managers? How, for example, do they shape the basic values of their management cadre? Our reason for asking the question at all is simply that no serious discussion of organization can afford to ignore it (although many do). Our reason for framing the question around the development of managers is our observation that the superbly performing companies pay extraordinary attention to managing what might be called the socialization process in their companies. This applies especially to the way they introduce young recruits into the mainstream of their organizations and to the way they manage their careers as the recruits develop into tomorrow's managers. . . .

Considering people as a pool of resources to be nurtured, developed, guarded, and allocated is one of the many ways to turn the "staff" dimension of our 7-S framework into something not only amenable to, but worthy of practical control by senior management.

We are often told, "Get the structure 'right' and the people will fit" or "Don't compromise the 'optimum' organization for people considerations." At the other end of the spectrum we are earnestly advised, "The right people can make any organization work." Neither view is correct. People do count, but staff is only one of our seven variables.

SKILLS

We added the notion of skills for a highly practical reason: It enables us to capture a company's crucial attributes as no other concept can do. A strategic description of a company, for example, might typically cover markets to be penetrated or types of products to be sold. But how do most of us characterize companies? Not by their strategies or their structures. We tend to characterize them by what they do best. We talk of IBM's orientation to the marketplace, its prodigious customer service capabilities, or its sheer market power. We talk of Du Pont's research prowess, Procter & Gamble's product management capability, ITT's financial controls, Hewlett-Packard's innovation and quality, and Texas Instruments' project management. These dominating attributes, or capabilities, are what we mean by skills.

Now why is this distinction important? Because we regularly observe that organizations facing big discontinuities in business conditions must do more than shift strategic focus. Frequently they need to add a new capability, that is to say, a new skill. . . . These dominating capability needs, unless explicitly labeled as such, often get lost as the company "attacks a new market" (strategy shift) or "decentralizes to give managers autonomy" (structure shift).

Additionally, we frequently find it helpful to *label* current skills, for the addition of a new skill may come only when the old one is dismantled. Adopting a newly "flexible and adaptive marketing thrust," for example, may be possible only if increases are accepted in certain marketing or distribution costs. Dismantling some of the distracting attributes of an old "manufacturing mentality" (that is, a skill that was perhaps crucial in the past) may be the only way to ensure the success of an important change program. Possibly the most difficult problem in trying to organize effectively is that of weeding out old skills—and their supporting systems, structures, and so on—to ensure that important new skills can take root and grow.

SUPERORDINATE GOALS

The word "superordinate" literally means "of higher order." By superordinate goals, we mean guiding concepts—a set of values and aspirations, often unwritten, that goes beyond the conventional formal statement of corporate objectives.

Superordinate goals are the fundamental ideas around which a business is built. They are its main values. But they are more as well. They are the broad notions of future direction that the top management team wants to infuse throughout the organization. They are the way in which the team wants to express itself, to leave its own mark. Examples would include Theodore Vail's "universal service" objective, which has so dominated AT&T; the strong drive to "customer service" which guides IBM's marketing. . . .

In a sense, superordinate goals are like the basic postulates in a mathematical system. They are the starting points on which the system is logically built, but in themselves are not logically derived. The ultimate test of their value is not their logic but the usefulness of the system that ensues. Everyone seems to know the importance of compelling superordinate goals. The drive for their accomplishment pulls an organization together. They provide stability in what would otherwise be a shifting set of organization dynamics.

Unlike the other six S's, superordinate goals don't seem to be present in all, or even most, organizations. They are, however, evident in most of the superior performers.

To be readily communicated, superordinate goals need to be succinct. Typically, therefore, they are expressed at high levels of abstraction and may mean very little to outsiders who don't know the organization well. But for those inside, they are rich with significance. Within an organization, superordinate goals, if well articulated, make meanings for people. And making meanings is one of the main functions of leadership.

CONCLUSION

We have passed rapidly through the variables in our framework. What should the reader have gained from the exercise?

We started with the premise that solutions to today's thorny organizing problems that invoke only structure—or even strategy and structure—are seldom adequate. The inadequacy stems in part from the inability of the two-variable model to explain why organizations are so slow to adapt to change. The reasons often lie among the other variables: systems that embody outdated assumptions, a management style that is at odds with the stated strategy, the absence of a superordinate goal that binds the organization together in pursuit of a common purpose, the refusal to deal concretely with "people problems" and opportunities.

At its most trivial, when we merely use the framework as a checklist, we find that it leads into new terrain in our efforts to understand how organizations really operate or to design a truly comprehensive change program. At a minimum, it gives us a deeper bag in which to collect our experiences.

More importantly, it suggests the wisdom of taking seriously the variables in organizing that have been considered soft, informal, or beneath the purview of top management interest. We believe that style, systems, skills, superordinate goals can be observed directly, even measured—if only they are taken seriously. We think that these variables can be at least as important as strategy and structure in orchestrating major change; indeed, that they are almost critical for achieving necessary, or desirable change. A shift in systems, a major retraining program for staff, or the generation of top-to-bottom enthusiasm around a new superordinate goal could take years. Changes in strategy and structure, on the surface, may happen more quickly. But the pace of real change is geared to all seven S's.

At its most powerful and complex, the framework forces us to concentrate on interactions and fit. The real energy required to redirect an institution comes when all the variables in the model are aligned. One of our associates looks at our diagram as a set of compasses. "When all seven needles are all pointed the same way," he comments, "you're looking at an *organized* company."

• STRATEGY AND ORGANIZATION PLANNING*

BY JAY R. GALBRAITH

. . . There has been a great deal of progress in the knowledge base supporting organization planning in the last twenty-five years. Modern research on corporate structures probably started with Chandler's *Strategy and Structure*. Subsequent research has been aimed at expanding the number of attributes of an organization beyond that of just structure. I have used the model shown in Figure 1 to indicate that organization consists of structure, processes that cut the structural lines like budgeting, planning, teams, and so on, reward systems like promotions and compensation, and finally people practices like selection and development (Galbraith, 1977). The trend lately is to expand to more attributes like the 7-S's (Waterman, 1980) and to "softer" attributes like culture.

All of these models are intended to convey the same ideas. First, organization is more than just structure. And, second, all of the elements must "fit" to be in "harmony" with each other. The effective organization is one that has blended its structure, management practices, rewards, and people into a package that in turn fits with its strategy. However, strategies change and therefore the organization must change.

The research of the past few years is creating some evidence by which organizations and strategies are matched. Some of the strategies are proving more successful than others. One of the explanations is organizational in nature. Also the evidence shows that for any strategy, the high performers are those who have achieved a fit between their strategy and their organization.

These findings give organization planning a base from which to work. The organization planner should become a member of the strategic team in order to guide management to choose the appropriate strategies for which the organization is developed or to choose the appropriate organization for the new strategy.

In the sections that follow, the strategic changes that are made by organizations are described. Then the strategy and organization evidence is presented. Finally the data on economic performance and fit is discussed.

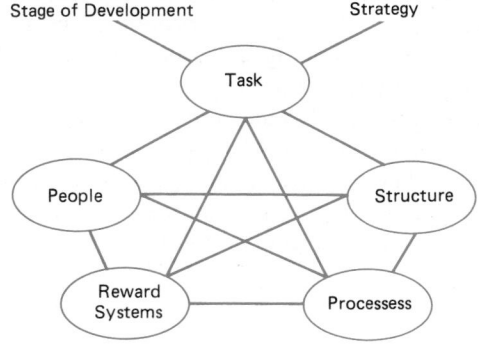

FIGURE 1
Model of Organization Structure

There has been a good deal of recent attention given to the match between strategy and organization. Much of this work consists of empirical tests of Chandler's ideas presented in *Strategy and Structure* (1962). Most of this material is reviewed elsewhere (Galbraith and Nathanson, 1978). However, some recent work and ideas hold out considerable potential for understanding how different patterns of strategic change lead to different organization structures, management systems, and company cultures. In addition, some good relationships with economic performance are also attained.

The ideas rest on the concept of an organization having a center of gravity or driving force. (Tregoe and Zimmerman, 1980). This center of gravity arises from the firm's initial success in the industry in which it grew up. Let us first explore the concept of center of gravity, then the patterns of strategic change that have been followed by American enterprises.

The center of gravity of a company depends on where in the industry supply chain the company started. In order to explain the concept, manufacturing industries will be used. Figure 2 depicts the stages of supply in an industry chain. Six stages are shown here. Each industry may have more or fewer stages. Service industries typically have fewer stages.

The chain begins with a raw material extraction stage which supplies crude oil, iron ore, logs, or bauxite to the second stage of primary manufacturing. The second stage is a variety-reducing stage to produce a standardized output (petrochemicals, steel, paper pulp, or aluminum ingots). The next stage fabricates commodity products from this primary material. Fabricators produce polyethylene, cans, sheet steel, cardboard cartons, and semiconductor components. The next stage is the product producers who add value, usually through product development, patents, and proprietary products. The next stage is the marketer and distributor. These are the consumer branded product manufacturers and various distributors. Finally, there are the retailers who have the direct contact with the ultimate consumer.

The line splitting the chain into two segments divides the industry into upstream and downstream halves. While there are differences between each of the stages, the differences between the upstream and downstream stages are striking. The upstream stages add value by reducing the variety of raw materials found on the earth's surface to a few standard commodities. The purpose is to produce flexible, predictable raw materials and intermediate products from which an increasing variety of downstream products are made. The downstream stages add value through producing a variety of products to meet varying customer needs. The downstream value is added through advertising, product positioning, marketing channels, and R&D. Thus, the upstream and downstream companies face very different business problems and tasks.

The reason for distinguishing between upstream and downstream companies is that the factors for success, the lessons learned by managers, and the organizations used are fundamentally different. The successful, experienced manager has

FIGURE 2
**Supply Stages in an
Industry Chain**

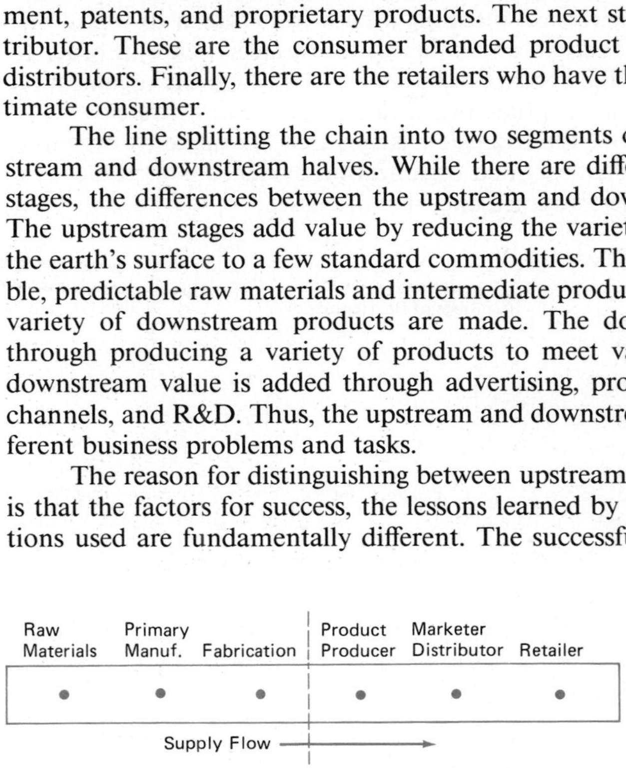

Raw Materials	Primary Manuf.	Fabrication	Product Producer	Marketer Distributor	Retailer
•	•	•	•	•	•

Supply Flow ⟶

316

been shaped and formed in fundamentally different ways in the different stages. The management processes are different, as are the dominant functions. In short, the company's culture is shaped by where it began in the industry chain. Listed are some fundamental differences that illustrate the contrast:

Upstream	*Downstream*
Standardize/homogenize	Customize/segment
Low-cost producer	High margins/proprietary positions
Process innovation	Product innovation
Capital budget	R&D/advertising budget
Technology/capital intensive	People intensive
Supply/trader/engineering	R&D/marketing dominated
Line driven	Line/staff
Maximize end users	Target end users
⋮	⋮
Sales push	Market pull

The mind set of the upstream manager is geared toward standardization and efficiency. They are the producers of standardized commodity products. In contrast, downstream managers try to customize and tailor output to diverse customer needs. They segment markets and target individual users. The upstream company wants to standardize in order to maximize the number of end users and get volume to lower costs. The downstream company wants to target particular sets of end users. Therefore, the upstreamers have a divergent view of the world based on their commodity. For example, the cover of the 1981 annual report of Intel (a fabricator of commodity semiconductors) is a listing of the 10,000 uses to which microprocessors have been put. The downstreamers have a convergent view of the world based on customer needs and will select whatever commodity will best serve that need. In the electronics industry there is always a conflict between the upstream component types and the downstream systems types because of this contrast in mind sets.

The basis of competition is different in the two stages. Commodities compete on price since the products are the same. Therefore, it is essential that the successful upstreamer be the low-cost producer. Their organizations are the lean and mean ones with a minimum of overheads. Low cost is also important for the downstreamer, but it is proprietary features that generate high margins. That feature may be a brand image, such as Maxwell House, a patented technology, an endorsement (such as the American Dental Association's endorsement of Crest toothpaste), customer service policy, and so on. Competition revolves around product features and product positioning and less on price. This means that marketing and product management sets prices. Products move by marketing pull. In contrast, the upstream company pushes the product through a strong sales force. Often salespeople negotiate prices within limits set by top management.

The organizations are different as well. The upstream companies are functional and line driven. They seek a minimum of staff, and even those staffs that are used are in supporting roles. The downstream company with multiple products and multiple markets learns to manage diversity early. Profit centers emerge and resources need to be allocated across products and markets. Larger staffs arise to assist top management in priority setting across competing product/market advocates. Higher margins permit the overhead to exist.

Both upstream and downstream companies use research and development. However, the upstream company invests in process development in order to lower costs. The downstream company invests primarily in product development in order to achieve proprietary positions.

The key managerial processes also vary. The upstream companies are driven by the capital budget and have various capital appropriations controls. The downstream companies also have a capital budget but are driven by the R&D budget (product producers) or the advertising budget (marketers). Further downstream it is working capital that becomes paramount. Managers learn to control the business by managing the turnover of inventory and accounts receivable. Thus, the upstream company is capital intensive and technological "know-how" is critical. Downstream companies are more people intensive. Therefore, the critical skills revolve around human resources management.

The dominant functions also vary with stages. The raw material processor is dominated by geologists, petroleum engineers, and traders. The supply and distribution function which searches for the most economical end use is powerful. The manufacturers of commodities are dominated by engineers who come up through manufacturing. The downstream companies are dominated first by technologists in research and product development. Farther downstream, it is marketing and then merchandising that emerge as the power centers. The line of succession to the CEO usually runs through this dominant function.

In summary, the upstream and downstream companies are very different entities. The differences, a bit exaggerated here because of the dichotomy, lead to differences in organization structure, management processes, dominant functions, succession paths, management beliefs and values or, in short, the management way of life. Thus, companies can be in the same industry but be very different because they developed from a beginning at a particular stage of the industry. This beginning, and the initial successes, teaches management the lessons of that stage. The firm develops an integrated organization (structure, processes, rewards, and people) which is peculiar to that stage and forms the center of gravity.

STRATEGIC CHANGE

The first strategic change that an organization makes is to vertically integrate within its industry. At a certain size, the organization can move backward to prior stages to guarantee sources of supply and secure bargaining leverage on vendors. And/or it can move forward to guarantee markets and volume for capital investments and become a customer to feed back data for new products. This initial strategic move does not change the center of gravity because the prior and subsequent stages are usually operated for the benefit of the center-of-gravity stage.

The paper industry is used to illustrate the concepts of center of gravity and vertical integration. Figure 3 depicts five paper companies which operate from different centers of gravity. The first is Weyerhauser. Its center of gravity is at the land and timber stage of the industry. Weyerhauser seeks the highest return use for a log. They make pulp and paper rolls. They make containers and milk cartons. But they are a timber company. If the returns are better in lumber, the pulp mills get fed with sawdust and chips. International Paper (the name of the company tells it all), by contrast, is a primary manufacturer of paper. It also has timber lands, container plants, and works on new products around aseptic packaging. However, if the pulp mills ran out of logs, the manager of the woodlands used to be fired. The raw material stage is to supply the manufacturing stage, not seek the highest return for its

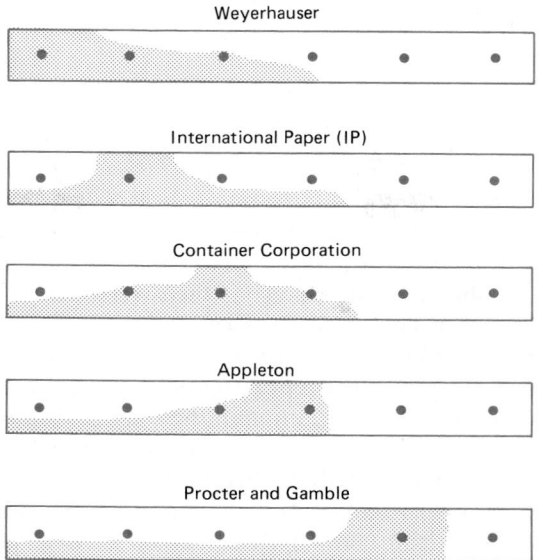

timber. The Container Corporation (again, the name describes the company) is the example of the fabricator. It also has woodlands and pulp mills, but they are to supply the container making operations. The product producer is Appleton. It makes specialty paper products. For example, Appleton produces a paper with globules of ink imbedded in it. The globules burst and form a letter or number when struck with an impact printer.

The last company is Procter & Gamble. P&G is a consumer products company. And, like the other companies, it operates pulp mills and owns timber lands. However, it is driven by the advertising or marketing function. If one wanted to be CEO of P&G, one would not run a pulp mill or the woodlands. The path to CEO is through the brand manager for Charmin or Pampers.

Thus, each of these companies is in the paper industry. Each operates at a number of stages in the industry. Yet each is a very different company because it has its center of gravity at a different stage. The center of gravity establishes a base from which subsequent strategic changes take place. That is, as a company's industry matures, the company feels a need to change its center of gravity in order to move to a place in the industry where better returns can be obtained, or move to a new industry but use its same center of gravity and skills in that industry, or make some combination of industry and center of gravity change. These options lead to different patterns of corporate developments.

By-products Diversification

One of the first diversification moves that a vertically integrated company makes is to sell by-products from points along the industry chain. Figure 4 depicts this strategy. These companies appear to be diversified if one attributes revenue to the various industries in which the company operates. But the company has changed neither its industry nor its center of gravity. The company is behaving intelligently by seeking additional sources of revenue and profit. However, it is still psychologically committed to its center of gravity and to its industry. Alcoa is such a firm. Even though they operate in several industries, their output varies directly with the aluminum cycle. They have not reduced their dependence on a single industry, as one would with real diversification.

319

FIGURE 4
By-product Diversification

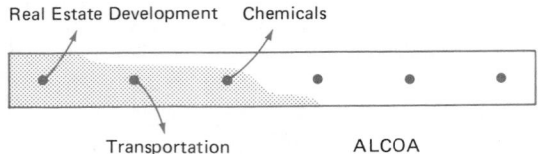

Real Estate Development   Chemicals

Transportation   ALCOA

Related Diversification

Another strategic change is the diversification into new industries but at the same center of gravity. This is called related diversification." The firm diversifies into new businesses, but they are all related. The relationship revolves around the company's center of gravity. Figure 5 depicts the diversification moves of Procter & Gamble. After beginning in the soap industry, P&G vertically integrated back into doing its own chemical processing (fatty acids) and seed crushing. Then, in order to pursue new growth opportunities, it has been diversifying into paper, food, beverages, pharmaceuticals, coffee, and so on. But each move into a new industry is made at the company's center of gravity. The new businesses are all consumer products which are driven out of advertising by brand managers. The 3M Company also follows a related diversification strategy, but theirs is based on technology. They have 40,000 different products which are produced by some seventy divisions. However, 95% of the products are based on coating and bonding technologies. Its center of gravity is a product producer, and it adds value through R&D.

Linked Diversification

A third type of diversification involves moving into new industries and operating at different centers of gravity in those new industries. However, there is a linkage of some type among various businesses. Figure 6 depicts Union Camp as following this pattern of corporate development. Union Camp is a primary producer of paper products. As such, it vertically integrated backwards to own woodlands. From there, it moved downstream within the wood products industry by running sawmills and fabricating plants. However, they recently purchased a retail lumber business.

They also moved into the chemical business by selling by-products from the pulping process. This business was successful and expanded. Recently, Union Camp was bidding for a flavors and fragrances (F & F) company. The F&F company is a product producer which adds value through creating flavors and fragrances for mostly consumer products companies.

Thus, Union Camp is an upstream company that is acquiring downstream companies. However, these new companies are in industries in which the company

FIGURE 5
Related Diversification

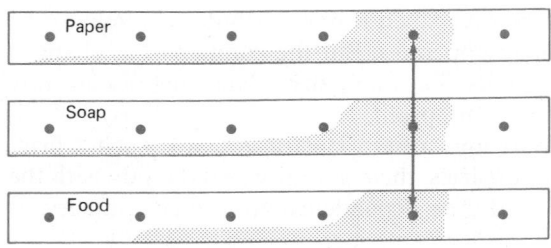

Paper

Soap

Food

Procter and Gamble

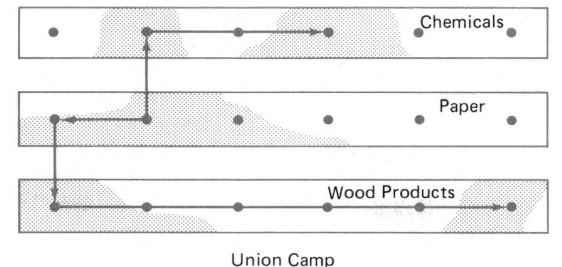

FIGURE 6
Linked Diversification

Union Camp

already diversified from its upstream center of gravity. But these new acquisitions are not operated for the benefit of the center of gravity but are stand-alone profit centers.

Unrelated Diversification

The final type of strategic change is to diversify into unrelated businesses. Like the linked diversifiers, unrelated diversifiers move into new industries often at different centers of gravity. They almost always use acquisition, while related and linked companies will use some acquisitions but rely heavily on internal development. There is often very little relation between the industries into which the unrelated company diversifies. Textron and Teledyne have been the paradigm examples. They operate in industrial equipment, aerospace, consumer products, insurance, and so on. Others have spread into retailing, services, and entertainment. The purpose is to insulate the company's earnings from the uncertainties of any one industry or from the business cycle.

Center of Gravity Change

Another possibility is for an organization to stay in the same industry but change its center of gravity in that industry. Recent articles describe the attempts of chemical companies to move downstream into higher margin, proprietary products. They went to move away from the overcapacity/undercapacity cycles of commodity businesses with their low margins and high capital intensity. In aerospace, some of the system integration houses are moving backward into making electronic components. For example, there are going to be fewer airplanes and more effort on the avionics, radars, weapons, and so on that go into airplanes. In either case, it means a shift in the center of gravity of the company.

In summary, several patterns of strategic change can occur in a company. These involve changes to the company's industry of origination, changes to the center of gravity of the company, or some combination of the two. For some of the strategic changes there are appropriate organizations and measures of their economic performance.

STRATEGY, ORGANIZATION, AND PERFORMANCE

For a number of years now, studies have been made of strategy and structure of the *Fortune* 500. Most of these were conducted by the Harvard Business School. These studies were reviewed in previous work (Galbraith and Nathanson, 1978). The current view is illustrated in Table 1. If one samples the *Fortune* 500 and categorizes them by strategy and structure, the following relationships hold.

TABLE 1

STRATEGY	STRUCTURE
Single business	Functional
Vertical by-products	Functional with P&Ls
Related businesses	Divisional
Linked businesses	Mixed structures
Unrelated businesses	Holding company

One can still find organizations staying in their same original business. Such a single business is Wrigley Chewing Gum. These organizations are run by centralized functional organizations. The next strategic type is the vertically integrated by-product seller. Again, these companies have some diversification but remain committed to their industry and center of gravity. The companies are also functional, but the sequential stages are often operated as profit and loss divisions. The companies are usually quite centralized and run by collegial management groups. The profit centers are not true ones in being independent to run their own businesses. These are almost all upstream companies.

The related businesses are those that move into new industries at their center of gravity. Usually these are downstream companies. They adopt the decentralized profit center divisions. However, the divisions are not completely decentralized. There are usually strong corporate staffs and some centralized marketing, manufacturing, and R&D. There may be several thousand people on the corporate payroll.

The clearest contrast to the related diversifier is the unrelated business company. These companies enter a variety of businesses at several centers of gravity. The organization they adopt is the very decentralized holding company. Their outstanding feature is the small corporate staff. Depending on their size, the numbers range between fifty and two hundred. Usually these are support staffs. All of the marketing, manufacturing, and R&D is decentralized to the divisions. Group executives have no staffs and are generally corporate oriented.

The linked companies are neither of these extremes. Often linked forms are transitory. The organizations that they utilize are usually mixed forms that are not easily classified. Some divisions are autonomous, while others are managed out of the corporate HQ. Still others have strong group executives with group staffs. Some work has been done on classifying these structures (Allen, 1978).

There has been virtually no work done on center of gravity changes and their changes in structure. Likewise, there has been nothing done on comparisons for economic performance. But for the other categories and structures, there is emerging some good data on relative economic performance.

The studies of economic performance have compared the various strategic patterns and the concept of fit between strategy and organization. Both sets of results have organization design implications. The economic studies use return on equity as the performance measure. If one compares the strategic categories listed in Table 1, there are distinct performance differences. The high performers are consistently the related diversifiers (Rumelt, 1974; Galbraith and Nathanson, 1978; Nathanson and Cassano, 1982; Bettis, 1981; Rumelt, 1982). There are several explanations for this performance difference. One explanation is that the related diversifiers are all downstream companies in businesses with high R&D and advertising expenditures. These businesses have higher margins and returns than other businesses. Thus, it may not be the strategy but the businesses the relateds happen to be in. However, if the unrelateds are good acquirers, why do they not enter the high-return businesses?

The other explanation is that the relateds learn a set of core skills and design an organization to perform at a particular center of gravity. Then, when they diversify, they take on the task of learning a new business, but at the same center of gravity. Therefore, they get a diversified portfolio of businesses but each with a system of management and an organization that is understood by everyone. The management understands the business and is not spread thin.

The unrelateds, however, have to learn new industries and also how to operate to a different center of gravity. This latter change is the most difficult to accomplish. One upstream company diversified via acquisition into downstream companies. It consistently encountered control troubles. It instituted a capital appropriation process for each investment of $50,000 or more. It still had problems, however. The retail division opened a couple of stores with leases for $40,000. It didn't use the capital process. The company got blindsided because the stores required $40 million in working capital for inventory and receivables. Thus, the management systems did not fit the new downstream business. It appears that organizational fit makes a difference. . . .

One additional piece of evidence results from the studies of economic performance. This result is that the poorest performer of the strategic categories is the vertically integrated by-product seller. Recall these companies are all upstream, raw material, and primary manufacturers. They make up a good portion of "Smokestack America." In some respects, these companies made their money early in the century, and their value added is shifting to lesser developed countries in the natural course of industrial development. However, what is significant here is their inability to change. It is no secret to anyone that they have been underperformers, yet they have continued to put money back into the same business.

My explanation revolves around the center of gravity. These previously successful companies put together an organization that fit their industry and stage. When the industry declined, they were unable to change as well as the downstream companies. The reason is that upstream companies were functional organizations with few general managers. Their resource allocation was within a single business, not across multiple products. The management skill is partly technological know-how. This technology does not transfer across industries at the primary manufacturing center of gravity. The knowledge of paper making does not help very much in glass making. Yet both might be combined in a package company. Also, the capital intensity of these industries limits the diversification. Usually one industry must be chosen and capital invested to be the low-cost producer. So there are a number of reasons why these companies have been notoriously poor diversifiers.

In addition, it appears to be very difficult to change centers of gravity no matter where an organization is along the industry chain. The reason is that a center of gravity shift requires a dismantling of the current power structure, rejection of parts of the old culture, and establishing all new management systems. The related diversification works for exactly the opposite reasons. They can move into new businesses with minimal change to the power structure and accepted ways of doing things. Changes in the center of gravity usually occur by new start-ups at a new center of gravity rather than a shift in the center of established firms. . . .

There are some exceptions that prove the rule. Some organizations have shifted from upstream commodity producers to downstream product producers and consumer product firms. General Mills moved from a flour miller to a related diversified provider of products for the homemaker. Over a long period of time they shifted downstream into consumer food products from their cake mix product beginnings. From there, they diversified into related areas after selling off the milling operations, the old core of the company. . . . [In these cases], however, new management was brought in and acquisition and divestment used to make the transition. So, even though vestiges of the old name remain, these are substantially different companies. . . .

The vast majority of our research has examined one kind of strategic change —diversification. The far more difficult one, the change in center of gravity, has received far less [attention]. For the most part, the concept is difficult to measure and not publicly reported like the number of industries in which a company operates. Case studies will have to be used. But there is a need for more systematic knowledge around this kind of strategic change.

● THE INTELLECTUAL HOLDING COMPANY: STRUCTURING AROUND CORE ACTIVITIES*

BY JAMES BRIAN QUINN, THOMAS L. DOORLEY,
AND PENNY C. PAQUETTE

Most companies primarily produce a chain of services and integrate these into a form most useful to certain customers. So dominant is this consideration that one questions whether many companies—like those in pharmaceuticals, computers, clothing, oil and gas, foods, office or automation equipment—should really be classified as "manufacturers" anymore. The vast majority of their systems costs, value-added profits, and competitive advantage grows out of service activities.

For example, the strategies of virtually all pharmaceutical companies are critically dependent on service functions. This is especially true of the top performers like $5-billion Merck and £1.7-billion Glaxo, and less true for lower profit generic drug producers. The direct manufacturing cost of most patented ethical drugs is trivial relative to their sale price. Value is added primarily by service activities— discovery of a drug through R&D, a carefully constructed patent and legal defense, rapid and thorough clinical clearance through regulatory bodies, or a strong preemptive distribution system. Recognizing this, in recent years Merck's strategy has focused on one portion of the value chain, a powerful research-based patent position. Glaxo has successfully targeted rapid clinical clearance as its key activity. Both strategies rest primarily on adding value through service activities. Merck and Glaxo outperform the industry in gross margins (71.5% and 79.6% versus an industry composite of 66.9%), in operating income margins (27.1% and 38.2% versus 21.2%), and in profits as a percentage of shareholders' equity (48% of 35% versus an industry average of 23%).

As manufacturing becomes more universally automated, the major value added to a product increasingly moves away from the point where raw materials are converted into useful form (that is, steel into an auto "body in white" or grain into edible cereals) and toward the styling features, perceived quality, subjective taste, and marketing presentation that service activities provide at all levels of the value chain. At each stage, technology had increased the relative power of services to the point where they dominate virtually all companies' value chains (see Figure 1).

* Originally published as "Technology in Services: Rethinking Strategic Focus," in *Sloan Managment Review* (Winter 1990). Copyright © 1990 by *Sloan Management Review*. Reprinted with deletions by permission of *Sloan Management Review*.

FIGURE 1
Make or Buy? Key Service Activities

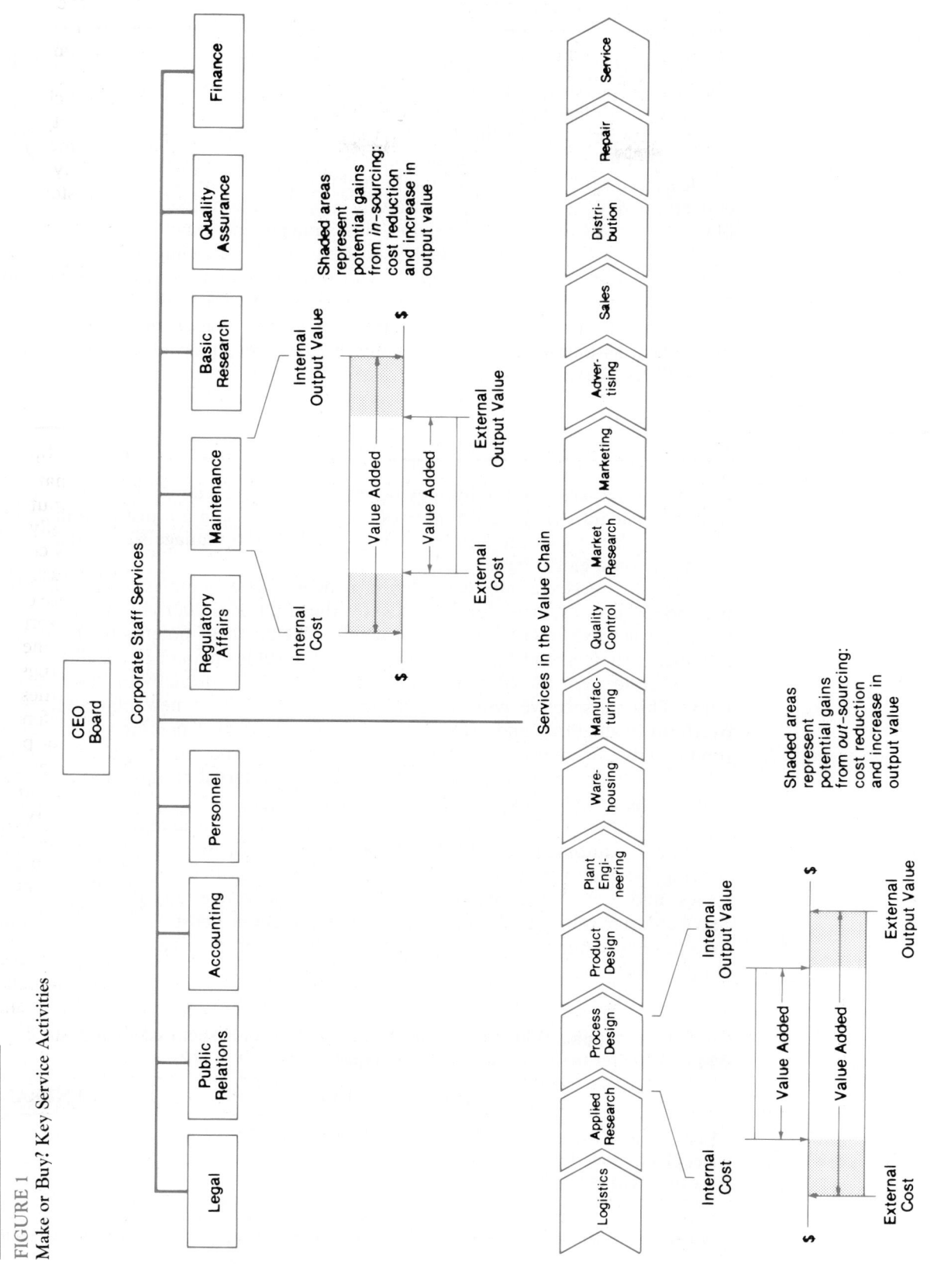

The fact is that many large companies, like Apple Computer and IBM, initially succeeded by recognizing and leveraging this concept—becoming essentially "intellectual holding companies," purposely manufacturing or producing as little product internally as possible. For example, until the early 1960s IBM was known as an "assembler," outsourcing up to 80 percent of its manufacturing costs. And Apple succeeded by masterminding the highly sophisticated interconnection of architectural, design, software, and hardware supply relationships that became its explosively successful Apple II system. This strategy may have been essential for Apple in its early years when it lacked both the time and capital to build factories or hire a salesforce. But even today—with three to four times the sales per employee and a third to a quarter the fixed investment per sales dollar of its competitors—Apple is structured less like a traditional "manufacturing" company and more like a $4-billion "service" company that happens to have three manufacturing facilities (see Table 1).

SMASHING OVERHEADS THROUGH OUTSOURCING

Because of the scale economies they permit, new service technologies also make it possible to achieve major economies of scale by purchasing not just manufactured parts, but also crucial services, externally—and also to manage such outsourcing effectively on a global basis.

Outside service groups can often provide greater economies of scale, flexibility, and levels of expertise for specialize overhead services than virtually any company can achieve internally. To thoroughly develop these potentials one should consider each overhead category—whether in the value chain or in a staff function—as a service that the company could either "make" internally or "buy" externally. This perspective will, at a minimum, introduce a new objectivity into overhead evaluations and create some strong competitive pressures for internal productivity. In many cases, companies find that specialized outside service sources can be much more cost effective than their internal groups. And they start outsourcing to lower costs or to improve value-added.

For example, $3-billion ServiceMaster Company can take over many of its customers' equipment and facilities maintenance functions, simultaneously improving the quality and lowering the costs of these activities through system economies and specialized management skills. So effective are its systems that ServiceMaster can not only lower absolute maintenance costs, it can often joint-invest in new equipment with its customers, sharing productivity gains to the benefit of both parties.

TABLE 1 **Apple, Which Outsources Extensively, Is Structured Less Like a Manufacturing than Like a Service Company**

	APPLE	IBM	DEC	DATA GENERAL
Sales per employee	$369,593	$139,250	$84,972	$81,243
Net plant, property, and equipment as % of sales[a]	18.4	63.0	44.6	56.7

[a] Net property, plant, and equipment figures have been adjusted to account for leased assets by multiplying the annual rental expense by 8.

Whenever a company produces a service internally that others buy or produce more efficiently or effectively externally, it sacrifices competitive advantage. Conversely, the key to strategic success for many firms has been their coalitions with the world's best service providers—their external product designers, advertising agencies, distribution channels, financial houses, and so on. How can companies best exploit such opportunities?

LEARNING TO LOVE THE "HOLLOW CORPORATION"

Considering the enterprise as an intellectual holding company (à la Apple Computer) restructures the entire way one attacks strategy. One needs to ask, activity by activity, "Are we really competitive with the world's best here? If not, can intelligent outsourcing improve our long-term position?" Competitive analyses of service activities should not consider just the company's own industry, but should benchmark each service against "best in class" performance among all potential service providers and industries that might cross-compete within the analyzed category—both in the United States and abroad.

As companies begin to outsource nonstrategic activities—particularly overheads—they often discover important secondary benefits. Managements concentrate more on their businesses' core strategic activities. Other internal costs and time delays frequently drop as long-standing bureaucracies disappear and political pressures decrease for annual increments to each department's budget. All this leads to a more compact organization, with fewer hierarchical levels. It also leads to a much sharper focus on recruiting, developing, and motivating the people who create most value in those areas where the company has special competencies.

DOMINATING THOSE ACTIVITIES CRUCIAL TO STRATEGY

Many have expressed concerns about the hollowing out and loss of strategic capability outsourcing could cause (*Business Week,* 1986). However, if the process is approached properly, careful outsourcing should increase both productivity and strategic focus. A company must maintain command of those activities crucial to its strategic position. If it does not, it has essentially redefined the business it is in. For all other activities, if the company cannot see its way to strategic superiority, or if the activity is not essential to areas where it can attain such superiority, the company should consider outsourcing. But it is essential that the company plan and manage its outsourcing coalitions so that it does not become overly dependent on —and hence dominated by—its partner. In some cases this means consciously developing and maintaining alternate competitive sources or even strategically controlling critical stages in an overall process that might otherwise be totally outsourced.

HIGHEST ACTIVITY SHARE, NOT MARKET SHARE, FOR PROFITS

Once a company develops great depth in certain selected service activities as its strategic focus, many individual products can spring off these "core" activities to give the firm a consistent corporate strategy for decades. Unfortunately, the true nature of these core capabilities is usually obscured by the tendency of organizations to think of their strengths in product—not activity or service—terms. The key point is that a few *selected activities should drive strategy*. Knowledge bases, skills sets, and service activities are the things that generally can create continuing added value and competitive advantage.

Too much strategic attention has been paid to having a high share of the market. High share can be bought by inappropriate pricing or other short-term strategies. High market share and high profitability together come from having the highest relevant *activity* share in the marketplace—in other words, having the most effective presence in a service activity the market desires and thus gaining the experience curve and other benefits accruing to that high activity share.

To be most effective, this service-activity dominance needs truly global development. As noted, the major value-added in most products today comes not from direct production or conversion processes, but from the technological improvements, styling, quality, marketing, timing, and financing contributions of service activities. Since these are knowledge-based intangibles that can be shipped cost-free anywhere, producers who expand their scope worldwide to tap the best knowledge and service sources available anywhere can obtain significant competitive advantage.

AVOIDING VERTICAL INTEGRATION

Since most firms cannot afford to own or internally dominate all needed service activities, they tend to form coalitions, linking their own and their partners' capabilities through information, communication, and contract arrangements—rather than through ownership (that is, vertical or horizontal integration). Because of their high value-added potentials, service companies and service activities within companies are central to many of these coalitions. An entirely new form of enterprise seems to be emerging, with a carefully conceived and limited set of "core strategic activities" (usually services) at its center, that allows a company to command and coordinate a constantly changing network of the world's best production and service suppliers on a global basis. This is a logical and most powerful extension of the Kieretsu concept (linked networks of banks, producers, suppliers, and support-distribution companies) that has long been at the heart of Japan's trading success.

Given today's rapid technological advances, many enterprises find they can lower their risks and leverage their assets substantially by *avoiding* investments in vertical integration and managing "intellectual systems" instead of workers and machines. The core strategy of a coordinating or systems company becomes: "Do only those things in-house that contribute to your competitive advantage, and try to source the rest from the world's best suppliers."

MANUFACTURING INDUSTRIES BECOME "SERVICE NETWORKS"

Many industries are becoming loosely structured networks of service enterprises that join together temporarily for one purpose—yet are each other's suppliers, competitors, or customers elsewhere.

Biotechnology, where highly specialized companies are developing at each level, providing "service" activities for one another and the industry, is becoming structured as a number of multiple-level consortia, offers an interesting example of this phenomenon. The semiconductor and electronics industries are moving toward a similar structure. Independent design, foundry, packaging, assembly, industrial distribution, kitting, configuration, systems analysis, networking, and value-added distributor groups do more than $15 billion worth of customized development, generating almost $140,000 of revenue per employee (*Electronic Business,* 1988). Even large OEMs are finding that these groups' specialization, fast turnarounds, advanced designs, and independent perspectives can lower costs, decrease investments, and increase value at all levels.

STRATEGICALLY REDEFINING THE "FOCUSED COMPANY"

Given the vast changes being wrought by new technologies, and the resulting potential for worldwide strategic outsourcing, the whole notion of what constitutes an "industry" or a "focused company" needs to be reexamined. True focus in strategy means the capacity to bring more power to bear on a selected sector than anyone else can.

Properly developed, a broad product or service line does not necessarily signify loss of focus if a firm can deploy especially potent service skills against selected marketplaces in a coordinated fashion. (In fact, a broad line may represent the leveraging of a less obvious strategic focus.) The key question is whether a company dominates a set of service skills that has importance to its customers—in other words, can bring more power to bear on this activity than anyone in the world. If so, the company can be a strategic success, provided it focuses its attention on that activity, obtains at least strategic parity through outsourcing elsewhere, and then blocks others from entering its markets by leveraging its skills across as broad a product line or customer base as it can dominate. Competitors must be defined as those with substitutable skill bases, not those with similar product lines. Product lines can be remarkably broad when the service skill base is deep enough to be dominating. Toys R Us, Procter & Gamble, McKesson, Matsushita, and 3M provide only a few of many excellent cases in point.

For example, Procter and Gamble (P&G) created a $15-billion corporation largely based on two central sets of service skills: its R&D capabilities in eight core technologies, and its superb marketing-distribution skills. Today its extremely broad product line flows naturally from the interaction of these two service activities. Figure 2 shows how skills associated with bar soup could lead P&G naturally to flaked soaps, Tide detergent, and many of its later products. P&G's research depth in surfactant chemistry provided the central linkage among products apparently as diverse as soap and acne or bone disease control drugs, while its marketing and distribution strength allowed P&G to move powerfully, but incrementally, from market to market.

CONCLUSIONS

Most companies create a major portion of their incremental value and gain their real competitive advantage from a relatively few—generally service—activities. Much of the remaining enterprise exists primarily to permit these activities to take place. Yet managements typically spend an inordinate amount of their time, energy, and company resources dealing with these latter support functions—all of which decrease their attention to the company's truly crucial areas of strategic focus. Virtually all managers can benefit from a more carefully structured approach to managing their service activities strategically. Doing so involves defining each activity in the value-creation system as a service; carefully analyzing each such service activity to determine whether the company can become the best in the world at it; and eliminating, outsourcing, or joint venturing the activity to achieve "best in world" status when this is impossible internally. Perhaps most important,

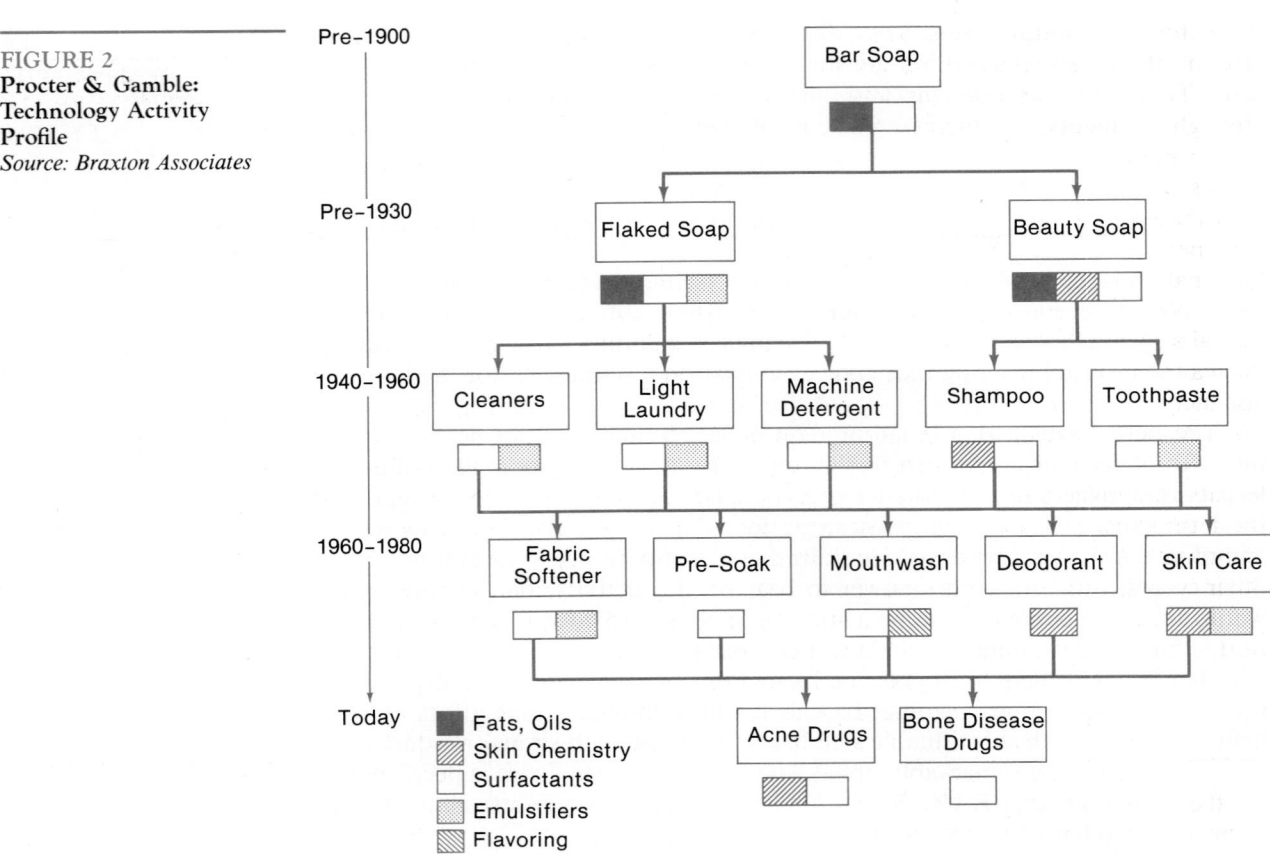

FIGURE 2
**Procter & Gamble:
Technology Activity
Profile**
Source: Braxton Associates

managers must recognize the cold reality that *not* achieving a strong enough competitive performance in each critical service activity will relegate the company to an inevitable loss of strategic advantage, provide lower profitability, and create a higher risk of takeover by those who do see the missed potentials.

● THE STRUCTURING OF ORGANIZATIONS*

BY HENRY MINTZBERG

The "one best way" approach has dominated our thinking about organizational structure since the turn of the century. There is a right way and a wrong way to design an organization. A variety of failures, however, has made it clear that organizations differ, that, for example, long-range planning systems or organizational development programs are good for some but not others. And so recent management theory has moved away from the "one best way" approach, toward an "it all depends" approach, formally known as "contingency theory." Structure should re-

---

* Excerpted originally from *The Structuring of Organizations* (Prentice Hall, 1979), with added sections from *Power in and Around Organizations* (Prentice Hall, 1983). This chapter was rewritten for this edition of the text, based on two other excerpts: "A Typology of Organizational Structure," published as Chapter 3 in Danny Miller and Peter Friesen, *Organizations: A Quantum View* (Prentice Hall, 1984) and "Deriving Configurations," Chapter 6 in *Mintzberg on Management: Inside Our Strange World of Organizations* (Free Press, 1989).

330

flect the organization's situation—for example, its age, size, type of production system, the extent to which its environment is complex and dynamic.

This reading argues that the "it all depends" approach does not go far enough, that structures are rightfully designed on the basis of a third approach, which might be called the "getting it all together" or, "configuration" approach. Spans of control, types of formalization and decentralization, planning systems, and matrix structures should not be picked and chosen independently, the way a shopper picks vegetables at the market. Rather, these and other elements of organizational design should logically configure into internally consistent groupings.

When the enormous amount of research that has been done on organizational structure is looked at in the light of this conclusion, much of its confusion falls away, and a convergence is evident around several configurations, which are distinct in their structural designs, in the situations in which they are found, and even in the periods of history in which they first developed.

To understand these configurations, we must first understand each of the elements that make them up. Accordingly, the first four sections of this reading discuss the basic parts of organizations, the mechanisms by which organizations coordinate their activities, the parameters they use to design their structures, and their contingency, or situational, factors. The final section introduces the structural configurations, each of which will be discussed at length in Section Three of this text.

SIX BASIC PARTS OF THE ORGANIZATION

At the base of any organization can be found its operators, those people who perform the basic work of producing the products and rendering the services. They form the *operating core.* All but the simplest organizations also require at least one full-time manager who occupies what we shall call the *strategic apex,* where the whole system is overseen. And as the organization grows, more managers are needed—not only managers of operators but also managers of managers. A *middle line* is created, a hierarchy of authority between the operating core and the strategic apex.

As the organization becomes still more complex, it generally requires another group of people, whom we shall call the analysts. They, too, perform administrative duties—to plan and control formally the work of others—but of a different nature, often labeled "staff." These analysts form what we shall call the *technostructure,* outside the hierarchy of line authority. Most organizations also add staff units of a different kind, to provide various internal services, from a cafeteria or mailroom to a legal counsel or public relations office. We call these units and the part of the organization they form the *support staff.*

Finally, every active organization has a sixth part, which we call its *ideology* (by which is meant a strong "culture"). Ideology encompasses the traditions and beliefs of an organization that distinguish it from other organizations and infuse a certain life into the skeleton of its structure.

This gives us six basic parts of an organization. As shown in Figure 1, we have a small strategic apex connected by a flaring middle line to a large, flat operating core at the base. These three parts of the organization are drawn in one uninterrupted sequence to indicate that they are typically connected through a single chain of formal authority. The technostructure and the support staff are shown off to either side to indicate that they are separate from this main line of authority, influencing the opening core only indirectly. The ideology is shown as a kind of halo that surrounds the entire system.

FIGURE 1
The Six Basic Parts of the
Organization

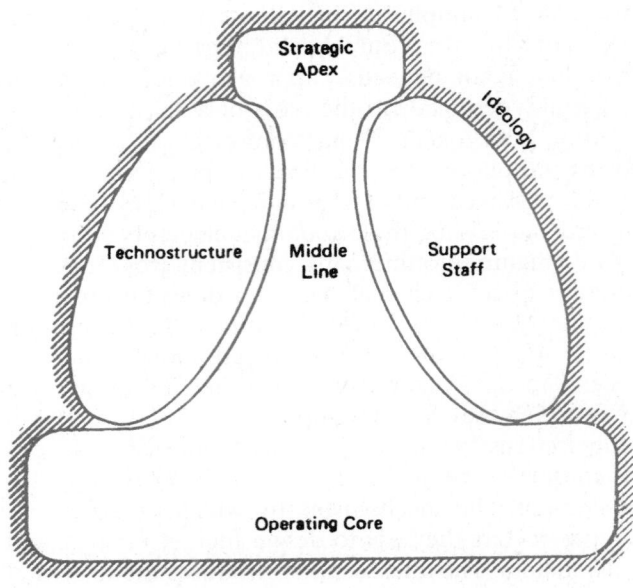

These people, all of whom work inside the organization to make its decisions and take its actions—full-time employees or, in some cases, committed volunteers —may be thought of as *influencers* who form a kind of *internal coalition*. By this term, we mean a system within which people vie among themselves to determine the distribution of power.

In addition, various outside people also try to exert influence on the organization, seeking to affect the decisions and actions taken inside. These external influencers, who create a field of forces around the organization, can include owners, unions and other employee associations, suppliers, clients, partners, competitors, and all kinds of publics, in the form of governments, special interest groups, and so forth. Together they can all be thought to form an *external coalition.*

Sometimes the external coalition is relatively *passive* (as in the typical behavior of the shareholders of a widely held corporation or the members of a large union). Other times it is *dominated* by one active influencer or some group of them acting in concert (such as an outside owner of a business firm or a community intent on imposing a certain philosophy on its school system). And in still other cases, the external coalition may be *divided,* as different groups seek to impose contradictory pressures on the organization (as in a prison buffeted between two community groups, one favoring custody, the other rehabilitation).

SIX BASIC COORDINATING MECHANISMS

Every organized human activity—from the making of pottery to the placing of a man on the moon—gives rise to two fundamental and opposing requirements: the *division of labor* into various tasks to be performed and the *coordination* of those tasks to accomplish the activity. The structure of an organization can be defined simply as the total of the ways in which its labor is divided into distinct tasks and then its coordination achieved among those tasks.

1. *Mutual adjustment* achieves coordination of work by the simple process of informal communication. The people who do the work interact with one another to coordinate, much as two canoeists in the rapids adjust to one an-

other actions. Figure 2a shows mutual adjustment in terms of an arrow between two operators. Mutual adjustment is obviously used in the simplest of organizations—it is the most obvious way to coordinate. But, paradoxically, it is also used in the most complex, because it is the only means that can be relied upon under extremely difficult circumstances, such as trying to figure out how to put a man on the moon for the first time.

2. *Direct supervision* in which one person coordinates by giving orders to others, tends to come into play after a certain number of people must work together. Thus, fifteen people in a war canoe cannot coordinate by mutual

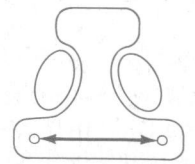

(a) Mutual Adjustment

FIGURE 2

The Basic Mechanisms of Coordination

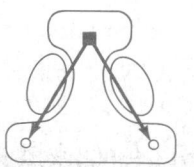

(b) Direct Supervision

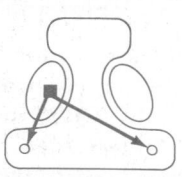

(c) Standardization of Work

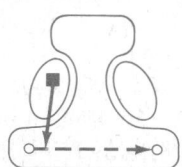

(d) Standardization of Outputs

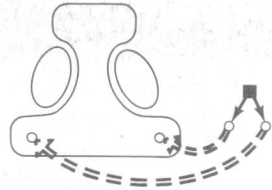

(e) Standardization of Skills

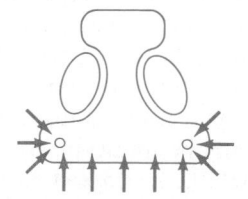

(f) Standardization of Norms

adjustment; they need a leader who, by virtue of instructions, coordinates their work, much as a football team requires a quarterback to call the plays. Figure 2b shows the leader as a manager with the instructions as arrows to the operators.

Coordination can also be achieved by *standardization*—in effect, automatically, by virtue of standards that predetermine what people do and so ensure that their work is coordinated. We can consider four forms—the standardization of the work processes themselves, of the outputs of the work, of the knowledge and skills that serve as inputs to the work, or of the norms that more generally guide the work.

3. *Standardization of work processes* means the specification—that is, the programming—of the content of the work directly, the procedures to be followed, as in the case of the assembly instructions that come with many children's toys. As shown in Figure 2c, it is typically the job of the analysts to so program the work of different people in order to coordinate it tightly.

4. *Standardization of outputs* means the specification not of what is to be done but of its results. In that way, the interfaces between jobs is predetermined, as when a machinist is told to drill holes in a certain place on a fender so that they will fit the bolts being welded by someone else, or a division manager is told to achieve a sales growth of 10% so that the corporation can meet some overall sales target. Again, such standards generally emanate from the analysts, as shown in Figure 2d.

5. *Standardization of skills,* as well as knowledge, is another, though looser way to achieve coordination. Here, it is the worker rather than the work or the outputs that is standardized. He or she is taught a body of knowledge and a set of skills which are subsequently applied to the work. Such standardization typically takes place outside the organization—for example in a professional school of a university before the worker takes his or her first job—indicated in Figure 2e. In effect, the standards do not come from the analyst; they are internalized by the operator as inputs to the job he or she takes. Coordination is then achieved by virtue of various operators' having learned what to expect of each other. When an anesthetist and a surgeon meet in the operating room to remove an appendix, they need hardly communicate (that is, use mutual adjustment, let alone direct supervision); each knows exactly what the other will do and can coordinate accordingly.

6. *Standardization of norms* means that the workers share a common set of beliefs and can achieve coordination based on it, as implied in Figure 2f. For example, if every member of a religious order shares a belief in the importance of attracting converts, then all will work together to achieve this aim.

These coordinating mechanisms can be considered the most basic elements of structure, the glue that holds organizations together. They seem to fall into a rough order: As organizational work becomes more complicated, the favored means of coordination seems to shift from mutual adjustment (the simplest mechanism) to direct supervision, then to standardization, preferably of work processes or norms, otherwise of outputs or of skills, finally reverting back to mutual adjustment. But no organization can rely on a single one of those mechanisms; all will typically be found in every reasonably developed organization.

Still, the important point for us here is that many organizations do favor one mechanism over the others, at least at certain stages of their lives. In fact, organizations that favor none seem most prone to becoming politicized, simply because of the conflicts that naturally arise when people have to vie for influence in a relative vacuum of power.

THE ESSENTIAL PARAMETERS OF DESIGN

The essence of organizational design is the manipulation of a series of parameters that determine the division of labor and the achievement of coordination. Some of these concern the design of individual positions, others the design of the super-structure (the overall network of subunits, reflected in the organizational chart), some the design of lateral linkages to flesh out that superstructure, and a final group concerns the design of the decision-making system of the organization. Listed as follows are the main parameters of structural design, with links to the co-ordinating mechanisms.

- **Job specialization** refers to the number of tasks in a given job and the workers's control over these tasks. A job is *horizontally* specialized to the extent that it encompasses a few narrowly defined tasks, *vertically* specialized to the extent that the worker lacks control of the tasks performed. *Unskilled* jobs are typically highly specialized in both dimensions; skilled or *professional* jobs are typically specialized horizontally but not vertically. "Job enrichment" refers to the enlargement of jobs in both the vertical and horizontal dimension.

- **Behavior formalization** refers to the standardization of work processes by the imposition of operating instructions, job descriptions, rules, regulations, and the like. Structures that rely on any form of standardization for coordination may be defined as *bureaucratic,* those that do not as *organic.*

- **Training** refers to the use of formal instructional programs to establish and standardize in people the requisite skills and knowledge to do particular jobs in organizations. Training is a key design parameter in all work we call professional. Training and formalization are basically substitutes for achieving the standardization (in effect, the bureaucratization) of behavior. In one, the standards are learned as skills, in the other they are imposed on the job as rules.

- **Indoctrination** refers to programs and techniques by which the norms of the members of an organization are standardized, so that they become responsive to its ideological needs and can thereby be trusted to make its decisions and take its actions. Indoctrination too is a substitute for formalization, as well as for skill training, in this case the standards being internalized as deeply rooted beliefs.

- **Unit grouping** refers to the choice of the bases by which positions are grouped together into units, and those units into higher-order units (typically shown on the organization chart). Grouping encourages coordination by putting different jobs under common supervision, by requiring them to share common resources and achieve common measures of performance, and by using proximity to facilitate mutual adjustment among them. The various bases for grouping—by work process, product, client, place, and so on—can be reduced to two fundamental ones—the *function* performed and the *market* served. The former (illustrated in Fig. 3) refers to means, that is to a single link in the chain of processes by which products or services are produced, the latter (in Fig. 4) to ends, that is, the whole chain for specific end products,

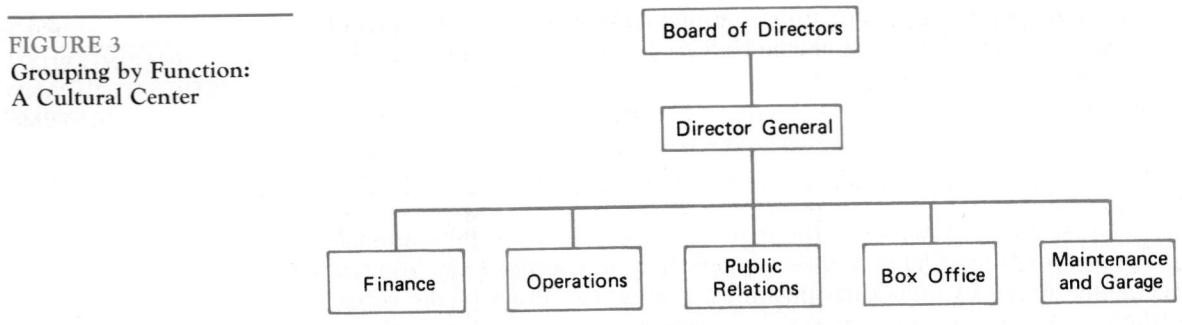

FIGURE 3
Grouping by Function:
A Cultural Center

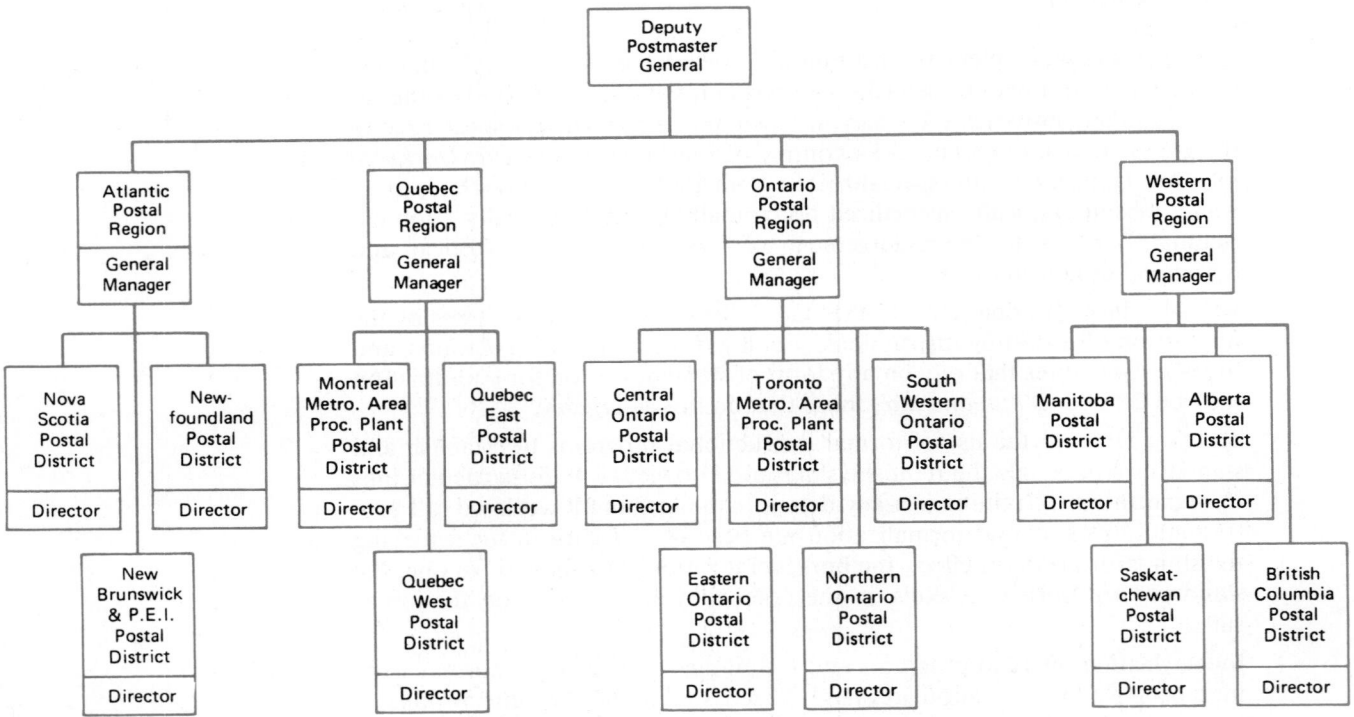

FIGURE 4
Grouping by Market: The Canadian Post Office

*Headquarter staff groups deleted.

services, or markets. On what criteria should the choice of a basis for grouping be made? First, there is the consideration of workflow linkages, or "interdependencies." Obviously, the more tightly linked are positions or units in the workflow, the more desirable that they be grouped together to facilitate their coordination. Second is the consideration of process interdependencies —for example, across people doing the same kind of work but in different workflows (such as maintenance men working on different machines). It sometimes makes sense to group them together to facilitate their sharing of equipment or ideas, to encourage the improvement of their skills, and so on. Third is the question of scale interdependencies. For example, all maintenance people in a factory may have to be grouped together because no single department has enough maintenance work for one person. Finally, there are the social interdependencies, the need to group people together for social reasons, as in coal mines where mutual support under dangerous working conditions can be a factor in deciding how to group people. Clearly, grouping by function is favored by process and scale interdependencies, and to a lesser extent by social interdependecies (in the sense that people who do the same kind of job often tend to get along better). Grouping by function also encourages specialization, for example, by allowing specialists to come together under the supervision of one of their own kind. The problem with functional grouping, however, is that it narrows perspectives, encouraging a focus on means instead of ends—the way to do the job instead of the reason for doing the job in the first place. Thus grouping by market is used to favor coordination in the workflow at the expense of process and scale specialization. In general, market grouping reduces the ability to do specialized or repetitive tasks well and is more wasteful, being less able to take advantage of economies of scale and often requiring the duplication of resources. But it enables the organization to accomplish a wider variety of tasks and to change its tasks more easily to serve the organization's end markets. And so if the workflow interdependencies are the important ones and if the organization cannot easily handle them by standardization, then it will tend to favor the market bases for grouping in order to encourage mutual adjustment and direct supervision. But if the workflow is irregular (as in a "job shop"), if standardization can easily contain the important workflow interdependencies, or if the process or scale interdependencies are the important ones, then the organization will be inclined to seek the advantages of specialization and group on the basis of function instead. Of course in all but the smallest organizations, the question is not so much *which* basis of grouping, but in what *order*. Much as fires are built by stacking logs first one way and then the other, so too are organizations built by varying the different bases for grouping to take care of various interdependencies.

- **Unit size** refers to the number of positions (or units) contained in a single unit. The equivalent term, *span of control,* is not used here, because sometimes units are kept small despite an absence of close supervisory control. For example, when experts coordinate extensively by mutual adjustment, as in an engineering team in a space agency, they will form into small units. In this case, unit size is small and span of control is low despite a relative absence of direct supervision. In contrast, when work is highly standardized (because of either formalization or training), unit size can be very large, because there is little need for direct supervision. One foreman can supervise dozens of assemblers, because they work according to very tight instructions.

- **Planning and control systems** are used to standardize outputs. They may be divided into two types: *action planning* systems, which specify the results of specific actions before they are taken (for example, that holes should be drilled with diameters of 3 centimeters); and *performance control* systems, which specify the desired results of whole ranges of actions after the fact (for example, that sales of a division should grow by 10% in a given year).

- **Liaison devices** refer to a whole series of mechanisms used to encourage mutual adjustment within and between units. Four are of particular importance:

  - *Liaison positions* are jobs created to coordinate the work of two units directly, without having to pass through managerial channels, for example, the purchasing engineer who sits between purchasing and engineering or the sales liaison person who mediates between the sales force and the factory. These positions carry no formal authority per se; rather, those who serve in them must use their powers of persuasion, negotiation, and so on to bring the two sides together.

- *Task forces and standing committees* are institutionalized forms of meetings which bring members of a number of different units together on a more intensive basis, in the first case to deal with a temporary issue, in the second, in a more permanent and regular way to discuss issues of common interest.

- *Integrating managers*—essentially liaison personnel with formal authority—provide for stronger coordination. These "managers" are given authority not over the units they link, but over something important to those units, for example, their budgets. One example is the brand manager in a consumer goods firm who is responsible for a certain product but who must negotiate its production and marketing with different functional departments.

- *Matrix structure* carries liaison to its natural conclusion. No matter what the bases of grouping at one level in an organization, some interdependencies always remain. Figure 5 suggests various ways to deal with these "residual interdependencies": a different type of grouping can be used at the next level in the hierarchy; staff units can be formed next to line units to advise on the problems; or one of the liaison devices already discussed can be overlaid on the grouping. But in each case, one basis of grouping is favored over the others. The concept of matrix structure is balance between two (or more) bases of grouping, for example functional with market (or for that matter, one kind of market with another—say, regional with product). This is done by the creation of a dual authority structure—two (or more) managers, units, or individuals are made jointly and equally responsible for the same decisions. We can distinguish a *permanent* form of matrix structure,

FIGURE 5
**Structures to Deal with
Residual Interdependencies**

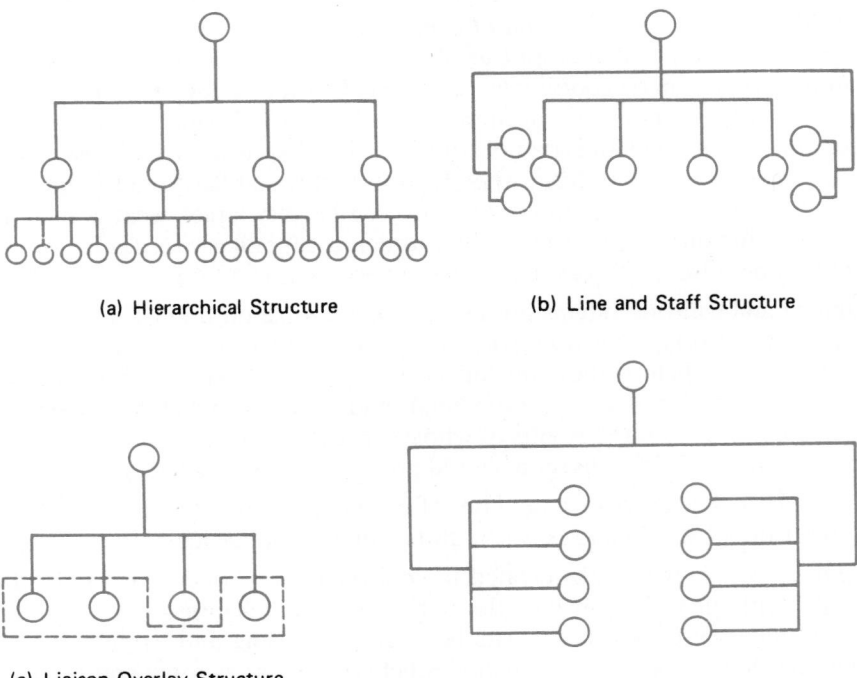

(a) Hierarchical Structure

(b) Line and Staff Structure

(c) Liaison Overlay Structure
(e.g., Task Force)

(d) Matrix Structure

where the units and the people in them remain more or less in place, as shown in the example of a whimsical multinational firm in Figure 6, and a *shifting* form, suited to project work, where the units and the people in them move around frequently. Shifting matrix structures are common in high-technology industries, which group specialists in functional departments for housekeeping purposes (process interdependencies, etc.) but deploy them from various departments in project teams to do the work, as shown for NASA in Figure 7.

- **Decentralization** refers to the diffusion of decision-making power. When all the power rests at a single point in an organization, we call its structure centralized; to the extent that the power is dispersed among many individuals,

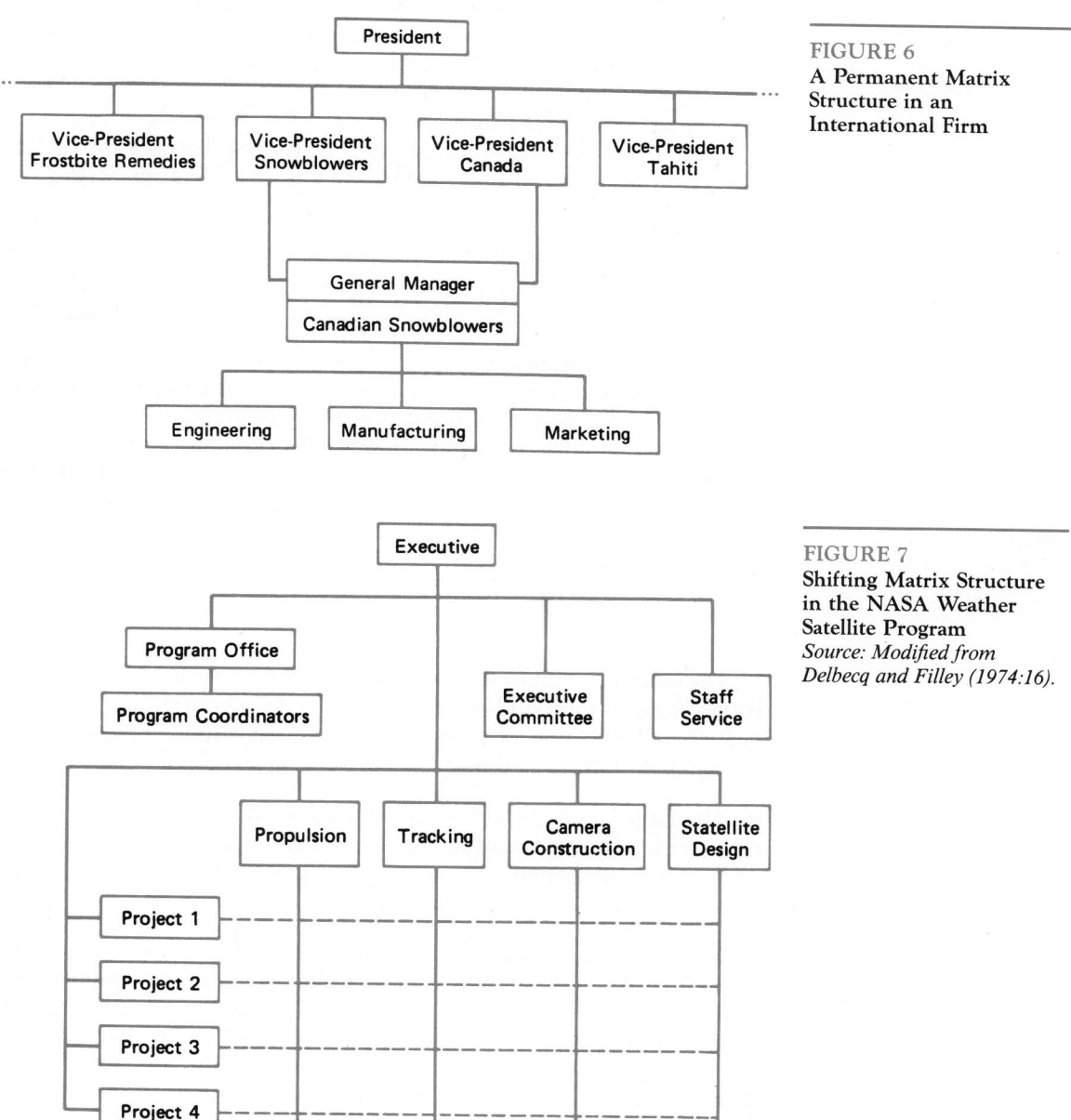

FIGURE 6
A Permanent Matrix Structure in an International Firm

FIGURE 7
Shifting Matrix Structure in the NASA Weather Satellite Program
Source: Modified from Delbecq and Filley (1974:16).

we call it relatively decentralized. We can distinguish *vertical decentralization* —the delegation of formal power down the hierarchy to line managers— from *horizontal decentralization*—the extent to which formal or informal power is dispersed out of the line hierarchy to nonmanagers (operators, analysts, and support staffers). We can also distinguish *selective* decentralization —the dispersal of power over different decisions to different places in the organization—from *parallel* decentralization—where the power over various kinds of decisions is delegated to the same place. Six forms of decentralization may thus be described: (1) vertical and horizontal centralization, where all the power rests at the strategic apex; (2) limited horizontal decentralization (selective), where the strategic apex shares some power with the technostructure that standardizes everybody else's work; (3) limited vertical decentralization (parallel), where managers of market-based units are delegated the power to control most of the decisions concerning their line units; (4) vertical and horizontal decentralization, where most of the power rests in the operating core, at the bottom of the structure; (5) selective vertical and horizontal decentralization, where the power over different decisions is dispersed to various places in the organization, among managers, staff experts, and operators who work in teams at various levels in the hierarchy; and (6) pure decentralization, where power is shared more or less equally by all members of the organization.

THE SITUATIONAL FACTORS

A number of "contingency" or "situational" factors influence the choice of these design parameters, and vice versa. They include the age and size of the organization; its technical system of production; various characteristics of its environment, such as stability and complexity; and its power system, for example, whether or not it is tightly controlled by outside influencers. Some of the effects of these factors, as found in an extensive body of research literature, are summarized below as hypotheses.

Age and Size

• **The older an organization, the more formalized its behavior.** What we have here is the "we've-seen-it-all-before" syndrome. As organizations age, they tend to repeat their behaviors: as a result, these become more predictable and so more amenable to formalization.

• **The larger an organization, the more formalized its behavior.** Just as the older organization formalizes what it has seen before, so the larger organization formalizes what it sees often. ("Listen mister, I've heard that story at least five times today. Just fill in the form like it says.")

• **The larger an organization, the more elaborate its structure; that is, the more specialized its jobs and units and the more developed its administrative components.** As organizations grow in size, they are able to specialize their jobs more finely. (The big barbershop can afford a specialist to cut children's hair; the small one cannot.) As a result, they can also specialize—or "differentiate"—the work of their units more extensively. This requires more effort at coordination. And so the larger organization tends also to enlarge its hierarchy to effect direct supervision and to make greater use of its technostructure to achieve coordination by standardization, or else to encourage more coordination by mutual adjustment.

- **The larger the organization, the larger the size of its average unit.** This finding relates to the previous two, the size of units growing larger as organizations themselves grow larger because (1) as behavior becomes more formalized, and (2) as the work of each unit becomes more homogeneous, managers are able to supervise more employees.

- **Structure reflects the age of the industry from its founding.** This is a curious finding, but one that we shall see holds up remarkably well. An organization's structure seems to reflect the age of the industry in which it operates, no matter what its own age. Industries that predate the industrial revolution seem to favor one kind of structure, those of the age of the early railroads another, and so on. We should obviously expect different structures in different periods; the surprising thing is that these structures seem to carry through to new periods, old industries remaining relatively true to earlier structures.

Technical System

Technical system refers to the instruments used in the operating core to produce the outputs. (This should be distinguished from "technology," which refers to the knowledge base of an organization.)

- **The more regulating the technical system—that is, the more it controls the work of the operators—the more formalized the operating work and the more bureaucratic the structure of the operating core.** Technical systems that regulate the work of the operators—for example, mass production assembly lines—render that work highly routine and predictable, and so encourage its specialization and formalization, which in turn create the conditions for bureaucracy in the operating core.

- **The more complex the technical system, the more elaborate and professional the support staff.** Essentially, if an organization is to use complex machinery, it must hire staff experts who can understand that machinery—who have the capability to design, select, and modify it. And then it must give them considerable power to make decisions concerning that machinery, and encourage them to use the liaison devices to ensure mutual adjustment among them.

- **The automation of the operating core transforms a bureaucratic administrative structure into an organic one.** When unskilled work is coordinated by the standardization of work processes, we tend to get bureaucratic structure throughout the organization, because a control mentality pervades the whole system. But when the work of the operating core becomes automated, social relationships tend to change. Now it is machines, not people, that are regulated. So the obsession with control tends to disappear—machines do not need to be watched over—and with it go many of the managers and analysts who were needed to control the operators. In their place come the support specialists to look after the machinery, coordinating their own work by mutual adjustment. Thus, automation reduces line authority in favor of staff expertise and reduces the tendency to rely on standardization for coordination.

Environment

Environment refers to various characteristics of the organization's outside context, related to markets, political climate, economic conditions, and so on.

• **The more dynamic an organization's environment, the more organic its structure.** It stands to reason that in a stable environment—where nothing changes—an organization can predict its future conditions and so, all other things being equal, can easily rely on standardization for coordination. But when conditions become dynamic—when the need for product change is frequent, labor turnover is high, and political conditions are unstable—the organization cannot standardize but must instead remain flexible through the use of direct supervision or mutual adjustment for coordination, and so it must use a more organic structure. Thus, for example, armies, which tend to be highly bureaucratic institutions in peacetime, can become rather organic when engaged in highly dynamic, guerilla-type warfare.

• **The more complex an organization's environment, the more decentralized its structure.** The prime reason to decentralize a structure is that all the information needed to make decisions cannot be comprehended in one head. Thus, when the operations of an organization are based on a complex body of knowledege, there is usually a need to decentralize decision-making power. Note that a simple environment can be stable or dynamic (the manufacturer of dresses faces a simple environment yet cannot predict style from one season to another), as can a complex one (the specialist in perfected open heart surgery faces a complex task, yet knows what to expect).

• **The more diversified an organization's markets, the greater the propensity to split it into market-based units, or divisions, given favorable economies of scale.** When an organization can identify distinct markets—geographical regions, clients, but especially products and services—it will be predisposed to split itself into high-level units on that basis, and to give each a good deal of control over its own operations (that is, to use what we called "limited vertical decentralization"). In simple terms, diversification breeds divisionalization. Each unit can be given all the functions associated with its own markets. But this assumes favorable economies of scale: If the operating core cannot be divided, as in the case of an aluminum smelter, also if some critical function must be centrally coordinated, as in purchasing in a retail chain, then full divisionalization may not be possible.

• **Extreme hostility in its environment drives any organization to centralize its structure temporarily.** When threatened by extreme hostility in its environment, the tendency for an organization is to centralize power, in other words, to fall back on its tightest coordinating mechanism, direct supervision. Here a single leader can ensure fast and tightly coordinated response to the threat (at least temporarily).

Power

• **The greater the external control of an organization, the more centralized and formalized its structure.** This important hypothesis claims that to the extent that an organization is controlled externally, for example by a parent firm or a government that dominates its external coalition—it tends to centralize power at the strategic apex and to formalize its behavior. The reason is that the two most effective ways to control an organization from the outside are to hold its chief executive officer responsible for its actions and to impose clearly defined standards on it. Moreover, external control forces the organization to be especially careful about its actions.

• **A divided external coalition will tend to give rise to a politicized internal coalition, and vice versa.** In effect, conflict in one of the coalitions tends to spill over to the other, as one set of influencers seeks to enlist the support of the others.

Fashion favors the structure of the day (and of the culture), sometimes even when inappropriate. Ideally, the design parameters are chosen according to the dictates of age, size, technical system, and environment. In fact, however, fashion seems to play a role too, encouraging many organizations to adopt currently popular design parameters that are inappropriate for themselves. Paris has its salons of haute couture; likewise New York has its offices of "haute structure," the consulting firms that sometimes tend to oversell the latest in structural fashion.

THE CONFIGURATIONS

We have now introduced various attributes of organizations—parts, coordinating mechanisms, design paramaters, situational factors. How do they all combine?

We proceed here on the assumption that a limited number of configurations can help explain much of what is observed in organizations. We have introduced in our discussion six basic parts of the organization, six basic mechanisms of coordination, as well as six basic types of decentralization. In fact, there seems to be a fundamental correspondence between all of these sixes, which can be explained by a set of pulls exerted on the organization by each of its six parts, as shown in Figure 8. When conditions favor one of these pulls, the associated part of the organization becomes key, the coordinating mechanism appropriate to itself becomes prime, and the form of decentralization that passes power to itself emerges. The organization is thus drawn to design itself as a particular configuration. We list here and then introduce briefly the six resulting configurations, together with a seventh that tends to appear when no one pull or part dominates.

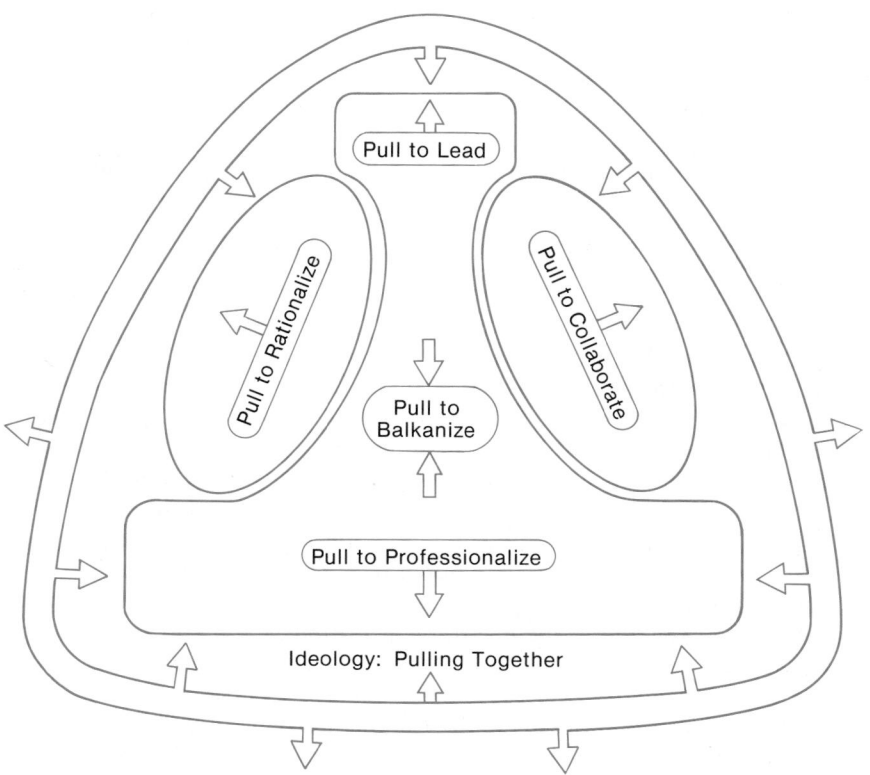

FIGURE 8
Basic Pulls on the Organization

CONFIGURATION	PRIME COORDINATING MECHANISM	KEY PART OF ORGANIZATION	TYPE OF DECEN-TRALIZATION
Entrepreneurial organization	Direct supervision	Strategic apex	Vertical and horizontal centralization
Machine organization	Standardization of work processes	Technostructure	Limited horizontal decentralization
Professional organization	Standardization of skills	Operating core	Horizontal decentralization
Diversified organization	Standardization of outputs	Middle line	Limited vertical decentralization
Innovative organization	Mutual adjustment	Support staff	Selected decentralization
Missionary organization	Standardization of norms	Ideology	Decentralization
Political organization	None	None	Varies

The Entrepreneurial Organization

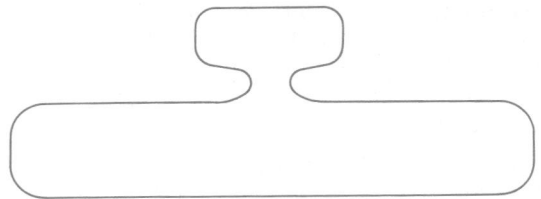

The name tells it all. And the figure above shows it all. The structure is simple, not much more than one large unit consisting of one or a few top managers, one of whom dominates by the pull to lead, and a group of operators who do the basic work. Little of the behavior in the organization is formalized and minimal use is made of planning, training, or the liaison devices. The absence of standardization means that the structure is organic and has little need for staff analysts. Likewise there are few middle line managers because so much of the coordination is handled at the top. Even the support staff is minimized, in order to keep the structure lean, the organization flexible.

The organization must be flexible because it operates in a dynamic environment, often by choice since that is the only place where it can outsmart the bureaucracies. But that environment must be simple, as must the production system, or else the chief executive could not for long hold on to the lion's share of the power. The organization is often young, in part because time drives it toward bureaucracy, in part because the vulnerability of its simple structure often causes it to fail. And many of these organizations are often small, since size too drives the structure toward bureaucracy. Not infrequently the chief executive purposely keeps the organization small in order to retain his or her personal control.

The classic case is of course the small entrepreneurial firm, controlled tightly and personally by its owner. Sometimes, however, under the control of a strong leader, the organization can grow large. Likewise, entrepreneurial organizations can be found in other sectors too, like government, where strong leaders personally control particular agencies, often ones they have founded. Sometimes under crisis conditions, large organizations also revert temporarily to the entrepreneurial form to allow forceful leaders to try to save them.

The Machine Organization

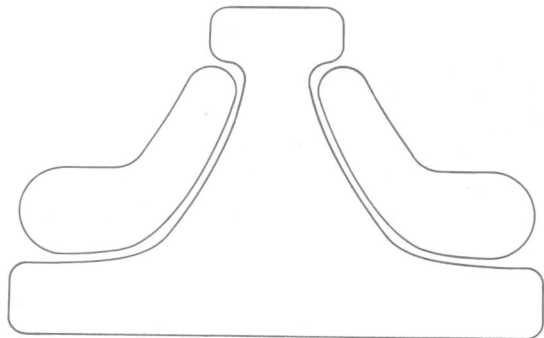

The machine organization is the offspring of the industrial revolution, when jobs became highly specialized and work became highly standardized. As can be seen in the figure above, in contrast to entrepreneurial organizations, the machine one elaborates is administration. First, it requires a large technostructure to design and maintain its systems of standardization, notably those that formalize its behaviors and plan its actions. And by virtue of the organization's dependence on these systems, the technostructure gains a good deal of informal power, resulting in a limited amount of horizontal decentralization, reflecting the pull to rationalize. A large hierarchy of middle-line managers emerges to control the highly specialized work of the operating core. But the middle line hierarchy is usually structured on a functional basis all the way up to the top, where the real power of coordination lies. So the structure tends to be rather centralized in the vertical sense.

To enable the top managers to maintain centralized control, both the environment and the production system of the machine organization must be fairly simple, the latter regulating the work of the operators but not itself automated. In fact, machine organizations fit most naturally with mass production. Indeed it is interesting that this structure is most prevalent in industries that date back to the period from the Industrial Revolution to the early part of this century.

The Professional Organization

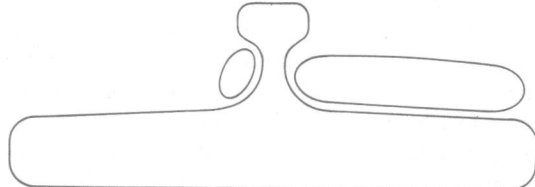

There is another bureaucratic configuration, but because this one relies on the standardization of skills rather than of work processes or outputs for its coordination, it emerges as dramatically different from the machine one. Here the pull to professionalize dominates. In having to rely on trained professionals—people highly specialized, but with considerable control over their work, as in hospitals or universities—to do its operating tasks, the organization surrenders a good deal of its power not only to the professionals themselves but also to the associations and institutions that select and train them in the first place. So the structure emerges as highly decentralized horizontally; power over many decisions, both operating and strategic, flows all the way down the hierarchy, to the professionals of the operating core.

Above the operating core we find a rather unique structure. There is little need for a technostructure, since the main standardization occurs as a result of training that takes place outside the organization. Because the professionals work so independently, the size of operating units can be very large, and few first line managers are needed. The support staff is typically very large too, in order to back up the high-priced professionals.

The professional organization is called for whenever an organization finds itself in an environment that is stable yet complex. Complexity requires decentralization to highly trained individuals, and stability enables them to apply standardized skills and so to work with a good deal of autonomy. To ensure that autonomy, the production system must be neither highly regulating, complex, nor automated.

The Diversified Organization

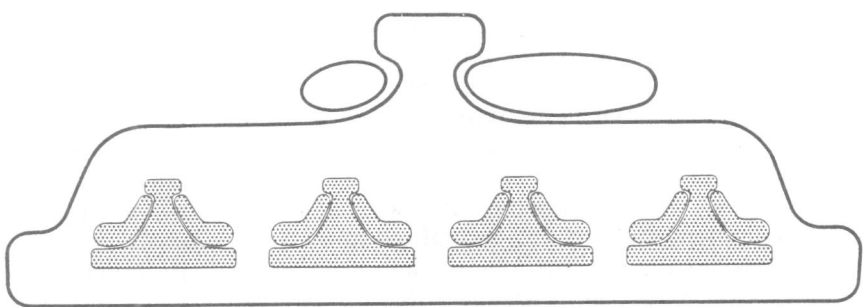

Like the professional organization, the diversified one is not so much an integrated organization as a set of rather independent entities coupled together by a loose administrative structure. But whereas those entities of the professional organization are individuals, in the diversified one they are units in the middle line, generally called "divisions," exerting a dominant pull to Balkanize. This configuration differs from the others in one major respect: it is not a complete structure, but a partial one superimposed on the others. Each division has its own structure.

An organization divisionalizes for one reason above all, because its product lines are diversified. And that tends to happen most often in the largest and most mature organizations, the ones that have run out of opportunities—or have become bored—in their traditional markets. Such diversification encourages the organization to replace functional by market-based units, one for each distinct product line (as shown in the diversified organization figure), and to grant considerable autonomy to each to run its own business. The result is a limited form of decentralization down the chain of command.

How does the central headquarters maintain a semblance of control over the divisions? Some direction supervision is used. But too much of that interferes with the necessary divisional autonomy. So the headquarters relies on performance control systems, in other words, the standardization of outputs. To design these control systems, headquarters creates a small technostructure. This is shown in the figure, across from the small central support staff that headquarters sets up to provide certain services common to the divisions such as legal counsel and public relations. And because headquarters' control constitutes external control, as discussed in the first hypothesis on power, the structure of the divisions tend to be drawn toward the machine form.

The Innovative Organization

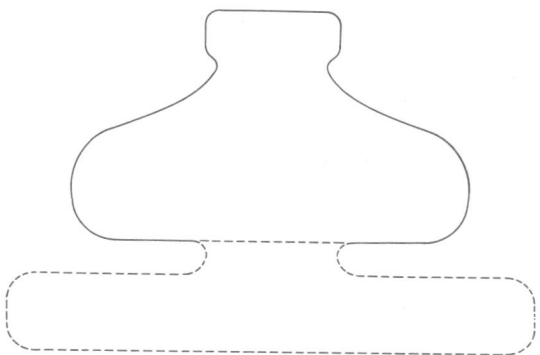

None of the structures so far discussed suits the industries of our age, industries such as aerospace, petrochemicals, think tank consulting, and film making. These organizations need above all to innovate in very complex ways. The bureaucratic structures are too inflexible, and the entrepreneurial one too centralized. These industries require "project structures," ones that can fuse experts drawn from different specialties into smoothly functioning creative teams. That is the role of our fifth configuration, the innovative organization, which we shall also call "adhocracy," dominated by the experts' pull to collaborate.

Adhocracy is an organic structure that relies for coordination on mutual adjustment among its highly trained and highly specialized experts, which it encourages by the extensive use of the liaison devices—integrating managers, standing committees, and above all task forces and matrix structure. Typically the experts are grouped in functional units for housekeeping purposes but deployed in small market based project teams to do their work. To these teams, located all over the structure in accordance with the decisions to be made, is delegated power over different kinds of decisions. So the structure becomes decentralized selectively in the vertical and horizontal dimensions, that is, power is distributed unevenly, all over the structure, according to expertise and need.

All the distinctions of conventional structure disappear in the innovative organization, as can be seen in the figure above. With power based on expertise, the line-staff distinction evaporates. With power distributed throughout the structure, the distinction between the strategic apex and the rest of the structure blurs.

These organizations are found in environments that are both complex and dynamic, because those are the ones that require sophisticated innovation, the type that calls for the cooperative efforts of many different kinds of experts. One type of adhocracy is often associated with a production system that is very complex, sometimes automated, and so requires a highly skilled and influential support staff to design and maintain the technical system of the operating core. (The dashed lines

347

of the figure designate the separation of the operating core from the adhocratic administrative structure.) Here the projects take place in the administration to bring new operating facilities on line (as when a new complex is designed in a petrochemicals firm). Another type of adhocracy produces its projects directly for its clients (as in a think tank consulting firm or manufacturer of engineering prototypes). Here, as a result, the operators also take part in the projects, bringing their expertise to bear on them; hence the operating core blends into the administrative structure (as indicated in the figure above the dashed line). This second type of adhocracy tends to be young on average, because with no standard products or services, many tend to fail while others escape their vulnerability by standardizing some products or services and so converting themselves to a form of bureaucracy.[1]

The Missionary Organization

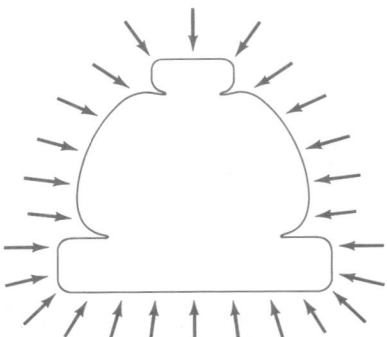

Our sixth configuration forms another rather distinct combination of the elements we have been discussing. When an organization is dominated by its ideology, its members are encouraged to pull together, and so there tends to be a loose division of labor, little job specialization, as well as a reduction of the various forms of differentiation found in the other configurations—of the strategic apex from the rest, of staff from line or administration from operations, between operators, between divisions, and so on.

What holds the missionary together—that is, provides for its coordination—is the standardization of norms, the sharing of values and beliefs among all its members. And the key to ensuring this is their socialization, effected through the design parameter of indoctrination. Once the new member has been indoctrinated into the organization—once he or she identifies strongly with the common beliefs —then he or she can be given considerable freedom to make decisions. Thus the result of effective indoctrination is the most complete form of decentralization. And because other forms of coordination need not be relied upon, the missionary organization formalizes little of its behavior as such and makes minimal use of planning and control systems. As a result, it has little technostructure. Likewise, external professional training is not relied upon, because that would force the organization to surrender a certain control to external agencies.

Hence, the missionary organization ends up as an amorphous mass of mem-

---

[1] We shall clarify in a later reading these two basic types of adhocracies. Toffler employed the term adhocracy is his popular book *Future Shock*, but it can be found in print at least as far back as 1964.

bers, with little specialization as to job, differentiation as to part, division as to status.

Missionaries tend not to be very young organizations—it takes time for a set of beliefs to become institutionalized as an ideology. Many missionaries do not get a chance to grow very old either (with notable exceptions, such as certain long-standing religious orders). Missionary organizations cannot grow very large per se —they rely on personal contacts among their members—although some tend to spin off other enclaves in the form of relatively independent units sharing the same ideology. Neither the environment nor the technical system of the missionary organization can be very complex, because that would require the use of highly skilled specialists, who would hold a certain power and status over others and thereby serve to differentiate the structure. Thus we would expect to find the simplest technical systems in these organizations, usually hardly any at all, as in religious orders or in the primitive farm cooperatives.

The Political Organization

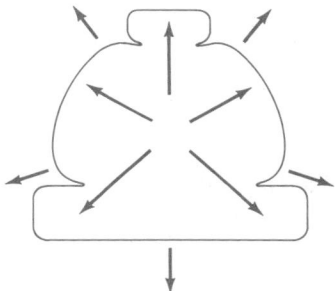

Finally, we come to a form of organization characterized, structurally at least, by what it lacks. When an organization has no dominate part, no dominant mechanism of coordination, and no stable form of centralization or decentralization, it may have difficulty tempering the conflicts within its midst, and a form of organization called the *political* may result. What characterizes its behavior is the pulling apart of its different parts, as shown in the figure above.

Political organizations can take on different forms. Some are temporary, reflecting difficult transitions in strategy or structure that evoke conflict. Others are more permanent, perhaps because the organization must face competing internal forces (say, between necessarily strong marketing and production departments), perhaps because a kind of political rot has set in but the organization is sufficiently entrenched to support it (being, for example, a monopoly or a protected government unit).

Together, all these configurations seem to encompass and integrate a good deal of what we know about organizations. It should be emphasized however, that as presented, each configuration is idealized—a simplification, really a caricature of reality. No real organization is ever exactly like any one of them, although some do come remarkably close, while others seem to reflect combinations of them, sometimes in transition from one to another.

The first five represent what seem to be the most common forms of organizations; thus these will form the basis for the "context" section of this book—labeled entrepreneurial, mature, diversified, innovation, and professional. There, a reading in each chapter will be devoted to each of these configurations, describing its structure, functioning, conditions, strategy-making process, and the issues that surround it. Other readings in these chapters will look at specific strategies in each of these contexts, industry conditions, strategy techniques, and so on.

The other two configurations—the missionary and the political—seem to be less common, represented more by the forces of culture and conflict that exist in all organizations than by distinct forms as such. Hence they will be discussed in the two chapters that immediately follow this one, on "Dealing with Power" and "Dealing with Culture." But because all these configurations themselves must not be taken as hard and fast, indeed because ideology and politics work within different configurations in all kinds of interesting ways, a final chapter in the context section, on managing change, will include a reading called "Beyond Configuration: Forces and Forms in Effective Organizations," that seeks to broaden this view of organizations.

DEALING WITH CULTURE

Culture arrived on the management scene in the 1980s like a typhoon blowing in from the Far East. It suddenly became fashionable in consulting circles to sell culture like some article of organizational clothing, much as "management by objectives" or "total information systems" were once sold. What gave this subject most impetus was Peter and Waterman's book *In Search of Excellence.* This depicted successful organizations as being rich in culture—permeated with strong and sustaining systems of beliefs. In our view—as in theirs—culture is not an article of fashion, but an intrinsic part of a deeper organizational "character," as Selznick described it (in Chapter 2). To draw on definitions introduced earlier, strategy is not just an arbitrarily chosen *position,* nor an analytically developed *plan,* but a deeply entrenched *perspective* which influences the way an organization develops new ideas, considers and weights options, and responds to changes in its environment.

Culture thus permeates many critical aspects of strategy making. But perhaps the most crucial realm is the way people are chosen, developed, nurtured, interrelated, and rewarded in the organization. The kinds of people attracted to an organization and the way they can most effectively deal with problems and each other are largely a function of the culture a place builds—and the practices and systems which support it.

In some organizations, the culture may become so strong that it is best referred to as an "ideology" that dominates all else—as in the "missionary" configuration introduced in the Mintzberg reading on structure in Chapter 6. But culture is generally an influencing force in all organizations, and so it is appropriately considered in this book as an element of organization, alongside structure, systems, and power. In a way, culture may be considered the mirror opposite of power exercised as politics. While the latter focuses on self-interest and the building of one's own power base through individual initiative, culture concentrates on the collective interest and the building of a unified organization, through shared systems of beliefs, habits, and traditions.

The readings in this chapter tend to focus on rich cultures—ideologies—and how these may promote "excellence" in certain situations. Later we shall consider how culture and ideology can discourage excellence by making organizations resistant to strategic change.

The first reading, drawn originally from two chapters of Mintzberg's book *Power in and Around Organizations,* traces how ideologies evolve through three stages: their rooting in a sense of mission, their development through traditions and sagas, and their reinforcement through various forms of identifications. Mintzberg then briefly considers the missionary type organization introduced in Chapter 6 and then shows how other organizations, for example regular business firms, sometimes overlay rich cultures on their more conventional ways of operating.

The second reading, by Pucik and Hatvany, focuses on one well-known example of this, the norm-driven Japanese business firm. The authors first investigate this much discussed organization's particular ways of functioning, its management practices and techniques. The authors then show how this organization's favored objectives and strategies—for example, its emphasis on market share, internal growth, and longer-term returns—grow directly out of its culture.

This chapter is supported by a number of case examples that give the reader a sense of the wide variety of cultures that can promote excellence. One should note the compatibilities and the contrasts between the Japanese cultures in Sony, Honda, and Matsushita; the highly innovative cultures of Intel, Hewlett-Packard, and Polaroid; the creative cultures of ARCOP and The New York Times; and the powerful competitive cultures of IBM, Zayre, Gallo, and Pillsbury. Each case offers an opportunity to investigate the important relationships among strategy, structure, systems, and style—four of the seven S's—that create and sustain a culture.

● IDEOLOGY AND THE MISSIONARY ORGANIZATION*

By Henry Mintzberg

We all know that $2 + 2 = 4$. But general systems theory, through the concept of synergy, suggests that it can also equal 5, that the parts of a system may produce more working together than they can apart. A flashlight and a battery add up to just so many pieces of hardware; together they form a working system. Likewise an organization is a working system that can entice from its members more than they would produce apart—more effort, more creativity, more output (or, of course, less). This may be "strategic"—deriving from the way components have been combined in the organization. Or it may be motivational: The group is said to develop a "mood," an "atmosphere," to have some kind of "chemistry." In organizations, we talk of a "style," a "culture," a "character." One senses something unique when one walks into the offices of IBM; the chemistry of Hewlett-Packard just doesn't feel the same as that of Texas Instruments, even though the two have operated in some similar businesses.

---

* Adapted from Henry Mintzberg, *Power in and Around Organizations* (copyright © Prentice-Hall, 1983), Chaps. 11 and 21; used by permission of the publisher; based on a summary that appeared in *Mintzberg on Management: Inside Our Strange World of Organizations* (New York: Free Press, 1989).

All these words are used to describe something—intangible yet very real, over and above the concrete components of an organization—that we refer to as its *ideology*. Specifically, an ideology is taken here to mean a rich system of values and beliefs about an organization, shared by its members, that distinguishes it from other organizations. For our purposes, the key feature of such an ideology is its unifying power: It ties the individual to the organization, generating an "esprit de corps," a "sense of mission," in effect, an integration of individual and organizational goals that can produce synergy.

THE DEVELOPMENT OF AN ORGANIZATIONAL IDEOLOGY

The development of an ideology in an organization will be discussed here in three stages. The roots of the ideology are planted when a group of individuals band together around a leader and, through a sense of mission, found a vigorous organization, or invigorate an existing one. The ideology then develops over time through the establishment of traditions. Finally, the existing ideology is reinforced when new members enter the organization and identify with its system of beliefs.

Stage 1: The Rooting of Ideology in a Sense of Mission

Typically, an organization is founded when a single prime mover identifies a mission—some product to be produced, service to be rendered—and collects a group around him or her to accomplish it. Some organizations are, of course, founded by other means, as when a new agency is created by a government or a subsidiary by a corporation. But a prime mover often can still be identified behind the founding of the organization.

The individuals who come together don't do so at random, but coalesce because they share some values associated with the fledgling organization. At the very least they see something in it for themselves. But in some cases, in addition to the mission per se there is a "sense of mission," that is, a feeling that the group has banded together to create something unusual and exciting. This is common in new organizations for a number of reasons.

First, unconstrained by procedure and tradition, new organizations offer wide latitude for maneuver. Second, they tend to be small, enabling the members to establish personal relationships. Third, the founding members frequently share a set of strong basic beliefs, sometimes including a sense that they wish to work together. Fourth, the founders of new organizations are often "charismatic" individuals, and so energize the followers and knit them together. Charisma, as Weber (1969:12) used the term, means a sense of "personal devotion" to the leader for the sake of his or her personal qualities rather than formal position. People join and remain with the organization because of dedication to the leader and his or her mission. Thus the roots of strong ideologies tend to be planted in the founding of organizations.

Of course, such ideologies can also develop in existing organizations. But a review of the preceding points suggests why this should be much more difficult to accomplish. Existing organizations *are* constrained by procedures and traditions, many are *already* large and impersonal, and their *existing* beliefs tend to impede the establishment of new ones. Nonetheless, with the introduction of strong charismatic leadership reinforced by a strong new sense of mission, an existing organization can sometimes be invigorated by the creation of a new ideology.

A key to the development of an organizational ideology, in a new or existing organization, is a leadership with a genuine belief in mission and an honest dedication to the people who must carry it out. Mouthing the right words might create the veneer of an organizational ideology, but it is only an authentic feeling on the part of the leadership—which followers somehow sense—that sets the roots of the ideology deep enough to sustain it when other forces, such as impersonal administration (bureaucracy) or politics, challenge it.

Stage 2: The Development of Ideology Through Traditions and Sagas

As a new organization establishes itself or an existing one establishes a new set of beliefs, it makes decisions and takes actions that serve as commitments and establish precedents. Behaviors reinforce themselves over time, and actions become infused with value. When those forces are strong, ideology begins to emerge in its own right. That ideology is strengthened by stories—sometimes called "myths"—that develop around important events in the organization's past. Gradually the organization establishes its own unique sense of history. All of this—the precedents, habits, myths, history—form a common base of tradition, which the members of the organization share, thus solidifying the ideology. Gradually, in Selznick's (1957) terms, the organization is converted from an expendable "instrument" for the accomplishment of externally imposed goals into an "institution," a system with a life of its own. It "acquires a self, a distinctive identity."

Thus Clark described the "distinctive college," with reference particularly to Reed, Antioch, and Swarthmore. Such institutions develop, in his words, an "organizational saga," "a collective understanding of a unique accomplishment based on historical exploits," which links the organization's present with its past and "turns a formal place into a beloved institution." (1972:178). The saga captures allegiance, committing people to the institution (Clark 1970:235).

Stage 3: The Reinforcement of Ideology Through Identifications

Our description to this point makes it clear that an individual entering an organization does not join a random collection of individuals, but rather a living system with its own culture. He or she may come with a certain set of values and beliefs, but there is little doubt that the culture of the organization can weigh heavily on the behavior he or she will exhibit once inside it. This is especially true when the culture is rich—when the organization has an emerging or fully developed ideology. Then the individual's *identification* with and *loyalty* to the organization can be especially strong. Such identification can develop in a number of ways:

- Most simply, identification occurs *naturally* because the new member is attracted to the organization's system of beliefs.
- Identification may also be *selected*. New members are chosen to "fit in" with the existing beliefs, and positions of authority are likewise filled from among the members exhibiting the strongest loyalty to those beliefs.
- Identification may also be *evoked*. When the need for loyalty is especially great, the organization may use informal processes of *socialization* and formal programs of *indoctrination* to reinforce natural or selected commitment to its system of beliefs.
- Finally, and most weakly, identification can be *calculated*. In effect, individuals conform to the beliefs not because they identify naturally with them nor because they even necessarily fit in with them, not because they have been

socialized or indoctrinated into them, but simply because it pays them to identify with the beliefs. They may enjoy the work or the social group, may like the remuneration, may work to get ahead through promotion and the like. Of course, such identification is fragile. It disappears as soon as an opportunity calculated to be better appears.

Clearly, the higher up this list an organization's member identifications tend to be, the more likely it is to sustain a strong ideology, or even to have such an ideology in the first place. Thus, strong organizational belief systems can be recognized above all by the presence of much natural identification. Attention to selected identification indicates the presence of an ideology, since it reflects an organization's efforts to sustain its ideology, as do efforts at socialization and indoctrination. Some organizations require a good deal of the latter two, because of the need to instill in their new members a complex system of beliefs. When the informal processes of socialization tend to function naturally, perhaps reinforced by more formal programs of indoctrination, then the ideology would seem to be strong. But when an organization is forced to rely almost exclusively on indoctrination, or worse to fall back on forms of calculated identification, then its ideology would appear to be weakening, if not absent to begin with.

THE MISSIONARY ORGANIZATION

While some degree of ideology can be found in virtually every organization, that degree can vary considerably. At one extreme are those organizations, such as religious orders or radical political movements, whose ideologies tend to be strong and whose identifications are primarily natural and selected. Edwards (1977) refers to organizations with strong ideologies as "stylistically rich," Selznick (1957) as "institutions." It is the presence of such an ideology that enables an organization to have "a life of its own," to emerge as "a living social institution" (Selznick 1949:10). At the other extreme are those organizations with relatively weak ideologies, "stylistically barren," in some cases business organizations with strongly utilitarian reward systems. History and tradition have no special value in these organizations. In the absence of natural forms of identification on the part of their members, these organizations sometimes try to rely on the process of indoctrination to integrate individual and organizational goals. But usually they have to fall back on calculated identifications and especially formal controls.

We can refer to "stylistically rich" organizations as *missionaries,* because they are somewhat akin in their beliefs to the religious organizations by that name. Mission counts above all—to preserve it, extend it, or perfect it. That mission is typically (1) clear and focused, so that its members are easily able to identify with it; (2) inspiring, so that the members do, in fact, develop such identifications; and (3) distinctive, so that the organization and its members are deposited into a unique niche where the ideology can flourish. As a result of their attachment to its mission, the members of the organization resist strongly any attempt to change it, to interfere with tradition. The mission and the rest of the ideology must be preserved at all costs.

The missionary organization is a distinct configuration of the attributes of structure, internally highly integrated yet different from other configurations. What holds this organization together—that is, provides for its coordination—is the standardization of its norms, in other words, the sharing of values and beliefs among its members. As was noted, that can happen informally, either through natural selection or else the informal process of socialization. But from the perspective of structural design the key attribute is indoctrination, meaning formalized programs to develop or reinforce identification with the ideology. And once the new member has been selected, socialized, and indoctrinated, he or she is accepted into the system as an equal partner, able to participate in decision making alongside everyone else. Thus, at the limit, the missionary organization can achieve the purest form of decentralization: All who are accepted into the system share its power.

But that does not mean an absence of control. Quite the contrary. No matter how subtle, control tends to be very powerful in this organization. For here, the organization controls not just people's behavior but their very souls. The machine organization buys the "workers' " attention through imposed rules; the missionary organization captures the "members' " hearts through shared values. As Jay noted in his book *Management and Machiavelli* (1970), teaching new Jesuit recruits to "love God and do what you like" is not to do what they like at all but to act in strict conformance with the order's beliefs (1970:70).

Thus, the missionary organization tends to end up as an amorphous mass of members all pulling together within the common ideology, with minimum specialization as to job, differentiation as to part, division as to status. At the limit, managers, staffers, and operators, once selected, socialized, and indoctrinated, all seem rather alike and may, in fact, rotate into each other's positions.

The traditional Israeli kibbutz is a classic example of the missionary organization. In certain seasons, everyone pitches in and picks fruit in the fields by day and then attends the meetings to decide administrative issues by night. Managerial positions exist but are generally filled on a rotating basis so that no one emerges with the status of office for long. Likewise, staff support positions exist, but they too tend to be filled on a rotating basis from the same pool of members, as are the operating positions in the fields. (Kitchen duty is, for example, considered drudgery that everyone must do periodically.) Conversion to industry has, however, threatened that ideology. As suggested, it was relatively easy to sustain the egalitarian ideology when the work was agricultural. Industry, in contrast, generally called for greater levels of technology, specialization, and expertise, with a resulting increase in the need for administrative hierarchy and functional differentiation, all a threat to the missionary orientation. The kibbutzim continue to struggle with this problem.

A number of our points about the traditional kibbutz are summarized in a table developed by Rosner, which contrasts the "principles of kibbutz organization"—classic missionary—with those of "bureaucratic organization," in our terms, the classic machine.

Principles of Bureaucratic Organization	*Principles of Kibbutz Organization*
1. Permanency of office	Impermanency of office
2. The office carries with it impersonal, fixed privileges and duties.	The definition of office is flexible—privileges and duties are not formally fixed and often depend on the personality of the official.
3. A hierarchy of functional authorities expressed in the authority of the officials.	A basic assumption of the equal value of all functions without a formal hierarchy of authority
4. Nomination of officials is based on formal objective qualifications.	Officials are elected, not nominated. Objective qualifications are not decisive, personal qualities are more important in election.

5. The office is a full-time occupation.	The office is usually supplementary to the full-time occupation of the official. (Rosner, 1969)

We can distinguish several forms of the pure missionary organization. Some are *reformers* that set out to change the world directly—anything from overthrowing a government to ensuring that all domestic animals are "decently" clothed. Other missionaries can be called *converters,* their mission being to change the world indirectly, by attracting members and changing them. The difference between the first two types of missionaries is the difference between the Women's Christian Temperance Union and Alcoholics Anonymous. Their ends were similar, but their means differed, seeking to reduce alcoholism in one case by promoting a general ban on liquor sales, in the other by discouraging certain individuals, namely joined members, from drinking. Third are the *cloister* missionaries that seek not to change things so much as to allow their members to pursue a unique style of life. The monasteries that close themselves off from the outside world are good examples, as are groups that go off to found new isolated colonies.

Of course, no organization can completely seal itself off from the world. All missionary organizations, in fact, face the twin opposing pressures of isolation and assimilation. Together these make them vulnerable. On one side is the threat of *isolation,* of growing ever inward in order to protect the unique ideology from the pressures of the ordinary world until the organization eventually dies for lack of renewal. On the other side is the threat of *assimilation,* of reaching out so far to promote the ideology that it eventually gets compromised. When this happens, the organization may survive but the ideology dies, and so the configuration changes (typically to the machine form).

IDEOLOGY AS AN OVERLAY ON CONVENTIONAL ORGANIZATIONS

So far we have discussed what amounts to the extreme form of ideological organization, the missionary. But more organizations have strong ideologies that can afford to structure themselves in this way. The structure may work for an Israeli kibbutz in a remote corner of the Negev desert, but this is hardly a way to run a Hewlett-Packard or a McDonald's, let alone a kibbutz closer to the worldly pressures of Tel Aviv.

What such organizations tend to do is overlay ideological characteristics on a more conventional structure—perhaps machinelike in the case of McDonald's and that second kibbutz, innovative in the case of Hewlett-Packard. The mission may sometimes seem ordinary—serving hamburgers, producing instruments and computers—but it is carried out with a good dose of ideological fervor by employees firmly committed to it.

Best known for this are, or course, certain of the Japanese corporations, Toyota being a prime example. Ouchi and Jaeger (1978:308) contrast in the table reproduced below the typical large American corporation (Type A) with its Japanese counterpart (Type J):

Type A (for American)	*Type J (for Japanese)*
Short-term employment	Lifetime employment
Individual decision making	Consensual decision making
Individual responsibility	Collective responsibility
Rapid evaluation and promotion	Slow evaluation and promotion

Explicit, formalized control   Implicit, informal control

Specialized career path   Nonspecialized career path

Segmented concern   Holistic concern

Ouchi and Jaeger (1978) in fact make their point best with an example in which a classic Japanese ideological orientation confronts a conventional American bureaucratic one:

> [D]uring one of the author's visits to a Japanese bank in California, both the Japanese president and the American vice-presidents of the bank accused the other of being unable to formulate objectives. The Americans meant that the Japanese president could not or would not give them explicit, quantified targets to attain over the next three or six months, while the Japanese meant that the Americans could not see that once they understood the company's philosophy, they would be able to deduce for themselves the proper objective for any conceivable situation. (p. 309)

In another study, however, Ouchi together with Johnson (1978) discussed a native American corporation that does resemble the Type J firm (labeled "Type Z"; Ouchi (1981) later published a best seller about such organizations). In it, they found greater loyalty, a strong collective orientation, less specialization, and a greater reliance on informal controls. For example, "a new manager will be useless for at least four or five years. It takes that long for most people to decide whether the new person really fits in, whether they can really trust him." That was in sharp contrast to the "auction market" atmosphere of a typical American firm: It "is almost as if you could open up the doors each day with 100 executives and engineers who had been randomly selected from the country, and the organization would work jut as well as it does now" (1978:302).

The trends in American business over several decades—"professional" management, emphasis on technique and rationalization, "bottom-line" mentality—have worked against the development of organizational ideologies. Certainly the missionary configuration has hardly been fashionable in the West, especially the United States. But ideology may have an important role to play there, given the enormous success many Japanese firms have had in head-on competition with American corporations organized in machine and diversified ways, with barren cultures. At the very least, we might expect more ideological overlays on the conventional forms of organizations in the West. But this, as we hope our discussion has made clear, may be both for better and for worse.

● MANAGEMENT PRACTICES IN JAPAN AND THEIR IMPACT ON BUSINESS STRATEGY*

BY VLADIMIR PUCIK AND NINA HATVANY

... we propose that a basic organizational paradigm in large Japanese organizations is the *focus on human resources*. Our understanding of this paradigm follows Kuhn's (1970) definition of it as an amalgamation of shared rules and common in-

---

* Originally published in *Advances in Strategic Management,* Vol. 1 (JAI Press, Inc., 1983), pp. 103–131. Copyright © 1983 by JAI Press, Inc. Reprinted with deletions by permission of JAI Press, Inc.

tuitions. The focus on human resources in Japanese firms reflects an explicit preference for the maximum utilization of available human assets as well as an implicit understanding of how an organization ought to be managed.

This paradigm translates into the three main interrelated strategic thrusts [which are in turn expressed in specific management techniques, as shown in Figure 1 and discussed in turn in the paragraphs that follow].

STRATEGIES

The Organization as an Internal Labor Market

As a rule, large Japanese companies hire a male employee just after graduation from high school or university with the expectation of retaining him for the rest of his working life (Yoshino, 1968). The policy of lifetime employment is not extended to females, who are generally expected to leave the company and the job market once they are married. The temporary nature of the female work force, as well as the use of part-time workers, gives employers flexibility in adjusting the size of their work force to adapt to current economic conditions and still maintain employment for regular workers. The widespread use of subcontracting serves a similar purpose....

Such a set of employment practices that price and allocate labor according to intraorganizational rules and procedures rather than according to external demand and supply conditions is described in the economic literature as an internal labor market (ILM) (Doeringer and Piore, 1971)....

The maintenance of a stable ILM requires that sufficient training is provided within the firm so that the company does not have to hire outside to satisfy its need for qualified personnel. Yet, when skills are learned on the job, they are largely "company specific," the employee cannot realize their full value outside the firm, and inter-firm mobility is again discouraged (Becker, 1964).

... job security has advantages for the organization. One, for example, is the reduction of employee hostility to the introduction of labor-saving technology or to organizational changes (Vogel, 1979). Employees know that they may be trans-

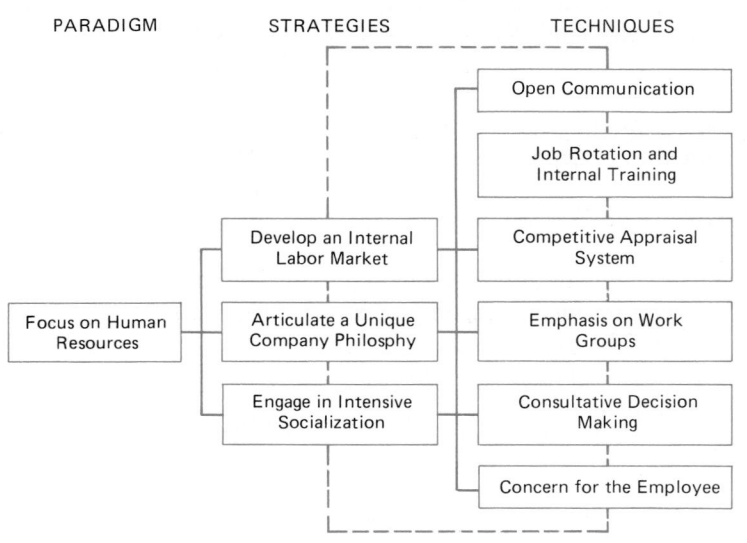

FIGURE 1
The Japanese Management System

ferred to new jobs but do not fear losing their jobs altogether. Another advantage . . . is that long tenure is positively associated with commitment to the organization. . . .

Articulated and Unique Company Philosophy

A philosophy that is both articulated and enacted may facilitate [the transformation of commitment to the organization into a productive effort] as it presents a clear picture of the organization's goals, norms, and values. Familiarity with the goals of an organization provides direction for individuals' actions, sets constraints on their behavior, and enhances their motivation (Scott, 1966). . . .

The personnel departments of large Japanese firms as well as many chief executives are actively engaged in promoting their company's philosophy of work and management (Rohlen, 1974). These philosophies frequently describe the firm as a family, unique and distinct from any other firm. This "family" is a social group into which one is carefully selected, but which, as in a real family, one is not supposed to leave, even if one becomes dissatisfied with this or that aspect of "family" life. The cultivation of a sense of "uniqueness" may provide an ideological justification of the limited possibilities for interfirm mobility.

At the same time, the articulation of concepts, such as "the family" embedded in a company philosophy, may change over time in order to fit the shifting values of a broader social environment. . . .

Among the norms of company life, *wa* (harmony), is still the single most popular component in company philosophies. The concept of *wa* expresses a "quality of relationship, particularly within working groups and it refers to the cooperation, trust, sharing, warmth, morale, and hard work of efficient, pleasant, and purposeful fellowship. Teamwork comes to mind as a suitable approximation" (Rohlen, 1974:74). *Wa* is the watchword for developing the group consciousness of the employees and enhancing cooperation within the work group. The ideal is to integrate two objectives: pursuit of profits and perpetuation of the company as a primary social group. The employees are asked to devote substantial effort to the company's well-being, and in return the company is expected to avoid layoffs and to contribute generously to its employees' welfare. Without reasonable employment security, the fostering of team spirit and cooperation would be a nearly impossible task.

The understanding of shared meanings and beliefs expressed in the company philosophy binds the individual to the collectivity (Pfeffer, 1979b) and at the same time stimulates the emergence of goals that are shared within an organization. This goal congruence provides one of the principal defenses against opportunistic behavior on the part of those members who, endowed with special skills, might be inclined to bargain for special rewards (Ouchi, 1980). . . .

Intensive Socialization

The benefits of an articulated company philosophy are lost, however, if not properly communicated to employees or if not visibly supported in management's behavior. Therefore, ensuring that employees have understood the philosophy and have seen it in action is one of the primary functions of the company's socialization effort.

The development of cohesiveness within the firm, based on the acceptance of common goals and values, is a major focus of personnel policies in a Japanese firm throughout the whole working life of an employee. . . . The basic criteria for hiring are moderate views and a harmonious personality. Ability on the job is obviously also a requirement, but at the same time applicants may be eliminated during the selection process if they arouse suspicion that they cannot get along with people, possess radical views, or come from an unfavorable home environment (Rohlen, 1974). It is only natural that, when employees are expected to remain the firm for most of their working lives, even top executives become intimately involved in the interviewing and assessment of new hires. To encourage recruitment into the company, employees' referrals are often actively solicited.

The socialization process begins with the initial training program, which is geared toward familiarizing new employees with the company, sometimes for as long as six months. During the course of the program the recruits learn about the business philosophy of the company and experience work on the factory floor as well as in the sales offices, disregarding their final vocational specialization. They are expected to assume the identity of a "company man," and in such a case their specialization becomes of secondary importance. Both careful screening and introductory training are designed to develop the homogeneity of the people in the firm.

In addition to this initial socialization, a "resocialization" (Katz, 1980) takes place each time the employee enters a new position, as he has to familiarize himself with a new set of people and tasks. Employees are transferred for two main reasons. First, they are assigned to new positions to learn additional skills in on-the-job training programs. Second, transfers are part of a long-range experience-building program, through which the organization grooms its future managers, which usually takes the form of periodic, lateral, interdepartmental transfers. (Yoshino, 1968). While employees rotate semilaterally from job to job, they become increasingly socialized into the organization, immersed in the company's philosophy and culture, as well as bound to a set of shared goals. It should be noted that such transfers are the prerogative of management, and unions are usually not involved....

TECHNIQUES

The basic management orientation and strategies are closely interrelated with [the following] management techniques used in Japanese firms....

Open Communication

If we had to stress one technique . . . it would be management's commitment to developing a climate of trust in the corporation, through sharing information across departmental boundaries. The emphasis on team spirit embodied in corporate philosophies and the network of contacts that employees develop during their long socialization in the organization encourage . . . extensive face-to-face communication. . . . Frequent and open communication is also an inherent part of the Japanese work setting. Work spaces are crowded with individuals at different levels of the hierarchy. Subordinates can do little that the supervisor is not aware of and vice versa. Even high-ranking office managers seldom have separate private offices. . . . Even senior plant managers spend as much time as possible on the shop floor.

Open communication is not limited to vertical exchanges. Periodic job rotation is instrumental in building extensive informal lateral communication networks across departmental boundaries. . . .

Job Rotation, Slow Promotion, and Internal Training

Under conditions of lifetime employment . . . [p]romotion is . . . unlikely to be rapid unless an organization is expanding dramatically. . . . [nevertheless] early informal identification of the "elite" is not unusual (Rohlen, 1974), and carefully planned lateral job transfers thereafter may add substantial flexibility to job reward and recognition (Ono, 1976). . . .

An additional feature adding flexibility to the promotion system is the emergence of a dual promotion system in many Japanese companies (Haitani, 1978). Promotion in "status" is based on the results of past evaluations and seniority within the firm; promotion in "position" is based on evaluation results and the availability of vacancies in the level above. Therefore, even if immediate upper-level positions are blocked by a cohort of seniors, promotion in status will provide an employe with more respect and money. Delegation of authority is also frequent, so a position of responsibility can be assigned to an outstanding employee who does not fulfill the seniority requirements for promotion in status (Tsurumi, 1977). . . .

The emphasis on job rotation creates an environment in which an employee becomes a "generalist," rather than a "specialist" in any functional area. . . .

Competitive Appraisal System

Employee evaluations in Japanese firms are usually conducted on an annual or semiannual basis. The evaluation criteria include not only "bottom-line" individual performance measures but also various desirable personality traits and behaviors, such as creativity, emotional maturity, and cooperation with others. . . . the employee is not made to feel that the "bottom-line," which may sometimes be beyond his control, is the key dimension of evaluation. Occasional mistakes, particularly for lower-level employees, are considered part of the learning process (Tsurumi, 1977).

At the same time, evaluations do clearly discriminate among employees, as each employee is compared to other members of an appropriate group (in age and status); and the competition is keen. Year after year, all managers at a given level are ranked according to their performance and future potential. This is done by the personnel department based on raw scores submitted by line superiors. For each manager, the scores from at last two superiors are required to assure objectivity, but the scores seldom differ substantially. . . .

A future- rather than a past-oriented evaluation system serves, however, as a powerful check in divisive competitiveness. What is rewarded is the credibility and ability to get things done in cooperation with others. Thus, the focal point of competition is building cooperative networks with the same people who are rivals for future promotions (Pucik, 1981). . . .

The Emphasis on Work Groups

Not only evaluation but many other company policies revolve around groups. Tasks are assigned to groups rather than individuals. (Rohlen, 1974). Group cohesion is stimulated by the delegation of responsibility to work groups as well as by other job design features such as job rotation and group-based performance feedback. . . .

Work-group autonomy is enhanced by not using experts to solve operational problems for specific groups. This would be regarded as outside interference, and the result would be to undermine morale and leadership (Rohlen, 1974). One widely used group-based technique is quality control (QC) circles (Cole, 1979). A QC circle has as its major function the uncovering and solving of a particular workshop's problem. However, fostering motivation by direct participation in the design of the work process is also a major consideration in the introduction of QC circles and similar activities to the factory floor. In principle, participation is voluntary, but in practice refusal to participate is unusual. The team operates autonomously, with an emphasis on self-improvement activities that will help the achievement of group goals. . . .

Consultative Decision Making

The extensive face-to-face communication observed in Japanese companies is often confused with participative decision making. . . . The usual procedure is that a formal proposal will be initiated by a middle manager, but often under the directive of top management (Hattori, 1977). Some observers of the Japanese decision-making process argue . . . that this process is not "bottom-up" but rather a top-down or interactive consultative process, especially when long-term planning and strategy are concerned (Kono, 1980).

The middle manager will usually engage in informal discussion and consultation about the decisions with his subordinates, peers, and supervisors. When all are familiar with the proposal, a request for a decision is made formally at an appropriate level, and because of the earlier discussions it is almost inevitably ratified, often in a ceremonial group meeting or through the *ringi* procedure. All this does not imply unanimous approval of the proposed decision, but it does imply consent to its implementation.

This kind of decision making is not "participative" in the Western sense of the word, which includes ideas of negotiations and bargaining between a manager and his subordinates. In the Japanese context the negotiations are primarily lateral, between the departments concerned with the decision. Within the work group, the emphasis is on inclusion of all group members in the process of decision making rather than on a consensus about the alternatives. However, the manager will usually not state his position "until others who will be affected have had sufficient time to offer their views, feel that they have been fairly heard, and are willing to support the decision even though they may not feel that it is the best one." (Rohlen, 1974:308). . . .

A frequently mentioned consequence of decision making in Japan is the avoidance of identifying responsibility for eventual mistakes. (Yoshino, 1968; Tsuji, 1968). However, Clark (1979) calls this "misleading," citing the large number of Japanese firms managed by a strong and powerful chief executive. . . .

Concern for the Employee

Informal communication not only facilitates decision making but it also forms a channel to express management concern for the well-being of employees. Managers invest a great deal of time in talking to employees about everyday matters, (Cole, 1971), and the quality of their relationships with subordinates is also an important part of their evaluation. They thus develop a feeling for their employees' personal needs and problems, as well as their performance. Obviously this intimate knowledge of each employe is facilitated by the employees' long tenure, but managers do consciously and explicitly attempt to get to know their employees and place a premium on having time to talk.

Deepening the company's involvement with employees' lives is the sponsoring of various cultural, athletic, and other recreational activities. There is usually a heavy schedule of company social affairs. These activities are ostensibly voluntary, but virtually all members participate. Rohlen (1974) describes an annual calendar of office events: it typically includes two overnight trips, monthly Saturday afternoon recreation, and an average of six office parties, all at company expense. At these events a great deal of drinking goes on and much good fellowship is expressed. Discussion in an informal atmosphere is also characteristic of evening social activities of the work team which are often subsidized by the manger's budget.

Finally, the company allocates substantial financial resources to pay for benefits that are given all employees such as a family allowance and commuting and other job-related allowances. Furthermore, there are various welfare systems that "penetrate every crack of workers' lives." (Hazama, 1978:43). These range from company housing, dormitories, and housing loans through company nurseries and company scholarships for employees' children, to credit extension, savings, and insurance. Thus, employees perceive their own welfare and the financial welfare of their company as being identical (Tsurumi, 1977). . . .

DISCUSSION

. . . There are indeed many cultural differences between people in Japan and Western countries. However, this should not distract our attention from the fact that people in any country also have a lot in common. In the workplace, they value decent treatment, security, and an opportunity for emotional fulfillment. It goes to the credit of Japanese managers that they have developed organizational systems which, even though far from perfect, respond to these needs to a great extent.

The strategies and techniques we have reviewed constitute a remarkably well-integrated system. The management practices are highly congruent with the way tasks are structured, with the goals of individual members, and with the climate of the organization. Such a "fit" is expected to result in a high degree of organizational effectiveness or productivity (Nadler and Lawler, 1977). . . .

There are, however, [certain] contingencies that may limit the applicability of [these] techniques. As we have indicated, the practices described and the resulting efficiency can be observed primarily in large Japanese manufacturing corporations. In the service industries, even among large firms as well as in parts of the public sector, the effectiveness of the system is markedly lower. . . .

The system also implicitly assumes the near equality of rights between the employees, management, and owners. The institutional arrangements in some countries may in fact operate against such equality. Moreover, general economic conditions are also obviously an important additional intervening variable. During recessions the system's stability in many Japanese firms relies to some degree on a reduction in a "buffer" labor force, be it women, reemployed retirees, or subscontractors. This pattern may be difficult to replicate in other countries, but, as the evidence shows, that does not preclude the emergence of the ILM structure (Doeringer and Piore, 1971). In addition, less overtime, hiring freezes, reduced bonuses, and temporary transfers are other effective and often used measures protecting basic job security while keeping labor costs flexible (Rohlen, 1979). . . .

IMPLICATIONS FOR BUSINESS STRATEGY

So far we have focused primarily on the relationship between Japanese human resource management practices and employee commitment and productivity. However, several important organizational characteristics directly tied to the area of business strategy are also heavily influenced by the management style described in detail above. . . .

Competitive Spirit

First of all, the long-term socialization of employees in combination with the articulated "distinct" company philosophy is conducive to the development of organizational culture emphasizing competition. The world outside of the firm is perceived in terms of foes and friends, markets to be captured or defended. The purpose of the organization is to survive as a group, a task possible only through besting its current and potential rivals, both in Japan and overseas.

Japanese managers are brought up in an atmosphere of a competitive rivalry that gradually permeates every action and decision they make. The activities of the firm are continuously scrutinized with respect to its impact on its major competitors (Ohmae, 1982). . . . gathered intelligence is distributed widely throughout the organization, accompanied by summaries pointing out its consequences for future market battles (Tsurumi, 1977).

Contrary to the popular image of "Japan, Inc." where the government and the private industry support each other in an oligopolistic collusion, competition in Japan is very keen. Often the foreign market strategies of Japanese firms are products of the competitive circumstances at home. For example, the heavy emphasis on export by relative newcomers in their respective fields, such as Sony on consumer electronics and Honda in automobiles, was to a large degree made imperative by the difficulties encountered in competition with the established domestic producers. . . .

Long-Term Perspective

It is not, as often thought, superior planning that enables the Japanese to execute consistent business strategies. Rather, it is the absence of short-term incentives that may otherwise distract managers from pursuing long-term corporate objectives. Although bonuses are usually tied to current performance, the fact that one cannot escape the consequences of one's decisions, as most employees are expected to remain in the organization for most of their working lives, tends to minimize the danger of taking advantage of the current circumstances at the expense of future goals.

In addition, the reliance on future company well-being to provide for individual welfare, coupled with the future-oriented appraisal system, makes it easier to incorporate long-term strategic objectives into the management of everyday operations, with a minimum of formality and complexity. There is no need for "sophisticated" reporting systems which attempt to use complex formulas to direct executives and managers in a proper direction. In this respect, "perseverance" and "commitment" are equal to "harmony" and "team spirit" in the arsenal of desired, and rewarded, corporate values.

The impact of a long-term strategic perspective is clearly visible in the way the Japanese on the one hand, and many Western firms on the other, view joint ventures and other kinds of technological and marketing tie-ups. Japanese perceive such relationships as a temporary arrangement to rectify some of their competitive weakness, and that should, in the long run, lead to their dominance in the partnership; the foreign firms are generally content with short-term gains from such endeavors, without considering the long-term competitive consequences. . . .

Emphasis on Market Share

... a market share orientation fits well into the system of Japanese management practices, as it provides an objective measure of competitive standing ... clear and understandable to anyone in the organization. At the same time, it has been shown that market share over the long run is a good predictor of corporate performance expressed in more traditional financial terms (Buzzell, Gale, and Sultan, 1975).

For most Japanese firms, driven by their competitive orientation, market share is ultimately a worldwide concept. To retreat from a market territory or product segment under challenge from a Japanese competitor will therefore do nothing more than buy time before the remaining markets also fall under siege. Just as self-defeating is attempting to piggyback onto Japanese manufacturing prowess and use them as OEM (original equipment manufacturer) suppliers for domestically well-established brands. Sooner or later they will go independent, with only crumbs left for their former partner. ... maintaining competitive parity is the only way to ensure fruitful long-term cooperation.

Internal Growth

The value system of Japanese managers and executives places a premium on maintaining the corporation as a semipermanent group of individuals tied together with lasting bonds. For that reason, divestitures, mergers, and acquisitions, especially affecting unrelated firms, are unusual in Japan, and hostile takeovers are for all practical purposes next to impossible (Clark, 1979).

This might be detrimental to the efficiency of resource allocation in the economy to some degree, but once it is clearly established that the only way to grow is from internal competitive strength, the strategic implications are clear: there is no shortcut, no other way, than concentrating on making a product which fits customers' needs and is cheaper and of better quality than the competitors'.

Under such conditions it is natural that production becomes a major strategic concern, resulting in an emphasis on continuous product and process innovation, on upgrading quality, and on lowering costs (Wheelwright, 1981). The production area is viewed as a key to corporate survival in the long run and is staffed by high-quality managers with good chances of advancing eventually to top executive positions.

Usually top management is also closely involved with production, and their staff are free from spending their time planning takeover strategies or putting together defenses against them. Given the limits on executive time, a contrast with the Japanese suggests that the acquisition route to growth may suffer from rather substantial opportunity costs.

In addition the focus on internal growth permits the organization to pursue strategic changes incrementally, so they can be more easily absorbed by the organization. The "logical incrementalism" advocated by Quinn (1980) is a concept familiar in practice to managers in many Japanese firms. Moreover, internal growth allows the organization to satisfy the career aspirations of many employees by opening additional vacancies in new areas of business to be staffed from within.

Aggressive Innovation

It was pointed out earlier that the nature of the competitive appraisal system in Japanese firms and the rapid reception and dissemination of new ideas possible in an "organic" firm should encourage innovation. This notion is contrary to the stereotypical image of the Japanese as poor innovators constrained in the exploration of new frontiers by a group desire to maintain consensus and harmony (Lohr, 1982). In this respect the evidence is clear: Japanese do innovate, and probably as fast, if not faster, than most businesses in other countries (Moritani, 1981).

One reason for the discrepancy between the stereotype and the reality is the misunderstanding of innovation processes in the organization. It is not only the bright idea that counts, it is also the process of bringing the product based on the new idea to market. In terms of winning the competitive game, the origin of the idea is often secondary. After all, computers, jet engines, or scanners were not invented in the United States. It is in the implementation process that the Japanese have an advantage with their carefully built worldwide monitoring systems on the outside, and high level of interface, coordination, and teamwork on the inside, which involve all those concerned with development, design, and manufacturing.

Second, it is widely believed that a lack of venture capital in Japan limits incentives for innovation, as it is very difficult for research and development (R&D) personnel to quit their employers and strike out on their own, a pattern common in the United States (*Business Week,* December 14, 1981). However, a closer look at the problem reveals this also to be to the advantage of the Japanese.

With their stable research teams shielded from the temptation of windfall profits as independent entrepreneurs, Japanese companies are well poised to capitalize quickly on newly acquired knowledge. Rather than working in the secrecy of the family garage, the Japanese engineer is working on a new invention in the corporate laboratory, in regular communication with those responsible for its future commercial adaptation. Then, once an innovative idea is proven to be potentially promising, the organization can move on very quickly to the adoption phase, as everyone concerned is already familiar with the new product's characteristics.

The close cooperation and communication between the research engineers on the one side, and production and market personnel on the other, built into the Japanese management system, greatly facilitates the commercialization of new innovations and assures the integration of research and development with other critical corporate functions. A steady feedback of market information to the research personnel makes it more likely that research and development result in products that will meet market needs. Participation of production engineers in the development process increases the likelihood that the newly designed product can be built efficiently with available production technologies or that new technologies will be available shortly. Thus, rather than remaining an exclusive domain of R&D professionals, the innovation process is diffused widely throughout the organization, enlarging the strategic alternatives available to the firm, especially in the high-technology area.

CONCLUSIONS

In many countries it is possible to observe firms as committed as the Japanese to growth through a superior product and process innovation. Well-run U.S. firms use management practices to a large degree similar to those we have pointed out as typical for the Japanese. What make the Japanese special, but by no means unique, is their concentrated effort to develop systemic solutions to managerial problems, to match cultural, organizational, and strategic imperatives in an integrated management system. . . .

. . . In our opinion . . . the Japanese will remain the principal challengers of any Western firm serious about world markets. There is no shortcut other than to meet this challenge. No concession bargaining, marketing gimmicks, or shuffling of assets through acquisitions will do more than provide a bit of breathing space. In the long run the only feasible response is to do better what the Japanese are doing well already—developing management systems that motivate employees from the top to the bottom to pursue growth-oriented, innovation-focused competitive strategies.

CHAPTER
8

DEALING WITH POWER

The readings to this point have, for the most part, dealt with organizations as rather rational and cooperative instruments. Strategies, whether formulated analytically or allowed to emerge in some kind of learning process, have nonetheless served for the good of the organization at large in a purely economic and competitive sense, as have the associated structures and systems. True, Wrapp's and Quinn's managers, for example, have consciously considered and dealt with potential resistance in creating and implanting their strategies. In doing so, they may have been forced to think in political terms. But the overt use of power and organized political action has largely been absent from our discussion.

An important group of thinkers in the field, however, have come to view the strategy process as an interplay of the forces of power, sometimes highly politicized. Rather than assuming that organizations are consistent, coherent and cooperative systems, tightly integrated to pursue certain traditional ends (namely the delivery of their products and services in the pursuit of profit, at least in the private sector), these writers start with quite different premises. They believe that organizations' goals and directions are determined primarily by the power needs of those who populate them. Their analyses raise all kinds of interesting and unsettled questions, such as: For whom does the organization really exist? For what purposes? If the organization is truly a political entity, how does one manage effectively in it? And so on.

No work in the literature sets this into perspective better than the famous study of the United States' response to the Cuban Missile Crisis by Graham Allison (1971) of Harvard's Kennedy School of Government. Allison believes that our conception of how decision making proceeds in organizations can be considered from three perspectives: a "rational actor" model (which is the concept he believes the American leaders had of the Soviets), an "organizations process" model, and a "bureaucratic politics" model (both of which Allison thinks could have been used as well to improve America's understanding of the Soviets' behavior). In the first model, power is embedded in a relatively rational and calculating center of action, much as strategy making was described in Chapters 3 and 4. In the second, it is entrenched in various organizational departments, each using power to further its own particular purposes. In the third model, "politics" comes into full play as individuals and groups exercise their influence to determine outcomes for their own benefits.

Our first reading focuses especially on the third model, but also incorporates aspects of the second. In parallel with Mintzberg's reading in the last chapter (and likewise based on two related chapters of his *Power In and Around Organizations* book), it considers first the general force of politics in organizations, what it is and what political "games" people play in organizations, and then the various forms taken by organizations that are dominated by such politics, the extreme one labeled the "political arena." This reading concludes with a discussion of when and why politics sometimes plays a functional role in organizations.

The second reading of the chapter brings us back to strategy, but in a kind of political way. You may recall one of the definitions of strategy introduced in Chapter 1 that was not heard from since—that of ploy. In this second reading, ploy comes to life in the context of "competitive maneuvering," various means strategists use to outwit competitors. This reading is based on two short articles entitled "Brinkmanship in Business" and "The Nonlogical Strategy" by Bruce Henderson, drawn from his book *Henderson on Corporate Strategy,* a collection of short, pithy, and rather opinionated views on management issues. Henderson founded the Boston Consulting Group, one of the early so-called "strategy boutiques," and built it into a major international force in management consulting. Now retired from there, he teaches strategy at the Vanderbilt University School of Management.

While the Mintzberg reading considers power and politics inside the organization, in terms of the maneuverings of various actors to gain influence, the Henderson one looks at the maneuverings of organizations at large, vis-à-vis their competitors. This second theme is pursued in the last two readings of this chapter, except that the context is extended beyond competitors to all of an organization's influencers (sometimes called "stakeholders," in contrast to only "shareholders"). To some observers, organizations are not merely instruments to produce goods and services, but also political systems that seek to enhance their own power. We might refer to this as *macro* politics, in contrast to the *micro* politics that takes place within organizations.

Some writers (e.g., Astley and Fombrun, 1983) have discussed the notion of *collective* strategy, concerning the management of external relationships in ways that are more cooperative (and perhaps social) than strictly competitive (and economic). This has become an important aspect of the strategy process in a world increasingly influenced by large multinational (or "global") corporations and by the joint ventures and other partnerships among such corporations and their associated coalitions with governments. The third reading of this chapter, by Jeffrey Pfeffer, a Stanford Business School professor and the researcher perhaps most identified with what we are here calling macro politics, goes beyond just the idea of collective strategy. It considers not only such legal, cooperative alignments, but also overt political behaviors for ends such as market collusion.

Note that Pfeffer is writing about *generic* strategies too, indeed some of the very same ones introduced earlier as competitive (such as acquisitions, or mergers, and joint ventures.) But in his work they are presented as *political* devices. Pfeffer's work, in some respects, can be viewed as a mirror image of Porter's. Perhaps you may want to go back to Chapter 4 and reread Porter, this time between the lines, about barriers to entry, bargaining power of suppliers, and so on—from Pfeffer's perspective. You may discover that "political" and "competitive" are not so distinct as they might at first seem.

You may not agree with Pfeffer who challenges some of the most cherished precepts about business. But it is difficult to deny the need to consider his point of view, which serves at the very least to balance the often overstated economic and competitive perspective. Pfeffer's views also deserve attention because they lie at the heart of many people's fears and concerns about business and the perceived need to regulate the behavior of large corporations.

The final reading of this chapter introduces another major theme about macro power, perhaps one that is really a composite of the issues raised in the other articles: For whom does or should the large business corporation exist? Mintzberg proposes a whole portfolio of answers around a "conceptual horseshoe." In so doing, he perhaps helps to reconcile some of the basic differences between those who view organizations as agents of economic competition and those who consider them to be instruments of the public will, or else as political systems in their own right. This reading also discusses the concept of *social responsibility,* one of the traditional topics covered in policy or strategy courses. But here the subject is treated not in a philanthropic or ethical sense, but as a managerial or organizational one. It also reviews the issues of corporate democracy, of regulation and pressure campaigns, and of "freedom" as described by Milton Friedman.

While no case deals solely with issues of power, many involve aspects of the concepts developed in these readings. ARCOP deals with the interface between personal power needs and the potentials for a cohesive strategy. IBM (A), Pillsbury, Gallo, and Mountbatten show how certain executives manage power relationships. The First Nationwide, General Motors (B), Royal Bank of Canada, Exxon, Continental Group, and Genentech cases raise questions about the relationship of corporations to outside sources having significant power to affect their actions. Almost all of the cases—notably The New York Times, Ford: Team Taurus, Biogen, and ARCOP—implicitly require that students deal with issues of personal power, organizationally entrenched power, and the power of opposing forces. Throughout the text, we emphasize that coping with power is one of the constant elements in any real-life strategic situation.

● POLITICS AND THE POLITICAL ORGANIZATION*

BY HENRY MINTZBERG

How does conflict arise in an organization, why, and with what consequences? Years ago, the literature of organizations avoided such questions. But in the last decade or so, conflict and politics that go along with it have become not just acceptable topics but fashionable ones. Yet these topics, like most others in the field, have generally been discussed in fragments. Here we seek to consider them somewhat more comprehensively, first by themselves and then in the context of what will be called the political organization—the organization that comes to be dominated by politics and conflict.

* Adapted from Henry Mintzberg, *Power in and Around Organizations* (Copyright © Prentice-Hall, 1983), Chaps. 13 and 23, used by permission of the publisher; based on a summary that appeared in *Mintzberg on Management: Inside Our Strange World of Organizations* (Free Press, 1989).

What do we mean by "politics" in organizations? An organization may be described as functioning on the basis of a number of systems of influence: authority, ideology, expertise, politics. The first three can be considered legitimate in some sense: Authority is based on legally sanctioned power, ideology on widely accepted beliefs, expertise on power that is officially certified. The system of politics, in contrast, reflects power that is technically illegitimate (or, perhaps more accurately, *a*legitimate), in the means it uses, and sometimes also in the ends it promotes. In other words, political power in the organization (unlike government) is not formally authorized, widely accepted, or officially certified. The result is that political activity is usually divisive and conflictive, pitting individuals or groups against the more legitimate systems of influence and, when those systems are weak, against each other.

POLITICAL GAMES IN ORGANIZATIONS

Political activity in organizations is sometimes described in terms of various "games." The political scientist Graham Allison, for example, has described political games in organizations and government as "intricate and subtle, simultaneous, overlapping," but nevertheless guided by rules: "some rules are explicit, others implicit, some rules are quite clear, others fuzzy. Some are very stable; others are ever changing. But the collection of rules, in effect, defines the game" (1971:170). I have identified thirteen political games in particular, listed here together with their main players, the main reasons they seem to be played, and how they relate to the other systems of influence.

- *Insurgency game:* usually played to resist authority, although can be played to resist expertise or established ideology or even to effect change in the organization; ranges "from protest to rebellion" (Zald and Berger, 1978:841), and is usually played by "lower participants" (Mechanic, 1962), those who feel the greatest weight of formal authority

- *Counterinsurgency game:* played by those with legitimate power who fight back with political means, perhaps with legitimate means as well (e.g., excommunication in the church)

- *Sponsorship game:* played to build power base, in this case by using superiors; individual attaches self to someone with more status, professing loyalty in return for power

- *Alliance-building game:* played among peers—often line managers, sometimes experts—who negotiate implicit contracts of support for each other in order to build power base to advance selves in the organization

- *Empire-building game:* played by line managers, in particular, to build power bases, not cooperatively with peers but individually with subordinates

- *Budgeting game:* played overtly and with rather clearly defined rules to build power base; similar to last game, but less divisive, since prize is resources, not positions or units per se, at least not those of rivals

- *Expertise game:* nonsanctioned use of expertise to build power base, either by flaunting it or by feigning it; true experts play by exploiting technical skills and knowledge, emphasizing the uniqueness, criticality, and irreplaceability of the expertise (Hickson et al., 1971), also by seeking to keep skills from being programmed, by keeping knowledge to selves; nonexperts play by attempting to have their work viewed as expert, ideally to have it declared professional so they alone can control it

- *Lording game:* played to build power base by "lording" legitimate power over those without it or with less of it (i.e., using legitimate power in illegitimate ways); manager can lord formal authority over subordinate or civil servant over a citizen; members of missionary configuration can lord its ideology over outsiders; experts can lord technical skills over the unskilled

- *Line versus staff game:* a game of sibling-type rivalry, played not just to enhance personal power but to defeat a rival; pits line managers with formal decision-making authority against staff advisers with specialized expertise; each side tends to exploit legitimate power in illegitimate ways

- *Rival camps game:* again played to defeat a rival; typically occurs when alliance or empire-building games result in two major power blocs, giving rise to two-person, zero-sum game in place of n-person game; can be most divisive game of all; conflict can be between units (e.g., between marketing and production in manufacturing firm), between rival personalities, or between two competing missions (as in prisons split between custody and rehabilitation orientations)

- *Strategic candidates game:* played to effect change in an organization; individuals or groups seek to promote through political means their own favored changes of a strategic nature; many play—analysts, operating personnel, lower-level managers, even senior managers and chief executives (especially in the professional configurations), who must promote own candidates politically before they can do so formally; often combines elements of other games —empire-building (as purpose of game), alliance-building (to win game), rival camps, line versus staff, expertise, and lording (evoked during game), insurgency (following game), and so on

- *Whistle-blowing game:* a typically brief and simple game, also played to effect organizational change; privileged information is used by an insider, usually a lower participant, to "blow the whistle" to an influential outsider on questionable or illegal behavior by the organization

- *Young Turks game:* played for highest stakes of all, not to effect simple change or to resist legitimate power per se, but to throw the latter into question, perhaps even to overthrow it, and institute major shift; small group of "young Turks," close to but not at center of power, seeks to reorient organization's basic strategy, displace a major body of its expertise, replace its ideology, or rid it of its leadership; Zald and Berger discuss a form of this game they call "organizational coup d'état," where the object is "to effect an unexpected succession"—to replace *holders* of authority while maintaining *system* of authority intact (1978:833).

Some of these games, such as sponsorship and lording, while themselves technically illegitimate, can nevertheless *coexist with* strong legitimate systems of influence, as found for example in the machine and missionary type organizations; indeed, they could not exist without these systems of influence. Other political games, such as insurgency and young Turks—usually highly divisive games—arise in the presence of legitimate power but are *antagonistic to it,* designed to destroy or at least weaken it. And still others, such as rival camps, often arise when legitimate power is weak and *substitute for* it, for example in the professional and innovative type organizations.

The implication of this is that politics and conflict may exist at two levels in an organization. They may be present but not dominant, existing as an overlay in a more conventional organization, perhaps a kind of fifth column acting on behalf of some challenging power. Or else politics may be the dominant system of influence, and conflict strong, having weakened the legitimate systems of influence or having arisen in their weakness. It is this second level that gives rise to the type of organization we call *political*.

FORMS OF POLITICAL ORGANIZATIONS

What characterizes the organization dominated by politics is a lack of any of the forms of order found in conventional organizations. In other words, the organization is best described in terms of power, not structure, and that power is exercised in ways not legitimate in conventional organizations. Thus, there is no preferred method of coordination, no single dominant part of the organization, no clear type of decentralization. Everything depends on the fluidity of informal power, marshaled to win individual issues.

How does such an organization come to be? There is little published research on the question. But some ideas can be advanced tentatively. First, conflict would seem to arise in a circumscribed way in an organization, say between two units (such as marketing and production) or between an influential outside group and a powerful insider (such as between a part owner and the CEO). That conflict may develop gradually or it may flare up suddenly. It may eventually be resolved, but when it becomes intense, it may tend to spread, as other influencers get drawn in on one side or the other. But since few organizations can sustain intense political activity for long, that kind of conflict must eventually moderate itself (unless it kills off the organization first). In moderated form, however, the conflict may endure, even when it pervades the whole system, so long as the organization can make up for its losses, perhaps by being in a privileged position (as in the case of a conflict-ridden regulatory agency that is sustained by a government budget, or a politicized corporation that operates in a secure cartel).

What we end up with are two dimensions of conflict, first moderate or intense and second confined or pervasive. A third dimension—enduring or brief—really combines with the first (intense conflict having to be typically brief, moderate conflict possibly enduring). Combining these dimensions, we end up with four forms of the political organization:

- *Confrontation,* characterized by conflict that is *intense, confined,* and *brief* (unstable)
- *Shaky alliance,* characterized by conflict that is *moderate, confined,* and possibly *enduring* (relatively stable)
- *Politicized organization,* characterized by conflict that is *moderate, pervasive,* and possibly *enduring* (relatively stable, so long as it is sustained by privileged position)
- *Complete political arena,* characterized by conflict that is *intense, pervasive,* and *brief* (unstable)[1]

---

[1] I do not consider conflict that is moderate, confined, and brief to merit inclusion under the label of political organization.

One of these forms is called *complete* because its conflict is both intense and pervasive. In this form, the external influencers disagree among themselves; they try to form alliances with some insiders, while clashing with others. The internal activities are likewise conflictive, permeated by divisive political games. Authority, ideology, and expertise are all subordinated to the play of political power. An organization so politicized can pursue no goal with any consistency. At best, it attends to a number of goals inconsistently over time, at worst it consumes all its energy in disputes and never accomplishes anything. In essense, the complete political arena is less a coherent organization than a free-for-all of individuals. As such, it is probably the form of political organization least commonly found in practice, or, at least, the most unstable when it does appear.

In contrast, the other three forms of political organization manage to remain partial, one by moderating its conflict, a second by containing it, and the third by doing both. As a result, these forms are more stable than the complete form and so are probably more common, with two of them in particular appearing to be far more viable.

In the *confrontational* form, conflict may be intense, but it is also contained, focusing on two parties. Typical of this is the takeover situation, where, for example, an outside stockholder tries to seize control of a closed system corporation from its management. Another example is the situation, mentioned earlier, of two rival camps in and around a prison, one promoting the mission of custody, the other that of rehabilitation.

The *shaky alliance* commonly emerges when two or more major systems of influence or centers of power must coexist in roughly equal balance. The symphony orchestra, for example, must typically combine the strong personal authority of the conductor (entrepreneurial orientation) with the extensive expertise of the musicians (professional orientation). As Fellini demonstrated so well in his film *Orchestra Rehearsal,* this alliance, however uncomfortable (experts never being happy in the face of strong authority), is nevertheless a necessary one. Common today is the professional organization operating in the public sector, which must somehow sustain an alliance of experts and government officials, one group pushing upward for professional autonomy, the other downward for technocratic control.

Our final form, the *politicized organization,* is characterized by moderate conflict that pervades the entire system of power. This would appear to describe a number of today's largest organizations, especially ones in the public sector whose mandates are visible and controversial—many regulatory agencies, for example, and some public utilities. Here it is government protection, or monopoly power, that sustains organizations captured by conflict. This form seems to be increasingly common in the private sector too, among some of the largest corporations that are able to sustain the inefficiencies of conflict through their market power and sometimes by their ability to gain government support as well.

THE FUNCTIONAL ROLE OF POLITICS IN ORGANIZATIONS

Little space need be devoted to the dysfunctional influence of politics in organizations. Politics is divisive and costly; it burns up energies that could instead go into the operations. It can also lead to all kinds of aberrations. Politics is often used to sustain outmoded systems of power, and sometimes to introduce new ones that are not justified. Politics can also paralyze an organization to the point where its effective functioning comes to a halt and nobody benefits. The purpose of an organization, after all, is to produce goods and services, not to provide an arena in which people can fight with one another.

What does deserve space, however, because they are less widely appreciated, are those conditions in which politics and the political organization serve a functional role.

In general, the system of politics is necessary in an organization to correct certain deficiencies in its other, legitimate systems of influence—above all to provide for certain forms of flexibility discouraged by those other systems. The other systems of influence were labeled legitimate because their *means*—authority, ideology, or expertise—have some basis of legitimacy. But sometimes those means are used to pursue *ends* that are illegitimate (as in the example of the lording game, where legitimate power is flaunted unreasonably). In contrast, the system of politics, whose *means* are (by definition) illegitimate, can sometimes be used to pursue *ends* that are in fact legitimate (as in certain of the whistle-blowing and young Turks games, where political pressures are used against formal authority to correct irresponsible or ineffective behaviors). We can elaborate on this in terms of four specific points.

First, politics as a system of influence can act in a Darwinian way to ensure that the strongest members of an organization are brought into positions of leadership. Authority favors a single chain of command; weak leaders can suppress strong subordinates. Politics, on the other hand, can provide alternate channels of information and promotion, as when the sponsorship game enables someone to leap over a weak superior (McClelland, 1970). Moreover, since effective leaders have been shown to exhibit a need for power, the political games can serve as tests to demonstrate the potential for leadership. The second-string players may suffice for the scrimmages, but only the stars can be allowed to meet the competition. Political games not only suggest who those players are but also help to remove their weak rivals from contention.

Second, politics can also ensure that all sides of an issue are fully debated, whereas the other systems of influence may promote only one. The system of authority, by aggregating information up a central hierarchy, tends to advance only a single point of view, often the one already known to be favored above. So, too, does the system of ideology, since every issue is interpreted in terms of "the word," the prevailing set of beliefs. As for the system of expertise, people tend to defer to the expert on any particular issue. But experts are often closed to new ideas, ones that developed after they received their training. Politics, however, by obliging "responsible men . . . to fight for what they are convinced is right" (Allison, 1971:145) encourages a variety of voices to be heard on any issue. And, because of attacks by its opponents, each voice is forced to justify its conclusions in terms of the broader good. That means it must marshal arguments and support proposals that can at least be justified in terms of the interests of the organization at large rather than the parochial needs of a particular group. As Burns has noted in an amusing footnote:

> It is impossible to avoid some reference from the observations made here to F. M. Cornford's well known "Guide for the Young Academic Politician." Jobs "fall into two classes, My Jobs and Your Jobs. My Jobs are public-spirited proposals, which happen (much to my regret) to involve the advancement of a personal friend, or (still more to my regret) of myself. Your Jobs are insidious intrigues for the advancement of yourself and your friends, spuriously disguised as public-spirited proposals." (1961–62:260)

Third, the system of politics is often required to stimulate necessary change that is blocked by the legitimate systems of influence. Internal change is generally threatening to the "vested interest" of an organization. The system of authority concentrates power up the hierarchy, often in the hands of those who were responsible for initiating the existing strategies in the first place. It also contains the established controls, which are designed to sustain the status quo. Similarly, the system of expertise concentrates power in the hands of senior and established experts, not junior ones who may possess newer, more necessary skills. Likewise, the system of ideology, because it is rooted in the past, in tradition, acts as a deterrent to change. In the face of these resistances, it is politics that is able to work as a kind of "invisible hand"—"invisible underhand" would be a better term—to promote necessary change, through such games as strategic candidates, whistle-blowing, and young Turks.

Fourth and finally, the system of politics can ease the path for the execution of decisions. Senior managers, for example, often use politics to gain acceptance for their decisions, playing the strategic candidates game early in promoting proposals to avoid having to play the more divisive and risky counterinsurgency game later in the face of resistance to them. They persuade, negotiate, and build alliances to smooth the path for the decisions they wish to make.

To conclude our discussion, while I am not personally enthusiastic about organizational politics and have no desire to live in a political organization, I do accept, and hope I have persuaded the reader to accept, that politics does have useful roles to play in a society of organizations. Organizational politics may irritate us, but it can also serve us.

● COMPETITIVE MANEUVERING*

BY BRUCE HENDERSON

BRINKMANSHIP IN BUSINESS

A businessman often convinces himself that he is completely logical in his behavior when in fact the critical factor is his emotional bias compared to the emotional bias of his opposition. Unfortunately, some businessmen and students perceive competition as some kind of impersonal, objective, colorless affair, with a company competing against the field as a golfer competes in medal play. A better case can be made that business competition is a major battle in which there are many contenders, each of whom must be dealt with individually. Victory, if achieved, is more often won in the mind of a competitor than in the economic arena.

I shall emphasize two points. The first is that the management of a company must persuade each competitor voluntarily to stop short of a maximum effort to acquire customers and profits. The second point is that persuasion depends on emotional and intuitive factors rather than on analysis or deduction.

The negotiator's skill lies in being as arbitrary as necessary to obtain the best possible compromise without actually destroying the basis for voluntary mutual cooperation of self-restraint. There are some commonsense rules for success in such an endeavor:

---

* "Brinkmanship in Business" and "The Nonlogical Strategy," in *Henderson on Corporate Strategy* (Cambridge, MA, Abt Books, 1979), pp. 27–33, title selected for this book; section on "Rules for the Strategist" originally at the end of "Brinkmanship in Business" moved to the end of "The Nonlogical Strategy;" reprinted by permission of publisher.

1. Be sure that your rival is fully aware of what he can gain if he cooperates and what it will cost him if he does not.

2. Avoid any action which will arouse your competitor's emotions, since it is essential that he behave in a logical, reasonable fashion.

3. Convince your opponent that you are emotionally dedicated to your position and are completely convinced that it is reasonable.

It is worth emphasizing that your competitor is under the maximum handicap if he acts in a completely rational, objective, and logical fashion. For then he will cooperate as long as he thinks he can benefit. In fact, if he is completely logical, he will not forgo the profit of cooperation as long as there is *any* net benefit.

Friendly Competitors

It may strike most businessmen as strange to talk about cooperation with competitors. But it is hard to visualize a situation in which it would be worthwhile to pursue competition to the utter destruction of a competitor. In every case there is a greater advantage to reducing the competition on the condition that the competitor does likewise. Such mutual restraint is cooperation, whether recognized as such or not.

Without cooperation on the part of competitors, there can be no stability. We see this most clearly in international relationships during times of peace. There are constant encroachments and aggressive acts. And the eventual consequence is always either voluntarily imposed self-restraint or mutual destruction. Thus, international diplomacy has only one purpose: to stabilize cooperation between independent nations on the most favorable basis possible. Diplomacy can be described as the art of being stubborn, arbitrary, and unreasonable without arousing emotional responses.

Businessmen should notice the similarity between economic competition and the peacetime behavior of nations. The object in both cases is to achieve a voluntary, cooperative restraint on the part of otherwise aggressive competitors. Complete elimination of competition is almost inconceivable. The goal of the hottest economic war is an agreement for coexistence, not annihilation. The competition and mutual encroachment do not stop; they go on forever. But they do so under some measure of mutual restraint.

"Cold War" Tactics

A breakdown in negotiations is inevitable if both parties persist in arbitrary positions which are incompatible. Yet there are major areas in business where some degree of arbitrary behavior is essential for protecting a company's self-interest. In effect, a type of brinkmanship is necessary. The term was coined to describe cold war international diplomacy, but it describes a normal pattern in business, too.

In a confrontation between parties who are in part competitors and in part cooperators, deciding what to accept is essentially emotional or arbitrary. Deciding what is attainable requires an evaluation of the other party's degree of intransigence. The purpose is to convince him that you are arbitrary and emotionally committed while trying to discover what he would really accept in settlement. The competitor known to be coldly logical is at a great disadvantage. Logically, he can afford to compromise until there is no advantage left in cooperation. If, instead, he is emotional, irrational, and arbitrary, he has a great advantage.

The heart of business strategy for a company is to promote attitudes on the part of its competitors that will cause them either to restrain themselves or to act in a fashion which management deems advantageous. In diplomacy and military strategy the key to success is very much the same.

The most easily recognized way of enforcing cooperation is to exhibit obvious willingness to use irresistible or overwhelming force. This requires little strategic skill, but there is the problem of convincing the competing organization that the force will be used without actually resorting to it (which would be expensive and inconvenient).

In industry, however, the available force is usually not overwhelming, although one company may be able to inflict major punishment on another. In the classic case, each party can inflict such punishment on the other. If there were open conflict, then both parties would lose. If they cooperate, both parties are better off, but not necessarily equally so—particularly if one is trying to change the status quo.

When each party can punish the other, the prospects of agreement depend on three things:

1. Each party's willingness to accept the risk of punishment
2. Each party's belief that the other party is willing to accept the risk of punishment
3. The degree of rationality in the behavior of each party

If these conclusions are correct, what can we deduce about how advantages are gained and lost in business competition?

First, management's unwillingness to accept the risk of punishment is almost certain to produce either the punishment or progressively more onerous conditions for cooperation—provided the competition recognized the attitude.

Second, beliefs about a competitor's future behavior or response are all that determine competitive cooperation. In other words, it is the judgment not of actual capability but of probable use of capability that counts.

Third, the less rational or less predictable the behavior of a competitor appears to be, the greater the advantage he possesses in establishing a favorable competitive balance. This advantage is limited only by his need to avoid forcing his competitors into an untenable position or creating an emotional antagonism that will lead them to be unreasonable and irrational (as he is).

The Nonlogical Strategy

The goal of strategy in business, diplomacy, and war is to produce a stable relationship favorable to you with the consent of your competitors. By definition, restraint by a competitor is cooperation. Such cooperation from a competitor must seem to be profitable to him. *Any competition which does not eventually eliminate a competitor requires his cooperation to stabilize the situation.* The agreement is usually that of tacit nonaggression; the alternative is death for all but one competitor. A stable competitive situation requires an agreement between competing parties to maintain self-restraint. Such agreement cannot be arrived at by logic. It must be achieved by an emotional balance of forces. This is why it is necessary to appear irrational to competitors. For the same reason, you must seem unreasonable and arbitrary in negotiations with customers and suppliers.

Competition and cooperation go hand in hand in all real-life situations. Otherwise, conflict could only end in extermination of the competitor. There is a point in all situations of conflict where both parties gain more or lose less from peace than they can hope to gain from any foreseeable victory. Beyond that point cooperation is more profitable than conflict. But how will the benefits be shared?

In negotiated conflict situations, the participant who is coldly logical is at a great disadvantage. Logically, he can afford to compromise until there is no advantage left in cooperation. The negotiator/competitor whose behavior is irrational or arbitrary has a great advantage if he can depend upon his opponent being logical and unemotional. The arbitrary or irrational competitor can demand far more than a reasonable share and yet his logical opponent can still gain by compromise rather than breaking off the cooperation.

Absence of monopoly in business requires voluntary restraint of competition. At some point there must be a tacit agreement not to compete. Unless this restraint of trade were acceptable to all competitors, the resulting aggression would inevitably eliminate the less efficient competitors leaving only one. Antitrust laws represent a formal attempt to limit competition. All antimonopoly and fair trade laws constitute restraint of competition.

Utter destruction of a competitor is almost never profitable unless the competitor is unwilling to accept peace. In our daily social contacts, in our international affairs, and in our business affairs, we have far more ability to damage those around us than we ever dare use. Others have the same power to damage us. The implied agreement to restrain our potential aggression is all that stands between us and eventual elimination of one by the other. Both war and diplomacy are mechanisms for establishing or maintaining this self-imposed restraint on all competitors. The conflict continues, but within the implied area of cooperative agreement.

There is a definite limit to the range within which competitors can expect to achieve an equilibrium or negotiate a shift in equilibrium even by implication. Arbitrary, uncooperative, or aggressive attitudes will produce equally emotional reactions. These emotional reactions are in turn the basis for nonlogical and arbitrary responses. Thus, nonlogical behavior is self-limiting.

This is why the art of diplomacy can be described as the ability to be unreasonable without arousing resentment. It is worth remembering that the objective of diplomacy is to induce cooperation on terms that are relatively more favorable to you than to your protagonist without actual force being used.

More business victories are won in the minds of competitors than in the laboratory, the factory or the marketplace. The competitor's conviction that you are emotional, dogmatic, or otherwise nonlogical in your business strategy can be a great asset. This conviction on his part can result in an acceptance of your actions without retaliation, which would otherwise be unthinkable. More important, the anticipation of nonlogical or unrestrained reactions on your part can inhibit his competitive aggression.

Rules for the Strategist

If I were asked to distill the conditions and forces described into advice for the business-strategist, I would suggest five rules:

1. You must know as accurately as possible just what your competition has at stake in his contact with you. It is not what you gain or lose, but what he gains or loses that sets the limit on his ability to compromise with you.

2. The less the competition knows about your stakes, the less advantage he has. Without a reference point, he does not even know whether you are being unreasonable.

3. It is absolutely essential to know the character, attitudes, motives, and habitual behavior of a competitor if you wish to have a negotiating advantage.

4. The more arbitrary your demands are, the better your relative competitive position—provided you do not arouse an emotional reaction.

5. The less arbitrary you seem, the more arbitrary you can in fact be.

These rules make up the art of business brinkmanship. They are guidelines for winning a strategic victory in the minds of competitors. Once this victory has been won, it can be converted into a competitive victory in terms of sales volume, costs, and profits.

● THE INSTITUTIONAL FUNCTION OF MANAGEMENT*

BY JEFFREY PFEFFER

Theory, research, and education in the field of organizational behavior and management have been dominated by a concern for the management of people *within* organizations. The question of how to make workers more productive has stood as the foundation for management theory and practice since the time of Frederick Taylor. Such an emphasis neglects the institutional function of management. While managing people within organizations is critical, managing the organization's relationships with other organizations such as competitors, creditors, suppliers, and governmental agencies is frequently as critical to the firm's success.

Parsons (1960) noted that there were three levels of organizations: (1) the technical level, where the technology of the organization was used to produce some product or service; (2) the administrative level, which coordinated and supervised the technical level; and (3) the institutional level, which was concerned with the organization's legitimacy and with organization-environment relations. Organization and management theory has primarily concentrated on administrative level problems, frequently at very low hierarchical levels in organizations.

Practicing managers and some researchers do recognize the importance of the institutional context in which the firm operates. There is increasing use of institutional advertising, and executives from the oil industry, among others, have been active in projecting their organizations' views in a variety of contexts. Mintzberg (1973a) has identified the liaison role as one of ten roles managers fill. Other authors explicitly have noted the importance of relating the organization to other organizations (Pfeffer and Nowak, n.d., Whyte, 1955). . . .

The purposes of this article are: (a) to present evidence of the importance of the institutional function of management, and (b) to review data consistent with a model of institutional management. This model argues that managers behave as if they were seeking to manage and reduce uncertainty and interdependence arising

---

* Originally published as "Beyond Management and the Worker: The Institutional Function of Management," in the *Academy of Management Review* (April 1976); copyright © *Academy of Management Review*. Reprinted with deletions by the permission of the *Academy of Management Review* and the author.

from the firm's relationships with other organizations. Several strategic responses to interorganizational exchange, including their advantages and disadvantages, are considered.

INSTITUTIONAL PROBLEMS OF ORGANIZATIONS

Organizations are open social systems, engaged in constant and important transactions with other organizations in their environments. Business firms transact with customer and supplier organizations, and with sources of credit; they interact on the federal and local level with regulatory and legal authorities which are concerned with pollution, taxes, antitrust, equal employment, and myriad other issues. Because firms do interact with these other organizations, two consequences follow. First, organizations face uncertainty. If an organization were a closed system so that it could completely control and predict all the variables that affected its operation, the organization could make technically rational, maximizing decisions and anticipate the consequences of its actions. As an open system, transacting with important external organizations, the firm does not have control over many of the important factors that affect its operations. Because organizations are open, they are affected by events outside their boundaries.

Second, organizations are interdependent with other organizations with which they exchange resources, information or personnel, and thus open to influence by them. The extent of this influence is likely to be a function of the importance of the resource obtained, and inversely related to the ease with which the resource can be procured from alternative sources (Jacobs, 1974; Thompson, 1967). Interdependence is problematic and troublesome. Managers do not like to be dependent on factors outside their control. Interdependence is especially troublesome if there are few alternative sources, so the external organization is particularly important to the firm.

Interdependence and uncertainty interact in their effects on organizations. One of the principal functions of the institutional level of the firm is the management of this interdependence and uncertainty.

THE IMPORTANCE OF INSTITUTIONAL MANAGEMENT

Katz and Kahn (1966) noted that organizations may pursue two complementary paths to effectiveness. The first is to be as efficient as possible, and thereby obtain a competitive advantage with respect to other firms. Under this strategy, the firm succeeds because it operates so efficiently that it achieves a competitive advantage in the market. The second strategy, termed "political," involves the establishment of favorable exchange relationships based on considerations that do not relate strictly to price, quality, service, or efficiency. Winning an order because of the firm's product and cost characteristics would be an example of the strategy of efficiency; winning the order because of interlocks in the directorates of the organizations involved, or because of family connections between executives in the two organizations, would illustrate political strategies.

The uses and consequences of political strategies for achieving organizational success have infrequently been empirically examined. Hirsch (1975) has . . . compared the ethical drug and record industries, noting great similarities between them. Both sell their products through gatekeepers or intermediaries—in the case of pharmaceuticals, through doctors who must write the prescriptions, and in the case of records, through disc jockeys who determine air time and, consequently, exposure. Both sell products with relatively short life cycles, and both industries place great emphasis on new products and product innovation. Both depend on the legal environment of patents, copyrights, and trademarks for market protection.

Hirsch noted that the rate of return for the average pharmaceutical firm during the period 1956–1966 was more than double the rate of return for the average firm in the record industry. Finding no evidence that would enable him to attribute the striking differences in profitability to factors associated with internal structural arrangements, Hirsch concluded that at least one factor affecting the relative profitability of the two industries is the ability to manage their institutional environments, and more specifically, the control over distribution, patent and copyright protection, and the prediction of adoption by the independent gatekeepers.

In a review of the history of both industries, Hirsch indicated that in pharmaceuticals, control over entry was achieved by (a) amending the patent laws to permit the patenting of naturally occurring substances, antibiotics and (b) instituting a long and expensive licensing procedure required before drugs could be manufactured and marketed, administered by the Food and Drug Administration (FDA). In contrast, record firms have much less protection under the copyright laws; as a consequence, entry is less controlled, leading to more competition and lower profits. While there are other differences between the industries, including size and expenditures on research and development, Hirsch argued that at least some of the success of drug firms derives from their ability to control entry and their ability to control information channels relating to their product through the use of detail personnel and advertising in the American Medical Association Journals. Retail price maintenance, tariff protection, and licensing to restrict entry are other examples of practices that are part of the organization's institutional environment and may profoundly affect its success.

MANAGING UNCERTAINTY AND INTERDEPENDENCE

The organization, requiring transactions with other organizations and uncertain about their future performance, has available a variety of strategies that can be used to manage uncertainty and interdependence. Firms face two problems in their institutional relationships: (a) managing the uncertainty caused by the unpredictable actions of competitors and (b) managing the uncertainty resulting from noncompetitive interdependence with suppliers, creditors, government agencies, and customers. In both instances, the same set of strategic responses is available: merger, to completely absorb the interdependence and resulting uncertainty; joint ventures; interlocking directorates, to partially absorb interdependence; the movement and selective recruiting of executives and other personnel, to develop interorganizational linkages; regulation, to provide government enforced stability; and other political activity to reduce competition, protect markets, and sources of supply, and otherwise manage the organization's environment.

Because organizations are open systems, each strategy is limited in its effect. While merger or some other interorganizational linkage may manage one source of organizational dependence, it probably at the same time makes the organizations dependent on yet other organizations. For example, while regulation may eliminate effective price competition and restrict entry into the industry (Jordan, 1972;

Pfeffer, 1974a; Posner, 1974), the regulated organizations then face the uncertainties involved in dealing with the regulatory agency. Moreover, in reducing uncertainty for itself, the organization must bargain away some of its own discretion (Thompson, 1967). One can view institutional management as an exchange process—the organization assures itself of needed resources, but at the same time, must promise certain predictable behaviors in return. Keeping these qualifications in mind, evidence on use of the various strategies of institutional management is reviewed.

Merger

There are three reasons an organization may seek to merge—first, to reduce competition by absorbing an important competitor organization; second, to manage interdependence with either sources of input or purchasers of output by absorbing them; and third, to diversify operations and thereby lessen dependence on the present organizations with which it exchanges (Pfeffer, 1972b). While merger among competing organizations is presumably proscribed by the antitrust laws, enforcement resources are limited, and major consolidations do take place. . . .

The classic expressed rationale for merger has been to increase the profits or the value of the shares of the firm. In a series of studies beginning as early as 1921, researchers have been unable to demonstrate that merger active firms are more profitable or have higher stock prices following the merger activity. This literature has been summarized by Reid (1968), who asserts that mergers are made for growth, and that growth is sought because of the relationship between firm size and managerial salaries.

Growth, however, does not provide information concerning the desired characteristics of the acquired firm. Under a growth objective, any merger is equivalent to any other of the same size. Pfeffer (1972b) has argued that mergers are undertaken to manage organizational interdependence. Examining the proportion of merger activity occurring within the same two-digit SIC industry category, he found that the highest proportion of within-industry mergers occurred in industries of intermediate concentration. The theoretical argument was that in industries with many competitors, the absorption of a single one did little to reduce competitive uncertainty. At the other extreme, with only a few competitors, merger would more likely be scrutinized by the antitrust authorities and coordination could instead be achieved through more informal arrangements, such as price leadership.

The same study investigated the second reason to merge: to absorb the uncertainty among organizations vertically related to each other, as in a buyer-seller relationship. He found that it was possible to explain 40% of the variation in the distribution of merger activity over industries on the basis of resource interdependence, measured by estimates of the transactions flows between sectors of the economy. On an individual industry basis, in two-thirds of the cases a measure of transactions interdependence accounted for 65% or more of the variation in the pattern of merger activity. The study indicated that it was possible to account for the industry of the likely merger partner firm by considering the extent to which firms in the two industries exchanged resources.

While absorption of suppliers or customers will reduce the firm's uncertainty by bringing critical contingencies within the boundaries of the organization, this strategy has some distinct costs. One danger is that the process of vertical integration creates a larger organization which is increasingly tied to a single industry.

The third reason for merger is diversification. Occasionally, the organization is confronted by interdependence it cannot absorb, either because of resource or legal limitations. Through diversifying its activities, the organization does not reduce the uncertainty, but makes the particular contingency less critical for its success and well-being. Diversification provides the organization with a way of avoiding, rather than absorbing, problematic interdependence.

Merger represents the most complete solution to situations of organizational independence, as it involves the total absorption of either a competitor or a vertically related organization, or the acquisition of an organization operating in another area. Because it does involve total absorption, merger requires more resources and is a more visible and substantial form of interorganizational linkage.

Joint Ventures

Closely related to merger is the joint venture: the creation of a jointly owned, but independent organization by two or more separate parent firms. Merger involves the total pooling of assets by two or more organizations. In a joint venture, some assets of each of several parent organizations are used, and thus only a partial pooling of resources is involved (Bernstein, 1965). For a variety of reasons, joint ventures have ben prosecuted less frequently and less successfully than mergers, making joint ventures particularly appropriate as a way of coping with competitive interdependence.

The joint subsidiary can have several effects on competitive interdependence and uncertainty. First, it can reduce the extent of new competition. Instead of both firms entering a market, they can combine some of their assets and create a joint subsidiary to enter the market. Second, since joint subsidiaries are typically staffed, particularly at the higher executive levels, with personnel drawn from the parent firms, the joint subsidiary becomes another location for the management of competing firms to meet. Most importantly, the joint subsidiary must set price and output levels, make new product development and marketing decisions and decisions about its advertising policies. Consequently, the parent organizations are brought into association in a setting in which exactly those aspects of the competitive relationship must be jointly determined.

In a study of joint ventures among the manufacturing and oil and gas companies during the period 1960–1971, Pfeffer and Nowak (1976a, 1976b) found that 56% involved parent firms operating in the same two-digit industry. Further, in 36% of the 166 joint ventures studied, the joint subsidiary operated in the same industry as both parent organizations. As in the case of mergers, the proportion of joint venture activities undertaken with other firms in the same industry was related to the concentration of the firm's industry being intermediate. The relationship between concentration and the proportion of joint ventures undertaken within the same industry accounted for some 25% of the variation in the pattern of joint venture activities.

In addition to considering the use of joint ventures in coping with competitive interdependence, the Pfeffer and Nowak study of joint ventures examined the extent to which the creation of joint subsidiaries was related to patterns of transaction interdependence across industries. While the correlations between the proportion of transactions and the proportion of joint ventures undertaken between industry pairs were lower than in the case of mergers, statistically significant relationships between this form of interorganizational linkage activity and patterns of resource exchange were observed. The difference between mergers and joint ventures appears to be that mergers are used relatively more to cope with buyer–seller interdependence, and joint ventures are more highly related to considerations of coping with competitive uncertainty.

Cooptation and Interlocking Directorates

Cooptation is a venerable strategy for managing interdependence between organizations. Cooptation involves the partial absorption of another organization through the placing of a representative of that organization on the board of the focal organization. Corporations frequently place bankers on their boards; hospitals and universities offer trustee positions to prominent business leaders; and community action agencies develop advisory boards populated with active and strong community political figures. . . .

Interlocks in the boards of directors of competing organizations provide a possible strategy for coping with competitive interdependence and the resulting uncertainty. The underlying argument is that in order to manage interorganizational relationships, information must be exchanged, usually through a joint subsidiary or interlocking directorate. While interlocks among competitors are ostensibly illegal, until very recently there was practically no prosecution of this practice. In a 1965 study, a subcommittee of the House Judiciary Committee found more than 300 cases in which direct competitors had interlocking boards of directors (House of Representatives, 1965). In a study of the extent of interlocking among competing organizations in a sample of 109 manufacturing organizations, Pfeffer and Nowak (n.d.) found that the proportion of directors on the board from direct competitors was higher for firms operating in industries in which concentration was intermediate. This result is consistent with the result found for joint ventures and mergers as well. In all three instances, linkages among competing organizations occurred more frequently when concentration was in an intermediate range.

Analyses of cooptation through the use of boards of directors have not been confined to business firms. Price (1963) argued that the principal function of the boards of the Oregon Fish and Game Commissions was to link the organizations to their environments. Zald (1967) found that the composition of YMCA boards in Chicago matched the demography of their operating areas, and affected the organizations' effectiveness, particularly in raising money. Pfeffer (1973) examined the size, composition, and function of hospital boards of directors, finding that variables of organizational context, such as ownership, source of funds, and location, were important explanatory factors. He also found a relationship between cooptation and organizational effectiveness. In 1972, Pfeffer (1972a) found that regulated firms, firms with a higher proportion of debt in their capital structures, and larger firms tended to have more outside directors. Allen (1974) also found that size of the board and the use of cooptation was predicted by the size of the firm, but did not replicate Pfeffer's earlier finding of a relationship between the organization's capital structure and the proportion of directors from financial institutions. In a study of utility boards, Pfeffer (1974b) noted that the composition of the board tended to correlate with the demographics of the area in which the utility was regulated.

The evidence is consistent with the strategy of organizations using their boards of directors to coopt external organizations and manage problematic interdependence. The role of the board of directors is seen not as the provision of management expertise or control, but more generally as a means of managing problematic aspects of an organization's institutional environment.

Executive Recruitment

Information also is transferred among organizations though the movement of personnel. The difference between movement of executives between organizations and cooptation is that in the latter case, the person linking the two organizations retains membership in both organizations. In the case of personnel movement, dual organizational membership is not maintained. When people change jobs, they take with themselves information about the operations, policies, and values of their previous employers, as well as contacts in the organization. In a study of the movement of faculty among schools of business, Baty et al. (1971) found that similar orientations and curricula developed among schools exchanging personnel. The movement of personnel is one method by which new techniques of management and new marketing and product ideas are diffused through a set of organizations.

Occasionally, the movement of executives between organizations has been viewed as intensifying, rather than reducing, competition. Companies have been distressed by the raiding of trade secrets and managerial expertise by other organizations. While this perspective must be recognized, the exchange of personnel among organizations is a revered method of conflict *reduction* between organizations (Stern, Sternthal, and Craig, 1973). Personnel movement inevitably involves sharing information among a set of organizations.

If executive movement is a form of interfirm linkage designed to manage competitive relationships, the proportion of executives recruited from within the same industry should be highest at intermediate levels of industrial concentration. Examining the three top executive positions in twenty different manufacturing industries, the evidence on executive backgrounds was found to be consistent with this argument (Pfeffer and Leblebici, 1973). The proportion of high level executives with previous jobs in the same industry but in a different company was found to be negatively related to the number of firms in the industry. The larger the number of firms, the less likely that a single link among competitors will substantially reduce uncertainty, but the larger the available supply of external executive talent. The data indicated no support for a supply argument, but supported the premise that interorganizational linkages are used to manage interdependence and uncertainty.

The use of executive movement to manage noncompetitive interorganizational relationships is quite prevalent. The often-cited movement of personnel between the Defense Department and major defense contractors is only one example, because there is extensive movement of personnel between many government departments and industries interested in the agencies decisions. The explanation is frequently proposed that organizations are acquiring these personnel because of their expertise. The expertise explanation is frequently difficult to separate from the alternative that personnel are being exchanged to enhance interorganizational relationships. Regardless of the motivation, exchanging personnel inevitably involves the transfer of information and access to the other organization.

Regulation

Occasionally, institutional relationships are managed through recourse to political intervention. The reduction of competition and its associated uncertainty may be accomplished through regulation. Regulation, however, is a risky strategy for organizations to pursue. While regulation most frequently benefits the regulated industry (Jordan, 1972; Pfeffer, 1974a), the industry and firms have no assurance that regulatory authority will not be used against their interests. Regulation is very hard to repeal. Successful use of regulation requires that the firm and industry face little or no powerful political opposition, and that the political future can be accurately forecast.

The benefits of regulation to those being regulated have been extensively reviewed (Posner, 1974; Stigler, 1971). Regulation frequently has been sought by the regulated industry. . . . Estimates of the effects of regulation on prices in electric utilities, airlines, trucking, and natural gas have indicated that regulation either increases price or has no effect.

The theory behind these outcomes is still unclear. One approach suggests that regulation is created for the public benefit, but after the initial legislative attention, the regulatory process is captured by the firms subject to regulation. Another approach proposes that regulation, like other goods, is acquired subject to supply and demand considerations (Posner, 1974). Political scientists, focusing on the operation of interest groups, argue that regulatory agencies are "captured" by organized and well-financed interests. Government intervention in the market can solve many of the interdependence problems faced by firms. Regulation is most often accompanied by restriction of entry and the fixing of prices, which tend to reduce market uncertainties. Markets may be actually allocated to firms, and with the reduction of risk, regulation may make access to capital easier. Regulation may alter the organization's relationships with suppliers and customers. One theory of why the railroads were interested in the creation of the Interstate Commerce Commission (ICC) in 1887 was that large users were continually demanding and winning discriminatory rate reductions, disturbing the price stability of railroad price fixing cartels. By forbidding price discrimination and enforcing this regulation, the ICC strengthened the railroads' position with respect to large customers (MacAvoy, 1965).

Political Activity

Regulation is only one specific form of organizational activity in governmental processes. Business attempts to affect competition through the operation of the tariff laws date back to the 1700's (Bauer et al., 1968). Epstein (1969) provided one of the more complete summaries of the history of corporate involvement in politics and the inevitability of such action. The government has the power of coercion, possessed legally by no other social institution. Furthermore, legislation and regulation affect most of our economic institutions and markets, either indirectly through taxation, or more directly through purchasing, market protection or market creation. For example, taxes on margarine only recently came to an end. Federal taxes, imposed in 1886 as a protectionist measure for dairy interests, were removed in 1950, but a law outlawing the sale of oleo in its colored form lasted until 1967 in Wisconsin.

As with regulation, political activities carry both benefits and risks. The risk arises because once government intervention in an issue on behalf of a firm or industry is sought, then political intervention becomes legitimated, regardless of whose interests are helped or hurt. The firm that seeks favorable tax legislation runs the risk of creating a setting in which it is equally legitimate to be exposed to very unfavorable legislation. After an issue is opened to government intervention, neither side will find it easy to claim that further government action is illegitimate.

In learning to cope with a particular institutional environment, the firm may be unprepared for new uncertainties caused by the change of fundamental institutional relationships, including the opening of price competition, new entry and the lack of protection from overseas competition.

CONCLUSION

. . . Considering its probable importance to the firm, the institutional function of management has received much less concern than it warrants. It is time that this aspect of management receives the systematic attention long reserved for motivational and productivity problems associated with relationships between management and workers.

• WHO SHOULD CONTROL THE CORPORATION?*

BY HENRY MINTZBERG

Who should control the corporation? How? And for the pursuit of what goals? Historically, the corporation was controlled by its owners—through direct control of the managers if not through direct management—for the pursuit of economic goals. But as shareholding became dispersed, owner control weakened; and as the corporation grew to very large size, its economic actions came to have increasing social consequences. The giant, widely held corporation came increasingly under the implicit control of its managers, and the concept of social responsibility—the voluntary consideration of public social goals alongside the private economic ones—arose to provide a basis of legitimacy for their actions.

To some, including those closest to the managers themselves, this was accepted as a satisfactory arrangement for the large corporation. "Trust it" to the goodwill of the managers was their credo; these people will be able to achieve an appropriate balance between social and economic goals.

But others viewed this basis of control as fundamentally illegitimate. The corporation was too large, too influential, its actions too pervasive to be left free of the direct and concerted influence of outsiders. At the extreme were those who believed that legitimacy could be achieved only by subjecting managerial authority to formal and direct external control. "Nationalize it," said those at one end of the political spectrum, to put ultimate control in the hands of the government so that it will pursue public social goals. No, said those at the other end, "restore it" to direct shareholder control, so that it will not waiver from the pursuit of private economic goals.

Other people took less extreme positions. "Democratize it" became the rallying cry for some, to open up the governance of the large, widely held corporation to a variety of affected groups—if not the workers, then the customers, or conservation interests, or minorities. "Regulate it" was also a popular position, with its implicit premise that only by sharing their control with government would the corporation's managers attend to certain social goals. Then there were those who accepted direct management control so long as it was tempered by other, less formal types of influence. "Pressure it," said a generation of social activists, to ensure that social goals are taken into consideration. But others argued that because the corporation is an economic instrument, you must "induce it" by providing economic incentives to encourage the resolution of social problems.

Finally, there were those who argued that this whole debate was unnecessary, that a kind of invisible hand ensures that the economic corporation acts in a socially responsible manner. "Ignore it" was their implicit conclusion.

This article is written to clarify what has become a major debate of our era, *the* major debate revolving around the private sector: Who should control the corporation, specifically the large, widely held corporation, how, and for the pursuit of

* Originally published in the *California Management Review* (Fall 1984), pp. 90–115, based on a section of Henry Mintzberg, *Power in and Around Organizations* (Prentice-Hall, 1983). Copyright © 1984 by The Regents of the University of California. Reprinted with deletions by permission of The Regents.

what goals? The answers that are eventually accepted will determine what kind of society we and our children shall live in. . . .

As implied earlier, the various positions of who should control the corporation, and how, can be laid out along a political spectrum, from nationalization at one end to the restoration of shareholder power at the other. From the managerial perspective, however, those two extremes are not so far apart. Both call for direct control of the corporation's managers by specific outsiders, in one case the government to ensure the pursuit of social goals, in the other case the shareholders to ensure the pursuit of economic ones. It is the moderate positions—notably, trusting the corporation to the social responsibility of its managers—that are farthest from the extremes. Hence, we can fold our spectrum around so that it takes the shape of a horseshoe.

Figure 1 shows our "conceptual horseshoe," with "nationalize it" and "restore it" at the two ends. "Trust it" is at the center, because it postulates a natural balance of social and economic goals. "Democratize it," "regulate it," and "pressure it" are shown on the left side of the horseshoe, because all seek to temper economic goals with social ones. "Induce it" and "ignore it," both of which favor the exclusive pursuit of economic goals, are shown on the right side.

This conceptual horseshoe provides a basic framework to help clarify the issues in this important debate. We begin by discussing each of these positions in turn, circling the horseshoe from left to right. Finding that each (with one exception) has a logical context, we conclude—in keeping with our managerial perspective—that they should be thought of as forming a portfolio from which society can draw to deal with the issue of who should control the corporation and how.

FIGURE 1
The Conceptual Horseshoe

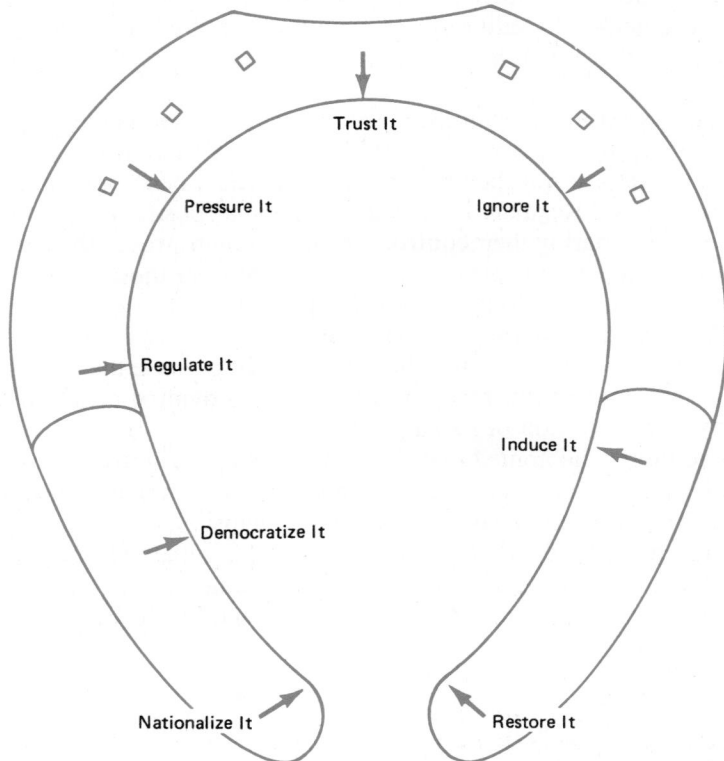

Nationalization of the corporation is a taboo subject in the United States—in general, but not in particular. Whenever a major corporation runs into serious difficulty (i.e., faces bankruptcy with possible loss of many jobs), massive government intervention, often including direct nationalization, inevitably comes up as an option. This option has been exercised: U.S. travelers now ride on Amtrak; Tennessee residents have for years been getting their power from a government utility; indeed, the Post Office was once a private enterprise. Other nations have, of course, been much more ambitious in this regard.

From a managerial and organizational perspective, the question is not whether nationalization is legitimate, but whether it works—at least in particular, limited circumstances. As a response to concerns about the social responsibility of large corporations, the answer seems to be no. The evidence suggests that social difficulties arise more from the size of an organization and its degree of bureaucratization than from its form of ownership (Epstein, 1977; Jenkins, 1976). On the other hand, contrary to popular belief in the United States, nationalization does not necessarily harm economic efficiency. Over the years, Renault has been one of the most successful automobile companies outside Japan; it was nationalized by the French government shortly after World War II. . . . When people believe that government ownership leads to interference, politicization, and inefficiency, that may be exactly what happens. However, when they believe that nationalization *has* to work, then state-owned enterprises may be able to attract the very best talent in the country and thereby work well.

But economic efficiency is no reason to favor nationalization any more than is concern about social responsibility. Nationalization does, however, seem to make sense in at least two particular circumstances. The first is when a mission deemed necessary in a society will not be provided adequately by the private sector. That is presumably why America has its Amtrak [and why Third World nations often create state enterprises]. . . . The second is when the activities of an organization must be so intricately tied to government policy that it is best managed as a direct arm of the state. The Canadian government created Petrocan to act as a "window" and a source of expertise on the sensitive oil industry.

Thus, it is not rhetoric but requirement that should determine the role of this position as a solution to who should control the corporation. "Nationalize it" should certainly not be embraced as a panacea, but neither should it be rejected as totally inapplicable.

A less extreme position—at least in the context of the American debate—is one that calls for formal devices to broaden the governance of the corporation. The proponents of this position either accept the legal fiction of shareholder control and argue that the corporation's power base is too narrow, or else they respond to the emergent reality and question the legitimacy of managerial control. Why, they ask, do stockholders or self-selected managers have any greater right to control the profound decisions of these major institutions than do workers or customers or the neighbors downstream.

This stand is not to be confused with what is known as "participative management." The call to "democratize it" is a legal, rather than ethical one and is based on power, not generosity. Management is not asked to share its power voluntarily; rather, that power is to be reallocated constitutionally. That makes this position a fundamental and important one, *especially* in the United States with its strong tradition of pluralist control of its institutions.

The debate over democratization of the corporation has been confusing in part because many of the proposals have been so vague. We can bring some order to it by considering, in organizational terms, two basic means of democratization and two basic constituencies that can be involved. As shown in Figure 2, they suggest four possible forms of corporate democracy. One means is through the election of representatives to the board of directors, which we call *representative democracy*. The other is through formal but direct involvement in internal decision making processes, which we call *participatory democracy*. Either can focus on the *workers* . . . or else on a host of outside interest groups, the latter giving rise to a *pluralistic* form of democracy. These are basic forms of corporate democracy in theory. With one exception, they have hardly been approached—let alone achieved—in practice. But they suggest where the "democratize it" debate may be headed.

The European debate has focused on worker representative democracy. This has, in some sense, been achieved in Yugoslavia, where the workers of all but the smallest firms elect the members of what is the equivalent of the American board of directors. In Germany, under the so-called *Mitbestimmung* ("codetermination"), the workers and the shareholders each elect half of the directors.

The evidence on this form of corporate democracy has been consistent, and it supports neither its proponents nor its detractors. Workers representation on the board seems to make relatively little difference one way or the other. The worker representatives concern themselves with wage and welfare issues but leave most other questions to management. Worker-controlled firms (not unlike the state-owned ones) appear to be no more socially responsible than private ones. . . .

On the other hand, worker representative democracy may have certain positive benefits. German Chancellor Helmut Schmidt is reported to have said that "the key to [his] country's postwar economic miracle was its sophisticated system of workers' participation" (in Garson, 1977:63). While no one can prove this statement, codetermination certainly does not seem to have done the German economy much harm. By providing an aura of legitimacy to the German corporation and by involving the workers (at least officially) in its governance, codetermination may perhaps have enhanced the spirit of enterprise in Germany (while having little real effect on how decisions are actually made). More significantly, codetermination may have fostered greater understanding and cooperation between the managers and the union members who fill most of the worker seats on the boards. . . .

. . . the embryonic debate over representative democracy in the United States

FIGURE 2
Four Basic Forms of Corporate Democracy

| | | GROUPS INVOLVED | |
		Internal Employees	External Interest Groups
FOCUS OF ATTENTION	Board of Directors	Worker Representative Democracy (European style, e.g., "co-determination" or worker ownership)	Pluralistic Representative Democracy (American style, e.g., "public interest" directors)
	Internal Decision-Making Process	Worker Participatory Democracy (e.g., works councils)	Pluralistic Participatory Democracy (e.g., outsiders on new product committees)

has shown signs of moving in a different direction. Consistent with the tradition of pluralism in America's democratic institutions, there has been increasing pressure to elect outside directors who represent a wide variety of special interest groups— that is, consumers, minorities, environmentalists, and so on. . . .

Critics . . . have pointed out the problems of defining constituencies and finding the means to hold elections. "One-person, one-vote" may be easily applied to electing representatives of the workers, but no such simple rule can be found in the case of the consumer or environmental representatives, let alone ones of the "public interest." Yet it is amazing how quickly things become workable in the United States when Americans decide to put their collective mind to it. Indeed, the one case of public directors that I came across is telling in this regard. According to a Conference Board report, the selection by the Chief Justice of the Supreme Court of New Jersey of 6 of the 24 members of the board of Prudential Insurance as public directors has been found by the company to be "quite workable" (Bacon and Brown, 1975:48). . . . [Note—see the associated box on "The Power of the Board."]

THE POWER OF THE BOARD

Proposals for representative democracy, indeed those for nationalization and the restoration of shareholder control as well, rest on assumptions about the power of the board of directors. It may, therefore, be worth considering at this point the roles that boards of directors play in organizations and the board's resulting powers.

In law, traditionally, the business of a corporation was to be "managed" by its board. But of course, the board does no such thing. Managers manage, although some may happen to sit on the board. What, then, are the roles of the board, particularly of its "outside" directors?

The most tangible role of the board, and clearly provided for in law, is to name, and of course to dismiss as well, the chief executive officer, that person who in turn names the rest of the management. A second role may be to exercise direct control during periods of crisis, for example when the management has failed to provide leadership. And a third is to review the major decisions of the management as well as its overall performance.

These three constitute the board's roles of control, in principal at least because there is no shortage of evidence that boards have difficulty doing even these effectively, especially outside directors. Their job is, after all, part-time, and in a brief meeting once in a while they face a complex organization led by a highly organized management that deals with it every day. The result is that board control tends to reduce to naming and replacing the chief executive, and that person's knowledge of that fact, nothing more. Indeed, even that power is circumscribed, because a management cannot be replaced very often. In a sense, the board is like a bee hovering near a person picking flowers. The person must proceed carefully, so as not to provoke the bee, but can proceed with the task. But if the bee does happen to be provoked, it only gets to sting once. Thus many boards try to know only enough to know when the management is not doing its job properly, so that they can replace it.

But if boards tend to be weaker than expected in exercising *control over* the organization, they also tend perhaps to be stronger than expected in providing *service to* the organization. Here board membership plays at least four other roles. First, it "co-opts" influential outsiders: The organization uses the status of a seat on its board to gain the support of people important to it (as in the case of the big donors who sit on university boards). Second, board membership may be used to establish contacts for the organization (as when retired military officers sit on the boards of weapons manufacturing firms). This may be done to help in such things as the securing of contracts and the raising of funds. Third, seats on the board can be used to enhance an organization's reputation (as when an astronaut or some other type of celebrity is given a seat). And fourth, the board can be used to provide advice for the organization (as in the case of many of the bankers and lawyers who sit on the boards of corporations).

How much do boards serve organizations, and how much do they control them? Some boards do, of course, exercise control, particularly when their members represent a well-defined constituency, such as the substantial owner of a corporation. But, as noted, this tends to be a loose control at best. And other boards hardly do even that, especially when their constituencies are widely dispersed.

To represent everyone is ultimately to represent no one, especially when faced with a highly organized management that knows exactly what it wants. (Or from the elector's point of view, having some distant representative sitting on a board somewhere hardly brings him or her closer to control over the things that impinge on daily life—the work performed, the products consumed, the rivers polluted.) In corporations, this has been shown to be true of the directors who represent many small shareholders no less than those who represent many workers or many customers, perhaps even those who represent government, since that can be just a confusing array of pressure groups. These boards become, at best, tools of the organization, providing it with the variety of the services discussed above, at worst mere façades of formal authority.

Despite its problems, representative democracy is crystal clear compared with participatory democracy. What the French call "autogestion" (as opposed to "cogestion," or codetermination) seems to describe a kind of bottom-up, grassroots democracy in which the workers participate directly in decision making (instead of overseeing management's decisions from the board of directors) and also elect their own managers (who then become more administrators than bosses). Yet such proposals are inevitably vague, and I have heard of no large mass production or mass service firm—not even one owned by workers or a union—that comes close to this. . . .

What has impeded worker participatory democracy? In my opinion, something rather obvious has stood in its way; namely, the structure required by the very organizations in which the attempts have been made to apply it. Worker participatory democracy—and worker representative democracy too, for that matter—has been attempted primarily in organizations containing large numbers of workers who do highly routine, rather unskilled jobs that are typical of most mass production and service—what I have elsewhere called Machine Bureaucracies. The overriding requirement in Machine Bureaucracy is for tight coordination, the kind that can only be achieved by central administrators. For example, the myriad of decisions associated with producing an automobile at Volvo's Kalmar works in Sweden cannot be made by autonomous groups, each doing as it pleases. The whole car must fit together in a particular way at the end of the assembly process. These decisions require a highly sophisticated system of bureaucratic coordination. That is why automobile companies are structured into rigid hierarchies of authority. . . .

Participatory democracy *is* approached in other kinds of organizations . . . the autonomous professional institutions such as universities and hospitals, which have very different needs for central coordination. . . . But the proponents of democracy in organizations are not lobbying for changes in hospitals or universities. It is the giant mass producers they are after, and unless the operating work in these corporations becomes largely skilled and professional in nature, nothing approaching participative democracy can be expected.

In principal, the pluralistic form of participatory democracy means that a variety of groups external to the corporation can somehow control its decision-making processes directly. In practice, of course, this concept is even more elusive than the worker form of participatory democracy. To fully open up the internal decision-making processes of the corporation to outsiders would mean chaos. Yet certain very limited forms of outside participation would seem to be not only feasible but perhaps even desirable. . . . Imagine telephone company executives resolving rate conflicts with consumer groups in quiet offices instead of having to face them in noisy public hearings.

To conclude, corporate democracy—whether representative or participatory in form—may be an elusive and difficult concept, but it cannot be dismissed. It is not just another social issue, like conservation or equal opportunity, but one that strikes at the most fundamental of values. Ours has become a society of organizations. Democracy will have decreasing meaning to most citizens if it cannot be extended beyond political and judicial processes to those institutions that impinge upon them in their daily lives—as workers, as consumers, as neighbors. This is why we shall be hearing a great deal more of "democratize it."

"REGULATE IT"

In theory, regulating the corporation is about as simple as democratizing it is complex. In practice, it is, of course, another matter. To the proponents of "regulate it," the corporation can be made responsive to social needs by having its actions subjected to the controls of a higher authority—typically government, in the form of a regulatory agency or legislation backed up by the courts. Under regulation, constraints are imposed externally on the corporation while its internal governance is left to its managers.

Regulation of business is at least as old as the Code of Hammurabi. In America, it has tended to come in waves. . . .

To some, regulation is a clumsy instrument that should never be relied upon; to others, it is a panacea for the problems of social responsibility. At best, regulation sets minimum and usually crude standards of acceptable behavior; when it works, it does not make any firm socially responsible so much as stop some from being grossly irresponsible. Because it is inflexible, regulation tends to be applied slowly and conservatively, usually lagging public sentiment. Regulation often does not work because of difficulties in enforcement. The problems of the regulatory agencies are legendary—limited resources and information compared with the industries they are supposed to regulate, the cooptation of the regulators by industries, and so on. When applied indiscriminately, regulation either fails dramatically or else succeeds and creates havoc.

Yet there are obvious places for regulation. A prime one is to control tangible "externalities"—costs incurred by corporations that are passed on to the public at large. When, for example, costly pollution or worker health problems can be attributed directly to a corporation, then there seems to be every reason to force it (and its customers) to incur these costs directly, or else to terminate the actions that generate them. Likewise, regulation may have a place where competition encourages the unscrupulous to pull all firms down to a base level of behavior, forcing even the well-intentioned manager to ignore the social consequences of his actions. Indeed, in such cases, the socially responsible behavior is to encourage sensible regulation. "Help us to help others," businessmen should be telling the government. . . .

Most discouraging, however, is Theodore Levitt's revelation some years ago that business has fought every piece of proposed regulatory or social legislation throughout this century, from the Child Labor Acts on up. In Levitt's opinion, much of that legislation has been good for business—dissolving the giant trusts, creating a more honest and effective stock market, and so on. Yet, "the computer is programmed to cry wolf" (Levitt, 1968:83). . . .

In summary, regulation is a clumsy instrument but not a useless one. Were the business community to take a more enlightened view of it, regulation could be applied more appropriately, and we would not need these periodic housecleanings to eliminate the excesses.

"PRESSURE IT"

"Pressure it" is designed to do what "regulate it" fails to do: provoke corporations to act beyond some base level of behavior, usually in an area that regulation misses entirely. Here, activists bring ad hoc campaigns of pressure to bear on one or a group of corporations to keep them responsive to the activists' interpretation of social needs. . . .

"Pressure it" is a distinctively American position. While Europeans debate the theories of nationalization and corporate democracy in their cafés, Americans read about the exploits of Ralph Nader et al. in their morning newspapers. Note that "pressure it," unlike "regulate it," implicitly accepts management's right to make the final decisions. Perhaps this is one reason why it is favored in America.

While less radical than the other positions so far discussed, "pressure it" has nevertheless proved far more effective in eliciting behavior sensitive to social needs . . . [activist groups] have pressured for everything from the dismemberment of diversified corporations to the development of day care centers. Of special note is the class action suit, which has opened up a whole new realm of corporate social issues. But the effective use of the pressure campaign has not been restricted to the traditional activist. President Kennedy used it to roll back U.S. Steel price increases in the early 1960s, and business leaders in Pittsburgh used it in the late 1940s by threatening to take their freight-haulage business elsewhere if the Pennsylvania Railroad did not replace its coal burning locomotives to help clean up their city's air.

"Pressure it" as a means to change corporate behavior is informal, flexible, and focused; hence, it has been highly successful. Yet it is irregular and ad hoc, with different pressure campaigns sometimes making contradictory demands on management. Compared to the positions to its right on the horseshoe, "pressure it," like the other positions to its left, is based on confrontation rather than cooperation.

To a large and vocal contingent, which parades under the banner of "social responsibility," the corporation has no need to act irresponsibly, and therefore there is no reason for it to either be nationalized by the state, democratized by its different constituencies, regulated by the government, or pressured by activists. This contingent believes that the corporation's leaders can be trusted to attend to social goals for their own sake, simply because it is the noble thing to do. (Once this position was known as *nobelesse oblige,* literally "nobility obliges.")

We call this position "trust it," or, more exactly, "trust the corporation to the goodwill of its managers," although looking from the outside in, it might just as well be called "socialize it." We place it in the center of our conceptual horseshoe because it alone postulates a natural balance between social and economic goals—a balance which is to be attained in the heads (or perhaps the hearts) of responsible businessmen. And, as a not necessarily incidental consequence, power can be left in the hands of the managers; the corporation can be trusted to those who reconcile social and economic goals.

The attacks on social responsibility, from the right as well as the left, boil down to whether corporate managers should be trusted when they claim to pursue social goals; if so, whether they are capable of pursuing such goals; and finally, whether they have any right to pursue such goals.

The simplest attack is that social responsibility is all rhetoric, no action. E. F. Cheit refers to the "Gospel of Social Responsibility" as "designed to justify the power of managers over an ownerless system" (1964:172). . . .

Others argue that businessmen lack the personal capabilities required to pursue social goals. Levitt claims that the professional manager reaches the top of the hierarchy by dedication to his firm and his industry; as a result, his knowledge of social issues is highly restricted (Levitt, 1968:83). Others argue that an orientation to efficiency renders business leaders inadept at handling complex social problems (which require flexibility and political finesse, and sometimes involve solutions that are uneconomic). . . .

The most far reaching criticism is that businessmen have no right to pursue social goals. "Who authorized them to do that?" asks Braybrooke (1967:224), attacking from the left. What business have they—self-selected or at best appointed by shareholders—to impose *their* interpretation of the public good on society. Let the elected politicians, directly responsible to the population, look after the social goals.

But this attack comes from the right, too. Milton Friedman writes that social responsibility amounts to spending other people's money—if not that of shareholders, then of customers or employees. Drawing on all the pejorative terms of right-wing ideology, Friedman concludes that social responsibility is a "fundamentally subversive doctrine," representing "pure and unadulterated socialism," supported by businessmen who are "unwitting puppets of the intellectual forces that have been undermining the basis of a free society these past decades." To Friedman, "there is one and only one social responsibility of business—to use its resources and engage in activities designed to increase its profits so long as it stays within the rules of the game" (1970). Let businessmen, in other words, stick to their own business, which is business itself.

The empirical evidence on social responsibility is hardly more encouraging. Brenner and Molander, comparing their 1977 survey of *Harvard Business Review* readers with one conducted fifteen years earlier, concluded that the "respondents are somewhat more cynical about the ethical conduct of their peers" than they were previously (1977:59). Close to half the respondents agreed with the statement that "the American business executive tends not to apply the great ethical laws immediately to work. He is preoccupied chiefly with gain" (p. 62). Only 5% listed social responsibility as a factor "influencing ethical standards" whereas 31% and 20% listed different factors related to pressure campaigns and 10% listed regulation. . . .

The modern corporation has been described as a rational, amoral institution —its professional managers "hired guns" who pursue "efficiently" any goals asked of them. The problem is that efficiency really means measurable efficiency, so that the guns load only with goals that can be quantified. Social goals, unlike economic ones, just don't lend themselves to quantification. As a result, the performance control systems—on which modern corporations so heavily depend—tend to drive out social goals in favor of economic ones (Ackerman, 1975). . . .

In the contemporary large corporation, professional amorality turns into economic morality. When the screws of the performance control systems are turned tight . . . economic morality can turn into social immorality. And it happens often: A *Fortune* writer found that "a surprising number of [big companies] have been involved in blatant illegalities" in the 1970s, at least 117 of 1,043 firms studied (Ross, 1980:57). . . .

How, then, is anyone to "trust it"?

The fact is that we have to trust it, for two reasons. First, the strategic decisions of large organizations inevitably involve social as well as economic consequences that are inextricably intertwined. The neat distinction between economic goals in the private sector and social goals in the public sector just doesn't hold up in practice. Every important decision of the large corporation—to introduce a new product line, to close an old plant, whatever—generates all kinds of social consequences. There is no such thing as purely economic decisions in big business. Only a conceptual ostrich, with his head deeply buried in the abstractions of economic theory, could possibly use the distinction between economic and social goals to dismiss social responsibility.

The second reason we have to "trust it" is that there is always some degree of discretion involved in corporate decision making, discretion to thwart social needs or to attend to them. Things could be a lot better in today's corporation, but they could also be an awful lot worse. It is primarily our ethics that keep us where we are. If the performance control systems favored by diversified corporations cut too deeply into our ethical standards, then our choice is clear; to reduce these standards or call into question the whole trend toward diversification.

To dismiss social responsibility is to allow corporate behavior to drop to the lowest level, propped up only by external controls such as regulation and pressure campaigns. Solzhenitsyn, who has experienced the natural conclusion of unrestrained bureaucratization, warns us (in sharp contrast to Friedman) that "a society with no other scale but the legal one is not quite worthy of man. . . . A society which is based on the letter of the law and never reaches any higher is scarcely taking advantage of the high level of human possibilities" (1978:B1).

This is not to suggest that we must trust it completely. We certainly cannot trust it unconditionally by accepting the claim popular in some quarters that only business can solve the social ills of society. Business has no business using its resources without constraint in the social sphere—whether to support political candidates or to dictate implicitly through donations how nonprofit institutions should allocate their efforts. But where business is inherently involved, where its decisions have social consequences, that is where social responsibility has a role to play: where business creates externalities that cannot be measured and attributed to it (in other words, where regulation is ineffective); where regulation would work if only business would cooperate with it; where the corporation can fool its customers, or suppliers, or government through superior knowledge; where useful products can be marketed instead of wasteful or destructive ones. In other words, we have to realize that in many spheres we must trust it, or at least socialize it (and perhaps change it) so that we can trust it. Without responsible and ethical people in important places, our society is not worth very much.

"Ignore it" differs from the other positions on the horseshoe in that explicitly or implicitly it calls for no change in corporate behavior. It assumes that social needs are met in the course of pursuing economic goals. We include this position in our horseshoe because it is held by many influential people and also because its validity would preempt support for the other positions. We must, therefore, investigate it alongside the others.

It should be noted at the outset the "ignore it" is not the same position as "trust it." In the latter, to be good is the right thing to do; in the present case, "it pays to be good." The distinction is subtle but important, for now it is economics, not ethics, that elicits the desired behavior. One need not strive to be ethical; economic forces will ensure that social needs fall conveniently into place. Here we have moved one notch to the right on our horseshoe, into the realm where the economic goals dominate. . . .

"Ignore it" is sometimes referred to as "enlightened self-interest," although some of its proponents are more enlightened than others. Many a true believer in social responsibility has used the argument that it pays to be good to ward off the attacks from the right that corporations have no business pursuing social goals. Even Milton Friedman must admit that they have every right to do so if it pays them economically. The danger of such arguments, however—and a prime reason "ignore it" differs from "trust it"—is that they tend to support the status quo: corporations need not change their behavior because it already pays to be good.

Sometimes the case for "ignore it" is made in terms of corporations at large, that the whole business community will benefit from socially responsible behavior. Other times the case is made in terms of the individual corporation, that it will benefit directly from its own socially responsible actions. . . . Others make the case for "ignore it" in "social investment" terms, claiming that socially responsible behavior pays off in a better image for the firm, a more positive relationship with customers, and ultimately a healthier and more stable society in which to do business.

Then, there is what I like to call the "them" argument: "If we're not good, *they* will move in"—"they" being Ralph Nader, the government, whoever. In other words, "Be good or else." The trouble with this argument is that by reducing social responsibility to simply a political tool for sustaining managerial control of the corporation in the face of outside threats, it tends to encourage general pronouncements instead of concrete actions (unless of course, "they" actually deliver with pressure campaigns). . . .

The "ignore it" position rests on some shaky ground. It seems to encourage average behavior at best; and where the average does not seem to be good enough, it encourages the status quo. In fact, ironically, "ignore it" makes a strong case for "pressure it," since the whole argument collapses in the absence of pressure campaigns. Thus while many influential people take this position, we question whether in the realities of corporate behavior it can really stand alone.

Continuing around to the right, our next position drops all concern with social responsibility per se and argues, simply, "pay it to be good," or, from the corporation's point of view, "be good only where it pays." Here, the corporation does not actively pursue social goals at all, whether as ends in themselves or as means to economic ends. Rather, it undertakes socially desirable programs only when induced economically to do so—usually through government incentives. If society wishes to clean up urban blight, then let its government provide subsidies for corporations that renovate buildings; if pollution is the problem, then let corporations be rewarded for reducing it.

"Induce it" faces "regulate it" on the opposite side of the horseshoe for good reason. While one penalizes the corporation for what it does do, the other rewards it for doing what it might not otherwise do. Hence these two positions can be direct substitutes: pollution can be alleviated by introducing penalties for the damage done or by offering incentives for the improvements rendered.

Logic would, however, dictate a specific role for each of these positions. Where a corporation is doing society a specific, attributable harm—as in the case of pollution—then paying it to stop hardly seems to make a lot of sense. If society does not wish to outlaw the harmful behavior altogether, then surely it must charge those responsible for it—the corporation and, ultimately, its customers. Offering financial incentives to stop causing harm would be to invite a kind of blackmail—for example, encouraging corporations to pollute so as to get paid to stop. And every citizen would be charged for the harm done by only a few.

On the other hand, where social problems exist which cannot be attributed to specific corporations, yet require the skills of certain corporations for solution, then financial incentives clearly make sense (so long, of course, as solutions can be clearly defined and tied to tangible economic rewards). Here, and not under "trust it," is where the "only business can do it" argument belongs. When it is true that only business can do it (and business has not done it to us in the first place), then business should be encouraged to do it. . . .

"RESTORE IT"

Our last position on the horseshoe tends to be highly ideological, the first since "democratize it" to seek a fundamental change in the governance and the goals of the corporation. Like the proponents of "nationalize it," those of this position believe that managerial control is illegitimate and must be replaced by a more valid form of external control. The corporation should be restored to its former status, that is, returned to its "rightful" owners, the shareholders. The only way to ensure the relentless pursuit of economic goals—and that means the maximization of profit, free of the "subversive doctrine" of social responsibility—is to put control directly into the hands of those to whom profit means the most.

A few years ago this may have seemed to be an obsolete position. But thanks to its patron saint Milton Friedman . . . , it has recently come into prominence. Also, other forms of restoring it, including the "small is beautiful" theme, have also become popular in recent years.

Friedman has written,

In a free-enterprise, private-property system, a corporate executive is an employee of the owners of the business. He has direct responsibility to his employers. That responsibility is to conduct the business in accordance with their desires, which generally will

400

be to make as much money as possible while conforming to the basic rules of the society, both those embodied in law and those embodied in ethical custom. (1970:33)

Interestingly, what seems to drive Friedman is a belief that the shift over the course of this century from owner to manager control, with its concerns about social responsibility, represents an unstoppable skid around our horseshoe. In the opening chapter of his book *Capitalism and Freedom,* Friedman seems to accept only two possibilities—traditional capitalism and socialism as practiced in Eastern Europe. The absence of the former must inevitably lead to the latter:

> The preservation and expansion of freedom are today threatened from two directions. The one threat is obvious and clear. It is the external threat coming from the evil men in the Kremlin who promised to bury us. The other threat is far more subtle. It is the internal threat coming from men of good intentions and good will who wish to reform us. (1962:20)

The problem of who should control the corporation thus reduces to a war between two ideologies—in Friedman's terms, "subversive" socialism and "free" enterprise. In this world of black and white, there can be no middle ground, no moderate position between the black of "nationalize it" and the white of "restore it," none of the gray of "trust it." Either the owners will control the corporation of else the government will. Hence: " 'restore it' or else." Anchor the corporation on the right side of the horseshoe, Friedman seems to be telling us, the only place where "free" enterprise and "freedom" are safe.

All of this, in my view, rests on a series of assumptions—technical, economic, and political—which contain a number of fallacies. First is the fallacy of the technical assumption of shareholder control. Every trend in ownership during this century seems to refute the assumption that small shareholders are either willing or able to control the large, widely held corporation. The one place where free markets clearly still exist is in stock ownership, and that has served to detach ownership from control. When power is widely dispersed—among stockholders no less than workers or customers—those who share it tend to remain passive. It pays no one of them to invest the effort to exercise their power. Hence, even if serious shareholders did control the boards of widely held corporations (and one survey of all the directors of the *Fortune* 500 in 1977 found that only 1.6% of them represented significant shareholder interests, [Smith, 1978]), the question remains open as to whether they would actually try to control the management. (This is obviously not true of closely held corporations, but these—probably a decreasing minority of the *Fortune* 500—are "restored" in any event.)

The economic assumptions of free markets have been discussed at length in the literature. Whether there exists vibrant competition, unlimited entry, open information, consumer sovereignity, and labor mobility is debatable. Less debatable is the conclusion that the larger the corporation, the greater is its ability to interfere with these processes. The issues we are discussing center on the giant corporation. It is not Luigi's Body Shop that Ralph Nader is after, but General Motors, a corporation that employs more than half a million people and earns greater revenues than many national governments.

Those who laid the foundation for conventional economic theory—such as Adam Smith and Alfred Marshall—never dreamed of the massive amounts now spent for advertising campaigns, most of them designed as much for affect as for effect; of the waves of conglomeration that have combined all kinds of diverse businesses into single corporate entities; of chemical complexes that cost more than a billion dollars; and of the intimate relationships that now exist between giant corporations and government, as customer and partner not to mention subsidizer. The concept of arm's length relationships in such conditions is, at best, nostalgic. What happens to consumer sovereignty when Ford knows more about its gas tanks than do its customers? And what does labor mobility mean in the presence of an inflexible pension plan, or commitment to a special skill, or a one-factory town? It is an ironic twist of conventional economic theory that the worker is the one who typically stays put, thus rendering false the assumption of labor mobility, while the shareholder is the mobile one, thus spoiling the case for owner control.

The political assumptions are more ideological in nature, although usually implicit. These assumptions are that the corporation is essentially amoral, society's instrument for producing goods and services, and, more broadly, that a society is "free" and "democratic" so long as its governmental leaders are elected by universal suffrage and do not interfere with the legal activities of businessmen. But many people—a large majority of the general public, if polls are to be believed—seem to subscribe to one or more assumptions that contradict these "free enterprise" assumptions.

One assumption is that the large corporation is a social and political institution as much as an economic instrument. Economic activities, as noted previously, produce all kinds of social consequences. Jobs get created and rivers get polluted, cities get built and workers get injured. These social consequences cannot be factored out of corporate strategic decisions and assigned to government.

Another assumption is that society cannot achieve the necessary balance between social and economic needs so long as the private sector attends only to economic goals. Given the pervasiveness of business in society, the acceptance of Freidman's prescriptions would drive us toward a one-dimensional society—a society that is too utilitarian and too materialistic. Economic morality, as noted earlier, can amount to a social immorality.

Finally, the question is asked: Why the owners? In a democratic society, what justifies owner control of the corporation any more than worker control, or consumer control, or pluralistic control? Ours is not Adam Smith's society of small proprietors and shopkeepers. His butcher, brewer, and baker have become Iowa Beef Packers, Anheuser-Bush, and ITT Continental Baking. What was once a case for individual democracy now becomes a case for oligarchy. . . .

I see Friedman's form of "restore it" as a rather quaint position in a society of giant corporations, managed economies, and dispersed shareholders—a society in which the collective power of corporations is coming under increasing scrutiny and in which the distribution between economic and social goals is being readdressed.

Of course, there are other ways [than Friedman's] to "restore it." "Divest it" could return the corporation to the business or central theme it knows best, restoring the role of allocating funds between different businesses to capital markets instead of central headquarters. Also, boards could be restored to positions of influence by holding directors legally responsible for their actions and by making them more independent of managers (for example, by providing them with personal staffs and by precluding full-time managers from their ranks, especially the position of chairman). We might even wish to extend use of "reduce it" where possible, to decrease the size of those corporations that have grown excessively large on the basis of market or political power rather than economies of scale, and perhaps to eliminate certain forms of vertical integration. In many cases it may prove advantageous, economically as well as socially, to have the corporation trade with its suppliers and customers instead of being allowed to ingest them indiscriminately.[1]

I personally doubt that these proposals could be any more easily realized in today's society than those of Friedman, even though I believe them to be more desirable. "Restore it" is the nostalgic position on our horseshoe, a return to our fantasies of a glorious past. In this society of giant organizations, it flies in the face of powerful economic and political forces.

CONCLUSION: IF THE SHOE FITS...

I believe that today's corporation cannot ride on any one position any more than a horse can ride on part of a shoe. In other words, we need to treat the conceptual horseshoe as a portfolio of positions from which we can draw, depending on circumstances. Exclusive reliance on one position will lead to a narrow and dogmatic society, with an excess concentration of power . . . the use of a variety of positions can encourage the pluralism I believe most of us feel is necessary to sustain democracy. If the shoe fits, then let the corporation wear it.

I do not mean to imply that the eight positions do not represent fundamentally different values and, in some cases, ideologies as well. Clearly they do. But I also believe that anyone who makes an honest assessment of the realities of power in and around today's large corporations must conclude that a variety of positions have to be relied upon [even if they themselves might tilt to the left, right or center of our horseshoe]. . . .

I tilt to the left of center, as has no doubt been obvious in my comments to this point. Let me summarize my own prescriptions as follows, and in the process provide some basis for evaluating the relevant roles of each of the eight positions.

First "trust it," or at least "socialize it." Despite my suspicions about much of the rhetoric that passes for social responsibility and the discouraging evidence about the behavior of large contemporary organizations (not only corporations), I remain firmly convinced that without honest and responsible people in important places, we are in deep trouble. We need to trust it because, no matter how much we rely on the other positions, managers will always retain a great deal of power. And that power necessarily has social no less than economic consequences. The positions on the right side of our horseshoe ignore these social consequences while some of those on the left fail to recognize the difficulties of influencing these consequences in large, hierarchical organizations. Sitting between these two sets of positions, managers can use their discretion to satisfy or to subvert the wishes of the public. Ultimately, what managers do is determined by their sense of responsibility as individual members of society.

Although we must "trust it," we cannot *only* "trust it." As I have argued, there is an appropriate and limited place for social responsibility—essentially to get the corporation's own house in order and to encourage it to act responsibly in its own sphere of operations. Beyond that, social responsibility needs to be tempered by other positions around our horseshoe.

Then "pressure it," ceaselessly. As we have seen, too many forces interfere with social responsibility. The best antidote to these forces is the ad hoc pressure campaign, designed to pinpoint unethical behavior and raise social consciousness

---

[1] A number of these proposals would be worthwhile to pursue in the public and parapublic sectors as well, to divide up overgrown hospitals, school systems, social service agencies, and all kinds of government departments.

about issues. The existence of the "pressure it" position is what most clearly distinguishes the western from the eastern "democracies." Give me one Ralph Nader to all those banks of government accountants.

In fact, "pressure it" underlies the success of most of the other positions. Pressure campaigns have brought about necessary new regulations and have highlighted the case for corporate democracy. As we have seen, the "ignore it" position collapses without "pressure it". . . .

After that, try to "democratize it." A somewhat distant third in my portfolio is "democratize it," a position I view as radical only in terms of the current U.S. debate, not in terms of fundamental American values. Democracy matters most where it affects us directly—in the water we drink, the jobs we perform, the products we consume. How can we call our society democratic when many of its most powerful institutions are closed to governance from the outside and are run as hierarchies of authority from within?

As noted earlier, I have no illusions about having found the means to achieve corporate democracy. But I do know that Americans can be very resourceful when they decide to resolve a problem—and this is a problem that badly needs resolving. Somehow, ways must be found to open the corporation up to the formal influence of the constituencies most affected by it—employees, customers, neighbors, and so on—without weakening it as an economic institution. At stake is nothing less than the maintenance of basic freedoms in our society.

Then, only where specifically appropriate, "regulate it" and "induce it." Facing each other on the horseshoe are two positions that have useful if limited roles to play. Regulation is neither a panacea nor a menace. It belongs where the corporation can abuse the power it has and can be penalized for that abuse—notably where externalities can be identified with specific corporations. Financial inducements belong, not where a corporation has created a problem, but where it has the capability to solve a problem created by someone else.

Occasionally, selectively, "nationalize it" and "restore it," but not in Friedman's way. The extreme positions should be reserved for extreme problems. If "pressure it" is a scalpel and "regulate it" a cleaver, then "nationalize it" and "restore it" are guillotines.

Both these positions are implicitly proposed as alternatives to "democratize it." One offers public control, the other "shareholder democracy." The trouble is that control by everyone often turns out to be control by no one, while control by the owners—even if attainable—would remove the corporation even further from the influence of those most influenced by it.

Yet, as noted earlier, nationalization sometimes makes sense—when private enterprise cannot provide a necessary mission, at least in a sufficient or appropriate way, and when the activities of a corporation must be intricately tied in to government policy.

As for "restore it," I believe Friedman's particular proposals will aggrevate the problems of political control and social responsibility, strengthening oligarchical tendencies in society and further tilting what I see as the current imbalance between social and economic goals. In response to Friedman's choice between "subversive" socialism and "free" enterprise, I say "a pox on both your houses." Let us concentrate our efforts on the intermediate positions around the horseshoe. However, other forms of "restore it" are worth considering—to "divest it" where diversification has interfered with capital markets, competition, and economic efficiency; to "*dis*integrate it" vertically where a trading network is preferable to a managerial hierarchy; to strengthen its board so that directors can assess managers objectively; and to "reduce it" where size represents a power game rather than a means to provide better and more efficient service to the public. I stand with Friedman in wishing to see competitive markets strengthened; it is just that I believe his proposals lead in exactly the opposite direction.

Finally, above all, don't "ignore it." I leave one position out of my portfolio altogether, because it contradicts the others. The one thing we must not do is ignore the large, widely held corporation. It is too influential a force in our lives. Our challenge is to find ways to distribute the power in and around our large organizations so that they will remain responsive, vital, and effective.

THE NEW YORK TIMES COMPANY

Despite persistent rumors that he would soon step down as Publisher of *The New York Times* while remaining Chairman of the Board of The New York Times Company, in early 1990 Mr. Arthur Sulzberger, Sr. (nicknamed Punch) was still very much in control. Nonetheless, as Deputy Publisher, Arthur Sulzberger, Jr.'s name appeared with his father's on the masthead of the paper, and he was actively involved in all areas of the management of the newspaper itself. The Sulzbergers and their management team were considering how to position the company and the newspaper given the complex and rapid changes occurring in the publishing, broadcasting, and information worlds the company spanned.

A PRESTIGIOUS HISTORY

The New York Times newspaper had been published continuously since 1851. In 1896 it was purchased by Adolph Ochs and incorporated as The New York Times Company. From that time through 1990, a member of the Ochs family had headed *The Times*. Adolph Ochs was Publisher for 39 years. Arthur Hays Sulzberger, his son-in-law, succeeded him in 1935. And Sulzberger's son-in-law, Orville Dryfoos, became President and Publisher from 1961 until his untimely death shortly after a disastrous 1963 union strike against *The Times*. Punch Sulzberger, then only 37, took over the reins and accomplished some major restructurings at *The New York Times*. Throughout this extensive period, all Adolph Ochs' successors had subscribed to the classic statement of philosophy and objectives which he had penned.

Copyright © 1990 by James Brian Quinn. This case was written by Penny C. Paquette under the supervision of Professor Quinn.

The generous cooperation of The New York Times Company is gratefully acknowledged.

It will be my earnest aim that *The New York Times* give the news, all the news, in concise and attractive form, in language that is permissible in good society, and give it as early, if not earlier, than it can be learned through any other medium. To give the news impartially, without fear or favor, regardless of party, section or interest involved; to make the columns of *The New York Times* a forum for the consideration of all questions of public importance, and to that end to invite intelligent discussion from all phases of opinion.[1]

More succinct—but not essentially different—is the motto on the masthead of the paper today: "All the news that's fit to print." Shortly before Punch Sulzberger took over at *The Times, Esquire* wrote an article which expounded *The Times* basic philosophies.

There is no need for ambiguity about what fashions *The Times*. It forms the paper's good qualities, explains its deficiencies, and charts it future course . . . in a deeper and more complete sense than any other journal that has ever existed, *The Times* is a record of events, a <u>news</u> paper.

If stressing the news is good business as well as good journalism, it also implies something much larger. It supposes, for one thing, that to make the truth known is to ensure its eventual triumph . . . it is a faith that enthrones goodwill, and accepts the rationality of humans and their ability to control the environment. For solid comfort and the views of the mighty, it maintains a healthy respect. . . . From such concepts as race, class, status, and the psyche, and from such weapons as wit and sarcasm, it shrinks as from the plague.

That is the creed that makes *The Times* good and grey, and it is in the paper every day. . . . Ochs had been so wary of seeming to color the news with bipartisanship that at one point he thought of doing away with editorials entirely. . . . A cartoon is no part of *The Times* editorial page precisely because of the slant. It can't, as Sulzberger once pointed out, say 'On the other hand.' This 'square' approach probably achieved its worst results in the handling of cultural affairs. All the fruitful critical attitudes—from wry sophistication to zest for the news—appeared to be out of bounds for *Times* men. . . .

Still, if news emphasis has its limitations, it also harbors an agent of change. Never in one place, altering in focus, volume, substance, and meaning, now solemn, now hilarious, what happened yesterday presents to those who would report it a constant challenge.[2]

Despite its dynastic ownership (The Times Company shares had been publicly traded since 1968, but its Class B shares that could elect a majority of the directors were controlled by several Sulzberger family members), *The Times* had long allowed professionals to dominate its various news departments. To an extent not achieved by any other newspaper, *The New York Times* was "a reporter's paper." According to its Annual Reports the reportorial watchwords were "enterprise, completeness, objectivity, and clarity." Its tradition of leadership had included acting as "the newspaper of record," publishing entire state documents of major speeches of Presidents or key Administration figures, producing the entire text of such matters as the Warren Report on President Kennedy's Assassination, always reporting the entire new cabinet of a newly-formed country, and so on. But such thorough journalism had proved no bar to criticism. In a mid-1960s jibe—picked up and quoted by *Newsweek* and *Time*—one English journalist complained that "*The New York Times* shoveled every flake of information at its readers in the trust that they could be their own snowplows."

However, when Punch Sulzberger took over as Publisher, he began a series of steps to enliven the newspaper, to expand its coverage, to deal with the complex and unhappy union situation he had inherited, and to diversify The New York

Times Company into other areas compatible with the interests of *The New York Times*. With many of these efforts reaching maturity in 1990, Mr. Sulzberger had to consider what other hallmarks he would like to leave as his legacy as he shaped The New York Times Company and *The New York Times* newspaper for a rapidly changing future.

A Time of Change

Early on, Mr. Sulzberger had determined not to be held hostage by the labor unions of *The New York Times*. Motivated in large part by this objective, he embarked upon a diversification strategy making acquisitions outside of the New York area or in other businesses which were not dominated by the *The New York Times'* labor unions. In the succeeding 20 years, the company spent about a billion dollars on such acquisitions. It acquired 35 regional newspapers, numerous magazines, 5 TV stations, and a variety of other related businesses. (See Table 1.) But in 1987, 65% of its profits were from *The New York Times,* approximately what they had been in the early 1970s. Business in the New York area simply had grown as rapidly as the very extensive diversification program. As Mr. David Gorham, chief financial officer of The New York Times Company said, "We thought we'd move away from dependence on New York, but New York just ran away with us."

Overall, the company's acquisitions in small city newspapers and specialized magazines (like *Golf Digest, Tennis,* and *Family Circle*) had done very well. And in 1989, The New York Times Company had closed a more than $80 million acquisition of *McCall's* magazine to add to its "women's service" group of magazines. (See Table 2 for details.) In other fields, Mr. Gorham said the company had pulled out of the cable television business, feeling that "continued growth there was inhibited by the tremendous prices necessary to buy new cable networks." In 1990 The New York Times Company's five TV stations were not growing strongly because of the fragmentation created by VCRs, cable networks, and the drop-off in national TV advertising. And it only kept constant its equity position in two Canadian newsprint companies. These were held both as a vertical integration and for security of paper supplies.

By 1990, The New York Times' Regional Newspaper Group had 26 dailies (with average weekday circulations of a little more than 33,000) and 9 weeklies. In Florida it had five of the six fastest growing newspapers; and in other areas of the South, Southwest, and California, it had developed other strong freestanding operations. As Mr. Gorham said, "Many people try to buy a newspaper and pull a lot of cash out of it. Our primary concern is to build a permanent business. It costs you a lot of money to expand circulation at first, because there is a long lag between such increases and getting the advertising to go with it. Competing acquirers have often pulled back on circulation and upped their advertising rates to cover their acquisition costs. We've gone completely the opposite way—to build circulation first, then be in a position to charge more for advertising. For example, in Sarasota, Florida, we spent about $100 million for a paper with a circulation in the high 90,000s which was losing money in 1982. That paper now has a circulation of over 180,000 and is making very good profits. We invested a lot of money in new plants, revised the paper's format, and built a genuine advertising strategy. In California, we're doing the same thing. However, to date we have allowed each of our operations to be run quite autonomously. We haven't forced similar distribution systems, editorial styles, formats, or anything else on the individual papers.

"We have also viewed ourselves primarily as a U.S. company. We have talked a lot about circulating *The Times* in Europe. We do, of course, have a 1/3 interest in the *International Herald Tribune (IHT)* which gives us a view into business in

TABLE 1   The New York Times Company
Acquisitions and Divestitures 1966–1989

NAME	TYPE OF BUSINESS	ACQUIRED	DIVESTED
Teaching Resources	Education	12/12/66	11/1/83
Microfilming Corporation of America	Microfilm	6/13/67	4/5/83
Arno Press (51%)	Books	3/5/68	6/30/82
Quadrangle Press	Books	2/25/69	11/30/84
Golf Digest	Magazine	2/28/69	
Malbaie (35%)	Newsprint	1/7/70	
Golf World (UK)	Magazine	2/19/70	
Educational Enrichment Materials	Filmstrips	6/30/70	1/17/83
Filmfax Productions	Filmstrips	7/10/70	1/17/83
Cowles:			
Cambridge	Books	4/30/71	8/29/80
Dental Survey	Magazine	4/30/71	1/11/77
Family Circle:			
United States	Magazine	4/30/71	
Great Britain	Magazine	4/30/71	7/11/72
Gainesville Sun (FL)	Newspaper	4/30/71	
Lakeland Ledger (FL)	Newspaper	4/30/71	
Lancet	Magazine	4/30/71	1/11/77
Modern Medicine:			
United States	Magazine	4/30/71	1/11/77
Australia	Magazine	4/30/71	4/10/81
Great Britain	Magazine	4/30/71	7/1/75
New Zealand	Magazine	4/30/71	4/10/81
Medimail	Magazine	4/30/71	1/11/77
Ocala Star Banner (FL)	Newspaper	4/30/71	
WREG-TV (Memphis)	Television	10/15/71	
Arno Press (49%)	Books	9/17/71	6/30/82
Leesburg Commercial (FL)	Newspaper	12/1/71	
Palatka Daily News (FL)	Newspaper	12/1/71	
Avon Park Sun (FL)	Newspaper	1/17/72	
Fernandina Beach Newsleader (FL)	Newspaper	1/17/72	
Lake City Reporter (FL)	Newspaper	1/17/72	
Sebring News (FL)	Newspaper	1/17/72	
Tennis	Magazine	10/30/72	
Marco Island Eagle (FL)	Newspaper	1/12/73	
Lexington Dispatch (NC)	Newspaper	11/1/73	
Hendersonville Times-News (NC)	Newspaper	5/31/74	
Metromedia Music Catalog	Music Publisher	12/28/74	2/7/77
Wilmington Star-News (NC)	Newspaper	1/17/75	
HFM Magazine	Magazine	4/14/75	11/1/77
Electronic Publishing Corp.	Education	6/28/78	5/16/79
Learning Concepts	Education	6/30/78	5/16/79
Zephyrhills News (FL)	Newspaper	12/15/78	1/31/84
KFSM (Ft. Smith, AR)	Television	10/1/79	
Madison Paper (40%)	Paper Mill	2/12/80	
US	Magazine	*	3/6/80
Anna Maria Islander (FL)	Newspaper	4/25/80	
WHNT-TV (Huntsville, AL)	Television	5/13/80	
Houma Courier (LA)	Newspaper	12/1/80	
Thibodaux Daily Comet (LA)	Newspaper	12/1/80	
Cable Systems, Inc. (Cherry Hill, NJ)	Cable TV	3/2/81	8/15/89

* Start-ups

TABLE 1 (continued)

NAME	TYPE OF BUSINESS	ACQUIRED	DIVESTED
Australia Family Circle	Magazine	*	4/10/81
Sarasota Herald Tribune (FL)	Newspaper	11/30/82	
Worrell Newspapers			
Florence Times Daily (AL)	Newspaper	12/3/82	
Opelousas Daily World (LA)	Newspaper	12/3/82	
Corinth Daily Corinthian (MS)	Newspaper	12/3/82	
Lenoir News-Topic (NC)	Newspaper	12/3/82	
Harlan Daily Enterprise (KY)	Newspaper	12/3/82	
Middlesboro Daily News (KY)	Newspaper	12/3/82	
Dyersburg State Gazette (TN)	Newspaper	12/3/82	
Madisonville Messenger (KY)	Newspaper	12/3/82	
Booneville Banner-Independent (MS)	Newspaper	12/3/82	
Claiborne Progress (TN)	Newspaper	12/3/82	
York County Coast Star (ME)	Newspaper	12/3/82	
Information Bank License	Elec Archive	*	2/3/83
Cruising World	Magazine	7/6/84	
Carney Point (NJ) Cable	Cable TV	10/15/84	8/15/89
Public Welfare:			
Gadsden Times (AL)	Newspaper	4/18/85	
Spartanburg Herald-Journal (SC)	Newspaper	4/18/85	
Tuscaloosa News (AL)	Newspaper	4/18/85	
Santa Rose Press-Democrat (CA)	Newspaper	4/30/85	
Santa Barbara News Press (CA)	Newspaper	6/21/85	
WQAD-TV (Moline, IL)	Television	10/3/85	
WNEP-TV (Scranton, PA)	Television	12/30/85	
Child	Magazine	5/15/87	
Gwinnett:			
Gwinnett Daily News (GA)	Newspaper	7/21/87	
Forsyth News (GA)	Newspaper	7/21/87	
Winder News (GA)	Newspaper	7/21/87	
Sailing World	Magazine	8/31/88	
Golf World	Magazine	12/29/88	
McCalls	Magazine	7/27/89	

* Start-ups

Europe. Although the *International Herald Tribune* is the only major profitable newspaper in Paris, there are many impediments for a newspaper company expanding in the international marketplace. For example, Canada has multiple laws against foreign press ownership, it's virtually impossible to do anything in Japan, and it is very difficult to enter most other areas. We currently print the *IHT* in Japan, Singapore, and Hong Kong as well as Europe and the U.S.[3] But many of the Asian markets are dominated by British newspapers like the *London Times* and *Financial Times*. In most foreign marketplaces, the newspapers make money on circulation, not advertising. This makes for a totally different business than the one we are used to." Investors and publishers indicated that while there is a global market for information, a newspaper is largely restricted by its place of origin.[4]

Although The New York Times Company had attempted a number of business ventures in related media areas, like videotext, an "information bank" (with extracts of *The New York Times* on line), and microfilming, it had sold off most of these ventures as money losers or unpromising. Nevertheless, as Mr. Gorham said, "We are still experimenting at various frontiers, seeing if we can find some way to

TABLE 2 The New York Times Magazine Group: Competitive Data

| | AVERAGE PAID SUBSCRIPTION (000) | | | ADVERTISING | | | | COMMENTS |
| | | | | NO. OF PAGES | | REVENUES ($MILLIONS) | | |
	1980	1985	1989	1980	1988	1980	1988	
Women's service magazines								
Family Circle	7,443	6,681	5,330	1,592	1,856	90.4	134.4	Acquired in 1971; 3/4 single copy
McCall's	6,237	6,272	5,120	1,228	1,035	64.0	62.6	Acquired in 1989; 85% subscript.
Good Housekeeping	5,215	5,180	5,134	2,006	1,621	90.2	129.3	Owned by Meredith Corp.
Redbook	4,294	4,149	3,904	1,368	1,213	51.0	68.6	Owned by Meredith Corp.
Ladies Home Journal	5,502	5,138	5,078	1,220	1,366	52.7	83.8	Owned by Hearst
Better Homes & Gardens	8,055	8,042	8,016	1,562	1,469	96.1	152.8	Owned by Hearst
Woman's Day	7,667	6,367	4,543	1,614	1,686	96.6	115.6	
First For Women	—	—	3,510	—	n/a	—	n/a	Owned by H. Bauer which also publishes Woman's World
Parenting magazines								
Child	—	—	335	—	n/a	—	n/a	
Parenting	—	—	489	n/a	n/a	n/a	n/a	Acquired in 1987; mainly subscript.
Parents	1,503	1,718	1,753	n/a	1,431	n/a	53.1	
Shelter magazines								
Decorating								
Remodeling	—	—	527	—	n/a	—	n/a	
Home	—	699	925	n/a	729	n/a	16.3	Acquired in 1986; 50% subscript.
Country	—	758	963	n/a	362	n/a	11.0	
Metropolitan Home	825	718	709	n/a	1,061	n/a	28.9	
1,001 Home Ideas	1,106	1,537	1,603	n/a	683	n/a	15.6	
House Beautiful	900	840	940	n/a	856	n/a	26.1	

TABLE 2 (continued)

	AVERAGE PAID SUBSCRIPTION (000)			ADVERTISING				COMMENTS
				NO. OF PAGES		REVENUES ($MILLIONS)		
	1980	1985	1989	1980	1988	1980	1988	
Golf magazines								
Golf Digest	1,011	1,231	1,364	822	1,266	15.1	55.3	Acquired in 1969 with circ. of 350k; almost exclusively subscription
Golf World	—	86	112	—	n/a	—	n/a	Acquired in 1989; subscription only
Golf	732	804	1,019	768	970	9.9	27.1	
Golf Illustrated	—	—	451	n/a	394	n/a	2.7	
Tennis magazines								
Tennis	479	507	603	787	918	7.1	16.7	Acquired in 1972 with circ. of 70k; mainly subscription
World Tennis	426	362	533	575	567	5.4	8.4	
Ski magazines								
Snow Country	—	—	225	n/a	n/a	n/a	n/a	Started up in 1988; 50% subscript.
Ski	419	420	465	n/a	993	n/a	17.5	
Skiing	434	440	447	n/a	868	n/a	17.7	
Powder	—	—	147	n/a	n/a	n/a	n/a	
Sailing magazines								
Cruising World	99	117	135	n/a	n/a	n/a	n/a	Acquired in 1984; 2/3 subscript.
Sailing World	37	46	58	n/a	n/a	n/a	n/a	Acquired in 1988; 2/3 subscript.
Sail	180	170	165	n/a	n/a	n/a	n/a	
Yachting	142	143	133	n/a	1,712	n/a	10.1	

Note: Publications in Bold face type are part of The New York Times Magazine Group.

Sources: Corporate records; "Leading National Advertisers," Publishers Information Bureau, Inc.; "1980 Magazine Service Supplement," Publishers Information Bureau and Leading National Advertisers, Inc.

expand beyond what we are now doing. We know there will be fascinating new opportunities out there for us. While we are trying to approach this creatively, there are certain inherent conflicts between our primary business of selling hard copy information to mass markets and making that information instantly available in an electronic format."

A Technology Revolution

During Mr. Sulzberger's era, the technology of news collection and delivery had radically changed. Punch Sulzberger had championed many changes for *The New York Times*, which had aggressively applied available technology in the newspaper field. And, as one of the largest combined daily and Sunday newspaper publishers, *The New York Times* had often had to push the limits of scale and complexity of newspaper publishing technologies.

When Mr. Sulzberger assumed office, news was assembled by reporters in the field taking hand notes, telephoning these to the head office, or later transcribing their notes directly on typewriters. All editing was done on paper using pencils. International communications had to be accomplished by telegraph or often unreliable telephone lines. Changing copy or checking back with the field was extraordinarily costly and time consuming. Graphics were an underdeveloped resource, and a color reproduction—which did not exist at *The New York Times*—was very cumbersome and inaccurate. The type for newspapers was laboriously put in place by large typewriter-like (linotype) machines which selected individual letters and symbols in the form of brass molds from huge racks, spaced the letters mechanically, and then held the molds together to produce lines (slugs) cast from molten lead, columns of which became the masters for producing each page. At the end of each press run, these lead masters had to be melted down to form new lead slugs so the process could be repeated. The skills of the linotype operators were central to the production of a newspaper, and the typesetters' union had become extraordinarily strong.

Computer and communication technologies were to change much of this. News could be assembled and typed on portable computers in the field, transmitted instantly by satellite to the central news room, editors could query field reporters directly for clarifications or corrections, layouts could be previewed on computer screens, and entire pages of text (in intended format) could be preset and communicated instantly to the press room by electronics. Perhaps the single most important technological change of recent decades was the shift from cold type to the computer. This became a burden on the news room in one sense, because reporters and editors suddenly became their own printers. It was a blessing in another sense; because it gave the news room much more control over all aspects of the final product. Yet, as one senior editor said, "As a writer myself I feel that writing on a computer is a liberating experience. It allows a more fluid and experimental style. It also allows more vigorous and experimental editing, because you can fix it, cancel it, and try it many other ways until you are happy. Many tasks have been simplified, like headline writing. The computer quickly tells us whether the headline will fit and how; in the past we used to sit there and actually count the widths of individual letters."

Perhaps the most important editorial movement was from what *The New York Times* referred to as "the front line," copy editing grammar, spelling, and forms of writing (etc.) to what it called the "back field." This was the appraisal group worrying about whether the story was right, was it fair, did it cover the subject the way *The Times* wanted to cover a story, was perhaps the real meaning of the story too far down in the copy, did the overall sequence need to be reorganized or reworked in light of developing space constraints. Increasingly, *The Times'* editors were doing these latter kinds of tasks. In part, this was because much of the news *The Times* covered was just more complicated. It was reporting on science and economics at a very high level, in a way that most reporters a generation ago could not have handled. Some editors felt that the more educated and complex the society and the story, the greater the demand for the kind of editorial appraisal and interpretation its audience expected of *The New York Times.*

But there were an increasing number of other important choices as well, such as when to use graphics instead of text or how to report stories with statistics in a much more vivid form than words allowed. In the past, it was rare if there were one or two graphs in the entire paper, and even then the Dow Jones stock market index was likely to be one of them. By the late 1980s virtually every other page had some kind of graphics element or artwork other than photographs. *The Times* was building up a large statistical department capable of presenting concepts in graphic form.

In addition, there was a whole new range of photographic technologies which allowed *The Times* a great deal more flexibility in the presentation of pictures. Once a photograph was reduced to digital components, it could be cropped, or enhanced, very quickly. But the technology had raised a host of new problems. It became easy to vary a background—say to put Gorbachev in China (when he really was in Thailand) and not only remove the spot on his head but to give him a set of hair, or anything else one desired. Photographs used to be documentation. Now a news group had to be very careful about each photo, its authenticity, and how to protect the integrity of the medium.

Each newspaper would have liked for all of its reporters and editors to be able to plug into each others' computers throughout the system. But, as in many other companies, they had found that even close colleagues might not be quite as respectful of privacy in a computer system as they had generally been in the file drawers of the past. Under the time pressures of a rapidly developing story being edited in real time, some difficult problems could easily arise, and new rules and practices needed to evolve.

By 1990 new technologies provided newspapers with the ability to "close" certain sections of the paper nearer and nearer to the printing deadlines. Pagination systems made it possible to change and test format and copy until the final electronic transmission over to the presses. Such systems also changed the way the make-up department and art directors interacted with the editorial staff. Introducing color into the production process would add other complexities since one could not print color back to back on the same sheet and the presence of color on one page changed the way the reader reacted to the opposing black and white page. *The New York Times* was in the process of deciding how and where to introduce color and how to handle the resulting needs for compromises among the editorial, advertising, and production people in terms of how and where they could place color elements.

At the production level press speeds had increased remarkably and color registration could be as accurate as newsprint paper itself allowed. Although the company and various newspaper unions (especially in the printing area) had had difficult negotiations over each major technological advance, *The New York Times* had slowly been able to make significant modernization changes throughout the composing and press room areas. But in 1990 the full implementation of many technologies in these and other areas of *The New York Times* was still underway. The most important program, in sheer scale, was the building of a new $450 million automated plant in Edison, New Jersey. At the Edison plant, newsprint would come in on rail cars from the paper mills in Canada in which The New York Times Company held minority interests. The plant was so large (23 acres) that 12 rail cars could be under its roof at a single time. Large robots would pluck rolls of newsprint off the cars and place them in a computer controlled warehouse. When the presses indicated that they needed newsprint, a signal would tell another robot to pluck the roll off the shelf, bring it into position and put it on the correct press. The Edison plant would produce all sections of the newspaper which could be printed in advance of the publication day. Instead of folding these and stacking them in "pre-printed sections," the Edison plant would collect them on huge wheels (some $9\frac{1}{2}$ feet in diameter) which other robots would then put into storage.

When the time came to insert the section into a particular day's newspaper, a computer system would automatically fetch the right roll, position it for the inserting machines, run the newspaper in which that specialized section fit, cut and fold the section in the right places, insert it in the newspaper, stack the collated papers on pallets, wrap the pallets with plastic, and position the pallets for forklifts to put directly on designated trucks. The Edison plant would be by far the largest such automated printing facility in the world. The New York Times Company had tested this concept at its Santa Rosa, California facility before beginning construction of the Edison plant. If Edison proved successful, The Times might build another plant inside the New York metropolitan area to serve its New York readers. However, like all such major technology introductions, the plant posed significant risks, opportunities, and challenges to management.

Mr. Lance Primis, President of The New York Times, noted, "Some of the more interesting questions about the new technologies concern amortizing the $450 million Edison investment much of which is in the press rooms. Others involve the stages which follow the press operations. Automation has made our press rooms relatively smaller than in the past, but the individual presses are getting larger as we begin to run color. The presses themselves are much faster. But the flexibility of the product is limited by the capacity to capture and store different versions of the paper in the mailroom, get these on the right trucks, and get the trucks to their distribution points. The complexities of doing this with existing technology are so great that today I still hire from a 'shape up' most nights, just like at the docks. We hope that the new technology will help us stabilize the workforce.

"Today, it is hard to get the commitment to performance and productivity that you could get with a more stabilized workforce. The new equipment and associated mailroom systems also need substantially fewer people for the same size press run. We have been able to introduce substantial incentives in other areas of the business like marketing, circulation, and advertising. I would like to see us have similar structures in production. The only incentive plans we have today are based essentially on revenues of the company; we don't have many based on savings to the company. Cost reduction is a big issue for us, not just in the production area, but across the entire company."

Gathering and Reporting the News

Mr. Sulzberger often said, "The heart of The New York Times is its news department" and, as testimony to that fact, the corridors to the executive dining room were lined with photographs of 61 Pulitzer Prize winning reporters from The New York Times. In 1990, The New York Times with 425 domestic and 35 foreign reporters, photographers, and artists had more reporters in the field than any other single newspaper. It was also tied into most of the major wire services, although it competed with these services as a news gathering entity itself.

But technology had revolutionized the nature and processes of gathering and disseminating the news. Television news teams could be at any crisis spot in a very short time. Using remote transmission techniques, they could then present the news in real time, and even shape the way in which the news itself developed—as they often did in hostage situations. Sporting events and the visible elements of crises, like the 1989 San Francisco earthquake, could be in millions of homes instantaneously. Radio and cable-news services, along with business wire-news services, intensified the urgency and availability of the news and the information bases that supported it. Computer and videotape capabilities enabled homeowners to store such news (for as long as they wished) before consumption or to select and analyze it in entirely new ways.

Newspaper reporting had changed remarkably rapidly. As Warren Hoge, Assistant Managing Editor of *The New York Times,* noted, "When I was on the Foreign Desk less than three years ago, I had to place telephone calls five or six hours ahead of time to reach the Soviet Union or other remote spots. Now instantaneous hard copy communications through fax machines and electronics are possible virtually anywhere. The reporter's job has changed enormously and most reporting jobs are highly specialized. Now we don't just look for a good writer willing to do anything to track down a story. We look for a Washington communications and legal reporter, a science and health writer, a consumer affairs reporter, a stock market or management writer, an advertising copy writer, a food specialist, a consumer-travel reporter, or an aviation writer.

"The recruiting you have to do to fill those kinds of holes is very different than just going out and trying to find the ten best reporters and writers in the world. There are now many doctors, lawyers, architects, and engineers in news rooms. The study of journalism alone is not enough. You have to understand a specialty in depth. Managing such a group is a very different task from managing a group of journalists, who in the past shared very similar educational backgrounds and experiences." The whole organization was concerned with standards for news presentation and the tone of the language it used. *The Times'* philosophy was expressed by one of the senior editors this way: "We try to maintain a slow evolution in style, control it, but make it hospitable to change. There are stylistic themes we adhere to as noble tradition, and these are important to *The Times.* We have the well known *New York Times Style Book,* which details our approach, but this is only reprinted every 10–15 years. How we can best handle the evolving nature of acceptable style is a continuing dilemma. We wage a constant battle to keep out opinion while allowing legitimate interpretation to occur. Just how to do this is very tricky."

By far the largest part of the mechanisms and rules by which *The New York Times* operated were unwritten and inherited, not only concerning what was a fair story, but how a reporter could use or not use an anonymous quote, the right of an individual to reply to an attack in a news article, and so on. There were thousands of such rules which were almost taken for granted at *The Times.* It was doubtful that any single person could write them down cohesively. And while *The Times* had documented as many of its rules for style as possible, these tended to be fluid; the actual style of writing and editing had to be personal. As one respected senior editor said, "*The Times* standards for responsible and effective presentation of the news evolves case by case, day by day."

The reporting, editorial, and layout choices were further complicated by concerns like the following. How would the timing of a *Times* story relative to its electronic and print competitors affect how it reported a particular story? What could make one assault case deserve page 1 coverage while most were placed back in local news? How could the viewpoints of *The Times* very strong Washington bureau be blended appropriately with those of other knowledgeable reporters, looking at the same national issue from different vantage points? Given the capacity to cover a story with so many more data and interested viewpoints, how could one define the desired coverage for a particular story? Setting up mechanisms to constantly monitor, update, and communicate about such choices within the organization had always been a central issue in the editorial control of the newspaper, but such efforts were made both simpler and more complex by new technologies. The phasing of "closing" times for the various sections of the paper and the sequencing of decisions required to make up an issue of any newspaper was extraordinarily complex, but that of *The New York Times* was even further complicated by the paper's size and its commitment to organize the news effectively for its readers. In the past, the newsroom had used a carefully negotiated and flexible schedule of closings for various aspects of the newspaper every few minutes from 5 P.M. to about 9 P.M. Efforts to use the instantaneous aspects of new technologies, including pagination and color, could necessitate far-reaching changes in the structure and processes of *The New York Times* news organization.

Meeting the New Competition

Along with all these changes came a number of important questions. If the reporter was to be the expert in the field, what would be the function of *The New York Times* editors? How could *The Times* obtain a consistent editorial philosophy among these many fragmented specialties? How could *The Times* position itself against the large number of specialist magazines, papers, and data bases which were appearing? No longer could *The New York Times* consider only the *Washington Post* or *Los Angeles Times* as its prime competitors. It had to position against many other high quality and specialized magazines (for example, in medicine, against *The New England Journal of Medicine, The Journal of the American Medical Association, Science Magazine,* and *Doctor's World*) which were the original sources of medical information as well as against the numerous public and private health magazines which had arisen to service specialized niches. As Mr. Hoge said, "A professional section like our law page obviously has to be sophisticated enough to appeal to well-educated lawyers, yet we must simultaneously try to make this field available and fascinating to people who are not lawyers. The university "law reviews" or Steven Brill's magazine, *The American Lawyer,* don't have to do that. You can imagine how difficult it is to define the role of our business sections against the *Wall Street Journal* and all the other excellent business publications there now are. We are trying to redefine our organizations and management structures now to do this." (See *The New York Times* news organization chart on page 425.)

Yet, while creating its own distinctiveness, *The Times* news department also had to learn to contain its costs. At one time, *The New York Times* had consciously put many more reporters on a major story than its competitors (especially in the New York area). With so many specialties to cover, this was no longer possible. As Mr. Hoge said, "In some respects, our reporting position is reversed. Our major competitors can often put in 2–3 times as much reporting time as we can on a particular specialty story. Trying to position our news and control its cost in this environment is a real problem."

CHANGING MARKETS

Positioning both The New York Times Company and *The New York Times* newspaper was made even more complex by the shifting nature of their markets. As Mr. Gordon Medenica, Vice President of Corporate Planning said, "We are basically in two different businesses: (1) gathering and packaging information, and (2) advertising. But every one of our information businesses is disproportionately dependent on advertising for its revenue. This is a major concern because of what's happening in the advertising field. For example, in an advertiser's budget the traditional ratios between media and promotion have flipped from 60/40% ten years ago to 40/60% today, with many more dollars being put into promotion, rather than advertising. Advertisers are consistently looking for better efficiencies, better targeting, and a closer link between their advertising budgets and the actual selling of products.

"For example, direct mail has become a huge business. Also, some entire magazines are given away to their readers, financed solely by their advertising revenues. There is a company named Whittle Communications which has a product that has grown from launch to $80 million in no time at all, based on this concept. They do a series of "mini-magazines" called "special reports" targeted especially for particular doctors' offices, like OB-GYN. The magazines go into doctors' waiting rooms for those people who are captive there for a half hour. Whittle is also

418

doing a special television broadcast format for high schools that contains 2 minutes of advertising in a 12 minute morning news show. There are a myriad of these specialist publications serving almost any need you can think of. While it is not clear if these products have long-term viability, they are certainly fragmenting advertising budgets today."

Advertising Competition

While *The New York Times* defined its major competition for newspaper advertising to be the very strong suburban newspapers around New York City, there were also 54 radio stations, a large number of TV signals off the air, over 50 cable stations, plus numerous demographic editions and regional editions of magazines available in the area. There were also videotext and home shopping experiments, but these had not yet affected *The New York Times* seriously in the advertising realm. In terms of readership, *The New York Times* enjoyed an enormous loyalty among influential, high income, intellectually curious people split roughly evenly between male and female readership. *The New York Times* readership profile was very attractive to advertisers. *The Times* considered anyone who met two out of three demographic criteria (income, professional status, and education) to be part of its target audience (see Table 3).

Mr. Primis commented, "Advertisers are asking us to do more for them within the local market. They are less interested in the potential expansion of this market than they are in penetration or coverage of the market. Penetration is the key word. Because of the density of our market, a lot of competitors are finding niched opportunities right underneath our coattails. We're too big to get small. Since it isn't easy for us to get smaller, the first challenge is how do we find ways of adding new readership inside this relatively mature market. Can we become important to people's lives nationally or regionally in ways which will attract new advertising revenues. I think the new technologies allow us some significant opportunities. An interesting question is whether our target audiences are really quite different in other markets than New York City. We need to think about this issue both as *The New York Times* newspaper and as The New York Times Company. There are some inherent conflicts of interest between *The New York Times* newspaper produced for the New York market, our regional and national editions, and the newspapers produced by our local newspaper subsidiaries."

Mr. Erich Linker, Executive Vice President of Advertising noted, "Of the top 20 newspapers in the country, approximately 5 of them are here in the New York market from a standpoint of advertising and lineage, including *Newsday, The Bergen Record, The Star Ledger,* and *Staten Island Advance* (see Table 4). We have very strong newspapers within the 27 county area in which we compete here. But in addition our strategy is keyed to building market share and advertising revenues in three different markets: Movie Show and Automotive National Advertising, the New York market, and the Northeast. National advertisers, like liquor producers, or technology companies are important categories. Local advertising comes largely from department stores, retail specialty stores, automotive dealers, help wanted, and real estate ads. Regional advertisers include financial institutions, retail chains, food chains, and some entertainment and large-scale retailer advertising." To capture special interests in depth, *The New York Times* published 70 complete magazines a year inside the newspaper alone—including its weekly Sunday magazine and 20 life style special interest magazines on Fashion, Entertaining, Health & Fitness, Travel, Home Design, and Business. Despite its regional and subject segmentation, two important trends were severely affecting *The New York Times'* advertising revenues. First, total advertising as a percentage of major companies' budgets was dropping. This had occurred largely because of the merger of multiple smaller companies into larger single corporations and the general shift from advertising to promotion. Second, while it continued to grow in absolute terms, newspaper advertising as a percentage of the total amount spent on advertising was declining steadily (see Table 5).

Mr. Primis continued, "What we have done is offer a number of choices for advertisers to be able to reach our audience selectively or en masse. Advertisers who find that their response comes from being in a certain location, or in a certain part of the paper are able to select those spots to the maximum extent possible. For example, in the business section there are opportunities for brokers and investment bankers in particular locations and for corporate advertisers in others. Similarly, we can offer special positions in the theme sections or specialized magazines we distribute with the newspaper from time to time. In addition, we have our regional (California) editions, and the developing national edition.

"In some areas, the advertising agencies can write and edit their copy right into our computers. In the film or amusement area, ADSAT provides a computerized hook-up which beams satellite copy to over 100 newspapers. All of these things give advertisers closer-to-closing-time opportunities to send in copy where fast-breaking product developments are important. Such immediacy is one of the strong viable products of a newspaper. But you can imagine the problems this can create for us in the make-up area. In fact, *The New York Times* newspaper may be the most complex single advertising institution in the world. Just our *New York Times Magazine* does over 4000 pages of advertising a year. Coordinating the strategies among all our different audience and advertising targets is one of the most interesting management problems we have. We have in total some 74 business areas in which we work, and each requires a quantitative and qualitative strategy. With the new plant in Edison we are looking at the possibility of even more flexibility and segmentation.

"One of these is the possibility of freestanding inserts. This is an $800 million business that is growing rapidly. Our home delivery area—approximately 500,000 subscribers—gives us an opportunity to do some interesting demographic segmentation. Some of the strongest advertising trends are toward personalized marketing, sales promotion, point of purchase displays, sweepstakes, cross-tie promotions, and multiple media usage—where advertisements in one medium are linked and referenced to other media presentations that are in electronic or printed media. We see all of this offering us enormous new advertising markets, if we can develop the right types of flexibilities in our production, mail room, and distribution capabilities."

To meet its competition, *The New York Times* was available to advertisers in a variety of forms. Its primary product was a "full run" offering to the Northeast in four sections—with a "theme section" every day, in addition to a business section and two main news sections, one of which began with a "metropolitan format." The theme section on Monday was sports, Tuesday science, Wednesday living, Thursday home, and Friday weekend. Each had a highly targeted editorial product. Within those sections, *The New York Times* could offer zones for specific advertisers in New Jersey, Westchester County, Long Island, Connecticut, Brooklyn, or Manhattan. In addition, advertisers could select a national edition projected at over 200,000 circulation or a California edition with 60,000 circulation.

In addition to the above, *The New York Times* Sunday edition was a separate mammoth production in itself. Readers received three to ten pounds of material every Sunday. The Sunday edition also had numerous special sections and its own Sunday *Magazine* which featured longer articles by well-known authors. Certain sections or pages of the Sunday *Times* were so prestigious that there was a competition by individual advertisers for special positions within the Sunday *Times'* various news sections. Entire sections, like those on real estate, could have a dominantly advertising content. All this made the packaging, formatting, and closing of the newspaper very complicated. One had to coordinate the unpredictability of late-breaking news, sudden changes in advertising copy for special sales or entertainment events, and the general unpredictability of classified and real estate advertising, which might vary enormously on any given day because of outside events, expected weather patterns, holidays, and so on.

Although national campaigns were planned long in advance, local advertisers liked to be able to place their ads as late as possible. Between 44-47% of the *Times* advertising revenue was from classified ads, many of which—oddly enough—were placed by some 1,000 advertising agencies. A major agency might place upward of 1,500 ads per week. On a peak weekend in the summer, there might be over 40 solid pages of help wanted ads. Although *The New York Times* had developed a number of rules and procedures for effectively allocating advertising and news space, it was constantly looking for new ways to make more effective use of the flexibilities new technologies offered.

Niche Competition

Within this complex structure, each of the sections had to compete against its own special subset of "niche players." For example, *The New York Times Book Review* section had its own very special marketplace, as did the sports section, the magazine section, the weekly news review section, the travel section, and so on. Within each of these, the advertising itself was becoming a major portion of the content information carried. But, as discussed above, *The New York Times* was fighting some strong negative trends in each area. For example, coupons, redemptions and point of sale promotions were growing at the expense of advertising. Such promotions were more efficiently distributed directly to households or retailers rather than through newspapers. In addition, cable TV, telemarketing, and other electronic techniques had created entirely new marketing modes. Using a home computer and a "900" number one could interactively obtain information on stocks, entertainment, rental cars, restaurants, etc.

Although there had been much discussion of potentially integrating its various media into a single corporate strategy, *The New York Times* had maintained its individual newspapers, magazines, and stations as independent businesses. In late 1989 the Time-Warner merger was much touted as creating a new form of "strongly integrated communications and media company." Rupert Murdoch had created a worldwide network of newspapers linked together by a "sky satellite" system and was moving into other media on a global basis. And others were looking at similar possibilities to exploit the new information and communications technologies.

What Next for *The New York Times?*

These various trends were expected to continue and to interact increasingly over the next decade, making it very difficult to position *The New York Times* for the future. Yet as Punch Sulzberger said, "We are in the process of building an enormous state-of-the-art production facility so, hopefully, there won't be too many new technology changes in the next five years. Right now, our task is to apply the technology that we have, not the technology that may be on the drawing boards. Besides printing and distribution technology, we must introduce news and advertising technology in the areas of pagination and the movement of copy. If we can accomplish this, I will be satisfied, for I do not see any other dramatic new devices or technologies that will impact too heavily over the next five years or so.

"Many people have predicted the demise of the American newspaper. I disagree. I do not see the news floating into the home each day in some mysterious way for a long time to come. Nevertheless, I think our business is going to change in many important ways. Of course, if you could tell me where the U.S. education system is going, I could make some better predictions. The decline in literacy, and reading skills in general, has me concerned as a citizen. But, as far as The New York Times Company is concerned, I believe the sophisticated, influential, upscale marketplace we serve will always contain plenty of readers. Our biggest problem will remain competition for their time. They are bombarded from so many different quarters that we must work to capture and maintain their interest. But we will not lower our sights to achieve this and are going to keep aiming for the top level of the marketplace."

However, within The New York Times organization, technology was obliterating many functions and changing the tasks of the people who remained. Direct access to databases was eliminating many complex archival and research tasks within The New York Times. Direct layout of entire pages on computers was consolidating the tasks of copy, photography, and art editors. Direct electronic connections from newsroom computers to the press rooms had already eliminated many blue-collar jobs. But The New York Times still faced strong union organizations in its remaining blue- and white-collar tasks, and the company had to deal with 17 different unions across its operations. Even in the newsroom, approximately 800 of the 950 professionals were unionized.

Major Issues Facing The New York Times

The 1990s promised to be an exciting time at The New York Times. As Mr. Arthur Sulzberger, Jr., Deputy Publisher, said, "There are some fundamental issues facing us. The most obvious is the national edition question. The technology to go national in a variety of ways is available now, whereas it was not a few years ago. We have been experimenting with a three-part newspaper which we will roll out across the entire country. But we have to decide whether we want to own the presses we print the paper on in various places around the country. We are feeling a number of pressures both in our local markets and from large national competitors like The Wall Street Journal.

"Other newspapers expand the paper depending on how advertising is running. We refuse to do this; we take the burden of organizing things for the reader, producing a four-section paper every day. The reader knows on any given day what sections will be there. We could run the paper "straight" every day on the presses; using this method you get two copies of the same page on each revolution of the press cylinder. But by running "collect," as we do, you run the corresponding pages of different sections (say A1 and C1) on a single revolution. The upshot is that we can produce twice the number of individual pages, but half the number of copies, in a press run of a given length. This puts an enormous burden on the planning of the whole paper and coordinating of all pages and sections. As you can imagine, orchestrating this each day is a major management challenge; the two sections produced together must be the same length, and the closing of all the different news and advertising segments must be carefully coordinated.

"In addition to variations in The New York Times and our national edition, we have to consider what other opportunities our unique news gathering capabilities, technologies, and data banks may offer us. And we have to consider how we can redefine the news itself. In the past, food was not news, now it is. There will be other changes the marketplace dictates. Some things we do because our advertisers want them, or they make money. For example, we do 'Fashions of *The Times*' because it is profitable. On the other hand, *The New York Times Book Review* has not made money for years, but it provides a service beyond the call of profits. There are just some things that are so fundamental that they make *The New York Times* what it is. For example, there are tremendous forces pressing for cuts in news room staff. But that depth in staffing is what we are. And *The Book Review* is, in a way, our flag. It is our bonus. Without *The Review,* we would be much less of a newspaper. Other concepts are similarly fundamental to *The New York Times,* and we must preserve them."

In talking about the first of these issues, a national edition of *The New York Times, Fortune* had noted:

> The demographics of national circulation are much more attractive than they used to be. In 1962 (when *The New York Times* had tested its Western edition concept) *The Times* envisioned 100,000 potential readers there with college educations and comfortable incomes. . . . That number has soared in California and across the nation. To gauge the promise of this, *The Times*—with a weekday circulation of slightly over 1 million—need only look to the success story of *The Wall Street Journal* whose nearly 2 million subscribers make up the largest newspaper readership in the country. For almost 30 years *The Journal* has published four U.S. editions: Eastern, Midwestern, Southwestern, and Western.
>
> If any newspaper can go head-to-head—and coast-to-coast—with *The Wall Street Journal, The Times* is the most imposing candidate. With its longstanding and plausible claim to being the nation's most comprehensive and influential daily—and its editorial staff of over 900, the largest in the world—*The Times* has both the stature and resources for such combat. . . . [However, the sobering fact of life for *The Times* is that it has rarely earned a very fat profit margin. Last year's pre-tax earnings came to around 10% of sales—a return high enough for *The Times* but far below that of many big-city dailies. For instance, one analyst estimated that the *Miami Herald* earned a 25% pre-tax margin and *The Washington Post* nearly a 20% margin.][5]

Storage and Retrieval System at the Edison Plant. Advance sections of the Sunday paper are temporarily stored on large wheels which each hold up to 234,000 pages of material. The wheels are automatically placed in storage and later retrieved for distribution by one of five computer-controlled systems. There is room for up to more than 1,000 "wheels" of stored papers in the Edison facility. *Source:* The New York Times Company

Technology Impacts

Through the 1980s *The Times* had been reluctant to be a technology leader, educating the market to new potentials. *The Times* was very large compared to most of its competitors, consequently its risk levels for any major moves were amplified. There was a tendency to say, "Don't send us a bread board, tell us when the technology is available and send us model #10". The goodwill and identity of *The Times* were clearly among its most important assets. Yet it constantly needed to innovate a new balance between the timing of its news, the accuracy and tone of its news versus its competitors, and the changing modes available for providing news to each of its many specialized audiences. Defining and maintaining this balance would be among the key strategic issues facing The New York Times Company and its prestigious newspaper in the 1990s.

All of this was occurring against a background in which mega-mergers like Time-Warner were occurring, and Wall Street was speculating about future deals. Would Coca-Cola sell Columbia Pictures to Telecommunications, Inc. (TCI), America's biggest cable operator—or perhaps to Japan's Sony which already owned CBS Records? Mr. Rupert Murdoch, the Australian newspaper entrepreneur, had bought Twentieth Century Fox, and the major book producers were merging madly. Large size was one way to absorb the risk of introducing new publications. People worldwide were reading much the same number of books and magazines, and watching the same amount of television and films each year in the industrialized countries.

However, the advantages of scale were beginning to show in this maturing industry. The big ten newspapers had moved from 37% to 43% of the U.S. market between 1980 and 1987, and the cost structure of the industry tended to favor larger newspapers. Papers with average circulations of 75,000 had variable costs of 26% while those with over 300,000 circulation had variable costs of 34%. However, broadcasting, newspapers, and other parts of the industry were surrounded by restrictions aimed to prevent huge companies from monopolizing the information content in particular industries or regions. The Federal Communication Commission's regulations covering multiple and cross ownership of various media, particularly within a single broadcast or circulation area, had been somewhat relaxed during the 1980s. For example, the number of television stations that could be owned by any single enterprise had increased from seven to twelve. However, as inter- and intra-media competition continued to increase, many expected the industry to be more seriously deregulated. *"The New York Times* is not a newspaper for everyone, but when I see two well dressed and apparently educated commuters on the railroad platform—one reading the paper and the other not—I wonder what we did wrong. For, there, without doubt, waits a member of our target audience. My problem is compounded early each morning when I leave my apartment house and see the number of families that seem able to do without *The Times*. What is it that these potential readers want that we are not supplying?

"As I look to the future, the problem becomes more difficult. Will the printed word be further battered by the electronic signal? Will the introduction of fiber optics to the home bring entire new competitive pressures? Just as important, will those of us who wish to venture into this electronic world be competitively disadvantaged by the big players who own the wires and the "gateways" that control the flow of information through those wires?

"The future is getting closer. It will be exciting and will force all of us in the print media to reassess our corporate strategies."

1. What do you see as the most important issues facing The New York Times Company and newspapers' management in 1990? What should Punch Sulzberger attempt to do about these?

2. What should be the strategy of The New York Times Company? What should be the relationship between The New York Times Company and *The New York Times* newspaper? How should their respective management structures be aligned to reflect this?

3. How should *The New York Times* be positioned in its marketplace? How should *The Times* be related to the company's other publications in terms of positioning, operating synergies, portfolio considerations, and organizational structure? What specific policy issues and solutions are needed within its news operations, production-distribution activities, and advertising areas? Why?

4. What have been the most important implications of technology for management of the newspaper? What new competitive issues and potentials will technology pose in the future? What should *The Times* and The New York Times Company do about these? To what extent should The New York Times Company develop a common technology strategy for all its operations? What should this consist of? Why?

The New York Times News Organization, 1990
Source: Corporate records

Executive Editor
Max Frankel — **Magazine Editor** James Greenfield

Managing Editor
Joseph Lelyveld — **Book Review Editor** Rebecca Sinkler

Assistant Managing Editor David Jones	**Assistant Managing Editor** John Lee	**Assistant Managing Editor** Warren Hoge	**Assistant Managing Editor** Allan Siegal	**Assistant Managing Editor** Carolyn Lee
Metropolitan Editor John Darnton	**Foreign Editor** Bernard Gwertzman	**Culture Editor** Marvin Siegel	**Senior Editor-Production** Robert Sheridan	**Senior Editor-Recruitment** Paul Delaney
National Editions Editor Donna Laurie	**Senior Editor-Nights** William Borders	**Arts & Leisure Editor** Constance Rosenblum	**Design Director** Tom Bodkin	**Senior Editor-Training/Development** William Connolly
Sports Editor Joseph Vecchione	**Senior Editor-Weekends** Mitchel Levitas	**Style Editor** Claudia Payne	**Picture Editor** Mark Bussell	**Business Manager** Penny Muse Abernathy
Real Estate Editor Michael Sterne	**National Editor** Soma Golden	**Travel Editor** Nancy Newhouse	**Technology Editor** Judith Wilner	
	Week in Review Editor Dan Lewis		**Information Services Director** Charles Robinson	
	Business/Finance Editor Fred Andrews			
	Washington Editor Howell Raines			
	Science/Health Editor Philip Boffey			
	Media Editor Martin Arnold			

TABLE 3A *The New York Times* Readership Profile, 1989

(in thousands of readers)

	Total U.S.	THE NEW YORK TIMES Weekday	THE NEW YORK TIMES Sunday	Total Northeast	THE NEW YORK TIMES Weekday	THE NEW YORK TIMES Sunday
Total Adults	178,193	3,303	3,604	39,614	2,557	3,018
Males	85,056	1,954	2,073	19,012	1,483	1,683
Females	93,136	1,350	1,567	20,602	1,074	1,335
Age						
18–34	68,997	1,108	1,238	14,438	838	961
35–54	58,707	1,332	1,451	13,151	1,039	1,211
55–64	21,733	464	493	5,167	366	465
65+	28,756	399	459	6,858	324	382
Education						
College graduate	32,799	1,978	2,258	8,494	1,513	1,819
<College graduate	145,394	1,325	1,381	31,121	1,044	1,200
Occupation						
Top management	14,772	554	768	3,255	431	681
Professionals/managers	29,483	1,619	1,740	8,022	1,247	1,440
Technical/clerical/sales	36,012	623	658	8,191	400	524
All other employed	45,205	297	353	8,412	240	309
Not employed	67,492	764	889	14,989	669	746
Household income						
$75,000+	10,406	717	971	3,328	567	875
$50,000+	31,697	1,458	1,834	9,309	1,211	1,632
$35,000+	68,015	2,364	2,668	18,646	1,842	2,267
$25,000+	99,581	2,838	3,188	25,035	2,222	2,717
<$25,000	78,612	465	452	14,579	335	301

Source: Simmons Market Research Bureau, 1989; corporate records.

TABLE 3B   Readership Profile of the New York ADI* and Major New York Newspapers, 1988
(in thousands of readers)

	Total NY ADI	WEEKDAY			SUNDAY	
		NY Times	*Daily News*	*NY Post*	*NY Times*	*Daily News*
Total adults	14,162	2,310	3,901	1,506	3,024	4,080
Males	6,522	1,281	1,971	775	1,545	1,825
Females	7,640	1,029	1,930	731	1,479	2,255
Age						
18–49	8,792	1,447	2,306	969	1,929	2,335
35–49	3,847	724	1,012	472	966	1,023
25–54	7,999	1,385	2,145	928	1,871	2,138
Occupation						
Top management	0,817	261	188	109	338	158
Prof./managerial	3,215	1,014	734	361	1,293	700
Other empl.	5,554	621	1,562	594	805	1,534
Education						
College grad+	3,243	1,231	642	363	1,537	593
Any college	5,775	1,660	1,341	635	2,122	1,315
HS grad+	10,747	2,133	2,939	1,179	2,790	2,963
Household income						
$100,000+	952	308	208	106	403	187
$75,000+	1,918	558	454	216	773	416
$50,000+	4,118	986	997	443	1,283	947
$35,000+	7,316	1,529	1,897	829	2,031	1,846
$25,000+	10,296	1,935	2,769	1,139	2,533	2,769
<$25,000	3,866	375	1,133	367	491	1,311
Place of residence						
NY City	5,685	1,226	2,518	0,982	1,541	2,775
Suburbs	8,478	1,084	1,384	0,524	1,483	1,305
Home ownership						
Own home	8,073	1,432	1,937	723	1,881	1,906
Value $300,000+	1,356	431	277	118	520	283
Value $250,000+	2,265	628	473	199	771	469
Value $200,000+	3,894	888	885	340	1,123	860

* ADI stands for Area of Dominant Influence as defined by the Arbitron rating service.

Source: 1988 *Scarborough Report,* corporate records.

TABLE 3C   Demographic and Readership Changes in the New York ADI*, 1980 to 1986
(in thousands of individuals)

	1980	1986
Population		
Manhattan	1,138	1,277
Rest of NYC	4,322	4,369
New Jersey	3,992	4,225
Long Island	1,928	1,995
Westchester/Rockland/ Putnam	896	927

TABLE 3C (Continued)

	1980	1986
Rest of ADI	1,133	1,213
College graduates		
Manhattan	320	435
Rest of NYC	642	873
New Jersey	702	994
Nassau-Suffolk	383	463
Westchester/Rockland/		
Putnam	204	278
Rest of ADI	256	284
Professional/managerial		
Manhattan	263	396
Rest of NYC	659	851
New Jersey	765	1,118
Nassau-Suffolk	441	517
Westchester/Rockland/		
Putnam	203	350
Rest of ADI	239	350
Individuals with a household income of $35,000+		
Manhattan	136	375
Rest of NYC	548	1,503
New Jersey	789	2,169
Nassau-Suffolk	455	1,162
Westchester/Rockland/		
Putnam	224	512
Rest of ADI	234	607
Weekday Times Readership	2,278	2,443
Sunday Times Readership	3,107	3,142
Newspaper readership in the New York ADI	1982	1986
Adults		
Sunday	80%	76%
Daily	78	74
Men		
Sunday	80	77
Daily	81	79
Women		
Sunday	79	76
Daily	76	71
Employment in the New York ADI	1982	1986
Adults	58%	59%
Men	74	73
Women	44	48
Median household size	1980	1986
ADI population	3.58	3.57
Sunday *Times*	3.53	3.21
Weekday *Times*	3.39	3.13

* ADI stands for Area of Dominant Influence as defined by the Arbitron rating service.

Source: 1980, 1982, and 1986 *Scarborough Reports;* corporate records.

TABLE 3D Demographic Trends in Readership, 1976 to 1986
(percentage of population or readers)

	TOTAL U.S.		WEEKDAY *TIMES*		SUNDAY *TIMES*	
	1976	1986	1976	1986	1976	1986
Male	48%	47%	65%	52%	49%	52%
Female	52	53	35	48	51	48
Median age	41	40	38	39	39	41
Race						
White			88	88	87	91
Non-white			12	12	13	9
Education						
College grad	13	17	36	60	40	61
Some college			23	20	23	18
H.S. grad			25	15	28	18
Marital status						
Single	17	21	31	36	27	31
Married	67	61	58	50	60	57
Div, sep, widowed	16	18	11	14	13	12
No. of children						
None	60	65	59	70	57	68
One	17	17	16	15	15	16
Two	15	15	14	11	14	13
Household size						
One	11	12	14	15	14	13
Two	31	31	28	34	29	35
Three/four	37	40	41	36	37	36
Five or more	21	17	17	15	21	17
Employed	59	61	71	75	68	73
Males employed			84	82	83	84
Females employed			45	69	53	65
Not employed			30	25	33	27
Prof/mgr'l	16	16	39	50	37	48
Own home	68	70	55	52	61	60
Place of residence						
Metro central city			50	42	43	38
Metro suburban			35	37	28	31
Median household Income (000)	$12.8	$25.4	$18.2	$42.7	$19.6	$45.5

Source: Simmons Market Research Bureau, 1976/77 and 1986; corporate records.

TABLE 3E   *Times* **Reader Profile**
(percent of readers)

	WEEKDAY		SUNDAY	
	1976	1986	1976	1986
Public activities (in past year)				
Voted	76%	48%	79%	52%
Written to editor	27	6	19	7
Written to elected official	25	13	26	16
Addressed a public meeting	27	9	27	9
Worked for a political party or candidate	14	5	15	5
Leisure activities, etc. (in past year)				
Played golf	12	11	16	12
Played tennis	26	15	26	17
Indoor gardening	43	23	43	27
Boating	21	11	19	10
Bicycling	36	15	33	14
Cooked for fun	36	26	41	29
Bought a paperback book	50	45	54	50
Bought a hardback book	32	32	33	35
Own a still camera	38	63	38	68
Travel (in past year)				
Took a foreign trip	23	35	23	37
Took 1 domestic trip	13	16	14	17
Took 2 domestic trips	11	11	11	11
Took 3 or more domestic trips	39	31	43	31
Other				
Own an automobile	81	72	87	73
Own securities worth $50,000+	8	10	8	9
Own or use any credit card	63	68	69	72
Own a dog	25	17	34	17
Own a cat	15	11	16	10

TABLE 4   **Competitor Profiles—Circulation**
(in thousands)

	DAILY		SUNDAY	
	1980	1989	1980	1989
New York Times	851	1,039	1,415	1,615
New York Daily News	1,619	1,282	2,273	1,623
New York Post	628	714	—	—
Newsday	506	633	554	681
Star Ledger (Newark)	408	465	569	676
Gannett (West/Rckl)	250	167	196	195
The Record (Bergen Co.)	151	157	213	228
Wall Street Journal	1,798	1,899	—	—
USA Today	—	1,329	—	—
Washington Post	588	789	815	1,122

Source: ABC Audit Data, March 1980 and March 1989; corporate records.

TABLE 4 (continued)
20 Largest U.S. Daily Newspapers: 1989
Circulation
(in thousands)

The Wall Street Journal	1,836
USA Today	1,326
New York Daily News	1,194
Los Angeles Times	1,108
The New York Times	1,068
The Washington Post	773
Chicago Tribune	720
Newsday	700
The Detroit News	690
Detroit Free Press	626
San Francisco Chronicle	556
Chicago Sun-Times	536
The Boston Globe	516
New York Post	508
The Philadelphia Inquirer	505
The Newark Star-Ledger	460
Houston Chronicle	437
The Cleveland Plain Dealer	437
The Miami Herald	413
The Baltimore Sun	409

Source: '90 Facts about Newspapers, American Newspaper
Publishers Association, Washington, D.C., April 1990.

TABLE 4   (Continued)
10 Largest U.S. Newspaper Companies: 1989 Circulation
(in thousands)

	DAILY CIRCULATION	NUMBER OF DAILIES	SUNDAY CIRCULATION	NUMBER OF SUNDAY EDITIONS
Gannett Co., Inc.	6,023	82	5,690	64
Knight-Ridder, Inc.	3,795	28	4,681	24
Newhouse Newspapers	2,998	26	3,785	21
Times Mirror Co.	2,627	8	3,144	7
Tribune Co.	2,698	9	3,429	7
Dow Jones & Co., Inc.	2,410	23	496	14
Thomson Newspapers, Inc.	2,127	122	1,682	70
The New York Times Co.	1,919	27	2,462	17
Scripps Howard	1,571	21	1,756	11
Cox Enterprises, Inc.	1,280	18	1,654	17

Source: '90 Facts about Newspapers, American Newspaper Publishers Association, Washington, D.C., April 1990.

TABLE 5 Trends in Annual U.S. Advertising Expenditures
(in millions of dollars)

	1950	1960	1970	1975	1980	1985	1989
Newspapers, of which	2,070	3,681	5,704	8,234	14,794	25,170	32,510
National	518	778	891	1,109	1,963	3,352	3,700
Local	1,552	2,857	4,813	7,125	12,831	21,818	28,810
Magazines, of which	478	909	1,292	1,465	3,149	5,155	6,750
Weeklies	261	525	617	612	1,418	2,297	2,950
Women's	129	184	301	368	782	1,294	1,645
Monthlies	88	200	374	485	949	1,564	2,155
Television, of which	171	1,627	3,596	5,263	11,469	21,022	27,215
Three networks	85	820	1,658	2,306	5,130	8,060	9,260
Cable networks	—	—	—	—	45	594	1,225
Syndication (nat'l)	—	—	—	—	50	520	1,215
Spot (nat'l)	31	527	1,234	1,623	3,269	6,004	7,400
Spot (local)	55	280	704	1,334	2,967	5,714	7,775
Cable (non-network)	—	—	—	—	8	130	340
Radio, of which	605	693	1,308	1,980	3,702	6,490	8,385
Network	—	43	56	83	183	365	475
Spot (nat'l)	196	222	371	436	779	1,335	1,560
Spot (local)	273	428	881	1,461	2,740	4,790	6,350
Yellow Pages, of which	—	—	—	—	2,900	5,800	8,355
National					330	695	1,040
Local					2,570	5,105	7,315
Direct Mail	803	1,830	2,766	4,124	7,596	15,500	22,175
Business Pubs.	251	609	740	919	1,674	2,375	2,765
Total National	3,260	7,305	11,350	15,200	29,815	53,355	69,500
Total Local	2,440	4,655	8,200	12,700	23,735	41,395	55,340
GRAND TOTAL	5,700	11,960	19,550	27,900	53,550	94,750	124,840

Source: Corporate records; derived from McCann-Erickson, Inc. figures published in *Advertising Age* for various years.

TABLE 6 Financial Highlights: The New York Times Company, 1985 through 1989
(dollars in thousands except per share data)

	YEAR ENDED DECEMBER 31				
	1989	**1988**	**1987**	**1986**	**1985**
Revenues and income					
Revenues	**$1,768,893**	$1,700,046	$1,642,424	$1,524,103	$1,357,699
Operating profit	**169,044**	251,065	283,656	266,373	209,645
Income from continuing operations before equity in operations of forest products group	**84,097**	132,033	138,274	110,165	93,223
Equity in operations of forest products group	**(15,922)**	28,928	17,990	19,560	21,387
Income from continuing operations	**68,175**	160,961	156,264	129,725	114,610
Gain on sale of cable television system and income from its operations, net of taxes	**198,448**	6,719	4,069	2,502	1,708
Net income	**266,623**	167,680	160,333	132,227	116,318
Cash flows from operations	**251,606**	254,631	270,285	249,024	200,367
Financial position					
Property, plant and equipment—net	**972,474**	814,739	644,253	483,988	437,712
Total assets	**2,187,520**	1,914,660	1,711,584	1,405,133	1,295,534
Long-term debt and capital lease obligations	**337,417**	377,527	390,630	216,515	273,611
Common stockholders' equity	**1,064,446**	872,937	823,093	704,744	585,575
Per share of common stock					
Continuing operations	**.87**	2.00	1.91	1.60	1.43
Discontinued operations	**2.52**	.08	.05	.03	.02
Net income	**3.39**	2.08	1.96	1.63	1.45
Dividends	**.50**	.46	.40	.33	.29
Common stockholders' equity (end of year)	**13.63**	11.02	10.04	8.59	7.24
Key ratios					
Operating profit to revenues	**10%**	15%	17%	17%	15%
Income from continuing operations before equity in operations of forest products group to revenues	**5%**	8%	8%	7%	7%
Return on average stockholders' equity	**27%**	20%	21%	20%	22%
Return on average total assets	**13%**	9%	10%	10%	11%
Long-term debt and capital lease obligations to total capitalization	**24%**	30%	32%	23%	32%
Current assets to current liabilities	**.86**	.70	1.03	.72	.77
Employees	**10,600**	10,700	10,500	10,000	10,350

Source: The New York Times Company, *Annual Report,* 1989.

TABLE 7 The New York Times Company: Segment Information, 1987 through 1989
(dollars in thousands)

	YEAR ENDED DECEMBER 31		
	1989	**1988**	**1987**
Revenues			
Newspapers[a]	$1,398,522	$1,380,080	$1,348,601
Magazines[b]	295,580	249,115	226,084
Broadcasting/Information Services[c]	74,791	70,851	67,739
Total	1,768,893	$1,700,046	$1,642,424
Operating profit (loss)			
Newspapers	$ 182,878	$ 231,450	$ 266,075
Magazines	(12,241)	20,887	22,800
Broadcasting/Information Services	12,729	12,647	12,062
Unallocated corporate expenses	(14,322)	(13,919)	(17,281)
Total operating profit	169,044	251,065	283,656
Interest expense, net of interest income	20,680	27,202	22,911
Income taxes	64,267	91,830	122,471
Income from continuing operations before equity in operations of forest products group	84,097	132,033	138,274
Equity in operations of forest products group	(15,922)	28,928	17,990
Income from continuing operations	68,175	160,961	156,264
Income from discontinued operations	198,448	6,719	4,069
Net income	$ 266,623	$ 167,680	$ 160,333
Depreciation and amortization			
Newspapers	$ 64,041	$ 60,885	$ 53,594
Magazines	19,820	3,934	3,529
Broadcasting/Information Services	14,199	12,203	11,597
Corporate	985	1,547	2,524
Discontinued operations	7,976	12,162	10,275
Total	$ 107,021	$ 90,731	$ 81,519

434

TABLE 7   (Continued)

	YEAR ENDED DECEMBER 31		
	1989	**1988**	**1987**
Capital expenditures			
Newspapers	$ **205,564**	$ 260,416	$ 180,926
Magazines	**3,088**	3,187	10,955
Broadcasting/Information Services	**7,911**	13,353	10,904
Corporate	—	22	4,605
Discontinued operations	**4,354**	8,989	10,206
Total	$ **220,917**	$ 285,967	$ 217,596
Identifiable assets at December 31			
Newspapers	**$1,460,429**	$1,317,414	$1,108,276
Magazines	**292,730**	173,828	141,604
Broadcasting/Information Services	**135,952**	136,360	126,721
Corporate	**109,441**	44,868	118,484
Investment in Forest Products Group[d]	**188,968**	179,635	145,212
Discontinued operations	—	62,555	71,287
Total	**$2,187,520**	$1,914,660	$1,711,584

Segment Information

[a] **Newspapers:** *The New York Times,* 35 regional newspapers and a one-third interest in the International Herald Tribune S.A.

[b] **Magazines:** Seventeen publications and related activities in the women's service and sports and leisure fields.

[c] **Broadcasting/Information Services:** Five network-affiliated television stations, two radio stations, a news service, a features syndicate and licensing operations of *The New York Times* databases and microfilm.

[d] **Forest Products Group:** Equity interests in three newsprint companies and a partnership in a supercalendered paper mill that together supply the major portion of the Newspaper Group's annual paper requirements.

Source: The New York Times Company, *Annual Report,* 1989.

MATSUSHITA ELECTRIC INDUSTRIAL COMPANY

In the mid-1980s Matsushita Electric Industrial Co. was often cited as one of the premier examples of the management practices and style that had made Japan into an industrial power, with a GNP second only to the United States. Matsushita's own brand names, Quasar, National, Panasonic, Victor (JVC), and Technic, were known around the world. Matsushita was Japan's largest producer of electric and electronic products and one of the world's largest firms in these fields. Why did its management practices work so well? To what extent were they applicable to other companies? What could be adopted outside Japan?

EARLY HISTORY

Matsushita (generally pronounced Mat*SOOSH*'ta) was started in 1918 by Mr. Konosuke Matsushita, one of Japan's now legendary entrepreneurs. In 1911, Mr. Matsushita had joined the Osaka Electric Light Company (at age 15), convinced that electricity had a great future in Japan. Seven years later, then the youngest inspector on Osaka's payroll, he resigned to form his own company.

At that time the few wired Japanese homes typically had only one circuit, and that usually emerged inconveniently from the center of the ceiling in one room. To

Case copyright © 1985 by James Brian Quinn. Research assistants—Penny C. Paquette and Allie J. Quinn.

Major sources for case were company interviews; company published records; and (1) T. Kono, *Strategy and Structure of Japanese Enterprises* (M. E. Sharpe, Armonk, N.Y., 1985); (2) J. Cruikshank, "Matsushita," *Harvard Business School Bulletin,* February 1983; and (3) R. Pascale and A. Athos, *The Art of Japanese Management* (Simon & Schuster, N.Y., 1981). Footnotes (x,xx) indicate cited references and page numbers in these sources. The generous cooperation of Matsushita Electric is gratefully acknowledged.

light another room or to use electricity meant using an awkward extension cord, dangling from the ceiling fixture. And the resident still had only one room lit. Mr. Matsushita, a tinkerer from his early days in his father's bicycle shop, conceived of a double-ended attachment for the outlet that permitted the main room to be lighted while a swivel socket allowed an extension cord to be guided elsewhere without tangling. When he offered his idea to Osaka Electric the company was not interested. Consequently, Mr. Matsushita took about $50 in savings and severance pay and—with his wife and brother-in law—began manufacturing his unique multiple socket in his own home. By using recycled light bulb bases, Matsushita was soon able to cut his already low costs (and prices) by some 30%, discouraging larger competitors from entering his market.

His next product was a bicycle lamp to replace the unreliable battery lamps (or in many cases small metal boxes with candles) then used by Japanese for cycling at night. Matsushita developed an improved battery, mounted his lamps in well-styled wooden casings, and left samples burning in Osaka's shop windows over weekends to prove that his lights would burn ten times longer than competitors'. From these humble beginnings began a great consumer electric products line. Matsushita became a public company in 1935. The National brand was registered in 1925; the first National radios were produced in 1930; washing machines, refrigerators, and televisions appeared in the post–World War II era; and a full range of high-fidelity electronics products in the 1960s through 1980s. In the 1960s and 1970s Matsushita added industrial equipment, communications devices, and measuring systems. Matsushita began producing television receivers in 1952, exported its first TVs to Thailand in 1956, and completed its 75 millionth set in 1985. A breakdown of its 1985 product line and summary financials appear in Exhibit 1.

A 250-Year Strategy

In 1932 Konosuke Matsushita noticed a tramp drinking water from a water tap on the street. He later said, "I began to think about abundance. And I decided that the task of an industrialist was to make his products widely available at the lowest possible cost to bring a better living to the people of the world." (2,63) This became his exhortation to his employees on the company's 14th anniversary in 1932—and the cornerstone of the company's "250-year corporate strategy." Exemplifying this philosophy was an incident in the early 1930s. There was a Japanese inventor/investor who then controlled most of the patents for radio circuitry, which was moving from the crystal set era toward the speaker radio. Mr. Matsushita approached this man—who intended to monopolize the new industry—and after lengthy negotiations bought out his patents for a huge price. Matsushita then opened the patents to the entire industry "so that everyone could manufacture in a more efficient way."

Mr. Matsushita's 250-Year Plan to eliminate poverty is divided into ten 25-year segments. In May 1982, Matsushita Company began the third 25-Year Plan which was to include "the true internationalization of the Matsushita Industrial Electric Company." (2,75) Shortly before Mr. Matsushita had noted in his book, *Japan at the Brink,* that "the Japanese miracle itself was on the verge of capsizing, politically, economically, and spiritually." He outlined problems of inflation, disaffected youth, what he called ineffective government, and a national lack of philosophical bearings. Among his many startling recommendations was the suggestion that Japan should abolish half of its universities. He felt much of the education was not worthwhile and that Japan's needs could be better provided by other institutions. Selling off the assets of Tokyo University (the nation's most prestigious university) alone would save the country some $500 million per year.

These incidents suggest the creative quality which Mr. Matsushita has lent to his company. When General MacArthur's advisors decided to eliminate the *zaibatsu* (or "financial clique") which had controlled Japanese industry prior to World War II, they removed Mr. Matsushita as head of his company. Numerous delegations of workers approached the authorities, saying Matsushita represented the very entrepreneurial spirit which the Americans were professing. While tolerated by the *zaibatsu,* they said Matsushita was distinctly not a part of it. He had welcomed a union in the postwar era, reiterating his conviction that labor and management must work together for a greater good. But the American authorities refused to listen to these supplications, and for four years during Mr. Matsushita's enforced exile, his company shrank from 20,000 to 3,800 employees, with many divisions closing permanently. Only when he was reinstated in 1951 did the company begin to return to its former strength.

Japan's Industry Structure

In this period, Japan was a nation still emerging from feudalism and a military system gone berserk. Its industrial infrastructure had been destroyed, its youth decimated, and its illusions of military conquest dashed. The nation had no significant energy resources, few natural resources, a small land mass relative to its population, and a very poorly paid labor force. Many ordinary amenities had disappeared and its social system verged on breakdown or revolution. But for 300 years, its dominant feudal and religious (Confucian and Shinto) groups had emphasized devotion to one's family and organization. Personal courtesy had been ingrained in numerous rituals and was a necessity for a large population living on a small land mass. But respect for laborers had not been a widely held value, nor had wealth been widely distributed.

In the disillusioned and labor-short postwar era, more democratic values began to appear. There began a concerted national effort to improve the ordinary Japanese person's standard of living. Through its Ministry for International Trade and Industry (MITI) the government targeted certain industries for expansion and assisted them in developing their own technologies and in importing foreign technologies. To stabilize the society large Japanese companies began to emphasize lifetime employment (to age 55) and to take over many of the social roles other institutions provide in western countries. Companies often provided employee housing, recreation facilities, and a focal point for sports activities. Even today the Japanese government provides few unemployment or retirement benefits to workers. Instead, it attempts to stabilize price levels, manages the economy to maintain employment and offers supplementary employment opportunities only when necessary—through the national railroad system, public works, and public service (sanitary, groundskeeping, etc.) activities. Income and social security taxes are low. In most large companies employees are considered partners in the enterprise, not interchangeable parts of production; and in recession times employment is continued at the sacrifice of profits or dividends. Japanese executives often say that since maintaining sales and profit levels is management's responsibility—not that of factory workers—management (not workers) should take the brunt of any layoffs which are unavoidable.

Another unique feature of Japanese industry has been its financial structures. Large Japanese companies are heavy users of loan capital, with an equity ratio of only 20% being average. The largest equity shareholders, however, are also banks and insurance companies, which are forbidden individually to own more than 10% of a given company. They hold stock to secure a long-term relationship more than to reap current profits. Other shareholders tend to be important suppliers or buyers from the companies. Only some 30% of all stock is held by individuals. Some illustrative financial data appear in Figure 1 and Tables 1–3.

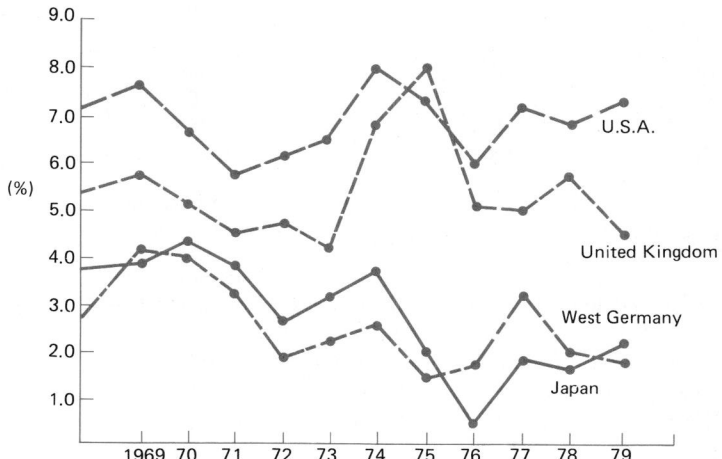

FIGURE 1

Corporate Profits in Four Countries—Average Return or Profits for Manufacturing Firms in the United States, the United Kingdom, West Germany, and Japan *Source:* From *Sekai no Kigyo no Keiei Bunseki.* Industrial Policy Bureau, MITI, Tokyo, 1980, p. 20, in William H. Davidson, *The Amazing Race,* copyright © 1984 John Wiley & Sons, Inc. Reprinted by permission of John Wiley & Sons, Inc.

TABLE 1   Financial Ratios for Selected U.S. and Japanese Firms, 1978

COMPANY	DEBT-EQUITY RATIO	PROFIT/SALES	INVENTORY TURN RATIO
Burroughs	0.538	10.46%	4.24
IBM	0.538	14.76	6.24
NCR	0.923	12.18	4.23
Control Data	0.786	4.65	4.38
DEC	0.639	9.90	3.58
Hitachi	2.99	2.56	5.45
Toshiba	5.08	1.52	3.56
Fujitsu	2.68	2.37	4.77
NEC	5.18	1.09	4.10
Oki	17.05	0.57	3.8
Mitsubishi Electric	5.67	1.71	3.78
Matsushita	1.01	3.34	16.47
Sanyo	2.02	1.93	21.32
Ricoh	1.43	4.15	12.10
Casio	1.60	3.54	7.82
Sony	0.923	4.35	5.65
Sharp	2.125	2.76	9.64

Source: Sekai no Kigyo no Keiei Bunseki, Industrial Policy Bureau, MITI, Tokyo, 1980, p. 29, in *William H. Davidson, The Amazing Race,* copyright © 1984 John Wiley & Sons, Inc. Reprinted by permission of John Wiley & Sons, Inc.

TABLE 2 A Comparison of Productivity-Adjusted Labor Costs in the United States and Japan, 1970–1980

YEAR	AVERAGE ANNUAL JAPANESE WAGES IN MANUFACTURING[a]	÷	JAPANESE OUTPUT PER LABOR HOUR DIVIDED BY U.S. OUTPUT PER LABOR HOUR[b]	=	ADJUSTED JAPANESE LABOR COST	U.S. LABOR COST[c]
1970	$ 1,787		0.508		$ 3,517	$ 7,439
1972	2,693		0.580		4,643	8,719
1974	4,224		0.649		6,508	9,947
1976	5,633		0.701		8,036	11,780
1978	10,009		0.782		12,799	14,063
1980	10,724		0.918		11,682	15,008

[a] These data cover the contracted cash payments to workers in manufacturing firms with 29 or more employees. From *Economic Statistics Annual,* Research and Statistics Department, Bank of Japan, 1981, pp. 293–294.

[b] This variable is created by dividing the average output per labor hour for Japanese industries by the average output in U.S. industries. Data are taken from the U.S. Department of Labor, Bureau of Labor Statistics.

[c] From Bureau of Labor Statistics, *Monthly Labor Review,* for manufacturing only.

Source: William H. Davidson, *The Amazing Race,* copyright © 1984 John Wiley & Sons, Inc. Reprinted by permission by John Wiley & Sons, Inc.

TABLE 3 Leading World Semiconductor Companies' Sales
(Discrete and Integrated Devices, 1982)

COMPANY	TOTAL ($ MILLION)
Motorola	1310
Texas Instruments	1227
Nippon Electric	1220
Hitachi	1000
Toshiba	810
National Semiconductor	690
Intel	610
Philips*	558
Fujitsu	475
Siemens*	420
Matsushita	340
Signetics (Philips)	384
Mitsubishi	380
Mostek	335
Advanced Micro Devices (Siemens)	282
Sanyo	260
AEG	196
Thomson-CSF	190
Sharp	155
SGS-ATES	150
Oki	125

*Not including U.S. affiliates.

Source: Annual Reports, Hambrecht and Quist "The Japanese Semiconductor Industry" in William H. Davidson, *The Amazing Race,* copyright © 1984 John Wiley & Sons, Inc. Reprinted by permission of John Wiley & Sons, Inc.

Within this general framework, Matsushita Company has developed its own unique and extraordinarily powerful philosophy. Matsushita's stated mission is "to contribute to the well being of mankind by providing reasonably priced products and services in sufficient quantities to achieve peace, happiness, and prosperity for all." This is supported by "5 Principles": (1) Growth through mutual benefit between the company and the consumer, (2) Profit as a result of contributions to society, (3) Fair competition in the marketplace, (4) Mutual benefit between the company, its suppliers, dealers, and shareholders, (5) Participation by all employees.

"Seven Spirits" then provide the code of behavior for employees to follow in making decisions. (1,50) They are the:

- Spirit of Service Through Industry
- Spirit of Fairness and Faithfulness
- Spirit of Harmony and Cooperation
- Spirit of Struggle for Betterment
- Spirit of Courtesy and Humility
- Spirit of Adaptation and Assimilation
- Spirit of Gratitude

Exercises and Discussions

Every morning at Matsushita's plants in Japan (and in most areas throughout the world) every employee attends a "morning meeting" at which the Matsushita creed, principles, and/or spirits are recited aloud. Only a skeleton force of telephone operators, guards, process controllers, and so on is not present. In Japan the meeting begins with prearranged exercises learned in early grade school. Then in "relaxation exercises" each person massages and pounds the back of another person, and then both turn around to give or receive similar benefits. Following the Company Song and these recitations, a discussion leader—a task rotated daily—poses a question for the group to discuss and try to resolve. This can be an operating problem, a new opportunity, an important philosophical issue (etc.) designed to promote interest. After 15 minutes or so, everyone goes off to work. At work stations the exercise routine is repeated for 5 minutes at the end of each hour and for 10–15 minutes at midmorning and afternoon.

In the company's early years, Mr. Matsushita used to interview all employees himself. This is no longer possible. But annually he and his wife host a gathering of newlywed employees. There are announcements and awards on "Adults Day" every January 15 to celebrate trainees becoming full employees. And there are constant company messages in each employee's paycheck to personalize the company-individual relationship. Mr. Niwa, chairman of Matsushita Electric Works, says, "We try to develop the supportive idea that 'we are always with you' psychologically." (2,65) Within most plants is a "trophy area" where individual and plant awards for outstanding performance are displayed. Much emphasis is given to company awards and to the performance of company sports teams competing with those of other companies.

Mr. Kosaka, head of Matsushita's Overseas Training Center says, "We feel you must create a spirit in which everyone can share. . . . It's not a theory, formulated after reading other people's books, but something based on *experience* itself.

441

Once the philosophy is clear, it talks to every individual, and all communication in the company can be based on it." (2,63) In Matsushita's Japan operations virtually all employees wear company-provided blue uniforms with white tennis shoes. Overseas the company provides the uniforms, but the choice is up to individuals.

AN ORGANIZED MAVERICK

Despite what appears to be conformity and regimentation in its philosophy, Matsushita has consistently been a maverick in Japanese industry. From the first, Matsushita violated the usual rules used by Japanese and American companies of the era. Rather than attempting to recoup investments as rapidly as possible, Matsushita has consistently cut its prices quickly and sought profits in the long run. While other companies used manufacturers' representatives to reach established retail channels, Matsushita set up its own distribution networks and went directly to retailers. Instead of an arms length transaction with retailers, Matsushita offered innovative trade financing for them and pioneered the use of installment sales and point-of-purchase advertising in Japan. Rather than using the Matsushita name, the company promoted its National, Victor, and Panasonic brands.

A Decentralization Pioneer

In the mid-1930s, paralleling Du Pont's pioneering efforts with a decentralized divisional structure, Matsushita and his talented controller, Takahashi, developed a similar concept with only 1,600 employees at the time. Matsushita was attracted not only to the organizational clarity and control the system offered, but to its motivational advantages as well. He wanted to keep things small, entrepreneurial, and market oriented in the rapidly emerging radio and small consumer appliance fields the company was in.

The decentralized divisional concept still dominates today's organization. But, recognizing the inherent disadvantages of this system, Matsushita also centralized four key functions which remain so to the present. First, he created a cadre of controllers reporting directly to headquarters and a centralized accounting system across the company. Second, he institutionalized a company "bank" into which 60% of all divisional profits flowed and from which divisions have to seek funds for capital improvements. Divisions have no bank accounts except for day-to-day transactions. Divisions' "float" must be cleared monthly, and borrowings beyond this are charged out at prime plus 2%. Third, Matsushita centralized the personnel function; no employee is hired without a central prescreening, and all management promotions are reviewed and monitored by headquarters. Fourth, he centralized the company's training system with its heavy emphasis on the values described above. Each university level employee goes through an approximately eight month training cycle to inspire them with the company's goals and philosophies, as well as to provide them with essential technical skills.

A Product Group Matrix

This basic organization has since oscillated back and forth with more (or less) autonomy given to the divisions depending on external economic or competitive conditions. In 1953 Matsushita introduced Product Groups with division heads reporting vertically to the president and horizontally to group vice presidents, who serve as specialists with detailed knowledge of a whole family of similar products. (3,33) This innovation was some ten years ahead of the widespread use of matrix organizations in the U.S. Matsushita tried not to take its formal organization charts too seriously and to "humanize" some of the inherent conflicts in the matrix structure. Controllers were called "coordinators" and housed directly in the factories they served. (3,35) To relieve some of the resistance to this matrix concept, Matsushita constantly reminded executives that everyone grew up with two bosses (a mother and a father), a situation that generally seemed quite tolerable. Even at the top level Matsushita established a three-person Executive Council to handle major decisions. He then slowly withdrew himself into a strategic role as chairman, although in times of crisis he reserved the right to reemerge to assume direct control.

Competition and Cooperation

Japanese corporations compete intensively with companies in the same line of business, but often cooperate extensively with other companies in a complementary relationship. For example, Matsushita has 120 "fully controlled" wholesalers selling only its products. It has 20% or more equity interest in all these distributors and serves them and other retailers through 100 sales offices which provide management assistance, showroom facilities, and other services to Matsushita's Japanese distribution network. Retailers include 25,000 National Shops, where Matsushita products account for 80% of sales and another 25,000 National Stores where its products exceed 50% of sales.

Matsushita does not hold shares in these retailers, but controls them by long term contracts and the special services it provides: management training, classes on new technologies, shared advertising, and some special rebates. Typically, products are sold at list in these channels, but they may have to meet the prices of the discount stores now becoming more common in Japan. Other separate channels exist for: (1) industrial and non-industrial construction products and (2) commercial, industrial, and government customers. Marketing for Matsushita is controlled from headquarters. Each product division can sell directly to its wholesalers or large customers like the government, but under rules established at headquarters. Export sales are handled by an independent subsidiary, Matsushita Trading Co., which has worldwide sales branches for all products.

TECHNOLOGY AND MANUFACTURING

Matsushita is heavily integrated on the components side. It produces its own batteries, vacuum tubes, integrated circuits, circuit boards, condensors, transformers, speakers, tuners, magnetic heads, and so on. But it buys standard raw materials (wire, steel, aluminum sheet, etc.) outside. Purchases from subsidiaries amount to about 80% of the value of all purchased materials. The company also sells components to outside groups. It only consumes about 50% of its component production, and is the largest single component manufacturer in Japan, with ¥386 billion sales in 1983. The manufacturing divisions are all profit centers, able to buy components outside if they so choose. These manufacturing divisions sell through the marketing channels described above. Products are sold by divisional salesmen, shipped directly to distributors or retailers, and transferred to Marketing at internal transfer prices. The Central Marketing group handles sales planning, marketing coordination, and promotional functions.

Although Matsushita started with two innovative products, it has rarely pioneered entirely new technologies. (3,30) Instead, it emphasizes quality and price. Its experience with video tape recorders (VTRs) is perhaps typical. SONY was generally acknowledged as the real pioneer of VTR technology with its Umatic and Betamax formats. While Matsushita had also done excellent early work on the technology, it took a license under SONY's early VHS-like format and turned its several divisions loose on improving the device for the marketplace. Discovering that customers wanted a 2–4 hour recording capacity (as opposed to SONY's 1-hour format), Matsushita designed this into a more compact VTR that was highly reliable and could be priced 10–15% below SONY. When SONY came up with its superior quality Beta format, Matsushita stayed with its well-developed VHS concept, got other major Japanese and U.S. firms to adopt its preferred format, and by the late 1970s manufactured two-thirds of all VTRs sold.

"FIGURE OUT HOW TO DO IT BETTER"

Matsushita consistently invested some 4% of sales in R&D, much of which went into production engineering. The company had some 20 production engineering laboratories equipped with the latest available technology. Most of these were attached to individual product divisions. But Matsushita's Central Production Engineering Laboratory at corporate level was one of the world's outstanding units. The company also had a Central (basic) Research Laboratory, Wireless Research Laboratory, and Research Institute Tokyo (which operated on an independent basis and conducted research for both company and outside groups). In addition, there were a Corporate Product Development Division, Corporate Quality Assurance Division, and Corporate Patent and Legal Division under the Central Engineering structure.

The company's focus in R&D was said to be "to analyze competing products and figure out how to do the job better." (3,31) Its Engineering and Research Laboratories were backed up by one of the world's most awesome production line suggestion systems. Matsushita processed some 460,000 employee generated suggestions or improvements per year. The company's motto was "Matsushita produces capable people before it produces products." Thus Matsushita's eight-month training for all university graduates involved: 3 weeks of headquarters training classes; 3 months in retail stores; one month in the factory; one month in cost accounting; and two months in marketing lectures and activities. Lesser time, but equal attention went into training rank and file workers. Job rotation was common throughout all ranks; 5% of all employees (comprised of $\frac{1}{3}$ managers, $\frac{1}{3}$ supervisors, and $\frac{1}{3}$ workers) rotated from one division to another each year, and some 80% of all employees participated in quality circle activities. About 15% of all suggestions were accepted and formally implemented, others were simply implemented by informal agreement among supervisors and employees. (1,304) Of these about 35 "super suggestions" occurred each year. These won coveted awards. And sponsors of patentable suggestions could receive patents and monetary awards in their own names. (2,71)

"Manage from Goodwill"

Not only could workers suggest improvements, they could stop the production line if they were not satisfied with quality. Production plants tended to be spotlessly clean. Cleanliness standards were dictated from headquarters and were not subject to interpretation anywhere in the world. Work stations were typically separated by 8–10 feet, aisles were extremely wide (15–30 feet), noise levels were relatively low around work stations, and the production line itself moved more slowly than was typical in western plants. A substantial amount of small-scale automation was generally visible at individual work stations. Individual workers were directly responsible for quality results at their own stations, but heavily automated quality control and test facilities were in evidence all along electronics and consumer products lines. Employee turnover in Japan was of course extremely low, but even overseas plants tended to have $\frac{1}{4}$ the turnover of comparable plants in their host countries—and often they rejected local unions.

Matsushita managers attributed this to the attempt to "manage from goodwill" and to "foster a homey, family atmosphere. We are first interested in nurturing a relationship of trust between management and labor. Once we achieve that goal, we can develop other things like suggestion systems, quality circles, and so on." North American employees responded, "You're not under a lot of pressure here; it's a comfortable place to work. You do the best you can. Everyone understands we're all here to help each other, and to put out the best product we can." (2,86) In 1974 Matsushita Electric Company of America (MECA) had bought a 25-year-old Westinghouse heavy equipment plant near Toronto. Although 7 of the 12 competitors in the market then had left by 1983, MECA had the highest growth rate in its industry in Canada over the decade.

PLANNING AND CONTROL SYSTEMS

Matsushita had derived its planning system from Phillips (NV), the Dutch electronics giant. On New Years day some 7,000 managers assembled to hear the chairman and president declare the basic policy for the year. This contained some key dimensions and figures, but more broadly it presented the important elements to be emphasized in the company during the year. These strategic directions were later conveyed to all employees through the company magazine.

Every six months each division manager presented three plans. The first was a long-term (five-year) plan, updated as new technologies and environmental events occurred. Second was a two-year (midterm) plan which stated how the division would translate its long-term plan into such things as plant capacity or specific new products. Neither was extensively reviewed by top line management, but each was scrutinized heavily by the product group side of the organization matrix. (3,36)

More attention was given to the Six-Month Operating Plan. Here the division stated its monthly forecasts of sales, market share, profits, inventories, accounts receivable, capital expenditures, head count, quality targets (etc). When variances occurred the division manager and his controller had to be prepared to explain them. Particular attention was given to market share, return on sales, asset turnover, and actual versus budgeted costs, since these were considered to be under the division managers' control. Matsushita had rigorous standards for collections from its customers and payments to its suppliers—normally both less than 30 days—but the corporation could extend long-term credit to build sales channels, develop new markets, or meet special competitive needs.

Everyone understood that key variables would be tracked monthly and reviewed scrupulously. Figures were available within a few days after the end of each month and were widely shared in Matsushita's "open information system." (3,39) Performance was judged and rewards made on the basis of actual versus planned results. Reviews were performed by three groups: corporate line officers, corporate staff, and "peer review" by the heads of other divisions. Matsushita expected every division to be completely self sustaining within five years and strongly resisted subsidizing losing divisions.

The 60% of each division's profits paid to headquarters covered Product Group Management, R&D, Production Engineering, and an equity return. The remaining 40% belonged to the divisions for facilities updating, production engineering, and new product development. But the funds were held at corporate and earned interest for the division. Matsushita expected each division to make sure its current and future product lines were healthy and did not use "portfolio" concepts favored in U.S. companies.

Performance Reviews

Corporate headquarters was kept deliberately lean, with only 1.5% of the company's total personnel there (excluding the Engineering Research Laboratories). However, each month the division manager spent several days at headquarters, going over each performance item and variance in detail with the Finance Office and with senior management. Key criteria were (1) the ability to stay on plan and (2) whether the division's management was "doing its best" and "as well as anyone in the market." If not, poor performers might be quickly transferred to other areas, "where their talents better fit circumstances." (3,37) In the "peer review" process (quarterly), summary operating results were shared before all divisions. Divisions were grouped A, B, C, or D; the A (outstanding) groups made their presentations first, D's last. Though individuals or divisions were not singled out for embarrassment, each group's relative performance was clear to all.

Matsushita's sales force and executives were monitored through exacting prospect lists and yield statistics. And the sales force was backed by the largest advertising budget in Japan. Senior sales executives were expected to visit retail outlets regularly and to seek group-level help when they needed it. To support its strong sales channels, Matsushita also operated an elaborate network of "customer clubs" to keep informed about its users' needs and to solicit ideas for improvement of products or services. Even top executives, like Mr. Matsushita and Mr. Yamashita (president), were expected to spend most of their time out of their offices and with customers. At various times both had gone into the field to solve specific crisis situations themselves. And in a 1970 recession, even assembly line workers were shifted to door-to-door selling to cut inventories and to bring costs into line.

Overseas Operations

Overseas, Matsushita operated 46 production facilities in 27 countries and 34 sales companies in 28 countries. In addition to marketing through its own affiliates, Matsushita also produced for private label distribution by OEMs abroad. In addition, it had a series of licensing arrangements with foreign companies, notably RCA (non exclusive) and Phillips (exclusive) with the latter owning a minority position in Matsushita Electric Company. Matsushita had a variety of ownership arrangements in various host countries from full ownership to join ventures, but never had less than a 50% board position.

Overseas units were almost always headed by a Japanese, and many middle managers were Japanese. Almost all managerial people—whether Japanese or not —were put through Matsushita's Overseas Training Center in Osaka, which offered specialized training in English, in overseas operations, in company policy, and in the company's value system. Because of scales of operation, tariff barriers, distances from Japan (etc.), the specific organization of each subsidiary might be quite different. For example the Malaysian subsidiary had a small local market, was close to Japan, was heavily protected by tariffs, and had to deal with significant "local content" rules. The U.K. and Canada plants were bound by few such rules, but served huge domestic markets. Because of the company's size, its stock was traded on several of the world's stock markets (including the United States) and it often raised funds locally.

A Pragmatic Approach

Matsushita had a pragmatic approach to all problems. The heart of its style was "to get to the problem and fix it." (3,43) There was much latent conflict between its competing divisions, its matrix units, and its "Venture Capital Fund," administered from the corporation's 60% of profits. Divisions made proposals asking the Fund's managers to support new products or concepts which did not fit normal capital allocation processes well. Yet Matsushita executives expressed surprise when asked if there was much interdivisional fighting. They said, "We conflict without conflicting. Our underlying premise is that in life we make adjustments. . . . We presuppose that parties will fundamentally strive to pull together rather than push apart." (3,43)

Employees were not viewed as "participating in management," but their opinions were sought. The company's books were open to the union, and the union was consulted directly as each division prepared its long-term and six-month plans. Matsushita encouraged long-term managerial continuity in its divisions with five to seven years in key spots being common. But the Central Personnel group also tracked the top several performers in each division and consciously moved these people to openings as they occurred. Matsushita's maxim was "extraordinary results from ordinary people." (3,47) It did not make particular efforts to hire from the elite schools and was willing to jump younger people over dozens of their seniors if their performance warranted. Another maxim was, "If you make an honest mistake, the company will be very forgiving. Treat it as a training experience and learn from it. You will be severely criticized [a euphemism for dismissed] however if you deviate from the company's basic principles." (3,51)

QUESTIONS

1. What is Japan's basic industrial strategy? Why has it chosen this strategy? How does it keep capital costs so low? What are the potential weaknesses in this strategy?

2. What is Matsushita's basic strategy? What are the most important policies involved in its implementation? Why were these chosen? What issues do they pose?

3. Based on the information in the case, draw an organization chart of Matsushita. What issues does this pose? How would you measure performance for each major unit? How should overseas operations be organized? Why?

4. What functions does Matsushita's elaborately developed value system perform? What problems does it pose?

EXHIBIT 1
Matsushita's Major
Products, 1983

The company is engaged in production and sales of electric and electronic products. For revenue reporting purposes, the company classified its products into the following categories.

VIDEO EQUIPMENT

Matsushita produces video tape recorders and related products (cameras, tapes, etc.) for home and professional use. For the year ended November 20, 1983, sales of video tape recorder products increased rapidly and accounted for ¥1,045 billion or 26% of total company sales.

The company manufactures a broad range of color and black-and-white television receivers designed to meet the demands of all segments of the Japanese and overseas markets. The company manufactures color and black-and-white television receivers with screens ranging from $1\frac{1}{2}$ to 25 inches and $1\frac{1}{2}$ to 19 inches respectively, measured diagonally. The company also manufactures large screen color projection TV systems. For the year ended November 20, 1983, sales of television receivers accounted for ¥399 billion or 10% of total sales of the company for that period.

AUDIO EQUIPMENT

The company produces a large variety of audio equipment, ranging from radio receivers, tape recorders and radio cassette combination models to stereo radio phonographs, hi-fi components and digital audio equipment. It also produces electronic organs. For the fiscal year 1983, total audio equipment sales represented ¥481 billion or 12% of the company total.

HOME APPLIANCES

The major products in this category include: refrigerators and freezers; home laundry equipment such as washing machines and dryers; cooking equipment such as microwave and other ovens, blenders, juicers, food processors, and rice cookers; air conditioners and electric fans; electric and kerosene heaters; vacuum cleaners; and electric irons. For fiscal 1983, total home appliance sales amounted to ¥596 billion or 15% of total sales of the company.

COMMUNICATION AND INDUSTRIAL EQUIPMENT

This category covers two-way communication equipment, including push-button telephones, community telephone systems and mobile communication equipment; broadcasting equipment, including radio and television broadcasting installations, broadcast television cameras and CATV systems; measuring instruments, including oscilloscopes and ultrasonic diagnostic systems; automotive accessories, including car radios and stereos; business equipment, including facsimile equipment, personal computers, word processors and plain paper copiers; and other products, including hearing aids, electronic calculators, traffic control systems, electronic educational systems,

EXHIBIT 1
(Continued)

point-of-sale systems and professional audio equipment. It also includes electric motors, micro motors, welding equipment, industrial robots, power distribution equipment, power transformers and capacitors, anti-pollution equipment, TLD irradiation measuring systems, vending machines and other electric and electronic industrial devices.

Sales of this product category were ¥588 billion, representing 15% of the company total, in 1983.

ENERGY AND KITCHEN-RELATED PRODUCTS

This category includes many types of batteries, among them manganese, nickel-cadmium, mercury, alkaline, silver oxide, lithium and air wet cells, storage batteries for automotive use, fuel cell batteries primarily for marine use, and solar cells. It also encompasses various battery appliances, gas appliances, kitchen sinks and cabinets, and solar energy equipment. Sales of these products as a whole reached ¥187 billion or 5% of the company's 1983 total.

ELECTRONIC COMPONENTS

This category includes a wide variety of transistors, diodes, ICs (integrated circuits) and LSIs (large-scale integrated circuits), as well as television picture tubes, other cathode ray tubes, image pickup tubes and magnetrons, for use by the company and other manufacturers. The company also manufactures a comprehensive line of incandescent, fluorescent, mercury and sodium lamps, speakers, audio accessories, TV tuners, resistors, capacitors, ceramic components, printed circuits, sensing devices and other parts. Total electronic components sales amounted to ¥386 billion or 9% of the company total for 1983.

OTHERS

This category includes phonograph records, prerecorded tapes, electric pencil sharpeners, bicycles, and photographic products, including cameras and flash units. Total sales of these miscellaneous products totaled ¥307 billion and accounted for 8% of total 1983 sales of the company.

Source: Matsushita Electric, SEC Form 20–F, November 20, 1983.

EXHIBIT 1 (Continued)
Main Products

Consumer Electronics

TV receivers
  Color
  Monochrone
  Industrial
Transistor radios
  Portables
  Clock radios
Headphones
Radio cassette recorders
Cassette recorders
Car audio
Transceivers
Music centers
Hi-fi components
  Turntables
  Tape decks
  Amplifiers
  Receivers
  Tuners
  Speaker Systems
Video tape recorders
Video cameras
Video projection systems
Video tape printers
Video editing machines
Video mixing apparatus
Electronic organs
Hearing aids

Industrial Equipment

Welding machines
  Light beam
  Electron beam
  Arc
  Automatic CO_2
Component insertion
  machines (PANASERT*)
Automatic riveting machines
Automatic screw feeding and
  driving machines
High-voltage transformers
Power capacitors
Power distribution equipment
Circuit breakers
TLD (Thermoluminescent
  dosimeter)

Medical equipment
  (PANAVISTA*)
Vending machines
Refrigerated showcases
Card readers
Measuring equipment
Elevators
Escalators
Antipollution equipment

Business Machines

Small business computers
Facsimile equipment
Plain paper copiers
Word processors
Electronic cash registers
Electronic calculators
Key telephones
Intercom systems
Automatic slide processors
Pencil sharpeners
Staplers
Letter openers

Home Appliances

Refrigerators
Microwave ovens
Gas and electric ovens
Rice cookers
Toasters
Blenders
Food processors
Coffee makers
Tempura-fondue cookers
Joy Cook (induction heating
  cooker)
Kitchen units
Water heaters
Dish washers
Disposers
Pumps
Washing machines
Dryers
Vacuum cleaners
Polishers
Electric fans
Ventilating fans
Air and water purifiers

Water coolers
Electric irons
Electric blankets
Air conditioners
Heating and cooling systems
  Electric
  Gas
  Kerosene
Dehumidifiers and humidifiers
Hair setters
Bicycles
Flash units
Clocks

Lighting Equipment

Incandescent lamps
Fluorescent lamps
Mercury discharge lamps
Metal halide lamps
Sodium lamps
Infrared ray lamps
Hologen lamps
Lighting fixtures

System Products

LL (Learning Laboratory)
  systems
Broadcasting systems
Sound systems
Traffic control systems
Tunnel systems
Disaster alert systems
Hotel service systems
Dam control systems
Meteorological robot buoy
  systems
CATV systems
POS (point-of-sale) systems
POSTA (post office service
  total automation) systems
Lighting systems
Surveillance systems
Public address systems
Mobile telephone systems

Electronic Components

Transistors
Diodes

EXHIBIT 1 (Continued)

ICs
LSIs
Thyristors
Cathode ray tubes
Image pickup tubes
    (NEWVICON*)
Receiving and transmitting
    tubes
Indicator tubes
Magnetrons
Hybrid microcircuits (Hi-
    MIC*)
Capacitors
Resistors
Ceramics (PCM*, ZNR*)
Printed circuit boards
Transformers
Coils
Switches
Connectors
Sensors
Display and graphic devices
System modules

Tuners
Speakers
Tape heads (HPF*)
Microphones
Antennas

Motors

DC motors
Micro motors
Transistor motors
Stepping motors
Servo motors
Coreless motors
Flat motors
Fan motors
Blower motors
Capacitor motors
Hermetically-sealed motors
Clutch motors
Needle positioning motors
Shaded pole motors
Synchronous motors
Geared motors

General purpose motors
Universal motors

Batteries

Manganese dioxide batteries
Alkaline manganese batteries
Lithium batteries
Mercury batteries
Silver oxide batteries
Air batteries
Paper-thin batteries
Lead-acid batteries
    Car batteries
    Storage batteries
    PANALLOID* batteries
Nickel-cadmium batteries
Battery chargers
Solar batteries
Fuel cells
Carbon electrodes
Battery operated golf carts
    and other appliances

* Trademark of Matsushita Electric.
Source: Matsushita Electric, Annual Report, 1983.

EXHIBIT 1 (Continued)

Sales Breakdown by Products and Geographic Areas
(Billions of Yen)

	Year Ended November 20					
	1981		1982		1983	
Video equipment	¥1,109	(32%)	¥1,329	(36%)	¥1,444	(36%)
Audio equipment	543	(16)	485	(13)	481	(12)
Home appliances	591	(17)	590	(16)	596	(15)
Communication and industrial equipment	429	(12)	464	(13)	588	(15)
Energy and kitchen-related products	166	(5)	181	(5)	187	(5)
Electronic components	313	(9)	310	(9)	386	(9)
Others	300	(9)	291	(8)	307	(8)
Total	¥3,451	(100%)	¥3,650	(100%)	¥3,989	(100%)

	Year Ended November 20					
	1981		1982		1983	
Japan	¥1,872	(54%)	¥1,965	(54%)	¥2,128	(53%)
North America (United States and Canada)	640	(19)	670	(18)	842	(21)
Others	939	(27)	1,015	(28)	1,019	(26)
Total	¥3,451	(100%)	¥3,650	(100%)	¥3,989	(100%)

Source: Matsushita Electric, *SEC Form 20–F,* November 20, 1983.

EXHIBIT 1 (Continued)

Selected Financial Data
(Billions of Yen, Except Per Share Amounts and Yen Exchange Rates)

	Year Ended November 20				
	1979	1980	1981	1982	1983
Net sales	2,363	2,916	3,541	3,650	3,989
Net income	98	125	157	157	183
Per common share:[a]					
Net income	69.54	87.13	101.48	100.79	116.29
Dividends[b]	8.26	8.26	9.09	10.00	12.50
	($0.036)	($0.038)	($0.038)	($0.041)	($0.053)
Net working capital	495	548	615	676	768
Total assets	2,139	2,478	2,946	3,174	3,451
Long-term indebtedness	68	59	35	49	40
Minority interests	200	242	302	339	377
Stockholders' equity	922	1,092	1,275	1,435	1,602
Yen exchange rates per U.S. dollar:					
Year end	246.20	213.70	218.65	257.85	235.95
Average	213.94	231.79	220.74	245.55	239.58
High	193.95	206.50	199.05	214.20	226.75
Low	247.00	261.40	246.10	277.65	257.05

[a] Per share amounts have been appropriately adjusted for free distributions of shares.
[b] Dividends per share are those declared with respect to the income for each fiscal year and dividends charged to retained earnings are those actually paid.

Source: Matsushita Electric, *SEC Form 20–F,* November 20, 1983.

EXHIBIT 1 (Continued)

Matsushita Electric Industrial Co., Ltd. and Consolidated Subsidiaries
Consolidated Balance Sheets November 20, 1983 and 1982

	Yen (millions)	
Assets	**1983**	**1982**
Current assets		
Cash (note 4)	553,998	492,509
Marketable securities, at cost, which approximates market	212,762	120,028
Trade receivables (note 4)		
Related companies (note 3)	75,321	78,044
Notes	118,386	112,186
Accounts	365,761	343,061
Allowance for doubtful receivables	(14,582)	(15,040)
Net trade receivables	544,886	518,251
Inventories (notes 2 and 4)	528,529	556,953
Other current assets (note 5)	179,179	158,577
Total current assets	2,019,344	1,846,318
Investments and advances (note 3)		
Nonconsolidated subsidiaries	164,281	169,235
Associated companies	76,054	71,762
Other investments and advances	590,942	508,061
Total investments and advances	831,277	749,058
Property, plant and equipment (note 4)		
Land	73,584	66,926
Buildings	330,193	308,874
Machinery and equipment	642,789	568,098
Construction in progress	22,168	17,540
	1,068,734	961,438
Less accumulated depreciation	603,709	508,942
Net property, plant and equipment	405,025	452,496
Other assets (note 5)	134,947	125,848

	Yen (millions)	
Liabilities and Stockholders' Equity	**1983**	**1982**
Current liabilities		
Short-term bank loans (note 4)	195,011	245,929
Current portion of long-term debt (note 4)	1,200	1,413
Trade payables		
Related companies (note 3)	36,959	32,991
Notes	82,325	75,101
Accounts	243,263	213,401
Total trade payables	362,547	321,493
Accrued income taxes (note 5)	161,253	113,187
Accrued payroll	114,892	104,918
Other accrued expenses	198,375	173,324
Deposits and advances from customers	76,956	75,536
Employees' deposits	83,107	76,374
Other current liabilities	58,453	57,725
Total current liabilities	1,251,794	1,169,899
Long-term debt (note 4)	40,405	49,158
Retirement and severance benefits	179,247	180,340
Minority interests		
Capital stock	39,273	38,082
Surplus	377,800	300,928
Total minority interests	377,073	339,010
Stockholders' equity		
Common stock of ¥50 par value (notes 4 and 6):		
Authorized—2,700,000,000 shares; issued—		
1,589,239,462 shares (1982—1,576,298,513 shares)	79,462	78,815
Capital surplus (note 6)	216,719	205,797
Legal reserve (note 7)	30,011	27,831
Retained earnings (notes 3, 4, 6, and 7)	1,282,536	1,117,689
Cumulative translation adjustments (note 1(d))	(3,820)	12,237
	1,606,908	1,442,369
Less cost of 7,005,397 shares (1982—16,641,324 shares) of common stock held by consolidated subsidiaries	2,834	7,056
Total stockholders' equity	1,602,074	1,453,313
Commitments and contingent liabilities (note 9)	3,450,593	3,173,720

Notes: Accompanying consolidated financial statements are provided in company's 20–F.
Source: Matsushita Electric, *SEC Form 20–F,* Nov. 1983

EXHIBIT 1 (Continued)

Matsushita Electric Industrial Co., Ltd. and Consolidated Subsidiaries
Consolidated Statements of Income
Years Ended November 20, 1983, 1982, and 1981

	Yen (Millions)		
	1983	1982	1981
Net sales			
Related companies (note 3)	958,972	772,326	732,492
Other	3,029,547	2,877,245	2,718,847
Total net sales	3,988,519	3,649,571	3,451,339
Cost of sales (note 3)	2,571,006	2,354,189	2,230,116
Gross profit	1,417,513	1,295,382	1,221,223
Selling, general and administrative expenses	990,987	917,552	848,483
Operating profit	426,526	377,830	372,740
Other income (deductions)			
Interest and dividend income	92,405	80,716	75,372
Equity in earnings of nonconsolidated subsidiaries and associated companies (note 3)	17,106	14,515	17,590
Interest expense	(50,257)	(54,958)	(44,742)
Other, net	12,294	10,830	10,969
	71,548	51,103	59,189
Income before income taxes	498,074	428,933	431,929
Provision for income taxes (note 5)			
Current	276,984	242,265	265,318
Deferred	(8,493)	(14,450)	(33,526)
	268,491	227,815	231,792
Income before minority interests	229,583	201,118	200,137
Minority interests	46,835	43,997	43,410
Net income	182,748	157,121	156,727
Net income per depositary share, each representing 10 shares of common stock (note 1(i))			
Assuming no dilution	1,163	1,008	1,015
Assuming full dilution	1,138	979	982

Notes: Accompanying consolidated financial statements are provided in company's 20-F.

Source: Matsushita Electric, *SEC Form 20-F,* November 20, 1983.

THE HEWLETT PACKARD COMPANY

The Hewlett Packard Company (HP) had been a dynamic business built around innovation. It had traditionally been a fast paced organization characterized by steady growth. From 1957 to 1984, sales increased from $28.1 million to $6 billion, and profits from $2.4 million to $665 million. In 1984 the company had close to 7,000 products on the market, and developed new products at a rate of 300 per year.

HP had become the world's leading manufacturer of electronic test and measurement equipment for engineers and scientists. Besides the electronics industry and scientific research programs, the principal markets for HP instruments included the telecommunications, aerospace, aircraft, and automotive industries. Its principal products were integrated instrument and computer systems, test and measurement instruments, computer systems and peripheral products, medical electronic equipment and systems, instrumentation and systems for chemical analysis, handheld calculators, and solid-state components. HP Laboratories, the company's common research facility, ranked as one of the world's leading electronics research centers.[1] HP was among the world's top ten companies in CAD/CAE/CAM sales. (See Table 1.)

Two Talented Cofounders

The two most influential people in HP's development had been its cofounders, William Hewlett and David Packard—in 1985 vice chairman and chairman of the board, respectively. Each was personally responsible for many of the company's most important products and diversification moves. Hewlett was an innovator

Case copyright © 1986 by Henry Mintzberg and James Brian Quinn. Case prepared by Maria G. Geretto and Penny C. Paquette under the supervision of Professors Mintzberg and Quinn. Case derived solely from secondary sources.

TABLE 1 The Top Ten in CAD/CAE/CAM Worldwide Sales
Revenue by application ($ million)

COMPANY	MECHANICAL ENGINEERING	ELECTRONIC/ ELECTRICAL ENGINEERING	ARCHITECTURAL/ ELECTRICAL/CIVIL ENGINEERING	MAPPING	SERVICES	TOTAL REVENUE
Computervision	272	111	56	6	111	556
IBM	391	13	16	—	109	529
Intergraph	64	20	178	89	52	403
Digital Equipment	107	103	22	32	37	301
Calma Corp. (GE)	70	90	28	—	47	235
McDonnell Douglas	94	—	24	—	16	134
Applicon	62	25	1	—	13	101
Hewlett Packard	45	36	6	—	10	97
Control Data	54	7	9	—	23	93
Prime Computer	53	3	14	—	20	90

Source: International Data Corp. in Paine Webber, Inc., *Hewlett Packard Company Report,* December 2, 1985.

with great technical expertise; he conceived of product lines and used parts of HP Labs for his own research. Packard was known for his sound business sense and outstanding managerial and administrative skills and was said to be the driving force behind such key decisions as HP's move into medical systems and its efforts to become a major factor in minicomputers.

Doing Things Well

For HP, growth came from doing things well and was not an objective in itself. The company did not stipulate long-term targets for expected profit or market share growth, having explicitly made the decision not to become dependent on such growth. Its focus was on making quality products that commanded a premium price in the marketplace. If it did this job well, the company believed profits would follow. The company's attitude toward long-term formal planning was stated by Mr. Hewlett, "We operate on a very short lead time, and don't have a master plan. In terms of next year's detailed plan we try and wait until the last possible moment to get that in place."[2]

EARLY HISTORY

Hewlett and Packard started what was to become HP in 1938, in a garage behind the Packards' home in Palo Alto, California. The two founders were both graduates of Standard University's engineering program. The company began with an audio oscillator—a high-quality electronic instrument for use in developing and testing sound equipment. Among the early customers for their product was Walt Disney Studios. In 1938, Walt Disney asked them to develop eight oscillators having different frequency characteristics and different physical configurations. One result was the HP Model 200A used in developing the soundtrack for the movie "Fantasia."

This large order provided a foundation for the company's early success. But growth was slow during World War II. Hewlett and Packard made a conscious decision not to pursue large military contracts because of their "boom or bust" possibilities. HP accepted only limited government work in microwave technologies and kept itself focused on instrumentation and microwave measurement.[3] HP operated as a partnership until 1947 when it incorporated.

An Expanding Product Line

After World War II the company began to expand its product line significantly and moved from being a focused instrument maker to a more diversified company. In 1957, when the organization reached 1,200 employees, this size was considered too large to manage by the informal methods HP had previously used.

For example, early in HP's history, two product development techniques had been prevalent. The first was known as the "next bench syndrome." A central strategy in the early years, this referred to listening to the problems of engineers on the next bench and finding ways to solve them. Since the company was working on the frontiers of its technologies, this approach helped the company identify new technical opportunities and needs; little market research was done, since the company could monitor most market needs internally.[4] A second approach was to design a machine specifically for one customer and then market it to others. This enabled the company to concentrate on products for a few customers, yet produce in volume and charge high margins. Rather than compete on price, the intention was to develop products so advanced and adapted to customers' needs that the market would be willing to pay a premium for HP performance.

Institutionalizing the HP Way

HP's "Corporate Objectives," embracing the company's basic values and philosophy, were put in writing in 1957 and became the "HP Way." (See Exhibit 1.) This same year the first personnel department was created. As Mr. Hewlett noted,

> Contrary to most companies at that time, we did not have a personnel department. We had strong convictions that one of a manager's most important jobs was to deal directly with his employees. We did not want to impose any artificial barriers to hinder direct communication.[3]

Mr. Hewlett later described the important organizational changes which were to occur in 1957 as follows:

> A real turning point for the company occurred in 1957, resulting in changes that would have a profound effect on the company in future years. Up to that time, HP was directed by the owner-founders operating in a single plant in Palo Alto, California. Most of the basic policies that directed the company were firmly in place, and we had a good team of people running the operation.
>
> But there were signs of strain appearing. I think the principal concern Dave and I had was that, as it increased in size, the company might lose the intimacy we felt was so important to the organization. Therefore, in January 1957, Dave and I took the top 10 or 12 people of the organization on a weekend retreat to discuss the future of the company, and to decide what action might be taken to insure its continued success.
>
> Several conclusions were reached. First, we decided to divisionalize the company along product lines. We felt that by reducing the size of the operating units and decreasing the span of control, we would provide an opportunity to recapture the personal touch that everyone felt was so important. The managers of these divisions would assume direct responsibility for the health and welfare of their charge, but they would need some guidance. Second, it seemed that this guidance could best be achieved with a simple set of policy statements. In fact, these statements consisted of no more than a codification of past company policies. Coupled with this belief was

the conviction that, with these guidelines, local managers could make better decisions than either Dave or me, because—if for no other reason—they would be closer to the problems.[3]

Corporate Culture and Organization

In order to appreciate the culture Hewlett and Packard attempted to foster, it is necessary to understand the founders' own backgrounds and beliefs. As Mr. Hewlett said,

> . . . it is important to remember that Dave and I were products of the Depression. We had observed its effects on all sides, and it could not help but influence our decisions on how a company should be run. Two thoughts were clear from the start. First, we did not want to run a hire and fire operation, but rather a company built on a loyal and dedicated work force. Further, we felt that this work force should be able to share to some extent in the progress of the company. Second, we wished to operate, as much as possible, on a pay-as-you-go basis, that our growth be financed by our earnings and not by debt.[3]

The new organization designed at the weekend retreat in 1957 was called the Product Division Structure. It separated the company into small divisions, which

EXHIBIT 1
The HP Way

Business Related

1. Pay as you go—no long-term borrowing
   - Helps to maintain a stable financial environment during depressed business periods.
   - Serves as an excellent self-regulating mechanism for HP managers.
2. Market expansion and leadership based on *new* product contributions
   - Engineering excellence determines market recognition of our new products.
   - Novel new product ideas and implementations serve as the basis for expansion of existing markets or diversification into new markets.
3. Customer satisfaction second to none.
   - We sell only what has been thoroughly designed, tested, and specified.
   - Our products have *lasting* value—they are highly reliable (quality) and our customers discover additional benefits while using them.
   - Best after-sales service and support in the industry.
4. *Honesty* and *integrity* in all matters
   - No tolerance for dishonest dealings with vendors or customers (e.g., bribes, kickbacks).
   - Open and honest communication with employees and stockholders alike; conservative financial reporting.

People Related

1. *Belief* in our people
   - Confidence in, and respect for, our people as opposed to depending upon extensive rules, procedures, and so on.
   - Depend upon people to do their job right (individual freedom) without constant directives.
   - Opportunity for meaningful participation (job dignity).

EXHIBIT 1
(Continued)

2. Emphasis on working *together* and *sharing* rewards (teamwork and partnership)
   - Share responsibilities; help each other; learn from each other, chance to make mistakes.
   - Recognition based on contribution to results—sense of achievement and self-esteem.
   - Profit sharing, stock purchase plan, retirement program, and so on; aimed at employees and company sharing in each other's successes.
   - Company financial management emphasis on protecting employee's job security.

3. A *superior* working environment which other companies seek but few achieve
   - Informality—open, honest communications; no artificial distinctions between employees (first-name basis); management by walking around; and open door communication policy.
   - Develop and promote from within—lifetime training, education, career counseling to help employees get maximum opportunity to grow and develop with the company.
   - Decentralization—emphasis on keeping work groups as small as possible for maximum employee identification with our businesses and customers.
   - Management by objectives (MBO)—provides a sound basis for measuring performance by employees as well as managers and is objective, not political.

Source: The Hewlett Packard Company.

were to become HP's fundamental business units. Each product division became an integrated, self-sustaining organization with a great deal of independence, similar in some ways to a company. Each division had its own engineering, manufacturing, and marketing organization. The divisions had considerable latitude in developing individual products and product line strategies, but they were not permitted to go outside their assigned markets or to raise money outside the corporation.

Technological leadership was to be a major goal for each production division.[1] Operations were pragmatically specialized around the division's technical focus. And what became known as HP's Originator/Producer strategy was introduced to move products to the marketplace. An idea's originator was expected to carry it through all stages of development and into the market if necessary. Bernard M. Oliver, vice president for R&D (in 1975) said,

> At the time we split R&D and product engineering. But we discovered that the only way to get things done in a timely fashion was to have the originator of an idea carry it through to the end. We've tried to remove the fences between research and production and make a chute that starts in the lab and ends at the shipping dock.[5]
>
> [To back up this concept] . . . [HP] Product Divisions are purposely kept small, seldom numbering more than 2000 people. This structure spurs entrepreneurship by allowing decisions to be made by the persons most responsible for putting them into action. Compact and action oriented, the HP division combines the flexibility of a small business with the resources of a large corporation.[1]

Key personnel worked together on projects without regard to their status in their own organizations. In developing new products, divisional project engineers organized technical development efforts, but product managers from Marketing joined the team early to provide inputs on design and price. For the most part, the early stage technical work done by the divisions was self-contained, requiring little communication across divisions. And the company tried to keep each division's product-technical-market focus as discrete as possible.

Management by Objectives and Involvement

Mr. Hewlett was later to say of the 1957 reorganization that:

> The recommendations of our 1957 meeting were quickly implemented by divisionalization and by wide distribution of the objectives. These objectives had an important role in training and guiding the new management teams. They served to reinforce the principles of cooperative management—the concept of leading, not directing. They stressed a management style that was informal, with give and take discussion, lack of private offices, casual dress and the universal use of first names.
> The informal structure of the company led to what was eventually known as its "open door" policy. In a sense this said that any employee who was unhappy could come in and talk with Dave or me or any other senior executive about his problems. Although such a technique could easily be abused, it never was, and it served as an excellent safety valve for the frustrations that occur in any organization.[3]

To back up this philosophy, the organization developed two important policies. The first was Management by Objectives (MBO). Mr. Packard believed this was the most effective way for an innovative company like HP to operate:

> You establish some objectives with people, provide some incentives, and try not to direct the detailed way in which they do their work. We've found you're likely to get a much better performance that way than if you have a more military-type procedure where somebody gives orders and expects them to be followed in every detail.[6]

The second was Management by Walking Around (MBWA), a term later popularized by *In Search of Excellence*. This was an extra step HP took to make sure the open door policy was truly effective. It involved a friendly, unfocused and unscheduled series of interactions with any employee with whom a manager from any level happened to stop by to chat. The result was an implicit invitation to repay this visit and walk through that manager's open door at any time—management by involvement.[4]

Expansion and Diversification

Also in 1957, HP's stock was first made available to the public. One year later the firm made its first acquisition, acquiring F. L. Moseley Co. of Pasadena, a producer of high-quality graphic recorders. By 1964, HP had acquired Sanborn Co. of Waltham, a pioneer in electrocardiography and a supplier of other recording instruments, and F. M. Scientific Corp., a manufacturer of chromatographic devices. Through these acquisitions HP entered medical electronics and analytic chemistry.

The first electronic calculator was designed at HP in 1966. An employee working for one of the calculator companies reportedly brought to HP a concept for an all electronic calculator. An HP team converted this concept into an electronic calculator to compete with the desk top mechanical calculators of that era. HP's calculator had a great deal of power, but was a large device measuring about one square foot.[4] HP successfully directed its early sales efforts toward educational, scientific, and engineering markets, where it was an established supplier of instruments.

Later, in 1972, HP introduced the first scientific handheld calculator, the HP-35. The original HP-35, championed and designed in part by Mr. Hewlett, went into production despite an outside market research study that scoffed at the idea. With no external marketing support, the company managed its own distribution. The HP-35 was introduced at a price of $395. It proved so popular that this price was maintained until mid 1973. The tremendous surge in calculator sales was accompanied by a 33% increase in employees as well as a rapid ballooning of inventories.

Complexity and Restructuring

As product complexities grew, in 1970 HP established its first product group structure. Some sales organizations were created at the group level, separate from those of the product divisions.[7] In years to come, these posed a number of communication and integration issues across divisions, but only within the product group. There the units could be coordinated by a vice president or general manager. There was little or no mandated communication across product groups.

HP's first period of significant difficulty occurred in 1970, triggered by economic downturns in both the computer and aerospace industries. The company's sales decreased by nearly $40 million, the first decrease since HP went public. Mr. Hewlett stated how the company dealt with the situation:

> One of the most dramatic examples of working with our employees occurred during the recession in early 1970. It became evident that we had about 10 percent more employees than we needed for the production schedule. Rather than lay off or furlough 10 percent of the work force, we simply decided that everyone in the company would take every other Friday off without pay. It worked very well. Employee after employee commented how much they appreciated the opportunity for continued employment, albeit at a reduced pay rate, when on all sides they saw people who were out of a job. After about six months, we were able to return to a full schedule. We helped our people and we preserved our work force, which was essential for continued development.[3]

Other policies characterized HP's approach to its people. Common coffee breaks were a ritual, and recreational facilities for all employees were available at every plant. Employees at all levels were entitled to use a cottage resort area on HP-owned land for vacations free of charge. HP still marks an employee's marriage with the gift of a silver bowl and the birth of a first child with a blanket,[8] and it has long done away with time clocks and rigid hours in favor of Flextime which it finds to be self-policing. Because HP believed that all employees contributed to the success of the organization and should be rewarded in good times, the company also had an attractive bonus plan for all employees. As of June 1985, the company had never had a union or an extensive layoff.

THE 1975 RESTRUCTURING

Mr. Packard began to perceive that HP had grown too fast in the boom years of 1972–1973. Business publications noted that inventories and accounts receivables were moving out of control, prices on new products were set too low to generate sufficient cash flows, and products often went into production before development was fully completed. Growth had been pursued vigorously without adequate concerns for profit. For the first time in the company's history, short-term borrowing had increased to the extent that long-term debt was considered.

Shaken by their need, in 1974, to become more personally involved in daily management, Hewlett and Packard wanted to develop an organization structure that could both respond better to growth and diversification needs and provide more effective management of day-to-day operations. Preparing the organization for an orderly management succession also became quite important; Mr. Packard would turn 65 in 1977 and Mr. Hewlett in 1978.

Accordingly, they restructured the organization in 1975. There were three main components to the change: (1) the basic product groups were expanded from four to six, (2) a new management level of top executives was added, and (3) an executive committee was established to oversee the day-to-day operations of the company.

Six Product Groups

Prior to 1975, HP's four product groups had consisted of: Test and Measurement, Data Products, Medical Equipment, and Analytical Instrumentation. The six groups created by the reorganization were: Electronic Test and Measurement Instruments, Computer and Computer Based Systems, Calculators, Solid-State Components, Medical Electronic Products, and Electronic Instrumentation for Chemical Analysis. (See Exhibit 2 for a diagram of the 1975 organization structure.)

Each of the product groups had both its own general manager and a sales service organization serving all the product divisions within that group. The product division marketing departments had as their responsibilities: order processing and shipping, sales engineering and contract administration, service engineering, technical writing, publications, and advertising and sales promotion. In addition, they provided sales forecasts and recommended and reviewed prices.

Nevertheless, because the actual selling and customer service activities were performed at the product group level, each division had to compete for the time of its group's field sales force. The objective of the more centralized sales organization was to increase cooperation and communication between divisional sales teams. Hewlett and Packard insisted that all customers receive similar treatment and be dealt with through consistent policies.[4]

The second element of the reorganization included the appointment of two executive vice presidents jointly responsible for operations—one was John Young who later became president—and a vice president for corporate administration. The new executive committee was made up of these three newly appointed executives and Mr. Hewlett and Mr. Packard. It was to meet weekly to coordinate all aspects of the company's operations.

Loss of Control and Regaining Direction

In early 1974, top management had made some basic strategy decisions. Long-term debt was to be avoided. Short-term debt would be decreased by controlling costs, managing assets and improving profit margins. Most importantly, top management began to realize that the company had somehow allowed market share to emerge as too strong an objective. To remedy this, Hewlett and Packard began a year-long campaign to reemphasize some principles they had developed when the partnership began. Packard was quoted as repeatedly telling company audiences:

Somewhere we got into the idea that market share was an objective. I hope that is straightened out. Anyone can build market share; if you set your prices low enough, you can get the whole damn market. But I'll tell you it won't get you anywhere around here.[5]

Two further strategies were used to get the company back on track: all prices were increased by 10% and R&D by 20% from the previous year. The intent was to improve the company's profits, while controlling a rate of growth which had more than doubled sales in three years. By early 1975, profit improvements were dramatic. The reaction to the Hewlett and Packard tour of the divisions was quick: inventories were slashed, accounts receivable tightened, productivity improved, and hiring was dramatically decreased to a total of only 1000 new employees in 1974 down from 7000 in the previous year. From 1973 to 1974 sales increased by $215 million and profits by $33 million.

For a brief period, HP had been the leader in the business and scientific handheld calculator field. In 1974 this market had yielded some 30% of the company's profits. However, HP's lead soon fell to competition led by Texas Instruments. HP chose not to compete across the board in calculators. Instead it decided to remain in the specialized upper end of the market. It preferred to develop products so advanced they could command a premium price. HP executives commented publicly that this philosophy fit the company's style of operation. They also indicated that the company was not geared to compete solely on a price basis but wanted to maintain its reputation by adding something that was not already available in competitive products.

To maintain coherence and a sense of personal communication despite the growth that was taking place, HP started an activity in the late 1970s that became known as "communication luncheons." Mr. Hewlett described the purpose and style of these luncheons as follows:

> You simply cannot run an operation and assume that everything is perfect. There are many ways to achieve this feedback. . . . One we have tried and which has been fairly successful, is a technique we call "communication luncheons." A senior executive will visit a division and ask to have lunch with a group of employees, 15 or 20 at most; no supervisors invited. Other employees know in advance who will be attending and very often they pass on their own questions or complaints. . . .
>
> This provides an opportunity to discuss company policy or company problems. . . . Sometimes you detect a pattern of problems—say, for example, inadequate supervisory training. Such problems can be dealt with on a broad company-wide basis. In any event you always learn more about how the company actually operates. Equally important, employees have a chance to hear first hand what is happening in the company and what management is trying to do.[3]

A NEW ERA

In 1978 when Mr. Hewlett stepped down as CEO, John Young, who had been groomed since 1975 to replace him, was appointed president and CEO. He was to lead HP into the rapidly changing computer marketplace, a relatively new major thrust for the company. (See Exhibit 2.)

Mr. Young launched several major programs designed to improve HP's planning, to coordinate its marketing efforts, and to strengthen its presence in computer markets. Specific strategy changes supported these important endeavors:

EXHIBIT 2
Simplified Organization Chart, 1975

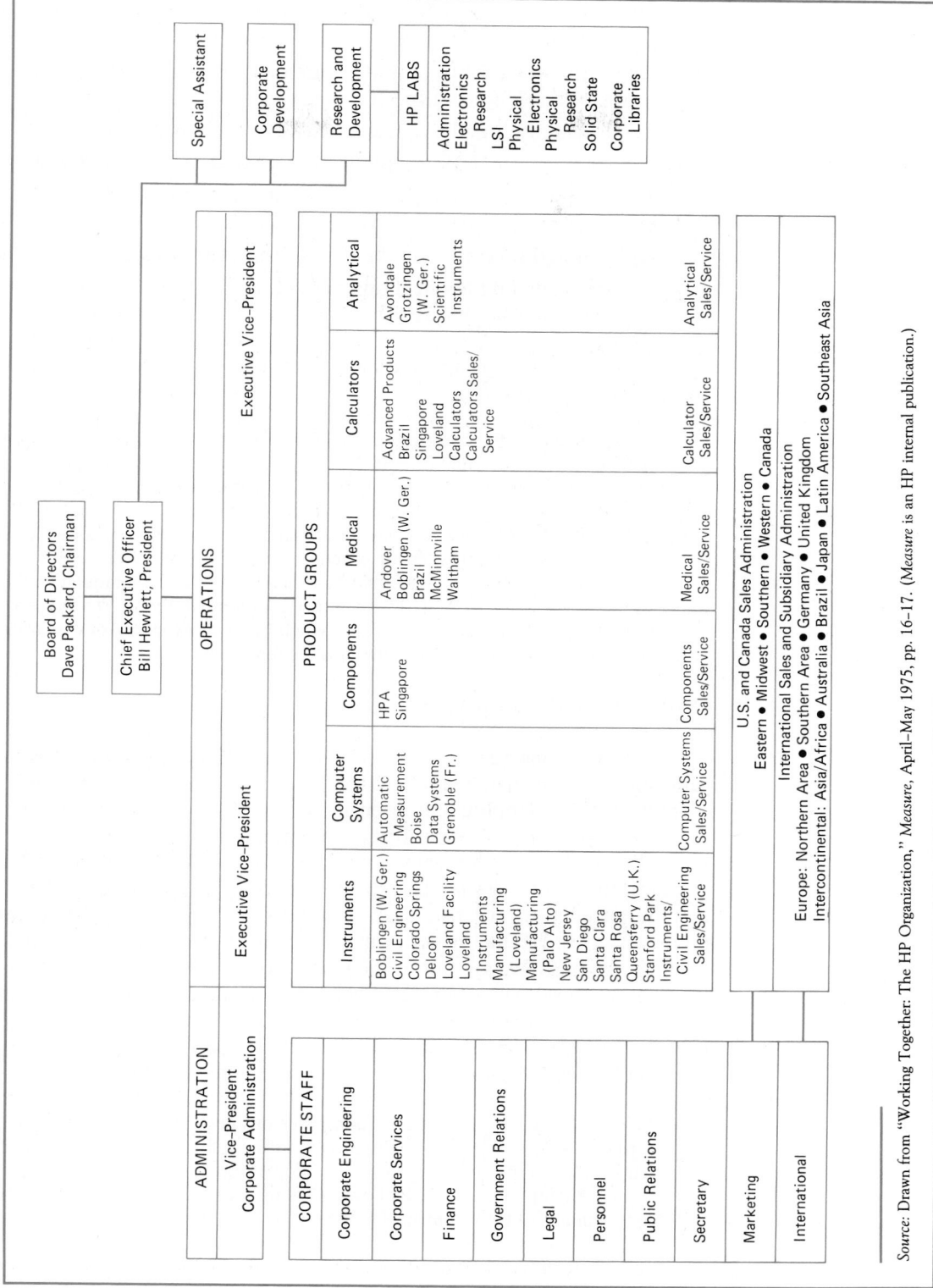

Source: Drawn from "Working Together: The HP Organization," *Measure*, April–May 1975, pp. 16–17. (*Measure* is an HP internal publication.)

- Mr. Young reorganized HP Laboratories after its R&D chief retired, replacing him with John Doyle, formerly HP's personnel executive. Young felt that the Labs needed management, not science, in its leadership. Doyle was particularly known for his ability to articulate HP's entrepreneurial culture.
- Doyle recruited 220 computer oriented professionals and several key researchers from other successful computer companies.
- The firm substantially increased its R&D spending.
- For the first time, HP started forming research partnerships with universities.
- The firm worked to couple HP Laboratories more closely to the strategies of its company operating groups.
- HP acquired several small companies to obtain specific applications skills.
- HP set up its first applications marketing division and staffed this with specialists from other industries.

In addition, Mr. Young felt that a focus on quality was one of the best ways to control costs. He said,

> A few years ago, the company did an internal study that had some surprising results. HP had always considered itself a quality leader in the industry—and indeed, it was. The company was therefore somewhat surprised when a study demonstrated that fully 25 percent of its manufacturing costs were involved in responding to bad quality.
> A "stretch objective" was announced. Employees were asked to improve on product failure rates by a factor of ten during the decade of the 1980s. . . .
> There has been a ripple effect of quality efforts throughout HP. The aggregate impact is large. In 1978, HP's inventory represented about 20.5 percent of sales. In 1983, it was down to 15.9 percent. Much of that reduction can be traced to better quality—less scrap, shorter cycles, and better flow.[9]

Problems with Computers

While these actions were having a positive impact, the effects of a decentralized organization were being adversely felt in its computer markets where HP's products —frequently overlapping and often incompatible in operation—were threatening the firm's fine quality and performance reputation.

HP faced conflicting demands, both within its organization and in the marketplace. In recent years HP had stressed profitability over market share. Of particular importance to HP had been creating unique products that commanded a premium price; HP had never been an organization to create "me-too" products. Said Mr. Young, "We are not in the clone business; we will differentiate our products." But according to *Fortune,* "Hewlett Packard's traditional approaches were all but useless in creating personal computers. In that business not being a clone—IBM compatible—was a good way to get clobbered in retail stores. . . .[2]

Yet as one HP corporate executive was quoted by *Forbes,*

> When it comes to the personal computer business, [HP has used] what I would describe as a very opportunistic approach to the marketplace. We have had several organizations in the company that were addressing the market. But none of them had it as their major focus . . . we had over $500 million sales in the personal computer market, which is not bad, but no significant focus on it.[10]

In addition, not many of HP's senior executives had specific experience in computer operations. In fact, most of HP's senior people had started with the organization on the instruments side, including those heading up the computer groups. Some believed this to be a problem, since the requirement of each business was rather distinct.

Past Principles and an Organization for the Future

Following is a 1983 description of the corporate objectives which encompassed HP's most important principles. Although there had been substantial change in the marketplace, few modifications had been made to the company's objectives since they were initially published in 1957.

1. *Profit:* to achieve sufficient profit to finance our company's growth and to provide resources we need to achieve our other corporate objectives.

2. *Customers:* to provide products and services of the highest quality and the greatest possible value to our customers, thereby gaining and holding their respect and loyalty.

3. *Fields of Interest:* to build on our strengths in the company's traditional fields of interest, and to enter new fields only when it is consistent with the basic purpose of our business and when we can assure ourselves of making a needed and profitable contribution to the field.

4. *Growth:* to let our growth be limited only by our profits and our ability to develop and produce innovative products that satisfy real customer needs.

5. *Our People:* to help HP people share in the company's success which they make possible: to provide job security based on their performance; to ensure them a safe and pleasant work environment; to recognize their individual achievements; and to help them gain a sense of satisfaction and accomplishment from their work.

6. *Management:* to foster initiative and creativity by allowing the individual greater freedom of action in attaining well-defined objectives.

7. *Citizenship:* to honor our obligations to society by being an economic, intellectual, and social asset to each nation and each community in which we operate.

HP's 1982 organization structure is outlined in Exhibit 3. In 1983 and again in 1984, the company restructured its organization in an attempt to deal with the issues posed by its move into computers. In Mr. Young's announcement of the organization changes of 1984, he spoke of this and previous fundamental reorganizations, ". . . each change has been a logical, evolutionary move that preserved the basic philosophy and integrity of the HP approach to business."[7]

Mr. Young further added,

Becoming a computer company has had a dramatic effect on our company, the biggest challenge is to orchestrate the divisions and provide a strategic glue and direction for the computer effort, while keeping the work units small.

Having small divisions is not the only way to organize a company, but having organizations that people can run like a small business is highly motivational, especially for professionals. Keeping that spirit of entrepreneurship alive is very important to us.[11]

When asked to compare his management style with that of HP's founders, Young said, "Bill is a brilliant engineer and Dave is a great businessman. I stress organization, planning, and the process." He further replied to the question of what he most hoped to achieve, by saying, "To show that it is worth institutionalizing

EXHIBIT 3
HP Organization Chart, 1982

ADMINISTRATION	OPERATIONS
Bob Boniface	Paul Ely,
Executive Vice President	Executive Vice President

EUROPE

Franco Mariotti
Vice President

Field Sales Regions
  France
  Germany
  Northern Europe
  South/East Europe
  United Kingdom

Manufacturing
  France
  Germany
  United Kingdom

INTERCONTINENTAL

Alan Bickell
Managing Director

Field Sales Regions
  Australasia
  Far East
  Japan
  Latin America
  South Africa
Manufacturing
  Brazil
  Japan
  Malaysia
  Mexico
  Puerto Rico
  Singapore

Corporate Controller
Jerry Carlson
Controller

Corporate Services
Bruce Wholey
Vice President

General Counsel
and Secretary
Jack Brigham
Vice President

International
Bill Doolittle
Senior Vice President

Government
Affairs
Bob Kirkwood
Director

Patents and Licenses
Jean Chognard
Vice President

Personnel
Bill Craven
Director

Public Relations
Dave Kirby
Director

Marketing
Al Oliverio
Senior Vice President

Treasurer
Ed van Bronkhorst
Senior Vice President

U.S./CANADA SALES

Field Sales Regions
  Eastern
  Midwest
  Neely (Western)
  Southern
  Canada

Corporate

  Marketing
  Operations
    ● Parts Center

COMPUTERS

TECHNICAL COMPUTER GROUP

Doug Chance
Vice President

■ Data Systems
■ Roseville
■ Desktop
  Computer
■ Engineering
  Systems
■ Böblingen
  Desktop
■ YHP Computer
■ Computer I.C.
  ● Cupertino I.C.
  ● Systems
    Technology

BUSINESS COMPUTER GROUP

Ed McCracken
General Manager
■ Computer Systems
  ● Roseville
■ Information Networks
  ● Office Systems
    Pinewood
  ● Office Systems
    Cupertino
  ● Grenoble
    Datacomm
■ Manufacturing Productivity
  ● Financial
    Systems
■ Böblingen
  General Systems
  ● Information Resources
  ● Guadalajara
    Computer

COMPUTER PERIPHERALS GROUP

Dick Hackborn
General Manager
■ Boise
■ Disc Memory
■ Greeley
  ● Singapore
■ Vancouver
  ● Bristol

COMPUTER TERMINALS GROUP

Cyril Yansouni
General Manager
■ Personal Office
  Computer
■ Roseville
  Terminals
■ Grenoble
  ● Puerto Rico

COMPUTER MARKETING GROUP
Jim Arthur, Vice President

■ Computer Support
■ Application Marketing
■ Personal Computer
  Marketing

● Systems
  Remarketing
● Computer
  Supplies

Source: **Hewlett Packard Company.**

EXHIBIT 3 (Continued)

BOARD OF DIRECTORS
Dave Packard, Chairman of the Board
Bill Hewlett, Chairman—Executive Committee

CHIEF EXECUTIVE OFFICER
John Young, President

OPERATIONS
Bill Terry,
Executive Vice President

OPERATIONS
Dean Morton,
Executive Vice President

INSTRUMENTS

MICROWAVE AND COMMUNICATIONS INSTRUMENT GROUP

Hal Edmondson
General Manager
- Colorado Telecom
- Queensferry Telecom
- Stanford Park
- Spokane
- Signal Analysis
- Network Measurements
- Santa Rosa Technology Center

ELECTRONIC MEASUREMENTS GROUP

G. B. Parzybok
General Manager
- Böblingen Instrument
- San Diego
- Colorado Springs
- Logic Systems
- YHP Instrument
- Loveland Instrument
- Lake Stevens Instrument
- New Jersey
- Santa Clara
- Integrated Circuits
  - Santa Clara
  - Loveland
  - Colorado Springs

INSTRUMENT MARKETING GROUP
Bob Brunner, General Manager

- Instrument Support

COMPONENTS GROUP

John Blokker
General Manager
- Microwave Semiconductor
- Optoelectronics
  - Visible Products
  - Interface Products
  - Singapore
  - Malaysia

Compents
Sales/Service

MEDICAL GROUP

Dick Alberding
Vice President
- Andover
- Böblingen Medical
- McMinnville
- Waltham
- Medical Supplies

Medical
Sales/Service

ANALYTICAL GROUP

Lew Platt
General Manager
- Avondale
- Scientific Instruments
- Waldbronn

Analytical
Sales/Service

PERSONAL COMPUTATION GROUP

Dick Moore
General Manager
- Corvallis
- Personal Computer
  - Corvallis Components
  - Brazil
  - Singapore

(Computer Marketing Group)

Key
- Division
- Operation (product line/ international locations)

HP LABORATORIES

Research and Development

John Doyle
Vice President

RESEARCH CENTERS

Computer Research

Physical Research

Technology Research

CORPORATE DEVELOPMENT

Dave Sanders
Director

INTERNAL AUDIT
George Abbott
Manager

CORPORATE MANUFACTURING SERVICES

Ray Démeré
Vice President

our founders' principles, hopefully by growing some and detracting nothing from the human elements that are so important."[8]

The Program Manager Concept

In response to these issues, a "program manager concept" had come into being at HP. Program managers had broad powers to tap various divisions for necessary support, components, or software. Previously, new products had always come from individual divisions, engineered typically in pursuit of the division's charter to "stay ahead of the game," or from HP Laboratories researchers who had "sold" their ideas and found a divisional sponsor.

The program manager concept was used for a special project called "Dawn." Under the direction of a program manager, half a dozen widely scattered HP divisions were coordinated on a $100 million project. On November 16, 1982, less than two years after "Dawn" began, the HP 9000, considered by many experts to be the ultimate in personal computers, was introduced. To succeed, the activities of the divisions had to be closely coordinated and the divisions' independence limited. As a target market for the HP 9000 (introduced in a remarkably short two years after a program manager was assigned), the company chose manufacturers, since these had been its primary customers for nearly ten years. It also selected four applications areas for focus: planning and control systems, factory automation, office systems, and engineering.

Traditionally, HP had marketed technologically sophisticated products and left applications details to its customers. That strategy worked well for many years because its customers were scientists who were often as sophisticated about applications as HP was. Yet computer customers were no longer necessarily scientists or engineers. As one corporate executive said, "I keep telling my engineers that they now have five minutes to make a sale, not five hours like we used to. We have to focus on apparent user benefits."[2] This executive's own experience typified the problem. While talking to a potential customer he became a bit rhapsodic about the HP 150's ability to process 2.2 megahertz faster than the IBM PC. "What's a megahertz?" asked the prospect, a lawyer. "I have to get out documents—what can you do for me?"

But technology was rapidly revolutionizing the small computer markets in which HP competed. In 1980 the 64K memory chip had made the desk-top *micro*-computer into one of the fastest growing markets in the United States. By 1985 the 256K chip allowed production of desk-top *mini*computers, powerful small lab computers, and engineering and production work stations of great complexity and power. By 1987 new megabit (one million bit) chips would permit mainframe powered computers to be produced in "micro" sizes. Pocket computers, electronic map navigators, and robots that could see and recognize some natural language commands were in the offing. By 1990 *micro-super*computers based on 4 megabit chips were expected with powers dwarfing all but the largest laboratory models. Yet these remarkable creations were likely to be so inexpensive that they would quickly become "commodity" items. Managing this degree of complexity in a commodity marketplace would become a singular challenge.

One analyst had earlier commented that over the past two decades HP had transitioned from a test instrument firm into a major systems company. By 1986 HP was involved in an even more complex shift toward multisystem networks—complete link ups between computers, instruments and peripherals—for laboratory, factory, hospital, or office automation systems.[12] An example of such a multisystem network is outlined in Exhibit 4.

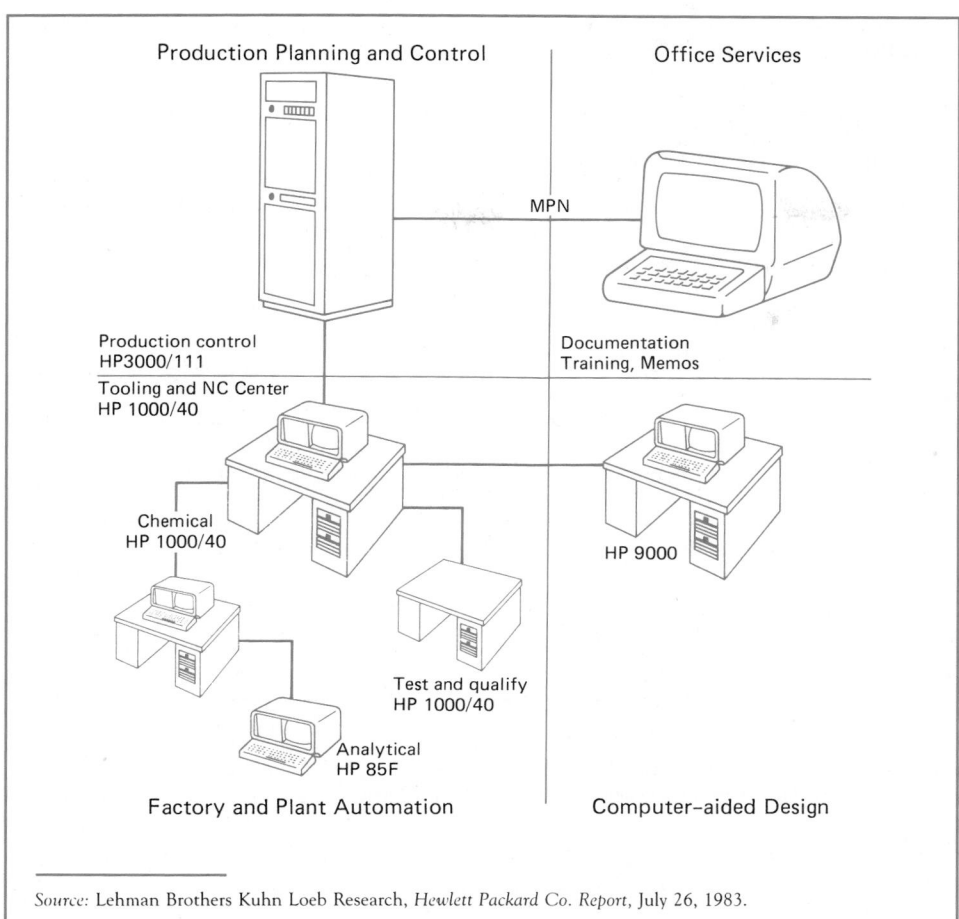

EXHIBIT 4
**Hewlett Packard's
Manufacturing
Productivity Network
(MPN)**

Source: Lehman Brothers Kuhn Loeb Research, *Hewlett Packard Co. Report,* July 26, 1983.

Finally HP had over 45 product divisions, of which at least 22 were directly related to computers. But in the burgeoning electronics markets of the mid-to-late 1980s increasing opportunities were appearing to link and relate what previously had been "stand alone" sensing, testing, measuring, processing, or controlling units. How HP could respond to these new needs, yet maintain its distinctive entrepreneurial style and culture was a critical issue for its management in the mid-1980s.

QUESTIONS

1. Why has HP been successful in the past? Why was its organization configured the way it was at each major transition point? Evaluate how well its structure and systems were adapted each time for their purposes.

2. What are the critical strategic issues facing HP in the mid 1980s? How should it respond to these? Key financial and operations data appear in the attached exhibits.

3. How should HP organize to meet its future challenges? Why? What changes in management style, control systems, and incentives should accompany these changes?

EXHIBIT 5
Hewlett Packard Company and Subsidiaries: Financials, 1980–1984

Consolidated Statement of Earnings, 1982–1984

For the years ended October 31 (millions except per share amounts)	1984	1983	1982
Net sales	$6,044	$4,710	$4,189
Costs and expenses:			
Cost of goods sold	2,865	2,195	1,967
Research and development	592	493	424
Marketing	1,066	771	631
Administrative and general	661	523	491
	5,184	3,982	3,513
Earnings before taxes	860	728	676
Provision for taxes	313	296	293
Reversal of DISC taxes*	(118)	—	—
	195	296	293
Net earnings	$ 665	$ 432	$ 383
Net earnings per share	$ 2.59	$ 1.69	$ 1.53

* Reversal of DISC taxes accrued prior to 1984 due to a change in U.S. tax law
The accompanying notes provided in the company's annual report are an integral part of these financial statements.

Selected Financial Data, 1980–1984

(Millions except per share amounts and employees)					
For the years ended October 31	1984	1983	1982	1981	1980
Domestic orders	$3,629	$2,901	$2,283	$1,918	$1,517
International orders	2,721	2,021	1,897	1,739	1,570
Total orders	$6,350	$4,922	$4,180	$3,657	$3,087
Net sales	$6,044	$4,710	$4,189	$3,528	$3,046
Earnings before taxes	860	728	676	567	513
Net earnings	665*	432	383	305	263
Per share					
Net earnings	$ 2.59*	$ 1.69	$ 1.53	$ 1.24	$ 1.09
Cash Dividends	$ 0.19	$ 0.16	$ 0.12	$ 0.11	$ 0.10
At year-end					
Total assets	$5,153	$4,161	$3,470	$2,782	$2,350
Employees (thousands)	82	72	68	64	57

* Includes a one-time increase in net earnings of $118 million (46 cents per share) resulting from a tax law change.
Source: Hewlett Packard Company, *Annual Report,* 1984.

EXHIBIT 5 (Continued)

Consolidated Balance Sheet, 1982–1984

October 31 (millions)	1984	1983	1982
Assets			
Current assets			
Cash and temporary cash investments	$ 938	$ 880	$ 684
Accounts and notes receivable	1,180	951	773
Inventories			
Finished goods	373	279	231
Purchased parts and fabricated assemblies	650	469	428
Other current assets	60	53	99
Total current assets	$3,201	$2,632	$2,215
Property, plant and equipment:			
Land	202	167	106
Buildings and leasehold improvements	1,416	1,102	940
Machinery and equipment	1,173	888	714
	2,791	2,157	1,760
Accumulated depreciation and amortization	923	726	589
	1,868	1,431	1,171
Other assets	84	98	84
	$5,153	$4,161	$3,470
Liabilities and shareholders' equity			
Current liabilities:			
Notes payable	$ 217	$ 148	$ 156
Accounts payable	281	203	139
Employee compensation and benefits	398	300	269
Other accrued liabilities	162	103	106
Accrued taxes on earnings	203	112	151
Other accrued taxes	61	54	42
Total current liabilities	$1,322	$ 920	$ 863
Long-term debt	81	71	39
Other liabilities	93	46	42
Deferred taxes on earnings	112	237	177
Shareholders' equity			
Common stock and capital in excess of $1 par value	775	733	587
Retained earnings	2,770	2,154	1,762
Total shareholders' equity	3,545	2,887	2,349
	$5,153	$4,161	$3,470

The accompanying notes provided in the company's annual report are an integral part of these financial statements.

Source: Hewlett Packard Company, *Annual Report,* 1984.

EXHIBIT 5 (Continued)

Segment Data, 1982–1984

Business Segments* (millions)	1984	1983	1982
Gross sales			
Computer products	$3,269	$2,476	$2,161
Electronic test and measurement	2,289	1,779	1,595
Medical electronic equipment	378	355	323
Analytical instrumentation	229	184	176
	$6,165	$4,794	$4,255
Intersegment sales			
Computer products	73	56	44
Electronic test and measurement	47	26	21
Medical electronic equipment	1	2	1
	121	84	66
Net sales	$6,044	$4,710	$4,189
Earnings before taxes			
Computer products	$ 439	$ 392	$ 370
Electronic test and measurement	514	381	339
Medical electronic equipment	41	61	60
Analytical instrumentation	37	23	28
Eliminations and corporate	(171)	(129)	(121)
	$ 860	$ 728	$ 676

* Sales between affiliates are made at market prices, less an allowance for subsequent manufacturing and/or marketing.

Source: Hewlett Packard Company, *Annual Report,* 1984.

Geographic Areas* (millions)	1984	1983	1982
Net sales			
United States	$3,527	$2,725	$2,270
Europe	1,620	1,392	1,318
Rest of world	897	593	601
	$6,044	$4,710	$4,189
Earnings before taxes			
United States	$ 768	$ 644	$ 554
Europe	138	148	157
Rest of world	110	59	95
Eliminations and corporate	(156)	(123)	(130)
	$ 860	$ 728	$ 676
Exports from			
United States	$1,420	$1,105	$1,081
Europe	145	100	61
Rest of world	277	160	164

* Net sales are based on the location of the customer. Earnings before taxes reflect the location of the company's facilities. Exports are primarily inter-area transfers to affiliates, which are made at market prices, less an allowance for subsequent manufacturing and/or marketing. Certain amounts have been reclassified to conform to the 1984 format.

EXHIBIT 5 (Continued)

Business Segments, 1982–1984

Identifiable assets (millions)	1984	1983	1982
Computer products	$2,182	$1,673	$1,358
Electronic test and measurement	1,379	1,022	903
Medical electronic equipment	268	224	191
Analytical instrumentation	154	133	104
Eliminations and corporate	1,170	1,109	914
	$5,153	$4,161	$3,470
Capital Expenditures (millions)	**1984**	**1983**	**1982**
Computer products	$ 330	$ 248	$ 215
Electronic test and measurement	202	108	104
Medical electronic equipment	27	37	18
Analytical instrumentation	14	18	7
Corporate	88	55	18
	$ 661	$ 466	$ 362
Depreciation and Amortization (millions)	**1984**	**1983**	**1982**
Computer products	$ 128	$ 105	$ 86
Electronic test and measurement	68	54	46
Medical electronic equipment	11	9	8
Analytical instrumentation	7	6	5
Corporate	23	17	13
	$ 237	$ 191	$ 158

* Direct and indirect sales to the U.S. Government amounted to approximately $550 million in 1984, $480 million in 1983 and $420 million in 1982. No other customer accounted for more than 5 percent of net sales.

Source: Hewlett Packard Company, *Annual Report,* 1984.

EXHIBIT 5
(Continued)

PRODUCTS AND BUSINESS SEGMENTS

The *Electronic Data Products* segment includes the following product groups: Business Computer, Technical Computer, Computer Peripherals, Computer Terminals, Computer Marketing and Personal Computation Groups. Products include small to medium-scale computer systems for business, scientific and industrial applications; desk-top, personal, and portable computers; personal scientific and business programmable calculators; computer peripherals; and a wide variety of software and support services.

The *Electronic Test and Measurement Products* segment includes the following product groups: Electronic Measurements, Microwave and Communication Instrument, Components, and Instrument Marketing. Products include instruments, systems and components for design, production and maintenance. Products used primarily in the communications, electronics manufacturing and aerospace industries.

Medical Electronic Equipment segment products perform a number of patient-monitoring, diagnostic, therapeutic, and medical and financial data-management functions for health care providers. Included are measurement and computation systems and a wide variety of software and support services.

Analytical Instrumentation segment products are used primarily to analyze chemical compounds. Products include gas and liquid chromatographs, mass spectrometers, spectrophotometers, laboratory automation systems, and integrators.

Source: Hewlett Packard Company, *Annual Report*, 1982.

EXHIBIT 5
(Continued)

Hewlett Packard Company Estimated Sales Breakdown, 1982–1984

	$ Million			The Market's
	1982	1983E	1984E	5-Yr. Growth
Computers				
Graphics/CAD	$ 730	$ 900	$1,090	20%
HP 3000 (MPN)	635	635	750	15
Peripherals	500	600	750	25
Calculators	117	90	115	10
Microcomputers	100	170	215	25
Software	35	50	70	35
HP1000 (Factory)	0	12	35	65
HP9000 (CAE)	0	30	75	70
Total	2,117	2,487	3,100	
Instruments				
Microwave/Comm.	470	500	590	15
Elec. Test	835	925	1,130	20
Automatic Test	45	56	70	25
Components	224	250	285	10
Total	1,574	1,731	2,075	
Medical				
Patient Monitoring	195	180	205	15
Diagnostic Instr.	127	150	180	20
Hospital Mgmt.	0	19	26	30
Total	322	349	411	
Analytical				
Gas Chromatographs	45	35	45	15
Data Stations	105	127	150	20
UV/Visible Spec.	15	20	25	20
Liquid Chromatog.	10	12	15	30
Biotechnology	1	1	5	50
Total	176	195	240	
Company Total	$4,189	$4,762	$5,826	

Source: E. F. Hutton, Inc., Equity Research, *Hewlett Packard Company Action Report,* June 28, 1983.

EXHIBIT 6
Comparative Financials

Electronic Business 200			Calendar 1984			
Rank			Electronics Sales ($ million)	Total Sales ($ million)	Net Income ($ million)	Return on Investment (%)
1984	1983	Company				
1	1	IBM	$45,937.0	$45,937.0	$6,582.0	21.8%
2	2	AT&T	17,406.7	33,187.5	1,369.9	5.9
3	3	General Electric	7,210.0	27,947.0	2,280.0	17.0
4	5	Xerox	6,981.0	8,791.6	375.6	6.0
5	4	ITT	6,589.0	12,701.0	302.5	3.4
6	8	Hewlett-Packard	6,297.0	6,297.0	564.0	18.2
7	9	Digital Equipment	6,229.6	6,229.6	486.9	7.4
8	6	Honeywell	6,073.6	6,073.6	334.8	10.9
9	10	Texas Instruments	5,741.6	5,741.6	316.0	16.4
10	12	Motorola	5,534.0	5,534.0	387.0	13.7
11	13	RCA	4,945.0	10,111.6	246.4	5.4
12	7	Hughes	4,925.0	4,925.0	300.0	NA
13	11	Burroughs	4,875.6	4,875.6	244.9	8.0
14	15	Sperry	4,648.0	5,370.0	262.2	5.6
15	16	Control Data	3,755.0	5,026.9	31.6	0.4
16	17	NCR	3,728.0	4,074.3	342.6	14.3
17	18	Raytheon	3,454.0	5,995.7	340.1	16.4
18	21	N. A. Philips	3,193.0	4,325.9	130.5	8.7
19	23	TRW	2,904.0	6,061.7	266.8	12.8
20	22	Tandy	2,771.1	2,771.1	234.9	21.1
27	29	Wang	2,421.1	2,421.1	231.0	12.9
31	49	Apple	1,897.9	1,897.9	104.3	13.8
34	38	Zenith	1,717.0	1,717.0	63.6	10.2
41	42	Tektronix	1,419.9	1,419.9	131.5	40.6
49	55	Perkin-Elmer*	1,169.0	1,255.5	79.2	10.2

* Leader in analytical instrumentation.
NA–Not available.

Source: Electronic Business, July 15, 1985.

EXHIBIT 6 (Continued)

Latest Fiscal Year			5-Year Growth (Compounded Growth Rate)		Capital Outlays to Net Cash Flow After Dividends	Debt as % of Total Capital
Cost of Goods as % of Sales	R&D as % of Sales	Net Income per Employee ($ thousand)	Sales (% per year)	Net Income (% per year)		
33.6%	9.1%	$16.7	15.0%	16.9%	83.1%	12.4%
50.5	7.2	3.8	NA	NA	190.1	41.0
69.6	3.7	6.9	4.5	10.1	101.6	6.4
39.4	6.4	3.6	4.6	−7.8	146.4	27.1
76.4	7.7	1.2	−5.9	−4.5	150.0	31.3
45.6	9.8	8.1	20.7	26.8	77.5	3.0
56.0	11.3	3.8	25.4	13.0	77.8	10.0
61.6	6.9	3.6	7.6	6.9	67.7	22.5
68.5	6.4	3.7	12.2	12.8	102.1	19.9
57.9	7.4	3.9	15.3	20.2	128.6	19.1
71.5	2.4	2.3	6.3	−2.8	131.3	41.5
NA	NA	NA	NA	NA	NA	NA
54.9	5.7	3.8	11.5	−4.3	113.4	25.0
59.3	8.4	2.7	3.3	−2.3	103.1	21.0
51.1	6.0	0.6	17.5	−23.2	94.8	76.6
43.7	7.1	5.5	6.3	7.9	61.7	13.1
77.4	3.9	4.6	10.0	11.5	105.7	4.6
74.3	2.3	2.3	12.4	9.8	92.4	34.0
73.3	2.4	2.9	5.9	6.5	113.2	15.7
43.4	0.0	8.3	17.6	27.6	25.1	26.1
47.6	7.3	6.9	46.7	49.0	155.3	23.3
55.5	4.7	11.9	99.5	66.1	38.8	0.0
77.2	5.1	2.2	9.8	27.4	69.5	28.8
50.5	11.2	5.7	11.1	8.9	54.9	68.2
55.3	6.7	4.3	10.0	5.6	68.3	12.9

EXHIBIT 7
Representative Market Share Data for HP Products

A. Worldwide 1985 Shares (%) Computers

Small Systems ($12K–350K)		Microsystems (< $12K)	
IBM	20.0	IBM	27.7
DEC	12.7	Apple	9.0
Nixdorf	6.0	Commodore	4.2
HP	5.8	HP	4.2
Wang	4.3	NEC	3.6
NEC	3.1	AT&T	3.5
AT&T	2.4	Wang	2.7

Source: The Wall Street Journal, April 7, 1986, p. 26.

B. Test & Measurement Shares (%) 1984

Logic Analyzers		Universal Microprocessor Development Systems	
HP	30	HP	61
Tektronix	29	Tektronix	32
Gould	7	Kontron	4
Phillips NV	7	Millenium	3

Source: F. Eberstadt & Co., Inc., *Test and Measurement Industry Report,* May 20, 1985.

FORD: TEAM TAURUS

In mid-1980, Ford Motor Company found itself with sales off 42% and a loss of $164 million for the quarter. Were it not for its profitable foreign operations, Ford's bottom line would have looked even worse. The auto sales slump that followed the gasoline shortages of 1979 deepened into a crisis as double-digit interest rates ascended. Ford was not alone in its suffering—in May 1980, Chrysler's sales were off 49%, and GM's 32%. Meanwhile, sales of small, fuel-efficient, well-made Japanese cars soared. Although the decline of the U.S. auto industry is a familiar story, what is less well known is how Ford arrived at this turning point and what it did to recover.

Ford's Early 1980s Style

Ford, founded in 1903 by Henry Ford, was one of a very few large U.S. corporations where the top management position was traditionally held by a descendant of the founder. With his family owning 40% of the voting stock, Henry Ford II led the company from 1945 until well into the early 1980s. He was CEO from 1945 until the fall of 1979 and, by all accounts, had a management style that could be described as "quite autocratic." While GM and the Japanese automakers had developed strategic decision-making processes that were intentionally depersonalized and based on a culture of consensus, Ford's strategic decisions had a more personalized character, because of Mr. Ford's presence, although formalized strategic planning existed in many areas.

Case copyright © 1988, James Brian Quinn. This case was developed by Penny C. Paquette under the guidance of Professor Quinn.

The help and cooperation of Ford Motor Co. are gratefully acknowledged. The special contributions of Mr. Dan Dimancescu of Cambridge, Mass., are especially acknowledged.

481

Ford had been the leading U.S. automaker in non-U.S. markets for the past three decades, successfully emphasizing the European market. Since the early 1970s Ford's non-U.S. operations had become increasingly important both in terms of volume and profitability. Yet strategy was made primarily from a "Detroit viewpoint," and the company did little to import experience or gain U.S. advantages from its worldwide operations. What went on in the rest of the world seemed to have little to do with the North American market, where big cars had always been status symbols and customers expected cars to "feel and handle like sofas with seat belts."

At Ford, the bottom line was all important. As in other old-line U.S. companies, blue-collar workers were generally considered as variable costs and laid off whenever cyclical downturns occurred. To obtain a measure of job security the unions resisted shifts among the very narrow job categories management itself had created to provide job ladders in the highly specialized mass production systems created by the "efficiency experts" of the past. Ford's CEO, Donald Petersen, in the mid-1980s acknowledged, "The old system had thought of the worker as primarily a single purpose machine tool."[1] A magazine article described the story of a plant manager who wanted to deliver a "state of the plant" message to all employees. An accountant protested saying that "with fringes, we're paying people $20 an hour. If the meeting lasts an hour, that's 5,000 hours times $20—$100,000." Given the need to control costs and meet production schedules, this was a message not to be ignored.

Centralization and Scale Economies

As in many other companies, Ford people were told what to do and were not expected to question it. The same article recounted another worker whose job in the 1950s involved lifting heavy transmissions. He approached his foreman and said "I've got an idea on how to improve this operation." The foreman stared at him incredulously. "You wanna work, kid, or don'tcha? You forget that stuff. We didn't hire you to think." When that worker came back to the plant as plant manager some 20 years later, he went to his station and found that nothing had changed. Often when plants had met their quotas, workers would be told to "go home" and lose their pay for the rest of the day.

Workers on the line were allowed little active input on quality; instead quality was controlled through inspection. A manager once described the operating style as "Management by exception. Watch for an error and then dive on it. We barked and they reacted."[2] First-run yields might only be 70% in spec. When things were going well, management felt it could rebuild the rejects. Marvin Runyon, who took early retirement from his job as vice president of Ford's Body and Assembly Manufacturing Operations in 1980 and ended up managing Nissan Motor's new U.S. plant, said he felt Ford had long-neglected manufacturing. The line was kept moving regardless of defects or machinery which might need repair. Runyon noted, "There never seemed to be enough money to maintain equipment or to improve the quality of Ford's cars, while advertising budgets seemed lush and marketing and finance executives earned considerably more than their manufacturing counterparts."[3]

Suppliers were given minimal lead times, and the low-cost bidder usually won the job. This often meant that several different suppliers would be given contracts for various parts within one section or subsystem of the car. One engineer recalled spending almost a year working with a supplier to design and develop a part only to have the buyer, whose performance was judged on finding the cheapest supplier, give the contract to another company. Little trust existed between

Ford and its suppliers, and communications with them usually began only after Ford's design teams had finalized the car's specifications and it was ready to go into production.

Unlike GM—which was highly decentralized in part because its major divisions had at one time been freestanding companies—Ford was very centralized. Within its major operational divisions—North American Automotive, International Automotive, and Diversified Products—Ford was vertically organized by function. These vertical organizations had become so powerful and self-contained that they were referred to as "chimneys" of power. Each function had its own goals and perspective, and each tended to view the others as part of any problem rather than as part of its solution. Design engineers looked down on manufacturing engineers, and both frequently disavowed the consequences when their elegant designs and processes passed into the grease-covered hands of the line.

As one former engineer put it, "When I was with Ford Manufacturing building the 1970's Mustangs, we didn't see the car we were going to make until eight or nine months before production was to start. And designers didn't want our ideas, either!" Each stage of product development—from research to design, to product engineering, to manufacturing, to assembly, to sales, to the dealer, and finally to the service units—was dominated by an individual functional department which seemed to be obsessed with why the preceding group's design would not work. When a downstream group encountered a problem, it was always the "fault" of a preceding group. Redos and changes proliferated and continued even past "Job 1," when the first new car rolled off the assembly line.

THE TURBULENT 1970s

The decade of the 1970s was turbulent at Ford, filled with internal upheavals and rapid changes in its external and regulatory environments. In 1970, an up-and-coming engineer named Lewis Veraldi, whose career up to this point had been in design engineering, began a three-year stint in Ford's manufacturing group. Working double shifts in manufacturing he soon gained a very different perspective on the design and product development process from other Ford engineers who tended to avoid associating with people on "the line." In 1973 when Ford embarked on its most expensive car program to date—the $840 million Fiesta small-car project in Germany—Philip Caldwell, then head of international operations, picked Veraldi to head the project. The car was to be a clean sheet project (not derived from an existing car platform). Ford's European engineering and manufacturing groups were then close to being at war with each other, and continuation of the internecine struggle could have been disastrous.[4]

Veraldi, a 25-year veteran of Ford's design systems, had just experienced the frustration of taking an engineering design to the plant only to have manufacturing reject it "because it wasn't designed right." He decided the time had come to bring the manufacturing people upstream into the design process. He started by asking them, "Before we put this design on paper, how do you, the manufacturing and assembly people, want us to proceed to make your job easier?" Bringing the two disciplines together and executing the program simultaneously rather than sequentially turned out to avoid a plethora of changes and saved Ford "a bundle of money."

By then the United States was experiencing its first oil price shock and was tumbling into an inflationary recession. Congress soon passed the 1975 Energy Policy and Conservation Act mandating fuel economy standards for 1978. In 1975 Ford was already committed to building the Fiesta in Europe, but the recession had brought operating losses that some thought might continue for a long time. In response the company cut capital spending by $2 billion, decided not to downsize as quickly as GM, and postponed the project for Ford's first small, front-wheel car then planned for introduction in 1978.

An Executive Response

Up to this point, Ford's executive management had not been directly involved in developing long-term product strategy alternatives. Division level managers had generally presented one or two alternatives for top management approval. But, because of the 1970s' new complexities, product design was elevated to the senior management level; and six more months were added to the implementation phase of Ford's already long product development cycle—then 5 to 6 years, as opposed to Japan's average of 43 months.

Serving in an advisory capacity to the Office of the Chief Executive was a product planning group, responsible for defining future product needs and assessing how changing internal and external factors might affect Ford's product line. Once broad product direction was determined, an Advanced Vehicle Development (AVD) group was responsible for assessing design feasibilities and trade-offs and recommending more specific car size; product configuration; and image, cost, and investment objectives. Engineering then designed the needed hardware and new engineering processes to convert AVD's approved prototype into manufacturable products. This began the lengthy sequential progress of the car through the various functional groups described above (see Figure 1).

But Henry Ford's own preferences vastly influenced outcomes. With big cars selling well, the company's top executives were in no hurry to design smaller cars. Consequently, Ford ended up behind its rivals in introducing front-wheel drive to the United States. Even when Ford finally downsized its biggest cars, it reduced fuel consumption but kept the larger look and feel of an earlier era. When, in 1979, gas lines reappeared and tastes suddenly shifted to smaller, fuel-efficient cars (both in style and reality), Ford did not have them to sell. Its market share in the United States plummeted from 23.6% in 1978 to 20.7% in 1979, to 17.3% by 1980. Not until the fall of 1980 was Ford able to introduce its first front-wheel drive cars to replace the Pinto and Bobcat. Although these cars, the Escort and Lynx, would help Ford regain some market share, they could not help its bottom line; Ford estimated that on a fully allocated basis it lost $400 every time it sold one. Ford ballyhooed the Escort as an example of a "world car," first designed in Europe. But it was reengineered in the United States by executives skeptical of their overseas counterparts, and the U.S. and European vehicles actually ended up with only one common part—a water pump seal![5]

Finally in March 1980 Henry Ford II stepped down as chairman of the board while remaining a member of the board and chairman of the finance committee. He was succeeded as CEO by Caldwell with Donald E. Petersen named president. At first, Philip Caldwell was underestimated by many people as a consummate company man who had gotten to the top by not crossing Henry Ford II—but he was the first non-family CEO. During his tenure, he transformed Ford from a family-run operation into one managed by professionals. He oversaw vast changes in Ford's management philosophy and its attitudes toward the market itself.

Petersen had been executive vice president of the profitable International Automotive Operations. A mechanical engineer with a Stanford MBA, Petersen had started his career at Ford in 1949 as a financial and product planning analyst and soon worked his way up through the product side. Over the years, he tried his hand at marketing, directed engineering and industrial design staffs, and managed

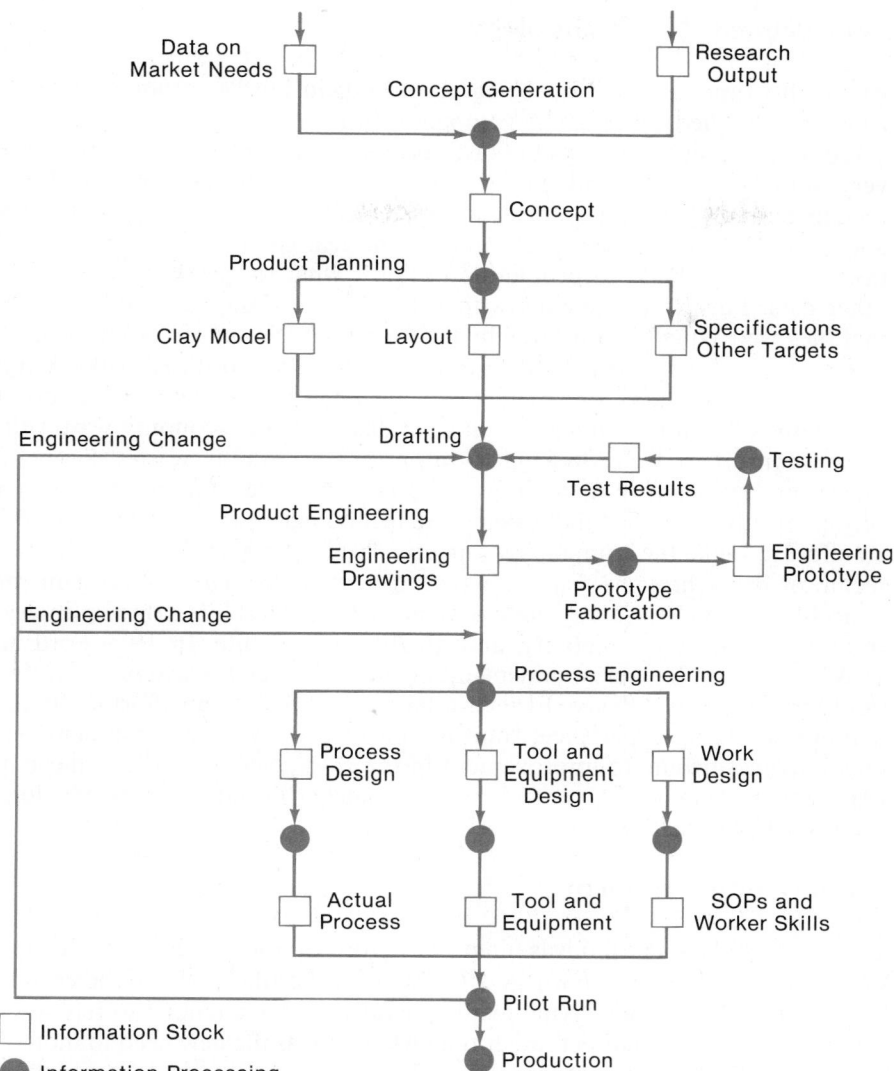

FIGURE 1
Typical Product Development Cycle
Source: Kim B. Clark and T. Fujimoto, Working Paper: "Overlapping Problem Solving in Product Development," April 1988, Harvard Business School, Division of Research.

Data on Market Needs

Research Output

Concept Generation

Concept

Product Planning

Clay Model   Layout   Specifications Other Targets

Engineering Change   Drafting   Test Results   Testing

Product Engineering

Engineering Drawings   Prototype Fabrication   Engineering Prototype

Engineering Change

Process Engineering

Process Design   Tool and Equipment Design   Work Design

Actual Process   Tool and Equipment   SOPs and Worker Skills

Pilot Run

Production

☐ Information Stock

● Information Processing

truck operations. He played a key part in developing the Mustang and got credit for Ford's Econoline, one of the most successful vans ever. During the 1970s, he served as head of Diversified Products as well as International Automotive Operations. Despite his financial orientation, Petersen was known as a product man—although he supposedly lacked the flamboyance and marketing flair Iacocca had shown at Ford.

Harold A. Poling, who had been vice president of finance and later chairman of Ford Europe, became head of the ailing North American Automotive Operations. With its product plans largely committed through the 1983 model year, Ford tried to staunch its losses in the United States with spending cuts. Poling slashed the payroll by 37,500 employees and permanently shut down two money-losing assembly plants, one of which did not have a reputation for producing high quality cars. During 1978 Ford United States had actually recalled more cars than it produced, and many thought it had become perhaps the worst U.S. producer in terms of quality.

Management, Not Technology

About this time, a scene was being played out in Ford's corporate design center which exemplified some of the company's problems. A few consumers had been asked in to get their reactions to Ford's prototype cars for the future. The cars were very similar to GM's and almost identical to Ford's own boxy-looking 1980 models currently rusting on dealers' lots. One member of the audience stood up and said, "I know, these are all phony. The real car is behind the curtain back there, isn't it." The Ford people didn't know what to say because there were no other cars. Further discussions with his corporate designers convinced Petersen that they were equally uninspired by the future models. At this point the new management decided to turn the designers loose to develop ideas, without trying to second-guess their bosses or merely copying what the competition was doing.

Ford's executives finally began to realize that fuel economy wasn't the only reason consumers were flocking to imports; Ford simply wasn't competitive in quality and styling with many imports. Quality became a top priority, as manufacturing executives studied the systems and technologies of automakers worldwide in an effort to make the company competitive again. They concluded that few major technical breakthroughs were either needed or likely. They could gain most by concentrating on improving management methods to achieve three primary goals: improved quality, productivity, and quality of work life. In 1979 Ford and the UAW had signed a letter of understanding on employee involvement (EI) in which both formally agreed to give EI their total commitment in an effort to "make work a more satisfying experience; improve the overall work environment; enhance creativity; contribute to improvement in the workplace; and help achieve quality, efficiency, and reduced absenteeism." Ultimately this led to a new Mission Statement for Ford. (See Exhibit 1.)

Employee Involvement

In early 1980 Pete Pestillo was hired away from BF Goodrich Co. to be vice president of labor relations at Ford. A colorful figure, Pestillo spoke of the need for new ways to manage people. "Americans generally . . . have tended to rely upon their ability to manage and direct rather than what I see as the new need to motivate and lead. We're dealing with a generation that saw dissent topple a government and change our foreign policy. These people are probably correct in paying limited attention to supposed authority." *Industry Week*[6] said, "Since the process of making a car offers 100,000 occasions for indifference, what Mr. Pestillo had in mind was a broad program that would involve everybody in the workplace on product quality —a system where everyone in an auto plant felt that the car at the end of the line bore a little part of him, so he wanted it done right." When Don Ephlin took over the Ford unit of UAW in May of the same year, the two of them saw a constructive opportunity to do things differently.

Neither Ford nor the UAW wanted to measure the economic results of EI, believing that "playing the numbers game" would kill the process.[7] In 1980, to prove its seriousness about employee involvement, Ford took an unprecedented step. It began sending drawings, parts, models, and mock-ups of its new Ranger truck to its Louisville plant, displayed them alongside the assembly lines, and invited workers to comment on how to improve what they might one day be building. Through the spring of 1983, the hourly employees had made 749 proposals for Ranger and Bronco II, and Ford adopted 542 of them.[8]

After a joint trip to Japan in 1981 to look at how the competition did things, Pestillo and Ephlin, with the support of Chairman Caldwell, were able to negotiate

EXHIBIT 1
Mission Statement

MISSION

Ford Motor Company is a worldwide leader in automotive and automotive-related products and services as well as in newer industries such as aerospace, communications, and financial services. Our mission is to improve continually our products and services to meet our customers' needs, allowing us to prosper as a business and to provide a reasonable return from our stockholders, the owners of our business.

VALUES

How we accomplish our mission is as important as the mission itself. Fundamental to success for the company are these basic values:

- *People*—Our people are the source of our strength. They provide our corporate intelligence and determine our reputation and vitality. Involvement and teamwork are our core human values.
- *Products*—Our products are the end result of our efforts, and they should be the best in serving customers worldwide. As our products are viewed, so are we viewed.
- *Profits*—Profits are the ultimate measure of how efficiently we provide customers with the best products for their needs. Profits are required to survive and grow.

GUIDING PRINCIPLES

- Quality comes first. To achieve customer satisfaction, the quality of our products and services must be our number-one priority.
- Customers are the focus of everything we do. Our work must be done with our customers in mind, providing better products and services than our competition.
- Continuous improvement is essential to our success. We must strive for excellence in everything we do: in our products, in their safety and value—and in our services, our human relations, our competitiveness and our profitability.
- Employee involvement is our way of life. We are a team. We must treat each other with trust and respect.
- Dealers and suppliers are our partners. The company must maintain mutually beneficial relationships with dealers, suppliers, and our other business associates.
- Integrity is never compromised. The conduct of our company worldwide must be pursued in a manner that is socially responsible and commands respect for its integrity and for its positive contribution to society. Our doors are open to men and women alike without discrimination and without regard to ethnic origin or personal beliefs.

Source: Ford Motor Company, *Annual Report,* 1984.

a new Ford-UAW contract in only 13 days—six months before the old one expired. This had never happened in the industry's history. They hammered out such precedent-setting new contract innovations as a joint UAW-Ford Employee Development and Training Program and various experiments with lifetime employment security, coupled with changes in job classifications and work rules. By 1982 some plants had even taken the unprecedented step of allowing hourly workers to stop the line to correct defects. At one plant, within four months after the stop buttons were installed, defects had dropped to fewer than 1 per car, down from 17.

Quality Improvement

Ford's began other programs as well. It instigated business plans which (instead of focusing on a target return on investment) called for improving quality on the theory that returns would follow. Ford not only began rigorously applying the statistical process control techniques and quality attitudes popularized by W. Edwards Deming in Japan, it also adopted the newer approaches to quality management developed by Genichi Taguchi.

Taguchi methods start with the premise that the quality goal should be to continually reduce variability around well-defined target specifications, rather than simply to ensure that the production process stays within specification limits. His rationale is developed in a formula called the "loss function curve," which proposes that the cost of deviating from the target specification increases quadratically (by squares) the further one gets away from the target. This formula not only allows engineers to set cost-justified specification tolerances but to figure out how much money they can spend to reduce variation in a process or product. Taguchi's other theories involve ways to design a product to be robust enough to achieve high quality despite fluctuations on the production line. Since designing a manufacturing process that makes a product with the highest possible uniformity at the lowest possible cost is complicated by the enormous number of alternatives available, Taguchi developed a statistical procedure called the "signal-to-noise ratio" to vastly reduce the number of options by grouping them and changing several variables at a time. Once engineers define an efficient production process, they can also design the product itself to be less sensitive to expected variations—especially those that are difficult or costly for the factory to regulate.

Ford's internal operation set up to train its engineers and suppliers in Taguchi methods was later spun off as the American Supplier Institute. Despite Mr. Poling's financial background and his diligence in cutting expenses, he emphasized that cutting costs and improving quality were not incompatible. In spite of formidable cost cutting, Ford North American spent around $3 billion during the early 1980s to completely renovate and expand its engine, transmission, stamping, and assembly plants. Ford's practice was to introduce new technology and new capacity in existing plants when new vehicles were introduced. This contrasted with GM's approach of bringing on new technology in new "green field" plants.

TAURUS RISES

In the midst of all these changes Ford sought to replace its midsized cars with innovative new products that would lure drivers back into the American fold and attack the heart of GM's market. The targeted segment, often called the "intermediate" car market, was the meat and potatoes of any full-line manufacturer's business. This was where volume sales and full profit margins met, and where Ford hoped that 40% of its sales would eventually lie.

What was to become the Taurus project began in earnest in 1979. The original designs were for a five-passenger, four-cylinder engine car about 170 inches long. It was to be a downsized replacement for the Ford LTD/Mercury Marquis as well as for the larger Crown Victoria/Marquis. In 1980, 64% of the U.S. market was in small cars. The product planning group was projecting fuel cost of $3 per gallon in the mid-1980s when the cars would go to market. When Lew Veraldi came back from Europe after the Fiesta project, he was assigned to Advanced Vehicle Development (AVD) where his job was to create advanced cars in hardware, not just on paper. It was there that he did his initial work on what became the Taurus/Sable cars.

In the summer of 1980 Veraldi and others made a presentation to senior management. The meeting was to make basic decisions about the cars' specifications, let management look at various designs, and settle on the critical path the Taurus project would take. A key question was whether it would be the costly, radical, clean sheet design AVD had come up with, or a low-investment program, with Taurus probably becoming a "muddle-through, parts bin car" liberally borrowing componentry from the Tempo and Topaz, which were to be introduced in 1983. Despite the fact that the company was treading water in red ink having lost over $1 billion two years in a row, Caldwell supported the clean sheet project—funding a $3.25 billion project for a brand-new, unproven car design.

Starting at this point, Caldwell asked the key questions he was to repeat again and again during the program, "Why should I buy this car? Specifically, why will this car be a success? What will Ford have to do to make the car absolutely world class in terms of quality and customer satisfaction?" By October 1982 when the project went to the board of directors for final approval it had become clear that the LTD and Marquis were ill equipped to meet the needs of the middle segment of the market. The board agreed that Ford had to become world class leader in this key segment, and that was not possible with what Ford then had.

At the critical 1980 meeting senior management agreed to the creation of a management team, later known as Team Taurus, to implement the concept of *concurrent* rather than sequential car design and development. This time, program management was to go even further than it had with the Fiesta project; representatives from *all* units—planning, design, engineering, manufacturing, marketing, and so on—would work together as a group and take final responsibility for the new vehicle. Veraldi even brought some team members over from Europe to help capture some of the luxury feel and nimble style of the European cars.

All decisions concerning the Taurus program would be made by the Team Taurus core group. The organization chart for Team Taurus resembled two large circular rings. (See Exhibit 2.) The inner ring contained the car program management (CPM) group of which Lew Veraldi was the head, with John Risk (Car Product Development planning director), A. L. Guthrie (chief engineer), John Telnack (chief designer), and Philip Benton (later president, Ford Automotive Group) among the other key players. In the various segments surrounding the inner CPM group were people from the various functional divisions within the company. Some of these worked full time with the Team Taurus core group. Others stayed in their respective functional divisions, but were committed to Team Taurus full time. The whole team was held together by common goals, keyed around the goal of Taurus being truly "world class in its segment."

Goals for the Team Taurus program management group eventually became

- Obtaining performance at "best in class"
- Getting 100% prototype parts on the first prototype in order to test designs and suppliers

EXHIBIT 2

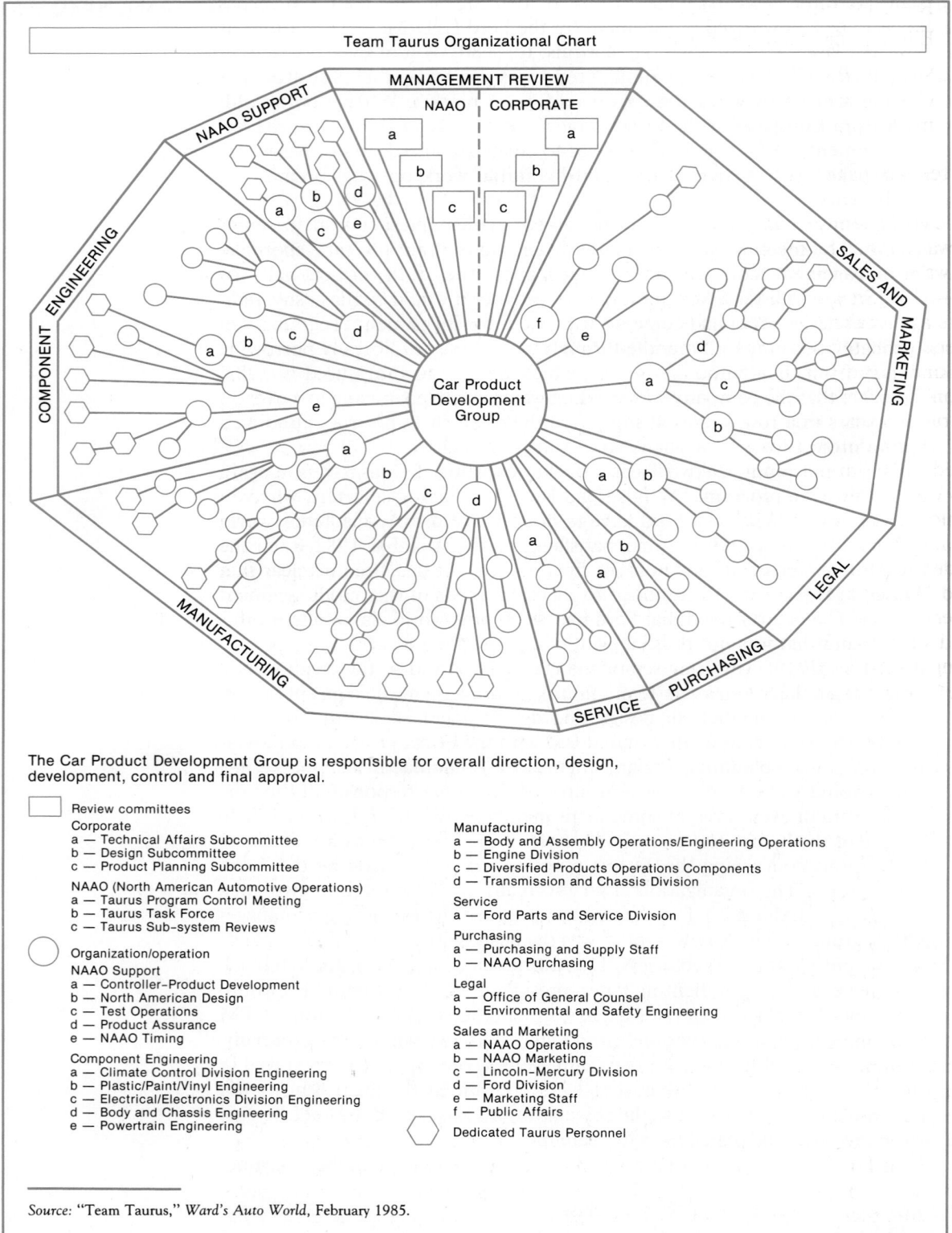

Team Taurus Organizational Chart

The Car Product Development Group is responsible for overall direction, design, development, control and final approval.

▢ Review committees

Corporate
a — Technical Affairs Subcommittee
b — Design Subcommittee
c — Product Planning Subcommittee

NAAO (North American Automotive Operations)
a — Taurus Program Control Meeting
b — Taurus Task Force
c — Taurus Sub-system Reviews

◯ Organization/operation

NAAO Support
a — Controller–Product Development
b — North American Design
c — Test Operations
d — Product Assurance
e — NAAO Timing

Component Engineering
a — Climate Control Division Engineering
b — Plastic/Paint/Vinyl Engineering
c — Electrical/Electronics Division Engineering
d — Body and Chassis Engineering
e — Powertrain Engineering

Manufacturing
a — Body and Assembly Operations/Engineering Operations
b — Engine Division
c — Diversified Products Operations Components
d — Transmission and Chassis Division

Service
a — Ford Parts and Service Division

Purchasing
a — Purchasing and Supply Staff
b — NAAO Purchasing

Legal
a — Office of General Counsel
b — Environmental and Safety Engineering

Sales and Marketing
a — NAAO Operations
b — NAAO Marketing
c — Lincoln–Mercury Division
d — Ford Division
e — Marketing Staff
f — Public Affairs

⬡ Dedicated Taurus Personnel

Source: "Team Taurus," *Ward's Auto World,* February 1985.

- Improving key decision timing for development
- Reducing product complexity
- Eliminating avoidable changes
- Controlling late program modifications
- Creating an atmosphere like a small business unit with identity and commitment

Systematic Planning and Tremendous Trifles

Little else was etched in granite at first. Instead the cooperative Team Taurus process was allowed to design the line. Before finalizing designs and $4\frac{1}{2}$ years before the car was introduced the team developed a "want" list by asking all the constituencies—Ford designers, body and assembly engineers, line workers, marketing managers and dealers, legal and safety experts, parts suppliers, insurance companies, independent service people, ergonomics experts, and consumers—"Considering the kind of car we're planning, what would you want to see included, changed, and so on?" The want list eventually included some 1,400 items—of which Team Taurus concentrated on 500.

At the Atlanta Assembly plant, chosen for Taurus, Team Taurus put the proposed car's initial drawings on a wall and said, "Tell us what you want to see in a new car for this plant, built with your current processes or with processes that you would like to develop." Examples of the suggestions given included (1) reducing the number of bodyside panels from the usual six or more—which had to be welded together and made it difficult to obtain integrity in the door margins or a good overall fit; (2) designing interior plastic trim pieces that were larger and thus easier to install, better fitting and better looking; (3) using one size screw head instead of many for fastening interior moldings so workers didn't have to keep changing the heads on their screw-torquing power tools. Mr. Veraldi described other cooperative measures as follows:

> We met with the legal and safety people very early in the project. Since the cars were expected to be on the market for a seven- or eight-year life cycle, we asked them to tell us what changes or additions to the laws and emission and safety regulations we should anticipate and "bake in" to the design and specifications of the car.[9] We did this for both the United States and Europe so the car could be easily adapted to the European market.
>
> The Service Managers Council was helpful in telling us what steps we could take to make the cars easier to service. We also looked very carefully at bodywork repairability by talking to independent repairmen and insurance companies. The repairmen came in and told us where in any body structure it was best to design in body integrity, ease of repair, and so on. For example, they showed us where to cut the car to get structural integrity after an accident or other repairs.

While many auto companies talked about being "best in their field," Team Taurus attempted a systematic follow through on that goal. The CPM group scrapped Ford's traditional "Detroit-knows-best" or "Not Invented Here" attitudes and methodically set out to identify 400 subsystems which comprised the world's best-designed and engineered automotive features, and tried to incorporate as many as possible into the Taurus. Starting in 1982, they selected cars, subsystems, and components from around the world with superior features and reverse engineered them to learn how they were designed, manufactured, and assembled. Mr. Veraldi continued:

For Taurus, suppliers were asked to participate early. If they shared their expertise with us, they would be guaranteed the business if we used their designs. But under Team Taurus we also made them accountable for quality and fit before producing the part. We instituted what I called the "Must See Before" program under which suppliers were required to show the Team the parts they were making and how they would make sure they fit right, functioned right, felt right, and looked right in the final product. We also used "system sourcing" for Taurus purchasing; instead of having different companies supply, say, interior trim moldings (leading to confusion and difficulty in resolving fit problems), only one company supplied all the moldings.

We tried to take time out of the project in ways that would take cost out as well. The car was sourced starting $3\frac{1}{2}$ years before Job 1. On average, sourcing was completed 26–29 months before production, letting suppliers plan their production and quality programs. We were even willing to make loans to qualified suppliers to help them get ready. Tooling was also planned far ahead for both stamping and assembly. Since we were always trying to come up with significant advantages for every component or feature in the car, we also tried to get suppliers to help us obtain "best-in-class" features for their products. We did this by getting the purchasing people to write long-term contracts with suppliers to create mutual trust.

Marketing Concentration

Many critics felt this process could only lead to a "copycat" car, but Team Taurus was determined to create Ford's first really distinctive car of the 1980s. John Telnack is often given credit for Ford's new "aero look" first introduced in the 1983 LTD. To implement this in the new line, Team Taurus launched Ford's largest ever series of market studies to determine customers' preferences and to respond to top management's instruction "to break with tradition and give us something uniquely Ford." This helped in determining which features should have highest priority in the new design and brought out myriad ideas for "customer appreciation items"— "tremendous trifles" as Lew Veraldi began to call them—which the Team found created a "halo effect" about the quality and comfort in the rest of the car. Examples included a net in the trunk to hold grocery bags upright, oil dipsticks painted a bright yellow for fast identification, and more width and height (footroom) under the front seat to make the back-seat ride more comfortable. On a broader scale engineers achieved a crisper, tauter, better tracking handling than other midsized U.S. cars. And a five-member ergonomics group undertook a systematic two-year task, scientifically studying ways to make the cars more comfortable and easier to operate.[10]

Based on the new inputs from consumers Team Taurus was able to reduce the marketing entities for Taurus (and the Mercury Division's version of the car, Sable) to the lowest number ever offered in this segment. Marketing entities are the models, series, or order specification groups production has to build. Taurus/Sable started out with about the same number (188) entities the preceding line had, and ended up with 37. Within these 37 marketing entities, the average build repeatability increased to 13,000. For comparison, Ford's 1985 LTD build repeatability was a little over 1,000. Comparable figures were about 7,000 for Toyota's entry in this segment, 2,300 for GM's Celebrity, and 11,500 for Nissan's Maxima.[11] While Team Taurus designed about 4,000 totally new parts for its cars, the line had some 1,700 fewer parts than its predecessors.[12] Eventually, the line had 95% new parts, and only 5% holdovers.

From a design viewpoint Mr. Veraldi said the program's toughest moment was in April 1981 when Team Taurus decided to increase the line's wheelbase, tread, and length. Oil prices appeared to be adjusting dramatically downward. Although the Team felt a year had been wasted, changed circumstances dictated a larger car. "We changed our strategy and decided to let the Crown Victoria and Grand Marquis stay in place and to reorient the new car as a sophisticated, family-oriented car. It grew into a six-passenger, six-cylinder, 188-inch car as fuel prices began to stabilize in the $1 to $1.25 range." A 2.5-liter, 4-cylinder base engine had been locked in from the start, but the optional V-6 grew from 2.8 to 3.0 liters as Ford adjusted its road performance requirements upward.

THE TEAM TAURUS MANAGEMENT APPROACH

After the crucial positioning of the car and its main performance characteristics were decided, Veraldi said,

> We established a key events schedule. There were two levels of activity for this, direct responsibilities—including business planning, product planning, design, technical engineering, and so on—and indirect responsibilities where we only determined the "what and when" issues. The line people determined the "who and how" issues. All the "key events" for each line function were set out on a chart with months across the top and functions down the side. A team member was assigned from each organization to sign off on the *entire* schedule on behalf of his department and to sign off on the *particulars of his own department's* key events schedule. The main program controls were getting these guys (1) to agree together on the overall schedule and (2) to agree to monitor it in their own organizations. There were over 1500 events on the way from concept to customer. The discipline of laying things down on the key events chart helped everyone to cut costs and increase value for each function. Team members were asked to sign off on these key events 3–4 years before production.

> Involving all groups in the process although seemingly more complicated, actually lowered costs because each group was not optimizing at its own level. It was much easier to get people to talk about and come up with constructive changes when they couldn't pass off responsibility by saying, "that's really a manufacturing problem not a design one." There were no specific incentives set up for this project other than pride of workmanship. We found out that most people want to do the job right when they get a chance. When they are given that chance they have as much of an "equity" in the project as any designer does. We motivated people by making sure they had an equity in the product—and then listened to them carefully. At every stage of the process we had inputs from customers and users. Customers and users were considered to be those in the later stages of the design and introduction process—as well as actual consumers in the marketplace. We even had the media in to tell us what consumers told them about models of the car, their own desires, and so on two years before the release of the car.

> My objective was to meet total returns on each design element. The only thing I looked at was total returns. When costs were higher than budgeted variable costs, the question was, "Could you price for the feature and meet 'returns' targets?" On earlier projects management used to give and get design targets as "less cost" for each element; now an element could cost more if value was added by the feature being introduced. We tried to put all members of the team in a position where they could measure themselves. If you measure yourself, you will be a lot tougher than your boss. We tried to indicate that arguments were okay—conflict and bargaining were permissible—as long as they increased the quality of the eventual output. Everything was done to direct ourselves toward the "best product." As the process went on, we tried to improve it each year by asking again how we could improve the product even more if we started over again from scratch.

The Manufacturing Process: The Livonia and Lima Plants

In 1981 designers decided a new front-wheel drive automatic overdrive (AXOD) transaxle was essential for the proposed 1986 family-sized cars. This transaxle would work as part of Ford's first electronically controlled powertrain and tie into the EEC-IV electronic engine controls being developed. These controls were eventually applied to the Vulcan 3, OL V-6 engines used in the Taurus/Sable cars. Some $1.2 billion was spent on new tools, facilities, and launch costs to build the new powertrain. Ford's Livonia Transmission plant and Lima Engine plant received approximately $700 million of that amount. With its existing operating procedures Ford's Powertrain and Chassis Division, which managed these plants, recognized how hard it would be to build the AXOD more efficiently than its Japanese competition. The 1,700 workers at the Livonia Transmission plant—which was currently building transmissions for Ford's rear-wheel cars—knew they could lose their jobs (and perhaps have their plant permanently closed in about five years) unless they could win the bid to build AXOD. Ford now made a regular practice of putting major new products out for bids both internally and externally.

Livonia's new manager and its union leader agreed that to win the contract away from Mazda (where Ford owned a 25% interest) they would have to work together to improve quality and cut costs sharply. They first agreed to put quality maintenance above production output, even if that meant shutting down the line. Employee involvement became a keystone at Livonia—during 1982 employees there earned $600,000 in cash and new cars for ideas that saved Ford $3.7 million.

The plant instituted a pilot program in which only two job classifications were used—"operator" and "manufacturing technician." The manufacturing technician was a new job classification—a multi-skilled worker with extensive training for responsibilities both on and off the plant floor. As the pilot programs proved effective, Ford and the union negotiated a series of cost-saving work rule changes—and 91% of the local union members approved. The final decision was made to award Livonia the contract when Ford's financial experts found costs could be cut by 25% and existing equipment could be upgraded enough to cut investment requirements from $1.5 billion to $1 billion. Quality improved simultaneously; post-assembly repair rates dropped from 23% to 11% and continued to decrease.

To launch AXOD, committees were created that crossed the organization lines normally separating division, product engineering, manufacturing, and purchasing personnel. Ergonomics experts designed all the workstations and job functions; and hourly and salaried employees worked together to plan machinery layout, work stations, equipment and job designs, supplier selection, personnel training, and so on. When asked why he was so sure quality would be achieved in the Taurus/Sable cars Mr. Veraldi said:

> I saw a dedication I had never seen before, especially when I visited the Livonia Transmission plant. The workers stayed until 8:00 P.M. to show me how they were building the parts. At each station the workers had small charts on easels or taped to desks—they were all different—and they would say, "This is how we are going to manufacture this part at this station—and this is how we're going to make it perfect." They all had their own way of showing you how they were doing statistical process control; the methods were common, but their individual applications were all different since the plant manager had given them the latitude to run their own businesses in the way they thought best.

After the AXOD launch, the Livonia plant received daily deliveries of parts from suppliers in a "just-in-time" system, and the parts were delivered to the line by computer-controlled driverless forklifts called automatic guided vehicles (AGVs). The revamped plant also utilized the world's largest known collection of laser welding systems and a "large area network" (LAN) connecting 650 computer-controlled machines and production controlling PCs—considered one of the largest and most complex installations in the worldwide auto industry. Among other things, these provided real-time linkages to suppliers on their products' quality performance.

The Lima engine plant also developed innovative procedures and processes to build the new Vulcan 3.0L V-6 engine. Management established a team approach for "consensus sourcing" in which the product engineering, manufacturing, and purchasing departments all had to agree on vendors selected. Each area represented its particular concerns: purchasing (price and availability), manufacturing (quality and ease of assembly), and engineering (design intent). The plant had a technical training committee made up of salaried and hourly workers who designed and coordinated the training of the work force to handle the complex new equipment being added—the number of robots on the Lima V-6 line was higher than any comparable line in the United States.

The launch team made a complete mock-up of the engine assembly line (including details of each workstation) where many operations could be simulated, videotaped, and revised before any expensive equipment was installed. The line itself was half the size of a normal line. There were to be no extra parts between sequential steps—that is, worker A had to produce a part every time worker B needed it. Since workers needed adequate time to do a quality job, the line was non-synchronized—that is, each station was not directly connected to other stations. Each worker maintained control over his own world with a "hold" switch to keep the work in position longer if necessary, although the power rollers continued to move elsewhere, keeping the whole line from being stopped.

Every station had full statistical process control and in some instances microprocessor-based computer programs allowing machines to measure and adjust their own performance. The rule was "only quality advanced, and anyone can stop the entire line to ensure quality." This attitude was exemplified by the fact that there were no repair bays along the line. To ensure quality further, dealers were given a hot-line to the Lima plant to report any engine problems so that manufacturing could make needed corrections immediately and ensure that no more faulty engines were shipped. Previously, this feedback had come only from after-the-fact warranty data.

Stamping and Vehicle Assembly

Taurus/Sable's outer body panels were designed on the CAD/CAM system. The design automatically produced an instruction tape which could be sent to the Buffalo stamping plant where it ran the milling machines making the dies from which panels would be stamped. Computers then checked the dies against the design specs before a single panel was struck. For final assembly, Team Taurus had some 100 "functional" cars built and tested with production parts, production tools, and processes to pretest the cars before full production. Previously, many major problems were discovered only after Job 1 rolled down the line.

The Atlanta and Chicago (Taurus/Sable) assembly plants were laid out with the advice of ergonomics experts and contained power and free-overhead conveyors to get workers out of the pits they had previously occupied—reaching up to do their work. In building Taurus/Sable, Ford made its most extensive use of automated, modular assembly. In modular assembly various subassemblies (or modules) are built on "feeder lines" connecting to the main line. This allows more fixed automation and hence tighter tolerances within each subsystem. Modular construction vastly simplifies the main line, allows a somewhat greater mix of flexibility in the subsystems, and creates added pockets of responsibility for cost and quality control. For example, doors and subframes were completed offline, allowing the interior to be completed with much easier access on the main line. Said Mr. Manoogian, quality control director, "Ten years ago 10–15 of every 100 cars built were diverted after assembly for repair. Now we have cut that to 1, and are shooting for 0." Both Taurus/Sable plants went from 53 to 63 jobs per hour, with only about 24 hours of labor being required per assembly. Yet the plants were so flexible they could go from Taurus to Sable or from sedans to wagons each hour-on-the-hour, if necessary.[13] Still, Petersen attributed 85% of Taurus' gains to "managing smarter" and only 15% to the new technology.

THE LAUNCH

Ultimately, Team Taurus built prototypes of the new cars seven months earlier than Ford's system normally would have. Both as a tribute to retiring Chairman Caldwell and to precondition the public to the "revolutionary" look of the cars, Taurus and Sable were unveiled at a Hollywood gala in December 1984—some ten months before they were due to hit dealer showrooms. Job 1 for Taurus/Sable was initially planned for July 1985, but was delayed until mid-October. Even then production was slower than planned, as Ford worked to iron out problems with some of its new equipment (notably its new robotic welding machinery) in the plants.[14] But the delay perhaps served the function of hammering home management's priorities better than any number of "Quality Is Job 1" posters could have.[15]

In early 1985 Mr. Petersen took over as chairman and CEO, and Poling moved up to the presidency. *Fortune*[16] later reported

> Petersen and Poling are examplars of Ford's new breed of manager. Both held big jobs overseas before landing top posts in the United States. . . . They also are the prime movers behind the team spirit that has overtaken the company since the man with his name on the building, the late Henry Ford II, stepped down as chief executive in 1979. . . . As the company's two top executives, they have done their jobs so well that Ford will make more money than GM and Chrysler combined this year, and Ford Division cars and trucks have passed Chevrolet's as the biggest-selling individual brand.

The New Line

Much of Ford's future was riding on the success of the $3 billion Taurus/Sable program, carrying Ford's aerodynamic styling into the crucial family car market. Ford aimed the new cars at families in their late thirties, whose income was rising, and who wanted to drive something more sophisticated than a traditional American family car. The cars were intended to catch the growing number of baby-boom parents "just before they settled into their first Volvo sedan, or Audi 5000."[17] The cars were designed to appeal more to young professionals with children than had the older Ford LTD and Mercury Marquis. But if the new models were not widely accepted by Ford's older, more traditional family car buyers—or if some import buyers were not won over by the radical design of the new models—analysts thought Ford could be in serious trouble.[18]

President Poling took care to note that although they looked like twins, Taurus and Sable shared no common body panels and that Sable was more than two inches longer with a larger trunk, a unique front end, hidden roof pillars, and its own instrument panel. Each line consisted of a four-door sedan and a four-door, two-seat wagon. All this was to emphasize that Lincoln Mercury's Sable was something more than a warmed over version of Ford Division's Taurus.[19]

Altogether Ford spent $100 million on its ad blitz for the introduction of Taurus/Sable;[20] and on the day they were first available Ford already had in hand more than 20,000 customer orders.[21] Taurus and Sable were the only domestically produced 1986 cars named by both *Car and Driver* and *Motor Trend* magazines as among the best cars available in the United States. Of the 400 "best-in-class" features studied, Ford claimed that 80% were met or exceeded in Taurus/Sable.

The cars gave Ford an aura of success, and they were good to Ford's earnings. (See Exhibits 3 and 4 for financial and sales data.) According to one analyst, Ford made $1,200 to $1,500 more on the Taurus and Sable than on the midsized cars they replaced. The cars, which offered "Japanese quality, European styling and ride for a modest price (of about $10,000)" lured the young professional market to Ford. The average age of the Ford Taurus buyer, for example was 47, compared to 59 for the replaced LTD. The buyers' median income was $38,000 for the Taurus owner versus $28,000 for the aged model; and a higher percentage (43%) had college degrees than the LTD buyers (29%). While only 5% of the trade-ins for a Marquis or LTD had come from former import owners, 15% did for the Taurus and Sable.[22]

The Team Taurus approach seemed to offer innumerable other benefits—including savings estimated at $250–400 million on the cars' development. One key item was that design changes after the start of production cost only $35 million, compared with at least $150 million in recent cars.[23] By reducing the number of bodyside panels, from six to two, Ford got an unexpected benefit of being able to use the same front panel on both its sedans and the wagons. And the cars improved repairability-after-accidents led Allstate and State Farm Mutual insurers to give 30% discounts to Taurus owners.

There were problems, however. Ford had to recall the new cars only a week after they were introduced to replace defective ignition switches that allowed the key to be removed without the ignition being locked. A second recall was necessary when some cars proved to have faulty window glass which broke into pieces too large to meet safety standards, because the glass had been improperly tempered. Other problems included a rotten egg smell coming from the catalytic converter and a minor engine surge which was corrected by replacing a microprocessor in the electronic engine control system. The most serious and publicized problem, however, was that the car scored poorly in 35 MPH crash tests.[24] And in 1987 Ford had to recall 4.3 million cars (including Taurus/Sables), light trucks, and vans to correct latent fuel system defects that had caused some 230 fires and injured 16 people. The recall was the largest by any U.S. automaker since 1981 and posed a threat to Ford's hard-won recognition for high quality.

The gains established by the Taurus/Sable program, nevertheless, had set new standards that the rest of the domestic industry (and Ford itself in its future introductions) would be hard pressed to duplicate. (See Table 1.)

TABLE 1

BEFORE TAURUS	TAURUS
188 market models	37 market models
1,000 ave. run per model	13,000 ave. run per model
30% defect rate	Zero defect goal
5–6 year model turnaround	4-year model turnaround
6 days of inventory	4 hours of inventory
Little training	400,000 hours training 1984–85
3500 suppliers	2300 suppliers

As a basis for comparison, a group under Professor Kim B. Clark at Harvard Business School had made a study of worldwide automotive practices in product development. Their data indicated some striking differences in performance among U.S. groups and those elsewhere in the world. Professor Clark's group compared data on passenger vehicle development from 20 automobile companies in Japan, Europe, and the United States. A brief summary of some key data is included in Exhibits 5–7.

Their analyses suggest that while differences in project scope and complexity explain part of the differences in product development performance, much more of the variation was determined by differences in the various companies' organization structures and processes for problem solving. They foresaw that understanding the need for better design practices and improving the U.S. companies' past engineering paradigms could substantially affect the competitiveness of the U.S. industry. Said Lew Veraldi, then vice president-Luxury and Large Car Engineering and Planning, "If we can keep on making things better, and keep on setting our sights higher on everything we do, we can compete with anyone in the world. Taurus is just a start. The next decade will see a lot more."

QUESTIONS

1. What were the key elements or conditions that made the Ford Team Taurus process successful?

2. What problems would you expect Ford to encounter in using this (simultaneous design) process? What are likely to be its main policy implications? How could the process be improved?

3. What are the potential explanations for and implications of the variations in competitive design processes illustrated in Exhibits 5–7?

4. What should Ford do in the future?

EXHIBIT 3
Ford Motor Company
Segment Data, 1985–1987

Structure The company and its consolidated subsidiaries comprise a vertically integrated business operating primarily in a single industry segment consisting of the manufacture, assembly, and sale of cars and trucks and related parts and accessories.

Intercompany sales among geographic areas consist primarily of vehicles, parts, and components manufactured by affiliated companies and sold to other affiliated companies. Transfer prices between affiliated companies are established through negotiations between the affected parties. Generally, the buying affiliate incurs additional costs following the purchase and prior to the sale of a product to an unaffiliated customer.

Geographic Area Sales

(in millions)	1987	1986	1985
Sales to unaffiliated customers			
United States	$47,688	$42,790	$36,779
Canada	3,942	3,158	2,901
Europe	15,731	12,481	8,745
Latin America	1,782	2,401	2,402
All other (primarily Asia-Pacific)	2,500	1,886	1,947
Total outside sales	$71,643	$62,716	$52,774

EXHIBIT 3
(Continued)

(in millions)	1987	1986	1985
Intercompany sales among geographic areas			
United States	$ 7,614	$ 7,244	$ 6,747
Canada	6,057	6,624	6,172
Europe	1,471	1,128	821
Latin America	1,386	885	705
All other (primarily Asia-Pacific)	347	160	81
Total intercompany sales	$16,875	$16,041	$14,526
Total sales revenue			
United States	$55,302	$50,034	$43,526
Canada	9,999	9,782	9,073
Europe	17,202	13,609	9,566
Latin America	3,168	3,286	3,107
All other (primarily Asia-Pacific)	2,847	2,046	2,028
Elimination of intercompany sales	(16,875)	(16,041)	(14,526)
Total sales	$71,643	$62,716	$52,774
Net income (loss)			
United States	$ 3,441	$ 2,460	$ 1,988
Canada	143	167	148
Europe	1,079	559	326
Latin America	(95)	66	(57)
All other (primarily Asia-Pacific)	57	33	110
Total net income	$ 4,625	$ 3,285	$ 2,515
Assets at December 31			
United States	$24,418	$22,701	$19,396
Canada	3,695	2,938	2,667
Europe	15,270	11,179	9,107
Latin America	1,865	2,501	2,131
All other (primarily Asia-Pacific)	3,247	2,224	1,820
Elimination of intercompany sales receivables	(3,539)	(3,610)	(3,517)
Total assets	$44,956	$37,933	$31,604
Capital expenditures (facilities, machinery and equipment, and tooling)			
United States	$ 2,108	$ 1,966	$ 2,553
Canada	242	174	180
Europe	853	720	620
Latin America	124	295	256
All other (primarily Asia-Pacific)	285	198	128
Total capital expenditures	$ 3,612	$ 3,353	$ 3,737

Source: Ford Motor Co., *Annual Report,* 1987.

EXHIBIT 4

10-Year Summary of Vehicle Factory Sales, 1978–1987
Ford Motor Company and Consolidated Subsidiaries

	1987	1986	1985	1984	1983	1982	1981	1980	1979	1978
U.S. and Canadian Cars and Trucks[a]										
Cars										
United States	2,171,442	2,093,698	1,940,662	2,047,671	1,671,837	1,270,519	1,385,174	1,397,431	2,044,461	2,632,190
Canada	187,840	188,887	194,540	167,295	143,425	118,721	148,515	162,576	236,437	248,285
Total cars	2,359,282	2,282,585	2,135,202	2,214,966	1,815,262	1,389,240	1,533,689	1,560,007	2,280,898	2,880,475
Trucks[b]										
United States	1,481,059	1,404,002	1,260,123	1,238,928	993,874	803,484	716,648	753,195	1,183,016	1,458,132
Canada	151,982	126,758	119,583	94,552	69,409	70,120	104,136	109,006	160,160	153,955
Total trucks	1,633,041	1,530,760	1,379,706	1,333,480	1,063,283	873,604	820,784	862,201	1,343,176	1,612,087
Total cars and trucks	3,992,323	3,813,345	3,514,908	3,548,446	2,878,545	2,262,844	2,354,473	2,422,208	3,624,074	4,492,562
Cars and Trucks Outside the United States and Canada[b]										
Germany	899,609	862,288	769,883	789,655	833,119	797,850	737,383	657,258	880,325	847,529
Britain	484,057	438,155	422,003	371,598	414,018	423,073	418,629	468,472	555,496	433,191
Spain	276,448	268,114	265,783	269,021	228,150	229,839	254,006	266,522	252,917	247,408
Australia	134,222	143,415	177,108	156,304	138,394	141,990	127,181	93,490	115,148	107,389
Mexico	34,495	43,601	70,238	50,560	47,670	90,478	107,312	84,668	74,703	68,009
Other countries[c]	230,220	346,827	330,577	399,067	394,335	321,513	314,204	335,832	307,641	265,977
Total outside United States and Canada	2,059,051	2,102,400	2,035,592	2,036,205	2,055,686	2,004,743	1,958,715	1,906,242	2,186,230	1,969,503
Total worldwide— cars and trucks	6,051,374	5,915,745	5,550,500	5,584,651	4,934,231	4,267,587	4,313,188	4,328,450	5,810,304	6,462,065
Tractors[b]										
United States	19,532	29,181	36,061	31,781	28,177	24,258	31,517	35,286	51,361	35,789
Overseas	44,382	39,155	47,787	50,730	39,141	48,905	57,757	62,415	82,267	59,448
Total worldwide— tractors	63,914	68,336	83,848	82,511	67,318	73,163	89,274	97,701	133,628	95,237
Total worldwide factory sales	6,115,288	5,984,081	5,634,348	5,667,162	5,001,549	4,340,750	4,402,462	4,426,151	5,943,932	6,557,302

[a] Factory sales are by source of manufacture, except that Canadian exports to the United States are included as U.S. vehicle sales, U.S. exports to Canada are included as Canadian vehicle sales, and Mexican exports to the United States are included as U.S. vehicle sales.

[b] Includes units manufactured by other companies and sold by Ford.

[c] Unit sales from Brazil and Argentina are included only through June 30, 1987.

EXHIBIT 4 (Continued)

Ford Shares of Major Car and Truck Markets, 1986–1987

| | CARS | | | | TRUCKS | | | |
| | 1987 | | 1986 | | 1987 | | 1986 | |
	Industry Unit Sales	Ford Market Share	Industry Unit Sales	Ford Market Share	Industry Unit Sales	Ford Market Share	Industry Unit Sales	Ford Market Share
United States	10,191,686	20.2%	11,405,235	18.2%	5,000,737	29.1%	4,921,213	28.1%
Canada	1,064,713	18.1	1,095,676	17.2	463,671	30.7	419,458	29.7
Mexico	154,365	10.7	160,664	12.1	93,705	18.6	98,425	21.4
Germany	2,807,318	10.4	2,734,735	10.6	262,277	8.2	238,029	7.6
United Kingdom	2,004,015	28.9	1,875,234	27.5	320,419	28.2	296,307	25.9
Other European markets*	7,289,834	8.1	6,792,973	8.0	1,150,339	6.4	1,043,527	5.4
Brazil	420,753	20.6	661,603	19.6	164,263	21.7	193,104	24.4
Argentina	156,199	12.3	137,016	14.2	34,733	39.8	32,730	39.3
Other Latin American markets*	310,898	6.5	333,129	10.1	140,144	16.2	166,378	12.7
Australia	358,755	31.1	392,862	30.8	93,110	18.7	137,389	16.3
All other markets*	5,103,694	2.9	4,753,042	2.3	3,764,222	1.2	3,482,705	1.1
Worldwide total*	29,862,230	13.8	30,342,169	13.4	11,487,620	16.8	11,029,265	16.5

* 1987 data estimated.

Source: Ford Motor Co., Annual Report, 1987.

EXHIBIT 5
Selected Design Profiles by Region

Variables	Total	Japan	United States	Europe
Number of projects	29	12	6	11
Year of introduction	1980–87	1981–85	1984–87	1980–87
Engineering hours (thousands)				
Average	2,577	1,155	3,478	3,636
Minimum	426	426	1,041	700
Maximum	7,000	2,000	7,000	6,545
Lead time* (months)				
Average	54.2	42.6	61.9	62.6
Minimum	35.0	35.0	50.2	46.0
Maximum	97.0	91.0	77.0	97.0
Product complexity indicators				
Average price				
(thousand 1987 U.S. $)	13,591	9,238	13,193	19,720
Body size				
(% in number of projects)				
Micro-mini	10%	25%	0%	0%
Small	56%	67%	17%	64%
Medium-large	34%	8%	83%	36%
Number of body types				
(Average)	2.1	2.3	1.7	2.2
Project scope indicators (average)				
Common parts ratio	19%	12%	29%	21%
Carried-over parts ratio	10%	7%	9%	14%
Unique parts ratio	74%	82%	62%	71%
Supplier design percentage	38%	52%	15%	35%

* Lead Time is the time elapsed between the start of the development project and market introduction.

Source: Kim B. Clark, W. Bruce Chew, and T. Fujimoto, "Product Development in the World Auto Industry: Strategy, Organization, and Performance," Working Paper, April 1988, Harvard Business School, Division of Research.

	Average No. of Engineers
Region	
Japan	485
United States	903
Europe	904
Organization	
Functional[a]	1,421
Project Manager[b]	573
Program Manager[c]	333

[a] Functional organization with no project manager.
[b] Functional teams coordinated by a project manager.
[c] Interfunctional team with strong directive control by program manager.

Source: Kim. B. Clark, W. Bruce Chew, and T. Fujimoto, "Product Development in the World Auto Industry: Strategy, Organization, and Performance," Working Paper, April 1988, Harvard Business School, Division of Research.

EXHIBIT 6
Number of Engineers per Project

503

EXHIBIT 7
Average Project Lead Time and Stage Length: European, United States, and Japanese Automakers

Development Phase	Japanese			United States			Europe		
	Begin	End	Stage Length	Begin	End	Stage Length	Begin	End	Stage Length
Concept study	42.6	34.3	8.3	61.9	44.0	18.0	62.6	49.6	13.1
Product planning	37.8	29.0	8.8	57.0	39.2	17.8	58.2	40.8	17.4
Advanced engineering	41.8	26.6	15.2	56.4	29.9	26.5	54.9	41.5	13.5
Product engineering	29.6	5.8	23.8	40.1	11.6	28.6	41.8	18.6	23.2
Process engineering	27.7	6.1	21.6	30.9	5.5	25.4	36.6	9.7	26.8
Pilot run	7.1	2.7	4.4	9.2	2.7	6.5	9.8	3.5	6.4
Total			82.2			122.6			100.3

Note: Data in months before Job 1
Sample size: Japan 12
United States 6
Europe 11

Source: Kim B. Clark and T. Fujimoto, "Overlapping Problem Solving in Product Development," Working Paper, April 1988, Harvard Business School, Division of Research.

POLAROID CORPORATION

Polaroid started as an inventor's story on the classical model.[1] A superbly gifted inventor and scientist, Edwin Land, created Polaroid in 1937 and remained its chairman and director of research until 1982, when he stepped aside to pursue his research interests full time and be available as a consultant to Polaroid. Mr. William McCune, CEO since 1980 and a longtime colleague and friend of Dr. Land, had to reposition the company in light of some powerful new competitive forces.

EARLY HISTORY

Edwin Land never graduated from Harvard, preferring to form a company with one of his professors. His doctorate was honorary. But his attachment to research and invention was inseparable and ultimately led to his acquiring over 500 patents. Dr. Land's innovative mind caused one associate to claim, in reference to Land's original instant photography work: "100 Ph.D.'s would not have been able to duplicate Land's feat in ten years of uninterrupted work."[2] Yet Land developed the basic physical elements of this process within six months. Polaroid was actually founded on Land's invention of a light-polarizing sheet material, which filtered out all light except that vibrating in a single plane. Normally light waves vibrate in myriad planes as they emanate from a source. By crossing these planes two polarized sheets could eliminate light or glare as desired.

Land's early efforts concentrated on manufacturing easily marketed products like sunglasses and scientific products. And almost from the beginning, his com-

Case copyright © 1985 by James Brian Quinn. Research associate—Penny C. Paquette. Case derived solely from secondary sources. Numbers in brackets indicate the reference page number for material from a previously footnoted source.

pany earned a profit. (2,154) In 1937 Land incorporated the company, selling common stock to the Rothschilds and Baron Schroder under an unusual agreement that allowed him to maintain control. The agreement gave Land power over a trust that held the majority of the stock. (1,116) With this unusual beginning, Polaroid issued no long-term debt for years, financing itself internally and through stock issues. Among other innovations, Polaroid was one of the first public companies to consciously adopt a "low-dividend" policy, offering its stockholders the opportunity of taking almost all their profits as capital gains. The company grew rapidly through the World War II period when it was a government supplier of specialized optical products.

But Land hoped to design his product into automobile headlights and windshields to reduce night driving glare. (2,157) With windshields polarized in one direction and headlights in another, each driver would have a full view of the road ahead with no glare from oncoming lights. In 1947 although Detroit had successfully tested the headlight polarizing system, the automakers turned them down. (2,157) The industry saw no practical way to equip the 33 million cars then on the roads and was concerned that owners of those vehicles might be handicapped by the somewhat brighter headlights needed on filter equipped cars.

INSTANT PHOTOGRAPHY

The year 1947 started dismally, but all that changed in February when Land disclosed his now famous 60-second photographic process. Land's inspiration came one day during World War II, as he was taking pictures of his daughter. She had asked impatiently why she could not see the finished picture right away. The question triggered Land's fertile imagination. And he soon conceptualized the basic idea for his revolutionary product. But he worked three long years before the process produced a sufficiently acceptable result. The secret lay in a self-developing film packet. Once he achieved initial success with this, Land moved quickly (in 1947) to design a camera to handle the film. William McCune, then a Polaroid engineer, and several associates contributed a series of important early inventions to support Land's work. (2,157) But this was only the beginning of a decades-long quest to develop improved films and cameras for instant photography.

The full requirements of the camera and film were beyond the financial capabilities of the young Polaroid Corporation, and it turned to outside contractors for much of its production. Protected by over 1000 patents, Polaroid ultimately had Bell & Howell and U.S. Time manufacture the camera, while Kodak supplied the negative film. Polaroid produced only the unique instant positive film and used its remaining manpower to market the camera.[3]

Sales grew from $1.5 million in 1947 to nearly $100 million by 1960. During this period Polaroid offered only black and white film—but vastly improved the quality of both its cameras and the film. It stayed strictly in the high (over $100) end of the camera market, while most of its potential competitors, including Kodak, scoffed at the idea of a large instant picture market. (2,125) In fact, Kodak worked with Polaroid, helping the growing fledgling introduce the world's first instant color film in 1963. This technological achievement spurred Polaroid's sales in the mid-1960s as Polaroid rode a burgeoning amateur photography market along with Kodak and its Instamatic line.

By 1963 Polaroid completely dominated the high-priced "instant" camera field and began to eye the much larger inexpensive segment controlled by Kodak. The Polaroid Swinger—a black and white camera selling under $20—introduced in the fall of 1965 was an immediate success.[4] Polaroid soon expanded its presence with the Big Swinger (in 1968) and Colorpak II in 1969. In each case, the new camera, priced within $5 of its predecessor, overwhelmed the former model, and large inventories of the older cameras were often sold below cost to discount houses.[4]

SX-70 AND SHOCKWAVES

Still, in this period Polaroid began to face some ominous problems. Its original patents for instant photography started to expire in 1965. While newer patents prevented immediate competition, other companies would be able to enter the instant picture market by 1970. And Polaroid's successful forays into the low price camera market had stimulated Kodak's interest in instant photography.[4]

In the early 1960s, Dr. Land began organizing a project team to revolutionize instant photography and leapfrog past his competition into another fortress of patents. As Land's project team pushed both film technology and the camera design art (Land called it forced evolution) Polaroid became involved in such seemingly unrelated fields as integrated circuits and batteries. Polaroid's new products had such demanding standards that they required significant design and manufacturing cooperation with suppliers. During this period, talented Polaroid engineers often "lived" with vendors to help them achieve new and rigorous design and production specifications. Virtually all of this project's work was performed without any market research except Polaroid's own confidence in knowing its customers' needs.[5]

Polaroid felt market research was only valid as a method of delineating an existing market, not for evaluating an entirely new concept. Land always held that Polaroid's product created the market, rather than the market dictating the product. This was in part why he could withstand the knee buckling skepticism and delays that accompanied the introduction of the revolutionary SX-70 line. He later scoffed at those who "couldn't see the potential of a $600 camera value marketed in the $100 range."[6]

In 1972, this project ("Aladdin") bore its professed creation, the SX-70. The camera offered startling improvements over previous models. Its color film literally developed before the customer's eyes. The distasteful refuse layers generated by the old "peel apart" process were eliminated. And the camera itself was a marvel of optical engineering. The SX-70's development costs had been staggering; some estimates were as high as $600 million (including buildings) over its full duration.

Polaroid initiated another important shift along with the introduction of the SX-70. Because of the camera's sophistication and Kodak's impending instant camera introduction, Polaroid decided to manufacture and assemble the major components of the camera "in house," as well as produce the negatives for its film. This decision not only required substantial investments in plant and equipment (over $200 million) between 1968 and 1972, but it strained the organization to adapt its highly unstructured management style to the routine operations of an assembly line.[7] The gamble also sent shockwaves down Wall Street, with many analysts doubting Polaroid's ability to maintain respectable earnings growth during this period. (3,125)

In fact, the SX-70's introduction was plagued with bad luck. The national introduction was delayed until late 1973, while engineers scrambled to solve its problems. Production difficulties caused product shortages in most locales. The 1974 recession cut deeply into the SX-70's potential sales, as its high price ($180) kept it from the volume markets. At the same time there were complaints about the quality of the SX-70's innovative self-developing pictures, and the sale of other Polaroid models fell off more than expected. Profits for 1974 dropped to $28.4 million, down $23.4 million from the previous year.

Land Changes Roles

In January 1975 Dr. Land stepped aside as president. Land wanted to get out of daily operations to concentrate on one of his favorite projects—instant movies—and he saw the need for a full-time operations manager. William McCune, who took over the presidency, was experienced in all phases of engineering and manufacturing and had spearheaded the project which removed Polaroid's color negative manufacturing from Kodak's benevolent control. "Bill" McCune had a warm, calm, and relaxed manner even in crisis situations. Slim and graying, McCune understood the unique Polaroid organization and Dr. Land's style well. He preferred to operate through consensus, but he was also demanding and wanted problems addressed. Said one executive at the time,

> He has known for years that certain things needed to be done around here, and now that he's got the charter he's doing them. . . . We had been trying to get certain product decisions for as long as two years before Bill became president," the executive added. "The routine had been that one top guy thought this and another top guy thought that and the boss (Mr. Land) was waffling. So we'd go back and get more data and do it all over again. Now Bill just says, "Okay, do it."[8]

McCune also removed some of the centralizing aura of Dr. Land's style from operating decisions.

> McCune's orders are usually clear, but if they aren't I can say, 'Bill, what are you trying to tell me? Exactly what do you want me to do?' I would never dare ask Land that.[8]

A NEW ERA BEGINS

Polaroid faced its first direct competitor in 1975. Pint-sized Berkey Photo introduced an instant picture camera which used SX-70 film.[9] Polaroid's reaction was prompt and predictable; it immediately filed a patent infringement suit against Berkey. Despite this unexpected intruder into its domain, Polaroid rebounded to near record profits of $62.5 million in 1975. But the prospects of a much bloodier battle seemed in prospect when Kodak marketed its entry in April 1976. Instead, the entire instant photo market exploded. Even with Kodak initially grabbing 25% of the market, Polaroid's sales grew to $950 million with record profits of $79.7 million by the end of 1976.

But the threat from the Rochester giant was lethal; and Polaroid, armed with its vast patent portfolio, pursued an injunction against Kodak to cease and desist from further manufacture of instant cameras and film. Similar actions in Canada and the United Kingdom temporarily prevented Kodak from offering its product, but Kodak's lawyers soon found a way out from each injunction.[9] Still, counter-punching effectively with Kodak, Polaroid's sales and profits grew while Kodak's instant camera division operated in the red.[10] Then from the east, a third challenger, Fuji Photo of Japan, reared its head and began its tentative probing of what had been Polaroid's exclusive domain only two years before.

As a partial counter to these entries, in 1977 Polaroid introduced instant movies. Dr. Land had been determined to provide a moving picture complement to his instant still pictures. But the initial product entry, Polavision, was expensive ($699) and was positioned at the high end of a stagnant home movie market, representing only 10% of the total photography market. Unlike SX-70, the camera and hardware were manufactured outside Polaroid. With his characteristic optimism, Dr. Land entered the new field hoping to generate the same response that occurred 30 years before. (9,45) As he had so many times before, Dr. Land made the announcement of this new product dramatically at the 1976 stockholders meeting (April 1977), a year before the product was to be fully available in the marketplace.

    Unfortunately, Polavision was a striking failure in both technology and marketing—the very areas in which the company had been so strong,[11] and it was financially costly with three years of "substantial" operating losses and a $68.5 million write off in 1979. But *Fortune* also noted,

> Polavision began in the late 1960s as part of Project Sesame, the code name the company used for experiments with film that is designed to be viewed by shining light through it (as opposed to film designed to produce printed pictures). One consolation for Polaroid is that Polavision is merely the first of the products that can be expected to grow out of Project Sesame . . . Polaroid may have discovered a way to reduce the cost of manufacturing all instant color film . . . In any case, there is an obvious application of the Polavision technology—instant slides.[11]

NEW COMPETITIVE FORCES

Instant cameras reached a peak of 41% of the still photographic market in 1978, with Polaroid selling a record 9.4 million cameras worldwide. Confident of future growth, it launched an extensive capital expenditure program to increase production of SX-70 cameras and film worldwide.[12] In 1979, after a 4 year growth of 41%, the U.S. camera market dropped 3%.[13] Polaroid's unit sales plummeted more than 22% just as its capital expansion projects neared completion. The worldwide recession of the following several years hurt the whole photographic industry, but even more so the instant cameras and films which had always sold to lower income groups than those who bought conventional cameras.[14]

    Polaroid fought to maintain and survive on its two-thirds share of the declining instant market. It introduced sonar automatic focusing, Time Zero Supercolor film, the Sun (light management system) cameras, and high-speed 600 ASA instant color film. Kodak's share dropped from 40% in 1978 to 30% in 1982. But by 1982 Polaroid's instant still sales had fallen to an estimated 4 million units annually.

    Fuji Photo's instant system was doing well in its Japanese home market, and Eastman upgraded its somewhat deficient instant line in 1982. In addition Kodak's new disc system had proved an immediate novelty and consumer success. Nimslo International had introduced a three dimensional still process, but its market was generally considered a novelty.[15] Sony too had announced its all electronic Mavica camera and system, but in 1982 this required several cabinets of complex backup equipment to manipulate and display its images. Other important market trends are shown in Exhibits 2–7.

Polaroid had for years marketed photographic products in non-consumer markets —such as instant cameras for use in hospitals and labs, microphotography cameras, panorama cameras, studio films, passport and drivers license photo equipment and special event cameras.[16] As the amateur market for instant photography declined, the company began to devote more of its energies toward expanding such markets and breaking into well-established (non-photography related) fields with spinoffs from its instant photographic and optical technology (such as a wafer thin battery, a filter for video display terminal screens, a curing agent for polyurethene, an anticounterfeit labeling material, a sonar transducer, and precision optical devices).[16]

These diversification efforts were beginning to bear fruit by mid 1982. Sales of such products constituted a growing percentage of Polaroid's revenues; although not yet the 50% that represented the goal that *Business Week* had earlier reported.[17] Intensified development efforts in these areas were also paying off. The company's 1982 *Annual Report* stated,

> The new 35mm Autoprocess color and black and white rapid access slide film system adds a new dimension to 35mm photography and marks the first time Polaroid will be marketing products in a conventional film format for use in existing cameras and instruments. [Our prototype of a new low-cost business graphics system for use with the Apple II and IBM Personal Computers] consists of a menu-driven software program (supplied on a diskette) and a tri-color videoprinter which can produce 4x5 inch format color prints and 35mm rapid-access color and black and white slides. These new Polaroid tabletop imaging and processing systems make Polaroid instant photography a part of the flow of immediate information in the office and laboratory. In their design, these self-contained systems become logical extensions of their host electronic imaging systems, and in operation they expand and complement the functions of those systems.

The graphics hardcopy system was an offshoot of Polaroid's 23% stake in a small company, Image Resource Corp. But these endeavors did not remedy the decline of Polaroid's primary market and the failure of its Polavision product. Polaroid saw its EPS drop from a high of $3.60 in 1978 to $0.95 in 1981. In the same period, return on assets fell from 9.3% to 2.2% and pretax profits as a percent of sales went from 14.1% down to 4.4%.

MANAGEMENT AND ORGANIZATIONAL CHANGES

In April 1980, Bill McCune took over as CEO, and Land became chairman of the board and consulting director of Basic Research in Land Photography. Soon after he took office, Mr. McCune began to change Polaroid's unique organization. *Business Week* had summarized some of the key philosophies under Dr. Land as follows:

> Seldom, if ever, has a large American company so faithfully reflected the substance and style of one man as does Polaroid Corp. under Dr. Edwin H. Land . . . Land thrives on informality; thus, Polaroid has no organization chart. Land is almost compulsively secretive; so is Polaroid. Land believes manufacturing is an extension of research; Polaroid employees often follow such projects as the new SX-70 camera from

laboratory to factory floor. Land works prodigious hours; so do key employees, who are resigned to taking phone calls from Land anytime.[18]

511

POLAROID
CORPORATION

Other philosophies of Dr. Land were still important factors in Polaroid's 1982 culture. (See Appendix A.) Under Dr. Land, Polaroid's commitment to research and development had dominated the organization's structure and approach. By providing exceptional work flexibility, Dr. Land attempted to create an innovative atmosphere where the corporate structure did not interfere with employees' motivation. Major divisions were organized simply along functional lines (i.e., marketing, manufacturing). The heart of the corporation's creative capability was the research division headed by Dr. Land. The manufacturing and operating divisions were coordinated by Mr. McCune. A Management Executive Committee (M.E.C.), comprised of Land, McCune, Julius Silver (corporate attorney) and the heads of the major divisions, served as a forum to discuss key aspects of corporate policy and to exchange information about major operating decisions.

McCune had coordinated the functional operations of the company. However, not being a detail man, he preferred to delegate to his young, aggressive divisional managers, who in turn assumed firm control over their areas and promoted strong divisional loyalties and even some degree of proprietary control over divisional information. All the division and senior managers were long-time Polaroid employees. And, although McCune could act as an effective coordinator and buffer, all understood that Land's word had been final on crucial issues, especially those associated with product offerings. In fact, Land had held strategic direction strictly to himself, and often preempted decisions or overturned operating management's consensus on issues of particular interest to him. Although no official organization chart existed prior to 1980, published information and informed outside observers estimated key relationships to be as shown in Exhibit 10. Some details about each major activity and player follow.

Manufacturing Division

Under the direction of I. M. "Mac" Booth, this division had responsibility for domestic camera and film pack production as well as all negative film coatings. Labor intensive operations such as the camera assembly were separated from the highly automated coating facilities for the negative and positive film production.

Polaroid had decided against consolidating all Boston area facilities into one giant Cambridge industrial complex, preferring to keep things in relatively smaller locations in Norwood, Needham, New Bedford, Freetown, and Waltham, Mass. It wanted to keep things more on a human and manageable scale, with workers having a greater opportunity to feel an integral part of what was happening. This dispersal also raised the company's profile in each community the way a single large Cambridge complex could not. (6,191)

In 1980 Booth (age 49) was a rising star at Polaroid. Tough, hard nosed, and inquiring, he often became the "devil's advocate" in top-level discussions. Booth had the difficult task of planning and operating the bulk of Polaroid's complex manufacturing facilities and coordinating them with the vagaries of the consumer marketplace and the magnificent spurts of inventiveness coming from Research. Booth believed in running a tight ship, was willing to experiment with new management techniques and prided himself on his capacities to select people. Booth had become the senior vice president of manufacturing after successfully developing and operating the company's new negative film manufacturing facilities. He had earlier served as an assistant to McCune and enjoyed excellent relationships with the president.

Marketing Division

Since the company's early beginnings, its marketing division had always played an important role. Polaroid's innovative product line had required an aggressive and intelligent marketing program which Edwin Land personally supported. In 1980 the division was headed by youthfully graying, dapper, soft spoken, Peter Wensberg (age 52) who had become senior vice president in 1971. More philosophical than "Mac" Booth in many ways, Wensberg liked to talk about the long-term market positioning and management needs of Polaroid amid a collection of historical instruments and nautical devices that artistically decorated his office. Nevertheless, within his division Wensberg was known as a hard driver. Along with Richard Young, head of Polaroid's International Division, Wensberg had been considered one of the three likely successors to Land, before McCune was named to the position. (6,216) He had complete control over marketing and was a powerful force throughout the corporation. However, his nontechnical background limited the depth of his influence in the more technical divisions.

The marketing division was responsible for all domestic marketing including advertising, customer service, and marketing/sales. The marketing/sales department was divided into a consumer and an industrial product group with a separate sales force for each. Consumer products were distributed directly to large retail, department, and discount stores and through selected wholesalers to smaller retail outlets. Polaroid's sales force handled both cameras and film supplies within their regional territories. Industrial products—designed for commercial photographers and industrial, scientific, or medical applications—were sold through an industrial sales force or independent industrial agents. In addition, the marketing division also had its own market research, marketing planning, advertising, promotion, order processing, internal bookkeeping, (etc.) groups.

Research Divisions

Since its inception Polaroid had been dominated by its research activities. And under Dr. Land's leadership research continued to be a major focal point of the corporation. No absolute delineation existed between applied and pure research; however, separate divisions had been set up to specialize in those two functions. The applied research division, referred to as the technology division, carried most new products or product improvements into production. It occasionally was responsible for manufacturing new products which either needed further design changes or whose market demand was not sufficient to justify transferring them to the huge manufacturing division. Dr. Sheldon Buckler (age 49), who had originally worked in pure research and had participated in a number of Land's entrepreneurial projects, had served as the division's manager since 1972. Dr. Land's great technical abilities and strong personality made this both a difficult and a highly rewarding role.

The research division worked primarily on more basic research projects and had fostered many major technological improvements in films and coatings. The division's close relations to Dr. Land gave it extremely high-level support in dealing with other divisions. In fact, some claimed that Research often had the controlling hand in such relationships. President McCune had also had a long association with research. When Land had come up with his early inventions McCune had been the one who followed up and built them. (6,216) In addition to McCune, research had served as an incubation ground for other senior managers, with three present members of the M.E.C.—Drs. Young, Buckler, and Bloom—each having at one time been Land's assistant director of research.

Land had philosophically conceptualized Polaroid as an extension of the scientific laboratory. He wanted to move the concept of scientific experimentation into the industrial sphere, with the same absence of guilt attached to business as to laboratory failures. In fact the company's success really came back to continual experiments and recombinations of technical work and business ventures that at many points in time had indeed been stopped or looked like failures. (6,184–5) Hence R&D teams were formed, dissolved and reformed with scientists and engineers fluidly following projects into development or production and then returning to the labs again.

Land believed in a strong relationship between the laboratory and the factory. In a manner reminiscent of Mao sending the intellectuals to the rice fields, he sometimes had research people "operating machines." He felt this exposure would give them a greater practical feel for their own theoretical work. In Land's vision, production was just a continuation of research and development, with McCune and Land participating (for example) in the design of machinery and components for SX-70. (6,190)

International Division

Dr. Richard Young (age 54) had managed the International division with an independence and feistiness sometimes envied by the domestic managers. His entrepreneurial talents were put to work in the division when he was appointed its president in 1969 after a very successful career in the research division. By early 1980 international sales had grown to nearly 40% of total corporate revenues and the division controlled all manufacturing and marketing outside the United States. The manufacturing capabilities of the division included positive film coating operations, camera and film pack assembly, and sunglass production. It relied on the U.S. operation for batteries, negative film and other proprietary items but used local contractors for other components. International had three manufacturing facilities—in Scotland, in Ireland, and the Netherlands. The facilities in Scotland and the Netherlands were involved with most phases of production, whereas the plant in Ireland was strictly for film pack assembly. No research had been conducted by the division. Almost all of its products had been first introduced in the United States. And its product line had been essentially the same as the domestic unit's, with some local adaptations to accommodate metric measures, special market conditions, or local regulations.

In 1980 International marketed the full line of Polaroid products directly through wholly owned subsidiaries in some 20 countries.[19] It hired independent distributors in most other areas of the world. The sales force also had a line of sunglasses which was marketed along with its other products; otherwise the sales organization operated in a manner similar to the domestic group's.

International was reportedly the only profit center within Polaroid in 1980. With this distinction, it seemed to operate somewhat more independently and aggressively within the corporation. Financial controls for all divisions were maintained by McCune and the finance division. Financial allocations had generally been based largely on the presentations of each functional group as reviewed by the finance division and the M.E.C. With the exception of major new products there had been little attempt to interrelate capital programs between divisions. And there had been significant reluctance to develop integrated five-year plans among the divisions because of the entrepreneurial nature of the company and the uncertainty of the marketplace.

Staff Divisions

The remaining divisions represented specialized staff activities which supported the line manufacturing, research, and marketing divisions. The largest were the engineering, finance, and legal divisions—although there were also personnel, planning, systems analysis, and public relations specialists at the corporate level. The company's accounting and financial controls tended to follow functional lines, with each division handling the bulk of its own detailed bookkeeping, systems development, and data generation internally. Of course, the finance division specified the records and reports needed for corporate purposes and coordinated all contracts with outside capital sources.[20]

A Smorgasbord of Talent

Dr. Land had used his flexible and creative organization as a "smorgasbord of talent." By selecting individuals with specific skills from any area in the corporation, Land could quickly assemble the highly diverse talents needed to handle desired tasks. For example, when he was confronted with an enormous project like "Aladdin" (SX-70), Land would reach into all his functional groups to gather the necessary people available within Polaroid. Then he would fill any gaps with outside specialists.

In such circumstances, Land reportedly maintained complete control over the project team's R&D activities, even to the information going to and from his team. Secrecy would often shroud his group's activities, and team members might purposely be kept isolated from nonessential contact with other groups in Polaroid. Land himself might be the only individual intimately aware of the entire project's work. (6,210) He would call for additional support work as necessary, and tried to make sure that each research task was the responsibility of a particular individual, rather than diffused as "an organizational responsibility."

As the project's concept crystalized into more definite shape, moved into development, or began scale-up, Dr. Land transferred his attention increasingly to marketing the evolving product. Individual technical team members usually followed their element of the project through full scale-up and debugging before returning to their former jobs. But occasionally, a team researcher or engineer ended up managing manufacturing for the developed component.

Under Land's care and feeding the Polaroid organization responded dynamically—and somewhat amorphously—to changing conditions. Teams formed and reformed around problems. (6,198) From the beginning Polaroid had encouraged employees to participate in decisions affecting their areas. In fact, innovation in organization and corporate human relations was a stated goal of the company. Employees were encouraged to take courses and advanced degrees at company expense. And many of Polaroid's more productive engineers were high school graduates or technicians who had never taken full time university training. Formal organizational constraints and authority relationships were kept to a minimum, and inconsistencies in managerial styles and even the corporation's functional setup were frequent. For example, digressions often arose when a development project moved into manufacturing or commercialization stages. At that point, the responsibility for the project's completion usually reverted to the team leader's division regardless of its function. Consequently, an applied research or engineering division might house manufacturing operations or a small commercial unit for some time. Eventually, however, the misplaced unit would be relocated to its proper functional area or occasionally operated as a small division more or less on its own.

Knowledgeable observers referred to the Polaroid organizations as a "moving target." The arrangement at any moment seemed to evolve naturally from the unstructured operational environment, and further adjustments might soon change any existing situation. The attached organizational charts indicate only those broad relationships which one could define from published data and external contacts with the company. And even these might change quickly with circumstances. There seemed to be substantial participation in decision making among affected parties *within* a division. But such participation *between* divisions was reportedly less common, and of course major interdivisional decisions had to be made at the very top level if substantial disagreements occurred.

The 1980 Reorganization

In October 1980, Mr. McCune began to restructure the top level activities of Polaroid, although many of its *operating* philosophies remained unchanged. He stated,

> Our goals are fourfold: to understand better our total potential, to encourage expanding fields such as our technical and industrial photographic businesses, to explore fields which are new for Polaroid such as batteries and the commercial chemical business; and to establish clear cut areas of responsibility for growth in both sales and profits.[21]

The office of the president was enlarged by the creation of four executive vice presidents. These were Drs. Buckler and Young, and Messrs. Booth and Wensberg. Major departments were consolidated on a worldwide basis to recognize global needs more fully in such areas as marketing, finance, manufacturing, and materials management.[21] This was widely recognized as the beginning of several phased moves which would ensure Polaroid's competitiveness and continued innovativeness in the 1980s. Mr. McCune wanted to be ready to announce his final organization concept in 1982.

QUESTIONS

1. In light of its changing competitive situation, what should Polaroid's strategy have been in 1982? Why?

2. Design an organization suited to support this strategy. Draw an organization chart showing critical relationships down through the departmental level. Who should occupy each position at the division level or above? Why?

3. What control system is needed to make your strategy and organization effective? Define key measures at each level down to departments.

4. What other steps are necessary to implement your strategy?

Polaroid Corporation Philosophy and Culture

In May 1967, Dr. Land wrote down some key points of the Polaroid philosophy. These were still widely accepted in Polaroid in 1982:

> We have two basic products at Polaroid: (1) Products that are genuinely unique and useful, excellent in quality, made well and efficiently, so that they present an attractive value to the public and an attractive profit to the Company; (2) A worthwhile working life for each member of the Company—a working life that calls out the member's best talents and skills—in which he or she shares the responsibilities and the rewards.
> These two products are inseparable. The Company prospers most, and its members find their jobs most worthwhile, when its members are contributing their full talents and efforts to creating, producing, and selling products of outstanding merit. (6,183)

In amplifying this Dr. Land was quoted as saying,

> "What we're after in America is an industrial society where a person maintains at work the full dignity he has at home. I don't mean that they will all be happy. They'll be unhappy—but in new, exciting, and important ways. [At Polaroid, people] would work happy for that time." Polaroid eliminated the time clock, provided extensive educational opportunities inside and outside the company, and allowed employees to "try out" for other jobs if they thought they would be more satisfying. (6,188–9)

In a *Harvard Business Review* article Dr. Land further stated his philosophies:

> I think whether outside science or within science there is no such thing as *group* originality or *group* creativity or *group* perspicacity.
> I do believe wholeheartedly in the individual capacity for greatness, in one way or another in almost any healthy human being under the *right* circumstances; but being part of a group is, in my opinion, generally the *wrong* circumstance. Profundity and originality are attributes of single, if not singular, minds. Two minds may sometimes be better than one, provided that each of the two minds is working separately while the two are working together; yet three tend to become a crowd.[22]

Dr. Land believed in mutual trust and commitment between employees and management; and he expected his people to actively participate in this opportunity:

> I don't regard it as normal for a human being to have an eight-hour day, with two long coffee breaks, with a martini at lunch, with a sleepy period in the afternoon and a rush home to the next martini. I don't think that can be dignified by calling it working, and I don't think people should be paid for it.[23]

In 1977 Dr. Land reaffirmed his commitment to a high corporate ethic in Polaroid's Annual Report:

> A company has as many aspects to its character as a person has, seeking fulfillment and self expression, power, friendship, creativity, immediate recognition and ultimate

significance. It has a conscience and high purpose and moral standards and vulnerability. It can sin, feel guilty and repent, it can love and it can hate, it can build and it can destroy. . . . Recognition of the analogs of human characteristics in corporate life will in my opinion rejuvenate the economy, regenerate national self-respect, initiate an intellectual renaissance, and reward us all with a vast family of blessings which in our blindness we hold stubbornly at arm's length. (9,3)

EXHIBIT 1

Polaroid Corporation and Subsidiary Companies Ten-Year Financial Summary (Unaudited)
Years Ended December 31, 1972–1981
(dollar amounts in millions, except per share data)

	1981	1980	1979
Consolidated Statement of Earnings			
Net sales:			
United States	$ 817.8	$ 791.8	$ 757.2
International	601.8	659.0	604.3
Total net sales	$1,419.6	$1,450.8	$1,361.5
Cost of goods sold	855.4	831.1	876.8
Marketing, research, engineering, and administrative expenses	520.8	483.9	449.4
Total costs	$1,376.2	$1,315.0	$1,326.2
Profit from operations	43.4	135.8	35.3
Other income	49.2	25.4	13.3
Interest expense	29.9	17.0	12.8
Earnings before income taxes	$ 62.7	$ 144.2	$ 35.8
Federal, state, and foreign income taxes (credit)	31.6	58.8	(0.3)
Net earnings	$ 31.1	$ 85.4	$ 36.1
Earnings per share	$0.95	$2.60	$1.10
Cash dividends per share	$1.00	$1.00	$1.00
Average number of shares (in millions)	32.9	32.9	32.9
Selected Balance Sheet Information			
Working capital*	$ 749.5	$ 721.9	$ 535.9
Net property, plant, and equipment	332.9	362.2	371.6
Total assets*	1,434.7	1,404.0	1,253.7
Long-term debt	124.2	124.1	—
Stockholders' equity*	958.2	960.0	907.5
Other Statistical Data			
Additions to property, plant, and equipment	$ 42.5	$ 68.1	$ 134.6
Depreciation	$ 69.2	$ 62.7	$ 51.7
Payroll and benefits	$ 550.5	$ 497.3	$ 464.1**
Number of employees, end of year	16,784	17,454	18,416
Return on equity* (two point average)	3.2%	9.1%	4.0

* Years 1972 through 1980 have been restated to reflect implementation of Financial Accounting Standards Board Statement No. 43 "Accounting for Compensated Absences."
** Restated.

Source: Polaroid Corporation, *Annual Report*, 1981.

EXHIBIT 1 (Continued)

1978	1977	1976	1975	1974	1973	1972
$ 817.4	$ 645.8	$ 586.7	$ 495.6	$ 487.3	$ 493.1	$ 417.5
559.2	416.1	363.3	317.1	270.0	192.4	141.8
$1,376.6	$1,061.9	$950.0	$812.7	$757.3	$685.5	$559.3
778.3	575.7	511.8	467.9	485.2	358.0	260.1
418.2	337.3	294.9	237.0	239.3	251.6	236.7
$1,196.5	$913.0	$806.7	$704.9	$724.5	$609.6	$496.8
180.1	148.9	143.3	107.8	32.8	75.9	62.5
20.3	19.0	14.4	16.8	13.4	14.2	13.5
5.9	6.4	3.3	1.3	1.1	.3	.8
194.5	161.5	154.4	123.3	45.1	89.8	75.2
76.1	69.2	74.7	60.7	16.7	38.0	32.7
$ 118.4	$ 92.3	$ 79.7	$ 62.6	$ 28.4	$ 51.8	$ 42.5
$3.60	$2.81	$2.43	$1.91	$0.86	$1.58	$1.30
$0.90	$0.65	$0.41	$0.32	$0.32	$0.32	$0.32
32.9	32.9	32.9	32.9	32.9	32.9	32.8
$ 609.5	$ 589.6	$ 546.4	$ 475.1	$ 402.0	$ 380.1	$ 341.7
294.8	225.9	198.2	203.3	224.3	228.3	224.5
1,276.0	1,076.7	959.0	843.7	777.8	751.0	661.2
—	—	—	—	—	—	—
904.3	815.5	744.6	678.4	626.3	608.4	566.2
$ 115.0	$ 68.7	$ 33.9	$ 21.8	$ 40.0	$ 40.3	$ 44.6
$ 43.0	$ 39.5	$ 38.3	$ 39.1	$ 39.6	$ 35.3	$ 32.0
$ 421.4**	$ 332.2**	$ 289.6**	$ 231.8**	$ 223.2	$ 191.3	$ 160.2
20,884	16,394	14,506	13,387	13,019	14,227	11,998
13.8%	11.8%	11.2%	9.6%	4.6%	8.8%	7.7%

* Years 1972 through 1980 have been restated to reflect implementation of Financial Accounting Standards Board Statement No. 43 "Accounting for Compensated Absences."
** Restated.

Source: Polaroid Corporation, *Annual Report,* 1981.

	Polaroid 1982			Kodak 1982
	Total	Nonamateur	Amateur	All Amateur
Sales	$1,294	$390	$904	$425
Cost of goods	741	211	530	264
% of sales	57.3%	54.0%	58.6%	62.0%
S & A.	473	128	345	162
% of sales	36.6%	32.8%	38.2%	38.2%
Operating profit	$ 80	$ 51	$ 29	$ (1)
margins	6.2%	13.1%	3.2%	—

Source: Donaldson, Lufkin & Jenrette, *Research Bulletin,* September 28, 1983.

EXHIBIT 3

Manufacturers' Shipments of Photographic Equipment and Supplies, 1977–1982
($ millions)

	1977		1978		1979		1980		1981		1982	
	$	%	$	%	$	%	$	%	$	%	$	%
Sensitized film and paper	$3,874.1	39.0%	$4,489.7	39.0%	$5,288.7	39.5%	$6,706.7	42.3%	$7,186.4	42.4%	$7,652.9	41.3%
Prepared photographic chemicals	695.6	7.0	805.4	7.0	937.2	7.0	1,030.6	6.5	1,033.9	6.1	1,080.4	5.8
Micrographic equipment	298.1	3.0	345.2	3.0	401.7	3.0	539.1	3.4	793.2	3.5	948.5	4.0
Motion picture equipment	198.7	2.0	230.1	2.0	267.8	2.0	269.5	1.7	220.3	1.3	298.3	1.6
Still picture equipment	993.7	10.0	1,150.6	10.0	1,405.9	10.5	1,442.8	9.1	1,271.2	7.5	1,466.5	7.9
Reprographic equipment	3,876.8	39.0	4,485.0	39.0	5,087.7	38.0	5,866.3	37.0	6,644.0	39.2	7,310.4	39.4
Total	$9,937.0	100%	$11,506.0	100%	$13,389.0	100%	$15,855.0	100%	$16,949.0	100%	$18,557.0	100%
Yr. to yr. change			15.8%		16.4%		18.4%		6.9%		9.5%	

Source: Lehman Brothers Kuhn Loeb, *The Photographic Products Market*, August 4, 1983.

521

EXHIBIT 4
U.S. Imports and Exports of Photographic Equipment and Supplies

Estimated Product Breakdown (1979–1982)
(*$ millions*)

	1979			1980			1981			1982		
	Exports	Imports	Net	Exports	Imports	Net	Exports	Imports	Net	Exports	Imports	Net
Sensitized film and paper	$1,074.2	$ 390.7	$683.5	$1,349.9	$ 532.7	$817.2	$1,346.1	$ 567.1	$779.0	$1,234.9	$ 607.7	$627.2
Prepared photographic chemicals	133.9	6.7	127.2	137.8	9.1	128.7	133.3	9.5	123.8	135.6	8.0	127.6
Micrographic equipment	77.3	1.6	75.7	90.9	1.9	89.0	110.0	5.0	105.0	86.1	2.7	83.4
Motion picture equipment	82.7	68.3	14.4	99.1	69.4	29.7	99.3	45.5	53.8	85.9	32.3	53.6
Still picture equipment	420.5	731.7	(311.2)	450.3	644.5	(194.2)	457.7	798.9	(341.2)	491.3	783.4	(292.1)
Reprographic equipment	358.4	358.3	0.1	331.7	497.0	(165.3)	361.5	721.1	(359.6)	423.6	676.4	(252.8)
Total	$2,147.0	$1,557.3	$589.7	$2,459.7	$1,754.6	$705.1	$2,507.9	$2,147.1	$360.8	$2,457.4	$2,110.5	$346.9

Source: Lehman Brothers Kuhn Loeb, *The Photographic Products Market*, August 4, 1983.

EXHIBIT 4 (Continued)

Estimated Regional Breakdown, 1979–1982
($ Millions)

	1979 Exports $	%	1979 Imports $	%	1980 Exports $	%	1980 Imports $	%	1981 Exports $	%	1981 Imports $	%	1982 Exports $	%	1982 Imports $	%
Europe	$ 972.6	45.3%	$ 294.3	18.9%	$1,167.7	45.4%	$ 352.7	20.1%	$ 969.4	38.7%	$ 329.7	15.3%	$1,069.7	43.5%	$ 373.2	17.7%
Canada	255.5	11.9	73.2	4.7	275.5	11.2	119.3	6.8	271.2	10.8	113.9	5.3	316.5	12.9	102.8	4.9
Latin America	188.9	8.8	1.6	0.1	206.6	8.4	1.8	0.1	376.2	15.0	1.8	0.1	287.5	11.7	3.0	.1
Asia	298.5	13.9	1,175.7	75.5	332.1	13.5	1,272.1	72.5	491.9	19.6	1,669.9	77.8	529.8	21.6	1,622.0	76.9
Other	431.5	20.1	12.5	0.8	528.8	21.5	8.7	0.5	399.2	15.9	31.9	1.5	253.9	10.3	9.5	.4
Total	$2,147.0	100.0%	$1,557.3	100.0%	$2,459.7	100.0%	$1,754.6	100.0%	$2,507.9	100.0%	$2,147.1	100.0%	$2,457.4	100.0%	$2,110.5	100.0%

Source: Lehman Brothers Kuhn Loeb, *The Photographic Products Market,* August 4, 1983.

EXHIBIT 5

Estimated Breakdown of Still Pictures Taken by U.S. Consumers
(Millions of Units)

	1977 Units	% Chg.	1978 Units	% Chg.	1979 Units	% Chg.	1980 Units	% Chg.	1981 Units	% Chg.	1982 Units	% Chg.
Color print negative	4,805	17.8%	6,010	25.1%	6,295	4.7%	6,645	5.6%	7,300	9.9%	7,950	8.9%
Slides (positive)	1,495	(4.4)	1,585	6.0	1,530	(3.5)	1,540	0.7	1,350	(12.3)	1,250	(7.4)
Instant	1,370	5.4	1,675	22.3	1,550	(7.5)	1,500	(3.3)	1,450	(3.3)	1,250	(13.8)
Black and white	660	(10.0)	600	(9.1)	575	(4.2)	565	(1.7)	525	(7.1)	500	(4.8)
Total	8,330	8.5%	9,870	18.5%	9,950	0.8%	10,250	3.0%	10,625	3.7%	10,950	3.1%

Source: Lehman Brothers Kuhn Loeb, *The Photographic Products Market,* August 4, 1983.

EXHIBIT 6

Estimated U.S. Consumer Purchases of Film, by Type, 1978–1982
(millions of units)

Film Type	1978	1979	1980	1981	1982	Change 1981–82
Instant B&W	18.8	12.8	7.9	5.8	4.4	(24.1)%
Instant color	119.6	124.1	124.2	126.0	110.9	(12.0)
35mm B&W	26.7	21.2	25.3	23.0	18.6	(19.1)
35mm color slide	61.3	56.2	55.3	57.0	52.0	(8.8)
35mm color print	84.8	98.5	119.9	137.0	146.8	7.2
110 cartridge B&W		18.4	14.0	10.0	13.9	39.0
110 cartridge color	16.1	170.7	182.3	193.0	196.5	1.8
126 cartridge B&W		14.3	9.2	8.0	9.0	12.5
126 cartridge color	221.6	104.2	103.1	105.0	90.0	(14.3)
Disc					21.0	
Other still B&W	20.0	8.2	6.9	6.7	6.5	(3.0)
Other still color	44.4	17.8	13.4	15.0	13.2	(12.0)
Movie	35.3	27.5	26.8	22.0	19.0	(13.6)
Total	648.6	673.9	688.3	708.5	701.8	(0.9)%

Source: Lehman Brothers Kuhn Loeb, *The Photographic Products Market,* August 4, 1983.

Estimated Breakdown of U.S. Consumer Camera Sales
(thousands of units)

	1974	1975	1976	1977	1978
Cartridge*	8,590	8,630	9,050	9,250	10,200
35mm (all types)	825	708	980	1,560	2,300
Instant	3,300	3,900	4,500	6,600	8,200
8mm Movie	636	392	450	609	525
Other**	12	15	20	22	23
Total	13,363	13,645	15,000	18,041	21,249

	1979	1980	1981	1982	Change 1981–82
Cartridge*	8,800	7,500	7,000	2,800	(60)%
Disc	—	—	—	3,900	—
35mm (all types)	2,600	2,900	3,400	3,700	8.8
Instant	6,600	5,700	5,000	4,500	(10.0)
8mm movie	300	230	180	100	(44.4)
Other**	30	33	36	35	(2.8)
Total	18,330	16,363	15,616	15,035	(3.7)%

* 110 and 126 combined.
** Roll and large format.
Source: Lehman Brothers Kuhn Loeb, *The Photographic Products Market,* August 4, 1983.

EXHIBIT 7
Polaroid Corp. Comparative Data, 1978–1982
($ millions, # millions)

	1977	1978	1979	1980	1981	1982
Sales						
Worldwide ($)	1,061.9	1,376.6	1,361.5	1,450.8	1,419.6	1,293.9
United States	645.8	817.4	757.2	791.8	817.8	752.5
Europe	274.2	364.9	383.3	436.8	369.2	333.2
Rest of world						
including Asia	141.9	194.3	220.9	222.2	232.6	208.2
Worldwide (no. of units)						
Cameras	7.0+*	9.4	7.3	6.6	5.6	4.0
Film packs	N/A	200+	205**	198**	194**	N/A
Tech/Ind Photo						
as % of Total $	N/A	N/A	N/A	25.30%	30%	33%
Financials ($)						
EPS	2.81	3.60	1.10	2.60	.95	.73
Dividends/share	.65	.90	1.00	1.00	1.00	1.00
R&D expense	88.9	86.5	109.6	114.0	121.4	118.4
Capital expense	68.9	115.0	134.7	68.1	42.5	31.5
Advertising expense	70.8	101.1	105.0	101.4	106.6	96.4
Return on assets	8.6%	9.3%	2.9%	6.1%	2.2%	1.8%
No. of employees	16,394	20,884	18,416	17,454	16,784	14,540

N/A–Not available.
* The Wall Street Journal, September 5, 1980.
** Merrill Lynch Securities Research Report, May 17, 1982, p. 3.

Source: All data not otherwise noted drawn from Polaroid Corporation, annual reports, 1978–1982.

EXHIBIT 8
Polaroid Executive Officers
1981

Name	Office	Age
Edwin H. Land	Chairman of the board	72
William J. McCune, Jr.	President and chief executive officer	66
I. M. Booth	Executive vice president	50
Sheldon A. Buckler	Executive vice president	50
Peter Wensberg	Executive vice president	53
Richard W. Young	Executive vice president	55
Milton S. Dietz	Senior vice president	50
Charles Mikulka	Senior vice president	68
Howard G. Rogers	Senior vice president and director of research	66
Harvey H. Thayer	Senior vice president, finance	54
Richard F. deLima	Vice president and secretary	51
Julius Silver	Vice president and chairman executive committee	81
Edward R. Bedrosian	Treasurer	49

Dr. Land, founder of the company, served as chairman of the board, chief executive officer and director of research from 1937 to 1980. In 1980, Dr. Land was reelected chairman of the board and assumed the new position of consulting director of basic research in Land photography. He is the inventor of synthetic sheet polarizer for light and of one-step photography. He is the holder of numerous honorary degrees and has been the recipient of many awards from various professional societies.

Mr. McCune joined the company in 1939 and has been a director since 1975. He was elected vice president, engineering in 1954, vice president, assistant general manager in 1963, executive vice president in 1969, president and chief operating officer in 1975 and to his present positions as president and chief executive officer in 1980.

Mr. Booth joined the company in 1958. He was elected assistant vice president and assistant to the president in 1975, vice president and assistant to the president in 1976, senior vice president in 1977, and to his present position as executive vice president in 1980.

Dr. Buckler joined the company in 1964. He was elected assistant vice president in 1969, vice president, research division in 1972, group vice president in 1975, senior vice president in 1977 and to his present position as executive vice president in 1980.

Mr. Wensberg joined the company in 1958. He was elected assistant vice president, advertising in 1966, vice president, advertising in 1968, senior vice president in 1971 and to his present position as executive vice president in 1980.

Dr. Young joined the company in 1962. He was elected vice president, assistant director of research in 1963, senior vice president in 1969 and to his present position as executive vice president in 1980.

Mr. Dietz joined the company in 1955. He was elected assistant vice president in 1975, vice president, engineering in 1977 and to his present position as senior vice president in 1980.

Mr. Mikulka joined the company in 1942. He was elected vice president, patents in 1960 and to his present position as senior vice president in 1975.

EXHIBIT 8 (Continued)

Mr. Rogers joined the company in 1937. He was elected vice president and senior research fellow in 1968, vice president, senior research fellow and associate director of research in 1975, senior vice president and associate director of research in 1979 and to his present positions as senior vice president and director of research in 1980.

Mr. Thayer joined the company in 1956. He was elected treasurer in 1970, vice president and treasurer in 1971, vice president, finance and treasurer in 1977 and to his present position as senior vice president, finance in 1980.

Mr. deLima joined the company as secretary in 1972. He was elected to his present positions as vice president and secretary in 1975.

Mr. Silver, a director and vice president since 1937 and chairman of the executive committee, is also a partner in the firm of Silver & Solomon, the company's general counsel.

Mr. Bedrosian joined the company in 1965. He was elected assistant treasurer in 1975 and to his present position as treasurer in 1980.

Source: Polaroid Corporation, *10K,* 1981.

EXHIBIT 9
Polaroid Corporation
Production Facilities as of
1981

Location	Function
Domestic	
Norwood, Mass.	Polarizer sheet production
Norwood, Mass.	Transparency film production
Norwood, Mass.	Camera assembly*
Waltham, Mass.	Battery assembly
Waltham, Mass.	Chemical production
Waltham, Mass.	Film pack production
Waltham, Mass.	Positive film production
Freetown, Mass.	Chemical production
Foreign	
Dumbarton, Scotland	Camera assembly, film pack assembly, positive film production, sunglass production
Enschede, Netherlands	Film pack assembly, positive film production, sunglass production
Newbridge, Ireland	Film pack assembly

* Highly labor intensive.

Source: Compiled from various annual reports.

EXHIBIT 10
Polaroid Corporation, 1980

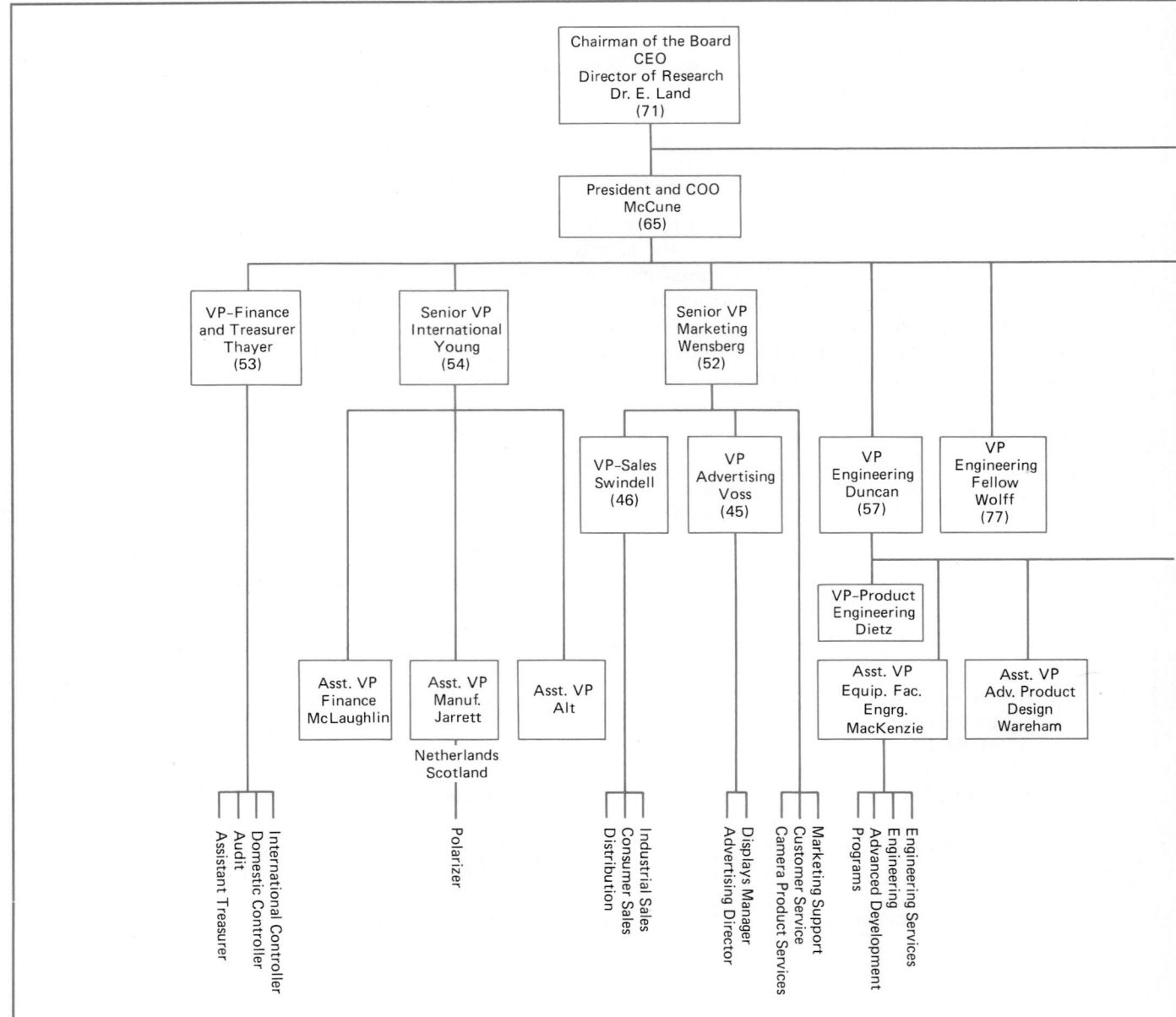

Note: Numbers in parentheses indicate the ages of the various executives.

Source: Approximate 1980, pre-reorganization, organizational chart drawn from various secondary sources. The company does not have an official organization chart.

EXHIBIT 10 (Continued)

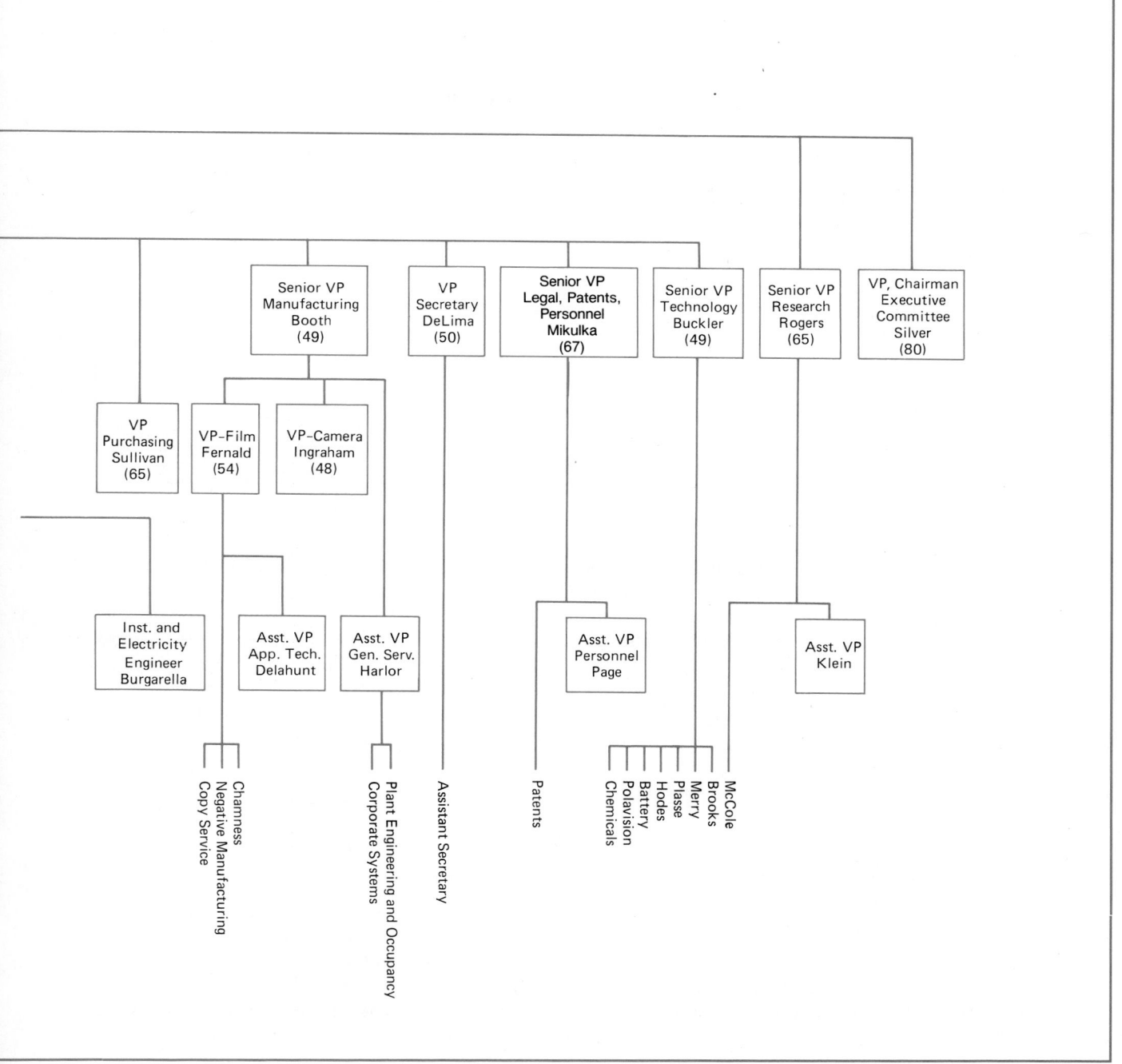

THE PILLSBURY COMPANY

"We laughed at Pillsbury ten years ago," said a General Mills executive as the 1980s began. "But now for better or for worse, Pillsbury seems to be getting all the action." [1] With fine performances by both companies over the preceding decade, this was rare praise in one of the strongest crosstown rivalries in the whole business world. What caused the spectacular turnaround at Pillsbury? What could be learned from these events? In May 1985, Mr. William Spoor, the man most associated with the changes at Pillsbury would step down as CEO and turn this authority over to his president, Jack Stafford. What actions should Stafford take to ensure the company's continuing success? And what should Pillsbury's strategies be for the late 1980s and early 1990s?

EARLY HISTORY AND BACKGROUND

Both companies had grown up in the burgeoning grain and flour markets of the mid-1800s. Both had headquarters in Minneapolis. And both began to diversify away from their stagnating flour milling activities in the early 1950s. In contrast to General Mills which moved into electronics, chemicals, and appliances (see General Mills, Inc., case), Pillsbury concentrated on flour, grains, baking mixes, and dough products through the 1950s. And it remained primarily a U.S.-based company.

Under President Paul S. Gerot, Pillsbury expanded in the 1960s into powdered drink mixes, calcium cyclamate, and poultry.[2] And it made some small re-

Case copyright © 1985 by James Brian Quinn. Material is partly adapted from an earlier case written by James Brian Quinn and Mariann Jelinek. Research associates—Penny C. Paquette and Allie J. Quinn.

The generous cooperation of the Pillsbury Company is gratefully acknowledged.

lated acquisitions in Canada and Latin America.[3] But earnings remained unstable; and when 1966 earnings dropped 3% despite a 9% sales growth, a new management team was named.

Robert J. Keith—who had engineered the company's 1940s entry into consumer baking mixes and 1950s expansion into refrigerated dough products—moved from president of the Consumer Division to chief executive officer. And Terrance Hanold, a lawyer with computer expertise, became president. Messrs. Keith and Hanold diversified Pillsbury further. In 1967, Call-A-Computer, a computer time sharing subsidiary, was formed; but more importantly, Burger King, a $12 million Miami restaurant chain, was acquired. Burger King expanded rapidly, growing by 150 restaurants in 1969 alone, to a total of 850 in 1972, when with less than one-sixth of Pillsbury's sales it began to provide more than one-fourth of total earnings.[4] In 1969, Pillsbury acquired majority interest in Poppin' Fresh Pie Shops. In 1970, J–M Poultry Packing was acquired, as were Pemton, Inc. (a residential and community developer of experimental housing),[5] *Bon Appetit,* (a gourmet foods magazine), and Bon Voyage (travel services). In 1971, Bachman's European Flower Markets (retail outlets for cut flowers, plants, and accessories) were added. In 1972, the company acquired Mallory Restaurants; Souverain Cellars, a California vintner; and Moline, Inc.

Messrs. Keith and Hanold also decentralized Pillsbury's organization, establishing Consumer Products, Agri-Products, Pillsbury Farms (poultry operations), Burger King, Food Service (commercial foods), and International as "freestanding businesses." But companywide profit margins hovered between 4.7% and 5.8% from 1967 to 1972 while rival General Mills achieved 7.8% to 11.4%. Consumer food sales stagnated at $267–$272 million for three years. And Pillsbury was a slow third behind General Mills' (Betty Crocker) and P&G's (Duncan Hines) brands in the crucial cake mix field.[6]

THE PILLSBURY DREAM

About this time (early 1972) CEO Robert Keith named an executive team to consider new goals and strategies for Pillsbury. As William Spoor, then vice president and general manager of international operations, recalls,

> The process kind of evolved in a natural way. I was talking to Bob Keith. I said, "You know, Bob, this is the fifth year of my stock options and they're all under water." He responded, "Bill, if you're dissatisfied with the results of the company, why don't you develop an alternate strategy?" I said, "Are you serious?" And he said, "Yes! You're free to use anyone you want in the company." So I got the general managers together and we agreed to meet 2–3 times a month to put together a preliminary plan.

A New Management Team

But Mr. Keith did not live to see the results of these deliberations. At the age of 59, he developed cancer, resigned in December 1972, and died only a few months later. In a move surprising to most outsiders, Mr. Hanold "stepped aside for youth." Bill Spoor (age 49), a tough numbers-oriented executive with acquisitions and overseas experience, was named chairman and CEO. James R. Peterson (age 45), a fast-rising grocery products and marketing executive, became president. Both had been hand-selected by Mr. Keith as potential contenders for the top job.

Mr. Spoor's strategy group had met over an eight-month period in 1972, before the seriousness of Mr. Keith's illness was known. In November, when

Mr. Keith's condition worsened, Spoor and Peterson were asked to prepare a strategy presentation for the Board. They were given 30 days. Mr. Peterson, on vacation, reportedly added a few comments to the draft Mr. Spoor worked up with the help of inside and outside experts. The presentation was a distillation of the general managers' strategy deliberations, what the new team would do with the company, Mr. Spoor's philosophy, and a bit about proposed management style:

> One executive who saw this document noted, "It talked about the kind of teamwork they were going to develop, the kind of company they would try to build, the kind of people they would try to acquire. It was on a high plane. It didn't say we were going to be $\frac{1}{3}$ restaurants, $\frac{1}{3}$ consumer, $\frac{1}{3}$ agri. It talked about the approach to the business, the strengthening of our staff, attracting stronger people through aggressive compensation, and good business planning . . . about the use of the executive committee as kind of the conscience and central nervous system of the company. It was seen on an informal basis—pieces of it—by senior management inside the company . . . [in addition to the Board's nominating committee]."

As a portion of drawing up the statement, Mr. Spoor asked each outside board member to identify the company's strengths and weaknesses and why each thought the company's performance had been so lackluster. He also asked 12 outside analysts both these questions and why Pillsbury wasn't more attractive to the investing public. Said Spoor,

> If you put them all together they said basically the same thing: inconsistent performance in earnings per share growth, poor profit record, a shotgun approach to our portfolio without the necessary resources to support all our businesses, the failure to make acquisitions in support of our basic businesses, which were then Agri-Products and Consumer Products. And last was a simple observation that we had some businesses making money, but too many that were losing money. With this in mind we sat down and laid out a plan that we knew would have the support of the general managers because, after all, they helped create it.

Setting Goals for a New Era

A portion of the process was the examination of other companies in the food business. Each member of the general managers' strategy group took three or four companies in the foods business and analyzed why they were successful. How they got there? What their performance measures were? Why they were great? Why the investors and analysts liked them? And so on. The general managers next extracted a composite of concepts they thought made attractive goals for Pillsbury and some things they were convinced the company really could do. Then, Mr. Spoor said,

> We laid out the key objectives of what we called "the Pillsbury dream." We said we wanted a five-year-record of consistent growth in sales and earnings per share. We wanted more than anything else, credibility, not only with our Board and ourselves, but with the investing public. We needed quality earnings, consistent, repetitive, growing. We wanted an average 10% growth per year in sales, minimum 10% growth in EPS, an ROE of 16%, an ROI on total capital employed of 20%, and a P/E ratio in the upper $\frac{1}{3}$ of the leading food companies. We felt if we had a record of performance [like that] the stock price would follow. We said that recruiting, development, and motivation of people was key. We wanted to be a quality company, first class in all respects—in our people, our products, our facilities, and our business conduct.

After almost a year of discussion there was a strong consensus. Of the goals, Mr. Spoor said, "There was no issue at all. The big issue became how do we know we're going to do it? What are our plans?" The next steps were unique. "We decided to really put ourselves on the spot. I suggested to the Board that we go public with our objectives, really lay the company out. . . . They said, 'Why? Why don't you just wait?' So we waited until the May Board meeting; then we laid out [for the Board] the presentation we wanted to take to the New York security analysts." Two months later (on July 19, 1973) Spoor, Peterson, and Arthur Rosewall (CEO of Burger King) publicly announced certain key strategies and objectives at a meeting of the New York Society of Security Analysts. Highlights are included in Exhibit 1. Mr. Spoor said, "I think people understood this was a different group [of managers] with different aspirations. But they still had doubts we could achieve what we said."

The Changeover

Certain actions were already under way. Organizationally, most of the operations now reported directly to Spoor: Wallin in Agriproducts, Elston (whom Spoor brought in from McKinsey) in International, Rosewall in Burger King, and most corporate staff units. Although Peterson had the title of president, he was not chief operating officer. His role was more that of group vice president over the consumer business. Spoor quickly started "Monday morning staff meetings" attended by these top line people and ultimately a few staff people. He made it clear that the style of Pillsbury had changed. He was going to be involved. He would call the shots. He would listen to people, but he was going to make the decisions. As one executive said, "Peterson didn't get to make many decisions—very aggravating to Jimmy," a man who had been considered a genuine candidate for the top spot.

According to some, "Pillsbury had become a bit inbred at this time." There was an inside Board with many Minneapolis people on it. The tenor of the company was described as "hold things the way they were." Sales growth had been largely through inflation. Relationships at the top level had been "very gentlemanly." In this milieu Spoor's style created a new driving force. His style was described as follows:

> He's a challenger. He really takes nothing at face value, even after you've worked with him for a long time. I'm as liable as ever to go up to his office and be really grilled. He's not doing it to grill me, but to really penetrate, to see how carefully an idea has been thought through, how ready it is to be hatched—and how strongly I believe it. He may oppose me and disguise his reason for opposition, just to see how deeply I feel about a thing. He's a challenger, a questioner. He's an options open kind of guy. . . . But he has very strong opinions on things. To change an opinion you just have to tackle him and break his shoulder.
>
> He's also very much a scorecard guy. He says, "I keep a scorecard, good and bad." Each time the Board meets, he says this is what I said I was going to do. This is what we've done. This is what we haven't done. This is what we're going to do the next period. And this is how I'll come to you to measure my and the corporation's performance. He has said, "I'm on this stage for awhile; then somebody else is going to have it. Some people have stayed here too long. I'm not going to. . . . I expect to be taken care of if I do a good job here, but don't keep me here a month longer than I am really contributing." He means it.
>
> He's not a gentle, caring, warm, human being. He's fun. He likes to have a drink, to tell a good story, to laugh. But he's an intensive, inward guy—very performance oriented. Unfortunately, there's a lot of fear of Bill Spoor too. Sometimes it costs him in terms of some people's willingness to really say where they are on issues. He seeks a lot of input, listens to people he respects and trusts, thinks. He doesn't make a decision until he has to. I don't mean that he procrastinates. He keeps every option open, whether it's who he'll have lunch with, who he'll name to the Board, or what or-

ganizational form he'll use. He doesn't commit his mind to a course of action until he has everything he can learn about it. He's a very bright guy, and a very clear thinker, especially on paper. Yet he's very low on self ego, very unselfish in his management style.

THE CHICKEN IS THE EGG

The first real test of the new management team was in stabilizing earnings. A key element in this had to be Pillsbury Farms' chicken business. Two years before Mr. Spoor's accession, *Financial World* had pointed out,

> [In 1971] Pillsbury's first half sales rose 4% from those in the corresponding period of fiscal 1969–70, but common share earnings fell from $2.34 to $1.30. This sharp drop would be startling enough even in a company dependent mainly on the badly depressed broiler market; but Pillsbury Farms, the chicken division, brought in only 16% of the sales in the fiscal 1969–70, so it's obvious that the chicken impact is really staggering.[7]

The Biggest Question

According to Mr. G. M. Donhowe, vice president and treasurer at the time,

> Bill knew before he took the job that the biggest question he'd have to face was to stay in or get out of chickens. Within a few months after taking over he asked a number of people who he knew were protagonists on one side or the other for whatever memoranda or position papers they had in their files on the subject. Then he invited any member of senior management who wanted to present a position paper to do so. He got papers from Terry Hanold, who was a strong advocate of the chicken business; Dean McNeal, who was on the Board and had formerly run our Agricultural Products group which included chickens; and Mike Harper, who had run the operation trying to sell branded chickens (fresh and frozen) and frozen processed chickens . . . I was a chief protagonist for getting rid of it. I was joined in that position substantially by Paul Kelsey, the controller. Just about everyone else was sitting in the wings. . . .

Spoor had purposely commissioned two papers on each side of the issue: Hanold and McNeal for retention, Harper and Donhowe for divestiture. But the decision was not easy. As Mr. Spoor said later, "Poultry was some $140 million of our [roughly] $700 million in sales, and in that particular year it was on an up cycle. In the last full year of our ownership, poultry made $6 million." Management was split on the issue. And to complicate matters, Mr. Hanold, the past president who had been largely responsible for the chicken business concept, was still on the Board and was chairman of the Executive Committee.

Debate and Decision

With the position papers as background, management debated the issue for 12 months "very hotly and under difficult circumstances." Spoor and Donhowe visited Ralston Purina which had recently made a similar divestiture. They invited consultants to look at the issue. And they asked Lehman Brothers what Pillsbury Farms' real value was. Lehman responded that they could sell it to a potential European buyer at a price higher "by some healthy margin" than the present value of the division's then projected five-year cash flows. Finally this information, the position papers, and management's own recommendation to divest went to the

Board. The Board continued the debate for some months. When the issue finally came to a vote, only Mr. Hanold voted against divestiture. According to some, this signaled Mr. Hanold's "break with management." And shortly afterward at his own request Hanold "went onto special assignment." Mr. Spoor later commented very sympathetically, "A very brilliant man! A shame, but that's just the way it went."

Following the Board's vote on March 6, 1974, Pillsbury Farms was sold to Imperial Group, Ltd., for over $20 million. Mr. Spoor later noted: "This really taught everyone a lesson—that anything that wasn't performing, that didn't have good long-range plans and prospects, was in trouble." But in his public announcement of the decision, he emphasized that,

> Pillsbury Farms is a good business directed by sound management. Our decision to sell is based on strategic fit and price—not inadequate performance.... To remain with Farms would call for a significant reinvestment program.... We do not believe that selection of broiler chickens for growth investments meets the corporate objectives we outlined to you in our meeting with the New York Society last July.[8]

The divested division had made $3 million net in fiscal 1974 before its sale.[9] In the next year, it reportedly lost money for its new owner, and in the words of one executive, "Spoor became an overnight hero. He gained a lot of ground with the Board."

A FOODS COMPANY

"By then, after a year," said Mr. Spoor, "we had decided that we wanted to be a foods company. As we looked back, that was the only thing that we'd really made money on. Once we'd agreed on that . . . we got rid of all the sideshows. We dumped housing, timesharing, the gourmet magazine, wines, and fresh flowers— all after careful study. But you have to give people a rationale—a truthful rationale —as to why you do these things. So we said, we want to be a foods company. We've agreed to that. This or that division or business doesn't fit, besides which it is losing money."

For example, housing had lost a lot of money. And, according to one major participant, "top management really didn't even know the vocabulary of the business." Time sharing had been created because the company had excess computer capacity and the former president—who was interested in computer applications[10] —had pushed the opportunity. This business clearly did not fit well into the "foods" concept. On the other hand, Spoor later said, "We should have been able to make *Gourmet* magazine go, but I couldn't find anyone who would take the challenge. That was an easy sale because the business could have been made profitable."

Out of Wine

Souverain Cellars was much more complicated because it involved big losses. In 1972 Pillsbury had bought Souverain in California's Napa Valley and had pumped in some $8 million to boost production from 12,000 cases toward 1978 goals of 570,000 cases. But the total industry overexpanded to an extent that it outran both consumer demand and its own storage facilities. By mid-1975 Souverain had lost money for two consecutive years, and its near term future looked just as bleak.[11]

Pillsbury tried several management teams in an attempt to turn the company around, but with little success. Finally Mr. Spoor asked the president of Souverain, "How much money could we make if every case was sold for margin." The president responded, "$2 million before taxes." At that time Pillsbury had already lost $6 million on Souverain. Shortly thereafter Souverain's president came back to Spoor and recommended, himself, that Pillsbury leave the wine business.

Several rationales presented themselves for this action in 1975. First, Souverain was a losing operation. Second, certain states prohibited alcoholic beverage producers from selling alcohol in their own restaurants. This would have prevented Burger King from ever selling beer. And it would have precluded an attractive potential acquisition, Steak and Ale, which suddenly appeared. But executives noted the divestiture decision was really underway much earlier. "We had a $1\frac{1}{2}\%$ market share and no real ability—without just mammoth investments—to become major. . . . Also, remember, Bill Spoor wants to be big and recognizable in anything he does, whether it's hitting a tennis ball or business. Steak and Ale just accelerated the decision. We had enormous earnings in 1975 so we could afford to take the bath then."

Of this early period, Mr. Spoor said,

I used to do quiet things at night. I was convinced if we could just turn off these loss divisions, we could really make some money. We were draining the company for no purpose at all. I've always got hedges in the back of my mind. I'm never overcommitted to a business unless I *know* there's something back there. I get surprised sometimes. But I knew if we got rid of all these, we'd have a better income later. Maybe that could give us 3–4% of our 10% target profit growth.

Mr. Spoor also noted that in this divestiture period,

In several cases the people who were directly involved in the management of troubled divisions—for example the president of Souverain—came in with recommendations that theirs were businesses we ought to get out of. In Souverain's case it was a major problem area. We had proven we couldn't manage it. We had made lots of fundamental managerial mistakes in terms of how we ran it.

But essentially the same thing occurred in the European Flower Markets. In its final year as a part of Pillsbury, that reported to me, I'd told the general manager that I'd like to have his recommendation for the future of the business. . . . And his recommendation was to get out of it. He has a very important role elsewhere in Pillsbury now.

Reinvestment and Diversification

With the cash freed up by divestitures, Pillsbury began to reinvest in growth opportunities. Primary among these, at the time, was Burger King. As Spoor said, "With cake mix you could only grow two ways—by a new product expanding the total market or by increasing your market share. But with Burger King we could grow these two ways, or we could grow geographically. Burger King was the throttle on our growth. [With care we could open it up a little or close it down] to control our growth rate and credibility." Another advantage of restaurants was that they could, in part, finance themselves without impairing the capital access of the rest of the company. All debt and lease obligations of the restaurant subsidiaries were obtained on the basis of their own credits and not guaranteed by the parent company. Eventually the company carried some 65% of its combined restaurant capitalization as debt or debt equivalent.[12]

In 1975 Pillsbury began another important entry into the restaurant field. As Mr. Spoor recalls,

I got a call from an outside director, John Whitehead, on Steak and Ale Restaurants of America. They were being courted and were almost at the point of being acquired by Ralston Purina . . . We were not looking [at Steak and Ale] at all. John Whitehead had just picked up signals about it informally . . . So I called Norm Brinker, who was a cofounder of Steak and Ale, and he and I talked very quietly. We hit it off. We talked the same way, we were trying to do the same things in life, and we had a similar up-bringing . . . We just clicked. Finally, during later negotiations, Brinker said, "Bill, if we can put this thing together, I'll go with Pillsbury. But I have one condition. I will only report to you."

It seems another top Pillsbury executive, after spending days looking at Steak and Ale Restaurants, had given up around 10:30 one night while Spoor had hung on for as long as Brinker wanted. Spoor said, "He was a nondrinker, so it was pretty dry at times. . . . But a sensitive guy like that is selling his life's blood. He wants to know he's loved, accepted, part of the organization. . . . Little things like that make a big difference."

Mr. Walter Scott, chief financial officer of Pillsbury, later noted,

At that stage we were not particularly out looking for new acquisitions in the restaurant business. We were concentrating our efforts on consumer products companies. Nevertheless through our acquisitions department we looked at the particular sector in which Steak and Ale was operating to determine whether (on a long-term basis) it looked like an interesting aspect of the restaurant business and what it would do for Pillsbury—positive and negative. We commissioned some outside studies to try to help us in developing a conviction as to whether we were on the right track. All this was orchestrated by the acquisition department with lots of plug-ins from other parts of the company.

By the end of 1976 the company had begun to assume a new shape. Pillsbury had pared off all its nonfood-related lines and some of its smaller food lines overseas. In addition to Pillsbury Farms, *Bon Appetit*, Pemton, Standard Computer, Souverain, and European Flower Markets, Pillsbury had divested McLaren's (Canadian—pickles and olives), Lara (Mexican—cookies), Calgary Mills (Canadian—flour), and Gringoire-Brossard (French bakery products). Spoor began to say publicly: "I'm only interested in businesses that fall into three categories . . . consumer foods, foods-away-from-home, and agri-products."[13]

The Consumer Group

Of these, Pillsbury's consumer foods activities posed special problems for Mr. Spoor. *Fortune* described some of the key issues this way:

In picking Pillsbury's new chief, Spoor's predecessor sidestepped his own protege, James R. Peterson, whose management skills were much admired by many Pillsbury executives despite the lackluster performance of the consumer group he headed. When Spoor was appointed CEO, Peterson was named President with continuing responsibility for consumer products.

It soon became apparent that neither man was too comfortable working with the other. Spoor gradually began to limit Peterson's role. Peterson sensed erosion in the high level support he was used to in previous jobs—and subordinates found him more difficult to work for. Ultimately, Peterson was forced out by pressures from above and below. In December, 1975, one of his ranking subordinates, George Masko, resigned. Using this resignation along with statements of dissatisfaction from another veteran consumer products executive, Raymond V. Kimrey, Spoor argued to the Board that Peterson's subordinates were up in arms. Confronted with an unappealing choice—the departure of the President or his two top lieutenants—the directors opted to get rid of Peterson.[14]*

When Mr. Peterson left in April 1976 (as executive vice president and director of R. J. Reynolds) Pillsbury's Consumer Group, which provided some 36% of fiscal 1976 profits, included Grocery Products, Refrigerated Products (largely dough), Frozen Foods (principally pizza), Wilton Enterprises (cake and party decorations), and Pillsbury's international consumer activities. According to *Fortune* the group "had seldom developed exciting new products or provided consistent marketing support for the winners it had."[14] To wake up the operation Spoor went after a new top man and recruited Raymond F. Good, who as its president had restored Heinz' domestic foods operations to profitability.

Each of the Consumer Group's divisions had its own problems. The Grocery Division was mired into cake mixes, flour, potatoes (etc.) with declining markets in which it held only a number two or three position. It had to accept price levels set by the leaders, but lacked their modern facilities and scale. The refrigerated dough business, where Pillsbury's market share was high, also appeared to be in a long-term declining industry. The only bright spot in Consumer was frozen foods; Totino's[15] pizza brand—acquired in 1975—was on its way to a strong second-place market share. Although frozen foods in general were declining, frozen pizzas were booming. Said *The Wall Street Journal,*

> Totino's is the market leader almost everywhere it competes. The frozen pizza market is growing rapidly and is already larger than the cake mix or refrigerated dough markets, previously Pillsbury's major consumer food areas.[16]

Good had a choice of two overall strategies: (1) put up the long-term massive advertising necessary to gain first-place penetration for more of his products or (2) manage the declining products for cash and build future businesses in other growth markets. Wishing to avoid the negative profit impact of the former course, Good chose the latter. He commissioned a McKinsey & Company study, which suggested positive consumer trends toward convenience foods, natural foods, more nutritious foods, snacks, and "foods-to-match-changing-lifestyles" where the sit-down family meal was becoming the exception rather than the rule. At Spoor's request Good presented the complete plan for Consumer's redevelopment to the Board. "You could have heard a pin drop. . . . It was so good," said Spoor soon afterward.

Good brought in Edgar Mertz, a former Heinz executive vice president, as his number two man and pressed hard on cost cutting programs to yield savings of 2–3% of sales. Then he plowed the margins into Totino's and selected acquisitions like Speas Farm (apple juice and vinegar) and American Beauty (macaroni). For a while these things seemed to work. By late 1978, however, company veterans were complaining about the new Consumer team's management style, and Good's relations with Spoor seemed to deteriorate. According to *Fortune* Spoor became progressively more insistent that Good clean up "the mess in grocery," show some dramatic financial improvements, and deal with Mertz's abrasive style which was becoming a "time bomb" about to explode the consumer operation.[14] When Spoor needed money to make up shortfalls elsewhere, Good grudgingly cut back on Consumer's advertising and promotional activities and slashed marketing budgets to meet short-term profit goals. On the other hand, while Spoor wanted more

---

profits from Consumer, he was reportedly reluctant to back away from its traditional baking products. So the division in 1979 began to press hard to increase its market share on those lines—with all that implied.[14]

Agri-Products

Agri-Products had provided the remaining quarter of Pillsbury's sales and earnings. Agri—which included mainly Industrial Foods (flour milling, baking mix, hydro-processing), Commodity Merchandising (of grain and feed ingredients), Food Service (volume feeding to institutions), and Export—had been the foundation of Pillsbury's original foods business. But by the late 1970s these activities were declining in relative importance to Pillsbury. In boom years Agri fared well as its grain merchandising and flour milling activities responded to industry cycles. But even as the largest flour producer, Pillsbury found it hard to maintain acceptable margins in bad years.

Nevertheless, Agri was one of the world's largest grain merchandising operations, and enjoyed gross sales of over $3 billion in 1983. Only gross margins from these operations appeared in consolidated sales. The industries on which Agri was based (especially grain production and feed ingredients) were huge and growing at some 3% per year. In summary, in 1983 Agri-Products was (1) the nation's largest flour miller, (2) its eighth largest rice miller, (3) its largest feed ingredient merchandiser, (4) its largest flour exporter, (5) among the top five in grain and oilseed origination, and (6) a major producer of bakery mixes.

Phase Two

In 1976–77 Pillsbury entered phase two of its overall plan. Most of its divestitures were complete, and a new management team was coming into place. About this time Spoor started to talk about becoming "a truly great corporation." How was this to be measured? "We have 12 foods companies we measure ourselves against —like General Mills, General Foods, Kraft, Ralston Purina. We want our P/E ratio to be in the upper one-third of these food companies," said Spoor. But he also wanted to have "the best management" of these companies and "to be number one or number two in every product category we compete in." Spoor continued, "I also want to leave the next management with the same kind of growth vehicle we inherited."[17]

The latter idea became known throughout the company as Spoor's "superbox." Anticipating that in a decade or so the fast-food market would be saturated, Spoor was planting the seeds for a totally new opportunity farther down the road. "It can be almost anything—food, non-food, or food related." This was the first official break with the "foods" concentration that had emerged from the divestiture period. In 1976–77 Spoor allocated some $350,000 to an open ended search for "superbox." The concept was not clearly specified—only that it was to be a large move and one that would provide the basis for growth in the late 1980s. Said Spoor at the time,

> "I deal in dreams. You can't deal just in the hard facts in this kind of job. Somebody's got to dream. And then you get some smart people to put meat on the dreams. . . ."[17]
> He observed: "We broke the initial Pillsbury Dream into sub-missions. We started out with the spirit of '76. We said by 1976, the 200th anniversary of our company, we can break $1 billion in sales and have a $5 EPS. We had things to talk about, magic things, because people need handles. We talked about the 'spirit of '76' first, which was a dream. And we hit that about a year in advance. That then let us push forward the fi-

nancial dream. We wanted to split the shares, call the converts, clean up the balance sheet, and really get a powerful balance sheet for the first time—all of which we did . . . zap! The next dream is superbox."

ORGANIZATION CHANGES

Mr. Spoor later said, "In terms of everything that's happened at Pillsbury, it's the people that make the big difference." The people changes began shortly after Spoor took office, and seven years later they were still a dramatic portion of Pillsbury's activities. Along with the early divestitures outlined above, Mr. Spoor quickly began to modify the company's overall organizational structure. He said,

> We inherited the "free standing business" concept which I felt was hurting the company more than anything we could have done organizationally. We took great strengths and fragmented them. So one of the early ideas was to pull the company back together. The idea of what specifically to do wasn't too far advanced at that time. . . . I couldn't just go to a lower-level unit and get anything [coordinated] done. I'd have to talk to Grocery or Refrigerated and so forth first. . . . Among other things the former management had delegated acquisitions to each of the businesses, but no one had made an acquisition. . . . And so on. The company was very split up; a "this is mine, that's yours idea" prevailed. We were really going to have to change the culture to get needed coordination.

Consolidation and Acquisition

Spoor immediately had most operations report directly to him: Rosewall of Burger King, Wallin in Agri-Products, Elston (whom Spoor brought in from McKinsey) in International, and Peterson in Consumer Products. In addition, the various corporate staff units reported to Spoor. Most important among these were Personnel and Finance where Spoor recruited two high-powered heads from outside the company —Walter D. Scott and Edwin H. Wingate. Both were top candidates from extensive head hunts. Like many others recruited later, both were reportedly extremely well paid and offered "the opportunity to fulfill their career objectives" with Pillsbury. In short order Spoor also brought in Philip D. Aines from Procter & Gamble to head up research and Jerry W. Levin to handle mergers and acquisitions. Most agree that these were all outstanding people, extremely talented. Commentary like that used about Mr. Scott would apply to many of these executives:

> Wally Scott was a gifted man—not just good—he was gifted. He had given up two years of his life at about one tenth of his industrial income to make his government better. He was then at OMB. He liked the Pillsbury Dream we had started by then and saw the challenge. At the time he was interviewed the head hunters said "These final two men are great men, but we think you'll find Mr. Scott head and shoulders above."

After Mr. Wingate had been aboard a short time, Spoor asked him to "Think about the kinds of businesses we are in, how we ought to be structured." With substantial impact from Mr. Willys H. Monroe, a Board member, the three began to discuss how to organizationally restructure Pillsbury. From the first, it was abundantly clear that we were in three businesses. Win Wallin had the agribusiness, Jimmy Peterson had the consumer business, and Arthur Rosewall had the restaurants (which was really Burger King at that time). The key questions then were: "How do we take best advantage of these businesses, use the people we've got, and develop succession management?" In response to these questions Wingate and Monroe wrote up "white papers" for Spoor. Finally the three men, working largely from the Monroe document, designed the basic outlines of the new organization. Mr. Wingate noted,

> These papers weren't done in a vacuum. They were reviewed with Spoor often, and we'd test different thoughts. It's hard to say which day it really happened. . . . There was talk even a year earlier in the consumer companies that some day it would be possible to take advantage of synergies that undoubtedly existed in production, sales, marketing, and research—to restructure activities so that this body of knowledge could be focused against the whole retail market.

Distron—which was part of Burger King and was the second largest food distribution system in the United States—could service 2–5 restaurant chains. Davmor, a manufacturer of kitchen equipment and furniture for restaurants, could also apply staff across the board. Real Estate could work across the various businesses. There was a lot of construction in the groups. And so on. Mr. Wingate later said,

> In developing the final format there were many discussions with corporate level people before the new organization could be officially put on paper. . . . There were extensive interchanges and seminar activities on "how this or that would work?" before anything was done. . . . There evolved a consensus understanding—if not a consensus agreement—on where we were heading. . . . Individuals might not even recall who articulated the concept to them or when. People simply gained an appreciation and were able to internalize the fact that some organization changes were going to take place. They knew what was being considered and could project how they would be affected.

In the area of what became the new senior management committee, there was serious opposition from the heads of the "free standing businesses" and staff people who would not be on that committee any more. The new group was line, just seven people: Spoor, Scott, Powell, and the four line executive vice presidents —instead of the 15 general managers who had previously funneled into the executive office. Most of these now reported to the executive VPs as staff heads or heads of individual product or activity centers. Support activities for each unit were consolidated at the group level whenever possible. Some of the very senior people reportedly found this quite hard to swallow. Nevertheless, by mid-1976 the new structure was largely in place. But it kept evolving over the next several years as pieces of Peterson's former activities were split between Spoor and Scott.

Changes at the Top

Meanwhile Spoor kept up his search for first-rate talent to run his line operations. As was noted, Ray Good had taken over Consumer Products. In 1977 Spoor hired Donald N. Smith (then 36 and McDonald's third-ranking executive) as CEO of Burger King, and the talented newcomer began to bring that diverse enterprise under more effective operating control. But Burger King had an uphill profitability fight against McDonald's larger distribution system and outlet size ($200,000 per year greater sales than the average Burger King unit).

Then unfortunately, after a glowing few years, Ray Good's relationship with Spoor began to deteriorate seriously as Consumer profit performance lagged and it developed internal management problems. When Spoor suddenly picked the much liked head of Agri-Products, Winston R. Wallin, to be president, both Good and

"Wally" Scott were deeply unsettled. In the process of selection the Board's nominating committee reviewed all the top line and staff people. Mr. Spoor later described events this way,

> I went to the Board in March (1978) and said, "We need a president of this company." They were absolutely aghast. They said, "But things are going so well. Why rush into naming a president now and risk losing all those top candidates you brought in? The reason they're good is they're scrambling for the open slot." I answered, "Because the company could be run more effectively." They replied, "Let us think about it." And basically they turned me down.
>
> In May I went back and I was irate . . . I said, "I want to set up the time this company can be managed more effectively; and frankly it can be. There's something called the concentration of power—in me. Everybody listens too carefully to what I say—and I'm not that good—it becomes 'Spoor said this, and Spoor said that.' I know what I can do and what I can't do within reason. . . . If you want to put this company at risk, just let me go on like this for another couple of years." . . . Zap! The situation changed in two seconds. We announced Wallin as president in June.

A few years before, Spoor and Wallin had participated in an encounter group at the National Training Laboratories. There they had spent a lot of time together and had gotten to know each other quite well. Spoor said, "Win has a marvelous sense of humor. He is very slow on the draw and will let people speak their piece. But when he comes out, he has a point of view that is absolutely spectacular. I have built up extreme confidence in Win."

The Green Giant Arrives

Then in late 1978 Spoor began negotiations with Green Giant Company, a large well-established foods company headed by Thomas H. Wyman, formerly second in command at Polaroid. Before the merger, Spoor reportedly told visitors, "No one at Pillsbury can run Green Giant." And Wyman—who was considered one of the rising stars of the U.S. executive world—was assured like other talented managers that his "career expectations could be fulfilled at Pillsbury."[14]

On completion of the merger, Wyman personally received a windfall of almost $1 million in salary, bonuses, and benefits. The question then became where to put Wyman in the Pillsbury structure. The solution was an executive office—with Wallin as president, Wyman as vice chairman, and Scott as executive vice president. Explained Spoor, "I had to offer Wyman the top job to keep him and to make the merger work."[18] Discouraged by these events, Good left the company in July 1979 and became president of Munsingwear in October of that year. When asked why he was willing to sacrifice Good, Spoor replied bluntly, "Tom's better."[19]

By March 1980 Spoor could report to analysts that Pillsbury had "the finest management team in the foods industry." Then began a series of high level defections that staggered the company. In early May, Wally Scott resigned to head Investors Diversified Services, Inc. Then shortly thereafter Don Smith left for the top spot at PepsiCo, Inc. *Business Week* noted however that: "Spoor had created an atmosphere of intense competition among the top officers, luring each initially with the promise of succession." But perhaps the biggest jolt came on May 23 when Tom Wyman agreed to become president and chief executive of CBS. While upset by the turmoil, Spoor responded philosophically, "There were solid reasons behind each of the moves. Tom Wyman couldn't turn down the offer CBS made him . . .

[reportedly a $1 million bonus and $800,000 per year guaranteed salary] . . . And we would have destroyed our pay structures trying to meet the offers."[20]

One consolation for Spoor was that along with Wyman, Pillsbury got Jack Stafford, Green Giant's chief operating officer. Stafford's background seemed ideal for Pillsbury. In addition to his success at Green Giant, he had spent 12 years in consumer advertising at Leo Burnett and had risen to senior vice president-marketing at Kentucky Fried Chicken Corporation. Stafford was named an executive vice president at Pillsbury in 1979, became head of Consumer Foods in 1981, and joined the board of directors in 1983.

CONTINUED PERFORMANCE

Despite the turmoil, Pillsbury's financial performance continued to be exceptionally strong. (See Exhibits 2–4). And the departed executives had all left their own positive imprints. Before leaving, Don Smith had brought a new discipline to Burger King. He had expanded menus and increased sales in real terms during a period when McDonald's and Wendy's real sales declined. Green Giant's Stafford had moved into the top slot at Consumer, and Spoor claimed "the company could now market in the league with Kraft and General Mills."

The company also continued both to acquire and divest operations in keeping with its extraordinary goals.

Acquisitions and Divestments Fiscal 1974–1983

DIVESTMENTS	ACQUISITIONS
Pillsbury Farms (poultry)	Wilton Enterprises (cake decorating)
Pemtom (housing development)	Totino's Finer Foods (frozen pizza)
Standard Computer (timesharing)	Steak & Ale Restaurants of America
Lara (Mexican cookie manufacturer)	American Beauty Macaroni Company
Bon Appetit (gourmet magazine)	Fox Deluxe Pizza
Souverain Wine	Green Giant
European Flower Markets	Wickes Agricultural
Calgary Flour Mill	Pioneer Rice
Wilson Enterprises	B & B Mushrooms
Poppin Fresh Pie Shops	Jokish
	Hoffman Menuü
	Hammonds
	Häagen-Dazs

The company had changed in important qualitative dimensions as well. At the time the Pillsbury Dream was first drawn up, the management group had decided it wanted to share its proposed successes with all important constituencies, including stockholders, the board of directors, employees, customers, suppliers, and especially the communities where the company operated. The management group set general goals in each area and resolved to monitor progress against these. As profits grew, the company multiplied its contributions to community causes to $3.5 million in 1983. Pillsbury occasionally bought out the remaining tickets to the Minnesota Vikings games and gave them to United Way so local people could see games which would have been blacked out on TV. During the Vietnam refugee crisis, company officers went to Washington to see what Pillsbury could do to help and gave every person in the company who would "adopt" a Vietnamese family $1,000—or a year's supply of food for the family.

In addition, top management engaged Survey Research, Inc., to do a series of employee attitude surveys to see how people at all levels regarded Pillsbury in terms of compensation, supervisory practices, planning, communications, and so on. The company changed a number of employee practices: better explaining each individual's compensation and role in the total enterprise, posting and allowing bidding for all internal openings, improving the house medium *The Pillsbury Reporter* to explain where the company was going, the progress it was making, and the reasons things were being done. Top executives noted, "Recruiting is a lot easier than it was. We have people coming to us now—good people—saying they hear what's happening here and want to be a part of it."

1985 AND BEYOND

In 1984–85 Mr. Spoor announced a new set of goals for Pillsbury. These were: annual growth rates of 12–15% for EPS, 25% for ROI, and 18% for ROE. How this should be accomplished was an open question. Mr. Spoor had told analysts and public audiences that Pillsbury wished to remain dominantly a foods company. But to achieve its goals it would consider: making tactical acquisitions, joining in major mergers where Pillsbury was the surviving entity, and entering nonfoods fields where Pillsbury could add significant value through use of its skills and resources. In keeping with this Pillsbury had recently acquired Häagen Dazs (a quality ice cream producer and distributor), Sedutto Ice Creams (for the food service market), Azteca Corn Products (refrigerated tortillas), Apollo Foods (high-quality ethnic foods), and Van de Kamps (frozen foods).

In June 1983, it had attempted to acquire Stokley-Van Camp, Inc., for a $62 per share tender offer. When the target company's management fought the offer and Quaker Oats put in a "friendly" tender of $77 per share, Pillsbury withdrew with a pretax gain of over $6 million.[21] A similar scenario occurred when Pillsbury made a bid for the Joan of Arc Co., a closely-held producer of specialty canned goods.[22]

Summary financial data for Pillsbury's major divisions are included in Exhibit 2. Burger King continued to be the most significant contributor to 1984 gains in sales (20%) and operating profit (60%). Its systemwide sales rose to $3.43 billion. Over the preceding two years, operating profit had increased 74% while return on invested capital had increased from 18% to nearly 26%. By year end Burger King had 3,827 restaurants worldwide, with 14% operating as company owned units. While experiencing losses during fiscal 1984, Burger King's international operations improved substantially over the preceding year, and it was making substantial progress with its institutional franchise program. By the end of fiscal 1984, Häagen Dazs had a total of 316 units located in 32 states. Steak & Ale Restaurants numbered 32, with average restaurant sales increasing to $1.5 million. Bennigan's, the popular fern bar, continued its growth with average unit sales of $2.3 million and instituted a number of programs to offer non-alcoholic drinks and to discourage intoxicated individuals from driving. By year end it had 148 units. J. J. Muggs, a gourmet hamburger restaurant concept that began in fiscal 1983, showed strong consumer acceptance and had been expanded to 5 units.

Pillsbury's Foods Group included Consumer Foods and Agri-Products. Overall sales increased 10% to $2.4 billion and operating profits rose 16% to $181 million. Agri-Products, aided by a large sale of flour to Egypt and the movement of grain as part of the government's Payment-in-Kind program to support farm prices, showed an increase of 111% over the preceding year's depressed profit levels. However, profits for fiscal 1984 remained below acceptable levels in barge transportation, grain exporting, rice milling, and edible beans.[23]

Consumer Foods 1984 performance was led by strong profit gains from Refrigerated Foods and Häagen Dazs with important volume growth in Frozen Foods. Partially due to the attention given to EDB, the Dry Grocery business experienced a marginal year with profits and volume somewhat below fiscal 1983. Häagen Dazs sales increased 22% during 1984, and Refrigerated Foods set new records for profits and sales. Within the Foods Group, all of International's wholly owned businesses finished fiscal 1984 ahead of the preceding year in their local currencies. However, the strength of the U.S. dollar resulted in operating profits below fiscal 1983.

Pillsbury's capital spending increased dramatically during fiscal 1984 to $282 million, a 16% increase over 1983. Restaurant expansion was the primary focus of investment, with other major capital projects supporting Häagen Dazs's major new production facilities and some tactical acquisitions domestically and abroad.

In his last two years as CEO, Mr. Spoor had emphasized both internal development of Pillsbury's three basic businesses (see Exhibit 4) and an aggressive acquisition program. He had formed a venture capital unit within Pillsbury to help it investigate and take positions in promising new areas and had commissioned studies by Stanford Research Institute (SRI) and Hudson Institute to define promising areas for future growth.

In early 1984 when Pillsbury announced that Jack Stafford (age 46) was moving up to president, replacing Win Wallin who became vice chairman, the press suggested that Spoor had identified his successor.[24] At that time Stafford took over responsibility for all foods operations while Wallin managed the restaurant businesses. Agri-Products was broken up into Commodities Marketing under Mr. Coonrod and Industrial Foods overseen by Kent Larson, who was responsible for the Dry Grocery portion of Consumer Foods.

As Mr. Stafford assumed the role of CEO, he faced a strong and much different Pillsbury than that of the early 1970s. Analysts, both within and outside the company, were wondering what he would make the hallmarks of his era. Mr. Spoor had worked hard to create a "superbox" for his successor, but what it should be and how Pillsbury should change its overall structure and portfolio to meet the opportunities and challenges of the late 1980s and 1990s were still unclear.

QUESTIONS

1. Evaluate Mr. Spoor's handling of the early stages in his strategy changes at Pillsbury. Why were these steps taken in this sequence? What could have been improved? How?

2. What do you think of the way Pillsbury's acquisition-expansion program was planned? Implemented? What changes would you have made? Why?

3. What should Mr. Stafford's strategy be for the late 1980s? Why? What should he do to implement it? What should Pillsbury's "superbox" be? How would you identify it? Implement it?

EXHIBIT 1

Highlights of a
Presentation by the
Pillsbury Company to
the New York Society
of Security Analysts
July 19, 1973

Strategic Posture (Mr. Spoor)

I believe I can best outline our strategic posture by simply stating a group of propositions about the kind of company we intend to be:

- We are and will continue to be a market- and marketing-oriented company.
- We will be international in scope.
- We will be diversified beyond our food base.
- We will be dominated by our brand-oriented businesses serving rapidly growing consumer needs.
- There remains an important place for the basic commodity oriented enterprises in Pillsbury, provided earnings can be demonstrated to meet corporate standards for volatility.

We selected this kind of company over other alternates for two reasons. First, this posture represents a natural extension of what we are and what we know how to do best. Secondly, we believe there are an ample number of investment opportunities available within this definition to satisfy our objectives. . . .

Corporate Objectives

In the general category

- We know that we must have a consistent record of growth in sales and earnings.
- We are hopeful of a price/earnings ratio in the upper one-third of a selected sample of food-based companies.
- We intend to continue our dividend policy.

If we can manage ourselves like that, in fiscal 1976 our sales would exceed $1 billion and earnings per share $5.00.

Applied against the base of fiscal 1973 results, this means we will have to grow at a compounded annual rate of 10% in both sales and earnings per share.

We recognize that these are demanding objectives, particularly for a company that historically has not operated at these levels. . . .

Agri-Products

The oldest business function of Pillsbury is our Agri-Products group, led by flour milling. Producing flour and selling it to the baker is a thoroughly mature business. We happen to be number one in this industry, and I think in more ways than capacity. Nonetheless we have in the past and will continue to employ a very disciplined allocation of capital for reinvestment in this business. Our objective is to sustain the most satisfactory earnings stream from flour milling on a constant or modestly declining capital base. . . .

EXHIBIT 1 (Continued)

International

Our International operations finished a fine year. Jim Peterson will comment on the momentum in our consumer businesses in Europe, all of which are healthy and growing. Economic nationalism in Latin America, however, points to some difficult times ahead. We do not intend to walk away from these investment areas which have been very good to us. However, the desire for local government participation in several of our businesses and the recent adoption of Andean Pact legislation in Venezuela suggest a reduction rather than expansion of our developing country investments. . . .

Pillsbury Farms

Finally, I want to report to you on Pillsbury Farms, our broiler poultry business. First, you should understand that after the pruning and re-direction of the business, which was begun two years ago, and included our recent withdrawal from further processed and microwave operations, Farms has become a healthy business. Aided by a strong price level, Farms turned in a record performance last year, delivering in excess of $5 million profit before tax. There is no doubt in my mind that this is an extremely well-run business with a management team second to none.

The question that we have been wrestling with is whether or not this well-run and profitable business fits the strategy we have laid out for Pillsbury. This is not an easy question to answer because one does not, with haste, decide to dispose of a major source of earnings per share where the likelihood for replacement is through internal development. . . .

So, at this point we are not prepared to make a definite statement as to what the answer to the question on Farms will be other than to say that all options remain open. . . .

Consumer Strategies (Mr. Peterson)

1. The importance of our consumer business in size, as well as in quality of earnings, identifies the fundamental need for accelerated growth here first if we are to move the total company.

2. The retail food industry with sales of over $100 billion in 1972 represents a broad array of opportunities for the mass marketing of branded consumer food products and an increasing opportunity in the 1970s for the mass marketing of non-food products.

3. We are keenly aware that to be a leader in our industry and to maintain the leverage that will ensure premium profitability, we must be both a leader in the markets in which we participate or plan to enter and that we must generate a growing share of retail grocery sales.

4. One's ability to grow in today's highly competitive food business and the rapidly emerging non-food areas of the supermarket depends on one's understanding of the consumer environment with its ever more rapidly increasing levels of personal income (both here and abroad), resulting in demands for ever-increasing levels of quality and convenience in both products and services.

EXHIBIT 1 (Continued)

We finally stated that we felt our plans for the future of our consumer businesses were soundly based on these principles, that they represented a balanced program and a continuing opportunity for premium growth.

Our four point strategy was stated as follows:

1. We are committed to a larger share of market in our current business areas. We will continue to place the investment of resources behind our fundamental consumer businesses to continue their share growth.
2. We believe that internal growth from new products can continue to be a source of increased earnings even in our mature areas.
3. The third part of our strategy involves the internal development of new businesses in areas that we are not in currently.
4. We will increase our acquisition activities and this will be a primary accountability of the executive office.

In February, I emphasized the importance of the development of brand franchises through the application of our marketing skills. We are giving great priority to the acceleration of this process. . . .

Consumer Orientation

As I stated earlier, we have based our consumer products efforts on the belief that the consumer is demanding rapidly increasing levels of quality and convenience and that this rate of change, fueled by increasing levels of personal income, provides an excellent opportunity for premium growth for those food companies that have the insight to identify the desired changes and are organized to commercialize them. We have reorganized our new products' teams to do both.

In each of the consumer business areas that I have discussed, branded products of high quality and convenience, keyed to contemporary life styles and value systems, clearly dominate our strategy. How we apply this philosophy to increase our share of market in our basic businesses, to accelerate our new product program, to develop products for new areas, and to acquire new consumer businesses will, in our view, determine our record in the months ahead. . . .

Burger King Restaurants (Mr. Rosewall)

Looking ahead for fiscal 1974 through fiscal 1977, our present planning horizon:

1. The fast-food industry is expected to grow at a compound rate of 11% per year, increasing from present annual sales of $5.9 billion to $9.9 billion.
2. The number of Burger King restaurants is expected to increase at a rate of 18% per year.
3. Total Burger King restaurant sales are expected to increase at a rate of 27% per year.

EXHIBIT 1 (Continued)

Attainment of these objectives would result in the number of restaurants increasing from the 982 in operation at the end of fiscal 1973 to 1,930. Company operated units would increase from 278 to 670, or to about 35% of the total.

Total restaurant sales would increase from last year's $338 million to $891 million, with average sales per store, for comparable stores, moving from fiscal 1973's $376,000 to $492,000.

We want to continue to be Pillsbury's major investment opportunity.

Social Responsibility (Mr. Spoor)

This discussion of our business performance would not be complete without reporting on that broad and important topic "social responsibility." We are convinced that excellence in performance in these areas is a requirement our customers, employees and stockholders expect if we intend to compete successfully in the marketplace. This is not an extracurricular activity, but rather an integral part of the practice of management. . . .

Source: Company records.

EXHIBIT 2

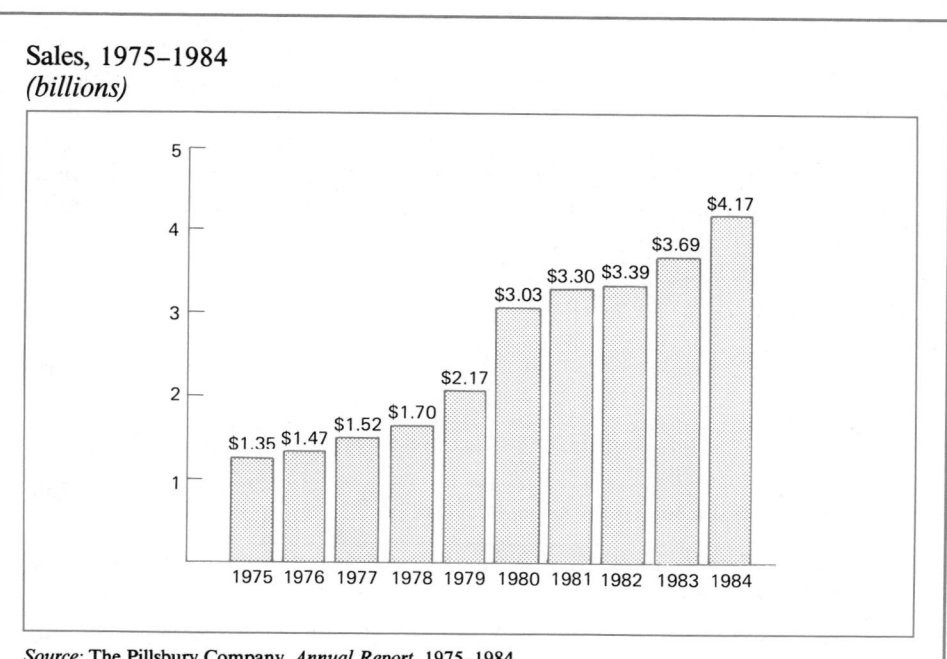

Sales, 1975–1984
(billions)

Source: The Pillsbury Company, *Annual Report,* 1975–1984.

EXHIBIT 2 (Continued)

Net Earnings, 1975–1984
(millions)

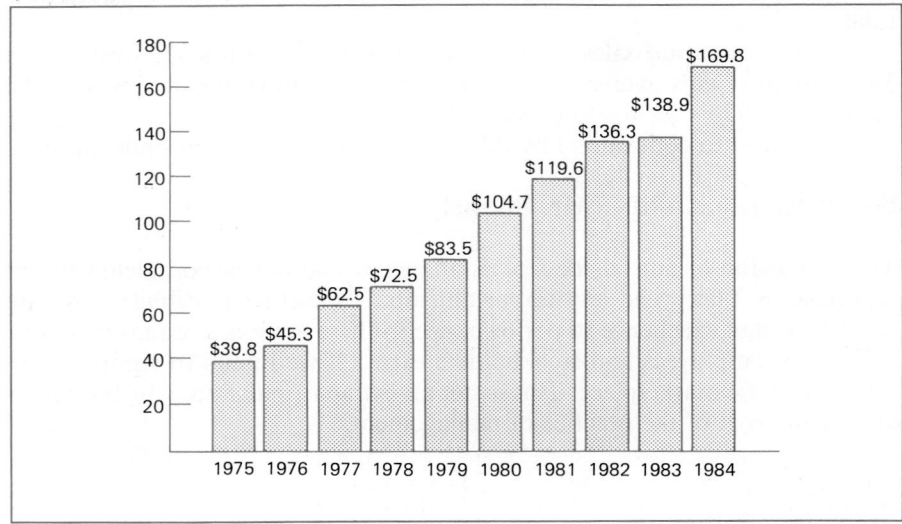

Source: The Pillsbury Company, *Annual Report,* 1975–1984.

Cash Dividends, 1975–1984
(per share)

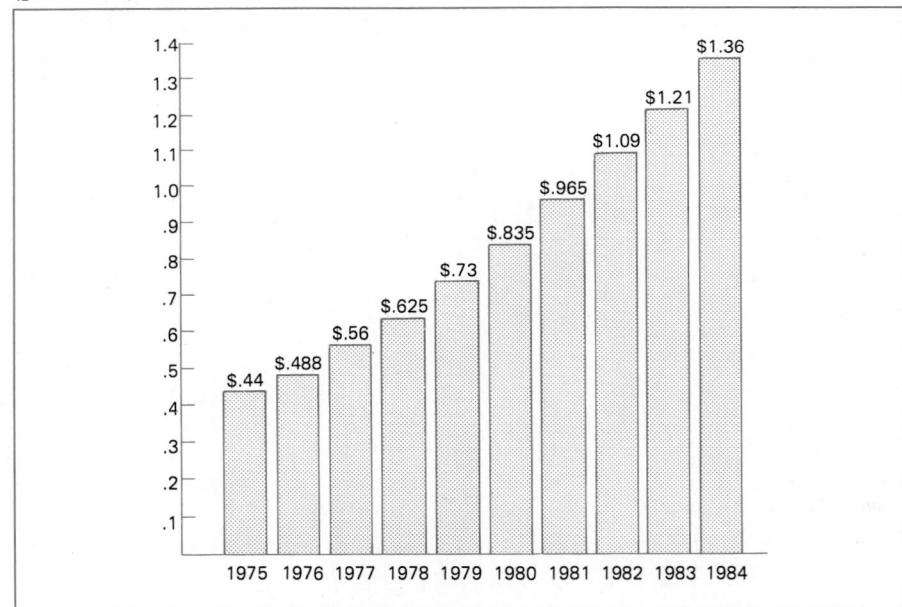

Source: The Pillsbury Company, *Annual Report,* 1975–1984.

EXHIBIT 2
(Continued)

The Pillsbury Company, Charitable Contributions, 1973 vs. 1983–1984
(millions)

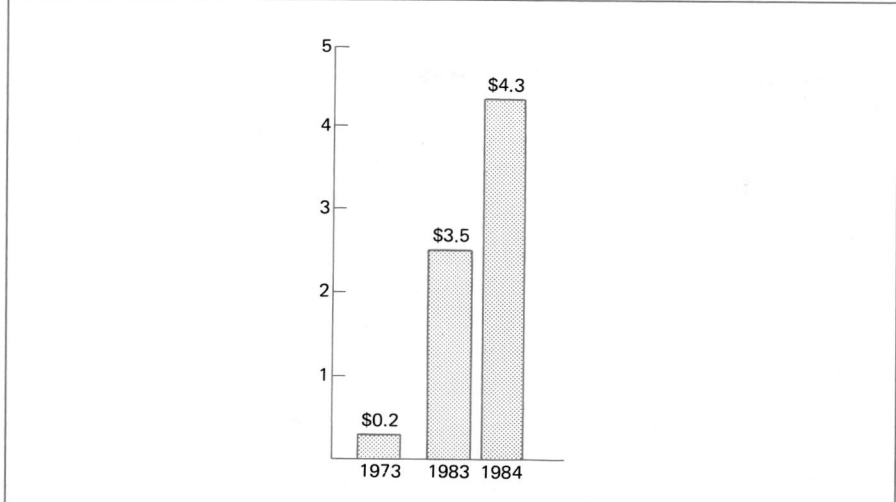

Source: The Pillsbury Company, *Annual Report,* 1973, 1983, 1984.

Consumer Foods Operating Profits 1979–1984
(millions)

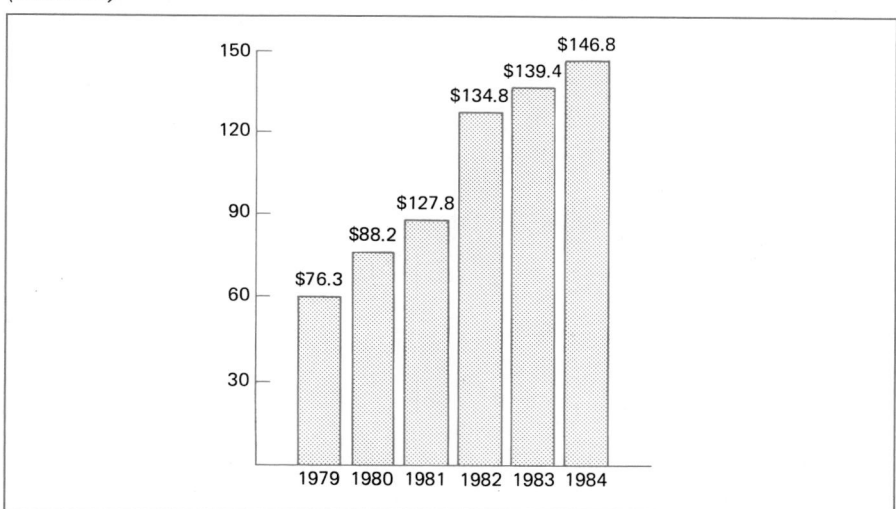

Source: The Pillsbury Company, *Annual Report,* 1979–1984.

551

EXHIBIT 2 (Continued)

Restaurant Operating Profit, 1979–1984
(millions)

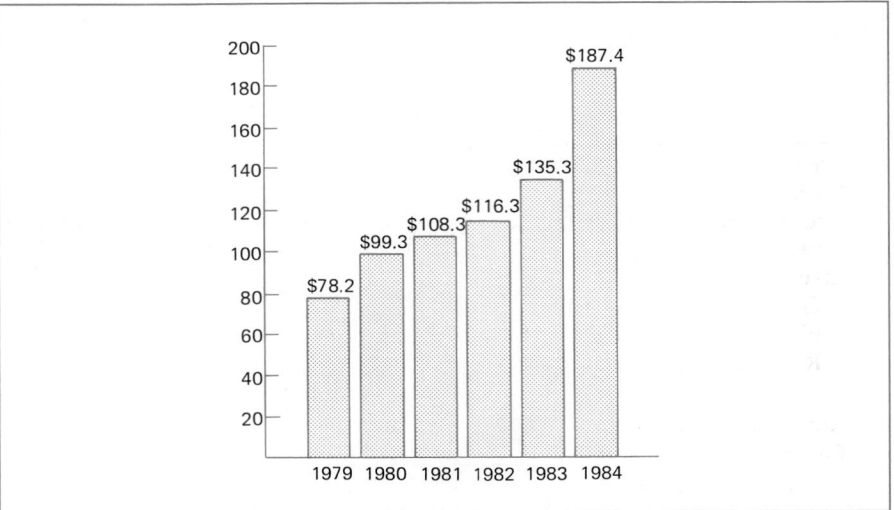

Source: The Pillsbury Company, *Annual Report,* 1979–1984.

Agri Products Operating Profit, 1979–1984
(millions)

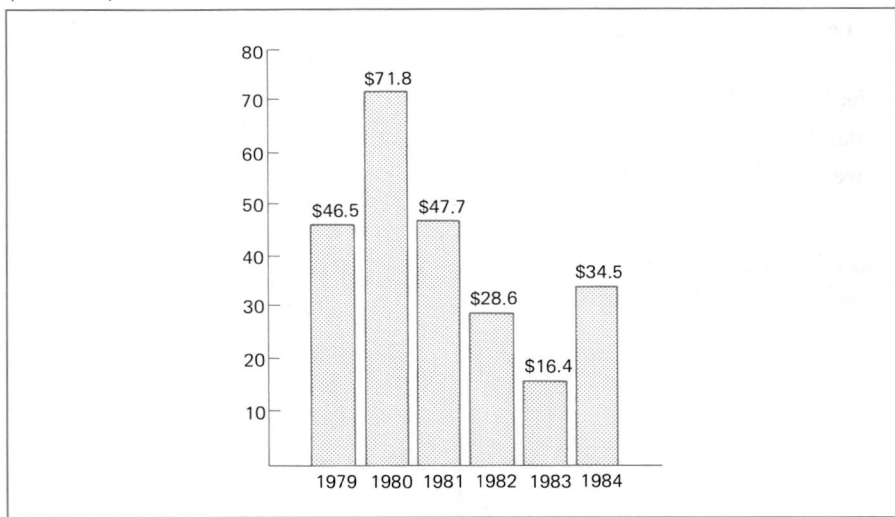

Source: The Pillsbury Company, *Annual Report,* 1979–1984.

EXHIBIT 3
The Pillsbury Company and Subsidiaries Consolidated Balance Sheets, 1983–1984

	May 31	
	1984	1983
	(In Millions)	
Assets		
Current assets		
Cash and equivalents	$ **142.5**	$ 129.6
Receivables, less allowance for doubtful accounts of $11.5 million and $12.9 million, respectively	**355.8**	350.6
Inventories		
Grain	**75.5**	52.9
Finished products	**214.1**	204.1
Raw materials, containers, and supplies	**150.6**	133.7
	440.2	390.7
Advances on purchases	**107.7**	128.4
Prepaid expenses	**25.6**	22.3
Total current assets	**1,071.8**	1,021.6
Property, plant, and equipment*		
Land and improvements	**199.2**	179.3
Buildings and improvements	**885.1**	788.2
Machinery and equipment	**692.5**	600.3
	1,776.8	1,567.8
Less: Accumulated depreciation	**583.8**	514.6
	1,193.0	1,053.2
Net investment in direct financing leases	**184.0**	178.7
Intangibles	**83.2**	21.6
Investments and other assets	**76.3**	91.5
	$2,608.3	$2,366.6

* See Summary of Significant Accounting Policies and Notes to Consolidated Financial Statements provided in company's annual report.

Source: The Pillsbury Company, *Annual Report,* 1984.

EXHIBIT 3 (Continued)

	May 31	
	1984	1983
	(In Millions)	
Liabilities and Stockholders' Equity		
Current liabilities		
Notes payable	$ 17.3	$ 10.5
Current portion of long-term debt	94.3	32.8
Trade accounts payable	369.2	279.6
Advances on sales	136.0	136.7
Employee compensation	83.8	72.4
Taxes on income	16.5	20.8
Other liabilities	169.3	152.1
Total current liabilities	886.4	704.9
Long-term debt, noncurrent portion	503.1	572.4
Deferred taxes on income	149.3	108.5
Other deferrals	22.3	24.4
Stockholders' equity		
Preferred stock, without par value, authorized 500,000 shares, no shares issued		
Common stock, without par value, authorized 80,000,000 shares, issued 43,516,019		
shares and 43,462,156 shares, respectively	306.2	284.1
Common stock in treasury at cost, 322,785 shares and 180,318 shares, respectively	(11.7)	(4.6)
Accumulated earnings retained and used in the business	792.4	704.9
Accumulated foreign currency translation	(40.7)	(28.0)
Total stockholders' equity	1,046.2	956.4
	$2,608.3	$2,366.6

* See Summary of Significant Accounting Policies and Notes to Consolidated Financial Statements provided in company's annual report.

Source: The Pillsbury Company, *Annual Report,* 1984.

554

	Year ended May 31		
	1984	**1983**	**1982**
		(In millions)	
Net Sales			
Consumer Foods	**$1,793.9**	$1,652.1	1,635.7
Restaurants	**1,768.7**	1,494.6	1,279.3
Agri-Products	**694.8**	627.5	568.6
Less Agri-Products intersegment sales	**(85.1)**	(88.3)	(98.5)
Total	**4,172.3**	3,685.9	3,385.1
Operating profit			
Consumer Foods	**146.8**	139.4	134.8
Restaurants	**187.4**	135.3	116.3
Agri-Products	**34.5**	16.4	28.6
Total	**368.7**	291.1	279.7
General corporate expense, net	**(20.8)**	(21.5)	(12.4)
Interest expense, net	**(44.2)**	(39.4)	(39.3)
Earnings before taxes on income	**303.7**	230.2	228.0
Identifiable assets			
Consumer Foods	**836.3**	725.4	747.9
Restaurants	**1,191.2**	1,025.7	993.3
Agri-Products	**498.2**	486.1	536.6
Corporate	**82.6**	129.4	150.5
Total	**2,608.3**	2,366.6	2,428.3
Capital expenditures			
Consumer Foods	**59.4**	48.7	50.0
Restaurants	**197.4**	164.0	126.8
Agri-Products	**13.8**	20.9	15.8
Corporate	**11.8**	10.3	15.9
Total	**282.4**	243.9	208.5
Depreciation expense			
Consumer Foods	**36.1**	33.0	30.3
Restaurants	**59.5**	54.7	48.6
Agri-Products	**14.2**	13.6	11.5
Corporate	**4.8**	4.2	2.4
Total	**114.6**	105.5	92.8
Foreign operations included in the above categories are as follows			
Net sales	**355.5**	360.1	357.9
Operating profit	**16.2**	18.0	22.8
Identifiable assets	**241.8**	212.8	241.8
Capital expenditures	**20.4**	16.3	22.6
Depreciation expense	**9.7**	10.3	8.8

Pillsbury is a diversified international food company operating in three major segments of the food industry. Net sales by segment include both sales to unaffiliated customers, as reported in the consolidated statements of earnings, and intersegment sales made on the same basis as sales to unaffiliated customers. Operating profit of reportable segments is net sales less operating expenses. In computing operating profit, none of the following items has been included: interest income and expense, general corporate income and expenses, equity in net earnings (losses) of unconsolidated affiliates, and income taxes.

Source: The Pillsbury Company, *Annual Report*, 1984.

EXHIBIT 4
Summary by Industry Segment; The Pillsbury Company and Subsidiaries, 1982–1984

EXHIBIT 5
10-Year Comparisons in Foods Industry, 1973–1983

Company Name	Annual Growth EPS	Annual Growth Net Sales	10 Year Change in ROE	10 Year Change in ROIC*
Pillsbury Co.	17.7%	17.0%	115.4%	76.8%
Heinz (J. J.) Co.	15.5	15.1	69.8	85.4
General Mills Inc.	14.7	15.8	31.9	48.7
Kellogg Co.	13.5	13.3	25.2	5.4
Carnation Co.	12.8	11.9	10.4	6.0
CPC International Inc.	12.5	11.6	35.3	41.0
Quaker Oats Co.	12.4	14.4	20.7	21.9
Ralston Purina Co.	11.6	11.6	9.1	22.8
Beatrice Foods Co.	10.2	17.0	(7.6)	(2.5)
General Foods Corp.	8.0	11.2	5.8	7.2

* Return on invested capital (pretax).

Source: Prepared Foods, September 1983.

EXXON CORPORATION

With total sales in1981 of $113.7 billion, Exxon Corp. was the largest oil company in the world. It held interests in a number of enterprises, mainly in the oil, gas, energy, and chemical industries. In most of its affiliates—with the notable exception of Aramco which was substantively controlled by Saudi Arabia—Exxon was the majority or sole shareholder. Exxon was a worldwide entity, with exploration activities on all continents, 54 refineries in 28 countries, and marketing activities in nearly 100 countries. Six million motorists stopped at its 65,000 service stations each day. In 1981, Exxon's holdings outside the U.S. comprised 55% of its assets; it obtained four times more oil from foreign than U.S. sources, and its overseas affiliates refined and sold twice its U.S. volume. Within the non-communist world Exxon sold some 4.6 million barrels per day (B/D) of petroleum products or 9.75% of the world's 47.1 million BPD demands.[1] The company's ownership was widely dispersed, with some 776,000 shareholders in many different countries throughout the world.

ORGANIZATION AND PHILOSOPHY

As a truly multinational company, Exxon attempted to decentralize operations as much as possible to its divisions and affiliates. These units were responsible for maintaining adequate returns on corporate investments in them. Since corporate policy was to staff each subsidiary with nationals of its host countries, it was rare to find more than a few Americans in any non-U.S. subsidiary. Wherever possible,

Case copyright © 1985 by James Brian Quinn. Research associates—Penny C. Paquette and Allie J. Quinn. Case derived solely from secondary sources.

the boards, CEOs, and key executives of each unit were also nationals of the host country.

The corporation maintained some centralized units to help allocate overall corporate resources and to coordinate activities of operating groups where necessary. Whenever possible, raw materials, supplies, intermediate products, and services were transferred among divisions at market prices. When these could not be readily determined, negotiated transfer prices were used. The corporation's policy was to transfer materials and services "at arm's length"—with divisions allowed to purchase outside the corporation if they so desired. Purchasing from and trading with other companies was common.

Certain major decisions were of course reserved to corporate headquarters. Operating heads were expected to clear major policy decisions having corporate-wide significance with their "contact member" on the Board of Directors or with the appropriate major Board committee. No single listing of such decisions existed in the corporation.

Exxon also had its own $7 billion Exxon Chemicals operation producing and supplying chemicals worldwide. Coordination between successive operations in both (petroleum and chemicals) groups was very important. Efficient plant sizes in either group were so large that their outputs could easily exceed the demands of smaller countries in which production occurred. Since petrochemicals and plastics were important inputs for many secondary and fabricating industries it was common to find large chemical-industrial complexes growing up around refineries or petrochemical plants—located even in the most remote areas of individual countries.

Exxon's size and complexity inevitably exposed the company to a variety of different national policies, nationalistic pressures, and risks of retaliation or expropriation by host countries. As a mature and progressive company, Exxon's management had given considerable attention to the problem of host country relationships. Its expressed policy was: "To perform as a responsible and desirable corporate citizen in all host countries . . . (since) Exxon's interests are inextricably linked to the interests of our host countries throughout the world. . . ." The company had purposely not tried to refine this broad policy into rigid rules, binding on all its affiliates.

RECENT HISTORY

Crude oil prices had been steady at less than $2 per barrel through the 1960s, reflecting a general surplus supply balance. They had crept up very slowly to approximately $3 per barrel when, in October 1973, Arab oil-producing nations imposed a total ban on petroleum exports to Israel, the United States, and other "supporters" of Israel in the 1973 Arab-Israeli War. Posted prices leapt to $10 per barrel (bbl) during January–February 1974, with some oil auctioned in the spot markets for $17. Nevertheless, after the initial 1973–1974 crisis subsided, oil prices increased only nominally until 1978. Inflationary pressures actually forced the real price of oil to drop some 10–15% during this period.

The next major jolt came on October 31, 1978 when oil workers in Iran went on strike—cutting production from 5.3 million barrels per day (B/D) to 2 million B/D. The workers demanded higher wages and an end to martial law. In December, OPEC ended an 18-month price freeze on crude oil by announcing increases that would boost the price from $12.70/bbl to $14.54/bbl by October 1979.

Iran announced price increases to $16.50/bbl. Saudi Arabia supported these prices by limiting its oil production in April to the ceiling of 8.5 million B/D imposed before the Iranian revolution. As production limits forced prices up, OPEC raised the posted price to $20/bbl in June 1979, approximately double the preceding year's prices. And a new era in oil began.

In 1978, Exxon's sales were $63.9 billion with profits of $2.7 billion reported. Sales had been growing at 9.1% per year rate and profits at 3.8%. The company and its affiliates accounted for about 9% of the industry's crude runs. Exxon expected its sales growth in the early 1980s to at least match industry averages and to be slightly above recent levels. The company deployed total assets of $41.5 billion against which it charged $1.7 billion in depreciation per year. Its announced proved reserves were 23 billion barrels of crude, offering it an 11.9-year coverage in terms of 1978 refinery runs. Chase Econometrics and industry sources estimated that the industry would invest over $1.5 trillion worldwide in the next decade to replace existing facilities and develop needed new resources.

Through 1980–1981 there had been no significant shifts in expected growth rates of oil use throughout the world. Most observers continued to forecast growth at 4–5% per year through the year 2000. Despite extensive exploration by oil companies and ministries throughout the world, only a few large new finds were developed between 1974–1981. Most publicized of these were the North Slope (Alaska), North Sea (Europe), and Mexican fields. North Slope (Canada-Alaska) fields were thought to contain some 20–50 billion barrels of ultimately exploitable oil. Because of price increases Mexico's estimated reserves expanded dramatically to some 200–300 billion barrels of petroleum liquids. Nevertheless most writers projected long-term shortages of crude at high prices. (See Figures 1 and 2). Exxon's own reserves are described in Appendix A.

By October 1981, Chase Econometrics and major banking institutions[2] were estimating that the industry would have to invest $2–3 trillion worldwide in the next decade to meet forecast demands. Each country had its own special interests in the developing worldwide energy situation. The differing postures of some example countries and areas are briefly described below. Appendix A summarizes their crude reserves and gives some brief economic comparisons.

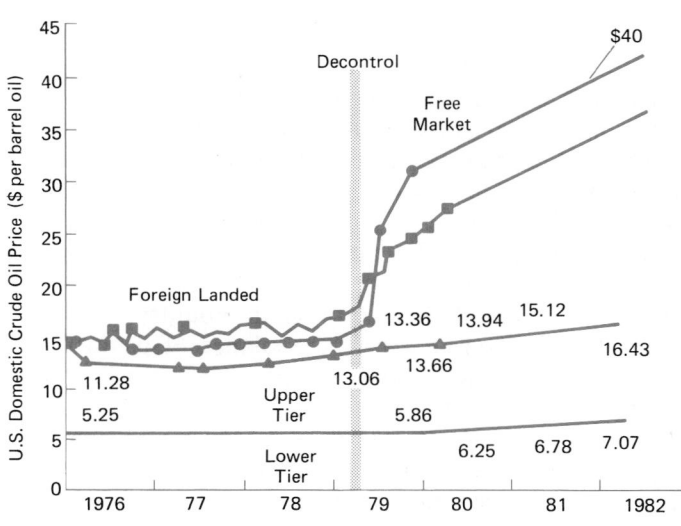

FIGURE 1
U.S. Domestic Crude Oil Prices, 1976–1979
Source: World Oil, February 15, 1981.

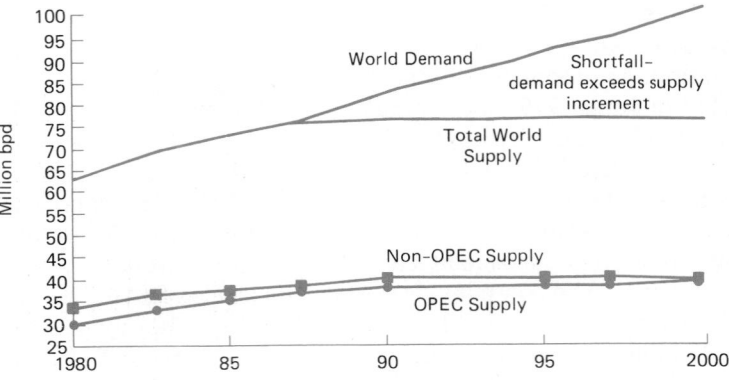

FIGURE 2
Oil Supply/Demand Shortfall, 1980–2000
Source: The Journal of Energy and Development, Autumn 1979, in *World Oil,* February 15, 1981.

EUROPE DISCOVERS OIL—THE NORTH SEA

Northeastern Europe had very limited oil and gas resources until November 10, 1969, when the *Oil & Gas Journal* noted: "Phillips confirmed the first huge oil discovery in the North Sea off Norway in field #2, Block 4, with its #2 Ekofisk well flowing high-gravity oil from tertiary sand at approximately 5,500 feet. The well—which produces highly desirable, low-sulfur crude—lies in an area with little open acreage around it, inside Norwegian territorial waters." Within a few months other finds and geological assessments indicated the probability of a very large play extending across both British and Norwegian waters. (See Map.) But costs of developing these fields were exceptionally high. The North Sea was one of the worst areas in the world for construction work. And the technical problems of laying, protecting, and inspecting underwater pipelines several hundred miles long were substantial.

THE NORWEGIAN SITUATION

North Sea oil led to wide ranging discussions in Norway about how to best exploit its resources in the national interest. Norway had essentially no domestic oil industry prior to the North Sea find. Abundant hydroelectric sources had fulfilled most central power needs, while imported oil and gas had met transportation and other demands. Norway's highly dispersed population of 4.1 million did not represent a major—or concentrated—market for petroleum products. In fact, a large modern refinery would have a throughput vastly in excess of the sales any company could reasonably expect in Norway.

Independence and Wealth

Government officials wanted to see the country's North Sea resources exploited in ways which improved Norway's balance of payments and offered flexibility in dealing with its major trading partners. The government was also concerned about the percentage of industry owned by foreigners. For centuries Norway had been controlled by Denmark and Sweden, and it had suffered severely during the Nazi occupation of World War II. When the North Sea find was announced, over 60% of Norway's large manufacturing industry was foreign held.

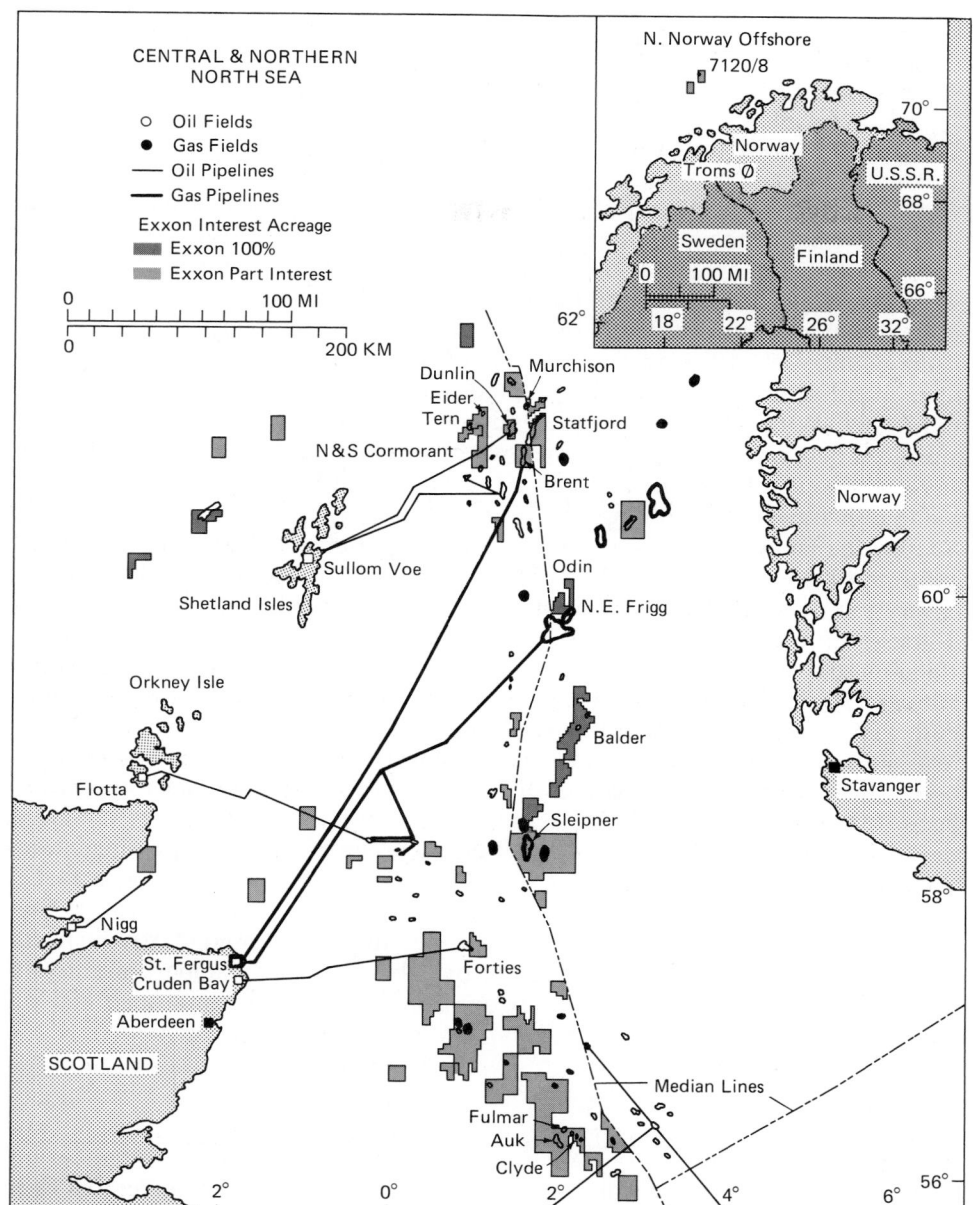

FIGURE 3

Central and Northern North Sea Oil and Gas Fields
Source: Exxon Corporation, *Financial and Statistical Supplement to the Annual Report,* 1981.

Inside the map:

CENTRAL & NORTHERN NORTH SEA

○ Oil Fields
● Gas Fields
— Oil Pipelines
━ Gas Pipelines

Exxon Interest Acreage
▓ Exxon 100%
░ Exxon Part Interest

0 — 100 MI
0 — 200 KM

Dunlin
Eider
Tern
N & S Cormorant
Murchison
Statfjord
Brent
Sullom Voe
Shetland Isles
Odin
N.E. Frigg
Orkney Isle
Balder
Flotta
Stavanger
Sleipner
Nigg
St. Fergus
Cruden Bay
Forties
Aberdeen
SCOTLAND
Median Lines
Fulmar
Auk
Clyde

Inset: N. Norway Offshore
7120/8
Norway
Troms Ø
U.S.S.R.
Sweden
Finland
Norway

Government policymakers wanted to shift exports away from the basic (wood products, mechanical products, electro-metallurgical, shipbuilding and ship operating) industries which had dominated the past and into the "knowledge industries" of the future. Norway's technical schools and institutions had been expanded in recent years, but were small by international standards. And petroleum engineering and petrochemical research and curricula were either nonexistent or quite underdeveloped when oil was found. To coordinate its oil activities, Norway formed a government owned company, Den Norske Stats Okjeselscap (called Statoil). Statoil was to take over operation of the Norwegian portion of all concession

561

rights and be solely responsible for drilling north of the 62nd parallel "in order to preserve relationships with Russia," which bordered Norway on the North and only had access to its year round Port of Murmansk through this area.

A Unique Quality of Life

Norwegians were fiercely proud of their national identity, their beautiful natural surroundings, and their "unique quality of life." No slums existed in the major cities, and full employment had been a policy for decades. To control the impact of North Sea oil, the government set a ceiling of 1.8 million B/D on production and set out on massive infrastructure investments to modernize the more remote areas of the country. By 1981 oil and gas accounted for 15% of GDP, as much as all other manufactures combined. Some predicted they would reach 20–25% by the mid-1990s.[3] With revenues from these sources, the government hoped to repay the enormous debts it had incurred earlier, when it had continued its planned high social investments despite the fact that oil revenues had been slow in materializing due to difficulties in developing the North Sea.[4]

By the late 1970s Norway had changed its initial concession rights. Statoil's 50% interest could be increased to 80%, if so desired. And starting with block 34/10 in 1978 it began its "Norwegian Solution." Only three companies—Statoil (100% government owned), Norsk Hydro (51% government owned), and Saga Petroleum (100% Norwegian privately owned)—could hold equity positions. Foreign companies could serve as "technical advisors" in exchange for access to petroleum.[5] In 1980, the Ministry of Petroleum and Energy issued a Parliamentary Report, outlining tax proposals to increase the government's share of oil revenues to levels which industry leaders said "would make Norway's tax laws onerous to a degree unparalleled in the world."[6]

As elections approached in the fall of 1981, Norway faced some difficult decisions. During the past two years substantial new discoveries had been made, which if exploited efficiently would result in production beyond the 1.8 million B/D ceiling.[7] In addition the three Norwegian companies allowed to explore north of the 62nd parallel had found enough recoverable reserves to support production at current rates for 25 years.[8] But only one-tenth of the continental shelf had yet been explored.

THE BRITISH SITUATION

Realizing that exploiting Britain's North Sea oil would require considerable cash and expertise, the government had awarded its first blocks to large companies for fast exploitation. But in 1974 as prices rose above $10/bbl the Wilson government actively discussed nationalizing the whole North Sea area. Instead it "restructured" the terms of earlier leases, calling for both majority government interest in *existing* concessions and a controlling interest in blocks *already* leased. It also formed the British National Oil Corporation (BNOC) to act as the vehicle for exercising the government's participation rights.

Britain's initial interest was to get the North Sea explored and producing as soon as possible because of its weak balance of payments situation. However, despite predictions of 2–3 million B/D production rates in the early 1980s, actual production by 1982 was only 1.5 million B/D.[9] In summer 1979, British motorists had suffered a shortage of gasoline while 45% of all production was being exported to the United States and Western Europe. This was partly a function of Britain's need for exports and partly the fact that private oil companies controlled refining activities.[10] At one point in 1980, Britain "found itself in the strange position of charging $30/bbl for its oil while Saudi Arabia's was pegged at $24/bbl."[11]

The Conservative (Thatcher) government tried to "privatize" some of BNOC's activities in 1980, but was thwarted by other political interests which feared a massive oil boom in the 1980s followed by an abrupt reentry to importation in the 1990s.[12] By mid-1980, 25 fields had been discovered in the U.K. North Sea. (See Map.) Predictions were that subsequent fields would be smaller and costs of developing them (excluding taxes and dry holes) soon would move from $11/bbl to over $15/bbl.[13] Shell Oil Co. estimated that to achieve full North Sea potentials would require £115 billion over the next 10–15 years.[14] But *Oil & Gas Journal* noted that proposed British tax actions would "raise the government's share of all revenues from U.K. North Sea oil production to more than 90%."[15] Fortunately, rising oil prices had changed the economics of developing smaller fields and could support the tertiary recovery necessary to keep oil fields in action.

JAPAN

Japan, with its powerful national economy, had very limited fossil fuel supplies. When the Iranian turmoil cut off 17% of this crucial supply in 1978, the government formed the Japan National Oil Company (JNOC), and MITI pressed for Japanese controlled oil sources to equal 30% of imports by 1985 (versus 8.5% in 1978). Nippon Oil, one of Japan's major refiners, boosted prices 15% immediately in response to government pressures, although Exxon's prices went up only 1–2%. Japan solved its immediate shortfall by going to the spot market and by direct "government-to-government" purchase agreements with exporting countries.[16]

For its longer term needs, it started a joint venture with China to develop oil in the latter's Bohai Sea and stepped up its financial and technical aid to poorer oil exporting nations, notably Mexico and Indonesia.[17] Because of its tight pollution standards Japan became the world's largest user (60% of all supplies) of liquified natural gas (LNG)—for central power production and for propane in automobiles.[18] Exxon's *Energy Outlook (1980)* predicted Japan would still be dependent on outside sources for 74% of its energy needs in the year 2000, despite its strong conservation and nuclear power programs.

RECENTLY DEVELOPED COUNTRIES

China: The size of the People's Republic of China's petroleum resources was largely unknown, although for over 25 years Peking (Beijing) had force fed the country's oil industry with funds and technical manpower. Knowledgeable observers, as reported in *The Wall Street Journal,* thought there could be several hundred billion barrels of potential oil in the China Sea. Other sources estimated some 40 billion more on shore. But there were severe financial, technological, and structural constraints on China's developing these services itself.

After a brief spurt (+11%) in 1978 production, China's oil and gas output rose at only a disappointing 1–2% per year. But China hoped to have eight to ten giant new fields opened by 1985. Its internal economic plans, however, keyed on doubling coal output to 1 billion tons/year in the late 1980s and to twice that in the

1990s. Oil was intended primarily as an export to generate capital needed for China's gigantic "Four Modernizations" programs. The world community's most serious concerns were that China might increasingly "press for its share" of world oil imports or come into conflict with its neighbors who were already developing oil in the very large coastal zone claimed by China.[19]

Indonesia: Indonesia had a population of some 150 million people, about half of OPEC's total. Despite increased oil revenues in recent years, Indonesia's $488 per person annual income in 1980 ranked it as one of Asia's poorest countries. About 50 million of its people subsisted on less than $100 a year. Its recent oil and economic history had been chaotic. The Sukarno regime of the 1960s had created inflation rates of 650% per year which it took successor regimes almost ten years to bring under control. Then in 1975 a series of disastrous ($10.5 billion) tanker deals by General Ibn Sutowo—head of the state oil company, Pertomina—brought on a late 1970s debt and currency crisis which was only handled by the "inspired management"[20] of the country's well-trained civil servants. By 1981 they had managed to balance the budget, increase capital spending, and increase GDP by some 40%.

Nevertheless, Indonesia faced the prospect of declining oil revenues as its big fields like Minas shifted to secondary recovery, and domestic energy needs grew at 13% per year.[21] The country's ambitious Five Year Plan (1979–1984) relied on "increased investment by local and foreign businessmen" to reduce the country's precarious dependence on oil and raw materials exports and to make a dent in its massive unemployment.[22] By mid-1980 the future looked brighter than ever as exploration picked up and the United States and Indonesia implemented new agreements, allowing dollar-for-dollar credits for U.S. companies on taxes paid to Indonesia for oil production.

Venezuela: Venezuela's oil had been originally developed by international oil companies. However, Venezuela nationalized substantially all of its very large oil resources in the mid-1970s. Its proved crude reserves of 18.0 billion barrels made it third in the western hemisphere. But it was well known that Venezuela also had "trillions" of barrels of heavy oil in identified formations. Estimates of ultimately exploitable potentials varied from 2 to 3 trillion bbl. This oil required an infusion of heat (or heat and chemicals) to make it flow through its sustaining formations. It also contained extraneous chemicals which had to be removed in a "preprocessing" stage before refining. By 1981 new refining methods increasingly allowed heavy oils to be processed competitively versus many crudes.

Venezuela had the largest refining capacity in Latin America, but its facilities had been built largely to supply the U.S. East Coast with fuel oil. During the early 1980s Venezuela planned to invest some $25 billion to upgrade these facilities for gasoline and other "high-end" products and to develop new capabilities for heavy oils.[23]

As the Venezuelan government put together its Sixth Plan (in 1980–1981) it was running large deficits in its 200-odd government businesses. And the Sixth Plan's emphasis on hospitals, schools, and housing (rather than industrial growth) seemed likely to create even larger deficits and international debts—despite an oil production rate of 2.2 million B/D and prices reaching $47/bbl.[24] Venezuela had the largest "steam flood" field in the world for processing heavy oil and was among the leaders in developing new heavy crude processing technologies. Observers said that, "Despite the politicization, corruption, and general lack of efficiency elsewhere, the oil industry is kept out of politics and is well run in Venezuela."[25]

Nigeria: Through the 1970s Nigeria had become second only to Saudi Arabia in its exports of oil to the United States. But Nigerian economic fortunes took a sudden reversal in 1978 when oil payments, which formed 85% of total government income, dropped to only three-fourths of 1977's levels. Nigeria's economy crashed, its trade balances went into deficit for the first time since the oil boom, and there were rumblings about maladministration of $ billions in the Nigerian National Petroleum Corp. (NNPC).[26]

Experts considered Nigeria "one of the best oil provinces in the world" with a superb sulfur free crude and potentials of up to 5 million B/D possible for export in the mid 1980s. Because of high quality and good location, Nigeria often priced its oil at premiums over other OPEC crudes.[27] And Nigeria faced further confrontation with some OPEC countries (particularly Iran) over their oil exports to South Africa.[28] In fact, the government had nationalized all the Nigerian assets of BP in retaliation for that company's breaking sanctions against South Africa.[29]

Although bribery remained a fact of life in Nigeria and getting money out of the country was difficult, foreign investors continued to participate there because, "This is a real free enterprise country." In 1980 foreign companies were invited to submit proposals for over 120,000 square miles of exploration, with much of the rich Niger basin and offshore areas yet to be explored. Although the latter was reserved for NNPC, it was widely recognized that NNPC lacked the resources for the task. And like other new or replacement supplies throughout the world these areas would cost considerably more than the ($0.30–$0.50 per barrel) finding and lifting costs then encountered in many Middle Eastern areas.

EXXON'S CURRENT OPERATIONS

In 1981, Exxon was the largest industrial company in the world, excluding certain Japanese banking and holding complexes. Key financial and operating data about the company are included as Appendix B. Exxon managed the world's largest tanker fleet, aggregating over 21 million tons. The company's own tankers were built to its specifications in shipyards throughout the world. In addition, Exxon owned or shared in the ownership of an extensive network of pipelines. Some of these carried crude from underdeveloped areas to coastlines. Some were undersea. Some carried chemical intermediates; others took finished products to distribution centers. Because of the size and complexity of its worldwide operations, Exxon had been forced to develop extremely sophisticated techniques for long-range planning, fleet operations and control, plant production allocation decisions, cost and management control, communications, data handling, and so on.

Exxon Research and Engineering (ER&E) was responsible for Exxon's long-term technological activities worldwide. Its laboratories performed research, engineering, and technical service activities in close coordination with the operating companies they supported. Royalty income received was deducted from the total cost of ER&E's operations to obtain a "net cost" which was allocated to affiliates roughly in proportion to their sales at point of manufacture. ER&E tried to allocate specific corporate R&D tasks to those laboratories in various countries which could most effectively perform on behalf of the total corporation. Whenever possible, ER&E tried to staff its research centers throughout the world with scientists and engineers representing many nationalities—not just those of the host country.

For almost a decade prior to 1973 Exxon's return on total assets had remained below 8%. But the 1970s had changed all that. 1981 was a banner year for Exxon. Over the past five years its sales had grown at an average 14.5% rate to

$113 billion and profits at 18.5% rates to $5.5 billion. Total assets had grown from $38.4 billion in 1978 to $62.9 billion in 1981—and employees from 127,000 to 180,000 in the same period. Exxon's own proved reserves of oil had dropped from some 45 billion barrels in 1972 to about 7 billion barrels in 1981, largely due to nationalizations. But its coal (10.6 billion tons) and uranium holdings were also substantial, and it had attempted to diversify into energy devices (Reliance Electric Co.) and other areas through Exxon Enterprises, Inc.

In late 1981, a worldwide recession began, triggered by high U.S. interest rates, disastrous U.S. trade balances, and widespread layoffs in a less competitive U.S. manufacturing base. Some expected a strong recovery by 1983–1984, others dismally predicted a continuing long-term world stagflation. Most agreed that world GDP growth to the end of the century would be less than the 5% per year experienced through the 1960s and mid 1970s, but published estimates placed real GDP growth at between 2.7% and 3.6% per year to the year 2000. However, China's sudden real growth at 7–8% per year (planned and actually experienced in (1978–1981) was pushing estimates upward. Since modernized agriculture and rapidly industrializing countries throughout the world called for substantially increased uses of energy, energy forecasts in 1981 usually indicated a "shortfall" of energy for the late 1980s and 1990s. (See Figure 1.) Combined with higher replacement costs for reserves and host governments' strong political interests in maintaining prices, many forecasters foresaw energy demand and prices significantly outpacing GNP growth through the mid 1990s.

QUESTIONS

1. Why should any of the above host countries allow Exxon to participate in their markets or the development of their resources? What are the most significant potential conflicts between Exxon's interests and those of these host countries?

2. What should have been the principal strategic concerns of Exxon from 1978–1982? What should its strategy have been in response to these? How should Exxon have dealt with its potential conflicts with host countries in this era?

3. How should Exxon's 1978–1982 strategy be modified for the future? What specific actions should be taken? Why? How should Exxon be organized for the future?

EXHIBIT 1
World Supply and Demand Situation

World Oil Production and Proved Reserves, 1978 versus 1982

	1978		1982	
	Prod. (million B/D)	Reserves (billion bbls)	Prod. (million B/D)	Reserves (billion bbls)
Western Hemisphere				
Total	14.8	75.7	16.0	115.3
United States	8.7	28.5	8.7	29.8
*Venezuela	2.2	18.0	1.8	21.5
Mexico	1.3	16.0	2.7	48.3
Canada	1.3	6.0	1.2	7.0
Western Europe				
Total	1.8	24.0	2.8	22.9
United Kingdom	1.1	16.0	2.1	13.9
Norway	0.4	5.9	0.5	6.8
Middle East				
Total	18.2	362.1	12.5	369.3
*Saudi Arabia	7.8	165.7	6.5	162.4
*Kuwait	1.9	66.2	0.7	64.2
*Iran	5.3	59.0	1.9	55.3
*United Arab Emirates	1.9	31.3	1.2	32.4
*Iraq	2.5	32.1	0.9	41.0
Africa				
Total	6.1	57.9	4.5	57.8
*Libya	2.1	24.3	1.1	21.5
*Nigeria	1.8	18.2	1.3	16.8
*Algeria	1.3	6.3	0.8	9.4
Asia-Pacific				
Total	2.8	20.0	2.6	19.8
*Indonesia	1.7	10.2	1.3	9.6
India	0.2	2.9	0.4	3.4
Australia	0.4	2.1	0.4	1.6
Malaysia	0.2	2.8	0.3	3.3
OPEC	29.4	438.5	17.5	434.1
Noncommunist World	46.2	547.6	38.4	585.1
Total World	60.0	641.6	53.0	670.2

* OPEC members.

Source: Oil & Gas Journal, December 25, 1978, and December 27, 1982.

EXHIBIT 1 (Continued)

International Petroleum Supply and Disposition, 1979
(thousand barrels per day)

	Crude Oil Prod.[a]	Crude Oil Imports	Refined Product Imports	Crude Oil Exports	Refined Product Exports	Apparent Consumption[b]
United States	10,136	6,519	1,937	235	236	18,513
Mexico	1,611	0	27	533	68	904
Brazil	171	1,026	19	5	22	1,175
Venezuela	2,436	0	2	1,412	618	279
France	46	2,555	242	0	434	2,385
West Germany	95	2,187	828	0	137	3,073
Italy	36	2,215	231	0	437	2,003
Norway	443	129	77	382	25	219
United Kingdom	1,613	1,157	286	796	272	1,930
Eastern Europe and USSR	12,176	2,020	184	2,603	1,015	10,762
Algeria	1,294	7	15	1,082	71	104
Libya	2,132	0	47	1,979	85	85
Nigeria	2,302	0	91	2,210	24	161
Middle East	22,045	531	158	19,311	1,173	1,774
China	2,122	0	1	190[c]	0[c]	1,851
Indonesia	1,631	52	39	1,233	108	367
Japan	8	4,834	770	0	16	5,480

[a] Data includes lease condensate and natural gas plant liquids.
[b] Data represents apparent consumption, which includes domestic consumption, refinery fuel and loss, and international bunkering.
[c] Estimated

Source: U.S. Department of Energy, *1981 Annual Report to Congress,* May 1982, pp. 75–77.

EXHIBIT 1 (Continued)

Price—Landed Cost of Crude Oil Imports from Selected Countries,[a] 1975–1981

Dollars per Barrel

		Algeria	Canada	Indonesia	Iran	Libya	Mexico	Nigeria	Saudi Arabia	United Arab Emirates	United Kingdom	Venezuela
1975	Average	12.72	12.72	13.79	12.21	12.35	NA	12.62	12.30	12.87	NA	11.65
1976	Average	13.81	13.57	13.82	12.82	13.58	NA	13.80	13.04	13.30	NA	11.80
1977	Average	15.20	14.21	14.63	13.80	14.87	13.75	15.25	13.61	14.04	NA	13.13
1978	Average	14.91	14.50	14.64	13.88	14.72	13.54	14.86	13.92	14.39	NA	12.83
1979	Average	21.90	20.43	20.69	25.02	23.68	20.86	22.96	19.15	21.90	22.16	18.18
1980	January	35.32	27.73	31.03	30.37	37.10	30.18	33.03	27.85	32.35	32.14	26.25
	February	35.28	28.60	32.95	NA	36.98	32.38	35.25	28.15	32.71	34.07	25.91
	March	38.54	30.75	33.04	b	37.18	31.17	36.93	28.26	30.96	35.73	24.97
	April	38.52	30.31	33.81	b	36.57	30.77	37.41	29.14	32.29	35.34	25.10
	May	38.54	31.16	33.73	b	37.36	31.22	37.53	30.30	34.06	35.82	25.93
	June	38.71	31.26	34.51	b	38.09	31.43	38.15	30.16	34.96	37.41	26.42
	July	39.60	31.31	34.81	b	38.39	32.60	38.23	30.04	NA	37.25	25.47
	August	38.60	31.44	34.81	b	38.38	32.62	37.77	31.24	NA	36.20	26.37
	September	38.28	30.97	34.64	b	38.30	31.93	37.60	31.86	NA	36.35	25.47
	October	38.77	29.22	33.65	b	38.53	31.96	37.75	31.73	NA	36.82	23.92
	November	38.41	28.81	34.55	b	38.22	32.42	37.97	32.86	NA	36.62	27.75
	December	38.63	32.72	34.64	b	39.04	33.76	38.11	33.40	NA	36.31	27.66
	Average	37.90	30.47	33.92	b	37.72	31.80	37.05	30.02	NA	35.88	25.86
1981	January	41.25	34.26	38.08	b	41.81	36.81	41.55	34.06	NA	39.90	33.80

NA–Not available.

[a] Landed cost of imported crude oil from selected countries does not represent the total cost of all imported crude.

[b] No crude oil was imported.

Source: U.S. Department of Energy, Energy Information Administration, *Monthly Energy Review,* October 1982.

EXHIBIT 2

Summary Financial Data For Exxon Corp
Comparative Financial Data, 1978 versus 1981

Company	Sales		Net Income		Return on Equity		Return on Net Assets	
	1978	1981	1978	1981	1978	1981	1978	1981
Exxon	60.3	108.1	2.8	5.6	13.7	19.5	6.7	8.8
Royal Dutch Shell Group	44.0	82.3	2.1	3.6	12.8	14.4	4.9	5.6
Mobil	34.7	64.5	1.1	2.4	12.6	16.6	5.0	7.0
General Motors	63.2	62.7	3.5	0.3	20.0	1.9	11.5	1.0
Texaco	28.6	57.6	0.9	2.3	9.0	16.8	4.2	8.4
British Petroleum	27.4	52.2	0.8	2.1	11.1	13.9	3.2	4.3
Standard Oil of Calif.	23.2	44.2	1.1	2.4	13.4	18.7	6.6	10.1
Ford Motor	42.8	38.2	1.6	(1.1)	16.4	(14.4)	7.2	(4.6)
Standard Oil of Indiana	15.0	29.9	1.1	1.9	15.1	18.0	7.6	8.4
Gulf Oil	18.1	28.3	0.8	1.2	12.0	12.3	5.3	6.0

Source of raw data: Fortune 500 Listings of 1978–1981.

EXHIBIT 2 (Continued)

Exxon Corporation: Consolidated Balance Sheet at Year-End, 1972–1981
(*millions of dollars*)

	1972	1973	1974	1975	1976	1977	1978	1979	1980	1981
Assets										
Current assets										
Cash	482	563	939	876	1,279	1,598	1,993	2,516	2,762	2,479
Marketable securities	1,211	2,525	3,819	3,773	3,795	3,086	2,763	1,991	2,164	1,404
Notes and accounts receivable	3,328	4,063	5,282	5,098	5,354	5,708	6,726	9,011	9,849	9,665
Inventories										
Crude oil	251	446	1,172	1,229	1,337	1,250	1,190	1,214	1,438	1,623
Products and merchandise	1,301	1,615	2,597	2,368	2,458	2,606	2,537	3,576	4,175	4,341
Materials and supplies	199	206	375	399	440	479	570	691	937	1,620
Prepaid taxes and expenses	333	424	603	262	389	605	590	1,479	2,134	2,716
Total current assets	7,105	9,842	14,787	14,005	15,052	15,332	16,369	20,478	23,459	23,840
Investments and advances	1,277	1,295	954	1,523	1,578	1,592	1,533	1,475	1,459	1,575
Property, plant & equipment, at cost, less accumulated depreciation and depletion	12,645	13,462	14,846	16,115	18,593	20,491	22,806	26,293	30,311	36,094
Other assets										
Deferred charges	163	139	193	262	275	316	274	246	221	581
Special deposits and funds	224	197	299	515	627	559	361	277	331	297
Intangibles and other assets	86	99	93	393	155	147	188	721	796	536
Total assets	21,500	25,034	31,172	32,813	36,280	38,437	41,531	49,490	56,577	62,931

Liabilities										
Current liabilities										
Notes and loans payable	1,161	1,127	1,729	1,598	1,860	1,385	1,401	1,868	1,537	**3,032**
Accounts payable	1,877	2,998	4,597	5,288	6,315	6,764	7,234	9,183	9,557	**9,536**
Accrued liabilities	857	996	1,307	1,198	1,399	1,586	1,881	2,662	2,925	**3,183**
Income taxes payable	812	1,187	1,913	1,261	947	978	1,525	2,170	2,865	**1,993**
Total current liabilities	4,707	6,308	9,546	9,345	10,521	10,713	12,041	15,883	16,884	**17,744**
Long-term debt										
U.S. dollars—Exxon Corporation	725	601	702	735	786	772	684	683	697	**627**
U.S. dollars—consolidated subsidiaries	833	978	1,177	1,554	1,697	1,640	2,085	2,574	3,052	**3,356**
Other currencies—consolidated subsidiaries	1,059	1,092	1,173	1,162	1,214	1,458	980	1,001	968	**1,170**
Total long-term debt	2,617	2,671	3,052	3,451	3,697	3,870	3,749	4,258	4,717	**5,153**
Annuity and other reserves	499	551	640	609	647	807	1,100	1,414	1,892	**2,041**
Deferred income tax credits	750	1,076	1,890	1,987	2,516	3,036	3,437	4,385	6,218	**7,959**
Deferred income	105	90	83	78	72	69	95	105	139	**144**
Equity of minority shareholders in affiliated companies	538	598	666	705	769	821	880	893	1,314	**1,373**
Total liabilities	9,216	11,294	15,877	16,175	18,222	19,316	21,302	26,938	31,164	**34,414**
Shareholders' equity										
Capital stock	2,637	2,595	2,578	2,583	2,608	2,572	2,389	2,136	1,695	**1,826**
Earnings reinvested	9,647	11,145	12,717	14,055	15,450	16,549	17,840	20,416	23,718	**26,691**
Total shareholders' equity	12,284	13,740	15,205	16,638	18,058	19,121	20,229	22,552	25,413	**28,517**
Total liabilities and shareholders' equity	21,500	25,034	31,172	32,813	36,280	38,437	41,531	49,490	56,577	**62,931**

EXHIBIT 2 (Continued)

Exxon Corporation: Consolidated Statement of Income, 1972–1981
(*millions of dollars*)

	1972	1973	1974	1975	1976	1977	1978	1979	1980	1981
Revenue										
Sales and other operating revenue										
Petroleum and natural gas										
Petroleum products, including excise taxes	16,072	20,681	31,597	33,040	36,867	40,739	45,216	59,458	77,910	79,674
Crude oil	3,177	3,985	8,488	9,548	8,474	9,628	10,340	11,968	14,784	17,117
Natural gas	646	748	903	1,262	1,509	1,791	2,123	2,517	3,034	3,167
Other	744	872	991	979	1,106	1,225	1,429	2,219	2,546	2,429
Total	20,639	26,286	41,979	44,829	47,956	53,383	59,108	76,162	98,274	102,387
Chemical products[a]	1,258	1,563	2,787	2,594	3,238	3,578	4,034	5,807	6,936	7,126
Other	174	173	255	373	432	568	754	1,586	3,239	3,684
Total sales and operating revenue	22,071	28,022	45,021	47,796	51,626	57,529	63,896	85,555	108,449	113,197
Earnings from equity interests and other revenues[b]	365	454	775	968	966	931	1,191	1,412	1,932	1,951
Total revenue	22,436	28,476	45,796	48,764	52,592	58,460	65,087	84,967	110,381	115,148
Costs and other deductions										
Crude oil and product purchases	6,022	7,456	18,607	21,702	26,776	29,274	34,677	45,746	60,915	64,324
Operating expenses	3,009	3,855	4,246	4,347	4,658	5,378	6,395	8,482	10,872	11,698
Selling, general and administrative expenses	2,104	2,277	2,439	2,628	2,719	2,955	3,640	4,292	5,461	5,231
Depreciation and depletion	1,059	1,136	1,231	1,471	1,392	1,494	1,678	2,027	2,282	2,948
Exploration expenses										
Dry holes	133	108	191	239	267	321	378	594	504	811
Other	132	147	240	246	260	321	397	458	648	842
Total exploration expenses	265	255	431	485	527	642	775	1,052	1,152	1,653

Income, excise and other taxes										
Income taxes, U.S. Federal	279	417	649	938	960	842	1,063	1,155	1,762	1,407
Income taxes, other	2,066	3,322	7,205	6,347	4,222	4,801	1,634	2,547	3,666	2,803
Total income taxes	2,345	3,739	7,854	7,285	5,182	5,643	2,697	3,702	5,428	4,210
Excise taxes	1,761	2,298	2,959	2,931	2,995	3,403	3,561	4,449	5,306	5,089
Other taxes and duties	3,989	4,558	4,460	5,116	5,323	6,545	8,190	10,184	12,474	14,025
Total taxes	8,095	10,595	15,273	15,332	13,500	15,591	14,448	18,335	23,208	23,324
Interest expense	251	280	366	385	396	399	425	494	728	843
Foreign exchange translation loss/(gain)[b]	(11)	44	82	(165)	(105)	186	186	103	(82)	(575)
Income applicable to minority interests	83	127	126	123	114	98	100	141	195	135
Total deductions	20,877	26,025	42,801	46,308	49,977	56,017	62,324	80,672	104,731	109,581
Net income	1,559	2,451	2,995	2,456	2,615	2,443	2,763	4,295	5,650	5,567
[a]		70	476	449	503	610	619	878	1,292	1,323
[b]		72	72	(50)	45	72	130	35	(112)	(135)

[a] Chemical products supplied to petroleum affiliates not included above.

[b] Foreign exchange loss/(gain) related to equity companies included in "Earnings from equity interests and other revenue."

Source: Exxon Corporation, Financial and Statistical Supplement to the Annual Report, 1981.

EXHIBIT 2
(Continued)

Exxon Corporation: Return on Average Capital Employed by Business
Segment (1977–1981)
(percent)

	1977	1978	1979	1980	1981
Energy operations					
Petroleum and natural gas					
United States					
Exploration and production	20.2	20.5	22.6	29.2	**24.8**
Refining and marketing	10.0	10.7	4.0	7.9	**3.5**
Foreign					
Exploration and production	25.9	25.7	30.5	36.7	**37.0**
Refining and marketing	8.9	10.5	24.1	22.6	**11.6**
International marine	1.0	—	—	2.4	**0.2**
Coal mining and development	—	—	—	0.8	**2.7**
Uranium mining and nuclear					
fuel fabrication	—	—	—	—	**—**
Other energy	8.7	5.2	4.9	2.5	**3.7**
Total energy operations	14.7	15.3	20.2	23.5	**18.4**
Chemical operations					
United States	18.0	14.6	16.1	8.7	**7.5**
Foreign	7.1	9.8	20.4	20.5	**8.9**
Total chemical operations	11.5	12.1	18.2	14.3	**8.1**
Reliance Electric Co. operations	—	—	—	—	**2.0**
Minerals mining and development	—	—	—	—	**—**
Other operations	4.8	—	—	—	**—**
Total operations	14.2	14.6	18.7	20.5	**15.7**
Corporate total	11.9	12.5	16.6	18.4	**14.4**

Source: Exxon Corporation, *Financial and Statistical Supplement to the Annual Report,* 1981.

EXHIBIT 2 (Continued)

Exxon Corporation: Petroleum Product Sales, Natural Gas Sales, 1972–1981

	1972	1973	1974	1975	1976	1977	1978	1979	1980	1981
Petroleum product sales[a] (thousands of barrels daily)										
Market sales										
Aviation fuels	318	329	277	266	285	298	309	320	311	294
Motor gasolines, naphthas	1,201	1,328	1,221	1,184	1,215	1,258	1,333	1,362	1,282	1,188
Heating oils, kerosene, diesel oils	1,211	1,322	1,087	1,034	1,154	1,160	1,192	1,200	1,110	1,047
Heavy fuels	1,487	1,543	1,392	1,168	1,212	1,143	1,131	1,089	946	836
Specialty petroleum products	441	479	429	396	408	408	396	405	378	355
Total market sales	4,658	5,001	4,406	4,048	4,274	4,267	4,361	4,376	4,027	3,720
Supply sales	1,043	1,177	1,099	942	1,079	999	1,029	943	926	881
Total market and supply sales	5,701	6,178	5,505	4,990	5,353	5,266	5,390	5,319	4,953	4,601
Natural gas sales[b] (millions of cubic feet daily)										
United States	5,952	5,758	5,312	4,937	4,673	4,476	4,348	4,007	3,729	3,364
Canada	423	477	419	410	376	361	343	367	314	299
Other Western Hemisphere	68	91	104	104	41	50	54	76	84	87
Europe										
Netherlands	2,319	2,814	3,409	3,579	3,807	3,756	3,505	3,630	3,396	3,127
West Germany	552	643	727	692	689	783	1,021	1,079	1,061	1,193
United Kingdom	367	398	477	502	613	515	486	456	362	443
Other	3	3	2	3	2	3	3	3	5	16
Total Europe	3,241	3,858	4,615	4,776	5,111	5,057	5,015	5,168	4,824	4,779
Other Eastern Hemisphere										
Libya	173	237	208	253	286	304	367	346	232	128
Australia	54	84	117	141	167	194	190	171	196	256
Other	12	12	17	24	24	46	51	46	83	67
Total other Eastern Hemisphere	239	333	342	418	477	544	608	563	511	451
Worldwide	9,923	10,517	10,792	10,645	10,678	10,488	10,368	10,181	9,462	8,980
European petroleum product price indices[c] (1980 = 100)										
Gasoline	17	21	40	45	46	47	51	69	100	102
Distillate	12	18	34	36	38	41	45	70	100	101
Fuel oil	12	14	35	41	40	46	47	66	100	110
Total product barrel (major fuels)	13	19	36	40	41	44	47	69	100	103

[a] Petroleum product sales include 100% of the sales of Exxon and majority-owned affiliates. Market sales are sales to service station dealers, consumers (including government and military), jobbers and small resellers. Supply sales are sales to large oil marketers, large unbranded resellers and other oil companies.

[b] Natural gas sales include 100% of the sales of Exxon and majority owned affiliates and Exxon's ownership percentage of sales by companies owned 50% or less. Natural gas sales for the Netherlands and West Germany have been restated for the years 1972–1975 to include Exxon's ownership share of sales by two additional companies owned less than 50%.

[c] The European product price index is the ratio of U.S. dollar realization per unit volume (excluding excise tax) from company sales to that obtained in the 1980 base period.

Source: Exxon Corporation, *Financial and Statistical Supplement to the Annual Report,* 1981.

EXHIBIT 2 (Continued)

Exxon Corporation: Proved Reserves and Supplies of Liquids, 1972–1981
(millions of barrels at year end)

	1972	1973	1974	1975	1976	1977	1978	1979	1980	1981
Net proved developed and undeveloped reserves										
United States	4,679	4,401	4,298	4,030	3,823	3,751	3,435	2,997	2,854	2,822
Canada	1,119	1,084	769	728	734	685	669	629	574	489
Other Western Hemisphere	6,226	6,463	7,045	47	40	34	30	26	21	36
Europe	331	490	734	878	791	991	972	1,157	1,765	1,646
Middle East and Africa	1,174	536	479	447	413	389	426	398	377	7[b]
Australia and Far East	652	758	845	801	788	751	981	1,088	1,139	1,157
Total consolidated affiliates	14,181	13,732	14,170	6,931	6,589	6,601	6,513	6,295	6,730	6,157
Proportional interest in reserves of equity companies	26,089	20,435	10,768	11,149	11,246	11,193	83[a]	67[a]	75	80
Supplies available under long-term agreements with foreign governments	4,570	3,965	2,966	1,859	1,702	1,565	1,255	608	593	544[b]
Oil sands reserves—Canada	—	—	—	—	—	—	355	295[d]	303	294
Total worldwide	44,840	38,132	27,904	19,939	19,537	19,359	8,206	7,265	7,701	7,075
Net proved developed reserves included above										
United States					2,836	2,965	2,900	2,347[c]	2,281	2,185
Canada					700	632	599	565	490	408
Other Western Hemisphere					36	30	26	23	20	19
Europe					131	139	192	273	316	470
Middle East and Africa					397	387	420	392	276	3[b]
Australia and Far East					518	589	595	599	551	551
Total consolidated affiliates					4,618	4,742	4,732	4,199[c]	3,934	3,636
Proportional interest in reserves of equity companies					7,612	7,511	70[a]	62[a]	71	66
Supplies available under long-term agreements with foreign governments					1,651	1,532	1,142	608	593	544[b]
Oil sands reserves—Canada					—	—	355	295[d]	249	240
Total worldwide	NA	NA	NA	NA	13,881	13,785	6,299	5,164	4,847	4,486

[a] Aramco data not included.

[b] Under the terms of an agreement effective December 1, 1981, Exxon assigned its rights, assets and properties in Libya to the National Oil Corporation. Consequently, no reserves for Libya are included in the year-end 1981 data.

[c] 291 million barrels of proved reserves, classified as developed in the 1979 data, were reclassified as undeveloped in the 1979 information.

[d] During 1979, the Alberta Energy Company Ltd., exercised its option to purchase 20% of the participating interests in the Syncrude project. As a result, Imperial Oil Limited's interest was reduced from 31.25% to 25%.

Source: Exxon Corporation, Financial and Statistical Supplement to the Annual Report, 1981.

EXHIBIT 2 (Continued)

Exxon Corporation: Proved Reserves and Supplies of Natural Gas, 1972–1981
(billions of cubic feet at year-end)

	1972	1973	1974	1975	1976	1977	1978	1979	1980	1981
Net proved developed and undeveloped reserves										
United States	28,656	26,040	24,061	22,655	20,696	19,489	18,170	17,200	16,687	16,924
Canada	2,590	2,426	2,021	1,909	1,513	1,361	1,338	1,495	1,358	1,293
Other Western Hemisphere	15,653	16,581	17,078	375	346	343	329	324	309	280
Europe	5,847	5,848	5,908	5,922	5,261	4,908	4,790	4,411	6,271	5,998
Middle East and Africa	3,238	1,528	1,467	1,311	1,240	1,160	1,459	1,382	1,322	5[b]
Australia and Far East	3,687	3,034	3,470	3,084	3,237	2,856	3,173	3,297	3,294	3,285
Total consolidated affiliates	59,671	55,457	54,005	35,256	32,293	30,117	29,259	28,109	29,241	27,785
Proportional interest in reserves of equity companies	34,289	30,647	25,798	25,650	24,771	24,041	17,231[a]	17,000[a]	16,194	16,067
Supplies available under long-term agreements with foreign governments	20,202	7,562	5,113	5,033	1,753	1,657	1,976	1,881	1,809	—[b]
Total worldwide	114,162	93,666	84,916	65,939	58,817	55,815	48,466	46,990	47,244	43,852
Net proved developed reserves included above										
United States					15,164	17,814	16,628	15,766	16,133	15,886
Canada					989	909	872	1,191	1,094	1,021
Other Western Hemisphere					279	272	257	252	238	208
Europe					3,124	2,759	3,241	2,944	3,006	3,097
Middle East and Africa					757	1,099	1,403	1,325	1,216	5[b]
Australia and Far East					2,262	2,108	2,238	1,981	2,035	2,689
Total consolidated affiliates					22,575	24,961	24,639	23,459	23,722	22,906
Proportional interest in reserves of equity companies					21,177	20,996	16,140[a]	15,938[a]	15,492	15,071
Supplies available under long-term agreements with foreign governments					1,753	1,657	1,976	1,881	1,809	—[b]
Total worldwide	NA	NA	NA	NA	45,505	47,614	42,755	41,278	41,023	37,977

[a] Aramco data not included.
[b] Under the terms of an agreement effective December 1, 1981, Exxon assigned its rights, assets and properties in Libya to the National Oil Corporation. Consequently, no reserves for Libya are included in the year-end 1981 data.
Source: Exxon Corporation, *Financial and Statistical Supplement to the Annual Report,* 1981.

FIRST NATIONWIDE FINANCIAL CORPORATION: THE SAVINGS AND LOAN CRISIS

First Nationwide started as Citizens Building & Loan Association in 1885. Its first chairman, Fremont Wood, saved the files of Citizens from fire during the great San Francisco earthquake by submerging them under water. No Citizens' depositor suffered lost funds in this catastrophe, beginning a long tradition of trust and continuity with the Association's depositors. By 1971 a series of mergers had helped raise assets to over $500 million.

In 1971 Mr. Anthony Frank became Citizens' fourth chairman. In that same year, Citizens converted from a federal mutual charter to a state stock charter company with initial market value of about $40 million. (See Appendix A for a description of the S&L industry's structure.) Some 85,000 of Citizens' depositors suddenly became shareholders. Shortly, thereafter, Citizens began a series of spectacular moves that brought the enterprise's assets to $11.5 billion in 1985, with 180 branches in New York, California, Florida, and Hawaii. In the process, the company had become truly the first "nationwide" savings and loan (S&L) institution.

MID-1970s TRANSITIONS

Congress had created the S&Ls, and their associated regulations, during the 1930s depression to encourage residential construction and to facilitate home ownership. For years, the S&L industry had been stable, borrowing money at low interest rates from depositors and lending long term to home owners for mortgages. However, the volatile and skyrocketing interest-inflation rates of the late 1970s and early

Case copyright © 1990 by James Brian Quinn. Case prepared by Penny C. Paquette under the supervision of Professor Quinn.

The generous cooperation of First Nationwide Financial Corporation is gratefully acknowledged.

1980s upset this tidy relationship. For years, the "yield curve"—the relationship between long-term rates and short-term rates—had held steady. However, after 1966 the yield curve was only positive about 50% of the time (see Figure 1), creating an intermittent, but progressively greater, drain on S&Ls' net worth.

S&Ls also suffered "disintermediation" as consumers eliminated their savings accounts and invested directly in money market funds paying higher market rates than the S&Ls were allowed to pay on deposits. As Mr. Frank later said, "How would you like to be in an industry that had 'one-day money' lent out for 30 years, then suddenly be told, 'Guess what, the signals have just changed.' There used to be an old joke in the industry called 3-6-3, meaning that you could buy money at 3%, lend it at 6%, and be on the golf course at 3. That was the way it was. . . . The industry was boring! I once left the industry because of that. There was nothing exciting, no choices, no decisions, nothing. Then suddenly in a few years time, the yield curve inverted—first in 1966, then in 1971, 1973, 1974. (See Figure 1.) I used to tell people, 'I'm a father and you know what happens when the contractions come closer together.' The industry wasn't dull anymore."

The Hot Breath of Change

Mr. Frank continued, "It became crystal clear that anyone who thought they could predict interest rates had to be an extraordinary genius, lucky, or a fool. I didn't feel we could be any one of those three. We started to think about how we could survive without knowing what interest rates were going to do. The answer to that, of course, changed our whole method of operation and became one of the cornerstones of how we operate today. We took a number of steps so that we did not have to predict interest rates anymore.

First, we changed our product and investment mix in creative ways. Second, we expanded our size through a merger with United Financial Corporation, a publicly

FIGURE 1
Long- and Short-Term Interest Rates
Source: Federal Reserve Board, *Historical Chart Book,* 1984, p. 96.

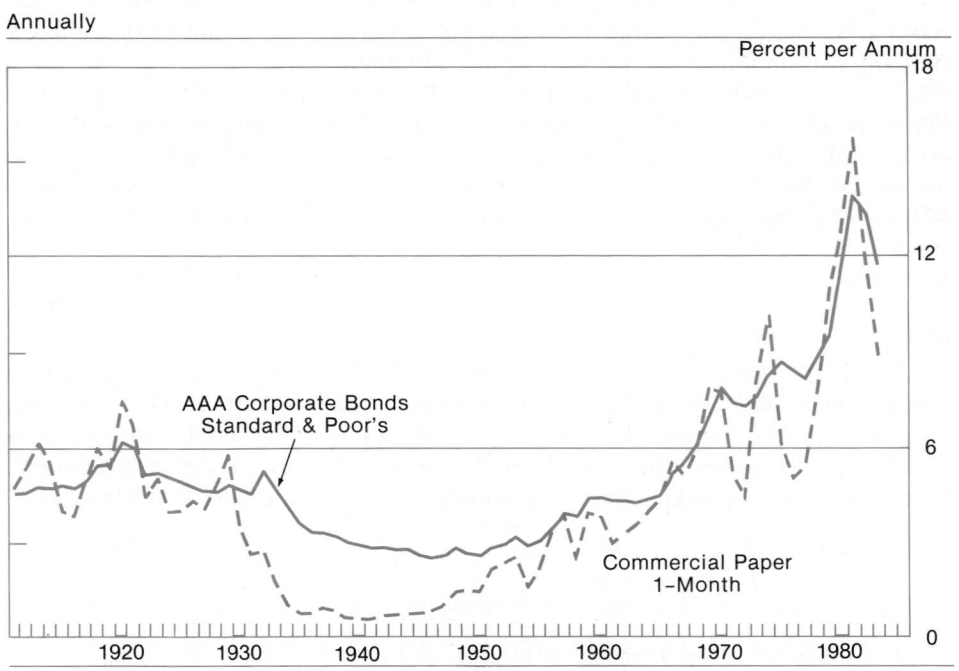

owned holding company listed on the big board, and having as its chief subsidiary the highly capitalized United Savings and Loan of California with over 20 branches in the Los Angeles area. The transaction had a total value of $41.2 million,[1] which gave United Financial a substantial premium over its calculated market value." Mr. Frank said, "We were heavily criticized for this at the time, but we were still an unknown quantity although the combined S&Ls had assets in excess of $1 billion. We could see even then the beginnings of deregulation, and I became absolutely convinced that this was (and is) going to lead to 20 major players in the financial services sector in this country. We had the ambition to be one of those players and the clear understanding that we never could be one of them without some dramatic moves. This same view has led to many of our later strategic actions."

For their part, many of the southern California associations at that time were looking northward and attempting to acquire northern associations. As Mr. Frank later said, "I could feel their hot breath on my neck."

DECISION POINT

1. Given the volatilities and trends noted above, what policies should Citizens undertake in the mid 1970s? What major strategic options did Citizens have?

2. What specific strategy should it follow in California? Why? How would you expect competitors to respond?

FIRST NATIONWIDE BEGINS

By 1981, the savings and loan (S&L) industry was in disarray. Nationally, thrift institutions were losing an average of $0.20 on each $100 in assets. In California, the average S&L lost $0.005 on each $100 in assets, but Citizens was among the most profitable of all thrift institutions. Its net income as a percentage of total average assets for the 12 months ending June 30, 1981 was 0.72%. Mr. Frank later said, "We seemed to have made many of the right moves in comparison with our competitors, and we had a jewel in California that would survive. I wanted to pursue that ambition of growing, without impacting what we already had. That was no small order." In 1980 United Financial (Citizens' parent holding company) had been acquired by National Steel Corporation, later called National Intergroup, Inc., a $3.7 billion diversified holding company. National Steel paid $238 million cash for 100% of the shares of United Financial in open market and tender transactions.

Nationally, however, many major savings and loan institutions were in deep trouble, and some were on their way to large-scale bankruptcies, threatening the nation's confidence in all S&Ls. As insurer for the industry, the Federal Savings and Loan Insurance Corporation (FSLIC) faced some extremely disquieting issues. Since FSLIC did not have the capability itself to manage ailing or bankrupt S&Ls, it tended to seek healthy thrift institutions in the same state as merger partners for troubled S&Ls. One of those in deepest difficulties was West Side Federal Savings & Loan Association of New York, the largest S&L in its state. West Side was losing $5–6 million per month and up to $10 million in net daily withdrawals; no S&L in New York had the capacity to take on its problems.

The West Side Story

Mr. Frank later said,

> We didn't have any private knowledge about the West Side situations. We just knew what we read in the paper. The *Daily News* ran a little box every day called the West Side Story ... imagine what that did for consumer confidence. Seeing some interesting possibilities in interstate moves, I went to my parent company and asked if they would give me $75 million more in capital if I could do a large interstate merger. They preferred that I find a partner somewhere else, but having tried several major partners, I just couldn't do it. Finally a deal was struck with the FSLIC whereby National Intergroup agreed to contribute $75 million in additional capital to United Financial over four years. This was a courageous things to do in 1981, when the investment community was snickering about a steel company having bought a savings and loan at exactly the wrong time.

Merger talks about West Side got started in May with a direct call from Mr. Frank to Mr. Pratt, the new head of the Federal Home Loan Bank Board, which regulates the S&L industry and operates FSLIC. Without mentioning any names Mr. Frank asked if "a proposal involving a capital infusion and an interstate merger would be so farfetched that I shouldn't even consider it." When Mr. Pratt said it was possible, Mr. Frank began to actively look for candidates. Frank thought that if he took over West Side, a difficult case for the Bank Board, he might be able to bundle in another unit having similar problems at the same time, Washington Savings & Loan of Miami, Florida. In late May he called FSLIC and made the proposal.[2]

Mr. Frank related,

> Essentially, I went to the regulators and asked, would you (1) be willing to do an interstate deal? (They had never done an interstate deal), (2) allow us to merge with both New York and Florida associations together?, and (3) give us a guarantee which protected our California jewel? The protection was to be in the form of a "breakeven spread" that would first bring the spread on any loan taken over by Citizens or its successor corporation to break even and then allow a $1\frac{1}{2}$% override, which is basically what it costs to run a savings and loan operation. (The annualized general and administrative expenses for Citizens in 1982 was actually 1.44%.) In addition, United Financial was fully protected by the FSLIC on all asset quality problems or adverse litigation. This arrangement was to last for ten years while we "worked out" the S&Ls.
>
> Ultimately the FSLIC said yes because they were under terrific pressure and wanted to show that there was new capital coming into the S&L business and that major *Fortune* 500 companies were interested. In one day, the Tuesday following Labor Day 1981, we went from $3 billion to $7 billion in assets and went from being in one state to being in three, none of which had ever been done before. We were prohibited from talking to or seeing the institutions until the deal was done. The arrangements were completed on Labor Day. We met our new associates on Labor Day, and on Tuesday morning we opened up for business with them. It went just beautifully.

The Wall Street Journal noted that in the negotiations which lasted all summer it was the FSLIC which sat across the table from United Financial. Mr. Frank reportedly lost 17 pounds during the long and arduous sessions needed to acquire two of the FSLIC's most pressing problems. From December 31, 1980, West Side's and Washington's combined net worth had fallen from $78.9 million to a stated deficit of $10.5 million by the merger date. In addition, West Side was losing $5–6 million and Washington $2.5–3 million per month. Washington was in trouble because it had many long-term large deposits, like jumbo CDs, for which it was paying 18% interest while its loan portfolio yield only averaged 10%.

In a follow-up article, *The New York Times* reported, "By the end of September (1981), the two acquired savings units, with $3.8 billion in assets between them had reported another $13.5 million in continuing losses, plus a $3.5 million write-down of overstated assets at West Side. Losses continued through the fourth quarter . . . [although sources] declined to specify the exact amount."[3] But any such losses were covered by First Nationwide's agreements with FSLIC. Although these arrangements virtually ensured First Nationwide of a break-even operation, there were some important strategic questions as to how to best manage and develop the two new entities in its portfolio. A major concern to First Nationwide, of course, was to obtain an attractive return on the added $75 million in capital its parent had invested to make the venture possible. Mr. Frank felt that a well-run S&L should be profitable in all markets and moved to rationalize operations to this purpose. But he said, "I had no intention of 'Californianizing' these two companies by forcing a lot of our people on them."

Management Philosophy

First Nationwide's acquisition of West Side and Washington Savings & Loan gave the company access to markets which in combination produced 30% of the nation's GNP and contained 23% of the nation's population. In integrating the new operations with First Nationwide, Mr. Frank explained some other aspects of his management philosophies rather colorfully as follows:

> My ambition is to run a great company that's fair to all of its constituencies—easy to say but hard to do. Savers want the most for their money, borrowers want to pay the lowest rates, and there you have a basic conflict. Employees, of course, want to make the most money they reasonably can, regulators want the most reserves, stockholders want the most dividends—those are all conflicting objectives. In addition, the community in general wants you to serve it well—and do all the above things at the same time. Somebody has to balance all of these items and do it in a fair way. I learned a lot about that from my predecessor. He really looked upon himself as the steward of the institution and infected me with that philosophy.
>
> On the other hand, I don't want to build a cult of personality in the company. I don't want to be the Iacocca of this company. I want it to have a broad capability in management and we do. We feature our officers in public relations, press releases, and so on. On the other hand, my mother always told me that fish begin to stink from the head, and they do so particularly in hierarchical organizations. Every S&L tends to take on the personality of its chief executive. If he is a sleazebag, it's a sleazebag company; if he is a gambler, it's a gambling company; and so on. I certainly want this company to have a very positive image, if only for that reason.
>
> We have to work hard with all our employees. Being in San Francisco, New York, and Miami, we really do have a lot of melting pot people. We try to work very hard at pushing our employees ahead and helping them learn English and other skills they will need. We like to make them feel good about where they work; but, of course, with 3,500 employees now it's getting increasingly impersonal and just very difficult to make all this work.
>
> I try to walk around our offices every day. They call me the walking boss. Nobody ever comes into my offices. I always try to go to theirs and just pop in. At first, it's no great fun to have your chairman pop in like that, but after he's done it 50 times or so, it becomes 'Oh, hi, Tony . . . how are you doing?' I never give orders to anybody that doesn't report to me. I really try to observe the chain of command even though I talk to everybody. I think people have a few inalienable rights, and one of them is to just have one boss.
>
> As far as incentives go, I think the biggest incentive you can give anyone is to let them within reason run their own show. That's the best incentive you can give to a

certain type of person, and we try to do that. We pay well. We pay about at market, I guess, for our top people, but we have two bonus programs. Anybody in our business can generate a profit at will for a short period of time. All you have to do is borrow from the future. But we want to make sure that we profit over a long period of time. We have an annual bonus based on this year's performance and a long term bonus that by itself can potentially contribute an additional 75% of people's income. Our top people can and do make a lot of money. That has been very helpful.

I think it's foolish that people argue about details of salaries for senior people in a savings and loan situation. The difference between an outstanding chief financial officer and a very good one is probably only $50,000 per year—yet the better person can, and will, make up that difference, every working day at the least. These major bonus programs only affect roughly the top 20 or 25 people. Remember S&Ls are very hierarchical. All other officers (300 people or so) are on a different incentive system. Giving bonuses to loan officers can be a very tricky thing. You don't want to motivate somebody to do something that is adverse for the entire company by taking an inappropriate risk to make a small gain. We are also starting bonuses for the rank and file aimed at getting them to cross sell the many services now available from the company.

One of our important policies is that we never want to have to buy lunch for a customer; which is a funny way of saying we never want to have any overwhelmingly important customers on either side of our balance sheet. In addition, we have a philosophy that we never want to bet the bank. Our attitude is that we don't necessarily want to be 100% right, because the reverse of being 100% right is being 100% wrong. We try not to take extreme positions.

DECISION POINT

1. How could First Nationwide financially benefit from its interstate acquisitions?

2. What steps should Mr. Frank take to integrate the New York and Florida operations? What problems would you expect it to encounter? What operating opportunities do the two new entities bring to First Nationwide. Mr. Frank was especially interested in developing any possible synergistic relationships between New York and Florida.

EARLY 1980s TRENDS

The skyrocketing interest rates of 1979–1981 led to two major pieces of legislation affecting S&Ls. These were the Depository Institutions Deregulation and Monetary Control Act of 1980 (DIDMCA) and the Garn-St Germain Depository Institutions Act of 1982. Both of these contained substantial elements of "deregulation." (See Appendix A.) With deregulation and "disintermediation" (the decline of intermediaries in financial transactions), consumers began to shop more for their financial services. A Stanford Research Institute study reported that a typical middle-class family dealt with 22 different kinds of financial institutions each year. And interestingly some 70% of all such transactions were made by women, more and more of whom were working. However, financial services companies had found it increasingly difficult to make money on this very diverse and transient middle-class group, and many were beginning to move "upscale" toward the upper-middle or multiple-income "yuppie" groups.

Mr. Frank was fascinated by the potentials this "middle-class" market represented. Mr. Frank said, "We do two things. One is to safeguard the savings of families and individuals, and the second is to finance the shelter of families and individuals. These are not fads or hula-hoops. They will be here 100 years from now. But they seem to be activities that competitors aren't very eager to undertake. Bankers hate making mortgages. For example, Citibank said you had to have $5,000 in an account before you could talk to a human being—otherwise you had to communicate through their ATMs. From my point of view, it is terrific to provide two of the most basic services that nobody else wants to provide. The question for us is: How can we make a reasonable margin on these two businesses with this middle class group of customers?"

Total home ownership was booming. But down payments had also soared, loan costs were high, and the consumer was increasingly asked to take on the added risk of adjustable mortgages or indexed interest rates. In addition, the consumer had burgeoning opportunities (and their associated problems) for borrowing through other credit instruments and for investing in a wide variety of savings, deferred income, or other investment instruments. As deregulation progressed, S&Ls could offer more of the services customers desired (see Table 1), but they still faced their traditional problems of maturity mismatch in their basic portfolios—personal savings accounts and home loans. And the S&L's traditional source of funds was threatened as electronic funds transfer (EFT) became increasingly possible. For years, various groups had talked about and studied the potential impact of EFT. Some estimates appear in Table 2.

TABLE 1 Types of Financial Services Likely to Be Used at One-Stop Provider of Choice

		INCOME IN THOUSANDS				
	Total	Under $10	$10.0–$17.5	$17.5–$24.9	$25.0–$34.9	$35 and Above
Checking	87	80	89	86	89	87
Passbook savings	70	70	74	77	70	63
Certificates of deposit	53	42	48	52	57	64
Money market funds accounts	44	27	38	43	48	58
Credit cards	60	39	58	64	64	72
Lines of credit	33	22	28	34	35	42
Consumer loans	33	20	31	37	37	39
Mortgages	43	23	39	46	52	52
Second mortgages	14	7	10	13	16	22
Life insurance	28	27	28	34	27	26
Property and casualty insurance	36	30	38	38	35	39
Real estate brokerage	18	13	16	18	20	21
Tax preparation service	33	28	35	35	32	37
Tax and investment planning and advice	27	13	19	24	30	42
Stock and bond brokerage	24	8	15	19	27	43
Managed investment funds	17	8	12	10	22	30
IRA/Keogh accounts	44	21	34	45	52	63
Estate planning, settlement, and trusts	21	14	16	16	23	33
Asset Management accounts	11	5	7	6	12	21
Total number of respondents	1,864	363	370	294	365	472

Source: "Consumer Demand for Product Deregulation," *Economic Review,* Federal Reserve Bank of Atlanta, May 1984, as shown in *Statistical Information on the Financial Services Industry,* 3rd ed., 1984. ©American Bankers Association. Reprinted with permission. All rights reserved.

TABLE 2   Expected Penetration of Selected EFT Services, 1978–1983 vs. 1990
(Average Estimates for 1990 and Historical Data Compared)

	PERCENTAGE OF ALL FINANCIAL INSTITUTION CUSTOMERS USING SERVICE				
	1978	**1980**	**1982**	**1983**	**1990**
Automated tellers	9%	14%	21%	28%	46%
Preauthorized payments	17	14	19	N/A	24
Direct deposit of payroll	8	10	N/A	11	21
Direct debit (POS)	2	2	5	6	17
Home banking	N/A	N/A	N/A	N/A	10
Telephone bill paying	2	2	N/A	N/A	5

N/A = Not available.

Source: Payment Systems Newsletter, Payment Systems, Inc., January 16, 1984, as shown in *Statistical Information for the Financial Services Industry,* 3rd ed., 1984. © American Bankers Association. Reprinted with permission. All rights reserved.

An Industry Restructures

As the services that customers demanded grew, there was also a trend toward consolidation in the S&L industry, which was typical of the consolidations following deregulation on other industries. (See Table 3.) Voluntary mergers accounted for some 65% of all mergers from 1980 through 1983. Mr. Frank noted, "There were hundreds of fine firms voluntarily leaving the industry by merging, thereby depriving their communities of locally owned and managed entities." Approximately 11% of all mergers were FSLIC assisted during this period. As in the commercial banking industry, certain economies of scale in product development, advertising

TABLE 3   Savings and Loan Association Merger Activity, 1970–1983

YEAR	TOTAL NUMBER FHLB MEMBERS	NUMBER OF FHLB MEMBERS MERGERS APPROVED	MERGER APPROVALS AS PERCENT OF FHLB MEMBERS
1970	4,792	79	1.65%
1971	4,649	110	2.37
1972	4,522	110	2.43
1973	4,412	74	1.68
1974	4,361	81	1.86
1975	4,340	130	3.00
1976	4,274	97	2.27
1977	4,238	80	1.89
1978	4,251	59	1.39
1979	4,242	51	1.20
1980	4,250	117	2.75
1981	4,244	315	7.42
1982	4,029	425	10.55
1983 (11 mos.)	3,555	122	3.43

Source: "The Merging of the Savings & Loan Industry," *Federal Home Loan Bank Board Journal,* January 1984.

services, and EFT capabilities were available to larger firms with wide distribution networks. "For example," said Mr. Frank, "We developed a 'sweep account' (which allowed First Nationwide to pay interest on checking accounts when this was not officially permitted by the regulators) in California. It cost us about $250,000 to develop all the legal work, procedures, and training films, and so on. Then we put it in New York, and the marginal cost of introduction was about $100 plus advertising."

Distribution related costs in the retail banking industry were high, averaging some 15–30% of total revenues for most financial products. They were particularly high for products that required personal interactions, and there was great interest in lowering such costs. Mr. Frank envisioned a national retail bank in the 1990s as follows, "It probably would look as if it had a branch in every town of more than 20,000 in the United States. It would be housed in somebody else's bricks and mortar so that it could (1) operate very inexpensively; (2) draw from the reputation of its host; (3) be open 12 hours a day, 7 days a week; (4) have free, lighted parking; and (5) have a friendly host institution which had a relationship with many Americans across the country."

Will S&Ls Survive?

Could S&Ls survive the new competitive environment? Some forces favored S&Ls. Some were countervailing. Banks had to have approximately $5\frac{1}{2}$% primary capital as a percentage of deposits, and there was some discussion of this going to 9%. Savings and loans had only been asked to have 3% capital, but in the late 1980s it appeared that S&L failures would cost $350 billion to rectify—over $1500 for every person in the United States. Many questioned why this should be. S&Ls' assets were typically fixed and secured. First Nationwide's foreclosed property was 0.2%. As Mr. Frank said, "There is nothing safer in this world than lending to a family that lives in its own house—nothing safer. If done right, mortgage lending can have a very low-risk level. Done wrong, of course, it can be a disaster. Commercial banks by their very nature are forced to higher risk levels by lending to people on their names and their futures. . . . If the people walk out or fail, they are left with some assets no one else wants. I don't like that very much."

But the S&L industry was more fragmented than banking. First Nationwide was the eighth or ninth largest S&L association, with only 1% of the industry's total assets. S&Ls worked under different rules than banks. Sometimes they seemed to enjoy more legislative favor because they were created by Congress and often served a wider base of constituents than commercial banks did. But commercial banks and insurance companies, with their higher concentration of resources, enjoyed very effective lobbies.

The success of any individual S&L depended largely upon its management's vision and the capabilities of that particular institution. As Mr. Frank said, "Naturally, we recognize that the risk/reward ratios of basic lending have changed dramatically. But we are always bemused that people in our industry think, when a loan is being considered that is not of standard quality, that it can be made of sufficient quality by charging a higher rate of interest or a higher fee. We've never understood how charging a higher rate or fee makes a bad loan into a good one. Obviously, the more you charge the borrower, the worse the loan gets in the first place. Just how a $\frac{1}{4}$-point shift makes a bad loan into a good one is baffling."

In the new deregulated environment, one source (Mortgage Guaranty Insurance Corporation) thought the S&L industry might mutate toward 3 basic types of structures with assets and loan structures roughly as in Table 4.

TABLE 4   Projected Asset/Liability Structure for Savings and Loan Types, 1990

	Classic Association	Mortgage Association	Consumer Bank
Assets			
Home mortgages	80%	40%	60%
Other real estate loans	0	22	13
Warehoused loans	0	10	0
Consumer loans	2	0	5
Municipal securities	0	10	5
Cash, securities	13	5	15
Other assets	5	13	2
Total	100%	100%	100%
Liabilities			
Savings accounts	60%	40%	35%
Demand deposits	10	2	35
Housing savings certificates	10	10	5
Borrowings	5	10	5
Subordinated capital notes	0	5	5
Mortgage-backed bonds	10	15	5
Other liabilities	0	8	4
Net worth	5	10	6
Total	100%	100%	100%

Source: Mortgage Guaranty Insurance Corporation. From "Major Issues for Thrifts in the 1980s," *Federal Home Loan Bank Board Journal*, February 1983.

DRAMATIC CHANGES

In December 1982, First Nationwide made a public offering of 2.7 million shares (1.215 million new shares and 1.485 million of National Intergroup's shares) reducing the latter's interest in First Nationwide to 82%. The shares would be traded on NASDAQ, over the counter. First Nationwide obtained a New York Stock Exchange listing in early 1985; and its stock jumped from $14 to $22 in the two weeks after the offering.

In late 1982 and early 1983, First Nationwide began a dual pilot program with J. C. Penney and Kmart to distribute some of its products through these retailers' stores in California. Penney's agreed to have First Nationwide offer money market accounts, checking, retirement accounts, mortgages, and other loans in five northern California stores. Penney's said it would evaluate the program over 12–18 months before deciding whether to expand it to other stores. The pilot program in Kmart involved offering a more limited set of services. By 1985, First Nationwide was represented in Kmart's ten stores in San Diego with an average account of $17,500. Mr. Frank said, "We were taking in an average of $500,000 per month per store, or $6 million a year per store—with one person. It was mind-boggling." In late 1985, it appeared that First Nationwide would enter into an agreement with Kmart to extend its pilot program within California and eventually to other states.

In a series of entrepreneurial moves, First Nationwide had entered several new business areas. In early 1981 it purchased 20% ownership in Charles Schwab, a discount brokerage house, for approximately $4 million. This interest was sold in early 1982 for approximately $10.6 million, after the Bank of America purchased Schwab. Later Mr. Frank said humorously, "I have three boasts about discount stock brokerage: namely, that we were the first in, the first out, and the only one to make money." In a similar move three years earlier, it had invested $175,000 in Grubb and Ellis, a publicly held real estate sales chain. By mid-1983 this investment was estimated to be worth more than $7 million.

In March 1985 First Nationwide agreed to buy TranSouth Financial Corporation, the consumer finance subsidiary of NCNB Corp., which operated banks in North Carolina and Florida. TranSouth was a South Carolina based consumer finance company with assets of about $400 million. It operated 144 branches in seven southeastern states. The price was $85 million. TranSouth was described as "a stable and well-managed consumer finance company, which NCNB was selling to concentrate on more fundamental banking activities complementing its long-term strategy."

As interest rates started to fall in 1983, First Nationwide had introduced the CAML (Certainly Affordable Mortgage Loan). Within the first year, over $1 billion of CAML loans were written. As Mr. Frank said, "It's a nice compromise between the institution taking all the interest rate risk and the borrower taking all the risk on an adjustable mortgage loan. It is assumable, it has a cap on it, and it has no negative amortization." [4] This was a unique substitute for adjustable rate mortgage loans which (when interest rates soared) sometimes led to significant rates of default. Thus both parties potentially benefitted.

The First Nationwide Network

In another creative move, First Nationwide made a 1983 arrangement with Bank Earnings International, a very large and well-known financial consulting house in Atlanta, to establish the First Nationwide Network, owned 80% by First Nationwide and 20% by Bank Earnings. What the Network offered to smaller S&Ls—bewildered by deregulation and the rapidly changing competitive situation—was a series of services that would help them stabilize their operations and increase their profitability. With the right services many of the smaller S&Ls could stay public or mutual, but local and independent, offering the wide variety of new products and services their customers now sought. Fees for the services of the Network ran approximately 7 basic points on assets.

Bank Earnings did management consulting and operational analyses for financial institutions and had a history of coming within 90%–100% of achieving all the earnings gains they projected. In 9 out of 10 cases, the savings identified in an initial consulting audit by Bank Earnings could be greater than the Network's fee. In December 1985 Mr. Frank said, "Now we have some 28 members with about $12 billion in assets, which is more assets than First Nationwide itself has. All of our members seem pleased with our service—which is of course terribly important —and they are our best salespeople. We have even found some significant savings for First Nationwide in the process. . . . One of the exciting things for me is to see two parallel lines of activity converge, namely our experiment with Kmart and our Network franchising efforts." In April 1985, First Nationwide took over another 20 branch operation in Hawaii owned by the failed State Savings & Loan Association of Salt Lake City. This brought its total branches to approximately 180 in four states, with franchise operations in 20 states.

ENTER FORD

In 1985, reportedly encouraged by Mr. Frank, National Intergroup, Inc., was considering selling its interest in First Nationwide in order to raise cash to support its other enterprises and to satisfy some dissident stockholders. In the past, First Nationwide had been allowed to keep all its earnings as a basis for its own growth, but National Intergroup had been limited in the amount of capital support it could provide, other than the $75 million for the West Side and Washington merger. By mid-1985, National Intergroup's discussions had begun to focus on the sale of First Nationwide to Ford Motor Co. for a total transaction value of over $490 million.

Ford was already involved in the financial services sector through its Ford Motor Credit Company, a wholly owned unconsolidated subsidiary with some $27 billion in assets. Ford Motor Credit Co. (FMCC) was the second largest consumer finance company in the United States. It provided wholesale financing and capital loans to franchised Ford vehicle dealers and purchased retail installment sales contracts from them. FMCC also offered diversified financial services (commercial, industrial, and real estate financing services), and engaged in direct consumer loan operations. FMCC also had five insurance subsidiaries which issued physical damage insurance, principally covering vehicles and equipment financed by Ford Credit. FMCC relied heavily on its ability to raise substantial amounts of funds, primarily through sales of commercial paper, issuance of term debt, and sales of receivables. Some summary information concerning Ford Motor Credit Co. is shown in Exhibit 2.

QUESTIONS

1. Why was First Nationwide so successful in this troubled industry? Why were other S&Ls doing so poorly? What should regulators have done? When? What could they do in 1985?

2. Assuming First Nationwide remained independent, what should its strategy be in 1985? What services should its Network provide and how could its potentials be expanded? What other actions should First Nationwide take? Why?

3. Why should First Nationwide be interested in merging with Ford? What would be Ford's interest in the arrangement? Assume the approximate price would be $490 million in cash to be paid by Ford to National Intergroup and the minority shareholders of First Nationwide.

4. If the transaction were to occur, how should it be implemented for maximum effectiveness? What should First Nationwide's role be within Ford? How can the mutual advantages and potentials of this merger best be developed?

EXHIBIT 1

First Nationwide Financial Corporation and Subsidiaries
Consolidated Statements of Financial Condition, 1984–1985
(Unaudited)

	June 30, 1985	December 31, 1984
	(000s omitted)	
Assets		
Cash, certificates of deposit, U.S. government and other securities	$ 891,206	$ 637,027
Loans receivable	9,073,072	8,193,456
Property held for investment and sale, at cost	325,140	305,023
Premises and equipment, net	119,463	111,868
Investment in capital stock of FHLB	104,080	104,080
Prepayments to FSLIC	11,526	10,361
Other assets	66,058	72,742
Receivable from FSLIC	9,719	14,419
Intangibles	87,521	11,974
Total assets	$10,687,785	$9,460,950
Liabilities, Preferred Stock and Stockholders' Equity		
Liabilities:		
Savings accounts	$ 7,718,919	$6,558,704
Accrued interest on savings accounts	8,716	6,989
Notes, bonds and other obligations	2,285,202	2,348,229
Advance payments by borrowers	33,864	25,953
Federal and state income taxes	13,153	10,741
Other liabilities	128,976	145,149
Deferred income	26,497	25,009
	10,215,327	9,120,774
Preferred stock of subsidiary	100,000	—
Stockholders' Equity:		
Capital stock and additional paid-in capital	87,106	83,285
Retained earnings	286,261	256,891
Valuation allowance—marketable equity securities	(909)	—
	372,458	340,176
Total liabilities, preferred stock, and stockholders' equity	$10,687,785	$9,460,950

Source: First Nationwide Financial Corporation, Form 10-Q, June 30, 1985.

EXHIBIT 1 (Continued)

First Nationwide Financial Corporation and Subsidiaries
Consolidated Statements of Operations, 1984–1985
(Unaudited)

	Three Months Ended June 30,		Six Months Ended June 30,	
	1985	1984	1985	1984
	(000s omitted)			
Revenue				
Interest on real estate loans	$228,412	$198,225	$449,817	$387,933
Interest on other loans	17,725	4,453	24,677	8,172
Loan origination fees	5,568	5,525	10,494	9,009
Other loan fees	3,389	2,350	6,436	4,681
Income on investments	22,349	19,700	39,452	40,995
Income from the sale of property held for investment	7,136	9,118	13,364	13,513
Payments from FSLIC	17,225	19,343	35,425	40,380
Other income	9,497	3,986	15,540	6,690
	311,301	262,700	595,205	511,373
Expense				
Interest on savings accounts	176,745	157,774	339,928	305,735
Interest on borrowings	61,173	56,738	126,442	113,241
General and administrative expenses	52,537	36,416	96,675	70,246
Dividends on preferred stock of subsidiary	1,193	—	1,193	—
	291,648	250,928	564,238	489,222
Earnings before income taxes	19,653	11,772	30,967	22,151
Federal and state income taxes	1,030	—	1,597	—
Net earnings	$ 18,623	$ 11,772	$ 29,370	$ 22,151
Earnings per common share	$ 1.21	$ 0.78	$ 1.92	$ 1.47

	At June 30,	
	1985	1984
	(000s omitted)	
Balance of non-FSLIC covered assets		
Loan portfolio	$6,453,951	$4,809,708
Investment portfolio	683,404	522,488
Combined	$7,137,355	$5,332,193
Yields on non-FSLIC covered assets		
Loan portfolio	12.47%	11.72%
Investment portfolio	8.53	11.10
Combined	12.07	11.66
Combined cost of money	9.41	9.94
Yield	2.66%	1.72%

At June 30, 1985, the loan portfolio includes $370 million of loans receivable acquired with the purchase of TranSouth at an average rate of 19.34%.

Source: First Nationwide Financial Corporation, Form 10-Q, June 30, 1985

Consolidated Income Statement, December 31, 1984	**Amount ($ millions)**
Financing revenue	
Retail	$ 2,189
Wholesale	638
Diversified and other	177
Insurance premiums earned	108
Investments and other income	71
Total revenue	3,183
Operating expenses	375
Provision for credit losses	178
Interest expense	1,932
Other expenses	162
Total expenses	2,647
Income before income taxes	535
Provision for income taxes	225
Net income	$ 310

Consolidated Balance Sheet, December 31, 1984	
Assets	
Cash	$ 143
Investment in securities	
Bonds and notes	420
Marketable equity securities	104
Net finance receivables	23,092
Other assets	277
Total assets	$24,036
Liabilities	
Short-term debt	8,602
Commercial paper	295
Borrowing agreements	39
Bank borrowing	1,468
Other	
Long-term debt payable within 1 year	1,406
Other current liabilities	1,742
Long-term debt	8,403
Total shareholders equity	2,082
Total liabilities and equity	$24,036

Source: Compiled from *Moody's Bank & Finance Manual,* 1985 edition.

593

EXHIBIT 3
Interest of Certain Persons
in the Proposed
Transaction

Messrs. Anthony M. Frank (Chairman of the Board and Chief Executive Officer of the Company), J. Clayburn LaForce, Jr., Howard M. Love and Richard S. Smith are each directors of both the company and N11. Messrs. Love and Smith are both directors of NHC.

Stock Options and Stock Appreciation Rights

As a condition to the consummation of the Merger, all outstanding stock options and stock appreciation rights must be extinguished. Accordingly, the Company has agreed to cause each holder of stock options and stock appreciation rights to enter into an agreement with the Company whereby such interests (and related performance units, if any) will be surrendered and cancelled. In exchange therefore, the Company, not later than 10 days after the effective date, will pay to each such holder cash in an amount equal to (a) the Merger Price, less (b) the exercise or determination price (the Merger Price less the exercise or determination price is hereinafter called the "spread"), times (c) the vested portion of such stock options or stock appreciation rights. . . .

Finder's Fee

In an agreement dated June 1, 1985, N11 agreed to pay Mr. Anthony M. Frank, chairman of the board and chief executive officer of both the Company and the Association and a director of N11, a finder's fee should Mr. Frank be successful in locating a buyer either for all or part of N11's interest in the company or for the company as a whole. The amount of the finder's fee paid will be based upon the purchase price actually received by N11; accordingly, if the Merger is consummated and N11 receives $32.00 per share, Mr. Frank will be entitled to receive $1.5 million from N11.

The following table sets forth, as to each executive officer of the Company, such person's holdings of stock options and stock appreciation rights (with percent vested in parentheses), the spread attributable to such holdings, and the date of original grant.

EXHIBIT 3 (Continued)

	Stock Options (% vested)	Stock Appreciation Rights (% vested)	Spread	Grant Date
Anthony M. Frank Chairman of the Board and Chief Executive Officer	-0-	100,000(50%) 50,000(0%)	$14.00 $18.25	12/19/82 1/1/85
William F. Ford President and Chief Operating Officer	-0-	75,000(50%) 37,000(0%)	(1) $18.25	9/30/83 1/1/85
John L. Carr Vice President, Secretary and General Counsel	-0-	50,000(50%) 26,763(0%)	$14.00 $18.25	12/19/82 1/1/85
Robert T. Barnum Vice President and Chief Financial Officer	-0-	30,000(0%)	$16.25	4/1/85
Donald R. Ansbro Vice President and Treasurer	5,555(50%) —	— 5,909(0%)	$14.00 $18.25	12/13/82 1/1/85
Neil F. M. McKay Vice President and Controller	5,555(50%) —	— 5,816(0%)	$14.00 $18.25	12/13/82 1/1/85
Paul D. Weinberg Vice President	5,555(50%) —	— 6,503(0%)	$14.00 $18.25	12/13/82 1/1/85

Source: First Nationwide Financial Corporation, *Notice of Action by Written Consent,* October 9, 1985.

APPENDIX A: SAVINGS AND LOAN (S&L) ASSOCIATIONS

Modern S&Ls—and the Federal Home Loan Bank System (FHLBS) which regulated them in much the same way the Federal Reserve Board did commercial banks—resulted from legislation passed during the Great Depression to stabilize residential construction and to encourage home ownership. In 1983 S&Ls held some $32 billion in residential mortgage loans or 43% of such private loans outstanding.[5]

The FHLB Board not only chartered and regulated the asset and liability powers of federal S&Ls but provided secondary liquidity to member associations through loans called "advances." States chartered and regulated S&Ls as well, often establishing more liberal powers than those granted by the FHLB Board. In the past the FHLB had frequently allowed federally chartered S&Ls to follow state rules where they were less restrictive. Recently, however, the FHLB Board had become concerned over the powers granted to state-chartered S&Ls. In California, for instance, state-chartered S&Ls could put up to 100% of their assets into almost any activity they chose, leading the FHLB Board to stop granting deposit insurance for new S&Ls in California and several similarly liberal states. All federally chartered S&Ls were required to be members of the Federal Savings and Loan Insurance Corporation (FSLIC) which insured deposits much as the FDIC did. State chartered S&Ls could join FSLIC or be part of the private insurance funds run by several states. (See Table 1.)

TABLE 1   State versus Federal Charters, 1973 vs. 1983

	1973	1983
Number of S&Ls		
Federal charters	2,404	1,553
State charters	3,130	1,960
Total	5,170	3,513
Assets ($ millions)		
Federal charters	$152,240	$499,254
State charters	119,665	272,451
Total	$271,905	$771,705

Source: United States League of Savings Institutions, *1984 Savings Institutions Sourcebook.*

To stimulate the market, some mortgages were insured by the Federal Housing Administration (FHA) or Veterans Administration. The Federal Home Mortgage Association (Fannie Mae) and Government National Mortgage Association (Ginnie Mae) were also developed later to assist mortgage financings. The Federal Home Loan Mortgage Corporation (Freddie Mac or FHLMC) was established to develop a secondary market for conventional and FHA- and VA-sponsored mortgages—and later other mortgage instruments. The existence of an active secondary market for mortgages meant that "lending strategy and portfolio strategy [could be] completely separate—what was originated need not be held, and what was held need not have been originated."[6] In fact, S&Ls were net sellers of mortgage loans in 1981.

Borrow Short and Lend Long?

S&Ls traditionally financed long-term assets (mortgages) with short-term liabilities (deposits). Regulations limiting the types of assets S&Ls could invest in made it extremely difficult for them to reduce their asset-liability maturity mismatch, and the fixed rate nature of their mortgages increased their interest rate exposure. Federal and state regulators responded to the problems these created for S&Ls by gradually removing S&L interest rate ceilings, broadening their asset and liability powers, and allowing them to issue alternative mortgage instruments and to fully utilize the financial futures market.

The Depository Institutions Deregulation and Monetary Control Act of 1980 (DIDMCA) (1) authorized S&Ls to increase their consumer loans and to issue credit cards, (2) authorized S&Ls to offer NOW accounts to individuals and not-for-profits and to establish remote service units (ATMs), and (3) subjected S&Ls and other thrifts to Federal Reserve Board reserve requirements for the first time. The Garn-St Germain Depository Institutions Act of 1982 continued the trend toward deregulation by (1) allowing S&Ls to offer two new liabilities which paid market rates—the Money Market Demand Account (MMDA) and the Super-Now account—and (2) permitting S&Ls to invest to varying degrees in commercial loans, commercial paper and debt securities, state and local debt obligations, and overdraft loans on any transaction account.[7]

As a group, thrifts did not make a big move into commercial lending—near the end of 1984 they held commercial loan assets equal to less than 2% of the amount held by commercial banks.[8] But S&Ls did begin to price their new MMDA and Super-Now accounts aggressively, and in short order the thrifts had collected some $150 billion in such deposits. About a third of these came from existing passbook savings and small time deposits.[9] In 1984 passbook deposits with restricted rates still accounted for $70 billion of the thrifts' assets and made a major contribution to S&Ls' earnings.[10]

Structural Changes and Current Problems

In the early 1980s the S&L segment underwent a steady series of mergers and conversions. The number of mergers rose to a peak of 425 in 1982 from 37 in 1979. The majority of mergers were voluntary, prompted by a desire to become larger and to spread risks further. S&Ls with federal charters were not allowed to become stock corporations until the mid-1970s. Mutual S&Ls converted to stock companies for a variety of reasons: (1) the potential of increasing reserves through increased capitalization; (2) a greater degree of familiarity, for both the public and directors, with the stock form; (3) ease of merging with another stock institution; (4) the ability to grant stock options to attract management talent; and (5) the capacity to issue stock.

Then deregulation and other changes brought major disasters. Growth in home values, which had increased an average 10.9% per year through the 1970s suddenly slowed to 3.3% in 1982–1985. Falling appreciation rates—and possibly a less than thorough screening of borrowers by lenders—led to sharp increases in default rates. Defaults, which averaged less than 1% in 1973, rose to 5.86% by the end of 1984.[11] In April 1985, Ohio's governor declared the first bank (S&L) holiday since the Great Depression. The collapse of a very large S&L (which had lost its money by investing in repurchase agreements from an unregulated securities dealer closed by the SEC) threatened the integrity of Ohio's entire state S&L deposit insurance fund—and presaged similar events in other parts of the country.

The FHLB Board (upset by such failures and the increasing liberalization of powers granted to state chartered S&Ls) began to consider what measures might be necessary to ensure the integrity of the S&L system. By late 1985 the FSLIC had been forced to "take over" some 17 S&Ls with assets totaling nearly $15 billion and foresaw the possibility of having to do the same with many others in the next several years. "The thrifts winding up in government hands now are very gravely ill. They hold billions in nonperforming loans carelessly made in the lending binge of the mid-1980s."[13]

Some regulators were convinced that deregulation—specifically the power to make direct investments (like ownership of land held for development, housing projects, and equity and service corporations)—had led to these failures. But some experts supported the view that such "direct investments considerably strengthened the [failed] thrifts' financial condition by letting them earn increased profits and by cutting their portfolios' vulnerability to interest rate risks . . . [and that] the major causes of S&L failures continued to be the traditional ones: negative interest rate spreads, bad loans, poor management, and outright fraud."[12] By the late 1980s coping with the flood of failures appeared likely to threaten the FSLIC insurance fund structure. And various corrective measures were being considered by Congress, including setting up an "asset management corporation" to sell off the real estate the FSLIC had inherited through bad loans from thrifts, or merging FSLIC with FDIC.

CONTEXT

THE ENTREPRENEURIAL CONTEXT

The text of this book really divides into two basic parts, although there are three sections. The first, encompassing Chapters 1 through 8 and Sections I and II, introduces a variety of important *concepts* of organizations—strategy, the strategist, process, structure, systems, culture, power. The second, beginning here with Section 3 and Chapter 9, considers how these concepts combine to form major *contexts* of organizations. In effect, a context is a type of situation wherein can be found particular structures, power relationships, processes, competitive settings, and so on.

Traditionally, policy and strategy textbooks divided themselves into two very different parts—a first on the "formulation" of strategy, a second on its "implementation" (including discussion of structure, systems, culture, etc.). As some of the readings of Chapter 5 have already made clear, we believe this is often a false dichotomy: in many situations (that is, contexts), formulation and implementation can be so intertwined that it makes no sense to separate them. To build a textbook around a questionable dichotomy likewise makes no sense to us, and so we have instead proceeded by introducing all the concepts related to the strategy process first and then considering the various ways in which they might interact in specific situations.

There is no "one best way" to manage the strategy process. The notion that there are several possible "good ways" however—various contexts appropriate to strategic management—was first developed in the Mintzberg reading in Chapter 6. In fact, his *configurations* of structure served as the basis for determining the set of contexts we include here. These are as follows:

We begin here in Chapter 9 with what seems to be the simplest context, certainly one that has had much good press in America since Horatio Alger first went into business—the *entrepreneurial* context. Here a single leader takes personal charge in a highly dynamic situation, as in a new firm or a small one operating in a growing market, or even sometimes in a large organization facing crisis.

601

We next consider in Chapter 10 a contrasting context that often dominates large business as well as big government. We label it the *mature* context, although it might equally be referred to as the stable context or the mass-production or mass-service context. Here rather formal structures combine with strategy-making processes that are heavily planning and technique oriented.

Third, we consider the context of the *diversified* organization, which has become increasingly important as waves of mergers have swept across various Western economies. Because product-market strategies are diversified, the structures tend to get divisionalized, and the focus of strategy shifts to two levels: the corporate or portfolio level and the divisional or business level.

Our fourth and fifth contexts are those of organizations largely dependent on specialists or experts. These contexts are called *professional* when the environment is stable, *innovation* when it is dynamic. Here responsibility for strategy making tends to diffuse throughout the organization, sometimes even lodging itself at the bottom of the hierarchy. The strategy process tends to become rather emergent in nature.

We complete our discussion of contexts with consideration of the problems of managing *change* from one of these contexts to another (often "cultural revolution") or from one major strategy and structure to another within a particular context.

In the chapter on each context, our intention was to include material that would describe all the basic concepts as they take shape in that context. We wished to describe the form of organizational structure and of strategic leadership found there, the nature of its strategy-making process, including its favored forms of strategy analysis and its most appropriate types of strategies (generic and otherwise), its natural power relationships and preferred culture, and the nature of its competition and industry structure as well as the social issues that surround it. Unfortunately, appropriate readings on all this are not available—in part we do not yet know all that we must about each context. But we believe that the readings that we have included in this section do cover a good deal of the ground, enough to give a real sense of each different context.

Before beginning, we should warn you of one danger in focusing this discussion on contexts such as these: it may make the world of organizations appear to be more pat and ordered than it really is. Many organizations certainly seem to fit one context or another, as numerous examples will make clear. But none ever does so quite perfectly—the world is too nuanced for that. And then there are the many organizations that do not fit any single context at all. We believe, and have included arguments in a concluding chapter to this section, that in fact the set of contexts altogether form a framework by which to understand better all kinds of organizations. But until we get there, you should bear in mind that much of this material caricatures reality as much as it mirrors it.

Of course, such caricaturing is a necessary part of formal learning: like the librarian's need for a cataloguing system to store books, we all need frameworks of categories in which to store the confusing set of experiences that the world throws at us. That is what theory is. Without it, we would simply be overwhelmed—and paralyzed. Managers, for example, would never get anything done if they could not use such simplified frameworks to comprehend their experiences in order to act on them. As we suggested in the introduction to this book, paraphrasing Keynes, the "practical" person who believes him or herself free of theory is simply the prisoner of some old theory buried deep in the subconscious mind. Moreover, as Miller and Mintzberg have argued in a paper called "The Case for Configuration," managers are attracted to a particular, well-defined context because that allows them to achieve a certain consistency and coherence in the design of their organization and so to facilitate its effective performance. Each context, as you will see, has its own logic, its own integrated way of dealing with its part of the world—that makes things more manageable.

This chapter of Section 3 discusses the entrepreneurial context. At least in its traditional form, this encompasses situations in which a single individual, typically with a clear and distinct vision of purpose, directs an organization that is structured to be as responsive as possible to his or her personal wishes. Strategy making thus revolves around a single brain, unconstrained by the forces of bureaucratic momentum.

Such entrepreneurship is typically found in young organizations, especially ones in new or emerging industries. Entrepreneurial vision tends to have a high potential payoff in these situations and may indeed be essential when there are long delays between the conception of an idea and its commercial success. In addition, in crisis situations a similar type of strong and visionary leadership may offer the only hope for successful turnaround. And it can thrive as well in highly fragmented industries, where small flexible organizations can move quickly into and out of specialized market niches, and so outmaneuver the big bureaucracies.

The word entrepreneurship has also been associated recently with change and innovation inside of larger, more bureaucratic organizations—sometimes under the label "intrapreneurship." In these situations, it is often not the boss, but someone in an odd corner of the organization—a "champion" for some technology or strategic issue—who takes on the entrepreneurial role. We believe, however, for reasons that will later become evident, that intrapreneurship better fits into our chapter on the innovation context.

To describe the structure that seems to be most logically associated with the traditional form of entrepreneurship, we open with material on the simple structure in Mintzberg's book *The Structuring of Organizations.* Combined with this is a discussion of strategy making in the entrepreneurial context, especially with regard to strategic vision, based on two sets of research projects carried out at McGill University. In one, the strategies of visionary leadership were studied through biographies and autobiographies; in the other, the strategies of entrepreneurial firms were tracked across several decades of their histories.

Then, to investigate the external situations that seem to be most commonly (although not exclusively) associated with the entrepreneurial context, we present excerpts from two chapters of Michael Porter's book *Competitive Strategy,* one on emerging industries, the other on fragmented industries.

A final reading of this chapter looks specifically at niche strategies, those most commonly associated with younger and smaller firms. Written by Cooper, Willard, and Woo of the Krannet Graduate School of Management at Purdue University, it "reexamines" this concept, suggesting some characteristics under which small and new firms can also compete directly with the larger bureaucracies.

Many of our cases in this section and the other two of this book deal with entrepreneurship in its classical and turnaround modes. The Genentech, Biogen, New Steel Corp., Federal Express, and Intel cases deal with some important new ventures of recent years. These involve the kinds of strategies and competitive situations described by Mintzberg and Porter. The Zayre, Gallo, Polaroid, and Pillsbury cases introduce the problems and potentials of a centrist entrepreneurial style during turnarounds in larger organizations. The Pilkington, Ford: Team Taurus, and Hewlett Packard cases suggest how intrapreneurship works and can be encouraged in large organizations. Entrepreneurship and entrepreneurial leadership provide much of the glamor of modern business. While we hope these cases and their counterpart readings will make the entrepreneurial juices run strong, we believe they also embrace some much needed caveats for the unwary.

• THE ENTREPRENEURIAL ORGANIZATION*

BY HENRY MINTZBERG

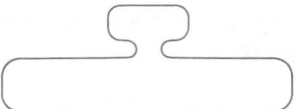

Consider an automobile dealership with a flamboyant owner, a brand-new government department, a corporation or even a nation run by an autocratic leader, or a school system in a state of crisis. In many respects, those are vastly different organizations. But the evidence suggests that they share a number of basic characteristics. They form a configuration we shall call the *entrepreneurial organization.*

THE BASIC STRUCTURE

The structure of the entrepreneurial organization is often very simple, characterized about all by what it is not: elaborated. As shown in the opening figure, typically it has little or no staff, a loose division of labor, and a small managerial hierarchy. Little of its activity is formalized, and it makes minimal use of planning procedures or training routines. In a sense, it is nonstructure; in my "structuring" book, I called it *simple structure.*

Power tends to focus on the chief executive, who exercises a high personal profile. Formal controls are discouraged as a threat to the chief's flexibility. He or she drives the organization by sheer force of personality or by more direct interventions. Under the leader's watchful eye, politics cannot easily arise. Should outsiders, such as particular customers or suppliers, seek to exert influence, such leaders are as likely as not to take the organizations to a less exposed niche in the marketplace.

Thus, it is not uncommon in small entrepreneurial organizations for everyone to report to the chief. Even in ones not so small, communication flows informally, much of it between the chief executive and others. As one group of McGill MBA students commented in their study of a small manufacturer of pumps: "It is not unusual to see the president of the company engaged in casual conversation with a machine shop mechanic. [That way he is] informed of a machine breakdown even before the shop superintendent is advised."

Decision making is likewise flexible, with a highly centralized power system allowing for rapid response. The creation of strategy is, of course, the responsibility of the chief executive, the process tending to be highly intuitive, often oriented to the aggressive search for opportunities. It is not surprising, therefore, that the re-

* Adapted from *The Structuring of Organizations* (Prentice Hall, 1979, Chap. 17 on "The Simple Structure"), *Power In and Around Organizations* (Prentice Hall, 1983, Chap. 20 on "The Autocracy"), and the material on strategy formation from "Visionary Leadership and Strategic Management," *Strategic Management Journal,* (1989, coauthored with Frances Westley); see also, "Tracking Strategy in an Entrepreneurial Firm," *Academy of Management Journal* (1982), and "Researching the Formation of Strategies: The History of a Canadian Lady, 1939–1976," in R. B. Lamb, ed., *Competitive Strategic Management* (Prentice Hall, 1984), the last two coauthored with James A. Waters. A chapter similar to this appeared in *Mintzberg on Management: Inside Our Strange World of Organizations* (Free Press, 1989).

sulting strategy tends to reflect the chief executive's implicit vision of the world, often an extrapolation of his or her own personality.

Handling disturbances and innovating in an entrepreneurial way are perhaps the most important aspects of the chief executive's work. In contrast, the more formal aspects of managerial work—figurehead duties, for example, receive less attention, as does the need to disseminate information and allocate resources internally, since knowledge and power remain at the top.

CONDITIONS OF THE ENTREPRENEURIAL ORGANIZATION

A centrist entrepreneurial configuration is fostered by an external context that is both simple and dynamic. Simpler environments (say, retailing food as opposed to designing computer systems) enable one person at the top to retain so much influence, while it is a dynamic environment that requires flexible structure, which in turn enables the organization to outmaneuver the bureaucracies. Entrepreneurial leaders are naturally attracted to such conditions.

The classic case of this is, of course, the entrepreneurial firm, where the leader is the owner. Entrepreneurs often found their own firms to escape the procedures and control of the bureaucracies where they previously worked. At the helm of their own enterprises, they continue to loathe the ways of bureaucracy, and the staff analysts that accompany them, and so they keep their organizations lean and flexible. Figure 1 shows the organigram for Steinberg's, a supermarket chain we shall be discussing shortly, during its most classically entrepreneurial years. Notice the identification of people above positions, the simplicity of the structure (the firm's sales by this time were on the order of $27 million), and the focus on the chief executive (not to mention the obvious family connections).

Entrepreneurial firms are often young and aggressive, continually searching for the risky markets that scare off the bigger bureaucracies. But they are also careful to avoid the complex markets, preferring to remain in niches that their leaders can comprehend. Their small size and focused strategies allow their structures to remain simple, so that the leaders can retain tight control and maneuver flexibly.

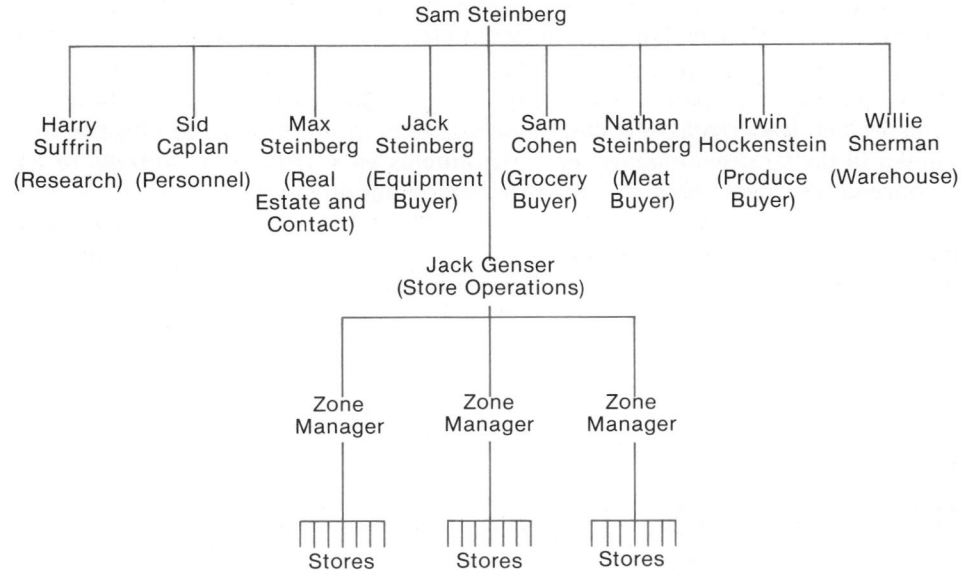

FIGURE 1
Organization of Steinberg's, an Entrepreneurial Firm (circa 1948)

Moreover, business entrepreneurs are often visionary, sometimes charismatic or autocratic as well (sometimes both, in sequence!). Of course, not all "entrepreneurs" are so aggressive or visionary; many settle down to pursue common strategies in small geographic niches. Labeled the *local producers,* these firms can include the corner restaurant, the town bakery, the regional supermarket chain.

But an organization need not be owned by an entrepreneur, indeed need not even operate in the profit sector, to adopt the configuration we call entrepreneurial. In fact, most new organizations seem to adopt this configuration, whatever their sector, because they generally have to rely on personalized leadership to get themselves going—to establish their basic direction, or *strategic vision,* to hire their first people and set up their initial procedures. Of course, strong leaders are likewise attracted to new organizations, where they can put their own stamp on things. Thus, we can conclude that most organizations in business, government, and not-for-profit areas pass through the entrepreneurial configuration in their formative years, during *start-up.*

Moreover, while new organizations that quickly grow large or that require specialized forms of expertise may make a relatively quick transition to another configuration, many others seem to remain in the entrepreneurial form, more or less, as long as their founding leaders remain in office. This reflects the fact that the structure has often been built around the personal needs and orientation of the leader and has been staffed with people loyal to him or her.

This last comment suggests that the personal power needs of a leader can also, by themselves, give rise to this configuration in an existing organization. When a chief executive hoards power and avoids or destroys the formalization of activity as an infringement on his or her right to rule by fiat, then an autocratic form of the entrepreneurial organization will tend to appear. This can been seen in the cult of personality of the leader, in business (the last days of Henry Ford) no less than in government (the leadership of Stalin in the Soviet Union). Charisma can have a similar effect, though different consequences, when the leader gains personal power not because he or she hoards it but because the followers lavish it on the leader.

The entrepreneurial configuration also tends to arise in any other type of organization that faces severe crisis. Backed up against a wall, with its survival at stake, an organization will typically turn to a strong leader for salvation. The structure thus becomes effectively (if not formally) simple, as the normal powers of existing groups—whether staff analysts, line managers, or professional operators, and so on, with their perhaps more standardized forms of control—are suspended to allow the chief to impose a new integrated vision through his or her personalized control. The leader may cut costs and expenses in an attempt to effect what is known in the strategic management literature as an *operating turnaround,* or else reconceive the basic product and service orientation, to achieve *strategic turnaround.* Of course, once the turnaround is realized, the organization may revert to its traditional operations, and, in the bargain, spew out its entrepreneurial leader, now viewed as an impediment to its smooth functioning.

STRATEGY FORMATION IN THE ENTREPRENEURIAL ORGANIZATION

How does strategy develop in the entrepreneurial organization? And what role does that mysterious concept known as "strategic vision" play? We know something of the entrepreneurial mode of strategy making, but less of strategic vision itself, since it is locked in the head of the individual. But some studies we have done at McGill do shed some light on both these questions. Let us consider strategic vision first.

Visionary Leadership

In a paper she coauthored with me, my McGill colleague Frances Westley contrasted two views of visionary leadership. One she likened to a hypodermic needle, in which the active ingredient (vision) is loaded into a syringe (words) which is injected into the employees to stimulate all kinds of energy. There is surely some truth to this, but Frances prefers another image, that of drama. Drawing from a book on theater by Peter Brook (1968), the legendary director of the Royal Shakespeare Company, she conceives strategic vision, like drama, as becoming magical in that moment when fiction and life blend together. In drama, this moment is the result of endless "rehearsal," the "performance" itself, and the "attendance" of the audience. But Brook prefers the more dynamic equivalent words in French, all of which have English meanings—"repetition," "representation," and "assistance." Frances likewise applies these words to strategic vision.

"Repetition" suggests that success comes from deep knowledge of the subject at hand. Just as Sir Laurence Olivier would repeat his lines again and again until he had trained his tongue muscles to say them effortlessly (Brook, p. 154), so too Lee Iococca "grew up" in the automobile business, going to Chrysler after Ford because cars were "in his blood" (Iococca, 1984:141). The visionary's inspiration stems not from luck, although chance encounters can play a role, but from endless experience in a particular context.

"Representation" means not just to perform but to make the past live again, giving it immediacy, vitality. To the strategist, that is vision articulated, in words and actions. What distinguishes visionary leaders is their profound ability with language, often in symbolic form, as metaphor. It is not just that they "see" things from a new perspective but that they get others to so see them.

Edwin Land, who built a great company around the Polaroid camera he invented, has written of the duty of "the inventor to build a new gestalt for the old one in the framework of society" (1975:50). He himself described photography as helping "to focus some aspect of [your] life"; as you look through the viewfinder, "it's not merely the camera you are focusing: you are focusing yourself . . . when you touch the button, what is inside of you comes out. It's the most basic form of creativity. Part of you is now permanent" (*Time,* 1972:84). Lofty words for 50 tourists filing out of a bus to record some pat scene, but powerful imagery for someone trying to build an organization to promote a novel camera. Steve Jobs, visionary (for a time) in his promotion, if not invention, of the personal computer, placed a grand piano and a BMW in Apple's central foyer, with the claim that "I believe people get great ideas from seeing great products" (in Wise, 1984:146).

"Assistance" means that the audience for drama, whether in the theater or in the organization, empowers the actor no less than the actor empowers the audience. Leaders become visionary because they appeal powerfully to specific constituencies at specific periods of time. That is why leaders once perceived as visionary can fall so dramatically from grace—a Steve Jobs, a Winston Churchill. Or to take a more dramatic example, here is how Albert Speer, arriving skeptical, reacted to the first lecture he heard by his future leader: "Hitler no longer seemed to be speaking to convince; rather, he seemed to feel that he was experiencing what the audience, by now transformed into a single mass, expected of him" (1970:16).

Of course, management is not theater; the leader who becomes a stage actor, playing a part he or she does not live, is destined to fall from grace. It is integrity—a genuine feeling behind what the leader says and does—that makes leadership truly visionary, and that is what makes impossible the transition of such leadership into any formula.

This visionary leadership is style and strategy, coupled together. It is drama, but not playacting. The strategic visionary is born and made, the product of a historical moment. Brook closes his book with the following quotation:

> In everyday life, "if" is a fiction, in the theatre "if" is an experiment.
> In everyday life, "if" is an evasion, in the theatre "if" is the truth.
> When we are persuaded to believe in this truth, then the theatre and life are one.
> This is a high aim. It sounds like hard work.
> To play needs much work. But when we experience the work as play, then it is not work any more.
> A play is play. (p. 157)

In the entrepreneurial organization, at best, "theater," namely strategic vision, becomes one with "life," namely organization. That way leadership creates drama; it turns work into play.

Let us now consider the entrepreneurial approach to strategy formation in terms of two specific studies we have done, one of a supermarket chain, the other of a manufacturer of women's undergarments.

The Entrepreneurial Approach to Strategy Formation in a Supermarket Chain

Steinberg's is a Canadian retail chain that began with a tiny food store in Montreal in 1917 and grew to sales in the billion-dollar range during the almost 60-year reign of its leader. Most of that growth came from supermarket operations. In many ways, Steinberg's fits the entrepreneurial model rather well. Sam Steinberg, who joined his mother in the first store at the age of 11 and personally made a quick decision to expand it 2 years later, maintained complete formal control of the firm (including every single voting share) to the day of his death in 1978. He also exercised close managerial control over all its major decisions, at least until the firm began to diversify after 1960, primarily into other forms of retailing.

It has been popular to describe the "bold stroke" of the entrepreneur (Cole, 1959). In Steinberg's we saw only two major reorientations of strategy in the sixty years, moves into self-service in the 1930s and into the shopping center business in the 1950s. But the stroke was not bold so much as tested. The story of the move into self-service is indicative. In 1933 one of the company's eight stores "struck it bad," in the chief executive's words, incurring "unacceptable" losses ($125 a week). Sam Steinberg closed the store one Friday evening, converted it to self-service, changed its name from "Steinberg's Service Stores" to "Wholesale Groceteria," slashed its prices by 15–20%, printed handbills, stuffed them into neighborhood mailboxes, and reopened on Monday morning. That's strategic change! But only once these changes proved successful did he convert the other stores. Then, in his words, "We grew like Topsy."

This anecdote tells us something about the bold stroke of the entrepreneur— "controlled boldness" is a better expression. The ideas were bold, the execution careful. Sam Steinberg could have simply closed the one unprofitable store. Instead he used it to create a new vision, but he tested that vision, however ambitiously, before leaping into it. Notice the interplay here of problems and opportunities. Steinberg took what most businessmen would probably have perceived as a *problem* (how to cut the losses in one store) and by treating it as a *crisis* (what is wrong with our *general* operation that produces these losses) turned it into an *opportunity* (we can grow more effectively with a new concept of retailing). That was how he got energy behind actions and kept ahead of his competitors. He "oversolved" his problem and thereby remade his company, a characteristic of some of the most effective forms of entrepreneurship.

But absolutely central to this form of entrepreneurship is intimate, detailed knowledge of the business or of analogous business situations, the "repetition" discussed earlier. The leader as conventional strategic "planner"—the so-called architect of strategy—sits on a pedestal and is fed aggregate data that he or she uses to "formulate" strategies that are "implemented" by others. But the history of Steinberg's belies that image. It suggests that clear, imaginative, integrated strategic vision depends on an involvement with detail, an intimate knowledge of specifics. And by closely controlling "implementation" personally, the leader is able to reformulate en route, to adapt the evolving vision through his or her own process of learning. That is why Steinberg tried his new ideas in one store first. And that is why, in discussing his firm's competitive advantage, he told us: "Nobody knew the grocery business like we did. Everything has to do with your knowledge." He added: "I knew merchandise, I knew cost, I knew selling, I knew customers, I knew everything . . . and I passed on all my knowledge; I kept teaching my people. That's the advantage we had. They couldn't touch us."

Such knowledge can be incredibly effective when concentrated in one individual who is fully in charge (having no need to convince others, not subordinates below, not superiors at some distant headquarters, nor market analysts looking for superficial pronouncements) and who retains a strong, long-term commitment to the organization. So long as the business is simple and focused enough to be comprehended in one brain, the entrepreneurial approach is powerful, indeed unexcelled. Nothing else can provide so clear and complete a vision, yet also allow the flexibility to elaborate and rework that vision when necessary. The conception of a new strategy is an exercise in synthesis, which is typically best carried out in a single, informed brain. That is why the entrepreneurial approach is at the center of the most glorious corporate successes.

But in its strength lies entrepreneurship's weakness. Bear in mind that strategy for the entrepreneurial leader is not a formal, detailed plan on paper. It is a personal vision, a concept of the business, locked in a single brain. It may need to get "represented," in words and metaphors, but that must remain general if the leader is to maintain the richness and flexibility of his or her concept. But success breeds a large organization, public financing, and the need for formal planning. The vision must be articulated to drive others and gain their support, and that threatens the personal nature of the vision. At the limit, as we shall see later in the case of Steinberg's, the leader can get captured by his or her very success.

In Steinberg's, moreover, when success in the traditional business encouraged diversification into new ones (new regions, new forms of retailing, new industries), the organization moved beyond the realm of its leader's personal comprehension, and the entrepreneurial mode of strategy formation lost its viability. Strategy making became more decentralized, more analytic, in some ways more careful, but at the same time less visionary, less integrated, less flexible, and ironically, less deliberate.

Conceiving a New Vision in a Garment Firm

The genius of an entrepreneur like Sam Steinberg was his ability to pursue one vision (self-service and everything that entailed) faithfully for decades and then, based on a weak signal in the environment (the building of the first small shopping center in Montreal), to realize the need to shift that vision. The planning literature makes a big issue of forecasting such discontinuities, but as far as I know there are no formal techniques to do so effectively (claims about "scenario analysis" notwithstanding). The ability to perceive a sudden shift in an established pattern and then to conceive a new vision to deal with it appears to remain largely in the realm of informed intuition, generally the purview of the wise, experienced, and energetic leader. Again, the literature is largely silent on this. But another of our studies, also concerning entrepreneurship, did reveal some aspects of this process.

Canadelle produces women's undergarments, primarily brassieres. It too was a highly successful organization, although not on the same scale at Steinberg's. Things were going well for the company in the late 1960s, under the personal leadership of Larry Nadler, the son of its founder, when suddenly everything changed. A sexual revolution of sorts was accompanying broader social manifestations, with bra burning a symbol of its resistance. For a manufacturer of brassieres the threat was obvious. For many other women the miniskirt had come to dominate the fashion scene, obsoleting the girdle and giving rise to pantyhose. As the executives of Canadelle put it, "the bottom fell out of the girdle business." The whole environment—long so receptive to the company's strategies—seemed to turn on it all at once.

At the time, a French company had entered the Quebec market with a light, sexy, molded garment called "Huit," using the theme, "just like not wearing a bra." Their target market was 15–20-year-olds. Though the product was expensive when it landed in Quebec and did not fit well in Nadler's opinion, it sold well. Nadler flew to France in an attempt to license the product for manufacture in Canada. The French firm refused, but, in Nadler's words, what he learned in "that one hour in their offices made the trip worthwhile." He realized that what women wanted was a more natural look, not no bra but less bra. Another trip shortly afterward, to a sister American firm, convinced him of the importance of market segmentation by age and life-style. That led him to the realization that the firm had two markets, one for the more mature customer, for whom the brassiere was a cosmetic to look and feel more attractive, and another for the younger customer who wanted to look and feel more natural.

Those two events led to a major shift in strategic vision. The CEO described it as sudden, the confluence of different ideas to create a new mental set. In his words, "all of a sudden the idea forms." Canadelle reconfirmed its commitment to the brassiere business, seeking greater market share while its competitors were cutting back. It introduced a new line of more natural brassieres for the younger customers, for which the firm had to work out the molding technology as well as a new approach to promotion.

We can draw on Kurt Lewin's (1951) three-stage model of unfreezing, changing, and refreezing to explain such a gestalt shift in vision. The process of *unfreezing* is essentially one of overcoming the natural defense mechanisms, the established "mental set" of how an industry is supposed to operate, to realize that things have changed fundamentally. The old assumptions no longer hold. Effective managers, especially effective strategic managers, are supposed to scan their environments continually, looking for such changes. But doing so continuously, or worse, trying to use technique to do so, may have exactly the opposite effect. So much attention may be given to strategic monitoring when nothing important is happening that when something really does, it may not even be noticed. The trick, of course, is to pick out the discontinuities that matter, and as noted earlier that seems to have more to do with informed intuition than anything else.

A second step in unfreezing is the willingness to step into the void, so to speak, for the leader to shed his or her conventional notions of how a business is supposed to function. The leader must above all avoid premature closure—seizing on a new thrust before it has become clear what its signals really mean. That takes a special kind of management, one able to live with a good deal of uncertainty and discomfort. "There is a period of confusion," Nadler told us, "you sleep on it . . . start looking for patterns . . . become an information hound, searching for [explanations] everywhere."

Strategic *change* of this magnitude seems to require a shift in mind-set before a new strategy can be conceived. And the thinking is fundamentally conceptual and inductive, probably stimulated (as in this case) by just one or two key insights. Continuous bombardment of facts, opinions, problems, and so on may prepare the mind for the shift, but it is the sudden *insight* that is likely to drive the synthesis—to bring all the disparate elements together in one "eureka"-type flash.

Once the strategist's mind is set, assuming he or she has read the new situation correctly and has not closed prematurely, then the *refreezing* process begins. Here the object is not to read the situation, at least not in a global sense, but in effect to block it out. It is a time to work out the consequences of the new strategic vision.

It has been claimed that obsession is an ingredient in effective organizations (Peters, 1980). Only for the period of refreezing would we agree, when the organization must focus on the pursuit of the new orientation—the new mind-set—with full vigor. A management that was open and divergent in its thinking must now become closed and convergent. But that means that the uncomfortable period of uncertainty has passed, and people can now get down to the exciting task of accomplishing something new. Now the organization knows where it is going; the object of the exercise is to get there using all the skills at its command, many of them formal and analytic. Of course, not everyone accepts the new vision. For those steeped in old strategies, *this* is the period of discomfort, and they can put up considerable resistance, forcing the leader to make greater use of his or her formal powers and political skills. Thus, refreezing of the leader's mind-set often involves the unfreezing, changing, and refreezing of the organization itself! But when the structure is simple, as it is in the entrepreneurial organization, that problem is relatively minor.

Leadership Taking Precedence in the Entrepreneurial Configuration

To conclude, entrepreneurship is very much tied up with the creation of strategic vision, often with the attainment of a new concept. Strategies can be characterized as largely deliberate, since they reside in the intentions of a single leader. But being largely personal as well, the details of those strategies can emerge as they develop. In fact, the vision can change too. The leader can adapt en route, can learn, which means new visions can emerge too, sometimes, as we have seen, rather quickly.

In the entrepreneurial organization, as shown in Figure 2, the focus of attention is on the leader. The organization is malleable and responsive to that person's initiatives, while the environment remains benign for the most part, the result of the leader's selecting (or "enacting") the correct niche for his or her organization. The environment can, of course, flare up occasionally to challenge the organization, and then the leader must adapt, perhaps seeking out a new and more appropriate niche in which to operate.

SOME ISSUES ASSOCIATED WITH THE ENTREPRENEURIAL ORGANIZATION

We conclude briefly with some broad issues associated with the entrepreneurial organization. In this configuration, decisions concerning both strategy and operations tend to be centralized in the office of the chief executive. This centralization has the important advantage of rooting strategic response in deep knowledge of the operations. It also allows for flexibility and adaptability: Only one person need act. But this same executive can get so enmeshed in operating problems that he or she loses sight of strategy; alternatively, he or she may become so enthusiastic about strategic opportunities that the more routine operations can wither for lack of attention and eventually pull down the whole organization. Both are frequent occurrences in entrepreneurial organizations.

This is also the riskiest of organizations, hinging on the activities of one individual. One heart attack can literally wipe out the organization's prime means of coordination. Even a leader in place can be risky. When change becomes necessary, everything hinges on the chief's response to it. If he or she resists, as is not uncommon where that person developed the existing strategy in the first place, then the organization may have no means to adapt. Then the great strength of the entrepreneurial organization—the vision of its leader plus its capacity to respond quickly—becomes its chief liability.

Another great advantage of the entrepreneurial organization is its sense of mission. Many people enjoy working in a small, intimate organization where the leader—often charismatic—knows where he or she is taking it. As a result, the organization tends to grow rapidly, with great enthusiasm. Employees can develop a solid identification with such an organization.

But other people perceive this configuration as highly restrictive. Because one person calls all the shots, they feel not like the participants on an exciting journey, but like cattle being led to market for someone else's benefit. In fact, the broadening of democratic norms into the sphere of organizations has rendered the entrepreneurial organization unfashionable in some quarters of contemporary society. It has been described as paternalistic and sometimes autocratic, and accused of concentrating too much power at the top. Certainly, without countervailing powers in the organization the chief executive can easily abuse his or her authority.

Perhaps the entrepreneurial organization is an anachronism in societies that call themselves democratic. Yet there have always been such organizations, and there always will be. This was probably the only structure known to those who first discovered the benefits of coordinating their activities in some formal way. And it probably reached its heyday in the era of the great American trusts of the late nineteenth century, when powerful entrepreneurs personally controlled huge empires. Since then, at least in Western society, the entrepreneurial organization has been on the decline. Nonetheless, it remains a prevalent and important configuration, and will continue to be so as long as society faces the conditions that require it: the prizing of entrepreneurial initiative and the resultant encouragement of new organizations, the need for small and informal organizations in some spheres and of strong personalized leadership despite larger size in others, and the need periodically to turn around ailing organizations of all types.

● COMPETITIVE STRATEGY IN EMERGING INDUSTRIES*

BY MICHAEL E. PORTER

Emerging industries are newly formed or reformed industries that have been created by technological innovations, shifts in relative cost relationships, emergence of new consumer needs, or other economic and sociological changes that elevate a new product or service to the level of a potentially viable business opportunity. . . .

The essential characteristic of an emerging industry from the viewpoint of formulating strategy is that there are no rules of the game. The competitive problem in an emerging industry is that all the rules must be established such that the firm can cope with and prosper under them.

THE STRUCTURAL ENVIRONMENT

Although emerging industries can differ a great deal in their structures, there are some common structural factors that seem to characterize many industries in this stage of their development. Most of them relate either to the absence of established bases for competition or other rules of the game or to the initial small size and newness of the industry.

Common Structural Characteristics

Technological Uncertainty: There is usually a great deal of uncertainty about the technology in an emerging industry: What product configuration will ultimately prove to be the best? Which production technology will prove to be the most efficient? . . .

Strategic Uncertainty: . . . No "right" strategy has been clearly identified, and different firms are groping with different approaches to product/market positioning, marketing, servicing, and so on, as well as betting on different product configurations or production technologies. . . . Closely related to this problem, firms often have poor information about competitors, characteristics of customers, and industry conditions in the emerging phase. No one knows who all the competitors are, and reliable industry sales and market share data are often simply unavailable, for example.

High Initial Costs but Steep Cost Reduction: Small production volume and newness usually combine to produce high costs in the emerging industry relative to those the industry can potentially achieve. . . . Ideas come rapidly in terms of improved procedures, plant layout, and so on, and employees achieve major gains in

---

* Excerpted from *Competitive Strategy: Techniques for Analyzing Industries and Competitors,* by Michael E. Porter. Copyright © 1980 by The Free Press, a division of Macmillan, Inc. Reprinted by permission of the publisher.

productivity as job familiarity increases. Increasing sales make major additions to the scale and total accumulated volume of output produced by firms. . . .

Embryonic Companies and Spin-Offs: The emerging phase of the industry is usually accompanied by the presence of the greatest proportion of newly formed companies (to be contrasted with newly formed units of established firms) that the industry will ever experience. . . .

First-Time Buyers: Buyers of the emerging industry's product or service are inherently first-time buyers. The marketing task is thus one of inducing substitution, or getting the buyer to purchase the new product or service instead of something else. . . .

Short Time Horizon: In many emerging industries the pressure to develop customers or produce products to meet demand is so great that bottlenecks and problems are dealt with expediently rather than as a result of an analysis of future conditions. At the same time, industry conventions are often born out of pure chance. . . .

Subsidy: In many emerging industries, especially those with radical new technology or that address areas of societal concern, there may be subsidization of early entrants. Subsidy may come from a variety of government and nongovernment sources. . . . Subsidies often add a great degree of instability to an industry, which is made dependent on political decisions that can be quickly reversed or modified. . . .

Early Mobility Barriers

In an emerging industry, the configuration of mobility barriers is often predictably different from that which will characterize the industry later in its development. Common early barriers are the following:

- proprietary technology
- access to distribution channels
- access to raw materials and other inputs (skilled labor) of appropriate cost and quality
- cost advantages due to experience, made more significant by the technological and competitive uncertainties
- risk, which raises the effective opportunity cost of capital and thereby effective capital barriers

. . . The nature of the early barriers is a key reason why we observe newly created companies in emerging industries. The typical early barriers stem less from the need to command massive resources than from the ability to bear risk, be creative technologically, and make forward-looking decisions to garner input supplies and distribution channels. . . . There may be some advantages to late entry, however. . . .

Strategic Choices

Formulation of strategy in emerging industries must cope with the uncertainty and risk of this period of an industry's development. The rules of the competitive game are largely undefined, the structure of the industry unsettled and probably changing, and competitors hard to diagnose. Yet all these factors have another side—the emerging phase of an industry's development is probably the period when the strategic degrees of freedom are the greatest and when the leverage from good strategic choices is the highest in determining performance.

Shaping Industry Structure: The overriding strategic issue in emerging industries is the ability of the firm to shape industry structure. Through its choices, the firm can try to set the rules of the game in areas like product policy, marketing approach, and pricing strategy. . . .

Externalities in Industry Development: In an emerging industry, a key strategic issue is the balance the firm strikes between industry advocacy and pursuing its own narrow self-interest. Because of potential problems with industry image, credibility, and confusion of buyers . . . in the emerging phase the firm is in part dependent on others in the industry for its own success. The overriding problem for the industry is inducing substitution and attracting first-time buyers, and it is usually in the firm's interest during this phase to help promote standardization, police substandard quality and fly-by-night producers, and present a consistent front to suppliers, customers, government, and the financial community. . . .

It is probably a valid generalization that the balance between industry outlook and firm outlook must shift in the direction of the firm as the industry begins to achieve significant penetration. Sometimes firms who have taken very high profiles as industry spokespersons, much to their and the industry's benefit, fail to recognize that they must shift their orientation. As a result, they can be left behind as the industry matures. . . .

Changing Role of Suppliers and Channels: Strategically, the firm in an emerging industry must be prepared for a possible shift in the orientation of its suppliers and distribution channels as the industry grows in size and proves itself. Suppliers may become increasingly willing (or can be forced) to respond to the industry's special needs in terms of varieties, service, and delivery. Similarly, distribution channels may become more receptive to investing in facilities, advertising, and so forth in partnership with the firms. Early exploitation of these changes in orientation can give the firm strategic leverage.

Shifting Mobility Barriers: As outlined earlier . . . the early mobility barriers may erode quickly in an emerging industry, often to be replaced by very different ones as the industry grows in size and as the technology matures. This factor has a number of implications. The most obvious is that the firm must be prepared to find new ways to defend its position and must not rely solely on things like proprietary technology and a unique product variety on which it has succeeded in the past. Responding to shifting mobility barriers may involve commitments of capital that far exceed those that have been necessary in the early phases.

Another implication is that the *nature of entrants* into the industry may shift to more established firms attracted to the larger and increasingly proven (less risky) industry, often competing on the basis of the newer forms of mobility barriers, like scale and marketing clout. . . .

Timing Entry

A crucial strategic choice for competing in emerging industries is the appropriate timing of entry. Early entry (or pioneering) involves high risk but may involve otherwise low entry barriers and can offer a large return. Early entry is appropriate when the following general circumstances hold:

- Image and reputation of the firm are important to the buyer, and the firm can develop an enhanced reputation by being a pioneer.
- Early entry can initiate the learning process in a business in which the learning curve is important, experience is difficult to imitate, and it will not be nullified by successive technological generations.
- Customer loyalty will be great, so that benefits will accrue to the firm that sells to the customer first.
- Absolute cost advantages can be gained by early commitment to supplies of raw materials, distribution channels, and so on. . . .

Tactical Moves: The problems limiting development of an emerging industry suggest some tactical moves that may improve the firm's strategic position:

- Early commitments to suppliers of raw materials will yield favorable priorities in times of shortages.
- Financing can be timed to take advantage of a Wall Street love affair with the industry if it happens, even if financing is ahead of actual needs. This step lowers the firm's cost of capital. . . .

The choice of which emerging industry to enter is dependent on the outcome of a predictive exercise such as the one described above. An emerging industry is attractive if its ultimate structure (not its *initial* structure) is one that is consistent with above-average returns and if the firm can create a defendable position in the industry in the long run. The latter will depend on its resources relative to the mobility barriers that will evolve.

Too often firms enter emerging industries because they are growing rapidly, because incumbents are currently very profitable, or because ultimate industry size promises to be large. These may be contributing reasons, but the decision to enter must ultimately depend on a structural analysis. . . .

COMPETITIVE STRATEGY IN FRAGMENTED INDUSTRIES*

BY MICHAEL E. PORTER

An important structural environment in which many firms compete is the fragmented industry, that is, an industry in which no firm has a significant market share and can strongly influence the industry outcome. Usually fragmented industries are populated by a large number of small- and medium-sized companies, many of them privately held. . . . The essential notion that makes these industries a unique environment in which to compete is the absence of market leaders with the power to shape industry events. . . .

Some fragmented industries, such as computer software and television program syndication, are characterized by products or services that are differentiated, whereas others, such as oil tanker shipping, electronic component distribution, and fabricated aluminum products, involve essentially undifferentiated products. Fragmented industries also vary greatly in their technological sophistication, ranging from high technology businesses like solar heating to garbage collection and liquor retailing. . . .

WHAT MAKES AN INDUSTRY FRAGMENTED?

. . . in many industries there are underlying economic causes [of fragmentation] and the principal ones seem to be as follows:

Low Overall Entry Barriers: Nearly all fragmented industries have low overall entry barriers. Otherwise they could not be populated by so many small firms. . . .

Absence of Economies of Scale or Experience Curve: Most fragmented industries are characterized by the absence of significant scale economies or learning curves in any major aspect of the business. . . .

High Transportation Costs: High transportation costs limit the size of an efficient plant or production location despite the presence of economies of scale. . . .

High Inventory Costs or Erratic Sales Fluctuations: Although there may be intrinsic economies of scale in the production process, they may be reaped if inventory carrying costs are high and sales fluctuate. . . . Small-scale, less specialized facilities or distribution systems are usually more flexible in absorbing output shifts than large, more specialized ones, even though they may have higher operating costs at a steady operating rate.

No Advantages of Size in Dealing with Buyers or Suppliers: . . . Buyers, for example, might be so large that even a large firm in the industry would only be marginally better off in bargaining with them than a smaller firm. . . .

Diseconomies of Scale in Some Important Aspect: [Rapid product changes or style changes, need to maintain low overhead, a highly diverse product line, heavy creative content, need for close local control (as in restaurants), personal service or local image or contacts are key.]

Diverse Market Needs: In some industries buyers' tastes are fragmented, with different buyers each desiring special varieties of a product and willing (and able) to pay a premium for it rather than accept a more standardized version. . . .

High Product Differentiation, Particularly if Based on Image: . . . Performing artists, for example, may prefer dealing with a small booking agency or record label that carries the image they desire to cultivate.

Exit Barriers: If there are exit barriers, marginal firms will tend to stay in the industry and thereby hold back consolidation. . . .

Local Regulation: Local regulation, by forcing the firm to comply with standards that may be particularistic, or to be attuned to a local political scene, can be a major source of fragmentation in an industry, even where the other conditions do not hold. . . .

Government Prohibition of Concentration: Legal restrictions prohibit consolidation in industries such as electric power and television and radio stations. . . .

Newness: An industry can be fragmented because it is new and no firm or firms have yet developed the skills and resources to command a significant market share, even though there are no other impediments to consolidation. . . .

COPING WITH FRAGMENTATION

It takes the presence of only one of these characteristics to block the consolidation of an industry. . . .

In many situations, industry fragmentation is . . . the result of underlying industry economics that cannot be overcome. Fragmented industries are characterized not only by many competitors but also by a generally weak bargaining position with suppliers and buyers. Marginal profitability can be the result. In such an environment, strategic *positioning* is of particularly crucial significance. The strategic challenge is to cope with fragmentation by becoming one of the most successful firms, although able to garner only a modest market share.

Since every industry is ultimately different, there is no generalized method for competing most effectively in a fragmented industry. However, there are a number of possible strategic alternatives for coping with a fragmented structure that should be considered when examining any particular situation. These are specific approaches to pursuing the low cost, differentiate, or focus generic strategies. . . .

Tightly Managed Decentralization: Since fragmented industries often are characterized by the need for intense coordination, local management orientation, high personal service, and close control, an important alternative for competition is tightly managed decentralization. Rather than increasing the scale of operations at one or a few locations, this strategy involves deliberately keeping individual operations small and as autonomous as possible. This approach is supported by tight central control and performance-oriented compensation for local managers. . . .

"Formula" Facilities: Another alternative, related to the previous one, is to view the key strategic variable in the business as the building of efficient, low-cost facilities at multiple locations. This strategy involves designing a standard facility, whether it be a plant or a service establishment, and polishing to a science the process of constructing and putting the facility into operation at minimum cost. . . .

Increased Value Added: Many fragmented industries produce products or services that are commodities or otherwise difficult to differentiate; many distribution businesses, for example, stock similar if not identical product lines to their competitors'. In cases such as these, an effective strategy may be to increase the value added of the business by providing more service with sale, by engaging in some final fabrication of the product (like cutting to size or punching holes), or by doing subassembly or assembly of components before they are sold to the customer. . . .

Specialization by Product Type or Product Segment: When industry fragmentation results from or is accompanied by the presence of numerous items in the product line, an effective strategy for achieving above-average results can be to specialize on a tightly constrained group of products. . . . [This] can allow the firm to achieve some bargaining power with suppliers by developing a significant volume of their products. It may also allow the enhancement of product differentiation with the customer as a result of the specialist's perceived expertise and image in the particular product area. . . .

Specialization by Customer Type: If competition is intense because of a fragmented structure, a firm can potentially benefit by specialization on a particular category of customer in the industry. . . .

Specialization by Type of Order: Regardless of the customer, the firm can specialize in a particular type of order to cope with intense competitive pressure in a fragmented industry. One approach is to service only small orders for which the customer wants immediate delivery and is less price sensitive. Or the firm can service only custom orders to take advantage of less price sensitivity or to build switching costs. Once again, the cost of such specialization may be some limitation in volume.

A Focused Geographic Area: Even though a significant industry-wide share is out of reach or there are no national economies of scale (and perhaps even diseconomies), there may be substantial economies in blanketing a given geographic area by concentrating facilities, marketing attention, and sales activity. This policy can economize on the use of the sales force, allow more efficient advertising, allow a single distribution center, and so on. . . .

Bare Bones/No Frills: Given the intensity of competition and low margins in many fragmented industries, a simple but powerful strategic alternative can be intense attention to maintaining a bare bones/no frills competitive posture—that is, low overhead, low-skilled employees, tight cost control, and attention to detail. This policy places the firm in the best position to compete on price and still make an above-average return.

Backward Integration: Although the causes of fragmentation can preclude a large share of the market, selective backward integration may lower costs and put pressure on competitors who cannot afford such integration. . . .

● A REEXAMINATION OF THE NICHE CONCEPT*

ARNOLD C. COOPER, GARY E. WILLARD, AND CAROLYN Y. WOO

. . . Despite the number and importance of new and small firms, there has been little explicit examination of their strategies. Founders of new firms must find ways to compete in a world which had gotten along without them before. Starting with no reputation and limited financial and human resources, they must seek out opportunities and develop strategies which enable them to compete, sometimes in industries dominated by large, established companies. Since almost any strategy involves competing with someone, they need to consider which established competitors might be challenged and whether sustainable competitive advantages could be achieved.

The extant literature generally advises small firms not to meet larger competitors head on. They should concentrate on specialized products, localize business

* Originally published in the *Journal of Business Venturing* (1986) under the title "Strategies of High-Performing New and Small Firms: A Reexamination of the Niche Concept." Copyright © 1986 by Elsevier Science Publishing Company, New York; reprinted with deletions by permission of the authors and publisher.

operations, and provide products which require a high degree of craftsmanship (Hosmer, 1957; Gross, 1967). Small businesses are also seen to benefit from the provision of customer service, product customization, and other factors which are inimical to large-scale production (Cohn and Lindberg, 1972). The above recommendations would often limit the opportunities open to new and small firms to "niches" too small to be of interest to larger firms. . . . We suggest that this concept of the niche, although descriptive of the strategies of many small firms, is unduly limiting; in fact, it does not describe the strategies of some of the most successful new and small companies. Under some conditions, and for some firms, exceptional opportunities exist for *competing directly* with large established companies. These smaller challengers pursue "niche" strategies in the sense of being focused and directed at serving the needs of a particular group of customers. However, they do not avoid direct competition with market leaders or confine themselves to segments of no interest to them. If we were to apply the test of asking who the young firm takes customers away from, the answer would be clear. It is the largest, the most established, often the most successful firms in the industry that the smaller firm is competing with. . . .

The objective of this article is to reexamine the concept of the niche strategy with particular attention to the new firms challenging industry leaders. In no sense do we argue that such strategies of direct competition are feasible under all conditions or should be undertaken by all new firms. In this article we will discuss what conditions might support the choice of this strategy. . . .

The concepts discussed will be illustrated by reference to five successful challenges which developed strategies of direct competition against much larger established industry leaders. These are

1. MCI, which competed directly with AT&T
2. Amdahl Corporation, which competed directly with IBM
3. Iowa Beef Processors, which competed directly against large meat packers such as Armour and Wilson
4. People Express Airline, which competed directly against larger airlines such as Eastern
5. Nucor, which competed directly against old-line steel companies such as US Steel and Bethlehem

CONDITIONS UNDER WHICH SUCCESSFUL DIRECT COMPETITION MAY BE POSSIBLE

Opportunities to compete directly with large firms vary widely across industries. Of particular importance is whether an industry is changing, the nature of those changes, and whether the managements of the leading firms recognize their implications. In any industry the leading companies have been the most successful in developing strategies to exploit previously existing opportunities. Over time they have mastered existing technologies, fine-tuned their strategies, and developed organizations trained and committed to these ways of competing. If there are no changes, there are few opportunities for challengers.

However, changes in the form of deregulation, new technology, organizational and management innovations, and changing consumer preferences create opportunities for new firms. Thus, deregulation in air transportation and telecommunications enabled People Express Airline and MCI to confront established firms not attuned to competing against new entrants. Nucor took advantage of technology in the form of electric furnaces and continuous casting which permitted it to compete directly against steel mills locked into old technology. . . .

Although change can create opportunities, other industry conditions may make it easier for a small firm to achieve advantages or to keep from being overwhelmed by larger competitors. If there are opportunities for differentiation, for offering a product or service which is somewhat different, then the small firm may be able to achieve an advantage in serving some segment of the market. Frequently, differentiation is perceived to be the process of adding services or product features which some customers value. But, differentiation may also be achieved by subtracting a feature or service included by large firms in their standard offering, but which a segment of the market does not value highly. People Express Airline, for example, eliminated the "meals-in-flight" feature and baggage handling from the standard airline product, reduced the price, and found a ready market from among the major airlines' price-sensitive passengers.

By contrast, if products are nondifferentiated—"commodity-like"—then alternative ways of competing are more limited. Although established firms may already be organized to compete on the basis of price, the new firm can, in certain cases, adopt a different (and inherently lower cost) technology for providing the commodity-like product. Nucor, a successful "mini-mill," adopted the electric furnace technology for making steel directly from scrap-iron, and avoided the heavy capital investments associated with making steel from ore. Low-cost technology similarly enabled Iowa Beef to undercut prices of industry leaders.

The relative importance of economies of scale and/or experience curve effects also bears upon the opportunities for direct competition. If it is possible to compete on a small scale or with little experience and not incur a substantial cost disadvantage, then small firms (with little volume) or new firms (with little experience) may be able to compete directly with success. Nucor and other mini-mills positioned themselves in a segment of the steel industry in which small scale was not a disadvantage. Mini-mills can achieve cost advantage despite annual tonnages of only 250,000 tons per year, a mere "drop in the ladle" in the steel industry.

NATURE OF SUCCESSFUL CHALLENGERS

Even within industries offering opportunities for direct competition, only some new firms may be in a position to adopt such strategies. There must be the right combination of insight, assets, and commitment.

Central to success is a concept, a strategy, which enables the new firm to earn a competitive advantage. Although all of the small firms considered here confronted much large companies, none competed in exactly the same way as their larger competitors. All were headed by entrepreneurs who innovated and challenged the conventional wisdom within their industries. At first, their strategies were untested and their potential was unclear. However, all saw possibilities not evident to others and all served as champions of the new strategies which their firms developed.

Financial and managerial resources are critical to all firms, but particularly to those following these strategies. The emphasis on innovation, the development of larger markets, and direct confrontation with powerful competitors all require more resources than needed for many small businesses. In addition, these strategies are characterized by experimentation, by feedback from the marketplace, and by adaptation to competitive response. All require time and sufficient capital to stay in the game. Some new firms run out of money (or credibility with investors) before they can perfect and implement their strategy. Thus, Amdahl, after developing its initial product line, but before market introduction, was confronted by a newly introduced IBM product in 1972. It was necessary for Amdahl to go back to its investors for an additional $16 million in order to upgrade its product line before it had realized any revenues.

The early capital of these five firms (after initial public offerings) ranged from $956 thousand to $105 million. Although these amounts were substantially more than the capitalization of most new firms, they were far less than those of their major competitors. For example, the initial capital of People Express Airline was $28 million versus $2 billion for Eastern Airline at that time, and that for MCI was $105 million, compared to $29 billion for AT&T. In no way were these challengers in a position to outspend their major competitors.

Those small competitors suited for strategies of direct confrontation must also be able to capitalize upon their potential for achieving organizational commitment and for shaping organizations attuned to these innovative strategies. A young firm, such as those considered here, does not have a stake in the status quo. Employees' security and influence are not tied to traditional ways of competing. If the young firm is led by management with vision and leadership ability, it may be possible to recruit, train, and motivate a cadre of people dedicated to the new strategy. Thus, the new employees of People Express knew they would be operating out of dingy headquarters in Newark, with "previously owned" aircraft, and a work schedule in which jobs would be rotated. An enthusiastic management, which led by example, was able to achieve a high degree of organizational commitment to the new strategy.

BARRIERS TO RESPONSE

In each of the five examples considered here, these young companies competed directly with established large firms. Despite limited finances, reputation, and organizations, they developed and implemented strategies which captured customers away from large, established competitors. We might have expected direct and massive retaliation. Yet, in many cases, this did not occur.

The literature on barriers that prevent response to competitive challenge offers some insights worth noting. MacMillan and Jones (1984) suggest that response will be difficult in situations in which the challenged firm is organized around a particular activity/output configuration. To the extent that response will divert the challenged firm from "doing what it does best," violate existing product-market boundary charters, or result in cannibalization of existing product offering, the competitive reaction will likely be delayed (Coyne, 1986; Kotter and Schlesinger, 1979; McIntyre, 1982).

If the response requires fundamental changes in the organizational or reporting relationships within the challenged firm, the response lag is likely to be greater (MacMillan, McCaffery, and Van Wijk, 1985). Coyne (1986) suggests that response may be delayed if "capability gaps" exist because of facility locations or regulatory/legal restrictions. MacMillan (1982) and Coyne (1986) refer to inertia barriers which may prevent competitive response.

The literature above suggests several reasons why the challenged firm may be unable to answer the competitive attack promptly. In our study of five focal firms, we found some support for these, as well as some additional considerations.

Standardized Products: Large firms often develop a common approach to serving broad markets, even though customer preferences may not be uniform. This practice enables firms to simplify the structure of their supporting organizations and to standardize policies with respect to production, customer services, distribution, pricing, and other functional activities. Thus, established airlines had developed strategies of providing full services for all of their customers. Organizations were developed and employees trained to provide ticketing assistance, baggage handling, and meals inflight. Having defined their "product" in this fashion, and having developed the supporting logistic structure, it was difficult for them to "unbundle" these services for those passengers who would rather not pay for them.

Pricing Distortions: Similar distortions may occur when one product is priced to recover the cost of another product. The unprofitable product may be justified on the basis of social benefits, attempt to gain distribution power, utilization of excess capacity or other reasons. AT&T, for example, had long used the profits from long-distance service to subsidize local telephone rates. As a regulated monopoly, it had been considered "in the public interest" to provide this subsidy, which was estimated to be as high as 35% of long-distance revenues. When MCI was permitted to compete in the long distance market, paying a much lower subsidy to local phone service than AT&T, the latter faced a competitive challenge which was difficult to respond to. This disparity was reported to account for 70% of MCI's ability to undercut AT&T. AT&T [was] bound to this local subsidy until 1988, when it [began to] be phased out. Meanwhile, they must rely on the short-term solution of emphasizing nonprice characteristics in the face of 15–50% price discounts offered by MCI and other new competitors.

Cannibalization of Existing Products: In meeting a confrontation, established firms are constrained by the extent to which their response would affect sales of products which are not directly challenged. Efforts to protect a particular product may lead to loss of sales on other products.

At IBM, the pricing policy reflected a constant price/performance ratio across the entire family of computers. This policy paid off for IBM inasmuch as the lineup of products was developed to derive maximum revenues. While still employed at IBM, Gene Amdahl proposed to IBM a large central processor which would be profitable under two conditions. First, to gain market acceptance, this machine would have to be priced lower than that stipulated by the existing pricing strategy. Second, two additional machines would have to be placed between the IBM 370 family and the largest processor to generate sufficient volume. These steps, however, would upset IBM's overall pricing ratio and threaten the demand for those machines for which the price/performance ratio would become less attractive. Thus, IBM rejected this proposal, and Amdahl subsequently left to found his own firm. He eventually gained success by offering an advanced central processor (the 470 V/6) priced at a level consistent with market demand and not hampered by consideration of whether it would cannibalize smaller machines.

Manufacturing Barriers

The challengers in our examples all demonstrated superior cost advantages. These became feasible through a combination of policies which departed from traditional industry practice. However, the established firms found themselves "locked into" higher cost positions, which reflected historic decisions about wages, work rules, locations, processes, and the skills needed to compete.

Wage Rates and Work Rules: At People Express, the salary structure was substantially lower than that of the established airlines. Initially, its pilots earned $30,000 per year and worked 70 hours per month, compared with industry averages of $60,000 and 45 hours.

Operating by work rules which were much more flexible than those of the industry, People Express promoted efficiency by rotating all its employees through different job assignments This practice extended to managers, pilots, maintenance personnel, and flight attendants (known as customer service managers at People Express). Hence, People Express "produced" at significantly lower costs than would have been the case had they accepted the high salary structures and rigid job classifications of their larger rivals. Its labor costs were about 20% of revenues, compared with 37% for major airlines as a group. The competing major airlines had wage contracts in place; they also had pilots and managers who would regard the rotation of job assignments as demeaning and unacceptable.

Existing Facilities and Processes: IBP's decision to locate its cattle slaughtering facilities in the heart of cattle feeding country, rather than only in the traditional stockyard terminal cities of Kansas City, St. Louis, or Chicago, not only resulted in lower wage rates, but also lower real estate and building costs. Moreover, this strategy drastically reduced the shrinkage normally experienced when livestock were transported long distances from the feedlot to the slaughter site.

And redefining the manner in which slaughter cattle were processed, IBP introduced the moving "disassembly" line. Unskilled or semiskilled laborers were used to perform simple repetitive tasks, replacing the skilled butchers required by the traditional meat packing process. The combination of efficient, one-story plants, redefined process operations and lower wage rates gave IBP a "kill" cost of around $18 per head compared to $30–35 per head for old-line packers.

IBP led the industry in cleaving and trimming carcasses into loins, ribs, and other cuts and boxing the pieces at the plant, which further reduced the transportation costs by removing excess weight. The innovative plastic packaging introduced by IBP virtually eliminated shrinkage due to refrigeration and quadrupled the shelf-life of fresh meat from 7 to 28 days. In fact, IBP claimed it could deliver boxed beef to a supermarket at prices as much as $36 less per head than the retailer could buy and process carcasses himself.

The established meat packers had commitments to existing plants and facilities. They had already trained skilled butchers, and were paying them accordingly. Their entire organizations were oriented toward the traditional way of slaughtering and shipping beef.

Joint Manufacturing: Components shared across product lines can give rise to economies of scale in production, lower design, engineering, and service costs. On the other hand, this practice often promotes standardization and exacts a compromise in product performance.

In IBM's case, the component division recognized that the largest mainframe computers represented only a small market. To attain economies of scale, components for the large processor would also be designed for use in the smaller computers in the company's line. This commonality would lead to lower production costs, particularly across the entire family of products, but also would lead to sacrifices in product performance. When Gene Amdahl proposed the development of a large cental processing unit, he could not obtain assurances that the components needed would not be downgraded. Yet without such guarantees, he felt that the desired performance specifications would be compromised. When Amdahl later left IBM and developed his own central processor, utilizing only those components appropriate to its design, IBM was faced with a dilemma. Should it retain emphasis on commonality, leading to lower development, manufacturing, and service costs across a family of products, or should it seek to match the price/performance ratios of the Amdahl computers through using components uniquely suited to large central processors?

Organizational Structure and Culture

Organizational Structures: The organizational structures of large companies influence their ability to respond to direct competition by small firms. High degrees of centralization and thick policy manuals make it more difficult to modify policies or respond quickly to the moves of smaller competitors. Layers of organization also are often associated with high overhead rates. AT&T was characterized by strong central staff groups, careful and deliberate study of proposed policy changes —including pricing, and concern about systemwide consistency. The corporation was noted for many strengths, but not for internal entrepreneurship. Thus, MCI's development of a lean, stripped-down organization with innovative pricing and marketing techniques, was difficult for AT&T to match.

Organization Cultures: The organizational cultures of established firms evolve through long periods of hiring, training, and motivating employees to implement particular strategies. Employees become proud of organizational capabilities, such as offering a full product line or excellent service.

The integrated steel companies competed on the basis of offering broad product lines. Many major steel companies had integrated backward to the point of iron and coal mining and forward to the point of steel service centers where structural shapes were prepared for individual customers. The traditional "big steel" claim of "If it's done in steel, we do it" required a large investment in metallurgical skills and facilities which had come to be accepted as a necessary requirement of being in the steel business.

But, at Nucor Steel, Iverson did not need or want a full product line. Hence, he had no requirement for the extensive staff, large-capacity furnaces, rolling equipment, reheating facilities, and other investments required of an integrated steel producer. In fact, the investment cost of Nucor's "mini-mills" ran only about $150 per ton of annual output, compared to the nearly $1400 per ton of annual output for an integrated mill.

The young firms in this study created cultures which were difficult for the large firms to replicate. In the early days of Amdahl, Gene Amdahl visited customers and closed the sale himself—an approach that was difficult for IBM to match. Nucor created a culture in which every employee was made to feel important. They even listed the name of every employee on the back page of their annual report!

Ability to Innovate: Innovation can vary widely across established firms. Often, they are well equipped to deal with incremental innovations leading to gradual improvements in cost or performance. However, dramatic changes in the concept of the products, services, or production systems may encounter significant organizational barriers. Initially, it is not clear whether the new concepts will be successful or how large their market potential might be. The methods of analysis used in large corporations often emphasize "hard data" and systematic analysis more suited to incremental innovation than to major changes in strategy. Moreover, innovative strategies often call into question the long-established success formula of the corporation. Such changes threaten managers whose power bases depend on the existing strategy and who may have spent careers developing skills which would no longer be valued.

By contrast, the entrepreneurs within these new companies were the product champions. Gene Amdahl of Amdahl Corporation and Gitner and Burr of People Express Airline had dreams of what they hoped to bring about through their new companies. They could rely upon their "feel" for the technology and marketplace based upon personal experience. Unencumbered by high administrative overhead and large organizations, they could achieve success at relatively low sales volumes. Thus, their small firms were almost ideal settings for experimentation with innovative strategies.

Barriers to Response: In examining these barriers to response, we should not underestimate the role of *government regulation* and *union contracts*. Established firms are visible and accumulate, over time, a history of agreements. AT&T certainly was subject to regulatory constraints, such as the requirement to provide low-cost local service. MCI was faced with no such requirement. Major airlines and old-line beef packers were obligated to labor agreements which restricted flexible work assignments and called for much higher hourly wage rates than those faced by competitors such as People Express or Iowa Beef.

FACTORS BEARING ON WHETHER CHALLENGER ADVANTAGES MAY BE ERODED

Young firms engaged in strategies of direct competition may achieve initial success, based upon some of the advantages just considered. The firms illustrated in this study . . . all achieved substantial growth. . . . Their 1984 sales ranged from more than $500 million to over $5 billion.

This is not to suggest that the conditions which give rise to this success, and the effectiveness of strategies which exploited these opportunities will persist permanently [as, for example, in the case of People Express]. Much depends on how the industry evolves and how established competitors respond. Responses may be of a short-term tactical nature, or they may involve basic changes in the large firms' strategies and organization structures.

Small firms must also be aware that, as they grow, they may lose some of the characteristics which contributed to their success. New players, encouraged by the visible success of challengers, may enter and crowd the markets. Managements of challenging firms must assess these developments and how they may threaten their competitive advantage.

The previous literature clearly notes that early success may not endure and that "sustainable competitive advantage" is required for continuing success (Coyne, 1986; Porter, 1985). The ability to sustain advantage may depend, in part, upon how well the new firm deals with the continuing crises of growth (Buchele, 1967; Baumback and Mancuso, 1975). Even as the firm grows to substantial size, management confronts a series of internal challenges, of evolutions and revolutions (Greiner, 1972). Outside the firm, continuing industry development may shift the focus of competition (Porter, 1980). In some cases early success may attract excessive numbers of competitors, which coupled with rapid change and customer instability, can lead to disappointing performance for many participants (Sahlman and Stevenson, 1985).

The five challengers considered here all had to deal with a succession of responses by established competitors, internal changes, and confrontations with new entrants.

Responses by Established Firms

Responses by established firms can be tactical or strategic. Tactical responses do not stem from fundamental changes in the firm's policies. They represent short term responses by established firms to protect critical segments, to test the commitment of challengers, or to buy time to implement new strategies or organizational changes. In certain key markets, established airlines slashed ticket prices by over 50% to meet People Express's low fares in an all-out price war. One United ad directly attacked the upstart with the slogan, "You can fly or you can be shipped." Established airlines also lobbied the CAB to eliminate subsidies relating to the lower penalties People Express faced if luggage was lost or confirmed passengers were bumped.

Strategic actions, on the other hand, involve major adjustments in the large competitors' products, processes, and organizational structures. Two years after Amdahl sold its first 470 V/6, IBM announced a radical new product, Model 3033, which would bring a price/performance improvement of some 140% over its predecessor. . . . Major efforts were also undertaken by leading airlines to pare down operations, evaluate route structures, and negotiate with unions for lower wage rates.

When faced with these tactical and strategic countermoves, what might challengers do? They must choose their battlefields carefully, taking into account their more limited resources. . . .

Challenging firms must also be prepared to compete more aggressively as established firms react. As MCI's cost advantage over AT&T began to slide, MCI increased its marketing emphasis and expanded its sales force to contact wavering customers. Moreover, it continued to adopt an aggressive posture, spending heavily to expand capacity, work force, and upgrade microwave transmitters.

Evolution of Small Firms

If challengers are successful in developing markets, they will eventually evolve into larger organizations. As these firms grow, they become more complex and the necessary administrative processes may cause such firms to take on characteristics of larger competitors, slowing response time and dulling the competitive edge they once held. . . .

Challengers must recognize those dimensions of their cultures which were relevant not only to their past success, but would be critical to their future performance as well. Only half-jokingly, McGowan said he would abolish the existing MCI to build a new company "to keep employees on their toes." This statement, albeit made in jest, reflected his acknowledgment of the need to maintain MCI's fighting spirit despite experiences of success. Nucor, to affirm its belief in the importance of its workers, has continued to print the names of employees on its annual reports. Only now the organization has grown so large that even the front cover is used for this purpose. Nucor's workers have always enjoyed generous bonuses based on production levels. The base levels on which such bonuses are calculated have remained unchanged despite significant technology-driven productivity gains.

Entrance of Other Firms

In the beginning, it is usually not clear whether innovative small firms are developing strategies with great potential. However, as their success becomes visible, other competitors, both established corporations and new ventures, may begin to copy their strategies. For example, MCI and AT&T subsequently competed not only with each other, but also with Sprint, Allnet, US Telephone, and SBS. In the meat-packing industry, IBP competed not only against the old-line packers, but also against such firms as MBPXL and Monfort, which were following strategies similar to their own. Suppliers of supercomputers subsequently included not only IBM and Amdahl, but Cray Research and Control Data as well.

The innovative small firm may thus confront a variety of competitors, with different strategies and strengths. Management must anticipate these competitive pressures. This may include being careful not to overextend the firm and developing the financial strength or competitive alliances needed to survive under more difficult conditions. It also means sharpening the distinctive skills which led to their early successes and being careful not to let creeping changes in strategy take the firm away from its core strengths. . . .

CONCLUSIONS

. . . The strategies considered here are niche strategies in the sense that they concentrate on serving the needs of limited groups of customers. They are also "focus strategies" as described by Porter (1980), in the sense of emphasizing lower costs, differentiation, or both, in dealing with a portion of the market. However, contrary to the prevailing thinking in much of the literature, these niche or focus strategies do not limit young firms to markets that are of no interest to leading competitors. Those firms with the right combination of corporate resources and industry opportunity may be able to develop strategies of direct competition which lead to continuing and enviable success.

In no way do we suggest that a direct confrontation strategy is appropriate for all small businesses. The sample considered is small and may not be broadly representative. However, these observations may challenge the dominant perspective and hopefully, invite future entrepreneurs and researchers to think more broadly and aggressively about the distinctive competencies of small and new businesses.

THE MATURE CONTEXT

In this chapter, we focus on one of the more common contexts for today's organizations. Whether we refer to this by its form of operations (usually mass production or the mass provision of services), by the form of structure adopted (machine-like bureaucracy), by the type of environment it prefers (a stable one in a mature industry), or by the specific generic strategy often found there (low cost), the context tends to be common and to give rise to a relatively well-defined configuration.

The readings on what we shall refer to as the *mature* context cover these different aspects and examine some of the problems and opportunities of functioning in this realm. The first reading, on the machine organization, from Mintzberg's work, describes the structure for this context as well as the environment in which it tends to be found, and also investigates some of the social issues surrounding this particular form of organization. This reading also probes the nature of the strategy making process in this context. Here we can see what happens when large organizations accustomed to stability suddenly have to change their strategies dramatically. The careful formal planning, on which they tend to rely so heavily in easier times, seems ill suited to dealing with changes that may require virtual revolutions in their functioning. A section of this reading thus considers what can be the role of planners when their formal procedures fail to come to grips with the needs of strategy making.

A second reading of this chapter probes more deeply into the nature of formal planning. A highly sophisticated piece by Brian Loasby who teaches management at the University of Sterling in the United Kingdom, considers in a balanced way the advantages of formal planning and a number of its dangers.

The third reading is a chapter from Michael Porter's book *Competitive Strategy* on how to deal with the transition to industry maturity. It describes the environment of this context and also probes some of its favored strategies, notably what Porter calls cost leadership.

A particular technique designed for use with this strategy, and the mature context in general, is the subject of the last reading. Called *Cost Dynamics: Scale and Experience Effects* and written by Derek Abell and John Hammond for a marketing textbook, it probes the "experience curve." Developed by the Boston Consulting Group some years ago, this technique became quite popular in the 1970s. Although its limitations are now widely recognized, it still has certain applicability to firms operating in the mature context.

Despite a preference for strategies of low cost in many cases (e.g. Exxon and Matsushita with regard to world networking), the cases will illustrate that other strategies can be pursued as well, including innovation on a large scale (Pilkington or Ford: Team Taurus), differentiation (Honda Motor and Gallo Wineries), aggressive penetration (First Nationwide Financial Corp. and *The New York Times*), automation and strong distribution (IBM (C) and General Motors (B)). Finally there are special exit or defensive strategies which companies like Continental Group and Gallo have to consider. These and other cases offer a wide variety of choice as to the handling of maturity problems.

● THE MACHINE ORGANIZATION*

BY HENRY MINTZBERG

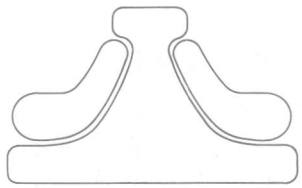

A national post office, a custodial prison, an airline, a giant automobile company, even a small security agency—all these organizations appear to have a number of characteristics in common. Above all, their operating work is routine, the greatest part of it rather simple and repetitive; as a result, their work processes are highly standardized. These characteristics give rise to the machine organizations of our society, structures fine-tuned to run as integrated, regulated, highly bureaucratic machines.

THE BASIC STRUCTURE

A clear configuration of the attributes has appeared consistently in the research: highly specialized, routine operating tasks; very formalized communication throughout the organization; large-size operating units; reliance on the functional

---

* Adapted from *The Structure of Organizations* (Prentice Hall, 1979), Chap. 18 on "The Machine Bureaucracy"; also *Power In and Around Organizations* (Prentice Hall, 1983), Chaps. 18 and 19 on "The Instrument" and "The Closed System"; the material on strategy formation from "Patterns in Strategy Formation," *Management Science* (1978); Does Planning Impede Strategic Thinking? Tracking the Strategies of Air Canada, from 1937–1976" (coauthored with Pierre Brunet and Jim Waters), in R. B. Lamb and P. Shrivastava, eds., *Advances in Strategic Management,* Volume IV (JAI press, 1986); and "The Mind of the Strategist(s)" (coauthored with Jim Waters), in S. Srivastva, ed., *The Executive Mind* (Jossey-Bass, 1983); the section on the role of planning, plans, and planners is drawn from a book in process on strategic planning. A chapter similar to this appeared in *Mintzberg on Management: Inside Our Strange World of Organizations* (Free Press, 1989).

basis for grouping tasks; relatively centralized power for decision making; and an elaborate administrative structure with a sharp distinction between line and staff.

The Operating Core and Administration

The obvious starting point is the operating core, with its highly rationalized work flow. This means that the operating tasks are made simple and repetitive, generally requiring a minimum of skill and training, the latter often taking only hours, seldom more than a few weeks, and usually in-house. This in turn results in narrowly defined jobs and an emphasis on the standardization of work processes for coordination, with activities highly formalized. The workers are left with little discretion, as are their supervisors, who can therefore handle very large spans of control.

To achieve such high regulation of the operating work, the organization has need for an elaborate administrative structure—a fully developed middle-line hierarchy and technostructure—but the two clearly distinguished.

The managers of the middle line have three prime tasks. One is to handle the disturbances that arise in the operating core. The work is so standardized that when things fall through the cracks, conflict flares, because the problems cannot be worked out informally. So it falls to managers to resolve them by direct supervision. Indeed, many problems get bumped up successive steps in the hierarchy until they reach a level of common supervision where they can be resolved by authority (as with a dispute in a company between manufacturing and marketing that may have to be resolved by the chief executive). A second task of the middle-line managers is to work with the staff analysts to incorporate their standards down into the operating units. And a third task is to support the vertical flows in the organization—the elaboration of action plans flowing down the hierarchy and the communication of feedback information back up.

The technostructure must also be highly elaborated. In fact this structure was first identified with the rise of technocratic personnel in early-nineteenth-century industries such as textiles and banking. Because the machine organization depends primarily on the standardization of its operating work for coordination, the technostructure—which houses the staff analysts who do the standardizing—emerges as the key part of the structure. To the line managers may be delegated the formal authority for the operating units, but without the standardizers—the cadre of work-study analysts, schedulers, quality control engineers, planners, budgeters, accountants, operations researchers, and many more—these structures simply could not function. Hence, despite their lack of formal authority, considerable informal power rests with these staff analysts, who standardize everyone else's work. Rules and regulations permeate the entire system: The emphasis on standardization extends well beyond the operating core of the machine organization, and with it follows the analysts' influence.

A further reflection of this formalization of behavior are the sharp divisions of labor all over the machine organization. Job specialization in the operating core and the pronounced formal distinction between line and staff have already been mentioned. In addition, the administrative structure is clearly distinguished from the operating core; unlike the entrepreneurial organization, here managers seldom work alongside operators. And they themselves tend to be organized along functional lines, meaning that each runs a unit that performs a single function in the chain that produces the final outputs. Figure 1 shows this, for example, in the organigram of a large steel company, traditionally machinelike in structure.

All this suggests that the machine organization is a structure with an obsession—namely, control. A control mentality pervades it from top to bottom. At the

FIGURE 1
Organigram of a Large Steel Company

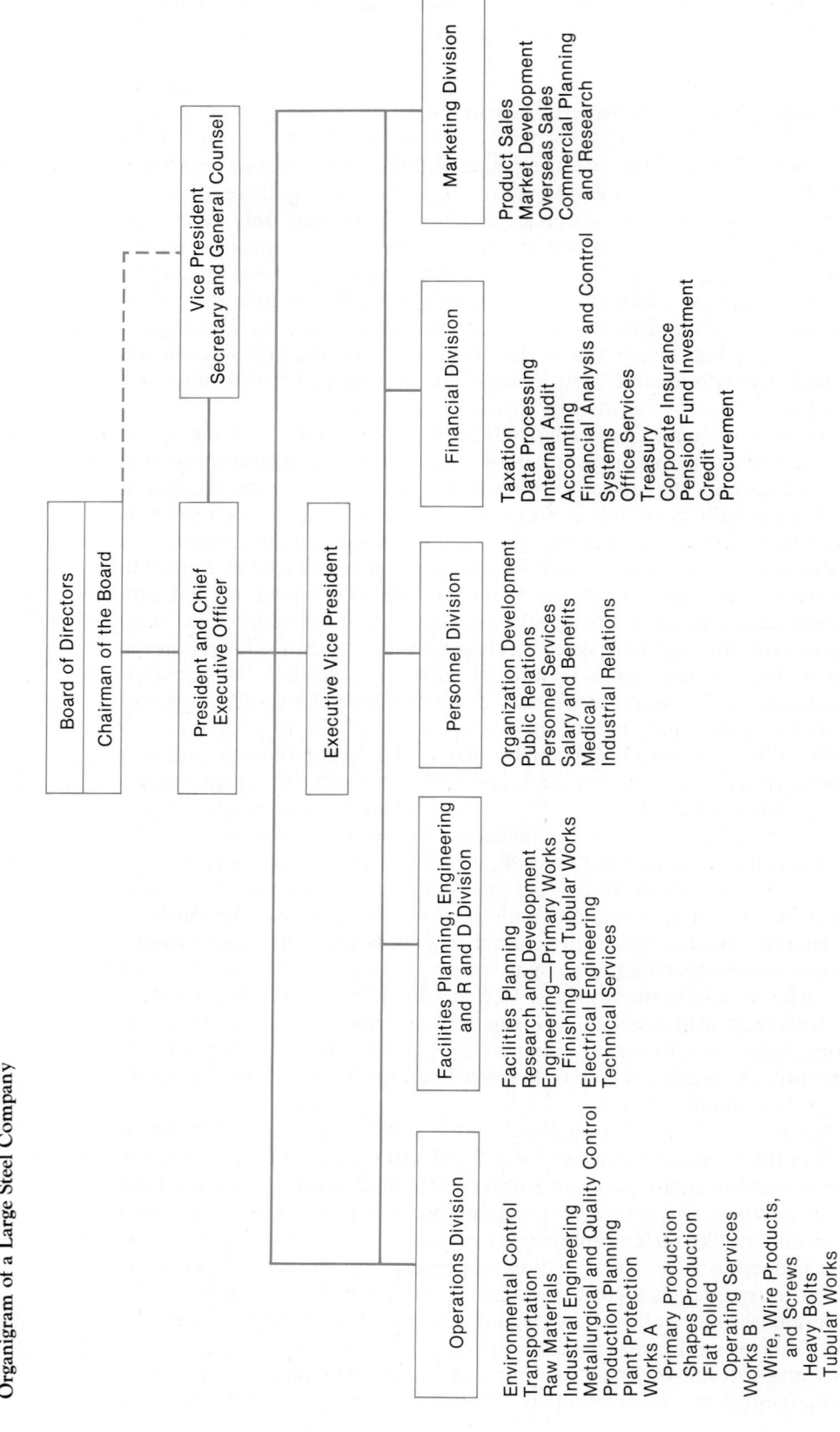

bottom, consider how a Ford Assembly Division general foreman described his work:

> I refer to my watch all the time. I check different items. About every hour I tour my line. About six thirty, I'll tour labor relations to find out who is absent. At seven, I hit the end of the line. I'll check paint, check my scratches and damage. Around ten I'll start talking to all the foremen. I make sure they're all awake. We can't have no holes, no nothing.

And at the top, consider the words of a chief executive:

> When I was president of this big corporation, we lived in a small Ohio town, where the main plant was located. The corporation specified who you could socialize with, and on what level. (His wife interjects: "Who were the wives you could play bridge with."). In a small town they didn't have to keep check on you. Everybody knew. There are certain sets of rules. (Terkel, 1972:186, 406)

The obsession with control reflects two central facts about these organizations. First, attempts are made to eliminate all possible uncertainty, so that the bureaucratic machine can run smoothly, without interruption, the operating core perfectly sealed off from external influence. Second, these are structures ridden with conflict; the control systems are required to contain it. The problem in the machine organization is not to develop an open atmosphere where people can talk the conflicts out, but to enforce a closed, tightly controlled one where the work can get done despite them.

The obsession with control also helps to explain the frequent proliferation of support staff in these organizations. Many of the staff services could be purchased from outside suppliers. But that would expose the machine organization to the uncertainties of the open market. So it "makes" rather than "buys," that is, it envelops as many of the support services as it can within its own structure in order to control them, everything from the cafeteria in the factory to the law office at headquarters.

The Strategic Apex

The managers at the strategic apex of these organizations are concerned in large part with the fine-tuning of their bureaucratic machines. Theirs is a perpetual search for more efficient ways to produce the given outputs.

But not all is strictly improvement of performance. Just keeping the structure together in the face of its conflicts also consumes a good deal of the energy of top management. As noted, conflict is not resolved in the machine organization; rather it is bottled up so that the work can get done. And as in the case of a bottle, the cork is applied at the top: Ultimately, it is the top managers who must keep the lid on the conflicts through their role of handling disturbances. Moreover, the managers of the strategic apex must intervene frequently in the activities of the middle line to ensure that coordination is achieved there. The top managers are the only generalists in the structure, the only managers with a perspective broad enough to see all the functions.

All this leads us to the conclusion that considerable power in the machine organization rests with the managers of the strategic apex. These are, in other words, rather centralized structures: The formal power clearly rests at the top; hierarchy and chain of authority are paramount concepts. But so also does much of the informal power, since that resides in knowledge, and only at the top of the hierarchy does the formally segmented knowledge of the organization come together.

Thus, our introductory figure shows the machine organization with a fully elaborated administrative and support structure—both parts of the staff component being focused on the operating core—together with large units in the operating core but narrower ones in the middle line to reflect the tall hierarchy of authority.

CONDITIONS OF THE MACHINE ORGANIZATION

Work of a machine bureaucratic nature is found, above all, in environments that are simple and stable. The work associated with complex environments cannot be rationalized into simple tasks, and that associated with dynamic environments cannot be predicted, made repetitive, and so standardized.

In addition, the machine configuration is typically found in mature organizations, large enough to have the volume of operating work needed for repetition and standardization, and old enough to have been able to settle on the standards they wish to use. These are the organizations that have seen it all before and have established standard procedures to deal with it. Likewise, machine organizations tend to be identified with technical systems that regulate the operating work, so that it can easily be programmed. Such technical systems cannot be very sophisticated or automated (for reasons that will be discussed later).

Mass production firms are perhaps the best-known machine organizations. Their operating work flows through an integrated chain, open at one end to accept raw materials, and after that functioning as a sealed system that processes them through sequences of standardized operations. Thus, the environment may be stable because the organization has acted aggressively to stabilize it. Giant firms in such industries as transportation, tobacco, and metals are well known for their attempts to influence the forces of supply and demand by the use of advertising, the development of long-term supply contacts, sometimes the establishment of cartels. They also tend to adopt strategies of "vertical integration," that is, extend their production chains at both ends, becoming both their own suppliers and their own customers. In that way they can bring some of the forces of supply and demand within their own planning processes.

Of course, the machine organization is not restricted to large, or manufacturing, or even private enterprise organizations. Small manufacturers—for example producers of discount furniture or paper products—may sometimes prefer this structure because their operating work is simple and repetitive. Many service firms use it for the same reason, such as banks or insurance companies in their retailing activities. Another condition often found with machine organizations is external control. Many government departments, such as post offices and tax collection agencies, are machine bureaucratic not only because their operating work is routine but also because they must be accountable to the public for their actions. Everything they do—treating clients, hiring employees, and so on—must be seen to be fair, and so they proliferate regulations.

Since control is the forte of the machine bureaucracy, it stands to reason that organizations in the business of control—regulatory agencies, custodial prisons, police forces—are drawn to this configuration, sometimes in spite of contradictory conditions. The same is true for the special need for safety. Organizations that fly airplanes or put out fires must minimize the risks they take. Hence they formalize their procedures extensively to ensure that they are carried out to the letter: A fire crew cannot arrive at a burning house and then turn to the chief for orders or discuss informally who will connect the hose and who will go up the ladder.

Control raises another issue about machine organizations. Being so pervasively regulated, they themselves can easily be controlled externally, as the *instruments* of outside influencers. In contrast, however, their obsession with control runs not only up the hierarchy but beyond, to control of their own environments, so that they can become *closed systems* immune to external influence. From the perspective of power, the instrument and the closed system constitute two main types of machine organizations.

In our terms, the instrument form of machine organization is dominated by one external influencer or by a group of them acting in concert. In the "closely held" corporation, the dominant influencer is the outside owner; in some prisons, it is a community concerned with the custody rather than the rehabilitation of prisoners.

Outside influencers render an organization their instrument by appointing the chief executive, charging that person with the pursuit of clear goals (ideally quantifiable, such as return on investment or prisoner escape measures), and then holding the chief responsible for performance. That way outsiders can control an organization without actually having to manage it. And such control, by virtue of the power put in the hands of the chief executive and the numerical nature of the goals, acts to centralize and bureaucratize the internal structure, in other words, to drive it to the machine form.

In contrast to this, Charles Perrow, the colorful and outspoken organizational sociologist, does not quite see the machine organization as anyone's instrument:

> Society is adaptive to organizations, to the large, powerful organizations controlled by a few, often overlapping, leaders. To see these organizations as adaptive to a "turbulent," dynamic, very changing environment is to indulge in fantasy. The environment of most powerful organizations is well controlled by them, quite stable, and made up of other organizations with similar interests, or ones they control. (1972:199)

Perrow is, of course, describing the closed system form of machine organization, the one that uses its bureaucratic procedures to seal itself off from external control and control others instead. It controls not only its own people but its environment as well: perhaps its suppliers, customers, competitors, even government and owners too.

Of course, autonomy can be achieved not only by controlling others (for example, buying up customers and suppliers in so-called vertical integration) but simply by avoiding the control of others. Thus, for example, closed system organizations sometimes form cartels with ostensible competitors or, less blatantly, diversify markets to avoid dependence on particular customers, finance internally to avoid dependence on particular financial groups, and even buy back their own shares to weaken the influence of their own owners. Key to being a closed system is to ensure wide dispersal, and therefore pacification, of all groups of potential external influence.

What goals does the closed system organization pursue? Remember that to sustain centralized bureaucracy the goals should be operational, ideally quantifiable. What operational goals enable an organization to serve itself, as a system closed to external influence? The most obvious answer is growth. Survival may be an indispensable goal and efficiency a necessary one, but beyond those what really matters here is making the system larger. Growth serves the system by providing greater rewards for its insiders—bigger empires for managers to run or fancier pri-

635

vate jets to fly, greater programs for analysts to design, even more power for unions to wield by virtue of having more members. (The unions may be external influencers, but the management can keep them passive by allowing them more of the spoils of the closed system.) Thus the classic closed system machine organization, the large, widely held industrial corporation, has long been described as oriented far more to growth than to the maximization of profit per se (Galbraith, 1967).

Of course, the closed system form of machine organization can exist outside the private sector too, for example in the fundraising agency that, relatively free to external control, becomes increasingly charitable to itself (as indicated by the plushness of its managers' offices), the agricultural or retail cooperative that ignores those who collectively own it, even government that becomes more intent on serving itself than the citizens for which it supposedly exists.

The communist state, at least up until very recently, seemed to fit all the characteristics of the closed system bureaucracy. It had no dominant external influencer (at least in the case of the Soviet Union, if not the other East European states, which were its "instruments"). And the population to which it is ostensibly responsible had to respond to its own plethora of rules and regulations. Its election procedures, traditionally offering a choice of one, were similar to those for the directors of the "widely held" Western corporation. The government's own structure was heavily bureaucratic, with a single hierarchy of authority and a very elaborate technostructure, ranging from state planners to KGB agents. (As James Worthy [1959:77] noted, Frederick Taylor's "Scientific Management had its fullest flowering not in America but in Soviet Russia.") All significant resources were the property of the state—the collective system—not the individual. And, as in other closed systems, the administrators tend to take the lion's share of the benefits.

SOME ISSUES ASSOCIATED WITH THE MACHINE ORGANIZATION

No structure has evoked more heated debate than the machine organization. As Michel Crozier, one of its most eminent students, has noted,

> On the one hand, most authors consider the bureaucratic organization to be the embodiment of rationality in the modern world, and, as such, to be intrinsically superior to all other possible forms of organizations. On the other hand, many authors—often the same ones—consider it a sort of Leviathan, preparing the enslavement of the human race. (1964:176)

Max Weber, who first wrote about this form of organization, emphasized its rationality; in fact, the word *machine* comes directly from his writings (see Gerth and Mills, 1958). A machine is certainly precise; it is also reliable and easy to control; and it is efficient—at least when restricted to the job it has been designed to do. Those are the reasons many organizations are structured as machine bureaucracies. When an integrated set of simple, repetitive tasks must be performed precisely and consistently by human beings, this is the most efficient structure—indeed, the only conceivable one.

But in these same advantages of machinelike efficiency lie all the disadvantages of this configuration. Machines consist of mechanical parts; organizational structures also include human beings—and that is where the analogy breaks down.

James Worthy, when he was an executive of Sears, wrote a penetrating and scathing criticism of the machine organization in his book *Big Business and Free Men.* Worthy traced the root of the human problems in these structures to the "scientific management" movement led by Frederick Taylor that swept America early in this century. Worthy acknowledged Taylor's contribution to efficiency, narrowly defined. Worker initiative did not, however, enter into his efficiency equation. Taylor's pleas to remove "all possible brain work" from the shop floor also removed all possible initiative from the people who worked there: the "machine has no will of its own. Its parts have no urge to independent action. Thinking, direction—even purpose—must be provided from outside or above." This had the "consequence of destroying the meaning of work itself," which has been "fantastically wasteful for industry and society," resulting in excessive absenteeism, high worker turnover, sloppy workmanship, costly strikes, and even outright sabotage (1959:67, 79, 70). Of course, there are people who like to work in highly structured situations. But increasing numbers do not, at least not *that* highly structured.

Taylor was fond of saying, "In the past the man has been first; in the future the system must be first" (in Worthy 1959:73). Prophetic words, indeed. Modern man seems to exist for his systems; many of the organizations he created to serve him have come to enslave him. The result is that several of what Victor Thompson (1961) has called "bureaupathologies"—dysfunctional behaviors of these structures—reinforce each other to form a vicious circle in the machine organization. The concentration on means at the expense of ends, the mistreatment of clients, the various manifestations of worker alienation—all lead to the tightening of controls on behavior. The implicit motto of the machine organization seems to be, "When in doubt, control." All problems have to be solved by the turning of the technocratic screws. But since that is what caused the bureaupathologies in the first place, increasing the controls serves only to magnify the problems, leading to the imposition of further controls, and so on.

Coordination Problems in the Administrative Center

Since the operating core of the machine organization is not designed to handle conflict, many of the human problems that arise there spill up and over, into the administrative structure.

It is one of the ironies of the machine configuration that to achieve the control it requires, it must mirror the narrow specialization of its operating core in its administrative structure (for example, differentiating marketing managers from manufacturing managers, much as salesmen are differentiated from factory workers). This, in turn, means problems of communication and coordination. The fact is that the administrative structure of the machine organization is also ill suited to the resolution of problems through mutual adjustment. All the communication barriers in these structures—horizontal, vertical, status, line/staff—impede informal communication among managers and with staff people. "Each unit becomes jealous of its own prerogatives and finds ways to protect itself against the pressure or encroachments of others" (Worthy, 1950:176). Thus narrow functionalism not only impedes coordination; it also encourages the building of private empires, which tends to produce top-heavy organizations that can be more concerned with the political games to be won than with the clients to be served.

Adaptation Problems in the Strategic Apex

But if mutual adjustment does not work in the administrative center—generating more political heat than cooperative light—how does the machine organization resolve its coordination problems? Instinctively, it tries standardization, for example, by tightening job descriptions or proliferating rules. But standardization is not suited to handling the nonroutine problems of the administrative center. Indeed, it only aggravates them, undermining the influence of the line managers and increasing the conflict. So to reconcile these coordination problems, the machine organization is left with only one coordinating mechanism, direct supervision from above. Specifically, nonroutine coordination problems between units are "bumped" up the line hierarchy until they reach a common level of supervision, often at the top of the structure. The result can be excessive centralization of power, which in turn produces a host of other problems. In effect, just as the human problems in the operating core become coordination problems in the administrative center, so too do the coordination problems in the administrative center become adaptation problems at the strategic apex. Let us take a closer look at these by concluding with a discussion of strategic change in the machine configuration.

STRATEGY FORMATION IN THE MACHINE ORGANIZATION

Strategy in the machine organization is supposed to emanate from the top of the hierarchy, where the perspective is broadest and the power most focused. All the relevant information is to be sent up the hierarchy, in aggregated, MIS-type form, there to be formulated into integrated strategy (with the aid of the technostructure). Implementation then follows, with the intended strategies sent down the hierarchy to be turned into successively more elaborated programs and action plans. Notice the clear division of labor assumed between the formulators at the top and the implementors down below, based on the assumption of perfectly deliberate strategy produced through a process of planning.

That is the theory. The practice has been shown to be another matter. Drawing on our strategy research at McGill University, we shall consider first what planning really proved to be in one machinelike organization, how it may in fact have impeded strategic thinking in a second, and how a third really did change its strategy. From there we shall consider the problems of strategic change in machine organizations and their possible resolution.

Planning as Programming in a Supermarket Chain

What really is the role of formal planning? Does it produce original strategies? Let us return to the case of Steinberg's in the later years of its founder, as large size drove this retailing chain toward the machine form, and as is common in that form, toward a planning mode of management at the expense of entrepreneurship.

One event in particular encouraged the start of planning at Steinberg's: the company's entry into capital markets in 1953. Months before it floated its first bond issue (stock, always nonvoting, came later), Sam Steinberg boasted to a newspaper reporter that "not a cent of any money outside the family is invested in the company." And asked about future plans, he replied: "Who knows? We will try to go everywhere there seems to be a need for us." A few months later he announced a $5 million debt issue and with it a $15 million five-year expansion program, one new store every two months for a total of thirty, the doubling of sales, new stores to average double the size of existing ones.

What happened in those ensuing months was Sam Steinberg's realization, after the opening of Montreal's first shopping center, that he needed to enter the shopping center business himself to protect his supermarket chain and that he could not do so with the company's traditional methods of short-term and internal financing. And, of course, no company is allowed to go to capital markets without a plan. You can't just say: "I'm Sam Steinberg and I'm good," though that was really the issue. In a "rational" society, you have to plan (or at least appear to do so).

But what exactly was that planning? One thing for certain: It did not formulate a strategy. Sam Steinberg already had that. What planning did was justify, elaborate, and articulate the strategy that already existed in Sam Steinberg's mind. Planning operationalized his strategic vision, programmed it. It gave order to that vision, imposing form on it to comply with the needs of the organization and its environment. Thus, planning followed the strategy-making process, which had been essentially entrepreneurial.

But its effect on that process was not incidental. By specifying and articulation the vision, planning constrained it and rendered it less flexible. Sam Steinberg retained formal control of the company to the day of his death. But his control over strategy did not remain so absolute. The entrepreneur, by keeping his vision personal, is able to adapt it at will to a changing environment. But by being forced to program it, the leader loses that flexibility. The danger, ultimately, is that the planning mode forces out the entrepreneurial one; procedure replaces vision. As its structure became more machinelike, Steinberg's required planning in the form of strategic programming. But that planing also accelerated the firm's transition toward the machine form of organization.

Is there, then, such a thing as "strategic planning"? I suspect not. To be more explicit, I do not find that major new strategies are formulated through any formal procedure. Organizations that rely on formal planning procedures to formulate strategies seem to extrapolate existing strategies, perhaps with marginal changes in them, or else copy the strategies of other organizations. This came out most clearly in another of our McGill studies.

Planning as an Impediment to Strategic Thinking in an Airline

From about the mid-1950s, Air Canada engaged heavily in planning. Once the airline was established, particularly once it developed its basic route structure, a number of factors drove it strongly to the planning mode. Above all was the need for coordination, both of flight schedules with aircraft, crews, and maintenance, and of the purchase of expensive aircraft with the structure of the route system. (Imagine someone calling out in the hangar: "Hey, Fred, this guy says he has two 747s for us; do you know who ordered them?") Safety was another factor: The intense need for safety in the air breeds a mentality of being very careful about what the organization does on the ground, too. This is the airlines' obsession with control. Other factors included the lead times inherent in key decisions, such as ordering new airplanes or introducing new routes, the sheer cost of the capital equipment, and the size of the organization. You don't run an intricate system like an airline, necessarily very machinelike, without a great deal of formal planning.

But what we found to be the consequence of planning at Air Canada was the absence of a major reorientation of strategy during our study period (up to the mid-1970s). Aircraft certainly changed—they became larger and faster—but the basic route system did not, nor did markets. Air Canada gave only marginal attention, for example, to cargo, charter, and shuttle operations. Formal planning, in our view, impeded strategic thinking.

The problem is that planning, too, proceeds from the machine perspective, much as an assembly line or a conventional machine produces a product. It all depends on the decomposition of analysis: You split the process into a series of steps or component parts, specify each, and then by following the specifications in sequence you get the desired product. There is a fallacy in this, however. Assembly lines and conventional machines produce standardized products, while planning is supposed to produce a novel strategy. It is as if the machine is supposed to design the machine; the planning machine is expected to create the original blueprint—the strategy. To put this another way, planning is analysis oriented to decomposition, while strategy making depends on synthesis oriented to integration. That is why the term "strategic planning" has proved to be an oxymoron.

Roles of Planning, Plans, Planners

If planning does not create strategy, then what purpose does it serve? We have suggested a role above, which has to do with the programming of strategies already created in other ways. This is shown in Figure 2, coming out of a box labeled strategy formation—meant to represent what is to planning a mysterious "black box." But if planning is restricted to programming strategy, plans and planners nonetheless have other roles in play, shown in Figure 2 and discussed alongside that of planning itself.

FIGURE 2
Specific Roles of Planning, Plans, Planners

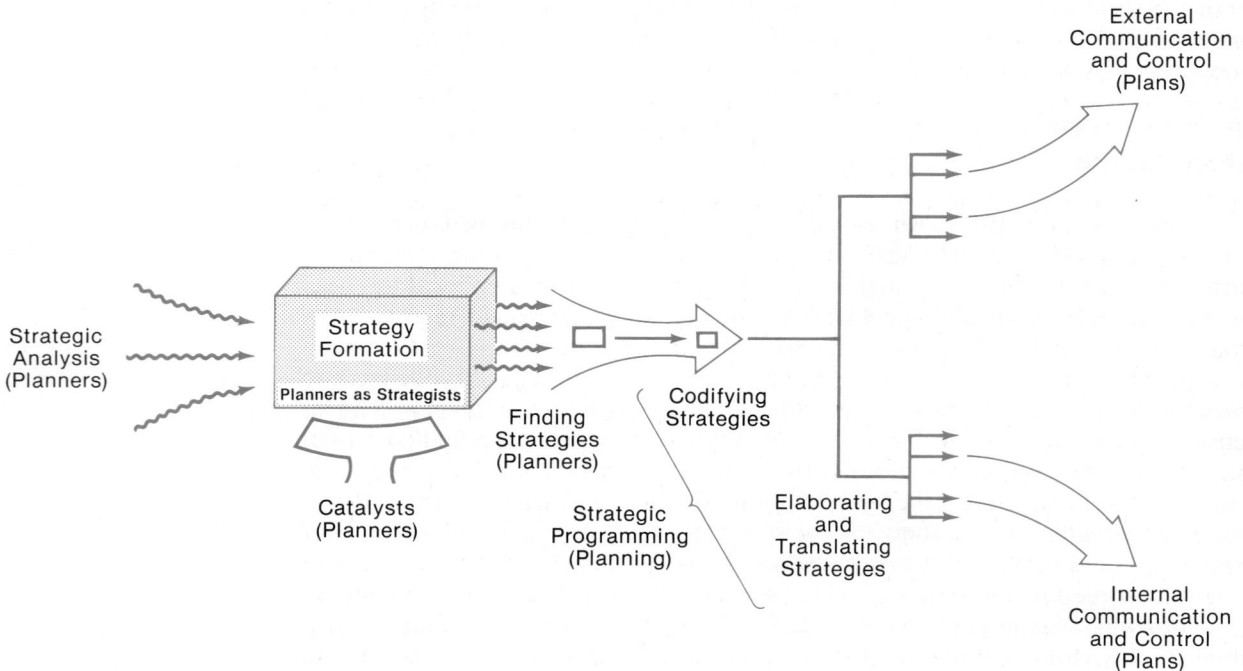

Role of Planning: Why do organizations engage in formal planning? The answer seems to be: not to create strategies, but to program the strategies they already have, that is, to elaborate and operationalize the consequences of those strategies formally. We should really say that *effective* organizations so engage in planning, at least when they require the formalized implementation of their strategies. Thus strategy is not the *consequence* of planning but its starting point. Planning helps to translate the intended strategies into realized ones, taking the first step that leads ultimately to implementation.

This *strategic programming,* as it might properly be labeled, can be considered to involve a series of steps, namely the *codification* of given strategy, including its clarification and articulation, the *elaboration* of that strategy into substrategies, ad hoc action programs, and plans of various kinds, and the *translation* of those substrategies, programs, and plans into routine budgets and objectives. In these steps, we see planning as an analytical process that takes over after the synthesis of strategic formation is completed.

Thus formal planning properly belongs in the *implementation* of strategy, not in its formulation. But it should be emphasized that strategic programming makes sense when viable intended strategies are available, in other words when the world is expected to hold still while these strategies unfold, so that formulation can logically precede implementation, and when the organization that does the implementing in fact requires clearly codified and elaborated strategies. In other circumstances, strategic programming can do organizations harm by preempting the flexibility that managers and others may need to respond to changes in the environment, or to their own internal processes of learning.

Roles of Plans: If planning is programming, then plans clearly serve two roles. They are a medium for communication and a device for control. Both roles draw on the analytical character of plans, namely, that they represent strategies in decomposed and articulated form, if not quantified then often at least quantifiable.

Why program strategy? Most obviously for coordination, to ensure that everyone in the organization pulls in the same direction, a direction that may have to be specified as precisely as possible. In Air Canada, to use our earlier example, that means linking the acquisition of new aircraft with the particular routes that are to be flown, and scheduling crews and planes to show up when the flights are to take off, and so on. Plans, as they emerge from strategic programming as programs, schedules, budgets, and so on, can be prime media to communicate not just strategic intention but also the role each individual must play to realize it.

Plans, as communication media, inform people of intended strategy and its consequences. But as control devices they can go further, specifying what role departments and individuals must play in helping to realize strategy and then comparing that with performance in order to feed control information back into the strategy-making process.

Plans can help to effect control in a number of ways. The most obvious is control of the strategy itself. Indeed what has long paraded under the label of "strategy planning" has probably had more to do with "strategic control" than many people may realize. Strategic control has to do with keeping organizations on their strategic tracks: to ensure the realization of intended strategy, its implementation as expected, with resources appropriately allocated. But there is more to strategic control than this. Another aspect includes the assessment of the realization of strategies in the first place, namely, whether the patterns realized corresponded to the intentions specified beforehand. In other words, strategic control must assess behavior as well as performance. Then the more routine and traditional form of control can come in to consider whether the strategies that were in fact realized proved effective.

Roles of Planners: Planners, of course, play key roles in planning (namely, strategic programming), and in using the resulting plans for purposes of communication and control. But many of the most important things planners do have little to do with planning or even plans per se. Three roles seem key here.

First, planners can play a role in finding strategies. This may seem curious, but if strategies really do emerge in organizations, then planners can help to identify the patterns that are becoming strategies, so that consideration can be given to formalizing them, that is, making them deliberate. Of course, finding the strategies of competitors—for assessment and possible modified adoption—is also important here.

Second, planners play the roles of analysts, carrying out ad hoc studies to feed into the black box of strategy making. Indeed, one could argue that this is precisely what Michael Porter proposes with his emphasis on industry and competitive analysis. The ad hoc nature of such studies should, however, be emphasized because they feed into a strategy-making process that is itself irregular, proceeding on no schedule and following no standard sequence of steps. Indeed, regularity in the planning process can interfere with strategic thinking, which must be flexible, responsive, and creative.

The third role of the planner is as a catalyst. This refers not to the traditional role long promoted in the literature of selling formal planning as some kind of religion, but to encourage strategic *thinking* throughout the organization. Here the planner encourages *informal* strategy making, trying to get others to think about the future in a creative way. He or she does not enter the block box of strategy making so much as ensure that the box is occupied with active line managers.

A Planner For Each Side of the Brain: We have discussed various roles for planning, plans, and planners, summarized around the block box of strategy formation in Figure 2. These roles suggest two different orientations for planners.

On one hand (so to speak), the planner must be a highly analytic, convergent type of thinker, dedicated to bringing order to the organization. Above all, this planner programs intended strategies and sees to it that they are communicated clearly and used for purposes of control. He or she also carries out studies to ensure that the managers concerned with strategy formation take into account the necessary hard data that they may be inclined to miss and that the strategies they formulate are carefully and systematically evaluated before they are implemented.

On the other hand, there is another type of planner, less conventional a creative, divergent thinker, rather intuitive, who seeks to open up the strategy-making process. As a "soft analyst," he or she tends to conduct "quick and dirty" studies, to find strategies in strange places, and to encourage others to think strategically. This planner is inclined toward the intuitive processes identified with the brain's right hemisphere. We might call him or her a *left-handed planner*. Some organizations need to emphasize one type of planner, others the other type. But most complex organizations probably need some of both.

Strategic Change in an Automobile Firm

Given planning itself is not strategic, how does the planning-oriented machine bureaucracy change its strategy when it has to? Volkswagenwerk was an organization that had to. We interpreted its history from 1934 to 1974 as one long cycle of a single strategic perspective. The original "people's car," the famous "Beetle," was conceived by Ferdinand Porsche; the factory to produce it was built just before the war but did not go into civilian automobile production until after. In 1948, a man named Heinrich Nordhoff was given control of the devastated plant and began the rebuilding of it, as well as of the organization and the strategy itself, rounding out Porsche's original conception. The firm's success was dramatic.

By the late 1950s, however, problems began to appear. Demand in Germany was moving away from the Beetle. The typically machine-bureaucratic response was not to rethink the basic strategy—"it's okay" was the reaction—but rather to graft another piece onto it. A new automobile model was added, larger than the Beetle but with a similar no-nonsense approach to motoring, again air-cooled with the engine in the back. Volkswagenwerk added position but did not change perspective.

But that did not solve the basic problem, and by the mid-1960s the company was in crisis. Nordhoff, who had resisted strategic change, died in office and was replaced by a lawyer from outside the business. The company then underwent a frantic search for new models, designing, developing, or acquiring a whole host of them with engines in the front, middle, and rear; air and water cooled; front- and rear-wheel drive. To paraphrase the humorist Stephen Leacock, Volkswagenwerk leaped onto its strategic horse and rode off in all directions. Only when another leader came in, a man steeped in the company and the automobile business, did the firm consolidate itself around a new strategic perspective, based on the stylish front-wheel drive, water-cooled designs of one of its acquired firms, and thereby turn its fortunes around.

What this story suggests, first of all, is the great force of bureaucratic momentum in the machine organization. Even leaving planning aside, the immense effort of producing and marketing a new line of automobiles locks a company into a certain posture. But here the momentum was psychological, too. Nordhoff, who had been the driving force behind the great success of the organization, became a major liability when the environment demanded change. Over the years, he too had been captured by bureaucratic momentum. Moreover, the uniqueness and tight integration of Volkswagenwerk's strategy—we labeled it *gestalt*—impeded strategic change. Change an element of a tightly integrated gestalt and it *dis*integrates. Thus does success eventually breed failure.

Bottleneck at the Top

Why the great difficulty in changing strategy in the machine organization? Here we take up that question and show how changes generally have to be achieved in a different configuration, if at all.

As discussed earlier, unanticipated problems in the machine organization tend to get bumped up the hierarchy. When these are few, which means conditions are relatively stable, things work smoothly enough. But in times of rapid change, just when new strategies are called for, the number of such problems magnifies, resulting in a bottleneck at the top, where senior managers get overloaded. And that tends either to impede strategic change or else to render it ill considered.

A major part of the problem is information. Senior managers face an organization decomposed into parts, like a machine itself. Marketing information comes up one channel, manufacturing information up another, and so on. Somehow it is the senior managers themselves who must integrate all that information. But the very machine bureaucratic premise of separating the administration of work from the doing of it means that the top managers often lack the intimate, detailed knowledge of issues necessary to effect such an integration. In essence, the necessary power is at the top of the structure, but the necessary knowledge is often at the bottom.

Of course, there is a machinelike solution to that problem too—not surprisingly in the form of a system. It is called a management information system, or MIS, and what it does is combine all the necessary information and package it neatly so that top managers can be informed about what is going on—the perfect solution for the overloaded executive. At least in theory.

Unfortunately, a number of real-world problems arise in the MIS. For one thing, in the tall administrative hierarchy of the machine organization, information must pass through many levels before it reaches the top. Losses take place at each one. Good news gets highlighted while bad news gets blocked on the way up. And "soft" information, so necessary for strategy information, cannot easily pass through, while much of the hard MIS-type information arrives only slowly. In a stable environment, the manager may be able to wait; in a rapidly changing one, he or she cannot. The president wants to be told right away that the firm's most important customer was seen playing golf yesterday with a main competitor, not to find out six months later in the form of a drop in a sales report. Gossip, hearsay, speculation—the softest kinds of information—warn the manager of impeding problems; the MIS all too often records for posterity ones that have already been felt. The manager who depends on an MIS in a changing environment generally finds himself or herself out of touch.

The obvious solution for top managers is to bypass the MIS and set up their own informal information systems, networks of contacts that bring them the rich, tangible, instant information they need. But that violates the machine organization's presuppositions of formality and respect for the chain of authority. Also, that takes the managers' time, the lack of which caused the bottleneck in the first place. So a fundamental dilemma faces the top managers of the machine organization as a result of its very own design: in times of change, when they most need the time to inform themselves, the system overburdens them with other pressures. They are thus reduced to acting superficially, with inadequate, abstract information.

The Formulation/Implementation Dichotomy

The essential problem lies in one of the chief tenets of the machine organization, that strategy formation must be sharply separated from strategy implementation. One is thought out at the top, the other then acted out lower down. For this to work assume two conditions: first, that the formulator has full and sufficient information, and second, that the world will hold still, or at least change in predictable ways, during the implementation, so that there is no need for *re*formulation.

Now consider why the organization needs a new strategy in the first place. It is because its world has changed in an unpredictable way, indeed may continue to do so. We have just seen how the machine bureaucratic structure tends to violate the first condition—it misinforms the senior manager during such times of change. And when change continues in an unpredictable way (or at least the world unfolds in a way not yet predicted by an ill-informed management), then the second condition is violated too—it hardly makes sense to lock in by implementation a strategy that does not reflect changes in the world around it.

What all this amounts to is a need to collapse the formulation/implementation dichotomy precisely when the strategy of machine bureaucracy must be changed. This can be done in one of two ways.

In one case, the formulator implements. In other words, power is concentrated at the top, not only for creating the strategy but also for implementing it, step by step, in a personalized way. The strategist is put in close personal touch with the situation at hand (more commonly a strategist is appointed who has or can develop that touch) so that he or she can, on one hand, be properly informed and, on the other, control the implementation en route in order to reformulate when necessary. This, of course, describes the entrepreneurial configuration, at least at the strategic apex.

In the other case, the implementers formulate. In other words, power is concentrated lower down, where the necessary information resides. As people who are naturally in touch with the specific situations at hand take individual actions—approach new customers, develop new products, et cetera—patterns form, in other words, strategies emerge. And this describes the innovative configuration, where strategic initiatives often originate in the grass roots of the organization, and then are championed by managers at middle levels who integrate them with one another or with existing strategies in order to gain their acceptance by senior management.

We conclude, therefore, that the machine configuration is ill suited to change its fundamental strategy, that the organization must in effect change configuration temporarily in order to change strategy. Either it reverts to the entrepreneurial form, to allow a single leader to develop vision (or proceed with one developed earlier), or else it overlays an innovative form on its conventional structure (for example, creates an informed network of lateral teams and task forces) so that the necessary strategies can emerge. The former can obviously function faster than the latter; that is why it tends to be used for drastic *turnaround,* while the latter tends to proceed by the slower process of *revitalization.* (Of course, quick turnaround may be necessary because there has been no slow revitalization.) In any event, both are characterized by a capacity to *learn*—that is the essence of the entrepreneurial and innovative configurations, in one case learning centralized for the simpler context, in the other, decentralized for the more complex one. The machine configuration is not so characterized.

This, however, should come as no surprise. After all, machines are specialized instruments, designed for productivity, not for adaptation. In Hunt's (1970) words, machine bureaucracies are performance systems, not problem-solving ones. Efficiency is their forte, not innovation. An organization cannot put blinders on its personnel and then expect peripheral vision. Managers here are rewarded for cutting costs and improving standards, not for taking risks and ignoring procedures. Change makes a mess of the operating systems: change one link in a carefully coupled system, and the the whole chain must be reconceived. Why, then, should we be surprised when our bureaucratic machines fail to adapt?

Of course, it is fair to ask why we spend so much time trying to make them adapt. After all, when an ordinary machine becomes redundant, we simply scrap it, happy that it served us for as long and as well as it did. Converting it to another use generally proves more expensive than simply starting over. I suspect the same is often true for bureaucratic machines. But here, of course, the context is social and political. Mechanical parts don't protest, nor do displaced raw materials. Workers, suppliers, and customers do, however, protest the scrapping of organizations, for obvious reasons. But that the cost of this is awfully high in a society of giant machine organizations will be the subject of the final chapter of this book.

Strategic Revolutions in Machine Organizations

Machine organizations do sometimes change, however, at times effectively but more often it would seem at great cost and pain. The lucky ones are able to overlay an innovative structure for periodic revitalization, while many of the other survivors somehow manage to get turned around in entrepreneurial fashion.

Overall, the machine organizations seem to follow what my colleagues Danny Miller and Peter Friesen (1984) call a "quantum theory" of organization change. They pursue their set strategies through long periods of stability (naturally occurring or created by themselves as closed systems), using planning and other procedures to do so efficiently. Periodically these are interrupted by short bursts of change, which Miller and Friesen characterize as "strategic revolutions" (although another colleague, Mihaela Firsirotu [1985], perhaps better labels it "strategic turn-around as cultural revolution").

Organization Taking Precedence in the Machine Organization

To conclude, as shown in Figure 3, it is organization—with its systems and procedures, its planning and its bureaucratic momentum—that takes precedence over leadership and environment in the machine configuration. Environment fits organization, either because the organization has slotted itself into a context that matches its procedures, or else because it has forced the environment to do so. And leadership generally falls into place too, supporting the organization, indeed often becoming part of its bureaucratic momentum.

This generally works effectively, though hardly nonproblematically, at least in times of stability. But in times of change, efficiency becomes ineffective and the organization will falter unless it can find a different way to organize for adaptation.

All of this is another way of saying that the machine organization is a configuration, a species, like the others, suited to its own context but ill suited to others. But unlike the others, it is the dominant configuration in our specialized societies. As long as we demand inexpensive and so necessarily standardized goods and services, and as long as people continue to be more efficient than real machines at providing them, and remain willing to do so, then the machine organization will remain with us—and so will all its problems.

FIGURE 3
Organization Takes Precedence

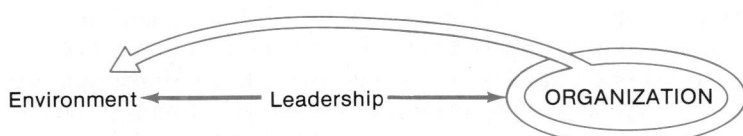

Environment ← Leadership → ORGANIZATION

• LONG-RANGE FORMAL PLANNING IN PERSPECTIVE*

BY BRIAN J. LOASBY

Planning has become a fashionable subject in American management literature, and shows some signs of becoming a fashionable managerial preoccupation in Britain. But the word 'planning' is currently used in so many and various senses that it is in some danger of degenerating into an emotive noise. . . . instead of succumbing to the slogan that "The Future Is Planning," [1] let us attempt to restore some content to the idea by examining the purposes of a formal procedure for long-range planning. . . .

---

* Originally published in *The Journal of Management Studies* (October 1967). Copyright © 1967 *The Journal of Management Studies;* reprinted by permission of the publishers.
[1]"The Past is History . . . The Future is Planning" is the title of an article (Rickard, 1965).

The basic question in considering any sort of planning is: why should a firm attempt to look into the future? Why not wait until it arrives? There seem to be three basic reasons.

The first reason for looking into the future in a systematic way is to understand the future implications of present decisions. What must a firm be prepared to do next year in order to gain the full advantage from what it decides to do now; what will be the effect of its current choice on the range of options available to it in the future; what problems may be created later on by choosing a particular course of action now? These questions need to be asked on a project-by-project basis; but the major advantage of a systematic procedure is that it also requires various projects to be looked at simultaneously. This is important if individual projects have important "external effects," that is, if one project is likely to assist or impede another—whether by their combined effects on the demand for the firm's resources (or the efficiency with which they are used), or by their effects outside the firm. The process by which two or more projects assist each other has been christened synergy (Ansoff, 1965:75); perhaps the opposite process by which they impede each other could be called allergy. It is hard to imagine a situation in which such effects are completely absent; if they are significant, then the agenda for considering one project is not wide enough unless it includes the implications of competitive or complementary projects. A formal procedure, by informing various levels and various sections of the firm of what other levels and other sections are proposing to do, and requiring such information to be taken into account when decisions are made, may be the most effective way of securing the necessary width.

The second reason for looking into the future in a systematic way is in a sense the obverse of the first. As well as considering the future implications of present decisions, it is necessary to examine the present implications of the future events. The question here is: 'What needs to be decided now in order to be prepared for what is expected to happen later on?' If the first question is concerned with the width of the agenda, the second is concerned with its length. When James P. McFarland of General Mills says that "effective long-range planning will probably be more useful in making problems apparent than in solving them"[2] he is pointing to the second purpose of looking into the future in a formal kind of way. The systematic attempt to forecast the future should help to reveal problems in time to anticipate them.

The future implications of present decisions and the present implications of future events cannot, obviously, be thoroughly considered every day; but without some specific motivation and mechanism they may never be adequately considered at all. The third reason for looking into the future in a systematic way is to provide such motivation and such a mechanism. The formal planning process should require an explicit review of the assumptions which underlie the limited agendas which are necessarily used for day-to-day decisions, in order to reduce the danger that "what look like rational decisions under limited agendas . . . (may) turn out to be disastrous." (Boulding, 1966:167).

Too many major issues, though obviously important, seem easily postponable in favor of immediate minor problems; they are therefore liable to be postponed either until they are decided by default, or, at best, until they have to be resolved by improvisation instead of by thoughtful and wide-ranging study. The

---

[2] James P. McFarland, "Planning and Control at General Mills," unpublished lecture notes, Harvard Business School, Cambridge, MA.

formal planning process should ensure an adequate commitment of management resources to these issues, and a commitment in time to allow such study. It should encourage the proper exploration of a range of genuine options, not merely a single proposal. A time to make choices is a time to offer alternatives: the final decision maker, of course, has the power to veto, but the power of veto is a very limited form of the power to choose.

It is not always easy for a manager to combine efficient day-to-day operation of a system with the review and redesign of that system; that he should be encouraged and assisted to combine them is clearly desirable for the reasons already given. There is another reason: this exercise of both widening and lengthening his agenda is the part of a manager's job that is most relevant to the requirements of a higher position, and is thus particularly useful in preparing him for greater responsibilities and in indicating his capacity to undertake them.

POTENTIAL DANGERS OF FORMAL PLANNING

It should be emphasized that the purposes identified so far all relate to present decisions for present action. ("I use long-range planning," says a senior I.C.I. manager, "to decide what to do tomorrow.") They imply no commitment to any future action, and do not in themselves require any planning document to be kept after the immediate decisions have been made. Short-term plans will presumably be prepared in the normal budgeting process, and performance will be evaluated against these. Why should managers be required to make decisions now about action to be taken in the future?

One obvious reason is that a comparison of performance with plan may be useful in revealing possible problems or opportunities—in other words, as a means of getting topics on the agenda. This is clearly useful in itself, though one must remember the danger with any incomplete automatic warning system—that it tends to divert attention from the danger that it does not signal.

Another possible reason is to secure a manager's commitment to an objective. But one must be very careful here. Commitment to making a proper job of today's decisions, based on careful and imaginative evaluation of their future implications, is certainly desirable. Some commitment to next year's plans may be desirable too—but not unquestioning commitment, because conditions may change. It is far from clear that any commitment that is at all precise is desirable beyond that. The fact that a firm should not, for example, start to develop a new product unless it is, at the time of the decision, prepared to launch a marketing effort at the appropriate time does not mean that is should decide now to launch that future effort. The attempt to develop a new product may fail; and even if it succeeds, the situation may have so changed by the time the decision to market needs to be taken that it may be best not to market. Just as by then the costs of development are sunk costs, so the earlier intention to market is a bygone intention; and sunk costs and bygone intentions are a poor basis for present decisions.

The third reason why a firm might want managers to make decisions now about future actions is to provide a basis for evaluation of their performance. This reason is subject to the same criticism as that advance against commitment, that action in accordance with a plan prepared long beforehand may well not be the action that is best for the firm.

It is not surprising that some companies should make the apparently natural progression for the annual budget to the "five-year forward look." It is not surprising, but it is dangerous. Any attempt to use a long-term plan for control purposes is liable to frustrate the valuable purposes of the planning process. Budgetary control is intended to ensure, by a system of rewards and penalties, the attainment of forecast results. As the penalty for failure is usually greater than the reward for success, the control system motivates a manager to promise no more than he is confident of performing.

This is quite the wrong apparatus for securing the advantages of formal planning. These advantages lie in the stimulus to fresh thought and imaginative ideas; but imaginative ideas involve risk, and risk implies the possibility of failure. To ask a man to commit himself, under threat of penalty, to the success of his proposed action is to ask him never to take a risk. It is therefore quite natural that, as Charles O. Rossotti (n.d.) observes, "one objection to action planning is that it makes an insufficient contribution to, or even hinders, the vital process of generating proposals for major policy changes and new opportunities" (p. 6). The allure of an integrated planning and control system should be resisted.

The fourth reason for requiring managers to decide now what they will do at specific points in the future is that it facilitates future decision making in other groups where external effects are important. Short-term decisions are made on the basis of two kinds of assumptions: one kind is about the outside world, the other is about what is happening in other parts of the organization. Whether the first kind of assumption turns out to be right or wrong cannot be controlled by the firm; but it does have the power to ensure that the assumptions of the second kind are right, by insisting that they be spelled out well in advance and adhered to. Thus the assurance which may be given in an action plan of what other parts of the organization will be doing helps to narrow the agenda for other decisions. It does not improve communications between parts of the organization; it eliminates the need for them. It makes it possible to allocate responsibilities in a pretty watertight way. This kind of planning is not an aid, but an alternative, to good communications.

Of course, the price of improving the compatibility between a decision made in one part of an organization and simultaneous decisions made elsewhere may be the reduction of compatibility between the decision and the outside environment. One way of dealing with this is to draw up a set of contingency plans, or conditional decisions, based on several different sets of assumptions; provided that the facts fit one set reasonably well, it is necessary only to make sure that everyone knows which set they are all to use. In some circumstances this may be a good method. But just how necessary is it to secure this coordination in advance? If these conditional decisions are to be intelligently prepared, with due regard for the interaction between various sections of the business, then while they are being prepared there has to be close contact between the sections (unless, of course, as may be the case, there really is very little cross-effect, in which case this reason for decisions about future action disappears). Why, then, should one design a system which appears to postulate very little contact in the intervals between the formulation of these decisions? Might one not get both better-integrated decision making and better-coordinated response to changing conditions by abandoning compartmentalization and not specifying responsibility so narrowly?

The apparent need to improve (but in fact to dispense with) communication and coordination is likely to be associated with what has been called a "mechanistic system of management" (Burns and Stalker, 1961), that is a system characterized by a well-ordered hierarchy of clearly defined responsibilities, so that everyone knows precisely what is—and also what is not—his business. In a situation where the interrelationships ignored by this formal structure are nevertheless important, the structure may appear to require equally formal planning procedures; and these procedures may appear to be facilitated by the structure. But instead of using formal planning procedures to reconcile the organization structure to the real needs of the company, it might be better to encourage the growth of a network structure of relationships, in which the active contacts at any time are determined by the task in hand, instead of being specified in advance. Such an "organic system" (Burns and Stalker, 1961) will be more responsive to changing circumstances, and might well produce better results for the organization than an attempt to predetermine future decisions.

An important virtue of a systematic look into the future is that it forces a company to make its forecasts more explicit. But even this virtue is not without its accompanying dangers. It is often argued that to make better decisions we need better information. Now it is certainly true that information can be improved. To take two examples: few firms apparently attempt to improve the accuracy of their forecasts by analyzing the reasons for past forecasting errors—even when the errors are as notorious as those made by American television manufacturers in the early days of color television; and few firms do as much as they could to assess the impact of known technological change. Better information is both desirable and obtainable. But—and here is a major source of error—better information does not necessarily mean more precise information. The demand for better information is often a demand for false certainty; and the institution of formal procedures for looking into the future may encourage this demand. Certainly one cannot make sensible decisions in ignorance; but uncertainty is not ignorance—it is knowledge. A seemingly precise forecast hides uncertainties, and therefore actually provides less information than a forecast which shows a range of possible values.

Thus the search for more information may be perverted into a search for false certainty. This is particularly likely if managers are asked to commit themselves to results at all far ahead. Such a pervasion may have two unfortunate consequences. Decisions may be made that do not properly reflect the possibility of error in the forecasts on which they are based; and overconfidence may produce excessive commitment to future action, and therefore a reluctance to take new decisions in the light of new information—indeed sometimes a reluctance even to notice new information.

The risk of domination by sophisticated techniques is serious. As a consequence of the emphasis on perfection of calculations, "computerized data processing rather than planning has (sometimes) become the major concern. Figures (have been) accepted without sufficient questioning" ("Little, Inc., 1966). At least one major British company has rejected the use of discounted cash flow for investment calculations because of the fear that its use will divert resources and attention from improving the quality of the basic data.

But these dangers are not inevitable. Instead of attempting to produce an optimum solution under given assumptions, formal procedures can be designed to force a "broadening of the planning agenda, . . . giving a means for exploring the meaning of changed assumptions and effects of changes in policy" (Magee, 1966). Its power to compel a systematic search, in situations where sequential search procedures may be inadequate, or even disastrous, is perhaps the most important virtue of the "decision tree" as an aid to management (Magee, 1964).

FORMAL PLANNING AND THE MANAGEMENT SYSTEM

Even if planning procedures are properly designed, however, there remains a deeper danger. Improving the quality of information is not the only way of improving the quality of decisions. If one asks what information is needed now to make the decisions that must be made now, one sometimes finds that some of the desired information is not really necessary. Some decisions are made too soon, even within the management system that a firm has at present. Others could be made later if the system were changed. Rossotti's statement that "the more efficiently . . . information is made available, presumably the more flexible the organization can be in adapting to it quickly" (p. 13) is precisely the reverse of the truth. Rossotti is confusing the speed of response with its timing. If reliable information is available well in advance, the organization can start to prepare well in advance. If one sets out early, one doesn't need to go very fast. Flexibility is not the result of good early warning, it is an alternative to it.

If one looks at the whole sequence between the emergence of information and the fruition of decisions, one may well see greater possibilities in reducing the delays in the system than in improving the quality of information. The Industrial Dynamics Group at M.I.T., investigating a successful company that was worried about the problem of predicting success for a new product, found not only that there were ways of reducing the interval between ordering equipment and getting it into production, but that half the total lapse of time between information and production was consumed in the decision process itself. In another instance, a company's production scheduling was improved by making more frequent but less accurate forecasts. A consulting team from Arthur D. Little, Inc., found a complex PERT chart, prepared for a highway agency, which showed a lead time of ten years between the results of traffic survey and the engineering drawing for the road; and not one input during that ten years represented any further information about traffic. A formal procedure which is directed at producing more information for earlier decisions is liable to channel efforts into refining forecasts and elaborating future action which could be better used in other ways.

The dangers of formal procedures outlined in the previous section may be summarized in two points: they may reduce the organization's flexibility (or in other words inhibit that initiation of a new decision process and reduce the speed with which new decisions can be made), and they may divert attention away from recognizing the need for flexibility. Perhaps the best way for firms to approach formal long-range planning is as something they should try to avoid. This does not mean as something they should try to dodge: it means so arranging the way they do things that as little as possible needs to be decided in advance. Of course, "as little as possible" will still be a good deal, but if, instead of asking how they can more accurately foresee future events and thus make better decisions further ahead, firms were to ask first what they can do to avoid the need to decide so far ahead, they might be led to discover important ways of improving their performance.

What is needed is not action planning but system planning: the question at issue is not only the adequacy of formal procedures but also the effectiveness (and especially the speed) of the decision process: these are by no means the same. The effectiveness of the decision process depends on information and organization. In assembling information, more emphasis should be placed on surveillance rather than sophistication. The valid arguments for sophistication should not be ignored, but nor should it be forgotten that effective monitoring is more useful than elaborate manipulation of data which is out of date before the manipulation is complete.

. . . the real problem is to design an organization that can cope with the amount of uncertainty that is inherent in its situation. To deal effectively with this problem requires a shift of emphasis for organizational structure to the decision process. . . . It is easy to become so absorbed in the details of devising an elaborate planning procedure as to forget that redesign of the information flow and of the management system may be more effective ways of achieving some of the objectives of formal long-range planning.

This article has been concerned with the purposes of formal planning, not with techniques. The great value of formal procedures—and their value can be very great—is in the raising and broadening of important issues that are liable otherwise to be inadequately considered. Much of this value can, however, be lost if these formal procedures are at all closely connected with the conflicting objective of controlling managerial performance. Planning procedures should be designed to illuminate, rather than obscure, the existence and implications of uncertainty. Finally, planning procedures should not concentrate on management action at the expense of the management system, and in particular should not be used to reconcile organization structure with the real situation: the design of a management system which facilitates quicker and more direct responses can be a better answer to some of the problems for which formal procedures offer only a second-best solution.

● THE TRANSITION TO INDUSTRY MATURITY*

BY MICHAEL E. PORTER

As part of their evolutionary process, many industries pass from periods of rapid growth to the more modest growth of what is commonly called industry maturity. . . . industry maturity does not occur at any fixed point in an industry's development, and it can be delayed by innovations or other events that fuel continued growth for industry participants. Moreover, in response to strategic breakthroughs, mature industries may regain their rapid growth and thereby go through more than one transition to maturity. With these important qualifications in mind, however, let us consider the case in which a transition to maturity is occurring. . . . .

INDUSTRY CHANGE DURING TRANSITION

Transition to maturity can often signal a number of important changes in an industry's competitive environment. Some of the probable tendencies for change are as follows:

1. *Slowing growth means more competition for market share.* With companies unable to maintain historical growth rates merely by holding market share, competitive attention turns inward toward attacking the shares of the others. . . . Not only are competitors probably going to be more aggressive, but also the likelihood of misperceptions and "irrational" retaliation is great. Outbreaks of price, service, and promotional warfare are common during transition to maturity.

2. *Firms in the industry increasingly are selling to experienced, repeat buyers.* The product is no longer new but an established legitimate item. Buyers are often increasingly knowledgeable and experienced, having already purchased the product, sometimes repeatedly. The buyers' focus shifts from deciding whether to purchase the product at all to making choices among brands. Approaching these differently oriented buyers requires a fundamental reassessment of strategy.

3. *Competition often shifts toward greater emphasis on cost and service.* As a result of slower growth, more knowledgeable buyers, and usually greater technological maturity, competition tends to become more cost and service-oriented. . . .

4. *There is a topping-out problem in adding industry capacity and personnel.* As the industry adjusts to slower growth, the rate of capacity addition in the industry must slow down as well or overcapacity will occur. . . . [But the necessary] shifts in perspective rarely occur in maturing industries, and overshooting of industry capacity relative to demand is common. Overshooting leads to a period of overcapacity, accentuating the tendency during transition toward price warfare. . . .

5. *Manufacturing, marketing, distributing, selling, and research methods are often undergoing change.* These changes are caused by increased competition for market share, technological maturity, and buyer sophistication. . . .

6. *New products and applications are harder to come by.* Whereas the growth phase may have been one of rapid discovery of new products and applications, the ability to continue product change generally becomes increasingly limited, or the costs and risks greatly increase, as the industry matures. This change requires, among other things, a reorientation of attitude toward research and new product development.

7. *International competition increases.* As a consequence of technological maturity, often accompanied by product standardization and increasing emphasis on costs, transition is often marked by the emergence of significant international competition. . . .

8. *Industry profits often fall during the transition period, sometimes temporarily and sometimes permanently.* Slowing growth, more sophisticated buyers, more emphasis on market share, and the uncertainties and difficulties of the required strategic changes usually mean that industry profits fall in the short run from the levels of the pretransition growth phase. . . . Whether or not profits will rebound depends on the level of mobility barriers and other elements of industry structure. . . .

9. *Dealers' margins fall, but their power increases.* For the same reasons that industry profits are often depressed, dealers' margins may be squeezed, and many dealers may drop out of business—often *before* the effect on manufacturers' profits is noticeable. . . . Such trends tighten competition among industry participants for dealers, who may have been easy to find and hold in the growth phase but not upon maturity. Thus, dealers' power may increase markedly.

SOME STRATEGIC IMPLICATIONS OF TRANSITION

. . . Some characteristic strategic issues often arise in transition. These are presented as issues to examine rather than generalizations that will apply to all industries; like humans, all industries mature a little differently. Many of these approaches can be a basis for the entry of new firms into an industry even though it is mature.

Overall Cost Leadership Versus Differentiate Versus Focus —The Strategic Dilemma Made Acute by Maturity

Rapid growth tends to mask strategic errors and allow most, if not all, companies in the industry to survive and even to prosper financially. Strategic experimentation is high, and a wide variety of strategies can coexist. Strategic sloppiness is generally exposed by industry maturity, however. Maturity may force companies to confront, often for the first time, the need to choose among the three generic strategies described (in Chapter 4 of this text). It becomes a matter of survival.

Sophisticated Cost Analysis

Cost analysis becomes increasingly important in maturity to (1) rationalize the product mix and (2) price correctly.

Rationalizing the Product Mix: . . . a quantum improvement in the sophistication of product costing is necessary to allow pruning of unprofitable items from the line and to focus attention on items either that have some distinctive advantage (technology, cost, image, etc.) or whose buyers are "good" buyers. . . .

Correct Pricing: Related to product line rationalization is the change in pricing methodology that is often necessary in maturity. Although average-cost pricing, or pricing the line as a whole rather than as individual items, may have been sufficient in the growth era, maturity often requires increased capability to measure costs on individual items and to price accordingly. . . .

We might summarize this and the other points in this section by saying that an enhanced level of "financial consciousness" along a variety of dimensions is often necessary in maturity, whereas in the developmental period of the industry areas such as new products and research may have rightly held center stage. . . .

Process Innovation and Design for Manufacture

The relative importance of process innovations usually increases in maturity, as does the payoff for designing the product and its delivery system to facilitate lower-cost manufacturing and control. . . .

Increasing Scope of Purchases: Increasing purchases of existing customers may be more desirable than seeking new customers. . . . Such a strategy may take the firm out of the industry into related industries. This strategy is often less costly than finding new customers. In a mature industry, winning new customers usually means battling for market share with competitors and is consequently quite expensive. . . .

Buy Cheap Assets

Sometimes assets can be acquired very cheaply as a result of the company distress that is caused by transition to maturity. A strategy of acquiring distressed companies or buying liquidated assets can improve margins and create a low-cost position if the rate of technological change is not too great. . . .

Buyer Selection

As buyers become more knowledgeable and competitive pressures increase in maturity, buyer selection can sometimes be a key to continued profitability. Buyers who may not have exercised their bargaining power in the past, or had less power because of limited product availability, will usually not be bashful about exercising their power in maturity. Identifying "good" buyers and locking them in . . . becomes crucial.

Different Cost Curves

There is often more than one cost curve possible in an industry. The firm that is *not* the overall cost leader in a mature market can sometimes find new cost curves which may actually make it a lower-cost producer for certain types of buyers, product varieties, or order sizes. This step is key to implementing the generic strategy of focus. . . .

Competing Internationally

A firm may escape maturity by competing internationally where the industry is more favorably structured. Sometimes equipment that is obsolete in the home market can be used quite effectively in international markets, greatly lowering the costs of entry there. . . .

STRATEGIC PITFALLS IN TRANSITION

In addition to failure to recognize the strategic implications of transition described above, there is the tendency for firms to fall prey to some characteristic strategic pitfalls:

1. *A company's self-perceptions and its perception of the industry.* Companies develop perceptions or images of themselves and their relative capabilities ("we are the quality leader"; "we provide superior customer service"), which are reflected in the implicit assumptions that form the basis of their strategies. . . . These self-perceptions may be increasingly inaccurate as transition proceeds, buyers' priorities adjust, and competitors respond to new industry conditions. Similarly, firms have assumptions about the industry, competitors, buyers, and suppliers which may be invalidated by transition. Yet altering these assumptions, built up through actual past experience, is sometimes a difficult process.

2. *Caught in the middle.* The problem of being caught in the middle described [earlier] is particularly acute in transition to maturity. Transition often squeezes out the slack that has made this strategy viable in the past.

3. *The cash trap—investments to build share in a mature market.* Cash should be invested in a business only with the expectation of being able to remove it later. In a mature, slow-growing industry, the assumptions required to justify investing new cash in order to build market share are often heroic. Maturity of the industry works against increasing or maintaining margins long enough to recoup cash investments down the road, by making the present value of cash inflows justify the outflows. Thus businesses in maturity can be cash traps, particularly when a firm is not in a strong market position but is attempting to build a large market share in a maturing market. The odds are against it.

A related pitfall is placing heavy attention on revenues in the maturing market instead of on profitability. This strategy may have been desirable in the growth phase, but it usually faces diminishing returns in maturity. . . .

4. *Giving up market share too easily in favor of short-run profits.* In the face of the profit pressures in transition, there seems to be a tendency for some companies to try to maintain the profitability of the recent past—which is done at the expense of market share or by foregoing marketing, R&D, and other needed investments, which in turn hurts future market position. . . . A period of lower profits may be inevitable while industry rationalization occurs, and a cool head is necessary to avoid overreaction.

5. *Resentment and irrational reaction to price competition ("we will not compete on price").* It is often difficult for firms to accept the need for price competition after a period in which it has not been necessary. . . .

6. *Resentment and irrational reaction to changes in industry practices ("they are hurting the industry").* Changes in industry practices, such as marketing techniques, production methods, and the nature of distributor contracts are often an inevitable part of transition. They may be important to the industry's long-run potential, but there is often resistance to them. . . .

7. *Overemphasis on "creative," "new" products rather than improving and aggressively selling existing ones.* Although past success in the early and growth phases of an industry may have been built on research and on new products, the onset of maturity often means that new products and applications are harder to come by. It is usually appropriate that the focus of innovative activity should change, putting standardization rather than newness and fine tuning at a premium. Yet this development is not satisfying to some companies and is often resisted.

8. *Clinging to "higher quality" as an excuse for not meeting aggressive pricing and marketing moves of competitors.* High quality can be a crucial company strength, but quality differentials have a tendency to erode as an industry matures. . . . Yet it is difficult for many companies to accept the fact that they do not possess the highest-quality product or that their quality is unnecessarily high.

9. *Overhanging excess capacity.* As a result of capacity overshooting demand, or because of capacity increases that inevitably accompany the plant modernization required to compete in the mature industry, some firms may have some excess capacity. Its mere presence creates both subtle and unsubtle pressures to utilize it, and it can be used in ways that will undermine the firm's strategy. . . .

• COST DYNAMICS: SCALE AND EXPERIENCE EFFECTS*

BY DEREK F. ABELL AND JOHN S. HAMMOND

Market share is one of the primary determinants of business profitability; other things being equal, businesses with a larger share of a market are more profitable than their smaller-share competitors. For instance, a study by the PIMS Program (Buzzell, Gale and Sultan, 1975) . . . found that, on average, a difference of 10 percentage points in market share is accompanied by a difference of about 5 points in pretax ROI ("pretax operating profits" divided by "long-term debt plus equity"). Additional evidence is that companies having large market shares in their primary product markets—such as General Motors, IBM, Gillette, Eastman Kodak, and Xerox—tend to be highly profitable.

An important reason for the increase in profitability with market share is that large-share firms usually have *lower costs*. The lower costs are due in part to econ-

---

omies of scale; for instance, very large plants cost less per unit of production to build and are often more efficient than smaller plants. Lower costs are also due in part to the so-called *experience effect,* whereby the cost of many (if not most) products declines by 10–30 percent each time a company's experience at producing and selling them doubles. In this context *experience* has a precise meaning: it is the cumulative number of units produced to date. Since at any point in time, businesses with large market shares typically (but not always) have more experience than their smaller-share competitors, they would be expected to have lower costs. . . .

This [reading] considers how costs decline due to scale and to experience, practical problems in analyzing the experience effect, strategic implications of scale and experience, and limitations of strategies based on cost reduction. . . .

SCALE EFFECT

As mentioned earlier, scale effect refers to the fact that large businesses have the potential to operate at lower unit costs than their smaller counterparts. The increased efficiency due to size is often referred to as "economy of scale"; it could equally be called "economy of size."

Most people think of economy of scale as a manufacturing phenomenon because large manufacturing facilities can be constructed at a lower cost per unit of capacity and can be operated more efficiently than smaller ones. . . .

Just as they cost less to build, large-scale plants have lower *operating* costs per unit of output. . . . While substantial in manufacturing, scale effect is also significant in other cost elements, such as marketing, sales, distribution, administration, R&D, and service. For instance, a chain with 30 supermarkets in a metropolitan area needs much less than three times as much advertising as a chain of 10 stores. . . . Economies of scale are also achieved with purchased items such as raw material and shipping. . . .

Although scale economies potentially exist in all cost elements of a business in both the short and long run, large size alone doesn't assure the benefits of scale. It is evident from the above illustrations that size provides an *opportunity* for scale economies; to achieve them requires strategies and actions consciously designed to seize the opportunity, especially with operating costs. . . .

EXPERIENCE EFFECT

The experience effect, whereby costs fall with cumulative production, is measurable and predictable; it has been observed in a wide range of products including automobiles, semiconductors, petrochemicals, long-distance telephone calls, synthetic fibers, airline transportation, the cost of administering life insurance, and crushed limestone, to mention a few. Note that this list ranges from high technology to low technology products, service to manufacturing industries, consumer to industrial products, new to mature products, and process to assembly oriented products, indicating the wide range of applicability. . . .

. . . it is only comparatively recently that this phenomenon has been carefully measured and quantified; at first it was thought to apply only to the labor portion of *manufacturing* costs. . . . In the 1960s evidence mounted that the phenomenon was broader. Personnel from the Boston Consulting Group and others showed that each time cumulative volume of a product doubled, total value added costs—including administration, sales, marketing, distribution, and so on in addition to manufacturing—fell by a constant and predictable percentage. In addition, the costs of purchased items usually fell as suppliers reduced prices as their costs fell, due also to the experience effect. The relationship between costs and experience was called the *experience curve* (Boston Consulting Group, 1972).

An experience curve is plotted with the cumulative units produced on the horizontal axis, and cost per unit on the vertical axis. An "85%" experience curve is shown in Figure 1. The "85%" means that every time experience doubles, costs per unit drop to 85% of the original level. It is known as the *learning rate*. Stated differently, costs per unit decrease 15 percent for every doubling of cumulative production. For example, the cost of the 20th unit produced is about 85% of the cost of the 10th unit. . . .

An experience curve appears as a straight line when plotted on a double log paper (logarithmic scale for both the horizontal and vertical axes). Figure 2 shows the "85 percent" experience curve from Figure 1 on the double logarithmic scale. . . . Figure 3 provides illustrations for [some specific] products.

FIGURE 1
A Typical Experience Curve [85%]

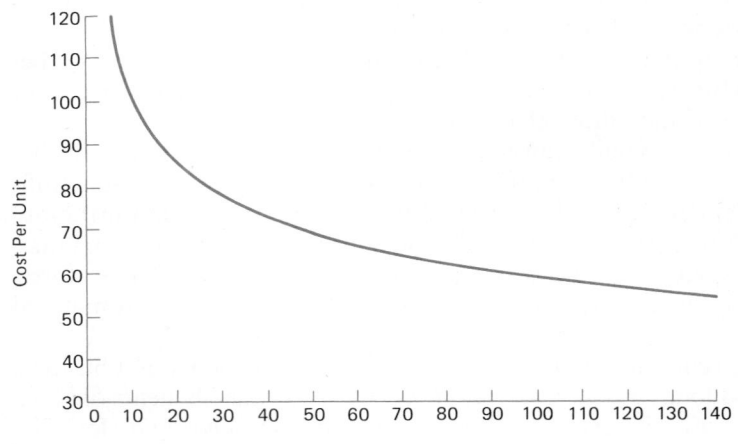

FIGURE 2
An 85% Experience Curve Displayed on Log-Log Scales

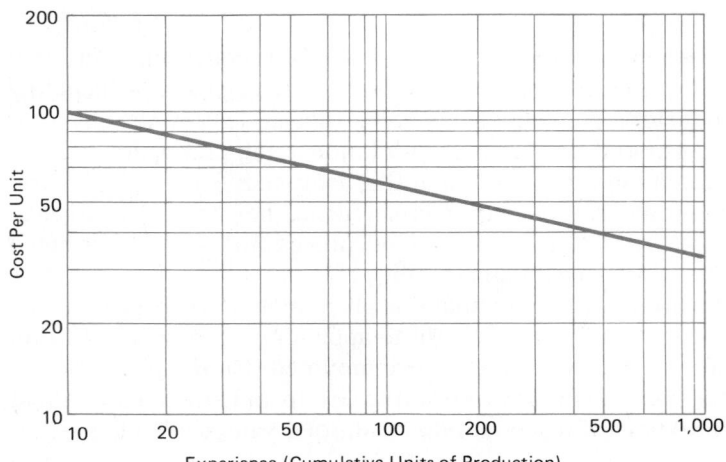

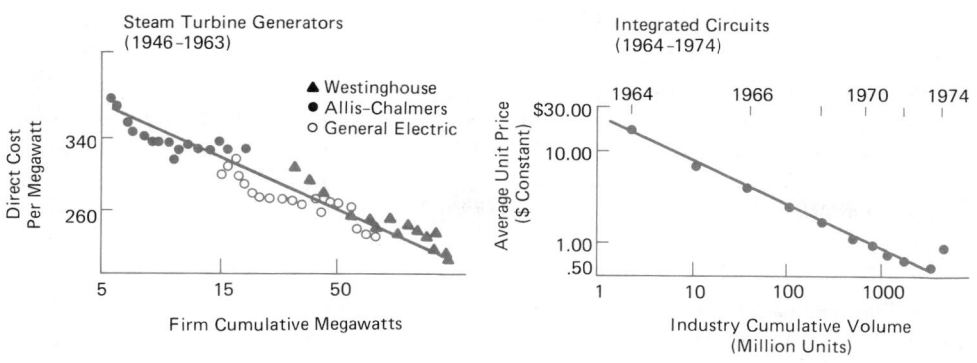

Steam Turbine Generators
(1946-1963)

▲ Westinghouse
● Allis-Chalmers
○ General Electric

Direct Cost Per Megawatt

340

260

5   15   50

Firm Cumulative Megawatts

Integrated Circuits
(1964-1974)

Average Unit Price ($ Constant)

1964   1966   1970   1974

$30.00

10.00

1.00
.50

1   10   100   1000

Industry Cumulative Volume
(Million Units)

FIGURE 3
Some Sample Experience Curves

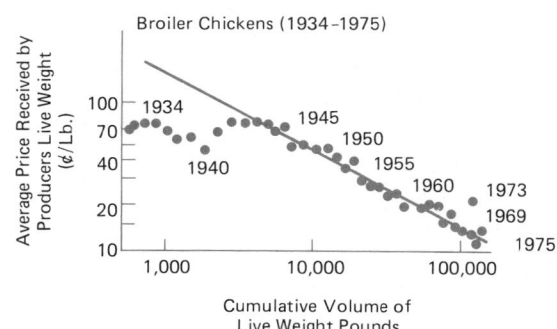

Broiler Chickens (1934-1975)

Average Price Received by Producers Live Weight (¢/Lb.)

100   1934   1945
 70   1950
 40   1940   1955
                                   1973
 20   1960   1969
 10   1975

1,000   10,000   100,000

Cumulative Volume of
Live Weight Pounds

Note: Technically an experience curve shows the relationship between cost and experience. However, cost figures are seldom publicly available; therefore most of the above experience curves show industry price (in constant dollars) vs. experience.

Source: The Boston Consulting Group.

SOURCES OF THE EXPERIENCE EFFECT

The experience effect has a variety of sources; to capitalize on it requires knowledge of why it occurs. Sources of the experience effect are outlined as follows:

1. *Labor efficiency.* . . . As workers repeat a particular production task, they become more dextrous and learn improvements and shortcuts which increase their collective efficiency. The greater the number of worker-paced operations, the greater the amount of learning which can accrue with experience. . . .

2. *Work specialization and methods improvements.* Specialization increases worker proficiency at a given task. . . .

3. *New production processes.* Process innovations and improvements can be an important source of cost reductions, especially in capital-intensive industries. . . .

4. *Getting better performance from production equipment.* When first designed, a piece of production equipment may have a conservatively rated output. Experience may reveal innovative ways of increasing its output. . . .

5. *Changes in the resource mix.* As experience accumulates, a producer can often incorporate different or less expensive resources in the operation. . . .

6. *Product standardization.* Standardization allows the replication of tasks necessary for worker learning. Production of the Ford Model T, for example, followed a strategy of deliberate standardization; as a result, from 1909 to 1923 its price was

659

repeatedly reduced, following an 85 percent experience curve (Abernathy and Wayne, 1974). . . .

7. *Product redesign.* As experience is gained with a product, both the manufacturer and customers gain a clearer understanding of its performance requirements. This understanding allows the product to be redesigned to conserve material, allows greater efficiency in manufacture, and substitutes less costly materials and resources, while at the same time improving performance on relevant dimensions. . . .

The foregoing list of sources dramatizes the observation that cost reductions due to experience don't occur by natural inclination; they are the result of substantial, concerted effort and pressure to lower costs. In fact, left unmanaged, costs rise. Thus, experience does not cause reductions but rather provides an opportunity that alert managements can exploit. . . .

The list of reasons for the experience effect raises perplexing questions on the difference between experience and scale effects. For instance, isn't it true that work specialization and project standardization, mentioned in the experience list, become possible because of the *size* of an operation? Therefore, aren't they each really scale effects? The answer is that they are probably both.

The confusion arises because growth in experience usually coincides with growth in size of an operation. We consider the experience effect to arise primarily due to ingenuity, cleverness, skill, and dexterity derived from experience as embodied in the adages "practice makes perfect" or "experience is the best teacher." On the other hand, scale effect comes from capitalizing on the size of an operation. . . .

Usually the overlap between the two effects is so great that it is difficult (and not too important) to separate them. This is the practice we will adopt from here on. . . .

PRICES AND EXPERIENCE

In stable competitive markets, one would expect that as costs decrease due to experience, prices will decrease similarly. (The price-experience curves in Figure 3 are examples of prices falling with experience.) If profit margins remain at a constant percentage of price, average industry costs and prices should follow identically sloped experience curves (on double logarithmic scales). The constant gap separating them will equal the profit margin percentage; Figure 4 illustrates such an idealized situation.

In many cases, however, prices and costs exhibit a relationship similar to the one shown in Figure 5, where prices start briefly below cost, then cost reductions exceed price reductions until prices suddenly tumble. Ultimately the price and cost curves parallel, as they do in Figure 4. Specifically, in the development phase, new product prices are below average industry costs due to pricing based on anticipated costs. In the price umbrella phase, when demand exceeds supply, prices remain firm under a price umbrella supported by the market leader. This is unstable. At some point a shakeout phase starts; one producer will almost certainly reduce prices to gain share. If this does not precipitate a price decline, the high profit margins will attract enough new entrants to produce temporary overcapacity, causing prices to tumble faster than costs, and marginal producers to be forced out of the market. The stability phase starts when profit margins return to normal levels and prices begin to follow industry costs down the experience curve. . . .

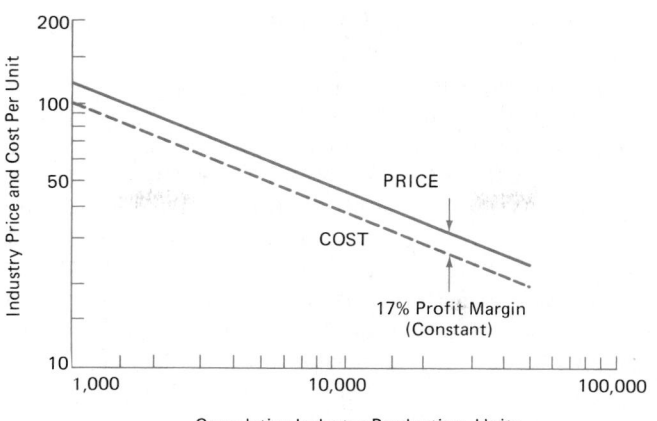

FIGURE 4
An Idealized Price-Cost
Relationship When Profit
Margin is Constant

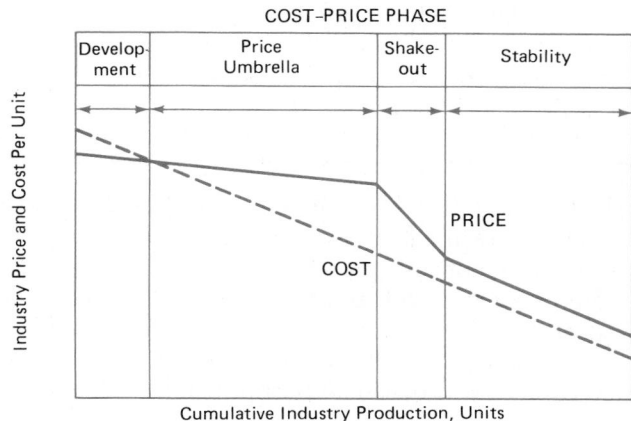

FIGURE 5
Typical Price-Cost
Relationship
Source: Adapted from
Perspectives on Experience
(Boston: The Boston
Consulting Group, 1972),
p. 21

STRATEGIC IMPLICATIONS

In industries where a significant portion of total cost can be reduced due to scale or experience, important cost advantages can usually be achieved by pursuing a strategy geared to accumulating experience faster than competitors. (Such a strategy will ultimately require that the firm acquire the largest market share relative to competition.).

The dominant producer can greatly influence industry profitability. The rate of decline of competitors' costs must at least keep pace with the leader if they are to maintain profitability. If their costs decrease more slowly, either because they are pursuing cost reductions less aggressively or are growing more slowly than the leader, then their profits will eventually disappear, thus eliminating them from the market.

. . . the advantage of being the leader is obvious. Leadership is usually best seized at the start when experience doubles quickly (e.g., experience increases tenfold as you move from the 20th to the 2,000th unit, but only doubles as you move from the 2,000th to the 4,000th unit.) Then a firm can build an unassailable cost advantage and at the same time gain price leadership. The best course of action for a product depends on a number of factors, one of the most important being the market growth rate. In fast-growing markets, experience can be gained by taking a disproportionate share of new sales, thereby avoiding taking sales away from competitors (which would be vigorously resisted). Therefore, with high rates of growth, aggressive action may be called for. But, share-gaining tactics are usually costly in the short run, due to reduced margins from lower prices, added advertising and marketing expense, new product development costs, and the like. This means that if it lacks the resources (product, financial, and other) for leadership and in particular if it is opposed by a very aggressive competitor, a firm may find it wise to abandon the market entirely or focus on a segment it can dominate. On the other hand, in no-growth or slowly growing markets it is hard to take share from competitors and the time it takes to acquire superior experience is usually too long and the cost too great to favor aggressive strategies.

In stable competitive markets, usually the firm with the largest share of market has the greatest experience and it is often the case that each firm's experience is roughly proportional to market share. A notable exception occurs when a late entrant to a market quickly obtains a commanding market share. It may have less experience than some early entrants. . . .

EFFICIENCY VERSUS EFFECTIVENESS: LIMITATIONS TO STRATEGIES BASED ON EXPERIENCE OR SCALE

The selection of a competitive strategy based on cost reduction due to experience or scale often involves a fundamental choice. It is the selection of cost-price *efficiency* over noncost-price marketing *effectiveness*. However, when the market is more concerned with product and service features and up-to-date technology, a firm pursuing efficiency can find itself offering a low-priced product that few customers want. Thus two basic questions arise: (1) when to use an efficiency strategy and (2) if used, how far to push it before running into dangers of losing effectiveness. . . .

Whether to pursue an efficiency strategy depends on answers to questions such as,

1. Does the industry offer significant cost advantages from experience or scale (as in semiconductors or chemicals)?
2. Are there significant market segments that will reward competitors with low prices?
3. Is the firm well equipped (financially, managerially, technologically, etc.) for or already geared up for strategies relying heavily on having the lowest cost . . .?

If the answer is "yes" to all these questions, then "efficiency" strategies should probably be pursued.

Once it decided to pursue an "efficiency" strategy a firm must guard against going so far that it loses effectiveness, primarily through inability to respond to changes. For instance, experience-based strategies frequently require a highly specialized work force, facilities and organization, making it difficult to respond to changes in consumer demand, to respond to competitors' innovations, or to initiate them. In addition, large-scale plants are vulnerable to changes in process technology, and the heavy cost of operation below capacity.

For example, Ford's Motel T automobile ultimately suffered the consequences of inflexibility due to overemphasizing "efficiency" (Abernathy and

Wayne, 1974). Ford followed a classic experience-based strategy; over time it slashed its product line to a single model (the Model T), built modern plants, pushed division of labor, introduced the continuous assembly line, obtained economies in purchased parts through high volume, backward integrated, increased mechanization, and cut prices as costs fell. The lower prices increased Ford's share of a growing market to a high of 55.4% by 1921.

In the meantime, consumer demand began shifting to heavier, closed-body cars and to more comfort. Ford's chief rival, General Motors, had the flexibility to respond quickly with new designs. Ford responded by adding features to its existing standard design. While the features softened the inroads of GM, the basic Model T design, upon which Ford's "efficiency" strategy was based, inadequately met the market's new performance standards. To make matters worse, the turmoil in production due to constant design changes slowed experience-based efficiency gains. Finally Ford was forced, at enormous cost, to close for a whole year beginning May 1927 while it retooled to introduce its Model A. Hence experience or scale-based *efficiency* was carried too far and thus it ultimately limited *effectiveness* to meet consumer needs, to innovate, and to respond.

Thus the challenge is to decide when to emphasize efficiency and when to emphasize effectiveness, and further to design efficiency strategies that maintain effectiveness and vice versa. . . .

11

THE DIVERSIFIED CONTEXT

A good deal of evidence has accumulated on the relationship between diversification and divisionalization. Once organizations diversify their product or service lines, they tend to create distinct structural divisions to deal with each distinct business. This relationship was perhaps first carefully documented in the classic historical study by Alfred D. Chandler, *Strategy and Structure: Chapters in the History of the Great American Enterprise.* Chandler traced the origins of diversification and divisionalization in Du Pont and General Motors in the 1920s which were followed later by other major firms. A number of other studies elaborated on Chandler's conclusions; these are discussed in the readings of this chapter.

The first reading, drawn from Mintzberg's work on structuring, probes the structure of divisionalization—how it works, what brings it about, what intermediate variations of it exist, and what problems it poses for organizations that use it and for society at large. It concludes on a rather pessimistic note about conglomerate diversification and about the purer forms of divisionalization.

The next set of readings on the diversified context probe issues of its strategy, generally referred to as "corporate," to be distinguished from the "business" strategies of specific divisions. This has to do with managing the "portfolio" of businesses—which to develop and acquire, which to close or divest, but more important as one of these readings makes clear, how to knit them into a viable corporate entity.

As diversification became an especially popular strategy among large corporations in the 1960s and 1970s, a number of techniques were developed to analyze strategies at the corporate level. Among the most widely used were a number labeled "portfolio," which viewed the businesses of a diversified company as a collection of investments whose return could be optimized by properly balancing their growth and maturity characteristics and by redeploying investments and cash flows among them.

To describe this, we turn to the words of Bruce Henderson, who built up the Boston Consulting Group in good part on the basis of the best known of these techniques, its "growth-share matrix." This offered corporate executives a way to think of managing an array of businesses, but it also came in for some sharp criticism, not the least of which came from John Seeger, a professor at Bentley College, who used his earlier journalistic skills to turn around BCG's images of businesses as question marks, cash cows, stars, and dogs. We reprint Seeger's article here not only to present another perspective on a famous technique but also to convey his broader message, one well worth bearing in mind throughout management education. "No management model can safely substitute for analysis and common sense." While techniques such as the experience curve and competitive and portfolio analysis can be very useful in understanding critical relationships and in making sure one touches all the right bases, they provide no substitutes for a thorough-going intellectual and intuitive understanding of the full complexity of a company's unique capabilities in its particular environments. Many of these cannot be captured in numerical analyses, but abide in the minds and motivations of the people in the organization.

Aspects of the diversified organization, particularly in its more conglomerate form, thus come in for some heavy criticism in this chapter. The next reading takes up that torch too, but it quickly turns to the more constructive questions of how to use strategy to combine a cluster of different businesses into an effective corporate entity. This is Michael Porter's award-winning *Harvard Business Review* article "From Competitive Advantage to Corporate Strategy." Porter discusses in a most insightful way various types of overall corporate strategies, including portfolio management, restructuring, transferring skills, and sharing activities (the last two referred to in his 1985 book *Competitive Advantage* as "horizontal strategies," the former dealing with "intangible," the latter "tangible" interrelationships among business units, and conceived in terms of his value chain [see pages 72–74]).

Finally, we close this chapter with a look at what might be thought of as an important subcontext of the diversified one. That is the so-called "global" context —diversification geographically across many parts of the globe with the various activities rationalized among many different countries. The recent article by George Yip, who now teaches management at Georgetown University after working for several years as a management consultant, provides an excellent summary of the issues surrounding "global strategies."

A wide variety of cases support these concepts. The Hewlett-Packard, Sony, Honda Motor, and IBM(C) cases deal largely with diversification through internal development and the divisional structures which accompany this. The New York Times, Pillsbury, General Mills, and Continental Group all provide examples of acquisition strategies which become overly diversified and need to be consolidated. Both groups of cases contain some excellent opportunities for portfolio analyses and discussions of the pros and cons of portfolio management in both a growth and maturing industry context. Matushita, Exxon, Honda Motor, and Royal Bank of Canada go beyond simple divisionalization into the complex multilayered matrix structures common in most global strategies. Each raises profound questions about how a large multinational corporation identifies its core skills, where it should focus its activities in the value chain, and how it can best coordinate its resources worldwide. The New York Times, PRA&D, and Royal Bank of Canada also raise many of the ticklish problems posed by advancing communications technologies and their capacity to create whole new organization forms with very wide spans of control, small remote nodes, and reversals in the role of management versus "front-line" personnel. Such organizations reach well beyond simple divisionalization.

THE DIVERSIFIED ORGANIZATION*

BY HENRY MINTZBERG

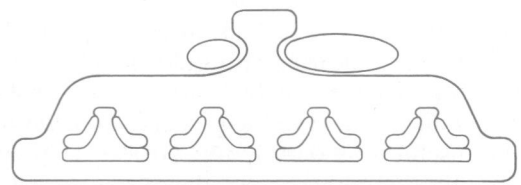

THE BASIC DIVISIONALIZED STRUCTURE

The diversified organization is not so much an integrated entity as a set of semiautonomous units coupled together by a central administrative structure. The units are generally called *divisions,* and the central administration, the *headquarters.* This is a widely used configuration in the private sector of the industrialized economy; the vast majority of the *Fortune* 500, America's largest corporations, use this structure or a variant of it. But, as we shall see, it is also found in other sectors as well.

In what is commonly called the "divisionalized" form of structure, units, called "divisions," are created to serve distinct markets and are given control over the operating functions necessary to do so, as shown in Figure 1. Each is therefore relatively free of direct control by headquarters or even of the need to coordinate

FIGURE 1

Typical Organigram for a Divisionalized Manufacturing Firm

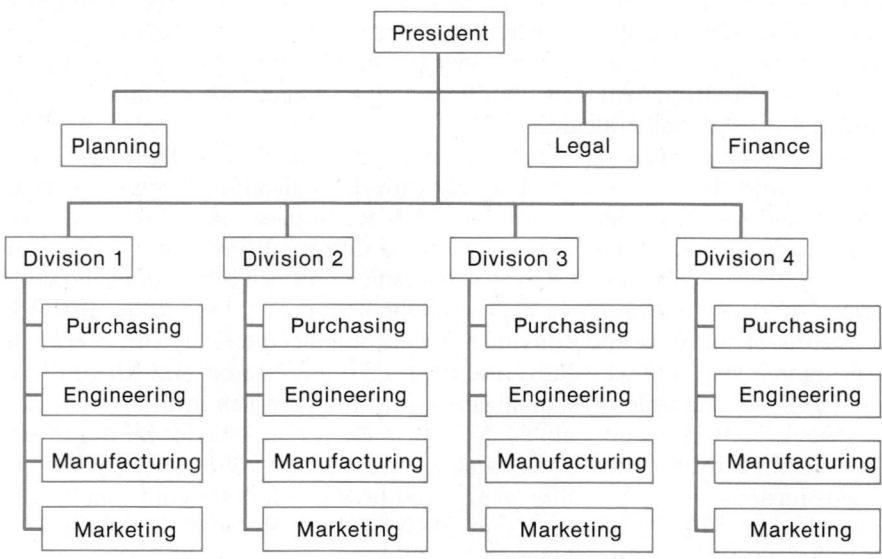

* Adapted from *The Structuring of Organizations* (Prentice Hall, 1979), Chap. 20 on "The Divisionalized Form". A chapter similar to this appeared in *Mintzberg on Management: Inside Our Strange World of Organizations* (Free Press, 1989).

activities with other divisions. Each, in other words, appears to be a self-standing business. Of course, none is. There *is* a headquarters, and it has a series of roles that distinguish this overall configuration from a collection of independent businesses providing the same set of products and services.

Roles of the Headquarters

Above all, the headquarters exercises performance control. It sets standards of achievement, generally in quantitative terms (such as return on investment or growth in sales), and then monitors the results. Coordination between headquarters and the divisions thus reduces largely to the standardization of outputs. Of course, there is some direct supervision—headquarters' managers have to have personal contact with and knowledge of the divisions. But that is largely circumscribed by the key assumption in this configuration that if the division managers are to be responsible for the performance of their divisions, they must have considerable autonomy to manage them as they see fit. Hence there is extensive delegation of authority from headquarters to the level of division manager.

Certain important tasks do, however, remain for the headquarters. One is to develop the overall *corporate* strategy, meaning to establish the portfolio of businesses in which the organization will operate. The headquarters establishes, acquires, divests, and closes down divisions in order to change its portfolio. Popular in the 1970s in this regard was the Boston Consulting Group's "growth share matrix," where corporate managers were supposed to allocate funds to divisions on the basis of their falling into the categories of dogs, cash cows, wildcats, and stars. But enthusiasm for that technique waned, perhaps mindful of Pope's warning that a little learning can be a dangerous thing.

Second, the headquarters manages the movement of funds between the divisions, taking the excess profits of some to support the greater growth potential of others. Third, of course, the headquarters, through it own technostructure, designs and operates the performance control system. Fourth, it appoints and therefore retains the right to replace the division managers. For a headquarters that does not directly manage any division, its most tangible power when the performance of a division lags—short of riding out an industry downturn or divesting the division— is to replace its leader. Finally, the headquarters provides certain support services that are common to all the divisions—a corporate public relations office or legal counsel, for example.

Structure of the Divisions

It has been common to label divisionalized organizations "decentralized." That is a reflection of how *certain* of them came to be, most notably Du Pont early in this century. When organizations that were structured functionally (for example, in departments of marketing, manufacturing, and engineering, etc.) diversified, they found that coordination of their different product lines across the functions became increasingly complicated. The central managers had to spend great amounts of time intervening to resolve disputes. But once these corporations switched to a divisionalized form of structure, where all the functions for a given business could be contained in a single unit dedicated to that business, management became much simpler. In effect, their structures became *more* decentralized, power over distinct businesses being delegated to the division managers.

But more decentralized does not mean *decentralized.* That word refers to the dispersal of decision-making power in an organization, and in many of the diversified corporations much of the power tended to remain with the few managers who ran the businesses. Indeed, the most famous case of divisionalization was one of relative *centralization:* Alfred P. Sloan introduced the divisionalized structure to General Motors in the 1920s to *reduce* the power of its autonomous business units, to impose systems of financial controls on what had been a largely unmanaged agglomeration of different automobile businesses.

In fact, I would argue that it is the *centralization* of power within the divisions that is most compatible with the divisionalized form of structure. In other words, the effect of having a headquarters over the divisions is to drive them toward the machine configuration, namely a structure of centralized bureaucracy. That is the structure most compatible with headquarters control, in my opinion. If true, this would seem to be an important point, because it means that the proliferation of the diversified configuration in many spheres—business, government, and the rest—has the effect of driving many suborganizations toward machine bureaucracy, even where that configuration may be inappropriate (school systems, for example, or government departments charged with innovative project work).

The explanation for this lies in the standardization of outputs, the key to the functioning of the divisionalized structure. Bear in mind the headquarters' dilemma: to respect divisional autonomy while exercising control over performance. This it seeks to resolve by after-the-fact monitoring of divisional results, based on clearly defined performance standards. But two main assumptions underlie such standards.

First, each division must be treated as a single integrated system with a single, consistent set of goals. In other words, although the divisions may be loosely coupled with each other, the assumption is that each is tightly coupled internally.[1]

Second, these goals must be operational ones, in other words, lend themselves to quantitative measurement. But in the less formal configurations—entrepreneurial and innovative—which are less stable, such performance standards are difficult to establish, while in the professional configuration, the complexity of the work makes it difficult to establish such standards. Moreover, while the entrepreneurial configuration may lend itself to being integrated around a single set of goals, the innovative and professional configurations do not. Thus, only the machine configuration of the major types fits comfortably into the conventional divisionalized structure, by virtue of its integration and its operational goals.

In fact, when organizations with another configuration are drawn under the umbrella of a divisionalized structure, they tend to be forced toward the machine bureaucratic form, to make them conform with *its* needs. How often have we heard stories of entrepreneurial firms recently acquired by conglomerates being descended upon by hordes of headquarters technocrats bemoaning the loose controls, the absence of organigrams, the informality of the systems? In many cases, of course, the very purpose of the acquisition was to do just this, tighten up the organization so that its strategies can be pursued more pervasively and systematically. But other times, the effect is to destroy the organization's basic strengths, sometimes including its flexibility and responsiveness. Similarly, how many times have we heard tell of government administrators complaining about being unable to control public hospitals or universities through conventional (meaning machine bureaucratic) planning systems?

This conclusion is, in fact, a prime manifestation of the hypothesis [discussed in Chapter 6] that concentrated external control of an organization has the effect of formalizing and centralizing its structure, in other words, of driving it toward the

---

[1] Unless, of course, there is a second layer of divisionalization, which simply takes this conclusion down another level in the hierarchy.

machine configuration. Headquarters' control of divisions is, of course, concentrated; indeed, when the diversified organization is itself a *closed system*, as I shall argue later many tend to be, then it is a most concentrated form of control. And, the effect of that control is to render the divisions its *instruments*.

There is, in fact, an interesting irony in this, in that the less society controls the overall diversified organization, the more the organization itself controls its individual units. The result is increased autonomy for the largest organizations coupled with decreased autonomy for their many activities.

To conclude this discussion of the basic structure, the diversified configuration is represented in the opening figure, symbolically in terms of our logo, as follows. Headquarters has three parts: a small strategic apex of top managers, a small technostructure to the left concerned with the design and operation of the performance control system, and a slightly larger staff support group to the right to provide support services common to all the divisions. Each of the divisions is shown below the headquarters as a machine configuration.

CONDITIONS OF THE DIVERSIFIED ORGANIZATION

While the diversified configuration may arise from the federation of different organizations, which come together under a common headquarters umbrella, more often it appears to be the structural response to a machine organization that has diversified its range of product or service offerings. In either case, it is the diversity of markets above all that drives an organization to use this configuration. An organization faced with a single integrated market simply cannot split itself into autonomous divisions; the one with distinct markets, however, has an incentive to create a unit to deal with each.

There are three main kinds of market diversity—product and service, client, and region. In theory, all three can lead to divisionalization. But when diversification is based on variations in clients or regions as opposed to products or services, divisionalization often turns out to be incomplete. With identical products or services in each region or for each group of clients, the headquarters is encouraged to maintain central control of certain critical functions, to ensure common operating standards for all the divisions. And that seriously reduces divisional autonomy, and so leads to a less than complete form of divisionalization.

Thus, one study found that insurance companies concentrate at headquarters the critical function of investment, and retailers concentrate that of purchasing, also controlling product range, pricing, and volume (Channon, 1975). One need only look at the individual outlets of a typical retail chain to recognize the absence of divisional autonomy: usually they all look alike. The same conclusion tends to hold for other businesses organized by regions, such as bakeries, breweries, cement producers, and soft drink bottlers: Their "divisions," distinguished only by geographical location, lack the autonomy normally associated with ones that produce distinct products or services.

What about the conditions of size? Although large size itself does not bring on divisionalization, surely it is not coincidental that most of America's largest corporations use some variant of this configuration. The fact is that as organizations grow large, they become inclined to diversify and then to divisionalize. One reason is protection: large organizations tend to be risk averse—they have too much to lose—and diversification spreads the risk. Another is that as firms grow large, they come to dominate their traditional market, and so must often find growth opportunities elsewhere, through diversification. Moreover, diversification feeds on itself. It creates a cadre of aggressive general managers, each running his or her own division, who push for further diversification and further growth. Thus, most of the giant corporations—with the exception of the "heavies," those with enormously high fixed-cost operating systems, such as the oil or aluminum producers—not only were able to reach their status by diversifying but also feel great pressures to continue to do so.

Age is another factor associated with this configuration, much like size. In larger organizations, the management runs out of places to expand in its traditional markets; in older ones, the managers sometimes get bored with the traditional markets and find diversion through diversification. Also, time brings new competitors into old markets, forcing the management to look elsewhere for growth opportunities.

As governments grow large, they too tend to adopt a kind of divisionalized structure. The central administrators, unable to control all the agencies and departments directly, settle for granting their managers considerable autonomy and then trying to control their results through planning and performance controls. Indeed, the "accountability" buzzword so often heard in governments these days reflects just this trend—to move closer to a divisionalized structure.

One can, in fact, view the entire government as a giant diversified configuration (admittedly an oversimplification, since all kinds of links exist among the departments), with its three main coordinating agencies corresponding to the three main forms of control used by the headquarters of the large corporation. The budgetary agency, technocratic in nature, concerns itself with performance control of the departments; the public service commission, also partly technocratic, concerns itself with the recruiting and training of government managers; and the executive office, top management in nature, reviews the principal proposals and initiatives of the departments.

In the preceding chapter, the communist state was described as a closed-system machine bureaucracy. But it may also be characterized as the ultimate closed system diversified configuration, with the various state enterprises and agencies its instruments, machine bureaucracies tightly regulated by the planning and control systems of the central government.

STAGES IN THE TRANSITION TO THE DIVERSIFIED ORGANIZATION

There has been a good deal of research on the transition of the corporation from the functional to the diversified form. Figure 2 and the discussion that follows borrow from this research to describe four stages in that transition.

At the top of Figure 2 is the pure *functional* structure, used by the corporation whose operating activities form one integrated, unbroken chain from purchasing through production to marketing and sales. Only the final output is sold to the customers.[2] Autonomy cannot, therefore, be granted to the units, so the organization tends to take on the form of one overall machine configuration.

As an integrated firm seeks wider markets, it may introduce a variety of new end products and so shift all the way to the pure diversified form. A less risky alternative, however, is to start by marketing its intermediate products on the open market. This introduces small breaks in its processing chain, which in turn calls for a measure of divisionalization in its structure, giving rise to the *by-product* form.

[2] It should be noted that this is in fact the definition of a functional structure: Each activity contributes just one step in a chain toward the creation of the final product. Thus, for example, engineering is a functionally organized unit in the firm that produces and markets its own designs, while it would be a market organized unit in a consulting firm that sells its design services, among other, directly to clients.

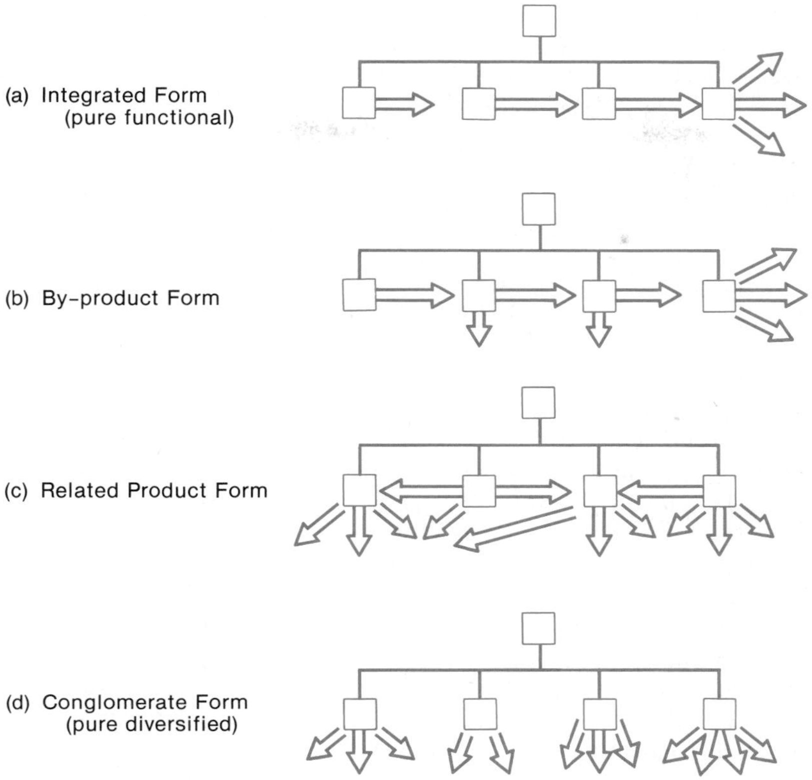

(a) Integrated Form
(pure functional)

(b) By-product Form

(c) Related Product Form

(d) Conglomerate Form
(pure diversified)

FIGURE 2
Stages in the Transition to the Pure Diversified Form

But because the processing chain remains more or less intact, central coordination must largely remain. Organizations that fall into this category tend to be vertically integrated, basing their operations on a single raw material, such as wood, oil, or aluminum, which they process to a variety of consumable end products. The example of Alcoa is shown in Figure 3.

Some corporations further diversify their by-product markets, breaking down their processing chain until what the divisions sell on the open market becomes more important than what they supply to each other. The organization then moves to the *related-product* form. For example, a firm manufacturing washing machines may set up a division to produce the motors. When the motor division sells more motors to outside customers than to its own sister division, a more serious form of divisionalization is called for. What typically holds the divisions of these firms together is some common thread among their products, perhaps a core skill or technology, perhaps a central market theme, as in a corporation such as 3M that likes to describe itself as being in the coating and bonding business. A good deal of the control over the specific product-market strategies can now revert to the divisions, such as research and development.

As a related-product firm expands into new markets or acquires other firms with less regard to a central strategic theme, the organization moves to the *conglomerate* form and so adopts a pure diversified configuration, the one described at the beginning of this reading. Each division serves its own markets, producing products unrelated to those of the other divisions—chinaware in one, steam shovels in a second, and so on.* The result is that the headquarters planning and

---

* I wrote this example here somewhat whimsically before I encountered a firm in Finland with divisions that actually produce, among other things, the world's largest icebreaker ships and fine pottery!

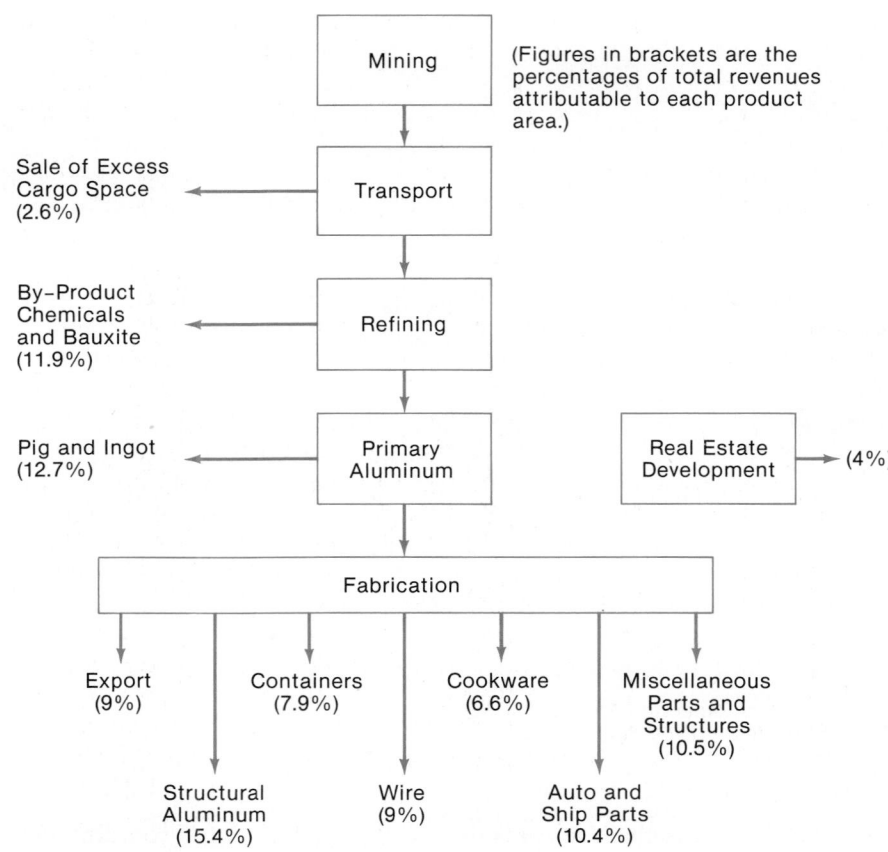

FIGURE 3
By-Product and End-Product Sales of Alcoa (from Rumelt, 1974:21)
Note: Percentages for 1969 prepared by Richard Rumelt from data in company's annual reports.

control system becomes simply a vehicle for regulating performance, and the headquarters staff can diminish to almost nothing—a few general and group managers supported by a few financial analysts with a minimum of support services.

SOME ISSUES ASSOCIATED WITH THE DIVERSIFIED ORGANIZATION

The Economic Advantages of Diversification?

It has been argued that the diversified configuration offers four basic advantages over the functional structure with integrated operations, namely an overall machine configuration. First, it encourages the efficient allocation of capital. Headquarters can choose where to put its money and so can concentrate on its strongest markets, milking the surpluses of some divisions to help others grow. Second, by opening up opportunities to run individual businesses, the diversified configuration helps to train general managers. Third, this configuration spreads its risk across different markets, whereas the focused machine bureaucracy has all its strategic eggs in one market basket, so to speak. Fourth, and perhaps most important, the diversified configuration is strategically responsive. The divisions can fine-tune their bureaucratic machines while the headquarters can concentrate on the strategic portfolio. It can acquire new businesses and divest itself of old, unproductive ones.

But is the single machine organization the correct basis of comparison? Is not the real alternative, at least from society's perspective, the taking of a further step

672

along the same path, to the point of eliminating the headquarters altogether and allowing the divisions to function as independent organization? Beatrice Foods, described in a 1976 *Fortune* magazine article, had 397 different divisions (Martin, 1976). The issue is whether this arrangement was more efficient than 397 separate corporations.[3] In this regard, let us reconsider the four advantages discussed earlier.

In the diversified corporation, headquarters allocates the capital resources among the divisions. In the case of 397 independent corporations, the capital markets do that job instead. Which does it better? Studies suggest that the answer is not simple.

Some people, such as the economist Oliver Williamson (1975, 1985), have argued that the diversified organization may do a better job of allocating money because the capital markets are inefficient. Managers at headquarters who know their divisions can move the money around faster and more effectively. But others find that arrangement more costly and, in some ways, less flexible. Moyer (1970), for example, argued early on that conglomerates pay a premium above stock market prices to acquire businesses, whereas the independent investor need pay only small brokerage fees to diversify his or her own portfolio, and can do so easier and more flexibly. Moreover, that provides the investor with full information on all the businesses owned, whereas the diversified corporation provides only limited information to stockholders on the details inside its portfolio.

On the issue of management development, the question becomes whether the division managers receive better training and experience than they would as company presidents. The diversified organization is able to put on training courses and to rotate its managers to vary their experience; the independent firm is limited in those respects. But if, as the proponents of diversification claim, autonomy is the key to management development, then presumably the more autonomy the better. The division managers have a headquarters to lean on—and to be leaned on by. Company presidents, in contrast, are on their own to make their own mistakes and to learn from them.

On the third issue, risk, the argument from the diversified perspective is that the independent organization is vulnerable during periods of internal crisis or economic slump; conglomeration offers support to see individual businesses through such periods. The counter-argument, however, is that diversification may conceal bankruptcies, that ailing divisions are sometimes supported longer than necessary, whereas the market bankrupts the independent firm and is done with it. Moreover, just as diversification spreads the risk, so too does it spread the consequences of that risk. A single division cannot go bankrupt; the whole organization is legally responsible for its debts. So a massive enough problem in one division can pull down the whole organization. Loose coupling may turn out to be riskier than no coupling!

Finally, there is the issue of strategic responsiveness. Loosely coupled divisions may be more responsive than tightly coupled functions. But how responsive do they really prove to be? The answer appears to be negative: this configuration appears to inhibit, not encourage, the taking of strategic initiatives. The problem seems to lie, again, in its control system. It is designed to keep the carrot just the right distance in front of the divisional managers, encouraging them to strive for better and better financial performance. At the same time, however, it seems to dampen their inclination to innovate. It is that famous "bottom line" that creates

---

[3] The example of Beatrice was first written as presented here in the 1970s, when the company was the subject of a good deal of attention and praise in the business press. At the time of this revision, in 1988, the company is being disassembled. It seemed appropriate to leave the example as first presented, among other reasons to question the tendency to favor fashion over investigation in the business press.

the problem, encouraging short-term thinking and shortsightedness; attention is focused on the carrot just in front instead of the fields of vegetables beyond. As Bower has noted,

> [T]he risk to the division manager of a major innovation can be considerable if he is measured on short-run, year-to-year, earnings performance. The result is a tendency to avoid big risk bets, and the concomitant phenomenon that major new developments are, with few exceptions, made outside the major firms in the industry. Those exceptions tend to be single-product companies whose top managements are committed to true product leadership. . . . Instead, the diversified companies give us a steady diet of small incremental change. (1970:194)

Innovation requires entrepreneurship, or intrapreneurship, and these, as we have already argued, do not thrive under the diversified configuration. The entrepreneur takes his or her own risks to earn his or her own rewards; the intrapreneur (as we shall see) functions best in the loose structure of the innovative adhocracy. Indeed, many diversified corporations depend on those configurations for their strategic responsiveness, since they diversify not by innovating themselves but by acquiring the innovative results of independent firms. Of course, that may be their role—to exploit rather than create those innovations—but we should not, as a result, justify diversification on the basis of its innovative capacity.

The Contribution of Headquarters

To assess the effectiveness of conglomeration, it is necessary to assess what actual contribution the headquarters makes to the divisions. Since what the headquarters does in a diversified organization is otherwise performed by the various boards of directors of a set of independent firms, the question then becomes, what does a headquarters offer to the divisions that the independent board of directors of the autonomous organization does not?

One thing that neither can offer is the management of the individual business. Both are involved with it only on a part-time basis. The management is, therefore, logically left to the full-time managers, who have the required time and information. Among the functions a headquarters *does* perform, as noted earlier, are the establishment of objectives for the divisions, the monitoring of their performance in terms of these objectives, and the maintenance of limited personal contacts with division managers, for example to approve large capital expenditures. Interestingly, those are also the responsibilities of the directors of the individual firm, at least in theory.

In practice, however, many boards of directors—notably, those of widely held corporations—do those things rather ineffectively, leaving business managements carte blanche to do what they like. Here, then, we seem to have a major advantage to the diversified configuration. It exists as an administrative mechanism to overcome another prominent weakness of the free-market system, the ineffective board.

There is a catch in this argument, however, for diversification by enhancing an organization's size and expanding its number of markets, renders the corporation more difficult to understand and so to control by its board of part-time directors. Moreover, as Moyer has noted, one common effect of conglomerate acquisition is to increase the number of shareholders, and so to make the corporation more widely held, and therefore less amenable to director control. Thus, the diversified configuration in some sense resolves a problem of its own making—it offers the control that its own existence has rendered difficult. Had the corporation remained in one business, it might have been more narrowly held and easier to understand, and so its directors might have been able to perform their functions more effectively. Diversification thus helped to create the problem that divisionalization is said to solve. Indeed, it is ironic that many a diversified corporation that does such a vigorous job of monitoring the performance of its own divisions is itself so poorly monitored by its own board of directors!

All of this suggests that large diversified organizations tend to be classic closed systems, powerful enough to seal themselves off from much external influence while able to exercise a good deal of control over not only their own divisions, as instruments, but also their external environments. For example, one study of all 5,995 directors of the *Fortune* 500 found that only 1.6 percent of them represented major shareholder interests (Smith, 1978) while another survey of 855 corporations found that 84 percent of them did not even formally require their directors to hold any stock at all! (Bacon, 1973:40).

What does happen when problems arise in a division? What can a headquarters do that various boards of directors cannot? The chairman of one major conglomerate told a meeting of the New York Society of Security Analysts, in reference to the headquarters vice presidents who oversee the divisions, that "it is not too difficult to coordinate five companies that are well run" (in Wrigley, 1970:V78). True enough. But what about five that are badly run? What could the small staff of administrators at a corporation's headquarters really do to correct problems in that firm's thirty operating divisions or in Beatrice's 397? The natural tendency to tighten the control screws does not usually help once the problem has manifested itself, nor does exercising close surveillance. As noted earlier, the headquarters managers cannot manage the divisions. Essentially, that leaves them with two choices. They can either replace the division manager, or they can divest the corporation of the division. Of course, a board of directors can also replace the management. Indeed, that seems to be its only real prerogative; the management does everything else.

On balance, then, the economic case for one headquarters versus a set of separate boards of directors appears to be mixed. It should, therefore, come as no surprise that one important study found that corporations with "controlled diversity" had better profits than those with conglomerate diversity (Rumelt, 1974). Overall, the pure diversified configuration (the conglomerate) may offer some advantages over a weak system of separate boards of directors and inefficient capital markets, but most of those advantages would probably disappear if certain problems in capital markets and boards of directors were rectified. And there is reason to argue, from a social no less than an economic standpoint, that society would be better off trying to correct fundamental inefficiencies in its economic system rather than encourage private administrative arrangements to circumvent them, as we shall now see.

The Social Performance of the Performance Control System

This configuration requires that headquarters control the divisions primarily by quantitative performance criteria, and that typically means financial ones—profit, sales growth, return on investment, and the like. The problem is that these performance measures often become virtual obsessions in the diversified organization, driving out goals that cannot be measured—product quality, pride in work, customers well served. In effect, the economic goals drive out the social ones. As the chief of a famous conglomerate once remarked, "We, in Textron, worship the god of New Worth" (in Wrigley, 1970:V86).

That would pose no problem if the social and economic consequences of decisions could easily be separated. Governments would look after the former, corporations the latter. But the fact is that the two are intertwined; every strategic decision of every large corporation involves both, largely inseparable. As a result, its control systems, by focusing on economic measures, drive the diversified organization to act in ways that are, at best, socially unresponsive, at worst, socially irresponsible. Forced to concentrate on the economic consequences of decisions, the division manager is driven to ignore their social consequences. (Indeed, that manager is also driven to ignore the intangible economic consequences as well, such as product quality or research effort, another manifestation of the problem of the short-term, bottom-line thinking mentioned earlier.) Thus, Bower found that "the best records in the race relations area are those of single-product companies whose strong top managements are deeply involved in the business" (1970:193).

Robert Ackerman, in a study carried out at the Harvard Business School, investigated this point. He found that social benefits such as "a rosier public image . . . pride among managers . . . an attractive posture for recruiting on campus" could not easily be measured and so could not be plugged into the performance control system. The result was that

> . . . the financial reporting system may actually inhibit social responsiveness. By focusing on economic performance, even with appropriate safeguards to protect against sacrificing long-term benefits, such a system directs energy and resources to achieving results measured in financial terms. It is the only game in town, so to speak, at least the only one with an official scoreboard. (1975:55, 56)

Headquarters managers who are concerned about legal liabilities or the public relations effects of decisions, or even ones personally interested in broader social issues, may be tempted to intervene directly in the divisions' decision-making process to ensure proper attention to social matters. But they are discouraged from doing so by this configuration's strict division of labor: divisional autonomy requires no meddling by the headquarters in specific business decisions.

As long as the screws of the performance control system are not turned too tight, the division managers may retain enough discretion to consider the social consequences of their actions, if they so choose. But when those screws are turned tight, as they often are in the diversified corporation with a bottom-line orientation, then the division managers wishing to keep their jobs may have no choice but to act socially unresponsively, if not actually irresponsibly. As Bower has noted of the General Electric price-fixing scandal of the 1960s, "a very severely managed system of reward and punishment that demanded yearly improvements in earnings, return and market share, applied indiscriminately to all divisions, yielded a situation which was—at the very least—conducive to collusion in the oligopolistic and mature electric equipment markets" (1970:193).

The Diversified Organization in the Public Sphere

Ironically, for a government intent on dealing with these social problems, solutions are indicated in the very arguments used to support the diversified configuration. Or so it would appear.

For example, if the administrative arrangements are efficient while the capital markets are not, then why should a government hesitate to interfere with the capital markets? And why shouldn't it use those same administrative arrangements to deal with the problems? If Beatrice Foods really can control those 397 divisions, then what is to stop Washington from believing it can control 397 Beatrices? After all, the capital markets don't much matter. In his book on "countervailing power,"

John Kenneth Galbraith (1952) argued that bigness in one sector, such as business, promotes bigness in other sectors, such as unions and government. That has already happened. How long before government pursues the logical next step and exercises direct controls?

While such steps may prove irresistible to some governments, the fact is that they will not resolve the problems of power concentration and social irresponsibility but rather will aggravate them, but not just in the ways usually assumed in Western economics. All the existing problems would simply be bumped up to another level, and there increase. By making use of the diversified configuration, government would magnify the problems of size. Moreover, government, like the corporation, would be driven to favor measurable economic goals over intangible social ones, and that would add to the problems of social irresponsibility—a phenomenon of which we have already seen a good deal in the public sector.

In fact, these problems would be worse in government, because its sphere is social, and so its goals are largely ill suited to performance control systems. In other words, many of the goals most important for the public sector—and this applies to not-for-profit organizations in spheres such as health and education as well —simply do not lend themselves to measurement, no matter how long and how hard public officials continue to try. And without measurement, the conventional diversified configuration cannot work.

There are, of course, other problems with the application of this form of organization in the public sphere. For example, government cannot divest itself of subunits quite so easily as can corporations. And public service regulations on appointments and the like, as well as a host of other rules, preclude the degree of division manager autonomy available in the private sector. (It is, in fact, these central rules and regulations that make governments resemble integrated machine configurations as much as loosely coupled diversified ones, and that undermine their efforts at "accountability.")

Thus, we conclude that, appearances and even trends notwithstanding, the diversified configuration is generally not suited to the public and not-for-profit sectors of society. Governments and other public-type institutions that wish to divisionalize to avoid centralized machine bureaucracy may often find the imposition of performance standards an artificial exercise. They may thus be better off trying to exercise control of their units in a different way. For example, they can select unit managers who reflect their desired values, or indoctrinate them in those values, and then let them manage freely, the control in effect being normative rather than quantitative. But managing ideology, even creating it in the first place, is no simple matter, especially in a highly diversified organization.

In Conclusion: A Structure on the Edge of a Cliff

Our discussion has led to a "damned if you do, damned if you don't" conclusion. The pure (conglomerate) diversified configuration emerges as an organization perched symbolically on the edge of the cliff, at the end of a long path. Ahead, it is one step away from disintegration—breaking up into separate organizations on the rocks below. Behind it is the way back to a more stable integration, in the form of the machine configuration at the start of that path. And ever hovering above is the eagle, representing the broader social control of the state, attracted by the organization's position on the edge of the cliff and waiting for the chance to pull it up to a higher cliff, perhaps more dangerous still. The edge of the cliff is an uncomfortable place to be, perhaps even a temporary one that must inevitably lead to disintegration on the rocks below, a trip to that cliff above, or a return to a safer resting place somewhere on that path behind.

THE PRODUCT PORTFOLIO* (GROWTH-SHARE MATRIX OF THE BOSTON CONSULTING GROUP)

BY BRUCE D. HENDERSON

To be successful, a company should have a portfolio of products with different growth rates and different market shares. The portfolio composition is a function of the balance between cash flows. High-growth products require cash inputs to grow. Low-growth products should generate excess cash. Both kinds are needed simultaneously.

Four rules determine the cash flow of a product:

Margins and cash generated are a function of market share. High margins and high market share go together. This is a matter of common observation, explained by the experience curve effect.

Growth requires cash input to finance added assets. The added cash required to hold share is a function of growth rates.

High market share must be earned or bought. Buying market share requires additional investment.

No product market can grow indefinitely. The payoff from growth must come when the growth slows, or it will not come at all. The payoff is cash that cannot be reinvested in that product.

Products with high market share and slow growth are "cash cows." (See Figure 1.) Characteristically, they generate large amounts of cash, in excess of the reinvestment required to maintain share. This excess need not, and should not, be reinvested in those products. In fact, if the rate of return exceeds the growth rate, the cash *cannot* be reinvested indefinitely, except by depressing returns.

Products with low market share and slow growth are "dogs." They may show an accounting profit, but the profit must be reinvested to maintain share, leaving no cash throwoff. The product is essentially worthless, except in liquidation.

All products eventually become either a "cash cow" or a "dog." The value of a product is completely dependent upon obtaining a leading share of its market before the growth slows.

Low-market-share, high-growth products are the "problem children." They almost always require far more cash than they can generate. If cash is not supplied, they fall behind and die. Even when the cash is supplied, if they only hold their share, they are still dogs when the growth stops. The "problem children" require large added cash investment for market share to be purchased. The low-market-share, high-growth product is a liability unless it becomes a leader. It requires very large cash inputs that it cannot generate itself.

The high-share, high-growth product is the "star." It nearly always shows reported profits, but it may or may not generate all of its own cash. If it stays a leader, however, it will become a large cash generator when growth slows and its reinvestment requirements diminish. The star eventually becomes the cash cow—providing high volume, high margin, high stability, security—and cash throwoff for reinvestment elsewhere.

678

* Originally published in *Henderson on Corporate Strategy* (Cambridge, MA; Abt Books, Copyright © 1979); reprinted by permission of the author and the publisher. pp. 163–166.

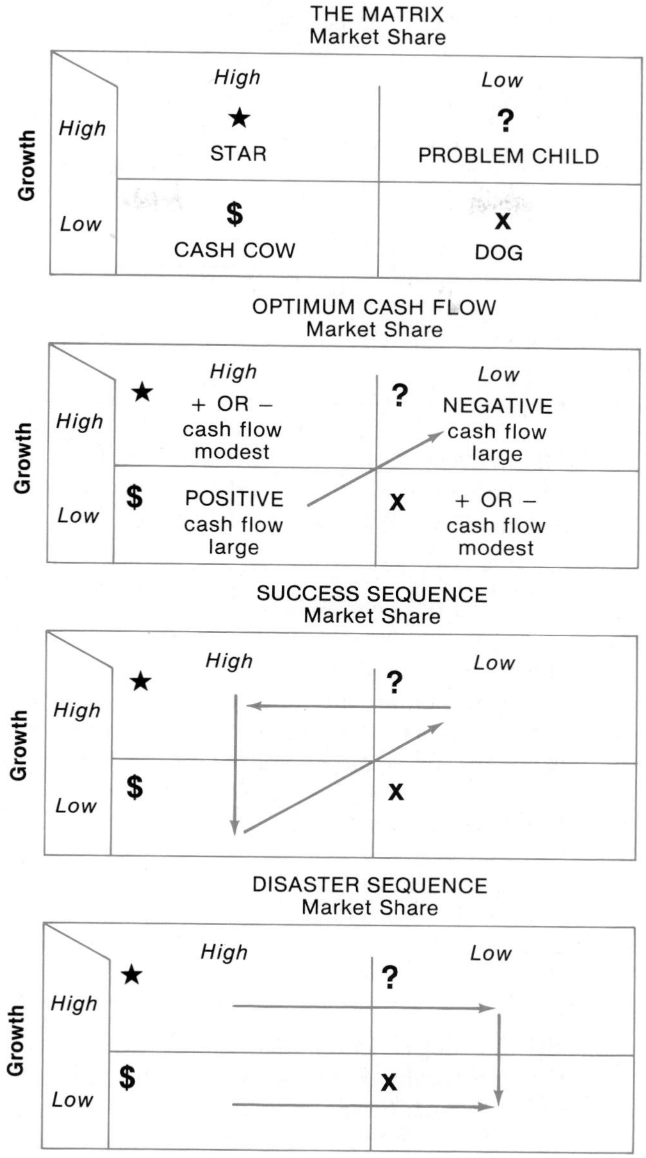

FIGURE 1
Boston Consulting Group
Growth-Share Matrix

The payoff for leadership is very high indeed, if it is achieved early and maintained until growth slows. Investment in market share during the growth phase can be very attractive—if you have the cash. Growth in market is compounded by growth in share. Increases in share increase the margin. Higher margin permits higher leverage with equal safety. The resulting profitability permits higher payment of earning after financing normal growth. The return on investment is enormous.

The need for a portfolio of businesses becomes obvious. Every company needs products in which to invest cash. Every company needs products that generate cash. And every product should eventually be a cash generator; otherwise, it is worthless.

Only a diversified company with a balanced portfolio can use its strengths to truly capitalize on its growth opportunities. The balanced portfolio has "stars," whose high share and high growth assure the future.

"cash cows," that supply funds for that future growth.

"problem children," to be converted into "stars" with the added funds.

"Dogs" are not necessary. They are evidence of failure either to obtain a leadership position during the growth phase, or to get out and cut the losses.

• REVERSING THE IMAGES OF BCG'S GROWTH SHARE MATRIX*

BY JOHN A. SEEGER

. . . Simple concepts can easily be oversimplified, and graphic descriptors can become stereotypes. Few current business concepts are more prone to oversimplification than the growth/share model, with its labeling of products or divisions or whole companies as "dogs," "question marks," "stars" or "cash cows." Three-quarters of those labels are subject to dangerous misapplication, because popularized versions of the BCG philosophy and its derivatives carry a handy prescription for each category: we should kick the dogs, cloister the cows, and throw our money at the stars. Only the question mark category demands management thought.

This commentary attempts to counter these superficial prescriptions by turning the BCG model's own images back upon themselves. If the tendency to oversimplify comes from the language's imagery, then we must make the images do double duty; they must remind the student and manager of the growth/share matrix's pitfalls as well as its presumptions.

EVERY DOG HAS ITS DAY

Consider the "dogs." In the BCG model these are the portfolio components which have low market shares and whose markets themselves are matured or shrinking; these are components we should dispose of, for they are going nowhere. The image conveyed by BCG's term is that of a feral beast preying on our resources or of a mangy cur slinking off with our picnic hotdogs.

But there are other kinds of dogs—warm, loving companions of humanity since the time of the caves. These dogs give unquestioning loyalty to their managers, serving as scouts or watchdogs, to spread the alarm if intruders threaten. By establishing a presence—with bared teeth if necessary—these friendly dogs prevent their wild cousins from approaching our picnic at all. They protect our weaker members and occupy the territory so that attackers will keep their distance. Our own dogs can repay handsomely a small investment in dog food and flea powder. . . .

"It's a dog," says [one CEO of his key] retail product line. "I only wish I could get rid of it." Such attitudes are easily sensed, by canines or humans. It is

* Originally published in the *Strategic Management Journal* Copyright © 1984 John Wiley & Sons; reprinted with deletions by permission of John Wiley & Sons Limited.

predictable that the managers of his company regard its retail division as the least attractive assignment in the company. Good managers do not willingly stay with an organization which is defined in the boss's eyes as hopeless.

Divesting this retail division would be analogous to a fire engine company's disposing of its Dalmation hound. The dog does not contribute much to the direct function of putting out fires. But it looks good in photographs; it makes life more pleasant for the firefighters during their boring waits for alarms; and it keeps other dogs from pissing on the equipment.

WHAT DO YOU GET FROM A CASH COW?

Consider the "cash cow." In the BCG model this is a business component which does dominate its market, but whose market is not growing. Since growth cannot logically be expected here, the consultant's advice is to operate the business as a cash flow generator. Management should deny requests for new resources from a cash cow component, and concentrate on milking it for the highest possible returns.

The imagery conveyed by this term is doubly unfortunate. In oversimplified form, the "cash cow" brand can result in the gradual wastage of both the physical and human resources of an organization, as operating management learns not to request new resources and top management learns not to demand continual replenishment of the unit's productive capacities. Where operations are measured in current profitability and growth aspirations are systematically throttled, it is natural for growth-oriented managers to leave the organization. They are replaced by people content to operate the business as it stands but uninterested and unskilled at changing the business. The creative energy required for continual renewal can decay as natural attrition suits the culture of the organization to its "cash cow" role.

In effect, classification as a cash cow may be the equivalent, over time, of placing the unit in a cloister where distractions of the outside world are minimized and all attentions are focused on the single goal, generation of high cash flows. "Milking managers" will be expert at feeding the cow and keeping it healthy in the short run. They may not be adept at maintaining the barn, however. Particularly where large outlays are needed for long term improvements, the cash cow manager is likely to postpone investments which would hurt cash flow in the short run.

Keeping creativity, innovation and energy at high levels in an organization designated as a cash cow is an unsolved problem. One possible solution is suggested by another look at the BCG symbolism. A cow can give more than milk; properly exposed to outside influences and environmental forces, a cow can also give calves.

The investment needed to produce a calf, given that you already have a cow, is incredibly small; without a cow, no amount of investment will do the job. Similarly, the investment needed to produce creative ideas, given a creative workforce, is small; where natural energy has burned out, however, no amount of effort will produce innovation. Recognition of the importance of new projects—even though the business unit itself lacks the resources to exploit them—might help retain the creativity needed in a naturally adaptive organization. Provision of exploitation channels outside the business unit itself—through transfer to other corporate units, new subsidiaries, joint ventures, or entrepreneurial sabbatical leaves—could help the unit's people see the utility of continued idea generation. In a time of diminished general economic growth, no company can afford to reject a good idea because it comes from a unit which is not "supposed to" grow. Neither can we afford to let the "cash cow" label stifle the creativity and adaptability which are vital to survival in increasingly competitive times.

The dairying analogy is appropriate for these organizations, so long as we resist the urge to oversimplify it. On the farm, even the best producing cows eventually begin to dry up. The farmer's solution to this is euphemistically called "freshening" the cow: he arranges a date with a bull; she has a calf; the milk begins flowing again. Cloistering the cow—isolating her from everything but the feed trough and the milking machines—assures that she will go dry.

THE FAULT LIES NOT IN OUR STARS, BUT IN OURSELVES . . .

Consider the "stars." In the BCG model, these are the business units with major shares of growing markets. These are the units which need resources and investments in order to exploit their opportunities. These are the units sought by aggressive, ambitious people, who crave the excitement and challenges of growth. It is in the stars that people blaze career reputations and become recognized as winners.

Unfortunately, however, not all stars turn out to be winners over the long term. Current market share and market growth rates are not sufficient criteria to justify investment, although they suffice to label the business unit as a star. Oversimplification of the BCG prescription can result in investing in situations whose growth rates cannot be sustained in the future for a variety of reasons not apparent in backward scanning market analysis. . . .

Investment based on growth rate and share, without regard for environmental constraints or market saturation, is encouraged by the oversimplification inherent in the popular two-by-two matrices.

Still, with proper qualification, the "star" analogy is appropriate. Think, for example, about the stars themselves. What we know of them is based on old information. When we observe a star through the telescope, we see evidence of an energetic past, but we have no knowledge of whether that same star is still producing energy now. The light we observe has been traveling towards us for eons—billions of years in some cases—and its source may have long since degenerated into a white dwarf or even a black hole, which would absorb any amount of resources we would care to throw at it without ever permitting any return.

Organizational stars, to, take their place in the BCG matrix based on their past performance. Whether they merit additional investment depends on their future potential, not upon their past.

CONCLUSION

I have no quarrel with the fourth BCG category, the "question mark" business unit. This unit, a nondominant participator in a growing market, requires management thought, says the BCG model. All the categories require management thought.

No management model can safely substitute for analysis and common sense. Models are useful to managers, to the extent that they can help provide order to the thinking process. Models are dangerous to managers, to the extent that they bias judgement or substitute for analysis. . . .

FROM COMPETITIVE ADVANTAGE TO CORPORATE STRATEGY*

BY MICHAEL E. PORTER

Corporate strategy, the overall plan for a diversified company, is both the darling and the stepchild of contemporary management practice—the darling because CEOs have been obsessed with diversification since the early 1960s, the stepchild because almost no consensus exists about what corporate strategy is, much less about how a company should formulate it.

A diversified company has two levels of strategy: business unit (or competitive) strategy and corporate (or companywide) strategy. Competitive strategy concerns how to create competitive advantage in each of the businesses in which a company competes. Corporate strategy concerns two different questions: what businesses the corporation should be in and how the corporate office should manage the array of business units.

Corporate strategy is what makes the corporate whole add up to more than the sum of its business unit parts.

The track record of corporate strategies has been dismal. I studied the diversification records of 33 large, prestigious U.S. companies over the 1950–1986 period and found that most of them had divested many more acquisitions than they had kept. The corporate strategies of most companies have dissipated instead of created shareholder value.

The need to rethink corporate strategy could hardly be more urgent. By taking over companies and breaking them up, corporate raiders thrive on failed corporate strategy. Fueled by junk bond financing and growing acceptability, raiders can expose any company to takeover, no matter how large or blue chip. . . .

A SOBER PICTURE

. . . My study of 33 companies, many of which have reputations for good management, is a unique look at the track record of major corporations. . . . Each company entered an average of 80 new industries and 27 new fields. Just over 70% of the new entries were acquisitions, 22% were start-ups, and 8% were joint ventures. IBM, Exxon, Du Pont, and 3M, for example, focused on startups, while ALCO Standard, Beatrice, and Sara Lee diversified almost solely through acquisitions. . . .

My data paint a sobering picture of the success ratio of these moves. . . . I found that on average corporations divested more than half their acquisitions in new industries and more than 60% of their acquisitions in entirely new fields. Fourteen companies left more than 70% of all the acquisitions they had made in new fields. The track record in unrelated acquisitions is even worse—the average divestment rate is startling 74%. Even a highly respected company like General Electric divested a very high percentage of its acquisitions, particularly those in new fields. . . . Some [companies] bear witness to the success of well-thought-out corporate strategies. Others, however, enjoy a lower rate simply because they have not faced up to their problem units and divested them. . . .

* Originally published in the *Harvard Business Review* (May–June 1987) and winner of the McKinsey Prize for the best in the *Review* in 1987. Copyright © 1987 by the President and Fellows of Harvard College; all rights reserved. Reprinted with deletions by permission of the Harvard Business Review.

I would like to make one comment on the use of shareholder value to judge performance. Linking shareholder value quantitatively to diversification performance only works if you compare the shareholder value that is with the shareholder value that might have been without diversification. Because such a comparison is virtually impossible to make, my own measure of diversification success—the number of units retained by the company—seems to be as good an indicator as any of the contribution of diversification to corporate performance.

My data give a stark indication of the failure of corporate strategies.[1] Of the 33 companies, 6 had been taken over as my study was being completed. . . . Only the lawyers, investment bankers, and original sellers have prospered in most of these acquisitions, not the shareholders.

PREMISES OF CORPORATE STRATEGY

Any successful corporate strategy builds on a number of premises. These are facts of life about diversification. They cannot be altered, and when ignored, they explain in part why so many corporate strategies fail.

Competition Occurs at the Business Unit Level: Diversified companies do not compete; only their business units do. Unless a corporate strategy places primary attention on nurturing the success of each unit, the strategy will fail, no matter how elegantly constructed. Successful corporate strategy must grow out of and reinforce competitive strategy.

Diversification Inevitably Adds Costs and Constraints to Business Units: Obvious costs such as the corporate overhead allocated to a unit may not be as important or subtle as the hidden costs and constraints. A business unit must explain its decisions to top management, spend time complying with planning and other corporate systems, live with parent company guidelines and personnel policies, and forgo the opportunity to motivate employees with direct equity ownership. These costs and constraints can be reduced but not entirely eliminated.

Shareholders Can Readily Diversify Themselves: Shareholders can diversify their own portfolios of stocks by selecting those that best match their preferences and risk profiles (Salter and Weinhold, 1979). Shareholders can often diversify more cheaply than a corporation because they can buy shares at the market price and avoid hefty acquisition premiums.

These premises mean that corporate strategy cannot succeed unless it truly adds value—to business units by providing tangible benefits that offset the inherent costs of lost independence and to shareholders by diversifying in a way they could not replicate.

---

[1] Some recent evidence also supports the conclusion that acquired companies often suffer eroding performance after acquisition. See Frederick M. Scherer, "Mergers, Sell-Offs and Managerial Behavior," in *The Economics of Strategic Planning,* ed. Lacy Glenn Thomas (Lexington, MA: Lexington Books, 1986), p. 143, and David A. Ravenscraft and Frederick M. Scherer, "Mergers and Managerial Performance," paper presented at the Conference on Takeovers and Contests for Corporate Control, Columbia Law School, 1985.

To understand how to formulate corporate strategy, it is necessary to specify the conditions under which diversification will truly create shareholder value. These conditions can be summarized in three essential tests:

1. *The attractiveness test.* The industries chosen for diversification must be structurally attractive or capable of being made attractive.

2. *The cost-of-entry test.* The cost of entry must not capitalize all the future profits.

3. *The better-off test.* Either the new unit must gain competitive advantage from its link with the corporation or vice versa.

Of course, most companies will make certain that their proposed strategies pass some of these tests. But my study clearly shows that when companies ignored one or two of them, the strategic results were disastrous.

How Attractive Is the Industry?

In the long run, the rate of return available from competing in an industry is a function of its underlying structure [see Porter reading in Chapter 4]. An attractive industry with a high average return on investment will be difficult to enter because entry barriers are high, suppliers and buyers have only modest bargaining power, substitute products or services are few, and the rivalry among competitors is stable. An unattractive industry like steel will have structural flaws, including a plethora of substitute materials, powerful and price-sensitive buyers, and excessive rivalry caused by high fixed costs and a large group of competitors, many of whom are state supported.

Diversification cannot create shareholder value unless new industries have favorable structures that support returns exceeding the cost of capital. If the industry doesn't have such returns, the company must be able to restructure the industry or gain a sustainable competitive advantage that leads to returns well above the industry average. An industry need not be attractive before diversification. In fact, a company might benefit from entering before the industry shows its full potential. The diversification can then transform the industry's structure.

In my research, I often found companies had suspended the attractiveness test because they had a vague belief that the industry "fit" very closely with their own businesses. In the hope that the corporate "comfort" they felt would lead to a happy outcome, the companies ignored fundamentally poor industry structures. Unless the close fit allows substantial competitive advantage, however, such comfort will turn into pain when diversification results in poor returns. Royal Dutch Shell and other leading oil companies have had this unhappy experience in a number of chemicals businesses, where poor industry structures overcame the benefits of vertical integration and skills in process technology.

Another common reason for ignoring the attractiveness test is a low entry cost. Sometimes the buyer has an inside track or the owner is anxious to sell. Even if the price is actually low, however, a one-shot gain will not offset a perpetually poor business. Almost always, the company finds it must reinvest in the newly acquired unit, if only to replace fixed assets and fund working capital.

Diversifying companies are also prone to use rapid growth or other simple indicators as a proxy for a target industry's attractiveness. Many that rushed into fast-growing industries (personal computers, video games, and robotics, for example) were burned because they mistook early growth for long-term profit potential. Industries are profitable not because they are sexy or high tech; they are profitable only if their structures are attractive.

What Is the Cost of Entry?

Diversification cannot build shareholder value if the cost of entry into a new business eats up its expected returns. Strong market forces, however, are working to do just that. A company can enter new industries by acquisition or start-up. Acquisitions expose it to an increasingly efficient merger market. An acquirer beats the market if it pays a price not fully reflecting the prospects of the new unit. Yet multiple bidders are commonplace, information flows rapidly, and investment bankers and other intermediaries work aggressively to make the market as efficient as possible. In recent years, new financial instruments such a junk bonds have brought new buyers into the market and made even large companies vulnerable to takeover. Acquisition premiums are high and reflect the acquired company's future prospects—sometimes too well. Philip Morris paid more than four times book value for Seven-Up Company, for example. Simple arithmetic meant that profits had to more than quadruple to sustain the preacquisition ROI. Since there proved to be little Philip Morris could add in marketing prowess to the sophisticated marketing wars in the soft drink industry, the result was the unsatisfactory financial performance of Seven-Up and ultimately the decision to divest.

In a start-up, the company must overcome entry barriers. It's a real catch-22 situation, however, since attractive industries are attractive because their entry barriers are high. Bearing the full cost of the entry barriers might well dissipate any potential profits. Otherwise, other entrants to the industry would have already eroded its profitability.

In the excitement of finding an appealing new business, companies sometimes forget to apply the cost-of-entry test. The more attractive a new industry, the more expensive it is to get into.

Will the Business Be Better Off?

A corporation must bring some significant competitive advantage to the new unit, or the new unit must offer potential for significant advantage to the corporation. Sometimes, the benefits to the new unit accrue only once, near the time of entry, when the parent instigates a major overhaul of its strategy or installs a first-rate management team. Other diversification yields ongoing competitive advantage if the new unit can market its product, through the well-developed distribution system of its sister units, for instance. This is one of the important underpinnings of the merger of Baxter Travenol and American Hospital Supply.

When the benefit to the new unit comes only once, the parent company has no rationale for holding the new unit in its portfolio over the long term. Once the results of the one-time improvement are clear, the diversified company no longer adds value to offset the inevitable costs imposed on the unit. It is best to sell the unit and free up corporate resources.

The better-off test does not imply that diversifying corporate risk creates shareholder value in and of itself. Doing something for shareholders that they can do themselves is not a basis for corporate strategy. (Only in the case of a privately held company, in which the company's and the shareholder's risk are the same, is diversification to reduce risk valuable for its own sake.) Diversification of risk should only be a by-product of corporate strategy, not a prime motivator.

Executives ignore the better-off test most of all or deal with it through arm waving or trumped-up logic rather than hard strategic analysis. One reason is that they confuse company size with shareholder value. In the drive to run a bigger company, they lose sight of their real job. They may justify the suspension of the better-off test by pointing to the way they manage diversity. By cutting corporate staff to the bone and giving business units nearly complete autonomy, they believe they avoid the pitfalls. Such thinking misses the whole point of diversification, which is to create shareholder value rather than to avoid destroying it.

CONCEPTS OF CORPORATE STRATEGY

The three tests for successful diversification set the standards that any corporate strategy must meet; meeting them is so difficult that most diversification fails. Many companies lack a clear concept of corporate strategy to guide their diversification or pursue a concept that does not address the tests. Others fail because they implement a strategy poorly.

My study has helped me identify four concepts of corporate strategy that have been put into practice—portfolio management, restructuring, transferring skills, and sharing activities. While the concepts are not always mutually exclusive, each rests on a different mechanism by which the corporation creates shareholder value and each requires the diversified company to manage and organize itself in a different way. The first two require no connections among business units; the second two depend on them. . . . While all four concepts of strategy have succeeded under the right circumstances, today some make more sense than others. Ignoring any of the concepts is perhaps the quickest road to failure.

Portfolio Management

The concept of corporate strategy most in use is portfolio management, which is based primarily on diversification through acquisition. The corporation acquires sound, attractive companies with competent managers who agree to stay on. While acquired units do not have to be in the same industries as existing units, the best portfolio managers generally limit their range of businesses in some way, in part to limit the specific expertise needed by top management.

The acquired units are autonomous, and the teams that run them are compensated according to unit results. The corporation supplies capital and works with each to infuse it with professional management techniques. At the same time, top management provides objective and dispassionate review of business unit results. Portfolio managers categorize units by potential and regularly transfer resources from units that generate cash to those with high potential and cash needs. . . .

In most countries, the days when portfolio management was a valid concept of corporate strategy are past. In the face of increasingly well-developed capital markets, attractive companies with good managements show up on everyone's computer screen and attract top dollar in terms of acquisition premium. Simply contributing capital isn't contributing much. A sound strategy can easily be funded; small to medium-size companies don't need a munificent parent.

Other benefits have also eroded. Large companies no longer corner the market for professional management skills; in fact, more and more observers believe managers cannot necessarily run anything in the absence of industry-specific knowledge and experience. . . .

But it is the sheer complexity of the management task that has ultimately defeated even the best portfolio managers. As the size of the company grows, portfolio managers need to find more and more deals just to maintain growth. Supervising dozens or even hundreds of disparate units and under chain-letter pressures to add more, management begins to make mistakes. At the same time, the inevitable costs of being part of a diversified company take their toll and unit performance slides while the whole company's ROI turns downward. Eventually, a new management team is installed that initiates wholesale divestments and pares down the company to its core businesses. . . .

In developing countries, where large companies are few, capital markets are undeveloped, and professional management is scarce, portfolio management still works. But it is no longer a valid model for corporate strategy in advanced economies. . . . Portfolio management is no way to conduct corporate strategy.

Restructuring

Unlike its passive role as a portfolio manager, when it serves as banker and reviewer, a company that bases its strategy on restructuring becomes an active restructurer of business units. The new businesses are no necessarily related to existing units. All that is necessary is unrealized potential.

The restructuring strategy seeks out undeveloped, sick, or threatened organizations or industries on the threshold of significant change. The parent intervenes, frequently changing the unit management team, shifting strategy, or infusing the company with new technology. Then it may make follow-up acquisitions to build a critical mass and sell off unneeded or unconnected parts and thereby reduce the effective acquisition cost. The result is a strengthened company or a transformed industry. As a coda, the parent sells off the stronger unit once results are clear because the parent is no longer adding value, and top management decides that its attention should be directed elsewhere. . . .

When well implemented, the restructuring concept is sound, for it passes the three tests of successful diversification. The restructurer meets the cost-of-entry test through the types of company it acquires. It limits acquisition premiums by buying companies with problems and lackluster images or by buying into industries with as yet unforeseen potential. Intervention by the corporation clearly meets the better-off test. Provided that the target industries are structurally attractive, the restructuring model can create enormous shareholder value. . . . Ironically, many of today's restructurers are profiting from yesterday's portfolio management strategies.

To work, the restructuring strategy requires a corporate management team with the insight to spot undervalued companies or positions in industries ripe for transformation. The same insight is necessary to actually turn the units around even though they are in new and unfamiliar businesses. . . .

Perhaps the greatest pitfall . . . is that companies find it very hard to dispose of business units once they are restructured and performing well. . . .

Transferring Skills

The purpose of the first two concepts of corporate strategy is to create value through a company's relationship with each autonomous unit. The corporation's role is to be a selector, a banker, and an intervenor.

The last two concepts exploit the interrelationships between businesses. In articulating them, however, one comes face-to-face with the often ill-defined concept of synergy. If you believe the text of the countless corporate annual reports, just about anything is related to just about anything else! But imagined synergy is much more common than real synergy. GM's purchase of Hughes Aircraft simply because cars were going electronic and Hughes was an electronics concern demonstrates the folly of paper synergy. Such corporate relatedness is an ex post facto rationalization of a diversification undertaken for other reasons.

Even synergy that is clearly defined often fails to materialize. Instead of cooperating, business units often compete. A company that can define the synergies it is pursuing still faces significant organizational impediments in achieving them.

But the need to capture the benefits of relationships between businesses has never been more important. Technological and competitive developments already link many businesses and are creating new possibilities for competitive advantage. In such sectors as financial services, computing, office equipment, entertainment, and health care, interrelationships among previously distinct businesses are perhaps the central concern of strategy.

To understand the role of relatedness in corporate strategy, we must give new meaning to this often ill-defined idea. I have identified a good way to start—the value chain. [See pp. 72–74] Every business unit is a collection of discrete activities ranging from sales to accounting that allow it to compete. I call them value activities. It is at this level, not in the company as a whole, that the unit achieves competitive advantage.

I group these activities in nine categories. *Primary* activities create the product or service, deliver and market it, and provide after-sale support. The categories of primary activities are inbound logistics, operations, outbound logistics, marketing and sales, and service. *Support* activities provide the input and infrastructure that allow the primary activities to take place. The categories are company infrastructure, human resource management, technology development, and procurement.

The value chain defines the two types of interrelationships that may create synergy. The first is a company's ability to transfer skills or expertise among similar value chains. The second is the ability to share activities. Two business units, for example, can share the same sales force or logistics network.

The value chain helps expose the last two (and most important) concepts of corporate strategy. The transfer of skills among business units in the diversified company is the basis for one concept. While each business unit has a separate value chain, knowledge about how to perform activities is transferred among the units. For example, a toiletries business unit, expert in the marketing of convenience products, transmits ideas on new positioning concepts, promotional techniques, and packaging possibilities to a newly acquired unit that sells cough syrup. Newly entered industries can benefit from the expertise of existing units, and vice versa.

These opportunities arise when business units have similar buyers or channels, similar value activities like government relations or procurement, similarities in the broad configuration of the value chain (for example, managing a multisite service organization), or the same strategic concept (for example, low cost). Even though the units operate separately, such similarities allow the sharing of knowledge. . . .

Transferring skills leads to competitive advantage only if the similarities among businesses meet three conditions:

1. The activities involved in the businesses are similar enough that sharing expertise is meaningful. Broad similarities (marketing intensiveness, for example, or a common core process technology such as bending metal) are not a sufficient basis for diversification. The resulting ability to transfer skills is likely to have little impact on competitive advantage.

2. The transfer of skills involves activities important to competitive advantage. Transferring skills in peripheral activities such as government relations or real estate in consumer goods units may be beneficial but is not a basis for diversification.

3. The skills transferred represent a significant source of competitive advantage for the receiving unit. The expertise or skills to be transferred are both advanced and proprietary enough to be beyond the capabilities of competitors. . . .

Transferring skills meets the tests of diversification if the company truly mobilizes proprietary expertise across units. This makes certain the company can offset the acquisition premium or lower the cost of overcoming entry barriers.

The industries the company chooses for diversification must pass the attractiveness test. Even a close fit that reflects opportunities to transfer skills may not overcome poor industry structure. Opportunities to transfer skills, however, may help the company transform the structures of newly entered industries and send them in favorable directions.

The transfer of skills can be one time or ongoing. If the company exhausts opportunities to infuse new expertise into a unit after the initial post-acquisition period, the unit should ultimately be sold. . . .

By using both acquisitions and internal development, companies can build a transfer-of-skills strategy. The presence of a strong base of skills sometimes creates the possibility for internal entry instead of the acquisition of a going concern. Successful diversifiers that employ the concept of skills transfer may, however, often acquire a company in the target industry as a beachhead and then build on it with their internal expertise. By doing so, they can reduce some of the risks of internal entry and speed up the process. Two companies that have diversified using the transfer-of-skills concept are 3M and PepsiCo.

Sharing Activities

The fourth concept of corporate strategy is based on sharing activities in the value chains among business units. Procter & Gamble, for example, employs a common physical distribution system and sales force in both paper towels and disposable diapers. McKesson, a leading distribution company, will handle such diverse lines as pharmaceuticals and liquor through superwarehouses.

The ability to share activities is a potent basis for corporate strategy because sharing often enhances competitive advantage by lowering cost or raising differentiation. . . .

Sharing activities inevitably involves costs that the benefits must outweigh. One cost is the greater coordination required to manage a shared activity. More important is the need to compromise the design or performance of an activity so that it can be shared. A salesperson handling the products of two business units, for example, must operate in a way that is usually not what either unit would choose were it independent. And if compromise greatly erodes the unit's effectiveness, then sharing may reduce rather than enhance competitive advantage. . . .

Despite . . . pitfalls, opportunities to gain advantage from sharing activities have proliferated because of momentous developments in technology, deregulation, and competition. The infusion of electronics and information systems into many industries creates new opportunities to link businesses. . . .

Following the shared-activities model requires and organizational context in which business unit collaboration is encouraged and reinforced. Highly autonomous business units are inimical to such collaboration. The company must put into place a variety of what I call horizontal mechanisms—a strong sense of corporate identity, a clear corporate mission statement that emphasizes the importance of integrating business unit strategies, an incentive system that rewards more than just business unit results, cross-business-unit task forces, and other methods of integrating.

A corporate strategy based on shared activities clearly meets the better-off test because business units gain ongoing tangible advantages from others within the corporation. It also meets the cost-of-entry test by reducing the expense of surmounting the barriers to internal entry. Other bids for acquisitions that do not share opportunities will have lower reservation prices. Even widespread opportunities for sharing activities do not allow a company to suspend the attractiveness test, however. Many diversifiers have made the critical mistake of equating the close fit of a target industry with attractive diversification. Target industries must pass the strict requirement test of having an attractive structure as well as a close fit in opportunities if diversification is to ultimately succeed.

CHOOSING A CORPORATE STRATEGY

. . . Both the strategic logic and the experience of the companies I studied over the last decade suggest that a company will create shareholder value through diversification to a greater and greater extent as its strategy moves from portfolio management toward sharing activities. . . .

Each concept of corporate strategy is not mutually exclusive of those that come before, a potent advantage of the third and fourth concepts. A company can employ a restructuring strategy at the same time it transfers skills or shares activities. A strategy based on shared activities becomes more powerful if business units can also exchange skills. . . .

My study supports the soundness of basing a corporate strategy on the transfer of skills or shared activities. The data on the sample companies' diversification programs illustrate some important characteristics of successful diversifiers. They have made a disproportionately low percentage of unrelated acquisitions, *unrelated* being defined as having no clear opportunity to transfer skills or share important activities. . . . Even successful diversifiers such as 3M, IBM, and TRW have terrible records when they strayed into unrelated acquisitions. Successful acquirers diversify into fields, each of which is related to many others. Procter & Gamble and IBM, for example, operate in 18 and 19 interrelated fields respectively and so enjoy numerous opportunities to transfer skills and share activities.

Companies with the best acquisition records tend to make heavier-than-average use of start-ups and joint ventures. Most companies shy away from modes of entry besides acquisition. My results cast doubt on the conventional wisdom regarding start-ups. . . . successful companies often have very good records with start-up units, as 3M, P&G, Johnson & Johnson, IBM, and United Technologies illustrate. When a company has the internal strength to start up a unit, it can be safer and less costly to launch a company than to rely solely on an acquisition and then have to deal with the problem of integration. Japanese diversification histories support the soundness of start-up as an entry alternative.

My data also illustrate that none of the concepts of corporate strategy works when industry structure is poor or implementation is bad, no matter how related the industries are. Xerox acquired companies in related industries, but the businesses had poor structures and its skills were insufficient to provide enough competitive advantage to offset implementation problems.

An Action Program

. . . A company can choose a corporate strategy by:

1. Identifying the interrelationships among already existing business units. . . .
2. Selecting the core businesses that will be the foundation of the corporate strategy. . . .
3. Creating horizontal organizational mechanisms to facilitate interrelationships among the core businesses and lay the groundwork for future related diversification. . . .
4. Pursuing diversification opportunities that allow shared activities. . . .
5. Pursing diversification through the transfer of skills if opportunities for sharing activities are limited or exhausted. . . .
6. Pursuing a strategy restructuring if this fits the skills of management or no good opportunities exist for forging corporate interrelationships. . . .
7. Paying dividends so that the shareholders can be the portfolio managers. . . .

Creating a Corporate Theme

Defining a corporate theme is a good way to ensure that the corporation will create shareholder value. Having the right theme helps unite the efforts of business units and reinforces the ways they interrelate as well as guides the choice of new businesses to enter. NEC Corporation, with its "C&C" theme, provides a good example. NEC integrates its computer, semiconductor, telecommunications, and consumer electronics businesses by merging computers and communication.

It is all too easy to create a shallow corporate theme. CBS wants to be an "entertainment company," for example, and built a group of businesses related to leisure time. It entered such industries as toys, crafts, musical instruments, sports teams, and hi-fi retailing. While this corporate theme sounded good, close listening revealed its hollow ring. None of these businesses had any significant opportunity to share activities or transfer skills among themselves or with CBS's traditional broadcasting and record businesses. They were all sold, often at significant losses, except for a few of CBS's publishing-related units. Saddled with the worst acquisition record in my study, CBS has eroded the shareholder value created through its strong performance in broadcasting and records.

Moving from competitive strategy to corporate strategy is the business equivalent of passing through the Bermuda Triangle. The failure of corporate strategy reflects the fact that most diversified companies have failed to think in terms of how they really add value. A corporate strategy that truly enhances the competitive advantage of each business unit is the best defense against the corporate raider. With a sharper focus on the tests of diversification and the explicit choice of a clear concept of corporate strategy, companies' diversification track records from now on can look a lot different.

GLOBAL STRATEGY . . . IN A WORLD OF NATIONS?*[1]

BY GEORGE S. YIP

Whether to globalize, and how to globalize, have become two of the most burning strategy issues for managers around the world. Many forces are driving companies around the world to globalize by expanding their participation in foreign markets. Almost every product market in the major world economies—computers, fast food, nuts and bolts—has foreign competitors. Trade barriers are also falling; the recent United States/Canada trade agreement and the impending 1992 harmonization in the European Community are the two most dramatic examples. Japan is gradually opening up its long barricaded markets. Maturity in domestic markets is also driving companies to seek international expansion. This is particularly true of U.S. companies that, nourished by the huge domestic market, have typically lagged behind their European and Japanese rivals in internationalization.

Companies are also seeking to globalize by integrating their worldwide strategy. Such global integration contrasts with the multinational approach whereby companies set up country subsidiaries that design, produce, and market products or services tailored to local needs. This multinational model (also described as a "multidomestic strategy") is now in question (Hout et al., 1982). Several changes seem to increase the likelihood that, in some industries, a global strategy will be more successful than a multidomestic one. One of these changes, as argued forcefully and controversially by Levitt (1983) is the growing similarity of what citizens of different countries want to buy. Other changes include the reduction of tariff and nontariff barriers, technology investments that are becoming too expensive to amortize in one market only, and competitors that are globalizing the rules of the game.

Companies want to know how to globalize—in other words, expand market participation—and how to develop an integrated worldwide strategy. As depicted in Figure 1, three steps are essential in developing a total worldwide strategy:

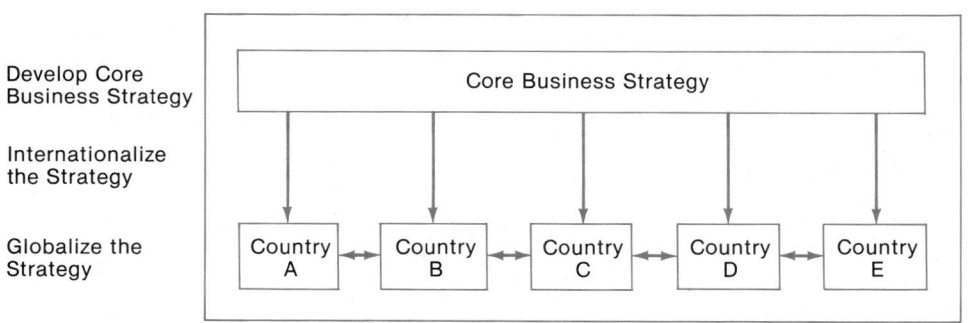

FIGURE 1
Total Global Strategy

Develop Core Business Strategy

Internationalize the Strategy

Globalize the Strategy

[1] My framework, developed in this article, is based in part on M. E. Porter's (1986) pioneering work on global strategy. Bartlett and Ghoshal (1987) define a "transnational industry" that is somewhat similar to Porter's "global industry."
* Originally published in the *Sloan Management Review* (Fall 1989). Copyright © *Sloan Management Review* 1989; reprinted with deletions by permission of the *Review*.

- Developing the core strategy—the basis of sustainable competitive advantage. It is usually developed for the home country first.
- Internationalizing the core strategy through international expansion of activities and through adaptation.
- Globalizing the international strategy by integrating the strategy across countries.

Multinational companies know the first two steps well. They know the third step less well since globalization runs counter to the accepted wisdom of tailoring for national markets (Douglas and Wind, 1987).

This article makes a case for how a global strategy might work and directs managers toward opportunities to exploit globalization. It also presents the drawbacks and costs of globalization. Figure 2 lays out a framework for thinking through globalization issues.

Industry globalization drivers (underlying market, cost, and other industry conditions) are externally determined, while global strategy levers are choices available to the worldwide business. Drivers create the potential for a multinational business to achieve the benefits of global strategy. To achieve these benefits, a multinational business needs to set its *global strategy levers* (e.g., use of product standardization) appropriately to industry drivers, and to the position and resources of the business and its parent company. The organization's ability to implement the strategy affects how well the benefits can be achieved.

WHAT IS GLOBAL STRATEGY?

Setting strategy for a worldwide business requires making choices along a number of strategic dimensions. Table 1 lists five such dimensions or "global strategy levels" and their respective positions under a pure multidomestic strategy and a pure global strategy. Intermediate positions are, of course, feasible. For each dimension, a multidomestic strategy seeks to maximize worldwide performance by maximizing local competitive advantage, revenues, or profits; a global strategy seeks to maximize worldwide performance through sharing and integration.

FIGURE 2
Framework of Global Strategy Forces

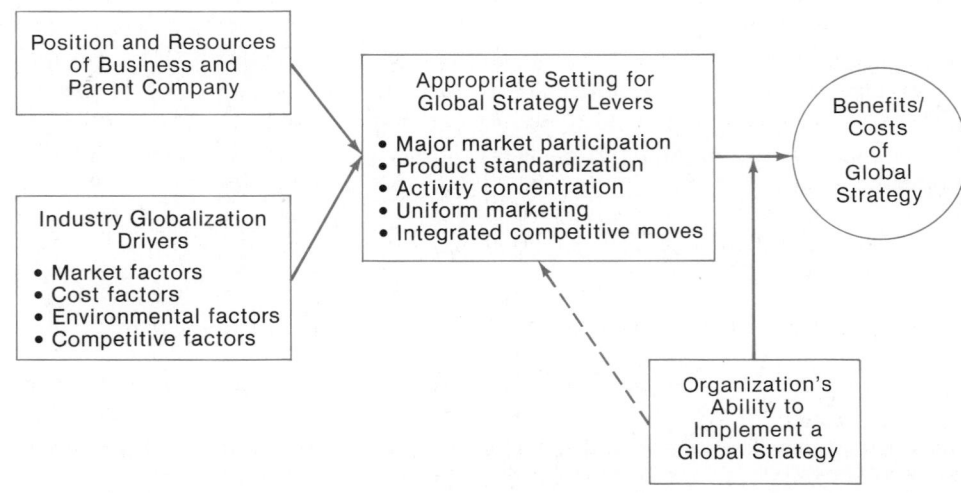

TABLE 1 **Globalization Dimensions/Global Strategy Levers**

DIMENSION	SETTING FOR PURE MULTIDOMESTIC STRATEGY	SETTING FOR PURE GLOBAL STRATEGY
Market Participation	No particular pattern	Significant share in major markets
Product Offering	Fully customized in each country	Fully standardized worldwide
Location of Value-Added Activities	All activities in each country	Concentrated—one activity in each (different) country
Marketing Approach	Local	Uniform worldwide
Competitive Moves	Stand-alone by country	Integrated across countries

Market Participation

In a multidomestic strategy, countries are selected on the basis of their stand-alone potential for revenues and profits. In a global strategy, countries need to be selected for their potential contribution to globalization benefits. This may mean entering a market that is unattractive in its own right, but has global strategic significance, such as the home market of a global competitor. Or it may mean building share in a limited number of key markets rather than undertaking more widespread coverage. . . . The Electrolux Group, the Swedish appliance giant, is pursuing a strategy of building significant share in major world markets. The company aims to be the first global appliance maker. . . .

Product Offering

In a multidomestic strategy, the products offered in each country are tailored to local needs. In a global strategy, the ideal is a standardized core product that requires minimal local adaptation. Cost reduction is usually the most important benefit of product standardization. . . . Differing worldwide needs can be met by adapting a standardized core product. In the early 1970s, sales of the Boeing 737 began to level off. Boeing turned to developing countries as an attractive new market, but found initially that its product did not fit the new environments. Because of the shortness of runways, their greater softness, and the lower technical expertise of their pilots, the planes tended to bounce a great deal. When the planes bounced on landing, the brakes failed. To fix this problem, Boeing modified the design by adding thrust to the engines, redesigning the wings and landing gear, and installing tires with lower pressure. These adaptations to a standardized core product enabled the 737 to become the best selling plane in history.

Location of Value Added Activities

In a multidomestic strategy, all or most of the value chain is reproduced in every country. In another type of international strategy—exporting—most of the value chain is kept in one country. In a global strategy, costs are reduced by breaking up the value chain so each activity may be conducted in a different country. . . .

Marketing Approach

In a multidomestic strategy, marketing is fully tailored for each country, being developed locally. In a global strategy, a uniform marketing approach is applied around the world, although not all elements of the marketing mix need be uniform. Unilever achieved great success with a fabric softener that used a globally common positioning, advertising theme, and symbol (a teddy bear), but a brand name that varied by country. Similarly, a product that serves a common need can be geographically expanded with a uniform marketing program, despite differences in marketing environments.

Competitive Moves

In a multidomestic strategy, the managers in each country make competitive moves without regard for what happens in other countries. In a global strategy, competitive moves are integrated across countries at the same time or in a systematic sequence: a competitor is attacked in one country in order to drain its resources for another country, or a competitive attack in one country is countered in a different country. Perhaps the best example is the counterattack in a competitor's home market as a parry to an attack on one's own home market. Integration of competitive strategy is rarely practiced, except perhaps by some Japanese companies.

Bridgestone Corporation, the Japanese tire manufacturer, tried to integrate its competitive moves in response to global consolidation by its major competitors. . . . These competitive actions forced Bridgestone to establish a presence in the major U.S. market in order to maintain its position in the world tire market. To this end, Bridgestone formed a joint venture to own and manage Firestone Corporation's worldwide tire business. This joint venture also allowed Bridgestone to gain access to Firestone's European plants.

BENEFITS OF A GLOBAL STRATEGY

Companies that use global strategy levers can achieve one or more of these benefits. . . .

- cost reductions
- improved quality of products and programs
- enhanced customer preference
- increased competitive leverage

Cost Reductions

An integrated global strategy can reduce worldwide costs in several ways. A company can increase the benefits from economies of scale by *pooling production or other activities* for two or more countries. Understanding the potential benefit of these economies of scale, Sony Corporation has concentrated its compact disc production in Terre Haute, Indiana, and Salzburg, Austria.

A second way to cut costs is by *exploiting lower factor costs* by moving manufacturing or other activities to low-cost countries. This approach has, of course, motivated the recent surge of offshore manufacturing, particularly by U.S. firms. For example, the Mexican side of the U.S.-Mexico border is now crowded with "maquiladoras"—manufacturing plants set up and run by U.S. companies using Mexican labor.

Global strategy can also cut costs by *exploiting flexibility*. A company with manufacturing locations in several countries can move production from location to location on short notice to take advantage of the lowest costs at a given time. Dow Chemical takes this approach to minimize the cost of producing chemicals. Dow uses a linear programming model that takes account of international differences in exchange rates, tax rates, and transportation and labor costs. The model comes up with the best mix of production volume by location for each planning period.

An integrated global strategy can also reduce costs by *enhancing bargaining power*. A company whose strategy allows for switching production among different countries greatly increases its bargaining power with suppliers, workers, and host governments. . . .

Improved Quality of Products and Programs

Under a global strategy, companies focus on a smaller number of products and programs than under a multidomestic strategy. This concentration can improve both product and program quality. Global focus is one reason for Japanese success in automobiles. Toyota markets a far smaller number of models around the world than does General Motors, even allowing for its unit sales being half that of General Motors's. . . .

Enhanced Customer Preference

Global availability, serviceability, and recognition can enhance customer preference through reinforcement. Soft drink and fast food companies are, of course, leading exponents of this strategy. Many suppliers of financial services, such as credit cards, must have a global presence because their service is travel related. . . .

Increased Competitive Leverage

A global strategy provides more points from which to attack and counterattack competitors. In an effort to prevent the Japanese from becoming a competitive nuisance in disposable syringes, Becton Dickinson, a major U.S. medical products company, decided to enter three markets in Japan's backyard. Becton entered the Hong Kong, Singapore, and Philippine markets to prevent further Japanese expansion (Var, 1986).

DRAWBACKS OF GLOBAL STRATEGY

Globalization can incur significant management costs through increased coordination, reporting requirements, and even added staff. It can also reduce the firm's effectiveness in individual countries if overcentralization hurts local motivation and morale. In addition, each global strategy lever has particular drawbacks.

A global strategy approach to *market participation* can incur an earlier or greater commitment to a market than is warranted on its own merits. Many American companies, such as Motorola, are struggling to penetrate Japanese markets, more in order to enhance their global competitive position than to make money in Japan for its own sake.

Product standardization can result in a product that does not entirely satisfy *any* customers. When companies first internationalize, they often offer their standard domestic product without adapting it for other countries, and suffer the consequences. . . .

A globally standardized product is designed for the global market but can seldom satisfy all needs in all countries. For instance, Canon, a Japanese company, sacrificed the ability to copy certain Japanese paper sizes when it first designed a photocopier for the global market.

Activity concentration distances customers and can result in lower responsiveness and flexibility. It also increases currency risk by incurring costs and revenues in different countries. Recently volatile exchange rates have required companies that concentrate their production to hedge their currency exposure.

Uniform marketing can reduce adaptation to local customer behavior. For example, the head office of British Airways mandated that every country use the "Manhattan Landing" television commercial developed by advertising agency Saatchi and Saatchi. While the commercial did win many awards, it has been criticized for using a visual image (New York City) that was not widely recognized in many countries.

Integrated competitive moves can mean sacrificing revenues, profits, or competitive position in individual countries, particularly when the subsidiary in one country is asked to attack a global competitor in order to send a signal or to divert that competitor's resources from another country.

FINDING THE BALANCE

The most successful worldwide strategies find a balance between overglobalizing and underglobalizing. The ideal strategy matches the level of strategy globalization to the globalization potential of the industry. . . .

INDUSTRY GLOBALIZATION DRIVERS

To achieve the benefits of globalization, the managers of a worldwide business need to recognize when industry globalization drivers (industry conditions) provide the opportunity to use global strategy levers. These drivers can be grouped in four categories: market, cost, governmental, and competitive. Each industry globalization driver affects the potential use of global strategy levers. . . .

Market Drivers

Market globalization drivers depend on customer behavior and the structure of distribution channels. These drivers affect the use of all five global strategy levers.

Homogeneous Customer Needs: When customers in different countries want essentially the same type of product or service (or can be so persuaded), opportunities arise to market a standardized product. Understanding which aspects of the product can be standardized and which should be customized is key. In addition, homogeneous needs make participation in a large number of markets easier because fewer different product offerings need to be developed and supported.

Global Customers: Global customers buy on a centralized or coordinated basis for decentralized use. The existence of global customers both allows and requires a uniform marketing program. There are two types of global customers: national and multinational. A national global customer searches the world for suppliers but uses the purchased product or service in one country. National defense agencies are a good example. A multinational global customer also searches the world for suppliers, but uses the purchased product or service in many countries. The World Health Organization's purchase of medical products is an example. Multinational global customers are particularly challenging to serve and often require a global account management program. . . .

Global Channels: Analogous to global customers, channels of distribution may buy on a global or at least a regional basis. Global channels or middlemen are also important in exploiting differences in prices by buying at a lower price in one country and selling at a higher price in another country. Their presence makes it more necessary for a business to rationalize its worldwide pricing. Global channels are rare, but regionwide channels are increasing in number, particularly in European grocery distribution and retailing.

Transferable Marketing: The buying decision may be such that marketing elements, such as brand names and advertising, require little local adaptation. Such transferability enables firms to use uniform marketing strategies and facilitates expanded participation in markets. A worldwide business can also adapt its brand names and advertising campaigns to make them more transferable, or, even better, design global ones to start with. Offsetting risks include the blandness of uniformly acceptable brand names or advertising, and the vulnerability of relying on a single brand franchise.

Cost Drivers

Cost drivers depend on the economics of the business; they particularly affect activity concentration.

Economies of Scale and Scope: A single-country market may not be large enough for the local business to achieve all possible economies of scale or scope. Scale at a given location can be increased through participation in multiple markets combined with product standardization or concentration of selected value activities. Corresponding risks include rigidity and vulnerability to disruption. . . .

Learning and Experience: Even if economies of scope and scale are exhausted, expanded market participation and activity concentration can accelerate the accumulation of learning and experience. The steeper the learning and experience curves, the greater the potential benefit will be. Managers should beware, though, of the usual danger in pursuing experience curve strategies—overaggressive pricing that destroyed not just the competition but the market as well. Prices get so low that profit is insufficient to sustain any competitor.

Sourcing Efficiencies: Centralized purchasing of new materials can significantly lower costs. . . .

Favorable Logistics: A favorable ratio of sales value to transportation cost enhances the company's ability to concentrate production. Other logistical factors include nonperishability, the absence of time urgency, and little need for location close to customer facilities. . . .

Differences in Country Costs and Skills: Factor costs generally vary across countries; this is particularly true in certain industries. The availability of particular skills also varies. Concentration of activities in low-cost or high-skill countries can increase productivity and reduce costs, but managers need to anticipate the danger of training future offshore competitors. . . .

Product Development Costs: Product development costs can be reduced by developing a few global or regional products rather than many national products. The automobile industry is characterized by long product development periods and high product development costs. One reason for the high costs is duplication of effort across countries. The Ford Motor Company's "Centers of Excellence" program aims to reduce these duplicating efforts and to exploit the differing expertise of Ford specialists worldwide. As part of the concentrated effort, Ford of Europe is designing a common platform for all compacts, while Ford of North America is developing platforms for the replacement of the mid-sized Taurus and Sable. This concentration of design is estimated to save "hundreds of millions of dollars per model by eliminating duplicative efforts and saving on retooling factories" (*Business Week,* 1987).

Governmental Drivers

Government globalization drivers depend on the rules set by national governments and affect the use of all global strategy levers.

Favorable Trade Policies: Host governments affect globalization potential through import tariffs and quotas, nontariff barriers, export subsidies, local content requirements, currency and capital flow restrictions, and requirements on technology transfer. Host government policies can make it difficult to use the global levers of major market participation, product standardization, activity concentration, and uniform marketing; they also affect the integrated-competitive moves lever. . . .

Compatible Technical Standards: Differences in technical standards, especially government-imposed standards, limit the extent to which products can be standardized. Often, standards are set with protectionism in mind. Motorola found that many of their electronics products were excluded from the Japanese market because these products operated at a higher frequency than was permitted in Japan.

Common Marketing Regulations: The marketing environment of individual countries affects the extent to which uniform global marketing approaches can be used. Certain types of media may be prohibited or restricted. For example, the United States is far more liberal than Europe about the kinds of advertising claims that can be made on television. The British authorities even veto the depiction of socially undesirable behavior. For example, British television authorities do not allow scenes of children pestering their parents to buy a product. . . .

Competitive Drivers

Market, cost, and governmental globalization drivers are essentially fixed for an industry at any given time. Competitors can play only a limited role in affecting these factors (although a sustained effort can bring about change, particularly in the case of consumer preferences). In contrast, competitive drivers are entirely in the realm of competitor choice. Competitors can raise the globalization potential of their industry and spur the need for a response on the global strategy levers.

Interdependence of Countries: A competitor may create competitive interdependence among countries by pursuing a global strategy. The basic mechanism is through sharing of activities. When activities such as production are shared among countries, a competitor's market share in one country affects its scale and overall cost position in the shared activities. Changes in that scale and cost will affect its competitive position in all countries dependent on the shared activities. Less directly, customers may view market position in a lead country as an indicator of overall quality. Companies frequently promote a product as, for example, "the leading brand in the United States." Other competitors then need to respond via increased market participation, uniform marketing, or integrated competitive strategy to avoid a downward spiral of sequentially weakened positions in individual countries.

In the automobile industry, where economies of scale are significant and where sharing activities can lower costs, markets have significant competitive interdependence. As companies like Ford and Volkswagen concentrate production and become more cost competitive with the Japanese manufacturers, the Japanese are pressured to enter more markets so that increased production volume will lower costs. Whether conscious of this or not, Toyota has begun a concerted effort to penetrate the German market: between 1984 and 1987, Toyota doubled the number of cars produced for the German market.

Globalized Competitors: More specifically, matching or preempting individual competitor moves may be necessary. These moves include expanding into or within major markets, being the first to introduce a standardized product, or being the first to use a uniform marketing program.

The need to preempt a global competitor can spur increased market participation. In 1986, Unilever, the European consumer products company, sought to increase its participation in the U.S. market by launching a hostile takeover bid for Richardson-Vicks Inc. Unilever's global archrival, Procter & Gamble, saw the threat to its home turf and outbid Unilever to capture Richardson-Vicks. With Richardson-Vicks's European system, P&G was able to greatly strengthen its European positioning. So Unilever's attempt to expand participation in a rival's home market backfired to allow the rival to expand participation in Unilever's home markets.

In summary, industry globalization drivers provide opportunities to use global strategy levers in many ways. Some industries, such as civil aircraft, can score high on most dimensions of globalization (Yoshino, 1986). Others, such as the cement industry, seem to be inherently local. But more and more industries are developing globalization potential. Even the food industry in Europe, renowned for its diversity of taste, is now a globalization target for major food multinationals.

Changes over Time

Finally, industry evolution plays a role. As each of the industry globalization drivers changes over time, so too will the appropriate global strategy change. For example, in the European major appliance industry, globalization forces seem to have reversed. In the late 1960s and early 1970s, a regional standardization strategy was successful for some key competitors (Levitt, 1983). But in the 1980s the situation appears to have turned around, and the most successful strategies seem to be national (Badenfuller et al., 1987).

In some cases, the actions of individual competitors can affect the direction and pace of change; competitors positioned to take advantage of globalization forces will want to hasten them. . . .

MORE THAN ONE STRATEGY IS VIABLE

Although they are powerful, industry globalization drivers do not dictate one formula for success. More than one type of international strategy can be viable in a given industry.

Industries vary across drivers: No industry is high on every one of the many globalization drivers. A particular competitor may be in a strong position to exploit a driver that scores low on globalization. . . . The hotel industry provides examples both of successful global and successful local competitors.

Global effects are incremental: Globalization drivers are not deterministic for a second reason: the appropriate use of strategy levers adds competitive advantage to existing sources. These other sources may allow individual competitors to thrive with international strategies that are mismatched with industry globalization drivers. For example, superior technology is a major source of competitive advantage in most industries, but can be quite independent of globalization drivers. A competitor with sufficiently superior technology can use it to offset globalization disadvantages.

Business and parent company position and resources are crucial: The third reason that drivers are not deterministic is related to resources. A worldwide business may face industry drivers that strongly favor a global strategy. But global strategies are typically expensive to implement initially even though great cost savings and revenue gains should follow. High initial investments may be needed to expand within or into major markets, to develop standardized products, to relocate value activities, to create global brands, to create new organization units or coordination processes, and to implement other aspects of a global strategy. The strategic position of the business is also relevant. Even though a global strategy may improve the business's long-term strategic position, its immediate position may be so weak that resources should be devoted to short-term, country-by-country improvements. Despite the automobile industry's very strong globalization drivers, Chrysler Corporation had to deglobalize by selling off most of its international automotive businesses to avoid bankruptcy. Lastly, investing in nonglobal sources of competitive advantage, such as superior technology, may yield greater returns than global ones, such as centralized manufacturing.

Organizations Have Limitations: Finally, factors such as organization structure, management processes, people, and culture affect how well a desired global strategy can be implemented. Organizational differences among companies in the same industry can, or should, constrain the companies' pursuit of the same global strategy. . . .

THE PROFESSIONAL CONTEXT

While most large organizations draw on a variety of experts to get their jobs done, there has been a growing interest in recent years in those organizations whose work, because it is highly complex, is organized primarily around experts. These range from hospitals, universities, and research centers to consulting firms, space agencies, and biomedical companies.

This context is a rather unusual one, at least when judged against the more traditional contexts discussed in previous chapters. Both its strategic processes and its structures tend to take on forms quite different from those presented earlier. Organizations of experts, in fact, seem to divide themselves into two somewhat different contexts. In one, the experts work in rapidly changing situations that demand a good deal of collaborative innovation (as in the biotechnology or semiconductor fields); in the other, experts work more or less alone in more stable situations involving slower-changing bodies of skill or knowledge (as in law, university teaching, and accounting). This chapter takes up the latter, under the label of the "professional" context; the next chapter discusses the former under the label of "innovation."

We open this chapter with a description of the type of organization that seems best suited to the context of the more stable application of expertise. Drawn from Mintzberg's work, primarily his original description of "professional bureaucracy," it looks at the structure of the professional organization, including its important characteristic of "pigeonholing" work, the management of professionals, the unusual nature of strategy in such organizations (drawing from a paper Mintzberg coauthored with Cynthia Hardy, Ann Langley, and Janet Rose), and some issues associated with these organizations.

The second article in this chapter, recently published in the *Sloan Management Review* and authored by Brian Quinn and his colleague Penny Paquette at the Dartmouth Amos Tuck School, focuses on the service sector, and especially changes that are now being rendered there as a result of technological developments. Not all service organizations fit into the professional context, by any stretch of the imagination, although many professional organizations do operate in the service sector, as will be evident from the examples of the first reading. Many services, such as retail banking, merchandise retailing, and fast-food restauranting, involve numerous unskilled jobs characteristic of the machinelike organizations described in the mature context. Nevertheless, many of the points made by Quinn and Paquette—about focusing on small units and empowering the operating people there, and about new organizational forms that invert the traditional pyramid, flatten the hierarchy, and create connections between relatively autonomous units —sound an awful lot like the professional form of organization described in the first reading. In other words, technological advances seem to have a professionalizing effect on many traditional machinelike services. And these advances seem to be rendering important changes in the more traditional professional services themselves, such as accounting and consulting. This reading, therefore, seems to provide us with glimpses of the professional organizations of the future.

Overall, these two readings suggest that the traditional concepts of managing and organizing simply do not work as we move away from conventional mass production—which has long served as the model for "one best way" concepts in management. Whether it be highly expert work in general or service work subjected to new technologies in particular, our thinking has to be opened up to very different needs. Several cases deal specifically with strategy in professional organizations per se. PRA&D and Blanchflower, White and Greaves are in this category. However, Biogen, Genentech, and The New York Times provide some even more complex issues where professional groups—like newspaper reporters or researchers—must interface with other elements of a company which are more business or production driven. These and cases like Hewlett-Packard, Intel, and Honda Motor pose some of the more profound questions managers face when they must manage in a multicultural setting.

THE PROFESSIONAL ORGANIZATION*

BY HENRY MINTZBERG

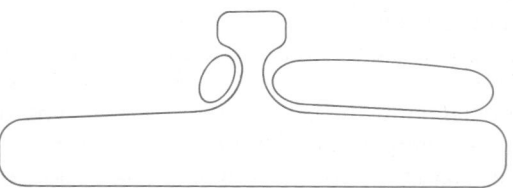

* Adapted from *The Structuring of Organizations* (Prentice Hall, 1979), Chap. 19 on "The Professional Bureaucracy"; also *Power In and Around Organizations* (Prentice Hall, 1983), Chap. 22 on "The Meritocracy"; the material on strategy formation from "Strategy Formation in the University Setting," coauthored with Cynthia Hardy, Ann Langley, and Janet Rose, in J. L. Bess (ed.) *College and University Organization* (New York University Press, 1984). A chapter similar to this one appeared in *Mintzberg on Management: Inside Our Strange World of Organizations* (Free Press, 1989).

An organization can be bureaucratic without being centralized. This happens when its work is complex, requiring that it be carried out and controlled by professionals, yet at the same time remains stable, so that the skills of those professionals can be perfected through standardized operating programs. The structure takes on the form of *professional* bureaucracy, which is common in universities, general hospitals, public accounting firms, social work agencies, and firms doing fairly routine engineering or craft work. All rely on the skills and knowledge of their operating professionals to function; all produce standardized products or services.

The Work of the Professional Operators

Here again we have a tightly knit configuration of the attributes of structure. Most important, the professional organization relies for coordination on the standardization of skills, which is achieved primarily through formal training. It hires duly trained specialists—professionals—for the operating core, then gives them considerable control over their own work.

Control over their work means that professionals work relatively independently of their colleagues but closely with the clients they serve—doctors treating their own patients and accountants who maintain personal contact with the companies whose books they audit. Most of the necessary coordination among the operating professionals is then handled automatically by their set skills and knowledge—in effect, by what they have learned to expect from each other. During an operation as long and as complex as open-heart surgery, "very little needs to be said [between the anesthesiologist and the surgeon] preceding chest opening and during the procedure on the heart itself . . . [most of the operation is] performed in absolute silence" (Gosselin, 1978). The point is perhaps best made in reverse by the cartoon that shows six surgeons standing around a patient on an operating table with one saying, "Who opens?"

Just how standardized the complex work of professionals can be is illustrated in a paper read by Spencer before a meeting of the International Cardiovascular Society. Spencer notes that an important feature of surgical training is "repetitive practice" to evoke "an automatic reflex." So automatic, in fact, that this doctor keeps a series of surgical "cookbooks" in which he lists, even for "complex" operations, the essential steps as chains of thirty to forty symbols on a single sheet, to "be reviewed mentally in sixty to 120 seconds at some time during the day preceding the operation" (1976:1179, 1182).

But no matter how standardized the knowledge and skills, their complexity ensures that considerable discretion remains in their application. No two professionals—no two surgeons or engineers or social workers—ever apply them in exactly the same way. Many judgments are required.

Training, reinforced by indoctrination, is a complicated affair in the professional organization. The initial training typically takes place over a period of years in a university or special institution, during which the skills and knowledge of the profession are formally programmed into the students. There typically follows a long period of on-the-job training, such as internship in medicine or articling in accounting, where the formal knowledge is applied and the practice of skills perfected. On-the-job training also completes the process of indoctrination, which began during the formal education. As new knowledge is generated and new skills develop, of course (so it is hoped) the professional upgrades his or her expertise.

705

All that training is geared to one goal, the internalization of the set procedures, which is what makes the structure technically bureaucratic (structure defined earlier as relying on standardization for coordination). But the professional bureaucracy differs markedly from the machine bureaucracy. Whereas the latter generates its own standards—through its technostructure, enforced by its line managers—many of the standards of the professional bureaucracy originate outside its own structure, in the self-governing associations its professionals belong to with their colleagues from other institutions. These associations set universal standards, which they ensure are taught by the universities and are used by all the organizations practicing the profession. So whereas the machine bureaucracy relies on authority of a hierarchical nature—the power of office—the professional bureaucracy emphasizes authority of a professional nature—the power of expertise.

Other forms of standardization are, in fact, difficult to rely on in the professional organization. The work processes themselves are too complex to be standardized directly by analysts. One need only try to imagine a work-study analyst following a cardiologist on rounds or timing the activities of a teacher in a classroom. Similarly, the outputs of professional work cannot easily be measured and so do not lend themselves to standardization. Imagine a planner trying to define a cure in psychiatry, the amount of learning that takes place in a classroom, or the quality of an accountant's audit. Likewise, direct supervision and mutual adjustment cannot be relied upon for coordination, for both impede professional autonomy.

The Pigeonholing Process

To understand how the professional organization functions at the operating level, it is helpful to think of it as a set of standard programs—in effect, the repertoire of skills the professionals stand ready to use—that are applied to known situations, called contingencies, also standardized. As Weick notes of one case in point, "schools are in the business of building and maintaining categories (1976:8). The process is sometimes known as *pigeonholing.* In this regard, the professional has two basic tasks: (1) to categorize, or "diagnose," the client's need in terms of one of the contingencies, which indicates which standard program to apply, and (2) to apply, or execute, that program. For example, the management consultant carries a bag of standard acronymic tricks: MBO, MIS, LRP, OD. The client with information needs gets MIS; the one with managerial conflicts, OD. Such pigeonholing, of course, simplifies matters enormously; it is also what enables each professional to work in a relatively autonomous manner.

It is in the pigeonholing process that the fundamental differences among the machine organization, the professional organization, and the innovative organization (to be discussed next) can best be seen. The machine organization is a single-purpose structure. Presented with a stimulus, it executes its one standard sequence of programs, just as we kick when tapped on the knee. No diagnosis is involved. In the professional organization, diagnosis is a fundamental task, but one highly circumscribed. The organization seeks to match a predetermined contingency to a standardized program. Fully open-ended diagnosis—that which seeks a creative solution to a unique problem—requires the innovative form of organization. No standard contingencies or programs can be relied upon there.

The Administrative Structure

Everything we have discussed so far suggests that the operating core is the key part of the professional organization. The only other part that is fully elaborated is the support staff, but that is focused very much on serving the activities of the operating core. Given the high cost of the professionals, it makes sense to back them up with as much support as possible. Thus, universities have printing facilities, faculty clubs, alma mater funds, publishing houses, archives, libraries, computer facilities, and many, many other support units.

The technostructure and middle-line management are not highly elaborated in the professional organization. They can do little to coordinate the professional work. Moreover, with so little need for direct supervision of, or mutual adjustment among, the professionals, the operating units can be very large. For example, the McGill Faculty of Management functions effectively with 50 professors under a single manager, its dean, and the rest of the university's academic hierarchy is likewise thin.

Thus, the diagram at the beginning of this chapter shows the professional organization, in terms of our logo, as a flat structure with a thin middle line, a tiny technostructure, but a fully elaborated support staff. All these characteristics are reflected in the organigram of a university hospital, shown in Figure 1.

Coordination within the administrative structure is another matter, however. Because these configurations are so decentralized, the professionals not only control their own work but they also gain much collective control over the administrative decisions that affect them—decisions, for example, to hire colleagues, to promote them, and to distribute resources. This they do partly by doing some of the administrative work themselves (most university professors, for example, sit on various administrative committees) and partly by ensuring that important administrative posts are staffed by professionals or at least sympathetic people appointed with the professionals' blessing. What emerges, therefore, is a rather democratic administrative structure. But because the administrative work requires mutual adjustment for coordination among the various people involved, task forces and especially standing committees abound at this level, as is in fact suggested in Figure 1.

Because of the power of their professional operators, these organizations are sometimes described as inverse pyramids, with the professional operators on top and the administrators down below to serve them—to ensure that the surgical facilities are kept clean and the classrooms well supplied with chalk. Such a description slights the power of the administrators of professional work, however, although it may be an accurate description of those who manage the support units. For the support staff—often more numerous than the professional staff, but generally less skilled—there is no democracy in the professional organization, only the oligarchy of the professionals. Such support units as housekeeping in the hospital or printing in the university are likely to be managed tightly from the top, in effect as machinelike enclaves within the professional configuration. Thus, what frequently emerges in the professional organization are parallel and separate administrative hierarchies, one democratic and bottom-up for the professionals, a second machinelike and top-down for the support staff.

The Roles of the Administrators of Professional Work

Where does all this leave the administrators of the professional hierarchy, the executive directors and chiefs of the hospitals and the presidents and deans of the universities? Are they powerless? Compared with their counterparts in the entrepreneurial and machine organizations, they certainly lack a good deal of power. But that is far from the whole story. The administrator of professional work may not be able to control the professionals directly, but he or she does perform a series of roles that can provide considerable indirect power.

708

FIGURE 1
Organization of a University Hospital

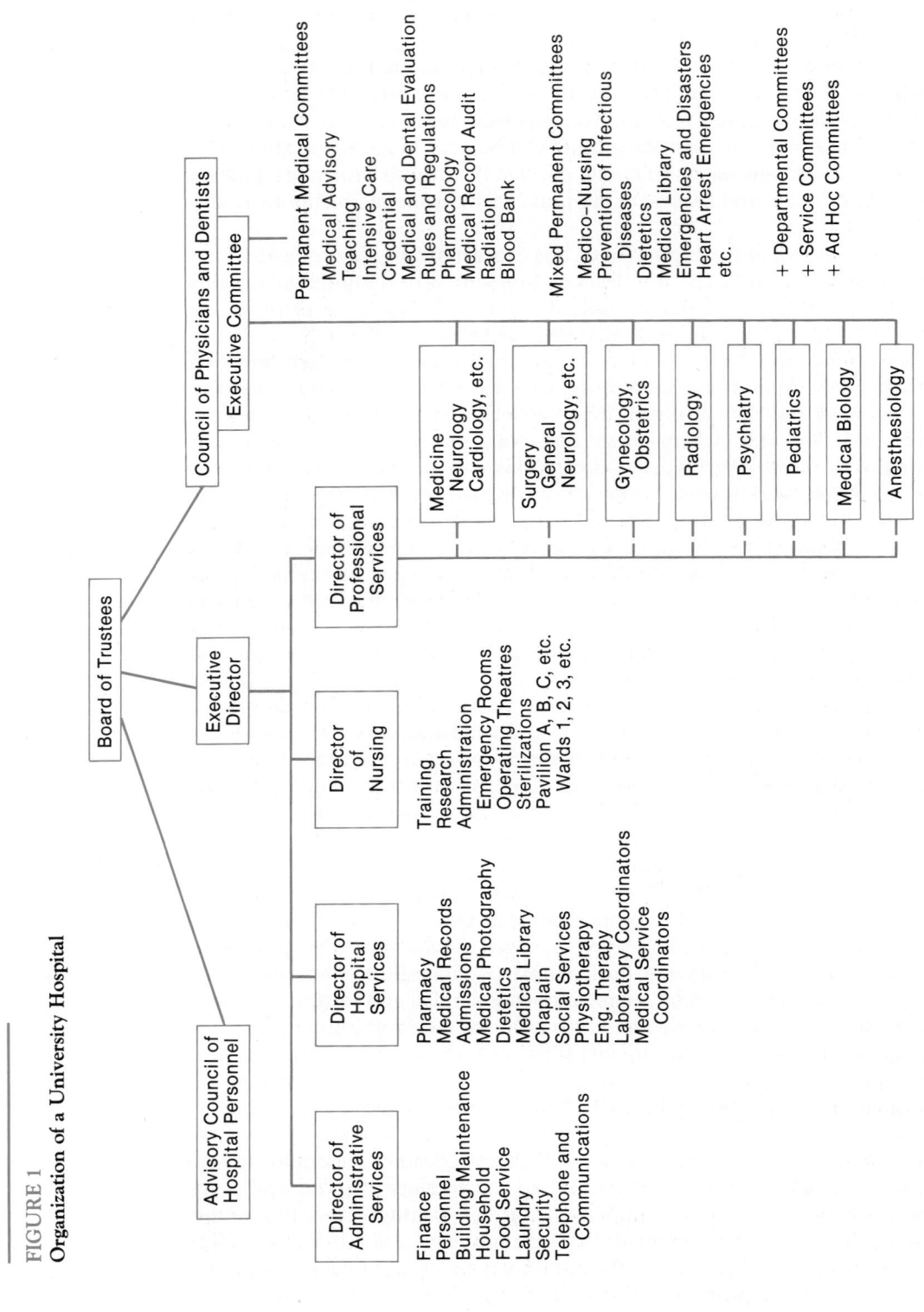

First, this administrator spends much time handling disturbances in the structure. The pigeonholing process is an imperfect one at best, leading to all kinds of jurisdictional disputes between the professionals. Who should perform mastectomies in the hospitals, surgeons who look after cutting or gynecologists who look after women? Seldom, however, can one administrator impose a solution on the professionals involved in a dispute. Rather, various administrators must often sit down together and negotiate a solution on behalf of their constituencies.

Second, the administrators of professional work—especially those at higher levels—serve in key roles at the boundary of the organization, between the professionals inside and the influencers outside: governments, client associations, benefactors, and so on. On the one hand, the administrators are expected to protect the professionals' autonomy, to "buffer" them from external pressures. On the other hand, they are expected to woo those outsiders to support the organization, both morally and financially. And that often leads the outsiders to expect these administrators, in turn, to control the professionals, in machine bureaucratic ways. Thus, the external roles of the manager—maintaining liaison contacts, acting as figurehead and spokesman in a public relations capacity, negotiating with outside agencies—emerge as primary ones in the administration of professional work.

Some view the roles these administrators are called upon to perform as signs of weakness. They see these people as the errand boys of the professionals, or else as pawns caught in various tugs of war—between one professional and another, between support staffer and professional, between outsider and professional. In fact, however, these roles are the very sources of administrators' power. Power is, after all, gained at the locus of uncertainty, and that is exactly where the administrators of professionals sit. The administrator who succeeds in raising extra funds for his or her organization gains a say in how they are distributed; the one who can reconcile conflicts in favor of his or her unit or who can effectively buffer the professionals from external influence becomes a valued, and therefore powerful, member of the organization.

We can conclude that power in these structures does flow to those professionals who care to devote effort to doing administrative instead of professional work, so long as they do it well. But that, it should be stressed, is not laissez-faire power; the professional administrator maintains power only as long as the professionals perceive him or her to be serving their interests effectively.

CONDITIONS OF THE PROFESSIONAL ORGANIZATION

The professional form of organization appears wherever the operating work of an organization is dominated by skilled workers who use procedures that are difficult to learn yet are well defined. This means a situation that is both complex and stable—complex enough to require procedures that can be learned only through extensive training yet stable enough so that their use can become standardized.

Note that an elaborate technical system can work against this configuration. If highly regulating or automated, the professionals' skills might be amenable to rationalization, in other words, to be divided into simple, highly programmed steps that would destroy the basis for professional autonomy and thereby drive the structure to the machine form. And if highly complicated, the technical system would reduce the professionals' autonomy by forcing them to work in multidisciplinary teams, thereby driving the organization toward the innovative form. Thus the surgeon uses a scalpel, and the accountant a pencil. Both must be sharp, but both are otherwise simple and commonplace instruments. Yet both allow their users to perform independently what can be exceedingly complex functions.

The prime example of the professional configuration is the personal-service organization, at least the one with complex, stable work not reliant on a fancy technical system. Schools and universities, consulting firms, law and accounting offices, and social work agencies all rely on this form of organization, more or less, so long as they concentrate not on innovating in the solution of new problems but on applying standard programs to well-defined ones. The same seems to be true of hospitals, at least to the extent that their technical systems are simple. (In those areas that call for more sophisticated equipment—apparently a growing number, especially in teaching institutions—the hospital is driven toward a hybrid structure, with characteristics of the innovative form. But this tendency is mitigated by the hospital's overriding concern with safety. Only the tried and true can be relied upon, which produces a natural aversion to the looser innovative configuration.)

So far, our examples have come from the service sector. But the professional form can be found in manufacturing too, where the above conditions hold up. Such is the case of the craft enterprise, for example the factory using skilled workers to produce ceramic products. They very term *craftsman* implies a kind of professional who learns traditional skills through long apprentice training and then is allowed to practice them free of direct supervision. Craft enterprises seem typically to have few administrators, who tend to work, in any event, alongside the operating personnel. The same would seem to be true for engineering work oriented not to creative design so much as to modification of existing dominant designs.

STRATEGY FORMATION IN THE PROFESSIONAL ORGANIZATION

It is commonly assumed that strategies are formulated before they are implemented, that planning is the central process of formulation, and that structures must be designed to implement these strategies. At least this is what one reads in the conventional literature of strategic management. In the professional organization, these imperatives stand almost totally at odds with what really happens, leading to the conclusion either that such organizations are confused about how to make strategy, or else that the strategy writers are confused about how professional organizations must function. I subscribe to the latter explanation.

Using the definition of strategy as pattern in action, strategy formation in the professional organization takes on a new meaning. Rather than simply throwing up our hands at its resistance to formal strategic planning, or, at the other extreme, dismissing professional organizations as "organized anarchies" with strategy-making processes as mere "garbage cans" (March and Olsen, 1976) we can focus on how decisions and actions in such organizations order themselves into patterns over time.

Taking strategy as pattern in action, the obvious question becomes, which actions? The key area of strategy making in most organizations concerns the elaboration of the basic mission (the products or services offered to the public); in professional organizations, we shall argue, this is significantly controlled by individual professionals. Other important areas of strategy here include the inputs to the system (notably the choice of professional staff, the determination of clients, and the raising of external funds), the means to perform the mission (the construction of buildings and facilities, the purchase of research equipment, and so on), the structure and forms of governance (design of the committee system, the hierarchies, and so on), and the various means to support the mission.

Were professional organizations to formulate strategies in the conventional ways, central administrators would develop detailed and integrated plans about these issues. This sometimes happens, but in a very limited number of cases. Many strategic issues come under the direct control of individual professionals, while others can be decided neither by individual professionals nor by central administrators, but instead require the participation of a variety of people in a complex collective process. As illustrated in Figure 2, we examine in turn the decisions controlled by individual professionals, by central administrators, and by the collectivity.

Decisions Made by Professional Judgment

Professional organizations are distinguished by the fact that the determination of the basic mission—the specific services to be offered and to whom—is in good part left to the judgment of professionals as individuals. In the university, for example, each professor has a good deal of control over what is taught and how, as well as what is researched and how. Thus the overall product-market strategy of McGill University must be seen as the composite of the individual teaching and research postures of its 1,200 professors.

That, however, does not quite constitute full autonomy, because there is a subtle but not insignificant constraint on that power. Professionals are left to decide on their own only because years of training have ensured that they will decide in ways generally accepted in their professions. Thus professors choose course contents and adopt teaching methods highly regarded by their colleagues, sometimes even formally sanctioned by their disciplines; they research subjects that will be

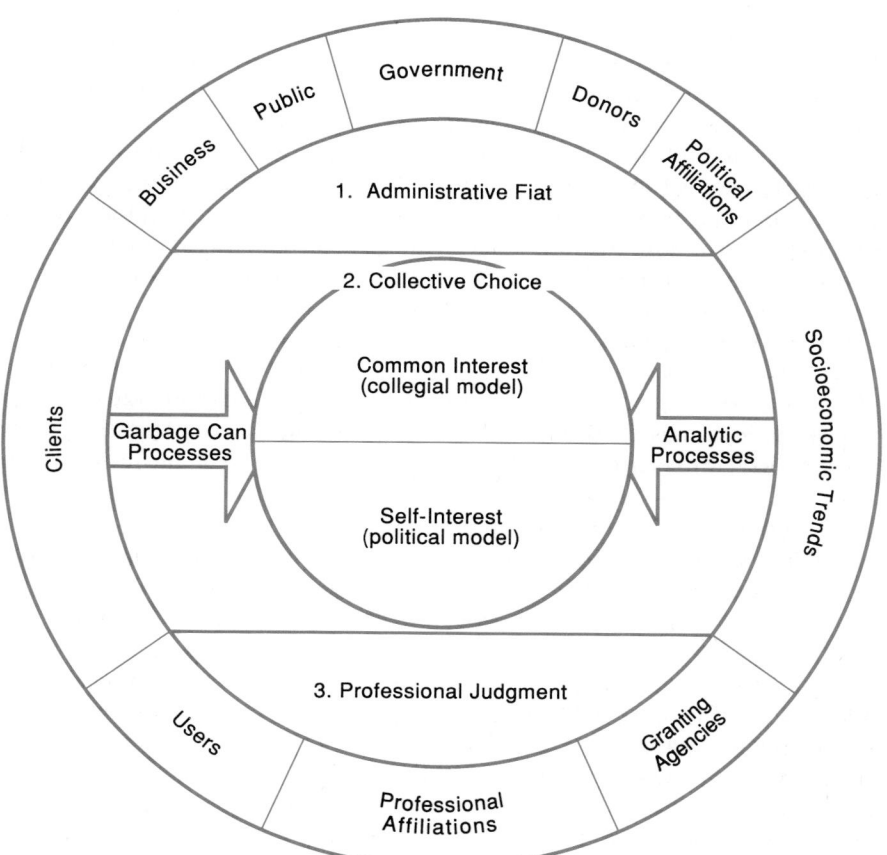

FIGURE 2
Three Levels of Decision Making in the Professional Organization

funded by the granting agencies (which usually come under professional controls); and they publish articles acceptable to the journals refereed by their peers. Pushed to the limit, then, individual freedom becomes professional control. It may be explicit freedom from administrators, even from peers in other disciplines, but it is not implicit freedom from colleagues in their own discipline. Thus we use the label "professional judgment" to imply that while judgment may be the mode of choice, it is informed judgment, mightily influenced by professional training and affiliation.

Decisions Made by Administrative Fiat

Professional expertise and autonomy, reinforced by the pigeonholing process, sharply circumscribe the capacity of central administrators to manage the professionals in the ways of conventional bureaucracy—through direct supervision and the designation of internal standards (rules, job descriptions, policies). Even the designation of standards of output or performance is discouraged by the intractable problem of operationalizing the goals of professional work.

Certain types of decisions, less related to the professional work per se, do however fall into the realm of what can be called administrative fiat, in other words, become the exclusive prerogative of the administrators. They include some financial decisions, for example, to buy and sell property and embark on fund-raising campaigns. Because many of the support services are organized in a conventional top-down hierarchy, they too tend to fall under the control of the central administration. Support services more critical to professional matters, however, such as libraries or computers in the universities, tend to fall into the realm of collective decision making, where the central administrators join the professionals in the making of choices.

Central administrators may also play a prominent role in determining the procedures by which the collective process functions: what committees exist, who gets nominated to them, and so on. It is the administrators, after all, who have the time to devote to administration. This role can give skillful administrators considerable influence, however indirect, over the decisions made by others. In addition, in times of crisis administrators may acquire more extensive powers, as the professionals become more inclined to defer to leadership to resolve the issues.

Decisions Made by Collective Choice

Many decisions are, however, determined neither by administrators nor by individual professionals. Instead they are handled in interactive processes that combine professionals with administrators from a variety of levels and units. Among the most important of these decisions seem to be ones related to the definition, creation, design, and discontinuation of the pigeonholes, that is, the programs and departments of various kinds. Other important decisions here include the hiring and promotion of professionals and, in some cases, budgeting and the establishment and design of the interactive procedures themselves (if they do not fall under administrative fiat).

Decision making may be considered to involve the three phases of *identification* of the need for a decision, *development* of solutions, and *selection* of one of them. Identification seems to depend largely on individual initiative. Given the complexities of professional work and the rigidities of pigeonholing, change in this configuration is difficult to imagine without an initiating "sponsor" or "champion." Development may involve the same individual but often requires the efforts of collective task forces as well. And selection tends to be a fully interactive process, involving several layers of standing committees composed of professionals and administrators, and sometimes outsiders as well (such as government representatives). It is in this last phase that we find the full impact and complexity of mutual adjustment in the administration of professional organizations.

Models of Collective Choice

How do these interactive processes in fact work? Some writers have traditionally associated professional organizations with a *collegial* model, where decisions are made by a "community of individuals and groups, all of whom may have different roles and specialties, but who share common goals and objectives for the organization" (Taylor, 1983:18). *Common interest* is the guiding force, and decision making is therefore by consensus. Other writers instead propose a *political* model, in which the differences of interest groups are irreconcilable. Participants thus seek to serve their *self-interest,* and political factors become instrumental in determining outcomes.

Clearly, neither common interest nor self-interest will dominate decision processes all the time; some combination is naturally to be expected. Professionals may agree on goals yet conflict over how they should be achieved; alternatively, consensus can sometimes be achieved even where goals differ—Democrats do, after all, sometimes vote with Republicans in the U.S. Congress. In fact, we need to consider motivation, not just behavior, in order to distinguish collegiality from politics. Political success sometimes requires a collegial posture—one must cloak self-interest in the mantle of the common good. Likewise, collegial ends sometimes require political means. Thus, we should take as collegial any behavior that is *motivated* by a genuine concern for the good of the institution, and politics as any behavior driven fundamentally by self-interest (of the individual or his or her unit).

A third model that has been used to explain decision making in universities is the *garbage can.* Here decision making is characterized by "collections of choices looking for problems, issues and feelings looking for decision situations in which they may be aired, solutions looking for issues to which they might be an answer, and decision makers looking for work" (Cohen, March, and Olsen, 1972:1). Behavior is, in other words, nonpurposeful and often random, because goals are unclear and the means to achieve them problematic. Furthermore, participation is fluid because of the cost of time and energy. Thus, in place of the common interest of the collegial model and the self-interest of the political model, the garbage can model suggests a kind of *disinterest.*

The important question is not whether garbage can processes exist—we have all experienced them—but whether they matter. Do they apply to key issues or only to incidental ones? Of course, decisions that are not significant to anyone may well end up in the garbage can, so to speak. There is always someone with free time willing to challenge a proposal for the sake of so doing. But I have difficulty accepting that individuals to whom decisions are important do not invest the effort necessary to influence them. Thus, like common interest and self-interest, I conclude that disinterest neither dominates decision processes nor is absent from them.

Finally, *analysis* may be considered a fourth model of decision making. Here calculation is used, if not to select the best alternative, then at least to assess the acceptability of different ones. Such an approach seems consistent with the machine configuration, where a technostructure stands ready to calculate the costs and benefits of every proposal. But, in fact, analysis figures prominently in the professional configuration too, but here carried out mostly by professional operators themselves. Rational analysis structures arguments for communication and debate and enables champions and their opponents to support their respective positions. In fact, as each side seeks to pick holes in the position of the other, the real issues are more likely to emerge.

Thus, as indicated in Figure 2, the important collective decisions of the professional organization seem to be most influenced by collegial and political processes, with garbage can pressures encouraging a kind of haphazardness on one side (especially for less important decisions) and analytical interventions on the other side encouraging a certain rationality (serving as an invisible hand to keep the lid on the garbage can, so to speak!).

Strategies in the Professional Organization

Thus, we find here a very different process of strategy making, and very different resulting strategies, compared with conventional (especially machine) organizations. While it may seem difficult to create strategies in these organizations, due to the fragmentation of activity, the politics, and the garbage can phenomenon, in fact the professional organization is inundated with strategies (meaning patterning in its actions). The standardization of skills encourages patterning, as do the pigeonholing process and the professional affiliations. Collegiality promotes consistency of behavior; even politics works to resist changing existing patterns. As for the garbage can model, perhaps it just represents the unexplained variance in the system; that is, whatever is not understood looks to the outside observer like organized anarchy.

Many different people get involved in the strategy-making process here, including administrators and the various professionals, individually and collectively, so that the resulting strategies can be very fragmented (at the limit, each professional pursues his or her own product-market strategy). There are, of course, forces that encourage some overall cohesion in strategy too: the common forces of administrative fiat, the broad negotiations that take place in the collective process (for example, on new tenure regulations in a university), even the forces of habit and tradition, at the limit ideology, that can pervade a professional organization (such as hiring certain kinds of people or favoring certain styles of teaching or of surgery).

Overall, the strategies of the professional organization tend to exhibit a remarkable degree of stability. Major reorientations in strategy—"strategic revolutions"—are discouraged by the fragmentation of activity and the influence of the individual professionals and their outside associates. But at a narrower level, change is ubiquitous. Inside tiny pigeonholes, services are continually being altered, procedure redesigned, and clientele shifted, while in the collective process, pigeonholes are constantly being added and rearranged. Thus, the professional organization is, paradoxically, extremely stable at the broadest level and in a state of perpetual change at the narrowest one.

SOME ISSUES ASSOCIATED WITH THE PROFESSIONAL ORGANIZATION

The professional organization is unique among the different configurations in answering two of the paramount needs of contemporary men and women. It is democratic, disseminating its power directly to its workers (at least those lucky enough to be professional). And it provides them with extensive autonomy, freeing them even from the need to coordinate closely with their colleagues. Thus, the professional has the best of both worlds. He or she is attached to an organization yet is free to serve clients in his or her own way, constrained only by the established standards of the profession.

The result is that professionals tend to emerge as highly motivated individuals, dedicated to their work and to the clients they serve. Unlike the machine organization, which places barriers between the operator and the client, this configuration removes them, allowing a personal relationship to develop. Moreover, autonomy enables the professionals to perfect their skills free of interference, as they repeat the same complex programs time after time.

But in these same characteristics, democracy and autonomy, lie the chief problems of the professional organization. For there is no evident way to control the work, outside of that exercised by the profession itself, no way to correct deficiencies that the professionals choose to overlook. What they tend to overlook are the problems of coordination, of discretion, and of innovation that arise in these configurations.

Problems of Coordination

The professional organization can coordinate effectively in its operating core only by relying on the standardization of skills. But that is a loose coordinating mechanism at best; it fails to cope with many of the needs that arise in these organizations. One need is to coordinate the work of professionals with that of support staffers. The professionals want to give the orders. But that can catch the support staffers between the vertical power of line authority and the horizontal power of professional expertise. Another need is to achieve overriding coordination among the professionals themselves. Professional organizations, at the limit, may be viewed as collections of independent individuals who come together only to draw on common resources and support services. Though the pigeonholing process facilitates this, some things inevitably fall through the cracks between the pigeonholes. But because the professional organization lacks any obvious coordinating mechanism to deal with these, they inevitably provoke a great deal of conflict. Much political blood is spilled in the continual reassessment of contingencies and programs that are either imperfectly conceived or artificially distinguished.

Problems of Discretion

Pigeonholing raises another serious problem. It focuses most of the discretion in the hands of single professionals, whose complex skills, no matter how standardized, require the exercise of considerable judgment. Such discretion works fine when professionals are competent and conscientious. But it plays havoc when they are not. Inevitably, some professionals are simply lazy or incompetent. Others confuse the needs of their clients with the skills of their trade. They thus concentrate on a favored program to the exclusion of all others (like the psychiatrist who thinks that all patients, indeed all people, need psychoanalysis). Clients incorrectly sent their way get mistreated (in both senses of that word).

Various factors confound efforts to deal with this inversion of means and ends. One is that professionals are notoriously reluctant to act against their own, for example, to censure irresponsible behavior through their professional associations. Another (which perhaps helps to explain the first) is the intrinsic difficulty of measuring the outputs of professional work. When psychiatrists cannot even define the words *cure* or *healthy,* how are they to prove that psychoanalysis is better for schizophrenics than is chemical therapy?

Discretion allows professionals to ignore not only the needs of their clients but also those of the organization itself. Many professionals focus their loyalty on their profession, not on the place where they happen to practice it. But professional organizations have needs for loyalty too—to support their overall strategies, to staff their administrative committees, to see them through conflicts with the professional associations. Cooperation is crucial to the functioning of the administrative structure, yet many professionals resist it furiously.

Problems of Innovation

In the professional organization, major innovation also depends on cooperation. Existing programs may be perfected by the single professional, but new ones usually cut across the established specialties—in essence, they require a rearrangement of the pigeonholes—and so call for collective action. As a result, the reluctance of the professionals to cooperate with each other and the complexity of the collective processes can produce resistance to innovation. These are, after all, professional *bureaucracies,* in essence, performance structures designed to perfect given programs in stable environments, not problem-solving structures to create new programs for unanticipated needs.

The problems of innovation in the professional organization find their roots in convergent thinking, in the deductive reasoning of the professional who sees the specific situation in terms of the general concept. That means new problems are forced into old pigeonholes, as is excellently illustrated in Spencer's comments: "All patients developing significant complications or death among our three hospitals . . . are reported to a central office with a narrative description of the sequence of events, with reports varying in length from a third to an entire page." And six to eight of these cases are discussed in the one-hour weekly "mortality-morbidity" conferences, including presentation of it by the surgeon and "questions and comments" by the audience (1978:1181). An "entire" page and ten minutes of discussion for a case with "significant complications"! Maybe that is enough to list the symptoms and slot them into pigeonholes. But it is hardly enough even to begin to think about creative solutions. As Lucy once told Charlie Brown, great art cannot be done in half an hour; it takes at least 45 minutes!

The fact is that great art and innovative problem solving require *inductive* reasoning—that is, the inference of the new general solution from the particular experience. And that kind of thinking is *divergent;* it breaks away from old routines or standards rather than perfecting existing ones. And that flies in the face of everything the professional organization is designed to do.

Public Responses to These Problems

What responses do the problems of coordination, discretion, and innovation evoke? Most commonly, those outside the profession see the problems as resulting from a lack of external control of the professional and the profession. So they do the obvious: try to control the work through other, more traditional means. One is direct supervision, which typically means imposing an intermediate level of supervision to watch over the professionals. But we already discussed why this cannot work for jobs that are complex. Another is to try to standardize the work or its outputs. But we also discussed why complex work cannot be formalized by rules, regulations, or measures of performance. All these types of controls really do, by transferring the responsibility for the service from the professional to the administrative structure, is destroy the effectiveness of the work. It is not the government that educates the student, not even the school system or the school itself; it is not the hospital that delivers the baby. These things are done by the individual professional. If that professional is incompetent, no plan or rule fashioned in the technostructure, no order from any administrator or government official, can ever make him or her competent. But such plans, rules, and orders can impede the competent professional from providing his or her service effectively.

Are there then no solutions for a society concerned about the performance of its professional organizations? Financial control of them and legislation against ir-responsible professional behavior are obviously in order. But beyond that, solutions must grow from a recognition of professional work for what it is. Change in the professional organization does not *sweep* in from new administrators taking office to announce wide reforms, or from government officials intent on bringing the professionals under technocratic control. Rather, change *seeps* in through the slow process of changing the professionals—changing who enters the profession in the first place, what they learn in its professional schools (norms as well as skills and knowledge), and thereafter how they upgrade their skills. Where desired changes are resisted, society may be best off to call on its professionals' sense of public responsibility or, failing that, to bring pressure on the professional associations rather than on the professional bureaucracies.

• TECHNOLOGY IN SERVICES: CREATING ORGANIZATIONAL REVOLUTIONS*

BY JAMES BRIAN QUINN AND PENNY C. PAQUETTE

Service technologies have radically reordered the power relationships, competitive environments, and leverageable opportunities in most industries—whether in services or manufacturing. In the process, they are obliterating long-held precepts about management itself and creating entirely new strategic, organizational, and control system options for achieving competitive advantage. What are some of the more important management insights from our research?

• Contrary to much popular dogma, well-managed service technologies can simultaneously deliver both *lowest cost outputs* and *maximum personalization and customization* for customers.

• In accomplishing this, enterprises generally obtain strategic advantage not through traditional economies of scale, but through *focusing on the smallest activity or cost units* that can be efficiently measured and replicated—and then *cloning and mixing these units* across as wide a geographical and applications range as possible.

• Instead of the dehumanization often experienced in other realms, well-implemented service automation actually *increases the independence* and value of lower-level jobs. At the same time, such automation *empowers contact people* to be much more responsive to customer needs.

• Such systems, when well implemented, frequently drive organizations toward entirely *new conceptual configurations*. These may assume "inverted pyramid," "infinitely flat," or "spider's web" characteristics in order to deliver outputs most effectively and flexibly to a widely distributed customer base.

• In the process, they often *disintermediate costly organizational bureaucracies,* dramatically *lower overhead costs, support rapid execution of strategies,* and substantially *increase the system's customer responsiveness.*

* Originally published in the *Sloan Management Review* (Winter, 1990). Copyright © 1990 by the Sloan Management Review. Reprinted by permission of the *Review.*

Creative use of technology in leading-edge companies has converted these concepts from theoreticians' fantasies into realistic strategic options for virtually any company.

OBTAINING BOTH CUSTOMIZATION AND LOWEST COST

Strategic dogmas exist that postulate an inherent conflict between obtaining lowest cost from a system and offering highest flexibility and customization (Porter, 1985). To achieve maximum value from service technologies, one must set these aside. By designing their systems properly, many well-run service companies both obtain optimal flexibility at the customer contact point and achieve maximum "production" efficiencies from constant repetition, experience curve effects, and cost-quality control. They accomplish this by first seeking the smallest possible core unit at which production can be replicated or repeated, then developing micromeasures to manage processes and functions at this level, and finally mixing these micro-units in a variety of combinations to match localized or individual customers' needs. What do these smallest replicable units look like? The nature of the unit, of course, varies by industry and by strategy.

- For Mary Kay Cosmetics or Tupperware, the sales presentation is such a unit; for accountants, audit check procedures, inventory control processes, or tax preparation subroutines may be critical; for lawyers, prepackaged documents, paragraphs, phrases, court opinions, or case briefings may be the leverageable unit. In financial services, elements of individual "transactions" (like buy/sell units, prices, times, names, customer codes, etc.) are core units; for information retrieval, it is the "key word"; for communications, it is the "packet" or the bit; and so on.

Early in the life cycle of many service industries, the smallest truly replicable unit seemed to be an individual office, store, or franchise location. Later, as volume increased, it often became possible for the parent to develop and replicate greater efficiencies within locations (Levitt, 1976). This was accomplished by managing and measuring critical performance variables at individual departmental, sales counter, activity, or stock-keeping unit (SKU) levels. Then the successful formula approaches of H&R Block, McDonald's, Mrs. Fields, and Pizza Hut pushed the repeatability unit to even smaller "micromanagement" levels. Replicating precisely measured activity cycles, personal selling approaches, inventory control patterns, ingredients, freshness and cooking cycles, counter display techniques, and cleanliness and maintenance procedures in detail became keys to success; lapses led to difficulties. So precise are many nationwide chains' measurement and feedback systems that their headquarters can tell within minutes when something goes wrong in a decentralized unit, and often precisely what the problem is.

Finally, in some industries—like banking, communications, structural design, or medical research—it has become possible to disaggregate the critical units of service production into packets, data blocks, or "bytes" of information. Accessing and combining such units on a large scale is emerging as the core activity in achieving flexibility and economies of scale on a level never before envisioned.

MANAGING AT THE MICRO-UNIT LEVEL

Most of the major strategic successes we observed in the use of service technologies came from defining and developing these replicability units and their associated micromeasures in careful detail. The exceptions were some large transportation companies (airlines or railroads) and utilities (electric power grids) that relied on more traditional economies from large-scale facilities. The ultimate purpose of focusing on the smallest replicable unit of operations, however, is not just the mass production benefit that standardization allows. Effectively combining these micro-units permits one to achieve the highest possible degrees of segmentation, strategic fine tuning, value-added, and customer satisfaction in the marketplace. Interestingly, the larger the organization, the more refined these replicability units may practically be—and the higher their leverage for creating value-added gains. Greater volume allows a larger company to collect more detail about its individual operating and market segments; analyze these data at more disaggregated levels; and experiment with more detailed segmentations in ways smaller concerns cannot. For example:

- American Express (AmEx) is the only major credit card company with a large travel service. By capturing in the most disaggregated possible form—essentially data bytes—the details that its various traveler, shopper, retailer, lodging, and transportation company customers put through its credit card and travel systems, AmEx can mix and match the patterns and capabilities of each group to add value for them in ways its competitors cannot. It can identify life-style changes (like marriage or moving) or match forthcoming travel plans with its customers' specific buying habits to notify them of special promotions, product offerings, or services AmEx's retailers may be presenting in their local or planned travel areas. From its larger information base AmEx can also provide more detailed information services to its two million retailer customers—like demographic and comparative analyses of their customer bases or individual customers' needs for wheelchair, pickup, or other convenience services. These can provide unique value for both consumer and retailer customers.

The key to micromanagement is breaking down both operations and markets into such detail that—by properly cross-matrixing the data—one can discern how a very slight change in one arena may affect some aspect of the other. The ability to micromanage, target, and customize operations in this fashion, because of the knowledge base that size permits, is becoming one of the most important uses of scale in services.

Critical to proper system design is conceptualizing the smallest replicable unit and its potential use in strategy as early as possible in system design. Summing disaggregated data later, if one so desires, is much easier than moving from a more aggregated system to a greater refinement in detail. And highly disaggregated data often capture unexpected experience patterns that summary data would obscure. Much of the later power and flexibility of American's SABRE, McKesson's ECONOMOST, or National Rental Car's EXPRESSWAY systems derived from making this choice correctly, while less successful competitors' systems did not.[1] Too many companies have chosen a larger replicability unit in order to save initial installation costs. In the process they have lost crucial detailed experience and segmentation data that should have become the core of their later strategies.

---

[1] McKesson's ECONOMOST system was planned from the beginning to collect such detailed information concerning item description, price, price changes, shelf location, sales rates, facings information, and so on, that the system could later be easily adapted for follow-on services like optimizing floor layouts, stock locations, reordering patterns, bill payments, accounting, credit, and insurance arrangements, market testing, and so on.

Well-designed technology systems for services not only increase efficiency, they empower employees to do their jobs better. Why is this so important in services? In most cases, a service must be produced simultaneously with its consumption—as a telephone call, a vacation, a restaurant meal, electrical energy, or a hospital stay would be. There is often no inventory potential, very little opportunity for later repair, and no resale market for the service. This means that much of a service's perceived value is created at the moment and place of contact. And the frontline person's willingness to handle that contact with diligence and flair is often critical to success of the enterprise.

Properly designed service technology systems allow relatively inexperienced people to perform very sophisticated tasks quickly—vaulting them over normal learning curve delays. Then by constant updating, the most successful technologies and systems automatically capture the highest potential experience curve benefits available in the entire system. This allows employees to take advantage of the total organization's constantly expanding capabilities, which they could not possibly learn first hand or be trained personally to execute. This is vital when so many service operations rely on entry-level, part-time, or relatively inexperienced workers to meet their needs at lowest cost. By increasing the value added per employee, the technologies also open possibilities for wage gains, as well as opportunities for many employees to own a profitable franchise or manage the very decentralized operations of automated service systems.

Interestingly, effective service automation generally encourages greater—rather than less—empowerment and decentralization at the contact level. This is true of both professional and more product-oriented service organizations—like restaurants, retailers, or postsale product support units. By routinizing the operating detail that it once took great effort to master, managers and workers can concentrate their attention on the more conceptual or personalized tasks only people can perform. An example will suggest how technology helps both decentralize and empower personnel in successful service organizations.

• Domino's Pizza, perhaps the fastest-growing food chain in history, encourages its local store managers to regard themselves as individual entrepreneurs. First, for each of its 4,500 highly decentralized outlets, industrial engineering and food science research automated the making of a pizza to as near a science as possible, eliminating much of the drudgery in such tasks, yet ensuring higher quality and uniformity. Then, finding that its store managers were still spending fifteen to twenty hours per week on paperwork, Domino's introduced NCR "minitower" systems at its stores to handle all of the ordering, payroll, marketing, cash flow, inventory, and work control functions. This freed store executives to perform more valuable supervisory, follow-up, menu experimentation, public relations, or customer service activities—expanding and elevating their management roles. Thus they could focus even more on founder Tom Monahan's goals: that they be independent entrepreneurs devoting themselves as much as possible to the company's highly developed customer service philosophies.

Some strategies, of course, call for more empowerment, some for more standardization of activity. Some service situations even require that technologies be used *primarily* to obtain uniformity, rather than flexibility. In some services, like bank accounting, film processing, or aircraft maintenance, one may actively discourage too much independence, because exactness and tight tolerances are required. Great service successes, however, generally exhibit a unique blend: a distinctly structured technology system and a carefully developed management style to support it. The subtle ways in which the two are developed and emphasized can lead to quite different market postures in the same industry.

- Federal Express (FedEx) has long emphasized the use of a friendly, people-oriented, entrepreneurial management style in conjunction with state-of-the-art technology systems. Its DADS (computer aided delivery) and COSMOS II (automated tracking) systems give FedEx maximum responsiveness. And its training programs, colorful advertising, decentralized operating style, and incentive systems stress the need to go to the limit personally in responding to customer needs and ensuring reliable, on-time delivery. By contrast, UPS has long utilized old-style trucks, hand sorting, lower-cost land transport, detailed time and motion study controls for its drivers, and a hard-headed control system that give it a lower cost—but considerably less customer responsive—market position. Both companies have been successful, FedEx by emphasizing "highest reliability and customer service" and UPS by emphasizing good service at low cost.

NEW ORGANIZATIONAL FORMS

In their efforts to gain the benefits of these two concepts—management at the micro-level and increased empowerment at the customer contact point—many service companies have developed strikingly new, and more effective, organizational modes. Several of the most important ones are described below.

Inverting the Organization

To the customer, the most important person in the company is very often the one at the point of contact. What happens in the usually brief one to three minutes of that contact will demonstrate—or destroy—for the customer all the value the company so expensively has sought to create through its product, quality, distribution, and advertising investments (Carlzon, 1987).

In some situations this consideration is so dominant that it has led to the concept of "inverting the organization" to make all systems and support staffs in the company "work for" the frontline person to deliver the company's full capabilities at the moment of customer contact. Managers in such enterprises try to make their organizations perform as if they were a series of pyramids focused on the frontline contact people. Some, like Toronto Dominion Bank and AIG, have formal organization charts with the customer at the top, the CEO at the bottom, and an inverted organization hierarchy in between.

Such techniques may be useful reminders, but it is really technology and an inversion of roles and attitudes that make such concepts work. The point person (e.g., a branch bank's customer service representative) cannot possibly know or control all the system details (investment options, differential interest rates, future values, etc.) necessary to deliver the organization's full power to the customer. Thus, successfully inverted organizations first capture and continuously update or monitor as many relevant service elements as possible by structuring data banks, "expert system" models, and interactive feedback and communication systems to make as much as possible of the firm's total expertise available instantly to the point person. Network technologies allow frontline personnel to call forth and cross-matrix whatever details their customers' specific needs may require—using collected micro-units of information either directly as data or indirectly to build unique solutions for customers even at the most remote locations. Within the data limits and decision rules defined by the system, nonroutine decisions are left as much as possible to local personnel. These individuals then call for help on those specialized issues they cannot handle themselves. And each person in the management hierarchy is expected to respond to this "order" for support.

As an interesting part of the inversion, it is usually the software or planning personnel (ordinarily considered "service" or "staff") who design "line" decisions. They do so by providing accessible answers to routinely asked questions or by simulating (through expert systems) many of the more sophisticated decisions line managers would normally make. To complete the inversion, intermediate line managers, rather than being order givers, become essentially expediters, information sources, and performance observers—roles frequently assumed to be "staff"—supporting the contact people. However, their other substantive line roles—particularly as arbiters of last resort for frontline personnel and as sensors of situations beyond the scope of the technological systems—take on even greater relative importance as routine activities decline. Because of the distortions that inevitably take place in human communication, eliminating the hierarchical layers between the central repository of information and the customer contact point becomes an important goal that a well-developed information technology system facilitates. When this occurs the few remaining line executives become even more important in their expanded roles—managing much wider areas of organizational contact and those more complicated issues where interpretation, intuition, creativity, and human motivation count.

"Infinitely Flat" Organizations

When technology is creatively implemented in services, companies often achieve other remarkable organizational configurations. For example, there now seems to be virtually no limit to the reporting span—the number of people reporting to one supervisor or center—that a service organization can make effective. While spans of twenty to fifty have become relatively common, spans of hundreds exist in some service organizations. Several examples will make the point.

• Shearson American Express's and Merrill Lynch's 310 to 480 domestic brokerage offices connect directly with their parents' central information offices for routine needs, yet can bypass the electronic system for personal access to individual experts in headquarters. In effect, technology permits the company to function in a coordinated fashion with the full power of a major financial enterprise, yet allows local brokers to manage their own small units independently. The result is to provide the most extensive possible local responsiveness and customization for the company's dispersed customer base.

• Federal Express, with 42,000 employees in more than 300 cities worldwide, has a maximum of only five organizational layers between its nonmanagement employees and its COO or CEO. Typical operating spans of control are 15–20 employees to one manager, with only 2.1 staff employees per million dollars in sales—about one-fifth the industry average. As many as 50 couriers are under the line control of a single dispatching center. FedEx's advanced DADS and COSMOS computer-communications capabilities allow it to coordinate its 21,000 vans nationwide to make an average of 720,000 "on call" stops per day. Because of its leading edge flight operations technologies and avionics controls, as many as 200 FedEx aircraft can be in the air simultaneously, but under the control of a single authority, should it become necessary to override flight plans because of weather or special emergencies.

There is no inherent reason that organizations cannot be made "infinitely flat"—in other words, with innumerable outposts guided by one central "rules-based" or "computer controlled inquiry" system. In designing service company systems, instead of thinking about traditional "spans of control," our study suggests that the terms "spans of effective cooperation," "communication spans," or "support spans" may have more meaning. By defining, routinizing, and automating operating parameters at their finest replicable level, companies can often obtain the thorough cost and quality controls they need for system coordination and productivity at each of many highly decentralized operating nodes. In these circumstances, the normal functions provided by personal hierarchical controls become almost irrelevant.

Extremely wide reporting spans work well when the following conditions exist: localized interactive contact is very important; each ultimate contact point or operations unit can operate independently from all others at its level; the critical relationship between decentralized units and the center is largely quantitative or informational; and the majority of the relationships with the information center can be routine or rules based. Although service units have generally pioneered such organizations, a few manufacturing enterprises have realized that the same characteristics occur in specific production situations and are beginning to implement similar approaches. The immediate economic impact of such systems is, of course, that they allow major investments in extremely sophisticated systems at the center, deliver this sophistication in highly customized form at remote points, eliminate overhead hierarchies, and add value (at lower unit costs) in both the center and the remote nodes. American Express—whose expertise at credit processing is so great that its competitors hire it to process their credit transactions—is one such example. AMRIS (described later) is another.

An often overlooked feature of these systems is the longer-term payoff potentials that carefully developed feedback loops from the decentralized nodes can offer to the center. By sophisticated segmentation and synthesis of data generated at the nodes—and the often much more detailed information about their customers they collect—the corporation's "information center" can develop a knowledge base with a power neither it nor any single outlet could possibly achieve alone. Aggregating and comparing detailed information from these sources, the center can often develop an ever-increasing set of higher value-added services and sell them back to its own nodes (or the latter's customers) to further increase its profits and those units' competitiveness. For example:

• American Airlines' parent recently created a sister company, AMR Information Services (AMRIS) to further leverage the knowledge, staff, facilities, and technologies its SABRE reservations system had built. Along with operating an offshore data entry business, AMRIS is entering a partnership with Hilton, Marriott, and Budget Rent-a-Car to handle their critical reservations and property management activities worldwide. AMRIS's system (called CONFIRM) will provide a single source with hundreds of remote nodes—in other words, a very flat organization—through which travel agents can make and confirm all desired reservations.

But CONFIRM will also provide its client industries with a much broader and deeper database to micromanage their yield strategies, for example, foreseeing unexpected shortfalls or special surges in occupancy or demand soon enough to target short-term promotional and pricing strategies. In time, comparative data across client companies will enable AMRIS to develop industrywide decision support models, further amplifying its own and its clients' competitive advantages. Yet each participant in this consortium (and their individual outlets) can operate as independently as they wish.

"Spider's Web" Organizations

When the highly dispersed nodes of service operations or customer contact must interact frequently, another startling organizational form begins to emerge. It is sometimes called a network, but is best described as a spider's web because of the light yet structured quality of its interconnections.

• Arthur Andersen and Company (AA&Co.,) a leader in applying technology to professional services, has to interlink its 40,000 knowledgeable professionals with thousands of clients, each with a mix of operations around the United States and in up to 200 other countries. The company's cumulative experience is growing so fast that, according to executives, "Even those in the know may not have the best answer to the totality of a complex question." Consequently, individuals in AA&Co. can no longer even rely on their personal knowledge of whom to call for information. So in addition to trying to capture the history of its contacts with major clients, keeping up electronically with changing IRS and FASB requirements, and attempting to catalogue where it has found solutions to particular problems, the firm is developing an electronic bulletin board to let any professional send out a query to the entire AA&Co. system to find useful solutions or knowledge that any other individual in the company may have for special problems.

The firm operates in a highly decentralized, real-time mode. Each local office is as independent as possible. Partners say that AA&Co.'s distinctive competency has become "empowering people to deliver better quality technology-based solutions to clients in a shorter time." Customers now look to the firm to deliver computer-based solutions to systems problems in a league competitive with EDS's and IBM's capabilities. Yet professionals who leave AA&Co. immediately lose access to its systems and accumulated experience.

Such open network formats increasingly characterize the way multinational or investment banks, financial or professional service companies, engineering and construction enterprises, research and health care, and accounting and advertising firms operate. Unlike the units of infinitely flat organizations, each of the nodes in the spider's web frequently needs, for effectiveness, to be in touch with the information or resources all other nodes contain. Within wide ranges, each node may function quite independently in serving a particular client base. However, in certain circumstances, the individual nodes may need to operate in a highly coordinated fashion to achieve strategic advantage for a specific purpose. To deal with this problem, companies with traditional organizational structures must resort to complex matrix organizations that allow the project leader to coerce resources, as needed, from the otherwise decentralized network. But this often creates very costly motivational, priority, turf, and transfer pricing issues. Others have found the flexibility, fast response, and opportunism of the spider's web concept so attractive that they have established entirely new management modes that allow it to operate.

CREATIVE MANAGEMENT FOR PROFITS

Managing these new organizational forms poses some interesting challenges. Yet we have observed some consistent patterns, problems, and benefits that seem to accompany development of these new modes. What are some of the most interesting themes?

Destruction of Bureaucracies

A common consequence of these new organizational strategies is their dramatic potential for reducing intermediate management—and other organizational—bureaucracies. This occurs in part because a customer's highly personalized perception of quality in services tends to demand as much customization at the point of sale as possible. Delivering reliably against this expectation requires that intermediate levels of interpretation or handling be avoided like the plague. Each transfer point or intermediary can introduce unintended errors, distort intentions, or create costly but unmeasured bureaucratic delays. Unfortunately, because the outputs of internal service functions are so difficult to measure, it is easy for such costs to balloon uncontrollably. Targeting internal, as well as external, service activities for substantial disintermediation (entire elimination of the function if possible) can lead to startling competitive gains, usually including more rapid response times and better service for customers.

• For major newspapers like *The New York Times,* electronic technologies are enabling editors and reporters to go directly to printable copy at their electronic work stations. While still in contact with their field sources, they can pretest spacings, enhance picture quality, and lay out entire pages without handling any hard copy. Through disintermediation of make up, type setting, and other proofing stages they cut costs, shorten cycle times, and deliver more current news to their customers. Electronic publishing also allows such newspapers to target the news for different localities, release multiple local editions on tight schedules, and serve their regional advertising customers more effectively. In many cases, outside suppliers like ADP Services (in payroll processing), ServiceMaster (in maintenance services), or Kelly Services (in temporary personnel services) can add more value and provide greater economies of scale through technology than any less specialized company can achieve internally. In these situations, a company will sacrifice competitive advantage if it does not outsource and eliminate as much of its internal bureaucracy as possible. Most overheads are merely services the company has chosen to produce internally. Approaching each such activity as a "make or buy" option (in light of new services technologies' potentials) will, at a minimum, stimulate creative strategic alternatives. In many cases it will lead to the dismantling of outmoded bureaucracies.

Leveraging and Keeping Key People

Many companies find that developing internal service technologies to a high level has become a critical factor in attracting, leveraging, and keeping key people. This is most obvious in the more professional service areas like research, design, engineering, finance, marketing, or public relations. In such fields, better qualified people will more readily join or stay with a company if it provides the most advanced technology systems for practicing their art. The concept has special power in independent professional service firms, where very talented people are essential but can easily move to other enterprises, often taking clients with them. Proper strategic use of technology in these situations increases the professionals' personal potentials within the firm—enabling higher billing rates and salaries—yet creates a dependency that ties them more tightly to the enterprise. Thus used, technology serves in both *offensive* and *defensive* roles.

• Advanced accounting, legal, consulting, and financial service houses use technology as a two-edged sword. First they capture and store updated regulations, legal opinions, and professional practice rules to ensure highest quality for their services. Then they attempt to automate their routine audit, client analysis, and repetitious operations (like contract boiler plate or tested clauses for public documents) and concentrate on the unique aspects of their clients' situations. This has progressed so far that some activities—like audit functions in CPA firms and portfolio or bubble chart analyses—that used to be the core offerings of many professional firms have become commodities with such low margins that they are often used primarily as promotions to obtain other business. As they are freed from overseeing these routine tasks, key people can benefit from the excitement of solving more challenging problems and from the higher revenues this allows. In fact, many professional services firms now find that the core of their distinctive competency lies in the accumulated knowledge in their databases and the capacity of their members to access and build solutions on those databases. The technology thus creates entry barriers for competitors, switching costs for clients, and (perhaps most important) switching costs for their own key personnel.

Successful use of technology in these situations is built around certain imperatives. First, the technology must leverage its users' personal capabilities and enhance their value to the greatest extent possible. Second, to capture the maximum benefits of the technology, quotes, billings, and internal controls need to shift from an hourly billing basis toward a value-added concept. Finally, while being simple to access, the technology's innards must be sufficiently complex that its reproduction becomes a genuine barrier to key individuals' leaving. This defensive consideration is especially critical for independent professional partnerships, but it is increasingly important in product-oriented companies where an individual's knowledge or contacts—for example, in research or marketing—are central to the enterprise's success.

Technology has also become strategically important in providing job satisfaction at all levels of service organizations. How well a company treats its key employees—whether they are high performing sales clerks, skilled technicians, or expensive professionals—will ultimately be reflected in how productive these employees are and how well they treat customers. Well-designed technology systems directly support desired motivational processes at all levels.

• For example, retail stores have found that some of the major benefits of their bar code scanning and price look-up systems come from a marked decrease in pricing and inventory identification errors and, even more important, a correspondingly improved morale among checkout personnel. Because there are no product identification errors, purchasing and stocking activities are more accurate, avoiding annoying stockouts and outdated merchandise. Checkout and salesclerks are less embarrassed by not knowing item descriptions or current prices, can speed up their service considerably (thus decreasing frustrated customers' antagonism), and have more time to spend on the more pleasant customer interactions they enjoy.

Precise and Swift Strategy Execution

Another important advantage accrues from proper exploitation of service technologies. As managers break their service production down to the smallest replicable units consistent with customers' varying needs, they must be able to measure performance in comparable detail. Assuming they install proper feedback mechanisms, this gives them the capability to execute their strategies quickly and precisely, maintaining a desired productivity, quality, and "product" mix even as demand fluctuates violently or new products are introduced.

- While insurance companies used to rewrite their offerings and rate books once or twice a year, they must now adjust to the constantly changing interest rates and offerings of other direct and functional competitors, like banks, money market funds, and the single-premium offers from brokerage houses. Insurance executives state flatly that their agents could not possibly understand or present the volatile complexity of their products without responsive on-line information connections with headquarters. Such connections are essential to calculate and immediately update the company's margins on each product, maintain desired spreads, and motivate agents to sell the most profitable current product mix.

Respondents in our study often asserted this theme: "In services, execution is everything. If you can't deliver what customers want, when they want it, with the personal touch they like, all your strategic thinking and investments won't amount to much. Our technology is one key factor in execution. The other is the management systems and culture that cause our people to react quickly and favorably to our offerings and to our customers' needs."

Managing Technologies and Attitudes

While many strategic analyses focus mostly on measurable economic factors, our study found that managing employee perceptions at the frontline level was among the most highly leverageable—and lowest-cost—activities service managers undertook. When strongly inculcated corporate values were made meaningful at the operating level, morale became higher, service levels improved, productivity went up, time horizons lengthened, increased delegation was possible, personal conflicts decreased, and control system costs dropped—all with high impacts on value added and profits. But it also turned out that a dual orientation toward technology and managing values was crucial. Together, in our sample, the two yielded some of the greatest successes in modern business history. But when one was ignored, disasters could happen.

- Many are familiar with the explosive growth Donald Burr created with his charismatic leadership of People Express. At first, the company's shared vision was fully communicated and internalized at virtually all levels of the organization. This and other personnel practices led to a highly committed, efficient, and responsive company. However, one of the reasons People Express failed was Mr. Burr's disdain, if not active dislike, for technology. Despite the pleading of some key people, People Express was not connected to the major automated reservation systems, key operations were not computerized, and flight services became ever more confused and difficult for passengers. Finally, other airlines with more sophisticated information about flight patterns and rate structures were able to chip away at People Express's niche without severe cost to themselves.

- By contrast, Wal-Mart stores, the last decade's fastest-growing and most profitable major retail chain, offers an excellent example of how the combination can be implemented well. Wal-Mart focuses its advanced technologies and all of its efficiency efforts on serving its customers better and lowering prices, not just on cost cutting or margin generating per se. To drive its customer-oriented value system, executives spend four to five days a week personally talking to customers and employees in the field, and then return for Friday/Saturday "idea sessions" to improve operations. To emphasize this orientation further, Wal-Mart often designates certain employees (who might otherwise have been displaced by technology or systems changes) as "people greeters" to increase customer satisfaction. It has also developed an extensive "Buy American Plan," which helps Wal-Mart's dominantly blue-collar customers by protecting their jobs. All these practices support the company's constantly reinforced theme that "serving the customer right is what makes profits" (Barrier, 1988).

The Company as a Voluntary Organization

Two of the most important strategic differences between large-scale services and manufacturing operations are the dependency of the entire system on the person at the contact point with the customer, and the very high degree of geographical dispersion among the points where the service is produced and delivered. The people who can and do create the greatest value in these situations are genuinely "volunteers"; they have often been described as "assets who walk out the door every night." And their skills, intrinsic attitudes, and knowledge are such that they rarely have to stay with the company unless they so choose. For a service company's core strategies to succeed, everyone in critical positions—especially those who deal directly with customers' concerns—must be in an environment where they want to perform well, and be trained and empowered to do so. Many of these people—often numbering in the thousands in large enterprises—tend to be at locations remote from the corporate center.

Realizing this, successful service companies focus on delivering empowering details—from required data to repair supplies—in a timely manner to key personnel and then cultivating their willingness and capabilities to use these to serve customers. In order to ensure maximum responsiveness at the contact point, however, one must also have the confidence that the frontline person will intuitively respond in the proper way when nonprogrammed situations occur. Empowerment with control entails many things. Critical among them are providing information, supplies, and performance measures with microprecision at the front-line level and paying special attention to values and attitude management—including the selection, indoctrination, skills training, and incentive processes converging on people at the point where the service is created and delivered.

One of the least glamorous services—hair dressing—shows dramatically how managing this combination can pay off.

• Visible Changes, in the fragmented hairdressing industry, achieves three and one-half times the turnover of its competitors, twice the average sales per customer, and almost four times the industry's average product sales in its outlets. Starting with hairdressers—who generally have no loyalty to their employers and see their profession as a low-paying dead end—Visible Changes tries to give its employees a sense of proprietorship, without stock equity. Employees make their own decisions, and always earn their rewards.

Nothing comes as a "benefit." People earn their health insurance from their sale of hair care products. They have to earn the right to go to advanced hair styling programs. But as a reward, hairdressers, when customers especially request them, receive a 35% commission and the right to raise service fees by up to 40%. Bonuses, based on performance ratings, can add another 10%, and profit sharing 15% more. A computer-based system helps measure and reward each individual's performance down to the finest detail; it maintains needed cost controls, points out where performance can be improved, and creates equity among individuals. The typical employee earns three times the industry's average wage.

The value of most service companies depends strongly on their managements' style and leadership qualities, the culture that management creates, and the way key people respond to these factors. No financial analysis of the "breakup" or "takeover" value of a service company means much without a realistic assessment of whether a new management could—and would—continue to build similar value through its people. To enhance a firm's market value, perhaps management should try to capitalize as much of a firm's uniqueness as possible into its operating systems and technologies, which are transferable on sale. But these will never quite capture that last, most important, ephemeral, and leverageable element in services—the skills and attitudes of key operating people and management.

KEY CHALLENGES

We have emphasized the reality and the success of these fascinating new organizational forms and strategies. Yet managements encounter many difficult issues in implementing them—particularly in settings where more traditional structures have enjoyed a long history. It is often easy to introduce a radical organization form in a well-conceived startup. Elsewhere, one can anticipate certain common complications.

• Intermediate management levels—whose very meaning is threatened by such configurations—will resist strongly, unless the firm's growth offers more productive havens.

• Especially in more professional service activities, those for whom information has been power will struggle against giving their newer colleagues access to client contacts, mentally stored solutions, or private files that have given senior members a competitive edge in the past.

• MIS people who have made their careers around large central computer systems often become unsettled centers of resistance when they realize that powerful desktop computers and decentralized networks will make their primary skills obsolescent and erode their power bases.

• Experienced line personnel may become frustrated and confused by the need to choose and compromise among the competing demands various important parties place on them.

By simplifying their organizations, companies can overcome many of these resistances while achieving much greater strategic focus. This article suggests that the opportunities for increased efficiency, flexibility, and responsiveness—with significantly lowered overheads—are very great. The question is no longer whether these potentials are real. The issue is whether, when, and how to begin moving toward those potentials—before or after one's competitors have seized the initiative.

13

THE INNOVATION CONTEXT

Although often seen as a high-technology event involving inventor-entrepreneurs, innovation may, of course, occur in high or low technology, product or service, large or small organizational situations. Innovation may be thought of as the *first reduction to practice* of an idea in a culture. The more radical the idea, the more traumatic and profound its impact will tend to be. But there are no absolutes. Whatever is most new and difficult to understand becomes the "high technology" of its age. As Jim Utterback of MIT is fond of pointing out, the delivery of ice was high technology at the turn of the century, later it was the production of automobiles. By the same token, fifty years from now, electronics and space stations may be considered mundane.

Our focus here, however, is not on innovation per se, but on the innovation *context,* that is the situation in which steady or frequent innovation of a complex nature is an intrinsic part of the organization and the industry segment of which it choses to operate. Such organizations depend, not just on a single entrepreneurial individual, but on teams of experts molded together for "intrapreneurship."

The innovation context is one in which the organization often must deal with complex technologies or systems under conditions of dynamic change. Typically, major innovations require that a variety of experts work toward a common goal, often led by a single champion or a small group of committed individuals. Much has been learned from research in recent years on such organizations. While this knowledge may seem less structured than that of previous chapters, several dominant themes have emerged.

This chapter opens with a description of the fifth of Mintzberg's structures, here titled the innovative organization, but also referred to as "adhocracy." This is the structure that, as noted, achieves its effectiveness by being inefficient. This reading probes into the unusual ways in which strategies evolve in the context of work that is both highly complex and highly dynamic. Here we see the full flowering of the notion of emergent strategy, culminating in a description of a "grass-roots" model of the process. We also see here a strategic leadership less concerned with formulating and then implementing strategies than managing a process through which strategies almost seem to *form* by themselves.

The second reading of this chapter, James Brian Quinn's "Managing Innovation: Controlled Chaos" (winner of the McKinsey prize for the best *Harvard Business Review* article of 1985), suggests how the spirit of adhocracy and strategy formation as a learning process can be integrated with some of the formal strategic processes of large organizations. To achieve innovativeness, other authors have advocated adhocracy with little or no reliance on planning. Quinn suggests that blending broad strategy planning with a consciously structured adhocracy gives better results. This reading also brings back the notion of "intrapreneurship," mentioned in the introduction to Chapter 9 on the entrepreneurial context. When it is successful, intrapreneurship—implying the stimulation and diffusion of innovative capacity throughout a larger organization, with many champions of innovations—tends to follow most of Quinn's precepts. As such, it seems to belong more to this context than the entrepreneurial one, which focuses on organizations highly centralized around the initiatives of their single leaders, whether or not innovative.

Again many cases support the development of these key concepts. In a smaller company setting we have the start up of Genentech, Biogen, Sony, Polaroid, and Hewlett-Packard. In the innovative services context we find ARCOP. And in the midsized to large company context one finds Intel and the very large projects of IBM's 360 program, Pilkington's float glass, and Ford's Team Taurus. The complexities of innovation thus can be viewed from many different perspectives.

• THE INNOVATIVE ORGANIZATION*

BY HENRY MINTZBERG

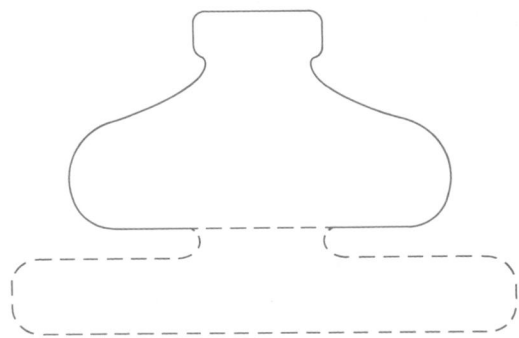

None of the organization forms so far discussed is capable of sophisticated innovation, the kind required of a high-technology research organization, an avant-garde film company, or a factory manufacturing complex prototypes. The

* Adapted from *The Structuring of Organizations* (Prentice Hall, 1979), Chap. 21 on the adhocracy; on strategy formation from "Strategy Formation in an Adhocracy," coauthored with Alexandra McHugh, *Administrative Science Quarterly* (1985: 160–197), and "Strategy of Design: A Study of 'Architects in Co-Partnership,' " coauthored with Suzanne Otis, Jamal Shamsie, and James A. Waters, in J. Grant (ed.), *Strategic Management Frontiers* (JAI Press, 1988). A chapter similar to this one appeared in *Mintzberg on Management: Inside Our Strange World of Organizations* (Free Press, 1989).

entrepreneurial organization can certainly innovate, but only in relatively simple ways. The machine and professional organizations are performance, not problem-solving types, designed to perfect standardized programs, not to invent new ones. And although the diversified organization resolves some problem of strategic inflexibility found in the machine organization, as noted earlier it too is not a true innovator. A focus on control by standardizing outputs does not encourage innovation.

Sophisticated innovation requires a very different configuration, one that is able to fuse experts drawn from different disciplines into smoothly functioning ad hoc project teams. To borrow the word coined by Bennis and Slater in 1964 and later popularized in Alvin Toffler's *Future Shock* (1970), these are the *adhocracies* of our society.

THE BASIC STRUCTURE

Here again we have a distinct configuration of the attributes of design: highly organic structure, with little formalization of behavior; specialized jobs based on expert training; a tendency to group the specialists in functional units for housekeeping purposes but to deploy them in small project teams to do their work; a reliance on teams, on task forces, and on integrating managers of various sorts in order to encourage mutual adjustment, the key mechanism of coordination, within and between these teams; and considerable decentralization to and within these teams, which are located at various places in the organization and involve various mixtures of line managers and staff and operating experts.

To innovate means to break away from established patterns. Thus the innovative organization cannot rely on any form of standardization for coordination. In other words, it must avoid all the trappings of bureaucratic structure, notably sharp divisions of labor, extensive unit differentiation, highly formalized behaviors, and an emphasis on planning and control systems. Above all, it must remain flexible. A search for organigrams to illustrate this description elicited the following response from one corporation thought to have an adhocracy structure: "[W]e would prefer not to supply an organization chart, since it would change too quickly to serve any useful purpose." Of all the configurations, this one shows the least reverence for the classical principles of management, especially unity of command. Information and decision processes flow flexibly and informally, wherever they must, to promote innovation. And that means overriding the chain of authority if need be.

The entrepreneurial configuration also retains a flexible, organic structure, and so is likewise able to innovate. But that innovation is restricted to simple situations, ones easily comprehended by a single leader. Innovation of the sophisticated variety requires another kind of flexible structure, one that can draw together different forms of expertise. Thus the adhocracy must hire and give power to experts, people whose knowledge and skills have been highly developed in training programs. But unlike the professional organization, the adhocracy cannot rely on the standardized skills of its experts to achieve coordination, because that would discourage innovation. Rather, it must treat existing knowledge and skills as bases on which to combine and build new ones. Thus the adhocracy must break through the boundaries of conventional specialization and differentiation, which it does by assigning problems not to individual experts in preestablished pigeonholes but to multidisciplinary teams that merge their efforts. Each team forms around one specific project.

Despite organizing around market-based projects, the organization must still support and encourage particular types of specialized expertise. And so the adhocracy tends to use a matrix structure: Its experts are grouped in functional units for specialized housekeeping purposes—hiring, training, professional communication, and the like—but are then deployed in the project teams to carry out the basic work of innovation.

As for coordination in and between these project teams, as noted earlier standardization is precluded as a significant coordinating mechanism. The efforts must be innovative, not routine. So, too, is direct supervision precluded because of the complexity of the work: Coordination must be accomplished by those with the knowledge, namely the experts themselves, not those with just authority. That leaves just one of our coordinating mechanisms, mutual adjustment, which we consider foremost in adhocracy. And, to encourage this, the organization makes use of a whole set of liaison devices, liaison personnel and integrating managers of all kinds, in addition to the various teams and task forces.

The result is that managers abound in the adhocracy: functional managers, integrating managers, project managers. The last-named are particularly numerous, since the project teams must be small to encourage mutual adjustment among their members, and each, of course, needs a designated manager. The consequence is that "spans of control" found in adhocracy tend to be small. But the implication of this is misleading, because the term is suited to the machine, not the innovative configuration: The managers of adhocracy seldom "manage" in the usual sense of giving orders; instead, they spend a good deal of time acting in a liaison capacity, to coordinate the work laterally among the various teams and units.

With its reliance on highly trained experts, the adhocracy emerges as highly decentralized, in the "selective" sense. That means power over its decisions and actions is distributed to various places and at various levels according to the needs of the particular issue. In effect, power flows to wherever the relevent expertise happens to reside—among managers or specialists (or teams of those) in the line structure, the staff units, and the operating core.

To proceed with our discussion and to elaborate on how the innovative organization makes decisions and forms strategies, we need to distinguish two basic forms that it takes.

The Operating Adhocracy

The *operating adhocracy* innovates and solves problems directly on behalf of its clients. Its multidisciplinary teams of experts often work under contract, as in the think-tank consulting firm, creative advertising agency, or manufacturer of engineering prototypes.

In fact, for every operating adhocracy, there is a corresponding professional bureaucracy, one that does similar work but with a narrower orientation. Faced with a client problem, the operating adhocracy engages in creative efforts to find a novel solution; the professional bureaucracy pigeonholes it into a known contingency to which it can apply a standard program. One engages in divergent thinking aimed at innovation, the other in convergent thinking aimed at perfection. Thus, one theater company might seek out new avant-garde plays to perform, while another might perfect its performance of Shakespeare year after year.

A key feature of the operating adhocracy is that its administrative and operating work tend to blend into a single effort. That is, in ad hoc project work it is difficult to separate the planning and design of the work from its execution. Both require the same specialized skills, on a project-by-project basis. Thus it can be difficult to distinguish the middle levels of the organization from its operating core, since line managers and staff specialists may take their place alongside operating specialists on the project teams.

Figure 1 shows the organigram of the National Film Board of Canada, a classic operating adhocracy (even though it does produce a chart—one that changes frequently, it might be added). The Board is an agency of the Canadian federal government and produces mostly short films, many of them documentaries. At the time of this organigram, the characteristics of adhocracy were particularly in evidence: It shows a large number of support units as well as liaison positions (for example, research, technical, and production coordinators), with the operating core containing loose concurrent functional and market groupings, the latter by region as well as by type of film produced and, as can be seen, some not even connected to the line hierarchy!

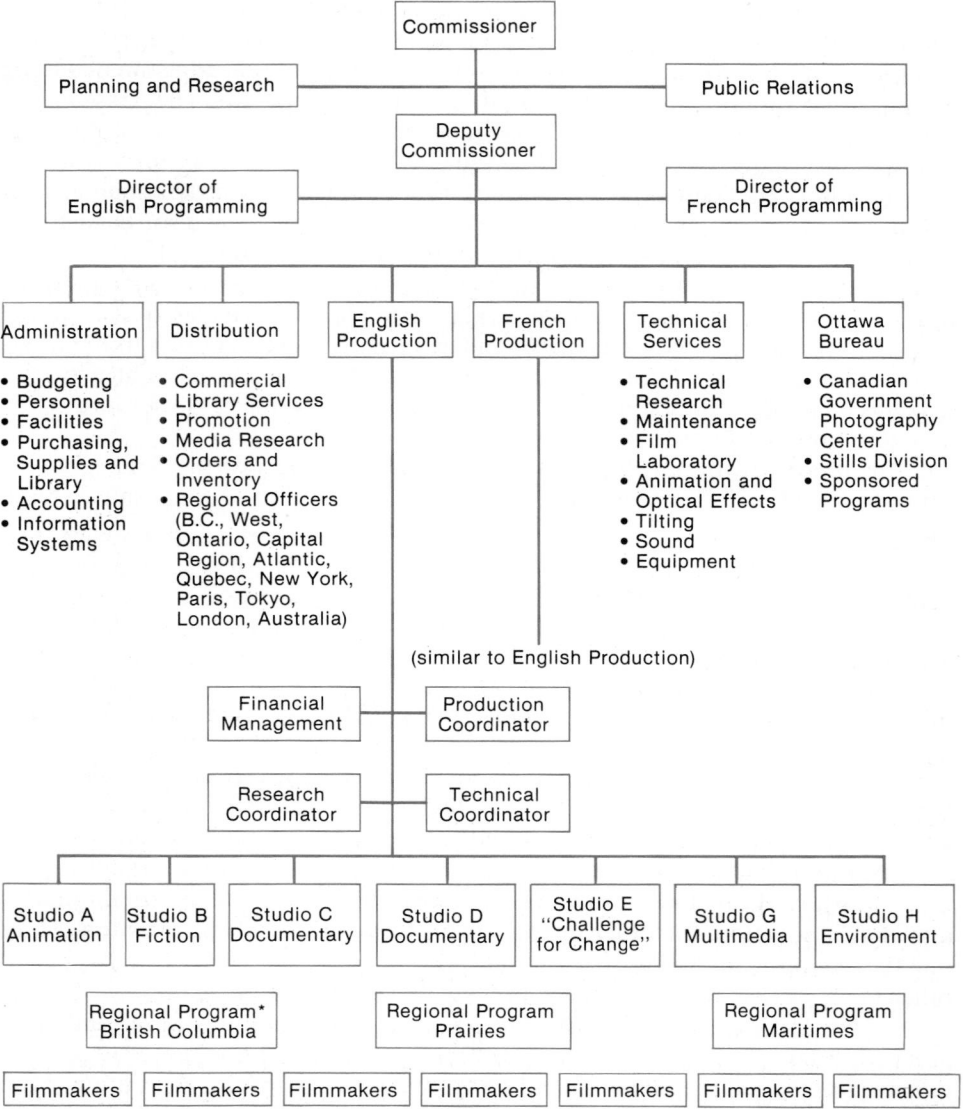

FIGURE 1

The National Film Board of Canada: An Operating Adhocracy (circa 1975; used with permission)
* *No lines shown on original organigram connecting Regional Programs to Studios or Filmmakers.*

The Administrative Adhocracy

The second type of adhocracy also functions with project teams, but toward a different end. Whereas the operating adhocracy undertakes projects to serve its clients, the *administrative adhocracy* undertakes projects to serve itself, to bring new facilities or activities on line, as in the administrative structure of a highly automated company. And in sharp contrast to the operating adhocracy, the administrative adhocracy makes a clear distinction between its administrative component and its operating core. That core is *truncated*—cut right off from the rest of the organization—so that the administrative component that remains can be structured as an adhocracy.

This truncation may take place in a number of ways. First, when the operations have to be machinelike and so could impede innovation in the administration (because of the associated need for control), it may be established as an independent organization. Second, the operating core may be done away with altogether—in effect, contracted out to other organizations. That leaves the organization free to concentrate on the development work, as did NASA during the Apollo project. A third form of truncation arises when the operating core becomes automated. This enables it to run itself, largely independent of the need for direct controls from the administrative component, leaving the latter free to structure itself as an adhocracy to bring new facilities on line or to modify old ones.

Oil companies, because of the high degree of automation of their production process, are in part at least drawn toward administrative adhocracy. Figure 2 shows the organigram for one oil company, reproduced exactly as presented by the company (except for modifications to mask its identity, done at the company's request). Note the domination of "Administration and Services," shown at the bottom of the chart; the operating functions, particularly "Production," are lost by comparison. Note also the description of the strategic apex in terms of standing committees instead of individual executives.

The Administrative Component of the Adhocracies

The important conclusion to be drawn from this discussion is that in both types of adhocracy the relation between the operating core and the administrative component is unlike that in any other configuration. In the administrative adhocracy, the operating core is truncated and becomes a relatively unimportant part of the organization; in the operating adhocracy, the two merge into a single entity. Either way, the need for traditional direct supervision is diminished, so managers derive their influence more from their expertise and interpersonal skills than from formal position. And that means the distinction between line and staff blurs. It no longer makes sense to distinguish those who have the formal power to decide from those who have only the informal right to advise. Power over decision making in the adhocracy flows to anyone with the required expertise, regardless of position.

In fact, the support staff plays a key role in adhocracy, because that is where many of the experts reside (especially in administrative adhocracy). As suggested, however, that staff is not sharply differentiated from the other parts of the organization, not off to one side, to speak only when spoken to, as in the bureaucratic configurations. The other type of staff, however, the technostructure, is less important here, because the adhocracy does not rely for coordination on standards that it develops. Technostructure analysts may, of course, be used for some action planning and other forms of analysis—marketing research and economic forecasting,

FIGURE 2
Organigram of an Oil
Company: An
Administrative Adhocracy

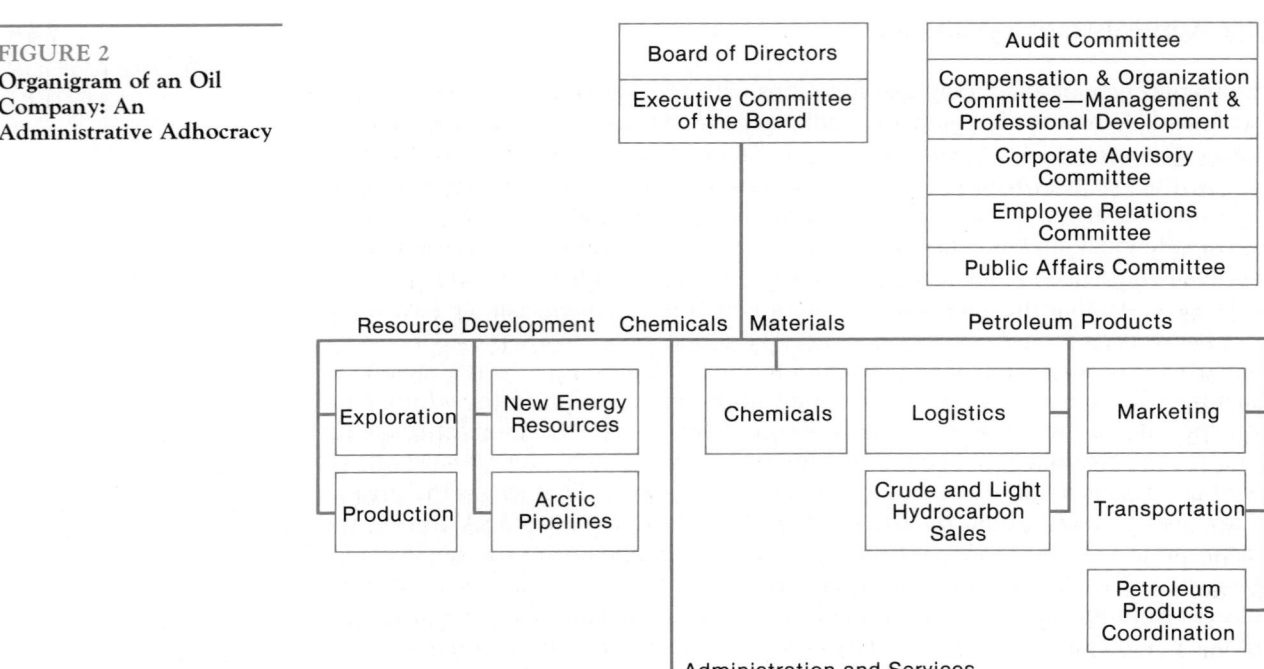

for example—but these analysts are as likely to take their place alongside the other specialists on the project teams as to stand back and design systems to control them.

To summarize, the administrative component of the adhocracy emerges as an organic mass of line managers and staff experts, combined with operators in the operating adhocracy, working together in ever-shifting relationships on ad hoc projects. Our logo figure at the start of this chapter shows adhocracy with its parts mingled together in one amorphous mass in the middle. In the operating adhocracy, that mass includes the middle line, support staff, technostructure, and operating core. Of these, the administrative adhocracy excludes just the operating core, which is truncated, as shown by the dotted section below the central mass. The reader will also note that the strategic apex of the figure is shown partly merged into the central mass as well, for reasons we shall present in our discussion of strategy formation.

The top managers of the strategic apex of this configuration do not spend much time formulating explicit strategies (as we shall see). But they must spend a good deal of their time in the battles that ensue over strategic choices and in handling the many other disturbances that arise all over these fluid structures. The innovative configuration combines fluid working arrangements with power based on expertise, not authority. Together those breed aggressiveness and conflict. But the job of the managers here, at all levels, is not to bottle up that aggression and conflict so much as to channel them to productive ends. Thus, the managers of adhocracy must be masters of human relations, able to use persuasion, negotiation, coalition, reputation, and rapport to fuse the individualistic experts into smoothly functioning teams.

Top managers must also devote a good deal of time to monitoring the projects. Innovative project work is notoriously difficult to control. No MIS can be relied upon to provide complete, unambiguous results. So there must be careful personal monitoring of projects to ensure that they are completed according to specifications, on schedule and within budget (or, more likely, not excessively late and not too far in excess of cost estimates).

Perhaps the most important single role of the top management of this configuration (especially the operating adhocracy form) is liaison with the external environment. The other configurations tend to focus their attention on clearly defined markets and so are more or less assured of a steady flow of work. Not so the operating adhocracy, which lives from project to project and disappears when it can find no more. Since each project is different, the organization can never be sure where the next one will come from. So the top managers must devote a great deal of their time to ensuring a steady and balanced stream of incoming projects. That means developing liaison contacts with potential customers and negotiating contracts with them. Nowhere is this more clearly illustrated than in the consulting business, particularly where the approach is innovative. When a consultant becomes a partner in one of these firms, he or she normally hangs up the calculator and becomes virtually a full-time salesperson. It is a distinguishing characteristic of many an operating adhocracy that the selling function literally takes place at the strategic apex.

Project work poses related problems in the administrative adhocracy. Reeser asked a group of managers in three aerospace companies, "What are some of the human problems of project management?" Among the common answers: "[M]embers of the organization who are displaced because of the phasing out of [their] work . . . may have to wait a long time before they get another assignment at as high a level of responsibility" and "the temporary nature of the organization often necessitates 'make work' assignments for [these] displaced members." (1969:463) Thus senior managers must again concern themselves with a steady flow of projects, although in this case, internally generated.

CONDITIONS OF THE INNOVATIVE ORGANIZATION

This configuration is found in environments that are both dynamic and complex. A dynamic environment, being unpredictable, calls for organic structure; a complex one calls for decentralized structure. This configuration is the only type that provides both. Thus we tend to find the innovative organization wherever these conditions prevail, ranging from guerrilla warfare to space agencies. There appears to be no other way to fight a war in the jungle or to put the first man on the moon.

As we have noted for all the configurations, organizations that prefer particular structures also try to "choose" environments appropriate to them. This is especially clear in the case of the operating adhocracy. Advertising agencies and consulting firms that prefer to structure themselves as professional bureaucracies seek out stable environments; those that prefer the innovative form find environments that are dynamic, where the client needs are difficult and unpredictable.[1]

A number of organizations are drawn toward this configuration because of the dynamic conditions that result from very frequent product change. The extreme case is the unit producer, the manufacturing firm that custom-makes each of its products to order, as in the engineering company that produces prototypes or the fabricator of extremely expensive machinery. Because each customer order constitutes a new project, the organization is encouraged to structure itself as an operating adhocracy.

Some manufacturers of consumer goods operate in markets so competitive that they must be constantly changing their product offerings, even though each product may itself be mass produced. A company that records rock music would be a prime example, as would some cosmetic and pharmaceutical companies. Here again, dynamic conditions, when coupled with some complexity, drive the organization toward the innovative configuration, with the mass production operations truncated to allow for adhocracy in product development.

Youth is another condition often associated with this type of organization. That is because it is difficult to sustain any structure in a state of adhocracy for a long period—to keep behaviors from formalizing and thereby discouraging innovation. All kinds of forces drive the innovative configuration to bureaucratize itself as it ages. On the other hand, young organizations prefer naturally organic structures, since they must find their own ways and tend to be eager to innovate. Unless they are entrepreneurial, they tend to become intrapreneurial.

The operating adhocracy is particularly prone to a short life, since it faces a risky market which can quickly destroy it. The loss of one major contract can literally close it down overnight. But if some operating adhocracies have short lives because they fail, others have short lives because they succeed. Success over time encourages metamorphosis, driving the organization toward a more stable environment and a more bureaucratic structure. As it ages, the successful organization develops a reputation for what it does best. That encourages it to repeat certain activities, which may suit the employees who, themselves aging, may welcome more stability in their work. So operating adhocracy is driven over time toward professional bureaucracy to perfect the activities it does best, perhaps even toward the machine bureaucracy to exploit a single invention. The organization survives, but the configuration dies.

Administrative adhocracies typically live longer. They, too, feel the pressures to bureaucratize as they age, which can lead them to stop innovating or else to innovate in stereotyped ways and thereby to adopt bureaucratic structure. But this

---

[1] I like to tell a story of the hospital patient with an appendix about to burst who presents himself to a hospital organized as an adhocracy: "Who wants to do another appendectomy? We're into livers now," as they go about exploring new procedures. But the patient returning from a trip to the jungle with a rare tropical disease had better beware of the hospital organized as a professional bureaucracy. A student came up to me after I once said this and explained how hospital doctors puzzled by her bloated stomach and not knowing what to do took out her appendix. Luckily, her problem resolved itself, some time later. Another time, a surgeon told me that his hospital no longer does appendectomies!

will not work if the organization functions in an industry that requires sophisticated innovation from all its participants. Since many of the industries where administrative adhocracies are found do, organizations that survive in them tend to retain this configuration for long periods.

In recognition of the tendency for organizations to bureaucratize as they age, a variant of the innovative configuration has emerged—"the organizational equivalent of paper dresses or throw-away tissues" (Toffler, 1970:133)—which might be called the "temporary adhocracy." It draws together specialists from various organizations to carry out a project, and then it disbands. Temporary adhocracies are becoming increasingly common in modern society: the production group that performs a single play, the election campaign committee that promotes a single candidate, the guerrilla group that overthrows a single government, the Olympic committee that plans a single games. Related is what can be called the "mammoth project adhocracy," a giant temporary adhocracy that draws on thousands of experts for a number of years to carry out a single major task, the Manhattan Project of World War II being one famous example.

Sophisticated and automated technical systems also tend to drive organizations toward the administrative adhocracy. When an organization's technical system is sophisticated, it requires an elaborate, highly trained support staff, working in teams, to design or purchase, modify, and maintain the equipment. In other words, complex machinery requires specialists who have the knowledge, power, and flexible working arrangements to cope with it, which generally requires the organization to structure itself as an adhocracy.

Automation of a technical system can evoke even stronger forces in the same direction. That is why a machine organization that succeeds in automating its operating core tends to undergo a dramatic metamorphosis. The problem of motivating bored workers disappears, and with it goes the control mentality that permeates the structure; the distinction between line and staff blurs (machines being indifferent to who turns their knobs), which leads to another important reduction in conflict; the technostructure loses its influence, since control is built into the machinery by its own designers rather than having to be imposed on workers by the standards of the analysts. Overall, then, the administrative structure becomes more decentralized and organic, emerging as an adhocracy. Of course, for automated organizations with simple technical systems (as in the production of hand creams), the entrepreneurial configuration may suffice instead of the innovative one.

Fashion is most decidedly another condition of the innovative configuration. Every one of its characteristics is very much in vogue today: emphasis on expertise, organic structure, project teams, task forces, decentralization of power, matrix structure, sophisticated technical systems, automation, and young organizations. Thus, if the entrepreneurial and machine forms were earlier configurations, and the professional and the diversified forms yesterday's, then the innovative is clearly today's. This is the configuration for a population growing ever better educated and more specialized, yet under constant encouragement to adopt the "systems" approach—to view the world as an integrated whole instead of a collection of loosely coupled parts. It is the configuration for environments that are becoming more complex and more insistent on innovation, and for technical systems that are growing more sophisticated and more highly automated. It is the only configuration among our types appropriate for those who believe organizations must become at the same time more democratic and less bureaucratic.

Yet despite our current infatuation with it, adhocracy is not the structure for all organizations. Like all the others, it too has its place. And that place, as our examples make clear, seems to be in the new industries of our age—aerospace, electronics, think-tank consulting, research, advertising, filmmaking, petrochemicals—virtually all of which experienced their greatest development since World War II. The innovative adhocracy appears to be the configuration for the industries of the last half of the twentieth century.

STRATEGY FORMATION IN THE INNOVATIVE ORGANIZATION

The structure of the innovative organization may seem unconventional, but its strategy making is even more so, upsetting virtually everything we have been taught to believe about that process.

Because the innovative organization must respond continuously to a complex, unpredictable environment, it cannot rely on deliberate strategy. In other words, it cannot predetermine precise patterns in its activities and then impose them on its work through some kind of formal planning process. Rather, many of its actions must be decided upon individually, according to the needs of the moment. It proceeds incrementally; to use Charles Lindblom's words, it prefers "continual nibbling" to a "good bite" (1968:25).

Here, then, the process is best thought of as strategy *formation,* because strategy is not formulated consciously in one place so much as formed implicitly by the specific actions taken in many places. That is why action planning cannot be extensively relied upon in these organizations: Any process that separates thinking from action—planning from execution, formalization from implementation—would impede the flexibility of the organization to respond creatively to its dynamic environment.

Strategy Formation in the Operating Adhocracy

In the operating adhocracy, a project organization never quite sure what it will do next, the strategy never really stabilizes totally but is responsive to new projects, which themselves involve the activities of a whole host of people. Take the example of the National Film Board. Among its most important strategies are those related to the content of the hundred or so mostly short, documentary-type films that it makes each year. Were the Board structured as a machine bureaucracy, the word on what films to make would come down from on high. Instead, when we studied it some years ago, proposals for new films were submitted to a standing committee, which included elected filmmakers, marketing people, and the heads of production and programming—in other words, operators, line managers, and staff specialists. The chief executive had to approve the committee's choices, and usually did, but the vast majority of the proposals were initiated by the filmmakers and the executive producers lower down. Strategies formed as themes developed among these individual proposals. The operating adhocracy's strategy thus evolves continuously as all kinds of such decisions are made, each leaving its imprint on the strategy by creating a precedent or reinforcing an existing one.

Strategy Formation in the Administrative Adhocracy

Similar things can be said about the administrative adhocracy, although the strategy-making process is slightly neater there. That is because the organization tends to concentrate its attention on fewer projects, which involve more people. NASA's Apollo project, for example, involved most of its personnel for almost ten years.

Administrative adhocracies also need to give more attention to action planning, but of a loose kind—to specify perhaps the ends to be reached while leaving flexibility to work out the means en route. Again, therefore, it is only through the making of specific decisions—namely, those that determine which projects are undertaken and how these projects unfold—that strategies can evolve.

Strategies Nonetheless

With their activities so disjointed, one might wonder whether adhocracies (of either type) can form strategies (that is, patterns) at all. In fact, they do, at least at certain times.

At the Film Board, despite the little direction from the management, the content of films did converge on certain clear themes periodically and then diverge, in remarkably regular cycles. In the early 1940s, there was a focus on films related to the war effort. After the war, having lost that raison d'être as well as its founding leader, the Board's films went off in all directions. They converged again in the mid-1950s around series of films for television, but by the late 1950s were again diverging widely. And in the mid-1960s and again in the early 1970s (with a brief period of divergence in between), the Board again showed a certain degree of convergence, this time on the themes of social commentary and experimentation.

This habit of cycling in and out of focus is quite unlike what takes place in the other configurations. In the machine organization especially, and somewhat in the entrepreneurial one, convergence proves much stronger and much longer (recall Volkswagenwerk's concentration on the Beetle for twenty years), while divergence tends to be very brief. The machine organization, in particular, cannot tolerate the ambiguity of change and so tries to leap from one strategic orientation to another. The innovative organization, in contrast, seems not only able to function at times without strategic focus, but positively to thrive on it. Perhaps that is the way it keeps itself innovative—by periodically cleansing itself of some of its existing strategic baggage.

The Varied Strategies of Adhocracy

Where do the strategies of adhocracy come from? While some may be imposed deliberately by the central management (as in staff cuts at the Film Board), most seem to emerge in a variety of other ways.

In some cases, a single ad hoc decision sets a precedent which evokes a pattern. That is how the National Film Board got into making series of films for television. While a debate raged over the issue, with management hesitant, one filmmaker slipped out and made one such series, and when many of his colleagues quickly followed suit, the organization suddenly found itself deeply, if unintentionally, committed to a major new strategy. It was, in effect, a strategy of spontaneous but implicit consensus on the part of its operating employees. In another case, even the initial precedent-setting decision wasn't deliberate. One film inadvertently ran longer than expected, it had to be distributed as a feature, the first for the organization, and as some other filmmakers took advantage of the precedent, a feature film strategy emerged.

Sometimes a strategy will be pursued in a pocket of an organization (perhaps in a clandestine manner, in a so-called "skunkworks"), which then later becomes more broadly organizational when the organization, in need of change and casting about for new strategies, seizes upon it. Some salesman has been pursuing a new market, or some engineer has developed a new product, and is ignored until the organization has need for some fresh strategic thinking. Then it finds it, not in the vision of its leaders or the procedures of its planners, not elsewhere in its industry, but hidden in the bowels of its own operations, developed through the learning of its workers.

What then becomes the role of the leadership of the innovative configuration in making strategy? If it cannot impose deliberate strategies, what does it do? The answer is that it manages patterns, seeking partial control over strategies but otherwise attempting to influence what happens to those strategies that do emerge lower down.

These are the organizations in which trying to manage strategy is a little like trying to drive an automobile without having your hands on the steering wheel. You can accelerate and brake but cannot determine direction. But there do remain important forms of control. First the leaders can manage the *process* of strategy-making if not the content of strategy. In other words, they can set up the structures to encourage certain kinds of activities and hire the people who themselves will carry out these activities. Second, they can provide general guidelines for strategy —what we have called *umbrella* strategies—seeking to define certain boundaries outside of which the specific patterns developed below should not stray. Then they can watch the patterns that do emerge and use the umbrella to decide which to encourage and which to discourage, remembering, however, that the umbrella can be shifted too.

A Grass-roots Model of Strategy Formation

We can summarize this discussion in terms of a "grass-roots" model of strategy formation, comprising six points.

1. *Strategies grow initially like weeds in a garden, they are not cultivated like tomatoes in a hothouse.* In other words, the process of strategy formation can be overmanaged; sometimes it is more important to let patterns emerge than to force an artificial consistency upon an organization prematurely. The hothouse, if needed, can come later.

2. *These strategies can take root in all kinds of places, virtually anywhere people have the capacity to learn and the resources to support that capacity.* Sometimes an individual or unit in touch with a particular opportunity creates his, her, or its own pattern. This may happen inadvertently, when an initial action sets a precedent. Even senior managers can fall into strategies by experimenting with ideas until they converge on something that works (though the final result may appear to the observer to have been deliberately designed). At other times, a variety of actions converge on a strategic theme through the mutual adjustment of various people, whether gradually or spontaneously. And then the external environment can impose a pattern on an unsuspecting organization. The point is that organizations cannot always plan where their strategies will emerge, let alone plan the strategies themselves.

3. *Such strategies become organizational when they become collective, that is, when the patterns proliferate to pervade the behavior of the organization at large.* Weeds can proliferate and encompass a whole garden; then the conventional plants may look out of place. Likewise, emergent strategies can sometimes displace the existing deliberate ones. But, of course, what is a weed but a plant that wasn't expected? With a change of perspective, the emergent strategy, like the weed, can become what is valued (just as Europeans enjoy salads of the leaves of America's most notorious weed, the dandelion!).

4. *The processes of proliferation may be conscious but need not be; likewise they may be managed but need not be.* The processes by which the initial patterns work their way through the organization need not be consciously intended, by formal leaders or even informal ones. Patterns may simply spread by collective action, much as plants proliferate themselves. Of course, once strategies are recognized as valuable, the processes by which they proliferate can be managed, just as plants can be selectively propagated.

5. *New strategies, which may be emerging continuously, tend to pervade the organization during periods of change, which punctuate periods of more integrated continuity.* Put more simply, organizations, like gardens, may accept the biblical maxim of a time to sow and a time to reap (even though they can sometimes reap what they did not mean to sow). Periods of convergence, during which the organization exploits its prevalent, established strategies, tend to be interrupted periodically by periods of divergence, during which the organization experiments with and subsequently accepts new strategic themes. The blurring of the separation between these two types of periods may have the same effect on an organization that the blurring of the separation between sowing and reaping has on a garden—the destruction of the system's productive capacity.

6. *To manage this process is not to preconceive strategies but to recognize their emergence and intervene when appropriate.* A destructive weed, once noticed, is best uprooted immediately. But one that seems capable of bearing fruit is worth watching, indeed sometimes even worth building a hothouse around. To manage in this context is to create the climate within which a wide variety of strategies can grow (to establish flexible structures, develop appropriate processes, encourage supporting ideologies, and define guiding "umbrella" strategies) and then to watch what does in fact come up. The strategic initiatives that do come "up" may in fact originate anywhere, although often low down in the organization, where the detailed knowledge of products and markets resides. (In fact, to be successful in some organizations, these initiatives must be recognized by middle-level managers and "championed" by combining them with each other or with existing strategies before promoting them to the senior management.) In effect, the management encourages those initiatives that appear to have potential, otherwise it discourages them. But it must not be too quick to cut off the unexpected: Sometimes it is better to pretend not to notice an emerging pattern to allow it more time to unfold. Likewise, there are times when it makes sense to shift or enlarge an umbrella to encompass a new pattern—in other words, to let the organization adapt to the initiative rather than vice versa. Moreover, a management must know when to resist change for the sake of internal efficiency and when to promote it for the sake of external adaptation. In other words, it must sense when to exploit an established crop of strategies and when to encourage new strains to displace them. It is the excesses of either—failure to focus (running blind) or failure to change (bureaucratic momentum)—that most harms organizations.

I call this a "grass-roots" model because the strategies grow up from the base of the organization, rooted in the solid earth of its operations rather than the ethereal abstractions of its administration. (Even the strategic initiatives of the senior management itself are in this model rooted in its tangible involvement with the operations.)

Of course, the model is overstated. But no more so than the more widely accepted deliberate one, which we might call the "hothouse" model of strategy formulation. Management theory must encompass both, perhaps more broadly labeled the *learning* model and the *planning* model, as well as a third, the *visionary* model.

I have discussed the learning model under the innovative configuration, the planning model under the machine configuration, and the visionary model under the entrepreneurial configuration. But in truth, all organizations need to mix these approaches in various ways at different times in their development. For example, our discussion of strategic change in the machine organization concluded, in effect, that they had to revert to the learning model for revitalization and the visionary model for turnaround. Of course, the visionary leader must learn, as must the learning organization evolve a kind of strategic vision, and both sometimes need planning to program the strategies they develop. And overall, no organization can function with strategies that are always and purely emergent; that would amount to a complete abdication of will and leadership, not to mention conscious thought. But none can function either with strategies that are always and purely deliberate; that would amount to an unwillingness to learn, a blindness to whatever is unexpected.

Environment Taking Precedence in the Innovative Organization

To conclude our discussion of strategy formation, as shown in Figure 3, in the innovative configuration it is the environment that takes precedence. It drives the organization, which responds continuously and eclectically, but does nevertheless achieve convergence during certain periods.[2] The formal leadership seeks somehow to influence both sides in this relationship, negotiating with the environment for support and attempting to impose some broad general (umbrella) guidelines on the organization.

If the strategist of the entrepreneurial organization is largely a concept attainer and that of the machine organization largely a planner, then the strategist of the innovative organization is largely a *pattern recognizer,* seeking to detect emerging patterns within and outside the strategic umbrella. Then strategies deemed unsuitable can be discouraged while those that seem appropriate can be encouraged, even if that means moving the umbrella. Here, then, we may find the curious situation of leadership changing its intentions to fit the realized behavior of its organization. But that is curious only in the perspective of traditional management theory.

FIGURE 3
Environment Taking the Lead in Adhocracy

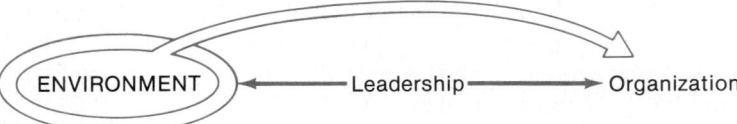

SOME ISSUES ASSOCIATED WITH THE INNOVATIVE ORGANIZATION

Three issues associated with the innovative configuration merit attention here: its ambiguities and the reactions of people who must live with them, its inefficiencies, and its propensity to make inappropriate transitions to other configurations.

---

[2] We might take this convergence as the expression of an "organization's mind"—the focusing on a strategic theme as a result of the mutual adjustments among its many actors.

Human Reactions to Ambiguity

Many people, especially creative ones, dislike both structural rigidity and the concentration of power. That leaves them only one configuration, the innovative, which is both organic and decentralized. Thus they find it a great place to work. In essence, adhocracy is the only structure for people who believe in more democracy with less bureaucracy.

But not everyone shares those values (not even everyone who professes to). Many people need order, and so prefer the machine or professional type of organization. They see adhocracy as a nice place to visit but no place to spend a career. Even dedicated members of adhocracies periodically get frustrated with this structure's fluidity, confusion, and ambiguity. "In these situations, all managers some of the time and many managers all the time, yearn for more definition and structure" (Burns and Stalker, 1966:122–123). The managers of innovative organizations report anxiety related to the eventual phaseout of projects; confusion as to who their boss is, whom to impress to get promoted; a lack of clarity in job definitions, authority relationships, and lines of communication; and intense competition for resources, recognition, and rewards (Reeser, 1969). This last point suggests another serious problem of ambiguity here, the politicization of these configurations. Combining its ambiguities with its interdependencies, the innovative form can emerge as a rather politicized and ruthless organization—supportive of the fit, as long as they remain fit, but destructive of the weak.

Problems of Efficiency

No configuration is better suited to solving complex, ill-structured problems than this one. None can match it for sophisticated innovation. Or, unfortunately, for the costs of that innovation. This is simply not an efficient way to function. Although it is ideally suited for the one-of-a-kind project, the innovative configuration is not competent at doing *ordinary* things. It is designed for the *extra*ordinary. The bureaucracies are all mass producers; they gain efficiency through standardization. The adhocracy is a custom producer, unable to standardize and so be efficient. It gains its effectiveness (innovation) at the price of efficiency.

One source of inefficiency lies in the unbalanced workload, mentioned earlier. It is almost impossible to keep the personnel of a project structure—high-priced specialists, it should be noted—busy on a steady basis. In January they may be working overtime with no hope of completing the new project on time; by May they may be playing cards for want of work.

But the real root of inefficiency is the high cost of communication. People talk a lot in these organizations; that is how they combine their knowledge to develop new ideas. But that takes time, a great deal of time. Faced with the need to make a decision in the machine organization, someone up above gives an order and that is that. Not so in the innovative one, where everyone must get into the act —managers of all kinds (functional, project, liaison), as well as all the specialists who believe their point of view should be represented. A meeting is called, probably to schedule another meeting, eventually to decide who should participate in the decision. The problem then gets defined and redefined, ideas for its solution get generated and debated, alliances build and fall around different solutions, until eventually everyone settles down to the hard bargaining over which one to adopt. Finally a decision emerges—that in itself is an accomplishment—although it is typically late and will probably be modified later.

The Dangers of Inappropriate Transition

Of course, one solution to the problems of ambiguity and inefficiency is to change the configuration. Employees no longer able to tolerate the ambiguity and customers fed up with the inefficiency may try to drive the organization to a more stable, bureaucratic form.

That is relatively easily done in the operating adhocracy, as noted earlier. The organization simply selects the set of standard programs it does best, reverting to the professional configuration, or else innovates one last time to find a lucrative market niche in which to mass produce, and then becomes a machine configuration. But those transitions, however easily effected, are not always appropriate. The organization came into being to solve problems imaginatively, not to apply standards indiscriminately. In many spheres, society has more mass producers than it needs; what it lacks are true problem solvers—the consulting firm that can handle a unique problem instead of applying a pat solution, the advertising agency that can come up with a novel campaign instead of the common imitation, the research laboratory that can make the really serious breakthrough instead of just modifying an existing design. The television networks seem to be classic examples of bureaucracies that provide largely standardized fare when the creativity of adhocracy is called for (except, perhaps, for the newsrooms and the specials, where an ad hoc orientation encourages more creativity).

The administrative adhocracy can run into more serious difficulties when it succumbs to the pressures to bureaucratize. It exists to innovate for itself, in its own industry. Unlike the operating adhocracy, it often cannot change orientation while remaining in the same industry. And so its conversion to the machine configuration (the natural transition for administrative adhocracy tired of perpetual change), by destroying the organization's ability to innovate, can eventually destroy the organization itself.

To reiterate a central theme of our discussion throughout this section: In general, there is no one best structure; in particular, there may be at a cost of something forgone, so long as the different attributes combine to form a coherent configuration that is consistent with the situation.

MANAGING INNOVATION: CONTROLLED CHAOS*

BY JAMES BRIAN QUINN

Management observers frequently claim that small organizations are more innovative than large ones. But is this commonplace necessarily true? Some large enterprises are highly innovative. How do they do it? . . . This article [reports on a] $2\frac{1}{2}$ year worldwide study . . . [of] both well-documented small ventures and large U.S., Japanese, and European companies and programs selected for their innovation records. . . . More striking than the cultural differences among these companies are the similarities between innovative small and large organizations and among innovative organizations in different countries. Effective management of innovation seems much the same, regardless of national boundaries or scale of operations.

There are . . . many reasons why small companies appear to produce a disproportionate number of innovations. First, innovation occurs in a probabilistic setting. A company never knows whether a particular technical result can be achieved and whether it will succeed in the marketplace. For every new solution that succeeds, tens to hundreds fail. The sheer number of attempts—most by small-scale entrepreneurs—means that some ventures will survive. The 90% to 99% that fail are distributed widely throughout society and receive little notice.

On the other hand, a big company that wishes to move a concept from invention to the marketplace must absorb all potential failure costs itself. This risk may be socially or managerially intolerable, jeopardizing the many other products, projects, jobs, and communities the company supports. Even if its innovation is successful, a big company may face costs that newcomers do not bear, like converting existing operations and customer bases to the new solution.

By contrast, a new enterprise does not risk losing an existing investment base or cannibalizing customer franchises built at great expense. It does not have to change an internal culture that has successfully supported doing things another way or that has developed intellectual depth and belief in the technologies that led to past successes. Organized groups like labor unions, consumer advocates, and government bureaucracies rarely monitor and resist a small company's moves as they might a big company's. Finally, new companies do not face the psychological pain and the economic costs of laying off employees, shutting down plants and even communities, and displacing supplier relationships built with years of mutual commitment and effort. Such barriers to change in large organizations are real, important, and legitimate.

The complex products and systems that society expects large companies to undertake further compound the risks. Only big companies can develop new ships or locomotives; telecommunication networks; or systems for space, defense, air traffic control, hospital care, mass foods delivery, or nationwide computer interactions. These large-scale projects always carry more risk than single-product introductions. A billion-dollar development aircraft, for example, can fail if one inexpensive part in its 100,000 components fails.

Clearly, a single enterprise cannot by itself develop or produce all the parts needed by such large new systems. And communications among the various groups making design and production decisions on components are always incomplete. The probability of error increases exponentially with complexity, while the system innovator's control over decisions decreases significantly—further escalating potential error costs and risks. Such forces inhibit innovation in large organizations. But proper management can lessen these effects.

OF INVENTORS AND ENTREPRENEURS

A close look at innovative small enterprises reveals much about the successful management of innovation. Of course, not all innovations follow a single pattern. But my research—and other studies in combination—suggest that the following factors are crucial to the success of innovative small companies:

Need Orientation

Inventor-entrepreneurs tend to be "need or achievement oriented." They believe that if they "do the job better," rewards will follow. They may at first focus on their own view of market needs. But lacking resources, successful small entrepreneurs soon find that it pays to approach potential customers early, test their solutions in users' hands, learn from these interactions, and adapt designs rapidly. Many studies suggest that effective technological innovation develops hand-in-hand with customer demand (Von Hippel, 1982:117).

Experts and Fanatics

Company founders tend to be pioneers in their technologies and fanatics when it comes to solving problems. They are often described as "possessed" or "obsessed," working toward their objectives to the exclusion even of family or personal relationships. As both experts and fanatics, they perceive probabilities of success as higher than others do. And their commitment allows them to persevere despite the frustrations, ambiguities, and setbacks that always accompany major innovations.

Long Time Horizons

Their fanaticism may cause inventor-entrepreneurs to underestimate the obstacles and length of time to success. Time horizons for radical innovations make them essentially "irrational" from a present value viewpoint. In my sample, delays between invention and commercial production ranged from 3 to 25 years.[1] In the late 1930s, for example, industrial chemist Russell Marker was working on steroids called sapogenins when he discovered a technique that would degrade one of these, diosgenin, into the female sex hormone progesterone. By processing some ten tons of Mexican yams in rented and borrowed lab space, Marker finally extracted about four pounds of diosgenin and started a tiny business to produce steroids for the laboratory market. But it was not until 1962, over 23 years later, that Syntex, the company Marker founded, obtained FDA approval for its oral contraceptive.

For both psychological and practical reasons, inventor-entrepreneurs generally avoid early formal plans, proceed step-by-step, and sustain themselves by other income and the momentum of the small advances they achieve as they go along.

Low Early Costs

Innovators tend to work in homes, basements, warehouses, or low-rent facilities whenever possible. They incur few overhead costs; their limited resources go directly into their projects. They pour nights, weekends, and "sweat capital" into their endeavors. They borrow whatever they can. They invent cheap equipment and prototype processes, often improving on what is available in the marketplace. If one approach fails, few people know; little time or money is lost. All this decreases the costs and risks facing a small operation and improves the present value of its potential success.

Multiple Approaches

Technology tends to advance through a series of random—often highly intuitive—insights frequently triggered by gratuitous interactions between the discoverer and the outside world. Only highly committed entrepreneurs can tolerate (and even enjoy) this chaos. They adopt solutions wherever they can be found, unencum-

---

[1] A study at Battelle found an average of 19.2 years between invention and commercial production. Battelle Memorial Laboratories, "Science, Technology, and Innovation," Report to the National Science Foundation, 1973; also Dean (1974:13).

bered by formal plans or PERT charts that would limit the range of their imaginations. When the odds of success are low, the participation and interaction of many motivated players increase the chance that one will succeed.

A recent study of initial public offerings made in 1962 shows that only 2% survived and still looked like worthwhile investments 20 years later.[2] Small-scale entrepreneurship looks efficient in part because history only records the survivors.

Flexibility and Quickness

Undeterred by committees, board approvals, and other bureaucratic delays, the inventor-entrepreneur can experiment, test, recycle, and try again with little time lost. Because technological progress depends largely on the number of successful experiments accomplished per unit of time, fast-moving small entrepreneurs can gain both timing and performance advantages over clumsier competitors. This responsiveness is often crucial in finding early markets for radical innovations where neither innovators, market researchers, nor users can quite visualize a product's real potential. For example, Edison's lights first appeared on ships and in baseball parks; Astroturf was intended to convert the flat roofs and asphalt playgrounds of city schools into more humane environments; and graphite and boron composites designed for aerospace unexpectedly found their largest markets in sporting goods. Entrepreneurs quickly adjusted their entry strategies to market feedback.

Incentives

Inventor-entrepreneurs can foresee tangible personal rewards if they are successful. Individuals often want to achieve a technical contribution, recognition, power, or sheer independence, as much as money. For the original, driven personalities who create significant innovations, few other paths offer such clear opportunities to fulfill all their economic, psychological, and career goals at once. Consequently, they do not panic or quit when others with solely monetary goals might.

Availability of Capital

One of America's great competitive advantages is its rich variety of sources to finance small, low-probability ventures. If entrepreneurs are turned down by one source, other sources can be sought in myriads of creative combinations.

Professionals involved in such financings have developed a characteristic approach to deal with the chaos and uncertainty of innovation. First, they evaluate a proposal's conceptual validity: If the technical problems can be solved, is there a real business there for someone and does it have a large upside potential? Next, they concentrate on people: Is the team thoroughly committed and expert? Is it the best available? Only then do these financiers analyze specific financial estimates in depth. Even then, they recognize that actual outcomes generally depend on subjective factors, not numbers (Pence, 1982).

Timeliness, aggressiveness, commitment, quality of people, and the flexibility to attack opportunities not at first perceived are crucial. Downside risks are minimized, not by detailed controls, but by spreading risks among multiple projects, keeping early costs low, and gauging the tenacity, flexibility, and capability of the founders.

---

[2] Business Economics Group, W. R. Grace & Co., 1983.

Less innovative companies and, unfortunately, most large corporations operate in a very different fashion. The most notable and common constraints on innovation in larger companies include the following:

Top Management Isolation

Many senior executives in big companies have little contact with conditions on the factory floor or with customers who might influence their thinking about technological innovation. Since risk perception is inversely related to familiarity and experience, financially oriented top managers are likely to perceive technological innovations as more problematic than acquisitions that may be just as risky but that will appear more familiar (Hayes and Garvin, 1982:70; Hayes and Abernathy, 1980:67).

Intolerance of Fanatics

Big companies often view entrepreneurial fanatics as embarrassments or troublemakers. Many major cities are now ringed by companies founded by these "non-team" players—often to the regret of their former employers.

Short Time Horizons

The perceived corporate need to report a continuous stream of quarterly profits conflicts with the long time spans that major innovations normally require. Such pressures often make publicly owned companies favor quick marketing fixes, cost cutting, and acquisition strategies over process, product, or quality innovations that would yield much more in the long run.

Accounting Practices

By assessing all its direct, indirect, overhead, overtime, and service costs against a project, large corporations have much higher development expenses compared with entrepreneurs working in garages. A project in a big company can quickly become an exposed political target, its potential net present value may sink unacceptably, and an entry into small markets may not justify its sunk costs. An otherwise viable project may soon founder and disappear.

Excessive Rationalism

Managers in big companies often seek orderly advance through early market research studies or PERT planning. Rather than managing the inevitable chaos of innovation productively, these managers soon drive out the very things that lead to innovation in order to prove their announced plans.

Excessive Bureaucracy

In the name of efficiency, bureaucratic structures require many approvals and cause delays at every turn. Experiments that a small company can perform in hours may take days or weeks in large organizations. The interactive feedback that fosters innovation is lost, important time windows can be missed, and real costs and risks rise for the corporation.

Inappropriate Incentives

Reward and control systems in most big companies are designed to minimize surprises. Yet innovation, by definition, is full of surprises. It often disrupts well-laid plans, accepted power patterns, and entrenched organizational behavior at high costs to many. Few large companies make millionaires of those who create such disruptions, however profitable the innovations may turn out to be. When control systems neither penalize opportunities missed nor reward risks taken, the results are predictable.

HOW LARGE INNOVATIVE COMPANIES DO IT

Yet some big companies are continuously innovative. Although each such enterprise is distinctive, the successful big innovators I studied have developed techniques that emulate or improve on their smaller counterparts' practices. What are the most important patterns?

Atmosphere and Vision

Continuous innovation occurs largely because top executives appreciate innovation and manage their company's value system and atmosphere to support it. For example, Sony's founder, Masaru Ibuka, stated in the company's "Purposes of Incorporation" the goal of a "free, dynamic, and pleasant factory . . . where sincerely motivated personnel can exercise their technological skills to the highest level." Ibuka and Sony's chairman, Akio Morita, inculcated the "Sony spirit" through a series of unusual policies: hiring brilliant people with nontraditional skills (like an opera singer) for high management positions, promoting young people over their elders, designing a new type of living accommodation for workers, and providing visible awards for outstanding technical achievements.

Because familiarity can foster understanding and psychological comfort, engineering and scientific leaders are often those who create atmospheres supportive of innovation, especially in a company's early life. Executive vision is more important than a particular management background—as IBM, Genentech, AT&T, Merck, Elf Aquitaine, Pilkington, and others in my sample illustrate. CEOs of these companies value technology and include technical experts in their highest decisions circles.

Innovative managements—whether technical or not—project clear long-term visions for their organizations that go beyond simple economic measures. . . . Genentech's original plan expresses [such a] vision: "We expect to be the first company to commercialize the [rDNA] technology, and we plan to build a major profitable corporation by manufacturing and marketing needed products that benefit mankind. The future uses of genetic engineering are far reaching and many. Any product produced by a living organism is eventually within the company's reach."

Such visions, vigorously supported, are not "management fluff," but have many practical implications.[3] They attract quality people to the company and give focus to their creative and entrepreneurial drives. When combined with sound internal operations, they help channel growth by concentrating attention on the ac-

---

[3] Thomas J. Allen (1977) illustrates the enormous leverage provided such technology accessors (called "gatekeepers") in R&D organizations.

tions that lead to profitability, rather than on profitability itself. Finally, these visions recognize a realistic time frame for innovation and attract the kind of investors who will support it.

Orientation to the Market

Innovative companies tie their visions to the practical realities of the marketplace. Although each company uses techniques adapted to its own style and strategy, two elements are always present: a strong market orientation at the very top of the company and mechanisms to ensure interactions between technical and marketing people at lower levels. At Sony, for example, soon after technical people are hired, the company runs them through weeks of retail selling. Sony engineers become sensitive to the ways retail sales practices, product displays, and nonquantifiable customer preferences affect success. . . .

From top to bench levels in my sample's most innovative companies, managers focus primarily on seeking to anticipate and solve customers' emerging problems.

Small, Flat Organizations

The most innovative large companies in my sample try to keep the total organization flat and project teams small. Development teams normally include only 6 or 7 key people. This number seems to constitute a critical mass of skills while fostering maximum communication and commitment among members. According to research done by my colleague, Victor McGee, the number of channels of communication increases as $n[2^{n-1}-1)$. Therefore:

For team size	=	1	2	3	4	5	6
Channels	=	1	2	9	28	75	186
		7	8	9	10	11	
		441	1016	2295	5110	11253	

Innovative companies also try to keep their operating divisions and total technical units small—below 400 people. Up to this number, only two layers of management are required to maintain a span of control over 7 people. In units much larger than 400, people quickly lose touch with the concept of their product or process, staffs and bureaucracies tend to grow, and projects may go through too many formal screens to survive. Since it takes a chain of yesses and only one no to kill a project, jeopardy multiplies as management layers increase.

Multiple Approaches

At first one cannot be sure which of several technical approaches will dominate a field. The history of technology is replete with accidents, mishaps, and chance meetings that allowed one approach or group to emerge rapidly over others. Leo Baekelund was looking for a synthetic shellac when he found Bakelite and started the modern plastics industry. At Syntex, researchers were not looking for an oral contraceptive when they created 19-norprogesterone, the precursor to the active ingredient in half of all contraceptive pills. And the microcomputer was born because Intel's Ted Hoff "happened" to work on a complex calculator just when Digital Equipment Corporation's PDP8 architecture was fresh in his mind.

Such "accidents" are involved in almost all major technological advances. When theory can predict everything, a company has moved to a new stage, from development to production. Murphy's law works because engineers design for what they can foresee; hence what fails is what theory could not predict. And it is rare that the interactions of components and subsystems can be predicted over the lifetime of operations. For example, despite careful theoretical design work, the first high performance jet engine literally tore itself to pieces on its test stand, while others failed in unanticipated operating conditions (like an Iranian sandstorm).

Recognizing the inadequacies of theory, innovative enterprises seem to move faster from paper studios to physical testing than do noninnovative enterprises. When possible, they encourage several prototype programs to proceed in parallel. . . . Such redundancy helps the company cope with uncertainties in development, motivates people through competition, and improves the amount and quality of information available for making final choices on scale-ups or introductions.

Developmental Shoot-outs

Many companies structure shoot-outs among competing approaches only after they reach the prototype stages. They find this practice provides more objective information for making decisions, decreases risk by making choices that best reflect marketplace needs, and helps ensure that the winning option will move ahead with a committed team behind it. Although many managers worry that competing approaches may be inefficient, greater effectiveness in choosing the right solution easily outweighs duplication costs when the market rewards higher performance or when large volumes justify increased sophistication. Under these conditions, parallel development may prove less costly because it both improves the probability of success and reduces development time.

Perhaps the most difficult problem in managing competing projects lies in reintegrating the members of the losing team. If the company is expanding rapidly or if the successful project creates a growth opportunity, losing team members can work on another interesting program or sign on with the winning team as the project moves toward the marketplace. For the shoot-out system to work continuously, however, executives must create a climate that honors high-quality performance whether a project wins or loses, reinvolves people quickly in their technical specialties or in other projects, and accepts and expects rotation among tasks and groups. . . .

Skunkworks

Every highly innovative enterprise in my research sample emulated small company practices by using groups that functioned in a skunkworks style. Small teams of engineers, technicians, designers, and model makers were placed together with no intervening organizational or physical barriers to developing a new product from idea to commercial prototype stages. In innovative Japanese companies, top managers often worked hand in hand on projects with young engineers. Surprisingly, *ringi* decision making was not evident in these situations. Soichiro Honda was known for working directly on technical problems and emphasizing his technical points by shouting at his engineers or occasionally even hitting them with wrenches!

The skunkworks approach eliminates bureaucracies, allows fast, unfettered communications, permits rapid turnaround times for experiments, and instills a high level of group identity and loyalty. Interestingly, few successful groups in my research were structured in the classic "venture group" form, with a careful balancing of engineering, production, and marketing talents. Instead they acted on an old truism: introducing a new product or process to the world is like raising a healthy child—it needs a mother (champion) who loves it, a father (authority figure with resources) to support it, and pediatricians (specialists) to get it through difficult times. It may survive solely in the hands of specialists, but its chances of success are remote.

Interactive Learning

Skunkworks are as close as most big companies can come to emulating the highly interactive and motivating learning environment that characterizes successful small ventures. But the best big innovators have gone even farther. Recognizing that the random, chaotic nature of technological change cuts across organizational and even institutional lines, these companies tap into multiple outside sources of technology as well as their customers' capabilities. Enormous external leverages are possible. No company can spend more than a small share of the world's $200 billion devoted to R&D. But like small entrepreneurs, big companies can have much of that total effort cheaply if they try.

In industries such as electronics, customers provide much of the innovation on new products. In other industries, such as textiles, materials or equipment suppliers provide the innovation. In still others, such as biotechnology, universities are dominant, while foreign sources strongly supplement industries such as controlled fusion. Many R&D units have strategies to develop information for trading with outside groups and have teams to cultivate these sources. Large Japanese companies have been notably effective at this. So have U.S. companies as diverse as Du Pont, AT&T, Apple Computer, and Genentech.

An increasing variety of creative relationships exist in which big companies participate—as joint venturers, consortium members, limited partners, guarantors of first markets, major academic funding sources, venture capitalists, spin-off equity holders, and so on. These rival the variety of inventive financing and networking structures that individual entrepreneurs have created.

Indeed, the innovative practices of small and large companies look ever more alike. This resemblance is especially striking in the interactions between companies and customers during development. Many experienced big companies are relying less on early market research and more on interactive development with lead customers. Hewlett-Packard, 3M, Sony, and Raychem frequently introduce radically new products through small teams that work closely with lead customers. These teams learn from their customers' needs and innovations, and rapidly modify designs and entry strategies based on this information.

Formal market analyses continue to be useful for extending product lines, but they are often misleading when applied to radical innovations. Market studies predicted that Haloid would never sell more than 5,000 xerographic machines, that Intel's microprocessor would never sell more than 10% as many units as there were minicomputers, and that Sony's transistor radios and miniature television sets would fail in the marketplace. At the same time, many eventual failures such as Ford's Edsel, IBM's FS system, and the supersonic transport were studied and planned exhaustively on paper, but lost contact with customers' real needs.

A STRATEGY FOR INNOVATION

The flexible management practices needed for major innovations often pose problems for established cultures in big companies. Yet there are reasonable steps managers in these companies can take. Innovation can be bred in a surprising variety of organizations, as many examples show. What are its key elements?

An Opportunity Orientation

In the 1981–1983 recession, many large companies cut back or closed plants as their "only available solution." Yet I repeatedly found that top managers in these companies took these actions without determining firsthand why their customers were buying from competitors, discerning what niches in their markets were growing, or tapping the innovations their own people had to solve problems. These managers foreclosed innumerable options by defining the issue as cost cutting rather than opportunity seeking. As one frustrated division manager in a manufacturing conglomerate put it: "If management doesn't actively seek or welcome technical opportunities, it sure won't hear about them."

By contrast, Intel met the challenge of the last recession with its "20% solution." The professional staff agreed to work one extra day a week to bring innovations to the marketplace earlier than planned. Despite the difficult times, Intel came out of the recession with several important new products ready to go—and it avoided layoffs.

Entrepreneurial companies recognize that they have almost unlimited access to capital and they structure their practices accordingly. They let it be known that if their people come up with good ideas, they can find the necessary capital—just as private venture capitalists or investment bankers find resources for small entrepreneurs.

Structuring for Innovation

Managers need to think carefully about how innovation fits into their strategy and structure their technology, skills, resources, and organizational commitments accordingly. A few examples suggest the variety of strategies and alignments possible:

Hewlett-Packard and 3M develop product lines around a series of small, discrete, freestanding products. These companies form units that look like entrepreneurial start-ups. Each has a small team, led by a champion, in low-cost facilities. These companies allow many different proposals to come forward and test them as early as possible in the marketplace. They design control systems to spot significant losses on any single entry quickly. They look for high gains on a few winners and blend less successful, smaller entries into prosperous product lines.

Other companies (like AT&T or the oil majors) have had to make large system investments to last for decades. These companies tend to make longterm needs forecasts. They often start several programs in parallel to be sure of selecting the right technologies. They then extensively test new technologies in use before making systemwide commitments. Often they sacrifice speed of entry for long-term low cost and reliability.

Intel and Dewey & Almy, suppliers of highly technical specialties to EOMs, develop strong technical sales networks to discover and understand customer needs in depth. These companies try to have technical solutions designed into customers' products. Such companies have flexible applied technology groups working close to the marketplace. They also have quickly expandable plant facilities and a cutting edge technology (not necessarily basic research) group that allows rapid selection of currently available technologies.

Dominant producers like IBM or Matsushita are often not the first to introduce new technologies. They do not want to disturb their successful product lines any sooner than necessary. As market demands become clear, these companies establish precise price-performance windows and form overlapping project teams to come up with the best answer for the marketplace. To decrease market risks, they use product shoot-outs as close to the market as possible. They develop extreme depth in production technologies to keep unit costs low from the outset. Finally, depending on the scale of the market entry, they have project teams report as close to the top as necessary to secure needed management attention and resources.

Merck and Hoffman-LaRoche, basic research companies, maintain laboratories with better facilities, higher pay, and more freedom than most universities can afford. These companies leverage their internal spending through research grants, clinical grants, and research relationships with universities throughout the world. Before they invest $20 million to $50 million to clear a new drug, they must have reasonable assurance that they will be first in the marketplace. They take elaborate precautions to ensure that the new entry is safe and effective, and that it cannot be easily duplicated by others. Their structures are designed to be on the cutting edge of science, but conservative in animal testing, clinical evaluation, and production control.

These examples suggest some ways of linking innovation to strategy. Many other examples, of course, exist. Within a single company, individual divisions may have different strategic needs and hence different structures and practices. No single approach works well for all situations.

Complex Portfolio Planning

Perhaps the most difficult task for top managers is to balance the needs of existing lines against the needs of potential lines. This problem requires a portfolio strategy much more complex than the popular four-box Boston Consulting Group matrix found in most strategy texts. To allocate resources for innovation strategically, managers need to define the broad, long-term actions within and across divisions necessary to achieve their visions. They should determine which positions to hold at all costs, where to fall back, and where to expand initially and in the more distant future.

A company's strategy may often require investing more resources in current lines. But sufficient resources should also be invested in patterns that ensure intermediate and long-term growth; provide defenses against possible government, labor, competitive, or activist challenges; and generate needed organizational, technical, and external relations flexibilities to handle unforeseen opportunities or threats. Sophisticated portfolio planning within and among divisions can protect both current returns and future prospects—the two critical bases for that most cherished goal, high price/earnings ratios.

AN INCREMENTALIST APPROACH

Such managerial techniques can provide a strategic focus for innovation and help solve many of the timing, coordination, and motivation problems that plague large, bureaucratic organizations. Even more detailed planning techniques may help in guiding the development of the many small innovations that characterize any successful business. My research reveals, however, that few, if any, major innovations result from highly structured planing systems. [Why?] . . .

The innovative process is inherently incremental. As Thomas Hughes says, "Technological systems evolve through relatively small steps marked by an occasional stubborn obstacle and by constant random breakthroughs interacting across laboratories and borders" (Hughes, 1984:83). A forgotten hypothesis of Einstein's became the laser in Charles Townes's mind as he contemplated azaleas in Franklin Square. The structure of DNA followed a circuitous route through research in biology, organic chemistry. X-ray crystallography, and mathematics toward its Nobel prize–winning conception as a spiral staircase of [base pairs]. Such rambling trails are characteristic of virtually all major technological advances.

At the outset of the attack on a technical problem, an innovator often does not know whether his problem is tractable, what approach will prove best, and what concrete characteristics the solution will have if achieved. The logical route, therefore, is to follow several paths—though perhaps with varying degrees of intensity—until more information becomes available. Now knowing precisely where the solution will occur, wise managers establish the widest feasible network for finding and assessing alternative solutions. They keep many options open until one of them seems sure to win. Then they back it heavily.

Managing innovation is like a stud poker game, where one can play several hands. A player has some idea of the likely size of the pot at the beginning, knows the general but not the sure route to winning, buys one card (a project) at a time to gain information about probabilities and the size of the pot, closes hands as they become discouraging, and risks more only late in the hand as knowledge increases. . . .

Chaos Within Guidelines

Effective managers of innovation channel and control its main directions. Like venture capitalists, they administer primarily by setting goals, selecting key people, and establishing a few critical limits and decision points for intervention rather than by implementing elaborate planning or control systems. As technology leads or market needs emerge, these managers set a few—most crucial—performance targets and limits. They allow their technical units to decide how to achieve these, subject to defined constraints and reviews at critical junctures.

Early bench-scale project managers may pursue various options, making little attempt at first to integrate each into a total program. Only after key variables are understood—and perhaps measured and demonstrated in lab models—can more precise planning be meaningful. Even then, many factors may remain unknown; chaos and competition can continue to thrive in the pursuit of the solution. At defined review points, however, only those options that can clear performance milestones may continue. . . .

Even after selecting the approaches to emphasize, innovative managers tend to continue a few others as smaller scale "side bets" or options. In a surprising number of cases, these alternatives prove winners when the planned option falls.

Recognizing the many demands entailed by successful programs, innovative companies find special ways to reward innovators. Sony gives "a small but significant" percentage of a new product's sales to its innovating teams. Pilkington, IBM, and 3M's top executives are often chosen from those who have headed successful new product entries. Intel lets its Magnetic Memory Group operate like a small company, with special performance rewards and simulated stock options. GE, Syntex, and United Technologies help internal innovators establish new companies and take equity positions in "nonrelated" product innovations.

Large companies do not have to make their innovators millionaires, but reward should be visible and significant. Fortunately, most engineers are happy with the incentives that Tracy Kidder (1981) calls "playing pinball"—giving widespread recognition to a job well done and the right to play in the next exciting game. Most innovative companies provide both. . . .

MATCH MANAGEMENT TO THE PROCESS

. . . Executives need to understand and accept the tumultuous realities of innovation, learn from the experiences of other companies, and adapt the most relevant features of these others to their own management practices and cultures. Many features of small company innovators are also applicable in big companies. With top-level understanding, vision, a commitment to customers and solutions, a genuine portfolio strategy, a flexible entrepreneurial atmosphere, and proper incentives for innovative champions, many more large companies can innovate to meet the severe demands of global competition.

MANAGING CHANGE

Strategy itself is really about continuity, not change: it is concerned with imposing stable patterns of behavior on an organization, whether these take the form of intentions in advance that become deliberate strategies or actions after the fact that fall into the consistent patterns of emergent strategies. But to manage strategy is frequently to manage change—to recognize when a shift of a strategic nature is possible, desirable, necessary, and then to act.

Managing such change is generally far more difficult than it may at first appear. The need for major strategic reorientation occurs rather infrequently, and when it does, it means moving from a familiar domain into a less well-defined future where many of the old rules no longer apply. People must often abandon the roots of their past successes and develop entirely new skills and attitudes. This is clearly a frightening situation—and often, therefore, the most difficult challenge facing a manager.

The causes of such change also vary, from an ignored steady decline in performance which ultimately demands a "turnaround" to a sudden radical shift in a base technology that requires a reconceptualization of everything the organization does; from the gradual shift into the next stage of an organization's "life cycle;" to the appearance of a new chief executive who wishes to put his or her particular stamp on the organization. The resulting strategic alignments may also take a variety of forms, from a shift of strategic position within the same industry to a whole new perspective in a new industry. Some changes require rapid transitions from one structural configuration to another, as in a machine organization that having diversified into new businesses suddenly switches to a divisionalized form of structure, while others are accompanied by slower structural change, as when a small entrepreneurial firm grows steadily toward a larger mature company. Each transition has its own management prerequisites and problems.

This chapter covers a number of these aspects of organizational change, presenting material on what evokes them in the first place, what forms they can take, and how they can and should be managed in differing situations. These readings appropriately cap the earlier chapters of this book: on strategy and its formation, structure and systems, power and culture, and the various contexts in which these come together. Major changes typically involve them all. Configuration, so carefully nurtured in earlier chapters, turns out to be a double-edged sword, promoting consistency on the one hand but sometimes discouraging change on the other.

We begin broadly and then focus, starting with some general theories of change in organizations and then consider views of how to manage crises brought on by change (or the lack of it) before closing with a specific set of ideas on how managers can deal with strategic change.

The first reading seeks to bring some closure to our discussion of the different configurations of structure presented in the last five chapters. Called "Beyond Configuration: Forces and Forms in Effective Organizations," it is, in a sense, Mintzberg's final chapter of his book on structure, except that it was written very recently, years after that book first appeared. It seeks to do just what its title says: make the point that while the different structural forms (configurations) of the last chapters can help us to make sense of, and to manage in, a complex world, there is also a need to go beyond configuration, to consider the nuanced linkages among these various forms. This he proposes be done by treating all the forms as a framework of forces that act on every organization and whose contradictions need to be reconciled. By so doing, we can begin to see the weaknesses in each form as well as the times when an organization is better off to design itself as a combination of two or more forms. Some organizations, to use a metaphor introduced in this reading, achieve greater effectiveness by playing "organizational LEGO"—creating their own form rather than letting themselves be put together like a jigsaw puzzle into a standard form. Finally, this reading discusses how the forces of ideology (representing cooperation—pulling together) and of politics (representing competition—pulling apart) work both to promote change and also to impede it, and how the contradictions among these two must also be reconciled if an organization is to remain effective in the long run.

Our second reading on managing the context of change considers the "unsteady pace of organizational evolution" in terms of distinct periods of "convergence" and "upheaval." Related to the literature on organizational life cycles, its three authors, Michael Tushman and William Newman of Columbia University's Graduate School of Business and Elaine Romanelli of Duke University's Fuqua School of Business, argue for what has also been referred to as a "quantum theory" or organizational change (Miller and Freisen, 1984). The essence of the argument is that organizations prefer to stay on course most of the time, accepting incremental changes to improve their strategies, processes, and structures, but that periodically they must submit to dramatic shifts in these—"strategic revolutions" of a sort—to realign their overall orientation.

This argument is obviously compatible with the earlier notion of configuration, which represents a form of alignment of strategy, structure, and processes that dictate a certain stability in an organization. But note that it differs from Quinn's concept of "logical incrementalism," introduced in Chapter 5, which argues for more of a gradual shift in strategic thinking as a way to achieve major change in an organization. There appears to be merit in both approaches and we shall return to some words of reconciliation between the two momentarily.

The next two readings share the quantum view, but approach it rather differently—one from the perspective of process and culture, the other from that of context and strategy. In "Responding to Crises," Starbuck, Greve, and Hedberg team up to explain why organizations need these dramatic revolutions—why they fall into crises, how they tend to cope with them, and how they should. This reading brings us back to the idea of culture, particularly why and how it acts as a deterrent to major strategic change, and discusses how a deeply engrained culture that is no longer viable might be changed. In fact, this paper reflects a most interesting body of research carried out in Sweden in the 1970s on the relationships between culture and strategy. (Two of the authors are Scandinavian—Arent Greve, an academic at the Bergen, Norway, business school, and Bo Hedberg, an ex-academic who now works for a Swedish banking federation—while the third, William Starbuck, is an American who teaches at the NYU Business School but who worked with the others in Europe.)

Starbuck and his colleagues deal with situations of quantum change—namely crisis—but their ideas nonetheless link up with those of Quinn as well, specifically on how to manage incrementally and above all how to work out difficulties through an interactive process of learning. This reading also challenges many conventional notions in management. For example, its final suggestion is that crises themselves can represent *opportunities* for those organizations prepared to exploit them. Often those who approach crises in this fashion earn critical strategic advantages in the next stage of their industry's development. Consider the emergence of entirely new dominant players in the deregulated transportation and financial services industries. Cases like Federal Express, First Nationwide Financial, Royal Bank of Canada, and Zayre offer interesting opportunities to investigate this theme.

The next reading considers crises too—specifically organizations in need of "turnaround"—but very differently, more in the spirit of strategy analysis discussed in Chapter 4. Written by Charles Hofer, who teaches business policy at the University of Georgia, this reading considers various strategies that organizations can use to turn themselves around. In so doing, it introduces the important distinction between "operating" and "strategic" turnaround.

These last two readings, in suggesting very different approaches to managing crisis, reflect what are probably the two major themes today in the literature of organizational effectiveness. Picking up on a point made in Mintzberg's reading, we can call them "Porterian" and "Peterian," after Michael Porter, who argues that effectiveness resides in choosing the right strategy (positioning right), and Tom Peters, who believes it resides in carrying out the operations excellently no matter what the strategy (executing right). As Peter Drucker commented long ago, organizations may do the right things or they may do things right.

Finally, we close the chapter with James Brian Quinn's reading on "Managing Strategies Incrementally." Here he offers specific advice of various kinds on how managers can deal with the practical realities of creating change. While the previous readings have tended to look at organizations through telescopes, Quinn puts the exigencies of strategic change under a microscope—from the senior managers' perspective. In fact, while the others argue for the need to change the management in order to significantly change an organization, the Quinn reading shows how a management in place can render important strategic change. Consciously moving incrementally allows them to cope with many of the informational, political, motivational, and commitment problems that often inhibit or prevent change in large organizations. While Quinn's prescriptions do not appear as neat and orderly as those that show up in the "planned change" literature, they have direct relevance to managers who must deal in a complex, somewhat politicized world, that is, the real world of most large organizations. This reading also closes various loopholes by relating both the emergent and deliberate aspects of strategy formation to the various articles which dealt with the politics and social dynamics of change.

How can we reconcile Quinn's logical incrementalism with the ideas of those authors who promote the quantum view? Perhaps these views are not as contradictory as they seem. Consider three dimensions: (1) the specific aspects of the strategy change process that each considers, (2) the time frames of the two viewpoints, and (3) the types of organizations involved. Quinn's incrementalist view focuses on the processes going on in senior managers' minds as they help create new strategies. Because of the complexities involved, effective strategic thinking requires an incremental, interactive, learning process for all key players. The quantum approach, in contrast, focuses, not on the strategists' intentions so much as on the strategies actually pursued by the organization (referred to in Chapter 1 as the realized strategies of the organization). It is these that often seem to change in quantum fashion. It may be, therefore, that managers conceive and promote their intended strategies incrementally, but once that is accomplished they change their organizations in rapid, integrated leaps, quantum fashion.

But then again, each of these two approaches may also occur in their own situations. For example, quantum changes may more often take place in crisis situations, when top managements change, or when external environments compress time frames—often caused by technological or regulatory shifts as in the Zayre, Ford: Team Taurus, First Nationwide Financial, Biogen, or Royal Bank of Canada cases. Incremental changes may, in contrast, be more common in large, healthy organizations with multiple power points as in the cases of IBM, General Mills, Pillsbury, or The New York Times. Most situations, however, are not "either-or" propositions. A program of radical change often takes place—as did Ford's Team Taurus or Pilkington's float glass—within a company where many other elements continue to perform along well-established norms.

● BEYOND CONFIGURATION: FORCES AND FORMS IN EFFECTIVE ORGANIZATIONS*

BY HENRY MINTZBERG

Charles Darwin once made the distinction between "lumpers" and "splitters."[1] Lumpers categorize; they are the synthesizers, prone to consistency. Once they have pigeonholed something into one box or another, they are done with it. To a lumper in management, strategies are generic, structures are types, managers have a style (X, Y, Z, 9–9, etc.). Splitters nuance; they are the analyzers, prone to distinction. Since nothing can ever be categorized, things are never done with. To a splitter in management, strategies, structures, and styles all vary infinitely.

I believe a key to the effective organization lies in this distinction, specifically in its simultaneous acceptance and rejection (which themselves amount to lumping and splitting). Both are right and both are wrong. Without categories, it would be impossible to practice management. With only categories, it could not be practiced effectively.

For several years I worked as a lumper, seeking to identify types of organizations. Much as in the field of biology, I felt we in management needed some categorization of the "species" with which we dealt. We long had too much of "one best way" thinking, that every organization needed every new technique or idea that came along (like MBO or formal planning or participative management).

* Adapted from a chapter of this title in *Mintzberg on Management: Inside Our Strange World of Organizations* (Free Press, 1989); an article similar to this chapter was recently published in the *Sloan Management Review*.
[1] See F. Darwin (ed.), *The Life and Letters of Charles Darwin* (London: John Murray, 1887), p. 105.

Thus, in my books on structure and power, I developed various "configurations" of organizations. My premise was that an effective organization "got it all together" as the saying goes—achieved consistency in its internal characteristics, harmony in its processes, fit with its context.

But then, a student of mine, Alain Noël, came along and asked me a question that upset this nice lumping. He wanted to know whether I was intending to play "jigsaw puzzle" or "LEGO" with all the elements of structure and power that I described in those books. In other words, did I mean all these elements of organizations to fit together in set ways—to create known images—or were they to be used creatively to build new ones? I had to answer that I had been promoting jigsaw puzzle even if I was suggesting that the pieces could be combined into several images instead of the usual one. But I immediately began to think about playing "organizational LEGO." All of the anomalies I had encountered—all those nasty, well-functioning organizations that refused to fit into one or another of my neat categories—suddenly became opportunities to think beyond configuration. I could become a splitter too.

This reading is presented in the spirit of playing "organizational LEGO." It tries to show how we can use splitting as well as lumping to understand what makes organizations effective as well as what causes many of their fundamental problems.

FORMS AND FORCES

I shall refer to the configurations of organizations as *forms*. The original five of my structure book—here labeled entrepreneurial, machine, diversified, professional, and adhocracy—are laid out at the nodes of a pentagon, shown in Figure 1.

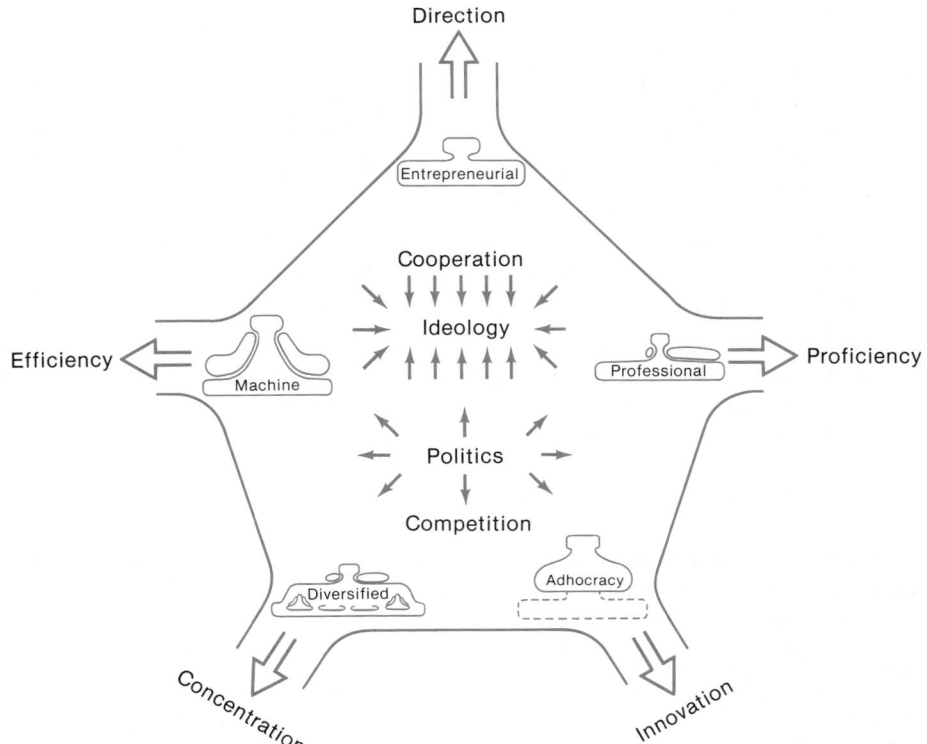

FIGURE 1
An Integrating Pentagon of Forces and Forms

Many organizations seem to fit naturally into one or another of these categories, *more or less.* We all know the small aggressive entrepreneurial firm, the perfectly machinelike Swiss hotel, the diversified conglomerate, the professional collegial university, the freewheeling intrapreneurial Silicon Valley innovator. But some organizations do not fit, much to the chagrin of the lumpers. And even many that may seem to, on closer examination reveal curious anomalies. It is difficult to imagine a more machinelike organization than McDonald's; why then does it seem to be rather innovative, at least in its own context? And why is it that whenever I mention to an executive group about a 3M or a Hewlett-Packard as innovative in form, someone from the audience leaps up to tell me about their tight control systems. Innovative adhocracies are not supposed to rely on tight controls.

All this of course pleases the splitters. "Come on, Henry," a colleague chided me recently, "in my consulting practice I never see any one of these forms. I can find all of them in all serious organizations." To him, organizations float around the inside of my pentagon; they never make it to any one node. In response, therefore, to the valid claims of the splitters, I recently added *forces* to the pentagon, shown as arrows emanating out from each of the forms. In other words, every form can be thought to represent a force too:

- First is the force for *direction,* represented by the entrepreneurial form, for some sense of where the organization must go. Without such direction—which today is apt to be called "strategic vision," years ago "grand strategy"—the various activities of an organization cannot easily work together to achieve common purpose.

- Next is the force for *efficiency,* represented by the machine form, for ensuring a viable ratio of benefits gained to costs incurred. Without some concern for efficiency, all but the most protected of organizations must eventually falter. Efficiency generally means standardization and formalization; often it reduces to economy. In current practice, it focuses on rationalization and restructuring, among other things.

- Across from the force for efficiency is the force for *proficiency,* represented by the professional form, for carrying out tasks with high levels of knowledge and skill. Without proficiency, the difficult work of organizations—whether surgery in the hospital or engineering in the corporation—just could not get done.

- Below efficiency is the force for *concentration,* represented by the diversified form, for individual units in an organization to concentrate their efforts on particular markets that it has to serve. Without such concentration, it becomes almost impossible to manage an organization that is diversified.

- At the bottom right of the pentagon is the force for *innovation,* represented by the adhocracy form. Organizations need central direction and focused concentration and they need efficiency and proficiency. But they also need to be able to learn, to discover new things for their customers and themselves—to adapt and to innovate.

I have so far left out the two forms from my book on power. We can certainly find examples of the missionary organization, as in the traditional Israeli kibbutz. Likewise, some regulatory agencies, sometimes even business corporations, become so captured by conflict for a time that they come to look like political organizations. But these forms are relatively rare, at least compared with the other five, and so I prefer to show them only as forces (placed in the middle of the pentagon for reasons to be discussed later).

- Ideology represents the force for *cooperation,* for "pulling together" (hence the arrows focus in toward the middle).
- And politics represents the force for *competition,* for "pulling apart" (hence the arrows flare out).

To recap to this point, we have two views of organizational effectiveness. One, for the lumpers, concentrates on a *portfolio of forms,* from which organizations are encouraged to choose if they wish to become effective. The other, for the splitters, focuses on a *system of forces,* with which organizations are encouraged to play in order to become effective.

The basis of my argument here is that both views are critical to the practice of management. One represents the most fundamental forces that act on organizations: All serious organizations experience all seven of them, at one time or another if not all the time. And the other represents the most fundamental forms that organizations can take, which some of them do some of the time. Together, as conceived on the pentagon, these forces and forms appear to constitute a powerful diagnostic framework by which to understand what goes on in organizations and to prescribe effective change in them.

My argument here will proceed as follows. First, I suggest that when one force dominates an organization, it is drawn toward a coherent, established form, described as *configuration.* That facilitates its management, but also raises the problem of *contamination,* which must be dealt with. When no one force dominates, the organization must instead function as a balanced *combination* of different forces, including periods of *conversion* from one form to another. But combination raises the problem of *cleavage,* which must also be dealt with. Both contamination and cleavage require the management of *contradiction,* and here the catalytic forces of the middle of the pentagon come into play: cooperation and competition both help to deal with it. But these two forces are themselves contradictory and so must be balanced as well. Put this all together and you get a fascinating game of jigsaw puzzle-cum-LEGO. It may seem difficult, but bear with me; reading it here will prove a lot easier than managing it in practice. And it may even help!

CONFIGURATION

When one force dominates the others, based on an organization's particular needs or perhaps just the arbitrary exercise of power, then we should look for the organization to fall close to one of the nodes, to take the form of one of our configurations, more or less. But these configurations are really pure types, what Max Weber once labeled "ideal types" (in Gerth and Mills, 1958). We must first ask whether they really do exist in practice.

In one sense, these configurations do not exist at all. After all, they are just words and pictures on pieces of paper, caricatures that simplify a complex reality. No serious organization can be labeled a pure machine or a pure innovator, and so on. On the other hand, managers who have to make decisions in their heads cannot carry reality around there either. They carry simplifications, called theories or models, of which these forms are examples. We must, therefore, turn to a second question: whether the forms are useful, real or not. And again I shall answer yes and no.

While no configuration ever matches a real organization perfectly, some do come remarkably close, as in the examples of the machinelike Swiss hotel or the freewheeling Silicon Valley innovator cited earlier. Species exist in nature in response to distinct ecological niches, likewise configurations evolve in human society to serve distinct needs. The Swiss hotel guest wants no surprises—no jack-in-the-box popping up when the pillow is lifted, thank you—just pure predictability, the efficiency of that wake-up call at 8:00, not 8:07. But in the niche called advertising, the client that gets no surprises may well take its business to another agency.

My basic point about configuration is simple: when the form fits, the organization is well advised to wear it, at least for a time. With configuration, an organization achieves a sense of order, of integration. There is internal consistency, synergy among processes, fit with the external context. It is the organization without configuration, much like the person without distinct character, that tends to suffer the identity crises.

Outsiders appreciate configuration; it helps them to understand an organization. We walk into a McDonald's and we know immediately what drives it, likewise a Hewlett-Packard. But more important is what configuration offers the managers: it makes an organization more manageable. With the course set, it is easier to steer, also to deflect pressures that are peripheral. No configuration is perfect—the professional one, for example, tends to belittle its clients and the machine one often alienates it workers—but there is something to be said for consistency. Closely controlled workers may not be happier than autonomous ones, but they are certainly better off than ones confused by quality circles in the morning and time study engineering in the afternoon. Better to have the definition and discipline of configuration than to dissipate one's energies trying to be all things to all people.

Moreover, much of what we know about organizations in practice applies to specific configurations. There may not be any one best way, but there are certainly preferred ways in particular contexts, for example time study in the machine organization and matrix structure in the innovative one.

Thus for classification, for comprehension, for diagnosis, and for design, configuration seems to be effective. But only so long as everything holds still. Introduce the dynamics of evolutionary change and, sooner or later, configuration becomes ineffective.

Contamination by Configuration

In harmony, consistency, and fit lies configuration's great strength. Also its debilitating weakness. The fact is that the dominant force sometimes dominates to the point of undermining all the others. For example, in a machine organization, the quest for efficiency can almost totally suppress the capacity for innovation, while in an adhocracy organization, it is the need to express some modicum of efficiency that often gets suppressed. I call this phenomenon *contamination,* although it might just as easily be called Lord Acton's dictum: among the forces of organizations too, power tends to corrupt and absolute power corrupts absolutely. For example, the story of medical care across the United States could well be described as the contamination of efficiency by proficiency. No one can deny the primacy of proficiency—who would go to a hospital that favors efficiency—but certainly not to the extent that it has been allowed to dominate.

Machine organizations recognize this problem when they put their research and development facilities away from head office, to avoid the contaminating effects of the central efficiency experts. Unfortunately, while lead may block X rays, there is no known medium to shield the effects of a dominant culture. The controller drops by, just to have a look: "What, no shoes?" Of course, the opposite case is also well known. Just ask the members of an innovative organization who's the most miserable person in adhocracy? Whenever I do this in a workshop with such an organization, the inevitable reply is a brief silence followed by a few smiles, then growing laughter as everyone turns to some poor person cowering in the corner. Of course, it's the controller, the victim of adhocracy's contamination. He or she may wear shoes, but that hardly helps him or her keep the lid on all the madness.

Contamination is another way of saying that a configuration is not merely a structure, not even merely a power system: each is a culture in its own right. Being machinelike or innovative is not just a way of organizing, it's a way of life!

Of course, given the benefits claimed for configuration, contamination may seem like a small price to pay for being coherently organized. True enough. Until things go out of control.

Configuration Out of Control

A configuration is geared not only to a general context but also to specific conditions—for example, a particular leader in an entrepreneurial organization, even a particular product and market in a machine one. Thus, when the need arises for change, the dominating force may act to hold the organization in place. Then other forces must come into play. But if contamination has worked its effects, the other forces are too weak. And so the organization goes out of control. For example, a machine organization in need of a new strategy may find available to it neither the direction of an entrepreneurial leader nor the learning of intrapreneurial subordinates. And so its internal consistency gets perpetuated while it falls increasingly out of touch with its context.

In addition, each configuration is also capable of driving itself out of control. That is to say, each contains the seeds of its own destruction. These reside in its dominating force, and come into play through the effects of contamination. With too much proficiency in a professional organization, unconstrained by the forces of efficiency and direction, the professionals become overindulged (as in many of today's universities), just as with too much technocratic regulation in a machine organization, free of the force for innovation, there arises an obsession with control (as in far too much contemporary industry and government).

My colleagues, Danny Miller and Manfred Kets de Vries (1987), have published an interesting book about *The Neurotic Organization*. They discuss organizations that become dramatic, paranoid, schizoid, compulsive, and depressive. In each case, a system that may once have been healthy has run out of control. Very roughly, I believe these five organizational neuroses correspond to what tends to happen to each of the five forms. The entrepreneurial organization tends to go out of control by becoming dramatic, as its leader, free of the other forces, takes the system off on a personal ego trip. The machine organization seems predisposed to compulsion once its analysts and their technocratic controls take over completely. Those who have worked in universities and hospitals well understand the collective paranoid tendencies of professionals, especially when free of the constraining forces of administration and innovation. I need not dwell on the depressive effects of that obsession with the "bottom line" in the diversified organization; the results on morale and innovation of the turning of the financial screws are now widely appreciated. As for the adhocracy organization, its problem is that while it must continually innovate, it must also exploit the benefits of that innovation. One requires divergent thinking, the other convergent. Other forces help balance that tension; without them, the organization can easily become schizoid.

In effect, each form goes over the edge in its own particular way, so that behaviors that were once functional when pursued to excess become dysfunctional.

This is easily seen on our pentagon. Remove all the arrows but one at any node, and the organization, no longer anchored, flies off in that direction.

Containment of Configuration

Thus I conclude that truly effective organizations do not exist in pure form. What keeps a configuration effective is not only the dominance of a single force but also the constraining effects of other forces. They keep it in place. I call this *containment*. For example, people inclined to break the rules may feel hard pressed in the machine organization. But without some of them, the organization may be unable to deal with unexpected problems. Similarly, administration may not be the strongest in the professional organization, but when allowed to atrophy, anarchy inevitably results as the absolute power of the professionals corrupts them absolutely. Thus, to manage configuration effectively is to exploit one form but also to reconcile the different forces. But how does the effective organization deal with the contradiction?

COMBINATION

Configuration is a nice thing when you can have it. Unfortunately, some organizations all of the time and all organizations some of the time cannot. They must instead balance competing forces.

Consider the symphony orchestra. Proficiency is clearly a critical force, but so too is direction: such an organization is not conceivable without highly skilled players as well as the strong central leadership of a conductor. The Russians apparently tried a leaderless orchestra shortly after their revolution, but soon gave it up as unworkable.

I shall use the word *combination* for the organization that balances different forces. In effect, it does not make it to any one node of the pentagon but instead finds its place somewhere inside.

How common are combinations as compared with configurations? To some extent the answer lies in the eyes of the beholder: what looks to be a relatively pure form to one person may look like a combination of forces to another. Still, it is interesting to consider how organizations appear to intelligent observers. For several years now, we have sent McGill MBA students out to study organizations in the Montreal area, having exposed them, among other things, to the five forms of organizations. At year end, I have circulated a questionnaire asking them to categorize the organization they studied as one of the forms, a combination of two or more, or neither. In just over half the cases—66 out of 123—the students felt that a single form fitted best. They identified 25 entrepreneurial, 13 machine, 11 diversified, 9 adhocracy, and 8 professional. All the rest were labeled combinations—seventeen different ones in all. Diversified machines were the most common (9), followed by adhocracy professionals (8), entrepreneurial professionals (6), and entrepreneurial machines (5).[2]

---

[2] The high incidence of entrepreneurial forms may be thought to reflect the students' bias toward studying small organizations, but I think not. There exist many more small organizations, in business and elsewhere, than large ones, usually entrepreneurial in nature. Of the larger ones, I would expect the machine form to predominate in any Western society. As for the incidence of combinations, I personally believe that the diversified and adhocracy forms are the most difficult to sustain (the former a conglomerate with no links between the divisions, the latter a very loose and freewheeling structure), and so these should be most common in hybrid combinations. Also some of the hybrids reflect common transitions in organizations, especially from the entrepreneurial to the machine form, as I shall discuss later.

Kinds of Combinations

Combinations themselves may take a variety of forms. They may balance just two main forces or several; these forces may meet directly or indirectly; and the balance may be steady over time or oscillate back and forth temporarily.

When only two of the five forces meet in rough balance, the organization might be described as a *hybrid* of two of our forms. This is the case of the symphony orchestra, which can be found somewhere along the line between the entrepreneurial and professional forms. Organizations can, of course, combine several of the forces in rough balance as well. In fact, five of the McGill student groups identified combinations of three forms and another a combination of four forms.

Consider Apple Computers. It seems to have developed under its founder, Steve Jobs, largely as an adhocracy organization, to emphasize new product development. The next CEO, John Sculley, apparently felt the need to temper that innovation with greater focus, to give more attention to efficiency in production and distribution. When I presented this framework at an executive program a couple of years ago, an employee of Apple Canada saw other things going on in his operation too: he added an entrepreneurial form in sales due to a dynamic leader, professional forms in marketing and training to reflect the skills there, and another adhocracy form in a new venture unit. Organizations that experience such multiple combinations are, of course, the ones that must really play LEGO.

Then there is the question of how the different forces interact. In some cases, they function on a direct steady basis; in others, they can be separated as to place or time. The combination in the symphony orchestra must be close and pervasive —leadership and professional skill meet regularly, face to face. In organizations like Apple, however, whose different units may reflect different forces, they can act somewhat independently of each other. In fact, some organizations are lucky enough to be able to achieve almost complete buffering between units representing different forces. In newspapers, for example, the more professional editorial function simply hands over its camera-ready copy to the machinelike plant for production, with little need for interaction.

Finally, in contrast to the combinations maintained on a steady-state basis are those that achieve balance in a dynamic equilibrium over time—power oscillates between the competing forces. In this regard, Richard Cyert and James March (1963) some years ago wrote about the "sequential attention to goals" in organizations, when conflicting needs are attended to each in their own turn—for example, a period of innovation to emphasize new product development followed by one of consolidation to rationalize product lines. (Might Apple Computers simply be in one of these cycles, the innovation of Jobs have been replaced by the consolidation of Sculley, or will Sculley himself be able to get the organization to balance these two forces?)

Cleavage in Combinations

Necessary as it may sometimes be, all is not rosy in the world of combination, however. If configuration encourages contamination, which can drive the organization out of control, then combination encourages *cleavage,* which can have much the same effect. Instead of one force dominating, two or more confront each other to the point of paralyzing the organization.

In effect, a natural fault line exists between any two opposing forces. Pushed to the limit, fissures begin to open up. In fact, Fellini made a film on exactly this with my favorite example. Called *Orchestra Rehearsal,* it is about musicians who revolt against their conductor, and so bring on complete anarchy, followed by paralysis. Only then do they become prepared to cooperate with their leader, who they realize is necessary for their effective performance.

But one need not turn to allegories to find examples of cleavage. It occurs commonly in most combinations, for example, in business in the battles between the R&D people who promote new product innovation and the production people in favor of stabilizing manufacturing for operating efficiency. Cleavage can, of course, be avoided when the different forces are separated in time or place, as in the newspaper. But not all organizations with combinations are so fortunate.

Combination of one kind or another is necessary in every organization. The nodes of our pentagon, where the pure configurations lie, are only points, imaginary ideals. Indeed, any organization that reaches one is already on its way out of control. It is the inside of the pentagon that has the space; that is where the effective organization must find its place. Some may fall close to one of the nodes, as configuration, more or less, while others may sit between nodes as combinations. But, ultimately, configuration and combination are not so very different, one representing more of a tilt in favor of one force over others, the other more of a balance between forces. In other words, there must always be the splitting of gray between the black and white of lumping. The question thus becomes again: how does the effective organization deal with the contradiction?

CONVERSION

So far our discussion has suggested that an organization finds its place in the pentagon and then stays there, more or less. But, in fact, few organizations get the chance to stay in one place forever: their needs change, and they must therefore undergo *conversion* from one configuration or combination to another.

Any number of external changes can cause such a conversion. An innovative organization may chance upon a new invention and decide to settle down in machine form to exploit it. Or a previously stable market may become subject to so much change that machine forms must become innovative. Some conversions are, of course, temporary, as in a machine organization in trouble that becomes entrepreneurial for a time to allow a forceful leader to impose new direction on it (usually called "turnaround"). This seems to describe Chrysler's experience when Iacocca first arrived, also that of SAS when Carlzon took over.

Cycles of Conversion

Of particular interest here is another type of conversion, however, somewhat predictable in nature because it is driven by forces intrinsic to the organization itself. Earlier I discussed the seeds of destruction contained in each configuration. Sometimes they destroy the organization, but other times they destroy only the configuration, driving the organization to a more viable form. For example, the entrepreneurial form is inherently vulnerable, dependent as it is on a single leader. It may work well for the young organization, but with aging and growth a dominant need for direction may be displaced by that for efficiency. Then conversion to the machine form becomes necessary—the power of one leader must be replaced by that of administrators.

The implication is that organizations often go through stages as they develop —*if* they develop—possibly sequenced into so-called life cycles. In fact, I have placed the forces and forms on the pentagon to reflect the most common of these, with the simple, earlier stages near the top and the more complex ones lower down.

What appears to be the most common life cycle, especially in business, occurs around the left side of the figure. Organizations generally begin life in the entrepreneurial form, because start-up requires clear direction and attracts strong leaders. As they grow and develop, many settle into the machine form to exploit increasingly established markets. But with greater growth, established markets eventually become saturated, and that often drives the organization to diversify its markets and then divisionalize its structure, taking it finally to the bottom left of our pentagon. Those organizations highly dependent on expertise, however, will instead go down the right side of the pentagon, using the professional form if their services are more standardized or the adhocracy form if these are more creative. (Some adhocracy organizations eventually settle down by converting to the professional form, where they can exploit the skills they have developed, a common occurrence, for example, in the consulting business.)

Ideology is shown above politics on the pentagon because it tends to be associated with the earlier stages of an organization's life, politics with the later ones. Any organization can, of course, have a strong culture, just as any can become politicized. But ideologies develop rather more easily in young organizations, especially with charismatic leadership in the entrepreneurial stage, whereas it is extremely difficult to build a strong and lasting culture in a mature organization. Politics, in contrast, typically spreads as the energy of a youthful organization dissipates with age and its activities become more diffuse. In fact, time typically blunts ideology as norms rigidify into procedures and beliefs become rules; then political activity tends to rise in its place. Typically, it is the old and spent organizations that are the most politicized; indeed, it is often their political conflict that finally kills them.

Cleavage in Conversion

Conversions may be necessary, but that does not make them easy. Some are, of course; they occur quickly because a change is long overdue, much as a supersaturated liquid, below the freezing point, solidifies the moment it is disturbed. But most conversions require periods of transition, prolonged and agonizing, involving a good deal of conflict. Two sides battle, usually an "old guard" committed to the status quo challenged by a group of "Young Turks" in favor of the change. As Apple Computer grew large, for example, a John Sculley intent on settling it down confronted a Steve Jobs who wished to maintain its freewheeling style of innovation.

As the organization in transition sits between its old and new forms, it becomes, or course, a form of combination, with the same problems of cleavage. Given that the challenge is to the very base of its power, there can be no recourse to higher authority to reconcile the conflict. Once again, then, the question arises: how does the effective organization deal with the contradiction?

CONTRADICTION

The question of how to manage contradiction has been the concluding point of each of the sections of this reading. I believe the answer lies in the two forces in the center of our pentagon. Organizations that have to reconcile contradictory forces, especially in dealing with change, often turn to the cooperative force of ideology or the competitive force of politics. Indeed, I believe that these two forces themselves represent a contradiction that must be managed if an organization is not to run out of control.

I have placed these two forces in the middle of the pentagon because I believe they commonly act in ways different from the other five. It is true that each can dominate an organization, and so draw it toward a missionary or political form, but more commonly I believe that these forces act differently. While the other forces tend to infiltrate parts of an organization (for example, direction in senior management, efficiency in accounting), and so isolate them, these tend instead to *infuse* the entire organization. Thus I refer to them as *catalytic,* noting that one tends to be centripetal, drawing behavior inwards toward a common core , and the other centrifugal, driving behavior away from any central place. I shall argue that both can act to promote change, also to prevent it, either way sometimes rendering an organization more effective, sometimes less.

Cooperation Through Ideology

Ideology represents the force for cooperation in an organization, for collegiality and consensus. People "pull together" for the common good—"we" are in this together.

I use the word ideology here to describe a rich culture in an organization, the uniqueness and attractiveness of which binds the members tightly to it. They commit themselves personally to the organization and identify with its needs.

Such an ideology can infuse any form of organization. It is often found with the entrepreneurial form, because, as already noted, organizational ideologies are usually created by charismatic leaders. But after such leaders move on, these ideologies can sustain themselves in other forms too. Thus we have the ideological machine that is McDonald's and the ideological adhocracy built up by Messrs. Hewlett and Packard. And one study some years ago (Clark, 1970) described "distinctive" colleges, such as Swarthmore and Antioch—professional forms infused with powerful ideologies.

Ideology encourages the members of an organization to look inward—to take their lead from the imperatives of the organization's own vision, instead of looking outward to what comparable organizations are doing. (Of course, when ideology is strong, there are no comparable organizations!) A good example of this is Hewlett Packard's famous "next bench syndrome"—that the product designer receives his or her stimulus for innovation, not from the aggregations of marketing research reports, but from the need of a particular colleague at the next bench.

This looking inward is represented by the direction of the halo of the arrows of cooperation on the pentagon. They form a circle facing inward, as if to shield the organization from outside influences. Organizational ideology above all draws people to cooperate with each other, to work together to take the organization where all of them, duly indoctrinated into its norms, believe it must go. In this sense, ideology should be thought of as the spirit of an organization, the life force that infuses the skeleton of its formal structure.

One important implication of this would appear to be that the infusion of an ideology renders any particular configuration more effective. People get fired up to pursue efficiency or proficiency or whatever else drives the organization. When this happens to a machine organization—as in a McDonald's, very responsive to its customers and very sensitive to its employees—I like to call it a "snappy bureaucracy." Bureaucratic machines are not supposed to be snappy, but ideology changes the nature of their quest for efficiency. This, of course, is the central message of the Peters and Waterman (1982) book, *In Search of Excellence,* that effectiveness is achieved, not by opportunism, not even by clever strategic positioning, but by a management that knows exactly what it must do ("sticks to its knitting") and then does it with the fervor of religious missionaries ("hands on, value driven").

There seems to be another important implication of this: ideology helps an organization to manage contradiction and so to deal with change. The different forces no longer need conflict in quite the same way. As an organization becomes infused with ideology, parts that reflect different forces can begin to pull together. As a result, forces that normally dominate or oppose each other begin to work together, thereby reducing contamination and cleavage and so facilitating adaptation.

I have always wondered why it is that McDonald's, so machinelike, is so creative in its advertising and new product development. Likewise, if 3M and Hewlett Packard really do conform largely to the adhocracy model, why do they have those tight control systems? I suspect we have the answer here. Their strong cultures enable these organizations to reconcile forces that work against each other in more ordinary organizations. People behind these different forces develop a grudging respect for one another: when it matters, they actively cooperate for the common good. "Old Joe, over there, that nut in R&D: we in production sometimes wonder about him. But we know this place could never function without him." Likewise in the great symphony orchestra, the musicians respect their conductor because they know that without him they could never produce beautiful music.

Such organizations can more easily reconcile their opposing forces because what matters to their people is the organization itself, not any of its particular parts. If it is IBM you believe in over and above marketing finesse or technical virtuosity per se, then when things really matter you will suspend your departmental rivalries to enable IBM to adapt. Great organizations simply pull together when they have to, because they are rooted in great systems of beliefs.

In his popular book, *Competitive Strategy,* Michael Porter (1980) warns about getting "stuck in the middle" between a strategy of "cost leadership" and one of "differentiation" (one representing the force for efficiency, the other including quality as well as innovation). How, then, has Toyota been able to produce such high-quality automobiles at such reasonable cost? Why didn't Toyota get stuck in the middle?

I believe that Porter's admonition stems from the view, prevalent in American management circles throughout this century and reflected equally in my own case for configuration, that if an organization favors one particular force, then others must suffer. If the efficiency experts have the upper hand, then quality gets slighted; if it is the elite designers who get their way, productive efficiency must lag; and so on. This may be true so long as an organization is managed as just a collection of different parts—a portfolio of products and functions. But when the spirit of ideology infuses the bones of its structure, an organization takes on an integrated life of its own and contradictions get reconciled. In Toyota, for example, one has the impression that each individual is made to feel like the embodiment of the entire system, that no matter what job one does, it helps to make Toyota great. Is that not why the assembly workers are allowed to shut down the line: each one is treated as a person capable of making decisions for the good of Toyota. Thus the only thing that gets stuck in the middle at Toyota is the conventional management thinking of the West!

I have so far discussed the reconciliation of contradictory forces between people and units. But even more powerful can be the effect of reconciling these forces within individuals themselves. That is what the concept of infusion really means. It is not the researchers who are responsible for innovation, not the accountants for efficiency; everyone internalizes the different forces in carrying out his or her own job. In metaphorical terms, it is easy to change hats in an organization when all are emblazoned with the same insignia.

Limits to Cooperation

Overall, then, ideology sounds like a wonderful thing. But all is not rosy in the world of culture either. For one thing, ideologies are difficult to build, especially in established organizations, and difficult to sustain once built. For another thing, established ideologies can sometimes get in the way of organizational effectiveness.

The impression left by a good deal of current writing and consulting notwithstanding, ideology is not there for the taking, to be plucked off the tree of management technique like just another piece of fashionable fruit. As Karl Weick has argued, "A corporation doesn't *have* a culture. A corporation *is* a culture. That's why they're so horribly difficult to change (in Kiechel, 1984:11). The fact is that there are no procedures for building ideologies, no five easy steps to a better culture. At best, those steps overlay a thin veneer of impressions that washes off in the first political storm; at worst, they destroy whatever is left of prevailing cultural norms. I believe that effective ideologies are built slowly and patiently by committed leaders who establish compelling missions for their organizations, nurture them, and care deeply about the people who perform them.

But even after an ideology is established, the time can come—indeed usually does eventually—when its effect is to render the organization ineffective, indeed sometimes to the point of destroying it. This is suggested in the comment above that ideologies are "so horribly difficult to change."

Just as I argued that ideology promotes change, by allowing an organization to reconcile contradictory forces, now I should like to argue the opposite. Ideology discourages change by forcing everyone to work within the same set of beliefs. In other words, strong cultures are immutable: they may promote change within themselves but they themselves are not to be changed. Receiving "the word" enables people to ask all kinds of questions but one: the word itself must never be put into question.

I can explain this in reference to two views of strategy, as position and as perspective. In one case, the organization looks down to specific product-market positions (as depicted in Michael Porter's work), in the other it looks up to a general philosophy of functioning (as in Peter Drucker's earlier writings about the "concept of a business"). In this regard, I like to ask people in my management seminars whether Egg McMuffin was a strategic change for McDonald's. Some argue yes, of course, because it brought the firm into the breakfast market. Others dismiss this as just a variation in product line, pure McDonald's, just different ingredients in a new package. Their disagreement, however, concerns not the change at McDonald's so much as their implicit definition of strategy. To one, strategy is position (the breakfast market), to the other it is perspective (the McDonald's way). The important point here is that change *within* perspective—change at the margin, to new position—is facilitated by a strong culture, whereas change *of* perspective— fundamental change—is discouraged by it. (Anyone for McDuckling à l'Orange?) The very ideology that makes an organization so adaptive within its niche undermines its efforts to move to a new niche.

Thus, when change of a fundamental nature must be made—in strategy, structure, form, whatever—the ideology that may for so long have been the key to an organization's effectiveness suddenly becomes its central problem. Ideology becomes a force for the status quo; indeed, because those who perceive the need for change are forced to challenge it, the ideology begins to breed politics!

To understand this negative effect of ideology, take another look at the penta-gon. All those arrows of cooperative ideology face inward. The halo they form may protect the organization, but at the possible expense of isolating it from the outside world. In other words, ideology can cause the other forces to atrophy: direction comes to be interpreted in terms of an outmoded system of beliefs, forcing effi-ciency, proficiency, and innovation into ever narrower corners. As the other arrows of the figure disappear, those of ideology close in on the organization, causing it to *implode*. That is how the organization dominated by the force of ideology goes out of control. It isolates itself and eventually dies. We have no need for the extreme example of a Jonestown to appreciate this negative consequence of ideology. We all know organizations with strong cultures that, like that proverbial bird, flew in ever diminishing circles until they disappeared up their own rear ends!

Competition through Politics

If the centripetal force of ideology, ostensibly so constructive, turns out to have a negative consequence, then perhaps the centrifugal force of politics, ostensibly so destructive, may have a positive one.

Politics represents the force for competition in an organization, for conflict and confrontation. People pull apart for their own needs. "They" get in our way.

Politics can infuse any of the configurations or combinations, exacerbating contamination and cleavage. Indeed, both problems were characterized as intrinsi-cally conflictive in the first place; the presence of politics for other reasons simply encourages them. The people behind the dominant force in a configuration—say, the accountants in a machine organization or the experts in a professional one—lord their power over everyone else, while those behind each of the opposing forces in a combination relish any opportunity to do battle with each other to gain advan-tage. Thus, in contrast to a machinelike Toyota pulling together is the Chrysler Iac-coca entered pulling apart; the ideology of an innovative Hewlett-Packard stands in contrast to the politics of a NASA during the *Challenger* tragedy; for every "dis-tinctive" college there are other "destructive" ones.

Politics is generally a parochial force in organizations, encouraging people to pursue their own ends. Infusing the parts of an organization with the competitive force of politics only reinforces their tendency to fly off in different directions. At the limit, the organization dominated by politics goes out of control by *exploding*. Nothing remains at the core—no central direction or even set of concentrations and no integrating ideology, and therefore, no directed effort at efficiency or profi-ciency or innovation.

In this respect, politics may be a more natural force than ideology in organi-zations. That is to say, organizations left alone seem to pull apart rather more eas-ily than they pull together. Getting a system of human beings to cooperate, on the other hand, seems to require continual effort on the part of a dedicated manage-ment.

Benefits of Competition

But we cannot dismiss politics as merely divisive. The constructive role that poli-tics can play in an organization is suggested by the very problems of ideology. If pulling together discourages people from addressing fundamental change, then pulling apart may become the only way to ensure that happens.

Change is fundamental to an organization because it upsets the deeply rooted status quo. Most organizations have such a status quo, reinforced especially by the forces of efficiency, proficiency, and ideology, all designed to promote development within an established perspective. Thus, to achieve fundamental change in an organization, particularly one that has achieved configuration and more so when that is infused with ideology, generally requires challenge of the established forces, and that means politics. In the absence of entrepreneurial or intrapreneurial capabilities, and sometimes despite them, politics may be the only force available to stimulate the change. The organization must, in other words, pull apart before it can again pull together. Thus, it appears to be an inevitable fact of life in today's organizations that a great deal of the most significant change is driven, not by managerial insight or specialized expertise or ideological commitment, let alone the procedures of planning, but by political challenge.

I conclude that both politics and ideology can promote organizational effectiveness as well as undermine it. Ideology infused into an organization can be a force for revitalization, energizing the system and making its people more responsive. But that same ideology can also hinder fundamental change. Likewise, politics often impedes necessary change and wastes valuable resources. But it can also promote important change that may be available in no other way, by enabling those who realize the need for it to challenge those who do not. There thus remains one last contradiction to reconcile in our story, between ideology and politics themselves.

Combining Cooperation and Competition

My final point is that the two catalytic forces of ideology and politics are themselves contradictory forces that have to be reconciled if an organization is to remain truly effective in the long run. Pulling together ideologically infuses life energy into an organization; pulling apart politically challenges the status quo; only by encouraging both can an organization sustain its viability. The centripetal force of ideology must contain and in turn be contained by the centrifugal force of politics. That is how an organization can keep itself from imploding or exploding—from isolating itself, on one hand, and going off in all directions, on the other. Moreover, maintaining a balance between these two forces—in their own form of combination—can discourage the other forces from going out of control. Ideology helps secondary forces to contain a dominant one; politics encourages them to challenge it. All of this—politics tempering the insularity of ideology, ideology restraining the divisiveness of politics, and both helping to limit the destructive power of the other forces—is somewhat reminiscent of that old children's game (with extended rules!): paper (ideology) covers scissors (politics) and can also help cover rocks (the force for efficiency), while scissors cut paper and can even wedge rocks out of their resting places.

Let me turn one last time to the arrows of the pentagon to illustrate. Imagine first the diverging arrows of competition contained within the converging circle of cooperation. Issues are debated and people are challenged, but only within the existing culture. The two achieve an equilibrium, as in the case of those Talmudic scholars who fight furiously with each other over the interpretation of every word in their ancient books yet close ranks to present a united front to the outside world. Is that not the very behavior we find in some of our most effective business corporations, IBM among others? Or reverse the relationship and put the arrows pulling apart outside those of the halo pulling together. Outside challenges keep a culture from closing it on itself.

Thus, I believe that only through achieving some kind of balance of these two catalytic forces can an organization maintain its effectiveness. That balance need not, however, be one of steady state. Quite the contrary, I believe it should constitute a dynamic equilibrium over time, to avoid constant tension between ideology and politics. Most of the time, to be preferred is the cooperative pulling together of ideology, contained by a healthy internal competition, so that the organization can pursue its established perspective with full vigor. But occasionally, when fundamental change becomes necessary, the organization has to be able to pull apart vigorously through the competitive force of politics. That seems to be the best combination of these two forces.

COMPETENCE

To conclude, what makes an organization truly effective? Two views tend to dominate much of the current management literature. I like to call them "Peterian" and "Porterian." Tom Peters implores managers to "stick to their knitting" and to be "hands on, value driven," among other best ways, while Michael Porter insists that they use competitive analysis to choose strategic positions that best match the characteristics of their industries. To Porter, effectiveness resides in strategy, while to Peters it is the operations that count—executing any strategy with excellence.

While agreeing that being effective depends on doing the right thing as well as doing things right, as Peter Drucker put it years ago, I believe we have to probe more deeply to find out what really makes an organization truly effective. We need to understand what takes it to a viable strategy in the first place, what makes it excellent there, and how some organizations are able to sustain viability and excellence in the face of change.

Let me close the reading by summarizing five increasingly developed views of organizational effectiveness.

Convergence: First is the *convergence* hypothesis. "One best way" is its motto, the single lens its image. There is a proper way to view, and so to design, an organization. This is usually associated with the machine form. A good structure is one with a rigid hierarchy of authority, with spans of control no greater than six, with heavy use of strategic planning, MIS, and whatever else happens to be in the current fashion of the rationalizers. In *In Search of Excellence,* in contrast, Peters and Waterman argued that ideology was the key to an organization's success. While we cannot dismiss this hypothesis—sometimes there *are* proper things to do in most if not all organizations—we must take issue with its general thrust. Society has paid an enormous price for "one best way" thinking over the course of this century, on the part of all its organizations that have been drawn into using what is fashionable rather than functional. We need to look beyond the obvious, beyond the convergence hypothesis.

Congruence: Beyond convergence is the *congruence* hypothesis, "it all depends" being its motto, the buffet table its image. Introduced in organization theory in the 1960s, it suggests that running an organization is like choosing dinner from such a table—a little bit of this, a little bit of that, all selected according to specific needs. Organizational effectiveness thus becomes a question of matching a given set of internal attributes, treated as a kind of portfolio, with various situational factors. The congruence hypothesis has certainly been an improvement, but like a dinner plate stacked with an old assortment of foods, it has not been good enough.

Configuration: And so the *configuration* hypothesis was introduced. "Getting it all together" is its motto, the jigsaw puzzle its image, the lumpers its champions. Design your organization as you would do a jigsaw puzzle, fitting all the pieces together to create a coherent, harmonious picture. There is certainly reason to believe that organizations succeed in good part because they are consistent in what they do; they are certainly easier to manage that way. But, as we have seen, configuration has its limitations too.

Contradiction: While the lumpers may like the configuration hypothesis, splitters prefer the *contradiction* hypothesis. Manage the dialectic, the dynamic tension, is their call, perhaps "to each his own" their motto, the tug of war their image. They point to the common occurrence of combinations and conversions, where organizations are forced to manage contradictory forces. This is an important hypothesis, together with that of configuration (in their own dynamic tension) certainly an important clue to organizational effectiveness. But still it is not sufficient.

Creation: The truly great organization transcends all of the foregoing while building on it to achieve something more. It respects the *creation* hypothesis. Creativity is its forte, "understand your inner nature" is its motto, LEGO its image. The most interesting organizations live at the edges, far from the logic of conventional organizations, where as Raphael (1976:5–6) has pointed out in biology (for example, between the sea and the land, or at the forest's edge), the richest, most varied, and most interesting forms of life can be found. These organizations invent novel approaches that solve festering problems and so provide all of us with new ways to deal with our world of organizations.

• CONVERGENCE AND UPHEAVAL: MANAGING THE UNSTEADY PACE OF ORGANIZATIONAL EVOLUTION*

By Michael L. Tushman, William H. Newman, and Elaine Romanelli

A snug fit of external opportunity, company strategy, and internal structure is a hallmark of successful companies. The real test of executive leadership, however, is in maintaining this alignment in the face of changing competitive conditions.

Consider the Polaroid or Caterpillar corporations. Both firms virtually dominated their respective industries for decades, only to be caught off guard by major environmental changes. The same strategic and organizational factors which were so effective for decades became the seeds of complacency and organization decline.

Recent studies of companies over long periods show that the most successful firms maintain a workable equilibrium for several years (or decades), but are also able to initiate and carry out sharp, widespread changes (referred to here as reorientations) when their environments shift. Such upheaval may bring renewed vigor to the enterprise. Less successful firms, on the other hand, get stuck in a particular pattern. The leaders of these firms either do not see the need for reorientation or they are unable to carry through the necessary frame-breaking changes. While not all reorientations succeed, those organizations which do not initiate reorientations as environments shift underperform.

This reading focuses on reasons why for long periods most companies make only incremental changes, and why they then need to make painful, discontin-

* Originally published in the *California Management Review* (Fall 1986). Copyright © 1986 by The Regents of the University of California. Reprinted with deletions by permission of the *Review*.

uous, system-wide shifts. We are particularly concerned with the role of executive leadership in managing this pattern of convergence punctuated by upheaval. . . .

The task of managing incremental change, or convergence, differs sharply from managing frame-breaking change. Incremental change is compatible with the existing structure of a company and is reinforced over a period of years. In contrast, frame-breaking change is abrupt, painful to participants, and often resisted by the old guard. Forging these new strategy-structure-people-process consistencies and laying the basis for the next period of incremental change calls for distinctive skills.

Because the future health, and even survival, of a company or business unit is at stake, we need to take a closer look at the nature and consequences of convergent change and of differences imposed by frame-breaking change. We need to explore when and why these painful and risky revolutions interrupt previously successful patterns, and whether these discontinuities can be avoided and/or initiated prior to crisis. Finally, we need to examine what managers can and should do to guide their organizations through periods of convergence and upheaval over time. . . .

The following discussion is based on the history of companies in many different industries, different countries, both large and small organizations, and organizations in various stages of their product class's life-cycle. We are dealing with a widespread phenomenon—not just a few dramatic sequences. Our research strongly suggests that the convergence/upheaval pattern occurs within departments at the business-unit level . . . and at the corporate level of analysis. . . . The problem of managing both convergent periods and upheaval is not just for the CEO, but necessarily involves general managers as well as functional managers.

PATTERNS IN ORGANIZATIONAL EVOLUTION: CONVERGENCE AND UPHEAVAL

Building on Strength: Periods of Convergence

Successful companies wisely stick to what works well. . . .

. . . convergence starts out with an effective dovetailing of strategy, structure, people, and processes. . . . The formal system includes decisions about grouping and linking resources as well as planning and control systems, rewards and evaluation procedures, and human resource management systems. The informal system includes core values, beliefs, norms, communication patterns, and actual decision-making and conflict resolution patterns. It is the whole fabric of structure, systems, people, and processes which must be suited to company strategy (Nadler and Tuchman, 1986).

As the fit between strategy, structure, people, and processes is never perfect, convergence is an ongoing process characterized by incremental change. Over time, in all companies studied, two types of converging changes were common: fine-tuning and incremental adaptations.

- *Converging change: Fine-tuning*—Even with good strategy-structure-process fits, well-run companies seek even better ways of exploiting (and defending) their missions. Such effort typically deals with one or more of the following:

  - *Refining* policies, methods, and procedures.
  - Creating *specialized units and linking mechanisms* to permit increased volume and increased attention to unit quality and cost.

- *Developing personnel* especially suited to the present strategy—through improved selection and training, and tailoring reward systems to match strategic thrusts.
- Fostering individual and group *commitments* to the company mission and to the excellence of one's own department.
- Promoting *confidence* in the accepted norms, beliefs, and myths.
- *Clarifying* established roles, power, status, dependencies, and allocation mechanism.

The fine-tuning fills out and elaborates the consistencies between strategy, structure, people, and processes. These incremental changes lead to an ever more interconnected (and therefore more stable) social system. Convergent periods fit the happy, stick-with-a-winner situations romanticized by Peters and Waterman (1982).

- *Converging change: Incremental adjustments to environmental shifts*—In addition to fine-tuning changes, minor shifts in the environment will call for some organizational response. Even the most conservative of organizations expect, even welcome, small changes which do not make too many waves.

A popular expression is that almost any organization can tolerate a "ten percent change." At any one time, only a few changes are being made; but these changes are still compatible with the prevailing structures, systems, and processes. Examples of such adjustments are an expansion in sales territory, a shift in emphasis among products in the product line, or improved processing technology in production.

The usual process of making changes of this sort is well known: wide acceptance of the need for change, openness to possible alternatives, objective examination of the pros and cons of each plausible alternative, participation of those directly affected in the preceding analysis, a market test or pilot operation where feasible, time to learn the new activities, established role models, known rewards for positive success, evaluation, and refinement.

The role of executive leadership during convergent periods is to reemphasize mission and core values and to delegate incremental decisions to middle-level managers. Note that the uncertainty created for people affected by such changes is well within tolerable limits. Opportunity is provided to anticipate and learn what is new, while most features of the structure remain unchanged.

The overall system adapts, but it is not transformed.

Converging Change: Some Consequences: For those companies whose strategies fit environmental conditions, convergence brings about better and better effectiveness. Incremental change is relatively easy to implement and ever more optimizes the consistencies between strategy, structure, people, and processes. At AT&T, for example, the period between 1913 and 1980 was one of ever more incremental change to further bolster the "Ma Bell" culture, systems, and structure all in service of developing the telephone network.

Convergent periods are, however, a double-edged sword. As organizations grow and become more successful, they develop internal forces for stability. Organization structures and systems become so interlinked that they only allow compatible changes. Further, over time, employees develop habits, patterned behaviors begin to take on values (e.g., "service is good"), and employees develop a sense of competence in knowing how to get work done within the system. These self-reinforcing patterns of behavior, norms, and values contribute to increased organizational momentum and complacency and, over time, to a sense of organizational history. This organizational history—epitomized by common stories, heroes, and standards—specifies "how we work here" and "what we hold important here."

This organizational momentum is profoundly functional as long as the organization's strategy is appropriate. The Ma Bell ... culture, structure, and systems—and associated internal momentum—were critical to [the] organization's success. However, if (and when) strategy must change, this momentum cuts the other way. Organizational history is a source of tradition, precedent, and pride which are, in turn, anchors to the past. A proud history often restricts vigilant problem solving and may be a source of resistance to change.

When faced with environmental threat, organizations with strong momentum

- may not register the threat due to organization complacency and/or stunted external vigilance (e.g., the automobile or steel industries), or
- if the threat is recognized, the response is frequently heightened conformity to the status quo and/or increased commitment to "what we do best."

For example, the response of dominant firms to technological threat is frequently increased commitment to the obsolete technology (e.g., telegraph/telephone; vacuum tube/transistor; core/semiconductor memory). A paradoxical result of long periods of success may be heightened organizational complacency, decreased organizational flexibility, and a stunted ability to learn.

Converging change is a double-edged sword. Those very social and technical consistencies which are key sources of success may also be the seeds of failure if environments change. The longer the convergent periods, the greater these internal forces for stability. This momentum seems to be particularly accentuated in those most successful firms in a product class ... in historically regulated organizations ... or in organizations that have been traditionally shielded from competition. ...

On Frame-Breaking Change

Forces Leading to Frame-Breaking Change: What, then, leads to frame-breaking change? Why defy tradition? Simply stated, frame-breaking change occurs in response to or, better yet, in anticipation of major environmental changes— changes which require more than incremental adjustments. The need for discontinuous change springs from one or a combination of the following:

- *Industry discontinuities*—Sharp changes in legal, political, or technological conditions shift the basis of competition within industries. *Deregulation* has dramatically transformed the financial services and airlines industries. *Substitute product technologies* ... or *substitute process technologies* ... may transform the bases of competition within industries. Similarly, the emergence of industry standards, or *dominant designs* (such as the DC-3, IBM 360, or PDP-8) signal a shift in competition away from product innovation and towards increased process innovation. Finally, *major economic changes* (e.g., oil crises) and *legal shifts* (e.g., patent protection in biotechnology or trade/regulator barriers in pharmaceuticals or cigarettes) also directly affect bases of competition.

- *Product life-cycle shifts*—Over the course of a product class life cycle, different strategies are appropriate. In the emergence phase of a product class, competition is based on product innovation and performance, where in the maturity stage, competition centers on cost, volume, and efficiency. Shifts in patterns of demand alter key factors for success. For example, the demand and nature of competition for mini-computers, cellular telephones, wide-body aircraft, and bowling alley equipment was transformed as these products gained acceptance and their product classes evolved. Powerful international competition may compound these forces.

- *Internal company dynamics*—Entwined with these external forces are breaking points within the firm. Sheer size may require a basically new management design. For example, few inventor-entrepreneurs can tolerate the formality that is linked with large volume. . . . Key people die. Family investors may become more concerned with their inheritance taxes than with company development. Revised corporate portfolio strategy may sharply alter the role and resources assigned to business units or functional areas. Such pressures especially when coupled with external changes, may trigger frame-breaking change.

Scope of Frame-Breaking Change: Frame-breaking change is driven by shifts in business strategy. As strategy shifts so too must structure, people, and organizational processes. Quite unlike convergent change, frame-breaking reforms involve discontinuous changes throughout the organization. These bursts of change do not reinforce the existing system and are implemented rapidly. . . . Frame-breaking changes are revolutionary changes *of* the system as opposed to incremental changes *in* the system.

The following features are usually involved in frame-breaking change:

- *Reformed mission and core values*—A strategy shift involves a new definition of company mission. Entering or withdrawing from an industry may be involved; at least the way the company expects to be outstanding is altered. . . .

- *Altered power and status*—Frame-breaking change always alters the distribution of power. Some groups lose in the shift while others gain. . . . These dramatically altered power distributions reflect shifts in bases of competition and resource allocation. A new strategy must be backed up with a shift in the balance of power and status.

- *Reorganization*—A new strategy requires a modification in structure, systems, and procedures. As strategic requirements shift, so too must the choice of organization form. A new direction calls for added activity in some areas and less in others. Changes in structure and systems are means to ensure that this reallocation of effort takes place. New structures and revised roles deliberately break business-as-usual behavior.

- *Revised interaction patterns*—The way people in the organization work together has to adapt during frame-breaking change. As strategy is different, new procedures, work flows, communication networks, and decision-making patterns must be established. With these changes in work flows and procedures must also come revised norms, informal decision-making/conflict-resolution procedures, and informal roles.

- *New executives*—Frame-breaking change also involves new executives, usually brought in from outside the organization (or business unit) and placed in key managerial positions. Commitment to the new mission, energy to overcome prevailing inertia, and freedom from prior obligations are all needed to refocus the organization. A few exceptional members of the old guard may attempt to make this shift, but habits and expectations of their associations are difficult to break. New executives are most likely to provide both the necessary drive and an enhanced set of skills more appropriate for the new strategy. While the overall number of executive changes is usually relatively small, these new executives have substantial symbolic and substantive effects on the organization. . . .

Why All at Once?: Frame-breaking change is revolutionary in that the shifts reshape the entire nature of the organization. Those more effective examples of frame-breaking change were implemented rapidly. . . . It appears that a piecemeal approach to frame-breaking changes gets bogged down in politics, individual resistance to change, and organizational inertia. . . . Frame-breaking change requires discontinuous shifts in strategy, structure, people, and processes concurrently—or at least in a short period of time. Reasons for rapid, simultaneous implementation include:

- *Synergy* within the new structure can be a powerful aid. New executives with a fresh mission, working in a redesigned organization with revised norms and values, backed up with power and status, provide strong reinforcement. The pieces of the revitalized organization pull together, as opposed to piecemeal change where one part of the new organization is out of synch with the old organization.

- *Pockets of resistance* have a chance to grow and develop when frame-breaking change is implemented slowly. The new mission, shifts in organization, and other frame-breaking changes upset the comfortable routines and precedent. Resistance to such fundamental change is natural. If frame-breaking change is implemented slowly, then individuals have a greater opportunity to undermine the changes and organizational inertia works to further stifle fundamental change.

- Typically, there is a *pent-up need for change.* During convergent periods, basic adjustments are postponed. Boat rocking is discouraged. Once constraints are relaxed, a variety of desirable improvements press for attention. The exhilaration and momentum of a fresh effort (and new team) make difficult moves more acceptable. Change is in fashion.

- Frame-breaking change is an inherently *risky and uncertain venture.* The longer the implementation period, the greater the period of uncertainty and instability. The most effective frame-breaking changes initiate the new strategy, structure, processes, and systems rapidly and begin the next period of stability and convergent change. The sooner fundamental uncertainty is removed, the better the chances of organizational survival and growth. While the pacing of change is important, the overall time to implement frame-breaking change will be contingent on the size and age of the organization.

Patterns in Organization Evolution: This historical approach to organization evolution focuses on convergent periods punctuated by reorientation—discontinuous, organizationwide upheavals. The most effective firms take advantage of relatively long convergent periods. These periods of incremental change build on and take advantage of organization inertia. Frame-breaking change is quite dysfunctional if the organization is successful and the environment is stable. If, however, the organization is performing poorly and/or if the environment changes substantially, frame-breaking change is the only way to realign the organization with its competitive environment. Not all reorientations will be successful. . . . However, inaction in the face of performance crisis and/or environmental shifts is a certain recipe for failure.

Because reorientations are so disruptive and fraught with uncertainty, the more rapidly they are implemented, the more quickly the organization can reap the benefits of the following convergent period. High-performing firms initiate reorientations when environmental conditions shift and implement these reorientations rapidly. . . . Low-performing organizations either do not reorient or reorient all the time as they root around to find an effective alignment with environmental conditions. . . .

EXECUTIVE LEADERSHIP AND ORGANIZATION EVOLUTION

Executive leadership plays a key role in reinforcing systemwide momentum during convergent periods and in initiating and implementing bursts of change that characterize strategic reorientations. The nature of the leadership task differs sharply during these contrasting periods of organization evolution.

During convergent periods, the executive team focuses on *maintaining* congruence and fit within the organization. Because strategy, structure, processes, and systems are fundamentally sound, the myriad of incremental substantive decisions can be delegated to middle-level management, where direct expertise and information resides. The key role for executive leadership during convergent periods is to reemphasize strategy, mission, and core values and to keep a vigilant eye on external opportunities and/or threats.

Frame-breaking change, however, requires direct executive involvement in all aspects of the change. Given the enormity of the change and inherent internal forces for stability, executive leadership must be involved in the specification of strategy, structure, people, and organizational processes *and* in the development of implementation plans. . . .

The most effective executives in our studies foresaw the need for major change. They recognized the external threats and opportunities, and took bold steps to deal with them. . . . Indeed, by acting before being forced to do so, they had more time to plan their transitions.

Such visionary executive teams are the exceptions. Most frame-breaking change is postponed until a financial crisis forces drastic action. The momentum, and frequently the success, of convergent periods breeds reluctance to change. . . .

. . . most frame-breaking upheavals are managed by executives brought in from outside the company. The Columbia research program finds that externally recruited executives are more than three times more likely to initiate frame-breaking change than existing executive teams. Frame-breaking change was coupled with CEO succession in more than 80% of the cases. . . .

There are several reasons why a fresh set of executives are typically used in company transformations. The new executive team brings different skills and a fresh perspective. Often they arrive with a strong belief in the new mission. Moreover, they are unfettered by prior commitments linked to the status quo; instead, this new top team symbolizes the need for change. Excitement of a new challenge adds to the energy devoted to it.

We should note that many of the executives who could not, or would not, implement frame-breaking change went on to be quite successful in other organizations. . . . The stimulation of a fresh start and of jobs matched to personal competence applies to individuals as well as to organizations.

Although typical patterns for the when and who of frame-breaking change are clear—wait for a financial crisis and then bring in an outsider, along with a revised executive team, to revamp the company—this is clearly less than satisfactory for a particular organization. Clearly, some companies benefit from transforming themselves before a crisis forces them to do so, and a few exceptional executives have the vision and drive to reorient a business which they nurtured during its preceding period of convergence. The vital tasks are to manage incremental change during convergent periods; to have the vision to initiate and implement frame-breaking change prior to the competition; and to mobilize an executive which can initiate and implement both kinds of change.

CONCLUSION

. . . Managers should anticipate that when environments change sharply

- Frame-breaking change cannot be avoided. These discontinuous organizational changes will either be made proactively or initiated under crisis/turnaround conditions.

- Discontinuous changes need to be made in strategy, structure, people, and processes concurrently. Tentative change runs the risk of being smothered by individual, group, and organizational inertia.

- Frame-breaking change requires direct executive involvement in all aspects of the change, usually bolstered with new executives from outside the organization.

- There are no patterns in the sequence of frame-breaking changes, and not all strategies will be effective. Strategy and, in turn, structure, systems, and processes must meet industry-specific competitive issues.

Finally, our historical analysis of organizations highlights the following issues for executive leadership:

- Need to manage for balance, consistency, or fit during convergent period.
- Need to be vigilant for environmental shifts in order to anticipate the need for frame-breaking change.
- Need to manage effectively incremental as well as frame-breaking change.
- Need to build (or rebuild) a top team to help initiate and implement frame-breaking change.
- Need to develop core values which can be used as an anchor as organizations evolve through frame-breaking changes (e.g., IBM, Hewlett-Packard).
- Need to develop and use organizational history as a way to infuse pride in an organization's past and for its future.
- Need to bolster technical, social, and conceptual skills with visionary skills. Visionary skills add energy, direction, and excitement so critical during frame-breaking change. . . .

● RESPONDING TO CRISIS*

BY WILLIAM H. STARBUCK, ARENT GREVE, AND BO L. T. HEDBERG

For nearly 50 years, Facit was regarded as a successful manufacturer of business machines and office furnishings. Facit grew until it operated factories in twenty cities and it maintained sales units in fifteen countries. Employment reached

---

* Originally published in the *Journal of Business Administration* (Spring 1978). Reprinted with deletions by permission of the *Journal of Business Administration*.

14,000. Suddenly, this success metamorphosed into impending disaster. For three consecutive years, gross profits were negative and employment and sales declined. Plants were closed or sold. Again and again, top managers were replaced and the managerial hierarchy was reorganized. Consultants were called in: they recommended that more operations should be closed and more employees should be fired. But after numerous meetings, the top managers could not decide whether to do what the consultants recommended. . . .

Facit . . . exemplifies organizations which encounter crises. Crises are times of danger, times when some actions lead toward organizational failure. . . .

Based on several case studies of organizations facing crises, this article explains what makes some organizations especially prone to encounter crises, it describes how organizations typically react to crises, and it prescribes how organizations ought to cope with crises.

WHY DO CRISES OCCUR?

One initial conjecture was that crises originate as threatening events in organizations' environments. A competing conjecture was that crises originate from defects within organizations themselves. Analyses of actual crises suggest that both conjectures are partly true and both are partly false. Organizations facing crises do perceive the crises as having originated in their environments. For example, Facit's top managers attributed many difficulties to temporary depressions of the firm's economic environment, and they often complained about the fierceness of market competition. At first, Facit's top managers thought that electronic calculators would replace mechanical calculators only very gradually; later, they saw electronic calculators as a technological revolution that was progressing too quickly for Facit to adapt to it (Starbuck and Hedberg, 1977).

And it was, in fact, true that national economic growth was sometimes faster and sometimes slower. There were indeed competing firms that were wooing Facit's customers. Electronic calculators actually did challenge and ultimately replace mechanical calculators. So the observations of Facit's top managers had bases in reality. But one would have to be quite gullible to accept such reasons as completely explaining Facit's crises.

Organizations' perceptions are never totally accurate. Organizations decide, sometimes explicitly but often implicitly, to observe some aspects of their environments and to ignore other aspects. They also interpret, in terms of their current goals, methods and competences, what they do observe. Such interpretation is evident in the statements about electronic calculators by Facit's top managers.

There are special reasons to question the perceptions of the top managers in organizations facing crises. If crises result partly from defects within organizations, these defects could distort the organizations' perceptions. Because distorted perceptions appear in all organizations, it may be overstatement to say that distorted perceptions are alone sufficient to cause crises. However, perceptual distortions do seem to contribute to crises by leading organizations to take no actions or inappropriate actions. . . .

Defects in organizations not only affect perceptions; they also affect the realities that are there to be perceived. Organizational defects are translated into environmental realities when organizations choose their immediate environments—by choosing suppliers, product characteristics, technologies or geographic locations—or when they manipulate their environments—by advertising, training employees, conducting research or negotiating cooperative agreements (Starbuck, 1976). . . .

Talk of organizational defects can, however, easily create misimpressions about the differences between those organizations which encounter crises and those which avoid crises. The organizations which encounter crises do not have qualitatively unusual characteristics, and they are not fundamentally abnormal. Probably the great majority of organizations have the potential to work themselves into crises, and the processes which produce crises are substantially identical with the processes which produce successes (Hedberg et al., 1976).

LEARNING/PROGRAMMING

These ironies arise from how organizations learn and from how they use their successes. The key process for organizational learning is programming: when organizations observe that certain activities appear to succeed, they crystallize these activities as standardized programs. These programs are built into the formalized roles assigned to organizations' members. Both programs and roles make activities consistent across different people and across different times. Programs generate activities that resemble those leading to good results in the past, and they do so efficiently. Organizations respond quickly to most environmental events because these events activate previously learned programs. Programs also loosen organizations' connections to their environments. Because environmental events fall into equivalence classes according to which programs they activate, organizations fail to perceive many of the small differences among environmental events. Because organizations indoctrinate their members and train them to perform roles, organizations fail to accommodate or utilize many of the differences among members who are recruited at various times in diverse locations (Nystrom et al., 1976).

Programming often facilitates success, and success always fosters programming. Success also produces slack resources and opportunities for buffering—both of which allow organizations to loosen their connections to their environments (Cyert and March, 1963; Thompson, 1967). Customers are clustered into equivalence classes, and products are standardized. Raw materials and products are stored in inventories, work activities are smoothed, and work schedules are stretched out into the future. Programs and roles are added rather frequently and discarded less frequently. Technologies are frozen by means of large capital investments. . . .

Programming, buffering, and slack resources are tools that cut on two sides. On one side, these tools enable organizations to act autonomously—to choose among alternative environments, to take risks, to experiment, to construct new environmental alternatives—and autonomous actions are generally prerequisites for outstanding successes. But on the other side, these tools render organizations less sensitive to environmental events. Organizations become less able to perceive what is happening, so they fantasize about their environments, and it may happen that realities intrude only occasionally and marginally on these fantasies. Organizations also become less able to respond to the environmental events they do perceive. . . .

WHAT REACTIONS DO CRISES EVOKE?

Explaining Crises Away

It seems that conventional accounting reports, and the ideology asserting that such reports should be bases for action, are among organizations' major liabilities. The more seriously organizations attend to their accounting reports, the more likely they are to encounter crises, and the more difficulty they have coping with crises.

Accounting reports are intentionally historical: at best they indicate what happened during the previous quarter, and even recent reports are strongly influenced by purchases of goods and equipment dating back many years and by inventories of unsalable products and obsolete components. The formats of accounting reports change very slowly. Accounting reports also intentionally focus upon formalized measures of well observed phenomena; the measures are always numerical, the importances of phenomena are appraised in monetary units, and the observations are programmatic. Much of the content in every report is ritualized irrelevance.

. . . The organizations which take their accounting reports very seriously are assuming that their worlds change slowly—that precedents are relevant to today's actions, that tomorrow's environments will look much like yesterday's, that current programs and methods are only slightly faulty at most (Hedberg and Jönsson, 1978; Thompson, 1967). Such organizations devote few resources to monitoring and interpreting unexpected environmental events; they do not tolerate redundant, ostensibly inessential activities; they guide their development by means of systematic long-range planning. . . .

All of these characteristics make it difficult for organizations to see unanticipated threats and opportunities. Many unanticipated events are never perceived at all; others are only perceived after they have been developing for some time. Then when unanticipated events are perceived, these characteristics introduce perceptual errors. One consequence is that organizations overlook the earliest signs that crises are developing. . . .

Those organizations which are strongly wedded to their pasts, naturally enough, fear rapid changes. They expect abrupt changes to produce undesirable consequences. This logic is often reversed when undesirable events occur: the undesirable events are hypothesized to be the consequences of rapid changes. The early signs of crises are attributed to the organizations' injudicious efforts to change—new markets, capital investments, inexperienced personnel, or product innovations. Such interpretations imply that no remedies are needed beyond prudent moderation, because performances will improve automatically as operations stabilize.

The idea that organizations ought to be stable structures also fosters another rationalization for early signs of crises—that poor performances result from transient environmental pressures such as economic recessions, seasonal variations in consumption, or competitors' foolish maneuvers. This rationale implies that no major strategic reorientations are called for; to the contrary, the current strategic experiments ought to terminate. Organizations decide that temporary belt-tightening is needed, together with some centralization of control and restraints on wasteful entrepreneurial ventures, but these are portrayed as beneficial changes that focus attention on what is essential (Beer, 1974; Nystrom et al., 1976; Thompson, 1967). . . .

. . . Managers who have helped to formulate strategies . . . resist strategic reorientations in order to retain power and status, and they try to persuade themselves and others that their strategies are appropriate . . . [they] may launch propaganda campaigns that deny the existence of crises. These propaganda efforts always include distortions of accounting reports: accounting periods are lengthened, depreciation charges are suspended, gains from sales or reevaluations of assets are included with operating profits. . . .

Facit's top managers made numerous efforts to persuade stockholders, employees, and the public that no crises existed, that the crisis was not serious, or that the crisis had ended. When poor performance first intruded into Facit's accounting reports, the top managers explained that this poor performance was the temporary product of currency devaluations and fierce competition. "Facit is well equipped to meet future competition. . . . Improvement is underway, but has not affected this year's outcome." Later, as the crisis deepened, Facit's managing director was replaced several times: each new managing director reported sadly that the situation was actually worse than his predecessor had publicly admitted, but he was happy to be able to announce that the nadir had been passed and the future looked rosy. Again and again, Facit's top managers announced that their firm was in sound condition and that improved performances were imminent; the chairman of the board and the managing director made such announcements even while they were secretly negotiating to sell the firm. After two years of serious difficulties, when plants were being closed, when hundreds of employees were losing their jobs, and when the top managers were privately in despair, the top managers announced that they intended to expand Facit's product line by sixty percent (Starbuck and Hedberg, 1977). . . .

Living in Collapsing Palaces

The organizations which encounter crises resemble palaces perched on mountain-tops that are crumbling from erosion. Like palaces, these organizations are rigid, cohesive structures that integrate elegant components. Although their flawless harmonies make organizational palaces look completely rational—indeed, beautiful —to observers who are inside them, observers standing outside can see that the beauty and harmony rest upon eroding grounds.

Organizational palaces are rigid because their components mesh so snugly and reinforce their neighbors. Perceptions, goals, capabilities, methods, personnel, products, and capital equipment are like stone blocks and wooden beams that interlock and brace each other. There are no chinks, no gaps, and no protruding beams because careful reason has guided every expansion and remodeling. Rationality is solidified in integrated forms that are very difficult to move: the components which blend smoothly in one arrangement fit badly in another, components which mesh tightly must be moved simultaneously, and movements fracture tight junctions. So the inhabitants' first reactions to crises are to maintain their palaces intact—they shore up shaky foundations, strengthen points of stress, and patch up cracks—and their palaces remain sitting beautifully on eroding mountaintops.

However, shoring up affords only temporary remedies against crumbling mountains, and eventually, the palaces themselves start falling apart. People begin to see that the top managers have been making faulty predictions: doubts arise that the top managers know how to cope with the crises, and the top managers usually end up looking like incompetent liars. Idealism and commitments to organizational goals fade; cynicism and opportunism grow; uncertainty escalates (Jönsson and Lundin, 1977; Kahn et al., 1964; Vickers, 1959). But cuts and reorganizations stir up power struggles that undermine cooperation. . . .

Two or three years after Facit's crisis became obvious, the top managers reached a state of paralysis. The managerial hierarchy had been reorganized repeatedly. Several small plants had been closed, and the main office-furnishings plant had been sold. But the situation had continued to get worse and worse. . . .

At this point, Electrolux bought Facit and achieved a dramatic turnaround. Eight-hundred employees were laid off right away, but these people were being re-hired within three months. It was discovered that Facit possessed a large, unfilled demand for typewriters: a mechanical-calculator plant was converted to typewriters, and the typewriter plants were expanded The demand for office furnishings was also found to exceed production capacity. Facit's research had developed electronic calculators, small computers, and computer terminals which had never been marketed aggressively; substantial demands existed for these products. During the second year after Electrolux stepped in, Facit's employment went up 10%, production increased 25%, and Facit earned a profit.

Facit's turnaround was made possible by the disintegration that preceded it. The impediments to learning usually grow very strong in organizations. Because organizations are intricate, they fear that changes would produce unforeseen disadvantages. Because organizations are logically integrated, they expect changes to initiate cascades of further changes. Because organizations are rational, they buttress their current programs and roles with justifying analyses. These impediments to learning grow strongest in the organizational palaces that emphasize rational analyses, reliable information, and logical consistency. Palaces have to be taken apart before they can be moved to new locations, and organizations have to unlearn what they now know before they can learn new knowledge. Organizations have to lose confidence in their old leaders before they will listen to new leaders. Organizations have to abandon their old goals before they will adopt new goals. Organizations have to reject their perceptual filters before they will notice events they previously overlooked. Organizations have to see that their old methods do not work before they will invent and use new methods (Cyert and March, 1963; Hedberg, 1981; Nystrom et al., 1976).

Unfortunately, crisis-ridden organizations may learn that their old methods do not work, and yet they may not learn new methods which do work.

HOW TO COPE WITH CRISES

Crises are dangerous, by definition. After crises have fully developed, organizations face serious risks of failure. To eliminate these risks is often difficult, and the remedies bring pain to some people. Consequently, the best way to cope with crises is to evade them.

Avoiding Excesses

. . . case studies suggest that many organizations adhere too strictly to those prescriptions which favor rationality, reliability, formality, logical consistency, planning, agreement, stability, hierarchical control and efficiency. All of these properties can bring benefits when they appear in moderation: organizations need some rationality, some formality, some stability, and so on. But excessive emphases on these properties turn organizations into palaces—palaces on eroding mountaintops. Organizations also need moderate amounts of irrationality, unreliability, informality, inconsistency, spontaneity, dissension, instability, delegation of responsibility, and inefficiency. These properties help to keep perceptions sharp, they disrupt complacency, and they nurture experimentation and evolutionary change (Hedberg et al., 1976; Miller and Mintzberg, 1974).

One sensible operating rule is that whenever organizations adopt one prescription, they should adopt a second prescription which contradicts the first. Contradictory prescriptions remind organizations that each prescription is a misleading oversimplification that ought not be carried to excess. For example, organizations should work toward consensus, but they should also encourage dissenters to speak out; organizations should try to exploit their strategic strengths, but they should also try to eliminate their strategic weaknesses; organizations should formulate plans, but they should also take advantage of unforeseen opportunities and they should combat unforeseen threats. It is as if each prescription presses down one pan of a balance: matched pairs of prescriptions can offset each other and keep a balance level. . . .

But balancing prescriptions is a defensive tactic that cannot rescue the organizations which already face crises. These organizations have been defending themselves—unsuccessfully—too long; they need to go on the offensive. The remainder of this article prescribes how organizations can terminate their crises and begin to rebuild themselves in viable forms.

Replacing Top Managers

When Electrolux took over Facit, it promptly fired all of Facit's top managers. This is exactly what Electrolux should have done. If Electrolux had not taken such drastic action, its intervention would probably have failed. . . .

Indiscriminate replacements of entire groups of top managers are evidently essential to bringing organizations out of crises. The veteran top managers ought to be replaced even if they are all competent people who are trying their best and even if the newcomers have no more ability, and less direct expertise, than the veterans. . . .

[In crises,] remedies are needed urgently. Perhaps the greatest need is for dramatic acts symbolizing the end of disintegration and the beginning of regeneration. Because propaganda and deceit have been rife, these symbolic acts have to be such that even skeptical observers can see they are sincere acts; and because the top managers represent both past strategies and past attempts to deceive, these symbolic acts have to punish the top managers. In addition, however, the organizations need new perceptions of reality, fresh strategic ideas, and revitalization. Since no one really knows what strategies will succeed, new strategies have to be discovered experimentally. Experimenting depends upon enthusiasm and willingness to take risks; people must have confidence their organizations can surmount new challenges and exploit discoveries. Experimenting also depends upon seeing aspects of reality which have been unseen and upon evaluating performances by criteria that differ from past criteria. . . .

. . . replacements of one or two top managers at a time are not enough. Such gradual replacements happen spontaneously while crisis-ridden organizations are disintegrating: if gradual replacements were sufficient to end crises, the crises would already have ended. But when top managers are replaced gradually, the newcomers are injected into ongoing, cohesive groups of veterans, and the newcomers exert little influence on these groups, whereas the groups exert much influence on the newcomers.

Group cohesion also impedes the veteran's own efforts to adopt remedies. Each member of a group is constrained by the other members' expectations, and cohesion draws these constraints tight. A group as a whole may bind itself to its current methods even though everyone in the group is individually ready to change; when a group includes one or two members who actively resist change, these resisters can control what happens. . . .

Rejecting Implicit Assumptions

One reason groups of top manages find change difficult is that many of the assumptions underlying their perceptions and behaviors are implicit ones. Explicit assumptions can be readily identified and discussed, so people can challenge these assumptions and perhaps alter them. But implicit assumptions may never be seen by the people who make them, and these unseen assumptions may persist indefinitely. . . .

Experimenting with Portfolios

. . . In order to escape from crises, organizations have to invest in new markets, new products, new technologies, new methods of operating, or new people. Diversification plays the same role in these investments as it does in other investments: expected returns are traded for protection against mistaken predictions. . . .

But crisis-ridden organizations find it difficult to pursue several alternatives simultaneously because they lack resources. Not many organizations start to develop alternatives while they are still [affluent]. . . .

Managing Ideology

Top managers are often the villains of crises. They are the real villains insofar as they steer their organizations into crises and insofar as they intensify crises by delaying actions or taking inappropriate actions. And they are symbolic villains who have to be replaced before crises end. But top managers are also the heroes when their organizations escape from crises. They receive the plaudits, and they largely deserve the plaudits because their actions have been the crucial ones.

Sometimes top managers contribute to escapes from crises by inventing new methods and strategies. Top managers have the best chance to do this effectively in small organizations . . . because small organizations do not make sharp demarcations among managers at different levels and they do not sharply distinguish managers from staff analysts. However, even in small organizations, the top managers should beware of relying on their own strategy-making skills. In large organizations where top management is a specialized occupation, it is generally a mistake for the top managers to act as strategy makers. . . .

. . . when top managers are occupied with strategy making, they are not doing the more important work which is their special responsibility: managing ideology. The low-level and middle managers do attend to ideological phenomena to some extent, but they focus their attentions upon visible, physical phenomena— the uses of machines, manual and clerical work, flows of materials, conferences, reports, planning documents such as schedules and blueprints, or workers' complaints. Top managers have the complementary responsibility: although they have to attend to visible, physical phenomena to some extent, they should concentrate their attentions on ideological phenomena such as morale, enthusiasm, beliefs, goals, values, and ideas. Managing ideology is very difficult because it is so indirect —like trying to steer a ship by describing the harbor toward which the ship should sail. But managing ideology is also very important because ideological phenomena exert such powerful effects upon the visible, physical phenomena.

Electrolux's turnaround of Facit was wrought almost entirely by managing ideology (Starbuck and Hedberg, 1977). Except for the replacements of top managers, Electrolux left Facit's organization largely alone. Electrolux did loan Facit approximately two million dollars so that actions would not have to be taken solely out of financial exigency, but this was a small sum in relation to the size of the company. What Electrolux did was to reconceptualize Facit and Facit's environment. Electronic calculators were no longer a technological revolution that was leaving Facit behind: Facit was making and selling electronic calculators. Typewriters and office furnishing became key product lines instead of sidelines to calculators. Competition stopped being a threat and became a stimulus. As Electrolux's managing director put it: "Hard competition is a challenge; there is no reason to withdraw." A newspaper remarked: "Although everything looks different today, the company is still more or less managed by the same people who were in charge of the company during the sequence of crises. It is now very difficult to find enough people to recruit for the factories. . . . All the present products emanate from the former Facit organization, but still, the situation has changed drastically." . . .

Facit . . . [is an organization that has] rediscovered the truth of an ancient, Chinese insight. The Chinese symbol for crisis combines two simpler symbols, the symbol for danger and the one for opportunity. Crises are times of danger, but they are also times of opportunity. . . .

● DESIGNING TURNAROUND STRATEGIES*

BY CHARLES W. HOFER

At some time in their history, most successful organizations suffer stagnation or decline in their performance. . . . Nevertheless, the Western ethic that "one must grow or die" causes psychological problems in such instances, much as the onset of middle age does in many individuals. . . .

This article will discuss turnarounds and turnaround strategies in business organizations. . . . [It will examine] turnarounds at the business-unit level. Its focus will be prescriptive rather than descriptive. Specifically, it will (1) analyze the nature of business-level turnaround situations, (2) discuss the types of turnaround strategies that are possible at this level, (3) present an analytical framework for deciding what type of turnaround strategy should be used in particular situations, and (4) discuss how to design and implement the various aspects of the indicated turnaround strategy.

THE NATURE OF TURNAROUND SITUATIONS

There are two factors that are important in describing turnaround situations. They are (1) the areas of organizational performance affected and (2) the time criticality of the turnaround situation.

In terms of organizational performance, the types of turnarounds that have been pursued and studied most frequently are those involving declines in organizational efficiency and/or profitability. Such declines usually have been measured by declining net income after taxes, although net cash flow and earnings per share have also been used.

The types of turnaround receiving next highest priority have been those involving stagnation or declines in organizational size or growth. The reason for such attention derives partly from the obvious link between size, growth, and net income, partly from the Western myth that one must grow or die, and partly from research findings linking profitability to relative market share. . . .

The third type of turnarounds to receive substantial management attention in the 1980s have been those involving poor organizational asset utilization. Such turnaround efforts have not received as much publicity or research attention as the first two, however, primarily because they have been pursued by firms that are performing reasonably well in terms of profits and growth. Thus, poor performance with respect to asset utilization does not *appear* to pose the same threat to organizational or management survival as poor performance in the former areas. Furthermore, such asset utilization turnaround strategies usually have not been discussed by the firms pursuing them outside of their management councils, primarily for competitive reasons. Asset utilization turnarounds are likely to receive far greater attention from top management in the late 1980s and early 1990s than they have to date, however, because the combination of reasonable profits and poor asset utilization provides an open invitation to corporate takeover and greenmail specialists. . . . Despite (or perhaps because of) such threats, it is still likely that most asset utilization turnaround efforts will continue to be pursued with a low profile.

The second characteristic of turnaround situations that is important to the design of effective turnaround strategies is the time criticality of the firm's current situation. If there is imminent danger to survival, it is almost always necessary to make an operational response to the situation in the near term even though a strategic response may eventually follow. The reason for this is the lengthy time delay that usually exists between the taking of a strategic action and the response that accompanies it. When the threat to organizational survival is not imminent (i.e., when there is some time to respond in a variety of ways), then it is possible to "customize" the turnaround strategy to the specific situation involved.

TYPES OF TURNAROUND STRATEGIES

There are two broad types of turnaround strategies that may be followed at the business-unit level: strategic turnarounds and operating turnarounds.

Strategic turnarounds are of two types: those that involve a change in the organization's strategy for competing in the same business, and those that involve entering a new business or businesses. The latter involve questions of corporation portfolio strategy and will not be discussed further here. Strategies for saving the existing business may be further subdivided according to the nature of the competitive position change desired, and by the core skills and competitive weapons around which the strategy is built. Most such strategic turnarounds can be classified into one of three categories:

1. Those that seek to move to a larger strategic group in the industry involved
2. Those that seek to compete more effectively within the business' existing strategic group through the use of different (or substantially modified) competitive weapons and core skills
3. Those that seek to move to a smaller strategic group in the industry involved

In terms of competitive weapons and core skills, most strategic turnarounds involve switches in the ways firms seek to achieve differentiation or cost effectiveness, rather than switches from a differentiation strategy to a cost effectiveness strategy, or vice versa.

Operating turnarounds are usually one of four types, none of which involves changing the firm's business-level strategy. These are nonstrategic turnarounds that emphasize: (1) increased revenues, (2) decreased costs, (3) decreased assets, or (4) a balanced combination of two or more of the preceding options. It should be noted that these categories could also be used to describe strategic turnarounds. In strategic turnarounds, though, the focus is on the strategy changes sought, with the performance produced being a derivative of the strategy change. In operating turnarounds, by contrast, the focus is on the performance targets, and any actions that can achieve them are to be considered whether they make good long-run strategic sense or not.

In practice, the distinction between strategic and operating actions and turnarounds becomes blurred because actions that substantially decrease assets also often require a change in strategy to be most effective, and so on. The distinction is still relevant, however, because of the different priorities attached to short-term versus long-term actions and trade-offs in the two types of strategies.

SELECTING THE TYPE OF TURNAROUND STRATEGY TO BE FOLLOWED

In trying to decide what type of turnaround strategy should be pursued in a particular situation, three questions should be asked:

1. Is the business worth saving? More specifically, can the business be made profitable in the long run, or is it better to liquidate or divest it now? And, if it is worth saving, then,
2. What is the current operating health of the business?
3. What is the current strategic health of the business?

Although one occasionally encounters turnarounds that involve long time horizons, the vast majority of turnaround situations involve severe constraints on the time available for action. In fact, in most turnaround situations there is some imminent danger to the firm's survival. For this reason, one must first check the current operating health of the business as longer-term considerations will be irrelevant if the firm goes bankrupt in the near term. For this same reason, the first step in assessing a firm's current operating health is an analysis of its current financial condition. The purpose of such analysis is to determine: (1) how probable it is that the firm may go bankrupt in the near term, (2) how much time it has to make needed changes before it goes bankrupt, (3) the magnitude of the turnaround needed to avoid bankruptcy, and (4) the financial resources that could be raised in the short term to aid in the battle. Once this analysis is completed, similar analyses must be conducted of the firm's current market, technological, and production positions in order to complete the determination of its current operating health.

After these analyses are completed, the task of selecting the optimal type of turnaround strategy can begin. In general, such optimal strategies will depend on the firm's current operating and strategic health. . . . If both are weak, then liquidation is probably the best option unless the firm has no other businesses in which it could invest. In the latter case, a combined operating/strategic turnaround with very tight controls might be possible. With a weak operating position and a moderate or strong strategic position, an operating turnaround strategy is usually needed, although divesture is also reasonable if the corporation has other businesses in which it might invest.

When the business is strong operationally but weak strategically, then a strategic turnaround is almost always indicated although the firm may have a grace period in which to decide what it will do. When both operating and strategic health are strong, turnaround strategies are seldom needed unless it is to improve asset utilization, which may sometimes lag. The approach to use for improving asset utilization in such cases will normally depend on the firm's current strategic health.

Once a business has selected the type of broad turnaround strategy it should use, that is, strategic or operating, it then needs to select the more specific aspects of its turnaround strategy. The details of these action plans will depend, of course, on the exact nature of the industry in which the business competes and on its strengths and weaknesses vis-à-vis its major competitors in that industry.

THE NEED FOR NEW TOP MANAGEMENT

Before discussing any specific turnaround options, though, one nearly universal generalization must be made. It is the "fact" that almost all successful turnarounds require the replacement of the business's current top management. There is, of course, no law written in stone that says a firm's current top management team cannot supervise a successful turnaround. Usually, however, the old management has such a strong set of beliefs about how to run the business in question, many of which must be wrong for the current problems to have arisen, that the only way to get a new view of the situation is to bring in new top management. There will, of course, be some exceptions to this generalization as there are to all generalizations. Nonetheless, in over 95% of the cases cited by Kami and Ross (1973) and by Schendel, Patton, and Riggs (1976), a change in top management did accompany a successful turnaround. Thus, one can say that a successful turnaround will require, almost without exception, either a change in top management or a substantial change in the behavior of the existing management team. Moreover, increasing evidence from the experiences of General Electric and other similar multi-industry companies indicates that different general managers are skilled at different types of tasks. Consequently, the new top management team should be selected to the degree possible with the skills appropriate to the type of turnaround strategy that will need to be followed. For instance, an entrepreneurial strategist should be chosen if a high-growth, strategic turnaround is to be pursued, while a hard-nosed, experienced cost cutter should be selected if an operating turnaround with a major cost-reduction effort is to be pursued.

STRATEGIC TURNAROUNDS

Strategic turnarounds are appropriate when the business has an average or strong current operating position, but a lost position strategically. Although it is possible that the business could be weak in its strategic technological, production, or financial positions (situations which usually produce declines in profits and ROI) but not its market share, such is not usually the case. Instead, most strategic turnarounds involve situations in which there has been a major decline in both sales and share position, and possibly even a change in the strategic group in which the business competes. Consequently, the principal method of differentiating among strategic turnarounds is according to the magnitude of the share reversal or strategic group change sought. Three options are possible: (1) a maintenance of the business's current share and/or strategic group position accompanied by a refocusing of the business on one or more easily defensible product-market segments or niches within the strategic group selected; (2) one-level shifts in share and strategic group position,[1] that is, movement from a dropout position to a follower position or from a follower position to a competitor position or from a competitor position to a leader position; or (3) two-level shifts in share and strategic group position, that is, from a dropout position to a competitor position or from a follower position to a leader position.

Usually, however, two-level shifts in share and strategic group position, or even one-level shifts that involve attempting to secure the leadership position, are not possible unless the business has unusual strategic resources that it has failed to exploit as well as access to discretionary strategic funds 50 to 100% more than it could normally generate on its own. (One such source is a corporate parent that is willing to fund heavy investments in areas of relative competitive advantage over moderately long periods of time, such as Phillip Morris was willing to do with Miller's.) The only other times when shifts of such magnitude are possible are (1) when the current leader slips, (2) when there is a major change in stage of product-market evolution, or (3) when the turnaround firm is the former leader who had recently fallen.

Normally, therefore, the choice of a strategic turnaround strategy is between a one-level shift in share and strategic group position (which might involve moving from fifth, sixth, or seventh position to a second, third, or fourth position in the industry), and a segmentation or niche strategy within the business' current strategic group. Again, unless the business has unusual resources or there is a shift in stage of product-market evolution, the segmentation/niche type strategy will normally be more profitable in terms of ROI, earnings per share, and other similar asset utilization measures of organizational performance. However, segmentation/niche strategies usually provide little or no opportunity for eventually seizing leadership in the industry involved and will usually produce lower total dollar sales and net income than a successful one-level share and strategic group shifting turnaround strategy—unless the segments selected for the new focus grow substantially. Most businesses, therefore, usually try strategic turnarounds that involve seeking higher dollar sales through one-level shifts in share and strategic group position, with a possible, even though remote, opportunity for seizing leadership should competitors slip or environmental challenges change.

Optimally, a strategic turnaround should attempt to combine the best features of both these approaches; that is, it should seek segmentation, but in such a way that overall sales and share would increase because of the strategic position or group change. Such an optimum strategic turnaround is usually not possible, however, unless there is a newly emerging segment to the market, and even then the turnaround business must be able to develop superior products for that segment, as well as upgrading its competences in the other functional areas important for serving that segment. Moreover, to be able to maintain any headstart it might get on its competitors, the firm involved needs to be able to differentiate itself from its key competitors in some relatively enduring way—a most difficult task if its competitors have superior resources.

The major conclusion that can be drawn from industry practice to date is that too much attention is given to strategic turnarounds that involve one-level increases in share and strategic group position, and not enough to strategic turnarounds that involve segmentation and niche hunting.

---

[1] Theoretically it would be possible, at least in some industries, to make a one-level shift in share position within the *same* strategic group. Practically, however, almost all efforts to achieve one- or two-level shifts in share position require a change in the strategic group in which the business competes.

There are four different types of operating turnaround strategies that are possible:

1. Revenue-increasing strategies
2. Cost-cutting strategies
3. Asset-reduction strategies
4. Combination strategies

While these turnaround strategies might seem to correspond in some ways to the three different types of strategic turnarounds noted above, attempts to make such a correspondence are really misleading since the correspondence is more one of results than of means, and as a consequence, usually exists only in the short term. A comparison of a typical strategic turnaround involving a one-level shift in the strategic group in which the firm competes with a typical revenue-increasing operating turnaround should help illustrate the differences. In the former instance, the business involved would normally develop a new line of products, alter the basic character of its production system, invest heavily in R&D, possibly even change its methods of distribution, and be slightly overstaffed in anticipation of future growth. In addition, that growth would start slowly since the efforts being undertaken are long-term ones. Later, however, the growth rate would take off for a period of several years before it slowed as the firm reached its new position.

In a typical revenue-generating operating turnaround, however, the firm would keep its existing line of products, although it might supplement these with products that it used to make but had discontinued—provided there was some indication this action would boost current sales. Also, the business might produce some products totally unrelated to its principal business if these required little start-up expense and helped utilize its facilities more fully in the short-term. In addition, both R&D and staffing would be at moderate or low levels relative to sales, while some major marketing efforts, such as price cutting, increased advertising, or increased direct sales calls, would be undertaken to stimulate current sales. One other difference would also exist. In a strategic turnaround designed to move a business to a larger strategic group, few activities would be undertaken that were not directly related to the business's long-term strategic thrust. At the same time, substantial attention would be given to *all* of the key success factors critical to the future health of the business. In a revenue-increasing operating turnaround, by contrast, almost total attention would be focused on short-term, revenue-generating actions with little or no attention to the other areas of the business. Moreover, several of the revenue-generating actions undertaken in such an operating turnaround might have no bearing on the long-term strategic health of the business. In short, strategic and operating turnarounds are really substantially different in character, even though there sometimes appears to be a similarity in the short-term results they produce.

Because of the primary focus on short-term operating actions, the first step in any operating turnaround should be to identify the resources and skills that the business will need to implement its long-term strategy so that these can be protected in the short-term action program that will follow. Once these resources have been identified, the type of operating turnaround strategy to be followed should be selected based primarily on the firm's current break-even position. . . .

If the firm is close to its current break-even point . . . but has high direct labor costs, high fixed expenses, or limited financial resources, then cost-cutting turn-around strategies are usually preferable because moderately large short-term decreases in fixed costs are usually possible and because cost-cutting actions take effect more quickly than revenue-generating actions. On the other hand, if the business is extremely far below its break-even point . . . then the only viable option is usually an asset-reduction turnaround strategy, especially if the business is close to bankruptcy. . . . If the firm's sales fall between the above ranges . . . then the most effective operating turnarounds usually involve revenue-generating or asset-reduction strategies, because in such circumstances there is usually no way to reduce costs sufficiently to reach a new break-even, and time and resources are typically not adequate to attempt a combination turnaround strategy. The choice between revenue-generating and asset-reduction strategies in such situations depends primarily on the longer-term potential of the business after turnaround, and the criticalness of the firm's current financial position. . . .

No matter what type of operating turnaround strategy is followed, though, the limited financial resources and time urgency associated with most operational turnaround situations require that particular attention be given to all actions that will have a major cash flow impact on the business in the short term. As a consequence, actions such as collecting receivables, cutting inventories, increasing prices when possible, focusing on high-margin products, stretching payables, decreasing wastage, and selling off surplus assets should almost always be pursued. . . .

SUMMARY AND CONCLUSIONS

Before closing, three other points deserve repeating. First, before starting any turn-around, an explicit calculation should be made to determine whether the turn-around effort will be worth it. Too often firms embark on turnaround efforts as a knee-jerk reaction to the myth that nothing can be worse than failure, that is, liquidation. Such is not the case, though, and in many instances, stockholders, employees, and other organizational stakeholders would be better served if management faced up to the true prospects and benefits of long-run survival and decided to liquidate the business for what it is worth now.

Second, before embarking on a strategic turnaround, an explicit investigation should be made of the conditions in the industry involved, and, in particular, of its competitive structure and stage of evolution. The reason for such analysis is quite simple. It is that industry structure is not uniformly flexible at all points in time. Thus, there are times when strategic changes abound within an industry. During such periods, shifts in relative competitive position occur moderately often. Consequently, during such times strategic turnarounds are relatively easy and inexpensive. At other times, however, it is almost impossible to make major shifts in competitive position with the resources available to most firms in the industry. During these periods, strategic turnarounds should not be attempted unless the organization has access to substantial outside resources or unless there are special circumstances, such as a competitor asleep at the switch, that provide unique opportunities in an otherwise barren situation.

Finally, it should be noted that the ideas presented in this article are based on limited research and study. It is, therefore, likely that some of them will be modified (or elaborated on) by future research.

● MANAGING STRATEGIES INCREMENTALLY*

BY JAMES BRIAN QUINN

MANAGING INCREMENTALISM

... [A section of the reading on "logical incrementalism" in Chapter 5 of this text states the logic for incremental management of strategies. But specifically] how can one proactively manage in this mode? One executive provided perhaps the most articulate short statement of the overall approach:

> Typically you start with a general concern, vaguely felt. Next, you roll an issue around in your mind until you think you have a conclusion that makes sense for the company. Then you go out and sort of post the idea without being too wedded to its details. You then start hearing the arguments pro and con, and some very good refinements of the idea usually emerge. Then you pull the idea in and put some resources together to study it so it can be put forward as more of a formal presentation. You wait for "stimuli occurrences" or "crises," and launch pieces of the idea to help in these situations. But they lead toward your ultimate aim. You know where you want to get. You'd like to get there in six months. But it may take three years, or you may not get there at all. And when you do get there, you don't know whether it was originally your own idea—or somebody else had reached the same conclusion before you and just got you on board for it. You never know.

Because of differences in organizational form, management style, and the content of individual decisions, no single paradigm holds for all strategic decisions (Quinn, 1977). But my study suggests that [many] executives [in large companies] tend to utilize somewhat similar incremental processes as they manage complex strategy shifts. [Some summary] glimpses follow:

Leading the Formal Information System

Rarely do the earliest signals for strategic change come from the company's formal horizon scanning, planning or reporting systems. Instead, initial sensing of needs for major strategic changes is often described as "something you feel uneasy about," "inconsistencies" or "anomalies" (Normann, 1977) between the enterprise's current posture and some general perception of its future environment (Mintzberg et al., 1976). Effective managers establish multiple credible internal and external sources to obtain objective information about their enterprise and its surrounding environments (Wrapp, 1967). They use these networks to short-circuit all the careful screens their organizations build up "to tell the top only what it wants to hear" (Argyris, 1977). They actively search beyond their organization's formal information systems, deeming the latter to be too historical, tradition oriented or extrapolative to pinpoint needed basic changes in time. For example,

* Originally published in modified form in *Omega: The International Journal of Management Science* (1982). Copyright © James Brian Quinn, all rights reserved. Adapted and reprinted by courtesy of *Omega*.

800

To avoid their own natural biases, executives who are aggressively seeking new potential opportunities or threats make sure their networks include people who look at the world quite differently from the dominating culture of the enterprise. Some companies have structured "devil's advocates" into their planning processes for this purpose. Others have undertaken "aggressor company" exercises to stimulate how intelligent aggressors could best attack their patents, markets, or desired future positions. Still others—like Xerox—have commissioned groups of known independent thinkers to make special studies, with the extensive help of outside consultants and authorities, to ensure top managers view changing environments analytically and creatively.

Building Organizational Awareness

This may be essential when key players do not have enough information or psychological stimulation to voluntarily change their past action patterns or to investigate options creatively. At early stages, successful change managers seem to consciously generate and consider a broad array of alternatives (Wrapp, 1967). While tapping the "collective wit" of the organization, they try to build awareness and concern about new issues. They assemble objective data to argue against preconceived ideas or blindly followed past practices. Yet they want to avoid prematurely threatening power centers that might kill important changes before potential supporters really know what is at stake and can bring broader interests to bear. At this stage, management processes are rarely directive. Instead they are likely to involve studying, challenging, questioning, listening, talking to creative people outside ordinary decision channels, generating options, but purposely avoiding irreversible commitments (Gilmore, 1973). . . .

Executives may want their colleagues to be more knowledgeable about . . . major issues and help think through ramifications clearly before taking specific actions. They want to avoid being the prime supporter of a losing idea or having the organization attack or slavishly adopt "the boss's solution" and having to change it as more evidence becomes available. Even though top executives may not have in mind specific solutions to an emerging problem they can proactively guide early steps in intuitively desired directions by defining the issues staffs investigate, selecting the people who make the investigations, and controlling the reporting process. They may not terminate this "diagnostic phase" (Mintzberg et al., 1976) until they have identified potential proponents and opponents of various positions and are sure that enough people will "get on board" to make a solution work.

Building Credibility/Changing Symbols

Symbols may help managers signal to the organization that certain types of changes are coming, even when specific solutions are not yet in hand. Knowing they cannot communicate directly with the thousands who must carry out a strategy, many executives purposely undertake a few highly visible symbolic actions which wordlessly convey complex messages they could never communicate as well, or as credibly, in verbal terms. Through word of mouth the informal grapevine can amplify signals of a pending change [with a power] no formal communication could (Rhenman, 1973). . . . Organizations often need such symbolic moves, or decisions they regard as symbolic, to verify the intention of a new strategy or to build credibility behind one in its initial stages. Without such actions people may interpret even forceful verbiage as mere rhetoric and delay their commitment to new thrusts.

Legitimizing New Viewpoints

[Strategy development] will often involve planned delays, since top managers may purposely create discussion forums or allow slack time [so that] their organizations can talk through threatening issues, work out the implications of new solutions, or gain an improved information base that permits new options to be evaluated objectively in comparison with more familiar alternatives. Because of familiarity, solutions which arise out of executives' prior experiences are perceived as having lower risks (or potential costs) than newer alternatives that are more attractive when viewed objectively. In many cases, strategic concepts which are at first strongly resisted can gain acceptance and positive commitment simply by the passage of time and open discussion of new information—when executives do not exacerbate hostility by pushing them too fast from the top (Cyert et al., 1958). Many top executives, planners, and change agents consciously arrange for such "gestation periods" and find that the concept itself is frequently made more effective by the resulting feedback and acceptance. . . . For example,

> When William Spoor took over as CEO as Pillsbury, one of the biggest issues he faced was whether to stay in or get out of the Pillsbury Farms' chicken business. Management was deeply split on the question. Spoor asked all key protagonists for position papers and purposely commissioned two papers on each side for the Board. He invited consultants' views and visited Ralston Purina, which had undergone a similar divestiture. He got an estimate from Lehman Brothers as to the division's value. All this went to the Board which debated the issue for months. A key event occurred when Lehman found a potential European buyer at a good price. Finally, when the vote was taken only one person—Pillsbury Farms' original champion—voted for retention.

Tactical Shifts and Partial Solutions

These are typical steps in developing a new overall strategic posture [when] early problem resolutions [need] to be partial, tentative, or experimental. Beginning moves are often handled as mere tactical adjustments in the enterprise's existing posture and as such they encounter little opposition. Executives can often obtain agreement to a series of small programs when a broad objective change would encounter too much opposition. Such programs allow the guiding executive to maintain the enterprise's ongoing strengths while shifting momentum—at the margin—toward new needs (Cyert and March, 1963). At this stage, top executives themselves may not yet comprehend the full nature or extent of the strategic shifts they are beginning. They can still experiment with partial new approaches without risking the viability of the total enterprise, while their broad early steps can legitimately lead to a variety of different success scenarios. . . .

As events unfurl, the solutions to several initially unrelated problems tend to flow together into a new synthesis. When possible, strategic logic (risk minimization) dictates starting broad initiatives that can be flexibly guided in any of several possible desirable directions (Wrapp, 1967).

Broadening Political Support

Broadening political support for emerging new thrusts is frequently an essential and consciously proactive step in major strategy changes. Committees, task forces or retreats tend to be favored mechanisms. By selecting such groups' chairmen, membership, timing, and agenda the guiding executive can largely influence and predict a desired outcome, yet nudge other executives toward a consensus. The careful executive, of course, still maintains complete control over these "advisory" processes through his various influence and veto potentials. In addition to facilitating smooth implementation, many managers report that interactive consensus building also improves the quality of the strategic decisions themselves and helps achieve positive and innovative assistance when things otherwise would go wrong.

Overcoming Opposition

Overcoming opposition is almost always necessary at some stage. Careful executives realize that they must deal with the support the preceding strategy had. They try not unnecessarily to alienate managers from the earlier era, whose talents they may need in future ventures, through a frontal assault on old approaches. Instead, they persuade individuals toward new concepts whenever possible, coopt or neutralize serious opposition if necessary (Sayles, 1964), or move through zones of indifference (Barnard, 1938) where early changes will not be disastrously opposed. Under the best circumstances, they find "no lose" situations that activate all important players positively towards new common goals. . . .

Successful executives tend to honor [and even stimulate] legitimate differences in views concerning even major directions and note that initial opponents often thoughtfully shape new strategies in more effective directions. Some may become active supporters as new information emerges to change their views. But consensus is not always possible. Strong minded executives sometimes disagree to the point where they must be moved to positions of less influence or stimulated to leave. And timing can dictate very firm top level direction at key junctures.

Consciously Structured Flexibility

Flexibility is essential in dealing with the many "unknowables" in the total environment. One cannot possibly predict the precise form or timing of all important threats and opportunities the firm may encounter. Logic dictates therefore that managers purposely design flexibility into their organizations and have resources ready to deploy incrementally as events demand. This requires

1. proactive horizon scanning to identify the general range, scale, and impact of the opportunities and threats the firm is most likely to encounter
2. creating sufficient resource buffers, or slacks, to respond as events actually do unfurl
3. developing and positioning "champions" who will be motivated to take advantage of specific opportunities as they occur
4. shortening decision lines between such persons and the top for rapid system response.

These—rather than precapsuled (and shelved) programs to respond to stimuli which never occur quite as expected—are the keys to real contingency planning. . . . With such flexible patterns designed into the strategy the enterprise is proactively ready to move on those thrusts that by their very nature may have to evolve incrementally.

Trial Balloons and Systematic Waiting

These are often the next steps for prepared strategists. As Roosevelt awaited a critical event like Pearl Harbor, [company] strategists may have to wait patiently for the proper option or precipitating event to appear. For example,

> The availability of desired acquisitions or real estate may depend upon a death, divorce, fiscal crisis, management change, or erratic economic break. Technological advances may await new knowledge, inventions, or lucky accidents. Or planned market entries may not be wise until new legislation, trade agreements or competitive shake outs occur. Very often the optimum strategy depends on the timing and sequence of such random events. For example the timing and nature of SDS Inc.'s availability was a proximate cause of both the date and results of this first Xerox entry into computers.

Executives may also consciously launch trial concepts . . . [like Mr. Spoor's "Super Box"] in order to attract options and concrete proposals. Usually these trial balloons are phrased in very broad contextual terms. Without making a commitment to any specific solution, the executive activates the organization's creative abilities. This approach keeps the manager's own options open until substantive alternatives can be evaluated against each other and against concrete current realities. And it prevents practical line managers from rejecting desirable strategic shifts because they are forced to compare "paper options" against what they see as well-defined, urgent needs.

Creating Pockets of Commitment

This may be necessary for entirely new strategic thrusts. The executive may encourage exploratory projects to test options, create necessary skills or technologies, or build commitment for several possible options deep within the organization. Initial projects may be kept small, partial, or ad hoc, not forming a comprehensive program or seeming to be integrated into a cohesive strategy. At this stage guiding executives may merely provide broad goals, a proper climate and flexible resource support, without being identified with specific projects (Soelberg, 1967). In this way they can avoid escalating attention to any one solution too soon or losing personal credibility if it fails. But they can stimulate those options which lead in desired directions, set higher hurdles for those that do not or quietly have them killed some levels below to maintain their own flexibility. Executives can then keep their own options open, control premature momentum, openly back only winners, and select the right moment to blend several successful thrusts into a broader program or concept (Witte, 1972). They can delay their own final decisions on a total thrust until the last moment, thus obtaining the best possible matchup between the company's capabilities, psychological commitments, and changing market needs. . . .

Crystalizing Focus

Crystalizing focus at critical points in the process is, of course, vital. Sometimes executives will state a few key goals at an early stage to generate action or cohesion in a difficult or crisis situation. But for reasons noted, guiding executives often purposely keep early goal statements vague and commitments broad and tentative (Quinn, 1977). Then as they develop information or consensus on desirable thrusts, they may use their prestige or power to push or crystalize a particular formulation. Despite adhering to the rhetoric of specific goal setting, most executives in my study were careful not to state many new strategic objectives in concrete terms until they had carefully built consensus among key players. To do otherwise might inadvertently centralize their organizations, preempt interesting options, provide a common focus for otherwise fragmented opposition, or cause the organization to undertake undesirable actions just to carry out a stated commitment. Because the net direction of an organization's goals ultimately reflects a negotiated balance among the imperatives felt by the dominant executive coalition (Perrow, 1961) and the most important power centers and stakeholders in the enterprise, the last thing an executive wants is to weaken his or her position by creating an unintended counter coalition. When to crystalize viewpoints and when to maintain open options is one of the true arts of strategic management. . . .

Formalizing Commitment

This is the final step in formulation. As partial consensus emerges, the guiding executive may crystalize events by stating a few broad goals in more specific terms for internal consumption. Finally when sufficient general acceptance exists and the timing is right, the decision may appear in more public pronouncements. For example, as General Mills divested several of its major "old line" divisions its annual reports began to state these as moves "to concentrate on the company's strengths" and "to intensify General Mills' efforts in the convenience foods field," statements which it would have been unwise or impolitic to make until many of the actual divestitures had taken place and a new management coalition and consensus had emerged.

As each major new thrust comes into focus, strategic managers ensure that some individual(s) feel responsible for its execution. Plans are locked into programs or budgets, and control and reward systems are aligned to reflect intended strategic emphases (Cohen and Cyert, 1973). Since so much has been written on this subject, I will avoid details here.

Continuing Dynamics and Mutating Consensus

[Unfortunately, old crusades can quickly become a] new conventional wisdom and the organization [can] fail to prepare itself for new concerns and concepts. In trying to build commitment, executives often surround themselves with people who strongly identify with the new strategy. These supporters can rapidly become systematic screens against new views. Even as the organization arrives at its new consensus, guiding executives must move to ensure that this too does not become inflexible. Effective strategic managers therefore immediately introduce new foc[i] and stimuli at the top to begin mutating the very strategic thrusts they have just solidified—a most difficult but essential psychological task. . . .

Not a Linear Process

While generation of a strategy generally flows along the sequence presented, stages are by no means orderly or discrete. Few executives manage the process through all phases linearly. . . . The strategy's ultimate development [usually] involves a series of nested partial decisions (in each strategic area) interacting with similar decisions in all other areas and with a constantly changing resource base. Pfiffner (1960) has aptly described the process as "like fermentation in biochemistry, rather than an industrial assembly line." The validity of a strategy lies not in its pristine clarity or rigorously maintained structure, but in its capacity to capture the initiative, to deal with unknowable events, to redeploy and concentrate resources as new opportunities and thrusts emerge, and thus to use resources most effectively toward selected goals.

Each major segment of a strategy is likely to be in a different phase of its development—from initial awareness to . . . ultimate commitment—at any given moment. The real integration of all these components into a total enterprise strategy takes place primarily in the minds of individual top executives. Some portions of the strategy may be seen the same way by all, but each executive may legitimately perceive the overall balance of goals and thrusts slightly differently. Some differences may be openly expressed as issues to be resolved when new information becomes available; others may remain unstated, hidden agendas to emerge at later dates; still others may be masked by accepting a broad statement of intention that accommodates many divergent views within its seeming consensus—while a more specific statement might be divisive. Events often move almost imperceptibly from awareness, to concern, to experiments, to options, to partial acceptance, to momenta, to consensus, to formal reinforcement. The process is so continuous that it may be hard to discern the particular point in time when specific clear-cut decisions are made.

INTEGRATING THE STRATEGY

Nevertheless, the total pattern of actions, though incremental, does not remain piecemeal in well-managed organizations. Effective executives constantly reassess the total organization, its capacities and needs as related to surrounding environment. . . .

Concentrating on a Few Key Thrusts

Strategic managers constantly seek to distil out a few (six to ten) "central themes" that draw the firm's diverse existing activities and new probes into common cause. Once identified, these help maintain focus and consistency in the strategy. They make it easier to discuss and monitor intended directions. In ideal circumstances, these themes can be converted into a matrix of strategic "thrusts" or "missions" cutting across divisional plans and dominating other criteria used to rank divisional commitments (see Quinn, 1980). Each division's plans have to show *enough* effort to accomplish its share of each thrust, even though this means overriding short-term present-value or rate-of-return rankings on projects within the division (Pfeffer et al., 1976). Texas Instruments and General Electric Company have provided some well-publicized formal models for doing this. Unfortunately, few companies seem able to implement such complex planning systems without generating voluminous paperwork, large planning bureaucracies and undesirable rigidities in the plans themselves. . . .

Coalition Management

[Nevertheless,] at the heart of all controlled strategy development lies coalition management. Top managers operate at a confluence of pressures from: stockholders, environmentalists, government bodies, customers, suppliers, distributors, producing units, marketing groups, technologists, unions, special issue activities, individual employees, ambitious executives, and so on, where knowledgeable people of good will can easily disagree on a proper balance of actions. In response to changing pressures and coalitions among these groups, the top management team continuously forms and reforms its own coalitions aligned around specific decisions. These represent various members' different values and interests concerning the particular issue at hand and are sources of constant negotiations and implied bargains among the leadership group (Sayles, 1964).

Most major strategic moves tend to assist some interests—and executives' careers—at the expense of others. Consequently, each set of interests can serve as a check on the others and thus help maintain the breadth and balance of the overall strategy. Some managements try to ensure that all important [polities] have representation or access at the top. And the guiding executive group may continuously adjust the number, power, or proximity of these access points to maintain a desired balance and focus (Zaleznik, 1970). People selection and coalition management are the ultimate controls top executives have in guiding and coordinating their companies' strategies.

15

THINKING STRATEGICALLY

We have made no secret of our intention in this text to upset many accepted and cherished notions about how organizations are supposed to work: what their strategies are supposed to be and how they are supposed to be formed, how structure and systems are supposed to coincide with these, and how managers are supposed to get their jobs done. We hope that we have succeeded not only in bringing conventional beliefs into question, but also in helping to replace them with broader, more insightful and useful ways to think about these phenomena.

The two readings we bring together in this last chapter on "thinking strategically" have been included to maintain this tone, but also to close with admonitions we believe are important for students about to embark on the world of organizations and management.

Tom Peters, the most popular of today's management "gurus," opens by warning about the whole idea of strategy. Don't think that just because you have *thought* it through you are through. Peters emphasizes that "execution is strategy," that it is in the hard work of *doing it*—something almost impossible to teach in a management school—that organizations succeed. As he stresses, it is in all those "boring" little details that the real effectiveness of an organization lies, and these depend on the distinctive competence that the organization builds up only slowly and carefully. Carrying beyond his best-seller *In Search of Excellence,* Peters presents its message for strategic management, and this served to admonish the management student from taking the excitement of managing the "big picture" too seriously. A good point for anyone finishing a course on the strategy process!

Finally, Sterling Livingston ends this text on a point that is important for everyone finishing an education in management in general: you are not finished, indeed you have barely begun. Livingston wrote this article many years ago, but the only thing dated about it is its gender. All managers-to-be, male and female, would be well warned to take its vital message seriously. Writing from his own experiences as a manager and entrepreneur as well as professor at the Harvard Business

School, Livingston cities evidence on the lack of association between how well a student does in business school and his or her later success on the job. He offers sage advice on how managers can learn from their own first hand experiences on the job, and on what kinds of people are suitable to becoming successful managers in the first place.

The message is clear, simple, and poignant: you have learned important things in school but that alone does not prepare you to manage an organization. A little humility can only help anyone who graduates from a business school today!

• STRATEGY FOLLOWS STRUCTURE: DEVELOPING DISTINCTIVE SKILLS*

BY THOMAS J. PETERS

. . . strategy follows structure. Distinctive organizational performance, for good or ill, is almost entirely a function of deeply engrained repertoires. The organization, within its marketplace, *is* the way it *acts* from moment to moment—not the way it thinks it *might* act or *ought* to act. Larry Greiner recently noted,

> Strategy evolves from inside the organization—not from its future environment. . . . Strategy is a deeply engrained and continuing pattern of management behavior that gives direction to the organization—not a manipulable and controllable mechanism that can easily be changed from one year to the next. Strategy is a nonrational concept stemming from the informal values, traditions, and norms of behavior held by the firm's managers and employees—not rational, formal, logical, conscious and predetermined thought processes engaged in by top executives. Strategy emerges out of the cumulative effect of many informal actions and decisions taken daily over the years by many employees—not a "one shot" statement developed exclusively by top management for distribution to the organization. (1983:13)

Of course we understand, at one level, exactly what Greiner is saying; few would disagree with it. At the same time, however, we more often than not manage as if the principal variable at our command—in order to bring about an adjustment to a changing environment—is the "strategy lever."

EXECUTION IS STRATEGY

SAS (Scandinavian Air System) [in the early 1980s] completed a monumental "strategic turnaround." In a period of 18 months, amid the worst recession in 40 years, it went from a position of losing $10 million a year to making $70 million a year (on $2 billion in sales), and virtually the entire turnaround came at the direct expense of such superb performers as SwissAir and Lufthansa. The "strategy" (he calls it "vision") of SAS's Jan Carlzon was "to become the premiere business person's airline." Carlzon is the first to admit that it is a "garden variety" vision: "It's everyone's aspiration. The difference was, we executed." Carlzon describes SAS as having shifted focus from "an aircraft orientation" to a "customer orientation," adding that, "SAS *is* the personal contact of one person in the market and one per-

---

* Originally published in the *California Management Review* (Spring 1984). Copyright © 1984 by The Regents of the University of California. Reprinted with deletions by permission of the *Review*.

son at SAS." He sees SAS as "50 million 'moments of truth' per year, during each of which we have an opportunity to be distinctive." That number is arrived at by calculating that SAS has 10 million customers per year, each one comes in contact with five SAS employees on average, which leads to a product of 50 million "opportunities."

Perdue Farms sells chickens. In the face of economists' predictions for over 50 consecutive years (according to Frank Perdue), Perdue Farms has built a three-quarter-billion-dollar business. Margins exceed that of its competitors by 700 or 800%. . . . Frank Perdue argues, and a careful analysis of his organization would lead one to argue, that his magic is simple: "If you believe there's absolutely no limit to quality [remember we're talking about roasters, not Ferraris] and you engage in every business dealing with total integrity, the rest [profit, growth, share] will follow automatically. . . ."

A colleague of mine once said, "Execution *is* strategy." The secret to success of the so-called excellent companies that Bob Waterman and I looked at, and the ones that I have looked at since, is almost invariably mundane execution. The examples—small and large, basic industry or growth industry— are too numerous to mention: Tupperware, Mary Kay, Stew Leonard's, Mrs. Field's Cookies, W. L. Gore, McDonald's, Mars, Perdue Farms, Frito-Lay, Hewlett-Packard, IBM, and on it goes.

My reason for belaboring this point is to suggest that, above all, the top performers—school, hospital, sports team, business—are a *package of distinctive skills.* In most cases, one particularly distinctive strength—innovation at 3M, J&J, or Hewlett-Packard; service at IBM, McDonald's, Frito-Lay, or Disney; quality at Perdue Farms, Procter & Gamble, Mars, or Maytag—and the distinctive skill—which in all cases is a product of some variation of "50 million moments of truth a year"—are a virtual unassailable barrier to competitor entry or serious encroachment. David Ogilvy quotes Mies van der Rohe as saying of architecture, "God is in the details" (1983:101). Jan Carlzon of SAS puts it this way, "We do not wish to do one thing a thousand percent better, we wish to do a thousand things one percent better." Francis G. (Buck) Rodgers, IBM's corporate marketing vice-president, made a parallel remark, "Above all we want a reputation for doing the little things well." And a long-term observer of Procter & Gamble noted, "They are so thorough, it's boring." The very fact that excellence has a "thousand thousand little things" as its source makes the word "unassailable" (as in "an unassailable barrier to entry") plausible. No trick, no device, no sleight of hand, no capital expenditure will close the gap for the also rans.

DISTINCTIVE COMPETENCE—THE FORGOTTEN TRAIL

The focus on execution, on distinctive competence is indeed not new. Philip Selznick, as far as I can determine, talked about it first:

> The term "organization" suggests a certain bareness, a lean, no-nonsense system of consciously coordinated activities. It refers to an *expendable tool,* a rational instrument engineered to do a job. An "institution," on the other hand, is more nearly a natural product of social needs and pressures—a responsive adaptive organism. The terms institution, organizational character, and distinctive competence all refer to the same basic process—the transformation of an engineered, technical arrangement of building blocks into a purposive social organization. (1957:5)

Early thinking about strategy, which was the focus of my MBA schooling a dozen years ago at Stanford, was driven by the industry standard: Edmund P. Learned and others's (1965) textbook, *Business Policy.* The focus of strategy making at that point was clearly on analyzing and building distinctive competences.

In the years since Selznick and Learned and others, the focus on distinctive competence has been downgraded. Analysis of strategic position within a competitive system has all but butted out concern with the boring details of execution (which sum up to that elusive competence). Presumably the "people types" (the OB faculty) take care of such mundane stuff. The experience curve, portfolio manipulation, competitive cost position analysis, and the like have reigned supreme for the last decade or so.

I have no problem with the usefulness of any of these tools. Each is vital, and a few of them, indeed, were used very thoughtfully or regularly just a dozen years ago. However, we seem to have moved (rushed?) from a position of "implementation without thought" (analyzing structures on the basis of span of control, rather than on the basis of external forces) to "thought without implementation." We have reached a wretched position in which Stanford, annually voted by the business school deans as America's leading business school (and thus the world's), has only *three* of 91 elective MBA courses focusing on the making (manufacturing policy) or selling (sales management) functions of business.[1] This distortion of priorities was poignantly brought home to me late last school year. A local reporter attended my last class (an elective based on *In Search of Excellence*) and asked my students if the course had been useful. One student, quoted in the subsequent article, tried to say the very most complimentary thing he could: "It's great. Tom teaches all that soft, intangible stuff—innovation, quality, customer service—that's not found in the hard P&L or balance statements." Soft? Hard? Has that youngster got it straight or backwards—is there a problem here? . . .

As best I can determine, there are only *three* truly distinctive "skill packages" . . .

Total Customer Satisfaction: . . . As Ted Levitt begins in his . . . very readable book, *The Marketing Imagination,* "There is no such thing as a commodity" (1983:72). The often slavish devotion to the experience curve effect is not responsible for our forgetting all of this counter evidence, to be sure. Making more (selling at a lower price to gain share) in order to achieve a barrier to entry via lowest subsequent industry cost is certainly not a bad idea. It's a great one. But the difficulty seems to be the unintended resultant *mind-set.* As one chief executive officer noted to me, "We act as if cost—and thus price—is the only variable available these days. In our hell bent rush to get cost down, we have given all too short shrift to quality and service. So we wake up, at best, with a great share and a lousy product. It's almost always a precarious position that can't be sustained." Also, I suspect, the relative ease of gaining dominant market position—first in the United States, and then overseas—by most American corporations in the 1950s through the 1970s (pre-OPEC, pre-Japan) led institutions to take their eye off the service and quality ball. The focus was simply on making a lot of it for ever-hungry markets. Moreover, this led to the executive suite dominance by financially trained executive-administrators, and the absence of people who were closer to the product (and thus the importance of quality and service)—namely, salespersons, designers, and manufacturers. . . .

Continuous Innovation: The second basic skill trait is the ability to constantly innovate. Virtually all innovations—from miracle drugs, to computers, to air-

---

[1] "Course Descriptions for Electives Taught in the 1983–84 Academic Year," Stanford University Graduate School of Business. [Peters later adds that 34 courses focus on accounting, finance, and decision analysis.]

planes, to bag size changes at Frito-Lay, to menu item additions at McDonald's—come from the wrong person, in the wrong division, of the wrong company, in the wrong industry, for the wrong reason, at the wrong time, with the wrong set of end-users. The assumption behind most planning systems, particularly the highly articulated strategic planning systems of the seventies, was that we could plan our way to new market successes. The reality differs greatly. Even at the mecca of planning systems, General Electric, the batting average of strategic planning was woefully low. In the 1970s (when planners were regularly observed walking on water at Fairfield), GE's major innovative, internally generated business successes—for example, aircraft engines, the credit business, plastics, and the information services company—came solely as a product of committed, somewhat irrational (assumed, inside, to be crazy) champions. When Jack Welch became GE's chairman in 1980—ending a 30-year reign by accountants—he moved to enhance entrepreneurship. One of his first steps was to reduce the corporate planning staff by more than 80 percent. The most truly innovative companies—Hewlett-Packard, the Raychem Corporation, 3M, Johnson & Johnson, PepsiCo, and the like—clearly depend upon a thoroughly innovative climate. Radical decentralization marks Johnson & Johnson. Both J&J and IBM (via its new Independent Business Unit structure) gives the innovating unit a Board of Directors with an explicit charter to "ignore the strictures of formal planning systems and to keep the bureaucrats out of the hair of the inventors." 3M is simply a collection of skunkworks. . . .

. . . A most unlikely vital company is U.S. Shoe, yet the entrepreneurial vigor of this billion-and-a-half-dollar company is extraordinary. A recent *Fortune* article attributed its success to "superior market segmentation." The next issue of *Fortune* carried a letter to the editor from the son of the founder which rebutted that argument: "My father's real contribution was not superior market segmentation. Rather, he created a beautiful corporate culture which encouraged risk taking. . . ."

All Hands: The third and final regularly found skill variable is the sine qua non that goes hand in glove with the first two. Superior customer service, quality, and courtesy (total customer satisfaction) is not a product of the executive suite—it's an all hands effort. Constant innovation from multiple centers is similarly not the domain of a handful of brilliant thinkers at the top. Thus, virtually all of these institutions put at the head of their corporate philosophies a bone-deep belief in the dignity and worth and creative potential of *all* their people. Said one successful Silicon Valley chief executive officer recently, "I'll tell you who my number one marketing person is. It's that man or woman on the loading dock who decides *not* to *drop* the box into the back of the truck." Said another, "Doesn't it follow that if you wish your people to treat your customers with courtesy that you must treat your people with courtesy?" Many sign up for these three virtues, but only the truly distinguished companies seem to practice them regularly.

COMMON THREAD: THE ADAPTIVE ORGANISM

These three skills—and these three alone—are virtually the *only* effective sources of sustainable, long-term competitive advantage. Notice that each suggests the essence of an adaptive organism. The organization that provides high perceived value—service, quality, courtesy—invariably does so by constantly listening and adapting to its customers' needs. The innovative company is similarly radically focused on the outside world. And the expectation that all people will contribute creatively to their jobs—receptionist and product designer alike—means similarly that each person is a source of external probing and a basis for constant renewal, fulfillment, and adaptation. These organizations, then, are alive and are excited—in both the "attuned" and the "enthusiastic" sense of that word. Moreover, such organizations are in the process of constant redefinition. The shared values surrounding these skills—customer listening and serving, constant innovation, and expecting all people to contribute—are rigid. But, paradoxically, the rigid values/skills are in service of constant externally focused adaptation and growth.

The excellent companies—chicken makers to computer makers—use their skills as the basis for continually reinventing adaptive strategies—usually on a decentralized basis—to permit them to compete effectively in both mature and volatile youthful markets. Skills, in a word, *drive* strategy in the best companies.

SKILLS VERSUS STRATEGY

I tend to see the word strategy, in the sense that it's currently taught in the business schools (or practiced by the leading consultants), as *not* having much meaning at the corporate or sector level at all, but as being the appropriate domain of the strategic business unit or other form of decentralized unit (the IBU at IBM, the division of Hewlett-Packard or J&J, the merchant organization at Macy's). To return to our 7-S model, this is the classic case for what we have constantly called "soft is hard." The driving variable in the model, which creates the preconditions for *effective* strategizing, is, above all, skills. Strategy is the dependent variable, operable at a lower level in the business.

We view the constantly innovating, constantly customer-serving organization as one that continually *discovers* new markets and new opportunities. The notion of the learning organization, the adapting organization, the discovering organization, reigns supreme.... By contrast, we watch the traditional "strategists" fall into the abyss time and again. Because a market looks good on paper, they believe the company should take it on. Yet they invariably underestimate the executional effort (skill base) required to do extremely well at *anything*.

PROACTIVE LEADERSHIP

If there is some sense to all the above, what then is the leader's role? If not master strategist, then what? He or she becomes, above all, a creator or shaper or keeper of skills....

Above all the leader's role becomes proactive rather than reactive.... The important people are those that view their prime role as protecting the champions from the silliness of inertial bureaucracies.... Sam Walton, founder of the remarkably successful WalMart Corporation, says, "The best ideas have always come and will always come from the clerks. The point is to seek them out, to listen, and to act...."

ENTHUSIASTS, PASSION, AND FAITH

Let's really stray afield from the world of traditional definitions of strategy formulation. Ray Kroc says, "You gotta be able to see the beauty in a hamburger bun." Recall that Debbie Fields of Mrs. Field's Cookies says, "I am not a business woman, I am a cookie person." Sam Walton loves retailing. From Steve Jobs to Famous Amos, the creators of effective organizations are unabashed *enthusiasts*. Bill Hewlett and Dave Packard had a passion for their machines. Herman Lay had a passion for his potatoes. Forrest Mars loved factories. Marvin Bower of McKinsey loved his clients. John Madden loved linebackers. The love was transmitted and transmuted into excitement, passion, enthusiasm, energy. These virtues infected an entire organization. They created the adaptive organization—the organization aimed externally, yet depending upon the full utilization of each of its people. This seemingly simple-minded definition of effective strategy for the ages even holds in mature organizations. The fervor with which Procter & Gamble revered quality has now been passed down through many generations. The "salesman's bias" of an IBM and 3M has similarly been maintained several generations beyond the founder. The passionate belief that the dominant skill reigns supreme is at the heart of business success. . . .

So where does all this leave us? The world of experience curves, portfolios, and 4-24 box matrices has led us badly astray. George Gilder notes in *Wealth and Poverty,*

> Economists who attempt to banish chance through methods of rational management also banish the only source of human triumph. The inventor who never acts until statistics affirm his choice, the businessman who waits until the market is proven—all are doomed to mediocrity by their trust in a spurious rationality. (1981:264)

The devilish problem is that there is nothing wrong with any of these strategy tools. In fact, each one is helpful! I think of the same thing in the area of quality: quality circles, automation, and statistical quality control are extraordinarily powerful tools—but *if and only if* a bone-deep belief in quality comes first. Given the 145-year tradition at Procter & Gamble, the tools are then helpful. Absent the faith, passion, belief, value, and skill, the tools become just one more manifestation of bureaucracy—another attempt to patch a fundamental flaw with a bureaucratic band-aid. . . .

But we should never forget for a moment that the analytic models are not neutral. Any analyst worth his salt, with anything from a decision tree to a portfolio analysis, can shoot down any idea. Analysts are well-trained naysayers, professional naysayers. Yet it turns out that only passion, faith, and enthusiasm win. Passion can also lead to losses—many of them, of that there is no doubt. Yet there is no alternative. We simply can't plan our way to certain success. John Naisbitt, *Megatrends* author, asserts: "Strategic planning turned out to be an orderly, rational way to efficiently ride over the edge of the cliff." I think he's not far off. Above all, the winning companies that we've observed—small and large, regulated or unregulated, mature or new—are ruled by somewhat channeled passion in pursuit of distinctive skill building and maintenance.

● MYTH OF THE WELL-EDUCATED MANAGER*

BY J. STERLING LIVINGSTON

How effectively a manager will perform on the job cannot be predicted by the number of degrees he holds, the grades he receives in school, or the formal management education programs he attends. Academic achievement is not a valid yardstick to use in measuring managerial potential. Indeed, if academic achievement is equated with success in business, the well-educated manager is a myth.

Managers are not taught in formal education programs what they most need to know to build successful careers in management. Unless they acquire through

* Originally published in the *Harvard Business Review* (January–February 1971). Copyright © by the President and Fellows of Harvard College; all rights reserved. Reprinted with deletions by permission of the *Harvard Business Review.*

their own experience the knowledge and skills that are vital to their effectiveness, they are not likely to advance far up the organizational ladder.

Although an implicit objective of all formal management education is to assist managers to learn from their own experience, much management education is, in fact, miseducation because it arrests or distorts the ability of managerial aspirants to grow as they gain experience. Fast learners in the classroom often, therefore, become slow learners in their executive suite.

Men who hold advanced degrees in management are among the most sought after of all university graduates. Measured in terms of starting salaries, they are among the elite. Perhaps no further proof of the value of management education is needed. Being highly educated pays in business, at least initially. But how much formal education contributes to a manager's effectiveness and to his subsequent career progress is another matter.

Professor Lewis B. Ward (1970) of the Harvard Business School has found that the median salaries of graduates of that institution's MBA program plateau approximately 15 years after they enter business and, on the average, do not increase significantly thereafter. While the incomes of a few MBA degree holders continue to rise dramatically, the career growth of most of them levels off just at the time men who are destined for top management typically show their greatest rate of advancement.

Equally revealing is the finding that men who attend Harvard's Advanced Management Program (AMP) after having had approximately 15 years of business experience, but who—for the most part—have had no formal education in management, earn almost a third more, on the average, than men who hold MBA degrees from Harvard and other leading business schools.

Thus the arrested career progress of MBA degree holders strongly suggests that men who get to the top in management have developed skills that are not taught in formal management education programs and may be difficult for many highly educated men to learn on the job. . . .

UNRELIABLE YARDSTICKS

Lack of correlation between scholastic standing and success in business may be surprising to those who place a premium on academic achievement. But grades in neither undergraduate nor graduate school predict how well an individual will perform in management.

After studying the career records of nearly 1,000 graduates of the Harvard Business School, for example, Professor Gordon L. Marshall concluded that "academic success and business achievement have relatively little association with each other" (Marshall, 1964). In reaching this conclusion, he sought without success to find a correlation between grades and such measures of achievement as title, salary, and a person's own satisfaction with his career progress. (Only in the case of grades in elective courses was a significant correlation found.)

Clearly, what a student learns about management in graduate school, as measured by the grades he receives, does not equip him to build a successful career in business.

Scholastic standing in undergraduate school is an equally unreliable guide to an individual's management potential. Professor Eugene E. Jennings of the University of Michigan has conducted research which shows that "the routes to the top are apt to hold just as many or more men who graduated below the highest one third of their college class than above (on a per capita basis)" (1967:21).

A great many executives who mistakenly believe that grades are a valid measure of leadership potential have expressed concern over the fact that fewer and fewer of those "top-third" graduates from the better-known colleges and universities are embarking on careers in business. What these executives do not recognize, however, is that academic ability does not assure that an individual will be able to learn what he needs to know to build a career in fields that involve leading, changing, developing, or working with people.

Overreliance on scholastic learning ability undoubtedly has caused leading universities and business organizations to reject a high percentage of those who have had the greatest potential for creativity and growth in nonacademic careers.

This probability is underscored by an informal study conducted in 1958 by W. B. Bender, Dean of Admissions at Harvard College. He first selected the names of 50 graduates of the Harvard class of 1928 who had been nominated for signal honors because of their outstanding accomplishments in their chosen careers. Then he examined the credentials they presented to Harvard College at the time of their admission. He found that if the admission standards used in 1958 had been in effect in 1928, two thirds of these men would have been turned down. (The proportion who would have been turned down under today's standards would have been even higher.)

In questioning the wisdom of the increased emphasis placed on scholastic standing and intelligence test scores, Dean Bender asked, "Do we really know what we are doing?"[1]

There seems to be little room for doubt that business schools and business organizations which rely on scholastic standing, intelligence test scores, and grades as measures of managerial potential are using unreliable yardsticks.

Career Consequences

.. **Arrested Progress and Turnover:** Belief in the myth of the well-educated manager has caused many employers to have unrealistic performance expectations of university graduates and has led many employees with outstanding scholastic records to overestimate the value of their formal education. As a consequence, men who hold degrees in business administration—especially those with advanced degrees in management—have found it surprisingly difficult to make the transition from academic to business life. An increasing number of them have failed to perform up to expectations and have not progressed at the rate they expected.

The end result is that turnover among them has been increasing for two decades as more and more of them have been changing employers in search of a job they hope they "can make a career of." And it is revealing that turnover rates among men with advanced degrees from the leading schools of management appear to be among the highest in industry.

As Professor Edgar H. Schein of the Massachusetts Institute of Technology's Sloan School of Management reports, the attrition "rate among highly educated men and women runs higher, on the average, than among blue-collar workers hired out of the hard-core unemployed. The rate may be highest among people coming out of the better-known schools" (1969:95). Thus over half the graduates of MIT's master's program in management change jobs in the first three years, Schein further reports, and "by the fifth year, 73% have moved on at least once and some are on their third and fourth jobs" (p. 90).

---

[1] Quoted in Anthony G. Athos and Lewis B. Ward, "Corporations and College Recruiting: A Study of Perceptions" (unpublished study prepared for the Division of Research, Harvard Business School), p. 14.

Personnel records of a sample of large companies I have studied similarly revealed that turnover among men holding master's degrees in management from well-known schools was over 50% in the first five years of employment, a rate of attrition that was among the highest of any group of employees in the companies surveyed.

The much publicized notion that the young "mobile managers" who move from company to company are an exceptionally able breed of new executives and that "job-hopping has become a badge of competence" is highly misleading. While a small percentage of those who change employers are competent managers, most of the men who leave their jobs have mediocre to poor records of performance. They leave not so much because the grass is greener on the other side of the fence, but because it definitely is brown on their side. My research indicates that most of them quit either because their career progress has not met their expectations or because their opportunities for promotion are not promising.

In studying the career progress of young management-level employees of an operating company of the American Telephone & Telegraph Company, Professors David E. Berlew and Douglas T. Hall of MIT found that "men who consistently fail to meet company expectations are more likely to leave the organization than are those who turn in stronger performances" (1964:36).

I have reached a similar conclusion after studying attrition among recent management graduates employed in several large industrial companies. Disappointing performance appraisals by superiors is the main reason why young men change employers.

"One myth," explains Schein, "is that the graduate leaves his first company merely for a higher salary. But the MIT data indicate that those who have moved on do not earn more than those who have stayed put" (p. 90). Surveys of reunion classes at the Harvard Business School similarly indicate that men who stay with their first employer generally earn more than those who change jobs. Job-hopping is not an easy road to high income; rather, it usually is a sign of arrested career progress, often because of mediocre or poor performance on the job.

WHAT MANAGERS MUST LEARN

One reason why highly educated men fail to build successful careers in management is that they do not learn from their formal education what they need to know to perform their jobs effectively. In fact, the tasks that are the most important in getting results usually are left to be learned on the job, where few managers ever master them simply because no one teaches them how.

Formal management education programs typically emphasize the development of problem-solving and decision-making skills, for instance, but give little attention to the development of skills required to find the problems that need to be solved, to plan for the attainment of desired results, or to carry out operating plans once they are made. Success in real life depends on how well a person is able to find and exploit the opportunities that are available to him, and, at the same time, discover and deal with potential serious problems before they become critical.

Problem Solving

Preoccupation with problem solving and decision making in formal management education programs tend to distort managerial growth because it overdevelops an individual's analytical ability, but leaves his ability to take action and to get things done underdeveloped. The behavior required to solve problems that already have been discovered and to make decisions based on facts gathered by someone else is quite different from that required to perform other functions of management.

On the one hand, problem solving and decision making in the classroom require what psychologists call "respondent behavior." It is this type of behavior that enables a person to get high grades on examinations, even though he may never use in later life what he has learned in school.

On the other hand, success and fulfillment in work demand a different kind of behavior which psychologists have labeled "operant behavior." Finding problems and opportunities, initiating action, and following through to attain desired results require the exercise of operant behavior, which is neither measured by examinations nor developed by discussing in the classroom what someone else should do. Operant behavior can be developed only by doing what needs to be done.

Instruction in problem solving and decision making all too often leads to "analysis paralysis" because managerial aspirants are required only to explain and defend their reasoning, not to carry out their decisions or even to plan realistically for their implementations. Problem solving in the classroom often is dealt with, moreover, as an entirely rational process, which, of course, it hardly ever is.

As Professor Harry Levinson of the Harvard Business School points out: "The greatest difficulty people have in solving problems is the fact that emotion makes it hard for them to see and deal with their problems objectively" (1070:109–110).

Rarely do managers learn in formal education programs how to maintain an appropriate psychological distance from their problems so that their judgments are not clouded by their emotions. Management graduates, as a consequence, suffer their worst trauma in business when they discover that rational solutions to problems are not enough; they must also somehow cope with human emotions in order to get results.

Problem Finding

The shortcomings of instruction in problem solving, while important, are not as significant as the failure to teach problem finding. As the research of Norman H. Mackworth of the Institute of Personality Assessment and Research, University of California, has revealed "the distinction between the problem-solver and the problem-finder is vital" (1969:242).

Problem finding, Mackworth points out, is more important than problem solving and involves cognitive processes that are very different from problem solving and much more complex. The most gifted problem finders, he has discovered, rarely have outstanding scholastic records, and those who do excel academically rarely are the most effective problem finders. . . .

. . . the [skill managers] need cannot be developed merely by analyzing problems discovered by someone else; rather, it must be acquired by observing firsthand what is taking place in business. While the analytical skills needed for problem solving are important, more crucial to managerial success are the perceptual skills needed to identify problems long before evidence of them can be found by even the most advanced management information system. Since these perceptual skills are extremely difficult to develop in the classroom, they are now largely left to be developed on the job.

Opportunity Finding

A manager's problem-finding ability is exceeded in importance only by his opportunity-finding ability. Results in business, Peter F. Drucker reminds us, are obtained by exploiting opportunities, not by solving problems. Here is how he puts it:

> All one can hope to get by solving a problem is to restore normality. All one can hope, at best, is to eliminate a restriction on the capacity of the business to obtain results. The results themselves must come from the exploitation of opportunities. . . . "Maximization of opportunities" is a meaningful, indeed a precise, definition of the entrepreneurial job. It implies that effectiveness rather than efficiency is essential in business. The pertinent question is not how to do things right, but how to find the right things to do, and to concentrate resources and efforts on them. (1964:5).

Managers who lack the skill needed to find those opportunities that will yield the greatest results, not uncommonly spend their time doing the wrong things. But opportunity-finding skill, like problem-finding skill, must be acquired through direct personal experience on the job.

This is not to say that the techniques of opportunity finding and problem finding cannot be taught in formal management education programs, even though they rarely are. But the behavior required to use these techniques successfully can be developed only through actual practice.

A manager cannot learn how to find opportunities or problems without doing it. The doing is essential to the learning. Lectures, case discussions, or text books alone are of limited value in developing ability to find opportunities and problems. Guided practice in finding them in real business situations is the only method that will make a manager skillful in identifying the right things to do.

Natural Management Style

Opportunities are not exploited and problems are not solved, however, until someone takes action and gets the desired results. Managers who are unable to produce effective results on the job invariably fail to build successful careers. But they cannot learn what they most need to know either by studying modern management theories or by discussing in the classroom what someone else should do to get results.

Management is a highly individualized art. What style works well for one manager in a particular situation may not produce the desired results for another manager in a similar situation, or even for the same manager in a different situation. There is no one best way for all managers to manage in all situations. Every manager must discover for himself, therefore, what works and what does not work for him in different situations. He cannot become effective merely by adopting the practices or the managerial style of someone else. He must develop his own natural style and follow practices that are consistent with his own personality.

What all managers need to learn is that to be successful they must manage in a way that is consistent with their unique personalities. When a manager "behaves in ways which do not fit his personality," as Rensis Likert's managerial research has shown, "his behavior is apt to communicate to his subordinates something quite different from what he intends. Subordinates usually view such behavior with suspicion and distrust" (1969:90).

Managers who adopt artificial styles or follow practices that are not consistent with their own personalities are likely not only to be distrusted, but also to be ineffective. It is the men who display the "greatest individuality in managerial behavior," as Edwin E. Ghiselli's studies of managerial talent show, who in general are the ones "judged to be best managers" (1969:236).

Managers rarely are taught how to manage in ways that are consistent with their own personalities. In many formal education and training programs, they are in fact taught that they must follow a prescribed set of practices and adopt either a "consultative" or "participative" style in order to get the "highest productivity, lowest costs, and best performance" (Likert, 1969:11).

The effectiveness of managers whose personalities do not fit these styles often is impaired and their development arrested. Those who adopt artificial styles typically are seen as counterfeit managers who lack individuality and natural styles of their own.

Managers who are taught by the case method of instruction learn that there is no one best way to manage and no one managerial style that is infallible. But unlike students of medicine, students of management rarely are exposed to "real" people or to "live" cases in programs conducted either in universities or in industry.

They study written case histories that describe problems or opportunities discovered by someone else, which they discuss, but do nothing about. What they learn about supervising other people is largely secondhand. Their knowledge is derived from the discussion of what someone else should do about the human problems of "paper people" whose emotional reactions, motives, and behavior have been described for them by scholars who may have observed and advised managers, but who usually have never taken responsibility for getting results in a business organization.

Since taking action and accepting responsibility for the consequences are not a part of their formal training, they neither discover for themselves what does—and what does not—work in practice nor develop a natural managerial style that is consistent with their own unique personalities. Managers cannot discover what practices are effective for them until they are in a position to decide for themselves what needs to be done in a specific situation, and to take responsibility both for getting it done and for the consequences of their actions.

Elton Mayo, whose thinking has had a profound impact on what managers are taught but not on how they are taught, observed a quarter of a century ago that studies in the social sciences do not develop any "skill that is directly useful in human situations" (1945:19). He added that he did not believe a useful skill could be developed until a person takes "responsibility for what happens in particular human situations—individual or group. A good bridge player does not merely conduct post mortem discussions of the play in a hand of contract; he takes responsibility for playing it" (p. 32).

Experience is the key to the practitioner's skill. And until a manager learns from his own firsthand experience on the job how to take action and how to gain the willing cooperation of others in achieving desired results, he is not likely to advance very far up the managerial ladder.

NEEDED CHARACTERISTICS

Although there are no born natural leaders, relatively few men ever develop into effective managers or executives. Most, in fact, fail to learn even from their own experience what they need to know to manage other people successfully. What, then, are the characteristics of men who learn to manage effectively?

The answer to the question consists of three ingredients: (1) the need to manage, (2) the need for power, and (3) the capacity for empathy. In this section of the article, I shall discuss each of these characteristics in some detail.

The Need to Manage

This first part of the answer to the question is deceptively simple: only those men who have a strong desire to influence the performance of others and who get genuine satisfaction from doing so can learn to manage effectively. No man is likely to learn how unless he really wants to take responsibility for the productivity of others, and enjoys developing and stimulating them to achieve better results.

Many men who aspire to high-level managerial positions are not motivated to manage. They are motivated to earn high salaries and to attain high status, but they are not motivated to get effective results through others. They expect to gain great satisfaction from the income and prestige associated with executive positions in important enterprises, but they do not expect to gain much satisfaction from the achievements of their subordinates. Although their aspirations are high, their motivation to supervise other people is low.

A major reason why highly educated and ambitious men do not learn how to develop successful managerial careers is that they lack the "will to manage." The "*way* to manage," as Marvin Bower has observed, usually can be found if there is the "*will* to manage." But if a person lacks the desire, he "will not devote the time, energy, and thought required to find the way to manage" (1966:6).

No one is likely to sustain for long the effort required to get high productivity from others unless he has a strong psychological need to influence their performance. The need to manage is a crucial factor, therefore, in determining whether a person will learn and apply in practice what is necessary to get effective results on the job.

High grades in school and outstanding performance as an accountant, an engineer, or a salesman reveal how able and willing a person is to perform tasks he has been assigned. But an outstanding record as an individual performer does not indicate whether that person is able or willing to get other people to excel at the same tasks. Outstanding scholars often make poor teachers, excellent engineers often are unable to supervise the work of other engineers, and successful salesmen often are ineffective sales managers.

Indeed, men who are outstanding individual performers not uncommonly become "do-it-yourself" managers. Although they are able and willing to do the job themselves, they lack the motivation and temperament to get it done by others. They may excel as individual performers and may even have good records as first-line managers. But they rarely advance far up the organizational hierarchy because, no matter how hard they try, they cannot make up through their own efforts for mediocre or poor performance by large numbers of subordinates.

Universities and business organizations that select managerial candidates on the basis of their records as individual performers often pick the wrong men to develop as managers. These men may get satisfaction from their own outstanding performance, but unless they are able to improve the productivity of other people, they are not likely to become successful managers.

Fewer and fewer men who hold advanced degrees in management want to take responsibility for getting results through others. More and more of them are attracted to jobs that permit them to act in the detached role of the consultant or specialized expert, a role described by John W. Gardner (1965) as the one preferred increasingly by university graduates. . . .

As Charlie Brown prophetically observed in a "Peanuts" cartoon strip in which he is standing on the pitcher's mound surrounded by his players, all of whom are telling him what to do at a critical point in a baseball game: "The world is filled with people who are anxious to act in an advisory capacity." Educational institutions are turning out scholars, scientists, and experts who are anxious to act as advisers, but they are producing few men who are eager to lead or take responsibility for the performance of others.

Most management graduates prefer staff positions in headquarters to line positions in the field or factory. More and more of them want jobs that will enable them to use their analytical ability rather than their supervisory ability. Fewer and fewer are willing to make the sacrifices required to learn management from the bottom up; increasingly, they hope to step in at the top from positions where they observe, analyze, and advise but do not have personal responsibility for results. Their aspirations are high, but their need to take responsibility for the productivity of other people is low.

The tendency for men who hold advanced degrees in management to take staff jobs and to stay in these positions too long makes it difficult for them to develop the supervisory skills they need to advance within their companies. Men who fail to gain direct experience as line managers in the first few years of their careers commonly do not acquire the capabilities they need to manage other managers and to sustain their upward progress past middle age.

"A man who performs nonmanagerial tasks five years or more," as Jennings discovered, "has a decidedly greater improbability of becoming a high wage earner. High salaries are being paid to manage managers (1967:15). This may well explain in part why the median salaries of Harvard Business School graduates plateau just at the time they might be expected to move up into the ranks of top management.

The Need for Power

Psychologists once believed that the motive that caused men to strive to attain high-level managerial positions was the "need for achievement." But now they believe it is the "need for power," which is the second part of the answer to the question: What are the characteristics of men who learn to manage effectively? . . .

Power seekers can be counted on to strive hard to reach positions where they can exercise authority over large numbers of people. Individual performers who lack this drive are not likely to act in ways that will enable them to advance far up the managerial ladder. They usually scorn company politics and devote their energies to other types of activities that are more satisfying to them. But, to prevail in the competitive struggle to attain and hold high-level positions in management, a person's desire for prestige and high income must be reinforced by the satisfaction he gets or expects to get from exercising the power and authority of a high office.

The competitive battle to advance within an organization, as Levinson points out, is much like playing "King of the Hill" (1969:53). Unless a person enjoys playing that game, he is likely to tire of it and give up the struggle for control of the top of the hill. The power game is a part of management, and it is played best by those who enjoy it most.

The power drive that carries men to the top also accounts for their tendency to use authoritative rather than consultative or participative methods of management. But to expect otherwise is not realistic. Few men who strive hard to gain and hold positions of power can be expected to be permissive, particularly if their authority is challenged.

Since their satisfaction comes from the exercise of authority, they are not likely to share much of it with lower-level managers who eventually will replace them, even though most high-level executives try diligently to avoid the appearance of being authoritarian. It is equally natural for ambitious lower-level managers who have a high need for power themselves to believe that better results would be achieved if top management shared more authority with them, even though they, in turn, do not share much of it with their subordinates.

One of the least rational acts of business organizations is that of hiring managers who have a high need to exercise authority, and then teaching them that authoritative methods are wrong and that they should be consultative or participative. It is a serious mistake to teach managers that they should adopt styles that are artificial and inconsistent with their unique personalities. Yet this is precisely what a large number of business organizations are doing; and it explains, in part, why their management development programs are not effective.

What managerial aspirants should be taught is how to exercise their authority in a way that is appropriate to the characteristics of the situation and the people involved. Above all, they need to learn that the real source of their power is their own knowledge and skill, and the strength of their own personalities, not the authority conferred on them by their positions. They need to know that overreliance on the traditional authority of their official positions is likely to be fatal to their career aspirations because the effectiveness of this kind of authority is declining everywhere —in the home, in the church, and in the state as well as in business.

More than authority to hire, promote, and fire is required to get superior results from most subordinates. To be effective, managers must possess the authority that comes with knowledge and skill, and be able to exercise the charismatic authority that is derived from their own personalities.

When they lack the knowledge or skill required to perform the work, they need to know how to share their traditional authority with those who know what has to be done to get results. When they lack the charisma needed to get the willing cooperation of those on whom they depend for performance, they must be able to share their traditional authority with the informal leaders of the group, if any exist.

But when they know what has to be done and have the skill and personality to get it done, they must exercise their traditional authority in whatever way is necessary to get the results they desire. Since a leader cannot avoid the exercise of authority, he must understand the nature and limitations of it, and be able to use it in an appropriate manner. Equally important, he must avoid trying to exercise authority he does not, in fact, possess.

The Capacity for Empathy

Mark Van Doren once observed that an educated man is one "who is able to use the intellect he was born with: the intellect, and whatever else is important" (1967:13). At the top of the list of "whatever else is important" is the third characteristic necessary in order to manage other people successfully. Namely, it is the capacity for empathy or the ability to cope with the emotional reactions that inevitably occur when people work together in an organization.

Many men who have more than enough abstract intelligence to learn the methods and techniques of management fail because their affinity with other people is almost entirely intellectual or cognitive. They may have "intellectual empathy" but may not be able to sense or identify the unverbalized emotional feelings which strongly influence human behavior (Paul, 1967:155). They are emotion-blind just as some men are color-blind.

Such men lack what Normal L. Paul describes as "affective empathy" (p. 155). And since they cannot recognize unexpressed emotional feelings, they are unable to learn from their own experience how to cope with the emotional reactions that are crucial in gaining the willing cooperation of other people.

Many men who hold advanced degrees in management are emotion-blind. As Schein has found, they often are "mired in the code of rationality" and, as a consequence, "undergo a rude shock" on their first jobs (p. 92). After interviewing dozens of recent graduates of the Sloan School of Management at MIT, Schein reported that "they talk like logical men who have stumbled into a cell of irrational souls," and he added,

> At an emotional level, ex-students resent the human emotions that make a company untidy. . . . [Few] can accept without pain the reality of the organization's human side. Most try to wish it away, rather than work in and around it. . . . If a graduate happens to have the capacity to accept, maybe to love, human organization, this gift seems directly related to his potential as a manager or executive" (p. 90).

Whether managers can be taught in the classroom how to cope with human emotions is a moot point. There is little reason to believe that what is now taught in psychology classes, human relations seminars, and sensitivity training programs is of much help to men who are "mired in the code of rationality" and who lack "affective empathy."

Objective research has shown that efforts to sensitize supervisors to the feelings of others not only often have failed to improve performance, but in some cases have made the situation worse than it was before (see Fleishmann et al., 1955). Supervisors who are unable "to tune in empathically" on the emotional feelings aroused on the job are not likely to improve their ability to emphathize with others in the classroom (Paul, pp. 150–157).

Indeed, extended classroom discussions about what other people should do to cope with emotional situations may well inhibit rather than stimulate the development of the ability of managers to cope with the emotional reactions they experience on the job.

CONCLUSION

Many highly intelligent and ambitious men are not learning from either their formal education or their own experience what they most need to know to build successful careers in management.

Their failure is due, in part, to the fact that many crucial managerial tasks are not taught in management education programs but are left to be learned on the job, where few managers ever master them because no one teaches them how. It also is due, in part, to the fact that what takes place in the classroom often is mis-education that inhibits their ability to learn from their experience. Commonly, they learn theories of management that cannot be applied successfully in practice, a limitation many of them discover only through the direct experience of becoming a line executive and meeting personally the problems involved.

Some men become confused about the exercise of authority because they are taught only about the traditional authority a manager derives from his official position—a type of authority that is declining in effectiveness everywhere. A great many become innoculated with an "antileadership vaccine" that arouses within them intense negative feelings about authoritarian leaders, even though a leader cannot avoid the exercise of authority any more than he can avoid the responsibility for what happens to his organization.

Since these highly educated men do not learn how to exercise authority derived from their own knowledge and skill or from the charisma of their own personalities, more and more of them avoid responsibility for the productivity of others by taking jobs that enable them to act in the detached role of the consultant or specialized expert. Still others impair their effectiveness by adopting artificial managerial styles that are not consistent with their own unique personalities but give them the appearance of being "consultative" or "participative," an image they believe is helpful to their advancement up the managerial ladder.

Some managers who have the intelligence required to learn what they need to know fail because they lack "whatever else is important," especially "affective empathy" and the need to develop and stimulate the productivity of other people. But the main reason many highly educated men do not build successful managerial careers is that they are not able to learn from their own firsthand experience what they need to know to gain the willing cooperation of other people. Since they have not learned how to observe their environment firsthand or to assess feedback from their actions, they are poorly prepared to learn and grow as they gain experience.

Alfred North Whitehead once observed that "the secondhandedness of the learned world is the secret of its mediocrity" (Whitehead, 1929:79). Until managerial aspirants are taught to learn from their own firsthand experience, formal management education will remain secondhanded. And its secondhandedness is the real reason why the well-educated manager is a myth.

3-1

PILKINGTON BROTHERS
P.L.C.

In 1826 William Pilkington—son of a surgeon cum wine and spirit merchant cum apothecary—joined with two well-known glassmakers to form the St. Helen's Crown Glass Company and later Pilkington Brothers, Ltd. (1894). The company remained privately held until 1970 when it offered some 5.7 million shares (10%) of its stock to the public. Then in 1973, after being honored as British Businessman of the Year, (Sir Harry) Lord Pilkington—the fourth generation direct descendant of the founder to head the company—retired. From 1974–1981 the company's next chairman Sir Alastair Pilkington—scientist, inventor, professional manager, but not a lineal descendant of the ownership group—led the company's transition to a diversified worldwide, technology leading, glass company. In 1981 when Sir Alastair stepped down as CEO, Pilkington's new management team had to design its strategies for a vastly changed world.

EARLY HISTORY

In 1894 Pilkington was the only British producer of both plate and sheet (window) glass, and it had diversified into other flat glasses. Because plate glass processes were so capital intensive, manufacturing was centralized at Pilkington's original St. Helens location, where all needed raw materials—coal, limestone, dolomite, alkali, and iron-free sand—were abundant within reasonable distance.

Case copyright © 1989 by James Brian Quinn. Research assistant—Allie J. Quinn.

The generous support of the International Management Institute, Geneva, Switzerland, is gratefully acknowledged. The generous cooperation of Pilkington Brothers is gratefully acknowledged.

The basic processes for making flat glass had remained substantially the same from the 1700s to the early 1900s. *Sheet* glass was drawn into a ribbon through a (slotted) block floating on the surface of the melted glass inside a glass furnace. The ribbon passed vertically upward through asbestos roller, a lehr which relieved stresses in the glass, and then into a cutting room where the cooled, hardened glass was cut and stacked. The process produced a good inexpensive window glass, but output was limited to relatively thin sheets of glass, subject to inhomogeneities and optical distortion.[1]

These properties were unacceptable for mirrors, automobile windows, and the large windows increasingly used for retail displays and architectural effects. *Plate* glass was required to meet these demands. To make plate, molten glass was rolled into a plate with a waffled surface and then, in a discontinuous process, was ground and polished until both surfaces were smooth and parallel. Grinding required several stages using a series of very large grinding wheels—or disks—with successively finer abrasive surfaces. Polishing was done with buffers and various powdered rouges. Gigantic factories and huge process investments were required. Because of this, plate manufacture slowly became concentrated in the hands of a few producers. And even these could survive only in countries with large markets.

Then in the early 1920s Ford Motor Company began to develop a flow process for continuous rolling of plate. At the same time, and quite independently, Pilkington had developed a continuous grinding process to replace the disk process. Pilkington stepped in to provide the needed technical expertise, joined its development capabilities with Ford, and in 1923—combining continuous rolling with continuous grinding—installed the industry's first continuous plate manufacturing process (at St. Helens). Twelve years later Pilkington pioneered a machine (the "twin") to grind both sides of a plate glass ribbon simultaneously. The machine ranked as one of the world's finest examples of large scale precision engineering and gave Pilkington world technological leadership in the manufacture of quality flat glass.

FLOAT GLASS DEVELOPMENT

Even the twin grinding process for making plate had substantial drawbacks. Tremendous equipment investments (of $30–$40 million) and sizable markets were required to support a single glass furnace and its associated plate line. Costs of operating and maintaining a grinding and polishing line were very high. Up to 800 people were necessary to keep a line operating continuously. Some 15–20% of the glass ribbon was ground away in the finishing processes. A plant discharged enough abrasives, polishing rouges, and glass to build waste mountains reminding one of the slag heaps of the steel industry. Plants were hundreds of yards long. The noise level of grinders, transfer machinery, and crashing cullet was formidable. And repairs often required costly shut downs or dangerous work in the grinding pits underneath the glass ribbon.

Many dreamed of combining the continuous flow, fire polish, and inexpensiveness of sheet with the distortion-free quality of polished plate. But the secret eluded the industry until the late 1950s when Lionel Alexander Bethune (Alastair) Pilkington* developed the float glass process. An intense and impatient but thor-

---

* Later Sir Alastair Pilkington, F.R.S.

oughly gracious man, Alastair had joined the company in 1947 after graduation from Cambridge with a degree in mechanical engineering and service in the Royal Artillery in World War II. He started in the sheet works technical development group, moved into plate works technical development, and by 1949 was production manager at the Doncaster works. At Doncaster Sir Alastair started some original experimental work involving interactions of glass and molten metals.

The Invention

Sir Alastair later described how he arrived at the basic idea for float glass:

> One quickly became aware that grinding and polishing was an extremely cumbersome way of making glass free from distortion. [You could see] that the window glass process produced a beautiful surface, which glass naturally has because it is a liquid. What you wanted to do was preserve the natural brilliance of molten glass and form it into a ribbon which was free from distortion. If you could do this you would have done something quite important. . . . A large part of innovation is, in fact, becoming aware of what is really desirable. [Then you] are ready in your mind to germinate the seed of a new idea. . . . You also must want to invent. This is terribly important. I don't know why, but I have always wanted to invent something.
>
> I was able to do some thinking about that time [June 1952] because I was bored. I had been very busy [in production operations at Doncaster and had been] brought back to work under the Technical Director . . . I was actually consciously bored. This gave me time to think about the problem. . . . The idea came to me when I was helping my wife to wash up [dishes], but it had nothing to do with the act of washing up. It was just one of those moments when your mind is able to think and then it was sort of "bang"—like that. Indeed the final solution was very similar to the original idea, though it was an awful long journey from the concept to making salable glass.[2]

Stage I—Experimentation

Alastair quickly drew up some sketches of the new process, which the Engineering Development Group converted into working drawings. The Board gave verbal approval to the project, and within three months a $70,000 pilot plant was built and operational. Fortunately some technical people were available for reassignment just then. Alastair—with a team of several engineers, a foreman, and workman sworn to secrecy—essentially knocked a hole in the side of a remote rolled glass furnace and tried to pour molten glass onto a bed of molten tin. He described this stage as follows:

> We got the cheapest flow of glass we could find in the company. At the earliest possible moment we made a box for the molten tin. The first one leaked like a sieve because we heated the tin by immersed tubes. We had to make gland joints at the end, and I can tell you molten tin goes through any gland joint. It just poured all over the ground. But it showed you could take a ribbon of glass, pass it over tin, at a relatively high temperature, and produce bright parallel surfaces. [The only answer] we wanted out of Stage I was: did the process look promising? Or would we crash up against some basic chemical or physical laws which would prevent the process from operating.
>
> The Pilkington Board decided to give the project the highest possible priority so that either success or failure would be decided as early as possible. My own greatest fear was that float would drag on for years being a near success; interesting enough to justify further work but never quite achieving satisfactory results.[3]

After some six months it appeared that it would be feasible to "fire finish" glass by floating it on a bath of molten tin. Once the process could be properly controlled, the bottom surface of the glass should be dead flat because it rested on the flat surface of the liquid tin. Natural forces of gravity and surface tension would tend to make the top surface flat too. And the glass should be of uniform thickness, with both surfaces completely parallel. There appeared to be no insurmountable barriers to achieving such results. But the process was far from producing commercial quality glass.

Still an important choice—that of tin as the support medium—had been made and was never changed. Only gallium, indium, and tin met the strict physical requirements for the process. The support medium had to be liquid from 1100°F to over 1900°F, the range necessary for melting and forming glass. The medium had to be more dense than glass. It needed a low vapor pressure at the 1900° end of the temperature range to avoid excess vaporization and contamination of the glass or the process. Finally the medium must not chemically combine with the glass during processing and had to be available at a reasonable price. Tin was the most attractive alternative on almost all counts. (See Exhibit 1A.)

EXHIBIT 1

A. Criteria Determining the Choice of a Support Metal for the Float Bath

	Melting Point °C	Boiling Point °C	Estimated Density at 1050°C g cm^{-3}	Vapour Pressure at 1027°C Torr
Required	<600	>1050	>2.5	<0.1
Bismuth	271	1680	9.1	27
Gallium	30	2420	5.5	7.6×10^{-3}
Indium	156	2075	6.5	7.9×10^{-2}
Lithium	179	1329	0.5	55
Lead	328	1740	9.8	1.9
Thallium	303	1460	10.9	16
Tin	232	2623	6.5	1.9×10^{-4}

B. The Roller Pouring Process

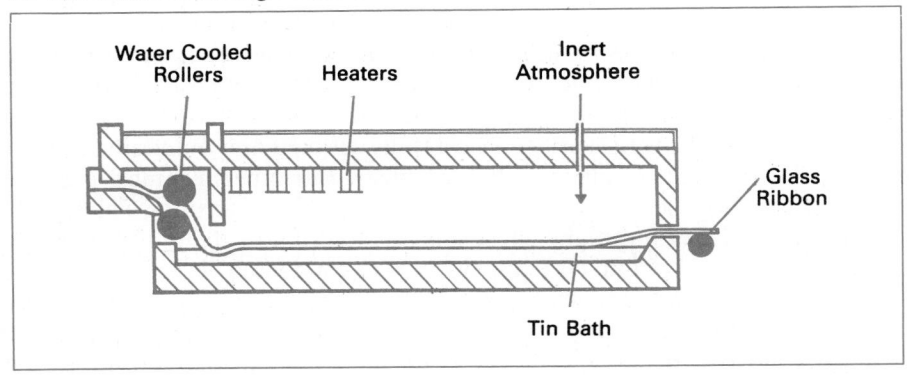

EXHIBIT 1
(Continued)

C. Direct Pouring with Spout Dipped Into the Tin Bath

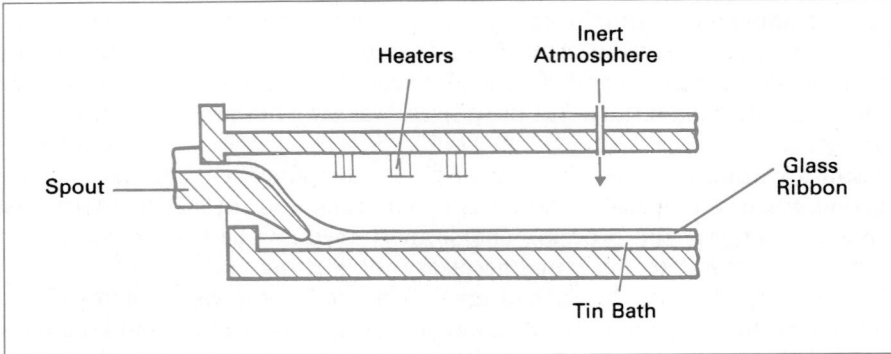

D. Direct Pouring with a Free Fall From the Spout

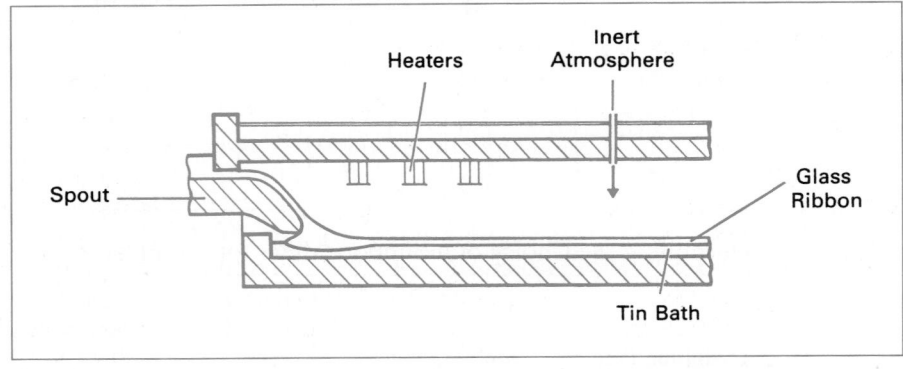

Source: L. A. B. Pilkington, "Review Lecture: The Float Glass Process," The Royal Society, February 13, 1969. Reproduced by special permission.

Stage II—Pilot Plants

Stage II was to make a ribbon 12″ wide under controlled atmospheric conditions. The experimental team hoped to learn more about controlling the quality of the glass. A new pilot plant was built in early 1954 to allow long enough runs to analyze and hopefully correct faults in the process. But technological problems were formidable. Upon exposure to the atmosphere the tin oxidized and produced a crystalline scale on the glass' surface. A carefully selected and maintained inert atmosphere slowly began to alleviate this problem. But other technical challenges rose to take its place. Because of the company's expertise in forming a glass ribbon through rollers, the team initially chose this method to flow the molten glass onto the tin surface. (See Exhibit 1B.) But tin vapors condensed on the water cooled rollers, which then imparted surface imperfections to the tin. Unless the tin was extremely pure it also reacted with the glass. Ultimately the team had to purify the tin well beyond the highest specifications for laboratory quality tin. Finally, the glass source, a rolled glass furnace for making patterned glass, did not provide molten glass of sufficient quality to judge just how well the process was working. Some $46,000 was charged against revenues for the 12″ experimental line, but no commercial quality glass was produced.

Still, progress was encouraging, and the team came upon one substantial bit of good fortune. When the glass was held for one minute at the 1900°F temperature needed to eliminate its surface irregularities, a combination of surface tension and gravity effects caused it to form at an equilibrium thickness of 7 mm (0.275″). By applying a tractive force from the annealing kiln (lehr) the glass might be thinned to 6.5 mm and sold as nominal $\frac{1}{4}$″ glass. As Sir Alastair later said, "This was a fantastic stroke of luck." Some 60% of Pilkington's plate sales at that time were in the $\frac{1}{4}$″ thickness.

In June 1953, upon the retirement of Mr. J. Meikle (former senior production director), Alastair Pilkington at age 33 became head of Pilkington's plate production and a subdirector of the company. He also continued to head the float glass experimental team. Despite the lack of progress in producing commercial quality glass, the board continued its confidence in the project, and in fall 1954 agreed to build a new pilot plant capable of producing a 30″ ribbon of glass. This experimental line was designed and built in the incredibly short span of only 3 months at a cost of $140,000. Molten glass for the line came from the same rolled plate tank as before. The glass made by the process was better than sheet for distortion, but its bubble count would have made it unsalable as plate.

Although roller forming of the glass into a ribbon had appeared more favorable at the outset, the development team continued a parallel project on the alternative possibility of pouring the glass directly onto tin. This approach would avoid roller contamination, but in experimental work tin compounds formed to contaminate the glass. Other major problems of glass flow, ribbon formation, and oxygen and sulfur contamination also persisted. These and high bubble counts from the rolled plate source kept the glass from approaching commercial quality. Nevertheless the technical team's enthusiasm and morale were very high. Sir Alastair said, "It was almost a crusade. Chaps were literally taken off on stretchers from heat exhaustion, yet came back for more. . . . We all thought the major faults in the glass were due to the glass source, not to the float process."

About this time the Board came to a very important decision. Float glass would only be launched on the world if it could replace plate glass. If float merely provided an improved sheet glass, it would occupy a peculiar position between two glasses with well-established positions, one of which (sheet) had very low margins. In describing this decision Sir Alastair said:

The forum for the decision was the Executive Committee of the Board. I was clearly a party to the decision and remember the discussions, but it is difficult to locate an exact moment when the decision was made. It was sometime during the discussions about whether to put down a production scale plant. There were no detailed calculations of such things as the ultimate capital implications of the process or its effects on our overall capital structure. Nevertheless, over a period of time a consensus crystallized with great clarity. This evolved from a series of formal and informal discussions among the members of the Executive Committee and the Board.

Once arrived at, I don't think anyone had any doubt this was the right decision. On the other hand, as technical director I was very disturbed to be expected to make such a tremendous jump forward in one enormous leap. It would have been easier for the technical group to learn about the process while making a better quality of sheet, then launch ourselves up the ladder from sheet to plate.

By April 1955 the three small pilot facilities had cost the company some $1.5 million. At this time Alastair Pilkington presented the Board a requisition for another $1.96 million to modify a redundant plate glass furnace and go to a full-scale production line capable of producing a 100″ ribbon. On it he hoped to achieve float glass of commercial quality. The cost of operating this full scale line would be £100,000 ($280,000) per month.

At that time 3 mm sheet glass sold for 3.34 pence (3.9¢) per ft^2, while 6 mm plate sold for 21.28 pence (24.9¢) per ft^2. Calculations showed the cost of float, if successful, would be closer to sheet than to plate. Sir Alastair later recalled:

> The early tests had been encouraging on surface quality and parallelism. But we didn't draw up any PERT charts or statements of probability. Nor did we run out detailed financial figures other than project costs. We knew if we could bring it through it would certainly be a world beater. . . . I suppose one should be able to face reality about a major development. But the reality may be difficult to bear in the early stages. You have to live it a bit from year to year.
>
> In the case of float, the figures are intriguing. It eventually took float 12 years to break even on cash flows. At one time it had a negative cash flow of £7 million ($19.6 million). Yet float was a commercial success immediately after we had solved its process problems. That's just how long it takes. If you went to an accountant and said, "I've got a great idea to create a massive negative cash flow for certain, and it may—if it's a great success—break even on its cash flows in 12 years," you wouldn't find many accountants who'd say "that's exactly what I want."
>
> But you can't look at development only on the basis of cash flows. If your company never does undertake major projects, then your standing is much lower. Some companies make things happen. They take really strategic decisions. Others aren't prepared to take big risks to [possibly] achieve great rewards.

The Board approved the expenditure, and Alastair's team modified an existing plate glass line at the Cowley Hill works. Cowley Hill people were used to change. Many had seen continuous rolling, continuous grinding and polishing, and twin grinding introduced. But the 100″ line immediately encountered enormous troubles. Many of the faults the team had attributed to the poor quality glass source on the 30″ line were actually caused by the float process. The controlled atmosphere then in use still did not maintain a clean glass-tin interface. But the biggest problems occurred in transferring the molten glass onto the tin. Contamination and bubbles plagued the process. Tin oxide condensed on the water cooled surfaces of the rollers metering the glass onto the tin, and this became imprinted on the glass surface. After some time the team made the momentous decision to move to direct pouring, even though this process was still unproved.[4]

In the early experiments with direct pouring the refractory spout dipped into the tin to provide a smooth glass contact. (See Exhibit 1C.) The chemical erosion on the refractory spout at the glass/tin interface was very rapid and contaminated the process. Glass that had been in touch with the refractory spout and then touched the tin bath created optical distortions called "music lines" in the glass. Removing the spout from the tin and pouring with a "free fall" of glass cured the interface wear problem. (See Exhibit 1D.) But the "music lines" doggedly persisted. Finally the team understood the scientific problems involved and made some key inventions to keep glass which touched the spout from contaminating the whole ribbon.

The team attacked each problem one at a time even though the process might be producing unsalable glass for a half dozen reasons at once. While they slowly solved other contamination problems, bubbles continued to appear in the glass. For 14 months the 100″ line ran 24 hours per day producing useless glass. Every month Alastair had to go to the Board to request another £100,000 ($280,000) to continue. He says of this period, "One of my records which will never be beaten is that of making more continuously unsalable glass than anyone in the history of the glass industry."

As technical director, Alastair discussed progress three times daily with the development team. Production executives in the plant were kept well informed. "We wanted the people who would operate the process to welcome it, not have it landed on them," said Sir Alastair. In addition, each morning Alastair would meet with the chief project engineer, Barradell Smith, to lay out strategy for the day:

> I took him away from the noise of crashing cullet so he could have a chance to think. A large pilot plant running 24 hours a day creates great stress and urgency. Glass making goes on around the clock; it never lets up. The heat and crashing glass is unbelievably disconcerting. We would discuss results, what was needed ahead, how the morale of the people was holding up. Every month I would write up a project report for the Board and ask for another £100,000. For 7 years it was an apologia as to why we weren't making salable glass, trying to explain the innumerable faults which occurred. But no single fault persisted. This is why we went ahead. When they would ask, "Can you make salable glass?" I would answer: "I don't know, but nothing has proved it's impossible." I couldn't recommend that we stop, because we had no reason to stop.
>
> The Board was remarkably understanding throughout all this. But it was very difficult for me at times. As the development leader I had to be an optimist and see problems as challenges to be overcome. I think this is crucial to the success of any development. As a Board member I had to be cold, analytical, and objective. It was hard to fulfill both roles.[5]

Magic and Agony

Finally a magical day came. In mid-1958, the process suddenly made its first salable glass. Unknown to the development team an accident had gone the right way for them. The pouring spout structure was in poor condition. Finally the spout's back broke, and the structure sagged badly in the middle. The bubbles which had plagued the process for 14 long months miraculously disappeared. The result was a beautiful plate of glass, which now came pouring off the line at the rate of roughly a thousand tons a week.

Fortunately, Pilkington could dispose of this vast outpouring. It quickly made arrangements with Triplex—in which Pilkington then owned a substantial interest—to sell the glass as windshields to British automotive companies. Triplex first tested the glass to ensure that it met their own strict standards. Then, because the surface characteristics of float plate differed slightly from those of ground plate, Triplex and Pilkington also let a few key procurement and quality control people in the automotive industry know that they were using "a new process." Otherwise the nature of the process was entirely secret. Pilkington actually sold over a million square feet of float glass before it publicly announced the process in January 1959. "One thing we were good at was security," said Sir Alastair. "People easily fail to understand that the greatest secret about a new process is not how to do it, but that it can be done." The process was a complete surprise to the industry. Even after the announcement, there were skeptics in other companies who wouldn't believe what had been accomplished.

Later in 1959 the float line was shut down for long overdue maintenance. The line was then carefully rebuilt with all that had been learned from the experimental line. There was agonizing disappointment when the new line was started up. The bubbles and crystals once again appeared. For several more months the team traced down every possible cause of the problem. Using a model in which silicone oil represented the glass and lead nitrate took the place of tin, they identified certain factors associated with the broken spout as keys to success. With new knowledge of the process the development team both captured the good features of the broken spout and designed a way to feed any contaminated glass to the edges of the ribbon. Although much more work was necessary, the process ultimately became self-cleaning and could run continuously for years without a shutdown for repairs.

The company had spent some £7.5 million ($21 million) over seven years' time. And it had chewed up more than 100,000 tons of glass. But in late 1959 Pilkington could make a glass of quality suitable for the market.

A STRATEGY FOR FLOAT

In October 1958 when the 100″ line was just beginning to produce salable plate, the Board formed a Directors Flat Glass Committee "to consider the broad issues of flat glass policy both in the present and the future." The committee* discussed all aspects of flat (rolled, sheet, wired, plate, etc) glass strategy worldwide, but by far the most important issue was float.

The Directors Flat Glass Committee tried to raise all the key issues about float. How should Pilkington use its technological advantage? What would its impact be on existing lines, competition, investments? How would float affect exports, employment, facilities, depreciation and tax structures, and so on? Not many detailed staff or financial projections were involved at this stage. Instead the Committee dominantly tried to deal in broad concepts, to identify alternate routes, and think through the potential consequences of each route for some ten years ahead. Sir Alastair later said, "You would be surprised how it sharpens your mind to be told you are only to think about the future." Members consciously tried to bring out different sides of each issue. At one stage, the Committee even hired a second patent attorney, gave him three of the people most knowledgeable about float, and invited him to attack the patent prepared (but not yet submitted) by the company's regular patent counsel. This helped sharpen and strengthen the ultimate application.

An interesting part of the deliberation was a series of process improvements made in the sheet glass division. Goaded by process on float, sheet glass engineers found a number of ways to improve the quality and lower the cost of their processes. In fact, for a while, the sheet and float glass teams were actively in competition with each other. The Directors Flat Glass Committee had to weigh the potential impact of these and future changes in sheet and plate technology.

They quickly agreed that float would surpass sheet's quality, but that it would not be sufficiently better than existing plate to demand a premium price because of its quality. On the other hand, a float line would ultimately more than halve labor requirements; it would lower energy costs by about 50%; the 15–25% of glass

---

* The Committee was composed of all the executive directors associated with float glass: Sir Harry (Lord) Pilkington, Arthur Pilkington, Alastair Pilkington, J. B. Watt, and D. V. Phelps.

ground away in earlier processes would be saved, as would be the cost of abrasives and rouges; equipment investment would be about one-third the (then) $40 million cost of a conventional line; production space requirements would drop by over 50%; and process interruption costs would virtually disappear. The Committee could not forecast the exact dimensions of these advantages. But it was clear that the process, if successful, would substantially lower existing plate costs. One director even predicted that float would be cost competitive with sheet by 1967–1968, but this opinion was not widely shared.

DECISION POINT

What should Pilkington's introduction strategy be? Should it license anyone? If so, whom? In what order? If not, how should it exploit float? What should have been the key considerations?

PATENTS AND LICENSING

Pilkington's goal was to see that float occupied its "right place" in the market place, to strengthen Pilkington's own position as a manufacturer, and to consolidate and extend Pilkington's own manufacturing interests throughout the world. Lord Pilkington later described certain key aspects of the resulting strategy as follows:

> We had the great benefit of time to decide upon our strategy. A great deal was said about ethics: that it was not our job to deliberately deny any existing glass competitor the opportunity of living in competition with us. I don't think we were shortsighted or rapacious. . . . There was a great deal of investment worldwide in plate, and people needed to have time to write off this plant or convert over. The alternative was chaotic disruption of a great industry.

Eventually Pilkington decided to license and licensees quickly lined up, until by the mid-1960s substantially all plate manufacturers used the process and royalty income began to roll in to Pilkington. But licensing was not all a bed of roses. Sir Alastair described a chastening experience from this period:

> "In the early sixties I was summoned with great urgency to a licensee's plant where an incredible thing was happening. The whole float bath was bubbling like a saucepan of boiling water. A unit which is normally calmer than a millpond was apparently on the verge of volcanic eruption! [The glass itself resembled swiss cheese.] . . . We were absolutely stumped. We had never seen anything like it and had no immediate answer. . . . Eventually we found that a thermal pump had been created in the bath because of the size of the pores in the refractory brick from which the bath was built."[4] Once the refractory brick was replaced the bath quieted down immediately.

After 1962, despite such temporary setbacks, *every new* plate glass facility built in the world used the float process. By 1968 float costs had become competitive with sheet glass in certain thicknesses. But float had much superior quality, and sheet manufacturers began to deluge the company with license applications. Since there were 20 to 30 times as many sheet manufacturers as there were plate producers, this created important policy dilemmas for Pilkington.

By 1974 the float glass process had virtually replaced polished plate glass worldwide. The plate glass industry had invested over £400 million (approximately $1 billion) in the process. 23 manufacturers in 13 countries (including Russia) operated some 51 float plants under Pilkington licenses, and float costs were very sensitive to scale of operations. Plants had to product at least 2000 tons of glass per week to be economical, and modern plants produced 5000 T/wk. Many of the OPEC countries, possessing sand and fuel, wanted the process. But these and other developing countries did not have large enough national markets to support a plant.

Nevertheless, a long development process was required before float could make a full range of commercial thicknesses. By the mid-1970s float's thickness range was 2.3 mm to 25 mm, with other thicknesses being made experimentally. And float had become cost competitive with sheet in thinner sections. Through 1981 development and experimentation on float continued. Sir Alastair noted,

> Everytime you made a move, you needed to optimize the plant for that particular thickness, width, or speed. It was a long, long learning process. How does the tin flow? How does it return through the bath? How does the constantly changing viscosity of the glass interact with the process? I don't know how many times I heard people over the years say, "We're just about on the limits of speed, or thickness, or something." Most times I said, "Rubbish! What you really mean is you've got to learn more or invent a new technique. You've reached the limits of your experience, not fundamental scientific limits."

Float opened new realms of chemical challenges to Pilkington's glass technologists. For example, they learned to introduce metal ions into the top surface of float glass. During the float process these ions were electrically attracted toward the tin bath. This penetration created a tinted plate extremely valuable in architectural and automotive uses. The technique, called Electrofloat, allowed the process to be switched from clear to tinted glass and back again in a fraction of the time needed for other processes. In 1967, Pilkington's Triplex subsidiary began work on its "Ten-Twenty" laminated glass for automobile windshields. This special plate made up from panels of thin float glass with a plastic interlayer was designed to greatly reduce laceration injuries in accidents. Pilkington hoped it would replace much of the "toughened" glass used for windshields throughout the world. A special high strength, low weight, Ten-Twenty (10/20) was developed for advanced aircraft. This led to Triplex receiving the Queen's Award for Industry in 1974.

CONSOLIDATION AND DIVERSIFICATION

In 1929 Pilkington and Triplex—the largest British safety glass producer—had formed a joint company, Triplex Northern, to produce laminate glass. In 1955 Pilkington and Triplex Safety Glass agreed that the latter should acquire Pilkington's 51% interest in Triplex (Northern) for which Pilkington received a block of Triplex Safety Glass shares. After 1955 Pilkington purchased Triplex stock at a steady rate as it came on the market, until in February 1965, Triplex became a subsidiary.

By 1967 Triplex controlled 85–90% of the English automotive safety glass market. Its main competitor was British IndesTructo Glass (BIG), which was controlled by four major auto companies. In early 1967 Triplex discussed with BIG's controlling owners the mutual advantages of a merger. Triplex took over BIG, and terminated all production in BIG's works in July 1967. But Pilkington and Triplex agreed with the automobile companies and the British Board of Trade that they would at all times maintain adequate capacity to meet the users' forecast demands.

Through its acquisition of Chance Brothers (1951) Pilkington had extended its entry into optical glass. In 1957, the optical business of both companies was merged into the Chance-Pilkington Optical Works. In 1966 a further company, Pilkington Perkin-Elmer (later Pilkington P. E., Ltd.) was set up to develop and produce electro-optical systems including specialized glasses for laser optics.

1971 saw the formation of the Chance-Propper Company to manufacture microscope slides, medical, surgical and laboratory equipment. In addition to ophthalmic glasses and lens systems, Chance Brothers had also led the company into television tubes, decorative glassware, and glass tubing for the fluorescent and incandescent light fields. In 1974 Pilkington added the Michael Birch group—lens prescriptions, sunglasses, safety glasses, and a microfilm equipment company. In 1977–1978 it acquired Barr and Stroud, a U.K. maker of periscopes and precision defense products and SOLA, an Australian-based maker of plastic opthalmic lenses. But the Monopolies Commission blocked its bid for U.K. Optical, the dominant British supplier of spectacle frames and glass lenses. In 1980–1981, the electro-optical and opthalmic businesses (including Pilkington's successful light sensitive Reactolite spectacle) were thought to each have revenues of over £30 million.

Fiberglass Products

Chance had been making glass fibers near Glasgow since the late 1920s. Pilkington acquired an interest in this activity in 1938 and eventually purchased the company from Chance Brothers. The company, reorganized as Fiberglass Ltd. in 1962–1963, extended its operations in the United Kingdom and abroad. In 1971 Fiberglass Ltd. announced the development of Cem-FIL fiber, the first glass fiber capable of enduring for any period as a reinforcement of portland cement. This product, jointly developed with the British National Research Development Corporation (NRDC), offered the possibility of lightweight, high-strength, concrete construction techniques not hitherto possible. The glass provided the tensile strength concrete lacked, and it avoided the weight, bulk, and chemical-oxidation problems inherent in steel reinforcing. As an alkali resistant fiber, Cem-FIL could replace asbestos in many of its uses. The development was a major breakthrough in glass chemistry, but in 1981 was only slowly working its way into a conservative marketplace.

Many of these successful diversifications became substantial businesses. But none compared in tonnage with the flat glass field. Here specialized glasses using float were developed for endless new uses: tinted windows, light-sensitive panes, special high-impact safety glass for vehicles, electroconducting glass for deicing, and specialized glass for air conditioning uses all entered the market. Perhaps the greatest potential impact lay in architectural glasses. Glass plates could be hung or suspended together to provide a wall with uninterrupted visibility. Pilkington's Armourplate glass was developed for high impact uses like doors or squash court walls. And solar control or insulated glasses provided new opportunities for energy conservation in construction.

The company also had its failures, largely in the field of pressed glass operations. While some were relatively small—pavement lights, glass blocks for buildings, and battery boxes—in 1975 the company had to withdraw from the television tube glass market after considerable investment. A high level of Japanese tube imports and a U.K. recession were given as the primary causes for withdrawal.

But the biggest disappointment was the late 1970s commerical failure of 10/ 20 windshield glass. The glass removed about 98% of risk of lacerations or head injuries from automobile windshield accidents. When hit by an object, the glass broke into fine particles that literally did not cut. Yet the plastic interlayer was strong enough to prevent a body going through the screen, and flexible enough to minimize brain injury. Still Pilkington could not get auto manufacturers to pay the 15% premium price over ordinary safety glass that made it economic to produce 10/20. Safety was not a great selling point, and the oil price increase put a premium on lightness and consequent fuel economy. The manufacturers said they could not pass costs on to consumers. Sir Alastair commented, "The program was one of those clear technical successes, but a commercial failure—most disappointing to all of us."

Geographical Expansion

In 1946 Pilkington had no glass production facilities outside the United Kingdom except a partly owned activity in Argentina. The 1950s and 1960s saw a great international expansion abroad. In 1951 Canada and South Africa started sheet production, followed by India (1965), Australia (1963), and New Zealand (1964). Vasa, in Argentina, became a subsidiary. Safety glass plants opened in New Zealand (1953), Australia (1965), Rhodesia (1961). During the same period the company acquired interests in other companies in Nigeria (1964), Mexico (1965), South Africa (1965), Sweden (1968), and Venezuela (1973). By 1981 Pilkington had nine float plants in other countries. (See Exhibit 2.) It had 25,000 employees and £515 million in sales overseas versus 20,000 people and £377 million in sales in the United Kingdom. Approximately one-half of the company's net trading assets were outside the United Kingdom. Exhibit 2 summarizes Pilkington's production operations outside the United Kingdom.

MANAGEMENT STYLE CHANGES

Through the 1970s much of St. Helens depended on Pilkington for employment. And the Pilkington family was conscious of this trust. Young Pilkingtons were looked over carefully before they entered the company and, once in, were expected to work doubly hard. Family members developed personal contacts with employees by living in the town and visiting the works regularly. The company had provided pension funds and hospital services, long before these were common in industry. The family also built and endowed theaters and recreation clubs for its employees in St. Helens. There was a personal touch too. For a long while, retired employees had been given vegetable seeds for their gardens and coal to warm them during the harsh midland winters. The company threw an annual employee party complete with dog shows, parachute jumping, and the like which someone described as "the finest blowout north of London."

A strong sense of morality and responsibility pervaded the company. As one director said,

> I think certainly the moral side does weigh with the company. If one runs a business one is to some extent one's brother's keeper. I think the company would still regard itself as being in business for something more than just money making, in the sense that it takes long-term views, and a long-term view is obviously that you have to look

after your human capital as well as your money. It isn't just what you do this year that matters, but what you are working on that is going to bear fruit in ten years' time. It is important that the company is not only profitable, but also has a "heart."[6]

In the mid-1970s, there were some 15,000 people in the St. Helens "family," many of them new members. General Board members were seen less regularly at the works. And lines of communication from shop floor to top management began to seem much longer. Diversification had led to anomalies between workers in different jobs and places.[7] And small incidents sometimes caused irritations. In a small community like St. Helens, one of these suddenly—a man's paycheck had been miscalculated, an error that was quickly corrected—amplified into a strike in early 1970. When management's hurt and shock subsided, the company recovered and learned from the strike. There were more formal procedures for negotiations and wage structures. Industrial relations professionals were brought into the corporate offices of Pilkington. And both union and management groups said relations improved markedly after the confrontation.

Regimes Change

During this difficult period another matter which would vastly affect the company's future had been quietly resolved: Pilkington Brothers became a public company in 1970. As Lord Pilkington said, "Modern taxation makes it very difficult to either pass on the wealth you have accumulated or keep it in the company. And without a public market for the stock, death duties could place large individual shareholders in an impossible cash bind."

Lord Pilkington had originally intended to retire on his 65th birthday which occurred in April 1970, right in the middle of the strike. But it was agreed that he should stay in order to pilot the change from private to public status and should retire after the annual meeting in 1973, when Sir Alastair Pilkington became chairman for a period of distinguished leadership, ending in 1981.

Sir Alastair continued the important processes of professionalizing and decentralizing Pilkington's management. Of his era he said,

> I think the company started to take a much wider view of itself in the world—in processes, products, and geography. I think it moved much more consciously to feeling that it could think out the future it wished to have, define what it meant by success in the future, and then lay out a route toward it. The company moved from feeling that it would essentially deal with situations and opportunities as they arose. We felt that we should create the future, rather than react to external circumstances.
>
> I am very strong on people and on success definition. My own feeling is that unless you decide where you want to go, you never arrive there. I don't set goals for other people. That is one of their key jobs—to define their goals, define success. I set goals for myself. I will set goals for the company, but not for other people. I set the company goals in my own mind, and then they come out in discussions. But I don't sort of lay them down. I've never taken a major decision without consulting my colleagues. It would be unimaginable to me, unimaginable. I can't even see any point to it. Firstly, they help me make a better decision in most cases. But secondly, if they know about it and agree with it, they'll back it. Otherwise, they might challenge it, not openly, but subconsciously.

Throughout Alastair wanted to avoid diversifications or any other moves that led to mediocrity. He said, "I'm absolutely obsessional on the subject of excellence. If you are going to work on a worldwide basis, you must have excellence. One of our most important policy statements was that we would only take on things where we intended to match or lead the world's best performers."

The 1981 Situation

By 1981 the company had changed substantially. Like others in the industry, Pilkington's volume had grown throughout the world. Capacity expanded by a factor of 3 times from 1971 to 1981. See Exhibits 3 and 3A. Pilkington had large new facilities outside the United Kingdom in Germany, Sweden, Australia, and Mexico. While other glass companies conglomerated and diversified into almost anything, in 1980 Pilkington bought Germany's Flachglas for £141M. *The Paper Clip* described how the new partners matched up: Pilkington had sales of £629M for 1980 and 35,000 employees while Flachglas had sales (unconsolidated) of £219M for 1979 from raw glass (approximately 35%) insulating glass (25%), safety glass (25%), plastics and other (approximately 15%) with 7,900 employees. In justifying further acquisitions in the industry, Antony Pilkington, who took over as chairman from Sir Alastair said, "If you are technologically excellent, you can maintain your position in your chosen market. Glass is not as narrow a field as some imagine."

Both parties moved carefully into the merger which had taken 4 years from concept to reality. The specific opportunity ultimately arose when BSN-Gervais-Danone, a French food company, decided to sell a large part of its glass-making operations. Many bizarre twists accompanied the purchase in which Pilkington could not—for competitive reasons—even investigate the facilities it was about to buy. For example, at the last moment due to legal considerations Pilkington had to come up with £28 million extra to up the percentage of stock bought from 55 to 62%. Then Pilkington had to learn to deal with the dual board and labor representation structures of German companies. But benefits accrued within a few months as Flachglas profits helped offset Pilkington's U.K. trading losses and Pilkington found new work practices to improve the productivity of its domestic plants. One special aspect of the merger was the fit between Pilkington's strength in process research and Flachglas' strength in product development.[8] The acquisition made Pilkington the largest flat glass manufacturer in the world.

This degree of diversification had worked well. License fees and oversees operations—and importantly the Flachglas group's profits—had bolstered Pilkington's lagging fortunes during the sharp downturn in Britain's 1981–1982 economy. The company's U.K. problems were compounded by a flood of glass imports from Europe, and the worldwide recession of those years. Pilkington's share of the U.K. flat glass market plummeted from 80% to a little over two-thirds in 1981–1982.

The European market was rapidly being restructured. Guardian—one of the most efficient operators in the industry—built a new plant in Luxembourg, turning over its stocks 10 times a year and reportedly making 20% on its capital before interest. Asahi Glass of Japan took over BSN's losing Belgium and Dutch plants, and PPG bought its French units. The new structure is outlined in Exhibit 3A. Much capacity was added while glass industry work forces plummeted—down 4,000 for St. Gobain and 3,000 for Pilkington in 2 years. Asahi controlled 50% of Japan's glass industry and was as efficient as Guardian. But the marketplace for flat glass in this period was over 50% in building and 20% in automobiles, both industries depressed by high interest rates. Overall demand was growing only 1% per year.

Although only 20% of Pilkington's flat glass output went to other divisions for processing, its optical business had moved steadily "down stream" through acquisitions. This division's growth rate led to its split into two divisions (ophthalmic and electro-optical) of some £30 million sales each in 1981. After 15 years of technical work, fiber optics were slowly working their way into advanced technology applications, and Pilkington's sunlight-sensitive Reactolite spectacles were a great market success especially in Japan. Many of these new high-technology businesses reported directly to Pilkington's technical board member, Dr. Oliver, who commented that, "Pilkington is still as prepared as ever to commit itself to long cycle developments like 'integrated optics' which may some day provide an optical replacement for silicon chips. Bread on the water for 1995," was the way he described such investments. "Waiting is the name of the game in high technology."[9]

Against this background of great success and increasing pressures, Pilkington's new management team—under tall, elegant, and marketing experienced Antony Pilkington—had to arrive at its new strategies for the 1980s.

QUESTIONS

1. What do you think of the way the float glass development project was managed?
2. What were the critical factors Pilkington should have considered when it arrived at its float strategy? What should it have done about these?
3. What crucial issues face the company at the end of the case? What should Antony Pilkington do?

BROTHERS P.L.C.

EXHIBIT 2
Pilkington Float Plants

Location		Date of Start-Up
UNITED KINGDOM	St. Helens	April 1962
	St. Helens	July 1963
	St. Helens	September 1972
	St. Helens	April 1981
GERMANY	Gladbeck	March 1974
	Gladbeck	December 1976
	Weiherhammer	October 1979
SWEDEN	Halmstad	July 1976
SOUTH AFRICA	Springs	April 1977
CANADA (49% owned)	Scarborough	February 1967
		December 1970
AUSTRALIA (50% owned)	Dandenong	February 1974
ICO (35% owned)	Mexico City, Villa de Garcia	November, 1981

Plants (owned in partnership with others) in Brazil, Venezuela, and Taiwan were scheduled to start-up during 1982.

Source: Company records.

EXHIBIT 3
**Clear Flat Glass
Salable Capacity, World,
Excl. Communist
Countries, 1971 vs. 1981**

('000 Tonnes per Annum)	1971			1981		
	Float/ Plate	Sheet	Total	Float	Sheet	Total
North America	1,488	714	2,202	3,869	35	3,904
Europe	1,048	1,842	2,890	3,896	588	4,484
Australasia (incl. Japan and India)	280	1,058	1,338	1,301	793	2,094
Africa		68	68	115	37	152
Middle East		114	114		365	365
South America	45	263	308	94	505	599
Total	2,861	4,059	6,920	9,275	2,323	11,598

The 1981 data excludes the three most recently opened float tanks, one in Europe (Luxguard), one in the Middle East (Turkey Sise), and one in Mexico.

Source: Company records supplied during interview.

**Two Years of Dramatic
Changes in Europe**

	Number of Float Lines		Capacity (Tons Per Day)	
Saint-Gobain	11.5	11.5	5,500	6,000
Pilkington	4	8	1,750	4,750
PPG	1	3	500	1,650
Asahi Glass	nil	2	nil	1,300
SIV (Italian govt.)	1.5	1.5	700	770
Luxguard	nil	1	nil	500
BSN-Gervais-Danone	7	nil	4,150	nil
Total	25	27	12,600	14,970

Source: La Compagnie de Saint-Gobain in *Financial Times*, January 25, 1982.

842

EXHIBIT 4

Pilkington Brothers P.L.C., 1981

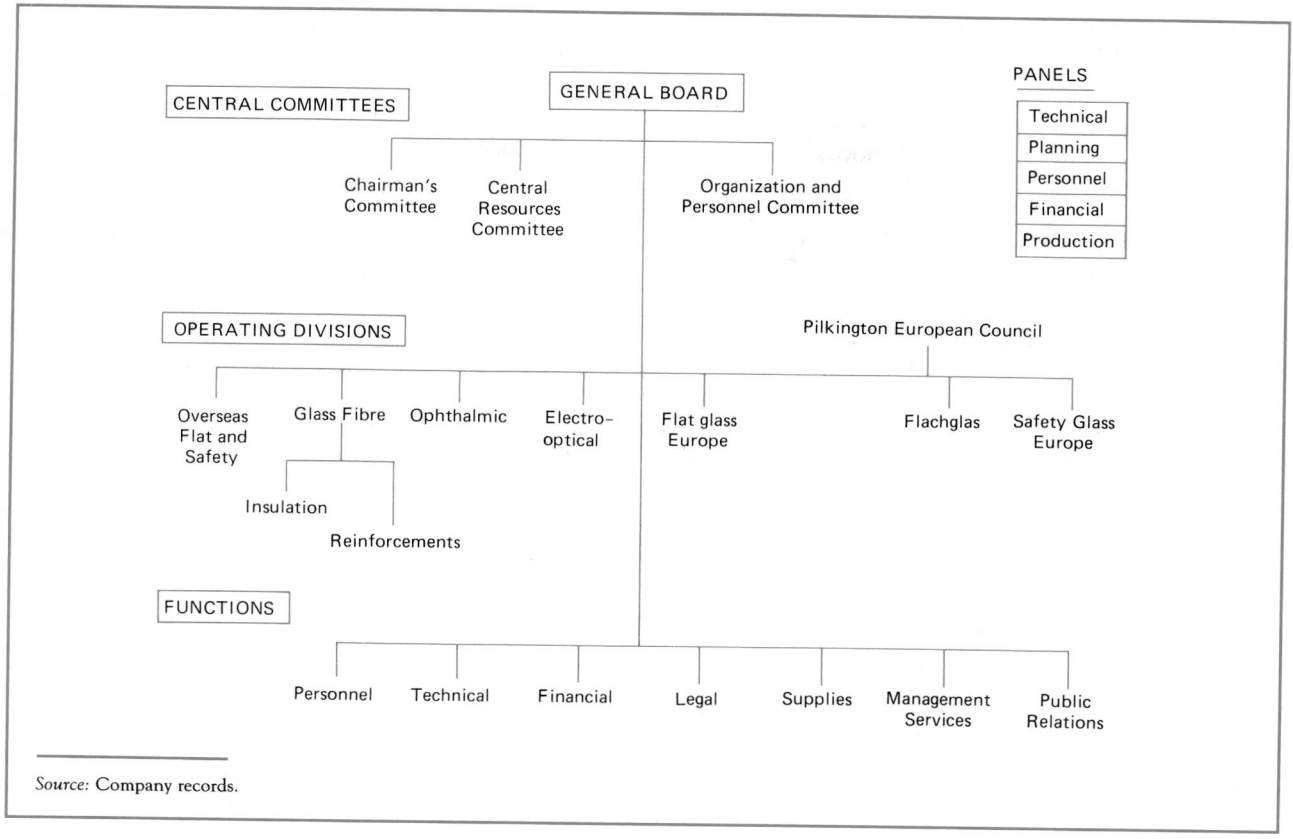

Source: Company records.

EXHIBIT 5

Pilkington Brothers
P.L.C.—Changes since
1961 (£ millions)

	1961	1971	1981
Group turnover			
Historical	58	123	786
In 1981 money terms	230	300, of which $\frac{2}{3}$ U.K., $\frac{1}{3}$ overseas	786, of which $\frac{1}{3}$ U.K., $\frac{2}{3}$ overseas
Group assets			
Historical	36	120	1,200
In 1981 money terms	150	300, of which $\frac{3}{4}$ U.K., $\frac{1}{4}$ overseas	1,200, of which $\frac{1}{2}$ U.K., $\frac{1}{2}$ overseas

Source: Compiled from company records.

843

EXHIBIT 6
Group Financial Record for the Years Ended March 31, 1978–1982
(£ millions)

	1978	1979	1980	1981	1982
Sales					
Sales to outside customers	469.5	548.8	629.0	786.8	958.9
Profits					
Trading profit	42.6	50.5	49.0	48.2	26.7
Licensing income	32.8	37.9	37.0	35.3	39.4
Related companies and other income less interest	(3.7)	1.9	5.4	(2.5)	(12.7)
Group profit before taxation	71.7	90.3	91.4	81.0	53.4
Taxation	36.3	42.7	20.5	32.2	49.9
Group profit after taxation	35.4	47.6	70.9	48.8	3.5
Profit attributable to shareholders of Pilkington Brothers P.L.C.	34.1	45.7	68.8	36.3	10.7
Dividends (net of taxation)	7.2	9.8	14.8	17.6	17.6
Profit/(loss) retained in the business	26.9	35.9	54.0	18.7	(6.9)
Assets employed					
Land, buildings, plant and equipment, less depreciation	338.4	385.6	455.3	852.0	924.7
Investments in related and other companies	35.8	49.1	53.1	60.6	70.6
Net current assets (before deducting bank overdrafts)	162.8	193.6	263.4	239.5	262.3
Assets employed	537.0	628.3	771.8	1,152.1	1,257.6
Financed by					
Ordinary share capital	62.2	124.4	155.8	167.7	167.7
Retained profits and reserves	300.9	298.5	426.1	568.4	624.0
	363.1	422.9	581.9	736.1	791.7
Minority interests in subsidiary companies	21.6	20.8	29.5	138.2	120.0
Loan capital and bank overdrafts	129.3	156.2	136.0	235.0	300.5
Deferred taxation and deferred income	23.0	28.4	24.4	42.8	45.4
Total funds invested	537.0	628.3	771.8	1,152.1	1,257.6

SONY CORPORATION

Sony Corporation began in the rubble and chaos of Japan at the end of World War II. Its first quarters were a small corner room of a burned out department store in Tokyo's Ginza district. Masaru Ibuka (age 37) had brought along seven young engineers to start "some sort of electronics laboratory or enterprise." His earlier company, Japan Precision Instrument Co., had supplied vacuum tube voltmeters and other instruments to the now defunct war effort, and Mr. Ibuka felt an obligation to provide continued work for his people. "We realized we could not compete against companies already in existence and against products in which they specialized. We started with the basic concept that we had to do something that no other company had done before."

From these inauspicious beginnings sprang one of the world's most innovative companies with worldwide sales in 1982 of $4.53 billion. In a nation not then known for product innovation, what had led to Sony's unique capabilities? Could its successful past policies survive the ferocious competitive atmosphere of the mid-1980s? A brief history of several of Sony's most important innovations provides an interesting basis for analysis.

MEAGER BEGINNINGS

Ibuka wanted to apply a mix of electronics and engineering to the consumer field, but Japan's banks and markets were anything but encouraging to a tiny upstart with no consumer experience. In August 1945, the group's first problem was to

Case copyright © 1986 by James Brian Quinn. Research associates—Penny C. Paquette and Roger Wellington.

The generous support of the Adolf H. Lundin Professorship at the International Management Institute, Geneva, Switzerland, is gratefully acknowledged. The generous cooperation of Sony Corporation is gratefully acknowledged.

find something to sell. The small group considered anything: bean paste soup, slide rules, an electric rice cooker Ibuka invented. Despite widespread fuel shortages, some electricity existed. Ibuka thought there was a genuine "need" for the innovative aluminum cooker. Technically it worked well—if the water levels and the rice were just right—but none sold. So Ibuka's team began to repair or modify wartime radios for a music and news hungry city. This barely enabled the company to survive as Ibuka slowly depleted his meager savings to keep his people employed during the first arduous year.

Then Akio Morita joined the company. He had been associated with Ibuka on thermal guidance and nocturnal vision projects during the war and had seen an article about his friend's shortwave adaptor and electronic repair business in October 1945. Though there was little money for a salary, Ibuka conveyed his missionary feelings about making electronics technology available to a peacetime civilian Japan. The talented Morita took a faculty appointment at the Tokyo Institute of Technology, but contributed part of his time to Ibuka's small company.

The Young Team

Like Ibuka, Morita had been an inveterate tinkerer as a child and was a descendant of a leading samurai family. As a student at Waseda University, Ibuka had won patents and international awards for a system to transmit sound by modulating neon light. Morita had ghost written articles for his professors at Osaka Imperial University where he had specialized in electronics. But there the similarities ended. Ibuka had failed his employment examination for a large Japanese electric company and only got his first job through the intervention of a friend. Morita's family company awaited him whenever he was ready.

Ibuka was passionate about invention, a humanist, a dreamer in many ways. Morita was a realist who had been trained in business by his father since birth. Ibuka had little interest in accounting and the intricacies of marketing. Morita was an administrator, as well as an enthusiastic, outgoing man who could charm or spellbind an audience. The two became the closest of friends.

Early Capitalization

When Morita decided to leave the University, Ibuka took an all-night train ride to persuade the elder Morita to let his son join the fledgling company. At first the senior Morita was not impressed. Later he not only acquiesced, but invested his own funds in the new firm. The banks were reluctant to lend even short-term money, so operating funds were constantly begged from the senior Morita and from personal friends. Eventually the elder Mr. Morita became the company's largest shareholder.

On May 7, 1946, the company was formally incorporated as Tokyo Telecommunications Engineering Co. (TTK being the Japanese acronym). Since companies capitalized at over 200,000 yen encountered more difficult incorporation regulations, TTK listed the company at 198,000 yen—$500-600 in exchange value—which was not much of an exaggeration.

The Purposes of Incorporation were listed in the Prospectus along with the new company's "Management Policies." Both of these remarkable statements— little changed since then—are shown in Exhibit 1. In 1983 Sony's Chairman Morita restated some of these basic principles:

> Young people who join our company next year will stay for 25 years. So that means for them the company should be prosperous for that period. All the top people feel responsible that the company live a long, long time, rather than making a big current

profit to make a very large bonus. That's why we don't pay bonuses to executives. We pay bonuses to employees because we like for the employees to feel and participate in the company's results.

Every year, when we receive our new graduate employees, I like to make a little speech to them. Now you have become a Sony employee. You will spend the most brilliant time of your life here. Nobody can live twice. This is the only life you can have, so I want you to become happy at Sony. If you don't feel happy, you better go out and change your job. But if you decide to stay with us, you must devote yourself to make your life happy and also to make your colleagues happy. People work together here for all of us in mutual benefit, mutual interest.*

Expansion with Umbrellas

When TTK surpassed its breakeven volume (primarily making voltmeters), Ibuka poured the cash flows into the introduction of an electrically heated cushion he had invented. TTK sold several hundred. Then Ibuka invented and produced a resonating sound generator that allowed operators trained with military telegraph equipment to hear their usual "dots and dashes" instead of the disconcerting "clicking" of the civilian systems. The American Occupation Forces (rebuilding Japan's destroyed communications systems to American standards) encountered some of TTK's equipment and were so impressed with its sophistication and quality that they began to order from the tiny company. By then TTK had expanded into some shacks in the Shinagawa district that were so dilapidated that executives had to use umbrellas during rainstorms. Nevertheless, Ibuka insisted on such rigorous design and quality standards that TTK—through clever use of a carefully developed supplier network—was soon performing almost all of Japan Broadcasting Network's (NHK's) revisions, converting its equipment to modern standards and building industrial and commercial electronic devices for other companies.

But TTK had no consumer products. Ibuka seriously considered a wire recorder, first introduced by the military in World War II. Japan's Dr. Kenzo Nagai held some key patents on the wire recorder, the device would be unique in consumer markets, and TTK had the proper skills to produce it. Ibuka was just about to commit his best resources to an onslaught on the wire recorder. Then one day as he was visiting the offices of NHK, a member of the Occupation Forces showed him a tape recorder from the United States, and history was made.

THE TAPE RECORDER

Tape recorders were unheard of in Japan—there wasn't even a word for them. Ibuka's team quickly checked the available patents and found Dr. Nagai held a key one here as well. They rapidly purchased the rights to it, knowing they had the magnetic and electrical skills to make a good machine. But there was little published information about either magnetic tapes or recorders. In Japan there was no plastic available to produce tape and no way to acquire any plastic through Japan's stringent import regulations. The TTK team tried cellophane; it stretched. They tried paper—Ibuka made tapes in his kitchen from rice paper and a paste of boiled rice—its edges caught and broke. Finally, Morita got a cousin in a paper manufacturing company to prepare a batch of specially calendered paper with a slick surface.

---

* All quotations not footnoted came from personal interviews with Professor Quinn.

Ibuka's group had to develop special techniques to cut the paper, hold it, and coat it uniformly with magnetic powder. They had to compensate for the less controllable paper base by designing extra quality into the circuitry, recording head, feed systems, and amplifiers in the recorder. It was a great struggle. The accounting manager constantly warned they were spending too much; they could bankrupt the company. Morita kept saying, "Be a little more patient and we will make a fortune." Finally after many months they created not just a new concept in tapes, but a new recorder, a new testing technology, and their own complete tape coating machine. Sony became perhaps the first company in the world to make the entire range of products from tapes to recorders, skills involving nearly a dozen basic technologies. In late 1949 they made their first unit, the G-type recorder, weighing over 100 pounds and selling for $400.

But would the device sell? Neither Ibuka nor Morita had marketing experience. After many months of effort the first unit sold to an *oden* shop—a kind of Japanese pub where people came to eat, sing, and talk noisily. Technically the expensive, cumbersome device performed well, but no one quite knew what to do with it. Ibuka's response was to take all his top engineers to an inn and work night and day to reduce the recorder's cost by 50% and to improve its size, weight, and portability. The result was a concept for a suitcase enclosed recorder at a reasonable price—and at less than one-half the G-type's weight.

As markets—at first to record NHK's English language programs for use in schools—opened, 3M began to sell its excellent magnetic tape to Japanese broadcasters and other large users. TTK tried to negotiate a license and reached a financially very attractive proposition. But in exchange for the license, 3M insisted that TTK drop its recorder manufacturing. After much consideration Morita and Ibuka said no, wanting no outside control over their product line. But this also meant TTK was now in competition with a much larger and very sophisticated world competitor, a very difficult situation for the young company.

TRANSISTOR RADIOS

In 1952 Ibuka went to the United States to explore possible markets for his tape recorder. While he was there, a U.S. friend told him that Western Electric was ready to license its transistor patent for the first time. Ibuka investigated, but when he heard the price was $25,000, he left the United States knowing the price was too much for TTK. Ibuka worried as he made the long trip home. He was convinced the transistor would revolutionize electronics, though no one then realized how. As he pondered what to do, another concern came into place. He had hired a number of young physicists. "Would tape recorders be challenge enough for them, motivate them to use their best abilities, or let them grow to their full potentials?" Ibuka was convinced they could not.

"A Pocketable Radio"

By the time Mr. Ibuka reached Tokyo, his questions had crystalized into a strategy to keep his people and his company growing. A short time later he announced, "We're going to use the transistor to make radios small enough so that each individual can carry them for his own use, but with a receiving ability that will enable civilization to reach areas that have no electric power." At that time "portable radios" weighed 10–20 pounds, were briefcase sized, and had batteries that lasted only a few hours. Ibuka spoke of a "pocketable transistor radio." But no one had applied transistors to radios—or much of anything else. The thought of a quality radio the size of a cigarette pack seemed almost beyond belief.

But Kazuo Iwama, a young geophysicist with no knowledge of transistors, was fired by Ibuka's enthusiasm. He left his job as tape recorder production head to lead the transistor task force. Morita had negotiated a license agreement with Western Electric whereunder the $25,000 patent was credited against potential future royalties. But the Ministry of International Trade and Industry (MITI) had to approve the release of the $25,000 in foreign currency. MITI was furious. If the big Japanese companies weren't interested in transistors, why should MITI support TTK? And why hadn't TTK come to MITI before *any* negotiations? They delayed approval for months until Ibuka's persuasiveness finally prevailed in early 1954.

Ibuka and Iwama immediately left for the United States, where they found that no one had achieved satisfactory yields on the high-frequency transistors needed for radio. Even lower-frequency transistors for hearing aids sold for $150–500. Ibuka and Iwama visited all the U.S. laboratories and plants they could, sending detailed letters to Iwama's task force each night. Months passed as the task force tried to reach the high frequencies needed for radio and the production yields required for commercial exploitation. Again the financial stability of the company was at risk as transistor program costs grew. Only an expanding tape recorder market kept it going.

Shock and a Market

Then came a shock. Texas Instruments announced the world's first transistorized radio, produced for Regency Co. In early 1955 TTK's team pulled out all stops, moving with what they had. In August they put their first radio on display. It was about $4'' \times 8'' \times 1\frac{1}{2}''$. They set a goal of 10,000 transistor radios in the first year and achieved 8,000. "The success of Sony is," said Iwama later, "that we produced a little less than was required. When there is enough, the market is saturated." Still Ibuka wanted a "pocketable radio." Despite the skepticism of marketing experts who thought the product would be too small, squeaky, and unreliable, Ibuka pushed on. TTK's component suppliers refused to modify their standard product lines, which were largely copied from world designs. They too were doubtful of the product's success. Ibuka single-handedly persuaded them to go ahead by offering Sony's technical support and production guidance. It was a momentous change for Japan. Japanese manufacturers had to become truly independent of foreign technology for perhaps the first time. In March 1957 the "pocketable" Type 63 radio was introduced using almost exclusively Japanese know-how. Since the Type 63 was still slightly larger than a shirt pocket, Sony made special shirts into which they would fit. Over a million Type 63s were soon sold.

Once the principle was proved, the bigger companies moved in. TTK changed its name to Sony, derived from the Latin *sonis* (for sound). The name had been carefully chosen to be simple, recognizable, and pronounceable in many languages. The Sony name became almost generic for transistor radios. "Sunny" and "Somy" trade names appeared and were fought off. Meanwhile, Sony had a two- to three-year technology lead and moved on to provide the world's first transistorized shortwave and FM receivers for consumers.

THE SONY SPIRIT

By now Sony was becoming known as a maverick among Japanese companies. It was not bound up in the traditions of older companies and relied as little as possible on the government or banks. Morita and Ibuka could make fast decisions, unhindered by the formalities of the *ringi* method of consensus building found in most larger companies. Over a single lunch Morita reached agreement with CBS for Sony to distribute CBS records in Japan. As the company grew at an amazing pace, it hired senior people away from other concerns—a practice frowned on by more traditional Japanese companies.

Some of the executives' backgrounds were unusual. Ibuka convinced Dr. Kikuchi, Sony's research head, to leave MITI after 26 years there. Shigeru Kobayashi was recruited from the printing industry, given charge of an ailing semiconductor plant, and told "do what you want." Norio Ohga—a music major destined to become a major opera baritone—was recruited upon his graduation from the university. He remained a consultant to Sony as he rose to operatic fame. When he returned from the stage—with no business training—he was made head of the tape recorder plant and rose to be a top board member of Sony. Morita and Ibuka always looked first for talent, not someone "to fill a job." Then with full trust they gave their selections a free hand. "I never knew what hidden abilities I had until I came to Sony," commented one of many so treated.

"Do Something Creative"

Sony's personnel grew over ten times in the 1950s and four times in the 1960s. Many of its personnel policies derived from its original goal to "establish an ideal factory—free, dynamic, and pleasant." To Ibuka this meant "to have fixed production and budgetary requirements but within these limits to give Sony employees the freedom to do what they want. This way we draw on their deepest creative potentials."[1]

Many more specific policies flowed from the remarkable experiences of Shigeru Kobayashi who took over Sony's Atsugi plant after its brief—and only—strike in 1961. Ibuka told Kobayashi, who knew nothing about semiconductor technology, "You are free to do there whatever you like. Try to do something truly creative." Kobayashi soon concluded the plant's problems derived from people feeling themselves insignificant there, what he called "a small pebble complex." He thought essential trust had been destroyed because management had tried to set up contrived Western methods for measuring output, increasing efficiency, and motivating people.

To eliminate cafeteria lines and to build trust Kobayashi removed all cashier attendants, letting people voluntarily place their meal coupons in appropriate boxes. He shut down the forbidding dormitories used by most Japanese companies then, built small prefabricated homes where a few employees could live together, and gave employees full autonomy over their premises. This had never been done in Japan. Next he eliminated time clocks, and created autonomy for Sony's recreation groups, moving away from the carefully controlled company teams so common in Japan.

Cells and Trust

Then Kobayashi developed a series of vertical and horizontal interconnecting teams or "cells" in the plant. Each was a specialized unit that could take charge of its own work. In these small (2 to 20 person) cells, workers could more easily develop a team spirit and help each other. Each cell would respond to input from all other cells above, below, on its sides. The cell would determine what methods to follow and evaluate its own output. Orders did not flow from above. Management's job was to assist the cells, to help them solve problems, to set overall goals, and to praise superior performances, while the cells were to control specific tasks at the workplace and group levels. The specifics of Kobayashi's "cell" system are different in each plant now, but the spirit and values it conveys continue.

In most areas, all new employees—whether law graduates or finance specialists—must spend several months on the production line learning to appreciate the company's products, practices, and culture. All engineers and scientists hired still must work in sales for several weeks or months. Promising people are shifted every two to three years to new areas to expand their knowledge and to identify their abilities for promotion. Typically workers learn several processes and are switched among tasks to keep up their interest. Production lines may be purposely segmented so they can be restructured rapidly if product mixes change. Rewards flow not to individuals, but to groups.

Morita recently said, "The best way to train a person is to give him authority. . . . We tell our young people: don't be afraid to make a mistake, but don't make the same mistake twice. If you think it is good for the company, do it. If something is wrong, I'm the man who should be accused. As CEO it's my job to take on the critics from the outside. For example, this year [1983] our profits are down, I tell my management, don't you worry about that, just do your job right."

Unlike other Japanese companies where seniority determines responsibility, young Sony employees were loaded with work and responsibility. But there was a complex "godfather system" in which a high executive watched over and specifically trained younger talent. A new executive interacted almost daily with his corporate mentor and received sophisticated insights and a corporate perspective. Mr. Morita expressed the overall philosophy this way, "Sony motivates executives not with special compensation systems but by giving them joy in achievement, challenge, pride, and a sense of recognition."

TUMMY AND OTHER TELEVISIONS

As its pocketable radio business boomed, Sony turned to all transistorized television. At first Sony's system could only drive small picture tubes, 5–8″ across, but not the larger tubes then popular. When Ibuka proposed to introduce a "mini-TV," the market experts again said, "It will never sell. RCA tried it and failed. The market wants big screens." Undeterred, Ibuka introduced an 8″ set in Japan (May 1960) and in the United States (June 1961). Again the road to the marketplace was complex and difficult, but Ibuka's "tummy television" sets became eminently successful.

During this rapid growth period Mr. Morita moved his family to New York so that Sony's top management would know the U.S. market, not through statistics, but through intuition. Although his wife and children could not speak English at first, he insisted that they meet and entertain Americans, enter American camps and schools. Their acculturation was rapid. Morita, himself, often helped sweep out the shabby rat-infested offices of Sony Corp. of America (Sonam), and worked 16-hour days and 7-day weeks. While joining in menial tasks, the distinguished Morita pushed Sonam to be the highest quality U.S. company. He insisted on "establishing proper servicing before distribution" and spent money to import more service engineers, rather than allowing Sonam to move into more acceptable sales headquarters in New York.

When offered a chance by a leading U.S. radio manufacturer to rebrand Sony transistor radios and have them introduced under the American company's well-accepted 50-year-old name, Morita refused. When asked how he could turn down the benefits of a fast start and 50 years' experience, Morita replied, "This is the first year of our 50 years' experience. If we do not do things ourselves, 50 years from now we will not be a great company like yours today."

"No Fun in Copying"

By 1964 color television had begun to take over the U.S. market. After some diverse experimentation, virtually every color manufacturer operated under RCA's "shadow mask" system using a triangle of three electron guns and a grid of tiny color "dots" to create color. But Ibuka said, "I could see no fun in merely copying their excellent system." In 1961 Ibuka had seen the Chromatron tube invented by Dr. O. E. Lawrence (world famous physicist and developer of the first cyclotron). The tube used a series of phosphor "stripes" to generate color, was potentially much simpler to manufacture than the shadow mask, and produced about three times the brightness of the RCA system. Sony had introduced the Chromatron in Japan, but it was plagued with defects, service costs were crushing, and losses were mounting daily on the product. Sonam was stridently pressing for a color system to sell in the United States—using the shadow mask.

Then some General Electric representatives came to license Sony a tube with three electron guns *in line,* not in the triangular configuration of the shadow mask. No one wanted after all their frustrations to be a mere licensee of a U.S. company, but Sony began investigating this and other possibilities. Engineering morale reached a low in the fall of 1966 after the GE approach. Ibuka came to the labs every day counseling, suggesting, experimenting, encouraging. He started small teams on different approaches in parallel and developed the backup technology for each. He quickly switched engineers from one project to another as roadblocks or leads developed for each alternative.

Ibuka said, "We must produce a product of our own. There is nothing more pitiable than a man who can't or doesn't dream. Dreams give direction and purpose to life, without which life would be mere drudgery." During this difficult period, Morita himself feared for the financial viability of the company, yet he had to calm his dealers. "Business should be considered in ten-year cycles," he explained. "If we wait and develop a unique product, we may start several years later, but we will be stronger than all the others in 10 years."

Then toward the end of 1966, a young engineer, Miyaoka, made a mistake while experimenting. Using a single gun and three cathodes, he had produced a blurred picture. "But it was a picture"—and a new concept. Intuitively, Ibuka recognized the promise of this approach and said, "This is it. This is the system to go with."

Ibuka became the project manager himself. His team often worked all night, taking a few hours off to rest on the sofa. By February they thought they had a better picture than the RCA tube, but for months they had problems with electron acceleration and control. Repeatedly experiments failed, and the engineers despaired. Finally, on October 16, 1967, the new "Trinitron" system really worked for the first time. It was a totally unique concept—using phosphor stripes, a one gun, three-beam system, and a vertical stripe aperture grille—in a market dominated worldwide by the shadow mask system.

In April Ibuka announced the Trinitron's availability in six months. The program's production head, Yoshida, didn't think that schedule was possible. He pleaded and convinced Ibuka to limit the size of the screen to 12″ because of fears that the Trinitron's glass bulb might fail in larger sizes. Again teams worked until they lost track of night and day. But after 6 months the first sets rolled off the assembly line. And within a year, the Trinitron dominated the small-screen market in Japan. After at first dismissing its added brightness as a function of its small 12″

size—"a clever marketing ploy" said U.S. competitors—the U.S. market responded. The Trinitron earned the first Emmy in the United States ever given to a product innovation. Although named for the prize himself, Ibuka saw that his key engineers shared in it. Sony could not catch up with world demand for the fabulously successful Trinitron until the late 1970s.

VIDEO TAPE RECORDERS

A final example, the video tape recorder (VTR), offers other insights about Sony's management of innovation. The first practical VTR, the Quadruplex, was introduced by Ampex in 1956. It set the standard for commercial television broadcasting for almost 20 years. NHK, Japan's national television network, bought a Quadruplex and (along with MITI) encouraged electronics manufacturers' engineers to become familiar with it. The "Quad" cost about $60,000 and was a complex machine filling several closet-sized equipment racks. In 1958, $3\frac{1}{2}$ months after Mr. Ibuka first saw the Ampex machine, a team under Dr. Nobutshu Kihara and Mr. K. Iwama completed an operating prototype using similar principles.

All the leading (six or seven) Japanese consumer electronics companies launched major VTR programs. In the United States, Ampex expanded its line into professional and industrial units. Philips dominated similar markets in Europe, but ignored consumer markets—perhaps because its VTR business was housed in a division with no consumer lines. No American consumer electronics company invested significantly in VTRs until after 1970, in part because their attention was riveted on surviving the 1950s and 1960s shakeout in the large U.S. TV market.

Sony Gears Up

Dr. Kihara, who headed Sony's VTR program, would later figure prominently in many of Sony's other famous innovations. When asked how Sony approached such radical innovations Dr. Kihara noted, "Mr. Ibuka would often come in with the 'seed or hint' of an idea and ask him to 'try it out.'" For example, shortly after Dr. Kihara had helped build the first VTR prototype (which would have to be priced at about 20 million yen or $55,000) Ibuka said, "We want to make commercial video recorders, can you develop one that will sell for 2 million yen ($5,500)?" After Kihara did that, Ibuka said, "Now can we make a color recorder for the home at 200,000 yen ($550). The complex sequence that ensued led to Sony's early preeminence in the home VTR market.

Sony's first commercial machine (in 1963) lacked Ampex's fidelity, but was one-twentieth of its size and sold for less than one-quarter of its $60,000 price. By 1965 Sony had the compact CV-2000 for $600, operating reel to reel in black and white to high commercial standards. Its U-Matic machine, the first video cassette recorder, became quite successful in commercial color markets in 1972 at $1,100. but Sony's target was the home market; its product was to be the legendary Betamax.

Early Stages

When did it all start? Mr. Ibuka says, "Around 1951–1952 I started to conceive of something called the video tape recorder; but at that time there was no TV broadcasting in Japan, there was no source to record from. Then we started the transistor radio project, and assigned all our engineers and technicians to it. So we stopped the video tape program until 1958, when Ampex began to deliver its video tape recorder. If we had worked on it steadily, I believe we would have been able to produce the tape recorder first. Within $3\frac{1}{2}$ months (after seeing the Ampex machine) we got an image. Ampex had invented a four-head machine. We invented the one-head machine. We developed our own system. I specifically ordered Sony engineers *not* to develop a broadcasting machine. Many engineers wanted to imitate the Ampex machine and make a good business in the broadcast field. I strongly ordered that we would make a $500 home machine."

The first all-transistorized VTR was the Sony PV100, a two-head 2″ tape machine. The biggest customers were an American medical X-ray company and American Airlines—to monitor landings. In 1965 Sony introduced its first home use VTR, the CV-2000. No formal market research studies were made. "After our experience with the micro-TV, I didn't believe the marketing research people. Merchandising and marketing people cannot envision a market that doesn't exist."

Mr. Ibuka continued, "We decided that the video tape recorder must be a cassette type. Our experience in audio said that open reel types were not good in the home market. We succeeded with the U-Matic, which was the first video cassette recorder in the world. When we decided on the U-Matic (U format) standard, Japan Victor and Matsushita agreed on it. We supplied our technology to both companies. Shortly after, we were able to come up with the Beta form of recording which is a helical system using all the space on the tape. All the relevant technologies were invented by us. We asked Matsushita to join us in that standard. But they had a license to operate with our original patent. So they denied us."

Instead, Matsushita changed the size of their cassettes for their VHS format (which depended in part on Sony's patents) so they could record twice as long, two hours. Other Japanese companies went to potential Japanese and American manufacturers to get them to join in their (VHS) standard, not Beta. They even convinced MITI to ask Sony to make the VHS format the national standard. But Sony already had some 200,000 recorders and many tapes in the marketplace. As one of the many alternatives it had looked at, Sony had actually tried the VHS format and was convinced that its BETA—meaning "full coverage" in Japanese—format was much superior. Sony stayed with the Beta system while may other Japanese companies and American consumer electronic companies adopted VHS. Zenith was the main U.S. exception.

The Design Approach

Dr. Kihara said, "My group started ten different major test options or approaches. Within these we developed two or three alternatives for each subsystem. . . . Much of the development process was trial and error. We did not have formal written plans. . . . For example, we developed a loading system with one reel and a leader, not two reels. We developed another where the wind up drum was inside the cassette. We developed the U-loading system, the M-loading system. We developed single heads, double heads, the skip system, and the asimuth system for reading and writing on the tapes. And so on. By taking the best of each option we ultimately developed Betamax."

In 1982 a development team member said, "Kihara was in charge of what kind of developments would be pursued, what systems to use. At Sony development moves fast. We make quick—but not rash—decisions. Kihara makes the decisions himself." This was reiterated. "Kihara believes there are only a few people directly involved in a new technology who have adequate information or knowledge about that technology. With new products one must create a new market. Not many people know how these new markets will develop, what a product can do, how well it will function, how it could be used by customers." Says Dr. Kihara, "We have never been told by Morita or Ibuka 'this product's sales will be this big or must make this much money.'"

"In my engineering intuition, something interesting comes to mind. I look at the unique things I can do. . . . I don't want to be a copycat. I want to be first, number one. I don't worry about marketing figures. At other companies, top executives expect their top engineers to do managerial chores. Here they do not. They give me a lot of time for development work."

"Produce Something New, Unique"

Dr. Kihara continued, "Most companies make profit the first priority. Sony's primary mission is to produce something new, unique, and innovative for the enhancement of people's lives. Technical people report right to the top of the organization. There is no formal technical committee, but many joint discussions. I like to make 'surprising reports' to Mr. Morita and Ibuka. If an idea is merely under development, I don't report it. After I obtain a working model, then I report it to Morita and Ibuka. I like to surprise the top. In the early development stages, there are typically only 5 or 6 people involved on a project team; for example in the Mavica camera there were 7 to 8. We work together until we have made a model. After we get the go ahead, the project may be expanded to perhaps 30 people."

At Sony there were no specific budgets for individual projects. Kihara reported to Morita once a year on his total budget. But most individual projects in Kihara's group were kept "beneath the surface," hidden in detail even from Morita and Ibuka. Dr. Kihara met with his younger engineers in a prolonged session at least every two months. Said Kihara, "I try to transfer my technical knowhow and to cultivate an atmosphere of innovation. The best reward system for a young engineer is the joy he gets from making products that are used and sold. The rate of new products from this area is the highest in the company. This gives the group confidence and satisfaction. Sometimes there may be some bonuses involved, but this is not as important as other things."

Research to Production

Sony consciously rotates its engineers to other divisions and back to engineering. In many large Japanese companies technology is transferred by drawings, prototypes, or production models. But in Sony people from other areas join the development team directly. They are trained on the spot by Research and Development people. Those most suited for production will go on with the project into production. This practice leaves a vacuum in development which can be filled by new people who infuse the department with fresh blood and ideas.

Dr. Kikuchi, director of research, said, "Everyone at the top has a strong interest in engineering and scientific problems and encourages people below to talk to them. And it is easy for us to talk to them. Even Sony's business people must talk technical languages, not just finance."

In 1982 Sony's President Iwama and Chairman Morita still visited the R&D labs frequently as did now honorary chairman, Ibuka. "Mr. Morita frequently telephones or brings in ideas from around the world on how to apply physics in new ways. And Mr. Ibuka visits many places in Sony randomly. After playing golf near the research center, he will drop in at the laboratory. He wants to see things, touch things. Recently he went to the laboratory and touched his tongue to a new tape compound, to taste it, to see what it was. He leaves people very excited."

There were monthly meetings between the top board and the technical section heads. But there was little calculation of projected financial ratios or returns for particular projects. Dr. Kikuchi said, "We as management must define the problems, but only with sufficient specificity to leave many directions open for technical work. The goal must be clear. It may not be expressed numerically. At first there may not even be a date attached. But it must be clear and not change easily. We let the technical leaders choose the approaches."

"Periodically, I give a 'crystal award' for highly evaluated work. Even if a team has lost a competition within Sony, we will still give them a crystal award if their quality of work is especially good. . . . We also may give engineers a certain percentage of a new product's first year's sales if their ideas had particular merit. The amount of money is significant, but not huge."

THE WALKMAN AND MAVICA

Through 1982, Sony continued its innovative ways. In the early 1980s two new products offered interesting examples of Sony's innovation capabilities, the Walkman sound system and the Mavica all-electronic still camera system.

As had happened so often before, the idea for Walkman (a compact cassette player with small earphones for highly portable listening) came from Ibuka and Morita. Mr. Morita, who purposely visited places where young people congregated, found that they wanted to listen to music on a very personal basis, especially if the sound was loud rock music. He also thought—as an avid golfer—that sportsmen would like a high-quality portable sound system. He gave the engineers a target of developing small high-quality earphones and a simple light tape player. When the marketing people heard of the project, they did not think such a system would sell well. They wanted to make the cassette record as well as play. Morita said, "No, Keep it small and simple." Despite marketing's skepticism, Mr. Morita was confident that there was a big market for the new concept. The Walkman sold out instantly upon introduction.

The Mavica Still Camera

In the fall of 1981, Sony had announced its revolutionary Mavica all-electronic camera for shooting still pictures. Exhibit 3 describes the way the system operated. The camera used no film or chemical developing processes. Images were recorded on a small magnetic disk called Mavipak and could be viewed immediately on a home TV set through a specially designed playback unit. The system also had a color printer called the Mavigraph which could electronically produce hard copy prints from the video signals developed by the Mavica.

The key technical developments for the system were (1) an electronic recording technique using very-high-density magnetic disks (developed in the 1960s by Sony), (2) the development of very high-quality charged couple devices (CCDs), which converted the optical image coming through the lens of the camera into a series of electrically charged spots on a semiconductor, and (3) the creation of high-density circuit boards small enough to operate the complex camera. Then the problem was to bring these together with optics into a quality system. Again there had been no market analysis on the project. "This was one of my dreams come true," said Kihara, "I wanted it to happen regardless of the marketplace."

Dr. Kihara said, "We got the original idea for the electronic still camera 25 years ago. But the technology did not exist to make it practical." Mr. Iwama, who later became president of Sony, had started the original research on the CCD around 1970. He judged the CCD to be a very important technology and backed it as one of the largest research projects Sony had in the 1970s. By 1982 the CCD was a small semiconductor device (about the size of a fingernail) on which several 100,000 individual pickup dots could convert optically focused light into individual electrical pulses.

Information from the CCD could be transferred directly to a magnetic storage device (disk or semiconductor RAM) from which the original image could be later retrieved, electronically enhanced, or eliminated to make room for another image. The resolution of individual pictures was of course limited by the density of information the camera could pick up and store. A color picture from a regular camera using regular instant film would contain about 100 million bits of information. CCDs, in 1981 could pick up about 200,000 bits of information for the same-sized black and white picture. But the density of information CCDs could pick up was doubling every two to three years, and image processing software could improve the picture's appearance even more. Electronically enhanced pictures from a 600,000-bit source would be difficult for the eye to discern from a regular film photograph.

The Mavica was no larger than a conventional 35mm single-lens reflex camera. Once its pictures were recorded on the Mavipak (or only on part of it), the disk could be removed from the camera and then inserted again with no fear of recording a new picture over a previous picture. Since the Mavipak could be erased, the memory disk could be used repeatedly with no deterioration of picture or color quality. Even small children could load a Mavipak into the camera. In 1982 a Mavipak memory medium could record 50 still color pictures. But this technology was rapidly advancing as well.

Dr. Kihara said, "Although the basic technologies were developed over the last 15 years, the real origin of the Mavica was October 1980. At that time I could see that all the technologies were available to make the idea concrete. We put a small team of seven to eight people on it. In August 1981 we unveiled the product. I did not talk to Mr. Ibuka about the Mavica in concrete form until winter 1980–1981 when I showed him the circuit board. Even then Ibuka didn't think it could be done. But we introduced the product with essentially the same circuit board." At one stage Mr. Ibuka had actually said the project should be stopped, but Dr. Kihara told his team to go ahead anyway. Dr. Kihara said Mr. Ibuka was "very fair" in his appraisal of the ultimate result.

The first official announcement of the Mavica system underlined its radical potentials: "Sony's new magnetic video still camera uses no photographic film and therefore does not require developing and printing processes which are indispensable to conventional chemical photography. This new still video camera represents an epic-making innovation in the history of still photography. For more than 104 years since the invention by Daguerre of France, there has been no fundamental change in the concept and technology of photography."

The Mavica Marketplace

The Mavica camera would move into a marketplace that was yet to be defined. Projected prices in Japan were $650 for the camera, $220 for the playback unit, and $2.60 for each magnetic disk. No price was initially announced for the printer, but it was expected to cost approximately $800–$1,000. The Mavica could also be used as a video camera. By attaching it to a portable Sony video tape recorder, one could make video films. Images could also be transmitted electronically over telephone lines. In addition, the Mavigraph allowed one to make hard copies of the graphics created on the Sony computer system, other compatible computer systems, and certain imaging equipment like Xrays, CAT scanners, or commercial graphic arts devices. While the initial image on a standard U.S. television set would be limited to the 350 horizontal lines on the tube, high-resolution screens of 1,500 lines were expected in the near future.

The investment community responded cautiously, but positively, concerning the product's impact. In its investment report, E. F. Hutton said, "In Hutton's view, the so-called photography industry is in the path of a tidal wave of digital electronic technology. In recent decades, digital electronics has revolutionized many industries that had been based on nonelectronic processes. And the processing display of scenes/images may become one of the most important uses of digital electronics yet seen. . . . The lion's share of the [photographic] industry profits have been from the sale of consumables (photographic film, paper, and chemicals) as opposed to hardware. The consumables are chemical based, reasonably proprietary, highly profitable—with film and paper made by the mile and sold by the millimeter."[2]

In its report on the photographic and imaging industry, Smith Barney noted,

- Recent developments, including the rapid growth of electronic home movies, have raised concerns about the impact of electronic imaging on current consumer photographic systems. . . .

- Silver halide technology [which currently dominates consumer imaging] will continue to improve in film sensitivity and sharpness, and hardware will become more compact, reliable, and convenient.

- We expect electronic cameras and other hardware to be more expensive than their silver halide counterparts, but the electronic consumables or recording media will be less costly to use.

- We project a total market for consumer electronic imaging of about $4–5 billion in 1990, accounting for about 39% of total consumer imaging expenditures.[3]

Electronics had already begun to erode the Super 8 movie camera marketplace: Smith Barney summarized shipments of Super 8 movie cameras as follows:

Super 8MM Movie Cameras

YEAR	SHIPMENTS (IN THOUSANDS)
1962	838
1967	1027
1972	1043
1977	609
1978	525
1979	280
1980	230
1981	180
1982	100 (est.)

Smith Barney further estimated that "approximately 11.5 billion conventional exposures, including color negative, slide, and black-and-white films, will require the purchase of about $1.2 billion of conventional film in 1984. Developing and printing will come to about $3 billion in the same year [with reprints and enlargements adding another $0.3 billion]. In addition to nearly $150 million for instant cameras, consumers will spend about $700 million in 1984 for 900 million instant exposures. . . . The [total] still photographic market in 1984 [will be] about $8.3 billion."[3] While the U.S. consumer would expend approximately $9.1 billion in 1984 for still photography and movies (both conventional and video), the worldwide market was estimated to be about $23 billion.

In responding to the Sony announcement, Kodak's president, Mr. Chandler, said, "People like color prints, . . . more than 85% of the amateur pictures taken are prints, rather than slides, up from about 66% 10 years ago. Traditional still photographs provide better images than those from electronic cameras, which at present can be viewed only over a television screen."[4] In October 1982, Kodak demonstrated a TV display device for displaying developed negatives from its disc cameras. This unit, informally dubbed the EkTViewer, used a 350,000-element CCD chip and provided a good-quality image on television. With a 2–1 zoom device, the unit allowed cropping into any quadrant of the original image with little loss of resolution. Kodak said the display unit would probably be priced around $300–400. Others speculated that commercial extensions of the EkTViewer could allow zooming, cropping, focus adjustments, contrast changes, and shifts in color balance on the monitor. The commercial units were forecast to handle both disc and 35mm films, but would probably cost well over $1,000.

Polaroid had taken equity positions in a number of smaller companies in the high-density magnetic recording, fiber optics, ink jet printing, and continuous tone color film recording fields. Polaroid's Palette, which sold for about $1,500, was the most successful color film recorder/printer introduced in the early 1980s. This system allowed the user to output digital images from IBM, Apple, and DEC PC's and record them on either instant print or 135 film.

Several Japanese competitors were also working on similar electronic camera and print systems, but none would divulge details. Canon said that it might have an electronic camera "in 2–3 years—but maybe not for 10 years." Even Sony's chairman Morita conceded that the initial Mavica posed little threat to conventional 35 millimeter cameras, but thought the Mavica would "open up a new market." Mr. Webster of Kodak further observed, "if you tie [the Mavica] in with the work that Sony and others are doing in high definition television—with a picture that has twice as many elements in both directions, or 4 times the current resolution—then you would be getting into the realm of what would compete with 35 millimeter and Polaroid cameras." In addition, as its resolution problems were resolved, Mavica might offer substantial cost advantages for the consumer. Estimated costs for the Mavica would be only 5–10 cents per picture against 80 cents for a Polaroid shot, or 42 cents for a pocket 110 shot on Kodak film. Even then, such prices assumed that silver costs would stay around $15 an ounce and not suddenly balloon as they recently had to around $48 an ounce.

Estimated U.S. retail still camera sales were as follows:

Estimated Domestic Retail Still Camera Sales
(units and $ in millions)

	1984	1983	1984	1983
Disc	5.2	4.9	$ 230	$ 225
Cartridge (110 and 126)	3.2	3.6	65	80
Instant	3.8	3.6	145	125
35 Range-finder	3.0	2.4	375	310
35 SLR	2.6	2.7	585	635
Other	0.1	0.1	80	80
	17.9	17.3	$1480	$1455

Source: P. J. Enderlin, Smith Barney, Harris Upham & Co., Inc., *Electronic Imaging—Impact on Consumer Photography,* December 20, 1984.

The biggest trend in camera sales was the growth of 35mm cameras from about 3% of the amateur market in the late 1970s to over 50% in the early 1980s. Much of this gain had come at the expense of instant cameras. This reflected the impact of the lower cost, more convenient, more compact, and more reliable equipment introduced and heavily promoted by its Japanese manufacturers. The best 35mm films far exceeded the resolving power of the human eye—and film performance had recently been accelerating its already impressive historical rate of improvement.

Initially magnetic disks would offer sufficient capability to store electronic images. Kodak's 5.25″ floppy disk could hold 3.3 megabytes. However, 3M estimated that with magneto-optics, a similar-size disk could hold 600 megabytes on each side. This technology was under rapid development. In estimating the potential markets for the Mavica, the sales patterns of video cassette recorders and color video cameras are instructive. See the accompanying tables.

U.S. Color Video Camera Market, 1979–1985E

YEAR	(UNITS 000)	YEAR-END PENETRATION % OF HOUSEHOLDS
1979	61	.1
1980	115	.3
1981	190	.5
1982	296	.9
1983	414	1.3
1984E	500	1.9
1985E	700	2.6

Source: P. J. Enderlin, Smith Barney, Harris Upham & Co., Inc., *Electronic Imaging—Impact on Consumer Photography,* December 20, 1984.

**U.S. Video Cassette Recorder Market Sales to Dealers,
1975–1985E**
(units 000)

YEAR	PORTABLE —(*)	TABLE MODEL	TOTAL	YEAR-END PENETRATION % OF HOUSEHOLDS
1975			20	0.03
1977			209	0.3
1980			805	2.4
1981			1,361	4.0
1982	436	1,599	2,035	6.4
1983	750	3,341	4,091	11.1
1984E	1,000	6,000	7,000	19.1
1985E	1,200	6,800	8,000	28.2

(*) Includes camcorders.

Smith Barney estimated the breakdown of the 1984 and 1990 markets as follows:

**Domestic Consumer Electronic Imaging
Market, 1984 vs. 1990**
($ billions)

	1990	1984
Still photography		
Silver halide	$11.0	$8.3
Electronic	1.0	0
Movies		
Silver halide	0	.1
Electronic	3.5	.7
Total consumer imaging	$15.5	$9.1
Total electronic	$ 4.5	$ .7
% electronic	29%	8%

Source: P. J. Enderlin, Smith Barney, Harris Upham & Co., Inc., *Electronic Imaging—Impact on Consumer Photography,* December 20, 1984.

As the mid 1980s emerged, most experts predicted a genuine revolution in the photographic and imaging industries led by new electronic and electro-optical technologies. The question was where Mavica would fit into this revolution and how each of the major players would respond to the challenge?

At this same time Sony was again about to pioneer with the first introduction of a compact disk (laser optical) audio record player which could record 100 billion bits of information on its 5″ disk and a small 8mm hand-held video camera (CAMCORDER) which could threaten all existing amateur (Super 8) film systems.

Despite these exciting developments, Sony's financial performance slowed markedly in the mid '80s. Mr. Morita, under fire from the press and investment analysts, had to review Sony's posture in the light of changing world electronic markets and determine how to position the company and its newest cluster of revolutionary products for the 1990s. Exhibit 4 shows Sony's mid 1980s financial position and product portfolio. Exhibit 5 shows the basic Mavica system and its potential extensions. The Polaroid case offers additional information on camera and imaging markets.

QUESTIONS

1. What are the most critical policies and practices which made Sony so innovative as a company? Can they be transferred to other companies? What problems do they pose for Sony?

2. How does Sony compare and contrast with conventional views of "the Japanese management style?" How did it compare and contrast with the American approach to "entrepreneurship" when it was a small company?

3. What overall strategy should Sony follow in the late '80s? Why?

4. How should Mavica fit into that strategy? What should be the specific strategy for introduction of Mavica? Why?

EXHIBIT 1
Sony Corporation

Purposes of Incorporation

- "The establishment of an ideal factory—free, dynamic, and pleasant—where technical personnel of sincere motivation can exercise their technological skills to the highest levels.

- Dynamic activities in technology and production for the reconstruction of Japan and the elevation of the nation's culture.

- Prompt application of the highly advanced technology developed during the war in various sectors to the life of the general public.

- Making rapidly into commercial products the superior research results of universities and research institutes, which are worth applying to the daily lives of the public."

Management Policies

- We shall eliminate any untoward profit-seeking, shall constantly emphasize activities of real substance, and shall not seek expansion of size for the sake of size.

- Rather, we shall seek a compact size of operation through which the path of technology and business activities can advance in areas that large enterprises, because of their size, cannot enter.

EXHIBIT 1
(Continued)

- We shall be as selective as possible in our products and will even welcome technological difficulties. We shall focus on highly sophisticated technical products that have great usefulness in society, regardless of the quantity involved. Moreover, we shall avoid the formal demarcation between electricity and mechanics, and shall create our own unique products coordinating the two fields with a determination that other companies cannot overtake.

- Utilizing to the utmost the unique features of our firm, which shall be known and trusted among the acquaintances in the business and technical worlds, we shall open up through mutual cooperation our production and sales channels and our acquisition of supplies to an extent equal to those of large business organizations.

- We shall guide and foster subcontracting factories in directions that will help them become independently operable and shall strive to expand and strengthen the pattern of mutual help with such factories.

- Personnel shall be carefully selected, and the firm shall be comprised of as small a number as feasible. We shall avoid mere formal position levels and shall place our main emphasis on ability, performance, and personal character, so that each individual can show the best in ability and skill.

Source: Sony Corporation of America.

EXHIBIT 2
Milestones in VTR Product Development

Market	Model	Company	Date of Commercial Introduction	Tape Width*	Tape Utilization (sq. ft./hour)	Price (in constant 1967 $)
Broadcast	VR–1000	AMPEX	1956	2″	747	$60,000
Professional	VR–1500	AMPEX	1962	2″	375	12,000
Industrial	PV–100	SONY	1962	2″	212	13,000
Industrial/professional	EL–3400	PHILIPS	1964	1″	188	3,500
Industrial/professional	CV–2000	SONY	1965	$\frac{1}{2}$″	90	600
Industrial/professional	N–1500	PHILIPS	1972	$\frac{1}{2}$″	70	1,150
Industrial/professional	U-Matic	SONY	1972	$\frac{3}{4}$″	70	1,100
Consumer	Betamax	SONY	1975	$\frac{1}{2}$″	20	850
Consumer	VHS	JVC	1976	$\frac{1}{2}$″	16	790
Consumer	VR2020	PHILIPS	1980	$\frac{1}{2}$″	6	520

* From 1972 onward, all models used cassettes instead of open reels and all used high-energy tape.
Source: Sony company records.

EXHIBIT 3
Perspective View of Mavica

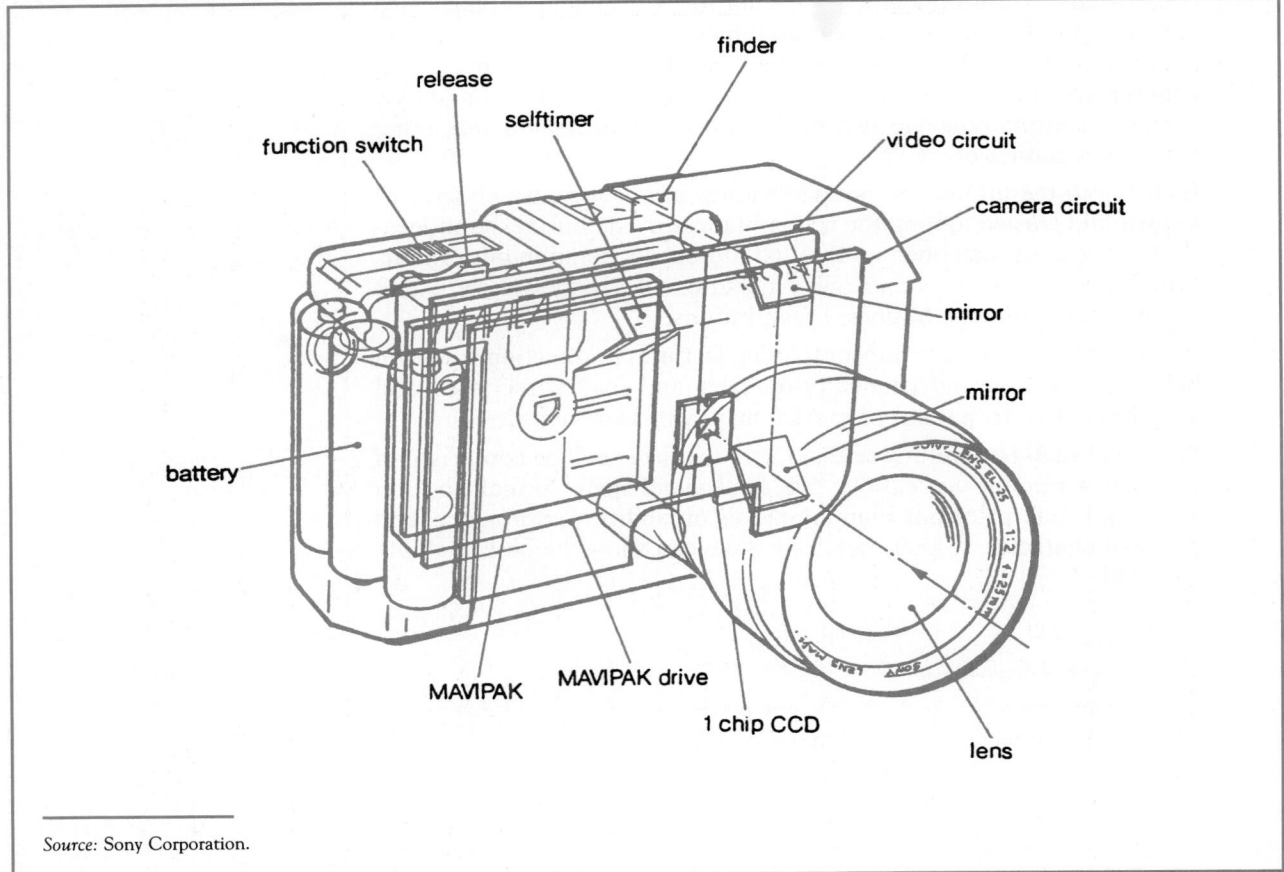

Source: Sony Corporation.

EXHIBIT 4
Sony Corporation (Sony Kabushiki Kaisha) Financials Consolidated Ten-Year Summary, 1973–1982

	Millions of yen except per share amounts (thousands of U.S. dollars except per share amounts)									
	1982	1981	1980	1979	1978	1977	1976	1975	1974	1973
Net sales										
Overseas	829,665 ($3,372,622)	744,775	610,545	394,554	320,085	310,721	272,455	224,248	198,939	148,653
Domestic	284,157 (1,155,110)	306,266	282,218	248,901	214,832	195,303	191,073	185,362	198,112	165,408
Total	1,113,822 (4,527,732)	1,051,041	892,763	643,455	534,917	506,024	463,528	409,610	397,051	314,061
Operating income	109,584 (445,464)	142,589	117,245	74,719	30,766	56,445	61,974	42,644	53,880	48,079
Income before income taxes	85,542 (347,732)	132,731	116,748	41,272	52,378	64,363	64,388	39,187	46,414	49,159
Income taxes	45,871 (186,468)	69,652	53,026	26,960	29,387	32,985	35,625	22,415	23,693	24,656
Net income	45,820 (186,260)	66,901	68,643	17,716	25,874	34,898	30,926	16,893	22,518	25,134
Per depositary share	198.67 (0.81)	291.67	318.34	82.16	120.00	161.85	143.42	78.34	106.55	121.40
Depreciation	48,229 (196,053)	32,421	24,703	20,086	15,844	12,992	10,778	10,850	10,298	7,586
Net working capital	195,240 ($793,859)	181,362	137,188	84,265	97,272	89,162	90,840	89,296	64,612	38,892
Capital investment (additions to fixed assets)	112,091 (455,654)	98,089	48,715	38,916	37,604	33,732	16,169	12,468	25,878	35,825
Shareholders' equity	474,592 (1,929,236)	425,765	325,523	263,349	251,024	230,541	201,034	174,421	160,115	119,988
Per depositary share	2,057.72 (8.36)	1,856.20	1,509.67	1,221.33	1,164.17	1,069.18	932.33	808.91	757.66	579.56
Total assets	1,240,355 (5,042,093)	1,152,655	877,413	763,907	618,854	552,138	509,859	423,123	416,681	344,194
Average number of shares (in thousands of shares)	230,639	229,375	215,625	215,625	215,625	215,625	215,625	215,625	211,328	207,031
Number of issued shares (as of end of fiscal year)	230,714	230,625	215,625	215,625	215,625	215,625	215,625	172,500	172,500	132,500
Number of employees	43,126	38,555	32,821	30,607	27,112	25,881	22,713	22,108	21,635	20,600

Notes: (1) Each Depository Share represents 1 share of Common Stock. Per share amounts are based on the average number of shares outstanding during each period, adjusted for all stock distributions. (2) 1981 amounts have been restated using FASB 52, as described in Note 1 of Notes to Consolidated Financial Statements. (3) U.S. dollar amounts for fiscal 1982 are translated for convenience from yen at the rate of Y246 = U.S. $1, the Tokyo foreign exchange market rate as of December 14, 1982, as described in Note 3 of Notes to Consolidated Financial Statements.

Source: Sony Corporation, *Annual Report*, 1982.

EXHIBIT 4 (Continued)

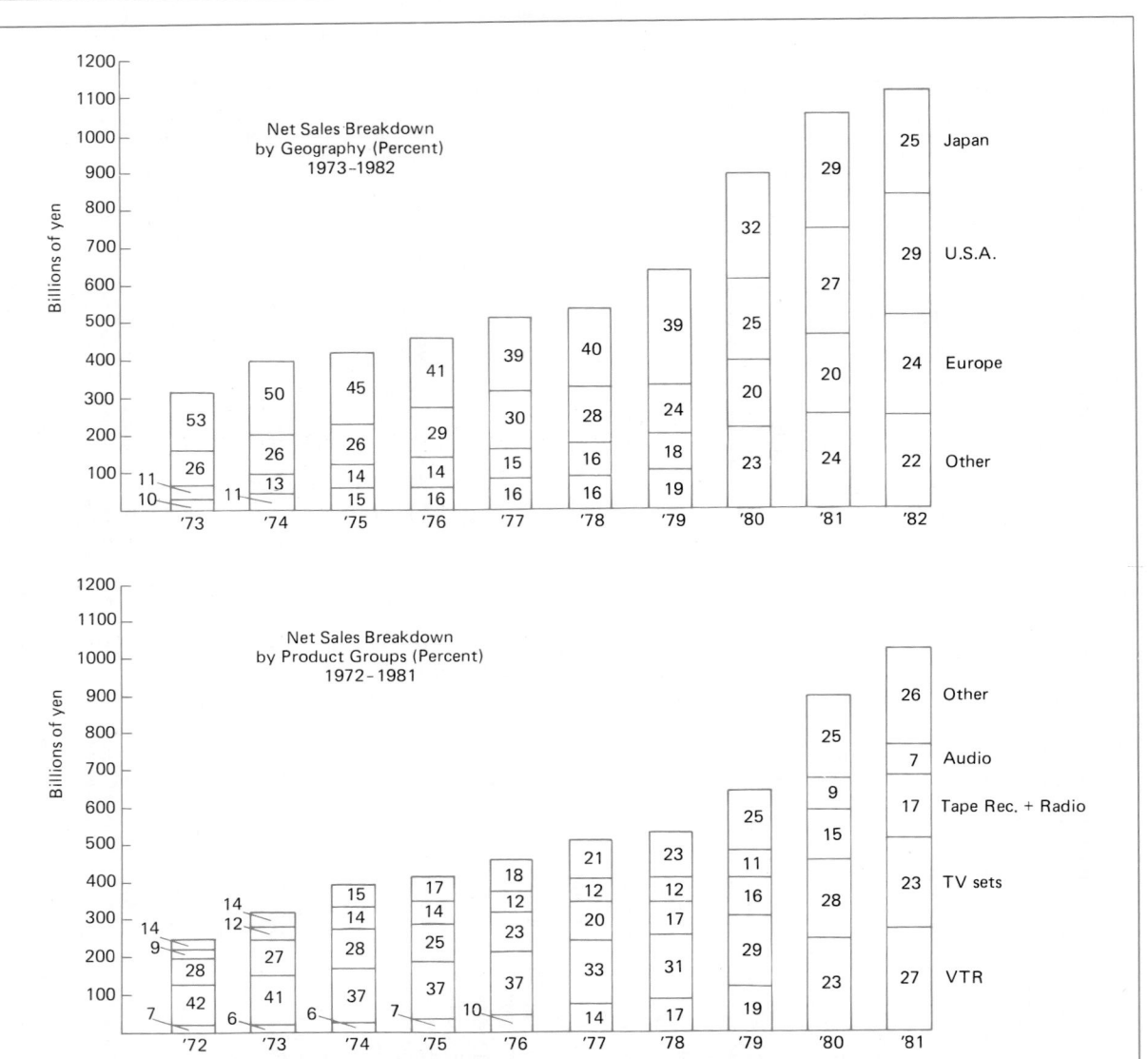

Note: In 1982 Sony changed its product groupings as follows: (1) Video Equipment (VTRs, video cameras, video tapes*, etc.); (2) Television Sets (color, black and white, projection*, etc.); (3) Audio Equipment (Hi-Fi audio products, tape recorders and radios, audio tapes*, etc.); (4) Others (Business Machines, etc.). The starred items were previously in the "Other" category. In 1982 Sony provided the following net sales breakdown by product groups:

	PERCENT OF NET SALES			
	Video	TV	Audio	Other
1981	34	26	29	11
1982	43	23	23	11

Source: Sony Corporation, *SEC Form 20F,* 1981 and 1982.

866

EXHIBIT 5
Mavica System

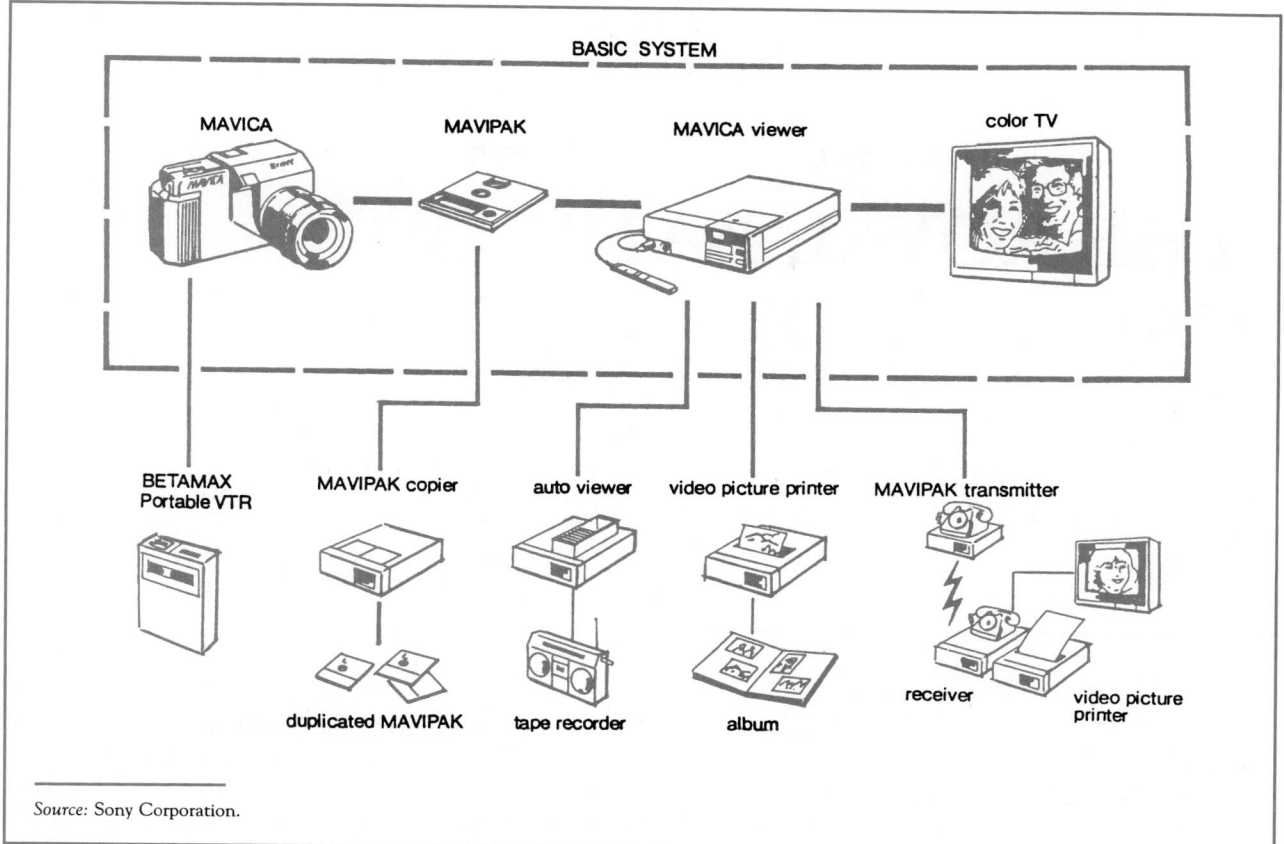

Source: Sony Corporation.

THE ROYAL BANK OF CANADA (B)

The Royal Bank of Canada (RBC) was founded (as the Merchants Bank) in 1894 to fund the Nova Scotian fishing trade. In 1985 it was the largest chartered bank in Canada, with operations in many other areas of the world. Although Canada is very large geographically (the second largest country in the world), it is sparsely settled in many areas, with its population concentrated along the Great Lakes–St. Lawrence waterways and in a few large western cities. Historically the western provinces have been especially strong raw material, energy, and agricultural producers, while the eastern provinces have dominated the manufacturing, retailing, financial, and service sectors of the economy. Significantly, however, Ontario produces 40% of Canada's minerals, and Quebec is noted for its extensive hydropower and forestry resources. Though similar to the U.S. banking system, Canada's structure differs in certain significant dimensions (see Appendix A). Its total domestic banking market is about the size of California's.

From 1961–1977 the Royal Bank was led by Mr. W. Earle McLaughlin. When Mr. McLaughlin took over in 1961, the bank had assets of just over $4 billion;* by 1977 its assets were $34 billion. Many changes, in addition to growth, occurred during the McLaughlin era. In 1967 the Bank Act of Canada was revised and among other things, eliminated the interest rate ceiling on bank loan charges

Case copyright © 1989 by James Brian Quinn. Case prepared by Penny C. Paquette under the supervision of Professor Quinn.

The generous cooperation of the Royal Bank of Canada is gratefully acknowledged.

* *Note:* All dollar figures are Canadian dollars unless otherwise indicated.

and eased the restrictions on residential mortgage lending by banks. Although the chartered banks vigorously pursued both deposits and consumer as well as commercial lending opportunities, "the near banks"** grew slightly faster than the banks.

For the Royal Bank, the decade 1967–1977 brought asset growth of 340% and the addition of some 50 new services. RBC became a large scale residential mortgage lender; moved firmly into consumer loans; developed specialized financial services for fishermen, farmers, professionals, and small businessmen; and took major steps in automation and international banking. In 1970, RBC was one of the founding partners of Orion Bank (with Chase Manhattan and others) formed to handle the growing consortium Eurodollar lending business. Orion eventually became RBC's main focus for merchant banking activities.

In June 1977, Mr. Rowland Frazee became president and heir apparent to Mr. McLaughlin and began the process of adjusting the bank's organization, culture, and strategy to cope with the massive changes in the world of banking.

EARLY 1980s ISSUES

By 1981, the Royal Bank had grown to $85 billion Canadian or U.S. $71 billion in assets at prevailing exchange rates, ranking it fourth in North America. One-third of its assets were foreign based. And its profits had grown at 16% compounded for the past five years. Income from international operations was growing at 26% compounded. Its international profits growth at 21.5% was better than twice the increase of Bank of America and four times that of Citicorp. As Canada's largest bank, RBC boasted a coast-to-coast retail network of 1,522 branches and held about $18 billion in secure retail deposits. This was twice the volume of Citicorp and almost half again as many branches as Bank of America.

The Bank enjoyed a good reputation internationally, but was still not considered "a first tier" bank. Domestically, it was strong in cash management and energy financing. Internationally, it was well known as a sound correspondent banker and merchant banker (through its Orion group). It had excellent funding strength in dollars and strong foreign exchange capabilities, especially in the $U.S./$Canadian and $U.S./Sterling markets. However, the whole world banking situation was changing rapidly. As the U.S. economy began to weaken in late 1981–1982, and the "energy shortage" faded, a variety of pressures developed for the world banking community. Most notable among these was the LDC debt crisis. May U.S. banks had lent sums in excess of their total reserves to developing countries. The Royal Bank's exposure in this area is shown in the next table. Because of U.S. inflation, interest rates had risen to all time highs in 1979–1980, placing intolerable debt burdens on many LDCs. The strong U.S. dollar and depressed world prices for raw materials made these debts increasingly difficult to repay as the decade of the 1980s developed.

** These include: trust companies, credit unions, some mortgage loan companies, and certain other institutions such as the Montreal City and District Savings Bank, the Province of Ontario Savings Office, and the Province of Alberta Treasury branches.

International Operations Distribution of Assets by Country Classification,* 1981–1982

($ BILLIONS AT OCTOBER 31)	1982	%	1981	%
Industrialized countries	$21.3	66.4%	$21.2	67.7%
Centrally planned countries	0.8	2.6	0.9	2.9
Oil exporting countries	1.2	3.7	1.0	3.2
Developing countries				
High income	1.3	4.0	1.4	4.5
Upper middle income	3.6	11.1	3.6	11.5
Intermediate middle income	3.0	9.5	2.4	7.7
Lower middle income	0.7	2.1	0.6	1.9
Low income	0.2	0.6	0.2	0.6
Total earning assets	$32.1	100.0%	$31.3	100.0%

* Based on International Bank for Reconstruction and Development classifications of per capita income.

Source: RBC internal report.

1983–1985 SITUATION

By 1983, the organization of the Royal Bank of Canada had slowly mutated to the form shown in Exhibit 1. Profiles of the key players are provided in Exhibit 2. In 1983–1985 the United States began to recover from its early 1980s recession, pulling the world economy up with it. Oil prices began to sag, offering the hope for a stronger long-term world growth pattern—but with some very great uncertainties facing the entire financial world. Mr. Frazee and his top management group began to work through the next important steps necessary to position the Royal Bank for its long term future. As they looked forward, they saw the following as the most important near-term and long-term changes in the Royal Bank's environment.

Deregulation Begins

By 1985, Canada would emerge from the severe recession of 1982 into an era of slower, but more evenly distributed regional growth. The National Energy Program had "backfired substantially" and raised serious doubts as to the merits of formalized sector planning. Loan demand sagged reaching such low levels at this time that some banks decreased their deposit interest rates below the market rate offered by other institutions. The Progressive Conservative party successfully pinpointed "unrestrained government interventionism" as the cause of Canada's faltering growth prospects. The country had elected a new government headed by a Progressive Conservative, Brian Mulroney; and prospects for improved relations and possibly even a free trade zone with the United States were fostered by a pulling back from some aspects of the Foreign Investment Review Act. An articulate internationalist constituency (including leading bankers) began to stress the concept of reciprocity versus that of "Canadianization."

The movement toward "constitutional reform" was put on a back burner, but provincial-federal rivalry over jurisdiction of the financial services industry continued. Quebec separatism had faded somewhat—key aspects of Bill 101 had been overturned by the Supreme Court of Canada, and Montreal was making a bid to recapture its position as a major international financial center. After the October Crisis of 1970 when some extremists set off bombs in Montreal, the financial industry had fled to Toronto and the Toronto Stock Exchange had boomed.

Euromoney noted that "deregulation is in the air in Canada; Canada's more adventurous banks are beginning to test the legal barriers that keep the main financial functions apart."[1] And pressure was building for changes in legislation governing the financial services industry as a whole. The Mulroney government, which had stressed cooperation versus rivalry between federal and provincial regulators, issued a white paper in the spring of 1985 laying out a plan (1) to allow holding companies to own banks as well as investment dealers if provincial legislation permitted and (2) to allow insurance and trust companies to make commercial loans. If this became policy, it would cast aside Canada's long standing "Four Pillars" concept—see Appendix A—and pit the big banks against large financial conglomerates, several of which (Trilon, Laurentian Group, Power Financial Corp.) were already in operation.

Such financial holding companies could already both sell stocks and perform some banking activities. But these companies would not be limited to the 10% ownership maximum imposed on other individual shareholders in banks. Trilon (owned by the Bronfman family) already controlled Canada's largest trust company, a number of real estate companies, and an insurance company. Through a subsidiary it had moved into merchant banking in a partnership with Merrill Lynch and Canadian Imperial Bank of Commerce (CIBC). The Government's White Paper would also permit life insurance and trust companies to make commercial loans—previously the exclusive domain of the banks. The Mulroney government was said to be "eager to bring free competition into the system, to lower borrowing costs, and to help spur lagging capital investment in the country."[2]

The Banks Respond

But the chartered banks were also responding. By purchasing Harris Trust in September 1984, the Bank of Montreal not only gained a foothold in the U.S. market, but created an opportunity to circumvent the Canadian law that prevented commercial banks from entering the trust business. No regulation forbade Harris Trust from managing Canadian pension fund money. CIBC used a loophole to arrange a $100 million convertible preferred private placement deal for Canadian Pacific. Toronto Dominion Bank had been in the stock brokerage business since 1983, after the Ontario Securities Commission allowed banks to register as brokers (but not to trade on the exchanges). For its part, the Royal Bank had opened an Orion Royal Bank representative office in Toronto, but its existence was being threatened by possible changes in Ontario Security Commission regulations.

As of late 1984, in Canada there were 13 "Schedule A" banks and 59 "Schedule B" banks, all of which were foreign based. (See Appendix A.) The foreign Schedule Bs soon introduced Canadian corporate treasurers to the "cost of funds" lending concept, which Canadian banks had successfully resisted until then. By early 1985 over 50% of the Schedule Bs' loans were on this cost-plus basis. The Schedule Bs had also driven down the price on bankers' acceptances, letters of credit, and stand-by lines of credit. Yet several of the Schedule Bs had achieved high ROAs and were going after more potentially lucrative or fee-based activities like factoring, venture capital, foreign exchange, and money-market transactions. The following table shows the Royal Bank's fee-based income.

Fee-Based Income, 1983–1984

($ millions)

	1984	1983	PERCENT CHANGE
Service charges	$212	$185	14.6%
Visa fees	98	84	16.7
Loan and commitment fees	105	108	(2.8)
Securities commissions	38	44	(13.6)
Foreign exchange revenue	101	93	8.6
Bankers' acceptances, letters of credit and guarantee fees	69	72	(4.2)
Sundry	86	81	6.2
Total	$709	$667	6.3%

Source: Royal Bank of Canada, *Annual Report,* 1984.

Merrill Lynch's Canadian subsidiary, although it was constrained to some extent by capital restrictions imposed in 1972, had been moving aggressively to regain a top position in Canada's capital markets. And new rules proposed by the Ontario government would allow additional foreign brokers to set up shop under similar capital restrictions, or to buy as much as 30% of a Canadian securities dealer—this would definitely heat up competition in the industry.[3] To complicate matters further, new electronics technologies were changing the financial services industry enormously. Non-banks were increasingly involved in banking type services. Credit cards had proliferated in retailing and similar institutions. Automated teller machines (ATMs) made it possible to obtain cash virtually anywhere. And in the United States, retail operations—like Sears, Roebuck, J. C. Penney, and others —were offering cash, insurance, and financial services through their retail outlets, a trend which might well spread to Canada.

THE ROYAL BANK IN 1985

From the Royal Bank Annual Report of 1984 and its March 1985 presentation to bank analysts, certain summary dimensions could be derived about RBC's internal operations. By mid-1985, The Royal Bank had grown to over $88 billion in assets, of which more than one-third were international. However, the severe recession of 1981–1983 and the LDC debt crisis had taken their toll on RBC's profits. The following tables give details of RBC's loan losses and nonperforming loans. (See Exhibit 3 for summary RBC financials.) RBC's prominent position as lender to major Canadian energy companies and to Latin American countries and corporations had put the bank in the uncomfortable position of having the highest loan loss experience on these accounts among the major Canadian banks. Profit margins had been squeezed by the competitive pressures outlined above (see Exhibit 4 for comparative data on RBC and other Canadian banks). But RBC continued to invest heavily in computer and automation equipment.

On the positive side, the Royal Banks's noninterest expenses (NIE) had increased by less than the inflation rate during 1984, and RBC ranked second best of the majors in NIE as a percent of income. Exhibit 3 shows the composition of RBC's NIE.

RBC had $16 billion in domestic consumer loans in Canada, representing a 25% market share for installment loans, mortgages, and credit card debt. Because of innovative new mortgage options and pricing structures, RBC's share of new commitments in mortgages was growing and was currently 29%. The bank's retail distribution network was made up of 1,440 branches and 750 automatic teller machines, representing the largest block of ATMs in Canadian banking. RBC's $28 billion in personal deposits comprised a 24.5% share of those held by chartered banks. And RBC's $4 billion in independent business loans represented a market share of 25%, up 300 basis points since 1982. The bank had $3.5 billion in agricultural loans to some 80,000 farmers, but about 5% of these were said to be in some difficulty because of the serious agricultural situation in Canada. In addition, the bank had $19 billion in commercial loans to some 8,000 large clients, including those managed by the National Accounts Division and Global Energy and Minerals (GEM).

Detail of Loan Losses, 1980–1984
($ millions)

	1984	1983	1982	1981	1980
Loan loss experience					
Domestic					
Consumer installment, Visa, mortgages, and other personal loans	$ 48	$ 92	$ 77	$ 43	$34
Agriculture and independent business	84	104	84	37	29
Large commercial and corporate	248	258	369	64	28
	$380	$454	$530	$144	$91
International					
Asia Pacific	22	14	—	3	2
Europe, Middle East, and Africa	48	85	57	31	19
Latin America and Caribbean	123	45	18	27	28
United States	169	174	75	14	7
	$362	$318	$150	$ 75	$56
Total	$742	$772	$680	$219	$147
Eligible loans					
Domestic	$45,476	$44,726	$47,178	$41,632	$29,568
International	21,281	20,529	20,904	19,222	12,706
Total	$66,757	$65,255	$68,082	$60,854	$42,274
Loss experience as a percent of eligible loans					
Domestic	0.84%	1.01%	1.12%	0.35%	0.31%
International	1.70	1.55	0.72	0.39	0.44
Total	1.11%	1.18%	1.00%	0.36%	0.35%
Provision for loan losses (five-year average)					
Domestic	$327	$309	$258	$135	$ 90
International	208	143	86	51	34
Total	$535	$452	$344	$186	$124

Source: Royal Bank of Canada, *Annual Report*, 1984.

RBC enjoyed the largest customer base of any financial services concern in Canada. However, competition was increasing faster than the total size of the market. By 1985 more than 60% of RBC's personal clients dealt with other financial service providers as well, and it was more and more important to provide a full array of products and services to retain their basic deposit business. These clients were also being heavily marketed by new competitors using careful niching strategies. These factors became of increasing importance as domestic margins were being squeezed on both fixed rate and prime-related business, due to a reduced differential between money market and prime rates. The foreign Schedule B banks, as noted above, were compressing margins in order to build market share during this period. And this pressure had increased in 1984 when the Schedule Bs allowable asset ceiling was raised to 16% of total banking assets.

Technology was also eroding the competitive advantages of traditional branch networks. Mr. Frazee noted in a 1984 interview that, "RBC does not make money on its depositors directly." ATMs could be easily installed at specific locations by competitors, near banks and non-banks. It was becoming increasingly difficult for RBC to support a full-service branch network as well as a growing ATM network. There was even some question as to whether RBC's traditional banking markets offered sufficient potential to utilize its extensive available distribution system.

International Operations

In the international realm, RBC had completed the purchase of Orion in 1981 and changed the name to Orion Royal Bank. Orion was in a lead or comanaged position in approximately 200 issues worth some $U.S. 38 billion or 50% of the total Euromarket. In Euro-Canadian and Euro-Australian dollar bonds, Orion Royal had 70% of the action on the Euromarket. Orion Royal Pacific managed the 10 largest syndicated credits in the Asian market. For the period January 1983 to May 1985, *Euromoney* listed Orion Royal Bank as the No. 1 bookrunner for private sector Canadian issues in the Eurobond market, as No. 8 for public sector Canadian issues, and as No. 4 for all Canadian issues combined. Only in the Eurocredits market did the other large Canadian banks factor heavily in the competition. The Bank of Montreal is ranked as the No. 2 lead manager to Canadian borrowers by a narrow margin over RBC-Orion Royal Bank as No. 3. Bank of Montreal also edged out RBC-Orion Royal Bank as the No. 1 Canadian lead manager to all borrowers in the Euromarkets.[4]

The total international division held over $18 billion in assets, managed over 5,000 correspondent relationships and employed some 6,000 people. RBC's international business was shifting from loan-oriented products toward a full array of capital market products. (See Canada's Financial Services Note.) The increasing interconnectedness among the world's capital markets was leading many of RBC's competitors to offer more extended global trading services and to provide their multinational clients access to all major capital markets as well as global account management services. In addition, as international trade balances and growth patterns changed, the positioning of RBC's extensive international distribution network became an issue. (See map—Exhibit 5.)

Organizational Issues

Despite a growing familiarity with its relatively new matrix organization, difficulties still arose for RBC in coordinating the efforts of its commercial and merchant bankers, especially on the international scene. Commercial bankers were increasingly being asked to "concept sell" complex capital market products such as interest and exchange rate swaps, note issuance facilities, and Eurobonds (which were delivered by the merchant banking group) as well as selling and managing the delivery of bread-and-butter banking products such as short term commercial loans, letters of credit, stand-by lines of credit, and international cash management services.

In a time of rapidly changing business environments and extremely tight operating margins, innovation and flexibility were essential to the Royal Bank. However, its very size and complexity created significant barriers to communications and serious concerns for top management. Executives in RBC's far-flung operations often complained of the complexity and length of time it took to make decisions and commitments. The Bank had conducted numerous experiments to understand changing customer patterns and how specific services would be received by its customers. But top management did not feel that it had found ultimate solutions to these complex problems in 1985. There was widespread discussion of the appropriate degree of decentralization needed by the bank. A crucial question was how this decentralization could be accomplished, yet maintain the essential controls required both by the banking laws and by prudent management.

Over the last decade differences in culture had become apparent between domestic bankers operating in the more restricted and conservative environment of Canada and international bankers, many of whom operated in markets where fewer barriers existed between the various segments of the financial services industry. There were also inherent differences in outlook between commercial bankers with a lending orientation and traders or merchant bankers with the more flamboyant style often required in the fast-paced capital markets. Although there were advantages (improved communications and support systems) to grouping each speciality together, such groupings also led to communication problems and potential value conflicts between groups with slightly different goals and quite different operating styles.

Values for the New Era

In dealing with the wide variety of issues facing the Royal Bank in 1985, its top management had developed a preliminary statement of values to serve as guidelines for any proposed solutions. The following statement seemed to meet with wide acceptance among key managers although it was under continuing review:

Our Values:

- The customer comes first.
- Integrity forms the foundation of our business.
- Trust, respect, and openness strengthen our relationships with customers and with each other.
- Quality and excellence are central to all that we do.
- Innovation and creativity give us the power to renew our business.
- Teamwork, we pull together for greater effectiveness.
- Community involvement strengthens our awareness and reputation.
- With our global presence we hope to build a strong Canada, competitive in a world economy.

EXHIBIT 1
RBC Organization, January 1982

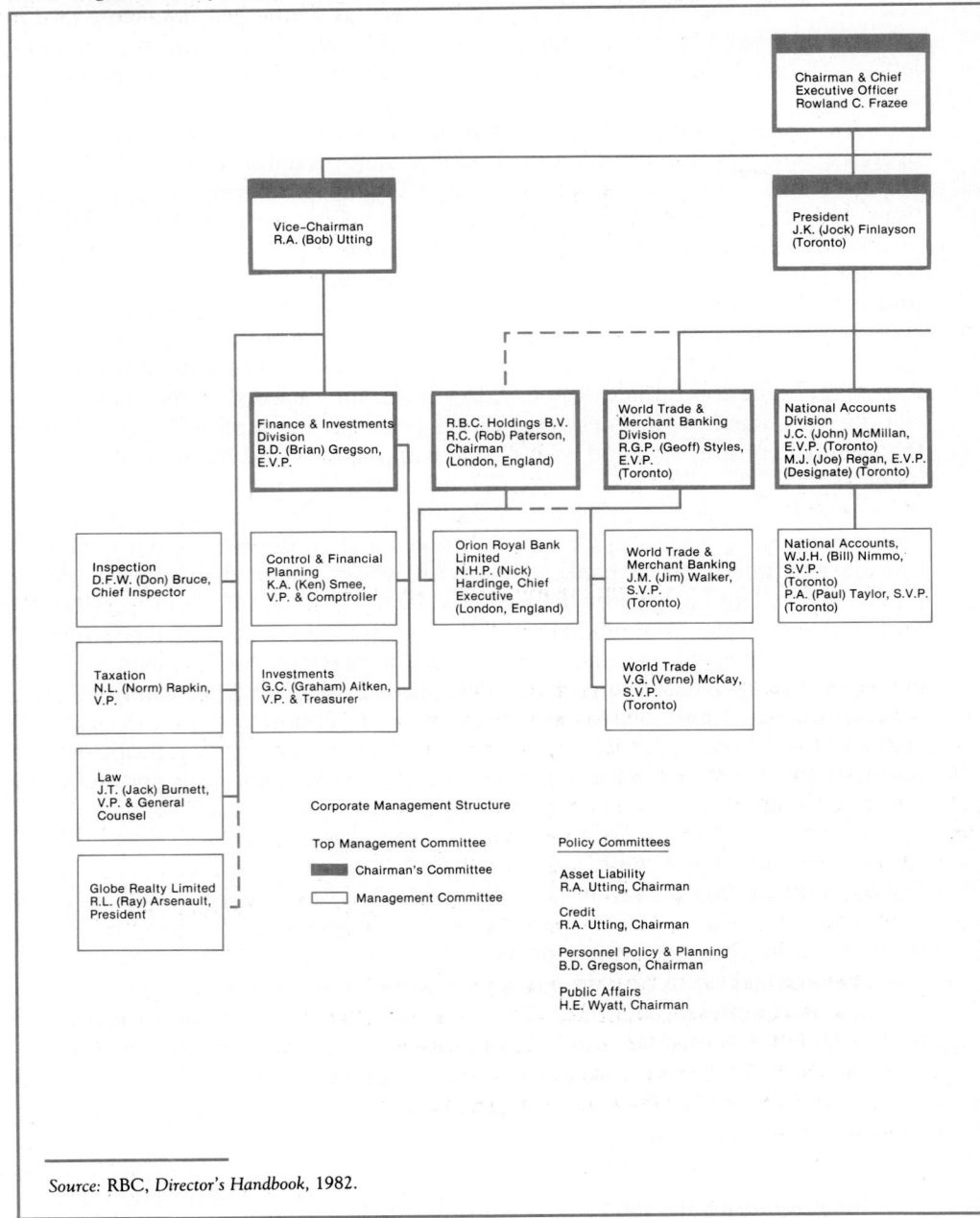

Source: RBC, *Director's Handbook*, 1982.

876

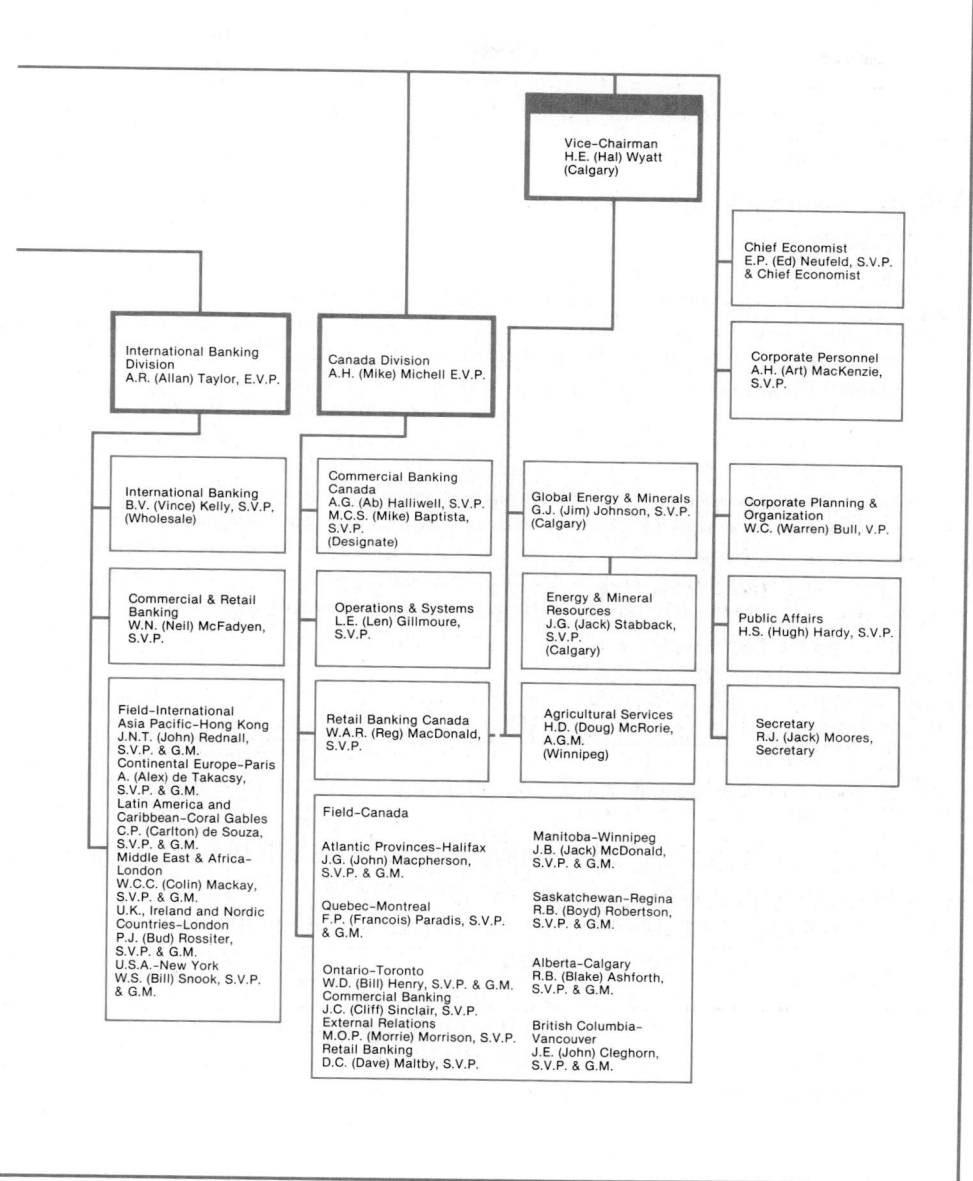

Vice-Chairman
H.E. (Hal) Wyatt
(Calgary)

Chief Economist
E.P. (Ed) Neufeld, S.V.P.
& Chief Economist

International Banking
Division
A.R. (Allan) Taylor, E.V.P.

Canada Division
A.H. (Mike) Michell E.V.P.

Corporate Personnel
A.H. (Art) MacKenzie,
S.V.P.

International Banking
B.V. (Vince) Kelly, S.V.P.
(Wholesale)

Commercial Banking
Canada
A.G. (Ab) Halliwell, S.V.P.
M.C.S. (Mike) Baptista,
S.V.P.
(Designate)

Global Energy & Minerals
G.J. (Jim) Johnson, S.V.P.
(Calgary)

Corporate Planning &
Organization
W.C. (Warren) Bull, V.P.

Commercial & Retail
Banking
W.N. (Neil) McFadyen,
S.V.P.

Operations & Systems
L.E. (Len) Gillmoure,
S.V.P.

Energy & Mineral
Resources
J.G. (Jack) Stabback,
S.V.P.
(Calgary)

Public Affairs
H.S. (Hugh) Hardy, S.V.P.

Field-International
Asia Pacific-Hong Kong
J.N.T. (John) Rednall,
S.V.P. & G.M.
Continental Europe-Paris
A. (Alex) de Takacsy,
S.V.P. & G.M.
Latin America and
Caribbean-Coral Gables
C.P. (Carlton) de Souza,
S.V.P. & G.M.
Middle East & Africa-
London
W.C.C. (Colin) Mackay,
S.V.P. & G.M.
U.K., Ireland and Nordic
Countries-London
P.J. (Bud) Rossiter,
S.V.P. & G.M.
U.S.A.-New York
W.S. (Bill) Snook, S.V.P.
& G.M.

Retail Banking Canada
W.A.R. (Reg) MacDonald,
S.V.P.

Agricultural Services
H.D. (Doug) McRorie,
A.G.M.
(Winnipeg)

Secretary
R.J. (Jack) Moores,
Secretary

Field-Canada

Atlantic Provinces-Halifax
J.G. (John) Macpherson,
S.V.P. & G.M.

Quebec-Montreal
F.P. (Francois) Paradis, S.V.P.
& G.M.

Ontario-Toronto
W.D. (Bill) Henry, S.V.P. & G.M.
Commercial Banking
J.C. (Cliff) Sinclair, S.V.P.
External Relations
M.O.P. (Morrie) Morrison, S.V.P.
Retail Banking
D.C. (Dave) Maltby, S.V.P.

Manitoba-Winnipeg
J.B. (Jack) McDonald,
S.V.P. & G.M.

Saskatchewan-Regina
R.B. (Boyd) Robertson,
S.V.P. & G.M.

Alberta-Calgary
R.B. (Blake) Ashforth,
S.V.P. & G.M.

British Columbia-
Vancouver
J.E. (John) Cleghorn,
S.V.P. & G.M.

877

Our Objectives:

- To be a consistent leader in providing customers with services and counseling of quality and value.
- To be viewed with respect and to be the leading financial services enterprise in Canada and the Canadian leader abroad.
- To be an enlightened employer known for quality of leadership and quality of people.
- To be one of the most profitable major financial enterprises in Canada and to have a top credit rating.

In summarizing the bank's aspirations in 1985 Mr. Frazee endorsed the following statement:

> From our modest beginning in 1864 in Halifax, we have become a world scale international bank. We succeeded by "serving the customer" well. We followed ships at sea and rails across continents. We pioneered with the pioneers. Since 1941 we have remained Canada's largest and most successful bank. This is our history as a bank.
>
> Let's turn to our future as a financial services enterprise. We have already entered a new era—an era which requires us to pioneer as never before in a world fast being reinvented. We will have to meet the changing needs of our customers quicker than ever before. We will continue to follow telecommunications to the perimeters of space. We will need to segment our markets, to serve our customers better, and to outpace our competitors—both new and old. If we actively seize every opportunity to serve our clients better, we will make more money, keep our jobs challenging, create new jobs for others, and be able to invest even more in improving our services to Canada and the world.

QUESTIONS

1. Evaluate RBC's responses to the challenges it faced in the late 1970s and early 1980s.
2. In 1985, what are the most critical factors which will determine the Royal Bank's future success in its changing environments?
3. How should the bank redeploy its resources to meet its future challenges? Specifically, how should it restructure its total organization to accomplish this effectively?
4. IF RBC is allowed to diversify into other financial services, which should be given highest priority? Why? How can RBC use its unique strengths and capabilities to maximum advantage?

EXHIBIT 2
Brief Personal Profiles of
Key Executives

Mr. Brian Gregson had been named executive vice president of finance and investments in September 1980. A line banker, he had come up through the Canada Bank and had been general manager of the large Toronto division and other central branches. Mr. Gregson was described as "having good business instincts, a good deal maker, and a skilled negotiator." He was known for his decisiveness and his directness in personal relationships. He tended to cut through to the core of issues and "to see things in clear terms." Friendly and distinguished in appearance, he took pains to get out of his office, to meet his people, and to work with them.

Mr. "Mike" Michell was a brawny, cigar-smoking analytical executive with a phenomenal appetite for numbers. He was highly respected as "a tremendously energetic person, who works 18-hour days, 8-day weeks." Mr. Michell had worked his way up through the ranks to become executive vice president of the Canada Division in 1978. Although he tended to manage from his office in a somewhat formal style, he was superb in one-on-one situations. He had a strong commitment to financial planning, drove himself hard in pursuit of objectives and had firm expectations of others. More formal than Mr. Gregson, he was known for his meticulous preparations for public appearances and his capacity to run his highly diverse empire in a manner totally dedicated and supportive of top management's goals. He had been a champion of the long-term development of RBC's electronic technology programs.

Mr. "Rob" Paterson had risen through various line positions in the domestic bank and a short stint in the New York unit of RBC. He then moved into the bank's head office investment department and rose to its top. From there he became executive vice president of the Finance and Investments Division. In 1980 he was posted to London as chairman, RBC Holdings B.V. He had spent most of his banking life in the money markets and investments side of the Royal Bank. A cultured, sophisticated man with an international perspective, Mr. Paterson had a trader's instincts for how money markets operated and an ability to see the bank's actions from the viewpoint of investors and depositors. On the personal level, he was said to have "a good sense of the market, what makes it tick. . . . Rob has a strong belief in people's willingness to perform. . . . His style is tolerant, helpful, not dictatorial."

Mr. "Joe" Regan's career had been primarily in the international area, dealing with "big ticket" loans and large clients. He had been involved in the United States, Carribean, and London markets and had been deputy to the head of the international division of RBC. He was a soft spoken, witty man of few words who had a distaste for those who might pontificate. In 1979 he was appointed senior vice president national accounts, and 1982 became executive vice president of the National Accounts Division. Mr. Regan was an experienced corporate-international banker who could think in non-traditional terms. He had headed up a bankwide task force on trends in the financial services industry and had developed a deep understanding of the fundamental changes occurring in this environment and their implications for the Royal Bank.

Mr. "Geoff" Styles was a tall, gregarious, outgoing, comfortable person who was very international in his viewpoint. He had represented the Royal

EXHIBIT 2
(Continued)

Bank at the founding of its Orion unit. Although he was an ardent "internationalist" in his viewpoint, he had moved back and forth between the European and Montreal units perhaps more than anyone in the upper levels in the bank. He was often described as "a visionary, very entrepreneurial, and perhaps the bank's best sponsor of the merchant-banking, investment-banking viewpoint." He tended to be very informal and approachable in his style. He was described as "a good communicator, encouraging freedom in thinking among his people." Despite his entrepreneurial flair, he was said "to have good balance sheet instincts and to be very effective with outside constituencies because of his deep knowledge of international banking and his dialoguing capabilities." He had been appointed executive vice president of the World Trade and Merchant Banking Division in June of 1980.

Mr. Allan Taylor was a very warm, open person. He had an extraordinarily high energy level, persistence, and an orderly mind that enabled him to digest the essence and dynamics of a complex issue and deal with it forthrightly. After working his way up the line in the domestic bank, Mr. Taylor spent three years in New York before returning to Montreal where he became the head of the International Division in 1977 and an executive vice president in 1978. Colleagues said, "Al Taylor relentlessly pursues his homework. Al says what he means and means what he says. He is known for his articulate, well-prepared, careful phrasings in public forums." Internally, he paid careful attention to details and expected clear commitments and carefully worked out plans from his subordinates. He was dedicated to the planning process, with accountability and commitment of individuals behind it. And his experiences had given him a well-balanced view of both Canadian and international operations.

Source: Author's interviews with various RBC executives.

EXHIBIT 3
Summary of Royal Bank Financial Structure, 1980–1984

Return on Assets (% of Average Assets)

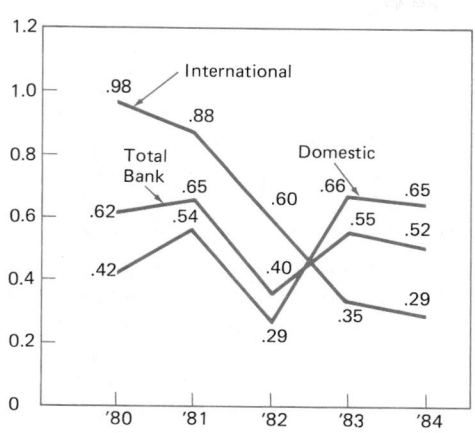

Net Interest Margin (% of Average Assets)

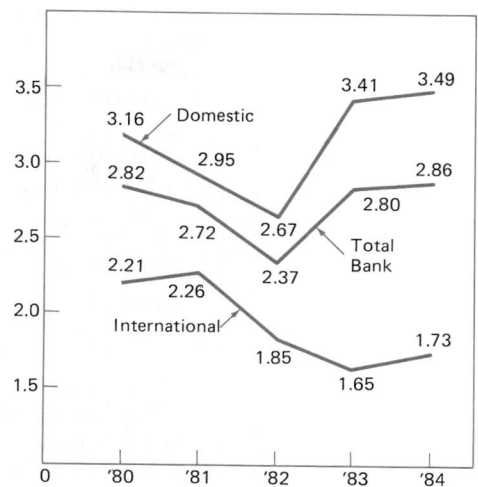

Composition of Average Domestic Deposits ($ Billions)

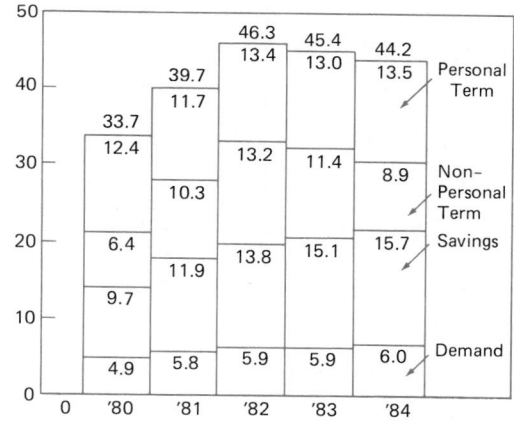

Fixed Rate Lending Portfolio Yield Versus Portfolio Cost of Personal Term Deposits (Including Reserve Costs) (Percent)

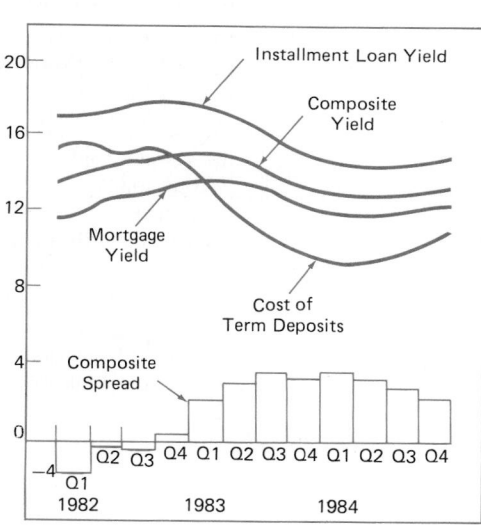

Source: Royal Bank of Canada, *Annual Report*, 1984.

EXHIBIT 3
(Continued)

Breakdown of Earning Assets,* 1983–1984

As at September 30 ($ Millions)	1984	Percent	1983	Percent
Loans				
Domestic				
Atlantic Provinces	$ 2,562	6.1%	$ 2,394	6.0%
Quebec	5,203	12.5	4,540	11.5
Ontario	13,070	31.3	11,968	30.3
Manitoba and Saskatchewan	4,862	11.6	4,327	11.0
Alberta	8,633	20.7	8,784	22.2
British Columbia	7,411	17.8	7,521	19.0
Total	$41,741	100.0%	$39,534	100.0%
Of which				
Mortgages	$ 8,990	21.5%	$ 8,004	20.2%
Loans to individuals	8,343	20.0	7,682	19.4
Agricultural	2,240	5.4	2,262	5.7
Financial institutions	2,866	6.9	2,446	6.2
Merchandisers	2,857	6.8	2,553	6.5
Manufacturing	3,704	3.9	4,108	10.4
Construction	1,959	4.7	2,359	6.0
Mining and energy	4,023	9.6	3,964	10.0
Other	6,759	16.2	6,156	15.6
Total	$41,741	100.0%	$39,534	100.0%
International				
Canadian risk	$ 659	3.7%	$ 739	4.1%
Asia Pacific	2,169	12.0	1,911	10.7
Europe, Middle East and Africa	5,227	28.9	5,927	33.3
Latin America and Caribbean	5,907	32.7	5,372	30.1
United States	4,102	22.7	3,874	21.8
Total	$13,064	100.0%	$17,823	100.0%
Total loans	$59,805	74.0%	$57,357	75.2%
Securities	6,867	8.5	7,092	9.3
Deposits with other banks	14,126	17.5	11,851	15.5
Total earning assets	$80,798	100.0%	$76,300	100.0%

* Earning assets are defined as all assets except cash and deposits with Bank of Canada, acceptances, land, buildings and equipment and other assets.

Source: Royal Bank of Canada, *Annual Report,* 1984.

EXHIBIT 3
(Continued)

Comparative Statistics for the Five Largest Canadian Banks

Asset Growth Rates (1980–1984 Compound Average)

Toronto-Dominion Bank	9.8%
Royal Bank of Canada	9.4
Bank of Nova Scotia	8.7
Bank of Montreal	8.6*
Canadian Imperial Bank of Canada (CIBC)	5.9

Pre-Tax Profits (as % shareholders' funds plus own account borrowing, 1980–1984 average)

Toronto-Dominion Bank	20.1
Bank of Nova Scotia	16.7
Royal Bank of Canada	14.6
CIBC	13.2
Bank of Montreal	13.2

Return on Assets (1980–1984 average—%)

	Domestic	International	Combined
Toronto-Dominion	0.74	0.73	0.73
CIBC	0.40	0.56	0.56
Royal Bank of Canada	0.51	0.62	0.55
Bank of Montreal	0.50	0.50	0.50
Bank of Nova Scotia	0.43	0.70	0.45

Lending as % of Deposits (1980–1984 average)

CIBC	83.1
Toronto-Dominion	82.1
Bank of Montreal	77.3
Royal Bank of Canada	75.7
Bank of Nova Scotia	73.2

* Excludes assets acquired with Harris Trust. Including Harris assets the rate is 12.6%.

Source: "An End to the Monopoly?" *Euromoney,* Supplement, July 1985.

EXHIBIT 3
(Continued)

Distribution of Domestic Lending by Category of Borrower (%, at Sept. 30, 1984)

	RBC	BOM	CIBC	BNS	TD
Personal loans	20.0	20.6	21.9	28.3	19.0
Residential mortgages	21.5	20.0	24.6	22.1	22.2
Primary producers	15.0	21.9	11.5	24.0	21.5
Trade & financial services	13.7	24.1	16.7		
Manufacturing	8.9		11.0	12.0	19.2
Construction and real estate	4.7	13.4	7.3	13.6	7.2
Other	16.2	—	7.0	—	10.9
	100.0	100.0	100.0	100.0	100.0

Distribution of Geographical Risk (% as of Sept. 30, 1984)

	RBC	BOM	CIBC	BNS	TD
North America					
Canada	61.8	55.0	70.2	48.1	65.6
United States	9.7	20.9	9.8	16.4	12.8
Europe, Middle East, Africa					
United Kingdom	4.9	3.4	2.1	4.5	1.8
France	1.7	1.3	0.9	3.1	1.4
Other	8.4	4.6	4.8	9.0	6.3
Latin America and Caribbean					
Mexico	1.8	2.3	1.4	2.0	2.1
Brazil	1.6	2.4	1.4	1.7	1.9
Other	4.6	2.2	2.2	7.5	2.1
Asia and Pacific					
Japan	2.3	5.5	1.1	4.2	2.7
Other	3.2	2.4	2.3	3.5	3.3

Source: "An End to the Monopoly?" *Euromoney,* Supplement, July 1985.

EXHIBIT 4

Competitive Summary—Financial 1981 vs. 1984

(*$ millions*)

	1981					1984				
	RBC	CIBC	BOM	BNS	TD	RBC	CIBC	BOM	BNS	TD
Total interest income	11037.1	9047.8	8713.6	6639.5	6007.9	9238.6	7233.3	7720.7	6014.4	4985.4
of which										
Loans	8193.5	7370.1	7028.3	4660.2	4934.9	6967.5	5988.0	5767.6	4328.2	3954.0
Securities	776.8	573.4	601.7	369.0	429.6	718.3	488.7	852.3	414.5	465.8
Bank deposits	1738.8	884.8	823.2	1448.7	476.1	1267.2	594.1	901.1	1148.6	407.5
Total interest expense	9038.7	7408.8	7133.4	5549.6	4977.1	6763.9	5435.1	5961.9	4623.3	3624.9
of which										
Deposits	8952.2	7337.1	7005.7	5500.2	4943.8	6605.1	5321.6	5769.9	4547.4	3584.5
Debentures	71.7	53.1	68.3	37.7	28.4	120.2	110.6	111.4	74.3	39.0
Tax equivalent spread	1998.4	1639.0	1580.2	1089.9	1030.8	2474.7	1798.2	1758.8	1391.1	1360.5
Loan loss provision	185.6	215.2	196.3	81.2	74.4	535.0	431.2	375.0	241.5	199.2
Other income	500.4	378.1	288.4	268.3	209.9	708.8	522.8	499.3	309.4	333.6
Net revenue	2313.2	1801.9	1672.3	1277.0	1166.3	2648.5	1889.8	1883.1	1459.0	1494.9
Total non-interest expense	1384.0	1175.1	1000.7	832.8	664.4	1803.5	1355.2	1384.2	1005.2	833.5
of which										
Staff costs	862.6	730.9	602.5	514.4	408.8	1105.8	840.0	777.6	611.0	512.6
Premises	203.0	199.9	184.7	144.6	114.7	294.0	233.7	287.8	190.0	154.5
Other operating	318.4	244.3	213.5	173.8	140.9	403.7	281.5	318.8	204.2	166.4
Net income before tax	929.2	626.8	671.6	444.2	501.9	845.0	534.6	498.9	453.8	661.4
Net income	478.2	320.1	352.9	244.1	285.4	405.1	282.3	283.4	271.7	355.9
Average assets	73,488	59,752	54,980	45,241	38,605	86,662	68,279	66,714	56,512	44,517
Total assets	85,360	65,698	62,374	49,067	43,249	88,003	68,118	76,491	59,124	46,597

Source: Competitive Summary by RBC's Control and Financial Planning Group, November 1984.

885

EXHIBIT 5
R.B.C. Global Network

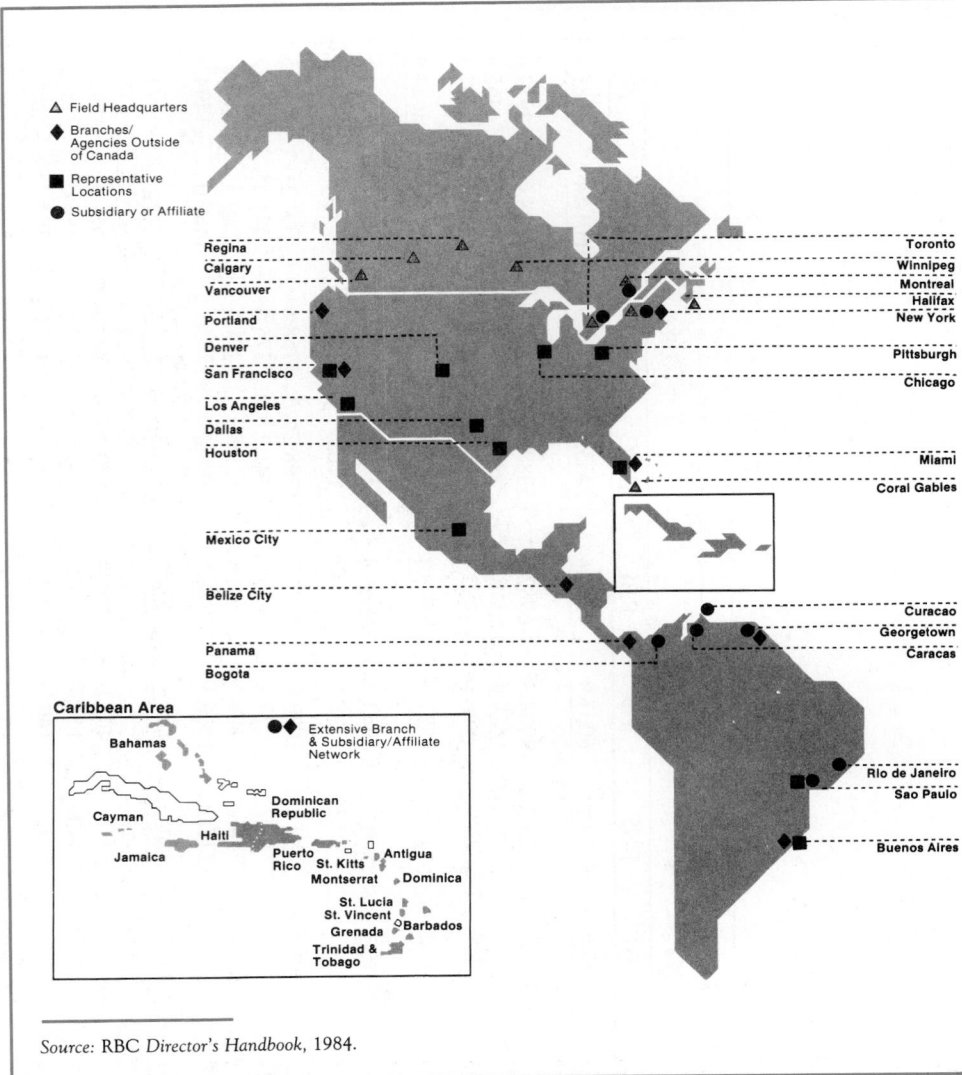

△ Field Headquarters
◆ Branches/
   Agencies Outside
   of Canada
■ Representative
   Locations
● Subsidiary or Affiliate

Regina
Calgary
Vancouver
Portland
Denver
San Francisco
Los Angeles
Dallas
Houston

Mexico City
Belize City
Panama
Bogota

Toronto
Winnipeg
Montreal
Halifax
New York
Pittsburgh
Chicago
Miami
Coral Gables
Curacao
Georgetown
Caracas
Rio de Janeiro
Sao Paulo
Buenos Aires

Caribbean Area

●◆ Extensive Branch
   & Subsidiary/Affiliate
   Network

Bahamas
Cayman
Jamaica
Haiti
Dominican
Republic
Puerto
Rico
St. Kitts
Montserrat
Antigua
Dominica
St. Lucia
St. Vincent
Grenada
Barbados
Trinidad &
Tobago

Source: RBC *Director's Handbook*, 1984.

EXHIBIT 5 (Continued)

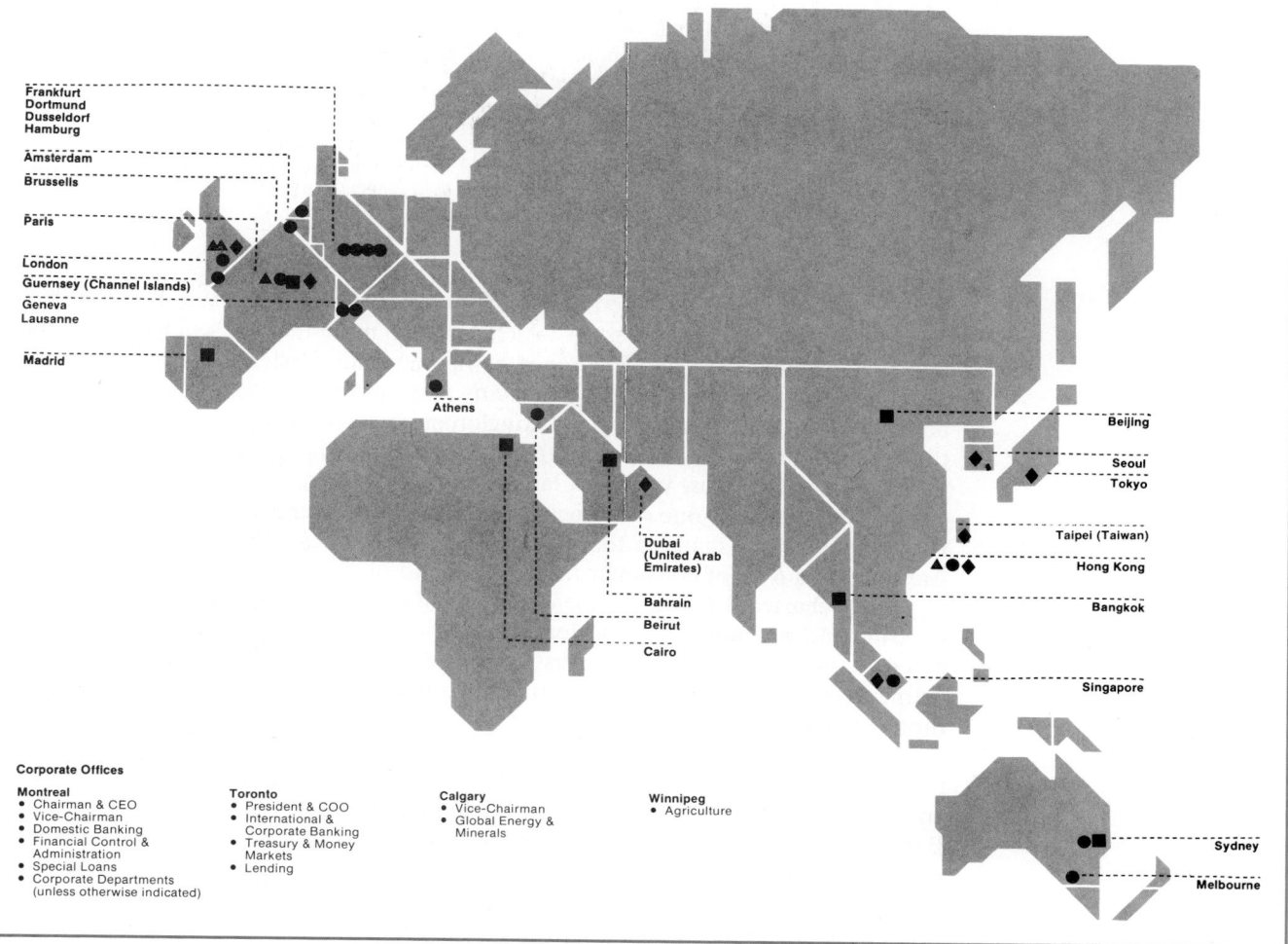

Corporate Offices

Montreal
• Chairman & CEO
• Vice-Chairman
• Domestic Banking
• Financial Control &
  Administration
• Special Loans
• Corporate Departments
  (unless otherwise indicated)

Toronto
• President & COO
• International &
  Corporate Banking
• Treasury & Money
  Markets
• Lending

Calgary
• Vice-Chairman
• Global Energy &
  Minerals

Winnipeg
• Agriculture

APPENDIX A—CANADA'S FINANCIAL SERVICES INDUSTRY

Competition and the Four Pillars: "The Canadian regulatory tradition had been to maintain institutional barriers around the 'core functions' performed by each of the four pillars of the Canadian financial system, primarily to prevent the conflicts of interest which can arise if these functions are combined under one roof."[5] The four pillars and their "core functions" are (1) the banks (chartered and regulated on the federal level) for commercial and consumer lending, (2) trust companies (chartered either on the federal or a provincial level) performing fiduciary activities, (3) insurance companies (chartered either on the federal or a provincial level) for insurance underwriting, and (4) investment dealers, (chartered and regulated on a provincial level) underwriting corporate securities.

The 1980 Bank Act changed much of this; the Canadian financial services industry became quite competitive with considerable overlap among the four pillars. The various key players had the following shares of total 1983 financial industry assets, using a global corporate asset measure:

887

Chartered banks	61.1%
Life insurance companies	11.8
Trust companies	8.7
Credit unions/caisses populaires	6.2
Investment dealers	1.4
Other financial corps., etc.	10.8
	100.0%

Source: Where's the Power in the Financial Services Industry?" *Canadian Banker,* June 1985.

These statistics overstate the banks' dominance within Canada because they include the foreign currency assets which make up more than 40% of banks' assets, and they exclude trust and insurance companies' administered assets. They also fail to take into account the fact that many trust and life insurance companies are actually divisions of large financial conglomerates, some of which are larger than the banks. The combined assets of the six largest financial holding companies total $142 billion while those of the six largest banks (excluding foreign currency assets) total $185 billion.[6] If one examines competition on a market-by-market basis, the banks held a 44% share of the personal savings market, 33% of mortgages outstanding, and 67% of consumer loans at the end of 1983.

The chartered banks compete to varying degrees with the "near banks" for deposits and for mortgages and loan (primarily consumer but some commercial) business. Banks compete with investment dealers in a more limited way. They can be members of selling groups for debt and equity securities and operate fully in the money market, but they can underwrite only certain government and bank related debt securities. More recently, many banks have pushed into private placements and one into discount brokerage while investment dealers have begun offering consumer banking services with Merrill Lynch-like cash management accounts. Banks compete with life insurance companies for mortgage and Registered Retirement Savings Plan (RRSP, the equivalent of an IRA) business and by selling credit-related life insurance. Trust companies, insurance companies, and investment dealers compete for pension fund management but trust companies are the only ones permitted to act in a fiduciary capacity. Banks compete directly with consumer loan companies on consumer loans and with sales finance, leasing, and factoring companies on sales-related and other commercial loans. Finally, there are a growing number of "merchant banking"* and venture capital firms in Canada which compete with the banks (and investment dealers in some areas) in: providing foreign exchange services, financing and facilitating international trade, bringing together buyers and sellers of listed and unlisted companies, providing financial advisory services, arranging long-term financing for governments and multinational corporations, and funding and nurturing of entrepreneurial enterprises.

Chartered Banking: Canada, unlike the United States, permits nationwide branch banking in the British tradition, and thus has relatively few banks. There

---

* *Note:* Merchant banking is a term used primarily in Great Britain and Europe to define the activities of such firms as Rothschilds which combine investment banking and parts of commercial banking as they have traditionally been practiced in the United States.

are five large banks with national branch systems which together hold 85% of all bank assets and have close to 7,000 branches—The Royal Bank of Canada, the Canadian Imperial Bank of Commerce, the Bank of Nova Scotia, the Bank of Montreal, and the Toronto Dominion Bank. In addition, there are other Schedule A banks which either have regional or specialized businesses, and 59 Schedule B banks chartered since the 1980 revisions to the Bank Act. Schedule A banks are widely held. No one interest can hold more than 10% of the voting shares. Schedule B banks can be closely held and are subsidiaries of foreign banks.

Foreign Schedule B banks have significant restrictions imposed on them by the Bank Act. They must obtain specific approval to operate from the Minister of Finance, based on their contribution to banking in Canada and reciprocity for Canadian banks in their home countries. Their license to operate is granted on an annual basis, and the Minister must approve their authorized capital. The domestic assets of any individual foreign B bank cannot exceed 20 times its authorized capital and the combined assets of Schedule Bs as a group cannot exceed 16% of all Canadian domestic banking assets. Only 17 of the 59 Bs offer any retail service. Nevertheless, the Bs represent a powerful competitive force since they have all the powers of Schedule A banks, most of them are subsidiaries of the largest banks in the world, and the 14 largest Bs account for 66% of Schedule B assets and 85% of Schedule B net income. In fact, B bank profits (excluding losses of Can. $2.5 million) increased by 14.4% in 1984 while the A banks had a fall of 7.7%.[7]

Given the scope of their operations, Canada's five big banks resemble the large New York City banks except that they have more extensive retail operations. The Canadian banks' international operations account for more than 40% of their total assets, and their role in relation to international financial markets is greater than that of Canada in relation to the world economy.[8] Domestic competition for commercial loan business is intense and until 1982 (when a 50% of equity limit was set) there was no legal lending limit. A single bank could, and often did, supply a large company with all its loans. All banks are members of the Canadian and/or Quebec Deposit Insurance Corporations and are subject to both primary cash reserve requirements set by the Bank Act and secondary reserve requirements set by the Bank of Canada. The chartered banks (and the Montreal City and District Savings Bank chartered under the Quebec Savings Bank Act) are the only institutions subject to such reserve requirements.

The Canadian payments system has one of the most efficient and effective check clearing systems in the world, making possible same-day credit and overnight clearing across a nation which covers six time zones. Prior to the 1980 establishment of the Canadian Payments Association, the banks controlled and operated the payments system with the Bank of Canada holding clearing accounts and making final interbank settlements. Now, other check-issuing institutions can gain direct access to the payments system through the Association, or continue to handle transactions through a clearing bank. The degree of internal automation and cooperation among the banks allows them to handle high value corporate payments, payrolls, and dividend credits on magnetic tape without intermediaries like automated clearing houses or Fed Wire. This also enables them to offer national cash management systems to corporations.

The Inspector General of Banks is responsible to the Minister of Finance for the administration of the Bank Act, including supervision of the banking system. He is assisted by and cooperates with the Canadian Deposit Insurance Corporation and the central bank, the Bank of Canada. The Bank of Canada's primary function is to formulate and execute monetary policy. In addition, the Bank holds the cash reserves of the banks, acts as fiscal agent for the federal government, provides liquidity for the banks, and acts as lender of last resort for the banks and investment dealers.

Trust Companies: At the end of 1982 there were 67 trust companies in Canada, about 25 of which were federally incorporated. While trusts have no reserve requirements per se, the Province of Ontario (in which most of them operate) requires them to have liquid assets equal to 20% of deposits. Most, if not all, trusts are members of the Canadian and/or Quebec Deposit Insurance Corporations. However, since most of their deposits are either non-checkable or have low turnover rates, few trusts maintain direct access to the payments system. The trusts' fiduciary business includes administration of estates and personal trust funds, management of pension funds, and administration of corporate funds set aside to repay bonded debt. As financial intermediaries, trusts operate much like savings and loan associations in the United States, having the vast majority of their liabilities in the form of term deposits and the majority of their assets in the form of mortgages.

Credit Unions/Caisses Populaires: Credit unions and their Quebec-style counterparts, Caisses Populaires, are cooperative, non-profit-seeking firms with autonomous local, normally (but not exclusively) single-office operations accepting deposits and lending money to members only. Overall, more than 32% of Canadians belong to a credit union and while much of their growth since the 1930s had been outside Quebec, Quebec's credit unions still represented 53% of all members and 46% of combined assets in 1975. There are many more Caisses Populaires than bank offices in Quebec, while in the rest of Canada bank offices outnumber credit unions 4 to 3. Credit unions tend to operate as mutual consumer loan societies where Caisses Populaires operate more like relatively conservative savings banks with more of their assets being in mortgages and "productive" loans to small independent proprietorships. Both types, because of their organizational form, can offer higher rates than banks on savings (or membership shares) while lending at low rates.

Credit unions have no reserve requirements, and except in Quebec, their deposits are not insured. While each credit union is independent in its operating policies, they almost all belong to a provincial federation or league which provides technical assistance, educational and public relations services, and a central credit society serving as a kind of central bank for its members. At present, no national link exists among the credit unions. However, the formation of shared ATM networks and syndicates for making commercial loans may be a step in that direction.

Life Insurance Companies: Canada's life insurance industry is made up of some 170 companies. But it is highly concentrated with more than 85% of all assets in 1980 being held by only 16 companies. Although insurance companies can be chartered by the provinces, more than 90% of all policies are written by federally registered companies. More than half of these companies are foreign based, and a third of Canada's life insurance policies are written by foreign companies. On the other hand, Canadian insurance companies (like the banks) have significant international operations with about 25% of their policies being written outside of Canada.

As in the United States, the importance of life insurance as a savings vehicle has waned because of high inflation and bank interest rates. But the industry has expanded its products and services to include mortgage loans, RRSPs, mutual funds, computer services, portfolio management, investment advice, and (through segregated funds) variable annuities, higher-yield life contracts, individual and group pension plans. Policy holders still invest 76% of their dividends in life insurance companies; and the industry finances 13% of all mortgages, 30% of all Canadian corporate bonds, and 10% of the Government of Canada's market securities.

Investment Dealers and Canada's Capital Markets: Canada has about 100 investment houses most of which are fully integrated, acting as brokers, dealers, and underwriters. With Canadian commission rates only unfixed in 1983, the investment houses still receive 56% of their income from brokerage compared to 32% from underwriting and trading. Competition in this sector is increasing substantially; discount brokers have sprung up and one bank now offers discount brokerage services. Competition for underwriting business has also increased rapidly, with investment dealers now targeting older Canadians (and those with high net worths) for money and cash management services. Despite some recent mergers, most investment dealers are thinly capitalized and are viewed by many as being too weak and reactionary to cope with the growing competition and internationalization in world capital markets.

Foreign dealer involvement in Canada's capital market peaked in 1971. In 1972 regulations were established which limited foreign shareholding in any Ontario-registered Securities Dealer to 10% for any one foreign shareholder and 35% for foreign shareholders in aggregate. At that time there were 26 affiliates of overseas firms in Canada with shareholdings in excess of the new rules. They were allowed to continue to do business subject to restrictions on the rate at which they could expand their business. In 1985 only three of the 26 affiliates were still in business, including a subsidiary of Merrill Lynch.[9] In February 1985 the Ontario Securities Commission proposed to allow additional foreign brokers to set up shop under similar restrictions, or to buy as much as 30% of a Canadian securities dealer.[10]

Canada has five stock exchanges—one in Toronto which accounts for nearly 80% of all trading, one in Montreal, and smaller exchanges trading mostly local stocks in Winnipeg, Calgary and Vancouver. There is also an extensive over-the-counter market in which all bonds and many stocks are traded. The combination of the five exchanges, the OTC market, and the nationwide branches of some of the investment houses provides Canada with something approaching a national capital market. However, private placements are very common and relatively few companies "go public" to raise equity capital. Only 9% of Canadians (as opposed to 22% of Americans) own shares directly; and the widespread use of nonvoting shares has led to 80% of the companies in the Toronto Stock Exchange's 300 index being controlled by a small (half dozen or so) group of investors.[11] The Montreal Stock Exchange, having dropped to only 8% of the share value traded in 1981, had increased its share by 1985 to more than 20%, by encouraging the number of Quebec companies going public to grow, by adding new products such as options and futures, and by attempting to become a connection point for the main international money centers.[12] Toronto is Canada's largest stock exchange and in the forefront of computer developments worldwide. Montreal is the innovator, introducing a widening range of new investment products. Vancouver for some years now has been carving out for itself a special niche as the market for new companies at an earlier stage of development than would qualify them for a listing on staider markets.

Profile of the Financial Services Industry in Canada: Financial Information, 1977–1983
($ billions)

Financial Institution	JUNE 1983 Assets	JUNE 1983 Market Share	December 1981–June 1983 Compound Annual Growth	DECEMBER 1981 Assets	DECEMBER 1981 Market Share	1977–1981 Compound Annual Growth	DECEMBER 1977 Assets	DECEMBER 1977 Market Share
Chartered banks								
Sch. A (Total)	368.7		3.6%	349.7		23.4%	150.5	
(Cdn. $ Assets)	213.5	45.2%	3.7	202.3	47.3%	18.4	102.8	46.7%
Insurance companies[a]	85.7	18.1	12.5	71.8	16.8	14.1	42.4	19.4
Trust companies	52.8	11.2	8.2	46.9	11.0	14.5	27.3	12.4
Mortgage loan companies[b]	94.4 (Adm.)		16.5	75.1 (Adm.)			N/A	
Credit Unions[c]	41.9	8.9	4.4	39.3	9.2	13.4	23.8	10.8
Other financial corp.[d]	30.7	6.5	(16.0)	39.9	9.3	35.0	12.0	5.4
Chartered banks								
Sch. B	20.1	4.3	108.0	6.7	1.6	24.4	2.8	1.3
Investment funds[e]	18.1	3.8	23.4	13.2	3.1	38.4	3.6[f]	1.6
Investment dealers	9.5	2.0	17.1	7.5	1.7	9.6	5.2	2.4
Total[g]	$472.3	100%	6.9%	$427.6	100%	24.6%	$219.9	100%

Notes: Information for all financial institutions is on a consolidated basis. In terms of compound annual growth Chartered Banks Schedule A had the smallest positive growth rate during the period 1981–83; other financial corporations experienced a negative compound annual growth for the same period; Chartered Banks Schedule B experienced the greatest growth.

[a] Includes life, accident and sickness, and property and casualty insurance companies.

[b] Excludes mortgage and loan companies associated with chartered banks.

[c] Includes credit union centrals.

[d] Includes acceptance, consumer loans, leasing, factoring, venture capital, term financing and merchant banking companies.

[e] Includes closed end funds, mutual funds, and segregated funds managed by insurance companies.

[f] Excludes segregated funds—information for that period not available.

[g] Excludes *Banks—Schedule A (Total) Assets, and Trust Companies and Mortgage Loan Companies administered total assets. Assets as at October 31, 1983 for Chartered Banks: Sch. A (Total)—$368.7; Schedule A (Cdn. $ Assets)—$217.6; Schedule B—$22.3.*

Source: RBC internal report.

GENERAL MILLS, INC.

In 1866, Mr. C. C. Washburn constructed a flour mill on the banks of the Mississippi River near Minneapolis. From these beginnings grew General Mills, the premier flour miller in the United States until it voluntarily sold approximately half its milling capacity in the mid-1960s. By the mid-1980s this and other strategic shifts had changed General Mills into a highly diversified consumer products company on the *Fortune* 100 list. How did these events occur? And what did they portend for the future of this once conservative, middle western, flour milling enterprise?

EARLY HISTORY

In 1928 Washburn Crosby's President, James Ford Bell, began to realize that the network of grain and flour mills he had merged to become General Mills was not going to have the kind of profitability he wanted for the company's future. He began to focus General Mills on more controllable, high-margin, consumer items, starting one of the country's first research operations dedicated to new product development. Bisquick, the nation's first prepared mix, grew from this effort in 1931, as did Cheerios, the world's first ready-to-eat oat cereal in 1941. By then major marketing efforts had made General Mills into the largest flour miller in the United States and its trade names—Wheaties (cereals), Gold Medal (flour), and Betty Crocker (mixes)—into household words.

Case copyright © 1989 by James Brian Quinn. Research associates—Penny C. Paquette and Allie J. Quinn.

Material is partly drawn from an earlier case written by James Brian Quinn and Mariann Jelinek. The generous cooperation of General Mills, Inc. is gratefully acknowledged.

The War, Electronics, and Chemicals

Then during World War II, General Mills diversified almost by accident into any field—lens coatings, sandbags, electronics, materials testing equipment, and torpedo direction devices—that helped support the war effort while keeping its own highly skilled technical teams intact. After the war it tried to use these same skills in small consumer appliances and started a line of coffee makers, toasters, pressure cookers, and steam irons in 1946. But General Mills soon discovered that it lacked the marketing ability and the trade outlets to compete with larger companies like GE and Westinghouse. And consumer appliances were sold off in 1954.

NEW DIRECTIONS

At about this time, a new management team joined the company, headed by General Edwin W. Rawlings, a dynamic, forceful man who had risen rapidly in the wartime Army Air Force to become one of the youngest four star generals in the nation's history.

The Changes Begin—Close Outs and Divestitures

Rawlings began to probe many of the areas that had concerned his predecessors—notably the commodity nature of the company's businesses and the wild and unpredictable swings caused by its dependency on grains and milling. At first he did this through a series of informal presentations. Later these became more formalized Management Operations Reviews—MORs as they were called—to reevaluate all aspects of the company's business.

In short order, General Mills sold off its Magnaflux Division to Champion Spark Plug Co., closed selected foods operations in Mexico and England (major soybean plants, various oil seed operations), and—perhaps most important—got out of the electronics business in 1964. All of this was backdrop for the most traumatic decision in General Mills' history. By the early 1960s worldwide overcapacity in flour milling was rampant. But the company had a strong internal need for flour, both for its institutional customers and for its consumer products like layer cakes and Bisquick.

Eventually, General Mills did not leave commodity (bakery) flour entirely. The consumer flour business was profitable enough to keep, but quite seasonal. Therefore the company maintained enough of a presence in bakery flour to even out the peaks and valleys of flour production and demand. The decision made in 1964 took the better part of a year and struck at the very heart of General Mills—no longer to be the world's largest flour miller.

Consumer Products

As milling capacity decreased to half its former size, the company's product mix changed markedly. And packaged foods soon provided some 75% of General Mills' total sales. About this time, General Rawlings announced a growth goal of 10% per year. And many shared the view that the central focus for expansion should be in *consumer products,* beginning with foods. As an executive commented,

> It made a lot of sense to us. . . . Here was a business—consumer products beginning with family flour, and progressing to cereals, cake mixes, and so on—that had showed a history of steady growth. With our marketing ability, it was obvious that we could

control our own destiny to a degree, there. . . . The philosophy was, "We're already there, and obviously we can sell things to the consumer. That's where our strength is."

General Mills' first nonfood consumer acquisition was Rainbow Crafts (a manufacturer of creative toys, including Play Doh), purchased in October 1965. An executive vice president of the Chemicals Division during this period recalled that the "toy and craft" involvement began almost casually, but quickly led to other things,

It seems to me that somebody came up with the idea that, "Look, there's a little company down in Cincinnati that makes Play Doh, and it's available." To my knowledge, it came to us. I don't think we found it. Rainbow Crafts just happened to be there, it happened to be a good idea, and we happened to get it. Then we started a real search (internally and externally) into other-than-food consumer areas. These quickly extended into the craft, game, toy, fashion, and jewelry businesses—all broad consumer lines other than food.

As background for this wider diversification program, the Acquisitions Group performed a major review of the consumer product industries of the United States. From this it distilled some six areas of major interest. These were: specialty retailing; restaurants; fashions; furniture; travel; and crafts, games, and toys. These investigations helped refine the company's acquisition criteria. Eventually, these criteria became to acquire consumer product or service companies: in low-technology fields, with the possibility of a brand franchise, growing faster than gross national product, in fragmented industries, in industries with at least $300 million total potential, and with the possibility of significant earnings-per-share impact. The intention was to build up a position over a period of time through acquisition of smaller units, rather than acquiring large single units.

The acquisition group presented these criteria and candidate industries to the Executive Council in fall 1967. It sanctioned looking into several industries further. The first of these was the fashion industry. The acquisition group then went through a full segmentation of that industry by customer age, type of product, price, style, distribution techniques, and so on. Following a full field investigation of some 200 companies, a few attractive and available candidates were brought in to top management. Even then, further education was needed. For example, one of the primary fashion candidates quickly left after he was asked in a top management interview to describe his five-year planning processes. He commented, "They really don't understand this industry, do they?" However, within a short while, these sorts of problems receded. One executive later recalled,

As part of the process, we did a very interesting thing, a sort of popularity contest. In effect each member ranked the presented areas in the order they thought we ought to consider them for diversification. As you might expect, the winners of the popularity contest were those most closely related to our existing businesses. The restaurant business got the most votes, the apparel industry very few. The next year was spent studying these industries and developing fairly comprehensive strategies for getting into them. . . . But many of the top managers were still not comfortable with the idea of investing significant amounts of money in unrelated new areas.

Nevertheless, in 1967 Craftmaster Corporation (maker of paint-by-number oil painting sets and other craft and hobby kits) was acquired, as was Kenner Products Corporation (maker of a broad line of innovative toys). Then in 1968, General Mills added Parker Brothers (makers of Monopoly and other games) and Model Products Corporation.

A prime mover in all this, Mr. James P. McFarland, was named president and chief operating officer in December 1967 to succeed General Rawlings, with Rawlings continuing as CEO. A 40 year veteran with General Mills, Jim McFarland had risen through marketing and general management positions in the Flour, Grocery Products, and later Consumer Products Divisions. *The Wall Street Journal* described him as "a man who had done well in every job he has been given." McFarland continued the strategy of making acquisitions in related areas, with Jesse Jones (maker of sausage and other meat specialities) and Gorton Corporation (a processor of seafoods) in 1968 and other Consumer Foods acquisitions on the Continent, in the United Kingdom, and Canada.

In addition, McFarland created a New Ventures Group "to form entrepreneurial teams that will conceive and develop new areas of profit growth." Acquisitions were stepped up with Monocraft Products (jewelry), Dexter Thread Mills (mail order crafts), Knothe Brothers (sleepwear), Donruss Co. (bubble gum), and David Crystal, Inc. (apparel) being added. Named Chief Executive Officer in 1969, Mr. McFarland could report the largest annual sales increase in the company's history, 18%—and a profit increase of 15%.

Establishing a Corporate Identity

Soon McFarland began a broad-based review of the company's overall direction. His own view was that the company should move from the assortment of businesses in which it then operated to "a family of businesses" which would offer more growth potential and possess greater balance. But he decided that the company's key managers should actively participate in this decision.

McFarland began by stating, for the first time, a corporate "mission." He felt that the real talent of the company rested in "its ability to market consumer products and/or services for which a brand franchise could be developed." Although the company had adequate skills in research, manufacturing, and technology, its critical edge lay in its marketing capability. The broad mission developed for General Mills became "to discern consumer wants and needs and convert those into products and services for which it could develop markets and a brand franchise."

The next step was to further develop, test, and communicate these concepts within the organization. McFarland took some 30–35 top managers "for a three-day retreat up north" which became known as the "goodness to greatness" conference. The company already had some broad financial and growth goals. The whole group first reviewed these and decided they still seemed appropriate. Next Mr. McFarland broke the total unit up into groups of 6 to 8 people. On the first day he asked them to define, "What are the characteristics of a great company?" Each group considered this from the viewpoint of stockholders, employees, suppliers, the public, and society—and reported back:

> Among characteristics agreed upon as keys to corporate greatness were: "A well-defined corporate purpose"; "A growth corporation in key leading indicators, including particularly earnings per share, sales and an overall increase in market penetration"; "An intense desire for greatness"; "An unusually high degree of creativity and innovation"; "The look of greatness, achieved through flair and imaginative and effective communication"; "Diversification," and "A participative, responsible internal climate."

The second day's discussions were devoted—in the same format—to the company's strengths and weaknesses relative to the defined posture of "greatness."

The third day focused on how to overcome the company's weaknesses and move from being a "very good company" toward being a "great company." At the end of each day, the whole group came together and tried to reach a broad consensus through further discussions. The Planning Director then distilled and summarized this consensus for the record. These meetings led to certain fundamental conclusions. In Mr. McFarland's words,

> We had this strong desire to grow. But the feeling was that we were not involved in enough areas of growth—industries or business activities of natural growth. We either had to go against the trends or be absolutely miracle-makers within our fields. Therefore, we decided that we should undertake and develop some new areas of activity. . . . There were also some more subjective elements [in our conclusions]; that we needed more flair in our business, more get up and go, and so on.

The "Comfort Factor"

Until 1969, most acquisitions, domestically and internationally, had been in the foods area. Some non-foods businesses appealed to management more than others. "The closer an item was to the core of the business, the more comfortable they would feel." Cosmetics were considered closer to foods than apparels. Broadcasting was closer than furniture because the company itself was spending so much on TV advertising. The company justified the consideration of non-food areas because of its deep seated faith in its ability to market consumer products to the homemaker and her family. This perception evolved into a "loose strategy" over a period of time through the interaction of key management personnel. Out of this came two thrusts. One was to expand in food-related sectors. The other was to develop new growth centers based on General Mills' marketing skills directed essentially at the homemaker. There was a strong informal feeling that the great majority of the company's resources should be used to expand in the food related areas.

Two Thrusts

Almost the reverse occurred. Over the next five years General Mills invested something like $400 million in new businesses, and the majority were not closely related to foods. A Direct Marketing Division was formed to include LeeWards Creative Crafts, Eddie Bauer (sports equipment and leisure wear), and The Talbots (fine clothing), all with both mail order and retail stores. And General Mills' fashion activities expanded to include Monet costume jewelry; Kimberly Knitwear; Picato; Alligator Company; Lord Jeff Knitting Company; and the Foot-Joy Company.

There were two main reasons why acquisitions were primarily outside the food area. First, the company was unable to continually develop good acquisition candidates in many food related sectors. The field was highly competitive, and acquisition opportunities tended to be marginal—that is, they either were not market leaders or their cost was prohibitive. Second, when candidate companies were strong in some areas, FTC restrictions prevented the company from acquiring them. In addition, there were two organizations whose sole responsibility was to find the develop new opportunities in the non-food sector. There was a strong bias for these groups to find interesting candidates, and they did.

Still in this same era, General Mills became vitally interested in the "away-from-home eating" market. Red Lobster Inns were acquired in January 1970. Betty Crocker Pie Shops—in the Minneapolis area—opened to feature a broad line of quality, fresh-baked pies. Betty Crocker Tree House restaurants were opened in four cities. And General Mills opened fish and chip shops in Arizona and take-out chicken shops in Britain. The Corporate Controller commented on General Mills' restaurant activities:

> Data indicated that more and more meals were being eaten away from home. Being a food company, we felt that we should and could participate [successfully] in this segment . . . Red Lobster Inns were acquired on a performance contract basis. And it was one of the best performance contracts we ever had. There were only about 6 outlets in the entire chain and they were all in central Florida. What we really acquired was three people who deeply understood the restaurant business—that is, the basic mathematics of that business. The real key to satisfactory return is capital turnover. They had built their restaurants so the sales/investment ratio was about 1.5 to 1. With inflation and the more or less sunk cost in investment, you can't go anywhere but up on returns.

Various executives noted that the company could start small in the restaurant business and use a "roll out" concept—that is, expand successful chains in discreet units, duplicating a local success in new geographical areas, with very little risk after the first few were proved. While the Red Lobster Inns proved successful, other efforts did not. Three of the four chains started internally were liquidated.

A Dazzling Array

By the mid-1970s General Mills businesses had proliferated into a fairly dazzling array. Table 1 shows how rapid growth was and how all this was financed. But some segments were not meeting profit goals. And others were competing for the same markets and resources.

The company had entered five new industries. Simultaneously, rising capital costs and the cash demands of many growing businesses made the Board of Directors and many securities analysts increasingly nervous. The company responded with two major steps. First, management changed its publicly stated strategy to one of consolidating the industries into which it diversified. Second, it placed new emphasis on internal growth as opposed to growth from external sources.

An All-Weather Company

Soon, however, acquisitions did continue with Harris Stamp, International Incentives, Feldbacher Backwarenfabrik (Austrian pretzels), David Reid, Bowers and Ruddy Galleries, General Interiors Corp., Clipper Games (Holland), Wallpapers-to-Go, and York Steak House Systems, Inc. becoming major acquisitions. By 1977

TABLE 1 **Income Statement**
(in $ millions)

	1967	1969	1971	1973	1975	1977
Sales	628	885	1120	1662*	2309*	2909*
COGS	401	579	724	1010	1532	1786
Depreciation	14	23	27	35	42	48
Net income	30	38	44	66	76	117
Total assets	367	622	750	909	1206	1447
Long-term debt	92	214	252	214	305	276
Common equity	194	281	329	426	560	725

* Restated for pooling of interest.

Source: Data drawn from various annual reports of General Mills, Inc.

General Mills, Inc. (GMI), had some 95 operating subsidiaries in which it held total or major equity positions. Some 30–35% of GMI's business came from non-foods products; its management had decided not to increase the ratio further for fear that General Mills would be considered a "conglomerate" and its P/E ratios would suffer accordingly.

During Mr. McFarland's eight years as Chief Executive Officer the company had grown spectacularly as shown below.

By 1977 top managers were confident that General Mills had developed into an "all weather" company, able—more than ever before—to maintain growth despite the buffets of politics, the economy, or other external environments. In spring 1977, as Mr. McFarland stepped down as chairman, General Mills signed a letter of intent to sell off its Chemical Division for $75 million, the last of the early post–World War II diversifications. Mr. McFarland said,

> We've gone through the wage and price controls period. We've gone through the recession. We went through the boom. We've gone through the energy crisis, and—I think because of our planning process and our understanding of our business—we've been able to maintain growth. We should constantly position ourselves to be a truly "all-weather growth company."
>
> I always believed that one of my greatest responsibilities as Chief Executive Officer was not only to use our physical facilities well, but more importantly, our human resources. For each individual, this meant to make a spot where he could effectively at least start things, implement them, and innovate. The more you use the thoughts of your vital organization, your human resources, the better off you are.

	1977	1969	1977 AS % OF 1969
Sales	$2,209M	$885M	328
Total assets	1,447M	662	232
Net income	117M	36.2M	323
Earnings per share	2.36	.89	265
Stock prices	26\frac{1}{2}$–35$\frac{1}{2}$	15\frac{3}{4}$–21$\frac{3}{4}$	165

Source: Data drawn from company's annual reports and various public sources.

A NEW MANAGEMENT FOR A NEW ERA

E. Robert Kinney became chairman of General Mills in early 1977. Mr. Kinney had come to GMI when it bought Gorton Corp. Prior to that time Kinney had built two small companies into thriving enterprises. Although not in General Mill's Midwest tradition, Kinney's "good gutsy Maine business sense"[1] fit well with General Mills' philosophy. Kinney had moved through several operations positions before becoming its chief financial officer and later president. Although General Rawlings and Mr. McFarland are given most credit for repositioning General Mills, Mr. Kinney continued the entrepreneurial flair that had characterized General Mills' preceding decades. During his five years as CEO, General Mills grew from $2.65 billion to $4.85 billion in sales at an annual average rate of 12.9%. Mr. Kinney further developed the basic strategies of his predecessors—primarily emphasizing and extending the successful and fast growing Consumer Foods and Restaurant lines. But much also happened in the Toys Group. The company gained the "galaxywide" rights to market products based on the Star Wars movies which it parlayed into a $100 million a year enterprise. In another arena, General Mills' Izod line suddenly became fashionable, and sales skyrocketed.

Organizationally, Kinney continued to maintain very loose reins on his subsidiary managements, a policy which was obviously favored by the various entrepreneurs who had sold their burgeoning businesses to General Mills and stayed on to make them grow rapidly with seemingly limitless cash.[2] However, by 1981 many of the original founders of General Mills' subsidiaries had retired, died, or gone on to other endeavors, including Darden of Red Lobster, Chernow of Monet, the Talbots, Feighner of Tom's Foods, the Hoffmans of Wallpapers-to-Go, Grayson of York Steak Houses, and Gallardo of Casa Gallardo.

After a short but successful reign, in April 1981 Kinney handed the mantle of CEO on to Mr. Bruce Atwater, a 23-year veteran of General Mills and president and COO since 1977. *Forbes,* which had disparaged General Mills' earlier diversification attempts in the mid-1970s as "disastrous," noted that "General Mills had doubled its return on equity and its earnings growth rates to 17.9% and 15.3%, respectively, and was now near the top of its industry."[3] While almost half of GMI's sales and earnings in fiscal year 1982 came from its four major areas of diversification—restaurants, toys and crafts, fashion goods, and specialty retailing—45% of its growth over the last decade had come from new products and services developed internally and only 10% from new acquisitions. Between 1967 and 1979 non-food acquisitions had cost General Mills some $335 million and 3.5 million shares, about the price of one good-sized acquisition, but in 1981 they contributed $2 billion in sales and $184 million in operating profits.

Interestingly, 13 of GMI's older (over 25 years) food lines tripled their volume in the same decade to some $2 billion, by responding rapidly and shrewdly to changing consumer tastes (low-calorie foods, specialty cake mixes, "healthy" breakfast cereals, and so on). With this strong base, Mr. Atwater predicated sales would double in five years to $8 billion and capital spending would rise to $1.4 billion. "Unlike some consumer companies we have more growth opportunities than we have capital to devote to growth."[3]

Managers and Entrepreneurs

In September 1981, *Business Week* noted,

> This year for the first time, General Mills is imposing stringent financial controls and restrictions on its once nearly autonomous subsidiary chiefs. . . . The corporation has increased internal working capital charges to 13% from 7%. And it has launched a study of the feasibility of taking a "balance sheet approach" to financial management that would look at the cost of financing fixed assets and would force each subsidiary to simulate intracompany dividends. . . . "We want the managers to look at after-tax results, not just pre-tax profits," explains Jane Evans.[2]

With Mr. Atwater firmly in charge, the company was reorganized with two vice-chairmen—one responsible for the Consumer Foods Group and the other the Fashion, Toys, Specialty Retailing, and Restaurant Groups. While wanting to avoid the evils of overcontrol, Mr. Atwater noted, "You've got to do things differently when you reach a certain size, or you're going to suffer." In the *1981 Annual Report* he noted,

> [Our strategy] demands intelligent and responsive employees who stay in close touch with the consumer. Employees of this calibre are also necessary to support our management philosophy of decentralized growth centers. A combination of decentralized operations, a strong financial reporting system, and heavy emphasis on long range planning are the basic elements of our strategy.

As the entrepreneurial founders of many of General Mills' business were replaced—often by managers who had progressed upward through the Consumer Foods Group—the product management system that worked so well in Consumer Foods was being adapted to nonfood areas as well. *Fortune* noted some of the impacts as follows, "While the product management system does create champions and encourages or at least rewards risk taking to some degree, it is also a relatively cumbersome process-oriented system in which the annual product plan follows a formula and the most common frustration of product managers themselves is how long it takes to get their proposed actions through the system."[4]

Mr. Atwater emphasized "we're trying to get things done as close to the market as we can. The object is to make running a General Mills Company as much like running a free standing business as possible." Nevertheless, *Business Week* noted in 1981,

> For some of the entrepreneurial managers, the jury remains out on whether General Mills will make good on its implied promise to keep strategic planning within the individual companies' domains. To them, the answer revolves around whether the corporate parent will remain as willing to accept variations in financial goals and performance as it said. "When you were by yourself, you set the standards," sums up Foot-Joy's Tarlow. "Here the standards are set and they're largely General Mills' standards."[2]

But like many other companies, General Mills had its problems with its entrepreneurs, too. When its Kimberly Division's founder had insisted that the division stick with its money-losing knitted products line, there were no experts in General Mills willing to second guess him. Ultimately, General Mills had to liquidate the operation when the division head's "knits strategy" caused excessive losses. In 1985, General Mills' very sophisticated management was still concerned with the problems of how to best utilize, motivate, and control a highly decentralized entrepreneurial management system.

A Long-Term Viewpoint

Nevertheless, General Mills had an important tradition of risk taking and patience in developing its enterprises. Tenacity in the face of problems had long permeated the Consumer Foods area where Atwater commented, "We judge people not on whether a product succeeded or failed, but on how well they approached the marketplace."[3] He also said, "We are long-term people . . . when we are convinced that consumer demand exists for a product, we constantly refine the product until it achieves marketing success. We never cut and run."[4] Applied to non-food areas this philosophy led to patience with such troublesome subsidiaries as Ship n' Shore, which plunged into the red in 1979 when it bet wrong on the potential popularity of Quiana, a synthetic silk. "I told them it would take two years to turn around Ship n' Shore, and there was no pressure (to speed that up)," said Stanley Gillette, the subsidiary's president.[2]

Atwater's style brought with it a new dedication to planning, careful market analyses, and targeted acquisitions programs. When *Dun's* selected General Mills as one of its five best managed companies, it stated, "Behind General Mills' success is its mastery of consumer marketing. It exhaustively researches the market potential of every new product considered, and, once the decision to go ahead is made, puts the product in the hands of a product manager whose single assignment is to make it a success. Management plows big bucks into its development and promotion and sticks with it until it turns a profit."[5] But flexibility was also needed. At the 1983 Annual Meeting Mr. Atwater added,

> General Mills intends to continue "our necessarily risk-oriented marketing activities" to execute its strategy of balanced diversification, aggressive consumer marketing, and entry into adjacent businesses. An overly cautious marketing approach would enable our competitors to move ahead more rapidly than General Mills in developing opportunities. On the other hand, a risk-oriented marketing approach inevitably results in a certain number of initiatives that don't work out. But, what the consumer wants and needs (and competitor's offerings) continually change. This is why it is far more risky to stay with the status quo than to continually experiment with changes and improvements.[6]

THE MID-1980s

1981 through early 1984 were hard years for the U.S. economy. And General Mills whose growth was intimately tied to consumer spending experienced a slower rise in sales. Nevertheless, return on average equity met or exceeded stated corporate goals, dividends per share continued to be raised, and earnings per share continued their 22-year record of increase. Within the five industry groups, however, unforeseen problems cropped up and were reflected in group level financial results. (See exhibits for a summary of group performance for the fiscal years 1979 through 1984.)

Consumer Foods led the company forward with its strategy of increased market share and profit growth in its traditional brands, introduction of meaningful new products in established categories, entry or creation of carefully selected new markets through internal development or acquisition, and concentration on productivity improvements in all areas. The other four groups each faltered, leading one analyst to comment that "A principal strength of General Mills has been its ability to diversify outside the consumer food business . . . This diversification is now being tested."[7]

The Restaurant Group which by 1984 accounted for nearly 20% of the company's sales was hard hit by a sudden decline in the Red Lobster chain's popularity and customer counts. As far back as 1982, research indicated to Joe Lee (manager of Red Lobster's first outlet and now the Restaurant Group president) that consumers were interested in a more casual dining experience, as well as lighter fresh food, and a greater variety of price points. "The research was telling him one thing; the Red Lobster books said something else. Doing very well—in the first year of the recession—hid the believability of the research. With 370 restaurants you didn't want to do the wrong thing," said Lee.[8]

During fiscal 1984 the company began a $100 million chainwide remodeling program and curtailed further expansion of Red Lobster until the remodeling was finished and earnings improved. The other four restaurants'—York Steak House, Casa Gallardo (Mexican foods), Daryll's (casual style, diverse menu), and Good Earth—concepts were constantly modified during this period with continuous expansion and improving results. Mr. Lee's philosophy—placing maximum responsibility and autonomy close to the restaurant—seemed to pay dividends. "Once Joe approves a plan, he lets the presidents do whatever is necessary to implement it," said one executive. But Lee also held personal quarterly meetings and had short monthly reports from each of his key people. He spent much of his time visiting individual restaurants around the country. "I've got to have a feel of the business myself. I can't get that in an office. I want to see what is actually happening in the restaurants and with the customers." Said an executive, "If Joe heard of a new restaurant concept or a new type of dishwasher, he would go miles out of his way to see it for himself. He almost got killed once when his airplane crash landed in Newfoundland because he wanted to visit his shrimp supplier personally." With high energy and standards, Lee had set a target of doubling his restaurants between 1982 and 1985.[9]

The Toy Group had suffered heavily from Parker Brothers entry into the video game market—which promptly went into a tailspin beginning in 1983. In 1982, its first year in the video business, Parker Brothers racked up earnings of $20 million on sales of $74 million. With such an auspicious start, the company geared up to produce $225 million of cartridges in fiscal 1983. Instead, it had to settle for revenues of $117 million and a loss.[8] Luckily, Parker had adopted basically a "software only" strategy and was able to scale down its operations and stem its losses somewhat. And the success of Star Wars toys and its line of licensed character products, Strawberry Shortcake and the Care Bears, balanced off its video game problems and some currency woes caused by its Mexican operations. In 1985 Parker and the entire Toys Group were trying hard to define how to recapture their lost volume and exploit the complex home entertainment marketplace.

The Fashion Group's Izod/LaCoste—while relatively small when acquired-had become the mainstay of GMI's fashion lines. Capitalizing on increased consumer interest in physical fitness, General Mills built Izod's alligator into a highly profitable symbol of quality and broadened its product line into a full range of leisure wear. At first the problem was to produce enough of Izod's classic shirt (the 2058) to meet orders. Izod's Ivy League look became the "sport shirt of choice" in the *Preppy Handbook* craze of the early 1980s, and competition copied the alligator concept and style with wild abandon. But it was Izod's failure to adapt its prep styles into other variations or a total "look" of shirts, pants, accessories (etc.) that gave others a chance to muscle out shelf space in retail stores. Under this impact, the Izod line began a steady decline in 1982. As Jane Evans, then the executive vice president of Fashion, said,

> "I think it is important to remember that fashion came to Izod. It was not because of anything we did as far as changing the shirt. All of a sudden we were reclassified as being a 'fashion line.' We didn't understand the implications of that." While some 20% of all knit shirts were brought by fad conscious teenage girls, Evans maintained, "Izod had no interest in chasing the juniors." She said flatly, "That is a huge business, it's a dangerous business, and it's not one we'll ever go after.[8]

The mainstream of GMI's David Crystal line—dressy sportswear geared to suburban activities—also proved to be out of tune with apparel market trends, as had Kimberly's double knit and synthetic fabrics.[10] While recognizing General Mills' impressive record and historical strengths, *The Wall Street Journal* summarized certain concerns as follows:

> The manner in which senior management disclosed Izod's problems also raises questions about how well it tracks General Mills' diverse operating units. Analysts say the Izod episode disclosed other potential problems: (1) Management's staple food heritage may prevent it from adapting to the faster paced marketing needs of nonfoods businesses . . . Fashion isn't like Wheaties and Cheerios. When you turn the key in the morning, you know you're going to sell cereals. But in the rag business, every day is really a new day. (2) The company's formal reporting systems may keep management in the dark until it's too late. And (3) entrepreneurship may be frustrated by great reliance on research and what one analyst calls "a typical large company monthly review

that looks at all the numbers. I'm not sure that breeds the kind of creativity you need to run a business," he says.[11]

Specialty Retailing had been developed by General Mills using "consumer trend analysis" to identify new distribution channels for conventional consumer products—chiefly mail-order marketing. The Talbots brought GMI into the fashion retailing market with a substantial mail order volume. First The Talbots' mail-order sales were extended out of The Talbots' traditional New England markets. Then as new customer loyalties developed, they were exploited with additional retail outlets in selected new areas. Eddie Bauer (quality, down insulated outdoor gear) followed the same strategy. And both brought General Mills into the new telecommunications, computer, and in-home shopping markets.

Overall in Specialty Retailing there were some success stories and some problems. The Talbots, Eddie Bauer, LeeWards retail operations, and Pennsylvania House furniture lines were gradually expanded and doing well. But LeeWards Creative Crafts mail-order business and two other furniture operations experienced serious setbacks and were eventually divested. And overall Specialty Retailing results were hurt by (1) the collapse of the Collectibles business, which was sold in 1983; (2) the sharp downturn in the housing market and hence sales at Wallpapers-to-Go outlets (these were either sold or remodeled and repositioned as full-service decorating stores); and (3) Wild West Stores' failure to react to changes in jeans fashions (The Wild West stores closed down and reopened as We Are Sportswear outlets in 1982–1984).

How Long Is the Primrose Path?

1984 may have been a watershed year for General Mills. Despite selling off its snack foods operation (Tom's Food) which increased its fiscal 1984 operating profits by more than $100 million, net earnings were down $11.7 million from 1983. Earnings per share would have been down also, except that the company bought back 3.2 million shares of common stock on the open market. Security analysts, most of whom had been as confident as management of the company's ability to correct its problems and continue its winning strategy, began in late 1984 to ask such questions as, "How long is the primrose path? Are the problems ahead or being put behind?" At General Mills Annual Meeting in September 1984, Mr. Atwater said that while Izod was troubled, it would "break even" for the fiscal year ending May 1985. But only a few weeks later he conceded that Izod would have a loss of millions of dollars and could take a 5 cent per share bite out of earnings.[11] This incident created a concern that General Mills might have some fundamental problems to grapple with before it resumed its strong recent growth history.

QUESTIONS

1. Evaluate General Mills implementation of its diversification program. To what extent can such a program be truly planned? How? How permanent can a strategy be in this kind of company? Why?

2. What are the main portfolio issues facing General Mills at the end of the case? What should it do about these?

3. What kind of organization and control systems should General Mills adopt? Why? How should it evaluate and reward managers in its various entrepreneurial endeavors? In its more mature lines?

EXHIBIT 1
General Mills, Inc.—Business Segment Data, 1980–1984

Fiscal Year	Sales ($ millions)	Percent of Total Sales	Pre-tax Operating Profits After Redeployment ($ millions)	Profits as Percent of Sales	Return on Identifiable Assets	Capital Expenditures ($ millions)	Depreciation Expense ($ millions)
Consumer Foods							
1980	$2,218.8	53.2%	$210.5	9.5%	27.7%	$80.6	33.6
1981	2,514.6	51.8	217.7	8.7	25.9	95.7	40.6
1982	2,707.4	51.0	263.0	9.7	28.9	96.2	46.6
1983	2,792.6	50.3	268.2	9.6	27.3	123.8	51.9
1984	2,713.4	48.4	383.0	14.1	41.0	130.3	53.9
Restaurants							
1980	525.7	12.6	52.7	10.0	19.6	49.8	14.3
1981	704.0	14.5	75.3	10.7	19.9	85.1	19.7
1982	839.4	15.8	79.2	9.4	16.0	122.4	24.4
1983	984.5	17.7	80.0	8.1	14.0	107.6	30.6
1984	1,079.7	19.3	37.3	3.5	6.4	82.3	34.7
Toys							
1980	647.0	15.5	60.1	9.3	13.6	34.7	19.2
1981	674.3	13.9	70.6	10.5	17.6	28.6	22.9
1982	654.8	12.3	79.2	12.1	19.6	30.6	20.7
1983	728.3	13.1	104.6	14.4	23.2	39.3	22.8
1984	782.7	14.0	51.0	6.5	9.4	36.3	22.2
Fashion							
1980	442.5	10.1	43.7	10.3	18.9	5.2	3.9
1981	580.5	12.0	87.5	15.1	27.0	14.4	5.0
1982	657.3	12.4	101.7	15.5	28.2	13.4	6.0
1983	616.3	11.1	75.9	12.3	21.9	17.3	6.2
1984	587.4	10.5	37.9	6.5	9.7	16.3	7.3
Specialty Retailing							
1980	365.3	8.5	26.4	7.4	14.5	19.3	4.1
1981	379.0	7.8	13.2	3.5	5.5	19.2	5.2
1982	453.2	8.5	(11.9)	−2.6	−4.6	21.8	7.7
1983	429.1	7.7	16.1	3.8	6.7	17.1	9.1
1984	437.6	7.8	(10.9)	−2.5	−5.2	14.3	9.2

Source of Raw Data: General Mills, Inc., Annual Report, 1980–1984.

EXHIBIT 2
Five-Year Financial Summary—Before Restatements (As Reported), 1980–1984
(amounts in millions, except per share data)

General Mills, Inc., and Subsidiaries

	May 27, 1984	May 29, 1983	May 30, 1982	May 31, 1981	May 25, 1980
Operating Results					
Earnings per share[a]	$ 4.98	$ 4.89	$ 4.46	$ 3.90	$ 3.37
Return on average equity	19.0%	19.9%	19.1%	18.2%[b]	17.6%[b]
Dividends per share[a]	$ 2.04	1.84	1.64	1.44	1.28
Sales	$5,600.8	5,550.8	5,312.1	4,852.4	4,170.3
Costs and expenses:					
Cost of sales, exclusive of items below	$3,165.9	3,123.3	3,081.6	2,936.9	2,578.5
Selling, general, and administrative[c]	$1,841.7	1,831.6	1,635.5	1,384.0	1,145.5
Depreciation and amortization	$ 133.1	127.5	113.2	99.5	81.1
Interest	$ 61.4	58.7	75.1	57.6	48.6
Earnings before income taxes	$ 398.7	409.7	406.7	374.4	316.6
Net earnings	$ 233.4	245.1	225.5	196.6	170.0
Net earnings as a percent of sales	4.2%	4.4%	4.2%	4.1%	4.1%
Weighted average number of common shares[a][e]	46.9	50.1	50.6	50.4	50.5
Taxes (income, payroll, property, etc.) per share[a]	$ 6.22	5.70	5.88	5.99	4.66
Financial Position					
Total assets	$2,858.1	2,943.9	2,701.7	2,301.3	2,012.4
Land, buildings, and equipment, net	$1,229.4	1,197.5	1,054.1	920.6	747.5
Working capital at year end	$ 244.5	235.6	210.7	337.3	416.3
Long-term debt, excluding current portion	$ 362.6	464.0	331.9	348.6	377.5
Stockholders' equity	$1,224.6	1,227.4	1,232.2	1,145.4	1,020.7
Stockholders' equity per share[a]	$ 27.03	25.68	24.50	22.75	20.32
Other Statistics					
Working capital provided from operations	$ 348.3	401.6	353.6	317.8	262.7
Total dividends	$ 96.0	92.7	82.3	72.3	64.4
Gross capital expenditures	$ 282.4	308.0	287.3	246.6	196.5
Research and development	$ 63.5	60.6	53.8	45.4	44.4
Advertising media expenditures	$ 349.6	336.2	284.9	222.0	213.1
Wages, salaries, and employee benefits	$1,121.6	1,115.2	1,028.4	907.0	781.2
Number of employees	80,297	81,186	75,893	71,225	66,032
Accumulated LIFO charge	$ 79.7	79.7	75.5	73.7	60.3
Common stock price range[a]	$ 57⅛–41⅝	$ 57¾–38⅝	$ 42⅛–32⅝	$ 35¾–23⅜	$ 28¼–19

[a] Years prior to fiscal 1976 have been adjusted for the two-for-one stock split in October 1975.
[b] Amounts not restated for vacation accrual accounting change made in fiscal 1982.
[c] Includes redeployment gains or losses.
[d] Before discontinued operations.
[e] Years prior to fiscal 1983 include common share equivalents.
[f] In fiscal 1975, we changed from the FIFO to the LIFO method of accounting for selected inventories.

Source: General Mills, Inc., *Annual Report,* 1980–1984.

EXHIBIT 3
General Mills, Inc. Operating Income 1980–1985
($ in millions, except earnings per share)

	1980	% Change	1981	% Change	1982	% Change	1983	% Change	1984E	% Change	1985E	% Change
Food Processing												
Cereals and granola products	$ 90.0	+ 10.8%	$ 99.7	+ 28.6%	$128.2	+ 2.3%	$131.2	+15.9%	$152.0	+ 8.6%	$165.0	
Snacks	38.0	+ 5.3	40.0	+ 10.0	44.0	+ 4.6	46.0	− 60.9	18.0	+ 16.7	21.0	
Flour baking mixes and deserts	55.0	− 5.5	52.0	+ 13.5	59.0	− 3.4	57.0	+ 5.3	60.0	+ 5.0	63.0	
Frozen and refrigerated products	6.0	− 50.0	3.0	+166.7	8.0	+ 25.0	10.0	+30.0	13.0	+ 30.8	17.0	
Consumer flour and commercial	21.5	+ 7.0	23.0	+ 4.4	24.0	−0−	24.0	+12.5	27.0	+ 7.4	29.0	
Total	$210.5	+ 3.4	$217.7	+ 20.9	$263.2	+ 1.9	$268.2	+ 0.7	$270.0	+ 9.3	$295.0	
Restaurants												
Red Lobster	$ 46.0	+ 52.2	$ 70.0	+ 6.0	$ 74.2	− 1.6	$ 73.0	−12.3	$ 64.0	+ 9.4	$ 70.0	
York Steak Houses	10.0	+ 10.0	11.0	+ 13.6	12.5	+ 4.0	13.0	+ 7.7	14.0	+ 7.1	15.0	
Other	(3.3)	+ 72.7	(5.7)	+ 31.6	(7.5)	− 20.0	(6.0)	−50.0	(3.0)	NM	−0−	
Total	$ 52.7	+ 42.9	$ 75.3	+ 5.2	$ 79.2	+ 1.0	$ 80.0	− 6.2	$ 75.0	+ 13.3	$ 85.0	
Crafts, Games, and Toys												
Parker Brothers	$ 26.0	+ 7.7	$ 28.0	− 35.7	$ 18.0	+142.2	$ 43.6	−77.1	$ 10.0	+100.0	$ 20.0	
Kenner	24.0	+ 8.3	26.0	+ 50.0	39.0	+ 18.0	46.0	+ 8.7	50.0	+ 20.0	60.0	
Fundimensions	−0−	NM	3.0	+ 33.3	4.0	NM	(3.0)	−33.3	(2.0)	NM	3.0	
International	10.1	+ 34.7	13.6	+ 33.8	18.2	− 1.1	18.0	−16.7	15.0	+ 13.3	17.0	
Total	$ 60.1	+ 17.5	$ 70.6	+ 12.2	$ 79.2	+ 32.1	$104.6	−30.2	$ 73.0	+ 37.0	$100.0	
Apparel and Accessories												
David Crystal	$ 31.0	+101.6	$ 62.5	− 4.0	$ 60.0	− 25.0	$ 45.0	−40.0	$ 27.0	− 7.4	$ 25.0	
Monet	21.7	+ 15.2	25.0	−0−	25.0	− 12.4	21.9	+ 5.0	23.0	+ 8.7	25.0	
Ship n' Shore and Other	(9.0)	NM	−0−	NM	16.7	− 46.1	9.0	+11.1	10.0	+ 20.0	12.0	
Total	$ 43.7	+100.2	$ 87.5	+ 16.2	$101.7	− 25.4	$ 75.9	−21.0	$ 60.0	+ 3.3	$ 62.0	
Specialty retailing	26.4	− 50.0	13.2	NM	(11.9)	NM	16.1	+73.9	28.0	+ 35.7	38.0	
Total operating profits	$393.4	+ 18.0	$464.3	+ 10.1	$511.4	+ 6.5	$544.8	− 7.2	$506.0	+ 14.6	$580.0	
Unallocated expenses	28.2	+ 14.5	32.3	− 8.4	29.6	+158.1	76.4[1]	−41.1	45.0	+ 11.1	50.0	
Interest expense	48.6	+ 18.5	57.6	+ 30.4	75.1	− 21.8	58.7	+2.2	60.0	+ 8.3	65.0	
Pretax income	$316.6	+ 18.3	$374.4	+ 8.6	$406.7	+ 0.7	$409.7	− 2.2	$401.0	+ 15.9	$465.0	
Taxes	146.6	+ 21.3	177.8	+ 1.9	181.2	+ 9.2	164.6	+ 2.2	168.3	+ 21.5	204.5	
Net income	$170.0	+ 15.6	$196.6	+ 14.7	$225.5	+ 8.7	$245.1	+ 8.7	$232.7	+ 11.9	$260.5	
Average shares (millions)	50.4	−0−	50.4	+ 0.4	50.6	+ 1.0	50.1	− 1.0	47.0	− 1.1	46.5	
Earnings per share	$3.37	+ 15.7	$3.90	+ 14.4	$4.46	+ 9.6	$4.89	+ 9.6	$4.95	+ 13.1	$5.60	

E—First Boston Corporation estimates.

[1] Includes $12 million of TRASOP and $15 million of currency translation losses.

Source: First Boston Corporation, *Research Progress Report*, April 3, 1984.

EXHIBIT 4

Family Spending Patterns by Age of Head of Household
Percentage of Average Annual Expenditures by Product Category

Item	Average All Families	Under 25	25–34	35–44	45–54	55–64	65 and Over
Food	19.4%	11.5%	15.9%	21.6%	20.5%	20.3%	22.8%
At home	17.0	9.1	13.3	18.7	18.0	18.1	21.1
Away from home	2.2	1.9	2.3	2.6	2.2	1.9	1.5
Other	0.2	0.5	0.3	0.3	0.3	0.3	0.2
Alcoholic Beverages	1.0	1.2	1.2	0.9	0.9	0.9	0.6
Tobacco	1.6	1.7	1.6	1.6	1.7	1.8	1.2
Housing	25.4	31.4	29.1	23.9	21.8	22.7	28.7
Shelter	16.2	24.5	20.3	15.2	13.4	12.9	15.8
Utilities	5.3	3.4	4.6	5.2	5.2	5.7	7.4
Other	3.9	3.5	4.2	3.5	3.2	4.0	5.5
Furnishings	5.1	5.4	6.1	5.6	4.7	4.3	4.0
Appliances	1.3	1.6	1.5	1.3	1.1	1.1	1.1
Furniture	1.8	2.3	2.4	2.1	1.6	1.2	1.1
Other	2.0	1.5	2.2	2.2	2.0	2.0	1.8
Clothing and Accessories	8.3	8.3	8.6	9.2	8.6	7.7	6.4
Men/boys	2.7	2.6	3.0	3.3	3.0	2.4	1.5
Women/girls	4.0	3.4	3.7	4.5	4.3	3.9	3.6
Materials, etc.	1.6	2.3	1.9	1.4	1.3	1.4	1.3
Transportation	20.2	25.5	20.1	19.2	22.0	21.3	14.9
Automobile	19.6	25.0	19.6	18.6	21.3	20.7	14.1
Other	0.6	0.5	0.5	0.6	0.7	0.6	0.8
Medical Care	6.1	3.8	5.1	5.1	5.7	7.0	10.2
Health insurance	2.5	1.6	2.0	1.9	2.2	3.0	4.8
Uninsured expense	3.6	2.2	3.1	3.2	3.5	4.0	5.4
Personal Care	1.3	0.5	0.8	1.2	1.4	1.7	1.7
Recreation	8.3	8.6	8.7	8.3	8.0	8.5	7.2
Vacation	3.1	2.0	2.6	2.6	3.1	3.8	4.0
Other	5.2	6.6	6.1	5.7	4.9	4.7	3.2
Reading	1.9	1.1	1.4	1.8	3.1	2.1	0.8
Other	1.3	0.9	1.2	1.4	1.4	1.6	1.4

Source: Equity Research, E. F. Hutton and Company, Inc., May 9, 1983.

EXHIBIT 5
Estimated Retail Food Dollar Sales, 1980–1982
($ millions)

Category	Industry			General Mills			Estimated Market Share		
	1982	1981	1980	1982	1981	1980	1982	1981	1980
Dry Packaged Foods									
RTE cereal	$3,260.0	$3,200.0	$2,420.0	$ 665.0	$ 610.0	$ 490.0	23.0%	19.1%	20.2%
Desserts	1,100.0	1,000.0	828.0	410.0	375.0	300.0	39.3	37.5	36.2
Family flour	460.0	470.0	427.0	155.0	160.0	180.0	33.7	34.0	41.2
Instant potatoes	190.0	195.0	140.0	90.0	60.0	50.0	47.4	30.8	35.7
Portable bars (granola)	220.0	200.0	104.0	145.0	110.0	45.0	65.9	55.0	43.3
Biscuit mixes	125.0	110.0	104.0	105.0	100.0	75.0	84.0	90.9	72.1
Helper dinners and casseroles	110.0	110.0	84.0	75.0	100.0	58.0	68.2	90.9	69.0
	$5,465.0	$5,285.0	$4,107.0	$1,645.0	$1,515.0	$1,198.0	30.1%	28.7%	29.2%
Frozen Foods									
Processed fish	$ 650.0	$ 650.0	$ 646.0	$ 130.0	$ 150.0	$ 140.0	20.0%	23.1%	21.7%
Pizza	780.0	950.0	667.0	50.0	40.0	25.0	6.4	4.2	3.7
	$1,430.0	$1,600.0	$1,313.0	$ 180.0	$ 190.0	$ 165.0	12.6	11.9	12.6
Refrigerated									
Yogurt	$ 550.0	$ 525.0	$ 450.0	$ 100.0	$ 80.0	$ 30.0	18.2%	15.2%	6.7%
Total	$7,445.0	$7,410.0	$5,870.0	$1,925.0	$1,785.0	$1,393.0	25.8%	24.1%	23.7%

Note: European, Canadian, Foodservice and Commercial flour and seafood sales represent the remainder of annual sales.

Source: Equity Research, E. F. Hutton and Company, Inc., May 9, 1983.

EXHIBIT 6

Other Market Statistics
Sales of Toys/Games by Major Categories, 1978–1982
(in millions of dollars—based on manufacturers' prices)

Category	1978	1979	1980	1981	1982
Dolls and accessories	$308	$288	$308	$395	$600
Games and puzzles	534	539	601	634	569
Preschool toys and playsets	365	388	386	404	376
Electronic games (nonvideo)	112	375	476	276	371
Video games	—	—	455	1,090	2,068
Stuffed animals and puppets	243	244	268	307	282
Unpowered toy cars, trucks, boats, and planes	155	190	256	331	279
Riding toys (excluding street bicycles)	154	178	176	230	254
Space toys	187	192	167	186	158

Source: Toy Manufacturers of America in "Basic Analysis—Leisure Time," Standard & Poor's *Industry Surveys,* October 13, 1983.

Food-Away-From-Home Market, 1981–1983
(food and drink sales, in billions of dollars)

Market	R1981	R1982	% chg. 1981–82	E1983
Commercial feeding				
Restaurants, lunchrooms	$ 39.3	$ 42.0	6.9%	$ 45.4
Limited menu restaurants	30.8	33.7	9.4	37.3
Bars and taverns	8.3	8.7	4.8	9.2
Hotel and motel restaurants	6.9	7.4	7.2	8.1
Cafeterias	2.3	2.4	4.3	2.6
Other	18.2	18.6	2.2	19.9
Total	$105.8	$112.8	6.6	122.5
Institutional feeding	18.6	19.6	5.4	20.7
Military feeding	0.7	0.7	—	0.8
Grand total	$125.1	$133.1	6.4	$144.0

E = estimated, R = revised.

Source: National Restaurant Association in "Basic Analysis—Retailing," Standard & Poor's *Industry Surveys,* January 26, 1984.

EXHIBIT 6
(Continued)

Child Population in the United States, 1983–1990
(in thousands)

Age	1983	1985	% Change 1983–85	1990	% Change 1983–90
Under 5	17,846	18,453	+3.4%	19,198	+ 7.6%
5–9	15,960	16,611	+4.1	18,591	+16.5
10–14	17,768	16,797	−5.5	16,793	− 5.5

Source: U.S. Department of Commerce, Bureau of the Census in "Current Analysis—Leisure Time," Standard & Poor's *Industry Surveys,* August 9, 1984.

Birth Statistics, 1970–1990E
(in thousands)

Year	Number of Births	Number of First Births	First Births as % of Total Births
1990E	3,849,000	—	—
1985E	3,826,000	—	—
1984E	3,788,000	—	—
1983E	3,614,000	—	—
1982E	3,704,000	—	—
1981	3,629,238	1,553,665	42.81
1980	3,612,258	1,545,604	42.79
1979	3,494,396	1,479,260	42.33
1978	3,333,279	1,401,491	42.05
1977	3,326,632	1,387,143	41.70
1976	3,167,788	1,324,811	41.82
1975	3,144,198	1,319,126	41.95
1974	3,159,958	1,314,194	41.59
1973	3,136,965	1,243,358	39.64
1972	3,258,411	1,289,257	39.57
1971	3,555,970	1,375,668	38.69
1970	3,731,386	1,430,680	38.34

Source: U.S. Department of Commerce, Bureau of the Census in "Current Analysis—Leisure Time," Standard & Poor's *Industry Surveys,* August 9, 1984.

EXHIBIT 7
Comparative Financials,
1982

	Revenues ($ billions)	Return on Assets	Return on Sales
Food Processing			
Beatrice	$ 9.19	0.9%	0.5%
Borden, Inc.	4.11	6.6	4.0
Campbell Soup	2.95	8.3	5.1
Carnation Co.	3.38	11.4	5.6
Consolidated Foods	6.04	6.6	2.5
Dart & Kraft	10.00	6.9	3.5
General Foods	8.25	6.9	3.5
General Mills	5.55	8.9	4.4
H. J. Heinz	3.74	9.9	5.7
International Multifoods	1.11	7.5	3.2
Kellogg Co.	2.37	17.7	9.6
Nabisco Brands	5.87	8.4	5.4
Pillsbury Co.	3.68	5.8	3.8
Quaker Oats	2.71	8.1	4.4
Ralston Purina	4.80	4.4	1.9
Toys			
Coleco Ind.	$ 0.51	23.3%	8.8%
Milton Bradley Co.	0.36	6.4	5.3
Restaurants			
Chart House	$0.38	6.3%	4.9%
Denny's, Inc.	0.96	6.4	3.8
Victoria Station	0.11	NM	—
Apparel Manufacturers			
Manhattan Ind.	$0.40	4.3%	1.9%
Philips-Van Heusen	0.46	4.1	1.9
Warnaco	0.50	8.5	4.7

Source: Data compiled from various analyses in Standard & Poor's *Industry Surveys.*

THE CONTINENTAL GROUP, INC.

The Continental Can Company began in 1904 in a former glass factory in Syracuse, New York. In October 1976 its name changed to the Continental Group, Inc., to reflect the shifting focus of its activities over the preceding 25 years. In 1984 its new CEO, Mr. Bruce Smart, after building Continental into a balanced and diversified giant, faced a challenge none of his predecessors had. How did Continental arrive at its current posture? And what should Mr. Smart do about the latest challenge to its existence?

PAST STRATEGIES

Coming out of World War II Continental's president, Hans Eggars, and sales vice president, Tom Fogarty, saw a need to focus on a market segment where the smaller company could distinctly surpass its larger rival, American Can Company. Recognizing an opportunity in the tin shortages of the war period, Eggars had put his research group to work to make beer cans with half the electrolytic plate then used. Customers soon got twice as many cans per pound of allocated tin as American could offer. Exploiting this innovation gave Continental the size and reputation to become an equal supplier with American in the burgeoning beer market of the postwar period.

Case copyright © 1989 by James Brian Quinn. Research associate—Penny C. Paquette.

The generous cooperation of the Continental Group is gratefully acknowledged.

Diversification and Packaging

Continental's next CEO, General Lucius Clay, was a forceful man of great quality and integrity, who saw matters on a grand strategic scale. He set out to make Continental the largest, most diversified packaging company in the world, striving as he phrased it within the company's walls "to become the General Motors of packaging." According to Raymond Fisher, later chairman of Continental's Executive Committee, "Clay set out on an acquisition campaign and, lo and behold, well before the end of the fifties Continental Can *was* the largest packaging company in the world. He had a clear and simple goal the organization understood. When people got up in the morning they weren't shocked to find that something had been purchased." During this period Continental acquired its initial entries into markets for: vacuum closures of jars, blow molded polyethylene, flexible plastic packaging materials, and paper packaging products.

"We Were Just Converters"

In its can businesses, the company increasingly found itself pitted squarely against American Can Company and sandwiched between its huge suppliers and its very large customers. Said one discouraged executive, "We were just converters . . . all we did was take a little steel and roll it into little circles." Of the 3 cents a pea can cost in 1961, 2.1 cents went to the steel companies for plate. That left 0.9 cents to fabricate, package, sell, and ship the can. At the other end were the processors and brewers who operated on fractional margins for products which sold in the 100 millions to billions of units per year. These customers often played off one supplier against another with dreadful effect. To minimize the cost of shipping empty cans, both Continental and American located plants near the big buyers, making themselves even more dependent on individual customers' whims. Still, as various customers' own scales of operation grew, they were even more tempted to make their own cans.

Consolidate and Weed

In September 1961, Tom Fogarty became chief executive and immediately began to consolidate the array of businesses that Clay had acquired and to weed out (or supply new management for) the poorest performers.

Mr. Fogarty concentrated efforts on the beer and soft drink sectors which were the glamor markets of that era. Mr. Fogarty was described as "more operationally oriented than General Clay had been," his leadership generated excellent financial results for the company. However, during this period the company's markets slowly began to change. As Mr. Hatfield, Continental's CEO from 1971 to 1981, said, "By 1969 we were all acutely aware of the probable topping out of the beverage market. Self-manufacture was in the minds of most of the large buyers. And the two-piece can brought new competition with it—Reynolds, Coors, and others."

THE SPRING FOR EUROPE

Continental had sold technology to European can groups ever since the 1930s. And in a dramatic move at the end of World War II, a Continental executive appeared at these European licensees' doors less than six weeks after the armistice to offer them the technology they had missed for some five years.[1] Through such actions Continental built close personal and business relationships with its European businesses over the years. Continental had licensing agreements with 51 companies and minority interests in 33 companies operating in some 100 countries worldwide. And by the end of the 1960s many of these had become major forces in their individual countries' can industries. Metal Box in Britain was the third largest can company in the world; Schmallbach-Lubeca-Werke (Germany), Carnaud (France), Sabigny (Belgium), and Thomassen & Drijver in Holland were among the strongest companies in their domestic markets. But through the 1960s Continental had invested in them only by invitation.

In a series of moves Continental formed a wholly owned subsidiary, Europemballage, for integrated management of its European operations—Schmallbach (86% owned) and Thomassen & Drijver (91% owned). Carnaud dropped out when a majority stockholder, a French steel company, objected that the takeover would violate the chauvanistic terms of its loan from the French government. Other diversification activities—like Tee Pak (sausage casings), Essco Stamping Products and SKD Manufacturing (both auto parts) of Canada and expansion of Continental's Canadian operations—complemented these international moves in 1970–1971. Along with other acquisitions in Mexico and expansion of its interests in South America, Continental's international operations grew to 25% of the business in 1971.

A Metals Strategy

Simultaneously, the domestic can business reached a critical stage. Attacks from conservationists and legislative threats to outlaw non-returnable containers escalated. The beverage market switched to two-piece aluminum cans.[2] And food processors, soft drink manufacturers, and brewers began increasingly to make their own cans. The company moved decisively to shift its investment patterns. Mr. Hatfield said,

> During this period, there was no long-range planning. The immediate task seemed quite clear. The domestic can company facilities had to be rationalized on an urgent time schedule, papermaking and converting facilities had to be brought to competitive positions in cost and product quality, and the efforts of the European can business redirected to the profit motive. After a nine-month study and appraisal, we reached the agonizing conclusion there was no choice but to take a major writeoff.

But as Mr. Smart, then head of Forest Products, noted,

> We had a devil of a time getting the can business in the U.S. to recognize its maturity, because this was perceived by its management to be an unacceptable situation. . . . This created a number of debates between New York's corporate Headquarters and Chicago's Metal's headquarters and most specifically between Metals and Hayford (then Financial V.P.) over what was a proper direction for that business. The culmination was a change in management at the division level.

With a younger leadership now under Warren Hayford and Donald Bainton, Domestic Metals began to turn toward cash generation. But maintaining its pride was a difficult task. Later Hayford said, "I didn't care how big we were as long as we were the most profitable company in the field. Once we were most profitable, we'd grow as fast as we could while maintaining that status."

Diversification Strategies

As Metals began to generate cash flows, funds became available for other activities. Mr. Smart's new management group now in power drew up a plan to invest some $700 million in Forest Products to utilize its full potentials and to bring better balance to the corporation's total portfolio. Mr. Smart, himself, moved to the president's office, and funds began to flow toward Forest Products. Said Mr. Hatfield,

> In capital intensive businesses during a period of heavy investment, the return on total corporate assets is adversely impacted. Our decision to invest in the paper business had the objective of developing a longer-term resource-based diversification for the company. With the other investment programs being undertaken, some financial creativity was required.

Diversified products was another area of investment. Tee Pak (sausage casings) was added to the old Plastics and Closures group, and "Diversified Industries" became a viable third leg for the total operation. This included White Cap (bottle tops), Plastic Containers (plastic bottles), Flexible Packaging (sheet and vacuum sealed plastic wrapping) and Tee Pak. By March 1975 *Business Week* reported Mr. Hatfield as saying, "We're looking to increase the diversity of our business and to broaden our product lines. The biggest challenge is to find the right segments, the right companies, the right time."[3]

By the late 1970s, Diversified Industries enjoyed some of the most profitable lines in the Continental portfolio and was in a strong net investment (negative cash flow) position. Although there were some acquisitions in the Diversified Industries area, most of the investment action and management focus continued to be packaging oriented. Said Mr. Hofmann,

> Over a long period of time there developed a management consensus to diversify, but not where to diversify. Sometime in the mid 1970s, Hatfield came to the conclusion that positive action on diversification was necessary—i.e. a fourth leg was needed. This was much in mind when he hired Donahue from Amax.

Mr. Donahue came on board in 1975 as vice chairman and chief financial officer after building a reputation as the creative deal maker in Amax's rapid expansion. A number of potential large acquisitions were considered. Several very large companies in such diverse areas as natural resources, energy, and insurance were tried on for size and fit. Acquisition of any one of these multibillion dollar companies would have preempted the purchase of the other. And each fitted some rationale as a "fourth leg for the stool" of Continental's stability and future growth.

Richmond Corporation

When Lazard Freres brokerage firm first brought Richmond Corporation (a $1.1 billion life, title, and casualty insurer) to his attention, Donahue was reportedly cool to the idea, "It certainly wasn't one of our priority areas . . . but the more I thought about it, the more I became convinced that Richmond was the best means of achieving a broader capital base." Mr. Smart perhaps best summarized top management's viewpoint when he said, "I think the growth of any company is best measured by the rate at which it adds to its equity base. Growth is not necessarily some hot new product."[2] The Richmond acquisition was closed in mid-1977 and consolidated with other insurance and real estate activities into Continental's Financial Services organization.

In 1979 Continental made its next major diversifying acquisition, Florida Gas Company, for some $351 million. Various components of this unit, which became Continental Resources Company (CRC), participated in different aspects of the energy field. Florida Exploration had five divisions engaged in exploration, development, and production of oil and gas. Florida Gas Transmission Co. operated an interstate natural gas pipeline system extending from the Texas-Mexico border to the southern tip of Florida. Another unit extracted and sold propane, butane, and natural gasoline. Prior to the acquisition Continental had working interests in offshore and onshore gas and oil properties in the Gulf of Mexico and Mississippi. These were merged into Florida Exploration Company.

Florida Gas Transmission Co. was the sole supplier of natural gas to peninsular Florida and was one of only six U.S. companies selected by PEMEX to purchase gas from that prime source. CRC was investigating several major projects including a 1,500-mile slurry pipeline that would transport coal from Eastern Appalachia and the Illinois basin to the Southeast. If approved, this project would call for $2–3 billion in financing over several years.

NEW STRATEGIES FOR THE 1980s

As the 1980s began, the Continental Group's *Annual Report* offered a concise summary of a decade of change:

> ... The decade just passed was probably the most eventful in Continental's history. But looking back from the perspective of 1980 it may be a bit difficult to remember the way things were for Continental 10 years ago. Known then as Continental Can, the Company was primarily a domestic can maker. It ended 1969 with earnings of $3.18 per share on sales that were just approaching $2 billion mark.
>
> Continental is still the world's largest diversified packaging company, but now its horizon has broadened to include major interests in financial services and energy, with a new emphasis on natural resources. ... The upshot of these evolutionary changes is a distribution of earnings contribution as follows: Can Company, 41%; Forest Industries, 19%; Diversified Businesses, 10%; Financial Services, 24%; and Continental Resources Company, 6% (representing only four full months of operation).
>
> ... The number of employees has actually decreased, down from the 1970 total by 10,000 people to a current payroll of 62,000 and the percentage of sales representing overseas operations is up to 31%, also a major change from 16% a decade ago. ...

When Mr. Bruce Smart took over from Mr. Hatfied as chairman and CEO, he outlined his goals for Continental in its *1981 Annual Report:*

> (1) to reduce holdings in operations that fall short of performance goals or do not fit the long-term strategy of the company; a target of realizing $400–500 million from such assets was established, (2) to reinvest these funds in areas promising profitable growth, principally in energy, (3) to improve return on equity over the long term as a consequence of this reinvestment strategy, and (4) to strengthen Continental Group's balance sheet and credit standing.

Divestitures

Continental purposely set out to sell certain businesses and to reduce its equity positions abroad. It took time and effort to find the right buyers and get the highest price possible. Although its original goal was to raise $400–500 million for redeployment, Continental eventually exceeded that goal. It accepted Stone Container's offer to buy its Brown System paper mills. Many of these had recently been upgraded and made energy efficient, but Continental had no real competitive edge in this segment of Forest Industries. The sale involved the assumption by Stone Container of some $120 million of debt associated with the divested businesses. More than $100 million of the cash received was used to retire long term debt, significantly reducing the company's interest costs and improving its fixed obligation ratio. Another $220 million of the proceeds went to repurchase 4.6 million shares of common stock, or 14% of those outstanding, at $48 per share further increasing earnings per share and strengthening the balance sheet.

The following table[4] outlines operations sold during this period of "redeployment." The company was committed to "achieving self-sufficiency in each of its subsidiary businesses. Performance in subsidiaries was measured by return on assets, further encouraging management to implement small scale asset redeployment within their segments."[5]

By 1984 these funds were redeployed into Continental's four main business groups, resulting in a strong, balanced portfolio (described in the following pages). Chairman Smart stated in the *1983 Annual Report* that Continental was ready to move on to a new phase:

> Our primary task is now the efficient production of quality goods and services within our restructured business competences—packaging, forest products, insurance, and energy. . . . Our overall strategy is to achieve the competitive advantages that can result from increased productivity, market focus, and innovation.

Operation Divested	GROSS PROCEEDS	AFTER-TAX GAIN (LOSS)
	($ millions)	
1981		
Teepak, Inc.	112	2
Canadian Paper Products	50	(2)
Other (including Morton G. Thalhimer—real estate brokerage)	39	16
	201	16
1982		
Containers Ltd. of Australia (20% equity interest)	45	13
Insurance Management Corp.	17	7
Other	16	8
	78	28
1983		
Brown System	525	80
Canadian Packaging	133	25
Plastic Beverage Bottle	31	(6)
Other	39	(8)
	728	91
	$1,007	$135

Packaging

In December 1983, Continental Packaging Company had been reorganized to facilitate a new strategy stressing market rather than product orientation. As Mr. Smart then told *New England Business:*

> We will start to look at our franchise not as the manufacture of blow-molded bottles, or two-piece aluminum cans, but as our relationship with the big package group marketers. Hitching Packaging's wagon to big customers like General Foods makes more sense than latching on to a particular technology or shape or structure that will inevitably change.[6]

The new organization operated in three major markets: Food and Beverage, Specialty Packaging, and International. Its cost reduction and productivity programs included closing a number of plants which were unable to meet long-term profitability standards, while improving capacity utilization and line efficiencies at other facilities. Basic research expenditures were reduced and emphasis directed towards business development and marketing. Continental Packaging had a major position in the fastest growing segment of the can industry—the two-piece aluminum can. However, the near-term results of the packaging business would be determined by (1) the success of new product introductions, (2) continued emphasis on cost cutting even after demand reaccelerated, and (3) whether or not metal cans would be besieged by another fundamental change in design.[4]

Forest Products

Smart had told *The Wall Street Journal* at the time of the Brown System sale,

> Our forest products business will be reduced in scale but will now be made up of specialty businesses in which we have world class and to some extent proprietary positions backed by a natural resource of immense and growing value.[7]

Continental was the world's largest producer of bleached folding carton board and ranked fourth in total production of bleached paperboard. Its modern bleached paperboard plant in Georgia had an annual capacity of 430,000 tons and was valued at more than $500 million.[8] It was also a major factor in the production of fiber drums with 12 plants. And it still owned 1.45 million acres of timberland located in the Southeast (of which 868,000 acres were in pine plantation targeted for continuing harvest beginning in 1988), carried on the books at $115 million but with a market value (conservatively) of at least $400 million.[9] Continental's *1983 Annual Report* noted that the timberland which previously supplied the Brown System mills could now be managed as a non-integrated profit center. Forest Products' activities were balanced as follows:[10]

Fibre Drum	25%	Fibre drum shipping containers, steel drums, plastic pails, laminator paper, fiber partition and DualPak (polyethylene bottle in corrugated box) for the chemical, pharmaceutical, plastic, food and other industries.
Bleach System	46%	Bleached folding carton grades for folding carton manufacturers; coated bleached bristols and cover stock for the domestic and international printing industry; and cup and other stock for the food service industry.
Woodlands	29%	Wood raw materials for paper mills and sawmills.

nancial Services

e Financial Services group had benefited substantially from the early 1980s re-
ployment program. In early 1981 Continental acquired Investors Mortgage In-
ance Company for $85.8 million. The company along with Lawyers Title
urance Company and Continental Land Title Company formed a core in the
al estate-related financial services area. Then in mid 1983 American Agency Life
Insurance Company, with its 49 master brokerage general agents and 13,000 independent brokers and agents, was acquired for $32 million, further extending Con-
tinental's distribution system for Life of Virginia's successful universal life
products. In 1984, Continental Financial Services underwrote insurance in three
broad segments: life, real estate, and property and casualty insurance.

Life of Virginia's traditional markets in the Southeast and Midwest had been
extended through a network of independent brokers and the acquisition of American Agency. Its universal life policy, the Challenger, had achieved rapid acceptance
but was being tested as large competitors introduced their own versions of the plan.

Lawyers Title Insurance, the nation's third largest title insurance company,
had concentrated on a broad independent agency network while stimulating productivity through special incentive programs. Investors Mortgage Insurance Company had been quite successful in facilitating innovative mortgage financing and in
decentralizing its sales force and operational responsibilities toward local levels.

Western Employers Insurance concentrated on underwriting workers' compensation coverage, but had recently expanded geographically into the Northeast
and Southwest and had established a division to sell Directors and Officers, Errors
and Omissions, and other related coverages.

Chairman Smart described the Insurance segment as,

> A surprisingly nimble and successful middleweight in the industry. There is no way
> our insurance division will ever be all things to all people in the sense of a Metropoli-
> tan or Prudential. . . . It has to pick its spots geographically, marketwise and product-
> wise and win by wit and innovation.[6]

Energy

The bulk of Continental's redeployment in the early 1980s had been into energy.
The company had joined with Shell and Mobil in the construction of a 502-mile
carbon dioxide pipeline in which the company had a 13% interest, had begun to
convert an 890-mile segment of its 4,300-mile natural gas pipeline to petroleum
products (while maintaining its natural gas deliveries to the Florida market), and
had participated in four major offshore natural gas pipeline projects in the Gulf of
Mexico to connect into the Florida Gas Transmission system.

In Exploration and Production, Continental undertook a joint acquisition
(with Applied Corporation) of Supron Energy Corp. at a cost of more than $400
million. This acquisition increased the company's proved reserves of oil and gas by
approximately 180% and its undeveloped acreage by 50%. Supron's emphasis on
development drilling also complemented Florida Exploration's activities and
strengthened its position in domestic natural gas.[11] In joint ventures with Shell Oil,
Continental acquired additional offshore leases and participated in extensive exploratory drilling activities. In 1981 it spent some $225 million on exploration, but
in 1983, due to changed energy prices, Continental was concentrating more on development of known resources.

Concerning Continental's Energy business, Mr. Smart said,

Although the company is a baby next to the industry giants, it dominates in the market segments it has chosen to exploit. It is the largest supplier of energy to the State of Florida, one of the nation's fastest growing states. When you're small you've got to focus and that's what we're trying to do in oil and gas.[6]

The company's pipeline operations offered a strong cash flow at relatively low risk, facilitating the expansion of other energy activities that were currently balanced between offshore exploration and development through Unicon Production Company (the operating company for the joint Allied and Continental Supron Energy acquisition).[4] Further details on Continental's posture are contained in the attached operating and financial statements.

SIR JAMES AND THE DEVOURING DRAGON

Just as Continental's long-sought goals of balance and competitiveness seemed within reach, a new jolt appeared from out of the blue. In early June, 1984, Sir James Goldsmith, a British financier, offered to buy Continental for about $2.1 billion in cash or $50 per share. Earlier, Goldsmith had made a bid for St. Regis Paper Co. and had lost out to another suitor, but only after realizing a $50 million personal profit in a month's time. Sir James' major American holdings in 1984 included the Grand Union Company (supermarkets) and Diamond International (forest products). He said that he wanted to increase his U.S. holdings and that a diversified company like Continental would be ideal. Analysts thought Continental's 1984 earnings would be up 20–30% over 1983. But the $50 per share offer (on June 6) contrasted sharply with the stock's price on June 1st of $34 and its book value of $38.75. Although Sir James said that he hoped Continental's management would stay on to manage the company and that he would "leave the company largely intact," *The Wall Street Journal* reported management was "adamantly opposed" to the takeover—which at that time would have been the largest private acquisition of a public company in history.[12]

When he made his takeover bid for Continental, Sir James Goldsmith (age 51) had an intricate web of investments both in the United States and in Europe. The son of a French mother and an English father, he dropped out of Eton at age 16 and started an ill-fated pharmaceutical company in France. At age 20 he eloped with an heiress to a Bolivian tin fortune and by 1964 he was in England starting to build Cavenham, Ltd., his main British holding company which was primarily in foods and publishing. During the 1970s Sir James shifted control of Cavenham to Occidentale in France and began his moves into the United States—prompted at least in part by Europe's drift toward socialism. In 1973 he purchased Grand Union, the seventh largest U.S. supermarket chain and concentrated on revamping that languishing enterprise.[13]

Then in the late 1970s he began the process of buying Diamond International Corporation, a wood, pulp, and paper firm. By 1980 he held 5% of Diamond and made a tender offer for up to 40% of its shares. The Board, knowing Sir James had a good chance of getting the 40%, negotiated a standstill agreement that prevented him from buying more than that for five years in exchange for seats on Diamond's Board. But the U.S. housing slump changed the situation; and by December 1981, with Diamond's profits at only a third of their 1979 level, the Board was prepared to recommend selling out for $44.50 a share. A year later, in December 1982, Sir James took the company private having financed the purchase by borrowing against the company's own assets. Many of Diamond's divisions were readily saleable and Sir James quickly began the process of dismembering the company to pay off his own and the corporation's debt. By early 1984, basically all that remained of what had been Diamond International was 1.7 million acres of timberland held by Diamond Land, Inc., which had an estimated value of over $700 million.[13] (See Exhibit 2 outlining the break-up of Diamond International.)

Exhibit 3 shows the complexity of Sir James' empire. While his businesses used to be concentrated in Britain and on the Continent, 70 to 80% of his holdings were now in the U.S. General Occidentale—Goldsmith's French holding company for Grand Union, Groupe Express (publishing) and his oil venture—earned approximately $29 million on sales of $3 billion in 1983. Basic Resources International was a joint oil-exploration venture with the French and Spanish governments whose Guatemalan oil fields had produced little but strife.[14] In June 1984 financial sources in London maintained that Sir James "owned less than 1% of Continental" and was "highly unlikely" to resort to "greenmail" or to swap any stock he might acquire in Continental for any of Continental's properties.[15]

QUESTIONS

1. Evaluate Continental's past strategies and current strategic posture. What other actions should it have taken in the past? When? Why?

2. What issues does Sir James' offer pose for Continental's management? For other companies' managers? What are management's main strategic options in June 1984?

3. What specific actions does each call for?

4. What should management do? Why?

EXHIBIT 1
Financial and Operating Statistics

Continental Group: Financial Statistics, 1955–1983
($ millions)

	1955	1957	1959	1961	1963	1965	1967	1969	1971	1973	1975	1977	1979	1981	1983
Operating revenues	929.4	1,046.3	1,146.5	1,153.3	1,154.0	1,225.6	1,397.6	1,780.0	2,081.6	2,539.7	3,101.9	3,660.9	4,510.9	5,194.4	4,820
Gross margin	148.5	149.6	150.8	154.9	171.4	207.8	245.5	312.8	306.9	374.7	396.1	462.4	540.0	650.4	446
Net (after tax) profit	38.7	41.0	40.0	36.1	40.1	59.2	78.1	90.4	72.9	97.0	107.2	143.8	184.6	234.0	199
Total assets	568.9	664.1	750.7	788.5	811.9	920.9	1,012.6	1,199.5	1,571.1	1,776.9	1,963.1	2,723.8	3,595.3	4,135.9	3,653
Long-term debt/equity	0.33	0.34	0.32	0.39	0.35	0.30	0.24	0.24	0.39	0.50	0.45	0.40	0.69	0.53	0.48
Return on sales	4.2	3.9	3.5	3.1	3.5	4.8	5.6	5.1	3.5	3.8	3.5	3.9	4.1	4.5	4.1
Return on assets	6.8	6.2	5.3	4.6	4.9	6.4	7.7	7.5	4.6	5.5	5.5	5.3	5.1	5.7	5.4
Return on equity	10.9	10.4	8.9	7.8	8.2	11.3	12.8	12.9	9.3	13.1	12.4	11.2	14.6	14.9	13
Share price (high-low)	$29\frac{1}{2}$–24	32–$25\frac{1}{4}$	39–$29\frac{1}{4}$	$32\frac{1}{2}$–$23\frac{1}{4}$	32–$27\frac{7}{8}$	$42\frac{1}{4}$–$32\frac{1}{4}$	$40\frac{5}{8}$–$27\frac{1}{4}$	$52\frac{1}{8}$–$41\frac{3}{8}$	$45\frac{1}{4}$–$26\frac{1}{8}$	$30\frac{7}{8}$–$19\frac{1}{2}$	$29\frac{5}{8}$–$22\frac{5}{8}$	$37\frac{3}{8}$–$30\frac{1}{4}$	$31\frac{7}{8}$–$25\frac{5}{8}$	$40\frac{1}{2}$–$30\frac{1}{4}$	$54\frac{1}{2}$–$32\frac{3}{4}$

Note: Share prices adjusted for 100% stock dividend in 1956 and 3-for-2 splits in 1966 and 1970.

Source: Data drawn from various years of *Moody's Industrial Manual.*

EXHIBIT 1
(Continued)

Five-Year Summary, 1979–1983
(dollars in millions, except per share amounts)

	1983	1982	1981	1980	1979
Results of Operations					
Revenues	**$4,820**	$5,012	$5,194	$5,120	$4,511
Net earnings	**199**	180	234	200	185
Per common share[a]					
Net earnings	**3.66**	3.20	4.24	3.57	3.42
Dividends	**1.73**	1.73	1.67	1.60	1.50
Financial Position at Year End					
Current assets	**$1,040**	$1,045	$1,249	$1,223	$1,238
Total assets	**3,653**	4,199	4,135	4,086	4,030
Current liabilities	**732**	778	835	870	844
Long-term debt	**726**	1,006	961	962	995
Redeemable preference shares	**249**	275	281	296	296
Common stockholders' equity per share[a]	**35.99**	33.19	31.87	30.16	28.70
Common shares outstanding (in thousands)	**42,428**	48,940	49,187	49,222	48,990
After-tax return on average common stockholders' equity[b]	**11.5%**	10.6%	15.0%	13.7%	14.1%
Number of Employees at Year End	**39,700**	46,900	51,400	56,700	59,800

[a] Restated for 3-for-2 stock split. In January 1984 Continental Group announced a 3-for-2 stock split which is reflected in all per share data. Net earnings were $3.66, $3.20, and $4.24 per share in 1983, 1982, and 1981, respectively. Significant asset sales and other major one-time events contributed $0.50, $0.49 and $0.53 per share during each of the three years.
[b] Computed excluding accumulated net unrealized investment gains and foreign currency adjustments from common stockholders' equity.

Source: The Continental Group, Inc., *Annual Report,* 1983.

EXHIBIT 1 (Continued)

Consolidated Balance Sheet, December 31, 1982–1983
(in millions)

ASSETS	1983	1982
Current assets		
Cash	$ 176	$ 66
Receivables	477	540
Inventories, at LIFO cost		
Current cost	642	756
Excess over LIFO cost	(332)	(384)
	310	372
Deferred income taxes and other assets	77	67
	1,040	1,045
Investments and advances		
Insurance operations	581	548
Unicon Producing Company	181	154
Other	98	166
	860	868
Property, plant, and equipment, at cost		
Buildings and equipment	1,909	2,716
Accumulated depreciation	(1,092)	(1,422)
	817	1,294
Oil and gas properties, net	576	624
Timberlands, net of timber harvested	138	114
Construction in progress	55	72
Land	17	20
	1,603	2,124
Other assets	150	162
	$3,653	$4,199

LIABILITIES AND EQUITY	1983	1982
Current liabilities		
Accounts payable	$ 372	$ 365
Short-term debt	29	32
Taxes payable	36	74
Accrued payrolls and employee benefits	174	160
Other	121	147
	732	778
Long-term debt, less current portion	726	1,006
Other liabilities		
Retirement benefits	276	258
Deferred income taxes	56	162
Other	82	91
	414	511
Redeemable preference shares	249	275
Preferred and common stockholders' equity		
$4.25 cumulative preferred stock	5	5
Common stock (issued: 1983—49,239,000 shares; 1982—48,940,000 shares adjusted for 3-for-2 stock split)	49	33
Paid-in surplus	343	347
Common stock in treasury	(219)	—
Net unrealized investment gains	72	40
Foreign currency adjustments	39	55
Retained earnings	1,243	1,149
	1,532	1,629
	$3,653	$4,199

See Statement of Significant Accounting Policies and Notes to Financial Statements provided in Company's Annual Report.

Source: The Continental Group, Inc., Annual Report, 1983.

EXHIBIT 1 (Continued)

Segment Earnings 1981–1983
(in millions)

Years Ended December 31	Packaging	Forest Products	Insurance	Energy — Pipeline Operations	Energy — Exploration and Production	Divested Operations	Combined
1983							
Revenues	$2,885	$517	$702	$722	$ 90*	$ 606	$5,522
Operating and equity earnings	$ 140	$ 41	$ 69	$ 77	$ 18	$ —	$ 345
Disposals/writedowns	(20)	—	—	—	(95)	111	(4)
Corporate expense	(19)	(4)	(3)	(4)	(2)	(3)	(35)
Realized investment gains, net of tax	—	—	8	—	—	—	8
Segment earnings	$ 101	$ 37	$ 74	$ 73	$(79)	$ 108	$ 314
1982							
Revenues	$2,882	$466	$575	$691	$ 80*	$ 903	$5,597
Operating and equity earnings	$ 114	$ 41	$ 59	$ 92	$ 19	$ 14	$ 339
Disposals/writedowns	—	—	—	—	—	52	52
Corporate expense	(20)	(5)	(3)	(3)	(1)	(8)	(40)
Realized investment gains, net of tax	—	—	—	—	—	—	—
Segment earnings	$ 94	$ 36	$ 56	$ 89	$ 18	$ 58	$ 351
1981							
Revenues	$2,917	$509	$576	$574	$ 67*	$1,151	$5,794
Operating and equity earnings	$ 75	$ 68	$ 80	67	$ 28	$ 102	$ 420
Disposals/writedowns	—	—	—	—	—	16	16
Corporate expense	(20)	(5)	(3)	(3)	(1)	(9)	(41)
Realized investment gains, net of tax	—	—	2	—	—	—	2
Segment earnings	$ 55	$ 63	$ 79	$ 64	$ 27	$ 109	$ 397

* Does not include revenues from sales to Pipeline Operations, which were $27 million in 1983; $32 million in 1982, and $22 million in 1981. Divested Operations includes the results from January 1, 1981 through the date of sale for businesses sold as a part of the asset redeployment program.

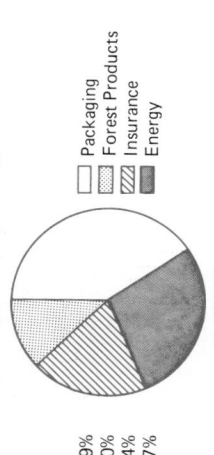

Operating and Equity Earnings

Packaging	41%
Forest Products	12%
Insurance	20%
Energy	27%

Revenues

Packaging	59%
Forest Products	10%
Insurance	14%
Energy	17%

Source: The Continental Group Inc. *Annual Report,* 1983.

EXHIBIT 1 (Continued)

Other Segment Information 1981–1983
(in millions)

	Packaging	Forest Products	Insurance	Energy — Pipeline Operations	Energy — Exploration and Production	Divested Operations	Corporate*	Consolidated
1983								
Identifiable assets	$1,109	$465		$293	$638	$ —	$320	$2,825
Equity investments	49	2	$581	—	181	—	15	828
Total assets	$1,158	$467	$581	$293	$819	$ —	$335	$3,653
Depreciation, depletion and amortization	$ 78	$ 27		$ 22	$ 66	$ 34	$ 3	$ 230
Capital expenditures	88	54		17	114	23	1	297
1982								
Identifiable assets	$1,158	$426		$285	$690	$645	$179	$3,383
Equity investments	41	20	$548	—	154	—	53	816
Total assets	$1,199	$446	$548	$285	$844	$645	$232	$4,199
Depreciation, depletion and amortization	$ 77	$ 25		$ 21	$ 55	$ 46	$ 3	$ 227
Capital expenditures	81	45		12	214	82	3	437
1981								
Identifiable assets	$1,152	$419		$306	$550	$651	$371	3,449
Equity investments	52	18	$545	—	—	21	50	686
Total assets	$1,204	$437	$545	$306	$550	$672	$421	$4,135
Depreciation, depletion and amortization	$ 80	$ 25		$ 23	$ 39	$ 62	$ 5	$ 234
Capital expenditures	65	37		41	185	62	16	406

* Corporate assets consist principally of cash and deferred income taxes.

Source: The Continental Group, Inc., *Annual Report,* 1983.

927

EXHIBIT 1
(Continued)

Insurance—Summary of Operations, 1981–1983
(in millions)

Years Ended December 31	1983	1982	1981
Revenues			
Life insurance	$372	$318	$298
Real estate insurance	228	163	167
Property and casualty insurance	97	100	113
Other	5	4	22
	$702	$585	$600
Operating earnings			
Life insurance	$ 47	$ 49	$ 53
Real estate insurance	18	2	18
Property and casualty insurance	4	7	10
Other	—	1	
	69	59	84
Gain on sale of subsidiaries	—	9	3
Interest expense*	(17)	(19)	(24)
Continental Group overhead	(3)	(3)	(3)
Earnings before income taxes	49	46	60
Income tax benefit (provision)	3	4	(13)
Net realized investment gains	8	—	2
Net earnings	60	50	49
Dividends on preferred shares	(1)	—	—
Company's equity in earnings	$ 59	$ 50	$ 49
Dividends paid to Continental Group	$ 50	$ 49	$ 19

* Includes intrasegment interest totaling $14 million in 1983, $17 million in 1982, and $13 million in 1981. The offsetting intrasegment interest income is included in operating earnings.
Condensed Financial Information Insurance includes the accounts of life insurance, real estate insurance, property and casualty insurance, and other operations. This information has been prepared on the basis of generally accepted accounting principles which differ from the statutory accounting practices prescribed by various state regulatory authorities. Net earnings determined in accordance with statutory accounting practices for the insurance subsidiaries were $33 million in 1983, $51 million in 1982, and $55 million in 1981.

Source: The Continental Group, Inc., *Annual Report,* 1983. Also see notes to table there.

EXHIBIT 1
(Continued)

Supplemental Oil and Gas Information, Pre-1981–1983
(in millions)

	1983	1982	1981	Prior to 1981	Total
Lease acquisition costs	$36	$20	$22	$31	$109
Exploration costs	6	5	—	—	11
Interest capitalized	10	11	7	2	30
	$52	$36	$29	$33	$150

An analysis of Florida Exploration Company's costs of offshore properties not being amortized at December 31, 1983 (by year incurred) appears above.

These offshore properties are part of an ongoing exploration and development program and are expected to be evaluated over the next several years. Onshore properties currently not being amortized were $39 million at December 31, 1983. These properties primarily represent lease acquisition costs in areas where the Company has an active exploration program.

Florida Exploration Company's depletion rate per gross revenue dollar was $0.56 in 1983, $0.49 in 1982 and $0.44 in 1981.

Florida Exploration Company's oil and gas activities are accounted for on the full-cost method. The SEC full-cost accounting rules require that a "ceiling test" be applied to the cost of properties capitalized. The ceiling test limits the amount of costs capitalized to the present value of future new revenues from only proved reserves and the lower of cost or estimated fair value of unproved properties. The present value of future net revenues was computed by applying prices for oil and gas based upon current market conditions to year-end quantities of proved reserves only, using a 10% discount factor. Future price increases were only considered to the extent they were fixed and determinable. For Florida Exploration Company, curtailments and declining prices in 1983 lowered projected future net revenues and made certain unproved properties uneconomical to develop resulting in a writedown of $95 million ($50 million after tax). Unicon's oil and gas activities are accounted for on the successful efforts method. The amount realizable exceeds the carrying value of the Unicon properties.

Source: The Continental Group, Inc., *Annual Report,* 1983.

EXHIBIT 1 (Continued)

Oil and Gas Reserves, 1981–1983

	1983		1982		1981	
	Oil (in thousands of barrels)	Natural Gas (in millions of cubic feet)	Oil (in thousands of barrels)	Natural Gas (in millions of cubic feet)	Oil (in thousands of barrels)	Natural Gas (in millions of cubic feet)
Proved Reserves						
Florida Exploration Company						
January 1	5,883	123,777	4,342	101,760	4,501	114,525
Revisions of previous estimates	(705)	10,479	942	7,671	(142)	(11,779)
Extensions, discoveries and other additions	1,334	31,686	1,510	35,610	591	20,132
Production	(1,463)	(20,100)	(911)	(21,264)	(608)	(21,118)
December 31	5,049	145,842	5,883	123,777	4,342	101,760
Unicon						
December 31	3,586	202,731	3,908	209,565		
Combined						
December 31	8,635	348,573	9,791	333,342		
Proved Developed Reserves at December 31						
Florida Exploration Company	3,845*	87,476*	5,696	116,349	3,953	83,940
Unicon	2,910	149,034	2,726	155,537		
Combined	6,755	236,510	8,422	271,886		

The Company's reserves are all within the United States and the Gulf of Mexico.
* Based upon the January 1, 1984 appraisal, 485,000 barrels of oil and 22.2 billion cubic feet of natural gas were reclassified from proved developed to proved undeveloped.

Source: The Continental Group, Inc., *Annual Report*, 1983.

EXHIBIT 2
Completed Divestitures of Diamond Divisions

Division	Buyer	Date	Price (millions)
Sales			
Neekim Can Division	Wearey Corp.	Dec. 1982	$ 98
Escher Wyss GambH	Sulzer Bros. Ltd. (Switzerland)	Feb. 1983	7
Diamond Automation	Leverage buyout by managers of Torok Co.	Mar. 1983	5
Diamond Match	80% sold to assorted investors	Mar. 1983	13
Calmar	83% sold in public offering	June 1983	62
Pulp and Paper	James River Corp. of Virginia	July 1983	149
Pending sales			
Retail lumber	Michigan General Corp.		$ 120
Sawmills and millwork plants	Buyer undisclosed		95
Diamond Fiber Products	Buyer undisclosed		38
		Subtotal	$ 587
Remaining assets (estimated value)			
Timberlands and one sawmill			$ 723
17% of Calmar			13
20% of Diamond Match			3
Total after divestitures			$1,326
Less: Goldsmith's cost of acquiring Diamond International			661
Diamond's Corporate Debt (estimated)			162
Goldsmith's potential gain			$ 503

Source: "Jimmy Goldsmith's U.S. Bonanza," *Fortune,* October 17, 1983.

EXHIBIT 3

The Goldsmith Empire

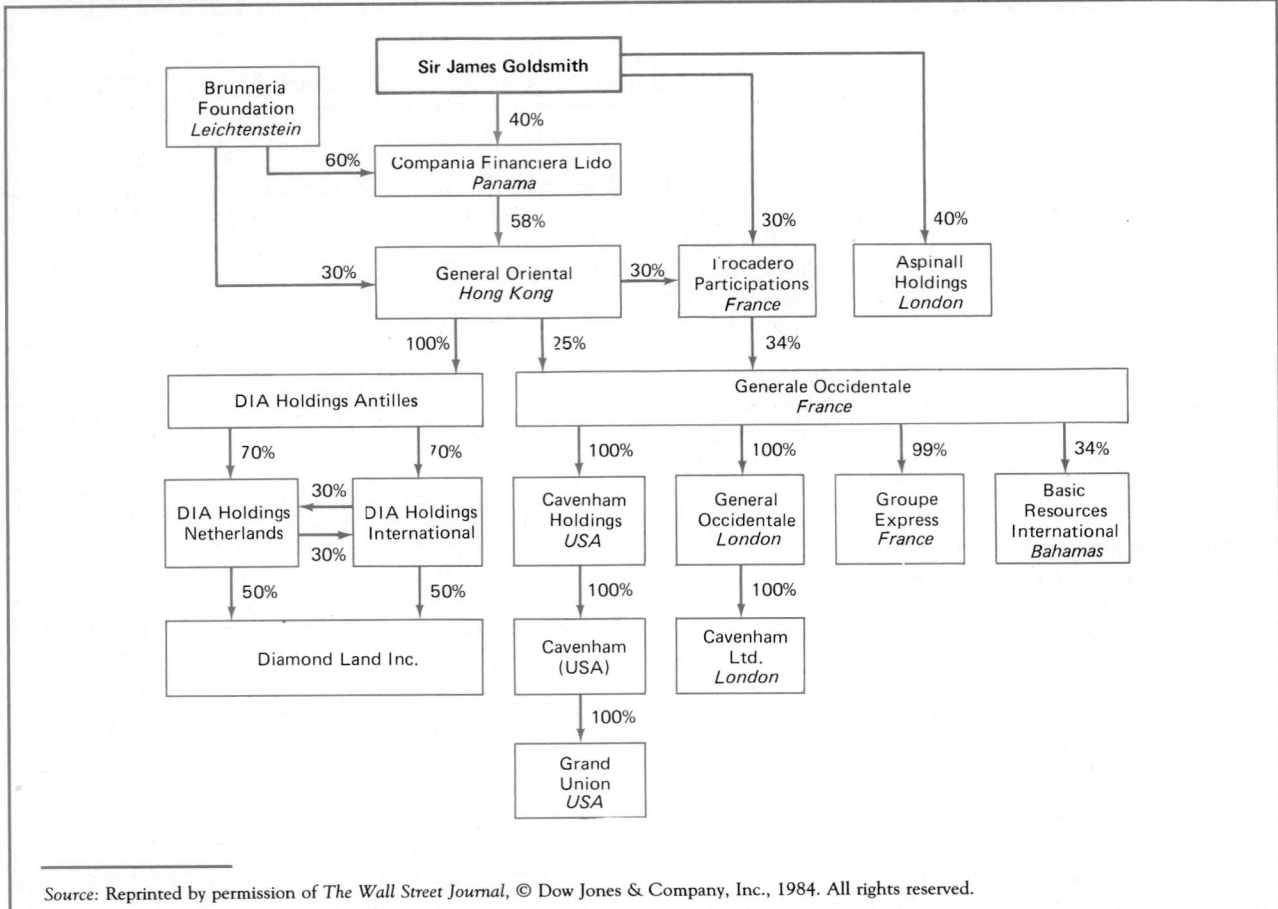

Many people live without changing their circumstances. We try different things. That is our strength. Once we get institutionalized, organized, paragraphed, that's when we are dead. The most important considerations for us are the preservation of our spirit . . . and the preservation of our quality.

This was the manner in which Fred Lebensold, one of the partners of ARCOP, described the firm that had surged to prominence in Canadian architecture during the 1960s. ARCOP ("Architects in Co-Partnership") had won several competitions for significant public buildings across Canada and received awards for many of the buildings that it had completed. Yet, there were underlying concerns about the ability of ARCOP to maintain the success that it had attained. Some of the partners wondered about the dramatic manner in which the volume of work seemed to grow and decline (see Exhibit 2) and about the strength and continuity of their partnership.

EVOLUTION OF THE PARTNERSHIP

The origins of ARCOP can be traced back to a group of aspiring young architects: Ray Affleck, Guy Desbarats, Hasen Size, and Jean Michaud. The four of them had met each other through the architecture department at McGill University, where they had been teaching on a part-time basis. They first began to pool resources in

Case copyright © 1986 Jamal Shamsie, McGill University. Material is partly adapted from H. Mintzberg, Suzane Otis, Jamal Shamsie, and James Waters, "Strategy of Design: A Study of 'Architects in Co-partnership'," in J. Grant, ed., *Strategic Management Frontiers* (JAI Press, 1987).

1953 with the intention of working independently on their own jobs. They started off sharing an office in the basement of a building in suburban Montreal. They also jointly employed a secretary and a draftsperson to assist them with their work.

At the outset, each partner obtained and conducted his own work, mostly in the form of small jobs. However, two larger jobs created the possibility of sharing work between them. Ray and Jean worked together on a post office building in a suburb of Montreal. Concurrently, Guy and Hasen jointly undertook the work on a service facility in centrally located Mont Royal Park, overlooking downtown Montreal. These joint efforts resulted in buildings that quickly gained recognition for excellence in architecture. The completed post office subsequently became the first public building to receive a prestigious Canadian Award for architecture.

These jobs also led these four individual architects to think about the possibility of all collaborating closely on a challenging job. In the meantime, they had come to know Fred Lebensold who was similarly teaching at McGill University and through him, Dimi Dimakopoulos who had been developing some preliminary drawings for a theater as part of his student course work. The six of them joined forces to prepare a submission for a national competition for a theatre complex in Vancouver. The group described their joint entry into the competition: "We tried to capture the timeless quality of a civic building at the same time creating the delight, contrast and visual excitement that is part of the experience of going to the theatre."[1]

The resulting design was awarded first place in the competition from over 60 submissions, some of which came from other larger firms that had already established themselves in Canada. However, the award confronted the group with the need to create an organization that could be contracted to carry out the job on the buildings to be known as the Queen Elizabeth and the Playhouse Theatres. As Fred noted: "We had never done a job of that size before . . . never."

Consequently, all of the six individuals formed a partnership that would be responsible for this single large job. The group also moved to larger premises and began hiring several architects and draftsmen to assist them in their work on the theatres.

Shortly afterwards, the developing organization received some visitors from I. M. Pei and Associates, a large U.S. architectural firm that was looking for help with the work on a major commercial complex that they had been designing for Montreal. Dimi recollected their meeting: "They came to see us in our building. . . . We had quickly fixed the office up, put pictures on the walls, tried to look proper. . . . While we were sitting around the conference table, I. M. Pei leaned back and one of the pictures we had stuck on the wall fell off and landed on his head. . . . There was a grim silence for a moment or two, then we all burst out laughing spontaneously. . . . It seemed to clinch the job."

The buildings, later called Place Ville Marie, consisted of a 50-story central tower surrounded by smaller office blocks that were all linked to each other by a shopping concourse at the lower levels. The project was centrally located in Montreal and became a driving force in the revitalization of the downtown core.

By 1958, the partners moved to a large office in downtown Montreal and decided to expand their partnership agreement to cover all their jobs. At this point, some questions were raised about the inclusion of Jean. Jean had been useful in bringing in some of the early work through his contacts, but he tended to be less active in the actual work. Guy commented: "We never saw him. . . . He would be away for months on end. But he was collecting full salary as a partner. We were all getting so busy we couldn't tolerate a partner that wasn't delivering anything." As a result, the partnership was reduced to five full-fledged architects by 1960.

All of the partners that constituted ARCOP shared a common enthusiasm for the modern movement in architecture which had only taken root in Canada in the 1950s. Each of them aspired to design buildings that would be unique and exciting. In an early promotional brochure, the partners expressed the objective of their firm as follows: "above all, to develop the utmost social and artistic values that represent the highest contribution of architecture to our civilization."

Their strong convictions led these budding architects to place a particularly strong emphasis on commitment to design excellence. Furthermore, all of the partners firmly believed that they could generate better designs through a collaborative problem solving approach to architecture as originally developed by Walter Gropius at the Bauhaus during the 1920s. An article in a leading U.S. architectural journal described them as follows:

> As their names suggest, the partners are of varied cultural backgrounds and share five languages among them. The firm's cosmopolitanism, and its juxtaposition of Turks, young and not so young, may account for the special quality of its work, which is marked by avoidance of fashionable cliches and scorn for the creation of monuments to individual self-expression—in favor of an emphasis upon inventive control of materials and construction processes, and fine detailing.[2]

The firm adopted the name ARCOP which stood for "Architects in Co-Partnership." It emphasized the values of equality and collaboration in the partnership. This ran contrary to most established architectural firms where the names of the partners identified the firm and the order of listing of the names represented the hierarchy or the status of the different partners. Furthermore, the partners decided that all of the work that they carried out would be attributed to their firm as a whole.

To their dismay, the partners discovered that the provincial laws governing professional practice required listing the names of the partners. Consequently, it was decided to place the names in alphabetical order to denote lack of hierarchy. Nevertheless, there were serious concerns about the possibility that the alphabetical order would not be recognized, leading clients to believe that those listed first represented the senior partners.

Acquisition of Work

The real impetus for ARCOP's growth came from the many different architectural competitions that were being organized all across Canada during these early years to support the development of domestic talent. Starting in 1958, the firm entered six competitions and won four of them.

The success of ARCOP in these competitions resulted in significant work on public buildings all across Canada. Some of these developed directly out of winning the competitions, while others came to the firm on the basis of the reputation that it was acquiring.

In particular, the firm was able to build up a string of jobs on civic complexes (see Exhibit 1). An early commission that came right on the heels of the job on the Queen Elizabeth Theatre was for a major concert hall as the first phase of a Place des Arts complex in Montreal.

Another major job resulted from a national competition for a complex of buildings that would commemorate the confederation of Canada. This complex was to be called the Confederation Centre and was located in Charlottetown on Prince Edward Island, off the eastern coast of Canada. It included a theatre, a museum and a library and was to have as its focal point the 1847 building which was the meeting place for the representatives who met to confederate the Canadian provinces.

Finally, ARCOP was asked to submit a design for the National Arts Centre in Ottawa. This led to a commission for the work on this prestigious building that was to consist of an opera house, a regular and an experimental theatre by the side of the Rideau Canal in the capital city of Canada.

In commenting on this type of work, an architectural critic wrote about the competition for the Confederation building:

> In the design of the . . . Confederation Memorial building, the architect has an opportunity, rare in any generation, of designing a building for centuries. The competitor is wasting his time who thinks of this building as anything but a national shrine to which Canadians will forever pay homage as the birthplace of their nation.[3]

Besides this type of work on public buildings, ARCOP was also building recognition in multi-use commercial complexes through its involvement in Place Ville Marie. The firm's best known job resulted from a subsequent collaboration with some developers. Ray recalled the events that led up to the job: "I remember seeing an advertisement asking developers to submit proposals for this property on Lagauchetiere and University Streets. I looked at it . . . we're not developers of course. A day or two later one of the developers who was involved with Place Ville Marie . . . asked if we would work with them in making a proposal. I was so busy with other things . . . somehow the whole idea didn't appeal to me tremendously . . . I don't know why, because it turned out to be one of the most fascinating jobs I have ever done. I must say they had an extremely imaginative proposal for building on that site. We put it together . . . our design and their concept . . . submitted it . . . and there was no contest."

This building, Place Bonaventure, was primarily a merchandise mart, the first of its kind in Canada. But it also contained a retail shopping concourse, an exhibition hall and a 400-room roof garden courtyard hotel. It generated the following comments:

> Place Bonaventure has no real plaza at all. One of the largest buildings in the world and relatively low in comparison to surrounding office and hotel towers, it is a dense monolith which almost completely covers its 6-acre site. As a building type it has no counterpart anywhere. As a prototype for the dense, multi-use urban complex of the future, Place Bonaventure's brilliant and unusual parti deserves careful study.[4]

Other significant types of work came to the firm through the personal contacts of the various partners. These included several educational buildings, among them the Leacock Social Sciences building and the Student Union building, both for McGill University. The firm also got involved in the design of some of the theme buildings for the world exhibition, Expo, that was slated to open in Montreal in 1967.

In 1967, ARCOP returned to competitions to try and generate new jobs, the first such effort since 1962. However, none of the partners showed much interest in either of the two competitions that were pursued and there was little effort to collaborate in the mode that had earlier been so successful. Much of the work was actually handled by some of the associates. As Guy put it, "We lost because we did not have our hearts in it."

Execution of Work

The partners quickly discovered that, with so many partners, someone had to take formal charge of each project or job, whether or not the work was shared. Moreover, they found that the clients usually preferred dealing with a single partner as primary contact. Hence there was an understanding that a single partner would take overall responsibility for each job and that the allocation of jobs would be worked out between the partners on an informal basis.

At the same time, an integral part of ARCOP's philosophy called for a close relationship between client, architect and contractor during the execution of jobs. This meant that the partner in charge had to personally get involved with the client and the contractor relatively early in the design stage. It signified a radical departure on the part of this firm away from the traditional practice of architecture where projects were passed from clients to architects to contractors in a sequential manner.

Ray elaborated upon the benefits of this method of working:

> An architect who is some sort of an isolated expert is a Don Quixote galloping around on a steed against windmills that aren't there. We really are nothing if we are not able to communicate with a great variety of people who are in many ways much more skilled in the areas in which we claim to be skilled. One of the great bogeymen that we must continually fight against . . . is the fragmented professional who sits in one area, is an expert in this and somebody else who sits in another area is an expert in that and both work in water-tight compartments. In today's world this will get us absolutely nowhere. . . .
>
> Basically it is important . . . to get all the significant entities, professionals and otherwise, involved together in the decision-making process and involved in a situation of simultaneity and not in a situation of linear sequence. It means bringing people together at the same time to collide with each other. One of the very important elements of this process is the exposure of conflict—conflicts between technically oriented people, esthetically oriented people and people who are experts at measuring things like money and time.
>
> A great deal of stalemate in creative work occurs when these diverse people do not interact soon enough. They collide when it is too late—they see each other in court or go behind each other's backs. This unfortunately is the traditional relationship between architect and contractor and often architect and client. If the conflicts aren't brought out in a controlled area of communication they will come up sooner or later to the detriment of action, rather than to its benefit. As we all know, in any dialectic process it is around the conflict that the real creative activity occurs. The exposure of conflict is a key thing.
>
> The process demands of the architect that he vacates his age old formalist prison and begins to perceive form as process, and accept that in dealing with extremely complex problems, . . . solutions—good ideas—can come from almost any source and are not locked into the narrow confines of the traditional professional disciplines. In our experience, this method has been an extremely rapid, often unpredictable but most creative mode of clarifying problems and finding solutions.[5]

However, this type of approach suggested that the partner in charge had to have sufficient control over the job so as to be able to engage in this creative problem solving process with the other parties. The collaboration between the partners on ongoing jobs began to depend upon the ability of the partner in charge of a project to draw in the other partners from time to time to consult on specific problems or issues.

Furthermore, the clients considered the partner that had worked with them as being primarily responsible for the final product. A problem with this occurred in 1963 when a plaque appeared at the completed Place des Arts building specifically crediting Fred, instead of the firm as a whole, as the architect. Although this plaque was subsequently removed, it created some tensions about the concept and role of the partner in charge, leading to an increase in lobbying for prestigious jobs within the partnership. In response to this growing conflict, Guy finally attempted to develop some formal criteria for the appointment of a partner in charge on new jobs, emphasizing rotation among the partners, depending upon their current workloads.

Another aspect of the job that was handled by the partner in charge was the organization of staff into teams that would undertake the job. The overall team on each job was headed by a project manager, whose principal responsibilities lay in the coordination and administration of the entire job. Additionally, larger jobs were broken down into sections based upon the actual physical parts of the structure as well as certain functional divisions of the work. Each of these sections was placed in the hands of a group of architects and draftsmen that was headed by a job captain.

Over time, the different partners also began to favor working with certain members of the staff, particularly those who acted as project managers and job captains. This led to occasional conflicts when another partner would want to use staff that had not previously worked with him. It is believed that on one occasion, a job was lost because a partner would not release a particular staff member who was requested by the potential client.

Growth and Organization

The team approach to job execution allowed the different partners to delegate a great deal of responsibility and provide tremendous challenge to the best young architectural talent that they had been hiring out of McGill University. Two of these were elevated to the position of associates of the partnership by 1961.

By 1963, ARCOP's billings had reached close to $1 million and the level of staff had risen to almost 60 members. A form of profit sharing plan was introduced by the partners for the associates and the senior staff. The firm also moved into a building that had been designed by the partners for the needs of their business.

With continued growth of work, the partnership also began to hire individuals with expertise in different areas such as design, drafting, graphics, specifications, field supervision and interior design. In something of a matrix management approach, individuals from these various areas worked closely with each other on job teams, coordinated by a project manager. Ray described the creation of the interior design group: "We got some young ladies . . . they had a little corner . . . They were not architects, they were specialists in furnishings, colors."

The firm's rapid growth also required increased attention to the management of the overall practice. The partners began to create some administrative management positions. A production manager was handed responsibility for scheduling and supervising the staff on the various jobs. The costing and accounting functions were vested in another position that was termed business manager. Finally, a construction manager was appointed to assist the supervision staff with the construction phase of jobs.

As the mid-1960s approached, the firm experienced its greatest spurt of growth, the result of the simultaneous occurrence of several very large jobs. The combination of these jobs resulted in a rise of billings to slightly over $3 million and a growth in staff to almost 150 people by 1966. The number of associates was increased to eight to handle the management of these jobs.

At the same time, the firm continued to add staff to fill in the various functional areas. This eventually forced the partners to make the role of these specialists clearer. The interior design group, in particular, began to lobby for a more independent practice. Its members wanted to take several steps, which included the possibility of setting themselves up in a separate location, that would allow them to solicit work for themselves. Guy most strongly favored the seeking of different kinds of work by these different areas, but Ray felt equally strongly that work should only be solicited by the firm as a whole. After much discussion, the partners eventually turned down the demands of the interior designers for a more autonomous operation.

But with the phenomenal rise in the volume of work, there was a growing belief among the managers and the associates that the firm was making insufficient profits and even losing money on the big jobs. Ray commented: "There was a feeling that we were inefficient. . . . We should be making more money. Everything should be going like clockwork." This led to frequent complaints from the associates and the managers whose bonuses were tied to the overall profitability of the practice. In order to deal with this growing dissatisfaction, the partners created another organization within their partnership that was controlled by the senior staff. This organization negotiated separately with the partners over fees that it charged for the work that it carried out on the jobs of the partnership. As such, it was also allowed to distribute among its employees any of the profits that it made on this work.

At around the same time, the partners asked the senior staff, mostly associates, to form a management committee to deal with the administration of the firm. The committee was headed by Roger Marshall, a senior associate who was appointed executive director. Roger was also pledged extensive powers to manage the daily operations. Under his direction, subcommittees were also established to deal with specific aspects of management such as reviewing job contracts, administering budgets, creating job descriptions and reviewing salaries.

However, the various partners differed radically in their enthusiasm for this growth in management structure. This was reflected in the following responses to the appointment of Roger Marshall as executive director. Ray: "It was a terrible disfavour we did to him. I found that he was trying to coordinate the uncoordinable." Guy: "It was a giant leap forward towards the possibility of setting up a properly managed firm."

The senior staff questioned the usefulness or effectiveness of the steps that had been taken. There were growing concerns about the relative indifference of most of the partners to issues other than their own jobs. One of the associates recollected later: "All of the partners were becoming decreasingly tolerant of any organizational decisions that would infringe upon their personal involvement with their own jobs."

Underlying all of this was a growing disagreement between Guy and Ray, in particular on the kind of organization that was desirable. Guy pushed for a larger tighter organization with increased formal controls, whereas Ray preferred a smaller looser organization with greater personal control. Dimi remarked of this growing confrontation: "Guy and Ray found themselves in boxes . . . with no windows or doors open."

THE LA CITE JOB

By 1968, the partnership had begun to show increasing signs of disintegration. The partners had started to hold some weekend retreats away from the office to try to recreate the earlier atmosphere. As Guy noted: "The more successful we were, the more tensions we created."

Subsequently, Guy chose to increase his teaching commitments at the University of Montreal and reduce his involvement with ARCOP. Hasen Size was retired from the partnership, though he continued to receive some benefits from the practice as his settlement.

The office was moved to another downtown location as the remaining partners decided to move out of the ARCOP-designed building, which was subsequently sold off.

In 1968, the partnership was approached regarding a job involving a multi-purpose commercial development in downtown Montreal. The complex that was being designed included separate buildings for offices, stores, a hotel and apartments. However, it involved the demolition of several blocks of housing and consequently generated organized protests from the residents of the area that were being forced out. The clients for the job were the developers who had worked with ARCOP on Place Bonaventure. Ray recalled his involvement with the project as follows: "It started as an interesting job . . . the notion of a great big development in an existing urban fabric. It involved a fair amount of demolition and of pushing people out. That kind of thing I don't think any developer would even try to do today. I attempted for quite a while to involve the citizens in the decision making. It ended up in quite a clash of values that I found myself very much caught in. I eventually resigned because I was pretty much divided in my loyalties. I couldn't perform with integrity and commitment, particularly with respect to the client." Dimi disagreed strongly with Ray and recalled his feelings: "I felt it was our duty to examine the situation properly. I think Ray abandoned the job without examining all the possibilities . . . it was easier pulling out."

Torn between this sense of commitment to client as well as to community, Dimi took over the job as Ray withdrew his services. The confrontation over the job on La Cite created more tensions in the partnership. As a result, the future of ARCOP was increasingly placed in doubt by late 1969, as the partners tried to seek a way out of their conflicts.

Through all of this, the level of work continued to decline with billings for 1969 dropping almost to $1 million. By the end of 1969, there were just over 30 people remaining with the firm. Most of the associates also left the firm during these years, and several of them were talented designers who subsequently started their own firms or became partners in already established competing firms. Yet, none of the partners, apart from Guy, seriously considered inviting any of these associates to join the partnership. Dimi justified this decision: "We had an element that made us successful. . . . The same magic could not be reproduced. We could not consider the associates to fill our ranks."

DECISION POINT

What are the critical issues that underlie the growing conflict in ARCOP? How can they be effectively addressed?

940

Ray Affleck and Fred Lebensold decided to continue working together after the decision was made to terminate the earlier partnership agreement. Two of the four associates remaining with the firm, Art Nichol and Ramesh Khosla, were also promoted to the status of new partners. Art had been the first associate appointed in the firm but Ramesh had only recently been hired and made an associate. As a result, Ray and Fred were viewed as the senior partners while Art and Ramesh were, in a sense, feeling their way into the partnership role. This move away from equality was clearly indicated by Fred's negotiated listing of his name first in the new partnership.

The immediate concern of all the partners was with the generation of work for their newly reorganized practice. Most of the new jobs obtained by ARCOP in the 1970s involved working with other architectural firms on multi-use commercial buildings (see Exhibit 2).

The search for more work also led the partners to think about opening another office in a different location, possibly Toronto. This move was made possible in 1973 when Paul Hughes, an established architect, approached ARCOP to open a separate office in Toronto under their name. Paul recalls, "I felt it would be more interesting, more challenging to practice with a firm that was already established . . . perhaps with a Montreal firm that I knew very well . . . I began talking to Ray about opening an office in Toronto. . . . As it developed, the new office in Toronto basically operated in an independent manner, obtaining and working on its own jobs.

Subsequently, both Paul and Ramesh spearheaded the effort to pursue more work for the two offices. Fred commented, "We all had to really look for work. We were not very good at that. We never did much of it. Work came to us. . . . We never had to chase work."

The firm began to increasingly seek jobs in the United States as well as in more distant overseas locations. Paul explained, "It seemed that the only way to survive was to go where the action was. We ended up having to go far afield to get to the action."

By 1975, the new partnership had built up enough work to generate close to $2 million in billings and the number of staff had increased to 70 employees, of which 45 were located in Montreal. But the partners had clearly moved away from hiring staff that were specialized in areas other than design or drafting. Ray explained the reasons for this change: "Our experience has been that the types of work we get has always been erratic. . . . Sometimes we get something to do requiring specifications or interiors, sometimes we don't."

The partners also tried to stay clear of the organizational issues which had created such conflict during the 1960s. Art, who had been substantially involved in administrative work even as an associate, assumed responsibility for most of the overall management functions. The partners continued to appoint project managers that took charge of individual jobs and to organize groups around the execution of work on these jobs. But they carefully avoided the recreation of the administrative management structure that had been previously developed. Ray justified this choice, "Managers tend to be too administratively oriented. They are not close enough to the work."

In 1976, ARCOP decided to enter a national competition, their first since the reorganization of their partnership. It was decided that the design work for this competition should be done in collaboration with another Montreal-based firm that had francophone partners. Art recalled the manner in which work progressed on the competition: "It was a great opportunity. There was a great desire for every-

941

one to get involved. However, there were sharp differences in the approaches of Fred and Ray to the job. Things went from bad to worse. Each partner pulled in his favorite staff members. It ended up as a competition within the office. Ray's design finally won out, but there was a great deal of bitterness created in the process. Needless to say, we lost the competition."

Meanwhile, annual billings for ARCOP dropped again to well below $1 million in 1977 resulting in the first loss ever registered by the partnership. The level of staffing was reduced to only 20 people distributed between the two offices at the start of 1978.

QUESTIONS

1. What kind of strategy did ARCOP pursue? What led to its early success?

2. What kind of conflicts did ARCOP face? Could these conflicts have been better resolved?

3. How were power and control exercised by the partners? by the associates? by the management staffs? by the departments?

4. Did the new firm effectively resolve the issues faced by the earlier partnership?

EXHIBIT 1

The jobs that represented the bulk of ARCOP's work over the years are listed below by the year in which work was started. Most jobs typically took three to five years to complete.

Name of Job	Location	Type of Work
1955 Queen Elizabeth Theater	Vancouver	Performing arts center
1958 Place Ville Marie[a]	Montreal	Office, retail complex
1958 Place des Arts	Montreal	Performing arts center
1961 McGill Leacock Building	Montreal	University building
1961 Confederation Center	P.E.I.	Theater, library, museum complex
1962 McGill Student Union	Montreal	University building
1962 Provincial Buildings	P.E.I.	Office complex
1963 Place Bonaventure	Montreal	Merchandise mart, retail, hotel complex
1964 National Arts Center	Ottawa	Performing arts center
1964 Arts and Culture Centre	St. Johns, Newfoundland	Performing arts center
1964 Expo Theme Buildings	Montreal	Exhibition buildings
1966 Polyvalente School	Montreal	High school buildings
1968 Dalhousie Life Sciences Building	Halifax	University building
1968 La Cite Complex[b]	Montreal	Residential, office, retail complex
1970 Onondaga County Centre	Syracuse	Theater, offices, retail complex
1970 World Trade Centre[a]	New York	Office, retail complex
1972 Museum of Fine Arts	Montreal	Art museum building
1972 Waterfront Study	Halifax	Master development plan for area
1973 Winnipeg Square	Winnipeg	Office, retail, hotel complex
1973 Sheraton Centre	Montreal	Hotel building
1973 Centrum Centre[b]	Los Angeles	Office, retail, hotel complex
1974 Harborfront Study	Toronto	Master development plan for area
1975 La Chaudiere	Ottawa/Hull	Office, retail, hotel complex
1977 Adeolo-Odeku Centre	Nigeria	Shopping center

[a] represents work carried out on parts of building.
[b] represents preliminary study and design work only.
Source: ARCOP records.

943

EXHIBIT 2

Financial Data in
Thousands of Dollars,
1958–1977

	Billings	Salaries[a]	Expenses[b]	Overhead[c]	Profit
1958	$ 85	$ 8	$ 7	$ 45	$ 25
1959	285	105	3	71	106
1960	692	299	52	129	212
1961	609	328	36	119	126
1962	970	389	247	175	159
1963	975	387	274	230	84
1964	1,411	465	467	314	165
1965	2,151	888	369	417	477
1966	3,085	1,137	867	483	598
1967	2,001	707	482	341	471
1968	1,602	529	442	314	317
1969	1,134	480	261	230	163
1970	953	418	171	198	166
1971	913	453	147	200	113
1972	985	457	141	227	160
1973	1,472	630	92	276	474
1974	1,449	681	118	349	301
1975	1,951	1,035	111	367	438
1976	1,324	697	124	341	162
1977	904	483	148	324	−51

[a] Covers architectural salaries applicable to jobs.
[b] Covers fees of consultants used that were not charged to client.
[c] Covers general and administrative expenses.

Source: ARCOP records.

EXHIBIT 3

The Architectural Industry
as of the Late 1970s

PRACTICE

Architects must be registered by provincial boards to be able to practice on their own in Canada. An individual architect is required to undergo a training period with practicing architects and to pass a board examination before he or she can be registered. An architect may, however, work with another firm under registered architects without obtaining registration.

Most Canadian architectural firms exist as individual proprietorships or as partnerships because most provinces do not allow incorporation. There were 57% individual proprietorships, 31% partnerships and 10% incorporated companies among architectural firms in Canada in 1977.

Incorporation has recently been permitted in some Canadian provinces, but an estimated 16% of firms in the other provinces have set up incorporated service companies to which they transferred all of the non-registered architectural staff.

FIRMS

The number of architectural firms has generally increased since the late 1950s and has doubled since the late 1960s. There were 1,707 firms registered in 1977, but only 1,283 firms were actually in operation. Architectural firms

EXHIBIT 3
(Continued)

have grown in all provinces, although in 1977, Quebec and Ontario still account for 63% and British Columbia and Alberta accounted for 26% of architectural firms in Canada.

The relative distribution of establishments in 1977 by volume of billings is indicated below:

Less than $100,000	646 firms	50.3%
$100,000–999,999	580 firms	45.2%
$1,000,000 and over	57 firms	4.5%

The firms in the smallest category generally employ less than five people, whereas those in the largest category usually carry more than 35 staff.

STAFF

Over two-thirds of the staff in architectural firms is generally evenly distributed between architects and drafting or technical people. The remainder of the staff carry out office and administrative functions. Staff are hired and laid off, for the most part, depending upon the volume and pressure of work. It is not uncommon for firms to hire certain people intermittently to help out during busy periods.

WORK

Architectural work is typically carried out in stages. In some instances, preliminary studies and planning work can be undertaken before any designs are produced. Otherwise, the work actually starts with the conceptual design stage, during which the basic design is developed in accordance with the client's needs and financial constraints. It subsequently moves into working drawings, which include all technical specifications that are necessary for construction. The final stage requires supervision of construction to ensure that it proceeds in accordance with the drawings.

CONTRACTED SERVICES

Architectural firms frequently hire external consultants from different areas during the course of work on jobs. For example, acoustical engineers can assist a firm with the design of an auditorium or theatre. Part of the cost of these consultants can be recovered from the client in addition to the regular fees for the architectural firm. The use of external consultants does, however, generally reduce the profits that can be made on a job. Nevertheless, most architectural firms do not carry in-house specialists because of their high salary expense and the fluctuating demand for their services.

EXHIBIT 3
(Continued)

MARKETING

Architectural firms acquire most of their work through the reputation that is generated as a result of their completed buildings. Nevertheless, this reputation can be built up and supported by a variety of marketing efforts. Firms can engage in promotional activities that are geared towards cultivating and maintaining contacts with prospective clients. Speculative work can also be done at minimal or no cost to the client on the understanding that if the client decides to proceed, further work at full cost will come to the firm. Finally, architectural firms can enter official competitions when these are announced to bid for work on specific jobs.

FEE STRUCTURE

Billings for a job are generally on a fixed fee basis, usually determined as a percentage of cost of construction, if construction activity is involved. It is sometimes charged on a cost plus basis, with an upset price determining the upper limit.

Profit margins have generally declined in the industry with average profits running from 11% to 17% of annual fees in 1977. These declines have occurred because of decline in larger jobs, tighter fee structures and increased client demands.

INDUSTRY BILLINGS

Overall billings in the Canadian architectural industry have shown periods of strong growth as indicated in the figures that follow:

1961	81 million	1970	186 million
1962	94 million	1971	185 million
1963	112 million	1972	181 million
1964	136 million	1973	194 million
1965	147 million	1974	233 million
1966	153 million	1975	291 million
1967	159 million	1976	324 million
1968	181 million	1977	326 million
1969	188 million	1978	329 million

Sources: "Offices of Architects 1977," *Statistics Canada*, Department of Industry Trade and Commerce, 1979; and P. Bernard Associates, "Survey of Canadian Architects' Services," Department of Industry, Trade and Commerce, 1979.

PEET, RUSS, ANDERSON, & DETROIT (PRA&D)*

The accounting profession, which had long been very stable and predictable, began changing dramatically during the 1970s and 1980s. First, the merger boom of the 1970s cut the ranks of publicly owned corporations normally served by the Big Eight accounting firms. The audit fee from a merged firm was usually about 65% of the combined fees the two firms had paid independently. While this saved the client companies substantial amounts, it cut dramatically into the fees of the accounting firms.

Then in the late 1970s the Federal Trade Commission (FTC), seeking to increase competition in the accounting profession, forced the profession to eliminate its self-imposed strictures against advertising and the solicitation of other firms' clients. Client corporations quickly learned they could radically reduce audit fees by replacing their auditors every few years. Reputation and long-standing client ties were no longer enough to attract or hold clients, or to shield accounting firms from price competition. As firms began actively courting competitors' clients, they also aggressively sought ways to cut their internal costs and to provide new client services. This led to substantial investments in computer and other technologies designed to reduce—or gain higher yields from—the high-priced labor involved in an audit. It also promoted further diversification into management consulting, tax counseling, systems design, and other services.

Case copyright © 1989, James Brian Quinn. This case was developed by Penny Paquette under the guidance of Professor Quinn.

* Disguised name of a real firm. Internal figures of PRA&D have been adjusted by constants in each exhibit.

Despite such efforts, *The Public Accounting Report* stated that revenues at the eight largest firms grew a total of only 22% from 1982–1985, down from 40% over the preceding two-year span. But accounting revenues rose only 14%; the biggest gains in the early 1980s came from consulting fees, up 33%. Simultaneously, net income per partner was being depressed by diminishing ratios of professional staff to partners (caused by the decreased demand in the audit area for ordinary "number crunchers"), by lower utilization rates (because more professional hours had to be spent on non-chargeable activities such as marketing or practice development as it was called in the industry), and by the increasing cost of recruiting and retaining the higher-quality professional staff firms now needed. So intense were the pressures on revenues that one of the larger firms took the unprecedented step of pushing out or retiring 10% of its partners.

Smaller and medium-sized firms either developed specialized niches or merged to broaden their services, gain expertise, or gain necessary economies of scale. In the mid-1980s some of the larger firms had even merged to gain the worldwide sales and expertise demanded by their large multinational clients. As such mergers increasingly divided the remaining members of the Big Eight from the smaller firms, their greater scale and potentials began raising antitrust issues.

The 1982 *Census of Service Industries* reported some 49,000 U.S. accounting firms, with revenues totaling $14.6 billion. The Big Eight among these firms (then Arthur Andersen; Peat Marwick; Ernst & Whinney; Coopers & Lybrand; Price Waterhouse; Arthur Young; Touche Ross; and Deloitte, Haskins, & Sells) earned more than 28% of all industry revenues, while the 12 largest firms received 32% of the total. Less than 3% of all firms had revenues of more than $1 million in 1982, and less than 1% had revenues exceeding $2.5 million. The Big Eight firms had an estimated $3.8 billion in non-U.S. billings in 1984, and foreign billings accounted for at least 25% of total billings for each of the Big Eight. (See Appendix A for a profile of the largest accounting firms.) Their international operations, originally established primarily to serve U.S.-based multinationals, tended to be organized abroad as loose collections of largely autonomous partnerships. Smaller accounting firms conducted considerably less international business. Table 1 breaks out revenues by type of service for the U.S. accounting profession as a whole and for a typical Big Eight firm in 1982. The size, number, ranking, and names of the largest accounting concerns actually shifted substantially as the 1980s emerged.

A study by the Congressional Research Service found that in 1980 clients of the then Big Eight accounted for 94% of all sales, 94% of all profits, 90% of all income taxes paid, 94% of all people employed, and 94% of all assets owned by New

TABLE 1   1982 Revenues by Type for Accounting Firms

TYPE OF SERVICE	U.S. ACCOUNTING PROFESSION AVERAGE	TYPICAL BIG EIGHT FIRM
Accounting/auditing	50.8%	50–75%
Tax preparation and consulting	26.8	15–25
Bookkeeping	11.9	
Management advisory	8.2	10–30
Other	2.4	

Source: Office of Technology Assessment, *Trade in Services,* OTA-ITE-316, September 1988, p. 48.

York Stock Exchange members. The eight to ten largest CPA firms tended to handle the preponderance of all *Fortune* 500 companies' business, but smaller companies and numerous not-for-profits and governmental organizations were also among their clients. Larger clients purchased tax and consulting services well in excess of what they spent on audits. But in the mid-1980s only about a fifth of the Big Eight's revenues were from nonaudit services.

TRENDS IN THE PROFESSION

The main focus of the profession's diversification efforts had been into management advisory or consulting services which in the United States yielded profit margins of about 20%, almost three times that on standard audits. While consulting competitors complained about unfair competition from auditing firms, the firms themselves felt that the experience they gained as auditors made them better consultants for their clients and that consulting improved the quality of their audits by helping them know more about their clients. The profession maintained that it had erected a careful "Chinese wall" between their auditing and consulting functions and cited the fact that only 10–40% of their audit clients ended up as consulting clients. But criticism was mounting against CPA firms for moving into specific areas of consulting some thought bordered on "conflicts of interest" with the objectivity needed in the auditing side of the business. For example, Peat Marwick had bought a major share in a public relations firm; Arthur Andersen had become a major factor in the asset-appraisal business; and Deloitte, Haskins, & Sells and Touche Ross were putting increased emphasis on consulting for investment bankers in corporate mergers, reorganizations, and bankruptcies. Others wondered openly whether an audit unit could really offer an unbiased appraisal of a system, major project, or decision its consulting group had recommended.

Aggravating matters was the fact that consultants in most firms were paid a bit more than auditors, and the disparate nature of the two activities often led to a culture clash. Public accountants had taken rigorous professional training and examinations to be certified as public accountants. They had to be not only knowledgeable about and adhere to the regulations of government bodies affecting financial and reporting matters but to the rules of the profession as interpreted by Generally Accepted Accounting Principles (GAAP) and the SEC in its Financial Accounting Standards Board (FASB) rulings. They had their own professional journals and looked to their professional colleagues for support and movement elsewhere in the industry.

The conflicts of this professionalism with the more freewheeling style of the consultants was further exacerbated by the partnership form that CPA firms followed. Accountants from the firms' earlier history usually dominated the partnership numerically. Consultants, who typically were not CPAs, could only be quasi-partners in that portion of the firm certifying audits. And disproportions between audit and consulting fees affected one group's willingness to share incomes and investments with the other. How these conflicts—and the power relationships they involved—could be resolved was an open question in the late 1980s.

Even so, the FTC was pushing for further sweeping changes in the professional codes which governed the accounting profession. The FTC was proposing that accountants would soon be free to draw contingent fees from sums recovered for clients as a result of audit work done in lawsuits, to accept commissions from the sellers of financial products the accountants had reviewed or recommended to customers, and to form private or even publicly held companies to process regular bookkeeping and accounting transactions for clients. The traditional partnership form the profession had adopted had made partners "fully and personally responsible" for their firm's CPA certifications and opinions. Many accountants were concerned that such moves would convert public accounting from its previous status as a "profession" with responsibilities beyond mere commercial concerns into "just another business." While the industry was fighting the FTC's efforts to promote harmful competition and to protect its image as a profession, legal actions against auditing firms had mounted, and most of the Big Eight had faced at least one potentially devastating lawsuit. Firms were hard pressed to get enough malpractice insurance to cover possible losses.

PRA&D POSITION

In the mid-1980s Peet, Russ, Anderson, & Detroit (PRA&D) sought to adjust its strategic position to respond to these changes in its industry and to the new global business environment it faced. PRA&D was among the largest and most prestigious of the public accounting firms. It was heavily represented among both manufacturing and service clients in the United States and in international markets. Well respected and conservative, PRA&D had so far moved cautiously in terms of diversification and marketing aggressiveness, but had developed strong consulting, tax, and systems units. PRA&D's headquarters were in a major Atlantic seaboard city, but it had branches or affiliates in most large U.S., European, Asian, Latin American, and Pacific Rim cities as well. Its past organization had given extensive autonomy to its partners in each local branch. But its central office had exerted strong policy controls in most functional areas, particularly those dealing with audit, tax, and ethical standards. Despite the presence of a Management Committee—elected by the partnership and usually containing the top functional and branch heads of the firm—PRA&D's Managing Partner, Henry Johnson, exercised very significant influence throughout the firm because of his personality and highly respected professional skills.

In 1989, concerned about the developing fragmentation resulting from its many specialized activities, its continued growth, and PRA&D's necessarily localized presence in so many different geographical areas, Mr. Johnson began to worry about how to reorganize and reposition his firm in light of the new competitive pressures. He wanted to establish a more focused organization and operating philosophy to deal with the complexities the firm then faced.

A considerable amount of self-analysis over the last two years had convinced the Management Committee that the 1980s' rapid rates of change, intense competition, new technology development, and needs for specialized skills would increase rather than decline. PRA&D felt it was well positioned in some market segments (notably with large traditional multinational manufacturers) and not as well in others (particularly smaller and mid-sized services companies). As a mid-sized member of the then Big Eight, PRA&D did not have the resources to develop a dominating presence in all areas. The gap in size between PRA&D and its largest competitors was already significant, and if past growth rates continued, the gap would increase in the future.

PRA&D's commitment to providing high-quality professional services through autonomous professional partners was fundamental to its culture. The firm had enjoyed well-deserved strengths in terms of its name recognition and its reputation for quality, integrity, and service, especially to its large clients. The latter were rather widely distributed both geographically and by industry classification.

However, PRA&D felt it lacked partner presence in many business segments and in some geographical areas which were likely to be important to its future. Over the last several years, growth pressures had been so great that the Management Committee was beginning to doubt whether there were an adequate number of partners to pursue its former highly decentralized strategy in the future. PRA&D's resources seemed spread among many smaller practice units, making it difficult to concentrate resources on a single client's needs, and indeed to provide the full array of services it wished in many markets.

Because of its highly decentralized partnership structure, PRA&D had often placed more emphasis on current profitability than on long-term investments in many of the growing areas of accounting and consulting. Although its client listings in the *Fortune* 500 was high relative to its competitors, there was some concern whether the firm was growing with the new clients who would become the next generation of *Fortune* 500 companies. Because of its highly decentralized structure and management philosophy, PRA&D found it difficult to develop the levels of specialization some of its stronger competitors had. As a consequence, PRA&D was suffering from lower billing rates and profitability in some key growth areas, especially in specialized industries like health care, financial services, and high-technology manufacturing. In the past, PRA&D had grown primarily by developing new business at its local geographic offices and by attempting to give each office the capability to deliver PRA&D's full range to all types of clients in its area.

While this strategy was extremely successful into the late 1970s, fragmentation and lack of coordination had become serious problems by the late 1980s. Only a few offices had the resources to carry out a full-service strategy across the full range of businesses in their areas. Because PRA&D was smaller than some of its major competitors, it had fewer partners, and its partnership skills were being badly stretched to meet the increasingly wide array of customer needs. Most of PRA&D's geographical offices and professional services were still very highly regarded in the industry, especially among its existing clients. However, it was becoming ever more difficult for its partners to find the time to generate new business or to focus on new emerging markets in any coordinated way across the United States—much less PRA&D's many international markets.

A MARKET-DRIVEN STRATEGY

Intuitively, Mr. Johnson and the Management Committee strongly preferred a "market-driven strategy," focusing PRA&D's efforts on the services, delivery needs, and specialized capabilities key growth markets would demand in the future. However, they were concerned that PRA&D did not have enough partners or associates in its development pipeline (1) to maintain its existing customer base with the kind of quality for which PRA&D was known and (2) to simultaneously develop new "key growth markets." Although they had generally risen through PRA&D's auditing ranks, most members of its Management Committee recognized that the increasing complexities of the CPA market place required greater specialization on many professional disciplines in their practice (like taxes, mergers, international regulations, and computer systems) as well as on the needs of specific types of clients (like not-for-profit, government, consortia, financial services, etc. groups). They also recognized that many organizational and incentive changes would be essential to shift PRA&D from its traditional stance into a market-driven enterprise.

In the past, PRA&D's partners had been primarily rewarded based upon the profitability and growth their particular geographical office generated. No special incentives existed to develop specific new markets or to cooperate with other offices on a large *Fortune* 500 client's audit which might need staffing support in their geographic area, yet be coordinated by a Practice Partner in another area. The local practice office and the disciplines (like audit, tax, or systems) within the office were the central organizational units in PRA&D. Regional, industry specialist, and other "specialized practice units" were generally subordinate to the practice offices. However, there had been much discussion about the desirability of centralizing some of the disciplines more or developing Regional Partners who would work with all the other partners in a designated geographical area. As envisioned, the Regional Partners would have primary responsibility (rather than simply a coordinating role) for regionwide strategy, planning, market development, and emphasis, and the allocation of many personnel and financial resources. The Regional Partners (reporting to the Management Committee) would be responsible for balancing the goals and needs of all "practice units" and geographical areas within their region into a consolidated strategy. Together, they would be responsible for drawing up a firmwide strategy and operating plan extending at least three years into the future. Although the development of such Regional Partners had been considered for some time, the concept had not been implemented.

The basic problem of organizing PRA&D—as with other major accounting firms—revolved around some very complex coordination and incentive issues. Within PRA&D there were at least seven levels of organization which needed to interact: (1) *Specialized Practice Units* focused on special issues, like government contracting, acquisitions and mergers, bankruptcies, or employee benefits and pensions; (2) *Industry Specialists Units* focused on particular industries like health care, law, retailing, minerals, or energy development; (3) *Practice Offices* having coordinative responsibilities for all local audit, law, systems, and specialized services activities; (4) *Regional Offices* which—if implemented—would be under a Regional Partner responsible for coordination, supervision, and operating performance of the overall practice within a large geographical area; (5) *Activity Partners* at both the national and major city offices, responsible for tax, systems, or management consulting services; (6) *Audit* or *Practice Partners* who coordinated large audits or consulting projects nationwide (or globally) and often had continuing responsibilities for client relationships with that customer; (7) the *Managing Partner* (and *Management Committee*) elected by all full partners.

COMMUNICATION AND COORDINATION AMONG GROUPS

Within PRA&D, as in other major accounting firms, the Management Consulting activity had grown rapidly. Although not as large as its biggest competitors in management consulting, PRA&D had developed a fine reputation for professional consulting. However, it had been unable to obtain substantial synergies between its Accounting and Management Consulting groups. At first, PRA&D had hoped that each group would be able to build the other's business by recognizing particular skills in its sister organization and recommending to clients that they enquire about PRA&D's capabilities in those areas. For example, an auditor might see a genuine inventory control problem developing in a client firm and suggest PRA&D Consulting's excellent inventory control group to work on it. Similarly, PRA&D's Consulting Group might develop an acquisition strategy for a client and recommend some of PRA&D Accounting's very sophisticated services at key junctures for the client. For a variety of reasons, this type of relationship had not developed well.

However, it had proved to be equally difficult for PRA&D to transfer specialized knowledge even within its Accounting Group or its Management Consulting Group. For example, the Accounting Group might develop an extremely sophisticated solution to a complex problem in Seattle, but other PRA&D offices might never hear about the solution. The Chicago Accounting Office might identify interesting new growth areas among high-technology or services companies in its area or develop a superb sales methodology for generating new clients. But such information was rarely effectively transmitted to or exploited by other offices. The Management Committee was deeply concerned that the firm was losing substantial profits by not utilizing its full capabilities and solutions to problems which existed inside PRA&D. The firm's highly decentralized, partner-centered, operating philosophy had dictated that all plans—for goals, client service activities, office or departmental operations be generated "bottom up." The Management Committee was concerned that these plans were not properly coordinated across the entire firm, nor did they serve well as the basis for PRA&D's most important strategic decisions: partner evaluation, business development, and partner deployment.

The Management Committee was also concerned that its current methodology of awarding partnership shares exacerbated local offices' independence, and hindered their coordination with others' activities. It also encouraged development of specialization at local levels, where it was difficult to find enough clients to justify the critical mass of people necessary to develop a specialty in real depth. Finally, it was extremely difficult to move a highly qualified specialist—or a partner with strongly developed client contacts—from one local office to another, either temporarily or permanently. Such people often had very strong personal preferences for a particular job location. In addition, they tended to be major contributors to local profitability. Consequently, practice offices were reluctant to transfer such people to other locations, or to lend them for any substantial period of time. And individuals hesitated to move to another location where they would lose income or partnership shares while they rebuilt their contacts and billing capabilities in the new area.

The reverse problem often occurred when another office asked a local practice office for support on a large client audit or consulting project which had a division or activity in its area. The local office might have its resources entirely deployed against its own high-priority client base, and be reluctant to take top-rated people from those clients to support another office's project. There were also great difficulties in stimulating local partners to invest substantial amounts of time or money in developing new skill sets or specialties which might not bring profits to their local office for many years. And, finally, many partners tended to resist investment in technologies (especially those they could not directly control) which were not immediately or solely related to their own particular practice's development and profitability. These were common problems for many CPA firms. But PRA&D, which had very sophisticated systems people and techniques for serving clients, had been slower than others to develop the coordinated computer, management information, incentives, and networking systems needed for its own operations.

The Management Committee was deeply aware of these problems and perplexed by them. Many of the specialist, practice, and local partners also shared these concerns, although many others were less worried. Because enough partners had been making very high incomes and were quite comfortable with existing practices, it had been extraordinarily difficult to develop an integrated strategy which could focus PRA&D's enormous potentials on selected markets either in the United States or worldwide.

QUESTIONS

1. What major strategic options exist for PRA&D? How can PRA&D evaluate those options effectively given the diverse interests of its various internal constituencies? What strategy would you recommend and why?

2. How does strategy in this professional environment differ from that in other fields? How does the interaction of Management Consulting, Accounting, and other specialist groups affect the decision?

3. What problems would you foresee in implementing your strategy? Specifically, how should PRA&D deal with these?

APPENDIX A—PROFILE OF THE MAJOR ACCOUNTING FIRMS

Growth and Source of International Versus U.S. Revenues, 1977 and 1986

U.S. VERSUS TOTAL REVENUES			Comp. Annual Growth Rate 1977–1986		Trend in Geographic Emphasis
Firm	1977	1986	Worldwide	U.S.	
Peat Marwick Main	71%	52%	20%	16%	Overseas
Arthur Andersen	75	76	16	16	Balanced
Coopers & Lybrand	52	56	14	15	Domestic
Price Waterhouse	51	53	12	13	Domestic
PRA&D	50	52	10	14	Overseas
Ernst & Whinney	74	68	15	14	Overseas
Arthur Young & Co.	54	47	15	13	Overseas
Touche Ross & Co.	53	53	14	14	Balanced
Deloitte, Haskins	54	55	12	12	Balanced

Source: 1977 figures from P. Bernstein, "Competition Comes to Accounting," *Fortune,* July 17, 1978; and 1986 figures from *Public Accounting Report,* as cited in "Peat Marwick and KMG Main Agree to Merge," *The Wall Street Journal,* September 4, 1986.

1986 Relative Market Positions International Versus U.S.

Firm	WORLDWIDE		UNITED STATES	
	Revenues ($ millions)	Relative Position	Revenues ($ millions)	Relative Position
Peat Marwick Main	$2,700	1.5	$1,400	1.0
Arthur Andersen	1,800	1.2	1,360	1.5
Coopers & Lybrand	1,550	1.1	865	1.2
PRA&D	1,450	1.0	790	1.1
Price Waterhouse	1,400	1.0	742	1.2
Ernst & Whinney	1,360	1.0	930	1.1
Arthur Young & Co.	1,330	1.2	625	1.0
Touche Ross & Co.	1,120	1.0	590	2.4
Deloitte, Haskins & Sells	1,100	2.6	610	1.0

Note: Relative market positions are calculated by dividing a firm's revenues by those of the next largest competitor.

Source: 1976 revenues from *Public Accounting Report,* as cited in "Peat Marwick and KMG Main Agree to Merge," *The Wall Street Journal,* September 4, 1986.

Consulting Practices of Major CPA Firms

FIRM	1987 WORLDWIDE CONSULTING REVENUES ($ MILLIONS)	% OF TOTAL REVENUES WORLDWIDE	NUMBER OF CONSULTANTS
Arthur Andersen	$838	36%	9,639
Peat Marwick Main	438	13	4,700
PRA&D	390	20	3,750
Coopers & Lybrand	381	18	4,712
Ernst & Whinney	374	21	3,255
Price Waterhouse	345	20	4,300
Touche Ross & Co.	248	17	2,142
Deloitte, Haskins & Sells	209	14	2,271
Arthur Young & Co.	204	12	2,443

Source: Consultants News and *Bowman's Accounting Report,* in "Cutting the Pie," *The Wall Street Journal,* July 26, 1988.

BLANCHFLOWER, WHITE AND GREAVES

"The problem we face can be simply described," noted Steven Perryman, managing partner of the law firm of Blanchflower, White and Greaves: "Among all the possible actions, what should we do to maintain and grow our partnership profits? It is reasonably clear that unless we make *some* changes in the way we run our affairs, we will be faced with, at best, flat income levels for the foreseeable future, particularly if you take inflation into account. Few of us in the firm are dissatisfied with our current compensation, but, as individuals, we naturally look forward to some growth in our incomes as our families get larger and as we learn to live up to our incomes. If we are to fulfill our collective income expectations, as well as those of our future partners (our current associates), we must find ways to increase our pool of profits."

Perryman made these comments after reviewing the 1984 Budget and Operating Plan prepared by his executive committee. The plan had projected a continued growth in firm revenues of 8%, based in part on adjustments averaging 4.5% in the firm's hourly rates. Revenue estimates had been compiled by polling each of the partners of the firm as to their estimates of work forthcoming from existing and new clients. Significant uncertainty existed about these revenue estimates. In recent years, gross fees per lawyer at Blanchflower, White and Greaves had, according to a survey conducted by a public accounting firm, corresponded to the median (approximately $200,000) for firms of its size and in its city. The executive committee expected that this would also be true in 1984.

Expenses in the 1984 budget were projected to increase by 12%, of which over half was attributable to increases in personnel costs, caused by staff increases, built-in salary increases and substantial increases in payroll taxes and health insurance costs. The cost structure of the firm was approximately as follows:

Associate Compensation	27% of total costs
Other Employee Costs	38% of total costs
Other Operating Costs	35% of total costs
Total	100% of total costs

Because expenses were projected to rise faster than revenues, the firm's margin (partnership profits as a percent of fees) was projected to decline in 1984, as it had done in each of the last three years. It was projected that over 20% of all the firm's attorney time would, as in the past years, be spent on non-billable matters such as administrative activities, leave and holidays, business solicitation, professional development, recruiting, and so on.

Blanchflower, White and Greaves had detected significant fee resistance from its corporate clients. While precise detail was not available, the firm believed its hourly rates were in line with those of other firms in the city, but its billing rates had not risen as rapidly as its expenses. Because of increased competition for the top graduates at the first-tier law schools from which the firm drew its new associates, associate salaries had grown faster than inflation. Occupancy costs had been held at a reasonable level, but there was a threat that these would jump significantly when the firm's lease on its current space expired in 18 months' time. With the introduction of word processing, computers, extended library resources, and so on, the firm's operating expenses per lawyer had grown rapidly. This not only affected the yearly income statement, but increased the firm's need for capital. In turn, this meant that an increasing percentage of yearly income was retained (and not distributed as partner income) in order to fund the firm's capital needs.

Steve Perryman reflected: "As I contemplated the means by which we could restore and promote the firm's economic health, I decided to sit down and make a list of all the possible actions we could take to improve profitability in both the short and long time-horizons. This exercise yielded the following list. We could:

(1) Raise Our Hourly Rates

"Obviously, this is the action we would do first if we could, but it seems the most unlikely to be successful. However, this may not be the case if we think about raising rates by *restructuring* them. While *some* clients have expressed concern about our fees, this is by no means true of all clients. Clients appear ready to pay top fees for truly superior legal advice; no one has ever complained about the fees charged by our most expert partners. Our hourly billing rates are basically set by seniority; the more senior the partner, the higher the rate. In consequence, all partners of roughly the same seniority bill at the same level. Perhaps we should look at whether this is wise. I have a suspicion that for some of our people we could raise rates fifty percent or more and the clients would never complain because those individuals are so valuable. Other partners may be overpriced at the level they are now at. Perhaps we should be more courageous in raising the rates of our best people. In the same spirit, perhaps we should look a little more carefully at the rates we charge for associates' time. It is there that we think the greatest fee resistance exists, so perhaps those fees could be reduced selectively: kept up for the best associates and reduced for the novices. We see greater demand for partner-intensive work and less for associate-intensive work, so a restructuring of our hourly rates could yield more revenues to the firm.

(2) Change Our Billing Practices

"Fundamentally, continued economic health must come from productivity improvements: accomplishing the same work with fewer resources. For us, this means spending less time to accomplish the same tasks. But since we bill according to the time we spend, better productivity would only mean we would bill less. For example, we could work to find ways to use associates and paralegals to do work now being done by partners. But if we do this, we just get paid less. We need to find some way to profit from any efforts at improved effectiveness or productivity. This would mean experimenting with such things as contingency fees, up-front negotiated flat fees, bonus payments, piece work rates or some form of "value billing." Of course, if we were successful in getting such arrangements with clients, we would then have to work at examining our methods of delivering legal services to indeed become more effective and efficient.

(3) Increase Our Billable Hours for Partners and/or Associates

"In recent years, our average billable hours per attorney have corresponded approximately to medians for firms of our size and location, i.e., in the high 1500s for partners and low 1700s for associates. I really don't know if these numbers can be increased. I suppose there are two basic ways to accomplish this: work more hours in total, or find ways to make more of our work billable. Since partners' billing rates are higher than those of associates, I would guess that working to improve *partner* billable hours is likely to have a bigger impact on our profits, but at what cost? There certainly are lifestyle considerations to take into account here.

(4) Drop Selected Unprofitable Clients

"I am personally convinced that some of our clients are unprofitable. However, I have no way of proving this, since we have never instituted any form of profitability accounting system. Naturally, we do get printouts of fees billed and collected to individual clients, as well as any write-down of hours worked on cases for those clients. However, we do not attempt to allocate any of our fixed costs (such as secretarial, word processing, occupancy, photocopying activities) to individual matters or clients. Similarly, we have no system for estimating the specific cost to us of the lawyer time spent working on cases. For example, not all of our associates are paid the same amount, even those in the same class. Accordingly, an hour of one associate's time does not cost us the same as an hour of some other associate's time. Should we attempt to calculate these costs (and hence profitability) on a case-by-case or client-by-client basis? If so, how? Should we attempt to estimate which clients (or lawyers) are making greatest use of our various fixed facilities and allocate a proportionate share of costs to them? How useful an exercise would this be? After all, even if we could show that some clients were unprofitable measured in this way, I know we'd have lots of fights about both the costing methodology and whether unprofitable clients could one day turn into profitable ones, and hence should be retained.

(5) Drop Selected Unprofitable Types of Work

"The same arguments about dropping unprofitable clients could be made about unprofitable matters. Our accounting system does not record revenues by type of matter, let alone costs. Yet I again suspect that some types of matters we handle are unprofitable. I would foresee that fights over dropping these would be even more rancorous. Should we refuse unprofitable work from otherwise profitable clients? Should we even collect the information in this form?

(6) Reduce Our Overhead

"Since 75 percent of our costs are either non-lawyer compensation costs or other operating expenses it would seem as if our greatest opportunities to keep more of our revenues lie in this area. I can think of at least three major actions:

1. cutting back on occupancy costs (move to less plush quarters);
2. make more efficient use of secretarial and other support staff;
3. get better control of unbilled telephone, photocopying, travel and other expenses.

"In the short term, there is perhaps not a lot we can do about occupancy costs. But our lease will shortly be up, and we do face the decision on what type of space we want to have. In the old days, we always treated ourselves generously in this regard: we have over 600 square feet per lawyer in very comfortable surroundings. But I suspect that the days of 'high living' in this regard are over. Similarly, we have always been generous with secretarial, photocopying, and other support personnel, on the theory that to skimp in this area would affect both the quality of our work life and, if we cut back too much, our timely responsiveness to clients. Yet we may be fooling ourselves here; there is probably some 'fat' to be cut. But how do you know when you've trimmed all the fat and started to cut into muscle? In a similar spirit, we have not been too tightfisted in overseeing cost expenditures such as telephones, taxis, travel, and entertainment made by lawyers, especially partners. Again, there is the quality-of-work-life issue. Our business manager (an ex-accountant) keeps proposing all sorts of tight control systems to keep track of these expenses, but I don't want to get to the point of partners having to obtain 'clearance' to spend money. After all, it's *their* firm.

(7) Improve Our Billing and Collection Performance

"At any given point in time, we have about 5 months' worth of 'unbilled work-in-progress' (time charges accumulated to client work but not yet billed). We understand this is in line with other firms, but it is *very* high compared to other professions. Perhaps, by greater use of 'progress billing' (sending bills out prior to the disposition of the matter) we could improve our cash flow. More timely billing might also improve our collections performance, which currently runs somewhere between two and three months' worth of our billings. This represents a lot of our money tied up. Yet to accomplish these changes would mean attempting to impose a new 'discipline' on both our billing partners (in getting bills out) and on our clients (paying us more promptly). We have exhorted each other repeatedly on this topic for years, but have not seen much improvement. Are there 'systems' we should consider to help us here?

(8) Reduce Our Write-offs

"Our write-offs of time worked approximate the averages for firms of our size (five to ten percent, depending upon how you calculate it), but I suspect there is room for improvement here. At the present time, each billing partner makes individual decisions on whether (and how much) to write down our time charges. Officially, they are supposed to consult with our 'Write-Down Committee' if they wish to exceed certain guidelines, but we are having difficulties in enforcing this. I suspect that attacking this problem means more than just exhorting partners. We really should examine *why* we incur write-offs, and attack the problem at its source. Do we staff our cases well? At present, we have a somewhat informal method of assigning associates to projects. Perhaps a more disciplined approach would pay off, as would better oversight on the part of partners as to how well they manage the time billed by associates to their projects.

(9) Increase Our Leverage

"It has always been conventional wisdom that, as partners, we make a lot of our money from our associates. Accordingly, we could try and improve our economic health by reaching for a higher associate-to-partner ratio. We could do this either by hiring more associates or making fewer partners. This latter solution might involve either just extending the time to partnership (officially or unofficially), or creating a category of principal between partners and associates. Of course, if we *do* increase our leverage, we'd have to go after more leveraged client work, which might not be the sort of work our partners want to do.

(10) Reduce Non-Billable Time

"If we could find a way to reduce our non-billable time, we could free up our partners either to bill more hours or spend more time on getting business. We really do not have a very good handle on where our non-billable time is going. It has been proposed by our business manager that we establish a large number of specific non-billable account numbers for specific activities (e.g., recruiting committee, facilities committee, professional development time, etc.) so that we can better track the time being invested in each of these areas. Presumably, this would also allow us to establish specific time budgets for each activity and hence not only control this time but actually calculate how much each activity is costing us. I'm somewhat afraid of this, because it could become an administrative nightmare keeping track of detailed billing codes. I'm not sure I could force my partners to do it, nor how much it would really help.

(11) Bill Overhead Costs Directly to Clients

"One way to attack our overhead costs would be to bill out to clients more of our secretarial, photocopying and other such costs. The first step would be to improve our controls on making sure we actually bill what we are supposed to. (I'm not sure my partners *are* doing this). The next step would be to consider 'marking up' some of these costs, instead of billing them out at cost. At the highest level, we could start billing out some things that we have traditionally absorbed ourselves.

(12) Get Rid of Non-Productive Partners

"Many of us suspect that this might be the most potent change we could make in affecting the long-run health of the firm. However, it is also the least easy to implement.

"Naturally, I don't mean cutting the salaries of our current associates. But we could reduce these costs in the long run by changing our recruitment practices. We could go after students at the best schools who are below the first tier, or go after students at the top of their class at second-tier schools."

As he concluded his list, Mr. Perryman reflected: "As you can see, this list is quite varied. Some of the actions represent one-time changes, others are more permanent. Some are easy to implement (in an organizational or political sense), others more difficult. Some will have a quick impact if we can implement them, others will only show benefit over an extended period of time. Some require negotiating new relationships with clients, others are purely internal. Some will require investments to be made, others can be implemented without adding to our costs. I could go on. In fact, I could easily draw up a long list of *criteria* by which we could assess the possible actions. Then we'd have two long lists instead of one! How do we think about this? What should be our plan of attack on this problem?"

QUESTIONS

1. For purposes of discussion and analysis, begin by making assumptions concerning data missing from the case study with respect to (a) the size of this firm (number of lawyers), (b) its associates-to-partner ratio, (c) its profitability margin (ratio of partnership profits to gross fees).

2. Examine the list of potential actions being considered by Steve Perryman. What, if anything, has he left out of his list of ways to improve the economic health of the firm?

3. At the end of the case, Steve Perryman points out that there are a number of criteria by which possible actions can be assessed. Make a list of all the possible criteria he could use in trying to decide which actions to take.

4. What information should Perryman collect to shed light on where economic improvements could best be made?

5. What analyses would you recommend that he make?

6. Which of the various actions being considered by Perryman do you think would be the most fruitful focus of attention in the firm (a) in the short run and (b) in the long run?

3-9

IBM (C)

The success of the 360 line was greater than anyone had predicted. In 1964 (at the time of the 360 announcement) management expected to place roughly 2,700 of the five largest models by 1970 and projected that only a third of these would be ordered with remote terminal and communications gear. In fact, shipments approached the 5,000 level with more than half demanding extra peripheral equipment. IBM's revenues exploded from $3.5 billion in 1965 to $7.5 billion in 1970. Peripheral equipment represented a large percentage of the customers' hardware dollar in 1970, and the high margins on these sales helped cover further massive R&D expenditures for future mainframes.

IBM has always used very conservative accounting in pricing leases—usually assuming a four-year life. Hence, a $1 million machine would rent for $250,000 per year. Over the long term, many customers naturally kept their machines longer which provided IBM with huge cash flows that dropped directly to the bottom line. For instance, in 1972 there were still about 3,900 Series 1400 computers on rental that were manufactured in the late 1950s. But the 360's very success threatened this carefully maintained structure, as independent leasing companies and "plug compatible" peripheral manufacturers (PCMs) moved in for the kill.

One of IBM's major concerns in the early 1970s was that an increasing number of its own customers would come to view IBM merely as another supplier of individual components rather than as a total system provider—an approach that IBM's marketing people had labored assiduously for years to create. To compound problems, on the last day of the Johnson administration in 1969, the Justice Department filed an antitrust suit against IBM, charging in part that the entire 360 line represented an effort to reduce competition. The government's goal was noth-

Case copyright © 1983 by James Brian Quinn. Research associate—Roger Wellington. Case derived primarily from secondary sources.

ing less than the breakup of IBM into several separate companies. IBM's response to these various threats had to be handled very carefully and with a long-term perspective.

THE 370 RESPONSE

One of its responses was the 370 series of computers. The 370s were designed to be compatible with the 360 machines in terms of software so that the users' huge investments in programming would be protected. Typically a user would invest $3-5 in software for each $1 in hardware. The 370 in essence was intended to make 360 programs run faster, and the transition to the new machines was intended to be painless compared to the disruptive way the 360 had been introduced.

Technical people at IBM would have preferred to equip the whole range of 370 computers with semiconductor memories at introduction. That would have made the 370 series much more versatile, more powerful, and technologically far ahead of any other computer. But IBM's marketing group pressed for earlier introduction with the first available quality product. The ultimate timing decision depended to a large extent on the fact that by 1970 most of the 370's building blocks were in hand, for development had begun as far back as 1965. "We had invested a few hundred million dollars in the 370," said Watson. "We might have been more prudent to upgrade the 360, but we thought a new line would be a stimulant for both the customer and the salesman." Unfortunately, the 370 strategy backfired. Customers often found they could replace two 360's with one 370 and save on monthly rental payments.

To compound difficulties, the medium- to large-sized mainframe market began to mature, and hardware prices dropped due to the rapid miniaturization of integrated circuits. To fill the gap in the low end of its line, IBM introduced the System/3, the result of an intensive development effort in the late 1960s headed up by the highest ranking line officer at IBM—Frank Cary, who later became IBM's chairman at age 52, when T. Vincent Learson stepped down in 1972. Although the System/3, first shipped in 1970, suffered in the recession of 1970–1971 just as the 370 did, it went on to become a best seller with more than 25,000 machines installed. But to achieve the breakthroughs in cost necessary to make it cheap enough for small users, the designers had to sacrifice compatibility with the 360/370 family. The System/3 spawned a new family of machines allowing all its new IBM users to trade up within the line. By 1983, the largest System/3 machines competed in price/performance with the smaller units in the 360/370 series.[1]

THE CARY YEARS

In 1975, an aggressive new company started by one of the designers of the System/360 (Gene Amdahl) and backed by Japan's Fujitsu, became the first to manufacture a "plug-compatible" mainframe computer. Amdahl's success in coming up with a cheaper and more sophisticated product targeted at high-powered users forced IBM to reevaluate its policy of introducing products at a controlled pace in order to extract maximum rental revenue from its already installed base.

A New Strategy

Every five or six years IBM had traditionally introduced a new generation of computers that outmoded its existing series. To convince customers to trade up to the new line, the company usually offered new machines with a lot more performance for only a little more money. One rule of thumb used in pricing a new mainframe was that a fourfold improvement in capacity would warrant only a doubling of price. And IBM's long-time pricing policy had been to keep the price/performance ratio constant across the entire line. In keeping with this tradition, IBM's labs developed an entirely new series of machines slated for introduction in 1975 known only by the somewhat cryptic designation "Future System." Future System was to have been a revolutionary technological leap, for the first time breaking away from the architecture of the 360/370 series in the main line of computers.

Future System was perhaps the most formally planned product line development in IBM's history. But it failed to materialize due to massive development difficulties and the prospect that many customers would hesitate to throw away a decade's worth of 360/370 programming investment. IBM had no choice but to extend the life of its existing computers by slightly enhancing them and lowering prices. Demand responded to price cuts more vigorously than IBM planners had assumed. IBM cut prices by one third on two aging models of the System 370, and sales exploded. In some cases, customers' data-processing departments had years of applications programs all coded and ready to run as soon as the cost dropped enough to justify new equipment.

The 4300

The next major step in IBM's product development was the 1979 launch of the 4300, a family of medium-sized computers. According to many estimates, in the first three weeks customers sent in an astounding $10 billion worth of orders for 42,000 machines, twice as many as IBM had expected to manufacture over the entire life of the series. Some customers were assigned delivery dates four years into the future, and places near the head of the line were traded for up to $15,000 each.[2]

The 4300s were priced so low that one model exceeded the computing power of an existing $560,000 machine, yet sold for only $69,000—an eightfold improvement in price/performance ratio. Users of bigger systems who assumed that IBM's future offerings at the high end of the market would be priced according to the same formula canceled orders for IBM's existing big machines, the 3030 series. Instead they turned to short-term leases which they could terminate when the new large-scale 3080 series computers came out.

The result was a terrific cash crunch. Not only did IBM have to fund the production of all those new 4300s, it had to finance $4.2 billion in new leased equipment in 1979 alone—a 55% increase over 1978. Profits in 1979 declined 3.2%—the first such drop in two decades. After trying to repurchase $700 million of its own stock in 1977–1978, the company had to go to the bond market in October 1979 with a $1 billion offering—the largest such public sale in history.

The Mini-Market

"Distributed processing"—connecting large central processors to a series of smaller, special purpose units in a single system—came into vogue in the mid-1960s as small stand-alone machines that could handle limited quantities of information and send it along to a larger central mainframe became available. As they gained popularity, these small units acquired the ubiquitous nickname of "minicomputers," like the miniskirts that appeared around the same time. The pioneer and leader in minicomputers was Digital Equipment Corp. (DEC), one of the greatest venture capital successes of all time.

Minis were marketed differently from "mainframes." They were sold, not rented, and the purchasers for minis were usually sophisticated companies who didn't need the systems engineers, software packages, and training programs that were IBM's trademark.

As hardware prices and sizes shrank in the 1970s, minis became more powerful, more flexible, and much cheaper. IBM found that many of its customers started practicing a technique called "off-loading." When a large central mainframe was operating at capacity, instead of upgrading or replacing the existing machine, they pushed off the extra jobs onto minis. This trend finally forced IBM to get serious about this rapidly growing segment. IBM had had small business systems since 1970 when it came out with the System/3, but it didn't announce a true minicomputer until 1976.

DEC, Hewlett Packard, Data General, Texas Instruments, and others offered quantity discounts on their minis of 30–40% to "systems houses"—sophisticated middlemen who bought components in bulk and packaged them into systems for various users. IBM, on the other hand, was used to letting its highly disciplined blue-suited sales force contact and service end users directly and refused to consider discounts of more than 15% for large orders of minis. In the words of a former IBM executive, "You really had to love the machine to take it at that price."

The Office of the Future

As a result of such practices, in 1980 IBM was still fifth in minicomputer sales but was finally learning and moving up fast. Its division responsible for small systems began discounting. And the 4300 series, which was designed with distributed processing applications in mind, helped strengthen IBM's hand. The company also introduced a high level software package called System Network Architecture (SNA) to help link together its minis, mainframes, word processors, smart copiers, and communication devices into the much discussed decentralized "office of the future."

Many firms had entered the battle to become the industry standard for this critical interface. Xerox, DEC, and Intel had teamed up to offer a local network package. And GTE and AT&T were working on global electronic mail and data transmission systems. Sperry and Burroughs were also in the hunt. But IBM's sheer market power if properly focused could ultimately overwhelm many of these efforts. By the end of 1981, 45% of all IBM computer users setting up new information networks had installed SNA. With more than 60% of the worldwide mainframe market in IBM's hands, there was a growing concern that incompatible machines could be frozen out of office network systems.[3]

Linking the World

IBM was also a partner in Satellite Business Systems, a joint venture (with Comsat and Aetna) that had three satellites providing interference-free data transmission capabilities. With the deregulation of the communications industry (occurring concurrently with the dropping of the Justice Department's antitrust suit against IBM in January 1982), IBM was cleared to move further in the direction of total systems services. But, so was AT&T.

As a result of its various actions, IBM's market share in minis had risen sharply from roughly 17% in 1980 to almost 25% in 1982. IBM's overall sales were $34.3 billion in 1982—a $5.3 billion increase from the previous year. By comparison, Digital Equipment Corp.'s 1982 revenues *totaled* only $3.8 billion.[4]

In 1981, 56-year-old John Opel became IBM's fifth chief executive officer. During his years of rising through the corporate ranks from his sales and marketing beginnings, Opel was often frustrated by the centralized management style at IBM. As CEO he promised to remedy that fault. Said Opel, "You have to leave people free to act, or they become dependent. They don't have to be told; they have to be allowed." A quiet, wiry, cerebral executive, who acquired the nickname "the brain" for his searching questions during a stint as Tom Watson, Jr.'s assistant during the 1970s, Opel would need all his powers of mind to confront the complex challenges facing IBM in the 1980s.

Shrinking Chips

Perhaps the biggest threat to IBM's preeminence came not from any particular competitor, but from changes in the computer technology itself. Integrated circuit (IC) capabilities were radically altering the size, speed, reliability and cost of all computers and accessories. For instance, a circuit package used in a 1983 top-of-the-line machine measured 4″ × 4″ × 2″ and contained over 100 chips interconnected through 33 layers. The same capacity required a space the size of a refrigerator for a 370 System model produced in the early 1970s. Until the 4300 Series, IBM had used ICs that could store 2,000 pieces of information although competitors had gradually introduced 16K chips. The 4300 leapfrogged the competition by using a 64K chip. In 1982, 256K chips were in production and some forecasters believed much denser circuits were feasible. If the automobile industry had developed at the same pace as the computer industry since 1960, a 1982 Rolls Royce would have cost only $2.75 and run 3 million miles on 1 gallon of gas.

The microprocessor, pioneered by Intel in the early 1970s, was the next logical challenge for IBM. Microprocessors were chips that contained both programmable logic and memory circuits as opposed to earlier "single-function" chips. The microprocessor was the engine driving the proliferation of electronic devices into home computers, "programmable" microwave ovens, "smart" machines, and so on worldwide. As one of the largest producers of ICs in the world—for its own use —IBM had to consider its possible role in such markets.

$10 Billion in Plant and Equipment

IBM's actions in the early 1980s indicated how seriously it took these challenges. Chairman Frank Cary said, "We've got to be price competitive, box by box (machine by machine). Nobody is going to pay us a 20% premium any more." To accomplish this, IBM invested heavily in increased capacity. Between 1977 and 1981 it added 22 million square feet of laboratory and manufacturing space, a staggering $10 billion in plant and equipment. Such additions accounted for roughly two-thirds of the gross asset value of plant and other property listed on IBM's balance sheet as of the end of 1982.

But these investments bucked two other important trends. In 1975, according to industry sources, the CPU represented 55% of a system's cost, the rest being terminals, printers, software and other peripherals. By 1980, that share had declined to 35%. Furthermore, systems with big CPUs made up a large but declining share of the market. In 1982 IBM received only 29% of its revenue from the sale or rental of central processors. At the same time, software, which had been only 10%

of development costs for early 1960s lines, became some 90% of such costs in the early 1980s.

In a vertically integrated firm like IBM, profits could often be shifted from one segment of the business that was attacked by competitors to areas where the company still retained a significant advantage. Sales and profits on various activities in IBM were heavily influenced by such choices. (Published data on 1982 lines are shown in Exhibit 2.) These same choices could also have devastating impact on smaller competitors—as for example, when IBM lowered the boom on plug-compatible memory producers by cutting memory prices while simultaneously increasing its prices on mainframes.

For a long time survival in the plug-compatible (PCM) market had depended on producers' ability to adapt swiftly to new offerings by IBM. This pressure made any information on future IBM technology extremely valuable. In 1982, IBM—with the help of the FBI—caught employees of several competing firms stealing proprietary information. Several of the companies involved were Japanese. The trade secrets that allegedly changed hands involved designs for IBM's top-of-the-line 3080 series of central processors.

Organizing for the Future

In a fast-changing, high-technology industry—where small companies have very real advantages over larger, more bureaucratic firms—IBM was often likened to a whale in a pool with lots of aggressive sharks. IBM had developed some specific techniques for countering a large company's natural propensity to minimize risk. In IBM's early computer years, when Tom Watson, Jr., was CEO, he encouraged the fresh thinking of people he called "wild ducks." Bob Evans said, "Watson, Jr., always felt the world is full of people who just don't see it the way most people do. More times than not they are probably wrong, but sometimes they are right, and we ought to have some mechanism for the wild ducks to have their fling. Watson encouraged this 'wild duckism.' He encouraged people, who normally would not be inclined to just go along with a team, to know there was an avenue where—if they wanted to express a different view—they'd be heard and maybe funded to do something by themselves."

To help coordinate its rapidly diversifying lines and complex presence in the marketplace, IBM reorganized in 1981. The most dramatic part of the shake-up occurred in IBM's three sales divisions which were folded into one integrated entity called the Information Systems Group. (See Exhibit 1.) This move was prompted in part by the confusion caused by IBM sales people from different divisions calling on the same company. The change further streamlined IBM's manufacturing operation by grouping all the computer related divisions together. It also set up 14 IBUs (independent business units) and SBUs (strategic business units) that could explore opportunities without the weight of the company's formal bureaucracy to hold them back. This strategy succeeded in shaking up traditional thinking at IBM. An SBU developed and built IBM's entry into the home computer market—the PC (personal computer). The rapid acceptance of the IBM PC was largely the result of several critical decisions that were significant departures from past company practice.

While IBM had recently tightened its control over systems software for its large computers (to make it tougher for the plug compatible manufacturers), the PC designers adopted an "open architecture," opening the machines' technical specifications to the public. They commissioned an independent software house

(Microsoft) to write the new operating system for the PC and quickly made it public too. Also breaking with tradition, many hardware components were standard units (including an Intel 8088 microprocessor CPU chip) sourced from outside vendors to ensure a faster start-up. Finally, instead of relying on IBM's sales force and 40 odd retail product centers, the PC's marketing people cut a deal with Sears and Computerland to sell IBM machines. The result—IBM's PC garnered 30% of the business microcomputer market in just two years. In late 1983 the PC manufacturing unit was allocating production by shipping only 1 unit for every 7 ordered—despite an assembly line that was so automated it took only 10 minutes of worker time to assemble a unit.[5]

Stiffer Competition

When the government announced settlement of its suits against AT&T and IBM, it provided for the spin-off of the local phone companies from AT&T. But AT&T would retain roughly $40 billion in assets including its long-distance lines, its manufacturing divisions (Western Electric), and Bell Laboratories. Many analysts thought AT&T would confront IBM with its first adequately financed, technologically adept competition. Bell Labs built one of the first computers in the 1940s and continued to be a leader in microelectronics development. American Bell, AT&T's recently chartered data communications subsidiary, would have $5 billion in assets to start with and would be backed up the world's most advanced global telecommunications system.

IBM also had to deal with the small chip manufacturers who were integrating forward into computers as they developed more powerful microprocessors. But perhaps the biggest threat to IBM's long-term dominance in computers might come from the Japanese. By 1983 the Japanese had entered every major segment of the office equipment industry with particular strength in printers and copiers. In addition, Japanese companies held some 10–15% of the worldwide computer market, although their national goal was a 30% share by 1990. Fujitsu, Nippon Electric Co., and Hitachi were the largest computer makers. Fujitsu had surpassed IBM as the number one computer supplier in Japan. All the Japanese manufacturers had standardized their current products around IBM 360/370 architecture. Although they sold primarily to their own domestic market, Japanese companies were actively pursuing new world markets through joint ventures and other agreements. Fujitsu was the largest shareholder in Amdahl, which held a 56% share of the IBM plug-compatible mainframe market, and it distributed its own equipment through TRW. Hitachi had a joint distribution agreement with National Advanced Systems, the number two PCM.

At the low end of the market, the Japanese presence in desk-top computers was small—less than 2% of the U.S. market in 1983. Their products to date had not been very impressive, and their lack of strong dealer networks and brand recognition had limited their sales growth. At the high end, the so-called "Fifth-Generation Project" was Japan's attempt to leap-frog established competition and become number one in computer technology by the 1990s. The Japanese envisioned a machine with humanlike reasoning capability (called artificial intelligence), and they committed $500 million to start it toward reality. Another related $100 million Japanese program called the National Superspeed Computer Project aimed to produce machines many times faster than 1983's best supercomputers. While many IBM experts doubted that these goals were achievable, they admitted that some major U.S. companies had recently refused to purchase more large IBM computers because they expected the Japanese would eventually dominate the field.

QUESTIONS

1. What should IBM's strategy for the future be? Why? What should be the structure of its portfolio?
2. How should it organize for this?
3. What are the most important changes in its industry IBM must deal with?
4. How should it meet the specific challenge of the Japanese in the future? AT&T? Smaller companies? Antitrust?

To conduct its business throughout the world, IBM is organized into the following groups, divisions, and wholly owned subsidiaries:

EXHIBIT 1
IBM Organization

Information Systems Group

Customer Service Division
Provides maintenance, related support and programming services within the United States and its territories for designated systems and products developed primarily by the Information Systems and Communications Group.

Federal Systems Division
Provides specialized information-handling and control systems to the Federal government for seaborne, spaceborne, airborne, and ground-based environments. Also participates in applied research and exploratory development.

Field Engineering Division
Provides maintenance and related services within the United States and its territories for all current IBM systems and products and designated new systems and products developed primarily by the Information Systems and Technology Group, as well as support for specified IBM program offerings. Has overall responsibility for the distribution of all hardware and software products and related publications. The division also provides maintenance, marketing support and central programming service for assigned products.

National Accounts Division
Has marketing and field administration responsibility within the United States and its territories for the full standard line of IBM products. Its assigned customers are selected large accounts with complex information processing needs.

National Marketing Division
Has marketing and field administration responsibility within the United States and its territories for the full standard line of IBM products. Its assigned customers are large, medium, and small accounts.

EXHIBIT 1
(Continued)

Systems Supplies Division

Has responsibility for formulating worldwide business strategy for information processing supplies and accessories; for manufacturing or procurement, and marketing within the United States and its territories of IBM supplies and services.

Information Systems and Technology Group

Data Systems Division

Has worldwide development and associated programming responsibility for large, complex systems, with primary emphasis on high-performance products, plus U.S. manufacturing responsibility for those systems.

General Products Division

Has worldwide development and U.S. manufacturing responsibility for storage systems, including tape units, disk products and mass storage systems, program products and product-related programming.

General Technology Division

Has worldwide development and product assurance and U.S. manufacturing responsibility for logic, memory, and special semiconductor devices and associated packaging. The division also procures components for the IBM World Trade Americas/Far East Corporation and U.S. operating units.

Information Systems and Communications Group

Communication Products Division

Has worldwide development and U.S. manufacturing responsibility for telecommunications systems, office systems, display products, distribution industry systems and related programming. The division serves as the worldwide architectural and systems focal point for office systems and Systems Network Architecture activities.

Information Products Division

Has worldwide development and related programming and U.S. manufacturing responsibility for typewriters, copiers and systems for banking and manufacturing industries, and for peripheral equipment, including printers, copier systems, keyboards, diskettes and associated supplies.

System Products Division

Has worldwide development and U.S. manufacturing responsibility for small and intermediate-sized general purpose systems, robotic systems and related programming. Its responsibility for the IBM Personal Computer also includes U.S. marketing through retail channels.

Other Divisions

Real Estate and Construction Division

Manages the selection and acquisition of sites, the design and construction of buildings and the purchase or lease of facilities for all IBM operations in the United States. The division has responsibility for assessing real estate projects outside the United States, as well as for IBM's worldwide energy and environmental programs. It also provides facility services to selected headquarters locations.

EXHIBIT 1
(Continued)

Research Division

Brings scientific understanding to bear on areas of company interest through basic research and development of technologies of potential long-range importance.

Subsidiaries

IBM Credit Corporation

Offers term leases and finances installment payment agreements on IBM information-handling equipment in the United States.

IBM Instruments, Inc.

Has responsibility for IBM's efforts in the analytical instruments field, including marketing and servicing selected products in the United States.

Science Research Associates, Inc.

Has worldwide development, publication and marketing responsibility for a wide range of educational and testing materials, services, and microcomputer software designed for use in elementary and secondary schools, colleges, businesses, and the home.

IBM World Trade Americas/Far East Corporation

With a territory extending across four continents, this subsidiary is responsible for IBM operations in 46 countries, including Australia, Brazil, Canada, and Japan.

IBM World Trade Europe/Middle East/Africa Corporation

Through its subsidiary, IBM Europe, located in Paris, it is responsible for IBM operations in 85 countries.

IBM World Trade Corporation

Provides designated support to IBM World Trade organizational units.

Source: IBM, *Annual Report*, 1982.

EXHIBIT 2
IBM Financial Data,
1979–1981

Gross Income by Segment*

	1981	1980	1979
	(Dollars in millions)		
Data Processing segment			
Equipment			
Sales	$ 9,449	$ 7,627	$ 6,335
Rentals	9,660	9,591	8,846
	19,109	17,218	15,181
Maintenance contracts, program products, parts, and supplies			
Sales	458	411	385
Rentals	24	25	24
Services	4,482	3,713	2,748
	4,964	4,149	3,157
	24,073	21,367	18,338
Office Products segment			
Sales	2,245	2,183	2,084
Rentals	1,155	1,253	1,199
Services	819	699	566
	4,219	4,135	3,849
All other segments			
Sales	749	698	669
Services	29	13	7
	778	711	676
Total	$29,070	$26,213	$22,863

* This information should be read in conjunction with the Industry Segments notes in the annual report. Gross income from rentals includes maintenance service on rented equipment. Gross income from services consists of maintenance service on sold equipment, program products, and other services.

Source: IBM, *Annual Report,* 1981.

EXHIBIT 2 (Continued)

Five-Year Comparison of Selected Financial Data, 1978–1982
(Dollars in millions except per share amounts)

	1982	1981[a]	1980[a]	1979	1978
For the year					
Gross income from sales, rentals and services	$34,364	$29,070	$26,213	$22,863	$21,076
Net earnings	4,409	3,610	3,397	3,011	3,111
Per share[b]	7.39	6.14	5.82	5.16	5.32
Cash dividends paid	2,053	2,023	2,008	2,008	1,685
Per share[b]	3.44	3.44	3.44	3.44	2.88
Investment in plant, rental machines and other property	6,685	6,845	6,592	5,991	4,046
Return on stockholders' equity	23.4%	21.1%	21.1%	21.2%	23.8%
At end of year					
Total assets	$32,541	$29,107	$26,831	$24,530	$20,771
Net investment in plant, rental machines and other property	17,563	16,797	15,200	12,193	9,302
Working capital	4,805	2,983	3,381	4,406	4,551
Long-term debt	2,851	2,669	2,099	1,589	285
Stockholders' equity	19,960	17,676	16,578	14,961	13,494

[a] Restated.
[b] Adjusted for 1979 stock split.

Source: IBM, *Annual Report,* 1982.

EXHIBIT 2
(Continued)

Industry Segments, 1979–1981

	1981	1980	1979
	(Dollars in millions)		
Information–Handling Business			
Data Processing			
Gross income—customers	$24,073	$21,367	$18,338
Operating income	5,832	5,330	4,737
Assets at December 31	23,846	21,088	17,373
Depreciation expense	2,576	2,061	1,683
Capital expenditures	6,094	6,027	5,359
Office Products			
Gross income—customers	4,219	4,135	3,849
Operating income	263	479	566
Assets at December 31	3,495	3,377	3,316
Depreciation expense	306	287	275
Capital expenditures	714	537	608
Federal Systems			
Gross income—customers	719	647	612
Operating income	56	37	35
Assets at December 31	436	371	329
Depreciation expense	16	13	11
Capital expenditures	37	27	23
Other Business			
Gross income—customers	59	64	64
Operating income	2	3	6
Assets at December 31	32	36	39
Depreciation expense	1	1	1
Capital expenditures	—	1	1
Consolidated			
Gross income—customers	$29,070	$26,213	$22,863
Operating income	$ 6,153	$ 5,849	$ 5,344
General corporate and interest expense	(533)	(382)	(240)
Other income, principally interest	368	430	449
Earnings before income taxes	$ 5,988	$ 5,897	$ 5,553
Assets identified to segments	$27,809	$24,872	$21,057
Assets not identified to segments, including marketable securities	1,777	1,831	3,473
Total assets at December 31	$29,586	$26,703	$24,530
Depreciation expense	$ 2,899	$ 2,362	$ 1,970
Capital expenditures	$ 6,845	$ 6,592	$ 5,991

IBM's operations, with very minor exceptions, are in the field of information–handling systems, equipment, and services. However, for purposes of segment reporting, IBM's information–handling business has been reported as three segments:

Data processing consists of information–handling products and services such as data processing machines and systems, computer programming, systems engineering, education and related services, and supplies for commercial and government customers.

Office products consists of information–handling products, systems, and services such as electric and electronic typewriters, magnetic media typewriters and systems, information processors, document printers, copiers, and related supplies and services for commercial and government customers.

Federal Systems consists of specialized information–handling products and services for U.S. space, defense, and other agencies and, in some instances, other customers.

Other Business consists of educational, training and testing materials and services for school, home, and industrial use.

Intersegment transfers of products and services similar to those offered to unaffiliated customers are not material.

Source: IBM, *Annual Report*, 1981.

EXHIBIT 2 (Continued)

Consolidated Statement of Financial Position at December 31, 1981–1982
International Business Machines Corporation and Subsidiary Companies

	(Dollars in millions)			
	1982		**1981***	
Assets				
Current assets				
Cash	$ 405		$ 454	
Marketable securities, at lower of cost or market	2,895		1,575	
Notes and accounts receivable-trade, less allowance				
1982, $216; 1981, $187	4,976		4,382	
Other accounts receivable	457		410	
Inventories	3,492		2,803	
Prepaid expenses	789		685	
		$13,014		$10,309
Rental machines and parts	16,527		16,599	
Less: Accumulated depreciation	7,410		7,347	
		9,117		9,252
Plant and other property	14,240		12,702	
Less: Accumulated depreciation	5,794		5,157	
		8,446		7,545
Deferred charges and other assets		1,964		2,001
		$32,541		$29,107
Liabilities and Stockholders' Equity				
Current liabilities				
Taxes	$ 2,854		$ 2,412	
Loans payable	529		773	
Accounts payable	983		872	
Compensation and benefits	1,959		1,556	
Deferred income	402		390	
Other accrued expenses and liabilities	1,482		1,323	
		$ 8,209		$ 7,326
Deferred investment tax credits		323		252
Reserves for employees' indemnities and retirement plans		1,198		1,184
Long-term debt		2,851		2,669
Stockholders' equity				
Capital stock, par value $1.25 per share	5,008		4,389	
Shares authorized: 750,000,000				
Issued: 1982—602,406,128; 1981—592,293,624				
Retained earnings	16,259		13,909	
Translation adjustments	(1,307)		(622)	
		19,960		17,676
		$32,541		$29,107

The notes on pages 35 through 42 provided in the company's annual report are an integral part of this statement.
* Restated. See Accounting Change—Foreign Currency Translation note on page 36 of annual report.
Source: IBM, *Annual Report,* 1982.

EXHIBIT 2
(Continued)

Geographic Areas, 1980–1982

	(Dollars in millions)		
	1982	**1981**	**1980**
United States			
Gross income—customers	$19,028	$15,088	$12,426
Interarea transfers	1,875	1,857	1,615
Total	$20,903	$16,945	$14,041
Net earnings	2,766	2,094	1,725
Assets at December 31	19,028	16,022	13,737
Europe/Middle East/Africa			
Gross income—customers	$10,260	$ 9,312	$ 9,932
Interarea transfers	337	383	491
Total	$10,597*	$ 9,695	$10,423
Net earnings	1,196	1,074	1,360
Assets at December 31	9,197	8,981	9,608
Americas/Far East			
Gross income—customers	$ 5,076	$ 4,670	$ 3,855
Interarea transfers	651	659	450
Total	$ 5,727	$ 5,329	$ 4,305
Net earnings	450	478	388
Assets at December 31	4,925	4,694	4,054
Eliminations			
Gross income	$ (2,863)	$ (2,899)	$ (2,556)
Net earnings	(3)	(36)	(76)
Assets	(609)	(590)	(568)
Consolidated			
Gross income	$34,364	$29,070	$26,213
Net earnings	$ 4,409	$ 3,610	$ 3,397
Assets at December 31	$32,541	$29,107	$26,831

* European operations account for some 95% of this total.

Source: IBM, *Annual Report,* 1982.

EXHIBIT 3
Market Data

Worldwide General-Purpose Computer Shipments and Installed Base—
December 1981
(U.S.-based manufacturers)

Company	1981 Shipments (million $)	% Chg. 1980–81	Installed Base	
			Units	Value (million $)
IBM	10,800	+1.4	61,109	74,560
IBM Compatible:				
Amdahl	345	−9.2	650	1,739
National	185	−2.6	702	928
Magnuson	40	+14.3	*	*
IPL	25	+150.0	*	*
Compatible peripherals	1,020	+45.7	*	*
Honeywell	1,590	+2.6	16,934	10,431
Sperry Univac	1,430	+1.4	7,255	8,346
Burroughs	1,190	+19.0	9,361	6,059
NCR	475	−1.0	7,226	2,354
Control Data	420	+5.0	1,272	3,893
Digital Equipment	165	−19.5	1,468	1,203
Gray	135	+170.0	*	*

* Insignificant.

Source: International Data Corporation.

General-Purpose Computer Shipments and Installed Base, 1972–1986E
(U.S.–based manufacturers—in billions of dollars)

	Shipments		Installed Base	
	United States	International	United States	International
1986E	$13.7	$11.0	$68.9	$71.8
1985E	13.0	10.3	65.9	68.2
1984E	12.4	9.7	62.3	64.0
1983E	11.4	8.9	59.0	60.4
1982E	10.3	8.2	56.4	57.2
1981R	9.6	7.7	55.6	54.6
1980R	8.8	7.8	55.0	55.7
1979	7.7	7.6	52.2	45.2
1978	7.5	7.1	48.3	40.1
1977	6.6	5.9	42.9	34.8
1976	5.5	5.3	37.9	30.6
1975	5.6	5.0	33.8	27.4
1974	6.2	4.4	30.2	23.9
1973	5.4	4.0	27.3	21.4
1972	5.0	3.5	24.7	18.8

E–estimated; R–revised.

Source: International Data Corporation.

977

3-10

GENERAL MOTORS (B)

The *General Motors Downsizing Decision* case describes the sequence of events leading to the restructuring of the General Motors product line in its automotive marketplace. After an initial strong surge of sales created for General Motors by its new lines, a combination of increasing import sales and a recessionary market made 1980 the worst year for the U.S. auto industry in six decades. General Motors lost over $760 million, and many were concerned that the U.S. auto industry would never again be competitive with foreign imports. Various studies showed that Japanese cars enjoyed a $2,000 lower production cost and a better quality performance than most U.S. cars (see Table 1).

MR. SMITH TAKES OVER

Mr. Roger B. Smith took over as chairman and CEO of GM on January 1, 1981. Mr. Smith had joined the company in 1949 as an accounting clerk and—like most of his predecessors as CEO—he had spent most of his career on GM's financial staff. He had a reputation as a dedicated company man who managed by the numbers. Smith went to work immediately, selling the General Motors Building in New York and laying off some 27,000 white-collar and 172,000 blue-collar workers. These and other cost cutting moves slashed $3 billion from the corporation's budget and (along with other events) produced a profit of $333 million in 1981—for which Roger Smith received little, if any, praise.

In April 1981, the United States had reached a "Voluntary Restraint Agreement" with Japan which was designed to give U.S. automakers time to adjust their

Case copyright © 1989 by James Brian Quinn. Case prepared by Penny C. Paquette under the supervision of Professor Quinn. Case derived solely from secondary sources.

TABLE 1 **The Japanese Advantage in Producing Small Cars**
(1983 Model Year)

Item	(1) COST ADVANTAGE PER SUBCOMPACT CAR, JAPAN VERSUS UNITED STATES	
	Amount	(2) % of Total
Lower wages and fringe benefits	$ 550	25.0%
Better inventory control	550	25.0
Better personnel management	478	21.7
Superior quality control	329	14.9
More flexible relief systems and allowances	89	4.0
Less absenteeism	81	3.7
Superior technology	73	3.3
Better materials handling engineering	41	1.9
Less interference from union representatives	12	0.5
Total Japanese cost advantage	$2,203	100.0%

Source: Grace Commission: President's Private Sector Survey on Cost Control, 1980–1984.

cost structures to the new international competition. While this gave the corporation some breathing room, one analyst pointed out that the four-year time frame of the agreement was not even long enough for the company to design and release a new model. In the meantime, GM was haunted by continuing quality problems in the downsized X–car line which was to have been its salvation. In August 1983 the U.S. Department of Justice filed a complaint against GM asking for $4 million in civil penalties for its actions concerning a recall of 1.1 million X–cars for brake defect problems. A consent decree settlement of the case led to the establishment of an arbitration process which itself became plagued by delays and other problems. In 1985 GM announced it was stopping production of the ill-fated X–cars— a year earlier than planned. In between, General Motors underwent some profound changes. Some of these and the issues they raised are here summarized briefly.

TECHNOLOGY AND CUSTOMER PREFERENCES

Early 1980s competition in automobiles was characterized by two powerful forces: (1) an increasing market fragmentation driven by swiftly changing customer preferences and (2) a much broadened and intensified worldwide cost and technological competition. After years of relatively slow change, technology was forcing rapid adaptations in every aspect of the automotive business. It affected how cars were made, what was put into them, and the way that companies interfaced with their marketplaces.[1]

Flexible Automation

For years auto manufacturing had been based on the traditional economies of scale—high volume, long production runs, rigid product specifications, and hard or fixed automated equipment. Computer-based manufacturing allowed production based on short machine setup times, flexible production of a variety of products on the same equipment, and more automated quality control. GM launched a large number of initiatives designed to help it adjust to this new reality and to reach its seeming goal of becoming the world's lowest cost producer of high-quality cars and trucks through the aggressive application of high technology. The company's expenditures for R&D and new plant and equipment totaled some $32 billion from 1979–1983, contrasted with a similar expenditure of only $15 billion from 1974–1978.[2]

By 1985 GM was using some 40,000 computer programmed devices on its plant floors and expected to be using 200,000 of them by 1990. In cooperation with computer, controls, and communications suppliers, GM had developed a Manufacturing Automation Protocol (MAP) program which would allow programmable devices to communicate with each other. In 1984, the Advanced Product and Manufacturing Engineering Group which had pushed for investments in artificial intelligence and machine-vision capabilities, proposed a Factory of the Future project. This $52 million project would use 70,000 square feet of an existing plant to test and develop highly flexible, automated production equipment, fully integrated as a system by computer controls. This plant, which would produce steering gears, was expected to perhaps double the cost of producing steering gears—but to speed up the adoption of new automated production technology in GM by five years.[3]

In addition, in 1982, GM invested $5 million and its own robotics expertise in a 50/50 venture with Fanuc Ltd. of Japan (a leading robot and computer controls manufacturer) to design, manufacture, and sell robotics systems. In 1984 and 1985, GM also took minority positions in several supplier companies having expertise in artificial intelligence and specialized areas of machine vision (see Table 2). General Motors saw potential internal applications for some 44,000 machine vision systems in the near future.

The Quality Push

General Motors attacked its problems of quality improvement in a variety of ways. In May 1984 it acquired a 10% interest in Philip Crosby Associates, Inc. (PCA), a recognized quality management training and consulting firm. Together they created the General Motors Quality Institute to train General Motors managers. GM implemented statistical process control techniques in many of its plants. This in-

TABLE 2 General Motors Minority Equity Investment in Technology Firms

COMPANY	PERCENT OWNERSHIP
Teknowledge	13%
Diffracto	30
Robotic Vision Systems	18
View Engineering	15
Applied Intelligent Systems	15
Automatix (option to purchase)	5

Source: "GM Moves Into a New Era," *Business Week,* July 16, 1984, and "High-Tech Drive," *The Wall Street Journal,* June 6, 1985.

volved rigid control of set ups and processing operations—and checking parts during production rather than randomly after they were finished. In some plants, the previously unthinkable became practice; any worker could halt the production line if defects were spotted. As part of its overall quality improvement program, GM demanded higher quality and consistency from its suppliers. Along with other automakers, General Motors was no longer asking suppliers to "make it to print," but rather "to make it right" and "make it the same every time." In 1984 General Motors revised its General Quality Standard to require suppliers to present a plan for quality improvement, and it established a supplier quality survey program and supplier quality rating system for incoming parts shipments.

As these quality improvement and automation programs came into place, they were expected to affect many aspects of GM's operations and strategy.

ON TO SATURN

General Motors' stated goal of offering a full product line—"a car for every purse and every purpose"—meant that the company had to solve the problem of competing with the Japanese in their stronghold, the subcompact and compact car market. Exhibit 2 outlines the structure of this segment of the U.S. marketplace. It was here also that the Japanese' cost advantages were greatest. In 1981, part way through the development of a new small car (the S-car), which was intended for the 1984 model year, General Motors conducted a detailed cost analysis which concluded that the *same car* could be built by a Japanese auto maker in Japan for *at least* $2,000 less than General Motors could build it. (See Table 3.)

GM's detailed figures were developed by its Japanese affiliate, Isuzu.[4] The average robot in a GM assembly plant would displace two workers. But in 1983 the Japanese used 6 times as many robots per million vehicles produced as the U.S. industry. Booz Allen & Hamilton also estimated that $800 of the Japanese production cost advantage was due to the simplicity of its product lines. In 1982 the Honda Accord offered 32 option combinations while the Ford Thunderbird offered 69,000.[5] The experts' view on how (on the average) Japanese producers achieved these cost advantages in 1982 is summarized in Table 3. The average cost of shipping a car from Japan to the United States in 1982 was about $400, while materials and components supplies cost Japanese producers about $700 less than their U.S. counterparts. American inventory practices were also substantially more costly than the Japanese. (See Table 4.)

The S-car never went into production. General Motors' X-cars (Citation, Phoenix, Omega, and Skylark) had been introduced in 1979. Its J-cars (Cavalier, 2000, Firenza, Skyhawk, and Cimarron) were added in 1981. GM's share of the small car market rose to 27.9% in 1980 but fell to 23.3% in 1983 despite the introduction of the J-cars and limitations on Japanese imports.[6] Meanwhile GM began to plan a totally integrated "Buick City" facility in Flint, Michigan, where steel blanks would enter one end of the line, bodies would be made, vehicles would be assembled, and cars would emerge from the far end.

In the early 1980s, General Motors responded to Japanese competition in several ways. In 1981 GM bought 5.3% of Suzuki Motor of Japan for $38 million. And in 1984 GM said it would invest another $100 million in a 50/50 joint venture with Korea's Daewoo Group to produce cars for potential import to the United States. In late 1983 it announced plans to invest some $100 million more in a joint venture with Toyota to build a version of Toyota's popular Corolla to be

TABLE 3 Factors Explaining the U.S—Japanese Productivity Gap: Rankings and Relative Weights from Expert Panel

PANEL MEMBERS

	A		B	C		D	E		Average	
Factor	Rank	Weight* (percentage)	Rank	Rank	Weight* (percentage)	Rank	Rank	Weight* (percentage)	Rank	Weight* (percentage)
1. Process yield	1	30	1	1	30	1	1	40	1	30–40
2. Absenteeism	3	20	3	1	30	2	2	25	2.2	20–30
3. Job structure	2	25	2	5	5	5	4	10	3.6	10–25
4. Process automation	6	6	4	3	15	4	3	15	4.0	6–15
5. Quality systems	7	5.5	5	4	10	6	4	10	5.2	5.5–10
6. Product design	4	7	7	4	10	3	7	0	5.0	0–10
7. Work pace	5	6.5	6	7	0	7	7	0	6.4	0–6.5

* Fraction of the differential explained by the factor.

Source: The Competitive Status of the U.S. Auto Industry, National Academy of Engineering, National Research Council, Washington, D.C., 1982.

TABLE 4   Inventory Comparisons—United States and Japan

LEVEL/PROCESS	JAPAN	UNITED STATES
1. Plant and process inventories		
Assembly plant component inventories (equivalent units of production)		
Heaters	1 hour	5 days
Radiators	2 hours	5 days
Brake drums	1.5 hours	3 days
Bumpers	1 hour	
Front-wheel-drive transfer case in process parts storage by operation (number of parts)		
Mill	7	240
Drill	11	200
Ream and chamfer	13	196
Drill	24	205
Mill, washer, test	10	40
Assemble	6	96
Finish	7	87
Total	79	1064
2. Company inventories		
Work-in-process inventories per vehicle		
1979	$80.2	$536.5
1980	$74.2	$584.3
Work in process turns[a]		
1979	40.0	12.1
1980	46.1	13.4

[a] Defined as cost of goods sold divided by work in process inventories.

Source: The Competitive Status of the U.S. Auto Industry, National Academy of Engineering, National Research Council, Washington, D.C., 1982.

sold as the Chevrolet Nova. Toyota was the world's lowest-cost auto producer, both dominating the Japanese market and reportedly being the only large auto producer to make money there. The deal was approved by the Federal Trade Commission in April 1984, despite protests by Chrysler Corporation. Plans called for production starting in late 1984 at an unused General Motors plant in Fremont (California) of up to 250,000 cars per year for the 12-year duration of the agreement.

The Nova was to fill a gap in GM's product line created by the phasing out of the 10-year-old Chevy Chevette. In exchange for wages and fringe benefits close to GM's national new hire rate, the UAW agreed to go along with many of Toyota's labor practices, allowing the use of only four classifications of workers—production workers and three types of skilled tradesmen. This would allow use of 5- to 10-person production teams within which all workers could rotate jobs regularly and be trained to do everyone else's job. The joint venture would provide jobs for some 12,000 U.S. workers (3,000 at Fremont and 9,000 elsewhere). About 50% of the vehicle's content would be American in origin.

Saturn

In November 1983, General Motors unveiled its most dramatic response to the Japanese challenge—the Saturn Project. Billed as a last-ditch effort to build a small car in the United States to compete successfully in cost and quality with Japanese small cars, the Saturn line was to begin with basic 2- and 4-door sedans in the $6,000 price range. But it might be expanded later to include liftbacks, station wagons, and possibly minivans. Ten percent of General Motors' total R&D budget was devoted to the project.[1] The lessons learned in many of GM's ongoing and planned plant modernizations (e.g., the Flint Assembly Complex, revamped Olds facilities, the Factory of the Future, and the Toyota Joint Venture) were all to be factored into the Saturn project. Although 80% of Saturn's technology was said to be in use somewhere, the rest had to be invented. The program expected to cut the man-hours required to build a small car from 200 to only 40, mainly by preassembling such components as doors and front ends and then plugging them together on a production line through "modular assembly."[7]

The Saturn's manufacturing complex was to be located in Spring Hill, Tennessee, less than 50 miles from Nissan's non-union plant in Smyrna. (Nissan had built the plant in response to a U.S. tariff interpretation which moved assembled car bodies and truck cabs from a "components" category (with a 4% tariff) to an "assembly" category (with a 25% tariff). This would be the most highly integrated and automated car operation in the United States. Its 6 million square foot complex, containing 150 acres under one roof, would include an assembly plant, stamping plant, engine and transaxle plant, forging operations for the powertrain, some component manufacturing facilities, and Saturn's administrative offices. The complex's projected cost of $3.5 billion (of the Saturn's estimated $5 billion capitalization) made it General Motors' most expensive facility. By contrast, a new assembly plant normally cost about $600 million; but Saturn not only included many other operations, it was designed to assemble 500,000 cars per year, nearly double the capacity of a normal assembly plant. Table 5 gives a sense of how manufacturing costs tended to change with volume in conventional plants.

GM included the UAW in all of its planning for Saturn. Initially, Saturn would employ about 6,000 workers, some 80% of whom would be protected from layoffs except in the case of "catastrophic events." Even then a joint committee could reject layoffs in favor of reduced hours or a temporary shutdown. Blue collar workers would be paid *salaries* "equal to 80% of prevailing wages." The remainder of their compensation would be "rewards" tied to productivity targets, quality goals, and Saturn's profits.[8]

As in the Toyota plant, only four to six job classifications would be used, teaming workers into "work units" of 6–15 people, self-managed by an elected

TABLE 5 Manufacturing-Cost Changes with Volume
(production cost as percent of minimum cost)

NUMBER OF UNITS	SUB-COMPACT	COMPACT	STANDARD
400,000	100.00	100.00	100.00
300,000	104.83	100.98	100.04
200,000	114.68	108.89	101.02
100,000	144.70	133.37	116.50
50,000	204.78	182.31	147.43

Source: J. Hunker, *Structural Change in the U.S. Automobile Industry,* D.C. Heath and Company, Lexington Books, 1983, p. 133—adapted from Eric J. Toder, *Trade Policy and the U.S. Automobile Industry* (New York: Praeger Special Studies, 1978).

UAW "counselor" rather than a company supervisor. Work units would be responsible for controlling their own variable costs and output quality. If a team came up with a better idea for a process or new piece of equipment, Saturn's finance and purchasing departments "had to respond" and reach a consensus with the team.[9] The contract with UAW also added a grievance system to parallel this consensus–decision-making process and tied job security guarantees to seniority. Significantly, to gain final agreement on its Saturn contract, GM was forced to cut a mission statement indicating its intention to implement Saturn ideas and methods throughout the company. And UAW's Bieber made it clear that "consideration for granting similar agreements would be limited to high quality, small car plants with high domestic content."[10]

GM insisted that Saturn was not just a small car—it was a whole new technology which could eventually be applied to bigger cars as well. Saturn was set up as a separate corporation to negotiate its new labor contracts and to rewrite dealer franchise agreements for its cars. GM made the decision to award Saturn franchises separately, rather than simply giving the car to any one of its existing dealer groups, like Chevrolet. Since the Saturn production and distribution system was designed to deliver a car 8 days (instead of six to eight weeks) after receipt of an order, the relationship between the dealer and General Motors would be much altered.[11] Saturn's designers were given a clean slate and told they could develop all its parts uniquely for the line (if they so desired) without accepting standard corporate components. Saturn's total projected cost was approximately $5 billion.

General Motors' domestic competitors lacked the scale and financial resources of General Motors. However, both Chrysler and Ford announced Saturn-like small-car projects in 1985. And Chrysler was planning a joint venture with Mitsubishi to build small cars in the United States. In 1985 Chrysler was already reportedly Detroit's lowest cost producer, in large part because it bought up to 70% of its parts from outside suppliers. GM historically bought 10–15% of its standard components outside, while Ford bought 40–50%. See Exhibit 3 for statistics on U.S. passenger car sales and production.

MAJOR DIVERSIFICATIONS

In a market protected from Japanese competition, average auto prices in the United States jumped by 50% from 1979 to 1985.[1] U.S. auto producers' profitability exploded, and GM built up a huge "war chest" of $8.6 billion in cash. (See Exhibit 4 for detailed financials.)

In October 1984 General Motors shocked the U.S. business community by announcing its acquisition of Electronic Data Systems, Inc. (EDS), for $2.55 billion financed with a combination of cash and a new class of General Motors' common stock, designated Class E. Holders of EDS stock were given a choice between accepting $44 for each EDS share, or a combination of $35.20 and 0.2 shares of General Motors Class E common, plus a non-transferrable contingent promissory note issued by GM. Class E's performance was to be linked to the new EDS subsidiary's performance within GM. EDS, founded in 1962 by H. Ross Perot, was described by General Motors as "a world leader in the design of large-scale data processing systems, the operation of cost effective data processing centers and networks, and the integration of large data processing and communications systems." From 1974 to 1984, EDS's revenues had grown from $119 million to $786 million.

Big Three Net Profits in Millions, 1980–1984

	1980	1981	1982	1983	1984
General Motors	$ (763)	$ 333	$ 963	$3,730	$4,516
Ford	(1,543)	(1,060)	(658)	1,867	2,907
Chrysler	(1,710)	(476)	(69)	302	1,496

Source: Company annual reports.

EDS Financial History, 1974–1984
($ million–except for per share figures)

	1974	1979	1982	1984
Revenues	$118.7	$274.2	$503.0	$786.1
Net income	15.3	23.7	75.0	71.1
Earnings per share	1.28	1.82	0.86	1.26*
Stock price range		$4\frac{5}{8}$–7	$9\frac{1}{2}$–25	$24\frac{1}{2}$–$46\frac{1}{4}$
General Motors EPS	3.27	10.04	3.09	14.22
General Motors stock price	$28\frac{7}{8}$–$55\frac{1}{2}$	$49\frac{3}{4}$–$65\frac{7}{8}$	34–$64\frac{1}{2}$	61–$82\frac{3}{4}$

* Adjusted for 2-for-1 stock splits in 1981 and 1983.

Source: Compiled from "GM and EDS," *Automotive News,* March 18, 1985 and various other sources.

1984 revenues of EDS were distributed as follows among different client industries as represented by EDS's five groups.

1984 EDS Systems Revenue by Group

INDUSTRY	PERCENT
Government	41%
Financial and Industrial	30
Insurance	23
Health Services	4
International	2

Source: Compiled from "GM and EDS," *Automotive News,* March 18, 1985.

Due to its emphasis on customer satisfaction, EDS had an 85% contract renewal rate and had recently won some extremely large contracts with U.S. military and other governmental agencies. With its business being concentrated mainly in services industries, EDS had little experience in manufacturing-related data processing systems, robotics, or CAD/CAM. Most of its large-scale computer integration work had been for the government. Following EDS's acquisition by General Motors, analysts predicted 1985 revenues of $1.8 billion for EDS and $3.6 billion by 1990.[11]

According to GM the acquisition of EDS offered "more effective control of health insurance costs, increased data processing capabilities, improved delivery of computer services throughout the corporation, and development of advanced computer systems for manufacturing process-control and order-entry for GM, its dealers, and suppliers. . . ." A *New York Times* article said: "Smith had no problem figuring out how EDS could help GM. What did present a problem was figuring out how to integrate the alien culture into a GM monolith without smothering the special qualities that made it successful."[3] Ross Perot had imbued EDS with a strongly individualistic culture. Its motto was "Eagles don't flock, they fly alone." Despite the fact that General Motors, before the merger, was the world's largest corporate user of computers and had some 10,000 data processing employees, one wit said, "EDS merging with GM is like a Green Beret outfit joining forces with the Social Security Administration."[12] Although EDS was set up as a separate, independent subsidiary with Mr. Perot reporting directly to GM's chairman, many wondered how the potential benefits of a merger could be realized for either party.

Hughes Aircraft

Then in June 1985, in the largest non-oil acquisition in history, GM agreed to acquire Hughes Aircraft from its parent, the Hughes Medical Institute, for $2.7 billion in cash plus 50 million shares of GM Class H common stock valued at $46 per share. Prior to the acquisition, Hughes stock had been privately held by the Institute and had no established market price. The acquisition created some $4 billion in goodwill, which the SEC insisted be charged against the subsidiary's income rather than against that of GM as a whole. The H stock, like its predecessor, Class E stock, was linked to the performance of the newly created GM subsidiary which housed it—GM Hughes Electronics Corporation. This would include not only Hughes Aircraft, but also Delco Electronics, Delco Systems Operations, and AC Spark Plug's Instrument and Display Systems Group. The combined 1984 sales of these units was estimated to have been $8.7 billion—$5.8 billion for Hughes and the rest for GM's various operations.[13] Credit for engineering GM's acquisition of Hughes went to Roger Smith's protege and heir apparent, F. Alan Smith (E.V.P., finance) and Courtney Jones (treasurer).

Hughes Aircraft was the nation's seventh largest defense contractor, deriving about 80% of its sales (versus GM's $1.3 billion) from the Pentagon and enjoying a $12 billion backlog in 1985. Hughes' earnings were $266 million in 1984. Its largest operation, the Ground Systems Group made such things as fire-finder radar sets which pinpointed enemy artillery fire and targeted a response. Other operations included Space and Communications Systems, Electro-Optical and Data Systems, and Radar Systems and Missile Systems. The various divisions frequently sold components to one another.[14] Advanced electronics was the fastest growing segment of the U.S. defense budget in 1985.

Hughes had a record of consistently high profitability and unusually low vulnerability to Defense Department program cuts. No single project of its 1,500 major programs accounted for more than 6% of sales, and the 10 largest programs together accounted for less than 40%. Hughes was known for its high concentration of engineering skills—one-third of its 73,000 employees were degreed scientists—and its strengths in systems engineering and artificial intelligence. Hughes had a history of expending large sums of money (some $250 million a year) for R&D, mostly of a high-risk nature. It was considered one of the premier high technology companies of the United States.

GM's spokesman said that Hughes could usefully (1) contribute its sophisticated technology to a number of advanced GM engineering projects including radar based collision-avoidance systems, satellite navigation systems, and advanced composite materials for lightweight vehicle strength; (2) team up with EDS in telecommunications and systems engineering; and (3) be a prime partner in the "Trilby" project to redefine the basic shape and function of post-Saturn cars and trucks "from mechanical products which include a few electrical subsystems to ones with major electromechanical and electronic elements."[15] Skeptics, however, pointed out that Hughes management knew very little about building basic transportation vehicles and that Hughes engineers were accustomed to working on advanced engineering projects like the Stealth Aircraft, the Space Shuttle, Deep Undersea Recovery Vehicles, Strategic Defense Initiative devices, and so on.

GMAC Acquisitions

General Motors Acceptance Corporation (GMAC), earning $1 billion per year, was the nation's largest finance company, with over $54 billion in assets and some 300 branches. Its primary function was to arrange financings for purchasers of GM cars and trucks. It also had an insurance subsidiary. In 1983, GMAC's profits had been increasing rapidly (46% since 1982) at an essentially noncyclical pace because of an extensive computerization program and gains in its share of financings.[2] F. Alan Smith (E.V.P., finance) oversaw GMAC and was given a mandate to seek compatible acquisitions for it. In 1985 GMAC acquired the Colonial Group of 7 mortgage banking and servicing companies (a $7.4 billion portfolio) and the rights to service Norwest Corp.'s $11 billion portfolio of mortgages. These acquisitions provided an expanded customer base and experience in secondary financings.

CAN GM DO IT?

While the business press generally responded favorably to General Motors' major moves during the early 1980s, many questioned whether GM could manage so much change. *The Wall Street Journal* noted, "No single overriding strategy [seems to] guide all these (technology) programs. Some activities overlap and GM is struggling to absorb the lessons learned."[16]

Even in its traditional operations, GM had trouble keeping up with demand for some models in 1985, while others languished on its dealers' lots. And the smaller engines GM had geared up to build were not well matched to the public's returning desires for greater power. While back in 1979 analysts had predicted that by 1985 as much as 25% of all U.S. passenger cars would be diesel-powered, GM had sold only 15,000 diesel cars in 1984. Its diesel engine plant was running at 9% of capacity[17] prior to being shut down in 1985. From 1974 to 1984, GM more than doubled the fuel economy of its fleet of cars primarily by expending over $40 billion on new products, plants, and equipment. As a result, it met or exceeded the CAFE standards from 1979 to 1982. Starting in 1983, however, falling fuel prices changed customer buying habits and GM as a full-line manufacturer fell more than 2 mpg below the standards. By 1985, due to the expiration of its accumulated fuel-economy credits, GM was at risk for huge fines. The Japanese who, up to this point, had exported mainly fuel efficient subcompacts and compacts, held substantial CAFE credits. By the fall of 1985, GM had increased its overall car production capacity by 15% as its new Hamtramck (Detroit) facility and its retooled Flint assembly complex—both geared to making larger cars—came on line. While some analysts predicted falling demand for U.S.-made cars in 1986, GM expected another boom year. But Japanese capacity had also been rising in recent years. (See Table 6.)

Despite its falling market share, GM (which was traditionally the domestic price leader) was planning to increase its base prices on 1986 models by an average of 3% over comparably equipped 1985 models.[18] Mid-1985 earnings at GM were 2.3% lower than comparable figures for a year earlier, and the company said it was feeling the impact of costs related to future model programs and its recent acquisition activities. Nevertheless, General Motors was still the largest auto producer on the world scene, dominating not just the United States, but increasingly the European markets. (See Table 7.)

TABLE 6   Japanese Automobile Production Capacity ($\times$ 1,000 units), 1979–1983

FIRM	1979	1980	1981	1982	1983
Toyota	2,782	2,902	3,040	3,305	3,430
Nissan	2,665	2,665	2,690	2,720	2,900
Mazda	885	910	960	1,070	1,250
Honda	770	880	1,010	1,110	1,290
Mitsubishi	1,000	1,000	1,000	1,000	1,000
Isuzu	320	340	400	520	600
Daihatsu	350	350	350	390	390
Fuji	280	300	320	320	320
Hino	65	66	6	66	66
Nissan diesel	30	35	35	48	50
Grand total	9,147	9,363	9,871	10,529	11,276

Source: Analysis by the U.S. Department of Transportation based upon published reports and estimates, as cited in U.S. Department of Transportation, The U.S. Automobile Industry, 1980, p. 62.

TABLE 7   Car Production by Major Manufacturer, 1984
(millions)

	1984
General Motors (U.S.)	6.33
Ford (U.S.)	3.62
Toyota (Japan)	2.49
Nissan (Japan)	2.05
Volkswagen-Audi (W. Ger.)	1.88
Renault (France)	1.55
Peugeot (France)	1.46
Fiat (Italy)	1.39
Chrysler (U.S.)	1.27
Honda (Japan)	1.02
Mazda (Japan)	0.77
Mitsubishi (Japan)	0.59
Daimler-Benz (W. Ger.)	0.48
Austin Rover (U.K.)	0.40

Source: DRI Europe in The Economist, March 2, 1985

EXHIBIT 1A
Old Organization*

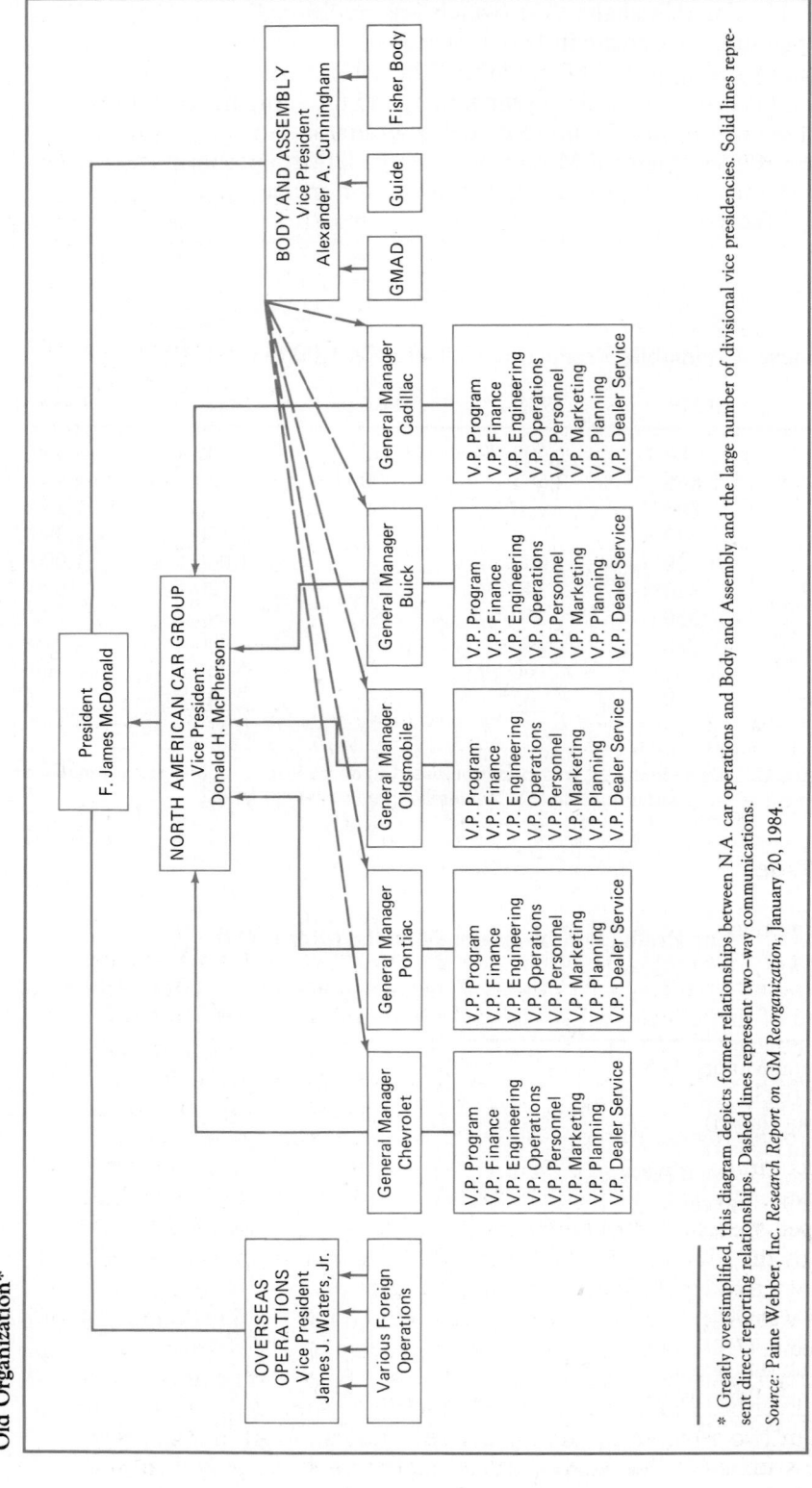

* Greatly oversimplified, this diagram depicts former relationships between N.A. car operations and Body and Assembly and the large number of divisional vice presidencies. Solid lines represent direct reporting relationships. Dashed lines represent two-way communications.

Source: Paine Webber, Inc. *Research Report on GM Reorganization,* January 20, 1984.

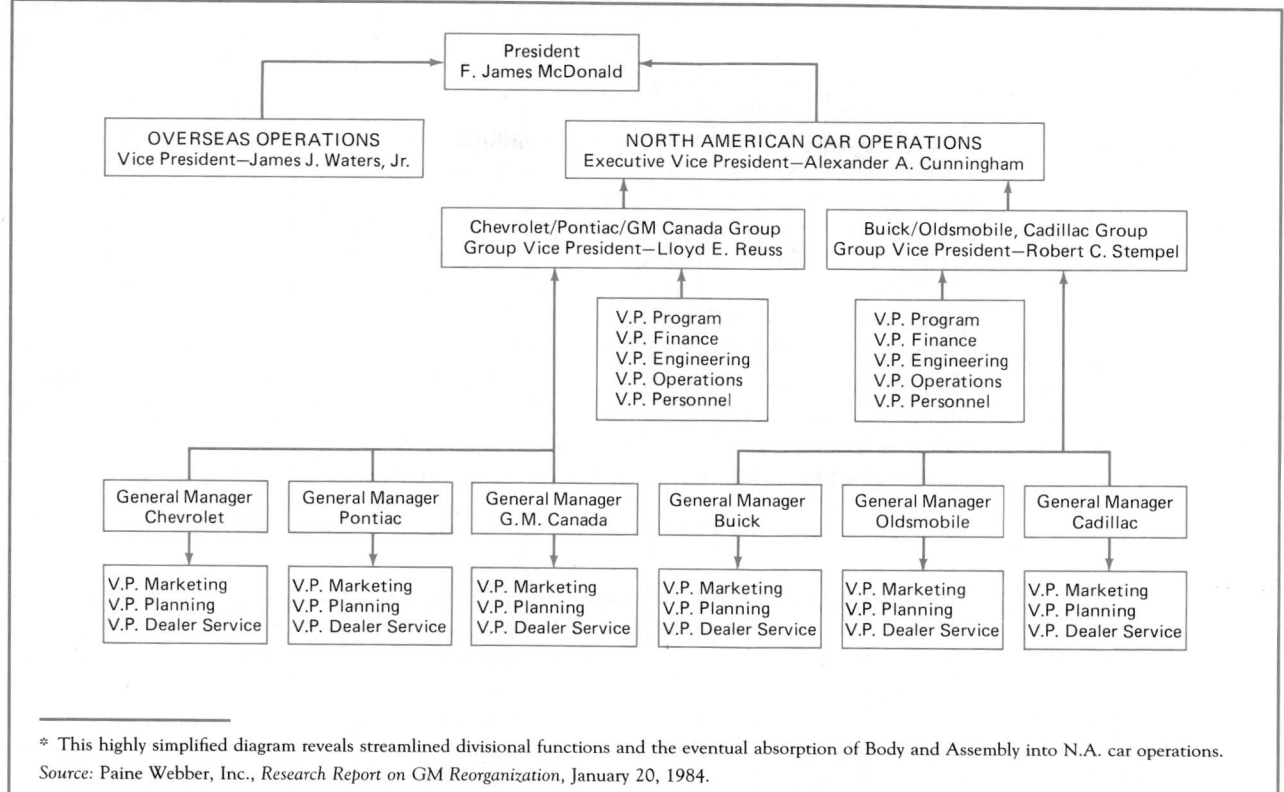

* This highly simplified diagram reveals streamlined divisional functions and the eventual absorption of Body and Assembly into N.A. car operations.
Source: Paine Webber, Inc., *Research Report on GM Reorganization*, January 20, 1984.

Organization Issues

GM's traditional management and decision making style had been one of centralized policy making and decentralized operating management, coupled with a separation of product policy and budgetary powers. GM's key management committee structure consisted of the following: "An Executive Committee which determined which products/programs as well as priorities to recommend to the Finance Committee and the Board; a Finance Committee which established corporate financial goals and determined whether products/programs would receive capital funding before they went to the Board; a Product Policy Committee which made the basic decisions and recommendations regarding development of standard corporate component hardware and engineering designs; and a Research Policy Committee which (1) developed specific R&D policies and priorities in response to corporate goals established by the Executive Committee and the Board and (2) reviewed and recommended new basic technologies. The decision-making process within committees or groups was described as consensus decision making."[19] (See Exhibit 2.)

For some years, GM had utilized the organization structure described in Exhibit 1A. In January 1984 after an extensive analysis, Mr. Roger Smith announced the organization described in Exhibit 1B. GM's committee structure remained essentially intact. But two separate car groups were established, functioning as fully integrated business units totally responsible for the engineering, manufacturing, and assembly of their products and for the performance and profitability of these products in the marketplace. The Chevrolet/Pontiac/GM of Canada group (CPC) was to target the smaller car, lower-cost marketplace, while the Buick/Oldsmobile/ Cadillac group (BOC) was to go after larger-car and premium-price buyers. Robert Stempel and Lloyd Reuss, the two prime contenders to succeed President F. James MacDonald, were named to head these two major operating groups. Reuss, who had been with Buick, took over CPC while Stempel, who had been with Chevrolet, led BOC. In keeping with these changes, Roger Smith attempted to introduce a "more hands on, more participatory approach for his managers, which included a total reevaluation of their responsibilities, increased authority for middle managers, and a speeded up process for promotions."[20] Mr. Smith's own compensation of $1.5 million in 1984 clearly left some upward mobility for other executives.

In 1985, this complex reorganization was "progressing slowly" and some analysts commented that the white-collar work force appeared to be growing rather than shrinking as predicted. Weaknesses in earnings and sales during the first half of 1985 raised questions about even so seasoned a management as GM's ability to manage all of these transitions simultaneously. While GM had made strides in labor relations and productivity within its newer plants, it still faced problems of changing long-standing practices in existing facilities.

Future Issues in the Auto Market

Pressures from imports were growing steadily. Many analysts predicted that sales of imports and cars made in the United States by foreign manufacturers would reach 4.5 million or 43% of the U.S. total by 1990.[7] See Exhibit 2 for statistics on U.S. passenger car sales and production. Worldwide sales of automobiles reached 35 million in 1983 and Mr. Smith expected the figure to hit 50 million in the 1990's.[20] Beginning with Honda, the Japanese had started to invest heavily in capacity to build cars in the United States. By 1990 Japanese production in the United States was expected to be at least 1 million cars (300,000 by Honda, 240,000 by Nissan, 250,000 by Toyota, and 240,000 by Mazda). While some observers thought the Japanese were just quota-jumping or attempting to improve trade relations, others believed the Japanese intended to grow into full-fledged U.S. auto companies like GM's Opel or Ford of Europe. Some 30 or so Japanese auto parts suppliers had begun setting up plants in the United States. While U.S. automakers had record profits during 1984, so had many of the Japanese.

Honda claimed its cost differential between U.S. and Japanese production was only $500 and that it could make money on even its small cars if built in the United States. Honda had 40% of its sales in the United States and derived 65% of its profits there.[21] While some of the Japanese producers had managed to maintain non-union plants, even those that had accepted the UAW enjoyed certain advantages from negotiating entirely new contracts and were not burdened with costs related to older workers and retirees. Despite the end of quotas the Japanese feared a renewal of U.S. protectionism and found it hard and expensive to expand capacity in Japan due to rapidly increasing land costs and scarcity of certain raw materials.

U.S. quotas had forced the Japanese to compete aggressively at home, and they had developed new products with much improved engines and drivetrains. Given the affluence of the Japanese market, they had progressed quickly down the experience curve for designing and producing intermediate sized cars. Data Resource, Inc. estimated that Toyota and Nissan made $5,800 on each mid-sized car versus $933 for each small car. And Toyota's planned new U.S. factory would build 200,000 intermediate-sized cars in 1988. *Business Week* commented, "[As] Japanese car makers face growing pressures to end their dependence on the increasingly cutthroat market for small cars . . . the real competition will be in the market for mid-sized cars."[22] While in the past the Japanese had concentrated on being cost leaders, many felt they were now moving ahead in the development and refining of auto technology. In the future they would rely ever more heavily on new technology they had developed themselves in response to very carefully estimated demands.

QUESTIONS

1. What specific organizational and strategic issues do these major new ventures pose for GM?

2. What are the most important external trends it should deal with? How should GM as a corporation position itself relative to competitors?

3. What important steps should management take to implement its strategy in the near future?

EXHIBIT 2
GM Decision-Making Style

It is difficult to pinpoint the precise time when many "decisions" in General Motors are actually made. Well prior to the presentation of matters at formal sessions of GM's governing committees and policy groups, a broad consensus is generally obtained among members of senior management. Part of this occurs as members of the executive committee sit along with other key staff and operating executives on various policy groups—subcommittees of the executive committee—where important topics are discussed. In addition, all top executives receive continuing input on significant matters from various levels of the organization outside of the formal setting of policy group meetings.

Informal Discussions

Another executive described the decision process as follows: "There were a lot of informal discussions going on among different people and small groups around the company. Even at the top level I don't think there was an attempt to get everybody together to analyze things as momentous issues. At the Product Policy Group level a lot of discussion always occurs before a formal meeting. From this perhaps six or seven key people will convince themselves —for a variety of reasons—that something must be done. That is where the crucial decisions are really made. In an organization as big as this, it is very important that the major decision makers appear to be together when a big decision is reached. They don't even want too much difference in viewpoint within the meeting as to the sense of direction their comments may convey. Otherwise there could be a lot of confusion throughout the design process. The major conceptual decisions are really thoroughly discussed and reviewed before the formal meeting.

The formal meeting is just to make sure everything gets looked at. One is forced to listen to a complete rationale. We get clear cost estimates and a thoroughly worked-out plan for a given product line. Everybody feels much more comfortable about the decisions after they have been discussed in a forum like that. More important, the line people know how we are planning to get where we are going. The more they understand this, the more they know what to do on their own as the program progresses.

There is a lot of moving out of channels in this organization. Product Planning knows in advance what is acceptable. People are involved in a lot of presentations at multiple levels. Everybody knows everyone. And the top decision makers have actually had a chance to meet and deal with a number of people on a person to person basis. We try to keep these key decision makers informed about the marketplace and who to go to for detailed information, and also bring to bear their own considerable experience garnered from a lifetime career in the transportation business.

994

EXHIBIT 3

Automotive News World Outlook, 1983–1990
Generated by Data Resources, Inc. (in millions)

	1983	1984	1985	1986	1987	1988	1989	1990
NEW CAR REGISTRATIONS								
Total Western Europe[a]	10,473	10,240	10,391	10,639	10,831	10,852	11,028	11,270
Germany	2,427	2,425	2,495	2,536	2,486	2,547	2,565	2,681
France	2,018	1,810	1,891	1,983	2,065	2,022	2,093	2,162
United Kingdom	1,792	1,733	1,698	1,742	1,782	1,724	1,768	1,809
Italy	1,582	1,629	1,662	1,645	1,676	1,702	1,712	1,693
Total U.S.	9,178	10,640	10,710	10,580	10,483	11,166	11,608	11,839
Asia-Pacific[b]	1,025	1,159	1,251	1,325	1,367	1,404	1,463	1,521
Japan	3,136	3,228	3,254	3,414	3,362	3,457	3,515	3,617
Total Africa-MidEast	1,271	1,242	1,305	1,450	1,575	1,635	1,603	1,645
Total Latin America	1,401	1,303	1,342	1,445	1,565	1,693	1,847	1,997
Total Eastern Bloc	2,085	2,118	2,155	2,222	2,302	2,366	2,407	2,457
CAR PRODUCTION								
Total Western Europe[a]	11,121	10,772	11,093	11,208	11,393	11,426	11,602	11,845
Germany	3,878	3,677	3,828	3,873	3,880	3,980	4,054	4,193
France	2,961	2,760	2,772	2,818	2,885	2,824	2,830	2,810
United Kingdom	1,045	981	1,016	1,001	1,010	995	1,028	1,050
Italy	1,396	1,493	1,504	1,498	1,518	1,521	1,562	1,594
Total North America	7,746	8,761	8,993	8,361	8,141	8,875	9,206	9,176
Asia-Pacific[b]	7,909	8,189	8,434	8,752	8,916	9,132	9,327	9,548
Japan	7,152	7,308	7,444	7,630	7,711	7,885	8,051	8,229
Total Latin America	1,113	1,094	1,144	1,247	1,407	1,559	1,670	1,826
Mexico	207	223	242	271	361	431	463	486
NEW TRUCK REGISTRATIONS								
Western Europe[c]	1,018	983	1,028	1,052	1,060	1,066	1,101	1,129
United States	3,161	4,164	4,373	4,342	4,390	4,537	4,624	4,767
TRUCK PRODUCTION								
Western Europe[c]	1,309	1,233	1,327	1,370	1,385	1,427	1,470	1,495
North America	2,971	4,017	4,166	4,004	3,991	4,122	4,232	4,421

[a] Includes Germany, France, United Kingdom, Italy, Netherlands, Belgium, Denmark, Ireland, Greece, Sweden, Norway, Finland, Switzerland, Austria, Spain and Portugal.
[b] Includes Taiwan, South Korea, Peninsular Malaysia, India, Australia, and New Zealand but excludes Japan, which is listed separately.
[c] Includes Germany, France, United Kingdom, Italy, Spain, Sweden, Netherlands and Belgium.

Source: Automotive News, 1985 Market Data Book Issue, April 24, 1985.

EXHIBIT 3 (Continued)

Ward's Import Car Market Segmentation, 1983–1984

	1984		1983			1984		1983	
	Units	% Tot.	Units	% Tot.		Units	% Tot.	Units	% Tot.
MINICOMPACT					Mitsubishi Starion	6,375	0.3	6,209	0.3
Honda Civic	137,401	5.8	137,747	5.9	Audi 4000 Quattro	3,923	0.2	577	0.0
Toyota Tercel	103,013	4.4	147,971	6.3	Dodge Conquest				
Mazda GLC	45,221	1.9	51,601	2.2	(Challenger)	3,725	0.2	14,024	0.6
Dodge Colt	36,560	1.6	39,158	1.7	Audi Coupe GT	3,508	0.1	3,349	0.1
Plymouth Colt	32,819	1.4	34,513	1.5	Plymouth Conquest				
Chevrolet Sprint	10,927	0.5	—	—	(Sapporo)	3,344	0.1	11,571	0.5
Mitsubishi Mirage	3,101	0.1	—	—	**Total specialty**	**294,874**	**12.6**	**307,723**	**13.1**
Toyota Starlet	260	0.0	6,717	0.3	**Total compact**	**689,542**	**29.4**	**716,182**	**30.7**
Nissan Pulsar	—	—	13,524	0.6					
Renault LeCar	—	—	11,148	0.5	**MIDSIZE**				
Total regular	**369,302**	**15.7**	**442,379**	**19.0**	Volvo DL/GL	68,610	2.9	60,932	2.6
Honda CRX	47,445	2.0	—	—	Nissan Maxima	68,209	2.9	76,209	3.3
VW Cabriolet	11,068	0.5	9,542	0.4	BMW 318i	28,661	1.2	34,619	1.5
Fiat X1/9	143	0.0	2,008	0.1	Toyota Cressida	34,466	1.5	39,755	1.7
Total specialty	**58,656**	**2.5**	**11,550**	**0.5**	Saab 900/900s	18,360	0.8	13,716	0.6
Total minicompact	**427,958**	**18.2**	**453,929**	**19.5**	Peugeot 505	19,723	0.8	14,791	0.6
SUBCOMPACT					VW Quantum	18,055	0.8	16,343	0.7
Toyota Corolla	157,875	6.7	143,430	6.1	Volvo Diesel	5,589	0.2	4,588	0.2
Nissan Sentra	189,488	8.1	209,889	9.0	Volvo 740 GLE	1,446	0.1	—	—
Subaru	152,543	6.5	150,943	6.5	**Total regular**	**263,119**	**11.2**	**260,953**	**11.2**
VW Jetta	37,750	1.6	21,736	0.9	Volvo GLT	9,866	0.4	13,198	0.6
Isuzu I-Mark	4,147	0.2	11,876	0.5	Saab 900 Turbo	14,408	0.6	12,117	0.5
Chevrolet Spectrum	2,077	0.1	—	—	Volvo 740 Turbo	47	0.0	—	—
Fiat Strada	40	0.0	659	0.0	**Total specialty**	**24,321**	**1.0**	**25,315**	**1.1**
Total regular	**543,930**	**23.2**	**538,533**	**23.0**	**Total midsize**	**287,440**	**12.2**	**286,268**	**12.3**
Nissan Pulsar NX	37,284	1.6	48,659	2.1					
Honda Prelude	66,924	2.9	41,188	1.8	**LUXURY**				
Mazda RX-7	54,310	2.3	52,226	2.2	Audi 5000	41,067	1.7	27,735	1.2
VW Scirocco	17,138	0.7	13,654	0.5	Mercedes 300-Series	33,552	1.4	42,765	1.7
Alfa Romeo Spider	2,783	0.1	1,931	0.1	Mercedes 190-Series	23,013	1.0	4,180	0.2
Fiat Spider 2000	208	0.0	3,513	0.2	BMW 325e	15,772	0.7	—	—
Total specialty	**178,647**	**7.6**	**161,171**	**6.9**	BMW 5-Series	15,409	0.7	16,004	0.7
Total subcompact	**722,577**	**30.8**	**699,704**	**29.9**	Jaguar XJ6	14,564	0.6	13,110	0.6
COMPACT					Mercedes 380/500SE	11,692	0.5	5,807	0.3
Honda Accord	123,049	5.2	171,735	7.3	BMW 7-Series	8,359	0.4	6,007	0.3
Toyota Camry	93,725	4.0	52,666	2.3	Volvo 760 GLE/Diesel	7,563	0.3	8,964	0.4
Mazda 626	70,135	3.0	69,561	3.0	Peugeot 604	284	0.0	450	0.0
Nissan Stanza	44,612	1.9	64,429	2.8	Mercedes 240D	26	0.0	9,728	0.4
Audi 4000	15,278	0.7	13,166	0.6	**Total regular**	**171,301**	**7.3**	**134,750**	**5.8**
Mitsubishi Tredia	13,724	0.6	13,747	0.6	Porsche	19,611	0.8	21,831	0.9
Mitsubishi Cordia	13,194	0.6	12,799	0.5	Mercedes 380 SL	9,288	0.4	9,255	0.4
Dodge Vista	7,805	0.3	2,311	0.1	Audi 5000 Turbo	6,380	0.3	1,928	0.1
Plymouth Vista	7,465	0.3	1,992	0.1	Volvo 760 Turbo	4,794	0.2	—	—
Mitsubishi Galant	2,710	0.1	—	—	Jaguar JX-S	3,480	0.1	2,705	0.1
Ren. Sportwagon (18i)	2,971	0.1	6,053	0.3	BMW 633/635 CSi	2,697	0.1	2,613	0.1
Total regular	**394,668**	**16.8**	**408,459**	**17.6**	Mercedes 500 SEC	1,651	0.1	1,957	0.1
Toyota Celica	85,213	3.6	117,836	5.0	Alfa Romeo GTV-6	919	0.1	1,071	0.1
Nissan 300 ZX	73,101	3.1	71,144	3.0	Ferrari	568	0.0	549	0.0
Nissan 200SX	63,466	2.7	31,158	1.3	Audi Quattro Turbo	64	0.0	240	0.0
Toyota Supra	29,871	1.3	26,972	1.2	Lancia	21	0.0	620	0.0
Isuzu Impulse	13,076	0.6	8,855	0.4	DeLorean	—	—	1,009	0.0
Renault Fuego	9,272	0.4	16,028	0.7	**Total specialty**	**49,473**	**2.1**	**43,778**	**1.8**
					Total luxury	**220,774**	**9.4**	**178,521**	**7.6**

Note: Segmemtation based on overall car size, marketing intent and price.
Source: Ward's Automotive Yearbook, 1985.

EXHIBIT 3 (Continued)

U.S. New Car Sales by Market Segments, 1984–1983 Calendar Years

Class/Model	1984	Share of Segment	1983	Share of Segment
Subcompact regular				
Chevette	164,917	13.5%	178,759	16.4%
1000	28,004	2.3	34,173	3.1
Escort	353,578	28.8	326,333	29.9
Lynx	67,725	5.5	78,876	7.2
Horizon	78,298	6.4	56,763	5.2
Omni	67,933	5.5	50,451	4.6
Renault Encore	69,235	5.6	20,182	1.9
Renault Alliance	100,366	8.2	126,008	11.6
Spirit	—	0.0	4,441	0.4
Golf (Rabbit)	73,844	6.0	85,042	7.8
Class Total	1,003,900	81.8	961,028	88.1
Subcompact specialty				
Fiero	93,485	7.7	22,591	2.1
EXP	31,213	2.5	19,574	1.8
LN7	—	0.0	4,694	0.4
Turismo	47,109	3.8	36,497	3.3
Charger	51,940	4.2	45,975	4.3
Class total	223,747	18.2	129,331	11.9
Total subcompact	1,227,647	100.0	1,090,359	100.0
Compact regular				
Cavalier	377,545	16.0	259,397	14.2
Citation	92,174	3.9	92,379	5.0
2000	126,916	5.3	88,313	4.8
Phoenix	13,202	0.6	24,362	1.3
Firenza	62,456	2.6	44,753	2.4
Omega	34,103	1.4	49,818	2.7
Skyhawk	121,858	5.1	72,998	4.0
Skylark	104,589	4.4	102,763	5.6

Class/Model	1984	Share of Segment	1983	Share of Segment
Intermediate regular (con't.)				
LTD	196,907	8.3%	165,396	7.6%
Granada	—	0.0	3,751	0.2
Marquis	103,722	4.4	65,184	3.0
Cougar '82	—	0.0	906	0.0
Caravelle	9,074	0.4	—	0.0
New Yorker (FWD)	53,698	2.3	50,091	2.3
E-Class	25,870	1.1	35,283	1.6
600 4 Dr.	36,872	1.6	33,882	1.6
Class total	1,701,779	71.7	1,470,082	67.8
Intermediate specialty				
Monte Carlo	115,930	4.9	105,797	4.9
Grand Prix	71,609	3.0	89,355	4.1
Regal	182,185	7.7	234,035	10.9
Thunderbird	154,865	6.5	134,710	6.2
Cougar	120,964	5.1	87,027	4.0
LeBaron GTS	2,494	0.1	—	0.0
Lancer	1,980	0.1	—	0.0
Cordoba	124	0.0	10,291	0.5
Mirada	250	0.0	4,417	0.2
Eagle	20,654	0.9	31,207	1.4
Class total	671,055	28.3	696,839	32.2
Total intermediate	2,372,834	100.0	2,166,921	100.0
Full-size				
Chevrolet	258,902	21.6	238,930	24.4
Pontiac	62,084	5.2	26,929	2.8
Oldsmobile 88	258,293	21.6	228,770	23.5
LeSabre	164,314	13.7	151,555	15.6
Ford	169,253	14.2	119,905	12.3

EXHIBIT 3 (Continued)

Class/Model	1984	Share of Segment	1983	Share of Segment
Tempo	256,532	10.9%	136,148	7.5%
Topaz	73,454	3.1	41,796	2.3
Fairmont	—	0.0	37,521	2.0
Zephyr	—	0.0	11,583	0.6
Reliant	138,154	5.8	157,247	8.6
Aries	111,984	4.7	119,400	6.5
Concord	—	0.0	11,513	0.6
Accord	133,601	5.6	50,402	2.7
Class total	**1,646,568**	**69.4**	**1,300,393**	**70.8**
Compact specialty				
Camaro	202,172	8.5	178,266	9.6
Firebird	101,414	4.3	90,777	4.9
Grand AM	16,751	0.7	—	0.0
Calais	14,881	0.6	—	0.0
Somerset	13,811	0.6	—	0.0
Mustang	138,296	5.8	116,976	6.4
Capri	17,739	0.7	22,708	1.2
Laser	53,131	2.2	11,097	0.6
Daytona	44,717	1.9	8,761	0.5
600 2 Dr.	24,956	1.1	28,593	1.6
LeBaron	98,842	4.2	80,309	4.4
Class total	**726,710**	**30.6**	**537,487**	**29.2**
Total compact	**2,373,278**	**100.0**	**1,837,880**	**100.0**
Intermediate regular				
Celebrity	322,189	13.6	180,627	8.3
Malibu	890	0.0	85,148	3.9
6000	125,823	5.3	92,513	4.3
Bonneville	65,396	2.8	84,122	3.9
Ciera	242,209	10.2	191,720	8.8
Supreme	302,087	12.6	331,179	15.4

Class/Model	1984	Share of Segment	1983	Share of Segment
Century (FWD)	217,042	9.1%	150,280	6.9%
Grand Marquis	143,594	12.0	96,659	9.9
Grand Fury	16,609	1.4	15,101	1.6
Fifth Avenue	94,340	7.9	73,729	7.6
Diplomat	28,623	2.4	22,498	2.3
Total full-size	**1,196,012**	**100.0**	**974,076**	**100.0**
Luxury regular				
Oldsmobile 98	34,284	4.4	119,528	16.5
Olds 98 (FWD)	66,135	8.5	—	0.0
Electra	32,578	4.2	80,106	11.0
Electra (FWD)	51,836	6.6	—	0.0
Cadillac (FWD)	77,117	9.9	—	0.0
Cadillac	118,060	15.0	176,003	24.2
Lincoln	90,869	11.6	59,626	8.2
Class total	**470,879**	**60.2**	**435,263**	**59.9**
Luxury specialty				
Corvette	30,424	3.9	28,144	3.9
Toronado	41,605	5.3	41,791	5.8
Riviera	53,398	6.8	53,346	7.3
Cimarron	18,014	2.3	19,188	2.6
Seville	36,249	4.6	33,522	4.6
Eldorado	70,577	9.1	71,624	9.9
Continental	31,110	4.0	13,691	1.9
Mark	29,496	3.8	28,257	3.9
Imperial	—	0.0	1,237	0.2
Class total	**310,873**	**39.8**	**290,800**	**40.1**
Total luxury	**781,752**	**100.0**	**726,063**	**100.0**
Total domestic	7,951,523	76.6	6,795,299	74.1
Total import	2,438,842	23.4	2,376,056	25.9
Grand total	10,390,365	100.0	9,171,355	100.0

Note: Segmentation is determined by size, price and marketing intent. With some exceptions, once a car bearing that nameplate and platform is placed in a category, it remains in the group as downsizing occurs unless significant changes are made in size or marketing intent. In general, specialty models are sportier, higher priced cars with separate nameplates. High-line versions of regular cars remain with the regular model. The Cougar name replaced the Monarch in 1980–1981, then became the downsized Marquis in 1983. The Cougar XR-7 is a specialty car in 1983. Rabbit and Accord are U.S.-built models only. Supreme and Regal 4-door models breakout estimated in 1983.

Source: Ward's Automobile Yearbook, 1985.

EXHIBIT 4

GM Financial and Operating Summary, 1982–1984
(dollars in millions except per share and hourly amounts)

	1984	1983	1982
Sales and Revenues			
U.S. operations			
Automotive products	$73,053.1	$63,665.0	$47,391.2
Nonautomotive products	2,107.6	1,670.3	2,138.9
Defense and space	1,322.7	826.8	793.8
Computer systems services (since October 18, 1984)	148.7	—	—
Total U.S. operations	76,632.1	66,162.1	50,323.9
Canadian operations	12,581.6	11,232.4	7,972.6
Overseas operations	11,345.5	11,955.5	12,212.8
Elimination of interarea sales and revenues	(16,669.3)	(14,768.4)	(10,483.7)
Total	$82,889.9	$74,581.6	$60,025.6
Worldwide automotive products	$80,499.3	$71,904.7	$56,676.8
Worldwide nonautomotive products	$ 3,390.6	$ 2,676.9	$ 3,348.8
Worldwide factory sales of cars and trucks			
(units in thousands)	8,256	7,769	6,244
Net income			
Amount	$ 4,516.5	$ 3,730.2	$ 962.7
As a percent of sales and revenues	5.4%	5.0%	1.6%
As a percent of stockholders' equity	18.7%	18.0%	5.3%
Attributable to			
$1⅔ par value common stock	$ 4,485.3	$ 3,717.3	$ 949.8
Class E common stock (issued in 1984)	$ 18.7		
Earnings per share of common stocks			
$1⅔ par value common	$14.22	$11.84	$3.09
Class E common (issued in 1984)	$1.03	—	—
Cash dividends per share of common stocks			
$1⅔ par value common	$4.75*	$2.80	$2.40
Class E common (issued in 1984)	$0.09	—	—
Taxes			
U.S., foreign, and other income taxes (credit)	$ 1,805.1	$ 2,223.8	($ 252.2)
Other taxes (principally payroll and property taxes)	3,572.4	2,675.8	2,470.3
Total	$ 5,377.5	$ 4,899.6	$ 2,218.1
Taxes per share of $1⅔ par value common stock	$16.98	$15.61	$7.22
Investment as of December 31			
Cash and marketable securities	$ 8,567.4	$ 6,216.9	$ 3,126.2
Working capital	$ 6,276.7	$ 5,890.8	$ 1,658.1
Stockholders' equity	$24,214.3	$20,766.6	$18,287.1
Book value per share of common stocks:			
$1⅔ par value common	$72.16	$64.88	$57.64
Class E common (issued in 1984)	$36.08	—	—
Number of Stockholders as of December 31			
(in thousands)			
$1⅔ par value common and preferred	957	998	1,050
Class E common	623	—	—

EXHIBIT 4 (Continued)

Financials By Segment, 1982–1984
(dollars in millions)

	United States	Canada	Europe	Latin America	All Other	Total*
1984						
Net sales and revenues						
Outside	$69,355.6	$ 4,411.6	$6,735.7	$1,642.0	$1,745.0	$83,889.9
Interarea	7,276.5	8,170.0	242.2	823.6	401.7	—
Total net sales and revenues	$76,632.1	$12,581.6	$6,977.9	$2,465.6	$2,146.7	$83,889.9
Net income (loss)	$ 3,872.0	$ 762.2	$291.1	$ 94.4	$ 61.5	$ 4,516.5
Total assets	$41,692.7	$ 2,833.5	$4,425.7	$2,874.0	$ 932.0	$52,144.9
Net assets	$22,149.7	$ 1,628.9	($ 439.2)	$1,016.7	$ 41.7	$24,214.3
Average number of employees (in thousands)	511	41	122	49	25	748
1983						
Net sales						
Outside	$59,668.7	$ 3,866.4	$7,761.7	$1,742.7	$1,542.1	$74,581.6
Interarea	6,493.4	7,366.0	208.6	653.1	295.4	—
Total net sales	$66,162.1	$11,232.4	$7,970.3	$2,395.8	$1,837.5	$74,581.6
Net income (loss)	$ 3,469.0	$ 592.3	($ 228.3)	($ 15.0)	($ 91.1)	$ 3,730.2
Total assets	$34,670.4	$ 2,385.5	$5,379.1	$2,834.3	$ 813.9	$45,694.5
Net assets	$18,749.3	$ 1,332.9	($ 120.5)	$ 919.6	$ 8.9	$20,766.6
Average number of employees (in thousands)	463	39	123	41	25	691
1982						
Net sales						
Outside	$45,650.1	$ 2,621.9	$7,150.5	$2,699.5	$1,903.6	$60,025.6
Interarea	4,673.8	5,350.7	234.3	310.2	192.9	—
Total net sales	$50,323.9	$ 7,972.6	$7,384.8	$3,009.7	$2,096.5	$60,025.6
Net income (loss)	$ 1,079.3	($ 33.5)	$ 6.2	($ 16.5)	($ 63.2)	$ 962.7
Total assets	$29,227.4	$ 2,299.0	$5,952.3	$2,973.3	$1,063.5	$41,397.8
Net assets	$15,756.0	$ 774.7	$ 803.3	$ 894.3	$ 170.7	$18,287.1
Average number of employees (in thousands)	441	34	114	38	30	657

* After elimination of interarea transactions.

Source: General Motors Corporation, *Annual Report*, 1984.

EXHIBIT 4 (Continued)

Summary Consolidated Balance Sheet, December 31, 1984 and 1983
(dollars in millions except per share amounts)

	1984	1983
Assets		
Current assets		
Total cash and marketable securities	8,567.4	6,216.9
Accounts and notes receivable	7,357.9	6,964.2
Inventories (less allowances)	7,359.7	6,621.5
Prepaid expenses and deferred income taxes	428.3	997.2
Total current assets	23,713.3	20,799.8
Equity in net assets of nonconsolidated subsidiaries and associates	4,603.0	4,450.8
Other investments and miscellaneous assets, (net)	2,344.4	1,221.2
Common stocks held for incentive program	144.2	56.3
Property		
Real estate, plants, and equipment—at cost	39,354.1	37,777.8
Less: Accumulated depreciation	21,649.8	20,116.8
Special tools, at cost (less amortization)	1,697.2	1,504.1
Total property	19,401.5	19,165.1
Intangible assets, at cost (less amortization)	1,938.5	1.3
Total assets	$52,144.9	$45,694.5
Liabilities and stockholders' equity		
Total current liabilities	17,436.6	14,909.0
Long-term debt	2,417.4	3,137.2
Capitalized leases	355.5	1,384.6
Other liabilities	1,749.2	1,798.9
Stockholders' equity		
Preferred stocks	255.6	283.6
Common stocks		
$1⅔ par value (issued, 317,504,133 and 315,711,299 shares)	529.2	526.2
Class E (issued, 29,082,382 shares in 1984)	2.9	—
Capital surplus (principally additional paid-in capital)	3,347.8	2,136.8
Net income retained for use in the business	20,796.6	18,390.5
Accumulated foreign currency translation and other adjustments	(717.8)	(570.5)
Total stockholders' equity	24,214.3	20,766.6
Total liabilities and stockholders' equity	$52,144.9	$45,694.5

Reference should be made to notes on pages 23 through 30 provided in company's annual report. Certain amounts for 1983 have been reclassified to conform with 1984 classifications.

Source: General Motors Corporation, *Annual Report,* 1984.

3-11

ZAYRE CORPORATION (A)

Discount retailing for broad ranges of nonfoods merchandise really began in the 1950s. The first stores—like Arlan's, Two Guys from Harrison, Kings, and J. M. Fields—moved into cheap vacated warehouse or mill spaces. Early discounters tended to be individual entrepreneurs with an intuitive sense of the new U.S. marketplace. Family sizes were exploding in the postwar baby boom; U.S. manufacturing efficiencies were creating millions of new jobs; the purchasing power of the working and middle classes had ballooned; national advertising media were stimulating widespread brand recognition and standardized tastes; and the automobile facilitated mobility, suburbanization, and mass purchasing on a scale never possible before. In 1956 Zayre Corporation became the first company to exploit these trends by building a complete newly constructed retail discount store and chain specially designed for self-service sales of general merchandise.

DISCOUNTERS TAKE OVER

The large department stores, which were then the dominant form of retail merchandising, ignored discounters at first. Most responded by upgrading their locations, displays, and services—and raising margins to cover the added costs. The three great national department store chains each reacted differently. Sears undertook an awesome branch rollout into the suburbs, aimed at the price-conscious

Case copyright © 1989 by James Brian Quinn. Research associate—Penny C. Paquette. Research assistant—Barbara Dixon.

The generous cooperation of the Zayre Corporation is gratefully acknowledged.

middle income market. J. C. Penney followed suit on a later and smaller scale. Montgomery Ward, anticipating a postwar recession, froze its posture, hoarded cash, and went into decline. In the early-to-mid-1960s S. S. Kresge and Woolworth's abandoned their early variety-store format (open counters, small items in jumbled displays) to build the Kmart and Woolco chains with a large range of merchandise and more sophisticated presentation. And discount sales boomed:

YEAR	NUMBER OF STORES	DISCOUNT SALES
1960	1,329	$ 2 billion
1970	5,000	19 billion
1980	8,300	45 billion
1984	8,600	56 billion

Discounters' 1984 sales represented 48% of all retail general merchandising sales. While there were several major shakeouts on the way, the top seven chains increasingly concentrated their share of the market from $11 billion in 1974, to $21 billion in 1978, to $34 billion in 1983. In New England, discounting accounted for an incredible 72% of full-line general merchandise sales, with five of the nation's largest 15 discounters headquartered there. Many of the top names of expansionary 1970s had essentially disappeared—including Woolco, Grants, Korvettes, Mammoth Marts, Two Guys, and Kings. Zayre Corp. had not only survived the rugged shakeout which had occurred, but had enjoyed record breaking growth in the early 1980s, and was positioning itself for the rigorous challenges of the late 1980s. What were the key events in Zayre's recent history? And what should its future strategy be?

ENTREPRENEURIAL TIMES

Mr. Stanley Feldberg, Zayre's first CEO, oversaw his company's growth from its 1950s birth to sales of $1.4 billion in 1978. By then there were 251 Zayre discount stores in major metropolitan areas, mainly east of the Mississippi. Like the discount field itself, Zayre had developed rapidly under the entrepreneurial styles of its founders, mostly Feldberg family members. (See organization chart.) The company had been privately held until it went public in 1962, and was still dominated by the founding group and their scions in the late 1970s. Together they held approximately 30% of Zayre's stock. The organization structure was both a cause and effect of Zayre's growth and management style. In the words of Mr. Stanley Feldberg,

> The original founders had always governed themselves as equal partners, and their successors had been groomed to think the same way. People were careful not to let a single person or position dominate the scene. It was often difficult to get a decision implemented in one area, if the head of that area disagreed. There tended to be management by committee and indeed management by consensus. One of the offshoots of this style was that there was not as much emphasis on profitability or "bottom line" as you might have found elsewhere. Profitability was important but could be sacrificed in the short run while you were seeking expansion opportunities.

Expansion Plans and Complications

Around 1969, Zayre went through a McKinsey & Co. organizational study in concert with a 5 year plan to double its stores (from 125 to 250) and its total volume (from $500 million to $1 billion). McKinsey suggested a much expanded executive force and a restructuring to increase Zayre's managerial depth and diversity. Zayre built up its organization rapidly in anticipation of its planned growth, causing a corresponding short-term buildup in overheads. While staying in its traditional market niches, Zayre attempted to decentralize the organization more extensively on a regional basis. Instead of reporting directly to headquarters, district managers began to report to six regional managers, who had their own staffs. These were very large businesses, with some 40–50 stores reporting to each regional manager. While Store Operations decentralized, Merchandising and Real Estate activities stayed centralized. (See organization chart.) And problems soon developed. Said Mr. Stanley Feldberg,

> Frankly, the Merchandising Department had not kept up with our changing customers of the 1960s. We had attempted to keep *absolute* price levels from increasing despite a mild inflation. It finally became impossible to do this and not lose quality in our merchandise lines at the very time our customers' capacity to buy higher quality was steadily growing. We kept advertising prices almost exclusively. In a practice that set my teeth on edge, we sometimes advertised specials with no more than a few days supply on hand to service customers. This brought customers in the door, and kept the store from losing too much on the margins of sale merchandise. But it alienated people who had expected a good buy and couldn't find it.

The merchandising problem was compounded by the fact that Zayre had started to build bigger 80,000 square foot stores (versus 65,000) and to move into

Zayre Corporation Organization Chart Mid-1976

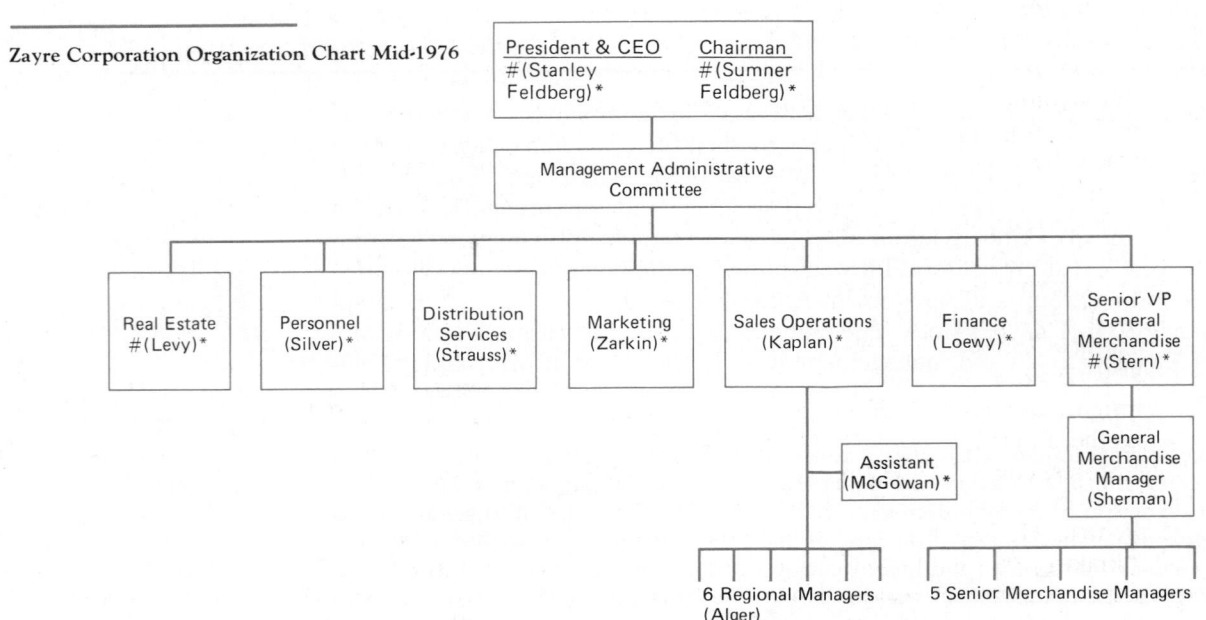

Family members.
* Member Management Administration Committee.

Source: *Company records.*

suburban areas. Zayre's product lines had to be spread over a larger physical area, creating the impression of thinner inventory coverage. Merchandising techniques of piling goods in aisle bins for quick sale—which had worked so well in lower income areas—failed in the more exclusive suburbs. Ads targeted solely at price didn't bring customers into these stores so readily. And new stores which had been budgeted for $3\frac{1}{2}$ to $4 million volumes, only brought in $1.5—$2 million. Meanwhile Kmart was opening stores budgeted for $9 million sales volumes and had Kresge's massive capital resources to help stock the stores and support them with advertising.

As one executive said, "All this killed our store productivity. As productivity declined, there wasn't enough income to keep the stores current. So we lost more sales. And so on. We wanted the stores to look a bit spartan, but soon our parking lots had potholes, maintenance had to be delayed, roofs began to leak, merchandise coverage dropped even more. Top management was deeply aware of the problem, but it was awfully hard to break out. Then along came the oil crisis and the 1974–1975 inflation-recession—fiscal 1975 (calendar 1974) earnings dropped to only $835,000."

Mr. Stanley Feldberg amplified, "As we disappointed customers at a merchandise level, store sales began to dry up, but overhead percentages began to escalate—not uncontrollably, but enough to hurt badly. Our first response was to cut back expenses at the stores, cleaning services, maintenance, even capital and investment payrolls. We cut back support services at home office too. But profits still dropped and we got into a vicious circle where it got even harder to correct things."

Race Tracks and Experiments

From this low point began one of the greatest turnarounds in retailing history. Zayre's top managers took a long view and began some experiments designed to reposition its stores for the future. They called in a consultant, Alton Doody, who said that while the Zayre Stores' format had been adequate for the 1960s, it was not well tuned to the future. In 1975 Stanley and Sumner Feldberg authorized a series of experimental layouts, presentations, display changes (etc.) that became known as the "Zayre '75" program. Mr. Doody brought in the concept of a "race track aisle" that carried the customers rapidly around the store to various departments. Each department was arranged around this aisle with "windows" on the aisle and "vistas" to invite the customer into the department. And new display techniques were developed to let each department put the "best foot forward" for its merchandise. Some experiments worked; others did not. "Zayre '75" was followed by another series of experiments in "Zayre '76" and again later in "Zayre '77." Sumner and Stanley Feldberg personally supported all these experiments, but they still had to be carried out with limited capital because of tight operating margins.

1976 brought several other major events. First, Zayre returned to stronger profitability, as the oil crisis receded. Second, Mr. Malcolm Sherman, later president of Zayre Stores, combined several features of the 1975–1976 experiments in some Indianapolis stores, along with a more complete inventory showing adapted to the local clientele. He later said, "I put together everything in this experiment I could without making capital demands." And store sales shot upward in this "Indy 1976" experiment. Another experiment in 1977 called the "loop design" led customers around its test stores—rather than through the central aisles—with good effect. And so on. But third, and perhaps most importantly, in 1975 Stanley and Sumner Feldberg had begun the search for a CEO to carry Zayre into the 1990s. And for the first time Zayre was looking seriously outside the family's ranks.

After an intensive three-year search Mr. Maurice Segall joined Zayre Corp. as its first nonfamily CEO in February 1978. Mr. Segall was a trained economist who had started his career as chief economist and director of planning and organization at Steinbergs, a large food supermarket operation headquartered in Montreal. He later became director of operations for the Treasure Island Stores chain of J. C. Penney, and finally (1974–1978) president of American Express' Credit and Card Division, where he is widely credited with tripling that organization's volume in a series of highly entrepreneurial and insightful moves. Mr. Segall said, "Many people thought I was crazy to go into a family-dominated situation in a difficult industry like retail discounting. But I had gotten to know Stanley and Sumner Feldberg very well over the last couple years. I knew they were people of quality and high integrity who would follow through on all commitments made to me—and they would not second-guess me. And frankly, while Zayre was a real challenge, I thought it had very high potentials for the future."

Mr. Segall's five-year contract called for a base salary of $300,000 a year plus substantial bonuses if he increased net income per share from continuing operations at rates of 10–20% a year in the first three years and 7.5–15% a year in the last two years. It also provided for a signing bonus of $200,000 in the first year, plus deferred compensation of $500,000. In an interview with *Chain Store Age Executive* Mr. Segall said, "The most successful retail executives are people with a real desire for continuing challenge. There are few companies where they can receive such stimulation year in and year out. . . . The people who have what it takes, the people who thrive on that challenge, are real risk takers. There are few industries other than retailing which offer these people such opportunities."[1]

First Steps

The Board had placed no constraints or set any specific goals for its new CEO. Mr. Segall immediately began a three-month series of travels around to all the stores. Knowing he would be gone constantly, he had kept his family home in Long Island, so his wife would have a familiar environment and close friends nearby while he traveled. In May 1978, Mr. Segall came back to Sumner and Stanley Feldberg and said, "Now I know what I have to do. I like all the experiments. But I want to stop the experiments, put them together, and do the chain."

There were many things that most agreed were crucial to getting Zayre stores back onto their growth curve again. Various executives and outside sources contributed the following composite view:

1. Because of the economic constraints and the corresponding morale problems of the cutback years, many of the stores had become unattractive and some were not well managed at the local level. Frequently, merchandise was not kept neatly arranged. In some cases store cleanliness was even a problem. Many stores did not have complete stock positions, and there was a lot of bickering between the field operations people and the home-office merchants. "When anything was wrong, some other party always seemed at fault."

2. Physically, many stores were in difficult shape. There were numerous stores with leaky roofs and peeling wallboard and plaster. Some of the store fronts

were run down and display fixtures were broken or in ill repair. Even stores which had been refurbished were often not properly maintained because of capital constraints. And it would cost millions to bring the chain up to a desired standard.

3. While Zayre had an outstanding financial control system, merchandising control had been a major problem. Merchandising had been centrally managed in detail. Stocking plans for each store were close to identical, even though store sizes and locations varied significantly. Zayre's merchandising group used mainly a "push" system of trying to get good buys on desired merchandise and then pushing goods out through the stores with a standardized plan. This approach had worked well enough when the chain was small, but it began to break down when the company had a complex group of some 250 stores.

4. Many of the stores' presentation techniques in terms of merchandise displays, lighting intensity, wall colors and floor coverings, were not up to date. Long checkout lines and service people not being available to assist on the floors were serious problems. Said one long time Zayre executive, "boxes often littered the floor, and you could look at shelves and see gaps in the merchandise lines. A facelift was necessary both in physical terms and in terms of the morale of employees who had been discouraged during the tight financial period by these surroundings."

Everything at Once

While these were widely recognized issues, action had been difficult to take because of both capital and organizational constraints. Mr. Segall said,

> First, it was evident we had to fix up our physical plant and keep it in shape. We needed enormous amounts of money to do the job. But it's not sufficient just to fix up a store. There are a lot of nice stores that go out of business. You have to update your marketing and advertising for that store, and you have to make sure you get the right merchandise in that store and maintain its stocks. None of this works without good people. The problem is you can't do it one step at a time. This chain had 250 stores, and it would take a lifetime to do it that way.
>
> But we had to do it right. And we didn't have the luxury of time. A key point in all this was to zero in on what our mission was and what our customer definition was. We agreed we should not change the definition of our target customer (the working class customer looking for good value), but would try to get to that customer more effectively. We were not going to suddenly become an upper middle class discount store.

Between May and September 1978, Mr. Segall—and a few people (notably Malcolm Sherman and Bob Alger) he had identified for their future executive potentials—developed a strategy called the Marketing Development Program (MDP) to present to the Board in September of that year. Before that meeting Mr. Segall decided to reorganize the entire field structure of Zayre Stores. He later said,

> You have to send some messages, and I decided the then executive vice president of Zayre Stores was not the right person to carry this out. There were any number of good people I could have hired from outside. But I decided to look around carefully inside the company and identified Bob Alger (age 39) as the right person for the job.

We had long discussions about what needed to be done, but I wanted Alger to find the players. Deciding that the whole thing should be done over one weekend, I asked Bob Alger, the V.P. of Personnel, and two promising young executive protégés of Mr. Alger to lock themselves in their hotel rooms at the Logan Hilton for three days and come out with names of all the new district and zone managers for the Zayre chain. It was done in three days without anyone knowing it. Then I asked Mr. Sherman and Mr. Zarkin to develop the kinds of merchandising and advertising strategies we had discussed. All this went into the fall Board presentation.

The proposal asked for $30 million (later $40 million) for a remodeling and updating program and another $25 million for an electronic point-of-sale (EPOS) program to convert all the cash registers and point of sale controls to a computer basis. Mr. Segall later said, "It was a bet-your-company strategy. It was either going to work and be successful, or it would drive us into bankruptcy." Exhibits 1 through 4 set forth some of the key background data for this 1978 strategy meeting.

Zayre Stores did not want to change its basic concept. Zayre was to remain a neighborhood, convenience, self-selection, general merchandise, discount department store chain. Its target customer was the lower part of the middle income class and the upper part of the lower income class—the great working class of America.

Other Zayre Operations

In 1976, Sumner Feldberg had been very impressed by the concept of off-price retailing which he saw at the then young ($120 million volume) Marshall's chain. Off-price stores sold quality brand-name merchandise at 20–60% below regular list prices. Zayre tried to buy Marshall's but was outbid by Melville's. Consequently Mr. Feldberg rapidly developed a similar concept for Zayre which became the T. J. Maxx chain, with ten stores in calendar 1977. T. J. Maxx's target was the middle-income customer who wanted a good value at a good price. It appealed to the female homemaker buying for a whole family. As *Forbes* said, "The chain catered to people who were snobby enough to want brand names, but didn't want to pay the full price for them."[2] T. J. Maxx carried brands like Calvin Klein, Gloria Vanderbilt, and Liz Claiborne for women; Arrow, Van Heusen, and Ralph Lauren for men; Carter's, Healthtex, and Izod for kids; and a wide selection of branded linens, towels, and housewares. T. J. Maxx stores operated in smaller (25,000 square foot) units in urban and suburban shopping malls. And like most start ups it had lost money in the first few years of operations.

Zayre's other off-price chain was Hit or Miss (H or M), originally acquired as a 10-store Boston chain in 1970, which grew to 17 units by year end. After a promising start, Hit or Miss had begun to top out in the mid-1970s. *Chain Store Age,* said, "In its first eight years, Hit or Miss had become a less than successful teenagers' and low-end girls' apparel chain which emphasized teeny bopper fads, accessories, and fringes."[3] In this very competitive market, H or M had operated 4,000 ft^2 shops in less expensive suburban strip malls where overheads were lower. Its format had been spartan, with bright exposed fluorescent lamps, lots of merchandise "up front" on racks, and heavy use of self-service promotional signage. Although by 1978, H or M was targeted more towards the price-conscious young woman buying for herself, in the words of *Chain Store Age* "Hit or Miss was missing more than hitting" and was a net money loser for the Zayre Corporation." Although its profitability figures were not broken out in Zayre's published statements, observers said H or M's problems were getting worse in the late 1970s.

The 1978 Competition

The major competitors of Zayre were positioned and moving roughly in the following directions in 1977–1978. Traditional department stores had moved to "top-of-the-line" positions in suburban areas or refurbished central cities—or by and large they had failed.

Sears, Roebuck: With sales of $17.2 billion and a 6.23% market share of U.S. general merchandise sales in 1977, Sears was the largest of the major chains. Its *Annual Report* in 1977 stated that its mission was "to provide quality merchandise at competitive prices across the nation." Its current sales distribution was 71% through store outlets, 20% catalogue sales, and 9% other. In the late 1960s Sears moved upscale to the middle- to upper-middle-income market vacated by the big full-line department stores. Sears anchored its big (up to 200,000 ft^2) full-line stores in the more expensive malls and backed its presentations with a greater number of service personnel than most of its chain competitors.[4] Part of the upscale move was toward fashion goods which some thought did not fit too well with Sears' strong (65% of sales) competitive hard goods image.[5] Sears had a strong private-label position especially in white goods, and with its high volume Sears could have quality merchandise made inexpensively with the special features it desired.

By 1978 Sears had 366 full-line (200,000 ft^2) stores, 371 semi-full-line (78,500 ft^2) stores, and 135 hard line (24,000 ft^2) outlets. Sears also held significant equity in some of its suppliers, and owned 49.9% of a Canadian chain, which had sales of $2 billion. And Allstate insurance contributed some $400 million to profits. Its catalogue sales were 55% from in-store centers; only 45% were handled by telephone or through free-standing catalogue stores.

Kmart: The second largest chain was Kmart with $9.9 billion in sales, 55% from hard goods and 45% soft lines. Kmart had outlets in 257 of the 275 SMAs of the U.S. Of its 1,395 stores, 795 had been built in the last five years and located mainly in high-growth suburban areas and smaller industrial or agriculturally based cities. Kmart used a one-story format in four basic store types (84,000, 68,000, 55,000, and 45,000 ft^2 formats). These could be "freestanding" stores—not necessarily tied into a shopping center—which could locate in any convenient, available space even in less populated rural or older, high-density city markets as well as in the suburbs. Kmart had grown at 20% per year mainly by opening new stores. Kmart had been S. S. Kresge's vehicle for diversifying out of the maturing variety store business in the 1960s. By 1977 Kmart accounted for 95% of Kresge's sales, and the parent had changed its own name.

J. C. Penney: Nearby was J. C. Penney with its $9.4 billion in sales, 59% from full-line stores, and 23% from soft line stores. In 1977 it had 460 full line stores (averaging 88,000 ft^2) mainly in shopping centers of major metropolitan markets. Its 1,226 soft line stores (average 12,000 ft^2) tended to be in the downtown areas of medium sized cities or the "main streets" of smaller communities, where J. C. Penney had built its reputation for reliable quality at a good price. In 1977 its expansion plans were focused around its full-line stores, with modernization and some relocation of its soft line outlets. Penney had recently begun a push toward higher profitability by adding more fashionware to its apparel lines and emphasizing home furnishings to combat the competition it faced from department stores in its shopping center locations.[6] Its other operations included 37 freestanding discount stores (the Treasury Stores) which averaged 97,000 ft^2 and were not very successful in 1977. Penney also had 229 drug store outlets (8,000 ft^2) which were performing adequately, a profitable $1 billion catalogue business, and a small insurance business which it was just beginning to integrate into its retail outlets.

Wal-Mart: A small but fast-growing regional chain was Wal-Mart with $900 million in sales, 68% in hard goods. Wal-Mart had 195 stores in a ten-state area (Texas to North Central states) located within 400 miles of its headquarters and distribution center. Its average store size was 43,000 ft^2, ranging from 30,000 to 60,000 ft^2. Wal-Mart was building 30 to 40 new stores a year in standardized formats built around 36 departments. Wal-Mart stressed rock-bottom priced staple goods and emphasized (68% of sales) its hard goods line.[7] Wal-Mart used a "big frog in little pond" philosophy, preferring to be the largest non-food retailer in the smaller 25,000–30,000-person communities. It targeted county seats where it often edged out older J. C. Penney stores by offering a wider selection with more hard goods.[8] Among discounters, department stores, and variety stores, *Forbes* ranked Wal-Mart first over the past five years in average ROE, return on invested capital, sales growth, and earnings growth. In its 1978 *Annual Report* CEO Sam Walton said the secret of success was "nothing more than bringing together men and women who are completely dedicated to their jobs, their company and their communities."

A New Strategy

Mr. Segall was deeply aware of these repositionings as well as the new modes of retailing that were beginning to emerge—especially those associated with direct-mail, "off-price" merchandising, the new wholesale clubs being formed, and the breakdown of traditional retailing structures (i.e., drugs, food supermarkets, merchandise chains) toward "mixed-line" merchandising. He was particularly concerned about the potential impact of the new electronics and communications technologies on retailing. But he had to deal with these from the limited resource base Zayre then had.

QUESTIONS

1. What should the early 1980s strategy of Zayre Corporation be? What are the critical action sequences?
2. How can Zayre acquire the capital needed for these moves?
3. How should Zayre be reorganized?
4. What other implementing actions must go along with these strategic changes?

Expense Analysis—Percent of Sales
(excluding lease or franchised departments)

	Fiscal 1976		Fiscal 1977	
	Cornell Excl. Zayre	Zayre	Cornell Excl. Zayre	Zayre
Total payroll	12.40%	12.76%	12.79%	12.72%
Supplies	0.75	0.87	0.66	0.91
Communications	0.23	0.78	0.25	0.40
Travel	0.21	0.38	0.20	0.39
Services purchased	0.74	0.50	0.67	0.52
Advertising	2.43	2.93	2.66	3.18
Taxes and licenses	1.17	1.33	1.12	1.35
Utilities	1.13	1.39	1.13	1.35
Insurance	0.57	0.70	0.66	0.71
Property rentals	3.21	3.36	3.09	3.56
Equipment rentals	0.35	0.31	0.33	0.30
Depreciation and amortization	0.85	1.13	0.76	1.00
Repair and maintenance	0.48	0.99	0.53	1.05
Donations	0.01	0.02	0.02	0.02
Professional services	0.24	0.17	0.22	0.18
Unclassified	1.05	1.08	1.09	1.11
Credits and allowances	(0.40)	(0.01)	(0.22)	—
Total expense	25.44%	28.39%	25.96%	28.75%

Source: Company records and analyses provided during interview.

Gross Margin, Expense, and Earnings Percent of Sales
(excluding leased or franchised departments)

	Fiscal 1976		Fiscal 1977	
	Cornell Excl. Zayre	Zayre	Cornell Excl. Zayre	Zayre
Gross margin	28.52%	30.15%	28.86%	30.61%
Leased department income	0.80	0.59	0.92	0.65
Gross income	29.32	30.74	29.78	31.26
Total expense	25.44	28.39	25.96	28.75
Net operating profit	3.88	2.35	3.83	2.51
Other income or deductions	(0.23)	(0.80)	(0.06)	(0.69)
Earnings before income taxes	3.65	1.55	3.77	1.82
Federal and state income taxes	1.84	0.78	1.84	0.92
Net earnings after taxes	1.81%	0.77%	1.93%	0.90%

Source: Company records and analysis provided during interviews.

1011

EXHIBIT 2
Zayre Corporation: Location of Operations, January 1978

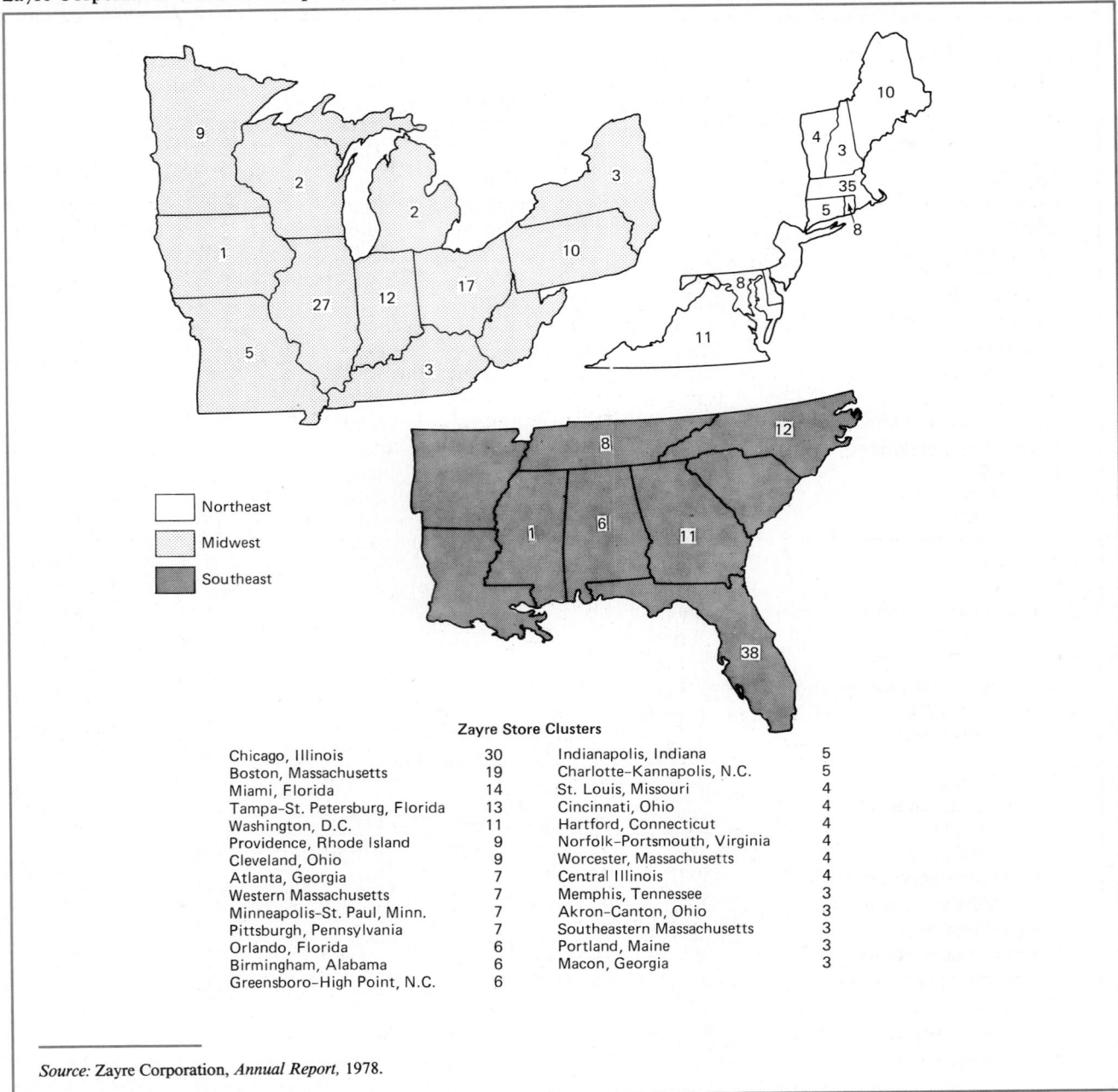

Zayre Store Clusters

Chicago, Illinois	30	Indianapolis, Indiana	5
Boston, Massachusetts	19	Charlotte-Kannapolis, N.C.	5
Miami, Florida	14	St. Louis, Missouri	4
Tampa-St. Petersburg, Florida	13	Cincinnati, Ohio	4
Washington, D.C.	11	Hartford, Connecticut	4
Providence, Rhode Island	9	Norfolk-Portsmouth, Virginia	4
Cleveland, Ohio	9	Worcester, Massachusetts	4
Atlanta, Georgia	7	Central Illinois	4
Western Massachusetts	7	Memphis, Tennessee	3
Minneapolis-St. Paul, Minn.	7	Akron-Canton, Ohio	3
Pittsburgh, Pennsylvania	7	Southeastern Massachusetts	3
Orlando, Florida	6	Portland, Maine	3
Birmingham, Alabama	6	Macon, Georgia	3
Greensboro-High Point, N.C.	6		

Source: Zayre Corporation, *Annual Report,* 1978.

EXHIBIT 3
Zayre Corporation Financials,* 1974–1979

Statement of Consolidated Earnings
($ millions)

	1979	1978	1977	1976	1975	1974
Net sales	$1,394.1	$1,261.3	$1,160.6	$1,084.0	$1.045.5	$996.4
Cost of sales	1,076.7	987.3	907.9	850.7	827.2	777.7
Gross profit	317.5	274.0	252.7	233.3	218.4	218.7
Operating expense	271.5	234.5	212.8	208.1	201.4	190.8
Interest expense	20.0	17.7	18.3	11.1	16.1	12.1
Income before tax	26.9	21.8	21.5	14.1	0.9	15.8
Federal income tax	12.9	10.8	11.3	7.2	0.2	7.2
Net income	$ 14.0	$ 11.0	$ 10.2	$ 4.9	$ 0.8	$ 9.1

Consolidated Balance Sheet
($ millions)

	1979	1978	1977	1976	1975	1974
ASSETS						
Cash	$ 23.0	$ 23.5	$ 25.9	$ 26.1	$ 38.7	$ 36.6
Accounts receivable	5.5	4.7	4.5	2.8	3.6	5.6
Inventories	254.0	242.3	211.0	187.8	177.6	191.5
Other current assets	19.9	17.9	16.8	15.0	13.6	3.9
Total current assets	302.4	288.5	258.2	231.6	233.5	237.6
Net fixed assets	173.8	168.2	96.0	102.5	112.0	118.5
Total assets	$476.2	$456.8	$354.2	$334.1	$345.4	$356.1
LIABILITIES						
Current installment, long-term debt	$ 9.2	$ 10.0	$ 11.4	$ 9.8	$ 13.7	$ 9.3
Accounts payable	73.3	76.1	57.6	52.0	60.4	70.6
Accrued expenses, taxes, etc.	62.5	53.7	44.2	35.8	30.5	31.0
Total current liabilities	145.1	139.8	113.1	97.6	104.6	110.9
Long-term debt	188.6	190.0	115.5	122.0	131.3	136.6
Stockholders' equity	142.5	128.0	125.5	114.5	109.5	108.7
Total liabilities and equity	$476.2	$456.8	$354.2	$334.1	$345.4	$356.1

* Fiscal year ends January of year designated, refers to operations of preceding calendar year.

Source: Company records.

EXHIBIT 3 (Continued)

Operating Results of the Zayre Company by Its Major Segments, 1978–1979
(amounts in thousands)

	January 27, 1979[a]			January 28, 1978[a]		
	Consolidated	Discount Dept. Stores	Specialty Stores	Consolidated	Discount Dept. Stores	Specialty Stores
Sales and operating revenues	$1,394,109	$1,222,900	$171,209	$1,261,301	$1,141,422	$119,879
Operating income	$ 46,778	$ 38,630	$ 8,148	$ 38,190	$ 33,542	$ 4,648
General corporate expense	7,941			6,695		
Interest expense	11,913			9,653		
Total income before income taxes	$ 26,924			$ 21,842		
Identifiable assets	$ 476,243	$ 401,376[b]	$38,214[b]	$ 456,754	$ 395,561[b]	$ 25,656[b]
Depreciation and amortization	$ 18,941	$ 17,738	$ 1,203	$ 17,561	$ 16,678	$ 883
Capital expenditures	$ 21,174	$ 17,108	$ 4,066	$ 10,536	$ 5,793	$ 4,743

[a] Includes the effect of SFAS 13. "Accounting for Leases." The prior year amounts have been restated accordingly. For further information see notes in company's annual report.
[b] Identifiable assets are those assets of the Company associated with an industry segment and do not include cash and marketable securities.
Source: Zayre Corporation, *Annual Report,* 1978.

EXHIBIT 4
Zayre Corporation 1978 Number of Retail Establishments in Operation

	Reported in January of Year Indicated					
	1965	1970	1975	1976	1977	1978
Zayre (discount dept. store)	72	153	258	254	255	252
Hit or Miss (apparel)			62	87	118	173
T J. Maxx (off price)						10
On Stage/Nugent's/Bell (apparel)	43	48	36	34	36	31
Beaconway (fabrics)		7	46	44	42	34
Gasoline stations	2	37	95	95	95	7
Shoppers City (food and nonfood supermarkets)		8	10	10	10	9
Spree! (discount toy stores)			6	5		

Source: Zayre Corporation, *Annual Report,* 1965, 1970, 1975–1978.

Merchandising involves the entire group of decisions and tasks involved in determining what merchandise is offered, acquiring it, and having it available in the right assortments at the right places to maximize the store's marketing objectives. In many retail operations merchandising includes the functions of buying, receiving, marketing, and handling all merchandise as well as controlling inventory levels and mixes in the stores. In some large or complex chains, some of these activities may be split off as specialized functions or be decentralized regionally.

Buying is a major line activity in retailing. Buying decisions include what merchandise should be purchased, in what quantities, at what prices, under what terms, and when it should be purchased and received. In some stores the buyer also determines prices, markups, markdowns, and closeouts and plans and coordinates a department's special sales. Buying can be organized according to the class of merchandise purchased, store type, or location served. In most department stores buyers are in charge of all merchandising for their particular departments as well as directing the sales force in these departments. In some decentralized operations, buying and local sales force management may be separated.

Operations include all those activities necessary to maintain the quality and appearance of the physical facilities of the enterprise. In some highly decentralized retail concerns, these activities as well as supervision and control of local salespeople and inventory handling functions are the responsibility of Operations. Service and support activities locally may report either to Operations or directly to other centralized line or administrative functions.

Sales is the face-to-face presentation of the product to the customer and the first recording of that transaction on the store's books through the cash register, sales slip, or electronic charge system. In some cases salespeople report to the buying or merchandise heads; in others they are separated from these functions and report either through Operations or a centralized sales unit.

Promotion generally includes advertising, publicity, displaying of merchandise, and any tactics (other than merchandise selection and pricing) which will induce profitable sales volume. Special attraction techniques like store signs, catalogues, premiums, trading stamps, and nonrecurring interest breaks are considered promotions. Store layout, design, traffic flow planning, rack displays, wall and floor coloring, lighting presentations, and so on are important aspects of in-store promotion which clearly impact the effectiveness of all other line activities.

3-12

MOUNTBATTEN AND INDIA

Louis Francis Albert Victor Nicholas Mountbatten, Viscount of Burma, was, at forty-six, one of the most famous men in England. He was a big man, over six feet tall, but not a trace of flab hung from his zealously exercised waistline. . . . Mountbatten knew perfectly well why he had been summoned to London. Since his return from his post as Supreme Allied Commander Southeast Asia, he had been a frequent visitor to Downing Street as a consultant on the affairs of the Asian nations that had fallen under S.E.A.C.'s command. On his last visit, however, the Prime Minister's questions had quickly focused on India, a nation that had not been a part of [Mountbatten's] theater of operations. The young admiral had suddenly had "a very nasty, very uneasy feeling." His premonition had been justified. Attlee intended to name him Viceroy of India. The viceroy's was the most important post in the Empire, the office from which a long succession of Englishmen had held domain over the destinies of a fifth of mankind. Mountbatten's task, however, would not be to rule India from that office. His assignment would be one of the most painful an Englishman could be asked to undertake—to give it up.

A HISTORIC TRAP

Mountbatten wanted no part of the job. He entirely endorsed the idea that the time had come for Britain to leave India, but his heart rebelled at the thought that he would be called on to sever the ancient links binding England and the bulwark of her empire. To discourage Attlee, he had produced a whole series of demands, major and minor, from the number of secretaries he must be allowed to take with him, to the make of the aircraft, the York MW-102 which had carried him around the world as Supreme Commander Southeast Asia, which would be placed at his disposal. The admiral still hoped somehow to resist Attlee's efforts to force the Indian assignment on him. . . .

There was much more to Mountbatten than his [impeccable] public image reflected; the decorations on his naval uniform were proof of that. The public might consider him a pillar of the Establishment, but the Establishment's members themselves tended to regard Mountbatten and his wife as dangerous radicals. His command in Southeast Asia had given him a vast knowledge of Asian nationalist movements, and there were few Englishmen who could match it. He had dealt with the supporters of Ho Chi Minh in Indochina, Sukharno in Indonesia, Aung San in Burma, Chinese Communists in Malaya, unruly trade unionists in Singapore. Realizing that they represented Asia's future, he had sought accommodations with them rather than try to suppress them as his staff and the Allies had urged. The nationalist movement with which he would have to deal if he went to India was the oldest and most unusual of them all. In a quarter of a century of inspired agitation and protest, its leadership had forced history's greatest empire to the decision that Attlee's party had taken to quit India in good time rather than to be driven out by forces of history and rebellion.

The Sublime Paradox

The Indian situation, the Prime Minister began, was deteriorating with every passing day, and the time for an urgent decision was at hand. It was one of the sublime paradoxes of history that at this critical juncture, when Britain was at last ready to give India her freedom, she could not find a way to do so. What should have been Britain's finest hour in India seemed destined to become a nightmare of unsurpassed horror. She had conquered and ruled India with what was, by the colonial standard, relatively little bloodshed. Her leaving threatened to produce an explosion of violence that would dwarf in scale and magnitude anything she had experienced in three and a half centuries there.

The root of the Indian problem was the age-old antagonism between India's 300 million Hindus and 100 million Moslems. Sustained by tradition, by antipathetic religions, by economic differences subtly exacerbated through the years by Britain's own policy of divide and rule, their conflict had reached a boiling point. The leaders of India's 100 million Moslems now demanded that Britain destroy the unity she had so painstakingly created and give them an Islamic state of their own. The cost of denying them their state, they warned, would be the bloodiest civil war in Asian history. Just as determined to resist their demands were the leaders of the Congress Party, representing most of India's 300 million Hindus. To them, the division of the subcontinent would be a mutilation of their historic homeland, an act almost sacrilegious in its nature.

Britain was trapped between those two apparently irreconcilable demands. Time and again British efforts to resolve the problem had failed. So desperate had the situation become that the present viceroy, an honest, forthright soldier, Field Marshal Sir Archibald Wavell, had just submitted to the Attlee government a final, and drastic, recommendation [called Operation Madhouse]. Should all else fail, he proposed, the British should "withdraw from India in our own method and in our own time and with due regard to our own interests; we will regard any attempt to interfere with our program as an act of war which we will meet with all the resources at our command. . . ."

Each morning brought a batch of cables to the India Office announcing an outburst of wanton savagery in some new corner of the subcontinent. It was, Attlee indicated, Mountbatten's solemn duty to take the post he had been offered. . . . Wavell had all the right ideas, Mountbatten thought. "If he couldn't do it, what's the point of my trying to take it on?" Yet he was beginning to understand that there was no escape. He was going to be forced to accept a job in which the risk of failure was enormous and in which he would easily shatter the brilliant reputation he'd brought out of the war.

Political Conditions

If Attlee was going to drive him into a corner, Mountbatten was determined to impose on the Prime Minister the political conditions that would give him some hope of success. His talks with Wavell had given him an idea what they must be. He would not accept, he told the Prime Minister, unless the government agreed to make an unequivocal public announcement of a precise date on which British rule in India would terminate. Only that, Mountbatten felt, would convince India's skeptical intelligentsia that Britain was really leaving and infuse her leaders with the sense of urgency needed to get them into realistic negotiations.

Second, he demanded something no other viceroy had ever dreamed of asking: full powers to carry out his assignment without reference to London, and above all, without constant interference from London. The Attlee government could give the young admiral his final destination, but he alone was going to set his course and run the ship along the way.

"Surely," Attlee said, "you're not asking for plenipotentiary powers above His Majesty's Government, are you?"

"I am afraid, sir," answered Mountbatten, "that that is exactly what I am asking. How can I possibly negotiate with the Cabinet constantly breathing down my neck?"

A stunned silence followed his words. Mountbatten watched with satisfaction as the nature of his breathtaking demand registered on the Prime Minister's face, and he hoped that it would prompt Attlee to withdraw his offer. Instead, the Prime Minister indicated with a sigh his willingness to accept even that. . . . As he got back into his Austin Princess, a strange thought struck Mountbatten. It was exactly seventy years to the day, almost to the hour, from the moment when his own great-grandmother had been proclaimed Empress of India on a plain outside Delhi. [16–20]

LAST TATTOO FOR A DYING RAJ

George VI [Lord Mountbatten's cousin] comprehended perfectly well that the great imperial dream had faded and that the grandiose structure fashioned by his great-grandmother's ministers was condemned. But if the empire had to disappear, how sad it would be if some of its achievements and glories could not survive, if what it had represented could not find an expression in some new form more compatible with a modern age. "It would be a pity," he observed, "if an independent India were to turn its back on the Commonwealth."

The Commonwealth could indeed provide a framework in which George VI's hopes might be realized. It could become a multiracial assembly of independent nations, with Britain *prima inter pares* at its core. Bound by common traditions, a common past, by common symbolic ties to his crown, the Commonwealth could exercise great influence in world affairs. If that ideal was to be realized, it was essential that India remain within the Commonwealth when she got her independence. If India refused to join, the Afro-Asian nations, which in their turn would accede to independence in the years to come, would almost certainly follow her example. That would condemn the Commonwealth to becoming just a grouping of the Empire's white dominions instead of the body the King longed to see emerge from the remains of his empire. . . .

Sitting there in their Buckingham Palace sitting room, Victoria's two great-grandsons reached a private decision that January day. Louis Mountbatten would become the agent of their common aspiration for the Commonwealth's future. In a few days Mountbatten would insist that Attlee include in his terms of reference a specific injunction to maintain an independent India, united or divided, inside the Commonwealth if at all possible. In the weeks ahead, there could be no task to which India's new viceroy would devote more thought, more persuasiveness, more cunning than the one conceived that afternoon in George VI's sitting room, that of maintaining a link between India and his cousin's crown. [45–46].

The Coronation

The closing chapter in a great story was about to begin. In a few minutes, on this morning of March 24, 1947, the last Englishman to govern India would mount his gold-and-crimson viceregal throne. Installed upon that throne, Louis Mountbatten would become the twentieth and final representative of a prestigious dynasty, his the last hands to clasp the scepter that had passed from Hastings to Wellesley, to Cornwallis and Curzon. The site of his official consecration was the ceremonial Durbar Hall of a palace whose awesome dimensions were rivaled only by those of Versailles and of the Peterhof of the Tsars. . . .

In Poona, Peshawar and Simla—wherever there was a military garrison in India—troops on parade presented arms as the first gun exploded in Delhi. Frontier Force Rifles, the Guides Cavalry, Hodsons and Skinners Horse, Sikhs and Dogras, Jats and Pathans, Gurkhas and Madrassis poised while the cannon thundered out their last tattoo for the British raj. As the sound of the last report faded through the dome of Durbar Hall, the new viceroy stepped to the microphone. The situation he faced was so serious that, against the advice of his staff, Mountbatten had decided to break with tradition by addressing the gathering before him.

"I am under no illusion about the difficulty of my task," he said. "I shall need the greatest good will of the greatest possible number, and I am asking India today for that good will." As he finished, the guards threw open the massive Assam teak doors of the Hall. Before Mountbatten was the breathtaking vista of Kingsway and its glistening pools, plunging down the heart of New Delhi. Overhead the trumpets sent out another strident call. . . . That brief ceremony, he realized, had turned him into one of the most powerful men on earth. He now held in his hand an almost life-and-death power over four hundred million people, one-fifth of mankind. [90–91]

Operation Seduction

India's last viceroy might, as he had glumly predicted at Northolt Airport, come home with a bullet in his back, but he would be a viceroy unlike any other that India had seen. Mountbatten firmly believed "it was impossible to be viceroy without putting up a great, brilliant show." He had been sent to New Delhi to get the British out of India, but he was determined that they would go in a shimmer of scarlet and gold, all the old glories of the raj honed to the highest pitch one last time.

He ordered all the ceremonial trappings that had been suppressed during the war restored—A.D.C.s in dazzling full dress, guard-mounting ceremonies, bands playing, sabers flashing—"the lot." . . . He intended to replace Wavell's "Operation Madhouse" with a kind of "Operation Seduction" of his own, a minirevolution in style directed as much toward India's masses as toward their leaders, with whom he would have to negotiate. It would be a shrewd blend of contrasting values, of patrician pomp and a common touch, of the old spectacles of the dying raj and new initiatives prefiguring the India of tomorrow.

Strangely, Mountbatten began his revolution with the stroke of a paint brush. To his aides' horror, he ordered the gloomy wooden panels of the viceregal study, in which so many negotiations had failed, covered with a light, cheerful coat of paint more apt to relax the Indian leaders with whom he would be dealing. He shook Viceroy's House out of the leisurely routine it had developed, turning it into a humming, quasi-military headquarters. He instituted staff meetings, soon known as "morning prayers," as the first official activity of each day.

Mountbatten astonished his new I.C.S. subordinates with the agility of his mind, his capacity to get at the root of a problem and, above all, his almost obsessive capacity for work. He put an end to the parade of *chaprassis*, who traditionally bore the viceroy his papers for his private contemplation in green leather dispatch boxes. He preferred taut, verbal briefings.

"When you wrote 'May I speak?' on a paper he was to read," one of his staff recalled, "you could be sure you'd speak, and you'd better be ready to say what was on your mind at any time, because the call to speak could come at two o'clock in the morning."

But it was, above all, the public image Mountbatten was trying to create for himself and his office that represented a radical change. For over a century, the viceroy of India, locked in the ceremonial splendors of his office, had rivaled the Dalai Lama as the most remote god in Asia's pantheon of ruling gods. Two unsuccessful assassination attempts had left him enrobed in a kind of security cocoon isolating him from all contact with the brown masses that he ruled. . . . Hundreds of bodyguards, police, and security men followed each of his moves. If he played golf, the fairways of his course were cleared and police were posted along them behind almost every tree. If he went riding, a squadron of the viceroy's bodyguard and security police jogged along after him.

Mountbatten's first announcement, that he and his wife or daughter would take their morning horseback rides unescorted, sent a shock wave of horror through the house. It took him some time to get his way, but suddenly the Indian villagers along the route of their morning rides began to witness a spectacle so wholly unbelievable as to seem a mirage: the Viceroy and Vicereine of India trotting past them, waving graciously, alone and unprotected.

Then he and his wife made an even more revolutionary gesture. He did something that no viceroy had deigned to do in two hundred years; he visited the home of an Indian who was not one of a handful of privileged princes. To the astonishment of all India, the viceregal couple walked into a garden party at the simple New Delhi residence of Jawaharlal Nehru. While Nehru's aides looked on dumb with disbelief, Mountbatten took Nehru by the elbow and strolled off among the guests casually chatting and shaking hands. The gesture had a stunning impact. "Thank God," an awed Nehru told his sister that evening, "we've finally got a human being for a viceroy and not a stuffed shirt."

Anxious to demonstrate that a new esteem for the Indian people now reigned in Viceroy's House, Mounbatten accorded the Indian military, two million of whom had served under him in Southeast Asia, a long-overdue honor. He had three Indian officers attached to his staff as A.D.C.s. Next, he ordered the doors of

Viceroy's House opened to Indians. Only a handful of Indians had been invited into its precincts before his arrival. He instructed his staff that there were to be no dinner parties in the Viceroy's House without Indian guests. And not just a few token Indians. Henceforth, he ordered, at least half the faces around his table were to be Indian. . . .

Not long after their arrival, *The New York Times* noted that "no viceroy in history has so completely won the confidence, respect and liking of the Indian people." Indeed, within a few weeks, the success of "Operation Seduction" would be so remarkable that Nehru himself would tell the new viceroy only half-jokingly that he was becoming a very difficult man to negotiate with, because he was "drawing larger crowds then anybody in India." [93–95]

STRAIGHT FOR CIVIL WAR

[But time was short. George Abell, whose reputation for brilliance and understanding of India was unsurpassed] told Mountbatten with stark simplicity that India was heading straight for a civil war. Only by finding the quickest of resolutions to her problems was he going to save her. The great administrative machine governing India was collapsing. The shortage of British officers, which was caused by the decision to stop recruiting during the war, and the rising antagonism between its Hindu and Moslem members meant that the rule of that vaunted institution, the Indian Civil Service, could not survive the year. The time for discussion and debate was past. Speed, not deliberation, was needed to avoid a catastrophe.

Coming from a man of Abell's stature, those words gave the new viceroy a dismal shock. Yet, they were only the first in a stream of reports and actions which engulfed him during his first fortnight in India. He received an equally grim analysis from the man he had handpicked to come with him as his chief of staff, General Lord Ismay, Winston Churchill's chief of staff from 1940 to 1945. A veteran of years on the subcontinent as an officer in the Indian Army and military secretary to an earlier viceroy, Ismay had concluded that "India was a ship on fire in mid-ocean with ammunition in her hold." The question, he told Mountbatten, was could they get the fire out before it reached the ammunition?

The first report that Mountbatten received from the British governor of the Punjab warned him that "there is a civil-war atmosphere throughout the province." It mentioned [in passing] a recent tragedy in a rural district near Rawalpindi. A Moslem's water buffalo had wandered onto the property of his Sikh neighbor. When its owner sought to reclaim it, a fight, then a riot erupted. Two hours later, a hundred human beings lay in the surrounding fields, hacked to death with scythes and knives because of the vagrant humors of a water buffalo. Five days after the new viceroy's arrival, incidents between Hindus and Moslems took ninety-nine lives in Calcutta. Two days later, a similar conflict broke out in Bombay, leaving forty-one mutilated bodies on its pavements.

Confronted by those outbursts of violence, Mountbatten called India's senior police officer to his study and asked if the police were capable of maintaining law and order in India. "No, Your Excellency," was the reply, "we cannot." . . .

Mountbatten quickly discovered that the government with which he was supposed to govern India, a coalition of the Congress Party and the Moslem League put together with enormous effort by his predecessor, was in fact an assembly of enemies so bitterly divided that its members barely spoke to one another. It was clearly going to fall apart, and when it did, Mountbatten would have to assume the appalling responsibility of exercising direct rule over one-fifth of humanity himself, with the administrative machine required for the task collapsing underneath him.

Confronted by that grim prospect, assailed on every side by reports of violence and the warnings of his most seasoned advisers, Mountbatten reached what was perhaps the most important decision he would make in India in his first ten days in the country; it was to condition every other decision of his viceroyalty. The date of June 1948 established in London for the transfer of power, the date that he himself had urged on Attlee, had been wildly optimistic. Whatever solution he was to reach for India's future, he was going to have to reach it in weeks, not months.

"The scene here," he wrote in his first report to the Attlee government on April 2, 1947, "is one of unrelieved gloom. . . . I can see little ground on which to build any agreed solution for the future of India." After describing the country's unsettled state, the young admiral issued an anguished warning to the man who had sent him to India. "The only conclusion I have been able to come to," he wrote, "is that unless I act quickly, I will find the beginnings of a civil war on my hands." [95–96]

THE FOUR INDIANS

Because of the urgency of the situation facing him, Mountbatten had decided to employ a revolutionary tactic in his negotiation with India's leaders. For the first time in its modern history, India's destiny was not being decided around a conference table, but in the intimacy of private conversations. . . . Five men would participate in them: Louis Mountbatten and four Indian leaders. The four Indians had spent the better part of their lives agitating against the British and arguing with one another. All were past middle age. All were lawyers who had learned their forensic skills in London's Inns of Court. . . .

In Mountbatten's mind, there was no question what the outcome of that debate should be. Like many Englishmen, he looked on India's unity as the greatest legacy Britain could leave behind. He had a deep, almost evangelical desire to maintain it. To respond to the Moslem appeal to divide the country was, he believed, to sow the seeds of tragedy. Every effort to persuade India's leaders to agree on a solution to their country's problems in a formal meeting had led to a deadlock. [But here in the privacy of his study] he was going to try to achieve in weeks what his predecessors had been unable to achieve in years—get India's leaders to agree on some form of unity. . . .

The Kashmiri Brahman

Nehru was the only Indian leader whom Mountbatten already knew. [At the end of World War II] to the horror of his staff Mountbatten rode through Singapore's streets in his open car with Nehru at his side. His action, his advisers had warned, would only dignify an anti-British rebel. "Dignify him?" Mountbatten had retorted, "It is he who will dignify *me*. Some day this man will be Prime Minister of India." [97–98]

There was a great deal to bind the scion of a three-thousand-year-old line of Kashmiri Brahmans and the man who claimed descent from the oldest ruling family in Protestantism. They both loved to talk, and they expanded in each other's company. Nehru, the abstract thinker, admired Mountbatten's practical dynamism, the capacity for decisive action that wartime command had given him. Mountbatten was stimulated by the subtlety of Nehru's thought. He quickly understood that the only Indian politician who would share and understand his desire to maintain a link between Britain and a new India was Jawaharlal Nehru.

With his usual candor, the Viceroy told Nehru that he had been given an appalling responsibility and he intended to approach the Indian problem in a mood of stark realism. As they talked, the two men rapidly agreed on two major points: a quick decision was essential to avoid a bloodbath and the division of India would be a tragedy. Then Nehru turned to the actions of the next Indian leader who would enter Mountbatten's study, the penitent Mohandas Gandhi marching his lonely path through Noakhali and Bihar. The man to whom he had been so long devoted was, Nehru said, "going around with ointment trying to heal one sore spot after another on the body of India instead of diagnosing the cause of the eruption of the sores and participating in the treatment of the body as a whole."

In offering a glimpse into the growing gulf separating the Liberator of India and his closest companions, Nehru's words provided Mountbatten with a vital insight into the form that his actions in Delhi should take. If he could not persuade India's leaders to keep their country united, he was going to have to persuade them to divide it. Gandhi's unremitting hostility to partition could place an insurmountable barrier in his path and confront him with a catastrophe. His only hope, then, would be to divorce the leaders of Congress from their aging leader. Nehru would be the key if that happened. He was the only ally Mountbatten must have; only he might have the authority to stand up against the Mahatma.

Now that words had revealed the discord between Gandhi and his party chief, Mountbatten might be forced to widen and exploit that gap to succeed. He needed Nehru, and he spared no effort to win his support. On none of India's leaders would Operation Seduction have more impact than on the realistic Kashmiri Brahman. . . . Taking Nehru to the door, Mountbatten told him, "Mr. Nehru, I want you to regard me not as the last British viceroy winding up the raj, but as the first to lead the way to a new India." Nehru turned and looked at the man he had wanted to see on the viceregal throne. "Ah," he said, a faint smile creasing his face, "now I know what they mean when they speak of your charm as being so dangerous." [101–102]

The Most Famous Asian Alive

[The next man to see Mountbatten was unique, a saint in his own time. He was Mohandas Gandhi—called Mahatma, meaning "Great Soul."] At every village, his routine was the same. As soon as he arrived, the most famous Asian alive would go up to a hut, preferably a Moslem's hut, and beg for shelter. If he was turned away, and sometimes he was, Gandhi would go to another door. "If there is no one to receive me," he had said, "I shall be happy to rest under the hospitable shade of a tree." Once installed, he lived on whatever food his hosts would offer: mangoes, vegetables, goat's curds, green coconut milk. Every hour of his day in each village was rigorously programmed. Time was one of Gandhi's obsessions. Each minute, he held, was a gift of God to be used in the service of man. . . . He got up at two o'clock in the morning to read his Gita and say his morning prayers. From then until dawn he squatted in his hut, patiently answering his correspondence himself with a pencil, in longhand. He used each pencil right down to an ungrippable stub, because he held that it represented the work of a fellow human being and to waste it would indicate indifference to his labors. . . .

The aging leader did not stop with words. Gandhi had a tenacious belief in the value of one concrete act. To the despair of many of his followers who thought a different set of priorities should order his time, Gandhi would devote the same meticulous care and attention to making a mudpack for a leper as preparing for an interview with a viceroy. So, in each village he would go with its inhabitants to their wells. Frequently he would help them find a better location for them. He would inspect their communal latrines, or if, as was most often the case, they didn't have any, he would teach them how to build one, often joining in the digging himself. [52]

Determined to convert [the Congress Party] into a mass movement attuned to his nonviolent creed, Gandhi presented the party a plan of action in Calcutta in 1920. It was adopted by an overwhelming majority. From that moment until his death, whether he held rank in the party or not, Gandhi was Congress's conscience and its guide, the unquestioned leader of the independence struggle. . . . Gandhi's tactic was electrifyingly simple, a one-word program for political revolution: non-cooperation. Indians, he decreed, would boycott whatever was British; students would boycott British schools; lawyers, British courts; employees, British jobs; soldiers, British honors. . . .

Above all, his aim was to weaken the edifice of British power in India by attacking the economic pillar upon which it reposed. Britain purchased raw Indian cotton for derisory prices, shipped it to the mills of Lancashire to be woven into textiles, then shipped the finished products back to India to be sold at a substantial profit in a market that virtually excluded non-British textiles. It was the classic cycle of imperialist exploitation, and the arm with which Gandhi proposed to fight it was the very antithesis of the great mills of the Industrial Revolution that had sired that exploitation. It was a primitive wooden spinning wheel. For the next quarter of a century Gandhi struggled with tenacious energy to force all India to forsake foreign textiles for the rough cotton khadi cloth spun by millions of spinning wheels. Convinced that the misery of India's half million villages was due above all to the decline in village crafts, he saw in a renaissance of cottage industry, heralded by the spinning wheel, the key to the revival of India's impoverished countryside. For the urban masses, spinning would be a kind of spiritual redemption by manual labor, a constant, daily reminder of their link to the real India, the India of half a million villages. [61–62]

"The British want us to put the struggle on the plane of machine guns where they have the weapons and we do not," he warned. "Our only assurance of beating them is putting the struggle on a plane where we have the weapons and they have not." Thousands of Indians followed his call, and thousands more went off to jail. The beleaguered governor of Bombay called it "the most colossal experiment in world history and one which came within an inch of succeeding."

It failed because of an outburst of bloody violence in a little village northeast of Delhi. Against the wishes of almost his entire Congress hierarchy, Gandhi called off the movement because he felt that his followers did not yet fully understand nonviolence. Sensing that his change of attitude had rendered him less dangerous, the British arrested him. Gandhi pleaded guilty to the charge of sedition, and in a moving appeal to his judge, asked for the maximum penalty. He was sentenced to six years in Yeravda prison near Poona. He had no regrets. "Freedom," he wrote, "is often to be found inside a prison's walls, even on a gallows; never in council chambers, courts and classrooms." [64]

"A leader," Gandhi replied, "is only a reflection of the people he leads." The people had first to be led to make peace among themselves. Then, he said, "their desire to live together in peaceful neighborliness will be reflected by their leaders." [53]

[Once Winston Churchill had called Mohandas Gandhi "a half-naked fakir."] Now that half-naked fakir was sitting in the viceregal study, "to negotiate and parley on equal terms with the representative of the King-Emperor." He's rather like a little bird, Louis Mountbatten thought, as he contemplated that famous figure at his side, a kind of "sweet, sad sparrow perched on my armchair." . . .

So important had Mountbatten considered this first meeting with Gandhi, that he had written the Mahatma inviting him to Delhi before the ceremony enthroning him as viceroy. Gandhi had drafted his reply immediately, then, with a chuckle, told an aide, "Wait a couple of days before putting it in the mail. I don't want that young man to think I'm dying for his invitation." That "young man" had accompanied his invitation with one of those gestures for which he was becoming noted and which sometimes infuriated his fellow Englishmen. He had offered to send his personal aircraft to Bihar to fly Gandhi to Delhi. Gandhi had declined the offer. He had insisted on traveling, as he always did, in a third-class railway car.

To give their meeting a special cordiality, Mountbatten had asked his wife to be present. Now, with the famous figure opposite them, worry and concern swept over the viceregal couple. The Mahatma, they both immediately sensed, was profoundly unhappy, trapped in the grip of some mysterious remorse. Had they done something wrong? Neglected some arcane law of protocol? . . .

[Finally] a slow, sorrowful sigh escaped the Indian leader. "You know," he replied, "all my life, since I was in South Africa, I've renounced physical possessions." He owned virtually nothing, he explained—his Gita, the tin utensils from which he ate, mementos of his stay in Yeravda prison, his three "gurus." And his watch, the old eight-shilling Ingersoll that he hung from a string around his waist because, if he was going to devote every minute of his day to God's work, he had to know what time it was.

"Do you know what?" he asked sadly. "They stole it. Someone in my railway compartment coming down to Delhi stole the watch." As the frail figure lost in his armchair spoke those words, Mountbatten saw tears shining in Gandhi's eyes. It was not an eight-shilling watch an unknown hand had plucked from him in that congested railway car, but a particle of his faith. After a long silence, Gandhi began to talk of India's current dilemma. Mountbatten interrupted with a friendly wave of his hand.

"Mr. Gandhi," he said, "first, I want to know who you are." He was determined to get to know these Indian leaders before allowing them to begin assailing him with their minimum demands and final conditions. By putting them at ease, by getting them to confide in him, he hoped to create an atmosphere of mutual confidence and sympathy in which his own dynamic personality could have greater impact. The Mahatma was delighted. He loved to talk about himself, and in the Mountbattens he had found a charming pair of people genuinely interested in what he had to say. He rambled on about South Africa, his days as a stretcher-bearer in the Boer War, civil disobedience, the Salt March. Once, he said, the West had received its inspiration from the East in the messages of Zoroaster, Buddha, Moses, Jesus, Mohammed, Rama. For centuries, however, the East had been conquered culturally by the West. Now the West, haunted by specters like the atomic bomb, had need to look eastward once again. There, he hoped, it might find the message of love and fraternal understanding that he sought to preach. [103–104]

[Much later] India's new viceroy moved into a serious exchange with Gandhi with trepidation. He was not persuaded that the little figure "chirping like a sparrow" at his side could help him elaborate a solution to the Indian crisis, but he knew that he could defeat all efforts to find one. The hopes of many another English mediator had foundered on the turns of his unpredictable personality. It was Gandhi who had sent Cripps back to London empty-handed in 1942. His refusal to budge on a principle had helped thwart Wavell's efforts to untie the Indian knot.

His tactics had done much to frustrate the most recent British attempt to solve the problem of liberation. Only the evening before, Gandhi had reiterated to his prayer meeting that India would be divided "over my dead body. So long as I am alive, I will never agree to the partition of India." . . .

It had always been British policy not to yield to force, he told Gandhi, by way of opening their talks on the right note, but his nonviolent crusade had won, and come what may, Britain was going to leave India. Only one thing mattered in that coming departure, Gandhi replied. "Don't partition India," be begged. "Don't divide India," the prophet of nonviolence pleaded, "even if refusing to do so means shedding rivers of blood."

Dividing India, a shocked Mountbatten assured Gandhi, was the last solution he wished to adopt. But what alternatives were open to him? Gandhi had one. So desperate was he to avoid partition that he was prepared to give the Moslems the baby instead of cutting it in half. Place three hundred million Hindus under Moslem rule, he told Mountbatten, by asking his rival Jinnah and his Moslem League to form a government. Then hand over power to that government. Give Jinnah all of India instead of just the part he wants, was his nonviolent proposal.

"Whatever makes you think your own Congress Party will accept?" Mountbatten asked.

"Congress," Gandhi replied, "wants above all else to avoid partition. They will do anything to prevent it."

"What," Mountbatten asked, "would Jinnah's reaction be?"

"If you tell him I am its author his reply will be, 'Wily Gandhi,' " The Mahatma said, laughing. [106–109]

The Bully

Why, this man is trying to bully me, an unbelieving Louis Mountbatten thought. His Operation Seduction had come to a sudden, wholly unexpected halt at the rocklike figure planted in the chair opposite his. With his Khadi dhoti flung about his shoulders like a toga, his bald head glowing, his scowling demeanor, his visitor looked to the Viceroy more like a Roman senator than an Indian politician.

Patel was Indian from the uppermost lump of his bald head to the calluses on the soles of his feet. His Delhi home was filled with books, but every one of them was written by an Indian author about India. He was the only Indian leader who sprang from the soil of India. Emotion, one of his associates once observed, formed no part of Patel's character. The remark was not wholly exact. Patel was an emotional man, but he never let those emotions break through the composed facade he turned to the world. If he gave off one salient impression, it was that of a man wholly in control of himself. In a land in which men talked constantly, threw their words around like sailors flinging away their money after three months at sea, Patel hoarded his phrases the way a miser hoarded coins. His daughter, who had been his constant companion since his wife's death, rarely exchanged ten sentences with him a day. When Patel did talk, however, people listened.

Vallabhbhai Patel was India's quintessential politician. He was an Oriental Tammany Hall boss who ran the machinery of the Congress Party with a firm and ruthless hand. He should have been the easiest member of the Indian quartet for Mountbatten to deal with. Like the Viceroy, he was a practical pragmatic man, a hard but realistic bargainer. Yet the tension between them was so real, so palpable, that it seemed to Mountbatten he could reach out and touch it. Its cause was in no way related to the great issues facing India. It was a slip of paper, a routine government minute issued by Patel's Home Ministry dealing with an appointment. But Mountbatten had read it as a calculated challenge to his authority.

Patel had a well-earned reputation for toughness. He had an almost instinctive need to take the measure of a new interlocutor, to see how far he could push him. The piece of paper on his desk, Mountbatten was convinced, was a test, a little examination that he had to go through with Patel before he could get down to serious matters. The Viceroy looked at the note which had offended him, then passed it across his desk to Patel. Quietly he asked him to withdraw it. Patel brusquely refused. Mountbatten studied the Indian leader. He was going to need the support of this man and the machinery he represented. But he was sure he would never get it if he did not face him down now.

"Very well," said Mountbatten. "I'll tell you what I'm going to do. I'm going to order my plane."

"Oh," said Patel, "why?"

"Because I'm leaving," Mountbatten replied. "I didn't want this job in the first place. I've just been looking for someone like you to give me an excuse to throw it up and get out of an impossible situation."

"You don't mean it," exclaimed Patel.

"Mean it?" replied Mountbatten. "You don't think I am going to stay here and be bullied around by a chap like you, do you? If you think you can be rude to me and push me around, you're wrong. You'll either withdraw that minute, or one of us is going to resign. And let me tell you that if I go, I shall first explain to your prime minister, to Mr. Jinnah, to His Majesty's Government, why I am leaving. The breakdown in India which will follow, the blood that will be shed, will be on your shoulders and no one else's." Patel stared at Mountbatten in disbelief. A long silence followed. "You know," Patel finally sighed, "the awful part is I think you mean it." "You're damned right I do," answered Mountbatten. Patel reached out, took the offending minute off Mountbatten's desk and slowly tore it up. [109–111]

The Father of Pakistan

The man who would ultimately hold the key to the subcontinent's dilemma in his hands was the last of the Indian leaders to enter the Viceroy's study. A quarter of a century later, an echo of his distant anguish still haunting his voice, Louis Mountbatten would recall, "I did not realize how utterly impossible my task in India was going to be until I met Mohammed Ali Jinnah for the first time."

Inside the study, Jinnah began by informing Mountbatten that he had come to tell him exactly what he was prepared to accept. As he had done with Gandhi, Mountbatten interrupted with a wave of his hand. "Mr. Jinnah," he said, "I am not prepared to discuss conditions at this stage. First, let's make each other's acquaintance." Then with his legendary charm and verve, Mountbatten turned the focus of Operation Seduction on the Moslem leader. Jinnah froze. To that aloof and reserved man who never unbent, even with his closest associates, the very idea of revealing the details of his life and personality to a perfect stranger must have seemed appalling. Gamely Mountbatten struggled on, summoning up all the reserves of his gregarious, engaging personality. For what seemed to him like hours, his only reward was a series of monosyllabic grunts from the man beside him.

The man who would one day be hailed as the Father of Pakistan had first been exposed to the idea at a black-tie dinner at London's Waldorf Hotel in the spring of 1933. His host was Rahmat Ali, the graduate student who had set the idea to paper. Rahmat Ali had arranged the banquet with its oysters on the half shell and un-Islamic Chablis at his own expense, hoping to persuade Jinnah, India's leading Moslem politician, to take over his movement. He received a chilly rebuff. Pakistan, Jinnah told him, was "an impossible dream." The man whom the unfortunate graduate student had sought to lead a Moslem separatist movement had, in fact, begun his political career by preaching Hindu-Moslem unity. . . . [115]

Like Gandhi, Jinnah had gone to London to dine in the Inns of Court and had been called to the bar. Unlike Gandhi, however, he had come back from London an Englishman. He wore a monocle, superbly cut linen suits, which he changed three or four times a day to remain cool and unruffled in the soggy Bombay climate. He loved oysters and caviar, champagne, brandy and good Bordeaux. A man of unassailable personal honesty and financial integrity, his canons were sound law and sound procedure. He was, according to one intimate, "the last of the Victorians, a parliamentarian in the mode of Gladstone or Disraeli."

A more improbable leader of India's Moslem masses could hardly be imagined. The only thing Moslem about Mohammed Ali Jinnah was the fact his parents happened to be Moslem. He drank, ate pork, religiously shaved his beard each morning, and just as religiously avoided the mosque each Friday. God and the Koran had no place in Jinnah's vision of the world. His political foe Gandhi knew more verses of the Moslem holy book then he did. He had been able to achieve the remarkable feat of securing the allegiance of the vast majority of India's ninety million Moslems without being able to articulate more than a few sentences in their traditional tongue, Urdu.

Jinnah despised India's masses. He detested the dirt, the heat, the crowds of India. Gandhi traveled India in filthy third-class railway cars to be with the people. Jinnah rode first-class to avoid them. Jinnah had only scorn for his Hindu rivals. He labeled Nehru "a Peter Pan;" a "literary figure" who "should have been an English professor, not a politician;" "an arrogant Brahman who covers his Hindu trickiness under a veneer of Western education." Gandhi, to Jinnah, was "a cunning fox," "a Hindu revivalist." The sight of Mahatma, during an interval in a conversation in Jinnah's mansion, stretched out on one of his priceless Persian carpets, his mudpack on his belly, was something Jinnah had never forgotten or forgiven. . . .

His disenchantment with the Congress Party dated from Gandhi's ascension to power. It was not the impeccably dressed Jinnah who was going to be bundled off to some squalid British jail half naked in a dhoti and wearing a silly little white cap. Civil disobedience, he told Gandhi, was for "the ignorant and the illiterate." The turning point in Jinnah's career came after the 1937 elections, when the Congress Party refused to share with him and his Moslem League the spoils of office in those Indian provinces where there was a substantial Moslem minority. Jinnah, a man of towering vanity, took Congress's action as a personal insult. It convinced him that he and the Moslem League would never get a fair deal from a Congress-run India. The former apostle of Hindu-Moslem unity became the unyielding advocate of Pakistan, the project that he had labeled an " impossible dream" barely four years earlier. [116–117]

Mountbatten and Jinnah held six critical meetings during the first fortnight of April 1947. They were the vital conversations—not quite ten hours in length—that ultimately determined the resolution of the Indian dilemma. Mountbatten went into them armed with "the most enormous conceit in my ability to persuade people to do the right thing, not because I am persuasive so much as because I have the knack of being able to present the facts in their most favorable light." As he would later recall, he "tried every trick I could play, used every appeal I could imagine," to shake Jinnah's determination to have partition. Nothing would. There was no trick, no argument that could move him from his consuming determination to realize the impossible dream of Pakistan. . . . He had made himself the absolute dictator of the Moslem League. There were men below who might have been willing to negotiate a compromise, but as long as Mohammed Ali Jinnah was alive, they would hold their silence. . . .

Mountbatten and Jinnah did agree on one point at the outset—the need for speed. India, Jinnah declared, had gone beyond the stage at which a compromise solution was possible. There was only one solution, a speedy "surgical operation" on India. Otherwise, he warned, India would perish. When Mountbatten expressed concern that partition might produce bloodshed and violence, Jinnah reassured him. Once his "surgical operation" had taken place, all troubles would cease and India's two halves would live in harmony and happiness. It was, Jinnah told Mountbatten, like a court case that he had handled, a dispute between two brothers embittered by the shares assigned them by their father's will. Yet two years after the court had adjudicated their dispute, they were the greatest friends. That, he promised the Viceroy, would be the case in India. . . .

. . . "India has never been a true nation," Jinnah asserted. "It only looks that way on the map. . . . The cows I want to eat, the Hindu stops me from killing. Every time a Hindu shakes hands with me he has to go wash his hands. The only thing the Moslem has in common with the Hindu is his slavery to the British." . . . . [118]

For Jinnah, the division that he proposed was the natural course. However, it would have to produce a viable state, which meant that two of India's great provinces, the Punjab and Bengal, would have to be included in Pakistan, despite the fact that each contained enormous Hindu populations. Mountbatten could not agree. The very basis of Jinnah's argument for Pakistan was that India's Moslem minority should not be ruled by its Hindu majority. How then to justify taking the Hindu minorities of Bengal and the Punjab into a Moslem state? If Jinnah insisted on dividing India to get his Islamic state, then the very logic he had used to get it would compel Mountbatten to divide the Punjab and Bengal.

Jinnah protested—that would give him an economically unviable, "moth-eaten Pakistan." Mountbatten, who didn't want to give him any Pakistan at all, told the Moslem leader that if he felt the nation he was to receive was as "moth-eaten" as all that, he would do well to abandon his plan.

"Ah," Jinnah would counter, "Your Excellency doesn't understand. A man is a Punjabi or a Bengali before he is Hindu or Moslem. They share a common history, language, culture and economy. You must not divide them. You will cause endless bloodshed and trouble." "Mr. Jinnah I entirely agree." "You do?" "Of course," Mountbatten would continue. "A man is not only a Punjabi or Bengali before he is a Hindu or a Moslem, he is an Indian before all else. You have presented the unanswerable argument for Indian unity." "But you don't understand at all," Jinnah countered—and the discussion would start again.

Mountbatten was stunned by the rigidity of Jinnah's position. "I never would have believed," he later recalled, "that an intelligent man, well educated, trained in the Inns of Court, was capable of simply closing his mind as Jinnah did. It wasn't that he didn't see the point. He did, but a kind of shutter came down. He was the evil genius in the whole thing. The others could be persuaded, but not Jinnah. While he was alive nothing could be done." [119]

If Louis Mountbatten, Jawaharlal Nehru, or Mahatma Gandhi had been aware in April 1947 of one extraordinary secret, the division threatening India might have been avoided. That secret was sealed onto the gray surface of a piece of film, a film that could have upset the Indian political equation and would almost certainly have changed the course of Asian history. Yet so precious was the secret which the film harbored that even the British C.I.D., one of the most effective investigative agencies in the world, was ignorant of its existence. The heart of the film was two dark circles no bigger than a pair of Ping-Pong balls. Each was surrounded by an irregular white border like the corona of the sun eclipsed by the moon. Above them, a galaxy of little white spots stretched up the film's gray surface toward the top of the thoracic cage. That film was an X ray, the X ray of a pair of human lungs.

The damage was so extensive that the man whose lungs were on that film had barely two or three years to live. . . . The lungs depicted on them belonged to the rigid and inflexible man who had frustrated Louis Mountbatten's efforts to preserve India's unity. Mohammed Ali Jinnah, the one unmovable obstacle between the Viceroy and Indian unity, was living under a sentence of death. . . . [124]

Meditating alone in his study after Jinnah's departure, Mountbatten realized that he was probably going to have to give him Pakistan. His first obligation in New Delhi was to the nation that had sent him there, England. He longed to preserve India's unity, but not at the expense of his country's becoming hopelessly entrapped in an India collapsing in chaos and violence. . . .

Military command had given Mountbatten a penchant for rapid, decisive actions, such as the one he now took. In future years, his critics would assail him for having reached it too quickly, for acting like an impetuous sailor and not a statesman, but Mountbatten was not going to waste any more time on what he was certain would be futile arguments with Jinnah. . . . Neither logic nor Mountbatten's power to charm and persuade had made any impact on him. The partition of India seemed the only solution. It now remained to Mountbatten to get Nehru and Patel to accept the principle and to find for it a plan that could get their support.

The Indian Rajahs

Yadavindra Singh presided over the most remarkable body in the world, an assembly unlike any other that man had ever devised. He was the Chancellor of the Chamber of Indian Princes (the fabled Rajahs). His state of Patiala in the Punjab, was one of the richest in India. He had an army the size of an infantry division, equipped with Centurion tanks to defend it if necessary.

The princes' anachronistic situation dated to Britain's haphazard conquest of India, when rulers who received the English with open arms or proved worthy foes on the battlefield were allowed to remain on their thrones provided that they acknowledged Britain as the paramount power in India. The system was formalized in a series of treaties between the individual rulers and the British Crown. The Princes had recognized the "Paramountcy" of the King-Emperor as represented in New Delhi by the viceroy, and they ceded to him control of their foreign affairs and defense. They received in return Britain's guarantee of their continuing autonomy inside their states. [See map.] . . .

Certain princes like the Nizam of Hyderabad or the Maharaja of Kashmir ruled over states which rivaled in size or population the nations of Western Europe. Others like those in the Kathiawar peninsula near Bombay lived in stables and governed domains no larger than New York City's Central Park. Their fraternity embraced the richest man in the world and princes so poor that their entire kingdom was a cow pasture. Over four hundred princes ruled states smaller than twenty square miles. A good number of them offered their subjects an administration far better than that the British provided. A few were petty despots more concerned with squandering their states' revenues to slake their own extravagant desires than with improving the lot of their peoples. Whatever their political proclivities, however, the future of India's 565 ruling princes, with their average of eleven titles, 5.8 wives, 12.6 children, 9.2 elephants, 2.8 private railway cars, 3.4

Roll-Royces, and 22.9 tigers killed, posed a grave problem in the spring of 1947. No solution to the Indian equation would work if it failed to deal with their peculiar situation. [165,166]

A SUBTLE MOSAIC

Inevitably, Mountbatten's decision would lead to one of the great dramas of modern history. Whatever the manner in which it was executed, it was bound to end in the mutilation of a great nation. . . . To satisfy the exigent demands of Mohammed Ali Jinnah, two of India's most distinctive entities, the Punjab and Bengal, would have to be carved up. The result would make Pakistan a geographic aberration, a nation of two heads separated by 1,500 kilometers (900 miles) of Himalayan mountain peaks, all purely Indian territory. Twenty days, more time than was required to sail from Karachi to Marseilles, would be needed to make the sea trip around the subcontinent from one half of Pakistan to the other. [120]. . .

The Punjab was a blend as subtle and complex as the mosaics decorating the monuments of its glorious Royal past. To divide it was unthinkable. Fifteen million Hindus, sixteen million Moslems, and five million Sikhs shared the neighborhoods and alleyways of its 17,932 towns and villages. Although divided by religion, they shared a common language, joint traditions, and a great pride in this distinctive Punjabi personality. Wherever the boundary line went, the result was certain to be nightmare for millions of human beings. Only an interchange of populations on a scale never effected before in history could sort out the havoc that it would create. From the Indus to the bridges of Delhi, for over 500 miles, there was not a single town, not a single village, cotton grove or wheat field that would not somehow be threatened if the partition plan were to be carried out.

The division of Bengal at the other end of the subcontinent held out the possibilities of another tragedy. Haboring more people than Great Britain and Ireland combined, Bengal contained thirty-five million Moslems and thirty million Hindus spread over an expanse of land running from the jungles at the foot of the Himalayas to the steaming marshes through which the thousand tributaries of the Ganges and Brahmaputra rivers drained into the Bay of Bengal. Despite its division into two religious communities, Bengal, even more than the Punjab, was a distinct entity of its own. Whether Hindu or Moslem, Bengalis sprang from the same racial stock, spoke the same language, shared the same culture. They sat on the floor in a certain Bengali manner, ordered the sentences they spoke in a peculiar Bengali cadence, each rising to a final crescendo, celebrated their own Bengali New Year on April 15. Their poets like Tabore were regarded with pride by all Bengalis. [122]

A land seared by droughts that alternated with frightening typhoon-whipped floods, Bengal was an immense, steaming swamp, in whose humid atmosphere flourished the two crops to which it owed a precarious prosperity, rice and jute. The cultivation of those two crops followed the province's religious frontiers, rice to the Hindu west, jute to the Moslem east. But the key to Bengal's existence did not lie in its crops. It was a city, the city that had been the springboard for Britain's conquest of India, the second city, after London, of the Empire, and the first port of Asia—Calcutta, site of the terrible Hindu-Moslem killings of August 1946.

Everything in Bengal—roads, railroads, communications, industry—funneled into Calcutta. If Bengal was split into its eastern and western halves, Calcutta, because of its physical location, seemed certain to be in the Hindu west, thus condemning the Moslem east to a slow but inexorable asphyxiation. If almost all of the world's jute grew in eastern Bengal, all the factories that transformed it into rope, sacks and cloth were clustered around Calcutta, in western Bengal. The Moslem east, which produced the jute, grew almost no food at all, and its millions survived on the rice grown in the Hindu west. . . .

Yet, no aspect of partition was more illogical than the fact that Jinnah's Pakistan would deliver barely half of India's Moslems from the alleged inequities of Hindu majority rule which had justified the state in the first place. The remaining Moslems were scattered throughout the rest of India so widely that it was impossible to separate them. Islands in a Hindu sea, even after the amputation, India would still harbor almost fifty million Moslems, a figure that would make her the third-largest Moslem nation in the world, after Indonesia and the new state drawn from her own womb. [123]

The Governors

The eleven men seated around the oval table in the conference chamber solemnly waited for Lord Mountbatten to begin the proceedings. They were, in a sense, the descendants of the twenty-four founding fathers of the East India Company, the men whose mercantile appetites had sent Britain along the sea lanes to India three and a half centuries earlier. . . . Their meeting was an awkward confrontation for Mountbatten. At forty-six, he was the youngest man at the table. . . . He was a comparative stranger in the India to which most of the eleven governors had devoted an entire career, mastering its complex history, learning its dialects, becoming, as some of them had, world-renowned experts on the phases of its existence. They were proud men, certain to be skeptical of any plan put before them by the neophyte in their midst. . . . [126]

Mountbatten began by asking each governor to describe the situation in his province. Eight of them painted a picture of dangerous, troubled areas, but provinces in which the situation still remained under control. It was the portrait offered by the governors of the three critical provinces, the Punjab, Bengal, and the Northwest Frontier Province, that sobered the gathering.

His features drawn, his eyes heavy with fatigue, Sir Olaf Caroe spoke first. He had been kept awake all night by a stream of cables detailing fresh outbursts of trouble in his Northwest Frontier Province. The labyrinth grottoes of his mountainous province sheltered scores of secret arms factories, from which flowed a profusion of ornate and deadly weapons to arm Mahsuds, Afridis, Wazirs, the legendary warrior tribes of the Pathans. The situation in the N.W.F.P. was close to disintegrating, he warned, and if that happened, the old British nightmare of invading hordes from the northwest forcing the gates of the Empire might be realized. The Pathan tribes of Afghanistan were poised to come pouring down the Khyber Pass to Peshawar and the banks of the Indus in pursuit of land they had claimed as theirs for a century. "If we're not jolly careful," he said "we are going to have an international crisis on our hands."

The portrait drawn by Sir Evan Jenkins, the taciturn governor of the Punjab, was even grimmer than Caroe's. . . . Whatever solution was chosen for India's problems, he declared, it was certain to bring violence to the Punjab. At least four divisions would be needed to keep order if partition was decided upon. Even if it was not, they would still face a demand by the Sikhs for an area of their own. "It's absurd to predict the Punjab will go up in flames if it's partitioned," he said; "its already in flames." [127]

The third governor, Sir Frederick Burrows of Bengal, was ill in Calcutta, but the briefing of the province's situation as offered by his deputy was every bit as disquieting as the reports from the N.W.F.P. and the Punjab. When those reporters were finally finished, Mountbatten's staff passed out a set of papers to each governor. They carried the details, Mountbatten announced, "of one of the possible plans under examination." It was called, "for easy reference," Plan Balkan, and it was the first draft of a partition plan that Mountbatten had ordered his chief of staff, Lord Ismay, to prepare a week earlier. . . . The plan, aptly named for the Balkanization of the states of Central Europe after World War I, would allow each of India's eleven provinces to choose whether it wished to join Pakistan or remain in India; or, if a majority of both its Hindus and Moslems agreed, become independent. Mountbatten told his assembled governors that he was not going to "lightly abandon hope for a united India." He wanted the world to know that the British had made every effort possible to keep India united. If Britain failed it was of the utmost importance that the world know it was "Indian opinion rather than a British decision that had made partition the choice." He himself thought a future Pakistan was so inherently unviable that it should "be given a chance to fail on its own demerits," so that later "the Moslem League could revert to a unified India with honor."

Those eleven men who represented the collective wisdom of the service that had run India for a century displayed no enthusiasm for the idea that partition might have to be the answer to India's dilemma. Nor did they have any other solution to propose. [128]

Visit to Peshawar

Louis Mountbatten had decided to suspend temporarily the conversations in his air-conditioned office while he, personally, took the political temperature of his two most troubled provinces, the Punjab and the N.W.F.P. The news that he was coming had swept over the Frontier. For twenty-four hours, summoned by the leaders of Jinnah's Moslem League, tens of thousands of men from every corner of the province had been converging on Peshawar. Overflowing their trucks, in buses, in cars, on special trains, chanting and waving their arms, they had spilled into the capital for the greatest popular demonstration in its history.

Now those tall, pale-skinned Pathans prepared to offer the Viceroy a welcome of an unexpected sort to Peshawar. . . . The police had confined them in an enormous low-walled enclosure running between a railroad embankment and the sloping walls of Peshawar's old Mogul fortress. Irritated and unruly, they threatened to drown the conciliatory tones of Operation Seduction with the discordant rattle of gunfire.

They were there because of the anomalous political situation of a province whose population was 93 percent Moslem, but was governed by allies of the Congress Party. . . . Stirred by Jinnah's agents, the population had turned against the Congress leader Ghaffar Khan who supported Gandhi and the government that he had installed in Peshawar. The huge, howling crowd greeting Mountbatten, his wife and seventeen-year-old daughter Pamela was meant to give final proof that it was the Moslem League and not the "Frontier Gandhi" that now commanded the province's support. [129] The crowd, growing more unruly by the hour, threatened to burst out of the area in which the police had herded them and start a headlong rush on the governor's residence. If they did, the vastly outnumbered military guarding the house would have no choice but to open fire. The resulting slaughter would be appalling. It would destroy Mountbatten, his hopes of finding a solution, and his viceroyalty in a sickening blood bath.

There was one way out, an idea condemned by the police and army commander as sheer madness. Mountbatten might present himself to the crowds, hoping that somehow a glimpse of him would mollify them. Mountbatten pondered a few moments. "All right, I'll take a chance and see them." To the despair of Caroe and his security officers, Edwina, his wife, insisted on coming with him. . . . A few minutes later, a jeep deposited the viceregal couple and the governor at the foot of the railway embankment. On the other side of that precarious dike, 100,000 hot, dirty, angry people were shouting their frustration in an indecipherable din. Mountbatten took his wife by the hand and clambered up the embankment. As they reached the top, they discovered themselves only fifteen feet away from the surging waves of the sea of turbans. The ground under their feet shook with the impact of the gigantic crowd stampeding forward in front of them. That terrifying ocean of human beings incarnated in their shrieks and gesticulations the enormity and the passions of the masses of India. Whirling spirals of dust stirred by thousands of rushing feet clotted the air. The noise of the crowd was an almost tangible layer of air crushing down on them. It was a decisive instant in Operation Seduction, an instant when anything was possible. . . . In that crowd were twenty, thirty, forty thousand rifles. Any madman, any bloodthirsty fool could shoot the Mountbattens "like ducks on a pond."

For the first few seconds Mountbatten did not know what to do. He couldn't articulate a syllable of Pushtu, the crowd's language. As he pondered, a totally unexpected phenomenon began to still the mob, stopping perhaps with its strange vibrations an assassin's hand. For this entirely unplanned meeting with the Empire's most renowned warriors, Mountbatten happened to be wearing the short-sleeved, loose-fitting bush jacket that he had worn as Supreme Allied Commander in Burma. Its color, green, galvanized the crowd. Green was the color of Islam, the blessed green of the hadjis, the holy men who had made the pilgrimage to Mecca. Instinctively, those tens of thousands of men read in that green uniform a gesture of solidarity with them, a subtle compliment to their great religion.

His hand still clutching hers, but his eyes straight ahead, Mountbatten whispered to his wife, "Wave to them." Slowly, graciously, the frail Edwina raised her arm with his to the crowd. India's fate seemed for an instant suspended in those hands climbing above the crowd's head. A questioning silence had drifted briefly over the unruly crowd. Suddenly, Edwina's pale arm began to stroke the sky; a cry, then a roaring ocean of noise burst from the crowd. From tens of thousands of throats came an interminable, constantly repeated shout, a triumphant litany marking the successful passing of the most dangerous seconds of Operation Seduction.

"Mountbatten Zindabad!" those embittered Pathan warriors screamed, "Mountbatten Zindabad!" ("Long live Mountbatten!") [130–131]

Slaughter at Kahuta

[Soon, however,] a shocked Mountbatten was to get his first direct contact with the horrors sweeping India in the cruel springtime of 1947. The naval officer who had seen most of his shipmates die in the wreck of his destroyer off Crete, the leader who had led millions through the savage jungle war in Burma, was overwhelmed by the spectacle he discovered in that village of 3,500 people, which had once been typical of India's half million villages.

For centuries, Kahuta's dirt alleys had been shared in peace by 2,000 Hindus and Sikhs and 1,500 Moslems. That day, side by side in the village center, the stone minaret of its mosque and the rounded dome of the Sikhs' gurudwara were the only identifiable remnants of Kahuta left on the skyline of the Punjab. Just before Mountbatten's visit, a patrol of the British Norfolk Regiment on a routine reconnaissance mission passed through the village. Kahuta's citizens, as they had been doing for generations, were sleeping side by side in mutual confidence and tranquility. By dawn, Kahuta had for all practical purposes ceased to exist, and its Sikhs and Hindus were all dead or had fled in terror into the night.

A Moslem horde had descended on Kahuta like a wolf pack, setting fire to the houses in its Sikh and Hindu quarters with buckets of gasoline. In minutes, the area was engulfed in fire and entire families, screaming pitifully for help, were consumed by the flames. Those who escaped were caught, tied together, soaked with gasoline and burned alive like torches. Totally out of control, the fire swept into the Moslem quarter and completed the destruction of Kahuta. A few Hindu women, yanked from their beds to be raped and converted to Islam, survived; others had broken away from their captors and hurled themselves back into the fire to perish with their families.

"Until I went to Kahuta," Mountbatten reported back to London, "I had not appreciated the magnitude of the horrors that were going on." This confrontation with the crowd in Peshawar and the atrocious spectacle of one devastated Punjabi village was the last proof Mountbatten needed. Speed was the one absolute, overwhelming imperative if India was to be saved. . . . And if speed was essential, then there was only one way out of the impasse, the solution from which he personally recoiled, but which India's political situation dictated—partition. [131–132]

THE SHATTERED DREAM

The last, painful phase in the lifelong pilgrimage of Mahatma Gandhi began on the evening of May 1, 1947, in the same spare hut in New Delhi's sweepers' colony in which a fortnight before he had unsuccessfully urged his colleagues to accept his plan to hold India together. Crosslegged on the floor, a water-soaked towel plastered once again to his bald head, Gandhi followed with sorrow the debate of the men around him, the high command of the Congress Party. The final parting of the ways between Gandhi and those men, foreshadowed in their earlier meeting, had been reached. All Gandhi's long years in jail, his painful fasts, his hartals and his boycotts had been paving stones on the road to this meeting. He had changed the face of India and enunciated one of the original philosophies of his century to bring his countrymen to independence through nonviolence; and now his sublime triumph threatened to become a terrible personal tragedy. His followers, their tempers worn, their patience exhausted, were ready to accept the division of India as the last, inescapable step to independence. . . .

Gandhi's tragedy was that he had that evening no real alternative to propose beyond his instincts, the instincts those men had so often followed before. This night, however, he was no longer a prophet. "They call me a Mahatma," he bitterly told a friend later, "but I tell you I am not even treated by them as a sweeper." Jinnah, he told his followers, will never get Pakistan unless the British give it to him. The British would never do that in the face of the Congress majority's unyielding opposition. They had a veto over any action Mountbatten proposed. Tell the British to go, he begged, no matter what the consequences of their departure might be. Tell them to leave India "to God, to chaos, to anarchy if you wish, but leave." . . .

Nehru was a torn and anguished man, caught between his deep love for Gandhi and his new admiration and friendship for the Mountbattens. Gandhi spoke to his heart, Mountbatten to his mind. Instinctively, Nehru detested partition; yet his rationalist spirit told him it was the only answer. Since reaching his own conclusion that there was no other choice, Mountbatten and his wife had been employing all the charm and persuasiveness of Operation Seduction to bring Nehru to their viewpoint. One argument was vital. With Jinnah gone, Hindu India could have the strong central government that Nehru would need if he was going to build the socialist state of his dreams. Ultimately, he too stood out against the man he had followed so long. With his and Patel's voices in favor, the rest of the high command quickly fell in line. Nehru was authorized to inform the Viceroy that while Congress remained "passionately attached to the idea of a united India," it would accept partition, provided that the two great provinces of Punjab and Bengal were divided. The man who had led them to their triumph was alone with his tarnished victory and his broken dream. [132–134]

"Sheer Madness"

All Mountbatten's hopes had foundered, finally, on the rock of Jinnah's determined, intransigent person. . . . For the rest of his life, Mountbatten would look back on that failure to move Jinnah as the single greatest disappointment of his career. His personal anguish at the prospect of going down in history as the man who had divided India could be measured by a document flown back to London with Ismay in Mountbatten's viceregal York, his fifth personal report to the Attlee government.

Partition, Mountbatten wrote, "is sheer madness," and "no one would ever induce me to agree to it were it not for this fantastic communal madness that has seized everybody and leaves no other course open. . . . The responsibility for this mad decision," he wrote, must be placed "squarely on Indian shoulders in the eyes of the world, for one day they will bitterly regret the decision they are about to make." [134]

More serious, however, was the real concern which underlay his growing apprehension. If the implications in the plan that he had sent to London were fully realized, the great Indian subcontinent would be divided into three independent nations, not two. Mountbatten had inserted in his plan a clause that would allow the sixty-five million Hindus and Moslems of Bengal to join into one viable country, with the great seaport of Calcutta as their capital.

Contrasted to Jinnah's aberrant, two-headed state, that seemed an entity likely to endure, and Mountbatten had quietly encouraged Bengal's politicians, Hindu and Moslem alike, to support it. He had even discovered that Jinnah would not oppose the idea. He had not, however, exposed it to Nehru and Patel, and it was this oversight that disturbed him now. Would they accept a plan that might cost them the great port of Calcutta with its belt of textile mills owned by the Indian industrialists who were their party's principal financial support? If they didn't, Mountbatten, after all the assurances he had given London, was going to look a bloody fool in the eyes of India, Britain, and the world.

A sudden inspiration struck Mountbatten. He would reassure himself privately, informally, with the Indian leader, whom, to the distress of his staff, he had invited to vacation with him in Simla, [Jawaharlal Nehru]. [159] To show the plan to Nehru without exposing it to Jinnah would be a complete breach of faith with the Moslem leader, they pointed out. If he discovered it, Mountbatten's whole position would be destroyed. For a long time, Mountbatten sat silently drumming the tabletop with his fingertips.

"I am sorry," he finally announced, "your arguments are absolutely sound. But I have a hunch that I must show it to Nehru, and I'm going to follow my hunch." That night, Mountbatten invited Nehru to his study for a glass of port. Casually, he passed the Congress leader a copy of the plan as it had been amended by London, asking him to take it to his bedroom and read it. Then perhaps he might let him know informally what reception it was likely to get from Congress. Flattered and happy, Nehru agreed.

[After a few hours], Nehru began to scrutinize the text designed to chart his country's future. He was horrified by what he read. The vision of the India that emerged from the plan's pages was a nightmare . . . an India divided, not into two parts but fragmented into a dozen pieces. Bengal would become, Nehru foresaw, a wound through which the best blood of India would pour. He saw India deprived of the port of Calcutta along with its mills, factories, steelworks; Kashmir, his beloved Kashmir, an independent state ruled by a despot he despised; Hyderabad become an enormous, indigestible Moslem body planted in the belly of India, half a dozen other princely states clamoring to go off on their own. The plan, he believed, would exacerbate all India's fissiparous tendencies of dialect, culture, and race to the point at which the subcontinent would risk exploding into a mosaic of weak, hostile states. White-faced, shaking with rage, Nehru stalked into the bedroom of his confidant V. P. Menon, who had accompanied him to Simla. With a furious gesture, he hurled the plan onto his bed. "It's all over!" he shouted. . . .

Mountbatten got his first intimation of his friend's violent reaction in a letter early the following morning. For the confident Viceroy, it was "a bombshell." As he read it, the whole structure he had so carefully erected during the past six weeks came tumbling down like a house of cards. The impression that his plan left, Nehru wrote, was one of "fragmentation and conflict and disorder." It frightened him and was certain to be "resented and bitterly disliked by the Congress Party." Reading Nehru's words, the poised, self-assured Viceroy, who had proudly announced to England that he was going to present a solution to India's dilemma in ten days' time, suddenly realized that he had no solution at all. The plan that the British Cabinet was discussing that very day, the plan that he had just assured Attlee would win Indian acceptance, would never get past the one element in India that had to accept it, the Congress Party.

Mountbatten's critics might accuse him of overconfidence, but he was not a man to brood at setbacks. Instead of descending into a fit of despondency at Nehru's reaction, Mountbatten congratulated himself on his hunch in showing him the plan, and set out to repair the damage. [161] To redraft his plan, Mountbatten called into his study the highest-ranking Indian in his viceregal establishment. It was a supreme irony that at that critical juncture the Indian to whom Mountbatten turned had not even entered that vaunted administrative elite, the Indian Civil Service. No degree from Oxford or Cambridge graced his office walls. No family ties had hastened his rise. V. P. Menon was an incongruous oddity in the rarefied air of Viceroy's House, a self-made man.

Mountbatten informed Menon that before nightfall he would have to redraft the charter that would give India her independence. Its essential element, partition, had to remain, and it must continue to place the burden of choice on the Indians themselves. Menon finished his task in accordance with Mountbatten's instructions by sunset. Between lunch and dinner, he had performed a tour de force. The man who had begun his career as a two-finger typist had culminated it by redrafting, in barely six hours on an office porch looking out on the Himalayas, a plan that was going to encompass the future of one-fifth of humanity, reorder the subcontinent, and alter the map of the world. [162–163]

A DAY CURSED BY THE STARS

[When the day came to approve this plan] the lusterless eyes of Robert Clive gazed down from the great oil painting upon the wall at the seven Indian leaders filing into the Viceroy's study. Representatives of India's 400 million human beings, those millions whom Gandhi called "miserable specimens of humanity with lusterless eyes," they entered Mountbatten's study on this morning of June 2, 1947, to inspect the deeds that would return to their peoples the continent whose conquest the British general had opened two centuries before. The papers, formally approved by the British Cabinet, had been brought from London by the Viceroy just forty-eight hours before. . . .

For the first time since he had arrived in Delhi, Mountbatten was now being forced to abandon his head-to-head diplomacy for a round-table conference. He had decided, however, that he would do the talking. He was not going to run the risk of throwing the meeting open for a general discussion that might degenerate into an acrimonious shouting match that could destroy his elaborately wrought plan. Aware of the poignancy and historic nature of their gathering, he began by noting that during the past five years he had taken part in a number of momentous meetings at which the decisions that had determined the fate of the war had been taken. He could remember no meeting, however, at which decisions had been taken whose impact upon history had been as profound as would be the impact of the decision before them.

Briefly, Mountbatten reviewed his conversations since arriving in Delhi, stressing the terrible sense of urgency they had impressed on him. Then, for the record and for history, he formally asked Jinnah one last time if he was prepared to accept Indian unity as envisaged by the Cabinet Mission Plan. With equal formality, Jinnah replied that he was not, and Mountbatten moved on to the matter at hand. Briefly, he reviewed the details of his plan. The dominion-status clause that had ultimately won Winston Churchill's support was not, he stressed, a reflection of a British desire to keep a foot in the door beyond her time, but to assure that British assistance would not be summarily withdrawn if it was still needed. He dwelt on Calcutta, on the coming agony of the Sikhs.

He would not, he said, ask them to give their full agreement to a plan, parts of which went against their principles. He asked only that they accept it in a peaceful spirit and vow to make it work without bloodshed. His intention, he said, was to meet with them again the following morning. He hoped that before that, before midnight, all three parties, the Moslem League, Congress, and the Sikhs, would have indicated their willingness to accept the plan as a basis for a final Indian settlement. If this was the case, then he proposed that he, Nehru, Jinnah, and Baldev Singh announce their agreement jointly to the world the following evening on All India Radio. Clement Attlee would make a confirming announcement from London.

"Gentlemen," he concluded, "I should like your reaction to the plan by midnight." [191–192]

A Nod of the Head

[That night] in Louis Mountbatten's study the lights still burned, illuminating the last meeting of his harrowing day. He stared at his visitor with uncomprehending disbelief. Congress had indicated in time their willingness to accept his plan. So, too, had the Sikhs. Now the man it was designed to satisfy, the man whose obdurate, unyielding will had forced partition on India, was temporizing. Everything Jinnah had been striving for for years was there, waiting only his acknowledgment. For some mysterious reason, Jinnah simply could not bring himself this night to utter the word that he had made a career refusing to pronounce—"yes."

Inhaling deeply one of the Craven A's that he chain-smoked in his jade holder Jinnah kept insisting that he could not give an indication of the Moslem League's reaction to Mountbatten's plan until he had put it before the League's Council, and he needed at least a week to bring its members to Delhi. All the frustrations generated by his dealings with Jinnah welled up in Mountbatten. Jinnah had gotten his damn Pakistan. Even the Sikhs had swallowed the plan. Everything he had been working for he had finally gotten, and here, at the absolute eleventh hour, Jinnah was preparing to destroy it all, to bring the whole thing crashing down with his unfathomable inability to articulate just one word, "yes."

Mountbatten simply had to have his agreement. Attlee was standing by in London waiting to make his historic announcement to the Commons in less than twenty-four hours. He had gone on the line personally to Attlee, to his government with firm assurances that this plan would work; that there would be no more abrupt twists like that prompted by Nehru in Simla; that this time, they could be certain they had approved a plan that the Indian leaders would all accept. He had, with enormous difficulty, coaxed a reluctant Congress up to this point, and, finally, they were prepared to accept partition. Even Gandhi, temporarily at least, had allowed himself to be bypassed. A final hesitation, just the faintest hint that Jinnah was maneuvering to secure one last concession, and the whole carefully wrought package would blow apart.

"Mr. Jinnah," Mountbatten said, "if you think I can hold this position for a week while you summon your followers to Delhi, you must be crazy. You know this has been drawn up to the boiling point. . . .The Congress has made their acceptance dependent on your agreement. If they suspect you're holding out on them, they will immediately withdraw their agreement and we will be in the most terrible mess."

No, No, Jinnah protested, everything had to be done in the legally constituted way, "I am not the Moslem League," he said. . . .

"Now, now, come on, Mr. Jinnah," said Mountbatten, icy calm, "don't try to tell me that. You can try to tell the world that. But don't kid yourself that I don't know what's what in the Moslem League. . . . Mr. Jinnah, I'm going to tell you something. I don't intend to let you wreck your own plan. I can't allow you to throw away the solution you've worked so hard to get. I propose to accept on your behalf.

"Tomorrow at the meeting," Mountbatten continued, "I shall say I have received the reply of the Congress, with a few reservations that I am sure I can satisfy, and they have accepted. The Sikhs have accepted. . . . Then I shall say that I had a very long, very friendly conversation with Mr. Jinnah last night, that we went through the plan in detail, and Mr. Jinnah has given me his personal assurance that he is in agreement with this plan.

"Now at that point, Mr. Jinnah," Mountbatten continued, "I shall turn to you. I don't want you to speak. I don't want Congress to force you into the open. I want you to do only one thing. I want you to nod your head to show that you are in agreement with me. . . . If you don't nod your head, Mr. Jinnah," Mountbatten concluded, "then you're through, and there'll be nothing more I can do for you. Everything will collapse. This is not a threat. It's a prophecy. If you don't nod your head at that moment, my usefulness here will be ended, you will have lost your Pakistan, and as far as I am concerned, you can go to hell." [196]

The meeting that would formally record the Indian leaders' acceptance of the Mountbatten plan to divide India began exactly as Mountbatten had said it would. Once again, on the morning of June 3, the Viceroy condemned the leaders to an unfamiliar silence by dominating the conversation himself. As he had expected, he said, all three parties had had grave reservations about his plan and he was grateful that they had aired them to him. Nonetheless Congress had signified its acceptance. So, too, had the Sikhs. He had had, he said, a long and friendly conversation the previous evening with Mr. Jinnah, who had assured him the plan was acceptable.

As he spoke those words, Mountbatten turned to Jinnah, seated at his right. At that instant Mountbatten had absolutely no idea what the Moslem leader was going to do. The captain of the *Kelly*, the supreme commander who had had an entire army corps encircled and cut off by the Japanese on the Imphal Plain, would always look back on that instant as "the most hair-raising moment of my entire life." For an endless second, he stared into Jinnah's impassive, expressionless face. Then slowly, reluctance crying from every pore, Jinnah indicated his agreement with the faintest, most begrudging nod he could make. His chin moved barely half an inch downward, the shortest distance it could have traveled consonant with accepting Mountbatten's plan. With that brief, almost imperceptible gesture, a nation of forty-five million human beings had received its final sanction.

A Sharp Crack

However abortive its form, however difficult the circumstances that would attend its birth, the "impossible dream" of Pakistan would at last be realized. Mountbatten had enough agreement to go ahead. Before any of the seven men could have a chance to formulate a last reservation or doubt, he announced that his plan would henceforth constitute the basis for an Indian settlement.

While the enormity of the decision they had just taken began to penetrate, Mountbatten had a thirty-four-page, single-spaced document set before each man. Clasping the last copy himself with both hands, the Viceroy lifted it over his head and whipped it back down onto the table. At the sharp crack that followed the slap of paper on wood, Mountbatten read out the imposing title on his equally imposing document—"The Administrative Consequences of Partition."

It was a carefully elaborated christening present from Mountbatten and his staff to the Indian leaders, a guide to the awesome task that now lay before them. Page after page, it summarized in its dull bureaucratic jargon the appalling implications of their decision. None of the seven was in even the remotest way prepared for the shock they encountered as they began to turn the pages of the document. Ahead of them lay a problem of a scope and on a scale no people had ever encountered before, a problem vast enough to beggar the most vivid imagination. They were now going to be called upon to settle the contested estate of 400 million human beings, to unravel the possessions left behind by thirty centuries of common inhabitation of the subcontinent, to pick apart the fruits of three centuries of technology. The cash in the banks, stamps in the post office, books in the libraries, debts, assets, the world's third-largest railway, jails, prisoners, inkpots, brooms, research centers, hospitals, universities, institutions and articles staggering in number and variety would be theirs to divide.

A stunned silence filled the study as the seven men measured for the first time what lay ahead of them. Mountbatten . . . had forced these seven men to come to grips with a problem so imposing that it would leave them neither the time nor the energy for recrimination in the few weeks of coexistence left to them.

"No Joy in My Heart"

Shortly after seven o'clock on that evening of June 3, 1947, in the New Delhi studio of All India Radio, the four key leaders formally announced their agreement to divide the subcontinent into two separate sovereign nations. As befitting his office, Mountbatten spoke first. His words were confident, his speech brief, his tones understated. Nehru followed, speaking in Hindi. Sadness grasped the Indian leader's face as he told his listeners that "the great destiny of India" was taking shape, "with travail and suffering." Baring his own emotions, he urged acceptance of the plan that had caused him such deep personal anguish, by concluding that "it is with no joy in my heart that I commend these proposals to you."

Jinnah was next. Nothing would ever be more illustrative of the enormous, yet wholly incongruous nature of his achievement than that speech. Mohammed Ali Jinnah was incapable of announcing to his followers the news that he had won them a state in a language that they could understand. He had to tell India's ninety million Moslems of the "momentous decision" to create an Islamic state on the subcontinent in English. An announcer then read his words in Urdu. . . . [197–199]

Gandhi walked into Mountbatten's study at 6 P.M. His prayer meeting was at seven. That left Mountbatten less than an hour in which to ward off a potential disaster. His first glance at the Mahatma told Mountbatten how deeply upset he was. Crumpled up in his armchair "like a bird with a broken wing," Gandhi kept raising and dropping one hand lamenting in an almost inaudible voice: "It's so awful, it's so awful."

In that state Gandhi, Mountbatten knew, was capable of anything. A public denunciation of his plan would be disastrous. Nehru, Patel, and the other leaders the Viceroy had so patiently coaxed into accepting it would be forced to break publicly with Gandhi or break their agreement with him. Vowing to use every argument his fertile imagination could produce, Mountbatten began by telling Gandhi how he understood and shared his feelings at seeing the united India he had worked for all his life destroyed by this plan. Suddenly as he spoke, a burst of inspiration struck him. The newspapers had christened the plan the "Mountbatten Plan," he said, but they should have called it the "Gandhi Plan." It was Gandhi, Mountbatten declared, who had suggested to him all its major ingredients. The Mahatma looked at him perplexed.

Yes, Mountbatten continued, Gandhi had told him to leave the choice to the Indian people, and this plan did. It was the provincial, popularly elected assemblies which would decide India's future. Each province's assembly would vote on whether it wished to join India or Pakistan. Gandhi had urged the British to quit India as soon as possible, and that was what they were going to do. "If by some miracle the assemblies vote for unity," Mountbatten told Gandhi, "you have what you want. If they don't agree, I'm sure you don't want us to oppose their decision by force of arms."

Approaching seventy-eight, Gandhi was, for the first time in thirty years, uncertain of his grip on India's masses, at odds with the leaders of his party. In his despair and uncertainty, he was still searching in his soul for an answer, still waiting for an illuminating whisper of the inner voice that had guided him in so many of the grave crises of his career. That June evening, however, the voice was silent, and Gandhi was assailed by doubt. Should he remain faithful to his instincts, denounce partition, even (as he had earlier urged) at the price of plunging India into violence and chaos? Or should he listen to the Viceroy's desperate plea for reason? . . .

Less than an hour later, cross-legged on a raised platform in a dirt square in the midst of his Untouchables colony, Gandhi delivered his verdict. Many in the crowd before him had come, not to pray, but to hear from the lips of the prophet of nonviolence a call to arms, a fiery assault on Mountbatten's plan. No such cry would come this evening from the mouth of the man who had so often promised to offer his own body for vivisection, rather than accept his country's division. It was no use blaming the Viceroy for partition, he said. Look to yourselves and in your own hearts for an explanation of what has happened, he challenged. Louis Mountbatten's persuasiveness had won the ultimate and most difficult triumph of his viceroyalty.

As for Gandhi, many an Indian would never forgive him his silence, and the frail old man whose heart still ached for India's coming division would one day pay the price of their rancor. [200]

The Announced Date

For Mountbatten the public announcement was the apotheosis, the consecration of a remarkable *tour de force*. In barely two months, virtually a one-man band, he had achieved the impossible, established a dialogue with India's leaders, set the basis of an agreement, persuaded his Indian interlocutors to accept it, extracted the whole hearted support of both the government and the opposition in London. He had skirted with dexterity and a little luck the pitfalls marring his route. And as his final gesture he had entered the cage of the old lion himself, convinced Churchill to draw in his claws and left him too, murmuring his approbation.

[As] Mountbatten concluded his talk to the assembled world press [there was] a burst of applause. He opened the floor to questions. He had no apprehension in doing so. "I had been there," he would recall later. "I was the only one who had been through it all, who'd lived every moment of it. For the first time the press were meeting the one and only man who had the whole thing at his fingertips." Suddenly, when the long barrage of questions began to trickle out, the anonymous voice of an Indian newsman cut across the chamber. His final question was the last square left to Mountbatten to fill in the puzzle he had been assigned six months before.

"Sir," the voice said, "If all agree that there is most urgent need for speed between today and the transfer of power, surely you should have a date in mind?"

"Yes, indeed," replied Mountbatten.

"And if you have chosen a date, sir, what is that date?" the questioner asked.

A number of rapid calculations went whirring through the Viceroy's mind as he listened to those questions. He had not, in fact, selected a date. But he was convinced it had to be very soon.

"I had to force the pace," he recalled later. "I knew I had to force Parliament to get the bill through before their summer recess to hold the thing together. We were sitting on the edge of a volcano, on a fused bomb and we didn't know when the bomb would go off." Like the blurred images of a horror film, the charred corpses of Kahuta flashed across Louis Mountbatten's mind. If an outburst of similar tragedies was not to drag all India into an apocalypse, he had to move fast. After three thousand years of history and two hundred years of *Pax Britannica,* only a few weeks remained, the Viceroy believed, between India and chaos. He stared at the packed assembly hall. Every face in the room was turned to his. A hushed, expectant silence broken only by the whir of the wooden blades of the fans revolving overhead stilled the room. "I was determined to show I was the master of the whole event," he would remember.

"Yes," he said, "I have selected a date for the transfer of power."

As he was uttering those words, the possible dates were still spinning through his mind like the numbers on a revolving roulette wheel. Early September? Middle of September, middle of August? Suddenly the wheel stopped with a jar and the little ball popped into a slot so overwhelmingly appropriate that Mountbatten's decision was instantaneous. It was a date linked in his memory to the most triumphant hours of his own existence, the day in which his long crusade through the jungles of Burma had ended with the unconditional surrender of the Japanese empire. A period in Asian history had ended with the collapse of that feudal Asia of the Samurai. What more appropriate date for the birth of the new democratic Asia arising to take its place than the second anniversary of Japan's surrender? His voice constricted with sudden emotion; the victor of the jungles of Burma, about to become the liberator of India, announced:

"The final transfer of power to Indian hands will take place on August 15, 1947." [201–202]

As soon as the radio announced Mountbatten's date, astrologers all over India began to consult their charts. Those in the holy city of Benares and several others in the South immediately proclaimed August 15 a date so inauspicious that India "would be better advised to tolerate the British one day longer rather than risk eternal damnation." . . .

"What have they done? What have they done?" one famous astrologer shouted to the heavens whose machinations he interpreted for man. Despite the discipline of his physical and spiritual forces acquired in years of yoga, meditation, and tantric studies in a temple in the hills of Assam, the astrologer lost control of himself. Seizing a piece of paper he sat down and wrote an urgent appeal to the man inadvertently responsible for this celestial catastrophe. "For the love of God," he wrote to Mountbatten, "do not give India her independence on August 15. If floods, drought, famine and massacres follow, it will be because free India was born on a day cursed by the stars."

QUESTIONS

1. What were the main forces that Mountbatten had to consider in his handling of the Indian situation?

2. Evaluate the way he handled each critical opponent and situation.

3. Evaluate the overall British strategy in leaving India.

4. What can one conclude about handling negotiation strategies from this case?

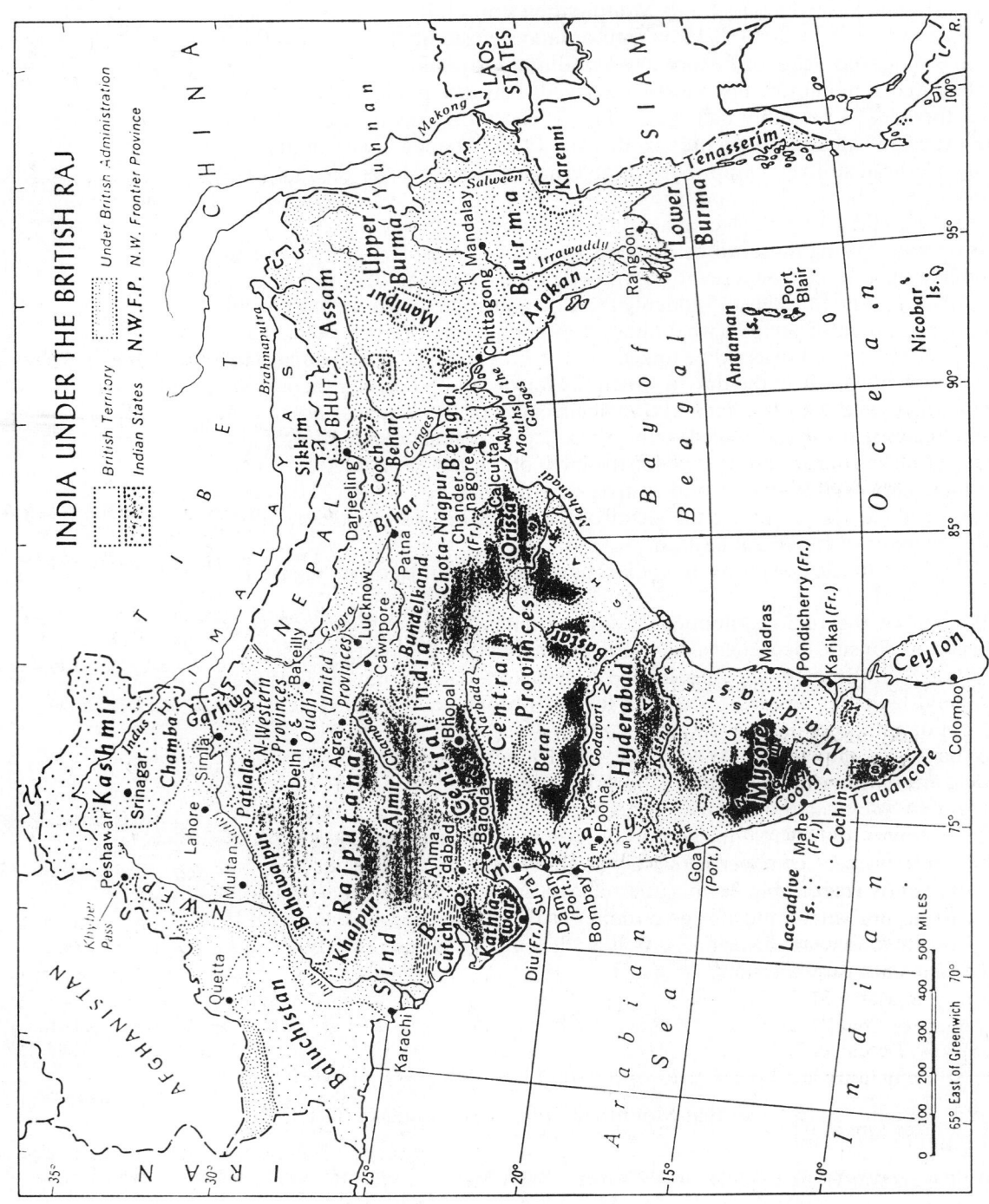

INDIA UNDER THE BRITISH RAJ

Legend:
- British Territory
- Indian States
- Under British Administration
- N.W.F.P. N. W. Frontier Province

AFGHANISTAN

IRAN

Khyber Pass

Peshawar

N.W.F.P.

Baluchistan

Quetta

Karachi

CHINA

TIBET

Yunnan

Mekong

LAOS STATES

SIAM

Tenasserim

Indus R.

Kashmir

Srinagar

Chamba

Garhwal

Simla

Lahore

Multan

Bahawalpur

Khaipur

Sind

Cutch

Kathiawar

HIMALAYAS

NEPAL

Sikkim

BHUT.

Darjeeling

Cooch Behar

Bihar

Brahmaputra

Assam

Upper Burma

Manipur

Salween

Mandalay

Burma

Arakan

Irrawaddy

Chittagong

Mouths of the Ganges

Bengal

Calcutta

Chander Nagore (Fr.)

Chota-Nagpur

Orissa

Bastar

Rangoon

Lower Burma

Karenni

N-Western Provinces

Delhi & Oudh

Agra (United Provinces)

Lucknow

Cawnpore

Bareilly

Gogra

Patna

Ganges

Rajputana

Ajmir

Bhopal

Central India

Narbada

Central Provinces

Berar

Hyderabad

Godavari

Krishna

Ahmadabad

Baroda

Daman (Port.)

Diu (Fr.) Surat

Bombay

Poona

Goa (Port.)

Mahe (Fr.)

Madras

Pondicherry (Fr.)

Karikal (Fr.)

Coorg

Mysore

Cochin

Travancore

Colombo

Ceylon

Bay of Bengal

Andaman Is.

Port Blair

Nicobar Is.

Arabian Sea

Indian Ocean

Laccadive Is.

65° East of Greenwich 70° 75°

MILES
0   100   200   300   400   500

1044

CASE
NOTES

1-2

1. Summarized from "A Market Milestone for DNA Research," *Business Week,* September 18, 1978.
2. "Bacteria Make Human Insulin," *Chemical and Engineering News,* September 11, 1978.

1-5

1. "The Five Best Managed Companies," *Dun's Review,* December 1980.
2. Gene Bylinsky, quoted from *The Innovation Millionaires.* Copyright © 1976, 1974, 1973, 1967 Gene Bylinsky. Reprinted with the permission of Charles Scribner's Sons.
3. *Electronic News,* December 27, 1974.
4. "Meet Bob Noyce," *Computer Decisions,* June 1974.
5. *The Wall Street Journal,* October 4, 1969.
6. "Special Report: Where the Action Is in Electronics," *Business Week,* October 4, 1969.
7. *Electronic News,* August 26, 1968.
8. *Electronics,* March 31, 1969.
9. "Why Cores Could Become Just a Memory," *Business Week,* December 26, 1970.
10. "American Industry and What Ails It," *The Atlantic,* May 1980.
11. "Intel Takes Aim at the '80's," *Electronics,* February 28, 1980.
12. "The Micro War Heats Up," *Forbes,* November 26, 1979.
13. "Intel Gambles for Continued Rapid Growth," *International Management,* November 1981.

14. "Creativity by the Numbers," *Harvard Business Review,* May–June 1980.

1-6

1. T.M. Powledge, "Biogen in Transition," *Bio/Technology,* July 1983, pp. 398–405.
2. "Flying Too High," *The Economist,* November 1, 1980, p. 96.
3. "Walter Gilbert Resigns as Chief...," *The Wall Street Journal,* December 18, 1984.
4. "Julian Davies' Farewell to Biogen," *Bio/Technology,* July 1985, p. 593.

1-7

1. Robert A. Sigafoos, *Absolutely Positively Overnight,* St. Luke's Press, Memphis, 1983, p. 25.
2. "A Business Visionary Who Really Delivered," *Nation's Business,* November 1981.
3. Robinson Humphrey Company, Inc., *Research Report on Federal Express Corporation,* April 1984.
4. "Redefining an Industry Through Integrated Automation," *Infosystems,* May 1985.
5. R. Levering, et al., *The 100 Best Companies to Work for in America,* Addison-Wesley, Reading, Mass., 1984, p. 114.
6. Rooney Pace, Inc., *Research Report-Federal Express Corporation,* June 18, 1984.
7. Robinson Humphrey Company, Inc., Equities Research, *Research Report-Federal Express Corporation,* April 1984.
8. Rooney Pace, Inc., *Research Report-Federal Express Corporation,* June 18, 1984.

1-10

1. T. Sakiya, *Honda Motor: The Men, The Management, The Machines.* Kodansha International, Ltd. Tokyo, 1982.
2. S. Sanders, *Honda: The Man and His Machines,* Little Brown, Boston, 1975.
3. Data in this section drawn in part from Richard Pascale, "Perspectives on Strategy," *California Management Review,* Spring 1984.
4. R. Guest, "The Quality of Work Life in Japan . . . ," *Hokudai Economic Papers,* Tokyo, Vol. XII, 1982–83.
5. "America's New No. 4 Automaker–Honda," *Fortune,* October 28, 1985.
6. "Toyota's Fast Lane," *Business Week,* November 4, 1985.
7. "Honda the Market Guzzler," *Fortune,* February 20, 1984.

2-1

1. E. Davis, *History of The New York Times,* The New York Times Company, New York, 1921, p. 194.
2. J. Kraft, "The Future of *The New York Times,*" *Esquire,* April 1961, pp. 121t.
3. C. David Rambo, "Lee Huebner: IHT publisher's talents match global challenges," *presstime,* February 1990, p. 34.
4. Mary A. Anderson, "Global Buying Spree Skips U.S. Dailies," *presstime,* February 1990, p. 8.
5. "*The New York Times?*" *Fortune,* July 28, 1980, pp. 84–85.

2-3

1. "Hewlett Packard in Brief," *Company Literature,* 1984.
2. "Hewlett Packard Discovers Marketing," *Fortune,* October 1, 1984.
3. William R. Hewlett, "The Human Side of Management," *Eugene B. Clark Executive Lecture,* March 25, 1982.
4. Thomas L. Wheelen and J. David Hunger, *Strategic Management and Business Policy,* Addison-Wesley Publishing Company, 1983.
5. "Hewlett Packard: Where Slower Growth is Smarter Management," *Business Week,* June 9, 1975.
6. "Hewlett Packard's Calculated Rise," *Management Today,* August 1977.
7. John Young, "HP White Paper on Organization Changes," *Company Literature,* July 19, 1984.
8. Bro Uttla, "Mettle-Test Time for John Young," *Fortune,* April 29, 1985.

9. John A. Young, "The Quality Focus at Hewlett Packard," *Journal of Business Strategy,* Winter 1985.
10. "Back Into the Race," *Forbes,* October 10, 1983.
11. "Can John Young Redesign Hewlett Packard?" *Business Week,* December 6, 1982.
12. E.F. Hutton, Inc., Equity Research, *Hewlett Packard Company Action Report,* June 28, 1983.

2-4

1. James W. Botkin, Dan Dimancescu, and Ray Stata, *The Innovators,* Harper & Row, New York, 1984, p. 22.
2. Ibid., p. 29.
3. "A Ford Man Tunes up Nissan," *Fortune,* November 24, 1986, pp. 140–144.
4. "Ford's Lewis Veraldi: Man of the Year," *Automotive Industries,* February 1987, pp. 64–68.
5. "In the Fast Lane," *Business Week,* February 11, 1985, pp. 48–52.
6. "A 'hot dog' tries to cut the mustard at Ford," *Industry Week,* August 18, 1980, pp. 76–82.
7. "What's Creating an Industrial Miracle at Ford?" *Business Week,* July 30, 1984, pp. 80–84.
8. "Ford's Drive for Quality," *Fortune,* April 18, 1983, pp. 62–70.
9. "Ford Team Taurus Concept is Blueprint for Future Cars," *Automotive News,* May 6, 1985, p. 2.
10. "Detroit Comes Through," *Business Week,* June 30, 1986, p. 69.
11. "Team Taurus," *Ward's Auto World,* February 1985, pp. 26–31.
12. "Ford's Mr. Turnaround: 'We Have More to Do,' " *Fortune,* March 4, 1985, pp. 83–89.
13. "Hot 'Lanta! Taurus Takes Off," *Automotive Industries,* November 1985, p. 46.
14. "Ford Motor Delays Introducing Data of Taurus Sable," *The Wall Street Journal,* September 20, 1985, p. 15.
15. "Can Ford Stay on Top?" *Business Week,* September 28, 1987, pp. 78–81.
16. "What's Ahead in the World Auto War?" *Fortune,* November 9, 1987, p. 74t.
17. "Ford Goes After Yuppies," *Christian Science Monitor,* February 1, 1985, p. 5.
18. "Ford Gambles on Styling to Regain Lost Consumers," *Los Angeles Times,* January 30, 1985, pp. 1–2.
19. "L-M Sees Sable Matching Taurus," *Automotive News,* August 19, 1985, p. 2.
20. "Ford Puts $100M on Table to Power Taurus and Sable," *Advertising Age,* November 18, 1985, p. 1.
21. "Ford to Introduce Taurus, Sable Today with High

Hopes Despite Short Supply," *The Wall Street Journal,* December 26, 1985, p. 2.

22. "The Road Warriors," *Marketing and Media Decisions,* March 1987, pp. 60–69.

23. "Now it's Simultaneous Car Design—," *Industry Week,* April 1, 1985, pp. 17–26.

24. Various *Wall Street Journal* articles.

2-6

1. *Wall Street Journal,* September 10, 1979, 1;8.

2. *Moody's,* 1970.

3. "The Name of the Game is Still General Mills," *Forbes,* April 1, 1970.

4. "An Unforeseen Succession at the Biggest Miller," *Fortune,* February 1973, p. 18.

5. "Pillsbury Mills Its Future," *Financial World,* February 3, 1971, p. 12.

6. "Pillsbury Turnaround . . ." *Advertising Age,* January 12, 1974.

7. "Pillsbury Mills Its Future," *Financial World,* February 3, 1971, p. 12.

8. *Transcript Consumer Analysts' Meeting,* New York, March 19, 1974.

9. "Recipe at Pillsbury Calls for Quick Results," *Barrons,* July 29, 1974, p. 25.

10. See T. Hanold, "An Executive View of MIS," *Datamation,* November 1972.

11. "Pillsbury's Winery," *Business Week.* September 8, 1975, p. 32.

12. Mr. W. Scott, Comments before Dain, Kalman & Quail Food Conference, March 1977.

13. "The One Man Show at Pillsbury," *Business Week,* January 19, 1976.

14. W. Kiechel, "Now for the Greening of Pillsbury," *Fortune,* November 5, 1979.

15. Acquired in November 1975 for 516,175 shares of Pillsbury with about $25 million. *Moody's,* 1976.

16. *The Wall Street Journal,* December 6, 1976, p. 24.

17. "William H. Spoor, Pillsbury Co.," *Financial World,* April 1, 1977, p. 20.

18. "Can Pillsbury Rise Above the Defections?" *Business Week,* June 9, 1980.

19. "CBS Chooses Wyman . . ." *The Wall Street Journal,* May 23, 1980.

20. "Can Pillsbury Rise Above the Defections?" *Business Week,* June 9, 1980.

21. *The Wall Street Journal,* July 20, 1983, p. 16.

22. "Pillsbury Co. Revives . . ." *The Wall Street Journal,* November 12, 1984.

23. "Friendly Whopper . . ." *Barron's,* September 10, 1984.

24. "Rising to the Top at Pillsbury," *Business Week,* March 12, 1984.

2-7

1. *Twentieth Century Petroleum Statistics,* by DeGolyer & MacNaughton, 1984.

2. *Oil & Gas Journal,* October 12, November 9, 1981.

3. "More Money Than it Properly Knows What to Do With," *The Economist,* April 8, 1981, p. 70.

4. "Will Norway Face Up to Being Rich?," *Euromoney,* November 1980, p. 42.

5. "Norway: Still Just Crumbs for Foreign Oil Companies," *World Oil,* October 1981.

6. *World Oil,* August 15, 1980, pp. 158 and 160.

7. "Norway: Still Just Crumbs for Foreign Oil Companies," *World Oil,* October 1981.

8. *Ibid.*

9. *World Oil,* March 1981, p. 31.

10. "Why North Sea Oil Gushes, But the Pumps Run Dry," *The Economist,* June 16, 1979.

11. "Problems of a European Oil Sheik," *The Economist,* January 12, 1980.

12. "U.K. Government Revenues from North Sea Oil," *The Banker,* July 1980.

13. *World Oil,* August 15, 1980, p. 153–56.

14. "U.K. North Sea Expenditures," *Ocean Industry,* November 1980, pp. 111–12.

15. "Prospects for the U.K. North Sea Suddenly Become Bleak," *Oil & Gas Journal,* March 23, 1981.

16. "Japan: Long-Term Oil Strategy Succeeding," *Petroleum Economist,* September 1979.

17. "Japanese Adjust to Oil Supply Changes," *Oil & Gas Journal,* January 26, 1981.

18. *Ibid.*

19. "China's Petroleum Surplus May Vanish in the 1980s," *Oil & Gas Journal,* October 6, 1980.

20. "Indonesian Survey," *Euromoney,* January 1979.

21. "Growing Problems Downstream," *Petroleum Economist,* November, 1979.

22. "Indonesia, A Plan Aimed at Cutting Overdependence on Oil," *Business Week,* April 9, 1979.

23. "Heavy Oil Revives Venezuelan Refining," *Oil & Gas Journal,* August 1980.

24. "The Risks in Recharging Venezuela's Economy," *Business Week,* September 1, 1980.

25. "Easy Come, Easy Go," *Forbes,* October 26, 1981.

26. "Nigeria Presses Claim for Reduced State Oil Sales," *Petroleum Economist,* September 1980.

27. "The Disaffection of Nigeria," *Oil & Gas Journal,* August 21, 1978, p. 25.

28. "West African Oil: At Last, an Alternative to the Mideast," *Business Week,* August 10, 1981, p. 52.

29. "Why the Spending Stopped in Nigeria," *Fortune,* July 16, 1979.

2-8

1. "United Financial Boosts . . . ," *The Wall Street Journal,* July 19, 1972, p. 5.
2. "Acquired Had Little to Say in S&L Merger," *The Wall Street Journal,* September 14, 1981, p. 33.
3. "First Nationwide: A New Era," *The New York Times,* January 4, 1982.
4. "A Talk with Anthony M. Frank . . . ," *Management,* Fall 1983, p. 4.
5. U.S. League of Savings Institutions, *1984 Savings Institutions Sourcebook,* p. 29.
6. "Thrifts and Deregulation: Freddie Mac's Role," *Federal Home Loan Bank Board Journal,* August 1983.
7. "Banks Feel Little Heat as Thrifts Warm to Business," *ABA Banking Journal,* March 1985, p. 93.
8. "The Financial Outlook for the Savings & Loan Industry," *Federal Home Loan Bank Board Journal,* January 1984.
9. "New Deposit Instruments," *Federal Reserve Bulletin,* May 1983, pp. 320–322.
10. "Hangover in the Mortgage Market," *Business Week,* April 8, 1985, p. 83.
11. "Uncle Sam Enters the S&L Business," *Fortune,* November 25, 1985, p. 69.
12. "Look Before Leaping to Regulate Thrifts," *The Wall Street Journal,* November 1985.

3-1

1. L.A.B. Pilkington, "Review Lecture, The Float Glass Process," The Royal Society, London, 13 February 1969.
2. J.J. Ermenc, "Interview with Sir Alistair Pilkington, June 25, 1968," edited transcript, Dartmouth College, Hanover, New Hampshire.
3. Sir Alistair Pilkington, Speech to Toledo Glass & Ceramics Award Ceremony, January 21, 1963.
4. Sir Alistair Pilkington, "Float: An Application of Science, Analysis, and Judgment, Turner Memorial Lecture," *Glass Technology,* August 1971.
5. Interview with James Brian Quinn, Spring 1978. All other quotations from Pilkington employees came from this same series of interviews unless otherwise footnoted.
6. T. Lane and K. Roberts, *Strike at Pilkingtons,* Collins/Fontana, London, 1971.
7. *Report of Joint Inquiry,* Dept. of Employment and Productivity, HMSO, p. 10.
8. *The Paper Clip,* Ford Glass Ltd., Toronto, Ontario, Number 28–62, June 22, 1982.
9. *Financial Times,* June 11, 1982, p. 16.

3-2

1. Nick Lyons, *The Sony Vision,* Crown Publishers, New York, 1976, p. 80.
2. R.D. Schwarz, E.F. Hutton, *Imaging Technology—Industry Report,* June 13, 1985.
3. P.J. Enderlin, Smith Barney, Harris Upham & Co., Inc., *Electronic Imaging—Impact on Consumer Photography,* December 20, 1984.
4. "Kodak President Says Concern Could Make Electronic Camera," *The Wall Street Journal,* October 29, 1981, p. 38.

3-2

1. Akio Morita. "International Marketing of Sony Corporation," monograph, Tokyo, July 14, 1969.
2. ———. "Decision Making in Japanese Business," monograph, Manila, September 30, 1975.
3. ———. "What Is the Difference Between the Japanese Management and the American?" Chicago, February 17, 1972.
4. ———. "Creativity in Modern Industry," Frank Nelson Doubleday Series, Smithsonian Institution, 1974.

GENERAL SOURCES

"Akio Morita: Chairman and CEO," *Director,* May 1982.
"The Americanization of Sony," *New York Times,* March 18, 1973.
"Another Revolution," *Economist,* June 4, 1983.
"A Diversification Plan Tuned to the People Factor," *Business Week,* February 9, 1981.
P. Drucker, *Management,* Harper and Row, 1974.
P.J. Enderlin, Smith Barney, Harris Upham & Co., Inc., *Electronic Imaging—Impact on Consumer Photography,* December 20, 1984.
"Even Sony Sometimes Stumbles," *Forbes,* April 25, 1983.
"The Giants in Japanese Electronics," *Economist,* February 20, 1982.
"Here Comes Projection Television," *Economist,* October 8, 1977.
"Horatio Alger Story with a Japanese Twist," *The New York Times Magazine,* September 10, 1967.
"How to Get Bigger with Smaller Products," *Business Week,* May 25, 1968.
Masaru Ibuka. "How Sony Developed Electronics for the World Market." *IEEE Transactions on Engineering Management,* Vol. EM-22, No. 1, February 1975.
"An Incongruous Search for Greener Pastures," *Business Week,* February 11, 1980.
Shigeru Kobayashi. *Creative Management,* American Management Association, 1971.
Nick Lyons. *The Sony Vision,* New York: Crown Publishers, Inc., 1976.
N. Pearlstine, "Blurred Image," *Forbes,* September 4, 1978.

1048

R.D. Schwarz, E.F. Hutton Group, Inc., *Imaging Technology—Industry Report*, June 13, 1985.

"Sony Levels Off," *Forbes*, September 9, 1978.

"Sony's Nearly 40 Years of Making It Better and Smaller," *Broadcasting*, May 16, 1983.

"Sony's Purposeful Dreams," *Fortune*, July 1964.

"Sony's US Operation Goes in for Repairs," *Business Week*, March 13, 1978.

"Talking Business With Akio Morita," *Business Week*, April 18, 1983.

R. Tanner and W. Ouchi, "Made in America: Under Japanese Management," *Harvard Business Review*, September–October 1974.

"Technology vs. Tariffs," *Forbes*, April 15, 1977.

"Video's New Frontier," *Newsweek*, February 9, 1976.

Wall Street Journal, November 2, 1981, p. 23.

3-3

1. "Canada Gets to Grips with Deregulation," *Euromoney*, November 1984.
2. "Mulroney Drops a Bombshell," *Business Week*, April 29, 1985.
3. "Merrill Lynch Canada. . . .," *The Wall Street Journal*, July 2, 1985, p. 10.
4. "Canada's Banks—A Decade of Change in the Euromarkets," *Euromoney*, Supplement, July 1985.
5. "The Four Pillars," *Canadian Banker*, February 1985.
6. "Where's the Power in the Financial Services Industry?" *Canadian Banker*, June 1985.
7. "Foreign Banks are Hopeful," *Euromoney*, Supplement, July 1985.
8. "An International Banking Centre in Canada," *Canadian Banker*, June 1983.
9. "Reconstruction of the Stockbroking Industry," *Euromoney*, Supplement, July 1985.
10. "Merrill Lynch Canada. . . ." *The Wall Street Journal*, July 2, 1985, p. 10.
11. "Canada's Fat Cats," *The Economist*, July 14, 1984.
12. "Montreal Attempts a Comeback," *Euromoney*, November 1984.
13. *op. cit.*, "Reconstruction of the Stockbroking Industry."

3-4

1. "A Dollop of 'Good, Gutsy Maine Business Sense,'" *Fortune*, July 1976, p. 27.
2. "How to Manage Entrepreneurs," *Business Week*, September 7, 1981, pp. 66–69.
3. "The Second Time Around," *Forbes*, March 2, 1981, p. 70.
4. "The General Mills Brand of Managers," *Fortune*, January 12, 1981.

5. "General Mills: An All-American Marketer," *Dun's Business Month*, December 1981, p. 72.
6. "General Mills Continues to Weed Knits," *Advertising Age*, October 3, 1983, p. 12.
7. Bear Stearns Research Report, September 30, 1982.
8. "When Business Got so Good it Got Dangerous," *Fortune*, April 2, 1983, p. 64.
9. "Farmer to President: Joe Lee of General Mills," *The Cornell Hotel and Restaurant Administration Quarterly*, November 1982.
10. "The Impact of Consumer Trends on Corporate Strategy," Sandra D. Kresch, *Journal of Business Strategy*, Winter 1983.
11. "General Mills' Izod Woes are Said to Reflect Broader Problems of Company Management," *The Wall Street Journal*, December 4, 1984.

3-5

1. "Continental Can's Continental Tribulations," *Fortune*, August 1973.
2. "How Continental Can is Packaging Growth," *Business Week*, March 3, 1975.
3. "Every Once in a While You Have to Buy a Bank," *Forbes*, September 15, 1976.
4. Donaldson, Lufkin, & Jenrette, *Research Report-Continental Group*, March 22, 1983.
5. Duff & Phelps, *Research Report-Continental Group*, March 3, 1983.
6. "Asset Redeployment Takes Continental Far Afield of Cans," *New England Business*, April 16, 1984.
7. "Major Sale Set of Continental Group Inc. Assets," *The Wall Street Journal*, August 31, 1983.
8. "Continental Group Sale . . . ," *New York Times*, September 21, 1984.
9. Donaldson, Lufkin, & Jenrette, *Research Report-Continental Group*, March 12, 1983.
10. Duff & Phelps, *Research Report-Continental Group*, September 16, 1983.
11. Butcher & Singer, *Research Report-Continental Group*, February 11, 1982.
12. "Goldsmith: I Wouldn't Cut Up Continental," *The Wall Street Journal*, June 1984.
13. "Jimmy Goldsmith's U.S. Bonanza," *Fortune*, October 17, 1983.
14. "How Sir Jimmy Builds His Global Empire," *Business Week*, May 14, 1984.
15. "Continental: Cans and More," *The New York Times*, June 6, 1984.

3-6

1. *The Canadian Architect*, January 1960, p. 51.
2. *Architectural Record*, February 1966, p. 137.

3. *Royal Architectural Institute of Canada Journal,* December 1964, p. 28.
4. *Architectural Record,* December 1967, p. 139.
5. *The Canadian Architect,* September 1966, pp. 46–50.

3-9

1. K.D. Fishman, *The Computer Establishment,* Harper & Row, 1981.
2. "IBM's Battle to Look Superhuman Again," *Fortune,* May 19, 1980.
3. "When IBM 'talks,' Everyone Now Listens," *Business Week,* September 20, 1982.
4. "The Lean, Mean New IBM," *Fortune,* June 13, 1983.
5. *Ibid.,* and "The Colossus That Works," *Time,* July 11, 1983.

3-10

1. "Another Turn of the Wheel," *The Economist,* March 2, 1985.
2. Research Report on General Motors Corporation, Nomura Securities International, Inc., March 12, 1984.
3. "The Innovator," *The New York Times Magazine,* April 21, 1985.
4. General Motors Corporation, *1984 General Motors Public Interest Report.*
5. "Where's the Niche?," *Forbes,* September 24, 1984.
6. Research Report on General Motors Corporation, Duff and Phelps, Inc., April 12, 1984.
7. "Can Detroit Cope This Time?," *Business Week,* April 22, 1985.
8. "GM's Saturn Unit . . . ," *The Wall Street Journal,* July 10, 1985.
9. "How Power Will be Balanced on Saturn's Shop Floor," *Business Week,* August 5, 1985.
10. "GM is Expected to Put Saturn Complex in Tennessee . . . ," *The Wall Street Journal,* July 29, 1985.
11. "GM and EDS," *Automotive News,* March 18, 1985.

12. "Perot's Singular Style . . . ," *The Wall Street Journal,* July 2, 1984.
13. "GM's Purchase of Hughes Aircraft . . . ," *The Wall Street Journal,* June 6, 1985.
14. "Pre-Sale Appraisal," *The Wall Street Journal,* March 27, 1985.
15. "Can Hughes Advance GM Car building," *The Los Angeles Times,* June 23, 1985.
16. "GM Struggles . . . ," *The Wall Street Journal,* June 6, 1985.
17. "Collapse of Diesel Car Market . . . ," *The Wall Street Journal,* July 11, 1984.
18. "Why GM is Risking Higher Prices," *Business Week,* September 16, 1985.
19. Harbridge House, Inc., *Corporate Strategies of the Automotive Manufacturers,* D.C. Heath and Company, 1979.
20. "Roger Smith—GM's Big Surprise," *Nation's Business,* February 1985.
21. "Made in the U.S.A.," *Forbes,* April 22, 1985.
22. "Japan vs. Detroit, Round 2: The Midsize Market," *Business Week,* July 22, 1985.

3-11

1. "Turnover at the Top: Cause and Effect," *Chain Store Age Executive,* May 1984.
2. "Making Money at the Low End of the Market," *Forbes,* December 17, 1984.
3. "Hit or Miss on Target with New Look," *Chain Store Age Executive,* February 1983.
4. "Too Big for Miracles," *Forbes,* June 15, 1977, p. 26.
5. "Sears' Strategic About-Face," *Business Week,* January 8, 1979.
6. "J.C. Penney's Fashion Gamble," *Business Week,* January 16, 1978, p. 66.
7. "Wal-Mart: A Discounter Sinks Deep Roots in Small Town, U.S.A.," *Business Week,* November 5, 1979, p. 145.
8. "A Day in the Life of Sam Walton," *Forbes,* January 1, 1977, p. 45.

BIBLIOGRAPHY FOR READINGS

ABELL, D.F., *Defining the Business: The Starting Point of Strategic Planning.* Englewood Cliffs, N.J.: Prentice Hall, 1980.

ABERNATHY, W.J. & K. WAYNE, "Limits on the Learning Curve," *Harvard Business Review,* September–October 1974: 109–119.

ACKERMAN, R.W., *The Social Challenge to Business.* Cambridge, MA: Harvard University Press, 1975.

ADVISORY COMMITTEE ON INDUSTRIAL INNOVATION: FINAL REPORT. Washington, D.C.: U.S. Government Printing Office, 1979.

AGUILAR, F.J., *Scanning the Business Environment.* New York: Macmillan, 1967.

ALLEN, M.P., "The Structure of Interorganizational Elite Cooptation: Interlocking Corporate Directorates," *American Sociological Review,* 1974: 393–406.

ALLEN, S.A., "Organizational Choices and General Management Influence Networks in Divisionalized Companies," *Academy of Management Journal,* 1978: 341–365.

ALLISON, G.T., *Essence of Decision: Explaining the Cuban Missile Crisis.* Boston: Little, Brown, 1971.

ANSOFF, H.I., *Corporate Strategy: An Analytic Approach to Business Policy for Growth and Expansion.* New York, McGraw-Hill, 1965.

ARGYRIS, C., "Double Loop Learning in Organizations," *Harvard Business Review,* September–October 1977: 115–125.

ASTLEY, W.G., & C.J. FOMBRUN, "Collective Strategy: Social Ecology of Organizational Environments," *Academy of Management Review,* 1983: 576–587.

BACON, J., *Corporate Directorship Practices: Membership and Committees of the Board.* Conference Board and American Society of Corporate Secretaries, Inc., 1973.

———, & J.K. BROWN, *Corporate Directorship Practices: Role, Selection and Legal Status of the Board.* New York: The Conference Board, 1975.

BADEN FULLER, C., et al., "National or Global? The Study of Company Strategies and the European Market for Major Appliances," London Business School Centre for Business Strategy, Working Paper series no. 28 (June 1987).

BARNARD, C.I., *The Functions of the Executive.* Cambridge, Mass.: Harvard University Press, 1938.

BARREYRE, P.Y., "The Concept of 'Impartition' Policy in High Speed Strategic Management." Working Paper, Institut d'Administration des Entreprises, Grenoble, 1984.

———, & M. CARLE, "Impartition Policies: Growing Importance in Corporate Strategies and Applications to Production Sharing in Some World-Wide Industries." Paper Presented at Strategic Management Society Conference, Paris, 1983.

BARRIER, M., "Walton's Mountain," *Nation's Business,* April 1988: 18–26.

BARTLETT, C.A., & S. GHOSHAL, "Managing Across Borders: New Strategic Requirements," *Sloan Management Review,* Summer 1987: 7–17.

BATY, G.B., W.M. EVAN, & T. W. ROTHERMEL, "Personnel Flows as Interorganizational Relations," *Administrative Science Quarterly,* 1971: 430–443.

BAUER, R. A., I. POOL, & L.A. DEXTER, *American Business and Public Policy.* New York: Atherton Press, 1968.

BAUMBACK, C., & J. MANCUSO, *Entrepreneurship and Venture Management.* Englewood Cliffs, N.J.: Prentice Hall, 1975.

BECKER, G., *Human Capital.* New York: National Bureau of Economic Research, 1964.

BEER, S., *Designing Freedom.* Toronto: CBC Publications, 1974.

BENNIS, W.G. & P.L. SLATER, *The Temporary Society.* New York: Harper & Row, 1964.

BERLEW, D.E. & D.T. HALL, "The Management of Tension in Organization: Some Preliminary Findings," *Industrial Management Review,* Fall 1964: 31–40.

BERNSTEIN, L., "Joint Ventures in the Light of Recent Antitrust Developments," *The Antitrust Bulletin,* 1965: 25–29.

BETTIS, R. A., "Performance Differences in Related and Unrelated Diversified Firms," *Strategic Management Journal,* 1981: 379–394.

BOSTON CONSULTING GROUP, *Perspectives on Experience.* Boston, 1972.

———, *Strategy Alternatives for the British Motorcycle Industry.* London: Her Majesty's Stationery Office, 1975.

BOULDING, K. E., "The Ethics of Rational Decision," *Management Science,* 1966: 161–169.

BOWER, J. L., "Planning within the Firm," *The American Economic Review,* 1970: 186–194.

BOWMAN, E.H., "Epistemology, Corporate Strategy, and Academe," *Sloan Management Review,* Winter 1974: 35–50.

BRAYBROOKE, D., "Skepticism of Wants, and Certain Subversive Effects of Corporations on American Values," in S. Hook, ed., *Human Values and Economic Policy.* New York: New York University Press, 1967.

——— & C.E. LINDBLOM, *A Strategy of Decision: Policy Evaluation as a Social Process.* New York: Free Press, 1963.

BRENNER, S.N. & E.A. MOLANDER, "Is the Ethic of Business Changing?" *Harvard Business Review,* January–February 1977: 57–71.

BROOK, P., *The Empty Space.* Harmondsworth, Middlesex: Penguin Books, 1968.

BROOM, H.N., J.G. LONGENECKER & C.W. MOORE, *Small Business Management.* Cincinnati, OH: Southwest, 1983.

BRUNSSON, N., "The Irrationality of Action and Action Rationality: Decisions, Ideologies, and Organizational Actions," *Journal of Management Studies,* 1982(1): 29–44.

BUCHELE, R. B., *Business Policy in Growing Firms.* San Francisco, CA: Chandler, 1967.

BURNS, T., "Micropolitics: Mechanisms of Institutional Change," *Administrative Science Quarterly.* December 1961: 257–281.

——— & G.M. STALKER, *The Management of Innovation,* 2d ed. London: Tavistock, 1966.

BUSINESS WEEK. "Japan's Strategy for the 80's," December 14, 1981: 39–120.

———. "The Hollow Corporation," March 3, 1986: Supplement.

BUZZELL, R. D., B.T. GALE, & R.G.M. SULTAN, "Market Share—A Key to Profitability," *Harvard Business Review,* January–February 1975: 97–106.

CARLZON, J., *Moments of Truth.* New York: Ballinger Press, 1987.

CHANDLER, A.D., *Strategy and Structure: Chapters in the History of the Industrial Enterprise.* Cambridge, Mass.: M.I.T. Press, 1962.

CHANNON, D.F., "The Strategy, Structure and Financial Performance of the Service Industries," Working Paper, Manchester Business School, 1975.

CHEIT, E.F., "The New Place of Business: Why Managers Cultivate Social Responsibility," in E.F. Cheit, ed., *The Business Establishment.* New York: John Wiley, 1964.

CHRISTENSON, C.R., K.R. ANDREWS, & J.L. BOWER, *Business Policy: Text and Cases.* Homewood, Ill.: Richard D. Irwin, 1978.

CLARK, B.R., *The Distinctive College: Antioch, Reed and Swarthmore.* Chicago: Aldine, 1970.

———, "The Organizational Saga in Higher Education," *Administrative Science Quarterly,* 1972: 178–184.

CLARK, R.C., *The Japanese Company.* New Haven: Yale University Press, 1979.

COHEN, K.J. & R.M. CYERT, "Strategy: Formulation, Implementation and Monitoring," *The Journal of Business,* 1973: 349–367.

——— & J.P. OLSEN, "A Garbage Can Model of Organizational Choice," *Administrative Science Quarterly,* 1972: 1–25.

COHN, T., & R.A. LINDBERG, *How Management is Different in Small Companies.* New York: American Management Association, 1972.

COLE, A.H., Business Enterprise in Its Social Setting. Cambridge, Mass.: Harvard University Press, 1959.

COLE, R.E., *Japanese Blue Collar: The Changing Tradition.* Berkeley: University of California Press, 1971.

———, *Work, Mobility and Participation.* Berkeley: University of California Press, 1979.

COPEMAN, G.H., *The Role of the Managing Director.* London: Business Publications, 1963.

COYNE, K.P., "Sustainable Competitive Advantage," *Business Horizons,* January–February 1986: 54–61.

CROZIER, M., *The Bureaucratic Phenomenon.* Chicago: University of Chicago Press, 1964.

CVAR, M.R., "Case Studies in Global Competition," in M.E. Porter, ed., *Competition in Global Industries.* Boston: Harvard Business School Press, 1986.

CYERT, R.M., W. R. DILL, & J.G. MARCH, "The Role of Expectations in Business Decision Making," *Administrative Science Quarterly,* 1958: 307–340.

CYERT, R.M. & J.G. MARCH, *A Behavioral Theory of the Firm.* Englewood Cliffs, N.J.: Prentice Hall, 1963.

DAVIS, R.T., *Performance and Development of Field Sales Managers.* Boston: Harvard Business School, 1957.

DELBECQ, A. & A.C. FILLEY, *Program and Project Man-*

agement in a Matrix Organization: A Case Study. Madison, Wis.: University of Wisconsin, 1974.

DOERINGER, P. & M. PIORE, *Internal Labor Market and Manpower Analysis.* Lexington, Mass.: Lexington Books, 1971.

DOUGLAS, S.P., & Y. WIND, "The Myth of Globalization," *Columbia Journal of World Business,* Winter 1987: 19–29.

DRUCKER, P.F., *The Practice of Management.* New York: Harper & Row, 1954.

———, *Management: Tasks, Responsibilities, Practices.* New York: Harper & Row, 1974.

———, "Clouds Forming Across the Japanese Sun," *Wall Street Journal,* July 13, 1982.

EDWARDS, J.P., "Strategy Formulation as a Stylistic Process," *International Studies of Management and Organization,* Summer 1977: 13–27.

ELECTRONIC BUSINESS, "Services Get the Job Done," September 15, 1988: 87–90.

EPSTEIN, E.M., *The Corporation in American Politics.* Englewood Cliffs, N.J.: Prentice Hall, 1969.

———, "The Social Role of Business Enterprise in Britain: An American Perspective; Part II," *The Journal of Management Studies,* 1977: 281–316.

ESSAME, H., *Patton: A Study in Command.* New York: Charles Scribner's Sons, 1974.

EVERED, R., *So What Is Strategy?* Working Paper, Naval Postgraduate School, Monterey, 1980.

FARAGO, L., *Patton: Ordeal and Triumph.* New York: I. Obolensky, 1964.

FIRSIROTU, M., "Strategic Turnaround as Cultural Revolution: The Case of Canadian National Express," doctoral dissertation, Faculty of Management, 1985.

FLEISHMANN, E.A., E.F. HARRIS, & H.E. BURT, *Leadership and Supervision in Industry: An Evaluation of Supervisory Training Program.* Columbus, Ohio: The Ohio State University, 1955.

FOCH, F., *Principles of War,* translated by J. DeMorinni. New York: AMS Press, 1970. First published London: Chapman & Hall, 1918.

FORRESTER, J. W., "Counterintuitive Behavior of Social Systems," *Technology Review,* January 1971: 52–68.

FRANKLIN, B., *Poor Richard's Almanac.* New York: Ballantine Books, 1977. First Published, Century Company, 1898.

FRIEDMAN, M., *Capitalism and Freedom.* Chicago: University of Chicago Press, 1962.

———, "A Friedman Doctrine: The Social Responsibility of Business is to Increase its Profits," *The New York Times Magazine,* September 13, 1970.

GALBRAITH, J.K., *American Capitalism: The Concept of Countervailing Power.* Boston: Houghton Mifflin, 1952.

———, *The New Industrial State.* Boston: Houghton Mifflin, 1967.

GALBRAITH, J. R., *Organization Design.* Reading, Mass.: Addison-Wesley, 1977.

———, "Strategy and Organization Planning." *Human Resource Management,* 1983: 63–77.

——— & D. NATHANSON, *Strategy Implementation.* St. Paul, Minn.: West Publishing, 1978.

GARDNER, J.W., "The Anti-Leadership Vaccine," in *Carnegie Corporation of New York Annual Report,* 1965.

GARSON, G.D., "The Codetermination Model of Worker's Participation: Where Is It Leading?" *Sloan Management Review,* Spring 1977: 63–78.

GERTH, H.H., & C. WRIGHT MILLS, eds., *From Max Weber: Essays in Sociology.* New York: Oxford University Press, 1958.

GHISELLI, E.E., "Managerial Talent," in D. Wolfe, ed., *The Discovery of Talent.* Cambridge, Mass.: Harvard University Press, 1969.

GILDER, G., *Wealth and Poverty.* New York: Basic Books, 1981.

GILMORE, F.F., "Overcoming the Perils of Advocacy in Corporate Planning," *California Management Review,* Spring 1973: 127–137.

GLUECK, W. F., *Business Policy and Strategic Management.* New York: McGraw Hill, 1980.

GOSSELIN, R., *A Study of the Interdependence of Medical Specialists in Quebec Teaching Hospitals.* Ph.D. thesis, McGill University, 1978.

GREEN, P., *Alexander the Great.* New York: Frederick A. Praeger, 1970.

GREINER, L.E., "Evolution and Revolution as Organizations Grow," *Harvard Business Review,* July–August 1972: 37–46.

———, "Senior Executives as Strategic Actors," *New Management,* Vol. 1, no. 2, Summer 1983.

GRINYER, P.H., & J.C. SPENDER, *Turnaround—Management Recipes for Strategic Success.* New York: Associated Business Press, 1979.

GROSS, W., "Coping with Radical Competition," in A. Gross & W. Gross, eds., *Business Policy: Selected Readings and Editorial Commentaries,* pp. 550–560. New York: Ronald Press, 1967.

GUEST, R.H., "Of Time and The Foreman," *Personnel,* May 1956: 478–486.

HAITANI, K., "Changing Characteristics of the Japanese Employment System," *Asian Survey,* 1978: 1029–1045.

HAMERMESH, R.G., M.J. ANDERSON, JR. & J.E. HARRIS, "Strategies for Low Market Share Business," *Harvard Business Review,* May–June 1978: 95–102.

HART, B.H.L., *Strategy.* New York: Frederick A. Praeger, 1954.

HATTORI, I., "A Proposition on Efficient Decision-Making in Japanese Corporation," *Management Japan,* Autumn 1977: 14–20.

HAYES, R.H. & W. J. ABERNATHY, "Managing Our Way to Economic Decline," *Harvard Business Review,* July–August 1980: 67–77.

———— & D.A. GARVIN, "Managing as if Tomorrow Mattered," *Harvard Business Review,* May–June 1982: 70–79.

HAZAMA, H., "Characteristics of Japanese-Style Management," *Japanese Economic Studies,* Spring–Summer 1978: 110–173.

HEDBERG, B.L.T., "How Organizations Learn and Unlearn," in P.C. Nystrom and W.H. Starbuck, eds., *Handbook of Organizational Design,* Volume 1. New York: Oxford University Press, 1981.

———— & S.A. JÖNSSON, "Designing Semi-confusing Information Systems for Organizations in Changing Environments," *Accounting Organizations and Society,* 1978: 47–64.

————, P.C. NYSTROM, & W.H. STARBUCK, "Camping on Seesaws: Prescriptions for a Self-designing Organization," *Administrative Science Quarterly,* 1976: 41–65.

HICKSON, D.J., C.A. LEE, R.E. SCHNECK & J.M. PENNINGS, "A Strategic Contingencies' Theory of Intraorganizational Power," *Administrative Science Quarterly,* 1971: 216–229.

HIRSCH, P.M., "Organizational Effectiveness and the Institutional Environment," *Administrative Science Quarterly,* 1975: 327–344.

HOFER, C.W. & D. SCHENDEL, *Strategy Formulation: Analytical Concepts.* St. Paul, Minn.: West Publishing, 1978.

HOSMER, A., "Small Manufacturing Enterprises," *Harvard Business Review,* November–December 1957: 111–122.

HOUSE OF REPRESENTATIVES, Staff Report to the Antitrust Subcommittee of the Committee on the Judiciary, *Interlocks in Corporate Management,* Washington, D.C.: U.S. Government Printing Office, 1965.

HOUT, T., M.E. PORTER & E. RUDDEN, "How Global Companies Win Out," *Harvard Business Review,* September–October 1982: 98–108.

HUGHES, T., "The Inventive Continuum," *Science 84,* November 1984.

HUNT, R.G., "Technology and Organization," *Academy of Management Journal,* 1970: 235–252.

IACOCCA, L., with W. NOVAK, *Iacocca: An Autobiography.* New York: Bantam Books, 1984.

IMAI, K., I. NONAKA & H. TAKEUCHI, "Managing the New Product Development Process: How Japanese Companies Learn and Unlearn," in K.B. Clark, R.H. Hayes, and C. Lorenz, eds., *The Uneasy Alliance.* Boston: Harvard Business School Press, 1985.

IRVING, D., *The Trail of the Fox.* New York: E.P. Dutton, 1977.

JACOBS, D., "Dependency and Vulnerability: An Exchange Approach to the Control of Organizations," *Administrative Science Quarterly,* 1974: 45–59.

JAMES, D.C., *The Years of MacArthur, 1941–1945.* Boston: Houghton Mifflin, 1970.

JANIS, I., *Victims of Group Think.* Boston: Houghton Mifflin, 1972.

JAY, A., *Management and Machiavelli.* New York: Penguin Books, 1970.

JENKINS, C., *Power at the Top.* Westport, Conn.: Greenwood Press, 1976.

JENNINGS, E.E., *The Mobile Manager.* Ann Arbor: University of Michigan, 1967.

JOHNSON, S.C., & C. JONES, "How to Organize for New Products," *Harvard Business Review,* May–June 1957: 49–62.

JOMINI, A.H., *Art of War,* translated by G.H. Mendell and W.P. Craighill. Westport, Conn.: Greenwood Press, 1971. Original Philadelphia: J. B. Lippincott, 1862.

JÖNSSON, S.A. & R.A. LUNDIN, "Myths and Wishful Thinking as Management Tools," in P.C. Nystrom and W.H. Starbuck eds., *Prescriptive Models of Organizations.* Amsterdam: North-Holland, 1977.

JORDAN, W.A., "Producer Protection Prior Market Structure and the Effects of Government Regulation," *Journal of Law and Economics,* 1972.

KAGONO, T., I. NONAKA, K. SAKAKIBARA & A. OKUMURA, *Strategic vs. Evolutionary Management: A. U.S.–Japan Comparison of Strategy and Organization.* Amsterdam: North-Holland, 1985.

KAHN, R. L., D.M. WOLFE, R.P. QUINN, J.D. SNOEK, & R.A. ROSENTHAL, *Organizational Stress.* New York: John Wiley, 1964.

KAMI, M.J. & J.E. ROSS, *Corporate Management in Crisis: Why the Mighty Fall.* Englewood Cliffs, N.J.: Prentice Hall, 1973.

KANO, T., "Comparative Study of Strategy, Structure and Long-Range Planning in Japan and in the United States," *Management Japan,* 1980(1): 20–34.

KATZ, R.L., *Cases and Concepts in Corporate Strategy.* Englewood Cliffs, N.J.: Prentice Hall, 1970.

————, "Time and Work: Towards an Integrative Perspective," in B.M. Staw and L.L. Cummings, eds., *Research in Organizational Behavior,* Vol. 1. Greenwich, Conn.: JAI Press, 1980.

KIDDER, T., *The Soul of a New Machine.* Boston: Little, Brown, 1981.

KIECHEL, W., III, "Sniping at Strategic Planning (interview with himself)," *Planning Review,* May 1984: 8–11.

KONO, T., "Comparative Study of Strategy, Structure and Long-Range Planning in Japan and in the United States," *Management Japan,* Spring 1980: 20–34.

KOTLER, P., & R. SINGH, "Marketing Warfare in the 1980s," *Journal of Business Strategy,* Winter 1981: 30–41.

1054

KOTTER, J.P., & L.A. SCHLESINGER, "Choosing Strategies for Change," *Harvard Business Review,* March–April 1979: 106–114.

KUHN, T., *The Structure of Scientific Revolutions.* Chicago: University of Chicago Press, 1970.

LAND, E., "People Should Want More from Life . . . ," *Forbes,* June 1, 1975.

LAPIERRE, L., "Le changement stratégique: Un rêve en quête de réel." Ph.D. Management Policy course paper, McGill University, Canada, 1980.

LEARNED, E.P., C.R. CHRISTIANSEN, K.R. ANDREWS & W.D. GUTH, *Business Policy: Text and Cases.* Homewood, IL: Richard D. Irwin, 1965.

———, D.N. ULRICH, & D.R. BOOZ, *Executive Action.* Boston: Harvard Business School, 1951.

LENIN, V.I., *Collected Works of V.I. Lenin,* edited and annotated. New York: International Publishers, 1927.

LEVINSON, H., "On Becoming a Middle-Aged Manager," *Harvard Business Review,* July–August 1969: 51–60.

———, *Executive Stress.* New York: Harper & Row, 1970.

LEVITT, T., "Marketing Myopia," *Harvard Business Review,* July–August 1960: 45–56.

———, "Why Business Always Loses," *Harvard Business Review,* March–April 1968: 81–89.

———, "Industrialization of Service," *Harvard Business Review,* September–October 1976: 63–74.

———, "Marketing Success Through Differentiation—of Anything," *Harvard Business Review,* January–February 1980: 83–91.

———, "The Globalization of Markets," *Harvard Business Review,* May–June 1983: 92–102.

———, *The Marketing Imagination.* New York: Free Press, 1983.

LEWIN, K., *Field Theory in Social Science.* New York: Harper & Row, 1951.

LIKERT, R., *New Patterns of Management.* New York: McGraw-Hill, 1969.

LINDBLOM, C.E., "The Science of 'Muddling Through,'" *Public Administration Review,* 1959: 79–88.

———, *The Policy-Making Process.* Englewood Cliffs, N.J.: Prentice Hall, 1968.

LITTLE, A.D., INC., *"Transportation Planning in the District of Columbia, 1955–65: A Review and Critique,"* Report to The Policy Advisory Committee to the District Commissioners. Washington, D.C.: U.S. Government Printing Office, 1966.

LODGE, G.C., *The New American Ideology.* New York: Alfred A. Knopf, 1975.

LOHR, S., "Japan Struggling With Itself," *New York Times,* June 13, 1982.

MACAVOY, P.W., *The Economic Effects of Regulation.* Cambridge, MA: M.I.T Press, 1965.

MACMILLAN, I.C., "Seizing Competitive Initiative," *Journal of Business Strategy,* Spring 1982: 43–57.

———, "Preemptive Strategies," *Journal of Business Strategy,* Fall 1983: 16–26.

———, & P.E. JONES, "Designing Organizations to Compete," *Journal of Business Strategy,* Spring 1984: 11–26.

———, M. MCCAFFERY & G. VAN WIJK, "Competitors' Responses to Easily Imitated New Products—Exploring Commercial Banking Product Introductions," *Strategic Management Journal,* 1985: 75–86.

MACE, M.L. & G.G. MONTGOMERY, *Management Problems of Corporate Acquisitions.* Boston: Harvard Business School, 1962.

MACHIAVELLI, N., *The Prince, and the Discourses.* New York: Modern Library, 1950.

MACKWORTH, N.H., "Originality," in D. Wolfe, ed., *The Discovery of Talent.* Cambridge, Mass.: Harvard University Press, 1969.

MAGEE, J.F., "Decision Trees for Decision Making," *Harvard Business Review,* July–August, 1964: 126–138.

———, *Desirable Characteristics of Models in Planning,* a paper delivered at the Symposium on the role of Economic Models in Policy Formulation, sponsored by the Department of Housing and Urban Development, Office of Emergency Planning, National Resource Evaluation Center, Washington, D.C., October, 1966.

MAJONE, G., "The Use of Policy Analysis," in *The Future and the Past: Essays on Programs,* Russell Sage Foundation Annual Report, 1976–1977.

MAO TSE-TUNG, *Selected Military Writings, 1928–1949.* San Francisco: China Books, 1967.

MARCH, J.G. & J.P. OLSEN, *Ambiguity and Choice in Organizations.* Bergen, Norway: Universitetsforlaget, 1976.

———, & H.A. SIMON, *Organizations.* New York: John Wiley, 1958.

MARSHALL, G.L., *Predicting Executive Achievement.* Ph.D. thesis, Harvard Business School, 1964.

MARTIN, L.C. "How Beatrice Foods Sneaked Up On $5 Billion," *Fortune,* April 1976: 119–129.

MATLOFF, M. & E.M. SNELL, *Strategic Planning for Coalition Warfare (1941–42).* Washington, D. C.: Office of Chief of Military History, Department of the Army, 1953.

MAYO, E., *The Social Problems of an Industrial Civilization.* Boston: Harvard Business School, 1945.

MCCLELLAND, D.C., "The Two Faces of Power," *Journal of International Affairs,* 1970: 29–47.

MCDONALD, J., *Strategy in Poker, Business and War.* New York: W.W. Norton, 1950.

MCINTYRE, S.H., "Obstacles to Corporate Innovation," *Business Horizons,* January–February 1982: 23–28.

MECHANIC, D., "Sources of Power of Lower Participants in Complex Organizations," *Administrative Science Quarterly,* 1962: 349–364.

MILLER, D., & P.H. FRIESEN, "Archetypes of Strategy Formulation," *Management Science,* May 1978: 921–933.

_____, *Organizations: A Quantum View.* Englewood Cliffs, N.J.: Prentice Hall, 1984.

_____, & M. KETS DE VRIES, *The Neurotic Organization.* San Francisco: Jossey-Bass, 1984.

_____, *Unstable at the Top.* New York: New American Library, 1987.

_____, & H. MINTZBERG, *Strategy Formulation in Context: Some Tentative Models.* Working Paper, McGill University, 1974.

MINTZBERG, H., "Research on Strategy-Making," *Academy of Management Proceedings,* 1972: 90–94.

_____, *The Nature of Managerial Work.* New York: Harper & Row, 1973.

_____, "Strategy Making in Three Modes," *California Management Review,* Winter 1973b: 44–53.

_____, "The Manager's Job: Folklore and Fact," *Harvard Business Review,* July–August 1975: 49–61.

_____, "Generic Strategies: Toward a Comprehensive Framework," *Advances in Strategic Management,* Vol. 5, pp. 1–67. Greenwich, CT: JAI Press, 1988.

_____, D. RAÌSINGNANÌ, & A. THÉORÊT, "The Structure of 'Unstructured' Decision Processes," *Administrative Science Quarterly,* 1976: 246–275.

_____ & J.A. WATERS, "Tracking Strategy in an Entrepreneurial Firm," *Academy of Management Journal,* 1982: 465–499.

_____, "Of Strategies, Deliberate and Emergent," *Strategic Management Journal,* 1985: 257–272.

MONTGOMERY, B.L., *The Memoirs of Field-Marshal The Viscount Montgomery of Alamein.* Cleveland: World Publishing, 1958.

MORITANI, M., *Japanese Technology: Getting the Best for the Least.* Tokyo: Simul Press, 1981.

MOYER, R.C., "Berle and Means Revisited: The Conglomerate Merger," *Business and Society,* Spring 1970: 20–29.

NADLER, D.A. & E.E. LAWLER, III, "Motivation—A Diagnostic Approach," in J.R. Hackman, E.E. Lawler, III, and L.W. Porter, eds., *Perspective on Behavior in Organizations.* New York: McGraw-Hill, 1977.

NADLER, D., & M.L. TUSHMAN, *Strategic Organization Design.* Homewood, IL: Scott Foresman, 1986.

NAISBITT, J., *Megatrends.* New York: Warner Books, 1982.

NAPOLEON, I., "Maximes de Guerre," in T.R. Phillips, ed., *Roots of Strategy.* Harrisburg, Pa.: Military Service Publishing, 1940.

NATHANSON, D. & J. CASSANO, "Organization Diversity and Performance," *The Wharton Magazine,* Summer 1982: 18–26.

NEUSTADT, R.E., *Presidential Power: The Politics of Leadership.* New York: John Wiley, 1960.

NONAKA, I., "Creating Organizational Order out of Chaos: Self-Renewal in Japanese Firms," *California Management Review,* Spring 1988: 57–73.

NORMANN, R., *Management for Growth,* translated by N. Adler. New York: John Wiley, 1977.

NYSTROM, P.C., B.L.T. HEDBERG, & W.H. STARBUCK, "Interacting Processes as Organization Designs," in R.H. Kilmann, L.R. Pondy, & D.P. Slevin, eds., *The Management of Organization Design,* Vol. 1. New York: Elsevier North-Holland, 1976.

OGILVY, D., *Ogilvy on Advertising.* New York: Crown, 1983.

OHMAE, K., *The Mind of the Strategist.* New York: McGraw-Hill, 1982.

ONO, H., "Nihonteki Keiei Shisutemu to Jinji Kettei Shisutemu," ("Japanese Management System and Personnel Decisions,") *Soshiki Kagaku,* 1976: 22–32.

OUCHI, W.G., "Market, Bureaucracies and Clans," *Administrative Science Quarterly,* 1980: 129–140.

_____, *Theory Z.* Reading, Mass.: Addison-Wesley, 1981.

_____, & A.M. JAEGER, "Type Z Organization: Stability in the Midst of Mobility," *Academy of Management Review,* 1978: 305–314.

_____, W.G., & B. JOHNSON, "Types of Organizational Control and Their Relationship to Emotional Well Being," *Administrative Science Quarterly,* 1978: 293–317.

PARSONS, T., *Structure and Process in Modern Societies.* Glencoe, Ill.: Free Press, 1960.

PASCALE, R.T., "Perspectives on Strategy: The Real Story Behind Honda's Success," *California Management Review,* Spring 1984: 47–72.

PAUL, N.L., "The Use of Empathy in the Resolution of Grief," in *Perspective in Biology and Medicine.* Chicago: University of Chicago Press, 1967.

PENCE, C.C., *How Venture Capitalists Make Venture Decisions.* Ann Arbor, Mich.: UMI Research Press, 1982.

PERROW, C., "The Analysis of Goals in Complex Organizations," *American Sociological Review,* 1961: 854–866.

_____, *Organizational Analysis: A Sociological Review.* Belmont, Calif.: Wadsworth, 1970.

_____, *Complex Organizations: A Critical Essay,* New York: Scott, Foresman, 1972.

PETERS, T.J., "A Style for All Seasons," *Executive,* Summer 1980: 12–16.

_____, & R.H. WATERMAN, *In Search of Excellence: Lessons from America's Best Run Companies.* New York: Harper & Row, 1982.

PFEFFER, J., "Size and Composition of Corporate Boards of Directors: The Organization and its Environment," *Administrative Science Quarterly,* 1972a: 218–228.

———, "Merger as a Response to Organizational Interdependence," *Administrative Science Quarterly,* 1972b: 382–394.

———, "Size, Composition and Function of Hospital Boards of Directors: A Study of Organization-Environment Linkage," *Administrative Science Quarterly,* 1973: 349–364.

———, "Administrative Regulation and Licensing: Social Problem or Solution?" *Social Problems,* 1974: 468–479.

———, *Management as Symbolic Action: The Creation and Maintenance of Organizational Paradigms.* Working Paper, Stanford University, 1979.

———, & H. LEBLEBICI, "Executive Recruitment and the Development of Interfirm Organizations," *Administrative Science Quarterly,* 1973: 449–461.

———, & P. NOWAK, "Patterns of Joint Venture Activity: Implications for Antitrust Policy," *The Antitrust Bulletin,* 1976: 315–339.

———, "Joint Ventures and Interorganizational Interdependence," *Administrative Science Quarterly,* 1976b: 398–418.

———, *Organizational Context and Interorganizational Linkages Among Corporations.* Working Paper, University of California at Berkeley, no date.

———, & H. LEBLEBICI, "The Effect of Uncertainty on the Use of Social Influence in Organizational Decision-Making," *Administrative Science Quarterly,* 1976: 227–245.

PFIFFNER, J.M., "Administrative Rationality," *Public Administration Review,* 1960: 125–132.

PHILLIPS, T.R. ED., *Roots of Strategy.* Harrisburg, Pa.: Military Service Publishing, 1940.

PORTER, M.E., *Competitive Strategy: Techniques for Analysing Industries and Competitors.* New York: Free Press, 1980.

———, *Competitive Advantage: Creating and Sustaining Superior Performance.* New York: Free Press, 1985.

———, "Generic Competitive Strategies," in M.E. Porter, *Competitive Advantage,* pp. 34–46. New York: Free Press, 1985.

———, "From Competitive Advantage to Corporate Strategy," *Harvard Business Review,* May–June 1987: 43–59.

———, "Competition in Global Industries: A Conceptual Framework," in M.E. Porter, ed., *Competition in Global Industries.* Boston: Harvard Business School Press, 1986.

POSNER, B., & B. BURLINGHAM, "The Hottest Entrepreneur in America," *Inc.,* January 1988, 44–58.

POSNER, R.A., "Theories of Economic Regulation," *Bell Journal of Economics and Management Science,* 1974: 335–358.

PRICE, J.L., "The Impact of Governing Boards on Organizational Effectiveness and Morale," *Administrative Science Quarterly,* 1963: 361–378.

PUCIK, V., "Getting Ahead in Japan," *The Japanese Economic Journal,* 1981: 970–971.

———, "Promotions and Intra-organizational Status Differentiation Among Japanese Managers," *The Academy of Management Proceedings,* 1981: 59–63.

PURKAYASTHA, D., *"Note on the Motocycle Industry—1975."* Copyrighted Case, Harvard Business School, 1981.

QUINN, J.B., "Strategic Goals: Process and Politics," *Sloan Management Review,* Fall 1977: 21–37.

———, *Strategies for Change: Logical Incrementalism.* Homewood, Ill.: Richard D. Irwin, 1980.

RAPHAEL, R., *Edges.* New York: Alfred A. Knopf, 1976.

REESER, C., "Some Potential Human Problems in the Project Form of Organization," *Academy of Management Journal,* 1969: 459–467.

REID, S.R., *Mergers, Managers, and the Economy.* New York: McGraw-Hill, 1968.

RHENMAN, E., *Organization Theory for Long-Range Planning.* New York: John Wiley, 1973.

ROHLEN, T.P., *For Harmony and Strength: Japanese White-collar Organization in Anthropological Perspective.* Berkeley: University of California Press, 1974.

ROSNER, M., *Principle Types and Problems of Direct Democracy in the Kibbutz.* Working Paper, Social Research Center on the Kibbutz, Givat Haviva, Israel, 1969.

ROSS, I., "How Lawless are the Big Companies?" *Fortune,* December 1, 1980: 56–64.

ROSSOTTI, C.O., *Two Concepts of Long-Range Planning.* Boston: The Management Consulting Group, The Boston Safe Deposit & Trust Company, no date.

RUMELT, R.P., *Strategy, Structure and Economic Performance.* Boston: Harvard Business School, 1974.

———, "A Teaching Plan for Strategy Alternatives for the British Motocycle Industry," in *Japanese Business: Business Policy.* New York: The Japan Society, 1980.

———, "Diversification Strategy and Profitability," *Strategic Management Journal,* 1982: 359–370.

SAHLMAN, W.A., & H.H. STEVENSON, "Capital Market Myopia," *Journal of Business Venturing,* Winter 1985: 7–30.

SAKIYA, T., "The Story of Honda's Founders," *Asahi Evening News,* June–August, 1979.

———, *Honda Motor: The Men, The Management, The Machines.* Tokyo, Japan: Kadonsha International, 1982.

SALTER, M.S., & W.A. WEINHOLD, *Diversification Through Acquisition.* New York: Free Press, 1979.

SAYLES, L.R., *Managerial Behavior: Administration in Complex Organizations.* New York: McGraw-Hill, 1964.

———, "How Graduates Scare Bosses," *Careers Today,* January, 1969.

SCHELLING, T.C., *The Strategy of Conflict,* 2nd. ed. Cambridge, MA: Harvard University Press, 1980.

SCHENDEL, D.G., R. PATTON, & J. RIGGS, "Corporate Turnaround Strategies: A Study of Profit Decline and Recovery," *Journal of General Management,* Spring 1976: 3–11.

SCOTT, W.E., "Activation Theory and Task Design," *Organizational Behavior and Human Performance,* September 1966: 3–30.

SELZNICK, P., *TVA and the Grass Roots.* Berkeley: University of California Press, 1949.

_____, *Leadership in Administration: A Sociological Interpretation.* New York: Harper & Row, 1957.

SHUBIK, M., *Games for Society, Business, and War: Towards a Theory of Gaming.* New York: Elsevier, 1975.

SIMON, M.A., "On the Concept of Organizational Goals," *Administrative Science Quarterly,* 1964–1965: 1–22.

SMITH, L., "The Boardroom Is Becoming a Different Scene," *Fortune,* May 8, 1978: 150–88.

SMITH, W.R., "Product Differentiation and Market Segmentation as Alternative Marketing Strategies," *Journal of Marketing,* July 1956: 3–8.

SOLZHENITSYN, A., "Why The West Has Succumbed to Cowardice," *The Montreal Star: News and Review,* June 10, 1978.

SPEER, A., *Inside the Third Reich.* New York: Macmillan, 1970.

SPENCER, F.C., "Deductive Reasoning in the Lifelong Continuing Education of a Cardiovascular Surgeon," *Archives of Surgery,* 1976: 1177–1183.

SPENDER, J.-C., *Industry Recipes: The Nature and Sources of Managerial Judgement.* London: Basil Blackwell, 1989.

STARBUCK, W.H., "Organizations and Their Environments," in M.D. Dunnette, ed., *Handbook of Industrial and Organizational Psychology.* Chicago: Rand McNally, 1976.

STARBUCK, W.H. & B.L.T. HEDBERG, "Saving an Organization from a Stagnating Environment," in H.B. Thorelli, ed., *Strategy + Structure = Performance.* Bloomington: Indiana University Press, 1977.

THE STATE OF SMALL BUSINESS, A REPORT TO THE PRESIDENT. Washington, D.C.: U.S. Government Printing Office, 1984.

STERN, L.W., B. STERNTHAL, & C.S. CRAIG, "Managing Conflict in Distribution Channels: A Laboratory Study," *Journal of Marketing Research,* 1973: 169–179.

STEVENSON, H.H., "Defining Corporate Strengths and Weaknesses," *Sloan Management Review,* Spring 1976: 51–68.

STEVENSON, W., *A Man Called Intrepid: The Secret War.* New York: Harcourt Brace Jovanovich, 1976.

STEWART, R., *Managers and Their Jobs.* London: Macmillan, 1967.

STIGLER, G.J., "The Theory of Economic Regulation," *Bell Journal of Economics and Management Science,* 1971: 3–21.

SUN TZU, *The Art of War,* translated by S.B. Griffith. New York: Oxford University Press, 1963. Original 500 B.C.

TAKEUCHI, H., & I. NONAKA, "The New New Product Development Game," *Harvard Business Review,* January–February 1986: 137–146.

TAYLOR, W.H., "The Nature of Policy Making in Universities," *The Canadian Journal of Higher Education,* 1983: 17–32.

TECHNOLOGICAL INNOVATION: ITS ENVIRONMENT AND MANAGEMENT. Washington, D.C.: U.S. Government Printing Office, 1967.

THOMPSON, J.D., *Organizations in Action.* New York: McGraw-Hill, 1967.

THOMPSON, V.A., *Modern Organizations.* New York: Alfred A. Knopf, 1961.

TILLES, S., "How to Evaluate Corporate Strategy," *Harvard Business Review,* July–August 1963: 111–121.

TIME. "The Most Basic Form of Creativity," June 26, 1972.

TOFFLER, A., *Future Shock.* New York: Bantam Books, 1970.

TREGOE, B., & I. ZIMMERMAN, *Top Management Strategy.* New York: Simon & Schuster, 1980.

TSUJI, K., "Decision-Making in the Japanese Government: A Study of Ringisei," in R.E. Wards, ed., *Political Development in Modern Japan,* Princeton: Princeton University Press, 1968.

TSURUMI, Y., *Multinational Management: Business Strategy and Government Policy.* Cambridge, Mass.: Ballinger, 1977.

TUCHMAN, B.W., *The Guns of August.* New York: Macmillan, 1962.

VANCIL, R.F., "Strategy Formulation in Complex Organizations," *Sloan Management Review,* Winter 1976: 1–18.

_____, & P. LORANGE, "Strategic Planning in Diversified Companies," *Harvard Business Review,* January–February 1975: 81–90.

VAN DOREN, M., *Liberal Education,* Boston: Beacon Press, 1967.

VARNER, V.J. & J.I. ALGER, EDS., *History of the Military Art: Notes for the Course.* West Point, N.Y.: U.S. Military Academy, 1978.

VICKERS, G., "Is Adaptability Enough?" *Behavioral Science,* 1959: 219–234.

VOGEL, E., *Japan as Number One.* Cambridge, Mass.: Harvard University Press, 1979.

VON BÜLOW, D.F., *The Spirit of the Modern System of War,* translated by C.M. deMartemont. London: C. Mercier, 1806.

VON CLAUSEWITZ, C., *On War,* translated by M. Howard

and P. Paret. Princeton, N.J.: Princeton University Press, 1976.

VON HIPPEL, E., "Get New Products From Customers," *Harvard Business Review,* March–April 1982: 117–122.

VON NEUMANN, J. & O. MORGENSTERN, *Theory of Games and Economic Behavior.* Princeton, N.J.: Princeton University Press, 1944.

WARD, L.B., *Analysis of 1969 Alumni Questionnaire Returns.* Unpublished Report, Harvard Business School, 1970.

WATERMAN, R.H., JR., T.J. PETERS & J.R. PHILLIPS, "Structure is Not Organization," *Business Horizons,* June 1980: 14–26.

WEBER, M., "The Three Types of Legitimate Rule," translated by H. Gerth, in A. Etzioni, ed., *A Sociological Reader on Complex Organizations.* New York: Holt, Rinehart and Winston, 1969.

WEICK, K.E., "Educational Organizations as Loosely Coupled Systems," *Administrative Science Quarterly,* 1976: 1–19.

WESTLEY, F., & H. MINTZBERG, "Visionary Leadership and Strategic Management," *Strategic Management Journal,* 1989: 17–32.

WHEELWRIGHT, S.C., "Japan—Where Operations Really are Strategic," *Harvard Business Review,* July–August 1981: 67–74.

WHITE, T.H., *In Search of History: A Personal Adventure.* New York: Warner Books, 1978.

WHITEHEAD, A.N., *Aims of Education and Other Essays.* New York: Macmillan, 1929.

WHYTE, W.F., *Street Corner Society.* Chicago: University of Chicago Press, 1955.

WILLIAMSON, O.E., *Markets and Hierarchies: Analysis and Antitrust Implications.* New York: Free Press, 1975.

———, *The Economic Institutions of Capitalism.* New York: Free Press, 1985.

WISE, D., "Apple's New Crusade," *Business Week,* November 26, 1984.

WITTE, E., "Field Research on Complex Decision-Making Processes—The Phase Theorem," *International Studies of Management and Organization,* Summer 1972: 156–182.

WODARSKI, J.S., R.L. HAMBLIN, D.R. BUCKHOLDT, & D.E. FERRITOR, "Individual Consequences versus Different Shared Consequences Contingent on the Performance of Low-Achieving Group Members," *Journal of Applied Social Psychology,* 1973: 276–290.

WOO, C., & A. COOPER, "Strategies of Effective Low Share Businesses," *Strategic Management Journal,* 1981: 301–318.

WORTHY, J.C., "Organizational Structure and Employee Morale," *American Sociological Review,* 1950: 169–179.

———, *Big Business and Free Men.* New York: Harper & Row, 1959.

WRAPP, H.E., "Good Managers Don't Make Policy Decisions," *Harvard Business Review,* September–October 1967: 91–99.

WRIGLEY, L., "Diversification and Divisional Autonomy," DBA dissertation, Graduate School of Business Administration, Harvard University, 1970.

YOSHINO, M., *Japan's Managerial System.* Cambridge, Mass.: MIT Press, 1968.

YOSHINO, M.Y., "Global Competition in a Salient Industry: The Case of Civil Aircraft," in M.E. Porter, ed., *Competition in Global Industries.* Boston: Harvard Business School Press, 1986.

YOUNG, D., *Rommel: The Desert Fox.* New York: Harper & Row, 1974.

ZALD, M.N., "Urban Differentiation, Characteristics of Boards of Directors and Organizational Effectiveness," *American Journal of Sociology,* 1967: 261–272.

———, & M.A. BERGER, "Social Movements in Organizations: Coup d'Etat, Insurgency, and Mass Movements," *American Journal of Sociology,* 1978.

ZALEZNIK, A., "Power and Politics in Organizational Life," *Harvard Business Review,* May–June 1970: 47–60.

SUBJECT INDEX

1075

NAME INDEX